STEPHEN KING'S THE DARK TOWER

THE COMPLETE CONCORDANCE

Robin Furth

FOREWORD BY
STEPHEN KING

SCRIBNER
New York London Toronto Sydney New Delhi

Scribner
A Division of Simon & Schuster, Inc.
1230 Avenue of the Americas
New York, NY 10020

First Scribner trade paperback edition November 2012

SCRIBNER and design are registered trademarks of The Gale Group, Inc. used under license by Simon & Schuster, Inc., the publisher of this work.

For information about special discounts for bulk purchases, please contact Simon & Schuster Special Sales at 1-866-506-1949 or business@simonandschuster.com.

Scribner originally published this book as two separate volumes entitled *Stephen King's The Dark Tower: A Concordance, Vol. I* copyright © 2003 by Robin Furth and *Stephen King's The Dark Tower: A Concordance, Vol. II* copyright © 2005 by Robin Furth.

The Simon & Schuster Speakers Bureau can bring authors to your live event. For more information or to book an event contact the Simon & Schuster Speakers Bureau at 1-866-248-3049 or visit our website at www.simonspeakers.com.

Manufactured in the United States of America

1   3   5   7   9   10   8   6   4   2

Library of Congress Control Number: 2012029819

ISBN 978-1-4516-9487-1
ISBN 978-1-4516-9504-5 (ebook)

We live our short lives on one side of the door; on the other is all of eternity.
Time is the wind that blows through the keyhole.
—Stephen King, e-mail correspondence
October 15, 2011

FOR MARK

FOR STEVE

FOR ROLAND

Commala-come-come,
A new journey has just begun!

ACKNOWLEDGMENTS

It takes many people to transform a manuscript into a book. I would like to thank the talented and hardworking people whose time, labor, and dedication helped to make this *Concordance* a reality. Here's a salute to the memory of Ralph Vicinanza, my agent who passed away in 2010. Thanks also to Eben Weiss and the people at Ralph Vicinanza Ltd. A huge thank you to Chris Lotts, my present agent, and all the great folks at the Lotts Agency. My profound gratitude goes to Brant Rumble (my U.S. editor), John Glynn, and all the folks at Scribner; Philippa Pride (my U.K. editor) and all the folks at Hodder and Stoughton; Marsha DeFilippo and Julie Eugley, for years of help and support; my husband, Mark, for living with me through all of this; and Burt Hatlen, who believed in me enough to recommend me for my job as Stephen King's research assistant. Finally, I'd like to give an extra-hearty thanks to Stephen King, who had faith in a struggling writer living in a secondhand trailer in the Maine woods.

CONTENTS

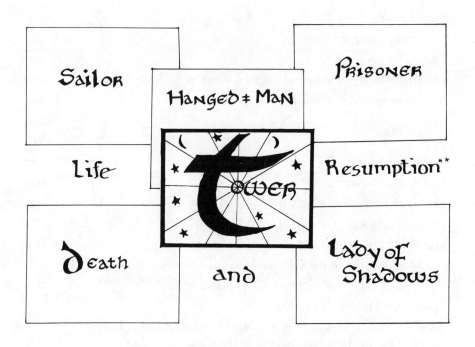

Sailor

Hanged ‡ Man

Prisoner

Life

Tower

Resumption**

Death

and

Lady of
Shadows

FOREWORD
BY STEPHEN KING

The tale of Roland of Gilead's search for the Dark Tower is a single tale, picaresque in nature (think *Huckleberry Finn* with monsters, and characters who raft along the Path of the Beam instead of the Mississippi), spanning seven volumes, involving dozens of plot twists and hundreds of characters. It's hard to tell how much time passes "inside the story," because in Roland Deschain's *where* and *when,* both time and direction have become plastic.[1] Outside the story—in what we laughingly call "the real world"—thirty-two years passed between the first sentence and the last one.

How long were the lapses between the individual books that make up the entire story? In truth, Constant Reader, I do not know. I think the longest lapse might have been six years (between *The Waste Lands* and *Wizard and Glass*). It is a miracle the story was ever finished at all, but perhaps an even greater one that a second volume ever followed the first, which was originally published in a tiny edition by Donald M. Grant, Publishers.[2] The manuscript of that first volume, wet and barely readable, was rescued from a mildewy cellar. The first forty handwritten pages of a second volume (titled, as I remember, *Roland Draws Three*) were missing. God knows where they wound up.

Will I tell you what happens to a story when it lies fallow over such long periods of time? Will you hear? Then close your eyes and imagine a vast department store, all on one level, lit by great racks of overhead fluorescent lights. You see every kind of item under those lights—underwear and automotive parts, TVs and DVDs, shoes and stationery and bikes for the kiddies, blue jeans and mattresses *(Oh look, Herbie, they're on sale, 40% off!),* cosmetics and air rifles, party dresses and picnic gear.

Now imagine the lights failing, one by one. The huge space grows darker; the goods so temptingly arrayed grow dimmer and harder to see. Finally you can hardly see your hand in front of your face.

That was the kind of room I came to when it was finally time to write *The Drawing of the Three,* except then the store wasn't so big—the first volume was less than three hundred pages long, so it was actually more of a mom n pop operation, do ya not see it. I was able to light it again simply by reading over the first volume and having a few ideas (I also resurrected a few old ones; I hadn't

---

1. This was a demand of the story, but I'd be less than honest if I didn't add that it also helps to foil the often troubling questions of copy editors such as those asked by Teddy Rosenbaum, who worked on the later volumes of the cycle.

2. The stories that made up the volume were issued in *The Magazine of Fantasy and Science Fiction,* then edited by Ed Ferman.

entirely forgotten what was in those handwritten pages, or the purpose of the tale).

Coming back to write the third volume *(The Waste Lands)* in the mid-eighties was harder, because the store was once again almost completely dark, and now it was much bigger. Once again I began by reading over what I'd written, taking copious notes, and filling paperback copies of the first two books with yellow highlighted passages and pink Post-it notes.

Another four years passed . . . or perhaps this time it was six. The store had once again grown dark, and by the time I was ready to write *Wizard and Glass,* it was bigger than ever. This time I wanted to add a whole new annex (call it Roland's Past instead of the Bridal Shoppe). Once again out came the books— three of them, this time—the yellow highlighter, and the packets of Post-it notes.

When I sat down to complete Roland's story in the year 2001, I knew that just rereading and writing myself Post-it notes wouldn't be enough. By now the store that was my story seemed to cover whole acres; had become a Wal-Mart of the imagination. And, were I to write three more volumes, I'd be adding dozens of characters (I actually ended up adding more than fifty), a whole new dialect (based on the pidgin English used by the natives of West Africa and first encountered by me in Richard Dooling's extraordinary *White Man's Grave*), and a backstory that would—I hoped—finally make Roland's wandering present clear to the patient reader.

This time, instead of reading, I listened to Frank Muller's extraordinary audio recordings of the first four Dark Tower stories. Unabridged audio forces the reader to slow down and listen to every word, whether he or she wants to or not. It also lends a new perspective, that of the reader and the audio director. But I knew even that would not be enough. I needed some sort of exhaustive written summary of *everything* that had gone before, a Dark Tower concordance that would be easy to search when I needed to find a reference in a hurry. In terms of the store metaphor, I needed someone to replace all the fluorescents, and inventory all the goods on offer, and then hand me a clipboard with everything noted down.

Enter Robin Furth. She came to me courtesy of my old friend and teacher at the University of Maine, Burton Hatlen. Burt is a wonderful scholar of poetry and popular fiction. He has written about Roland for several scholarly journals, and was sympathetic to what I was up to with the books (indeed, he seemed to understand what I was up to better than I did myself). So I gave him my list of requirements with some confidence (some hope, at least) that he would find the right person.

Someone who was bright and imaginative.

Someone who had read a good deal of fantasy (although not necessarily the Tower books themselves), and was therefore familiar with its rather unique language and thematic concerns.

Someone who could write with clarity and verve.

Someone who was willing to work hard and answer arcane and often bizarre questions *(Who was the mayor of New York in 1967? Do worms have teeth?)* on short notice.

He found Robin Furth, and my wandering gunslinger had found his Boswell. The concordance you hold in your hands—and which will surely delight you as it has delighted me—was never written to be published. As a writer I like to fly by the seat of my pants, working without an outline and usually without notes. When I have to slow down to look for something—a name in Volume III, say, or a sequence of events way back in Volume I—I can almost *feel* the story growing cold, the edge of my enthusiasm growing blunt and flecking out with little blooms of rust. The idea of the concordance was to limit these aggravating pauses by putting Roland's world at my fingertips—not just names and places, but slang terms, dialects, relationships, even whole chronologies.

Robin provided exactly what I needed, and more. One day I walked into my office to discover her down on her knees, carefully sticking photographs to a huge piece of poster paper. It was, she explained, a "walking tour" of Second Avenue in New York, covering the avenue itself and all the cross streets from Fortieth to Sixty-sixth. There was the U.N. Plaza Hotel (which has changed its name twice since I started writing Roland's story); there was Hammarskjöld Plaza (which did not even exist back in 1970); there was the spot where Tom and Jerry's Artistic Deli ("Party Platters Our Specialty") once stood. That poster eventually went up on the wall of my writing room in Florida, and was of invaluable help in writing *Song of Susannah* (The Dark Tower VI). In addition to the "walking tour" itself, Robin had patiently winkled out the history of the key two blocks, including the real shops and buildings I'd replaced with such fictional bits of real estate as Chew Chew Mama's and The Manhattan Restaurant of the Mind. And it was Robin who discovered that, across the street from 2 Hammarskjöld Plaza, there really is a little pocket park (it's called a "peace garden") that does indeed contain a bronze turtle sculpture. Talk about life imitating art!

As I say, her concordance was never meant to be published; it was created solely as a writer's tool. But, even with most of my mind preoccupied by the writing of my tale, I was aware of how good it was, how interesting and *readable* it was. I also became aware, as time passed and the actual publication of the final three volumes grew closer, of how valuable it might be to the Constant Reader who'd read the first three or four volumes of the series, but some years ago.

In any case, it was Robin Furth who inventoried the goods I had on sale, and replaced all the dim overhead lights so I could see everything clearly and find my way from Housewares to Appliances without getting lost . . . or from Gilead to Calla Bryn Sturgis, if you prefer. That in no way makes her responsible for my errors—of which I'm sure there are many—but it *is* important that she receive credit for all the good work she has done on my behalf. I found this overview of In-World, Mid-World, and End-World both entertaining and invaluable.

So, I am convinced, will you.

January 26, 2003

ABOUT THIS BOOK

This book had its first stirrings more than twenty years ago. I was fourteen, and I was spending the summer with my grandparents in Maine. I have always been obsessed by books, and so that July I arrived with a stack of them. Top of the pile wasn't *The Gunslinger*. No. Not yet. But it was a novel called *'Salem's Lot*.

I can still remember the feeling I had when I read that book. My body was on the tiny, weedy beach of Patten Pond, but the rest of me was in the Marsten House, or crouched by Mark Petrie's side as he held up a glow-in-the-dark cross to ward off the vampire at his window. I climbed on the Greyhound Bus behind Father Callahan—my hand burned and my mouth still tasting Barlow's blood—and the two of us set off for that unknown destination of Thunderclap, a haunted place on the lip of End-World.[1]

I closed the novel and, still caught in that dream-web, I began to walk back toward home. And there, in the pine woods, with my feet deep in leaf mould and my skin still smelling of pond water, I saw myself as an adult. I was grown-up, and I was working for Stephen King. I didn't know exactly what I was doing, but I knew it had to do with books, and Father Callahan, and with that dreaded place called Thunderclap. The vision was so vivid, so convincing, and so quickly over. I held on to the feeling of it long enough to write my first horror story (it wasn't very good), but as the vision faded, I began to doubt what I had seen. I buried that vision, lost the story, and didn't think about either for two decades. That is, until one day when I went to check my mail in the English department office at the University of Maine. As I was sorting through the grade sheets and memos, I felt a tap on my shoulder. It was Burt Hatlen, one of my professors. Stephen King needed a temporary research assistant, he said. Would I be interested . . .

Sometimes, art imitates life, and sometimes life imitates art, and sometimes the two of them blend to such a degree that we can't figure out where one ends and the other begins. For months before my chat with Burt, I'd been dreaming about roses, moons with demon faces, and huge, imposing, smoke-colored Towers. I didn't think I was losing my mind, but then there was the tall, lanky, ghostlike man pacing at my writing-room door. He seemed to want to get through to our world, to *need* to get through to our world, and for some reason he thought I

---

1. Believe it or not, the copy of *'Salem's Lot* that I had as a teenager actually mentioned Thunderclap. I spent years wondering where that place was—it didn't sound like any city in our world. I read the book several times as an adult and never saw this reference again. Recently I asked Steve whether he had deleted Thunderclap from later editions and he told me it was never there in the first place. But it should have been. How can I explain this weird occurrence? I can't.

could help him. And every time I laid out my tarot cards, my future came out Towers.

Ka is a wheel, its one purpose is to turn, and so often it brings us back to just where we started. Twenty years had passed since I boarded that bus to Thunderclap, but in Roland's world, in the world of the Tower quest, twenty years in the past, or twenty years in the future, are only just a doorway apart. I climbed back on that Greyhound Bus only to find myself, as a young girl, still sitting behind Callahan. I'd never really disembarked in the first place.

Pere Callahan waited in Calla Bryn Sturgis, on the border of Thunderclap, and Roland had to reach him. All he needed was somebody from our world to help crack open Steve's doorway. I knew many of Steve's other works, I loved fantasy and horror, and I had those rather sinister initials that implied I might be good for writing something other than academic essays. All that remained for me to do was open Roland's biography and read that first, all-important line. *The man in black fled across the desert, and the gunslinger followed . . .*

It is now 2012, and I have lived in Roland's world for more than twelve years. During that time I've collected much of the myth, history, and folklore of Mid-World. Just as, when you wake up from a dream, you try to capture what you saw during your night travels, the book that follows is my attempt to capture my journey with Roland. My goal, when I started, was to make a doorway between worlds. I hope that I have, at least, made a small window.

R.F.
March 12, 2003
(revisited July 16, 2006
and again, June 27, 2012)

THE WIND THROUGH THE KEYHOLE
AND THE WINDS OF MID-WORLD

"There's nothing like stories on a windy night when folks have found a warm place in a cold world."

> Roland Deschain
> *The Wind Through the Keyhole*, 31

Like all Dark Tower fans, I always hoped that Stephen King would return to Mid-World after the seventh, and seemingly final, installment of the Dark Tower saga. Hence, in 2009, when Steve told me that he had another idea for a Dark Tower story, I was delighted. At that point, the novel had the working title *Black Wind*. The title alone was intriguing, since as every Tower junkie knows, the winds of Mid-World are intrinsically linked to *sai* King's artistic inspiration. As he says in *Song of Susannah*, "the wind blows and the story comes." In *Black Wind*, however, that wind would have special significance, since it linked three stories, three eras of Mid-World history, and two vastly different periods in Roland's life.

By 2010, Steve had begun writing in earnest. The title, *Black Wind*, had become *The Wind Through the Keyhole*, and the story was firmly placed between *Wizard and Glass* and *Wolves of the Calla*. Since it wasn't technically a gunslinger novel—Steve had set out instead to write a fairy tale—he thought that the subtitle would be *A Novel of Mid-World*. In those early days, Steve sent me a beautiful epigraph that he wanted to place at the beginning of the book:

> We live our short lives on one side of the door; on the other is all of eternity. Time is the wind that blows through the keyhole.

Eventually both the subtitle and the epigram were cut, but I wanted to record them here, in this guide to all things Mid-World. Hence, the epigram appears at the beginning of this volume, and the old title is here too, along with *The Wind Through the Keyhole*'s many new characters, magical objects, fantastic places, games, words, and maps. Longtime readers will notice that my map of Mid-World's Beams has also altered. The Lion-Eagle Beam now runs north to south, which is fitting, since the starkblasts of North'rd Barony begin in the land of endless snows, which is also where Aslan, Guardian of Gilead's Beam, resides.

To me, *The Wind Through the Keyhole* is a very special novel. Throughout so much of the Dark Tower series Roland remains aloof: a character we love but don't fully understand, a reticent loner whose battle scars are so numerous that we can't help but feel that he has a thick layer of protective scar tissue over his heart. Yet in *The Wind Through the Keyhole* we not only see the world through Roland's eyes, but we gain a sense of how Roland sees himself. In both *Wizard and Glass* and *The Wind Through the Keyhole*, Roland's adventures with his American *ka-tet* serve as frame stories for tales about Roland's younger days. But while in *Wizard and Glass* Roland's autobiographical adventure is recounted in the third person by an unseen narrator, in *The Wind Through the Keyhole*, Roland tells his story in his own voice. In this novel, Roland is not just a young gunslinger-prodigy with dazzlingly quick reflexes and a precociously subtle sense of battle strategy. He is a young man struggling to make sense of the decisions he has made in his life, and to cope with the terrible consequences of his actions. Over the course of the novel, he comes closer to making peace between his conflicting emotions and allegiances. Somehow, his rigid sense of duty to the way of the gun and his resulting rage against Gabrielle Deschain for betraying her husband and her Barony, must sit beside the profound but confusing grief he feels over the accidental shooting of his mother.

Just as in *Wizard and Glass,* Roland's encounter with a thinny prompts him to tell his American *ka-tet* about his coming-of-age test and the trials he faced in Hambry soon after he won his guns, so in *The Wind Through the Keyhole,* the starkblast which sweeps along the Path of the Beam inspires Roland to recount two interlinked tales. All three narratives—the frame story of Roland's *tet* traveling along the path of the Beam, the autobiographical adventure in which Roland and his *ka*-mate Jamie DeCurry hunt for the skin-man of Debaria, and the folktale about Tim Ross, who discovered that his father had been murdered by his jealous best friend, are all linked by the sound of Mid-World's winds. But to Roland, the ferocious starkblast is not merely a catalyst for talespinning. That powerful storm is intrinsically bound to his memory of his mother and to his guilt over her death.

All that Roland knows about starkblasts—from the unseasonable warmth that precedes them to the erratic behavior of bumblers that warns farmers of impending disaster—was passed on to him by Gabrielle. Hence it is not surprising that, at the beginning of the novel, everything that Roland knows about starkblasts has been suppressed, just as his grief and guilt over his matricide has been suppressed. It is not until the ferryman Bix points out the approaching storm's many warning signs that the door of memory opens and Roland recalls both the autobiographical tale of "The Skin-Man," which took place shortly after Gabrielle's passing, and "The Wind Through the Keyhole," the folktale which his mother often read to him in the tower bedroom of his childhood.

From the outset of "The Skin-Man," we know that fifteen-year-old Roland is struggling with an overwhelming grief. Though he has not been back from Hambry for very long, Roland has appointed himself as nurse to his old teacher Cort. Roland claims that he nurses Cort out of respect (after all, Cort never recovered from Roland's coming-of-age battle against him), but his father suspects a darker motivation. Roland is searching for absolution for his accidental murder of his mother. In order to remove Roland from the unhealthy atmosphere of Gilead, and to try to get the boy to expiate his sense of sin in a more fitting manner, Steven Deschain sends Roland and his *ka*-mate Jamie DeCurry to Debaria, so that the boys can track down the bloodthirsty skin-man who has been terrorizing that western barony.

On the way to Debaria, Roland and Jamie stop at Serenity, the women's retreat where Roland's mother stayed after her betrayal of her husband and her city. There they not only see the terrible wounds inflicted upon one of the skin-man's few surviving victims, but they meet the retreat's prioress, the flamboyant but warm giantess, Everlynne of Serenity. Even this early in the tale, Roland begins to question the view of reality imparted to him by his father and the other gunslingers. After all, Everlynne is not the man-hating vixen that he has been led to believe she would be, but a vivacious, brave, and welcoming woman who maintained her respect for Roland's dead mother despite her crimes. In fact, she calls our young gunslinger *son-of-Gabrielle* rather than *son-of-Steven,* which is the more usual form of address in patriarchal Mid-World.

Once in Debaria, Roland must once again face the division between his mind and his heart. In order to catch the skin-man, he must play the role of adult gunslinger. This means operating with the intellect and instincts of a hunter, though it goes against the more humane instincts of the boy. Faced with the horrors of the skin-man's attacks, Roland decides that the only way he will be able to catch the shapeshifting killer is by setting a trap, baited with the only living person to have seen the skin-man in his human form—an eleven-year-old boy named Bill Streeter. Roland's *ka*-mate, Jamie DeCurry, is very uncomfortable with Roland's decision to use Young Bill in this way. As Roland says, "It was a thing [Jamie]'d never have done himself, even if he'd though of it. Which is why my father had put me in charge. Not because I'd done well in Mejis—I hadn't, not really—and not because I was his son, either. Although in a way, I suppose that was it. My mind was like his: cold."

Like any general, Roland-the-gunslinger knows that in war, the innocent are often sacrificed. But the way he describes the reason for his position of leadership is harsh. Though he was the youngest gunslinger ever to win his guns, and though as little more than an adolescent, he had defeated the brutal Big Coffin Hunters of Hambry, Roland does not think it is his bravery or his heroism or his skill that has made Steven Deschain put him in charge of this mission. Gilead's *dinh* let him lead the hunt for Debaria's skin-man because Roland is cold-minded and cold-blooded, just like the best of the *tet* of the gun.

But despite the coldness required by his calling, the young Roland tries to keep alive his own humanity. Although Roland puts Young Bill at risk, he tries to minimize that risk. He takes the boy to Debaria's jail—the most defendable building in the town—and locks the two of them in together. (If the skin-man tries to attack Billy, then Roland will defend the boy with his life.) While in that jail cell, listening to the wailing of the simoom outside, Roland tells Young Bill the story of another young boy—Tim Ross—who like Billy had to face terrible dangers in order to bring his father's killer to justice. Like Bill Streeter, Tim Ross was of low birth, but because of his bravery he not only became a gunslinger, but became the legendary hero, Tim Stoutheart. It is little wonder then, that in order to screw up his courage and face the skin-man, Young Bill pretends that he is Tim Stoutheart.

In many ways, *The Wind Through the Keyhole* is an exploration of how we deal with grief. All of the young protagonists—Roland, Bill Streeter, and Tim Ross—are forced to come to terms with the violent death of a parent. But the novel is not just about grief, it is also about how we react to the unfair vicissitudes of life. Roland has committed a crime, but he must come to accept that the death of his mother was an accident. Bill Streeter's father was brutally murdered by a shapeshifter who was not a mindless beast, but a human being who took some form of pleasure from his kills. Bill cannot bring his father back to life, but by identifying the killer he can bring some form of closure to the horrors he has faced, and he can also help to prevent future massacres. Similarly, Tim Ross discovers that his father—whom he has been told was incinerated by a dragon—was in truth slaughtered by his partner and best friend, Bern Kells, who coveted Tim's mother. Tim cannot wind back time any more than he can untie the knot that binds his mother to her violent and drunken new husband, but he can expose his stepfather's crime and also minimize the impact that Kells has on his own, and his mother's, life.

As well as the personal traumas that Roland, Bill, and Tim must face, there are the greater social injustices that echo throughout the three tales. On his way to Debaria, Roland is made uncomfortably aware of how successful his mother's lover, Marten Broadcloak, has been in turning the people of Mid-World against the gunslingers. (In Debaria, too many people have secretly given their allegiance to the mad harrier, John Farson.) As the adult Roland of the frame story knows, Farson's destiny is to bring about Mid-World's second destruction. In Tim Ross's world, the greedy Covenant Man (who is but another face of Roland's eternal enemy, Marten Broadcloak/Walter O'Dim) has poisoned the reputation of Gilead by squeezing as much tax as possible out of the people of Tree. Even in the land of fairytale, people whisper that Gilead's taxes are unfair, and that the people's covenant with the Eld has been paid a dozen times over, in blood as well as silver. As when he is in his Broadcloak disguise, the Covenanter knows full well that he is destroying the fabric of Mid-World society, but this is exactly what he wants to do. The wastelands that Roland and his American *tet* traverse are as much the fault of O'Dim as they are the fault of Mid-World's Old People.

Although the emotions explored in *The Wind Through the Keyhole* are dark ones, the novel's closure is redemptive. Before Roland leaves Debaria, Everlynne of Serenity gives him a note penned by Gabrielle before she left the women's retreat. Though the letter is as disjointed and distraught as the mind of the woman who had written it, Gabrielle tells her son that she knew she was destined to die by his hand, but returned to Gilead anyway. Although Gabrielle has already entered the clearing at the end of the path, from beyond the grave she offers her son absolution. The final words of her letter, written in High Speech, say, *I forgive you everything. Can you forgive me?* At the end of the novel, Steven King states that the two most beautiful words in any language are *I forgive*. I must say, I agree. Unless we are able to open our hearts and forgive others, we can never learn to forgive ourselves.

For all of us who have waited so long for another tale about our favorite wandering gunslinger, *The Wind Through the Keyhole* is a gift. Thank you, Steve. And thank you, my fellow Constant Readers, for perusing yet another version of my *Concordance,* this massive book which I regard as my travel log for Mid-World.

Long days and pleasant nights, and may the sun never fall in your eyes.

Robin Furth
August 6, 2012

ABBREVIATIONS AND TEXT GUIDE

ABBREVIATIONS USED FOR PRIMARY TEXTS BY STEPHEN KING

I: *The Gunslinger*. 1982. New York: Plume-Penguin, 1988. *The Gunslinger*. 2003 (revised edition). New York: Plume-Penguin, 2003. (*See* Please Note)

II: *The Drawing of the Three*. 1987. New York: Plume-Penguin, 1989.

III: *The Waste Lands*. 1991. New York: Plume-Penguin, 1989.

IV: *Wizard and Glass*. New York: Plume-Penguin, 1997.

V: *Wolves of the Calla*. New Hampshire: Donald M. Grant in association with Scribner, 2003.

VI: *Song of Susannah*. New Hampshire: Donald M. Grant in association with Scribner, 2004.

VII: *The Dark Tower*. New Hampshire: Donald M. Grant in association with Scribner, 2004.

E: "The Little Sisters of Eluria." *Everything's Eventual: 14 Dark Tales*. New York: Scribner, 2002.

W: *The Wind Through the Keyhole*. New Hampshire: Donald M. Grant in association with Scribner, 2012.

SECONDARY TEXTS BY STEPHEN KING

Bag of Bones. New York: Scribner, 1998.

Desperation. New York: Viking-Penguin, 1996.

"Everything's Eventual." *Everything's Eventual: 14 Dark Tales*. New York: Scribner, 2002.

The Eyes of the Dragon. New York: Viking-Penguin, 1984.

Insomnia. New York: Viking-Penguin, 1994.

It. New York: Viking-Penguin, 1986.

"Low Men in Yellow Coats." *Hearts in Atlantis*. New York: Scribner, 1999.

"The Mist." *Skeleton Crew*. New York: Putnam, 1985.

The Regulators (Stephen King as Richard Bachman). New York: Viking-Penguin, 1996.

'Salem's Lot. New York: Doubleday, 1975.

The Stand. New York: Doubleday, 1978.

SECONDARY TEXTS BY STEPHEN KING AND PETER STRAUB

Black House. New York: Random House, 2001.
The Talisman. New York: Viking-Penguin, 1984.

PLEASE NOTE

1. *Stephen King's The Dark Tower: A Concordance, Volume I* went to press before a paginated copy of the new version of *The Gunslinger* was available. As a result, all *Gunslinger* page references refer to the original version of the novel. All entries that contain material drawn from the 2003 *Gunslinger* are marked with a double asterisk (**). In the 2012 updated edition of this *Concordance,* I have included some page references from the revised 2003 edition of *The Gunslinger.* These page references are followed by the following: (*2003 edition*).
2. Page references are as follows:
    V:199
    (volume):(page number)
3. Although Mid-World was the name of a specific historical kingdom, Stephen King also uses this term when he needs to refer (in general terms) to Roland's version of Earth. I have followed this practice.
4. In Volume I of this *Concordance,* I often capitalized the term *Our World.* In the last three books of the series, we find out that there are many, many versions of our world, so I no longer use capitals. However, when I refer specifically to the world in which Stephen King writes his novels (and where I'm fairly certain you and I are reading them), I use the term *Keystone Earth.*
5. Constant Readers will notice that the Map of the Beams, located in Appendix VII, has changed so that it can remain consistent with the information imparted in *The Wind Through the Keyhole.* The Lion Eagle Beam, which passes through the Endless Forest of North'rd Barony, now flows north-south.

Commala, come-come,
Journey's almost done . . .

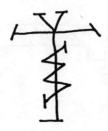

TRAVELLER, BEYOND LIES MID-WORLD

GILEAD FAIR-DAYS

WINTER

WIDE EARTH
Riddling

SOWING
(**New Earth)
(**Fresh Commala)
The Sowing Night Cotillion
called Commala
a courting rite dance
celebrating spring

MID-SUMMER

FULL EARTH
Riddling
Full Earth babies born

REAPING
Charyou Tree and burning of stuffy-guys,
Reaping lass and Reaping lad, Reap charms.
In the Outer Arc, a prize is given on Reap Day to the person or group
that collects the greatest number of rattlesnake skins.
Children planted on Reap come due on Full Earth.
This is the true Year's End.
Reap kisses
Orgy of Reap
Propitiating old gods
Reap Morn: First day of Winter

YEAR'S END

MID-WORLD MOONS

KISSING MOON
A perfect disk of silver
Moon of Romance
Shadows of lovers
On its bright skin

PEDDLER'S MOON
Late-summer moon
Huge and orange
And the Peddler, who comes out of the Nones
With his sack of squealing souls

HUNTRESS MOON
Last moon of summer, first moon of autumn
Picking apples, cutting hay
Snakes and scorpions wander east from the desert
Day moon
The huntress fills her belly
And becomes
A pallid, vampire woman
Season of Reap
The beginning of endings
Clearer and clearer on each starry night
The Huntress pulls back her bow

DEMON MOON
Blood red
Death moon
Closing of the year
Blade nose
Bone grin
Reap's scythe
Above
He grins and winks
Though a scarlet
Shifting
Scrim

STEPHEN KING'S THE DARK TOWER

THE COMPLETE CONCORDANCE

INTRODUCTION PART ONE
VOLUMES I–IV
ROLAND, THE TOWER,
AND THE QUEST

Spoiler's Warning: Read this essay only after you have read the first four books of Roland's saga. Otherwise, you'll get more than a glimpse of what is to come . . .

To any reader of the Dark Tower series, Roland Deschain is an instantly recognizable character. As I write this, I see him in my mind's eye, striding across the yellowing grasses of the River Barony savannah, his black hair threaded with gray, his body tall and lanky, his holster and gun belt strapped to his hips. Only one of those fabled sandalwood-handled six-shooters is with him; it rests against his left thigh. The other is back at camp, secure in the docker's clutch strapped to Eddie Dean's side. As I stare, Roland turns his head and regards me pragmatically. *If you need to talk to me,* he says, *then come.* Time may be a face on the water, but in Roland's world, water is scarce.

Roland watches as I pass through the doorway of the page. His pale blue eyes really are like those of a bombardier, both cool and assessing. By necessity, this meeting will be brief. I'm another one of Roland's secrets, and he thinks it better to keep me that way. He's not certain what level of the Tower I come from, but he knows one thing. I am mapping his travels.

Finding some shade, Roland hunkers. I hand him one of the rolling papers I've brought, and he accepts it silently. Unlacing the leather thongs of his traveling purse, he removes his tobacco poke and rolls a smoke. Despite the missing fingers on his right hand, he works the paper dexterously, licking the gummed side with a grimace. He strikes a match against the seam of his jeans and lights his cigarette. For a moment his face is illuminated with an eerie glow that makes his features look drawn and more than a little haggard. He has a few days' worth of stubble on his cheeks, and his lips are chapped. Once again I try to show him this concordance, but he waves the bound manuscript away as he exhales a cloud of smoke. As always, he thinks that my constant revisions waste paper. Besides, he's only interested in the maps. But today I've brought a short piece, and this he has agreed to hear. It's my interpretation of his epic journey. Taking another deep drag, Roland rolls his hand in that gesture which means only one thing, in any world. *Get on with it.* So I clear my throat and (rather nervously) begin.

ROLAND, THE TOWER, AND THE QUEST

Roland Deschain is Mid-World's final gunslinger. Like a knight from the Arthurian legends of our world, Roland is on a quest. His "grail" is the Dark Tower, the linchpin of the time/space continuum, and his goal is to climb to its very top and question the god or demon who resides there. Roland's world is unraveling. The Beams that maintain the proper alignment of time, space, size and dimension are breaking down and the Tower itself is foundering. This structural instability affects all worlds, but in Roland's, the symptoms are dramatic. As the fabric of reality wears away, thinnies form and spread. These squalling mist bogs swallow all those that stumble into them, letting their captives fall into the dark no-places between worlds. As the landscape stretches, directions drift. What is west today may be southwest tomorrow and southeast the day after. A goal that lay only fifty miles away can suddenly become a hundred, or even a thousand, miles distant.

As the direct descendant of Arthur Eld, King of All-World-that-was, and as Mid-World's last *dinh,* Roland must rescue his land from annihilation. But his task is gargantuan. He must find a way to safeguard the framework, the loom, upon which the interpenetrating realities are woven. But to do so—in order to shore up that central Tower and the Beams which radiate out from it—he must find his way across a landscape so fragmented that neither map nor memory can help him pinpoint his destination. In fact, Roland does not even know where the Tower stands. He realizes that he must head toward a place called End-World, but where does that land lie? How can he find it? During the early stages of his journey, Roland the warrior chooses the path of the ascetic. Believing he can only reach his goal as a solitary traveler, he sacrifices all human relationships, even when it means betrayal, because he thinks such sacrifice will speed him along his way. Comrades and lovers are left behind like abandoned water skins.

Roland believes that to climb the Tower he must have no ties holding him to Mid-World. He must be isolated, self-sufficient, cut off from the nurturing tides of relationship. Thinking in terms of conquest and battle, Roland follows the duplicitous Walter across the deserts of Mid-World, believing that this enemy will eventually lead him to his goal. Similarly, as a boy, he followed the path set for him by Maerlyn's Grapefruit, a magic ball whose evil, distorting visions tricked him into first sacrificing his lover, Susan Delgado, and then murdering his own mother.

What Roland doesn't at first realize is that, like any young knight, he is being tested. The initial path he chooses is a false start, no more than a *glammer* thrown by the enemies who want to thwart him. What their treachery exposes is that the young Roland is driven by ambition, personal glory, and revenge as much as he is by a desire to fulfill his destiny as the last warrior of the White. By tempting him to betray all that a knight should hold sacred, Roland's enemies ensure that Roland will repeat the mistakes of his fathers and either abandon his quest as hopeless or become lost in the deserts and golgothas of Mid-World which, in the end, but mirror the dry wreckage of his heart.

Roland, the young warrior, does not understand the ultimate nature of his quest. He does not realize that, as the trickster Walter says in the golgotha, he already stands so close to the Tower that worlds turn about his head.[1] Because of his own preconceptions, his inherited worldview, he does not understand that his fate, and the fate of Mid-World, are one and the same.

Roland's story is not just an adventure tale; it is one with symbolic meaning. His pilgrimage is intrinsically linked to a legend from our world, a legend which was an important influence upon the Modernists and which formed the basis for a famous poem by T. S. Eliot. That legend is the story of the Waste Land. In its incarnation in the Dark Tower series, this legend is bound to another belief, one that dates back to the time when men and women thought that their kings and queens were appointed by God. According to this worldview, the body of the king is the body of the land, and the well-being of one is indivisible from the well-being of the other. If the king is sick, in body or in mind, then the land falls to ruin. To cure the land, you must first cure the king. The one will only flourish if the other is in balance.

As above, so below. The disease of the larger is the same as that of the smaller, and they both progress according to the same principle. To understand what dries and devastates the land, what threatens the very fabric of the universe and the stability of the interpenetrating worlds, one must also understand what ails the king. All are affected by the same illness, but to cure this illness we must discover its underlying cause. And this is the true purpose of Roland's journey.

We all know that as the Beams snap, the Tower falters. But what is its equivalent on the human plane? What malaise weakens the bonds of Mid-World's culture? What disease affects Roland, the foremost representative of his fragmenting world?

High Speech, the tongue of gunslingers, is a subtle and complex language. Its words are difficult to define because they are so full of nuance. Each word has multiple meanings which refer, simultaneously, to ordinary human interaction, to the web that joins the interacting individuals, and to the greater pattern of humanity's past and future movements. No human interaction, then, is meaningless. They all reflect both individual and cultural *ka*.

Ka, we know, resembles a wheel. In fact, it looks much like the wheel Roland draws in *The Waste Lands,* a wheel meant to represent the Tower, the Beams, and the Portals in and out of Mid-World. In Roland's map, the hub of the wheel is the Tower, the spokes are the Beams, and the rivets are the Guardians, who are the Portals' sentries. Some Guardians, like the Turtle, are protective, while others, like the Bear Guardian Shardik, are downright dangerous. But they all serve the Beams, the Beams serve the Tower, and the Tower is what keeps the universe united. And perhaps these Beams work like Batteries, with positive and negative charges, the one balancing the other. That would explain why the Turtle is kind and the Bear—the opposite end of the Beam—is negative. Even polarity has its place, like light and darkness. That is, as long as the whole remains in balance.

Although it would be difficult to map the wheel of *ka* in this way—it is much too big—we can, at least, map the forces of *ka-tet*, remembering that the small is a miniature of the larger. As *dinh* of his *ka-tet* and as *dinh* of Mid-World, Roland sits at the center of the wheel. The Guardians of his present *ka-tet* are his companions Jake, Susannah, Eddie, and Oy. The sorcerer Walter—who plays a large

1. I:200

part in the drawing and binding of this *ka-tet*—can also be placed as one of the Guardians, though his polarity is negative.

Just as there is a word for the pattern of *ka-tet,* there is a word for the bonds (or Beams) that hold the *tet* together. This word is *khef.* Like almost all the words of High Speech, *khef* has multiple meanings, including birth and life force, but perhaps the most ubiquitous of these meanings is also the simplest. And that meaning is water.

As Roland knows all too well from his journey in the Mohaine Desert, a human will die much sooner from dehydration than he will from lack of food. The same can be said about the land, about society, and about the individual soul. Once again, the patterns and forces remain the same; what changes are the superficial forms. *Khef* can be literal water, the essence of life, but it can also mean emotion, the essence and bond of relationship. Whether this bond is one of loyalty or hatred, it always binds. That is, as long as the forces of the positive and the negative remain in dynamic balance. A certain amount of conflict is necessary for growth and change, but too much of the negative—too much repellent—and the *ka-tet* ceases to exist.

The patterns of *ka-tet* can be used to describe the subtle interactions which hold a society together. Without these emotional interactions, which create dynamic and forceful cohesion, society devolves and disintegrates; it becomes a mass of warring individuals, or warring clans. The beneficial interconnectedness of the whole is lost.

The bonds of *khef* are reciprocal. Both parties must contribute or else the connection is at best unstable, at worst illusory. Each side must give of itself. The unity of *ka-tet* depends on the forces of *khef.* In order for the *ka-tet* to survive, the Guardians of *ka-tet* must remain true, but their loyalty depends, in turn, upon the truth and honesty of the center. When the center does not hold true, the fabric begins to unravel, and this is exactly what has happened to Roland's world, and what has, in turn, happened over and over in Roland's life.

Ka is a wheel; its one purpose is to turn. The spin of *ka* always brings us back to the same place, to face and reface our mistakes and defeats until we can learn from them.[2] When we learn from the past, the wheel continues to move forward, toward growth and evolution. When we don't, the wheel spins backward, and we are given another chance. If once more we squander the opportunity, the wheel continues its rotation toward devolution, or destruction. While the High Speech terms for life and relationship have multiple meanings and subtle nuances, *char,* the Tongue's word for Death, has no other meaning. *Char* is bleak and final. The wheel continues to turn, but we are forcefully removed from it. Since we each have a place in the greater pattern, breaking of *khef* rends the fabric of the All.

What can be said of individuals can also be said of societies, and Roland's society is no exception. Although Mid-World enjoyed periods of stability, its history remains predominantly a story of sacrifice and bloodshed. Although High Speech shows that unity and relationship were valued, in the everyday of life they were, more often than not, forgotten. Many of Mid-World's sins were sins against *khef,* the bonding force of *ka* and culture. In Mid-World-that-was, the balance

2. As Steve mentioned when he read this essay, he first began to articulate this idea in *The Stand.*

between positive and negative was lost; creating and maintaining *khef* became less important than the propagation of *char*. Just as the Beams began to weaken, the *khef* which was meant to unite began to repel. The waters of life withdrew, and Mid-World became a desert. The result? Fragmentation and dehydration on all levels of reality, and on all levels of the Tower.

In "The Little Sisters of Eluria," Roland says that the religions of his world taught that "love and murder were inextricably bound together—that in the end, God always drank blood."[3] Upon intensive scrutiny, Roland's statement certainly seems to hold true. The Druits, the most ancient of Mid-World's people, raised the stones of the Speaking Rings in order to have temples devoted to human sacrifice. Although these practices may have drawn some of the people together, giving them a sense of unity and strength, they would have also created a blood-debt to the victim, and the victim's *ka-tet*, rending the fabric of the All. Even at this early stage of Mid-World's cultural evolution, the negative energy released by these acts began to thin reality. The forces of *char* became more powerful and the forces of *khef* were weakened. Within these circles doorways formed, but the sentries of these lesser portals were demons, not Guardians.

Although technologically advanced, the later generations of Mid-World gave little more thought to the forces of *khef*, or life-water, than their ancestors. The Great Old Ones created computerized wonders, such as Blaine, and accomplished amazing engineering and architectural feats, such as the building of Lud and the laying of the train lines deep below the Cyclopean Mountains, but even these seemingly "good" things were eventually tainted by the death-drive of their makers. Blaine developed a psychotic personality and drove the people of Lud on to Mid-World's oldest practice—human sacrifice. The city of Lud, once the gem of the Imperium, fell into the hands of diseased and warring gangs, and the train lines of the mountains seethed with Slow Mutants, those terrible creatures who were once human but who had been completely mutated by the Old Ones' poisons. No matter what grand plan they had for the future of the interpenetrating universes, the Old Ones worshiped the gods of *char*, the gods of destruction. The Old Ones' technological wizardry was focused on one endpoint, and that endpoint was the creation of more and more dangerous weapons. In this they succeeded. In fact, they succeeded so completely that they wiped out their own civilization and transformed Mid-World into a poisoned, desiccated wasteland.

As Susan Delgado says to Roland when they stand, horrified, by a line of resurrected war tankers, the ways of the Great Old Ones were the ways of death.[4] But over the course of the series we learn that the ways of death are, and always have been, the ways of Mid-World. Even during the time of Arthur Eld, Mid-World's greatest hero, human beings were thrown onto Charyou Tree fires to appease the gods of Reap, and in Roland's day those old ways were not completely abandoned. As we see when Susan Delgado is made into such a scapegoat, having the blame for her town's sins heaped upon her innocent head, such sacrifice and hypocrisy undermine all human relationships. No matter what their stated aims might be, such practices breed duplicity and mistrust and treachery, all of which are the opposite of *khef*.

3. E:147
4. IV:302

In the more central parts of Roland's world, stuffy-guys were usually burned in lieu of men and women, but life was still harsh and leaders were bred to be killers before they were taught to be statesmen. All that the ruling gunslingers had to do to justify this sacrifice of *khef* was to point west to the lands that were already torn apart by anarchy and rebellion. In Gilead, the light of civilization was championed, but its ideals of fairness, justice, compassion—of fundamental human worth whatever class or land that person might come from—were left to the gentle and the lame, like Roland's old tutor, Vannay, to promulgate. Although Roland loved Vannay, by far his most influential teacher was Cort, who taught him how to survive in a world where a knife would constantly be at his back, or at his throat.

In Gilead, the sons of the aristocracy trained to be an Eye and a Hand, an aim and a trigger, before they were trained to be a heart and a mind. And often, as Roland found to his later distress, such training meant that the hand could act before the mind had time to think. Gilead's coming-of-age battles were brutal, and the cost of defeat was banishment, a complete destruction of the *khef* that linked the young apprentice gunslinger to his society. The end—the creation of a strong, fearless, hardened gunslinger elite that could keep the anarchic darkness at bay—justified both the violence and the humiliation of the means. But *ka* makes no exceptions. As one sows, so one reaps, and the harvest is not always pleasant. Those trained killers—such as Eldred Jonas—who were banished from their society became the foot soldiers of Mid-World's next apocalypse.

The gunslingers could not see that the rot eating away at the fabric of their world was also at work upon the *khef* of their city, and upon the *khef* of their personal relationships. Roland's father, Steven Deschain, is a prime example. Trained as he was in the ways of *char,* the waters of *khef* dried up in him, and around him. He was bound to his fellow gunslingers, his fellow human hawks, but the bond he had with his wife became arid and his relationship with his magician (who also happened to be his foremost councillor) was duplicitous. Even his relations with Roland—whom he obviously loved—were gruff and distant. The situation was no better in the castle, or the kingdom. Hax, the head cook, turned traitor, as did at least some of the guards. All bonds of loyalty were broken, there was no longer a sense of cultural *ka-tet,* so many turned away to serve the forces of the enemy. Farson's propaganda about equality and democracy was only effective because it contained the grains of truth and exploited the alienation and anger of a society out of balance.

In the end, the gunslingers were destroyed and their city razed, its former castle becoming the filthy nest of a band of Slow Mutants. The forces of dissolution gained their coveted ground, and the universal waters of *khef* drew back a little more. With the fall of Gilead, the *ka-tet* of the Affiliation finally collapsed, and another part of the world stretched and unraveled.

As we have seen in the case of Steven Deschain, the reserved and isolated ruler who does not serve the greater *ka-tet* does not create the reciprocity and empathy needed to bind the parts of society into a whole. He is not behaving as a true *dinh* should. Although the disease predates him, and though he is, ultimately, another victim of the universal malaise, as the heir to the throne he carries the sins of both past kings and past kingdoms. As the center of cultural *ka-tet,* he must choose: either he must become the stable center of his kingdom and combat the malady of fragmentation or he must suffer the ultimate fate of his ancient forefathers. He can either perpetuate a cycle or pay penance, atone, and change. The disease of the land, and the disease of society, mirror the king's *ka.* In order to reverse the spin of the wheel and halt the process of dissolution, the king must look into the world-mirror but see the reflection of his own face, and the faces of his fathers.

When we first meet Roland in *The Gunslinger,* he is an anti-hero every bit as much as he is a hero. He is a man willing to sacrifice the members of his *ka-tet* in pursuit of his personal vision, just as his ancestors justified the drying of *khef* in the name of "progress" or "necessity." Susan Delgado, Roland's first and only true love, burns on a Charyou Tree fire because he will not be swayed from his quest long enough to save her. Jake Chambers falls into the abyss beneath the Cyclopean Mountains because Roland refuses to pause in his pursuit of the Man in Black. Even Roland's mother dies under his guns, those symbolic weapons of his fathers. As the trickster Walter hints during Roland's tarot reading in the golgotha, unless he, the Hanged Man, occupies the symbolic, central place of the Tower—unless he surrenders to the need of the world and focuses on the forces of *khef* which unite him to The Prisoner, The Lady of Shadows, The Sailor—his *ka* will encompass only Death, not Life. Unless he reclaims his humanity—which is, by its very definition, benevolence and respect for the needs of life—he will never reach the Tower, he will only be oppressed by its weight.

Roland, the isolated individual, is a survivor, but he is no more than a fragment of a larger, lost mosaic. He has no meaning. Like the landscape he travels, his soul has become a Wasteland. As we see in both *The Gunslinger* and the beginning of *The Drawing of the Three,* every time Roland betrays *khef,* he finds himself in an increasingly barren landscape. After his misadventures in Tull, Roland is almost killed by the parching dryness of the Mohaine Desert. After he lets Jake fall into the abyss, he finds himself first in the golgotha, an ancient bone-strewn killing ground, and then on the purgatorial beach of the Western Sea where lobstrosities devour two of his fingers and a chunk of one of his toes. It is only when Roland draws companions to him—first Jake, then Eddie and Susannah—that the landscape becomes more hospitable. At these points Roland, the isolated warrior focused only on himself and his desires, rediscovers his humanity. Significantly, it is at these points that he actually moves closer to the fulfillment of his quest. It is no accident that Roland discovers Jake at the Way Station, the place where he finds the water he needs to survive, and that with Jake he catches up with the Man in Black. Similarly, it is only after he has drawn Eddie and Susannah into his world (and out of their own personal hells) that he escapes the lobstrosity-infested beach of the Western Sea. And it is with Eddie and Susannah that he discovers the Bear-Turtle Beam, which will eventually lead him directly to his destination.

Unlike his ancestors, Roland is beginning to understand the relationship between his world and himself. He is beginning to learn from both his personal past and the past of Mid-World. Throughout the series, Eddie Dean accuses Roland of being a Tower-obsessed killing machine, but as Roland progresses on his journey, this accusation becomes less and less accurate. This Roland is determined to maintain his humanity despite the perils along his path. This Roland wants to live honorably, to live well and to live justly. And this is, in large part, what he strives to do over the course of the series.

In *The Gunslinger*, Roland lets Jake fall into the abyss beneath the Cyclopean Mountains, but in *The Waste Lands,* he risks his own life to save him from the Dutch Hill Mansion Demon and then from the boy-hungry gangs of Lud. When the wheel of *ka* turns and brings him back to a thinny so like the one he knew as a boy in Hambry, Roland tells his new companions about his betrayal of Susan Delgado, and then about the murder of his mother. It is almost as if he needs to confess his own sins against *khef* before he can move beyond them. This later Roland is conscious of himself and acknowledges his past mistakes. He recognizes his potential for treachery and fights against it. He is evolving, despite the twittering, goading, vindictive voice of the Man in Black. He is evolving from a mere warrior into a king.

Ka is destiny, but it is not just individual destiny. The sins Roland must expiate are not just his own, but those of all the rulers and cultures that came before him. *Ka* encompasses the past. Hence Roland's pilgrimage through the wastelands is also a penance for the human sacrifice of Arthur Eld's time, and for the time of the Speaking Rings. It is for the Great Old Ones and their hunger for power and their hubris, which drove them on to destroy the very fabric of the world. It's for the hierarchical inflexibility of Gilead-that-was, and the violent, destructive rebellion staged by Farson's army. It is his penance for, and his weapon against, the fragmentation generated by that gloating Prince of Chaos, the Crimson King.

Khef is what unites *dinh* and *ka-tet,* what unites king and kingdom, but it is also, ultimately, the force of the Beams and the force that keeps the multiple universes spinning like sequins around the needle of the Tower. In order to save the Tower, and in order to save all of the worlds that depend upon it, Roland must preserve the waters of *khef.* He must reenvision the world, redefine the cultural meaning of progress, and return to his lands a sense of what is truly sacred. In order to maintain the purity and strength of *khef,* he must, somehow, lessen the atrocity of Mid-World's history.

If each decision—personal, national, global—has a thousand different possible outcomes, each of those outcomes presents another possible future. Each of those futures will be different, and each will spin a unique timeline which exists only in that newborn world. But each of those future worlds remain linked, though they have no awareness of each other. Their link is the seed-moment that they came from, a seed held in the Eternal which encompasses every moment that ever has been or ever will be. They are all linked by the Tower.

In order to save the Tower, in order to ensure that there is a future for all these worlds and to ensure that more and more worlds are born, Roland must journey into the mythic history of his world—he must journey into our world. His quest, in the books to come, will be to save not a king or a kingdom but a single rose. A rose which sits in a vacant lot of a city which will someday become the technological Oz of the Great Old Ones, the foundation of their pride and the seed of their Fall. Before Roland, the great Warrior of the White, can save the Tower, he will have to risk his life to save a delicate flower whose yellow center is the womb of all worlds, and whose voice is the voice of *Yes* and of *Always*. He must save a simple rose which is, in our world, the symbol of unity and the symbol of love.

In their very imagery, the Tower and the Rose unite the symbolic male and the symbolic female, the two parts that join to give birth to the universe, and to life. In this unity they become One, which is simultaneously the center of all existence and the center of the integrated self. These two polarities, which seem so separate, bring together aggressive adventuring and passive nurturing, that within us which strives to conquer, to hold fast to high ideals, and that which is flexible enough to allow for human foibles, in ourselves and in others. They unite us with ourselves, our personal pasts, but also with the greater world. Although the Tower may reach higher than the heavens, and though the Rose may sing a single aria that rises from the deepest well of the universe, both are—as Roland sees and hears in his visions and his dreams—woven of many voices and faces. The Tower and Rose unite to form the self's axis, but they also function as a brutally honest mirror, exposing where we have betrayed both ourselves and the world. The two, which are One, contain the voices and faces of Roland's betrayed loves, the reminders of his sins against *khef*. And it is these, in the final reckoning, that Roland will have to face.

Roland journeys through the purgatorial wastelands of his world as both sinner and redeemer. He is simultaneously the king, the land, and the Everyman. Through the course of his journey he must come to Know Himself. And only in this way can he begin to approach the Tower.

INTRODUCTION PART TWO
VOLUMES V–VII
FOUR CHARACTERS
(AND A BUMBLER) IN SEARCH OF
AN AUTHOR: OR, A FEW REFLECTIONS
ON THE SIMILARITIES BETWEEN
FICTION AND REALITY

Spoiler's Warning: This Concordance *keeps no secrets. Read it only after you have finished all seven of the Dark Tower books.*

For those of us who have traveled with Roland Deschain from the wastes of the Mohaine Desert to the Castle of the Crimson King and then beyond, to the farthest reaches of End-World, the journey has been a long one, say thankya. For many Constant Readers, it has taken more than twenty years; for *sai* King, the travels have spanned more than thirty. And for Roland, who is able to leap over whole generations in pursuit of his quarry and his quest, the pilgrimage has lasted more than three hundred.[1] Yet as Eddie Dean points out at the beginning of *Wolves of the Calla,* time is elastic. Despite what we've been told about the accuracy of clocks, no two sixty-second periods are ever identical. Although a minute may move like dried mud while we're waiting or when we're bored, it speeds to the point of invisibility when we're in the throes of change. And what is a novel but a tale of transformation and discovery?

Over the course of the Dark Tower series, we witness tremendous transformation, both in our characters' natures and in the parameters of their quest. What began, in *The Gunslinger,* as the story of one man's obsessive pursuit of a goal becomes, in the final three books of our story, a tale of personal, and universal, redemption. By the time we reach the final page of our saga, we have witnessed so much. Roland, once a lone traveler willing to sacrifice anything and anyone to the achievement of his end, has drawn three companions to him[2] and has trained them to be gunslingers. With his new *tet*-mates, Roland discovers the Bear-Turtle

---

1. For an explanation, see my timeline, listed in Appendix II.

2. The three companions are Eddie, Susannah, and Jake. Roland's fourth companion is the billy-bumbler Oy. Although Oy doesn't train to be a gunslinger, he is an important member of Roland's *ka-tet.*

Beam and follows it to the haunted regions of End-World, where the Dark Tower sits. Along the Path of the Beam, the bonds of *khef,* which unite his new *ka-tet,* are tested and proved strong. And Roland, always an emotionally reticent man, rediscovers his ability to trust and to love. With this newfound knowledge, he can finally admit, and repent, all of his previous betrayals.

In many ways, the Dark Tower series falls into two parts: the adventures that Roland and his companions have in Mid-World (all of which were written before Stephen King's accident in 1999) and those that take place in the borderlands and End-World, which were penned after our author began to recover from the accident that almost claimed his life. The adventures our *ka-mates* have in both halves of their tale are dramatic, but the nature of the changes they undergo as a result are quite different. In the first four Tower books, the transformations our *tet* experiences are, in large part, personal. As well as bonding as a group, united in their vision of one day reaching the Dark Tower, each member has to battle his or her own demons. Eddie overcomes heroin addiction. Susannah's dual personalities of Detta and Odetta merge into a unified whole. Jake abandons his lonely life in New York to join his adopted father's quest, and Roland, who up until this point has been a self-obsessed loner, learns to value his *tet* as highly as he values his search for the linchpin of existence.[3] Yet if the first four Dark Tower books are about the *khef*[4] that binds self to *ka-tet,* in the final three novels, the responsibilities of *khef* ripple outward, encompassing not just the debt the individual owes to his *tet*-mates but the responsibilities each of us has to the greater world—or, in the case of the Dark Tower series, to the multiple worlds.

In the final three books of the Dark Tower series, Roland and his friends extend the scope of their quest. While keeping their ultimate goal in mind, they set out to accomplish a number of specific tasks that, when taken together, simultaneously halt the erosion of the Beams, frustrate the apocalyptic plans of the Crimson King, and work for the common good. First, in *Wolves of the Calla,* they destroy the robotic, green-cloaked horsemen who have been stealing children from Mid-World's borderlands for more than six generations.[5] By so doing, they not only liberate the people of the Callas but undermine the efficiency of the Breakers—those prisoners of the Crimson King who have been forced to erode the Beams with the equivalent of psychic battery acid. Second, in *Song of Susan-*

---

3. As Constant Readers will remember, in *The Gunslinger,* Roland allowed Jake to tumble into the abyss below the Cyclopean Mountains so that he could pursue the Man in Black. However, by the time he reaches the city of Lud in *The Waste Lands,* Roland puts his own life in danger to save Jake from the child-hungry gang of Grays.

4. The High Speech word *khef* means many different things, including water, birth, and life force. It implies all that is essential to existence. *Khef* is both individual and collective; it is the web that binds a *ka-tet.* Those who share *khef* share thoughts. Their destinies are linked, as are their life forces. Behind the multiple meanings of this term lies a philosophy of interconnectedness, a sense that all individuals, all events, are part of a greater pattern or plan. Our fates, for good or dis, are a result of both our own and our shared *khef.*

5. The Wolves steal one of every pair of prepubescent twins born in the Callas so that their masters in Thunderclap can extract the chemical that causes twin-telepathy. This chemical is then fed—in pill form—to the Breakers. (It increases their psychic abilities.) Unfortunately, once this chemical is removed from a child's brain, the child is roont, or ruined.

nah, Jake and Callahan manage to put Black Thirteen, the most evil of Maerlyn's magic balls, out of commission. And third, with the help of John Cullum (their Stoneham, Maine, *dan-tete*), Roland and Eddie begin to lay plans for the Tet Corporation, a company created to undermine the powers of the evil Sombra Corporation and to protect both the wild Rose, found in New York City's Vacant Lot, and our *kas-ka Gan,* Stephen King, creator of our tale.[6]

By accomplishing these tasks, our *tet* remains true to the Way of Eld, which demands that gunslingers protect the weak and vulnerable from those who would oppress or exploit them. Yet in defending the White against the ever-encroaching tide of the Outer Dark, our *tet* (like our author) comes under the shadow of *ka-shume,* the shadow of death.[7] In *The Dark Tower,* Roland and his friends destroy the Devar-Toi, or Breaker prison, and free the Breakers.[8] They halt the erosion of the Beams (which we are assured will regenerate), but Eddie Dean pays for this victory with his life. Not long after, when Roland and Jake travel to the year 1999 so that they can save their maker, Stephen King, from his predetermined collision with a Dodge minivan, Jake Chambers heaves his last breath. It seems that *ka* demands a life for a life, and though Stephen King survives his terrible accident, Jake does not.

And it is here, on Slab City Hill in Lovell, Maine, by the prostrate and profoundly injured body of our *kas-ka Gan,* and by the side of our gunslinger Roland, who grieves over the corpse of his adopted son, that I would like to pause. It is not a comfortable place to be—either for *sai* King, who lies bleeding in a ditch, or for us, who are unable to help—but it is an important place. Like Detta Walker's *Drawers,* this little patch of road in the year 1999 (when the *ka* of our world and the *ka* of Roland's world are united) is a place of power. It is a doorway between the rational and irrational worlds, a place where the veil is at its thinnest. And it is in this place where life and death meet that Roland accomplishes something worth discussing. By sacrificing what he loves above all else in order to save the life of the man who created his universe—a man who must live if the story of the Dark Tower is to exist in any world—Roland does what we assume is impossible. He stops the wheel of *ka* and alters its path.

Throughout the final three books of the Dark Tower series, we are told that, in the Keystone World we inhabit, there are no do-overs. Once an event has taken place, it cannot be changed. Yet it seems that this "truth" is not necessarily true. At the end of *Song of Susannah,* we are given Stephen King's obituary—ostensibly taken from the *Portland Sunday Telegram*—which states that King died at 6:02 PM on Saturday, June 20, 1999, at Northern Cumberland Memorial Hospital in Bridgton, Maine. Yet Stephen King didn't die. As we all know, he survived (albeit with terrible injuries) and returned to his computer keyboard to finish the last three books of his Dark Tower saga. On one level of the Tower, King's life was saved by paramedics and doctors, and that most fickle of mistresses, Lady Luck. But on another level, the one that we all inhabit when our

---

6. As Constant Readers all know, on Keystone Earth, the Dark Tower takes the form of a magical wild rose.

7. *Ka-shume* is the price one pays for altering *ka,* or the course of destiny.

8. Unfortunately, many of the Breakers don't appreciate this newfound freedom.

rational minds switch off and our imaginations wake up, Stephen King was saved by his characters.

When I was nineteen, I read a play by the Italian playwright Luigi Pirandello. The play was called *Six Characters in Search of an Author*. In it, six characters— all of whom have been abandoned by their original creator—go in search of a new person to pen their story. The person they turn to is a theater manager, already in the process of staging a different play. At first, the theater manager thinks these characters are either mad or joking, but as their traumatic story begins to unfold, he finds himself drawn into it. But no matter how the new playwright (for that is what he becomes) tries to bend the plot or alter the char- acters' temperaments, he can't. You see, the story already exists, from beginning to end, and the characters who live within its unwritten pages stubbornly hold on to their unique identities. What they want, and what they demand, is a writer who is willing to stand and be true—a person able to *facilitate* their tale and give it life, tragic as that tale turns out to be.

A number of years ago, in a writers' magazine, I read a firsthand account of an author's experience creating a character, and that, too, has remained with me. The author of the article (who was writing for an audience of apprentice authors) told of her experience with a character she called Bird. And though I lost the article long ago (which, like so many things in my life, I put in a place that at the time I had deemed "safe"), I still remember Bird. You see, Bird saved his author's life.

The story began when the author in question received a grant to finish her novel. She and her husband went to a remote cottage where the isolation and quiet would be perfect for the task at hand. However, it was winter, the cottage was old and cold, and the journey had been long. The woman and her husband shut the door and windows, turned on the stove, and decided to take a nap.

What felt like hours later, the writer was roused by Bird shaking her. Groggily, she opened her eyes and there was her character, standing by the bed. Bird put his hands by his throat. "I can't breathe!" he said. And then suddenly, the author realized what had happened. The old cottage was much less drafty than it had originally seemed, and the fire had eaten almost all of the oxygen. She and her husband, unconscious beside her, were asphyxiating.

Almost unable to move, the writer rolled onto the floor, crawled to the door, and managed to push it open. Fresh winter air wafted into the room, and both she and her husband survived. But only because of Bird. The explanation this author gave for her paranormal experience was this: She hadn't finished telling Bird's story yet, and Bird couldn't survive without the umbilical cord of thought which connected them. In order to live, Bird needed *her* to live, and Bird was determined to exist in the world. Self-serving heroism? Perhaps. But does that lessen the act's importance? Definitely not. Especially as far as the author was concerned.

I once read an article about the early-twentieth-century French explorer Alex- andra David-Neel. Evidently, while she studied with monks in Tibet, she learned how to create thought-forms by focused concentration. These thought-forms, which spring from the imagination of the creator, eventually gain an independent existence and can even (if they are especially powerful) become visible to other people. For me, characters are a kind of thought-form. An author creates them (or facilitates their passage into our world), but then the characters exist in the minds of many. They can live well beyond the lifespan of their creators; they can even exist independently of the book or story they originally inhabited. Think of Hamlet or Heathcliff or Dracula. Or of Roland Deschain.

There are some Dark Tower fans out there (including some very close to my heart) who like it when Stephen King appears in his films, but who are not comfortable with him entering his fiction. The reason? When King enters his own stories and his characters are shown to be just characters, it breaks the spell. When you think about it, such a reaction—even among devoted Tower junkies—isn't so surprising. Given the world we are expected to live in, where fact is supposed to be fact and fiction is supposed to be fiction, the two of them as separate as our waking lives and our dreaming lives, the events that take place in the final two books of the Dark Tower cycle are bound to confound us. The traditional *suspension of disbelief*, which we put on like a thinking cap whenever we sit down to read a fantasy adventure of any kind, isn't enough anymore. We have to allow the magic of *that* world—the world of the book—into *our* world, where we must earn a living, pay rent, eat, argue, and worry. In other words, those barriers we erect for our self-protection—barriers which separate our imaginative lives from our mundane ones—begin to break down. And if we're not careful, the guardrails of the rationalist, no-nonsense universe begin to snake out of control. And if those rails disappear, then we can free-fall into *todash* space, that no-place between worlds where monsters lurk.

As normal, functioning adults, we can't believe in surreal experiences any more than we can maintain that clapping our hands will bring Tinkerbell back to life. After all, we left all that behind in grade school. Or did we?

For me, the scenes where Stephen King's characters enter his life, *and change it*, are very powerful. They are powerful because they express the secret relationship King has with his creations. As every writer knows, writing is a two-way street. We may give birth to our characters, but our characters also change us. When Steve King writes about Eddie and Roland visiting him in Bridgton and then, many years later, Roland and Jake coming to him in his hour of deepest need, he is spinning a yarn, but he is also sharing with us the secret story that, in some deep part of his mind, he is telling himself. For the members of Roland's *ka-tet*, saving Stephen King is essential. But for Stephen King, his characters call him back from the void. Their need explains his survival. Some people have guardian angels. Authors have characters. This may be a strange thing to say, but all of you out there who write know it's true.

I suppose I have always believed that reality is a subjective affair. Of course, there are always events outside ourselves that are concrete and real, and that—small as we are—we cannot change. Yet in the backs of our minds, there is a voice that takes our experience in the world and weaves a story from it, for good or dis. And I suppose that it is this doorway, the doorway of the imagination, that is the ultimate Door to Anywhere. It gives us hope when there seems to be no hope, and it allows us to enter worlds that our rationalist culture tells us are unreal. I don't know about you, but I'm certainly glad the rationalists are wrong.

And so, my fellow Constant Readers, on this note, I will leave you. During my

1,396 days living and working in Mid-World,[9] I, too, have changed. But that's the nature of both life and fiction, isn't it? *Ka* turns, and the world moves on. If we're lucky, we move on with it.

Cam-a-cam-mal,
Pria-toi,
Gan delah.
(White Over Red,
Thus Gan Wills Ever.)

I wish you well.

Robin of the Calvins
January 26, 2005
Tell Gan Thankya.

---

9. 1+3+9+6=19. Are you surprised?

CHARACTERS,[1] MAGICAL OBJECTS, MAGICAL FORCES

. . . finally only three remained of the old world, three like dreadful cards from a terrible deck of tarot cards: gunslinger, man in black, and the Dark Tower.

I:140*

There's only three boxes to a man. . . . Best and highest is the head, with all the head's ideas and dreams. Next is the heart, with all our feelings of love and sadness and joy and happiness. . . . In the last box is all what we'd call low-commala: have a fuck, take a shit, maybe want to do someone a meanness for no reason . . .

V:630–31

A

AARON JAFFORDS
See JAFFORDS, AARON

ABAGAIL, MOTHER
In the alternate version of KANSAS which our *tet* traveled through in *Wizard and Glass*, JAKE CHAMBERS found a note tucked under a camper windshield. The note read, "The old woman from the dreams is in Nebraska. Her name is Abagail." Although our *tet* never meets this 108-year-old black woman, her path is nevertheless linked to Roland's. In STEPHEN KING's novel *The Stand*, this daughter of a former slave is a Warrior of the WHITE, and her archenemy is the evil RANDALL FLAGG.

In *Song of Susannah*, we discover that Mother Abagail's world is definitely linked to Roland's. Both the Red Death (the plague which devastated the END-WORLD town of FEDIC) and the superflu (the disease which wiped out

---

1. As all CONSTANT READERS know, the Dark Tower books contain many references to political and cultural figures from our world. Unless these figures play a central part in the narrative, they have been relegated to Appendix VI.

* This line comes from the 1982 version of *The Gunslinger*. It was cut from the revised 2003 edition.

99 percent of the people in Abagail's version of Earth) are both physical manifestations of a metaphysical illness. As the GREAT OLD ONES' technology fails
and the mechanical BEAMS collapse, such viruses and plagues are breaking out
on many levels of the TOWER.

IV:624, VI:405

ABRAHAM, DAUGHTER OF
See TASSENBAUM, IRENE

ADAMS, DIEGO
See CALLA BRYN STURGIS CHARACTERS: RANCHERS

ADAMS, RICHARD
See GUARDIANS OF THE BEAM: SHARDIK

ADAMS, SAREY
See ORIZA, SISTERS OF

**AFFILIATION
The Affiliation was the name given to the network of political and military alli-
ances that united MID-WORLD's baronies during Roland's youth. By the time
Roland reached adulthood, the Affiliation was in tatters, due in large part to the
bloody rebellions and terrible betrayals staged by THE GOOD MAN (JOHN
FARSON) and his followers.

The Affiliation—which played such a large part in *Wizard and Glass*—does
not figure directly in the following three books of the Dark Tower series. However, we can guess that the gunslingers who fought beside Roland in the final
battle of JERICHO HILL were all that remained of the Affiliation's forces. *See
also* DEMULLET'S COLUMN.

IV:148–49, IV:150, IV:151 *(in trouble because of Farson)*, IV:163 *(gunslingers' attitude toward it)*, IV:174–78 *(general info)*, IV:180 *(and Mejis's loyalty)*,
IV:181, IV:182, IV:189, IV:191, IV:199, IV:201, IV:204, IV:206, IV:211 *(hint
something is wrong in Hambry)*, IV:219 *(when Gilead falls, the Affiliation
ends)*, IV:221, IV:224, IV:225, IV:228, IV:229, IV:231–32, IV:250–51 *(Roland
asks Susan if she supports it)*, IV:255, IV:260 *("Affiliation brats")*, IV:277,
IV:302, IV:344, IV:350–51 *(implied—Inner Crescent)*, IV:359, IV:378, IV:381,
IV:411, IV:417 *(and the power of the White)*, IV:423, IV:430, IV:433, IV:438,
IV:501 *(Roland's ka-tet accused of being traitors)*

**AGELESS STRANGER (LEGION, MAERLYN)
In the original version of *The Gunslinger*, we learned that the Ageless Stranger
was actually just another name for the great sorcerer MAERLYN. Like WAL-
TER, he was a minion of the TOWER, only a more powerful one. As Walter said
in the GOLGOTHA, the Ageless Stranger *darkled* and *tincted*—in other words,
he could live simultaneously in all times. According to Walter, if Roland wanted
to reach the Tower, he would have to slay this formidable enemy.

In the new version of *The Gunslinger*, we learn something quite different
about this strange being. According to Walter the true name of the Ageless

Stranger is not Maerlyn but Legion, and he is a creature of END-WORLD. Roland must slay him in order to meet the Tower's present controller—the CRIMSON KING. Like Roland, we don't yet know whether slippery Walter is telling the truth or is spreading lies for his own ends.

See also MAERLYN *and* CRIMSON KING.

I:211–12, III:261, III:387

AIDAN
See TET CORPORATION: FOUNDING FATHERS: CULLUM, JOHN

**AILEEN OF GILEAD (AILEEN RITTER)
In the original version of *The Gunslinger*, we learned that Aileen was Roland's second important lover. He became intimate with her after his return from MEJIS but before GILEAD's fall. However, Aileen plays a smaller role in the 2003 version of *The Gunslinger*. Instead of remembering his love for beautiful, bright-eyed Aileen, Roland longingly recalls SUSAN DELGADO of HAMBRY. In the updated *Gunslinger*, Aileen becomes Roland's dancing companion, not his beloved, and the woman his parents want him to marry, not the girl he chooses to be his lover.

I:86, I:88, I:131, I:137, I:140

ALAIN JOHNS
See JOHNS, ALAIN

**ALAN
See ALLEN. *See also* DESCHAIN, GABRIELLE

ALBINO BEES
See MUTANTS

ALBRECHT
See VAMPIRES: TYPE THREE

ALEXANDER, BEN
See CAN-TOI

ALEXANDER, TRUMAN
See ENRICO, BALAZAR: BALAZAR'S MEN

ALIA (NURSE)
See TAHEEN: RAT-HEADED TAHEEN

**ALICE OF TULL (ALLIE)
In both versions of *The Gunslinger*, Roland meets Alice when she serves him from behind the plank bar of SHEB'S honky-tonk in TULL. Although she may once have been beautiful, by the time we see her she is straw-haired and scarred. Like so many people in MID-WORLD, Alice has been sucked dry—both physically and emotionally—by the sterile hardpan of the desert. The overall impression she gives is of a woman who has been worn down into an early

menopause. Her dirty blue dress is held at the strap by a safety pin and the livid scar corkscrewing across her forehead is emphasized, rather than hidden, by her face powder.

Although she initially reacts to him with hostility, Alice soon becomes Roland's lover. Unfortunately, she also becomes his victim. During the battle between Roland and SYLVIA PITTSTON's followers, Allie's former lover SHEB uses Alice as a human shield. Like so many of Roland's other friends and confidants, Alice dies under Roland's guns.

In the 2003 version of *The Gunslinger,* Allie still dies under Roland's guns, but before that she is the psychological victim of the MAN IN BLACK, also known as WALTER O'DIM. After he brings the weed-eater NORT back to life, Walter gives Nort a note for Allie. The note confides that Walter has planted a magical word in Nort's mind. The word is NINETEEN. If Allie says this word to him, the weed-eater will blurt out all that he saw in the world beyond.

But this message is a cruel trick, a Catch-22. Alice has always wanted to know what comes after this life, but attaining such forbidden knowledge will drive her mad. However, knowing the word, and not being able to speak it, is also guaranteed to drive her mad. In the end, Alice cannot control her curiosity and she says "Nineteen" to Nort, forcing him to spill forth all of his terrible, repressed secrets. Hence, when Roland aims his gun at her, a distressed Allie does not beg to be spared but begs to be killed so that her psychic torture will come to an end. Unfortunately for Alice, she ends up in the very place she wanted her imagination to escape—the LAND OF NINETEEN.

I:26–43 *(Nort's story 33–41),* I:45–47, I:52–54, I:58–59 *(dies),* I:60, I:64, I:77, I:78, I:79, I:118, I:131, I:143, I:156, II:231, III:42, III:44, III:127, VI:288

**ALLEN
In the original version of *The Gunslinger,* Allen was part of Roland's *ka-tel,* or class of apprentice gunslingers, and was one of the boys who witnessed Roland's battle with CORT. In the 2003 version of *The Gunslinger,* Allen's name is replaced with that of ALAIN JOHNS.

I:162, I:167–73 *(witnesses Roland's coming of age)*
SPELLED **ALAN:** II:121

**ALLGOOD, CUTHBERT (ARTHUR HEATH, LAUGHING BOY)
Talkative, brown-haired Cuthbert Allgood was Roland's beloved but restless childhood friend. Under the name Arthur Heath, he accompanied Roland and ALAIN JOHNS on Roland's dangerous MEJIS adventure, which figured so prominently in *Wizard and Glass.* Despite the comma of brown hair always falling over his forehead and his anarchic sense of humor, tall, narrow-hipped Bert was quite handsome. His dark, beautiful eyes made SUSAN DELGADO wonder whether—under different circumstances—she would have fallen in love with Cuthbert rather than with Roland.

Cuthbert had a kind nature but a complex and at times unpredictable character. Despite his constant stream of jokes and his deep-seated belief in human dignity (after all, it was Cuthbert who saved vulnerable SHEEMIE from the deadly bullying of the BIG COFFIN HUNTERS), Cuthbert's vision often took a dark turn. Like other apprentice gunslingers, Cuthbert was bred to be a killer, an instinct which showed itself when he secretly raged against CORT's chastisement in *The Gunslinger*. It also arose when, at age eleven, he and Roland informed upon the traitorous cook HAX and then watched him hang upon the gallows tree. (Cuthbert said he liked watching the dead man's jig.) Although our gunslinger Roland was Cuthbert's best friend, on occasion Cuthbert even felt a jealous rage rise up against his more ambitious companion.

Although Roland loved Cuthbert more than any of his other old friends, he also found Bert's constant humor irritating. Long before EDDIE DEAN took the job of being Roland Deschain's wisecracking mouthpiece, thin, dark-haired Cuthbert held that position. In fact, in *Song of Susannah* we find out that Eddie and Bert—both considered by Roland to be *ka-mais*, or *ka*'s fools—are actually twins. The two of them appeared to seven-year-old STEPHEN KING, who was on punishment duty in his uncle's barn. They saved him from the CRIMSON KING (who appeared in the form of tiny red spiders) and won him over to the cause of the WHITE.

Roland once predicted that Bert would die laughing, and so he did, on the battlefield of JERICHO HILL. Still holding the HORN OF ELD, the horn of Roland's fathers, a laughing but badly wounded Bert accompanied his friend in a final, suicidal charge against the legions of GRISSOM'S MEN. Unlucky Cuthbert was shot through the eye by RUDIN FILARO (another manifestation of Roland's longtime nemesis, WALTER) and entered the clearing at the end of the path at the much too young age of twenty-four. The Horn of Eld tumbled into the dust and Roland, perhaps out of grief, did not bother to retrieve it, a decision which he regrets greatly by the time he reaches the TOWER.

I:86, I:95, I:96–111, I:113, I:119, I:140, I:149 *(flashback)*, I:150–51 *(flashback: Cuthbert on Great Hall balcony with Roland)*, I:160, I:162, I:167–74 *(Roland's coming of age)*, I:197, II:52, II:121, II:176–77, II:207, II:231, II:355, II:394, III:33, III:41, III:60, III:124, III:242, III:268, III:270, III:278, III:346, III:377, III:417, IV:7, IV:57, IV:58, IV:59, IV:65, IV:119, IV:148 *("Mr. Arthur Heath")*, IV:151–53 *(Roland mentions him to Susan)*, IV:160–63 *(Rook skull prank and analysis of character. Physical description)*, IV:164, IV:174, IV:179–80 *(Mayor Thorin's party)*, IV:181–89 *(flashback to Sheriff Avery visit and false papers)*, IV:190–91, IV:191–210 *(Mayor Thorin's party cont., 192, raises eyebrow instead of nodding)*, IV:211, IV:218 *(physical description)*, IV:218–221 *(Travellers' Rest standoff)*, IV:224–30 *(Travellers' Rest standoff, 226–30 Sheriff Avery's office)*, IV:241, IV:245, IV:248, IV:255, IV:259–60 *("Little Coffin Hunters")*, IV:261–64 *(pigeons and message)*, IV:266–71 *(Depape learns true identity of Roland's ka-tet)*, IV:271–77, IV:282–89, IV:291 *(indirect reference)*, IV:336, IV:344–46, IV:347, IV:357–64 *(tension with Roland)*, IV:367, IV:368–69, IV:371, IV:380, IV:388–89, IV:392–93, IV:398–403, IV:408–19, IV:420, IV:426–42 *(428 described, 432 Roland's plan of attack; 436–39 flashback to Steven Deschain and Maerlyn's Grapefruit, 439 father, Robert Allgood)*, IV:450, IV:454–56, IV:463 *(indirect reference)*, IV:465, IV:473 *(Rook's skull left by Thorin's body)*, IV:474–80 *(taken for murder)*, IV:483, IV:487, IV:500, IV:503, IV:504 *(as Sheemie's savior)*, IV:505, IV:506, IV:508–13, IV:514–19, IV:523–24, IV:525 *(mentioned)*, IV:526, IV:529–32, IV:533–35 *(Jonas discovers part of plan)*, IV:535–36, IV:539, IV:540, IV:547–48, IV:549 *(indirect)*, IV:552–60 *(attacking Jonas's company)*,

IV:561 *(indirect)*, IV:573–75, IV:579–81, IV:583–84, IV:588–602 *(driving Farson's men into thinny)*, IV:608–11 *(Roland unconscious because of Maerlyn's ball)*, IV:620, IV:649, IV:658, IV:663, IV:664, E:150, E:187, V:59, V:78, V:79, V:84, V:85, V:164, V:170–72, V:182, V:218, V:240, V:347 *(Jericho Hill)*, V:400 *(indirect)*, V:410, V:590, VI:16 *(experienced a beamquake)*, VI:132 *(and Eddie)*, VI:292, VI:293, VII:118, VII:174 *(killed by an arrow through his eye, shot by Rudin Filaro)*, VII:219 *(Arthur Heath)*, VII:220, VII:270, VII:404, VII:465, VII:497, VII:552, VII:585, VII:695, VII:758, VII:762, VII:801, VII:819, VII:825, VII:829, W:38, W:39, W:41, W:42, W:65, W:269, W:276 *(knows that Roland doesn't joke)*

CUTHBERT'S FAMILY AND ASSOCIATES:

ALLGOOD, ROBERT (CUTHBERT'S FATHER): I:104, IV:225 *(fathers in general)*, IV:286, IV:399 *(fathers in general)*, IV:430 *(fathers in general)*, IV:435 *(fathers in general)*, IV:436–39, IV:547 *(fathers in general)*, IV:580 *(fathers in general)*, IV:620, V:85 *(father)*, V:590 *(indirect)*

CUTHBERT'S MOTHER: IV:282, IV:391 *(general)*

GLUEBOY: Glueboy was the horse Cuthbert rode during his MEJIS adventures. *For page references, see entries for* ALLGOOD, CUTHBERT, *Volume IV.*

HEATH, GEORGE: "Arthur Heath's" father. IV:152

THE LOOKOUT (ROOK'S SKULL): While in HAMBRY, Bert keeps this skull perched on the horn of his saddle. He also occasionally wears it as a comical pendant. Unfortunately, the BIG COFFIN HUNTERS use the Lookout to frame Cuthbert and the others for MAYOR HART THORIN's murder. IV:119, IV:160–61, IV:163 *(lookout)*, IV:180, IV:189, IV:190, IV:191, IV:218 *(as pendant)*, IV:224, IV:227, IV:233, IV:245, IV:259, IV:261, IV:273, IV:276, IV:344–45 *(lost)*, IV:380 *(Jonas finds)*, IV:409, IV:473, V:170

ALLGOOD, ROBERT
See ALLGOOD, CUTHBERT, *above*

ALORA FARM CHARACTERS
See SKIN-MAN: SKIN-MAN'S VICTIMS

AM
See PRIM

AMMIES, WHITE
See GILEAD'S WHITE AMMIES

AMOCO PREACHER
This hermit gained a quasi-religious following because of the wild sermons he preached while holding an ancient gasoline hose between his legs. (We don't know which was more popular among his followers—the sermons or the hose.) The words on the pump (AMOCO UNLEADED) were pretty much indecipherable, but this weird cult made AMOCO into the totem of a thunder god. They worshiped this destructive force with a mad slaughter of sheep.
I:154, III:97

ANDERSON, DELBERT
See DEAN, SUSANNAH: ODETTA HOLMES AND THE CIVIL RIGHTS
MOVEMENT: ODETTA'S "MOVEMENT" ASSOCIATES

ANDERSON, JUSTINE
See MAINE CHARACTERS: TOOTHAKER, ELVIRA

ANDERSON, RUPERT
See TREE VILLAGE CHARACTERS: ANDERSON, RUPERT

ANDOLINI, CLAUDIO
See BALAZAR, ENRICO: BALAZAR'S MEN

ANDOLINI, JACK
See BALAZAR, ENRICO: BALAZAR'S MEN

ANDREW (ANDREW FEENY)
See DEAN, SUSANNAH: ODETTA HOLMES'S ASSOCIATES

ANDREW (LOW MAN IN TUX)
See CAN-TOI

ANDRUS, CORTLAND
See CORT

ANDY
See NORTH CENTRAL POSITRONICS

ANGSTROM, JUNIOR
See MAINE CHARACTERS

ANSELM, HUGH
See CALLA BRYN STURGIS CHARACTERS: FARMERS (SMALLHOLD)

ANTASSI, OFFICER PAUL
See GUTTENBERG, FURTH, AND PATEL: DAMASCUS, TRUDY

APON
See GODS OF MID-WORLD: OLD STAR

ARDELIA SMACK
See WIDOW SMACK

ARMANEETA
The first time we hear about the existence of the SIGHE, or Mid-World's fairy-folk, is in the folktale which ROLAND recounts in *The Wind Through the Keyhole*. "Watch for the green sighe," the tax-collecting COVENANT MAN says to the tale's young hero, TIM ROSS. "She glows, so she does!" The sighe that the

Covenant Man mentions is actually his lovely but wicked little co-conspirator, Armaneeta.

Much like a sensual Tinkerbell, green little Armaneeta is four inches tall and has transparent wings on her back. These wings beat so quickly when she flies that they are almost invisible. (Their beating makes a purring sound.) Unlike Tinkerbell, Armaneeta is naked. (Tim can't tell whether her skin is green or it is just tinted by the bright green light that surrounds her.) Armaneeta's upturned, almond-shaped eyes are pupilless, and her laughter sounds like distant bells.

If the rest of the sighe are like Armaneeta, they are wonderful fliers. Despite her small size, she can soar upwards in dizzying spirals, higher than the tallest IRONWOODS, and then somersault down like a girl diving into a pool. Unfortunately, she is as treacherous as she is beautiful. At the Covenant Man's direction, flirtatious little Armaneeta leads Tim into the middle of the FAGONARD, and leaves him there.

W: 164 *(sighe)*, W:170 *(sighe)*, W:182–83 *(sighe)*, W:190–96 *(191—described, 193—named & deserts Tim)*, W:198, W:203, W:206 *(indirect)*, W:217, W:224, W:226, W:236 *(indirect)*, W:237

ARMITAGE, FRANK
See WARRIORS OF THE SCARLET EYE: DEVAR-TOI CHARACTERS: HUMANS

ARN
See DEBARIA CHARACTERS: JEFFERSON RANCH CHARACTERS

ARRA
See MANNI: CANTAB; *see also* CALLA BRYN STURGIS CHARACTERS: FARMERS (SMALLHOLD)

ARTHUR, KING
In our world, King Arthur (also known as King Arthur of the Round Table) was the legendary King of the Britons whose men went in search of the Holy Grail. In Roland's world, he was the ancient King of ALL-WORLD and the ancestor of the line of DESCHAIN. In *Song of Susannah,* pregnant MIA searches SUSANNAH DEAN's memory for a name for her CHAP and settles on one from the Arthurian storycycle. She chooses MORDRED, the name of Arthur's betraying son-nephew who was born to Arthur's sister after their incestuous coupling.

I:94, III:72, V:111 *(Tales of Arthur)*, VI:107 *(indirect)*

ARTHUR ELD
See ELD, ARTHUR

ASLAN
In *The Chronicles of Narnia,* Aslan is the great lion—King of the wood and the son of the great Emperor-Beyond-the-Sea. In the Dark Tower series, Aslan is a GUARDIAN OF THE BEAM.

According to the NORTH CENTRAL POSITRONICS Portable Guidance Module, DARIA, if Aslan is still alive he lives in the LAND OF ENDLESS

SNOWS. It is possible that the BLEEDING LION, which the TAHEEN FINLI O'TEGO says has been seen stalking to the north, is none other than Aslan.
W:234, W:250

ATWOOD, TIM
See BREAKERS: BRAUTIGAN, TED

AUNT BLUE
See DEAN, SUSANNAH: ODETTA HOLMES'S ASSOCIATES: SISTER BLUE

AUNT CORDELIA
See DELGADO, CORDELIA

AUNT MOLLY
See BREAKERS: BRAUTIGAN, TED

AUNT TALITHA
See RIVER CROSSING CHARACTERS

AVEN KAL
See APPENDIX I; see also BEAMS, PATH OF THE, in PORTALS

AVERY, BONNIE
See PIPER SCHOOL CHARACTERS

AVERY, HERK
See HAMBRY CHARACTERS: SHERIFF'S OFFICE

B

BABY MICHAEL
See MIA: MIA'S ASSOCIATES

BACHMAN, CLAUDIA Y INEZ
See CHARLIE THE CHOO-CHOO

BACHMAN, RICHARD
Richard Bachman began life as one of STEPHEN KING's pseudonyms, but as often happens with fictional characters, he soon assumed his own identity and made a break for freedom by taking up residence on one of the other levels of the DARK TOWER. During his lifetime, Bachman published five novels. These were *Rage, The Long Walk, Roadwork, The Running Man,* and *Thinner.* Although Bachman, a survivor of adult-onset leukemia, died of cancer of the pseudonym in 1985, additional manuscripts (including *The Regulators*) were discovered by

his widow, CLAUDIA INEZ BACHMAN (now Claudia Inez Eschelman), as late as 1994. This raises the inevitable question—did all of the Richard Bachmans, on all levels of the Tower, actually reach the clearing at the end of the path? Or is it possible that at least one Bachman still lives on? If so, we will see more of his books mysteriously appearing in our world.

VI:288, VI:392

BADMOUTH KING
See WARRIORS OF THE SCARLET EYE: CASSE ROI RUSSE: HUMANS: FEEMALO/FIMALO/FUMALO

BAEZ, VAN GOGH
See CAN-TOI

BAJ
See BREAKERS

BALAZAR, ENRICO (EMILIO BALAZAR, IL ROCHE)
In *The Drawing of the Three,* Enrico Balazar (also known as Emilio Balazar and *"Il Roche")* is a high-caliber big shot in New York's drug world. For a very short while, EDDIE DEAN works for him as a drug runner. Although his mob is based in BROOKLYN, Balazar's headquarters are in a Midtown bar called THE LEANING TOWER. The first time Roland sees the neon sign for this bar he thinks he is approaching the DARK TOWER itself.

Balazar is a second-generation Sicilian who looks like both a fat Italian peasant and a small-time Mafioso. However, despite his looks (and his nasty business methods), he has a quiet and cultured voice. He also has an associate's degree from the New York University Business School. One of Balazar's passions is building houses (or perhaps I should say palaces) out of cards. In fact, he once shot a man (THE MICK) for blowing down his creation.

In *The Drawing of the Three,* a very ill Roland and a naked Eddie Dean have a shoot-out with Balazar's men in the Leaning Tower. They escape after killing Balazar and his thugs. One of the most grisly weapons launched at Eddie during this fray is the decapitated head of his brother, HENRY DEAN. This shoot-out left some mighty bad *ka* between Eddie and this short, chubby, but murderous second-generation Sicilian, a *ka* destined to replay between Eddie and all of the Balazars on all levels of the Dark Tower.

At the beginning of *Wolves of the Calla,* Eddie Dean and JAKE CHAMBERS return to a TODASH version of NEW YORK and witness a much younger Balazar and two of his men harassing CALVIN TOWER, owner of the MANHATTAN RESTAURANT OF THE MIND. It turns out that Balazar has been hired by the SOMBRA CORPORATION (one of the many companies serving the CRIMSON KING) to "persuade" Tower to sell them the Vacant LOT, home of the ROSE. Caught in the invisible (or *dim*) *todash* state, neither Jake nor Eddie can intervene on Tower's behalf. However, they do get a good look at the document which Tower signed almost a year previously, promising not to sell the Lot for twelve months but giving Sombra first right of purchase after that time.

Deciding that the Rose must be kept safe from the WOLVES of New York every bit as much as the children of CALLA BRYN STURGIS must be kept safe from the Wolves of THUNDERCLAP, Eddie returns to New York (this time via the UNFOUND DOOR) to persuade Tower to sell the Lot to him rather than to Sombra. However, when he arrives at Tower's bookshop, he finds two of Balazar's "gentlemen"—namely JACK ANDOLINI and GEORGE BIONDI—leaning over Tower in his office, threatening to burn his precious books unless he agrees to sell. With a skillful use of Roland's gun (both the firing end and the sandalwood butt) Eddie sends a double message to Balazar, courtesy of his two thugs. First, Tower isn't selling the Lot to Sombra because he has already decided to sell to the TET CORPORATION. Second, Calvin Tower is now under the protection of people who make Balazar and his cohorts look like hippies attending WOODSTOCK.

Not surprisingly, Balazar doesn't listen. Acting on a tip given to the agents of the Crimson King by MIA, SUSANNAH DEAN's demon possessor, he sends his gunmen to EAST STONEHAM, MAINE, both to flush Tower out of hiding and to give Eddie and Roland (destined to enter our world here through the Unfound Door) an unpleasantly warm welcome. Thanks to Roland and Eddie's amazing gunslinger reflexes, they survive Balazar's ambush. They even manage to persuade an anally retentive Calvin Tower to sell them his Lot.

II:47, II:48, II:50, II:61, II:70, II:91–92, II:96, II:100, II:106, II:107–13 *(under discussion)*, II:113–20, II:121, II:124, II:125–35, II:137, II:140, II:142–50 *(shot)*, II:156, II:179, II:204, II:205, II:206, II:244, II:309, II:349, II:369, II:398, III:17, III:51, III:67, III:68, III:180, III:262, III:340, III:346, V:60, V:61, V:62–68, V:91, V:93, V:96, V:104, V:164, V:167, V:178, V:180, V:393, V:396, V:453, V:504, V:519, V:522, V:525, V:527 *(Il Roche)*, V:528, V:535–37, V:542, V:544, V:550, V:627–28, V:705, VI:28, VI:128, VI:139, VI:140, VI:142, VI:144, VI:146, VI:189, VI:277, VI:334

BALAZAR'S ENEMIES:
   MICK, THE: Fourteen years before our story takes place, this Irishman made the mistake of blowing down one of Balazar's card houses. Balazar shot him in the head with a .45 and instructed 'CIMI DRETTO and TRUMAN ALEXANDER to bury him under a chicken house somewhere outside of SEDONVILLE, CONNECTICUT. II:116–17

BALAZAR'S FAMILY:
   TIO VERONE: Balazar's uncle who told him never to trust a junkie. II:118
BALAZAR'S MEN: V:91, V:393, V:519, V:520, V:525 *(tet)*, V:535, V:542 *(goons)*, V:550, V:705, VI:129–48, VI:154 *(indirect)*, VI:162 *(indirect)*, VI:185, VI:194, VI:215
   ALEXANDER, TRUMAN: Truman Alexander died four years before our story takes place. He was one of the thugs who buried THE MICK under a chicken house in SEDONVILLE, CONNECTICUT. II:117
   ANDOLINI, CLAUDIO: JACK ANDOLINI's brother. He is also one of Balazar's bodyguards. II:113–14, II:115–20 *(watching Balazar build with cards)*, II:125–35, II:142–47 *(shot)*, II:150, V:528
   ANDOLINI, JACK (OLD DOUBLE-UGLY): Jack Andolini is known to his enemies as "Old Double-Ugly." Although his bulging forehead, bulky body, and tufted ears make him look like a Cro-Magnon, he's anything but stupid. Jack is Balazar's number-one lieutenant. Unfortunately for him,

Andolini meets an especially nasty end. Told by his boss to follow Eddie into the headquarters' lavatory, he ends up being pulled by Eddie onto the monster-infested beach of the WESTERN SEA, where he is devoured by LOBSTROSITIES.

In *Wolves of the Calla*, Old Double-Ugly is the man the big boss Balazar puts in charge of working over CALVIN TOWER and then ambushing EDDIE and Roland in EAST STONEHAM, MAINE. During the battle at the EAST STONEHAM GENERAL STORE, Andolini takes to calling Eddie "Slick." However, his sticks and stones break no one's bones, and at the end of the day, Andolini—a NEW YORK big shot—ends up sitting in a Maine county jail. Humiliating as Andolini might find this particular fate, it's better than the one that awaits one of his other selves on the *Drawing of the Three* level of the DARK TOWER, where he becomes a lobstrosity dinner special. II:91–95 *(tailing)*, II:105 *(in truck)*, II:106–13, II:115, II:122, II:125–41 *(eaten by lobstrosities)*, II:142, II:143, II:144, II:154, II:297, III:52, III:53, V:61, V:62–68, V:169, V:518–28, V:529, V:530 *(hoodlum)*, V:531, V:535, V:536, V:544, V:548, V:550, V:623, VI:130–48 *(present from 129; calls Eddie "Slick")*, VI:150, VI:154 *(indirect)*, VI:162, VI:164, VI:166, VI:168, VI:183, VI:184, VI:185, VI:189, VI:191, VI:192, VI:193, VI:194, VI:196, VI:211, VI:215, VII:40, VII:118, VII:396, VII:418, VII:426, VII:495

ANDOLINI FAMILY: V:527, V:582

BERNIE (OF BERNIE'S BARBER SHOP): EDDIE DEAN briefly considers holding up Bernie's Barber Shop (home of Balazar's weekend poker games) in order to scrape funds together so that CALVIN TOWER can leave NEW YORK CITY and escape the serious maiming that Balazar is sending his way. Instead, Tower borrows money from his old friend AARON DEEPNEAU and the two of them flee to MAINE. V:537

BIONDI, GEORGE (BIG NOSE): George Biondi is known as "Big George" to his friends and "Big Nose" to his enemies. During a game of Trivial Pursuit, he gives heroin-addicted HENRY DEAN his final deadly fix. "Big Nose" Biondi isn't as intelligent as his gun-bunny workmate, JACK ANDOLINI. When EDDIE sees this particular piece of pond scum during the battle at the EAST STONEHAM GENERAL STORE, he's still blue from the bruises Eddie gave him in the backroom office of CALVIN TOWER's bookshop. Biondi doesn't have to worry about his looks for long, though. Eddie uses Roland's gun to (literally) blow the bruises away. (And the rest of his face as well.) II:114, II:119–20, II:123–24, II:132–33, II:150–51, V:61, V:62–68, V:93 *(Big Nose)*, V:98, V:518–28, V:530 *(hoodlum)*, V:535, V:536, V:548, VI:140 *(present from 129; Eddie blows his face off)*, VI:143, VI:166, VII:397, VII:495

MOTHER: VI:140

BLAKE, KEVIN: In *The Drawing of the Three*, redheaded Kevin Blake is one of the hit men who plays a final (and deadly) game of Trivial Pursuit with HENRY DEAN. During the shoot-out which follows, he lobs Henry's decapitated head at EDDIE. II:123–24, II:151–52, II:153, V:61, V:544

DARIO: Although he is one of Balazar's "gentlemen," during the LEAN-

ING TOWER'S shoot-out he is accidentally killed by TRICKS POSTINO's incredible Rambo machine. II:148–49

DRETTO, CARLOCIMI ('CIMI): One of Balazar's personal bodyguards. In *The Drawing of the Three* we learn that 'Cimi and ALEXANDER TRUMAN buried THE MICK under a chicken house in CONNECTICUT. The Mick's crime? Blowing down Balazar's house of cards. II:113–14, II:115–20 *(watches Balazar build a house of cards)*, II:124, II:125, II:129, II:133, II:142–47 *(shot)*, V:528, V:544

> **BITCH-OF-A-WIFE:** II:115–16

> **FATHER:** II:116

> **LA MONSTRA:** 'Cimi's much-hated mother-in-law. II:115–16

GINELLI: Ginelli owns both the FOUR FATHERS Restaurant and the Ginelli's Pizza truck. He is a mobster in cahoots with Balazar. II:91–95 *(his truck follows Eddie)*, II:105, II:349

HASPIO, JIMMY: II:123–24, II:150 *(shot)*

POSTINO, TRICKS: One of Balazar's thugs. With a name like Tricks, this guy couldn't become anything other than a hit man. He is part of the deadly Trivial Pursuit game that takes place in Balazar's headquarters. II:114, II:123–24, II:132–33, II:142–49 *(shot)*, II:151, V:528, V:536, VI:134 *(present from 129; dies in this section)*, VI:135

VECHHIO, RUDY: II:151

VINCENT, COL: Col Vincent is a "glorified goofer" with a big yellow-toothed grin. He smells like old sweat. II:91–95 *(tailing)*, II:105 *(in truck)*, II:106–13, II:120, II:122, II:125–35 *(present)*

BALAZAR'S NASSAU CONNECTION:

SALLOW BRITISH MAN: While working as Balazar's cocaine mule in NASSAU, EDDIE DEAN has to have dealings with this unsavory and untrustworthy character. This guy tries to give Eddie Dean poison rather than a heroin fix. He hopes to kill Eddie or at least screw up his drug run and rob him. Eddie wins out. II:47–51, II:58, V:453 *(sallow thing)*

WILSON, WILLIAM: William Wilson is a soft-spoken American who specializes in strapping drugs onto smugglers. Although he doesn't know it, he shares a name with the narrator of Edgar Allan Poe's famous story entitled "William Wilson." II:57, II:74

BALDY ANDERSON
   See TREE VILLAGE CHARACTERS: ANDERSON, RUPERT

'BAMA
   See CHAMBERS, JAKE

BAMBRY, JOHN
   See DEAN, SUSANNAH: ODETTA HOLMES AND THE CIVIL RIGHTS MOVEMENT: ODETTA'S "MOVEMENT" ASSOCIATES

BAMBRY, LESTER
   See DEAN, SUSANNAH: ODETTA HOLMES AND THE CIVIL RIGHTS MOVEMENT: ODETTA'S "MOVEMENT" ASSOCIATES

BANDERLY
　　See DEBARIA CHARACTERS: SALT MINE CHARACTERS

BANDY BROOKS
　　See CALLAHAN, FATHER DONALD FRANK: CALLAHAN'S HIDDEN HIGHWAYS ASSOCIATES

BANGO SKANK
　　See SKANK, BANGO

BARBARIANS WITH BLUE FACES
　　See FARSON, JOHN: FARSON'S MEN

BARKER, JUNIOR
　　See MAINE CHARACTERS

BARLOW, KURT
　　See VAMPIRES: TYPE ONE

BARONY COVENANT MAN
　　See WALTER: WALTER'S ALIASES

BARONY TAX MAN
　　See WALTER: WALTER'S ALIASES

BASALE, MIGUEL
　　See DEAN, SUSANNAH: DETTA WALKER'S ASSOCIATES

BEAM BOY
In the seventh book of the Dark Tower series, SHEEMIE RUIZ (now a BREAKER in THUNDERCLAP) meets this human incarnation of the BEAM. To Sheemie, the Beam Boy looks like JAKE CHAMBERS, only his face is covered with blood, one of his eyes has been poked out, and he limps. Although this dream-creature was beautiful when he arose from the PRIM, by the time Sheemie sees him he is near collapse. Despite the torture he has undergone, the Beam Boy still loves the world. If our *tet* can save him, he promises to bring magic back to the multiverse.
　　VII:333–36, VII:338, VII:378 *(Beam says thankya)*, VII:389 *(Beam says thankya)*, VII:391 *(Beam speaks to Sheemie)*, VII:400

BEAM BREAKERS
　　See BREAKERS

BEAMS
　　See entry in PORTALS

BEAMS, GUARDIANS OF THE
　　See GUARDIANS OF THE BEAM

BEAR GUARDIAN
See GUARDIANS OF THE BEAM

BEASLEY, JESSICA
See DEAN, SUSANNAH: ODETTA HOLMES'S ASSOCIATES

BEAST, THE
See GUARDIANS OF THE BEAM

BECKHARDT, DICK
See MAINE CHARACTERS

BEECH, MRS.
See HAMBRY CHARACTERS: OTHER CHARACTERS

BEELIE TOWN CHARACTERS
Beelie Town played a small but important role in the story of the SKIN-MAN, which ROLAND recounts in *Wind Through the Keyhole*. According to STROTHER and PICKENS, DEBARIA's two not-so-good deputies, Beelie was once a MILITIA OUTPOST and the location of BEELIE STOCKADE. It was here that Debaria's circuit judge sent thieves, murderers, and card cheats. According to Pickens, witches and warlocks were sent here too. Anyone who spent time in the stockade had a blue ring tattooed around his ankle, though whether the tattoo was part of a convict's punishment or just identification to prevent him from running away from his work gang, no one can remember.
   Not only was Beelie the location of the stockade, but it was also a hanging ground. Beelie's hangings were like carnivals, complete with jugglers and booths and dogfights. Many of those who came to witness the executions brought picnic lunches and made a day of it. Five years after the close of the stockade and the departure of the militia, Beelie died a final death. Since the town was no longer protected by fighting men, harriers tore through it. Some say that the harriers worked for JOHN FARSON. By the time ROLAND DESCHAIN and JAMIE DeCURRY began their search for any tattooed SALTIES who spent time in BEELIE STOCKADE, the stockade had been closed for ten years.
   CANNIBAL WHO ATE HIS WIFE: This hungry fellow was hanged for his crime. W:103
   CARD CHEADS: W:102
   CIRCUIT JUDGE: Once upon a bye, the circuit judge sent thieves, murderers, and card cheats to BEELIE STOCKADE. According to PICKENS, he sent witches and warlocks here too. W:102
   HARRIERS WHO TORE THROUGH IT: After the MILITIA left BEELIE STOCKADE, these harriers tore through the town. Some people say that the harriers were JOHN FARSON's MEN. W:102
   MILITIA: Once upon a bye, there was a militia outpost in BEELIE, and the BEELIE STOCKADE was their place of business. W:102, W:103
   MURDERERS: W:102
   THIEVES: W:102

WITCHES AND WARLOCKS: According to the CIRCUIT JUDGE, practicing magic was a crime. Hence, he sent witches and warlocks to the BEELIE STOCKADE. W:102

BEEMAN
See CAN-TOI

BEEMER, CHARLIE
See MAINE CHARACTERS

BEEMER, RHODA
See MAINE CHARACTERS

BEEMER, RUTH
See MAINE CHARACTERS

BEESFORD-ON-ARTEN, CHARACTERS
See FARSON: FARSON SUPPORTERS; see also DESCHAIN, GABRIELLE

BENDS O' THE RAINBOW
See MAERLYN'S RAINBOW

BENZYCK, OFFICER (BENZYCK O' THE WATCH)
Benzyck is a rather chubby officer of the law. Each day he gives a ticket to REVEREND EARL HARRIGAN (CHURCH OF THE HOLY GOD-BOMB) for parking illegally on the corner of SECOND AVENUE.
    VI:258–59, VI:260 (Benzyck o' the Watch), VI:313, VI:316, VI:319, VI:320

BERNARDO
See CALLA BRYN STURGIS CHARACTERS: OTHER CHARACTERS

BERNIE'S BARBER SHOP
See BALAZAR, ENRICO: BALAZAR'S MEN

BERNSTEIN, MRS.
See DEAN, EDDIE: EDDIE'S PAST ASSOCIATES

BERTOLLO, DORA
See DEAN, EDDIE: EDDIE'S PAST ASSOCIATES

BESSA
See GODS OF MID-WORLD

BESSIE
See DANDELO

BIBLICAL FIGURES (OUR WORLD)
See APPENDIX VI

BIG COFFIN HUNTERS

The Big Coffin Hunters (also known as REGULATORS) were the nasty harriers that Roland and his childhood friends CUTHBERT ALLGOOD and ALAIN JOHNS were forced to fight in HAMBRY. Their name came from the blue coffin-shaped tattoos located on the webbing between right thumb and forefinger. Although they initially hid their true allegiance from Roland and his friends, Roland's *ka-tet* eventually found out that the Big Coffin Hunters worked for FARSON. Despite appearances, the Big Coffin Hunters held much of the power in MEJIS (much more than the mayor, HART THORIN) and were working to bring down the AFFILIATION.

In *Wolves of the Calla*, we find out that many of PERE CALLAHAN's LOW MEN bear similar coffin-shaped tattoos. Evidently, this sinister insignia is a *sigul* of the CRIMSON KING. EDDIE DEAN believes that BALAZAR and his associates are our world's version of the Big Coffin Hunters.

IV:65, IV:115–16, IV:142 *(as harriers and outlaws)*, IV:144, IV:154–55 *(hired by Rimer)*, IV:155 *(coffin tattoo)*, IV:177, IV:214, IV:225, IV:228, IV:234, IV:260, IV:265–66 *(tied to Vi Castas Mining Co.)*, IV:266 *(regulator tattoos)*, IV:285, IV:290, IV:292, IV:301, IV:305, IV:327, IV:342, IV:344 *(indirect reference)*, IV:347, IV:360, IV:374, IV:376, IV:424, IV:453, IV:468, IV:470, IV:472, IV:473, IV:487, IV:488, IV:498, IV:506, IV:508, IV:509, IV:546, IV:645, V:100, V:104, V:291, V:469, V:516

INDIVIDUAL BIG COFFIN HUNTERS:

DEPAPE, ROY: Roy Depape was a twenty-five-year-old redhead who wore gold-rimmed glasses. His laughter sounded like the braying of a loud donkey. Roy was obsessed with a fifteen-year-old whore named DEBORAH who wouldn't give up working. This often put Roy in a foul humor. In fact, the standoff at The TRAVELLERS' REST was the direct result of Depape's black mood and his desire to vent his rage on innocent SHEEMIE. As punishment for the events at the Rest, ELDRED JONAS, leader of the Coffin Hunters, sent Depape to the town of RITZY. While there, Depape learned Roland's true identity.

Although not particularly clever, Depape had plenty of spite in him. On Jonas's orders, he killed HART THORIN and then framed Roland, CUTHBERT, and ALAIN for the murder. To incriminate the boys, he left both Cuthbert's LOOKOUT and a drawing of FARSON's *sigul* next to Thorin's corpse. IV:65, IV:116, IV:119 *(age)*, IV:141, IV:142 *(indirect reference)*, IV:154–55, IV:172, IV:173, IV:175–76, IV:214–22 *(Travellers' Rest standoff. 214 blue coffins. 215 described)*, IV:224–32 *(Travellers' Rest standoff continued. 230 red hair, 231 glasses)*, IV:265–71 *(goes to Ritzy and learns Roland's identity)*, IV:271, IV:285, IV:286, IV:292 *(red hair)*, IV:301, IV:305, IV:318, IV:347–49, IV:350, IV:352, IV:363, IV:371, IV:377, IV:378, IV:382, IV:385, IV:386, IV:403–5, IV:420–25, IV:451, IV:462–63, IV:472–73 *(kills Thorin. Leaves Cuthbert's Lookout and Farson's sigul)*, IV:478, IV:480, IV:483–85, IV:487–93, IV:498–99, IV:503, IV:522, IV:528, IV:539, IV:542–46 *(present for action)*, IV:553–57 *(557 killed by Roland)*, VI:187, VI:242, VII:220

DEBORAH (GERT MOGGINS): Deborah (whose real name was Gert Moggins) was Depape's fifteen-year-old whore. Deborah was also known as "Her Nibs," "Her Majesty," and "Roy's Coronation Cunt." Gert preferred to call herself a "cotton-gilly." IV:173 *(described)*, IV:214–15, IV:266, IV:447, IV:605

DEPAPE, AMOS: Brother of ROY DEPAPE. Roland thought he was stung to death by a snake. Actually, he was fucked to death by SUSANNAH DEAN's demon possessor, MIA, who (while still a wraith) functioned as a kind of sexual VAMPIRE. VI:242

JONAS, ELDRED: Eldred Jonas was the leader of the Big Coffin Hunters. He was a failed gunslinger who was lamed in one leg by CORT's father, FARDO, in GILEAD. Like other failed gunslingers, limping Jonas was sent west, and in bitterness he forsook the WHITE and took up the cause of JOHN FARSON and the OUTER DARK.

Jonas had tufted eyebrows, long silky white hair, and a white mustache. Often described as a white-haired wolf, he seemed to have held some palaver with the MANNI since he knew about travel between worlds. Jonas's back was covered with scars which he said were inflicted in GARLAN. We don't know why. Jonas became CORAL THORIN's lover. Roland killed him after taking MAERLYN'S GRAPEFRUIT from him. I:86, IV:65, IV:115–17 *(described)*, IV:119, IV:121, IV:130 *(indirect reference)*, IV:141, IV:142, IV:154 *(described)*, IV:155, IV:172–78 *(failed gunslinger. 175 travels through "special doors" to other worlds!)*, IV:191–210 *(Thorin's party. 195–97 described; 206–8; 209)*, IV:211, IV:213 *(called "Il Spectro")*, IV:214, IV:220, IV:221–22 *(joins standoff at Travellers' Rest)*, IV:224–32 *(227 with Sheriff Avery; 230–32 Big Coffin Hunters' palaver)*, IV:235, IV:245, IV:249, IV:266, IV:269, IV:270, IV:271, IV:285, IV:286, IV:292, IV:301, IV:318, IV:327, IV:328–29 *(with Cordelia)*, IV:330, IV:331, IV:336, IV:342, IV:347–53 *(349 tufted eyebrows)*, IV:356, IV:358, IV:362–64, IV:367–68, IV:371–74 *(Cordelia tells him about Roland and Susan)*, IV:375–80 *(as white-haired wolf; 380 finds rook's skull!)*, IV:384–87, IV:388, IV:390–92 *(defaces Bar K)*, IV:393–94 *(defacement continued)*, IV:399–400, IV:401, IV:403–8 *(sent west by Fardo)*, IV:411, IV:420–25, IV:434, IV:443, IV:448, IV:453, IV:456, IV:460, IV:466, IV:472, IV:473, IV:474, IV:478–80 *(479 Roland reveals that Jonas is a failed gunslinger)*, IV:483–85, IV:487–93, IV:496, IV:500, IV:501, IV:502, IV:515, IV:519–23, IV:525 *(mentioned)*, IV:527–29, IV:530, IV:532–35, IV:536, IV:537–46, IV:548, IV:553–60 *(attacked by Roland's ka-tet; 559 killed by Roland)*, IV:561–62, IV:570, IV:579, IV:586, IV:592, IV:628, IV:645, IV:646, IV:649, IV:664, E:195, V:187, VI:242, VII:175, VII:297, VII:336

REYNOLDS, CLAY: Although not as sly as JONAS, Clay Reynolds— the final member of the Coffin Hunter *ka-tet*—was smarter than ROY DEPAPE. Although he walked with his left foot turned in, Reynolds was a vain womanizer who liked to swirl his fancy silk-lined cloak. He was either a redhead (see IV:173 and IV:537) or black-haired (IV:226).

Along with CORAL THORIN, Reynolds was one of the few of Roland's enemies to escape HAMBRY alive. Clay and Coral became lovers and formed a gang of professional bank robbers. Their gang was eventually trapped by a sheriff in the town of OAKLEY. Reynolds ended up dancing the hanged man's jig. IV:65, IV:116, IV:119, IV:141, IV:142

(indirect reference), IV:154–55, IV:173–78 *(173 red hair)*, IV:214–22 *(Travellers' Rest standoff)*, IV:224–32 *(standoff continued. 226 black hair)*, IV:245, IV:265, IV:269, IV:270, IV:272, IV:292, IV:298 *(tracks and left foot)*, IV:301, IV:347–49 *(more intelligent than Depape)*, IV:352, IV:363–64, IV:367–68, IV:371, IV:377, IV:378, IV:383, IV:385–86, IV:404, IV:420–25, IV:451–52, IV:470–71 *(stabs Rimer)*, IV:480, IV:483–85, IV:487–93, IV:521–23, IV:527–29, IV:532–35, IV:537–46, IV:548–49, IV:558, IV:565–70 *(Sheemie follows Reynolds and Susan)*, IV:585–87, IV:603–8 *(puts rope around Susan's neck. Present as she burns)*, IV:623 *(Bank robber and Coral Thorin's lover. Both killed)*, V:187

LITTLE COFFIN HUNTERS: This is the term HAMBRY folk used for Roland's *ka-tet*. Needless to say, Roland didn't like it much. IV:260, IV:287

BIG SKY DADDY
See GODS OF MID-WORLD

BILLY-BUMBLERS/THROCKEN (GENERAL INFORMATION)

A billy-bumbler looks like a cross between a raccoon, a woodchuck, and a dachshund. Bumblers have black-and-gray-striped fur and lovely gold-ringed eyes. Although they sometimes wag their tails like dogs, they are much more intelligent than canines. Before the world moved on, every barony castle in MID-WORLD kept a dozen or so. They were excellent ratters and sheep herders.

In the days they lived with men, bumblers could parrot the words they heard; some could even count and add. By the time Roland draws his American *ka-tet* into Mid-World, most bumblers wander the land in wild but harmless packs. Few remember their old skills, though Jake's pet OY does.

According to BIX, the ferryman whom we meet in *The Wind Through the Keyhole,* a bumbler's bright (or talent) is his ability to predict the coming of the terrible storm known as a STARKBLAST. In olden days, bumblers' strange pre-storm behavior was often the only warning farmers had about this impending disaster. Several days before a starkblast was due to roll along the PATH OF THE BEAM, a bumbler would sit down and turn to face the direction of the coming storm. He would lift his nose to the wind, prick his ears, and curl his tail around himself. When the storm was about to blow, the throcken would begin turning in circles. This advance warning was urgently needed by farmers in places frequently hit by starkblasts, such as those living in the GREAT WOODS north of NEW CANAAN.

Because of their special talent, Bumblers play a large role in *The Wind Through the Keyhole.* In the folktale which young Roland recounts to the young BILL STREETER in DEBARIA's JAIL, the youthful hero TIM ROSS met a throcket of bumblers in the forest beyond the FAGONARD. While traveling along the PATH OF THE BEAM toward the NORTH FOREST KINNOCK DOGAN, Tim spotted a half dozen of these pretty creatures sitting on a fallen ironwood tree, their snouts raised to the crescent moon, their eyes gleaming like jewels. Thanks to the warning given to him by the WIDOW SMACK, Tim understood that the bumblers' behavior indicated that a deadly starkblast was on its way. Roland's vivid description of these bumblers is drawn from a hand-colored woodcut which he remembers from his childhood days. It was one of a dozen well-loved illustrations from *Magic Tales of the Eld,* a book that his mother, GABRIELLE DESCHAIN, read to him when he was a boy.

III:18, III:159, III:164, III:220–22, III:253, III:327, W:3, W:4, W:5, W:7 *(throcken),* W:8, W:9, W:13, W:14 *(throcken never wrong about starkblast),* W:15, W:16, W:17, W:18, W:23 *(Oy and starkblast),* W:26, W:28, W:68 *(and starkblast),* W:151 *(many bumblers is a throcket)* W:166 *(dancing throcken),* W:218 *(runs from light),* W:220–21 *(dancing throcken),* W:224, W:225, W:226, W:227, W:232, W:305

See also OY

OLD GROOM FROM ROLAND'S YOUTH WHO PRAISED BUMBLERS: III:221, III:253–54

BILL STREETER
See STREETER, YOUNG BILL; *for Young Bill's father, see* SKIN-MAN: SKIN-MAN'S VICTIMS: JEFFERSON RANCH; *see also* DEBARIA CHARACTERS

BILLY THE KID
See GUNSLINGERS (OUR WORLD)

BIONDI, GEORGE
See BALAZAR, ENRICO: BALAZAR'S MEN

BIRD GUARDIAN
See GUARDIANS OF THE BEAM

BIRDMEN
See TAHEEN

BISHOP DUGAN
See CALLAHAN, FATHER DONALD FRANK: CALLAHAN'S OTHER PAST ASSOCIATES

BISSETTE, LEN
See PIPER SCHOOL CHARACTERS

BIX
ROLAND, EDDIE, SUSANNAH, JAKE, and OY come across Bix's bright green boathouse and red-and-yellow striped ferry near the beginning of *The Wind Through the Keyhole.* (At this particular point in the tale, our *tet* has just left the GREEN PALACE and is traveling southeast along the PATH OF THE BEAM toward CALLA BRYN STURGIS.) When Bix sees the big guns that Roland and Eddie wear, he drops to one knee, puts an arthritis-swollen fist to his forehead And cries, "Hile gunslinger. I salute thee." Obviously, Bix is loyal to both the WHITE and to GILEAD-that-was.

In the conversation that follows, Bix states that he has been running his ferry across the RIVER WHYE for ninety years. Once upon a bye, there had been farms and trading posts on both sides of the river, but by the time our *tet* arrives and asks for passage, his services have not been needed for years. Although he has lost count of his birthdays, Bix knows that he is over a hundred-and-twenty years old. Considering his age, Bix is doing extremely well. Although he has trouble carrying heavy picnic baskets, he still manages to work his ferry. Bix wears a vast straw hat, baggy green pants, and longboots. On the top half of his body he wears a thin white slinkum.

After feeding our *tet* some well-stuffed fish popkins (the river is full of shannies), Bix takes them across the river. In order to do this Bix attaches a ringbolt to the top of the post which sits like a mast in the center of the ferry, then he hooks the ringbolt to the cable which runs across the river. To move the ferry, he cranks a large metal crank shaped like a block Z. Not surprisingly, the crank is stamped with the NORTH CENTRAL POSITRONICS logo. According to Bix, both the steel cable and the crank were at the ferry when he took his job more than ninety years previously. He thinks that they came from an underground BUNKER or DOGAN, located near the GREEN PALACE. Bix says that this underground area goes on for miles, and that it is full of things that belonged to the OLD PEOPLE. Strange, tooth-rattling music still plays from overhead speakers. If you stay there too long, you break out in sores, puke, and start to lose your teeth.

During the hour it takes to cross the river, Bix asks our *tet* about the fate of LUD. (Long ago, Bix had a woman in that city and so he remembers both BLAINE the Insane Mono, and Blaine's suicidal twin, PATRICIA.) As our *tet* disembarks, he warns them about the ASIMOV ROBOT, ANDY, whom our friends are destined to meet in Calla Bryn Sturgis. ("If you see that cussed Andy, tell him I don't want no songs, and I don't want my gods-damned horrascope read!") It is Bix who reminds Roland about the coming of the STARKBLAST, and who tells our *tet* about the GOOK meetinghouse where they can rest and be safe from the storm. Unfortunately, the storm comes much more quickly than anyone expects. We can only hope that Bix made it back to his boathouse in time to take cover.

W:6 *(indirect),* W:7 *(indirect),* W:8–16, W:21, W:29

BLACK AMMIES
See SERENITY, SISTERS OF

BLACKIE
See WALTER: WALTER'S ALIASES: COVENANT MAN

BLACK MAN IN GRAY FATIGUES
See HARRIGAN, REVEREND EARL: CROWD

BLACK MAN IN JAIL CELL
See GAN

BLACK MAN WITH WALKMAN
EDDIE DEAN and JAKE CHAMBERS first see this man singing along with his Walkman when they travel via TODASH to 1977 NEW YORK. While preparing himself to travel back to 1977 through the magical UNFOUND DOOR, Eddie fixes the date in his mind by imagining this man walking in front of CHEW CHEW MAMA'S.
V:48, V:231, V:514

BLACK THIRTEEN
   See MAERLYN'S RAINBOW

BLACKBIRD, LADY
   See DEAN, SUSANNAH

BLACKBIRD MOMMY
   See DEAN, SUSANNAH

BLAINE
   See NORTH CENTRAL POSITRONICS

BLAKE, KEVIN
   See BALAZAR, ENRICO: BALAZAR'S MEN

BLEEDING LION
Even though the CRIMSON KING's followers in END-WORLD are systemati-
cally and purposefully eroding the final two BEAMS so that the DARK TOWER
will collapse and the macroverse will blink out of existence, they have their own
set of superstitions concerning the fearful end of the world and about how their
master's plans may yet be thwarted. Though we don't know the details of these
superstitions, we do know that at least one concerns a Bleeding Lion stalking
to the north. Another is about a gunslinger-man coming out of the west to save
the Tower. There is a good chance that the Bleeding Lion is none other than the
LION GUARDIAN, ASLAN.
   VII:238, VII:239

BLUE
   See SUSANNAH DEAN: ODETTA HOLMES'S ASSOCIATES

BLUE DEER
   See MUTANTS: ANIMALS, BIRDS, REPTILES

BLUE-FACED BARBARIANS
   See FARSON, JOHN: FARSON'S MEN

BLUE LADY
   See DEAN, SUSANNAH: ODETTA HOLMES'S ASSOCIATES: SISTER
BLUE

BOOM-FLURRY
Boom-flurry is a Calla term for the fantastically misshapen organ-pipe cacti
that live in the desert dividing CALLA BRYN STURGIS from THUNDERCLAP.
Their thick barrel arms are covered with long, nasty needles and they smell of
gin and juniper. Unlike the cacti of our world, boom-flurry are sentient, vicious,
and carnivorous. Hence, they make remarkably good sentries. JAKE and OY
encounter some boom-flurry on their way to the CALLA DOGAN. Luckily, the
salivating plant-monsters don't manage to pierce them with any of their spikes,

but they are plenty fashed by the time ANDY the Messenger Robot and the treacherous BEN SLIGHTMAN come upon them.
V:561, V:562, V:567–68, V:571, V:577

BORDER DWELLERS
Border Dwellers were the people who lived beyond TULL, just on the edges of the MOHAINE DESERT. Their partially submerged huts had low sod roofs and were designed to retain nighttime coolness. Dwellers burned devil grass for fuel, though they refused to look into the flames, which they believed contained beckoning devils. Their main crop was corn, though they occasionally grew peas. All of these meager crops had to be watered from deep hand-dug wells.

Many dwellers were either madmen or lepers, suffering from a disease known as the rot. The mad preacher SYLVIA PITTSTON was originally a Border Dweller.
I:12, I:15, I:44, II:32, III:42
INDIVIDUAL BORDER DWELLERS:
BROWN: Roland met Brown the Border Dweller after his disastrous experience in the town of TULL and before his long and almost deadly journey into the MOHAINE DESERT. Although his long, strawberry-colored hair was ringleted and wild, Brown was neither a madman nor a rotter. He lived with his pet raven, ZOLTAN, and his thin, thirsty corn crop. In *The Dark Tower* he is mistakenly called a weed-eater.

In the 2003 version of *The Gunslinger,* we learn that Brown's wife was MANNI and that he spent some time living with this sect. When Roland met him, Brown's speech was still peppered with terms such as "thee" and "thou." I:15–22, I:64–65, I:72, I:85, III:42, IV:570, IV:628, VI:283, VII:826 *(mistakenly called a weed-eater)*

PAPPA DOC: Pappa Doc brought beans to Brown. His name is very close to that of the Haitian despot Papa (Poppa) Doc Duvalier. I:16, I:18, I:20

ZOLTAN: Zoltan, the scrawny talking raven, was the rather sinister companion of Brown, the redheaded Border Dweller that Roland met in *The Gunslinger.* Zoltan's favorite sayings were "Beans, beans, the musical fruit, the more you eat the more you toot" and "Screw you and the horse you rode in on." He ate the eyes of Roland's dead mule. Zoltan was also the name of a folksinger and guitarist that STEPHEN KING knew at the UNIVERSITY OF MAINE. I:16–22, I:64–65, I:72, I:85–86, III:42, IV:628, VI:283, VII:826

BOSCO BOB
See DEAN, EDDIE: EDDIE'S PAST ASSOCIATES: OFFICER BOSCONI

BRANDON
See GRAYS: GRAY HIGH COMMAND

BRANNI BOB
See MANNI

BRANNIGAN, SKIPPER
  See DEAN, HENRY: HENRY DEAN'S KA-TET

BRASS
  See WARRIORS OF THE SCARLET EYE: CASSE ROI RUSSE: HUMANS: FEEMALO/FIMALO/FUMALO: FEEMALO

BRAUTIGAN, TED
  See BREAKERS

BRAVE BILL
  See MID-WORLD FOLKLORE

BRAWNY MAN
  See CALLAHAN, FATHER DONALD FRANK: CALLAHAN'S HIDDEN HIGHWAYS ASSOCIATES

BREAKERS (BEAM BREAKERS)
The Breakers of THUNDERCLAP are both the prisoners and the servants of the CRIMSON KING. Imprisoned in the DEVAR-TOI, located in the poisoned land of END-WORLD, they use their psychic abilities to weaken the BEAMS, which hold the DARK TOWER in place. Although few (if any) of the Breakers willingly undertook the job of destroying the macroverse (most were tricked into accepting *an offer-of-a-lifetime*—an offer which really *did* turn out to be for a lifetime, since most of the MECHANICAL DOORS leading into Thunderclap are one-way only), almost none of them complain once they experience the diverse pleasures available beneath the Devar's artificial sun.

"To break is divine," or so we are told. The Devar's 307 Breakers make use of their so-called wild talents in the STUDY, a room which looks like a richly endowed library in a nineteenth-century gentlemen's club. They work in shifts of thirty-three individuals, each sitting in his or her accustomed place, seemingly reading magazines or contemplating pictures, while actually their minds are rising, reaching the Beams, searching out cracks and crevices, and expanding those fault lines as much as they possibly can. Although the damage done by this activity is almost incomprehensible, the act of Breaking is intensely pleasurable, both for the Breakers who are doing it and for the balcony guards who relax in the "good mind" vibe which rises from below.

Even if an individual doggedly ignores the moral (or perhaps I should say immoral) implications of Breaking, this act has another very human cost. To keep their skills at top form, the Breakers are regularly fed pills which contain a chemical culled from the brains of prepubescent twins, a chemical which causes "twin-telepathy" and which, once removed, leaves the culled child ROONT, or ruined. Although few Breakers know exactly what they are being fed, many have their suspicions but choose to ignore their consciences. Why worry when the accommodation is classy, the food is great, and the sim sex is almost as good as the real thing? As the Breaker saying goes, "Enjoy the cruise, turn on the fan, there's nothing to lose, so work on your tan."

According to TED BRAUTIGAN, most of the Breakers are able to turn off guilt at will because they are *morks* (a term taken from the 1970s sitcom *Mork & Mindy*) and so don't readily form deep attachments to other people. It's not that morks are antisocial—in fact many of them are very sociable—it's just that their "friendships" are based on convenience rather than emotional compatibility. For example, if you have a pack of cigarettes in your pocket, a mork who is jonesing for a smoke will suddenly be your greatest buddy. Although this emotional coldness is disturbing to contemplate, it serves a protective purpose. Most of the Breakers spent their KEYSTONE EARTH lives (and most of them are from Keystone Earth) as the butt of jokes. Their talents have forced them to be perennial outsiders, freaks, and they have always been treated (as DINKY EARNSHAW so aptly puts it) like "Carrie at the fuckin prom." Hence, emotional distance from their fellow humans has been a matter of survival. It's not surprising, then, that for most Breakers, existence in the Devar is preferable to life on ordinary Earth. (That is, once they get used to the eczema, acne, and multiple illnesses which come from inhabiting a poisoned land.)

In the final book of the Dark Tower series, Roland's *ka-tet* arrives in Thunderclap and—with the help of a number of rebel Breakers—puts an end to the abominable practices of the Devar-Toi. Although they slaughter most of the Devar's CAN-TOI, TAHEEN, and hume (or human) guards, they do not harm the Breakers themselves, but tell them to make their way to the CALLAS and beg the *folken*'s forgiveness. (Their only other option is to stay in the ruins of the Devar.) Needless to say, most of the mork Breakers are incensed at such a suggestion, claiming that they had no idea what they were *really* doing in the Study. Rather than taking responsibility for their past actions, they choose to blame Roland's *ka-tet* as well as those Breakers who joined forces with the "enemy."

We never find out what happens to the majority of Breakers, but those who aided our *ka-tet* in their time of need decide to go to CALLA BRYN STURGIS. Once there, they hope to pass through the UNFOUND DOOR and back to America-side. We can only hope that the Calla *folken* help them achieve their goal.

V:659–60, VI:16, VI:18, VI:110, VI:111, VI:114, VI:115, VI:245, VI:246, VI:255, VI:378, VII:58, VII:121, VII:148, VII:150, VII:152, VII:153, VII:178, VII:180, VII:187, VII:211, VII:212–13, VII:214 *(indirect)*, VII:230, VII:232, VII:234, VII:235, VII:236–37, VII:238, VII:239, VII:241–45 *(study)*, VII:251, VII:256, VII:262, VII:288–89 *(rhyme)*, VII:291, VII:292, VII:293, VII:294, VII:295, VII:296, VII:307, VII:311, VII:312, VII:326–27, VII:332, VII:338, VII:343, VII:344, VII:349, VII:356–85 *(Devar-Toi battle)*, VII:388–90, VII:391–93, VII:394–95 *(accusing Roland)*, VII:399, VII:406, VII:407, VII:408, VII:411–14, VII:416, VII:505, VII:507, VII:510, VII:532, VII:563, VII:577, VII:595

INDIVIDUAL BREAKERS:

ADDICTS: Addiction of any kind is not tolerated in the DEVAR, since addiction can interfere with Breaking. Those Breakers who arrive at the Devar hooked on drugs or booze are quickly detoxed. However, those who can't seem to give up their habits simply disappear. VII:211

BAJ: Like SEJ, gentle little Baj is a hydrocephalic savant. In other words, he is a person who has hydrocephalus (enlargement of the head due to water collecting in the brain) but who is amazingly gifted. Baj has no arms, and so has no way to protect himself from the dangers of falling. During the DEVAR's final battle, eleven-year-old DANI ROSTOV tries to save both Baj and Sej from choking to death in the smoke of DAMLI HOUSE. However, while she is pulling them on wagons, Baj tumbles out and falls on his head. He doesn't survive. VII:212 *(indirect)*, VII:375–76 *(dies)*, VII:377

BANKERLY LOOKING BREAKER NUMBER ONE: *See* WORTHINGTON, FRED, *listed below*

BANKERLY LOOKING BREAKER NUMBER TWO: Despite holding our *ka-tet* personally responsible for destroying his life in the DEVAR-TOI, this morose, gray-haired gentleman has a certain amount of courage. Acting as a group spokesman, he confronts Roland with the ruination of the Breakers' lives. Roland reminds him what terrible crimes he and the other Breakers have been committing and tells him that he and his friends should travel to the CALLAS and beg the *folken*'s forgiveness. VII:412

BRAUTIGAN, TED STEVENS: To STEPHEN KING's CONSTANT READERS, the *totally eventual* Ted Brautigan is a familiar, well-loved character. We first met Ted in "Low Men in Yellow Coats," the opening story of *Hearts in Atlantis*. In that tale, Ted was a powerful psychic who could pass his talent on to others when he touched them. Because of this unusual ability, he was pursued by the CAN-TOI (referred to in the context of the story as the LOW MEN) who wanted to force him to use his skill for evil ends. Trying to remain unseen, a fugitive Ted moved into a CONNECTICUT boardinghouse already occupied by a young boy named BOBBY GARFIELD and his young but bitter widowed mother, LIZ. Thanks to their shared love of books, Ted and Bobby became friends. Bobby agreed to work for Ted, ostensibly to read the paper to him each day, but actually to act as a spotter for the garishly dressed low men and for the lost-pet posters and strange, occult designs which they used to hunt for their prey.

At the end of "Low Men in Yellow Coats," Ted was betrayed by Bobby's mother, Liz, who wanted to collect the low men's reward money. The last distressing glimpse Bobby had of Ted was of him sitting in the backseat of a huge DeSoto, surrounded by low men. He was on his way back to END-WORLD and a job he despised. However, he agreed to Beam-Break, as long as the low men left Bobby and his other young friends alone.

When we meet up with Ted again in *The Dark Tower*, he is imprisoned once more in the DEVAR-TOI in End-World. We also learn that he has not kept his promise to his captors. Although he appears to Break willingly enough, he and two of his fellow inmates—DINKY EARNSHAW and STANLEY RUIZ (otherwise known as SHEEMIE)—are preparing for the arrival of Roland Deschain, the savior-gunslinger whose appearance he predicted at the end of "Low Men in Yellow Coats."

In *The Dark Tower*, we find out that although Ted isn't from KEYSTONE EARTH, he is much more than a run-of-the-mill Breaker. He is a *facilitator*, or a psychic whose special skill is his ability to increase the power of other psychics. This, we learn, is why the servants of the RED KING were so determined to bring Ted back to the Devar, and why he was not severely punished for his "little vacation" in Connecticut. While the other Breakers work shifts in the STUDY, Ted comes and goes as he pleases. But whenever he arrives, the number of *darks* generated by the Breakers increases exponentially. Much to his chagrin, Ted's special skill has taken years off the Red King's work, and by the time our *tet* arrives in THUNDERCLAP, only two of the BEAMS are still intact.

Like his twinner, FATHER CALLAHAN, Ted Stevens Brautigan becomes a temporary member of Roland's *ka-tet*. He, Dinky, and Sheemie help our *tet* destroy the Devar and begin the healing of the Beams. Not only does Ted use his psychic abilities to help confuse both guards and Breakers during our *tet*'s attack, but he also employs his deadly mind-spear to kill the *can-toi* guard TRAMPAS. When we finally take leave of Ted in the twisting corridors beneath the FEDIC DOGAN, he, Dinky, FRED WORTHINGTON, and DANI ROSTOV are on their way to the CALLAS. From there they hope to pass through the UNFOUND DOOR to one of the MULTIPLE AMERICAS. VI:407, VI:408, VII:197–220, VII:233, VII:234, VII:238, VII:243–45, VII:247, VII:249, VII:261, VII:265–302 *(twin of Pere Callahan)*, VII:304, VII:306, VII:307, VII:315, VII:318–24, VII:326, VII:327–36, VII:337–42, VII:349, VII:356–58, VI:359, VII:366, VII:370, VII:372, VII:374–75, VII:376–77, VII:380, VII:382, VII:384, VII:388–90, VII:391, VII:392, VII:393, VII:394, VII:400–401, VII:404–8, VII:409, VII:411–17, VII:532, VII:535, VII:536–37, VII:538, VII:539, VII:540–41, VII:560, VII:563, VII:802

TED BRAUTIGAN'S ASSOCIATES:

ATWOOD, TIM: Tim Atwood was Ted's wealthy, childless uncle. He paid for Ted's education, hoping that Ted would take over his furniture business. Needless to say, Ted didn't. VII:273, VII:276

AUNT MOLLY: Ted's Aunt Molly and UNCLE JIM lived in BRIDGE-PORT, CONNECTICUT. VII:415

DALE, MR.: A butcher. VII:277

DOCTOR NUMBER ONE (SAM): This doctor gave Ted a 4F when he tried to enlist as a soldier during the First World War. He was deeply disturbed by Ted's psychic abilities. VII:274–75, VII:280

  GUY: Doc Number One's brother. VII:275

DOCTOR NUMBER TWO: This doctor consciously undermined Ted's "proof" of his psychic ability. VII:274–75, VII:277, VII:280, VII:286

GARFIELD, BOBBY: Redheaded Bobby Garfield was Ted's eleven-year-old CONNECTICUT friend, and the main character of the story "Low Men in Yellow Coats." Despite the difference in hair color, he and JAKE CHAMBERS are practically identical twins. PIMLI PRENTISS, the Devar Master, and FINLI O'TEGO, his security chief, have both made it clear to Ted that if he tries to run away again, Bobby will be put to death. VI:407, VI:408, VII:197, VII:199, VII:207, VII:215 *(indirect)*, VII:218, VII:234, VII:288, VII:298

  GARFIELD, LIZ: Bobby's young but bitter mother. She never forgave Bobby's dad for dying of a heart attack at age thirty-six. She turned Ted in to the LOW MEN for the reward money they offered. VII:218

GERBER, CAROL: Carol Gerber was BOBBY GARFIELD's friend/

girlfriend in "Low Men in Yellow Coats," the first story in *Hearts in Atlantis*. Carol also appears in "Why We're in Vietnam," "Heavenly Shades of Night Are Falling," and the book's title story. Like Bobby, Carol would have been killed by the LOW MEN had Ted attempted to escape from the DEVAR-TOI. VII:234, VII:298

MOTHER: VII:298

KIDS PLAYING KICK-THE-CAN: These kids in AKRON, OHIO, witnessed the first throw of Ted's deadly mind-spear. VII:277, VII:278

MUGGER: Directly after attacking Ted, this fleeing mugger dropped dead. The reason? Ted had arrowed a thought in his direction. This event changed Ted's life and made him fear his psychic ability. VII:277–78, VII:279, VII:376

SERGEANT AT ARMS: This sergeant at arms threw Ted out of a First World War recruiting station. VII:275–76

SOUTH AMERICAN SEABEES: *Listed separately*

SULLIVAN, JOHN (SULLY JOHN): Sully John was friends with both BOBBY GARFIELD and CAROL GERBER. He and Carol became a couple after Bobby left town, but Carol later abandoned the relationship. In the story "Why We're in Vietnam," found in STEPHEN KING's novel *Hearts in Atlantis,* we learn that Sully John had one of his testicles shot off in VIETNAM. VI:407, VII:288, VII:298

UNCLE JIM: Ted's AUNT MOLLY and Uncle Jim lived in BRIDGE-PORT, CONNECTICUT. VII:415

DICK: We never learn Dick's last name, even though he arrived at the DEVAR on the same day as TED BRAUTIGAN. Dick died six months after entering THUNDERCLAP. HUMMA O'TEGO insisted he died of pneumonia, but Ted thinks he committed suicide. VII:283 *(not yet named),* VII:286–90

EARNSHAW, DINKY: CONSTANT READERS know Dinky Earnshaw (born Richard Earnshaw) from "Everything's Eventual," the autobiographical tale he narrated in STEPHEN KING's book of the same name. At the time "Everything's Eventual" was written, Dinky worked for a POSITRONICS subsidiary as a psychic assassin. His method of attack was a personalized letter (either posted or sent via computer) which contained strange shapes and designs, the meanings of which not even Dinky seemed to know. Dinky's death-magic was incredibly powerful, and his employers rewarded him well for his services. Dinky's only problem was that he wasn't a full mork. When he began to admit to himself what he was doing—and when he started to learn about the people he was employed to kill—he decided to cut and run. Dinky sent one final personalized death letter (this time to his control, the sinister MR. SHARPTON) before trying to retire in obscurity. However, to the WARRIORS OF THE SCARLET EYE, psychics stand out like blazing fires. He was recaptured and sent to the DEVAR-TOI, where his skills were used to help destroy the BEAMS.

Like many of the other Breakers, Dinky is a precog. However, since the future is always a multi-forked path, Dinky cannot always tell which particular future will manifest. Despite this uncertainty, he joins forces with TED BRAUTIGAN, SHEEMIE RUIZ, and Roland's *ka-tet* to end the horrors of the Devar. After the future of the Beams is assured, he, Ted, FRED WORTHINGTON, and DANI ROSTOV set off for CALLA BRYN STURGIS. Once there, they hope to pass through the UNFOUND DOOR to one of the MULTIPLE AMERICAS. VII:197–220, VII:228, VII:231–32, VII:247, VII:267–70, VII:271, VII:272, VII:273, VII:276, VII:279, VII:285, VII:288, VII:290, VII:291, VII:292, VII:293, VII:296, VII:300, VII:318–36, VII:337–42, VII:356–57, VII:359–61, VII:363, VII:364–65, VII:371, VII:374, VII:375–77, VII:380, VII:384, VII:388–90, VII:392, VII:395, VII:396, VII:397–99, VII:400–401, VII:405–8, VII:409, VII:411–17, VII:532, VII:535, VII:536–37, VII:538, VII:539, VII:540 *(indirect)*, VII:541 *(indirect)*, VII:560, VII:561, VII:563, VII:802

DINKY EARNSHAW'S ASSOCIATES:

> **J.J. THE BLUE JAY:** VII:325
>
> **SHARPTON, MR.:** Mr. Sharpton was a talent scout for a NORTH CENTRAL POSITRONICS subsidiary. His specialty was recruiting psychic assassins. Before going *alleyo,* Dinky sent Mr. Sharpton a death letter. He personalized it with the word EXCALIBUR—the magical sword which was printed on Mr. Sharpton's ties. VII:232, VII:398

ITTAWAY, DAVE: Dave Ittaway was recruited to be a Breaker at the same time as TED BRAUTIGAN. VII:283 *(not yet named)*, VII:286–90

LEEDS, TANYA (TANYA LEEDS RASTOSOVICH): Like DAVE ITTAWAY, JACE McGOVERN, and DICK of the unknown last name, Tanya Leeds of BRYCE, COLORADO, was recruited to be a Breaker at the same time as TED BRAUTIGAN. Tanya is a tough young woman, but though she may once have been willing to join forces with Roland, by the time our *ka-tet* arrives in THUNDERCLAP she is newly married and wants only to snuggle with her fella, JOEY RASTOSOVICH. Unfortunately, during the DEVAR's battle chaos, Joey is run over by a robotic fire truck. VII:230–31, VII:283 *(Bryce, Colorado)*, VII:286–90, VII:293, VII:295, VII:337–38, VII:373, VII:393 *(indirect)*

McCANN, BIRDIE: Birdie is an ex-carpenter with a receding hairline. VII:370–71

McGOVERN, JACE: Jace entered the service of the CRIMSON KING at the same time as TED BRAUTIGAN. VII:283 *(not yet named)*, VII:286–90

RAPED BREAKER: This unnamed Breaker was raped by a LOW MAN called CAMERON, who said that the act was required of him by the CRIMSON KING and that it was part of his process of *becoming* (or becoming human). The DEVAR MASTER sentenced Cameron to death, and the Breakers were invited to watch. VII:326–27

RASTOSOVICH, JOSEPH: Joseph Rastosovich (never Joey, at least to his face) married TANYA LEEDS in the DEVAR-TOI. Although the Devar Master PIMLI PRENTISS performed the official ceremony, the couple asked TED BRAUTIGAN to marry them in secret, since Ted's blessing meant a lot more to them. During the chaos of the final Devar battle, Joseph is run over by a robotic fire truck. VII:230–31, VII:295, VII:337–38, VII:356, VII:371, VII:373

ROSTOV, DANEEKA (DANI): As far as we know, eleven-year-old Daneeka Rostov is the youngest of the Breakers. She is also Russian, which sets her apart from most of the others we've met. Unlike the selfish mork Breakers, Dani has a good heart. During the DEVAR's final battle, she tries to save BAJ and SEJ from the smoking wreck of DAMLI HOUSE. After EDDIE DEAN's death, she also helps TED BRAUTIGAN, DINKY EARNSHAW, SHEEMIE RUIZ, and FRED WORTHINGTON send Roland and JAKE back to NEW YORK. (At this time, she gives Jake his first and only romantic kiss.) Like her Breaker friends, Dani hopes to travel to CALLA BRYN STURGIS so that she can enter one of the MULTIPLE AMERICAS via the UNFOUND DOOR. VII:243, VII:375–77, VII:393, VII:404–8, VII:415–17, VII:536–37, VII:538, VII:539, VII:540 *(indirect)*, VII:541 *(indirect)*, VII:560, VII:563

**RUIZ, STANLEY (SHEEMIE): We first met the mildly mentally handicapped (but extremely sweet) Sheemie in *Wizard and Glass*. In that novel, we learned that Sheemie was the bastard offspring of DELORES SHEEMER and STANLEY RUIZ. He worked at the TRAVELLERS' REST and was described as having black kinky hair which he often topped with a pink sombrero. After CUTHBERT ALLGOOD saved Sheemie from the BIG COFFIN HUNTERS, Sheemie became devoted to Roland's *ka-tet*. In the 2003 version of *The Gunslinger,* Roland remembers Sheemie and his humorous relationship with the mule CAPRICHOSO.

When we meet Sheemie again in *The Dark Tower,* he is one of the most powerful Breakers in THUNDERCLAP. At this point he appears to be about thirty-five years old and mute. However, the arrival of Roland (good old WILL-DEARBORN-that-was) cures Sheemie of his muteness. Once Sheemie's voice returns, he confesses his love for SUSAN DELGADO and the terrible guilt he feels about her death.

Sheemie possesses the one wild talent which is absolutely forbidden in the DEVAR-TOI—the ability to teleport. With the help of his friends TED BRAUTIGAN and DINKY EARNSHAW, he uses this skill to transport our *ka-tet* from THUNDERCLAP STATION to the relative safety of STEEK-TETE, located several miles from the Devar-Toi. Unfortunately, teleportation has its own risks. When Sheemie teleports himself, Ted, and Dinky to Steek-Tete to see how Roland and his friends are progressing with their war plans, he suffers a mild stroke. It turns out that Sheemie has had four such strokes already, the first of which hit him when he helped Ted escape to 1960 CONNECTICUT. (The tale of Ted's Connecticut adventure is told in the short story "Low Men in Yellow Coats," found in STEPHEN KING's book *Hearts in Atlantis*.) However, Sheemie's teleportation skill is not his only unusual psychic talent. Unlike any other person in the Devar, Sheemie can make fistulas in time, or balconies on the edifice of the DARK TOWER. The fistula which Sheemie creates for his friends Ted and Dinky looks like a GINGERBREAD HOUSE out of a child's fairy tale.

Although Sheemie survives the Devar's final battle, during the resulting chaos he steps on a tainted piece of glass. Sheemie dies on a train heading for FEDIC. Roland never gets to say good-bye to him. IV:172, IV:190 *(described)*, IV:214, IV:215–22 *(cause of standoff at Travellers' Rest; 217 maternity/paternity discussed)*, IV:226 *(end of fight)*, IV:228–29,

IV:240–42, IV:244–45, IV:254, IV:287–88, IV:327, IV:336, IV:343–44, IV:382, IV:384–85, IV:389–90, IV:394–98 (*graf to Rhea. 396 she calls him "son of Stanley"*), IV:402–3, IV:413, IV:433–34, IV:443, IV:447–50 (*getting firecrackers with Susan*), IV:497, IV:504, IV:505–7, IV:512, IV:514–19, IV:523–24, IV:525, IV:526, IV:529, IV:536–37, IV:539–40, IV:546, IV:565–70 (*following Susan*), IV:571, IV:579–80, IV:581–83 (*583 he loves Susan*), IV:585, IV:594, IV:624, VII:84, VII:197–220, VII:228, VII:233, VII:234, VII:247, VII:256, VII:266, VII:267–71 (*Cappi mentioned on 270*), VII:272, VII:273, VII:279, VII:290, VII:296, VII:307, VII:308, VII:318–24, VII:326–36, VII:337–42, VII:356, VII:357, VII:359, VII:366, VII:378, VII:388, VII:389, VII:391–92, VII:393, VII:400–401, VII:404–8, VII:409, VII:411–17, VII:532, VII:535, VII:538, VII:705 (*idiot savant*), VII:802

SHEEMIE RUIZ'S ASSOCIATES:

CAPPI: Sheemie's mule from the TRAVELLERS' REST in HAMBRY. *For page references, see* SHEEMIE RUIZ, *above, volume IV as well as* VII:270.

RUMBELOW, GRACE: Grace Rumbelow was originally from ALDERSHOT, ENGLAND. She reminds JAKE CHAMBERS of the lifetime president of his mother's garden club. Grace is a true mork. VII:394

SEJ: Like BAJ, Sej is a hydrocephalic savant. However, unlike Baj, Sej has arms. Sej survives the DEVAR-TOI battle, although we don't know what becomes of him later. VII:375–77

SHEEMIE: *See* RUIZ, STANLEY, *listed above*

WAVERLY: Waverly is a fat Breaker who was a bookkeeper in his former life. VII:372

WORTHINGTON, FRED (BANKERLY LOOKING BREAKER NUMBER ONE): Fred Worthington looks like a banker, but despite his staid appearance he is willing to take risks. After the DEVAR's final battle, he helps TED BRAUTIGAN, DINKY EARNSHAW, DANI ROSTOV, and SHEEMIE RUIZ teleport Roland and JAKE to KEYSTONE EARTH so that they can save the life of STEPHEN KING. Fred hopes to eventually make his way to one of the MULTIPLE AMERICAS. VII:393, VII:404, VII:408, VII:538, VII:539, VII:540 (*indirect*), VII:541 (*indirect*), VII:560, VII:561, VII:563

YOUNG WOMAN ON MALL: JAKE sees this young woman forming what seems to be a séance circle with TED BRAUTIGAN and the other members of his Breaker *ka-tet*. Although we can't say for certain, it seems likely that she is actually TANYA LEEDS. *See* LEEDS, TANYA, *listed above*

BRIANA OF SERENITY
See SERENITY, SISTERS OF

BRICE, MR.
See TOWER, CALVIN

BRIGGS, MR.
See CHARLIE THE CHOO-CHOO

**BROADCLOAK, MARTEN
See WALTER: WALTER'S ALIASES

BROTHER OUTFIT
See CALLAHAN, FATHER DONALD FRANK: CALLAHAN'S HIDDEN HIGHWAYS ASSOCIATES: COVAY MOVERS

BROWN
See BORDER DWELLERS

BRUMHALL, DR.
See KATZ: KATZ'S EMPLOYEES, CUSTOMERS AND COMPETITORS

BUCKSKIN
See JOHNS, ALAIN

BUFFALO STAR
See GODS OF MID-WORLD

BUGS, FLESH-EATING
See ROSS, BIG JACK

BULLET
See KING, STEPHEN: SMITH, BRYAN

BUNKOWSKI, DEWEY
See DEAN, EDDIE: EDDIE'S ASSOCIATES, PAST AND PRESENT

BUNKOWSKI, MRS.
See DEAN, EDDIE: EDDIE'S ASSOCIATES, PAST AND PRESENT

BURKE, DAVID
See WARRIORS OF THE SCARLET EYE: DEVAR-TOI CHARACTERS: HUMANS

BURKE, MATTHEW
See CALLAHAN, FATHER DONALD FRANK: 'SALEM'S LOT CHARACTERS

BURLINGTON ZEPHYR
See CHARLIE THE CHOO-CHOO

BUSINESSMAN (MARK CROSS BRIEFCASE)
See VAMPIRES: TYPE THREE: MARK CROSS BRIEFCASE BUSINESSMAN

BUSKER
See DEAN, SUSANNAH: SUSANNAH'S PRESENT ASSOCIATES

C

C3PO
See NORTH CENTRAL POSITRONICS: ANDY

CAGNEY, JAMES
See CAN-TOI

CALDERWOOD, FLOYD
See KING, STEPHEN

CALLA BRYN STURGIS CHARACTERS
Near the beginning of *Wolves of the Calla*, our *ka-tet* is approached by six representatives from the town of Calla Bryn Sturgis—TIAN JAFFORDS, ZALIA JAFFORDS, WAYNE OVERHOLSER, BEN SLIGHTMAN, BENNY SLIGHTMAN, and PERE CALLAHAN. The Calla *folken* are in dire need of help, and at least three of their representatives believe that our posse of gunslingers is their only hope of salvation.

Although the Calla has been settled for more than a thousand years, over the last six generations it has been plagued by giant, green-cloaked marauders riding out of THUNDERCLAP. These predators (called WOLVES because of the terrible snarling masks that they wear) sweep down on the BORDERLAND CALLAS each generation to steal one of every pair of prepubescent twins. Although none of the Calla *folken* understand exactly what is being done to their children, they do know that when the children are finally returned to them, their minds and bodies are ruined, or ROONT.

The people of the Callas realize that in most parts of the world, twins are rarities and singletons are common, and that it is only in the arc of the borderlands that this natural phenomenon is reversed. It has led some among them to conclude that their children are being taken to the dark land so that a chemical which causes twin-telepathy can be culled from their brains. When our story begins, twenty-three years have passed since the last invasion. According to the town's one Messenger Robot, called ANDY, by the rise of the coming Demon Moon, the Wolves will be upon them once more.

The Calla *folken* are farmers and ranchers, not fighters. Most of the 140 men tend smallhold patches of rice near the river, and the majority of them are relatively poor. Only the wealthiest—such as the rancher VAUGHN EISENHART—have any guns at all, and everyone knows that those rusty shooting-irons are no match for the light-sticks, fire-hurling weapons, and sneetches wielded by the Greencloaks.

Although most of the Calla's attempts to stand up to the Wolves have ended in death and disaster, seventy years before Roland and his friends entered the borderlands, one of the SISTERS OF ORIZA, accompanied by a small group of friends, managed to bring a Greencloak down with one of her sharpened flying plates. The only member of that posse to survive (now an ancient old man) remembers all too well what the twitching Greencloak looked like behind its mask. According to GRAN-PERE JAFFORDS, the Wolf looked just like Andy.

By sending false battle plans to the Wolves via Andy and the traitorous Ben Slightman, Roland, EDDIE, SUSANNAH, JAKE, and the Sisters of Oriza defeat their enemies despite being vastly outnumbered. In the battle of the EAST ROAD, MARGARET EISENHART and Jake's friend Benny Slightman are killed. However, their deaths are not in vain since the Calla's children are saved.

As well as the Wolf battle, many important events take place in this small town located on the lip of END-WORLD. Roland and his friends meet a final (if temporary) member of their *tet*, FATHER DONALD FRANK CALLAHAN, whom CONSTANT READERS know from STEPHEN KING's novel *'Salem's Lot*. It is here that Susannah Dean's haunting demon, MIA, begins to get the upper hand and finally absconds with the body they share. It is also in the Calla that our *ka-tet* begins to suspect just how closely their *khef* is tied to that of the writer Stephen King.

GENERAL REFERENCES: V:13–31 *(men in Gathering Hall)*, V:123–24, V:209, V:211–34 *(Calla fiesta)*, V:238, V:402–6, V:479, V:490, V:562, V:572, V:581, V:585, V:601–17, V:643, V:648, V:649, V:650, V:654, V:659, V:689, V:693–97 *(present)*, VI:6, VI:9, VI:10, VI:14, VI:17, VI:24, VI:131, VI:350, VII:120, VII:173, VII:207, VII:233, VII:398, VII:412, VII:473, VII:540, W:9

CHILD-MINDERS: Early on the morning that the WOLVES are due to arrive in Calla Bryn Sturgis, these characters travel with Roland's *ka-tet* and the SISTERS OF ORIZA to the ARROYOS northeast of the Calla. Although they initially believe that Roland plans to hide the children in the arroyos, they find out that they are actually to be hidden in LADY ORIZA's rice.

The child-minders are SAREY ADAMS, HUGH ANSELM, KRELLA ANSELM, FATHER DONALD FRANK CALLAHAN, VAUGHN EISEN-HART, JORGE ESTRADA, TIAN JAFFORDS, ANNABELLE JAVIER, BUCKY JAVIER, BEN SLIGHTMAN, and CANTAB and ARA of the MANNI. REUBEN CAVERRA was supposed to be among them, but he busted a gut the night before and could not take part. WAYNE OVERHOL-SER takes his place. V:483–84 *(indirect; Roland asks Callahan for names)*, V:608, V:615, V:643, V:662–67, V:677, V:689 *(folken)*, V:693–97 *(folken)*

CHILDREN OF THE CALLA: *See also* CALLA BRYN STURGIS CHAR-ACTERS: ROONTS, *listed below.* V:132, V:139, V:143 *(twins)*, V:150, V:151, V:152, V:206, V:211, V:214, V:217, V:220, V:222, V:225, V:341, V:362, V:508, V:575, V:584, V:585–89 *(singing)*, V:602, V:607, V:609, V:629, V:636, V:637, V:643, V:646, V:650, V:654, V:658, V:662–67, V:671, V:677, V:689 *(part of folken)*, V:693–97, VI:6, VI:80, VI:115, VI:237, VI:243 *(indirect)*, VI:247, VI:378 *(victims of the Wolves)*, VII:75, VII:142, VII:152, VII:153, VII:173, VII:206, VII:213, VII:214 *(indirect)*, VII:339, VII:412

  PUDGY BOY: V:588

  TWIN SINGERS: V:227

FARMERS (LARGE FARMS):

  OVERHOLSER, WAYNE DALE: Wayne Dale Overholser, the Calla's most successful farmer and one of its most important citizens, is the owner of SEVEN MILE FARM, located just west of Calla Bryn Sturgis. His major crop is wheat. Wayne is about sixty years old, has heavy cheeks scarred with "I-want" lines, and a vast, sloping belly. Despite wearing a white Stetson like a good guy from a cowboy film, Overholser is initially dubious about the chances four gunslingers and a BILLY-BUMBLER have against more than sixty WOLVES. Obviously, he doesn't know Roland.

Although his two grown children were both singletons, Overholser himself had a twin named WELLAND. Like so many others, Welland was taken by the Wolves and returned ROONT. Despite his initial cynicism, Overholser is eventually won over to Roland's way of seeing and even acts as one of the CHILD-MINDERS during the battle of the EAST ROAD. According to CALVIN TOWER, in our world, Wayne D. Overholser is also the name of a cowboy novelist. V:20–31 *(Town Gathering Hall; present)*, V:44 *(following* ka-tet*)*, V:45 *(following* ka-tet*)*, V:47 *(following* ka-tet*)*, V:57 *(Wayne D)*, V:88 *(friends)*, V:92 *(indirect)*, V:106 *(indirect)*, V:109 *(indirect)*, V:111–13, V:116, V:117–18, V:122–37, V:142–60, V:162, V:165, V:166, V:201–10 *(present—mentioned directly on 205, 206, 208–9)*, V:211–34 *(present for fiesta—mentioned directly on 212, 213–14, 216, 217, 222, 223, 224)*, V:237, V:321 *(not as shrewd as Eisenhart)*, V:329, V:340, V:404, V:488, V:497, V:509, V:557, V:572, V:576, V:601–17 *(present—mentioned directly on 604, 606)*, V:651–52, V:654, V:656, V:661, V:662–67, V:677, V:681, V:689 *(folken)*, V:693–97 *(folken)*, VI:9, VI:92, VI:303 *(the writer)*

> **MOTHER (UNNAMED):** V:130 *(folks)*, V:147 *(ma)*, V:150 *(ma)*
>
> **OVERHOLSER, ALAN:** Alan was the father of Wayne and WELLAND OVERHOLSER. He died long before our story takes place. V:128, V:130 *(folks)*, V:147 *(pa)*
>
> **OVERHOLSER, MRS.:** Wayne's wife. We never learn her full name. V:651
>
> **OVERHOLSER, WELLAND:** *See* CALLA BRYN STURGIS CHARACTERS: ROONTS, *listed below*

FARMERS (SMALLHOLD):

ANSELM, HUGH: Hugh Anselm owns a smallhold just south of TIAN JAFFORDS's place. Tian wants to buy it. Anselm is one of the CHILD-MINDERS during the final battle with the WOLVES. V:349, V:587, V:589, V:662–67 *(not mentioned here, but we find out on 677 that he must have been present)*, V:677

> **ANSELM, KRELLA:** Krella is Hugh Anselm's wife. She also acts as a CHILD-MINDER during the final battle with the WOLVES. V:662–67 *(mentioned on 666)*, V:677, V:689 *(folken)*, V:693–97 *(folken)*
>
> **ANSELM TWINS:** The Anselm twins are about thirteen or fourteen years old. V:587–88

ARRA: During GRAN-PERE JAFFORDS's youth, Arra owned a smallhold patch just east of the Calla. It was near this smallhold that Gran-pere and the other members of the WOLF POSSE lay in ambush for their green-cloaked enemies. V:361

CAVERRA, REUBEN: Reuben Caverra is a plump man with a round, cheerful face. Later in the story he is described as a "hulk of a man" and is said to be fearless. The year the WOLVES took his twin, RUTH, he made a mark on the big pine tree in his front yard. He continued to make a mark each succeeding year. By his reckoning, the Calla had twenty-three years of peace between invasions from THUNDERCLAP. Reuben Caverra is one of the *folken* chosen to act as a CHILD-MINDER during the standoff against the Wolves. Unfortunately, Reuben busts a gut and is too ill to participate. WAYNE OVERHOLSER takes his place. *See also* CALLAHAN, FATHER DONALD FRANK: CALLAHAN'S HIDDEN HIGHWAYS ASSOCIATES: MEXICAN IMMIGRANTS (ILLEGAL). V:15–31 *(Town Gathering Hall; present)*, V:483, V:651

> **CAVERRA, DIANE:** Diane Caverra is Reuben's wife. CALLAHAN names her as another possible CHILD-MINDER. However, due to her husband's illness, she does not participate either. V:483
>
> **CAVERRA, RUTH:** *See* CALLA BRYN STURGIS CHARACTERS: ROONTS, *listed below*

ESTRADA, JORGE: Like many of the other smallhold farmers, Jorge Estrada has children young enough to be taken by the WOLVES. He acts as one of the CHILD-MINDERS during the EAST ROAD battle. *See also* CALLAHAN, FATHER DONALD FRANK: CALLAHAN'S HIDDEN HIGHWAYS ASSOCIATES: MEXICAN IMMIGRANTS (ILLEGAL). V:16–31 *(Town Gathering Hall; present)*, V:211–34 *(present; mentioned directly on 222)*, V:488–92 *(present)*, V:656, V:662–67 *(present)*, V:677, V:689 *(folken)*, V:693–97 *(folken)*

> **ESTRADA, DEELIE:** She is the wife of Jorge Estrada. V:488–92 *(present)*

FARADAY, NEIL: Squat, cynical Neil Faraday owns a smallhold rice patch far to the South'ards. He is a hard worker but an even harder drinker, a fact easily discerned from the dark circles under his eyes and the burst of purplish veins on his cheeks. When TIAN JAFFORDS calls a meeting to discuss fighting the WOLVES, Faraday (holding his filthy sombrero) counsels caution. Later, during the Calla meeting where Roland tells everyone to bring their children to the PAVILION on the eve of the Wolf attack, Faraday refuses. He will not allow his three children (or his wife) to take part in Roland's plan. V:18–31 *(Town Gathering Hall; present)*, V:211–34 *(present; mentioned directly on 222)*, V:601–17 *(present; mentioned directly on 611–12, 614)*

> **GEORGE:** *See* CALLA BRYN STURGIS CHARACTERS: ROONTS, *listed below*
>
> **GEORGINA:** Faraday's daughter. Her twin became ROONT. V:18
>
> **THREE CHILDREN:** V:612
>
> **WIFE:** V:612

HAYCOX, LOUIS: Haycox is a dark-skinned man with a black mustache. His farm is just west of TIAN JAFFORDS's, near the edge of the Calla. He has four-year-old twins. He is afraid of the WOLVES, but willing to fight for his family. V:19–31 *(Town Gathering Hall; present)*, V:211–34 *(present; mentioned directly on 222, 227)*, V:601–17 *(present; mentioned directly on 606, 608)*

> **TWINS:** V:19

JAFFORDS FAMILY: *See* JAFFORDS FAMILY, *listed separately*

JAVIER, BUCKY: Bucky Javier has bright little blue eyes in a small head that seems to slope back from his goateed chin. Although he is not the most landed of the smallhold farmers, he is powerful. He owns eighty acres; the rest he gave to his younger sister ROBERTA as a wedding present. His ROONT twin was named BULLY. He and his wife ANNABELLE are both CHILD-MINDERS during the final battle against the WOLVES. *See also* CALLAHAN, FATHER DONALD FRANK: CALLAHAN'S HIDDEN HIGHWAYS ASSOCIATES: MEXICAN IMMIGRANTS (ILLEGAL). V:17–31 *(Town Gathering Hall; present)*, V:159 *(owns eighty acres)*, V:483, V:489–92 *(present)*, V:601–17 *(present; mentioned directly on 602)*, V:654, V:662–67 *(present)*, V:689 *(folken)*, V:693–97 *(folken)*

JAVIER, ANNABELLE: She is Bucky's wife. She and her husband are two of the CHILD-MINDERS during the final battle against the WOLVES. V:483, V:489–92 *(present)*, V:601–17 *(not yet named, but present and mentioned on 602)*, V:654, V:662–67 *(present)*, V:689 *(folken)*, V:693–97 *(folken)*

JAVIER, BULLY: *See* CALLA BRYN STURGIS CHARACTERS: ROONTS, *listed below*

JAVIER, ROBERTA: Roberta is Bucky's younger sister. She and her twin were only a year old when the WOLVES last invaded the Calla, so the two of them were passed over. Since his own twin died, Bucky dotes on his younger siblings. When Roberta married, Bucky gave her half of what he owned. V:159

HUSBAND (UNNAMED): V:159

ROSARIO, FREDDY: Freddy Rosario owns the farm closest to TIAN JAFFORDS's land. He has fathered one set of twins, but since the children are still nursing, they are probably safe from the WOLVES. V:24–31 *(Town Gathering Hall; present)*, V:211–34 *(present; mentioned directly on 222, 225)*, V:601–17 *(present; mentioned directly on 602)*

TWINS: V:24

STRONG, GARRETT: Garrett Strong is a smallhold farmer with the face of a pug dog. During the men's meeting at the Calla GATHERING HALL at the beginning of *Wolves of the Calla*, he is outraged by the MANNI's suggestion that the people of the Calla should kill their children and kill themselves rather than face the WOLVES. His farmhand's name is ROSSITER. V:17–31 *(Town Gathering Hall; present)*, V:211–34 *(present; mentioned directly on 222)*, V:486, V:601–17 *(Strongs)*

ROSSITER: Garrett Strong's farmhand. V:20–31 *(Town Gathering Hall; present)*, V:601–17 *(present; mentioned directly on 602)*

MANNI: *See* MANNI, *listed separately*

RANCHERS:

ADAMS, DIEGO: Diego Adams has intense black eyes. Like OVERHOLSER and EISENHART, he is a wealthy man and so has much to lose should the WOLVES burn down the town. He does not want to fight the Wolves, though his own children are prepubescent and at risk. His wife, on the other hand, is one of the SISTERS OF ORIZA. She wants to fight alongside Roland during the EAST ROAD battle, but is not accurate enough with the plate to take part in the ambush. Instead, Roland puts her in charge of the CHILD-MINDERS and the twins they guard. V:17–31

(Town Gathering Hall; present), V:211–34 *(present; mentioned directly on 214, 230)*, V:489–92 *(present)*

ADAMS, SAREY: *See* ORIZA, SISTERS OF

EISENHART, VAUGHN: Vaughn Eisenhart is one of the most important men of the Calla. His ranch, called the ROCKING B, is located south of town. Eisenhart's foreman is BEN SLIGHTMAN, whose son, BENNY, becomes a close friend of JAKE's. Unfortunately, Slightman the elder turns out to be a traitor to his town.

Unlike most of the other men of the BORDERLANDS, Eisenhart owns three guns, all of which have been in his family for seven generations. The best of the shooting-irons is an ancient rifle, which he brings to important meetings, such as the one TIAN JAFFORDS calls at the GATHERING HALL at the outset of *Wolves of the Calla*. The other two are barrel-shooters, and only one of them is in good enough condition to fire.

Although Eisenhart, like the other wealthy men of the Calla, is initially skeptical about our *tet*'s ability to best the WOLVES, he eventually has a change of heart. This change comes about because of his wife, MAR-GARET (originally of the MANNI clan), who is one of the SISTERS OF ORIZA. Margaret wants to stand with Roland's *tet* and fight the Wolves, and her husband, who knows how much she has given up for him and their six children, agrees to let her take part in the EAST ROAD battle. During the Calla's final stand against the invaders from THUNDERCLAP, Vaughn acts as one of the CHILD-MINDERS. Unfortunately, his wife does not survive the fray, but is decapitated by one of the Wolves' light-sticks. In our last glimpse of Vaughn, he is cradling his dead wife's head. V:13–31 *(Town Gathering Hall; present)*, V:153, V:158, V:169, V:205, V:211–34 *(present; mentioned directly on 219, 223, 224)*, V:234, V:244, V:294, V:302, V:313, V:318–25 *(321—shrewder than Overholser)*, V:328–42, V:345, V:404 *(countryman's sense of humor)*, V:407–8 *(heathen man)*, V:495, V:497–98, V:572, V:601–17 *(present; mentioned directly on 602, 605, 608–9, 613)*, V:655, V:662–67 *(present; mentioned directly on 666)*, V:677, V:689, V:690–94, VI:9, VI:17, VI:25 *(indirect)*

COOKIE: The cook at ROCKING B. V:553

EISENHART, MARGARET: *See* ORIZA, SISTERS OF

EISENHART, VERNA: *See* CALLA BRYN STURGIS CHARACTERS: ROONTS, *listed below*

EISENHART CHILDREN (TOM AND TESSA, SECOND SET OF TWINS, FIFTEEN-YEAR-OLD TWINS): There are six Eisenhart children. The eldest two—Tom and Tessa—were born less than a month before the last WOLF invasion. The youngest pair is fifteen. Although none of the Eisenhart children have been made ROONT, all have left the Calla in search of a place free from THUNDERCLAP's marauders. In MARGARET's opinion, she and her husband didn't lose three children to the Wolves—they lost all six. V:328–29

EISENHART'S DA: V:319

EISENHART'S GRAND-DA: V:319

RANCH COWPOKES: V:321, V:334, V:336–37, V:489, V:495, V:553 *(hands)*

SLIGHTMAN, BEN (EISENHART'S FOREMAN): Ben Slightman is the father of BENNY, also called BENNY THE KID *(listed below)*. We are told that Slightman, an earnest-looking man in spectacles and farmer's clothes, does not suffer fools lightly. In the GATHERING HALL meeting where TIAN JAFFORDS suggests that the Calla *folken* stand up to the WOLVES, Slightman counsels caution. Later we learn the true reason for Slightman's fears.

Four years before the beginning of our story, Slightman (a widower) lost Benny's twin sister to a disease called hot-lung. The child was probably infected by ANDY, but grieving Slightman didn't know this. He agreed to betray his fellow townsfolk for a pair of spectacles, a music machine which he hides in his saddlebag, and a promise that his one remaining child would be kept safe from the Greencloaks. Slightman's secret is discovered by JAKE CHAMBERS while he is hiding in the CALLA DOGAN. Jake informs Roland, who then feeds false battle information to Slightman and Andy so that the two of them will misdirect the coming Wolves. Roland's plan works, but during the EAST ROAD battle Benny is killed. A distraught Slightman (also one of the CHILD-MINDERS) blames Roland for his son's death, screaming that Roland wanted vengeance on him. Roland manages to silence him before others can hear his confession of guilt. V:19–31 *(Town Gathering Hall; present)*, V:44 *(follows* ka-tet*)*, V:45 *(follows* ka-tet*)*, V:47 *(follows* ka-tet*)*, V:88 *(new friends)*, V:92 *(indirect)*, V:106 *(indirect)*, V:109, V:111–13, V:116, V:122, V:142–60, V:165, V:166, V:167, V:201–10, V:211–34 *(present; mentioned directly on 211, 216, 218)*, V:234, V:294, V:302, V:313, V:323 *(da)*, V:340–42, V:384–86, V:391, V:495–96, V:533 *(indirect)*, V:534, V:551, V:552, V:553, V:554, V:555, V:558, V:559, V:561, V:567–77, V:578, V:579–80, V:581, V:585, V:586, V:590, V:601–17 *(present; mentioned directly on 602, 607, 608, 610, 611, 614–16)*, V:637, V:638, V:641, V:654, V:655–61, V:662–67, V:683, V:687, V:689, V:690–97, V:704, VI:17, VI:25, VI:67, VI:167 *(or Benny)*, VI:168 *(or Benny)*, VI:205, VII:191, VII:508

SLIGHTMAN, BENNY (BENNY THE KID): Although Benny Slightman is a few years older than JAKE CHAMBERS, Jake is the more experienced of the two boys. Hence, the pair become well-matched friends. Ben's twin sister died of hot-lung four years before our story takes place, and so no one knows if he counts as a twin or a singleton. (We find out later that Benny's twin was probably infected by ANDY.) Benny does not know that his father is a traitor, a fact which saves brave young Ben a lot of pain. During the final stand against the WOLVES, Benny, along with the TAVERY twins, hides in the fighter's ditch located on the front line of the East Road battle. After MARGARET EISENHART's death, Benny is killed by one of the Wolves' flying sneetches.

When Eddie returns to NEW YORK 1977 via BLACK THIRTEEN, he finds out that in our world, Ben Slightman Jr. (or "Benny the Kid," as Eddie tends to call him) had a namesake who grew up to be a cowboy novelist. This other Ben Slightman Jr. settled in MONTANA, but was killed during an argument with some Indians in front of a local general store. In *The Dark Tower*, we find out that this Ben Slightman also wrote science fiction under the pen name DAN HOLMES, a name shared by SUSANNAH DEAN's father. V:29, V:44 *(following* ka-tet*)*, V:45 *(following* ka-tet*)*, V:47 *(following* ka-tet*)*, V:88 *(new friends)*, V:92 *(indirect)*, V:106 *(indirect)*, V:109 *(indirect)*, V:109 *(indirect)*, V:111–13, V:116, V:122–37, V:142–60, V:165, V:169, V:201–10, V:211–34 *(present; mentioned directly on 212, 216, 218, 221, 225 as Jake's friend, 227, 228, 233, 234)*, V:235, V:238, V:294, V:302, V:313, V:318–24, V:328, V:332–34 *(watches Margaret Eisenhart throw)*, V:340, V:341, V:381, V:385, V:386, V:487, V:495, V:496, V:501, V:532–34 *(namesake author; nineteen letters)*, V:552, V:553–56, V:557, V:558, V:559, V:568, V:571, V:572, V:574, V:575, V:577, V:578, V:579–80, V:586, V:601–17 *(present; mentioned directly on 602, 614, 615, 616)*, V:636–38, V:654, V:656, V:657 *(Jake's friend)*, V:658, V:660, V:661, V:662–73, V:675–76, V:679–82 *(hiding, killed on 682)*, V:683, V:687, V:688–97, V:700, V:705 *(friend)*, VI:3, VI:11, VI:24, VI:25, VI:27, VI:32, VI:167, VI:168, VI:205, VI:269, VI:340, VII:137, VII:191, VII:396, VII:398, VII:403, VII:473, VII:508

> **TWIN SISTER:** Benny's sister died of hot-lung four years before our story begins. Both she and Benny were ten at the time. At the end of *Wolves of the Calla*, we find out that she was probably purposefully infected by ANDY, who needed one vulnerable parent to become an informer for the WOLVES. V:112–13, V:204, V:385, V:495, V:554, V:580, V:660

SLIGHTMAN, EDNA: Benny's aunt. V:323

TELFORD, GEORGE: George Telford, owner of BUCKHEAD RANCH, is silver-haired, tanned, weather-beaten, and handsome. (In EDDIE DEAN's opinion, he strongly resembles Pa Cartwright from the television program *Bonanza*.) Although his ranch is not as large as EISENHART's, Telford is gifted with both a silver tongue and a smooth voice, powerful weapons which he uses against TIAN JAFFORDS in the GATHERING HALL battle for hearts and minds. Like the other wealthy men of the Calla, Telford does not want the Calla *folken* to stand up against the WOLVES. He is afraid of losing his home and his land. Unlike Eisenhart, who stands with Roland in the end, Telford remains staunchly opposed to our *tet*'s battle plan. After their victory, he probably has a change of heart. V:24–31 *(Town Gathering Hall; present)*, V:211–34 *(present; mentioned directly on 214, 218, 221, 223–26, 227, indirect, 230)*, V:244, V:509, V:553 *(Buckhead Ranch)*, V:601–14 *(present; mentioned directly on 602, 606–7, 608–9, 611, 612, 614)*, V:619

> **ELDEST SON:** V:601–17 *(present; mentioned directly on 608)*

> **TELFORD, MRS.:** George Telford's wife. She is described as a plump but hard-faced woman. V:601–17 *(present; mentioned directly on 602, 606)*

> **TELFORD FAMILY:** V:606

ROONTS: In Calla Bryn Sturgis, as in the other Callas of the CRESCENT, twins are the norm and singletons are rarities. However, this birthing anomaly has a hidden horror. Once a generation, the WOLVES sweep out of THUN-DERCLAP and take one of every pair of prepubescent twins over the age of three. The stolen children are almost always returned (they make the journey back to the Calla upon two flatcars drawn by a train), but when they come back from Thunderclap, they are ruined (roont). No matter how clever they were before they were taken, they return intellectually devastated. Few have the ability to do physical labor and even fewer can speak. Though they grow to prodigious size (some are as tall as seven feet), they are sexually dead. Those who understand at least part of what has happened to them, or who were old enough when they were taken to comprehend some of what they have lost, suffer from terrible depression. Some even commit suicide.

At the end of *Wolves of the Calla*, we learn that the Calla's twins are taken to Thunderclap so that the chemical (or perhaps enzyme) which causes "twin-telepathy" can be extracted from their brains. The servants of the CRIMSON KING transform this substance into pills and feed it to the psychic BREAK-ERS who are eroding the BEAMS. Hence, it seems that *ka*, not random chance, has brought Roland and his friends to the BORDERLANDS.

Upon reaching their thirties, the roonts grow old with shocking rapid-ity. They die in terrible physical agony. V:2, V:3, V:11, V:14, V:23, V:24, V:139 *(ruined)*, V:143–47, V:152, V:220, V:319, V:589, V:609, V:630, V:658, V:660, VI:152 *(Cullum speaks of roont walk-ins)*, VI:238 *(indirect)*, VII:173, VII:206, VII:339, VII:532

CAVERRA, RUTH: Twin of REUBEN CAVERRA. V:15, V:483

DOOLIN, MINNIE: Minnie Doolin was the twin sister of MOLLY DOO-LIN, the only person in the Calla ever to have killed one of the WOLVES. When Molly hurled that deadly ORIZA, she called out Minnie's name. V:361, V:363

EISENHART, VERNA: VAUGHN EISENHART's twin. V:319

FARADAY, GEORGE: Son of NEIL FARADAY, twin brother of GEOR-GINA FARADAY. V:18

HOONIK, ZALMAN: Twin of ZALIA JAFFORDS. He lives with the JAF-FORDS FAMILY. Zalman is seven feet tall. V:10–11, V:146, V:147, V:150, V:344–46, V:349, V:351–57, V:489–92 *(present)*, V:649, V:681 *(indirect; brother)*

JAFFORDS (GRAN-PERE'S TWIN): V:11, V:362

JAFFORDS, TIA: Tia is TIAN JAFFORDS's roont twin. She is six and a half feet tall and has enormous breasts. Unlike many of the roonts, she is able to talk. Although she functions at the mental level of a young child, Tia has the uncanny ability of avoiding holes in "loose ground." She wears one of FATHER CALLAHAN's Jesus-trees. V:2–9, V:10–11, V:144, V:147, V:150, V:344–46, V:349–50, V:351–57, V:368, V:489–92 *(present)*, V:649

JAVIER, BULLY: Twin of BUCKY JAVIER. He died. V:159

OVERHOLSER, WELLAND: Twin of WAYNE OVERHOLSER. V:144, V:147, V:150

SLIDELL (POKEY SLIDELL'S SON): V:362

SLIDELL (POKEY SLIDELL'S TWIN): V:362

SISTERS OF ORIZA: *See* ORIZA, SISTERS OF, *listed separately*

WOLF POSSE: Seventy years before the beginning of our story, a small band of Calla *folken* stood up to the WOLVES of THUNDERCLAP. One of their number (a redheaded SISTER OF ORIZA named MOLLY DOOLIN) killed one of these Greencloaks, but this victory came at a great cost. JAMIE JAF-FORDS was the only human survivor.

DOOLIN, EAMON: Balding, mild-mannered Eamon Doolin was the husband of the fiery MOLLY DOOLIN, the only person in the Calla ever to have killed one of the invading WOLVES. He stood true, but was killed by a sneetch which exploded in his face. He was twenty-three. V:358–63

DOOLIN, MOLLY: *See* ORIZA, SISTERS OF, *listed separately*

    MINNIE: *See* CALLA BRYN STURGIS CHARACTERS: ROONTS, *listed above*

JAFFORDS, JAMIE: *See* JAFFORDS FAMILY, *listed separately*

SLIDELL, POKEY: Pokey Slidell, best friend of JAMIE JAFFORDS, was the oldest member of the Wolf Posse. Pokey had already lost a brother and a young child to the WOLVES. Like EAMON DOOLIN, Pokey was killed by a sneetch. V:358–64, V:365

    POKEY'S SON: *See* CALLA BRYN STURGIS CHARACTERS: ROONTS, *listed above*

    POKEY'S TWIN: *See* CALLA BRYN STURGIS CHARACTERS: ROONTS, *listed above*

OTHER CHARACTERS:

    ANDY THE ROBOT: *See* NORTH CENTRAL POSITRONICS, *listed separately*

    BERNARDO: Bernardo is the town tosspot. V:601–17 *(mentioned on 602)*

    CALLAHAN, FATHER: *See* CALLAHAN, FATHER DONALD FRANK, *listed separately*

    CASH, BENITO: V:16–31 *(Town Gathering Hall; present),* V:211–34 *(present; mentioned directly on 222)*

    COWBOYS (UNNAMED): V:601–17 *(present; named on 602)*

    ECHEVERRIA: *See also* CALLAHAN, FATHER DONALD FRANK: CALLAHAN'S HIDDEN HIGHWAYS ASSOCIATES: MEXICAN IMMI-GRANTS (ILLEGAL). V:211–34 *(Town Gathering Hall; present)*

    FARMWORKERS (UNNAMED): V:402

    HAGGENGOOD TWINS: These twenty-three-year-old twins were born in the year that the WOLVES last invaded Calla Bryn Sturgis. They are incredibly ugly but are hard workers. V:601–17 *(present; mentioned directly on 603)*

    HANDS FAMILY: V:601–17 *(present; mentioned directly on 602)*

    MUNOZ, ROSALITA: *See* ORIZA, SISTERS OF, *listed separately*

    POSELLA, FARREN: A farmhand. V:22–31 *(Town Gathering Hall; present),* V:211–34 *(present; mentioned directly on 222, 225),* V:601–17 *(present; mentioned directly on 602)*

    SLIGHTMAN, BEN: *See* CALLA BRYN STURGIS CHARACTERS: RANCHERS: EISENHART, VAUGHN

    SLIGHTMAN, BENNY: *See* CALLA BRYN STURGIS CHARACTERS: RANCHERS: EISENHART, VAUGHN

    SPALTER: Cousin of WAYNE OVERHOLSER. V:211–34 *(present; mentioned directly on 222)*

TAVERY, FRANCINE: The talented Tavery twins draw Roland a map of the Calla and its surrounding countryside. This map proves useful when Roland plans his battle strategy. The Taverys are beautiful prepubescent children. They both have black hair, large blue eyes, clear skin, and cheeks with a smattering of freckles. If the raids from THUNDERCLAP had not been stopped, either Francine or Frank would have ended their days ROONT. V:242 *(indirect)*, V:249 *(indirect)*, V:250–51, V:294, V:310–12, V:337, V:340, V:351, V:388, V:399, V:490, V:512, V:575, V:601–17 *(present; mentioned directly on 603)*, V:649, V:662–73, V:675–76, V:677, V:679–82 *(hiding in fighter's hole; mentioned again 682)*, V:692, V:693–97 (folken), VI:24 *(indirect)*, VI:27 *(indirect)*

TAVERY, FRANK: Frank and FRANCINE TAVERY draw the map which Roland uses to plan his *tet*'s stand against the WOLVES. Like his sister, Francine, Frank is a beautiful prepubescent child. His hair is black, his eyes are blue, and his clear, smooth cheeks are covered with a smattering of freckles. Just before the battle of the EAST ROAD commences, Frank and Francine help JAKE CHAMBERS and BENNY SLIGHTMAN strew children's toys along the ARROYO path to divert the coming Wolves. However, Frank steps in a hole and breaks his ankle. After much struggle, Jake, Benny, and Francine manage to move him, but just in time. Jake's three companions are forced to hide in the gunslingers' fighting ditch with Roland, EDDIE, SUSANNAH, and the SISTERS OF ORIZA rather than in the rice with the other children. This unplanned frontline hiding place leads indirectly to Benny's death. V:242 *(indirect)*, V:249 *(indirect)*, V:250–51, V:294, V:310–12, V:337, V:340, V:351, V:399, V:490, V:512, V:575, V:601–17 *(present; mentioned directly on 603)*, V:649, V:662–73, V:675–76, V:679–82 *(hiding in fighters' hole; mentioned again 682)*, V:692, V:693–97 (folken), VI:11, VI:24, VI:27, VI:205

TOOK, EBEN: Shrewd, fat Eben Took is the present owner of TOOK'S GENERAL STORE. In his high, womanish voice, he makes it clear that he does not want to stand up to the WOLVES. (He is afraid they will burn down his store and ruin his profits.) Not surprisingly, none of the Tooks have children at risk. V:18–31 *(Town Gathering Hall; present)*, V:158–59, V:205, V:294, V:388, V:400, V:401, V:402–6, V:417, V:418, V:472, V:479, V:487 *(store)*, V:497, V:601–14 *(present; mentioned directly on 604, 608, 609, 611, 612, 613, 614)*, V:695, VI:130 *(shop)*, VI:162, VII:423

TOOK FAMILY (GENERAL): The Tooks are one of the wealthiest and most important families in the Calla. They own both TOOKY'S (the Calla's general store) and the TRAVELLERS' REST (the town's boardinghouse and restaurant). They also own half interest in the LIVERY and have loan papers on most of the smallhold farms in the Calla. In the distant past, some of the Tooks tried to hide children in their store so that the WOLVES would not find them. As punishment, the Wolves burned the store down to the ground and took the children anyway. Now no Took will stand up to the Wolves. V:13 *(store)*, V:14 *(store)*, V:19 *(Tooky's)*, V:158–59, V:331, V:359, V:487, V:497 *(store)*, V:534 *(store)*, V:566 *(store)*, V:585, V:601–17 *(clan present; mentioned directly on 602, 606, 621)*

CALLAHAN, FATHER DONALD FRANK (PERE CALLAHAN, FATHER CALLAHAN, THE OLD FELLA, CALLAHAN O' THE ROADS)

Before the publication of *Wolves of the Calla*, many CONSTANT READERS probably assumed that Father Donald Frank Callahan was wandering the Earth as cursed as Cain. Our last sight of him in the novel *'Salem's Lot* was of a broken man, abandoned by his God, waiting for the driver of his NEW YORK CITY–bound bus to return with a bottle of cheap hooch so that he could burn the terrible, damning taste of the VAMPIRE BARLOW's blood from his mouth.

Along with his companions BEN MEARS, JIM CODY, MATT BURKE, and MARK PETRIE, Callahan had dared to stand up to an ancient TYPE ONE VAMPIRE living in the town of JERUSALEM'S LOT, MAINE. But in his personal confrontation with that force of the Outer Dark, Callahan's faith had failed him. In the wreckage of the Petries' kitchen, Barlow challenged Callahan to throw down his cross, but Callahan did not have enough faith in the WHITE, that elemental force behind all religious trappings, to confront the vampire without it. But even as he hesitated, the said crucifix's blinding white fire faltered and went out. As a result, Callahan was forced to take part in Barlow's unholy communion and became unclean, both in his own eyes and in the eyes of God.

After fleeing 'Salem's Lot but before arriving in CALLA BRYN STURGIS, Pere Callahan traveled the HIGHWAYS IN HIDING, which connect the MULTIPLE AMERICAS on all levels of the DARK TOWER. Often he would "flip" between one level of the Tower and another. (For example, he would fall asleep in FORT LEE, NEW JERSEY, but wake up in one of its twinners named LEABROOK.) During his wanderings, Callahan had two brief periods of grace, first in the HOME shelter, located on FIRST AVENUE of New York City, and then in the LIGHTHOUSE SHELTER of DETROIT. However, his first hiatus ended with the death of his beloved friend LUPE DELGADO, and the second was clipped short by his own death on December 19, 1983. (He jumped out a window to save himself from RICHARD P. SAYRE, CAN-TOI servant of the CRIMSON KING, and his horde of AIDS-carrying vampires.)

When we meet Callahan in the town of Calla Bryn Sturgis, his God has taken him back into the fold, at least on a trial basis. He has been in the Calla long enough to build a church and to convert many of the townsfolk to his particular brand of Christianity. Beneath the floor of his church sleeps BLACK THIRTEEN, the most dangerous seeing sphere of MAERLYN'S RAINBOW. The powerful magic of Black Thirteen opened the UNFOUND DOOR in the WAY STATION between life and death and transported both Callahan, and itself, to the CAVE OF VOICES in the Calla.

Although many years have passed, the Calla's Callahan still bears the scars of his confrontation with the vampire Barlow—a burned hand from when he tried to reenter his church but was blasted away from it by the power of the White, and a disturbing ability to detect all otherworldly creatures, including both vampires and the VAGRANT DEAD. Callahan also bears a brand on his forehead (in the shape of a cross), which the people of the Calla think was self-inflicted. How-

ever, this scar was the result of mortal demons, namely the HITLER BROTH-
ERS, who were hired by the LOW MEN to hunt Callahan down and kill him.

At the end of *Wolves of the Calla,* a shaky Callahan finds out that he is actually a character in a novel by STEPHEN KING. The name of the novel? *'Salem's
Lot.* It is quite possible that rereading his own story reinforces Callahan's decision not to give in to doubt again. In *The Dark Tower,* as in *'Salem's Lot,* Callahan's faith in the White is put to the test. However, this time he triumphs. When
Callahan faces down the blood-drinkers of the DIXIE PIG with JAKE CHAM-
BERS, he does not lose faith. With first Susannah's SCRIMSHAW TURTLE, then
his cross, and then with just the little CAN-TAH (another symbol of the White),
he holds off the forces of darkness so that Jake and OY can escape. In the end,
Callahan is attacked by the low men, but before the vampires can approach and
feed upon him, Callahan ends his own life with Jake's Ruger. Callahan dies by
his own hand, but in his final desperate hour he redeems himself in his own eyes,
and in the eyes of his God.

V:2 *(Old Fella),* V:6, V:8, V:11, V:16–31 *(on 16 enters Gathering Hall; present
for action),* V:44 *(following our* ka-tet*),* V:45 *(following our ka-tet),* V:47 *(following our* ka-tet*),* V:106–16, V:117, V:118, V:119, V:122–37, V:138, V:139,
V:142–60, V:165, V:175, V:176, V:180, V:196, V:201–10 *(present; mentioned
on 204, 205, 206, 208),* V:211–34 *(Calla fiesta; mentioned on 211, 212, 214,
216, 218–19, 221, 225, 227–87),* V:234–37, V:238, V:240, V:241 *(the religious),* V:242, V:243, V:244–45, V:248, V:249, V:250, V:252–53, V:254–309
(Priest's tale), V:309–17, V:338, V:341, V:381, V:383, V:393, V:396, V:399,
V:400, V:401, V:402, V:403, V:409, V:411, V:412, V:413, V:414, V:415,
V:417, V:418, V:419, V:420, V:421–72 *(466; the Walking Old Fella),* V:475,
V:476–85, V:487, V:494, V:497–500, V:503, V:504, V:510, V:512, V:543
(indirect), V:549, V:550–51, V:552, V:574, V:581–600, V:601–17 *(present
at Calla gathering; mentioned on 601, 603, 604),* V:618–28, V:634, V:636,
V:639, V:641–44, V:647, V:653, V:654, V:655, V:662–67, V:685, V:689 *(one
of* folken*),* V:693–97 *(one of* folken; *mentioned on 693, 695),* V:699–705,
VI:3–8, VI:4, VI:11, VI:13–43, VI:80–82, VI:122, VI:123, VI:133, VI:143,
VI:147, VI:168, VI:169, VI:170, VI:177–78, VI:185, VI:198, VI:200, VI:202,
VI:206, VI:208, VI:210, VI:211, VI:215, VI:216, VI:224, VI:225, VI:231,
VI:245, VI:248, VI:253, VI:269, VI:271, VI:281, VI:288, VI:307–44, VI:360,
VII:3–16, VII:19, VII:23, VII:24–28, VII:31–33, VII:36, VII:55, VII:70, VII:81,
VII:85 *(indirect),* VII:86, VII:90, VII:93 *(faddah),* VII:111 *(faddah),* VII:129,
VII:134 *(indirect),* VII:143, VII:145, VII:146, VII:147, VII:152, VII:189,
VII:194, VII:259, VII:275 *(twin of Ted Brautigan),* VII:281, VII:303–4,
VII:310, VII:473, VII:503, VII:523, VII:525, VII:593, VII:689, VII:802

CALLAHAN'S PRESENT ASSOCIATES:

HIPPIE WITH ACNE/HAPPY COWBOY: See ROSE, *listed separately*

MUNOZ, ROSALITA (ROSITA): See ORIZA, SISTERS OF, *listed separately*

POSTMISTRESS IN STONEHAM, MAINE: See MAINE CHARAC-
TERS, *listed separately*

SNUGGLEBUT: Callahan's cat. V:566

CALLAHAN'S HIDDEN HIGHWAYS ASSOCIATES:

BANDY BROOKS: Just as Callahan crossed the NEW YORK CITY

FOOTBRIDGE, which spanned the HUDSON RIVER in his version of the Big Apple, he saw a huge vehicle on treads crossing the GEORGE WASHINGTON BRIDGE. This bizarre sight was the first indication that Callahan had entered one of the MULTIPLE AMERICAS. V:298

BARTENDER (AMERICANO BAR): This bartender served Callahan his first drink after LUPE DELGADO's death. Many more followed. V:285

BLACK DRIVER IN STRAW HAT: This man gave Callahan a lift in his beat-up Ford. Before dropping him off in SHADY GROVE, he gave Callahan five dollars and a spare baseball cap. V:304–5, V:445

BOY IN HARTFORD: After his terrible confrontation with the VAMPIRE BARLOW, Callahan saw this unhappy boy sitting by himself on a porch at four thirty in the morning. Callahan describes him as a silent essay in pain. V:263

BRAWNY MAN: Brawny Man was one of the day-labor companies that Callahan worked for during his years traveling the HIDDEN HIGHWAYS of America. V:292, V:444, V:467

CASTILLO, JUAN: Juan Castillo was one of the Mexican men Callahan worked with in CALIFORNIA. V:309

CHADBOURNE: In one of the ALTERNATIVE AMERICAS, a former U.S. president named Chadbourne appears on the ten-dollar bill. V:300, V:309, V:444

CHILD SKIPPING ROPE: Callahan saw this child in FOSSIL, OREGON. It is one of the vivid, snapshotlike memories he has of his time on the roads. V:305

CHUMM, GREG (CHUMM'S TRAVELING WONDER SHOW): Greg Chumm was the greasy-haired owner of Chumm's Traveling Wonder Show. While employed by Chumm, Callahan posed as MENSO THE ESP WONDER. V:302, V:303

COVAY MOVERS (THE BROTHER OUTFIT): After the death of LUPE DELGADO, Callahan worked as a day laborer for this outfit for five straight days. (It was his soberest period that summer.) However, as soon as they offered him steady work, he went out and got drunk. He never returned to their work site. V:286–87

CRAZY MARY'S: *See* CALIFORNIA (STATE OF): SACRAMENTO: CRAZY MARY'S, *in* OUR WORLD PLACES

FORT LEE REGISTER AMERICAN: The local paper which Callahan reads while staying in FORT LEE is the *Fort Lee Register American*. On the days when he finds himself in LEABROOK, he reads the LEABROOK REGISTER. V:300

HOLLINGS, ERNEST "FRITZ": In one of the MULTIPLE AMERICAS which Callahan traveled through during his years bumming it along the HIGHWAYS IN HIDING, Ernest "Fritz" Hollings was elected president. V:305

LARS: While traveling through one of the MULTIPLE AMERICAS, Callahan met this little boy and fixed his radio. In thanks, Lars's mother packed Callahan a wonderful lunch that seemed to last for days. V:302

   LARS'S MOM: V:302

LEABROOK REGISTER: This is the local newspaper of LEABROOK,

NEW JERSEY. Unfortunately you'll never be able to read it since Leabrook doesn't exist on our level of the DARK TOWER. V:297, V:300

MANPOWER: Manpower was another of the day-labor companies that Callahan worked for during his years traveling the HIDDEN HIGHWAYS of America. V:266, V:286, V:292, V:444, V:467

MENSO THE ESP WONDER: While working for CHUMM'S TRAVEL-ING WONDER SHOW, Callahan played Menso the ESP Wonder. He was disconcertingly good at it. V:302, V:303

MEXICAN IMMIGRANTS (ILLEGAL): ESCOBAR, ESTRADA, JAVIER, ESTEBAN, ROSARIO, ECHEVERRIA, CAVERRA: Callahan met these men while traveling through TODASH America. Strangely, he met them again later (or, to borrow a term from *The Talisman* and *Black House*, he met their twinners later) in CALLA BRYN STURGIS. V:306, V:307, V:308

> **"CAN'T DANCE" ANGLO WOMAN:** This snooty woman looked down her nose at Callahan's Mexican companions. It was in her copy of the SACRAMENTO BEE that Callahan found out about ROWAN MAGRUDER's death. V:307–8

OLD GEEZER: This old geezer came across Callahan just after Pere saw his first VAGS. He tried to warn Callahan that some cops were coming, but Callahan had other things on his mind! V:284–85

> **COPS IN RADIO CAR:** V:284–85

PETACKI, PETE: Pete Petacki was a KENTUCKY grave digger who had a taste for seventeen-year-old jailbait. At least one of the girls who caught his eye was a TYPE THREE VAMPIRE. Luckily for Petacki, Callahan killed her before she could sink her teeth into Pete's all-too-willing throat. Pete never found out. V:302

> **VAMPIRE GIRL:** *See* VAMPIRES: TYPE THREE: INDIVIDUAL TYPE THREE VAMPIRES AND THEIR VICTIMS: PETE PETACKI'S VAM-PIRE GIRL

POST, THE: A newspaper. V:448

ROLL CALL: This is the list of names Callahan heard while having a sei-zure in a TOPEKA jail cell: Nailor, Naughton, O'Connor, O'Shaugnessy, Oskowski, Osmer, Palmer, Palmgren, Peschier, Peters, Pike, Polovik, Rance, Rancourt, Ricupero, Robillard, Rossi, Ryan, Sannelli, Scher, Seavey, Shar-row, Shatzer, Sprang, Steward, Sudby. V:446–48

RUDEBACHER, DICKY: Dicky Rudebacher owned a diner in LEABROOK, NEW JERSEY. On a different level of the TOWER, another version of Dicky owned a diner in FORT LEE. Callahan worked for both of them. Like Callahan, Dicky was fond of drink. He also occasionally suffered from "itchy-foot," or the call of the roads, but unlike Callahan, he stayed put. V:300–301

RUTA: Ruta was one of the "lost pets" that the LOW MEN were after. Callahan came across a poster for her that read:

LOST! SIAMESE CAT, 2 YRS OLD
ANSWERS TO THE NAME OF RUTA
SHE IS NOISY BUT FULL OF FUN

LARGE REWARD OFFERED
$ $ $ $ $ $
DIAL 764, WAIT FOR BEEP, GIVE YOUR NUMBER
GOD BLESS YOU FOR HELPING

Callahan doesn't know who Ruta is, but he's fairly certain that she isn't a cat, and that she won't be much fun once the low men get hold of her. V:303, V:445, V:446

SACRAMENTO BEE: This newspaper carried an article about the HITLER BROTHERS and the injury they caused to Callahan's old friend ROWAN MAGRUDER. V:296, V:307–9

SLEEPY JOHN'S: *See* CALIFORNIA (STATE OF): SACRAMENTO: SLEEPY JOHN'S, *in* OUR WORLD PLACES

TEENAGE VICTIM: See VAMPIRES: TYPE THREE: INDIVIDUAL TYPE THREE VAMPIRES AND THEIR VICTIMS

CALLAHAN'S HOME SHELTER ASSOCIATES:

CHASE, FRANKIE: Frankie Chase worked at HOME. VI:332

DANCING WOMAN: V:272

DELGADO, LUPE: Although ROWAN MAGRUDER founded HOME, it was Lupe Delgado—a thirty-two-year-old former alcoholic—who invested the place with life and purpose. When Callahan first met Lupe, the younger man hadn't had drink or taken drugs for five years. Although he'd been spending evenings at Home since 1974, he still kept his day job, which was working as part of the maintenance crew at the PLAZA HOTEL on FIFTH AVENUE (not to be confused with the PLAZA–PARK HYATT on FIRST AVENUE, where SUSANNAH-MIO takes refuge during *Song of Susannah*). Like Roland's love, SUSAN DELGADO, Lupe was both honest and attractive. Callahan grew to love him, and it was a love threaded with sexual attraction, though nothing physical (besides one brotherly kiss on the cheek) ever came of it.

In March of 1976, after Callahan had been working at Home for about five and a half months, he saw the telltale dark blue glow (a little bit like electric blueberry juice) around Lupe's neck and smelled the revolting scent of burning onions mixed with hot metal. Horrified, Callahan realized that his friend had been preyed upon by a TYPE THREE VAMPIRE. By April, Lupe had become a regular hit for the vampires, and finding one actually drinking Lupe's blood made Callahan begin killing the bloodsuckers.

Although it is doubtful whether Type Three vampires can develop AIDS (they are as phantasmal as they are physical), they can carry HIV, and one such infected monster fed upon Lupe. By mid-May, Lupe was so ill that he couldn't bear the smells of the Home kitchen. By the end of June, he was dead. Lupe's death plunged Callahan into deep despair and sent him reeling along the HIDDEN HIGHWAYS of America, bottle in hand. V:267–68, V:271–83, V:285, V:293, V:304, V:423, V:424, V:428, V:429, V:445, V:456, V:464, V:591

MARK CROSS BRIEFCASE BUSINESSMAN: *See* VAMPIRES: TYPE THREE: INDIVIDUAL TYPE THREE VAMPIRES AND THEIR VICTIMS

GUY WITH D.T.'S: This man was shaking so badly that ROWAN MAGRUDER had to feed him coffee laced with whiskey. V:272
ILLITERATE (OR SEMILITERATE) MAN: V:272
JEFFY: Jeffy was one of the more psychotic residents of the HOME shelter. He used a switchblade to slit the throat of a fellow resident who was disgusted by his nose-picking habit. V:428–29
  JEFFY'S VICTIM: V:428–29
LISA: Lisa was one of HOME's residents. She was attending AA. V:272
MAGRUDER, ROWAN (THE STREET ANGEL, *also called* **GEORGE MAGRUDER):** Rowan Magruder founded the HOME shelter. Along with LUPE DELGADO, he crafted its "wet" policy, which basically meant that men and women were allowed in through Home's doors whether they were drunk or sober. As a young man, Rowan had been an aspiring writer and academic, but he gave up both potential professions for his true calling, which was to help the down-and-out. Although the nature of his work earned him the nickname The Street Angel, and though he was visited by Mother Teresa and was praised by magazines such as *Newsweek,* his sister, ROWENA MAGRUDER RAWLINGS, never forgave him for abandoning his more respectable (not to mention more potentially lucrative) interests.

Callahan worked at Home for nine months, and during that time he and Magruder became friends. In 1981, after five years on the road, Callahan hurried back to NEW YORK to see Magruder, who was critically ill in RIVERSIDE HOSPITAL. He had been attacked by the HITLER BROTHERS, whose intended prey had been Callahan himself. Not long after Callahan's visit, Magruder died. However, the orderlies barely had time to change the sheets before Callahan landed in the same bed as yet another victim of the disgusting duo. V:267–68, V:271, V:272, V:279, V:280, V:281, V:282–83, V:288, V:292, V:293, V:308–9 *("Man of the Year"),* V:422–27, V:430, V:436, V:441, V:442, V:445, V:449, V:591 *(says George should read Rowan. Left over from earlier version of manuscript),* VI:332, VI:338, VII:281 *(George)*

RAWLINGS, ROWENA MAGRUDER: Rowena Magruder Rawlings was Rowan Magruder's twin sister. She flew to NEW YORK from CHICAGO once she found out that her brother had been attacked by the HITLER BROTHERS. Rowena thought that her brother had given up a literary career to help bums, and when she met Callahan, she slapped him across the face out of sheer spite. Rowan, who was conscious though silent during this interchange, was less than impressed by his sister's behavior. V:422–26, V:436 *(indirect),* V:442, V:445, V:465
SPINELLI, FRANK: Frank Spinelli was one of HOME's residents. He wanted Callahan to write him a letter of recommendation. V:272
CALLAHAN AND THE HITLER BROTHERS:
HITLER BROTHERS (NORTON RANDOLPH AND WILLIAM GARTON): The Hitler Brothers were a couple of racist thugs who attacked Jewish people and black people. Sometimes they did it for money, but most of the time they did it for fun. Their calling card was a swastika carved upon the forehead. While Callahan was traveling through the MULTIPLE

AMERICAS, the Hitler Brothers attacked his former boss ROWAN MAGRUDER.

The Hitler Brothers' real names were Norton (Nort) Randolph and William (Bill) Garton. Because of the discrepancy in their sizes, Callahan secretly renamed them George and Lennie, after the odd-sized traveling companions in Steinbeck's novel *Of Mice and Men*. However, unlike the characters in Steinbeck's tale, it was the big Hitler Brother (six-foot-six Nort) who had all the brains. Five-foot-two Bill didn't have any brains worth mentioning. In fact, he couldn't even tell the difference between a crucifix and a swastika. Even more unpleasant, he became sexually aroused whenever he contemplated cutting someone up.

The Hitler Brothers were hired by the LOW MEN to find and kill Callahan. When they failed (thwarted by "MR. EX LIBRIS" CALVIN TOWER and his pal "MR. GAI COCKNIF EN YOM" AARON DEEPNEAU), they were assassinated. For once, the servants of the CRIMSON KING did the world a favor. V:265–66, V:308–9, V:424 *(indirect)*, V:426, V:427, V:430–42, V:443, V:447–48, V:450, VI:202, VI:269

> **MEDICAL AND LEGAL PERSONNEL:** These people had to deal with the Hitler Brothers' victims—first ROWAN MAGRUDER and then Callahan.
>
> > **DOCTORS:** V:308 *(Magruder)*, V:424, V:427
> > **NURSES:** V:427, V:442
> > **POLICE OFFICERS:** V:424, V:432, V:439, V:445
>
> **MR. EX LIBRIS (VOICE NUMBER ONE):** *See* TOWER, CALVIN, *listed separately*
>
> **MR. GAI COCKNIF EN YOM (VOICE NUMBER TWO):** *See* TET CORPORATION: FOUNDING FATHERS: DEEPNEAU, AARON
>
> **TWO YOUNG COUPLES:** These two couples witnessed the Hitler Brothers dragging a vomit-covered Callahan up SECOND AVENUE. However, they didn't realize what was really going on. V:432

CALLAHAN'S LIGHTHOUSE SHELTER ASSOCIATES:

> **HUCKMAN, WARD:** Ward Huckman and AL McCOWAN ran the LIGHTHOUSE SHELTER in DETROIT, MICHIGAN. It was while Callahan worked for them that the LOW MEN (working for the CRIMSON KING's company, the SOMBRA CORPORATION) finally tracked him down.
>
> Under the pretense of awarding a million-dollar grant to Lighthouse, Sombra's executive vice president (the evil RICHARD P. SAYRE) invited Callahan and his friends to his headquarters. Instead of awarding the money, Sayre's cohorts knocked out Huckman and McCowan. Sayre then tried to sic his HIV-infected VAMPIRES on Callahan. Pere jumped out of the window to avoid the terrible death that had claimed his friend LUPE DELGADO. He awoke in the company of Roland's nemesis, WALTER. V:450–55
>
> **LIGHTHOUSE CLIENTS:** V:450–51
>
> **McCOWAN, AL:** Al McCowan and WARD HUCKMAN ran the LIGHTHOUSE SHELTER in DETROIT, MICHIGAN, which was Callahan's final place of employment before the servants of the CRIMSON KING tracked him down. RICHARD P. SAYRE and his fellow LOW MEN tricked Calla-

han and his friends into visiting SOMBRA's Detroit offices. The three unsuspecting men thought that they were going to receive a million-dollar grant for Lighthouse. Instead, they were greeted by the nasty servants of the Red King. McCowan and Huckman were knocked unconscious, and Callahan jumped out of the window to escape the clutches of Sayre's VAMPIRES. Callahan didn't exactly die; instead, he got a one-way ticket to visit WALTER in the WAY STATION, and then a transfer to CALLA BRYN STURGIS. V:450–55

AL'S MOTHER: Al's mother always maintained that one should arrive five minutes early for an important appointment—no more, no less. Her son and his friends followed her advice for their meeting with SOM-BRA, but it didn't do them any good. V:453

SAYRE, RICHARD P.: *See* CAN-TOI, *listed separately*

CALLAHAN'S OTHER PAST ASSOCIATES:

BISHOP DUGAN: Bishop Dugan approved Father Callahan's transfer from his LOWELL, MASSACHUSETTS, parish. Little did he know it, but Callahan's restlessness was not due to urban malaise but to the malaise of the bottle. V:254

CALLAHAN, GRANDFATHER FRANK: Pere Callahan's middle name came from this grandfather. V:108

CALLAHAN, MR.: When Callahan was a boy, his father (Mr. Callahan) discovered some of his son's hidden *Playboy* magazines. He made Pere burn them in the incinerator, then pray by the foot of his bed. One can't help but wonder whether this influenced Callahan's decision to join the priesthood. V:254 *(indirect)*, V:599

CALLAHAN, MRS.: Callahan's mother bought the crucifix whose arms were broken by the VAMPIRE BARLOW. One of the reasons that Calla-han finds the CAVE OF VOICES so distressing is that his mother calls to him from the pit's deep throat, asking why he let that nasty bloodsucker break her cross. V:28, V:254 *(indirect)*, V:259, V:264, V:280, V:465, V:591, V:599, V:619, V:624, V:708

CROWD THAT GATHERS UPON ENTRY TO 1999 NEW YORK: *See* HARRIGAN, REVEREND EARL, *listed separately*

'SALEM'S LOT CHARACTERS:

BARLOW, KURT: *See* VAMPIRES: TYPE ONE

BURKE, MATTHEW: On a level of the DARK TOWER not far from ours, Matthew Burke taught high school English in the town of JERUSALEM'S LOT, MAINE, a town which (as we learned in the novel *'Salem's Lot*) became infested with VAMPIRES.

Not long after becoming friends with the writer BEN MEARS, Burke invited a former student (who seemed ill) to stay overnight at his house. This student died in Matt's spare bedroom and his body was hauled away. However, not long after this, he returned for another visit, this time as a vampire. Not surprisingly, Burke suffered a massive heart attack. Until his second heart attack (which happened in his hospital bed), Matthew Burke acted as a stable contact for Ben Mears's (and Callahan's) posse of vampire hunters. V:256

BUS DRIVER: After Callahan's horrific confrontation with the VAMPIRE

BARLOW, Pere boarded a bus for NEW YORK. Although it was officially against the rules to let passengers drink alcoholic beverages while riding on Greyhound, this Big Apple–bound driver bought Callahan a bottle of cheap booze. However, his motives were anything but altruistic—he earned himself a twenty-eight-dollar tip. Callahan didn't mind the driver's mercenary motives. He was desperate to get the taste of Barlow's blood out of his mouth. V:262–64

CODY, DR. JAMES (JIMMY): Jimmy Cody was the doctor who helped BEN MEARS, Donald Callahan, and MARK PETRIE stand up to the VAMPIRES of 'SALEM'S LOT, MAINE. In the end, Cody didn't succumb to the VAMPIRE BARLOW's teeth but to his treachery. He died while trying to descend stairs that led to the cellar where Barlow was hiding. Unbeknownst to him, the stairs had been sawed away by Barlow's vampire-servants, and Jimmy Cody was impaled upon knives inserted in the floor below.

On the flap of the original printing of *'Salem's Lot,* Callahan was accidentally called FATHER CODY. V:257, VI:208 *(Father Cody)*

CODY, FATHER: *See* CODY, DR. JAMES, *listed above*

COOGAN, LORETTA: Loretta Coogan worked in SPENCER'S, which was the drugstore and soda fountain of 'SALEM'S LOT. Spencer's also doubled as the town's bus station. V:262

FLIP, MR.: Mr. Flip was the name of the bogeyman that lived in Callahan's childhood closet. In the novel *'Salem's Lot,* we find out that the VAMPIRE BARLOW resembled him. V:708

FOYLE, FRANKIE: When Callahan was in the seminary, Frankie Foyle gave him a blasphemous crewelwork sampler which read, "God grant me the SERENITY to accept what I cannot change, the TENACITY to change what I may, and the GOOD LUCK not to fuck up too often." Although we learn about this gift in *'Salem's Lot,* we don't learn Frankie Foyle's name until *Wolves of the Calla.* V:708

GLICK, DANNY: Twelve-year-old Danny Glick was one of the first victims of vampirism in the town of JERUSALEM'S LOT, MAINE. (See the novel *'Salem's Lot* by STEPHEN KING.) He was also one of the Lot's first new VAMPIRES. Danny's initial victim was the young grave digger Mike Ryerson. On a midnight adventure several evenings later, he visited the bedroom window of his friend MARK PETRIE. Mark (well versed in horror stories) invited Danny in but then burned his cheek with a plastic crucifix from his toy graveyard. Danny's undead flesh turned to smoke. V:257, V:265, V:299

MEARS, BEN: On another level of the DARK TOWER, Ben Mears was the author of the book *Air Dance.* Along with Father Callahan, JIM CODY, MARK PETRIE, and MATTHEW BURKE, Ben fought the VAMPIRES of 'SALEM'S LOT, MAINE. (See STEPHEN KING's novel *'Salem's Lot.*) When BARLOW (a TYPE ONE VAMPIRE) turned Ben's lover, SUSAN NORTON, into one of his own, Ben hammered a stake through her heart. (Love has many manifestations.) With the help of Mark Petrie, Ben eventually destroyed Barlow and the two of them fled to MEXICO. Later, they returned to the still-infested Lot to burn it to the ground. V:256, V:257–58, V:291, V:469–70

NORTON, SUSAN: Pretty Susan Norton was a literary fan of BEN MEARS's before she became his girlfriend. Although lovely and wholesome, Susan did not achieve true beauty until the VAMPIRE BARLOW turned her into a vampire. At Callahan's insistence, Ben drove a stake through her heart. V:257–58

PETRIE, MARK: Twelve-year-old Mark Petrie was one of the fearless VAMPIRE hunters of *'Salem's Lot*. Although he managed to evade the toothy hunger of his friend DANNY GLICK, Mark couldn't save his parents from the TYPE ONE VAMPIRE BARLOW. While saving Mark from Barlow, Callahan was forced to take the vampire's communion. Although Callahan was devastated by this, Mark escaped. He and BEN MEARS destroyed Barlow and then, after fleeing to MEXICO, returned to the LOT ('SALEM'S LOT, not the magic LOT!) to burn its remaining vampires. Years later, Callahan traveled via TODASH to LOS ZAPATOS, Mexico. There he witnessed Ben Mears's funeral and heard Mark's eulogy for his dear friend. V:257 *(indirect)*, V:258–59, V:261 *(boy)*, V:280 *(family kitchen)*, V:469–70, VI:329, VII:11

    PARENTS: V:258, V:259, V:280 *(family kitchen)*, VI:329

    STRAKER: *See* VAMPIRES: TYPE ONE: BARLOW, KURT

CALLAHAN, GRANDFATHER FRANK
    See CALLAHAN, FATHER DONALD FRANK: CALLAHAN'S OTHER PAST ASSOCIATES

CALVINS
    See TET CORPORATION

CAM TAM
    See ELURIA CHARACTERS

CAMERON
    See CAN-TOI

CAN CALAH
GAN speaks through the voices of the *can calah*, who (in our world at least) are called angels.
    VI:318

CANARYMAN
    See TAHEEN: BIRDMEN TAHEEN

CANDOR THE TALL
    See DESCHAIN, GABRIELLE

CANFIELD, BILL
    See DEBARIA CHARACTERS: JEFFERSON RANCH

CANFIELD'S TRAILMATES
    See DEBARIA CHARACTERS: JEFFERSON RANCH CHARACTERS

CANNIBAL FISH OF THE FAGONARD
See FAGONARD CHARACTERS

CANTAB OF THE MANNI
See MANNI

CAN-TAH
CONSTANT READERS will recognize the *can-tah* (or little gods) from STE-PHEN KING's novel *Desperation*. In that book, the *can-tah* (spelled without the hyphen) are ugly composite animals carved from stone. One is a coyote with a snake-tongue; yet another is a pitted gray spider with a coyote-head poking out just above its mandibles. In both novels, the *can-tah* can mesmerize, but there the similarity between the two types of carved creatures ends. In *Desperation,* the *can-tah* depict little demons, but the one SUSANNAH-MIO finds in *Song of Susannah* serves the WHITE and is in the form of the TURTLE GUARDIAN.
    For page references, see GUARDIANS OF THE BEAM: TURTLE

CAN-TOI (LOW MEN)
The *can-toi* are none other than the LOW MEN who stalked TED BRAUTIGAN in "Low Men in Yellow Coats," the opening story of *Hearts in Atlantis*. Although they look more or less like men (despite their outrageously loud clothes), these particular WARRIORS OF THE SCARLET EYE are actually human/TAHEEN hybrids. Like the *taheen,* the *can-toi* have hume bodies but the heads of beasts. However, while the nature of *taheen* heads varies (some look like birds, others like mammals), in the case of the low men, the heads are almost invariably those of louse-infested, red-haired rats with multiple rows of teeth.
    The *can-toi* hide their rat-heads behind humanoid masks (can you blame them?), but up close, their faces are rarely that convincing. *Can-toi* masks are formed from a kind of living latex which cannot be manufactured but must be grown. As living things in their own right, the masks have to breathe. They do this through a red hole (which looks like a bleeding red eye) located on the forehead. These red holes usually dry up when their masters cross over to our world, which is probably a good thing. Otherwise, they'd never even begin to pass for human.
    While *taheen* look upon humans as an inferior race, the *can-toi* worship the human form as divine. They even believe that they are *becoming* human, and that after the fall of the DARK TOWER, they will replace mankind. It seems that they are having at least minor success in their endeavor to become like men, since their minds can be progged (or read) by psychics. (The thoughts of true *taheen* sound like white noise.) At a certain point in his or her development, each low man or low woman is given a human name by their clan-fam. These names often sound absurd to actual humans. For example, one *can-toi* has the name VAN GOGH BAEZ. Another is called JAMES CAGNEY.
    The *can-toi*'s primary job is to take care of the psychic BREAKERS in the DEVAR-TOI, or Breaker prison, located in THUNDERCLAP. However, their duties also include hunting down escapees with their duplicitous lost-pet post-ers and their secret pavement messages coded as moon-and-star designs. Some *can-toi,* such as RICHARD P. SAYRE, vice president of the SOMBRA CORPO-

RATION, even live in our world and pass for hume much of the time. Like the BIG COFFIN HUNTERS (or REGULATORS), who also ultimately serve the CRIMSON KING, many of the *can-toi* have blue coffins tattooed on their hands.

Although they occasionally get up to other nasty mischief in our world (as both PERE CALLAHAN and CALVIN TOWER can testify), when relaxing at home in ALGUL SIENTO or BLUE HEAVEN (the *taheen* and *can-toi* term for the Devar-Toi), the low men live in HEARTBREAK HOUSE. Despite their devotion to the Crimson King, the poisonous air of END-WORLD has as terrible an effect upon the low men as it does upon ordinary humes. End-World's poisons give the *can-toi* skin sores and nosebleeds. Even the smallest wounds they suffer can become infected and deadly.

When our *ka-tet* attacks the Devar-Toi, their policy is to save the Breakers but to kill the *taheen* and *can-toi* guards. The world won't miss these latter monsters much, especially since they have such a pathetic sense of humor. To a *can-toi*, hanging a picture of NIAGARA FALLS upside down is the height of comedy.

Like the CAN-TAH, the *can-toi* also appear in KING's novel *Desperation*. In that book, the *can-toi* are the animal servants of the demon Tak (short for Can-Tak, or big god). Unlike our *can-toi*, the *can-toi* of *Desperation* have neither human bodies nor the ability to reason or speak.

V:289 *(lost-pet posters)*, V:290–91, V:297 *(indirect)*, V:299, V:302–3 *(indirect; lost-pet posters)*, V:304, V:306, V:426–27 *(indirect)*, V:429, V:430, V:435, V:443, V:449 *(lost-pet posters)*, V:451 *(lost-pet posters)*, V:452, V:455–57, V:549, V:591, VI:64, VI:95, VI:111, VI:244–45 *(their job is the Breakers)*, VI:248, VI:278–79, VI:318, VI:320, VI:326, VI:337, VI:353, VI:364–84 *(Dixie Pig)*, VI:407, VII:5, VII:10, VII:14, VII:25 (can-toi), VII:26 (can-toi), VII:51 (can-toi), VII:55–71 *(five in birth room)*, VII:81, VII:83 *(came through door after Jake)*, VII:85, VII:86–87, VII:88, VII:90, VII:93, VII:101, VII:104–9 *(following Jake)*, VII:111 *(posse)*, VII:133–35, VII:146, VII:209, VII:222, VII:223, VII:226, VII:230, VII:235–36, VII:237, VII:238, VII:241, VII:269, VII:272, VII:281, VII:286, VII:288, VII:292, VII:293, VII:297, VII:300, VII:326–27, VII:334, VII:337, VI:556–82 *(Devar-Toi battle)*, VII:393, VII:407, VII:448, VII:476, VII:498

INDIVIDUAL CAN-TOI/LOW MEN:

ALEXANDER, BEN: Ben Alexander is one of the guards at the DEVAR-TOI. VII:372

ALIA (NURSE): *See* TAHEEN: RAT-HEADED TAHEEN

ANDREW: When we meet him in the DIXIE PIG, just before SUSAN-NAH/MIA gives birth, this obese low man is wearing a tux with plaid lapels and a red velvet bow tie. (His jilly, TIRANA, looks equally hideous in her strapless, silver evening dress.) Andrew is shot by FATHER CALLA-HAN. VI:365–71, VII:9–15

BAEZ, VAN GOGH: One of the strange human names adopted by a *can-toi*. VII:294

BEEMAN: A security guard at ALGUL SIENTO. VII:235–36, VII:239–40

CAGNEY, JAMES: James Cagney (named after a famous hume actor) is a red-haired *can-toi* who stands five feet five inches tall and who likes Western-style shirts and boots. (He prefers footwear that makes him seem much taller.) During the final DEVAR-TOI battle, his mask rips and (at one point) he is mistaken for a TAHEEN. VII:356–57, VII:371–74, VII:379–82 *(called* taheen*)*

CAMERON (THE RAPIST): This *can-toi* raped a BREAKER. His defense was that the CRIMSON KING commanded him to do it as part of his process of "becoming" human. *(See* BECOMING, *listed in the* END-WORLD *section of* APPENDIX I.*)* Luckily for the other female Breakers, the former Devar Master, HUMMA O'TEGO, thought Cameron's defense was preposterous and put him to death. The Breakers were invited to watch. VII:326, VII:344, VII:385

CARLYLE, THOMAS: One of the unexpected human names adopted by a *can-toi*. VII:294

CONROY: A technician at the DEVAR-TOI. VII:241

DIXIE PIG GUARDS: VI:377

DOORMEN AT THE DIXIE PIG: VI:364

GANGLI, DR.: *See* TRISTUM, DR. GANGLI, *listed below*

HABER: Haber is one of the *can-toi* who accompany SUSANNAH DEAN from the DIXIE PIG to the FEDIC DOGAN, where she and MIA give birth to the CHAP. Haber has a bulldoggy face, gray, luxurious curls, and a slanted hole in his forehead. Susannah shoots him in the chaotic battle following the birth of baby MORDRED. VI:370–84, VII:55–70

LONDON, JACK: Like so many of the *can-toi,* Jack London took a human name (in this case, the name of a famous hume writer). London is DR. GANGLI's assistant in the third-floor infirmary of DAMLI HOUSE in ALGUL SIENTO. VII:367

RANDO HATTEN LOOK-ALIKE: VII:293–94

SAYRE, RICHARD P.: The nasty *can-toi* Richard Patrick Sayre is the executive vice president of SOMBRA CORPORATION, one of the many companies in our world (and our world's twinners) serving the CRIMSON KING. On July 15, 1976, he signed a contract on behalf of Sombra with CALVIN TOWER, owner of the MANHATTAN RESTAURANT OF THE MIND. Tower was paid one hundred thousand dollars in exchange for his written consent to hold on to the magic LOT for one year, and then, at the end of that time, to give Sombra first right of purchase. However, as soon as the said year began to wind down (and as soon as he knew that Tower had blown the money), Sayre began to sic BALAZAR and his hoods on the chubby bookshop owner, figuring they could bully him into selling. (Thanks to EDDIE DEAN, this tactic doesn't work.)

With the help of his VAMPIRES and LOW MEN, Sayre brought about the death of FATHER DONALD FRANK CALLAHAN in the early 1980s. He was also in charge of the sting operation which lured MIA and an unwilling SUSANNAH DEAN to the DIXIE PIG so that Mia could give birth to her CHAP. (Susannah takes revenge by shooting him.) When we see Sayre in the Dixie Pig, he appears to be about sixty years old with white hair, a double row of teeth, and outrageously loud clothes. His humanoid mask looks lean and predatory.

Our final insight into Sayre's dirty work doesn't come from the *can-toi* himself, but from the bric-a-brac in his office, located below the FEDIC DOGAN. Here Roland and Susannah find files on themselves and their two dead *ka-tet* mates, as well as two significant oil paintings, both painted by PATRICK DANVILLE. One is of the DARK TOWER, and the other is a symbolic depiction of the Crimson King's triumph over ALL-WORLD-that-was. This second painting shows black-haired, blue-eyed MORDRED with one triumphant foot atop ARTHUR ELD's dead horse, LLAMREI. V:95, V:451, V:455–57, V:460, V:464, VI:119–24, VI:125, VI:228, VI:231, VI:234, VI:239, VI:240, VI:251, VI:254, VI:364–84, VII:8, VII:13, VII:14, VII:55–70 *(shot)*, VII:84, VII:104, VII:105, VII:106, VII:107, VII:108, VII:149, VII:240, VII:549–51 *(office)*, VII:703, VII:783

STRAW: Straw is a low man with flabby hands and many rings. Along with SAYRE and a number of other WARRIORS OF THE SCARLET EYE, he attends the birth of MORDRED, son of both the CRIMSON KING and Roland Deschain. SUSANNAH DEAN shoots him. VII:58–68, VII:71

TIRANA: When we meet this obese low woman in the DIXIE PIG, she is wearing a strapless, silver evening dress. DETTA WALKER rips off her mask and exposes the rat beneath. VI:365–71, VII:13–15, VII:25

TRAMPAS: In the final book of the Dark Tower series, we find out that all things, even eczema, can ultimately serve the BEAM. In *The Dark Tower,* we find out that Trampas, one of the few *can-toi* who are actually succeeding in the process of *becoming* human, has a terribly itchy scalp. Every time he lifts his beanie-like thinking cap, his thoughts can be read by his BREAKER friend TED BRAUTIGAN. Although Trampas does not mean to leak the CRIMSON KING's secrets, it is while scanning Trampas's thoughts that Ted realizes just what he and his fellow psychics are doing in the DEVAR-TOI's STUDY. It is also by listening to the radio-like broadcasts of Trampas's thoughts that Ted learns what part he—a facilitator—is playing in the untimely collapse of the Beams.

Although Ted's escape from the Devar is temporary, his distressing new knowledge strengthens his resolve to oppose the Lord of Discordia's plans for the macroverse. Ted helps Roland and his friends destroy the Devar and its guards. Unfortunately, Ted also ends up killing Trampas—who ultimately obeys the orders of the enemy—with one of his deadly thought-spears. VII:292, VII:293–96, VII:298, VII:299–302, VII:306, VII:356, VII:370–71, VII:375–77, VII:407

TRELAWNEY: Security guard at ALGUL SIENTO (the DEVAR-TOI). VII:239–40, VII:325–26

TRISTUM, DR. GANGLI: The much-feared Dr. Gangli is the DEVAR's sawbones. According to the BREAKERS, the dark, squat, heavily jowled Gangli looks like John Irving after a bad face-lift. However, none of them would dare say this to his face any more than they'd make fun of the roller skates he uses to sail through his rounds.

Dr. Gangli (who took a TAHEEN name even though he is *can-toi*) rules his third-floor surgery in DAMLI HOUSE with an iron fist. Because of the frequent infections that plague END-WORLD's denizens, Dr. Gangli prescribes many antibiotics. His prescriptions are losing their effectiveness, but Gangli isn't around to see them stop working completely. When the gas-pods behind the Damli House kitchens blow up during the Devar's final battle, Gangli (roller skates still spinning) is blown skyward along

with all of his paperwork. For Gangli, the end of life in the macroverse comes earlier than expected. VII:223, VII:239, VII:356, VII:367–68, VII:374
>   **GANGLI'S ORDERLIES:**
>   **LONDON, JACK:** *Listed above*
>   **NAMELESS ORDERLIES:** VII:367

CANTORA, IRENE
  See TASSENBAUM, IRENE

CAPRICHOSO (CAPI)
  See HAMBRY CHARACTERS: TRAVELLERS' REST: SHEEMIE; *see also* BREAKERS: RUIZ, STANLEY

CARLINER, MARK
  See KING, STEPHEN

CARLYLE, THOMAS
  See CAN-TOI

CARTOON CHARACTERS (OUR WORLD)
  See APPENDIX VI

CARVER, MARIAN ODETTA
  See TET CORPORATION

CARVER, MOSES
  See TET CORPORATION: FOUNDING FATHERS

CASH, BENITO
  See CALLA BRYN STURGIS CHARACTERS: OTHER CHARACTERS

CASSIDY, BUTCH
  See GUNSLINGERS (OUR WORLD)

CASSIOPEIA
  See MID-WORLD FOLKLORE

CASTNER
  See TULL CHARACTERS: SYLVIA PITTSTON'S REVIVAL

CASTILLO, JUAN
  See CALLAHAN, FATHER DONALD FRANK: CALLAHAN'S HIDDEN HIGHWAYS ASSOCIATES

CAT GUARDIAN
  See GUARDIANS OF THE BEAM

CAVERRA, DIANE
See CALLA BRYN STURGIS CHARACTERS: FARMERS (SMALLHOLD):
CAVERRA, REUBEN

CAVERRA, REUBEN
See CALLA BRYN STURGIS CHARACTERS: FARMERS (SMALLHOLD)

CAVERRA, RUTH
See CALLA BRYN STURGIS CHARACTERS: ROONTS

CHADBOURNE
See CALLAHAN, FATHER DONALD FRANK: CALLAHAN'S HIDDEN
HIGHWAYS ASSOCIATES

CHAMBERS, ELMER
Elmer Chambers is the father of our dear friend JAKE CHAMBERS. He is a
TV network big shot who works at 70 Rockefeller Plaza. His job is to destroy
other networks and he is very good at it. In fact, he is a self-proclaimed master
of "The Kill."
Elmer is five-foot-ten, and is both a chain-smoker and a coke fiend. He
smokes three packs of unfiltered Camels a day and has been known to snort
cocaine until his nose bleeds. His black crew cut bolts straight up from his head.
Jake thinks he looks like a man who has just suffered some tremendous, galva-
nizing shock. Elmer is living proof of Jake's theory that adults don't really know
any better than kids do. They just pretend to. In *Wind Through the Keyhole*, we
learn that Elmer Chambers knows great swear words.
    I:81, I:82, I:180, III:89–91, III:92, III:93, III:94, III:99, III:100, III:102,
III:103, III:108, III:121–22, III:126, III:129–35, III:136, III:137–38,
III:156–58, III:168, III:194, III:256, III:315, III:355, III:376, III:380, IV:21,
IV:31, IV:32 *(indirect),* IV:80 *(parents),* IV:85 *(parents),* IV:93, IV:655, V:40
(Jake's parents), V:46, V:104, V:155 *(father),* V:187, V:204 *(dad),* V:215,
V:382, V:471, V:559 *(dad),* V:561 *(father),* V:565–66, V:567, V:577, V:590,
V:617, V:637, V:656 *(father),* V:705, VI:11, VI:32, VI:41, VI:320, VI:324,
VII:7, VII:15, VII:84, VII:94, VII:95, VII:98, VII:110, VII:138 *(parents),*
VII:144, VII:191, VII:299, VII:310, VII:398, VII:399, VII:473, VII:535, W:21
(knows lots of great swears), W:30 *(son of Elmer)*
ELMER CHAMBERS'S ASSOCIATES:
    GIRL WITH BODACIOUS TA-TAS: "Bodacious ta-tas" is Elmer Cham-
    bers's term for a pair of really nice breasts. Hence, "a girl with boda-
    cious ta-tas" is a young woman who is well stacked. The girl in the film
    The Lost Continent fits this description. VII:97, VII:99, VII:103–4

****CHAMBERS, JAKE ('BAMA, TOM DENBY, KID SEVENTY-SEVEN,
JOHN "JAKE" CHAMBERS, JAKE TOREN, HYPERBOREAN WAN-
DERER)**
At eleven years old, John "Jake" Chambers is the youngest member of Roland's
present *ka-tet*. Jake is small for his age and (in his previous life) was often mis-
taken for a girl. However, his time in MID-WORLD has toughened him up.

Before being brought to Mid-World, blond, blue-eyed Jake was in the sixth grade at PIPER, his expensive private middle school. A loner, he had few friends and felt estranged from his parents, who were always too busy for him. His only close companion was GRETA SHAW, the family housekeeper. Jake spent most of his time under the care of professional people, even though he despised all professional people. At that point in his life, Jake was dangerously close to despising himself.

Unlike the other members of Roland's *ka-tet* whom Roland "draws" into his world over the course of the second book of the Dark Tower series, Jake enters Roland's world in *The Gunslinger*. (Unfortunately he doesn't last very long.) Roland and Jake's initial meeting takes place in the WAY STATION, an abandoned coach house in the MOHAINE DESERT, while Roland is pursuing the MAN IN BLACK. When Roland first discovers Jake, the boy can't remember who he is or where he came from. However, under hypnosis Jake reveals that he entered Mid-World by dying in his own *where* and *when*, namely in NEW YORK CITY on May 9, 1977, at 8:25 AM. Jake had been hit by a 1976 blue Cadillac (a Sedan de Ville) while standing on the corner of FIFTH AVENUE and Forty-third Street. Although Roland initially believes that Jake was pushed by the Man in Black, he later discovers that he was killed by JACK MORT, a psychopath whom we meet again in *The Drawing of the Three*.

Just as Jake is the first of Roland's American *ka-tet* to be drawn into Mid-World, he is also the first to discover Roland's potential for treachery. While Jake and Roland pursue the Man in Black, Roland lets Jake fall into a deep river chasm below the CYCLOPEAN MOUNTAINS so that he can get closer to their quarry. As Jake falls he utters the famous line, "There are other worlds than these." It turns out that Jake is right. There are many other worlds, and alternative Jakes exist in almost all of them. In fact, near the end of *The Drawing of the Three* Roland returns to one of these worlds in order to protect his young friend from Mort's dire schemes. Although Roland's motives are admirable, the consequences are dire. He creates a split in the time/space continuum, and both he and Jake end up traumatized by two conflicting sets of memories—one where Jake died and entered Mid-World, and one where he didn't.

The next time we meet Jake is in *The Waste Lands*. At the beginning of this book, both Jake and Roland are suffering from a kind of psychosis brought on by these double memories. The psychosis is cured when Roland, with the help of his new *tet*-mates EDDIE and SUSANNAH DEAN, draws Jake into Mid-World once more. Jake's second Mid-World birth takes place on June 1, 1977, the day after he finds both the MANHATTAN RESTAURANT OF THE MIND (where he buys *Charlie the Choo-Choo* and *Riddle-De-Dum!*) and the Vacant LOT, where he discovers the ROSE.

Although Jake's second entry into Mid-World is not as traumatic as his first, it is still difficult. To access Roland's world, Jake must travel to the haunted DUTCH HILL MANSION located in BROOKLYN and unlock one of the many DOORWAYS BETWEEN WORLDS which is located within it. This door is linked to one drawn by Eddie in the dirt of a SPEAKING RING located on the GREAT ROAD leading to LUD. Although each of these linked doorways is protected by a doorkeeper (on Jake's side it is the DUTCH HILL MANSION DEMON or PLASTER-MAN, and on Roland's it's the sinister SPEAKING

RING DEMON), our young friend passes over and is reunited with his adopted father, Roland.

Although Jake Chambers is eleven years old when we leave him at the end of *Wizard and Glass,* by the time he reaches CALLA BRYN STURGIS in *Wolves of the Calla,* he is twelve. Exposure to the ROSE has made Jake strong in "the touch." In fact, his psychic abilities are so formidable that when the MANNI help Roland, Jake, Eddie, and CALLAHAN to reactivate the UNFOUND DOOR at the beginning of *Song of Susannah,* HENCHICK (the Manni's *dinh*) places Jake directly in front of the door so that he can find its psychic "hook," or opening mechanism. In another *where* and *when,* Jake would probably have made a spectacular BREAKER.

Over the series, we watch Jake mature—a process filled with painful lessons. From Roland, he learns betrayal, but he also learns to forgive those he loves, and to accept that—although people make mistakes—they can change. In Lud (found in *The Waste Lands*) he discovers that adults can be sexually predatory, and that often the objects of their sadistic fantasies are vulnerable young boys. In *Wizard and Glass,* Jake gains insight into what Roland was like as a boy and begins to understand the forces which shaped the man he so loves into the obsessive being that Roland has become.

In the final three books of the Dark Tower series, Jake—now an accomplished gunslinger in his own right—continues to experience life's less savory lessons. While in Calla Bryn Sturgis, Jake witnesses another adult's betrayal (this time BEN SLIGHTMAN THE ELDER's betrayal of an entire community) and then learns to keep secrets, both from his *tet* and from his friend BENNY SLIGHT-MAN. Although no stranger to death, Jake has the distressing misfortune of having to witness the deaths of two who are dear to him. First, he sees his friend Benny blown apart by one of the WOLVES' sneetches, and then, in *The Dark Tower,* he watches as his *ka*-brother Eddie Dean is shot in the head by PIMLI PRENTISS, the Devar Master in THUNDERCLAP.

Perhaps it is this familiarity with death, as well as his own experience of it, which makes Jake so determined to sacrifice his own life to save STEPHEN KING rather than to witness the death of his *dinh,* Roland. On SLAB CITY HILL in LOVELL, MAINE, Jake—fresh from the horrors of the DEVAR-TOI—leaps out in front of an oncoming van, grabs King around the waist, and shields the writer with his own body. Hence it is Jake who is killed, not King, though our beloved *kas-ka Gan* suffers terrible injuries anyway. Blond-haired, blue-eyed Jake dies for a third time in the KEYSTONE EARTH occupied by his maker, Stephen King. Roland buries his adopted son in the Maine woods and makes IRENE TASSENBAUM promise to plant a rosebush over his grave.

Luckily for us, *ka* is sometimes kind. At the end of *The Dark Tower,* a trail-frayed Susannah Dean leaves Mid-World through the ARTIST'S DOOR (another manifestation of the UNFOUND DOOR, but this time drawn by PATRICK DANVILLE) and finds both Jake and Eddie alive and well in yet another version of NEW YORK. Although it's not the Keystone Earth (here they drive Takuro Spirits and drink Nozz-A-La cola), Susannah is still delighted to find herself in this snowy twinner of CENTRAL PARK. In this *where* and *when,* Eddie and Jake are brothers from WHITE PLAINS and their last name is TOREN. It seems only a matter of time before Susannah Dean becomes Susannah Toren, and that our *ka-tet,* reunited as family, will find a strange-looking canine named OY to join them.

As CONSTANT READERS will recognize, Jake Chambers is another manifestation of the brave and talented prepubescent/adolescent hero who can be found in a number of King's novels. In *'Salem's Lot* the boy is MARK PETRIE; in "Low Men in Yellow Coats" (the first story of *Hearts in Atlantis*) he's called BOBBY GARFIELD; in *Desperation* his name is David Carver; and in *It* he is the young Bill Denbrough. The boy-hero also appears in the King/Straub collaborative novel *The Talisman.* Although these boys have different appearances, personalities, and talents, they all prove that the adult world isn't always as wise as it thinks it is. It is the young boy (or the boy who still lives within the body of the man) who tries to remain true to his quest.

In *Wind Through the Keyhole,* Roland's American *ka-tet* plays a small role. In fact, their tale is but a frame story for the two interlinked narratives which Roland recounts during their stay in the village of GOOK, where our friends are forced to wait out the killing winds of a STARKBLAST. However, within this frame story, Jake and his pet BILLY-BUMBLER, OY, play important roles. While they are gathering wood to keep the town meetinghouse warm during the icy winds of the starkblast, Oy becomes mesmerized by the energy of the coming storm and Jake must risk his own life to carry Oy to safety. This event—and the powerful relationship between bumblers and starkblasts—is what inspires Roland to recount both his autobiographical tale about the SKIN-MAN, and the fairy tale called "The Wind Through the Keyhole," from which the novel takes its name.

I:74–95, I:112–13, I:117–26, I:129, I:132–44, I:149–58, I:174–92, I:198 *(indirect),* I:215, I:216, II:15 *(as sailor),* II:31, II:32 *(Isaac),* II:37, II:101, II:105, II:203, II:231, II:254, II:315–18 *(and Jack Mort),* II:319, III:29–30, III:35–36, III:41–48, III:50, III:51, III:59, III:78, III:86, III:89–146 *(89–102 looking for magic door),* III:149, III:151, III:152–58, III:162, III:165–70 *(169 as Tom Denby),* III:172–73, III:175–76, III:176–78, III:179, III:180, III:181 *(coming into Mid-World),* III:182–88, III:190–92, III:193–94 *(born),* III:194–96, III:197, III:198–201, III:202, III:203–4, III:205–13, III:219–67, III:268, III:269, III:273–81, III:283–303 *(294 Oy almost falls off bridge; 300 Gasher),* III:304–7, III:307–8 *(Roland follows),* III:312–14, III:314–16 *(Roland follows),* III:323 *(indirect),* III:325–28, III:328–31 *(Roland follows),* III:334–39, III:340, III:341, III:342, III:349, III:350–61, III:364, III:365–72, III:373–85 *(Roland and Jake escape Grays. Run to Blaine's cradle),* III:389, III:393–420, IV:3–10 *(Blaine),* IV:13–42 *(30 Edith Bunker, sex goddess; 31–35 Falls of the Hounds),* IV:44–70 *(61 leave Blaine; 64 sound of thinny; 64 and 67 saw player, Central Park),* IV:71–112 *(Topeka train station; 72–77 Topeka Capital Journal; 83 reflects on Forty-Sixth and Second; 86–87 roses; 87–89 Charlie the Choo-Choo in Topeka; 91 sign of Crimson King; 95 enters thinny; 97 Oz palace in distance; 106–12 Roland begins story),* IV:335–37 *(interlude in Kansas),* IV:414, IV:570 and 572 *(Roland's vision),* IV:615–25 *(end of Roland's story; back in Topeka),* IV:626–68 *(626 ruby Oxfords; 632 Green Palace; 634 gate like Wizard's Rainbow; 646 Tick-Tock; 648 Flagg; 652 Roland's matricide),* V:8 *(strangers from Out-World),* V:29–31 *(gunslingers),* V:35, V:36, V:38–47, V:48–70 *(visits New York via todash),* V:77, V:78, V:80, V:81, V:84, V:87, V:88–119, V:121, V:123–37, V:138, V:142–60, V:162, V:163, V:165,

V:167–69, V:176–85, V:187–98, V:201–34, V:235, V:238, V:239, V:241, V:246, V:249, V:257, V:258, V:266, V:291, V:294, V:302, V:313, V:318–24, V:325, V:328, V:329, V:330, V:332–34 *(watches Margaret Eisenhart throw)*, V:340, V:341, V:371–76 *(following Mia)*, V:378, V:380–87, V:388–406, V:408 *(indirect)*, V:412 *(ka-tet mate)*, V:417–19, V:420, V:421–23, V:428–30, V:437–38, V:442–45, V:448–49, V:452–54, V:457, V:460, V:461, V:462 *(indirect)*, V:466–72, V:476, V:479, V:480, V:485, V:487, V:488–96, V:496–505, V:506, V:511, V:514, V:519, V:534, V:552, V:553–80, V:581–90, V:592 *(indirect)*, V:601–17, V:621, V:636–39, V:641–44, V:652–53, V:656–57, V:659, V:660, V:661, V:662–73, V:675–76, V:678, V:679–705, VI:3–8, VI:10, VI:11–43, VI:64, VI:67, VI:68, VI:71, VI:79, VI:84, VI:85, VI:107, VI:121, VI:130, VI:143, VI:147, VI:199, VI:200, VI:205, VI:210, VI:216, VI:222, VI:224–25, VI:231, VI:247, VI:268, VI:284, VI:285, VI:288, VI:290, VI:298, VI:299, VI:302, VI:303 *(kid)*, VI:307–44, VI:360, VI:389, VI:391, VI:399, VI:400, VI:402, VII:3–11, VII:13, VII:14, VII:15, VII:19, VII:23, VII:24–28, VII:34, VII:36, VII:52, VII:59, VII:61, VII:63, VII:72, VII:78, VII:80, VII:81–104 *(100 changes places with Oy!)*, VII:104–5, VII:106 *(snot-babby)*, VII:107 *(brat)*, VII:108 *(snot-babby)*, VII:109–12, VII:114, VII:126, VII:129, VII:134 *(snot-babby)*, VII:136–38, VII:141–59, VII:164–65, VII:168, VII:169, VII:173, VII:177, VII:186 *(ka-tet)*, VII:187, VII:188, VII:189–220, VII:247–61, VII:262 *(indirect)*, VII:265–73, VII:276 *(indirect)*, VII:279–324 *(279–302 listening to Ted's story)*, VII:325, VII:329–42, VII:350, VII:351–52, VII:362–63, VII:368–70, VII:378–85, VII:387–418, VII:421–33, VII:441–43, VII:444–45, VII:448, VII:449–67 *(dies)*, VII:470, VII:472–75 *(a rose to be planted on his grave)*, VII:476, VII:477, VII:478, VII:485, VII:487, VII:503, VII:509, VII:510, VII:520, VII:523, VII:525, VII:526, VII:527, VII:528, VII:532, VII:533, VII:534–35, VII:538, VII:541, VII:542–43, VII:544, VII:549, VII:554–56, VII:559, VII:585, VII:630, VII:633, VII:643, VII:645–46, VII:649, VII:657, VII:662, VII:670, VII:697, VII:724–25, VII:727, VII:728, VII:729, VII:731, VII:733, VII:740, VII:744, VII:746, VII:747, VII:748, VII:758, VII:762, VII:769, VII:785, VII:797, VII:802, VII:809, VII:812–13, VII:818, VII:819, W:3–31, W:303–7

CHARACTERS JAKE MEETS WHEN HE RUNS AWAY TO THE LOT, TO BROOKLYN, AND TO MID-WORLD:

DEEPNEAU, AARON: *See* TET CORPORATION: FOUNDING FATHERS

DUTCH HILL CHARACTERS (JAKE MEETS THESE FOLKS DURING HIS JOURNEY):

DELIVERY VAN DRIVER: III:204–5

LITTLE LEAGUE PLAYERS: III:204

WOMEN OUTSIDE OF DUTCH HILL USED APPLIANCES: III:204–5

ELI: Jake met this guy—who happened to have dreadlocks and a canary yellow suit—while he was sitting in TIMES SQUARE. III:168

GUARD AT MET: III:167

MAN WHO BUMPS INTO PROSTITUTE: III:169

MARK CROSS PEN BUSINESSMEN: Jake saw two of these guys playing tic-tac-toe on a wall. One of them was named BILLY. III:110–11, V:51–52

MESSENGER BOY ON BIKE: III:111

OLD MAN FROM BROOKLYN: This old guy told Jake that there was no such thing as a MARKEY ACADEMY. III:177–78

PRETTY BLACK TEACHER AT THE MET: This woman discovered Jake while he was on "French leave." She told him to rejoin his class, not realizing just how far Jake was from it. III:166–67

TIMES SQUARE COP: While Jake was wasting time in TIMES SQUARE, this cop pegged him as a runaway. Jake mesmerized the bluecoat with his magic key and hid his true identity by giving the false name TOM DENBY. III:167–69

TIMES SQUARE PROSTITUTE: Jake wasn't certain what this woman did for a living, but he was fairly certain that she wasn't a librarian. III:169

TOWER, CALVIN: *See* TOWER, CALVIN, *listed separately*

UPS GUY: In *The Waste Lands,* Jake jumped over this man's dolly as he sprinted toward the Vacant LOT. While traveling via TODASH in 1977 NEW YORK, Jake recalls this incident. III:120, V:61

YOUNG PUERTO RICAN LADY: III:120

CHARACTERS JAKE MEETS WHEN HE TRAVELS TODASH:

BALAZAR'S MEN: *See* BALAZAR, ENRICO: BALAZAR'S MEN, *listed separately*

DEEPNEAU, AARON: *See* TET CORPORATION: FOUNDING FATHERS, *listed separately*

NEW YORK WOMAN: When Jake and OY visit 1977 TODASH NEW YORK, this woman hitches up her straight black skirt so that she can step over Oy. Even though she can't see our travelers, she can sense them. V:49, V:57

TOWER, CALVIN: *See* TOWER, CALVIN, *listed separately*

CHARACTERS WHO WITNESS JAKE'S DEATH:

BLACK MAN SELLING PRETZELS: I:83, III:103–7, III:112

BUSINESSMAN IN BLUE HAT WITH JAUNTY FEATHER: This man ran over Jake with his 1976 Sedan de Ville Cadillac. I:83, III:104–6

CHICANO GUY: III:104–6

FAT LADY WITH BLOOMINGDALE'S BAG: III:103–6, III:112

TALL MAN IN NAILHEAD WORSTED SUIT: III:103–6

TOOKER'S WHOLESALE TOYS (DRIVES BY): III:104

WHITE GIRL IN SWEATER AND SKIRT: III:104–6

WOMAN IN BLACK HAT NET: I:83

CHARLIE THE CHOO-CHOO CHARACTERS: *See* CHARLIE THE CHOO-CHOO, *listed separately*

CROWD THAT GATHERS UPON ENTRY TO 1999 NEW YORK: *See* HARRIGAN, REVEREND EARL, *listed separately*

JAKE'S FAMILY, FRIENDS, ASSOCIATES AND ALIASES:

CHAMBERS, ELMER: *See* CHAMBERS, ELMER, *listed separately*

CHAMBERS, JOHN: This is Jake's real name. III:89

CHAMBERS, LAURIE: *See* CHAMBERS, LAURIE, *listed separately*

DENBY, TOM: In *The Waste Lands,* Jake Chambers uses this alias during his NEW YORK wanderings. III:169

DOORMAN, JAKE'S APARTMENT BUILDING: III:129

MUCCI, TIMMY: Timmy Mucci was one of Jake's friends from MID-TOWN LANES. He liked comic books. Once, when Jake bowled a 282, Timmy gave him a bowling bag that said, "Nothing but Strikes at Mid-Town Lanes." Jake picks up a version of this bag when he and our *ka-tet* travel via TODASH to the magic LOT in NEW YORK CITY. The only difference between the bags is that the one Jake finds in *todash* New York says, "Nothing but Strikes at Mid-World Lanes." When Jake began to suffer from a split psyche in *The Waste Lands,* Timmy told him to go home and drink plenty of clear fluids, like gin and vodka. III:107, V:198, V:694

OY: *See* OY, *listed separately*

PIPER SCHOOL CHARACTERS: *See* PIPER SCHOOL CHARACTERS, *listed separately*

**SHAW, GRETA: Greta Shaw (who happened to look a lot like Edith Bunker) worked as a housekeeper for the Chambers family. Mrs. Shaw was one of the few professional people that Jake actually liked. In fact, she qualified as one of his "almost" friends. In many ways, she was more of a mother to Jake than Jake's biological mother. Greta Shaw gave Jake the nickname 'Bama, and little Jakey thought she would save him from the DEATHFLY. I:81–82, III:91, III:102, III:106, III:107–8, III:129–30, III:133–37, IV:30 *(and Edith Bunker),* IV:64 *(Central Park saw player),* V:42, V:187, V:382 *(housekeeper),* V:419, V:460, V:637, VII:89, VII:94–97, VII:381, W:305 *(housekeeper)*

CHAMBERS, LAURIE (MEGAN)

Laurie Chambers is JAKE's mother. In *Wizard and Glass,* she is called Megan. We are told that Laurie Chambers has a cultured Vassar voice and is "scrawny in a sexy way." She also tends to go to bed with her sick friends. In *Wolves of the Calla,* we find out that she slipped between the sheets with her masseuse as well. Jake found this affair especially depressing since the masseuse had lots of muscles but few brains.

Laurie Chambers's lullabies gave Jake the creeps. One of her favorites was "I heard a fly buzz, when I died," the upshot of which was that Jake developed a terrible fear of a monstrous creature he named the DEATHFLY.

I:81, I:82, I:135, III:89–90, III:92, III:99, III:100, III:102, III:106, III:108, III:129–35, III:137–38, III:156, III:157–58, III:168, III:186, III:355, IV:80 *(parents),* IV:85 *(parents),* IV:655 *(Megan),* V:40 *(Jake's parents),* V:42 *(Jake's mother),* V:187, V:382, VI:324, VII:94, VII:95, VII:96, VII:98, VII:111, VII:138 *(parents),* W:305 *(mother)*

LAURIE CHAMBERS'S ASSOCIATES:

MASSEUSE (BIG MUSCLES): Big muscles, no brains. V:382

CHANEY, JAMES

See DEAN, SUSANNAH: ODETTA HOLMES AND THE CIVIL RIGHTS MOVEMENT: VOTER REGISTRATION BOYS

CHAP, THE

See MORDRED

**CHARLES SON OF CHARLES
In the 2003 version of *The Gunslinger,* Charles son of Charles is the unlucky gunslinger who "drew the black stone" and so had to act as HAX's hangman.

CHARLIE THE CHOO-CHOO
Our first glimpse of Charlie the Choo-Choo comes in *The Waste Lands* when JAKE bought *Charlie the Choo-Choo*—a children's book about a talking 402 Big Boy Steam Locomotive—at the MANHATTAN RESTAURANT OF THE MIND. Charlie (whom Jake finds sinister despite his apparent friendliness) prefigures BLAINE the Insane Mono. Like Blaine, Charlie is part of the MID-WORLD RAILWAY and terminates in TOPEKA.

Throughout *Charlie the Choo-Choo,* Charlie sings this song:

> Don't ask me silly questions,
> I won't play silly games.
> I'm just a simple choo-choo train
> And I'll always be the same.
> I only want to race along
> Beneath the bright blue sky,
> And be a happy choo-choo train
> Until the day I die.

Charlie's nasty double, Blaine, actually likes silly games, if not EDDIE DEAN's silly questions. Both versions of the Mid-World Railway seem to be connected to the ATCHISON, TOPEKA, AND SANTA FE RAILROAD that once crossed much of the American West on our level of the TOWER.
III:114, III:116, III:125, III:128, III:129, III:133, III:134, III:138–46, III:153, III:156, III:186, III:254, III:255, III:263, III:265–67, III:270, III:278, III:343, III:400, IV:71, IV:87–89 *(in Reinisch Rose Garden, Topeka)*, V:54, V:55, V:57, V:91, V:104, V:118, V:152, V:167, V:600, V:709, VI:84, VI:154, VI:162, VI:168, VII:335
CHARLIE THE CHOO-CHOO'S ASSOCIATES:
BACHMAN, CLAUDIA Y INEZ: Claudia Inez Bachman was the widow of the author RICHARD BACHMAN. In the TODASH version of NEW YORK CITY, which JAKE CHAMBERS and EDDIE DEAN visit at the beginning of *Wolves of the Calla,* she was also the author of *Charlie the Choo-Choo.* On the levels of the DARK TOWER where Claudia Bachman is a published writer, her name contains a *y,* transforming her into one of the members of the *tet* of NINETEEN. V:57, V:59, V:92, V:93, V:94 *(nineteen letters),* V:600 *(author),* V:709 *(author)* VI:84, VI:154, VI:200, VI:214, VI:288
BRIGGS, MR.: Roadhouse manager. III:141–42
BURLINGTON ZEPHYR: He's the 5,000-horsepower diesel engine who is supposed to be Charlie's replacement. III:141–45, III:254–55
ENGINEER BOB: Engineer Bob was Charlie's driver and friend. III:139–46, III:245, III:255, III:266, IV:87–88, IV:101 *(and Eddie's bull-dozer dream),* V:91

DECEASED WIFE: III:141, III:146

EVANS, BERYL: On at least one level of the DARK TOWER, Beryl Evans was the author of *Charlie the Choo-Choo*. However, on KEYSTONE EARTH she was one of the victims of the 1940s British serial killer John Reginald Halliday Christie. Cristie killed both Beryl and her baby daughter. It's no wonder one of Beryl's twinners wrote scary books. III:114, III:139–45, IV:71, IV:88, V:57, V:59, V:91, V:93, V:119, V:600 *(indirect, as author),* V:709 *(indirect, as author),* VI:84, VI:154, VI:200, VI:214–15, VI:288

MARTIN, RAYMOND: President of MID-WORLD RAILWAY CO. III:141–42, III:143–46, III:255

MARTIN, SUSANNAH: Daughter of RAYMOND MARTIN. III:142, III:143–45, III:146

MID-WORLD RAILWAY CO.: *Also see entry in* PORTALS. III:139–46

CHAS
See ELURIA: CHARACTERS

CHASE, FRANKIE
See CALLAHAN, FATHER DONALD FRANK: CALLAHAN'S HOME SHELTER ASSOCIATES

CHASSIT
See NINETEEN

CHEVIN OF CHAYVEN
See MUTANTS: CHILDREN OF RODERICK

CHILDREN OF RODERICK
See MUTANTS: CHILDREN OF RODERICK

CHIP
See MAINE CHARACTERS: McAVOY, CHIP

CHLOE
See GODS OF MID-WORLD

CHUMLEY
See NORTH CENTRAL POSITRONICS: NIGEL THE BUTLER

CHUMM, GREG
See CALLAHAN, FATHER DONALD FRANK: CALLAHAN'S HIDDEN HIGHWAYS ASSOCIATES

CHUMM'S TRAVELING WONDER SHOW
See CALLAHAN, FATHER DONALD FRANK: CALLAHAN'S HIDDEN HIGHWAYS ASSOCIATES: CHUMM, GREG

CHURCH OF THE WALK-INS
See WALK-INS *and* MAINE CHARACTERS: PETERSON, REVEREND; *see also* MAINE (STATE OF): STONEHAM: STONEHAM CORNERS: LOVELL-STONEHAM CHURCH OF THE WALK-INS, *in* OUR WORLD PLACES

CLAY, ANNIE
See SERENITY, SISTERS OF: FORTUNA

CLAYPOOL, FRANK
See HAMBRY CHARACTERS: SHERIFF'S OFFICE

CLEMENTS, JUSTIN (ARNOLD CLEMENTS)
Justin Clements (also known as Arnold Clements) owns CLEMENTS GUNS AND SPORTING GOODS, a shop which Roland visits in *The Drawing of the Three*. Clements also happens to be one of BALAZAR's associates. (The police have been after him for years.) His brother-in-law, FAT JOHNNY HOLDEN, runs the shop for him.

   II:343, II:347, II:348–49, II:376

CLEMMIE
See SERENITY, SISTERS OF

CODY, DR. JAMES
See CALLAHAN, FATHER DONALD FRANK: 'SALEM'S LOT CHARACTERS

CODY, FATHER
See CALLAHAN, FATHER DONALD FRANK: 'SALEM'S LOT CHARACTERS: CODY, DR. JAMES

COLLINS, FLORA
See DANDELO

COLLINS, FRED
See DANDELO

COLLINS, HENRY
See DANDELO

COLLINS, JOE
See DANDELO

COMPSON
See WARRIORS OF THE SCARLET EYE: CASSE ROI RUSSE: HUMANS: FEEMALO/FIMALO/FUMALO: FUMALO

CONROY
See CAN-TOI

CONSTABLE HOWARD
  See TREE VILLAGE CHARACTERS: TASLEY, HOWARD

CONSTANT READER
STEPHEN KING's Constant Readers. This means you and me, folks!
  VI:406, VII:818

CONVEIGH, REVEREND
  See MAINE CHARACTERS

COOGAN, LORETTA
  See CALLAHAN, FATHER DONALD FRANK: 'SALEM'S LOT CHARAC-
TERS

COOKIE (CALLA BRYN STURGIS)
  See CALLA BRYN STURGIS CHARACTERS: RANCHERS: EISENHART,
VAUGHN

COOKIE (JEFFERSON RANCH, DEBARIA)
  See SKIN-MAN: SKIN-MAN'S VICTIMS: JEFFERSON RANCH CHAR-
ACTERS

CÖOS, RHEA
  See RHEA OF THE CÖOS

COPPERHEAD
  See GRAYS: GRAY HIGH COMMAND

COQUINA, SISTER
  See ELURIA, LITTLE SISTERS OF

CORCORAN, JOHN
  See TOPEKA CHARACTERS

CORNWELL, AUSTIN
  See WARRIORS OF THE SCARLET EYE: CASSE ROI RUSSE: HUMANS:
FEEMALO/FIMALO/FUMALO: FIMALO (RANDO THOUGHTFUL)

CORT (CORTLAND ANDRUS)
Muscular, scarred Cortland Andrus was Roland Deschain's mentor. Like his
father FARDO before him, Cort trained generations of gunslingers in the art of
war. Not only did Cort teach the apprentice gunslingers to battle with a variety
of weapons, but he also taught them to navigate by the sun and stars, and to keep
a clock ticking inside their heads. Described as a bald, squat man with bowlegs
and a bulging belly of solid muscle, he was a violent carouser who frequented the
brothels of GILEAD's lower town. He also happened to be blind on one side—
most likely the result of an ancient battle, brawling, or teaching injury. Cort called
the apprentices "maggots." Coming from him, it was an almost affectionate term.
His job was to train young gunslingers as killers, and he was excellent at it. In

The Gunslinger, we witness Roland's coming-of-age battle with his teacher. If all gunslingers enter manhood with such a fierce fight, it is surprising that Cort has reached middle age at all. Throughout the Dark Tower series, Roland hears Cort's cajoling, critical, and often observant voice inside his head. One of Cort's sayings was "Never speak the worst aloud." Another was "Always con your vantage."

Evidently, Cort had a philosophical side. Roland believes that he often held palaver with the mystical MANNI. He was also Gilead's finest riddler, though he was intolerant of cheaters. During one of the Fair-Day riddling contests, Cort stabbed a wandering singer and acrobat who had stolen the judge's answers.

In *The Drawing of the Three,* we're told that Roland's *ka-tel,* or class of apprentice gunslingers, was Cort's last group of students. On the day of the Presentation Ceremonies, Cort was too ill to attend, and so his final crop of pupils had to go to his cottage to kneel at his feet so that their teacher could load their guns for the first time. Nine weeks later, Cort was dead, probably of poison. Beautiful Gilead did not survive much longer. Two years after Cort's death, In-World's final bloody civil war had begun.

In *The Wind Through the Keyhole,* we learn that Cort had quite a different fate from the one we had previously suspected. Although in the revised version of *The Gunslinger* we're told that Cort was in a coma for a week after Roland defeated him in GILEAD's SQUARE YARD, in *Wind Through the Keyhole* we discover that Cort's injuries in that coming-of-age battle were much more severe. According to *Wind,* Cort's destruction of Roland's hawk David was the old teacher's last kill. Cort must have suffered brain damage during that final battle, since a full year after Roland won his guns Cort still had not regained his wits. (*Wind* begins after Roland's return from MEJIS, and after his tragic matricide.) In the months after Roland's mother's death and before Roland traveled to DEBARIA, Roland spent much time in Cort's hut, feeding him and changing his dirty clouts. (As Roland told his father, sometimes Cort couldn't get to the jakes and sometimes he forgot he had to go.) Despite Roland's almost constant attention, Cort only occasionally recognized his former student.

Although Roland claimed that he nursed Cort out of respect, STEVEN DESCHAIN believed that Roland was actually performing a self-imposed penance for murdering his mother, GABRIELLE DESCHAIN. We can't help but wonder whether Steven sent his son to investigate the SKIN-MAN killings in Debaria to free Roland from his self-imposed responsibility to his old teacher. After Roland's departure, Cort was cared for by the castle's WHITE AMMIES.

I:65, I:86, I:95, I:96–100, I:104, I:107, I:108–9, I:110, I:124 *(creation of mescaline),* I:127, I:135, I:137, I:149, I:162–73 *(Roland's coming of age),* I:213, II:16, II:28, II:36, II:66, II:104, II:166, II:167, II:174, II:177, II:180, II:249, II:250, II:251, II:304, II:309, II:361, II:383, III:11, III:13 *(indirect),* III:14, III:41, III:259, III:276, III:277, III:280, III:328, III:418–19, IV:8 *(Gilead riddling),* IV:9, IV:33–34 *(knowledge of other worlds),* IV:70, IV:107, IV:109, IV:110, IV:160 *(described),* IV:178 *(his father lamed Jonas),* IV:197, IV:286, IV:321, IV:325, IV:326, IV:344, IV:407 *(see Cort's father, Fardo),* IV:436, IV:479, IV:523, IV:650, IV:664, E:163–64, V:78 *(taught navigation and fighting),* V:86, V:169, V:204, V:240, V:245, V:248, V:383, V:392, V:476, V:597, V:675, VI:203, VII:21, VII:34, VII:148, VII:247, VII:250, VII:473, VII:587, VII:589 *(saying),* VII:778 *(always con yer vantage),* VII:779, VII:801 *(Cortland Andrus),* VII:824, VII:829; W:35–38 *(discussed),* W:76, W:79, W:287–88

CORT'S ASSOCIATES:

FARDO: Like his son, Cort, Fardo taught generations of apprentice gunslingers how to fight, but he was also responsible for sending many boys west in disgrace. During ELDRED JONAS's test of manhood, Fardo had broken the boy's leg with his ironwood club and had sent him, gunless, into exile. Like so many other failed gunslingers, Jonas eventually joined forces with Gilead's great enemy, JOHN FARSON.

**MARK: In the 2003 version of *The Gunslinger,* we learn that Cort's predecessor was named Mark. He died in the yard behind the GREAT HALL, stabbed to death by an overzealous student.

WANDERING SINGER AND ACROBAT: This man was cross-eyed and wore a cap of bells. Cort killed him for attempting to cheat in a riddling contest. III:277

COSINGTON, ADA
See TREE VILLAGE CHARACTERS:WOODSMEN: COSINGTON, PETER

COSINGTON, PETER
See TREE VILLAGE CHARACTERS: WOODSMEN

COTER, CHUGGY
See DEAN, EDDIE: EDDIE'S PAST ASSOCIATES

COUNCIL OF ELD
See GUNSLINGERS

COUNTESS JILLIAN OF UP'ARD KILLIAN
See HAMBRY CHARACTERS: TRAVELLERS' REST

COVAY MOVERS
See CALLAHAN, FATHER DONALD FRANK: CALLAHAN'S HIDDEN HIGHWAYS ASSOCIATES

COVENANT MAN
See WALTER: WALTER'S ALIASES

COWPUNCHERS ATTACKED BY SKINMAN
See SKIN-MAN: SKIN-MAN'S VICTIMS

CRAZY MARY'S
See CALIFORNIA (STATE OF): SACRAMENTO: CRAZY MARY'S, *in* OUR WORLD PLACES

CRESSIA CHARACTERS
In *Wizard and Glass* we learn that during Roland's youth, the rebel JOHN FARSON attacked the Barony of Cressia and burned its Barony seat of INDRIE to the ground. Before leaving the area, he slaughtered hundreds of people and beheaded all of the Barony officials.

IV:163
CRESSIA'S BARONY GOVERNOR: Beheaded by FARSON. IV:163
HIGH SHERIFF: Beheaded by FARSON. IV:163
INDRIE'S MAYOR: Beheaded by FARSON. IV:163

**CRIMSON KING (THE RED KING, LORD OF THE SPIDERS, LOS THE RED, LORD OF DISCORDIA)

CONSTANT READERS are already familiar with the Lord of Chaos known as the Crimson King. We met him in one of STEPHEN KING's other novels, namely *Insomnia*. If Roland is a soldier of the WHITE, then the Crimson King is his natural enemy. This prince of chaos is a shape-shifter whose true dual form vacillates between that of a satanic red-eyed Santa Claus and a scuttling spider.

In the 2003 version of *The Gunslinger,* SYLVIA PITTSTON claims that the Crimson King is the Antichrist who will lead men into the flaming bowels of perdition. He is behind every fleshly pleasure and is the wicked force that created the destructive machines imprinted with LaMERK FOUNDRY. However, despite her sermons, Sylvia Pittston has already been seduced by the Crimson King's power. Believing that WALTER was the King's angel, she let him impregnate her with his master's demonic child. Roland removes the demon by inserting his gun into Pittston's vagina and screwing her with it. The child dies, but in response, Pittston raises her congregation against Roland.

In the 2003 version of *The Gunslinger,* Walter tells Roland that the Red King already controls the DARK TOWER and that the Earth has been delivered into his hand. Although the Crimson King may turn his blazing red eyes toward the kingdoms of the mortal worlds, he is far from mortal himself. Roland has a larger and more powerful enemy than he ever imagined, and that enemy has opposed him from the beginning. Even FARSON, who bore the Red King's *sigul* of the staring red eye, was but a pawn of this destructive monster.

In *Song of Susannah* we learn that our favorite *kas-ka Gan* has also had a long and involved history with this most unsavory of were-spiders. The first time Stephen King encountered Los the Red—in the form of tiny red spiders feeding on the intestines of dead chickens—King was seven years old and sawing wood in his aunt and uncle's barn. The young King was saved from the spiders (and from their deadly bites, which would have turned him into a VAMPIRE) by CUTHBERT ALLGOOD and EDDIE DEAN. Needless to say, the Crimson King never forgave Stephen King for evading his clutches, or for converting to the cause of the White.

It is probably safe to assume that, like his half-son MORDRED, the Crimson King is able to transform his shape at will. He is also probably the BEAST and Keeper of the Tower that Walter spoke of in the original version of *The Gunslinger.* As the artist PATRICK DANVILLE realizes when he tries to draw him perched on a balcony of the Dark Tower, the Red King *darkles* and *tincts* like the AGELESS STRANGER, whom Walter also mentioned during his long palaver with Roland in the GOLGOTHA.

As was stated earlier, in his human form the Crimson King resembles a satanic Santa Claus, with a huge hooked nose, full red lips (overhung by a single tusk-like tooth), an enormous white beard, and long, snowy-white hair. Like Saint Nick, he wears a red robe, though Los's is dotted with lightning bolts and kabbalistic symbols, not cuffed and trimmed with fur. Although in *Wolves of the Calla* we came to suspect that BLACK THIRTEEN, the nastiest ball of the WIZARD'S RAINBOW, was actually one of the Red King's eyes, in *The Dark Tower* we learn that it isn't. The Crimson King's eyes are as red as the roses of CAN'-KA NO REY, and when Roland sees him shouting from a balcony of the Dark Tower, he is still in possession of both of them.

Not only is the Red King ugly, but he is also completely mad. Many years before our story began, he flooded THUNDERCLAP with poison gas, darkening the land and killing everything that lived there. Although he probably originally had an hourglass-shape on his back (a *sigul* which Mordred still has and which is the *dan-tete*'s key to the Dark Tower) somehow or other, the Red King managed to destroy his. Hence, he cannot enter the Tower proper without some *sigul* of the ELD—either his half-son's mark or Roland's guns.

Although the Red King is Roland's nemesis, he is also Roland's kinsman. According to Walter (the Crimson King's prime minister), they are both descended from ARTHUR ELD. However, whereas Roland's family branch is dedicated to the protection of the Tower, the Red King (always Gan's crazy side) is focused on its destruction. It is he, the Lord of Chaos, who enslaves the BREAKERS and who forces them to destroy the BEAMS that hold the Tower in place.

Just as the gunslingers serve the White, the WARRIORS OF THE SCARLET EYE serve the Crimson King and the cause of the Outer Dark. These servants include the WOLVES, VAMPIRES, TAHEEN, and CAN-TOI (or LOW MEN) of END-WORLD. Companies such as NORTH CENTRAL POSITRONICS, the SOMBRA CORPORATION, and LaMERK INDUSTRIES (all existing in versions of our world) also owe allegiance to the Crimson King.

When Roland and SUSANNAH journey to LE CASSE ROI RUSSE (the Red King's palace) on their way to the Dark Tower, they find out from AUSTIN CORNWELL that while they were battling the Wolves in CALLA BRYN STURGIS, the Red King foresaw their victory—both in the Calla and in the DEVAR-TOI—in one of MAERLYN's magic seeing spheres. (Six of them were in his possession at the time.) Enraged, Los forced all but three of his castle servants to eat rat poison. After watching them die from his throne of skulls, he smashed the six globes of Wizard's Rainbow and killed himself by swallowing a sharpened spoon. In his new undead form—which was safe even from Roland's guns (the barrels of which were made from Arthur Eld's sword EXCALIBUR)—he mounted his gray horse NIS and galloped for the Tower. Although he could not enter the Tower proper, he took up a position on one of its balconies. From there, he hoped to keep his fearsome enemy Roland at bay with his huge supply of sneetches. Luckily, the Crimson King was not destined to succeed.

Although the Red King may not have foreseen it, by the time Roland reaches his life's goal, he no longer has a *ka-tet* but is in the company of the mute but magical artist Patrick Danville, whom the Red King was so eager to destroy in the novel *Insomnia*. Patrick's pencils can change reality, so Roland has the younger man draw the Crimson King as he stands on the balcony of the Tower, complete with nose hair and snaggletooth. Once the picture has achieved the required verisimilitude (created by dabs of red for the eyes—pigment made from the petals of Can'-Ka No Rey mixed with Roland's blood), Roland has Patrick erase his drawing, and in so doing, he erases the Red King himself. As Roland mounts the steps of the Tower, all that remains of his enemy are two enraged red eyes.

In *The Wind Through the Keyhole,* the wizard MAERLYN calls the Crimson King the Great One. According to Maerlyn, the COVENANT MAN (otherwise known as WALTER O'DIM and MARTEN BROADCLOAK) is only capable of a little magic and long life. The Tower-pent Red King is Walter's true master, and when the Red King points his finger, the Broad Cloak scurries.

IV:91 *("WATCH FOR THE WALKIN' DUDE"; "ALL HAIL THE CRIMSON KING "),* IV:100 *(Eddie's bulldozer dream),* IV:111 *(creature that rules Farson and Marten),* IV:632, IV:666, V:236, V:291, V:366 *(Red King),* V:413 *(and the Dark Tower),* V:452, V:456, V:463, V:465, V:468, V:470, V:539, V:549, V:550, VI:13, VI:22, VI:95, VI:102, VI:105, VI:110, VI:111, VI:120, VI:121, VI:169, VI:171, VI:199, VI:231, VI:232, VI:233, VI:238, VI:239, VI:244–55 *(Walter and the Crimson King's plans),* VI:259 *(as Devil),* VI:269, VI:287, VI:293 *(as Lord of Spiders; Tower-pent),* VI:294 *(Lord of Discordia),* VI:295, VI:296, VI:318, VI:326, VI:328–31 *(voice of Black Thirteen),* VI:336, VI:337, VI:350, VI:374, VI:380 *(Eye),* VI:384, VI:407, VII:13, VII:25, VII:47, VII:62, VII:70 *(King),* VII:76 *(Big Red Daddy),* VII:89, VII:92, VII:111, VII:127, VII:133, VII:134, VII:141, VII:149, VII:150, VII:161, VII:173, VII:174, VII:175, VII:176, VII:177, VII:179, VII:188, VII:202, VII:210, VII:229, VII:238, VII:261, VII:262, VII:266, VII:281, VII:285, VII:298, VII:300, VII:301, VII:326–27, VII:406, VII:447, VII:498, VII:506, VII:512, VII:513, VII:514, VII:515–16, VII:539, VII:549–52 *(red goblin),* VII:559, VII:563, VII:578, VII:580, VII:581, VII:589, VII:591 *(indirect),* VII:593, VII:595, VII:603, VII:604 *(Los),* VII:605 *(killed castle staff with rat poison; throne made of skulls; has six of the Wizard's Glasses),* VII:605–10, VII:612, VII:613, VII:614, VII:615, VII:617–18, VII:619, VII:620, VII:621, VII:622, VII:623, VII:626, VII:650 *(mad guardian of the Tower),* VII:670–71 *(six months in Tower),* VII:703, VII:711, VII:717, VII:721, VII:724, VII:725, VII:754, VII:755, VII:757 *(indirect),* VII:759, VII:766, VII:767–68, VII:770–71, VII:772, VII:781, VII:782–800, VII:819–20, VII:823, W:140 *(Red King),* W:148–49 *(red eye behind Tim & Covenant Man),* W: 250–51 *(Great One),* W:253

THE CRIMSON KING'S ASSOCIATES:

BANGO SKANK: *See* SKANK, BANGO, *listed separately*

NIS: Nis is the Crimson King's horse. His name comes from the land of sleep and dreams. *See also* GODS OF MID-WORLD. VII:607

PEDDLER: W:253

CROSS DOG
See JESUS DOG, *in* ELURIA CHARACTERS

CROW, ALLAN
See DEBARIA CHARACTERS: CROW GANG

CROW GANG
See DEBARIA CHARACTERS

CROW, JIM
See "JIM CROW"

CROWELL, GARY
See MAINE CHARACTERS

CROYDEN, JOHN
See HAMBRY CHARACTERS: HORSEMEN'S ASSOCIATION

CUJO
See APPENDIX I

CULLUM, JOHN
See TET CORPORATION: FOUNDING FATHERS

CUSTOMS
See DEAN, EDDIE: DELTA FLIGHT 901 CHARACTERS

CUTHBERT ALLGOOD
See ALLGOOD, CUTHBERT

D

DADDY MOSE
See TET CORPORATION: FOUNDING FATHERS: CARVER, MOSES

DALE, MR.
See BREAKERS: BRAUTIGAN, TED

DAMASCUS, TRUDY
See GUTTENBERG, FURTH, AND PATEL

DAME, MARY
See MID-WORLD FOLKLORE: MARY DAME

DANDELO (JOE COLLINS, ODD JOE OF ODD LANE, ODD JOE OF ODD'S LANE, OLD MAN-MONSTER)
As he lies dying in the PROCTOR'S SUITE in the DEVAR-TOI, EDDIE DEAN whispers a final warning to JAKE CHAMBERS. He tells his young friend that he must protect their *dinh* from Dandelo. Unfortunately, by the time Roland reaches Dandelo's den, Jake is already dead. The boy's pet BILLY-BUMBLER passes the message on to Roland telepathically, and Eddie appears in dreams to warn SUSANNAH DEAN about this particular monster, but nothing prepares the two remaining members of our *ka-tet* for what they are about to encounter.

When Roland and Susannah arrive at Dandelo's home on ODD LANE, located just off TOWER ROAD in the WHITE LANDS OF EMPATHICA, Dandelo is posing as Joe Collins from America-side. Odd Joe of Odd's Lane (*s* added to throw our *tet* off the scent) appears to be a harmless retired comedian whose only companions are his blind horse LIPPY and his cane, BESSIE. However, in the land of Empathica nothing is as it seems.

In his true form, Dandelo (an anagram of *Odd Lane*) looks like a giant insect. Like the giant spider It (found in STEPHEN KING's novel of the same name), Dandelo feeds on human emotion. But while It feeds on faith, usually the faith of children, Dandelo's favorite emotional flavors are laughter and fear. However, there is a good chance that these two monsters are (to borrow a term from the King/Straub novel *The Talisman*) twinners of each other. As Susannah kills Dandelo (clued in to his real identity by a note left for her by Stephen King), he momentarily takes the shape of a psychotic clown. As CONSTANT READERS will remember, Pennywise the Clown was one of It's favorite forms.

Dandelo grows younger as he feeds, but it seems that in the White Lands, meals don't pass by that frequently. Hence, despite his ability to sleep for long periods, Dandelo has to keep a human "cow" for nourishment. That cow is the artist PATRICK DANVILLE, whom we met as a child in the novel *Insomnia*. When Roland and Susannah free Patrick from his prison in Dandelo's basement, they discover that Patrick is mute. However, Patrick's muteness isn't congenital. Dandelo pulled out his tongue.

VII:403, VII:411, VII:520, VII:541, VII:556, VII:645, VII:653–707, VII:708, VII:709, VII:710, VII:711, VII:719, VII:723, VII:731, VII:732, VII:734, VII:736, VII:739 *(indirect)*, VII:751, VII:754 *(old man-monster)*, VII:755, VII:761, VII:774

DANDELO'S ASSOCIATES AND "JOE COLLINS'S" ASSOCIATES:
AGENT: VII:668
BESSIE: Joe Collins's name for his walking stick. VII:657
COLLINS, FLORA: Joe Collins's mother. VII:657, VII:663 *(ma and pa)*
COLLINS, HENRY: Joe Collins's father. VII:657, VII:663 *(ma and pa)*
GRANDMOTHER: VII:674, VII:675
GRANDPA FRED: VII:674
LIPPY: This is Dandelo's demonic horse, though he is probably not a horse at all but some other kind of creature disguised by *glammer*. When MORDRED eats dead Lippy's flesh, he contracts food poisoning. VII:653–59, VII:660, VII:664, VII:667, VII:670, VII:682 *(wonder-nag)*, VII:693–94, VII:702, VII:708, VII:755 *(gave Mordred food poisoning)*

DANDO (KING DANDO)
King Dando had lots of rubies in his vault. We don't learn anything else about him.
VII:794

DAN-TETE
See MORDRED; *see also* APPENDIX I

DANVILLE, PATRICK (THE ARTIST)
We first met Patrick Danville in STEPHEN KING's novel *Insomnia*. At that time, four-year-old Patrick and his mother SONIA were attending a pro-choice rally at the DERRY Civic Center, where the feminist Susan Day was about to give a speech. Although still a child, talented little Patrick was already the focus of an assassination attempt by ED DEEPNEAU, a mad follower of the CRIMSON

KING.[2] The reason? At the age of twenty-two, Patrick was destined to save the lives of two men, one of whom is key to the Purpose[3] and to the stability of the TOWER. In *The Dark Tower*, we find out that Patrick's fate is even greater. He is destined to save the life of Roland Deschain as well.

At four years old, Patrick—enveloped in an aura of pink roses—was already an accomplished artist. But by the time he reaches adulthood, his pencils are, literally, magic. Patrick has an amazing talent which sets him above even the most skilled painters and draftsmen of our world. He can transform reality by drawing it in the configurations of his choosing, then "uncreate" with his nifty little erasers. This talent alone would be enough to put him on the Crimson King's hit list, but in the end, it isn't the Red King who captures him.

By the time he is in his late teens, Patrick—himself the child of an abused mother—is the prisoner of the sadistic DANDELO, a giant, emotion-eating were-insect living in the WHITE LANDS OF EMPATHICA, not far from the red fields of CAN'-KA NO REY, which surround the Tower. After killing Dandelo, Roland, OY, and SUSANNAH DEAN rescue Patrick from a cage in Dandelo's basement. But by the time they find him, Patrick is exhausted and weak from years of being "milked" of his emotions. Thanks to Dandelo's cruelty, he is also tongueless and mentally wounded. However, despite the torture he has endured, his artistic talents are intact. In fact, he manages to "draw" the UNFOUND DOOR and bring it into END-WORLD, giving Susannah Dean an escape route from the inevitable death which seems to await all those who become *ka-tet* with Roland.

In the end, it is Patrick—not Oy or Susannah—who is Roland's final companion on his journey through End-World. And as it turns out, it is Patrick's magical artistic skills, and not fast guns, which ultimately defeat the Lord of Discordia.

When Roland and Patrick approach the Tower, the Red King is standing on one of its balconies. Mad as a hatter, he is determined to thwart Roland's lifelong desire and prevent our gunslinger from entering that linchpin of existence. Since he is already undead (he swallowed a sharpened spoon while still resident in his palace, LE CASSE ROI RUSSE), Roland cannot shoot this Lord of Discordia. The only other option is to have Patrick draw the Red King and then erase him. By the time Roland begins to mount the first of those legendary spiral stairs, all that is left of the Crimson King is a pair of floating red eyes.

VII:514–15, VII:550–57, VII:646, VII:685, VII:695–710 *(crying before this, but Susannah/Roland thought it was the wind; 698—called Dandelo's cow)*, VII:716–24, VII:725, VII:726, VII:729–50, VII:751, VII:752 *(the Artist)*, VII:754, VII:756–65, VII:767–801, VII:802–3, VII:807

PATRICK DANVILLE'S ASSOCIATES:

DANVILLE, SONIA: Patrick's mother. VII:514 *(mother)*, VII:709, VII:773 *(mother)*, VII:774

2. Ed Deepneau thinks that he is destroying the "baby-killing" pro-choicers. However, he has been duped by the Crimson King into causing utter mayhem so that one four-year-old child will cease breathing.

3. In the novel *Insomnia*, two forces battle over the fate of the macroverse. These forces are the Random and the Purpose. Generally speaking, the Crimson King is aligned with the chaotic Random, while the White is aligned with the Purpose.

DANVILLE, SONIA
See DANVILLE, PATRICK

DARIA (NORTH CENTRAL POSITRONICS PORTABLE GUIDANCE MODULE)
See NORTH CENTRAL POSITRONICS

DARIO
See BALAZAR, ENRICO: BALAZAR'S MEN

DARK TOWER
See DARK TOWER in PORTALS section; *see also* GAN

DARRYL
See DEAN, SUSANNAH: ODETTA HOLMES AND THE CIVIL RIGHTS MOVEMENT: ODETTA'S "MOVEMENT" ASSOCIATES

DAVID (HAWK)
David—named for the young boy in the biblical story of David and Goliath—was Roland's trained falcon. He was a pet, a comrade at arms, and a weapon. Roland used him in his coming-of-age battle against CORT. Cort said that hawks were God's gunslingers. In many ways, David was the first of Roland's companions to be sacrificed to his ambition.
     I:95, I:96–98, I:104, I:105, I:160, I:165–74, II:19, II:180, III:174, IV:107, IV:344, IV:547, V:383, V:491, V:492, VII:802, VII:824, W:36

DAVID AND GOLIATH
See MID-WORLD FOLKLORE: PERTH, LORD

DAVID QUICK
See GRAYS: GRAY HIGH COMMAND

DEAN, EDDIE (THE PRISONER, EDDIE CANTOR DEAN, EDDIE TOREN)
Although he was born during the 1960s in BROOKLYN, NEW YORK, and spent most of his youth in CO-OP CITY, Eddie Dean reminds Roland of his two earlier *ka-tet* mates, CUTHBERT ALLGOOD and ALAIN JOHNS. Like Cuthbert, Eddie's sense of humor often borders on the silly (at least in Roland's estimation), and like Alain, he has deep flashes of intuition. Although Roland sometimes thinks Eddie is weak and self-centered, he appreciates the younger man's deep reservoirs of courage and his tremendously generous heart.
     When we first meet Eddie he is in his early twenties and has unruly black hair and hazel eyes. He is also running cocaine for the drug king ENRICO BALAZAR, in large part to support the heroin habit of his beloved but bullying older brother, HENRY DEAN. By the time Roland enters Eddie's mind on a DELTA flight from NASSAU to New York in 1987, Eddie is already addicted to smack. Despite Eddie's nasty habit, Roland knows that Eddie is a born gunslinger. At the beginning of their relationship, Roland compares him to a good gun sinking in quicksand. As the human embodiment of the tarot card called The Prisoner

(in this case, the prison is drugs), Eddie is an integral part of Roland's destiny, a future foretold by the sinister wizard WALTER (aka THE MAN IN BLACK) in the GOLGOTHA located near the shores of the WESTERN SEA.

Eddie Dean is the maverick of Roland Deschain's *ka-tet*. Roland often calls him *ka-mai*, or *ka*'s fool, and in many ways this assessment seems fairly accurate. In *The Drawing of the Three,* Eddie chose the love of ODETTA HOLMES/ DETTA WALKER over caution and thus almost lost his face to a LOBSTROS- ITY. Yet it is Eddie's anarchic sense of humor that fried the circuits of BLAINE the Insane Mono, allowing our *ka-tet* to win their riddling contest and outwit this seriously suicidal machine. Each member of Roland's *ka-tet* has at least one special talent, and Eddie's skills go beyond making bad jokes. In *The Waste Lands,* his hidden artistic vision shines forth, and he is able both to draw a magic door to bring JAKE CHAMBERS into Roland's world, and to fashion a key to open that door.

Eddie becomes an even more important character in the final books of the series. Of all the people we meet during our travels through IN-WORLD, MID- WORLD, THE BORDERLANDS, and END-WORLD, Eddie is the most remi- niscent of the traditional Arthurian knight. By his own admission, Eddie needs to be needed. While he shares Roland's desire to reach the DARK TOWER, unlike Roland, Eddie believes that his ultimate purpose is not to serve his *ka-tet,* or even his wife, SUSANNAH DEAN, but to protect the ROSE, which is (on our level of the Tower at least) one of the most fundamental symbols of love.

When Roland and Eddie visit STEPHEN KING in the *when* of 1977, they learn that Eddie is actually the twin of Cuthbert Allgood, Roland's old friend from GILEAD. According to King (speaking in a deep trance state), he saw both Cuthbert and Eddie when he was seven years old. They saved him from the clutches of the CRIMSON KING, Lord of the Spiders, and turned him from the grim seductions of DISCORDIA.

Without Eddie's intuition to guide him, Roland would never have seen the formation of the TET CORPORATION, the company which protects the Rose on our level of the Tower. Nor would he have met his maker, Stephen King, in the town of BRIDGTON, MAINE. In fact, he may not even have survived the onslaught of BALAZAR'S MEN in EAST STONEHAM, if he'd made it to that town at all. However, like those of all *ka-mais,* Eddie's days are numbered. Once our *tet* defeats the WOLVES of CALLA BRYN STURGIS and destroys the DEVAR-TOI where the BREAKERS are eroding the BEAMS, Eddie is shot in the head by PIMLI PRENTISS, the Devar Master. As GRAN-PERE JAFFORDS predicted, for men like Eddie Dean it is always a bullet that opens the way to the clearing at the end of the path.

One of the wonderful aspects of the macroverse is that somewhere, on some other level of the Tower, another version of us always survives. This is as true for Eddie Dean as for anyone else. When Susannah Dean leaves End-World through the UNFOUND DOOR, she finds herself in an alternative version of New York City. Although it is not 1987 of the KEYSTONE EARTH—people here drive Takuro Spirits and drink Nozz-A-La cola, and Gary Hart is president—she is still overjoyed to be there. The reason is simple. Waiting for her in a snowy CEN- TRAL PARK is none other than her beloved husband, Eddie Dean.

It seems that—on some levels of the Tower at least—stories can have happy endings. In this *where* and *when,* Eddie is from WHITE PLAINS, not Co-Op City. His brother isn't the bossy Henry Dean but his *ka*-mate, mate Jake Chambers. In fact, the two of them aren't Eddie Dean and Jake Chambers at all, but Eddie and Jake TOREN—descendants of the family which (on our level of the Tower) are the custodians of the Vacant LOT and of the magic Rose.

Like Susannah Dean, Jake Chambers, and Jake's bumbler Oy, Eddie plays a small part in *The Wind Through the Keyhole.* In fact, their tale (which is set just before *The Wolves of the Calla*) is essentially a frame story. In *Wind,* Roland and his American *tet* have just left the GREEN PALACE and are journeying southeast along the PATH OF THE BEAM toward CALLA BRYN STURGIS when they are beset by a STARKBLAST. They are forced to haul up in the stone meetinghouse of an abandoned village called GOOK so that they can wait out the storm. While the starkblast rages outside, Roland tells his *tet* two stories. The first tale is autobiographical, and tells of Roland's adventure with JAMIE DeCURRY in the town of DEBARIA where the two of them hunted down a murderous shapechanger called a SKIN-MAN. The second story is a folktale called "The Wind Through the Keyhole," and it is from this narrative that the novel takes its name.

I:130 *(Prisoner in prophecy of drawing),* II:25 *(Prisoner),* II:34–62 *(Prisoner's door; 38–57 Delta Flight 901),* II:63–84, II:85–157 *(85 twenty-one years old; 85–90 Customs; 121–57 Balazar's),* II:161–82 *(Lobstrosity Beach),* II:201–9, II:225–305 *(235 twenty-three years old, born 1964),* II:306–7 *(Detta thinks about him),* II:307–12, II:315, II:316 *(Prisoner),* II:324–26, II:327–38, II:339, II:357, II:359–61, II:367, II:371, II:379, II:386, II:387–90, II:393–99, III:11, III:12, III:13, III:16, III:18–19, III:21–86 *(25 Shardik/Mir attacks; 37 Roland's story; 51–54 dream),* III:96, III:97 *(Prisoner),* III:149–52, III:153–55 *(in Jake's dream),* III:158–66, III:170–76 *(171 he is twenty-three years old),* III:177–78 *(thirteen years old),* III:178–82, III:183–88, III:189–90 *(drawing Jake),* III:190–92 *(thirteen years old),* III:193–94 *(drawing Jake),* III:201–3, III:204, III:206–13, III:219–54, III:256–67, III:268–70, III:273–85, III:286–300 *(Gasher),* III:302–4, III:308–12, III:316–25, III:329, III:331–34, III:340–50, III:361–65 *(363 says Eddie was a junkie for six years. In earlier books he'd been shooting up for less than a year),* III:372–73, III:378, III:382–85 *(Blaine),* III:393–420, IV:3–10, IV:13–70 *(riddling; 42–45 flashback to own past; 49 decides to piss off Blaine; 51 begins to do it; 58–59 crash; 64 first thinny sound),* IV:71–112 *(Topeka train station. 72–77 Topeka Capital Journal and superflu; 79 Beam disappears; 87 Charlie the Choo-Choo in Topeka; 91 The Crimson King; 95 entering thinny; 97 Oz in distance; 99–101 Eddie's dream of bulldozer and rose; 102–3 discusses rose and Tower with Roland; 106 Roland begins his story),* IV:335–37 *(interlude in Kansas),* IV:570 and 572 *(Roland's vision),* IV:581, IV:615–25 *(end of Roland's story; back in Topeka),* IV:626–68 *(627 ruby Beatle-boots; 632 Green Palace; 634 gate like Wizard's Rainbow; 646 Tick-Tock; 648 Flagg; 652 Roland's matricide),* V:8 *(strangers from Out-World),* V:29–31 *(gunslingers),* V:35–47, V:49–70 *(New York and Jake—1977),* V:71, V:77, V:78, V:80, V:81, V:84, V:87, V:88–119, V:122, V:123–64, V:176–85, V:187–98, V:201–39, V:241, V:242, V:243, V:244, V:245–53, V:256–57 *(listening to Pere Callahan's tale),* V:258 *(listening),* V:260 *(listening),* V:262 *(listening),* V:264–71 *(listening),* V:273–74 *(listening),* V:275 *(listening),* V:281 *(listening),* V:284 *(listening),* V:285 *(listen-*

ing), V:290 *(listening)*, V:291–96 *(listening)*, V:301–2 *(listening)*, V:309–12, V:318, V:321, V:322, V:325, V:341, V:343–60, V:365–69, V:376–80, V:381, V:382, V:384, V:388, V:392, V:394, V:396–406, V:408, V:412 *(ka-tet mates)*, V:417–20, V:421–23, V:428–30, V:437–38, V:442–45, V:448–49, V:452–54, V:457, V:466–72, V:478, V:479, V:480, V:482, V:485–86, V:487, V:488–505, V:506–52, V:555, V:563, V:573–74 *(younger one)*, V:576, V:581–90, V:592, V:597, V:598, V:601–28 *(waiting for Callahan)*, V:629–35, V:639–40, V:641–50, V:652–53, V:654, V:658, V:662–74, V:679–705, VI:3–8, VI:10–18, VI:22, VI:24–43, VI:63, VI:64, VI:68, VI:69, VI:70, VI:71, VI:74, VI:80–82, VI:98, VI:117, VI:122, VI:123, VI:124, VI:129–216, VI:222, VI:224, VI:225, VI:230 *(indirect)*, VI:231, VI:233, VI:240, VI:246, VI:248, VI:259, VI:265–303 *(Eddie is Cuthbert's twin)*, VI:307, VI:320, VI:324, VI:348, VI:360, VI:365, VI:373, VI:374, VI:395, VI:399, VI:404, VII:1–3, VII:17–53, VII:57–58, VII:114–32, VII:134–38, VII:141–59, VII:168, VII:169, VII:173, VI:177 *(indirect)*, VII:186 *(ka-tet)*, VII:187, VII:188, VII:189–220, VII:247–61, VII:262 *(indirect)*, VII:265–73, VII:276 *(indirect)*, VII:279–309 *(297–302 listening to Ted's story)*, VII:316, VII:318–42, VII:350, VII:351–52, VII:362–63, VII:369–70, VII:378–85 *(Eddie is shot)*, VII:387, VII:388–90, VII:391, VII:392, VII:393, VII:394, VII:395 *(indirect)*, VII:396–97, VII:398, VII:401–4, VII:407, VII:408–10, VII:413 *(indirect)*, VII:416 *(indirect)*, VII:427, VII:428, VII:435, VII:438, VII:448, VII:453, VII:455, VII:464, VII:477, VII:485, VII:487, VII:488, VII:491, VII:495, VII:504, VII:508, VII:510, VII:518, VII:520, VII:533, VII:541, VII:549, VII:554–56, VII:559, VII:562, VII:569, VII:571, VII:601, VII:603, VII:604, VII:608, VII:629, VII:630, VII:633, VII:641, VII:642, VII:645–46, VII:662, VII:668, VII:674, VII:681, VII:683, VII:690, VII:708, VII:724–25, VII:727, VII:728, VII:729, VII:731, VII:733, VII:740, VII:744, VII:747, VII:748, VII:758, VI:762, VII:772, VII:785, VII:802, VII:807–13, VII:818, VII:819, W:3–31, W:303–7

EDDIE'S ASSOCIATES, PAST AND PRESENT:

BERNSTEIN, MISS: Miss Bernstein (we never learn her actual name) was paralyzed in a car accident. VII:103

BERNSTEIN, MRS.: Mrs. Bernstein's daughter was paralyzed in a car accident in MAMARONECK. VII:103

BERTOLLO, DORA (TITS BERTOLLO): Dora Bertollo was Eddie's mother's friend. The kids on Eddie's block called her Tits Bertollo because her breasts were the size of watermelons. V:187

BOY WITH BASKETBALL: This young black boy witnessed Eddie's interactions with BALAZAR'S MEN in CO-OP CITY. Thinking the boy might get into trouble if he talked too much, Eddie told the kid to forget everything he'd seen. II:110, II:113

BUNKOWSKI, DEWEY: Dewey was one of Eddie and HENRY DEAN's friends. III:187

BUNKOWSKI, MRS.: She was DEWEY's mom. III:187

COTER, CHUGGY: The Chugster was one of Eddie's old friends. While HENRY DEAN was in VIETNAM, Eddie and Chuggy went to the movies together. They liked Westerns. VI:285

DEAN, GLORIA: *See* DEAN, GLORIA, *listed separately*

DEAN, HENRY: *See* DEAN, HENRY, *listed separately*

DEAN, MRS.: *See* DEAN, MRS., *listed separately*

DEAN, WENDELL: *See* DEAN, WENDELL, *listed separately*

HATHAWAY, MISS: Eddie's third-grade teacher. II:295

KENOPENSKY, MARY LOU: While Eddie was still at school, he had a crush on this girl and wrote her name all over his books. VII:144

KIDS FROM NORWOOD STREET (MURDERED BY MANSION DEMON): According to HENRY DEAN, two kids from Norwood Street went to the haunted DUTCH HILL MANSION to bump uglies. By the time the police found them, all the blood had been drained from their bodies and their eyes were wide open, as if they'd died terrified. III:187

LOONY KIDS: When Eddie was young, these kids used to run around the neighborhood shouting, "I'm the Barber of Seville-a, You must try my fucking skill-a." The comedy entitled *The Barber of Seville* was written by Pierre Beaumarchais and was produced in Paris in 1775. It later gave rise to several operas. The kids were probably actually thinking of Sweeney Todd, the demon barber, who killed his customers and had his baker-accomplice turn them into meat pies. V:631–32

LUNDGREN, DAHLIE: Dahlie Lundgren owned a shop that made great fried dough. He also sold comic books, which were fairly easy to steal. Eddie, HENRY, and their friends used to smoke cigarettes behind Dahlie's shop. We don't know whether Dahlie approved or not. V:187, V:203, V:257

MARYANNE (MAJESTIC THEATER): *See* DEAN, HENRY: HENRY DEAN'S ASSOCIATES

McGURSKY, MRS.: Eddie and HENRY DEAN's neighbor. II:175

MISLABURSKI, MRS.: Mrs. Mislaburski was a large-bosomed old lady from CO-OP CITY who wore pink support hose. Mrs. Mislaburski would brave the icy sidewalks of Co-Op City to attend Mass and to visit the CASTLE AVENUE MARKET. VII:102–3

MR. "FUTURE CORONARY" BUSINESSMAN: Eddie bumps into this anally retentive businessman during his first solitary sojourn (via BLACK THIRTEEN) into 1977 NEW YORK. The man's attitude reminds Eddie of the punch line of an old New York joke: "Pardon me, sir, can you tell me how to get to City Hall, or should I just go fuck myself?" V:516–17

MR. RELAXED WINDOW-SHOPPER: Eddie meets this guy when he travels through the UNFOUND DOOR to 1977 NEW YORK. Mr. Relaxed (but somewhat sarcastic) Window-Shopper tells Eddie the date. V:517

OFFICER BOSCONI (BOSCO BOB): ANDY, the smiling but treacherous robot of CALLA BRYN STURGIS, reminds Eddie of Bosco Bob, the cop who had the BROOKLYN AVENUE beat in Eddie's old neighborhood. When you met him casually, Bosco Bob was friendly and happy to see you. However, if he thought you'd done something wrong, he'd turn into a dangerous robot-of-the-law. V:140, V:141, V:633

PERTH OIL AND GAS: VII:324–25

POTZIE: Eddie Dean's cat. II:111

SALLOW BRITISH MAN: *See* BALAZAR, ENRICO: BALAZAR'S NASSAU CONNECTION

SOBIESKI, MARY JEAN: Mary Jean Sobieski was one of Eddie's high school girlfriends. He lost his high school ring in the CONEY ISLAND sand the summer he was dating her. We can only imagine how that might have happened. V:701

TUBTHER, MR.: Mr. Tubther was Eddie's fifth-grade teacher and one of the voices-of-doom which Eddie hears in the CAVE OF VOICES. Mr. Tubther believed that Eddie's potential was ruined by his brother, HENRY DEAN. V:512

TURNPIKIN' FRIENDS: *See* DEAN, HENRY: HENRY DEAN'S TURN-PIKIN' FRIENDS

UNCLE REG: Eddie's uncle. He worked as a painter on both the TRIBOR-OUGH BRIDGE and the GEORGE WASHINGTON BRIDGE. III:292

DELTA FLIGHT 901 CHARACTERS, NASSAU TO JFK:

ANNE: Stewardess, Delta flight 901. II:58

CABBIE: He helped Eddie make a quick getaway from the "Priests of Customs." II:90–91, II:95

CUSTOMS OFFICIALS: Roland called these guys the "Priests of Customs." II:40, II:41, II:42, II:46, II:47, II:58, II:61–62, II:63, II:64, II:69, II:70, II:75 *(DEA)*, II:76, II:78, II:79–84, II:85–90 *(seven of them)*, II:91, II:92–95 *(following cab)*, II:96–99, II:104, II:111, II:112, II:119, II:205, II:239, II:241

DEERE: Copilot, 727 Delta flight 901. II:74–76, II:78–84

DORNING, JANE: Stewardess, Delta flight 901. Jane Dorning was the first member of the flight crew to notice that something was not quite right with Eddie. She thought that Eddie was a terrorist. Her friend SUSY DOUGLAS realized that he was a drug smuggler. II:38–39, II:45–46, II:52–55, II:56, II:58–60, II:61, II:64–69, II:75–76, II:78–83, II:86

> **BATTLE-AXE FLIGHT SCHOOL INSTRUCTOR:** She taught Jane how to spot potential terrorists. She was old enough to have flown with Wiley Post. II:53–54, II:59

DOUGLAS, SUSY: Susy Douglas was also a stewardess on Eddie's fateful flight, and was friends with JANE DORNING. She spotted the cocaine bulges under Eddie's armpits. II:59–60, II:64–69, II:75–76, II:78–83

FLIGHT ENGINEER: II:75–76

McDONALD, CAPT.: Pilot of Delta Flight 901. II:60, II:64, II:66, II:69, II:71, II:74–76, II:78–84

NAVIGATOR: II:75–76, II:78–84

OLD WOMAN EN ROUTE TO MONTREAL: II:78–79

PAULA: Stewardess, Delta flight 901. II:53

PETER: Steward, Delta flight 901. II:58

SALLOW BRITISH MAN: See BALAZAR, ENRICO: BALAZAR'S NAS-SAU CONNECTION

WILSON, WILLIAM: See BALAZAR, ENRICO: BALAZAR'S NASSAU CONNECTION

DEAN, GLORIA (SELINA)

Gloria Dean was EDDIE and HENRY DEAN's sister. She was run over by a drunk driver when she was six and Eddie was two. (She was standing on the sidewalk at the time, watching a game of hopscotch.) In *Song of Susannah*, Eddie refers to Gloria as his "little sister." Although this isn't technically correct—Eddie was two when she died—he has a point. The dead don't age. Gloria is, was, and will eternally be six years old.

II:68 *(Selina)*, II:172, III:22, VI:277

GLORIA DEAN'S ASSOCIATES:
DRUNK DRIVER WHO KILLED HER: III:22

DEAN, HENRY (GREAT SAGE AND EMINENT JUNKIE)
Henry was EDDIE DEAN's bossy and manipulative older brother. Eddie often refers to him as "the great sage and eminent junkie." Henry served in VIETNAM and returned home with a bad knee and a worse habit. Acne-scarred Henry was neither very attractive nor very bright, but he had one outstanding skill—he could make Eddie do whatever he wanted. Hence, he convinced Eddie to become a drug-runner for the dangerous mobster BALAZAR.

In many ways, Henry was the bane of Eddie's youth. Whenever Eddie tried to do something well—anything from playing basketball to woodcarving—Henry made fun of him for it. While under Balazar's "protection," Henry died of an overdose. During Roland and Eddie's final shoot-out with Balazar's gang at the LEANING TOWER, one of Balazar's thugs used Henry's head as a missile and lobbed it at Eddie.

Despite Henry's nasty end, which we witness in *The Drawing of the Three*, the great sage and eminent junkie doesn't rest easy. Eddie Dean's bullying older brother continues to make cameo appearances in the final three books of the Dark Tower series, usually in the form of a nasty, nagging, or teasing voice at the back of Eddie Dean's mind. (In *Wolves of the Calla*, Henry's taunts also rise up from the noxious pit found in the DOORWAY CAVE.)

In the final book of the series, we find out that—on at least one level of the DARK TOWER—Henry Dean was never born. In that *where* and *when*, Eddie Dean is Eddie TOREN, from WHITE PLAINS, and his beloved bro is actually JAKE CHAMBERS (Jake TOREN), not Henry.

II:41–42, II:46, II:47, II:48, II:51, II:52, II:61, II:68, II:71–72, II:77, II:81, II:86, II:87, II:88, II:95, II:97, II:99, II:106, II:107, II:108–9 *(Balazar has him)*, II:111–12, II:114, II:118–20, II:123–24, II:126–27, II:128, II:129, II:132–33, II:134, II:144–45, II:148, II:152 *(head only)*, II:154–56, II:169, II:171–76, II:178, II:206, II:207, II:209, II:233–34, II:237, II:239, II:254, II:276, II:287, II:309, II:337–38, II:398, III:21–23, III:24, III:26, III:27, III:41, III:59, III:72, III:75–76, III:84, III:85, III:150–51, III:154, III:161, III:162, III:174, III:179, III:180, III:183–88, III:189, III:190–92, III:207, III:333, III:344, III:348, IV:19, IV:25, IV:42–45 *(saying Eddie can talk the Devil into setting himself on fire)*, IV:49–50, IV:60, V:61, V:68, V:104 *(Eddie's brother)*, V:140 *(goodfornothin bro)*, V:152, V:163, V:183, V:187, V:203, V:216, V:221 *(indirect)*, V:284, V:292, V:349, V:509, V:510, V:512, V:514, V:524, V:618, V:619 *(indirect)*, V:704–5, VI:28, VI:80–81, VI:142, VI:157–58, VI:184, VI:204, VI:212–14, VI:277, VI:285, VII:43, VII:44 *(great sage and eminent junkie)*, VII:103, VII:118, VII:148, VII:289, VII:328, VII:336, VII:396, VII:812

HENRY DEAN'S ASSOCIATES:
  GOLDOVER, SYLVIA: Sylvia Goldover was Henry Dean's great love. According to EDDIE, she was a skank *El Supremo*, complete with bad breath and smelly armpits. Eventually, she deserted Henry and went off

with her old boyfriend. The only memento she left was a note tucked into Henry's wallet in place of the ninety dollars she'd stolen. The note said, "I'm sorry Henry." VI:157–58

    OLD BOYFRIEND: VI:158

    MARYANNE: Maryanne was a blonde who worked at the MAJESTIC THEATER box office in CO-OP CITY. Henry probably had a crush on her, but instead of being nice he teased her until she cried. III:182–84, III:185, III:186

HENRY DEAN'S KA-TET: IV:43–45, IV:60

    BRANNIGAN, SKIPPER: IV:43–45, IV:60, V:187

    DRABNIK, CSABA (THE MAD FUCKIN' HUNGARIAN): V:187, V:510

    DUGANELLI, FRANK: IV:43–45, IV:60

    FREDERICKS, TOMMY (HALLOWEEN TOMMY): Tommy Fredericks's nickname came from his habit of making faces during stickball games. The faces weren't purposeful but were the result of overexcitement. IV:43–45, IV:60, V:187

    McCAIN, LARRY: IV:43–45, IV:60

    PARELLI, JOHN: IV:43–45, IV:60

    POLINO, JIMMIE (JIMMIE POLIO): Jimmie had a clubfoot. IV:43–45, IV:60, IV:90, V:187

    PRATT, GEORGIE: IV:43–45, IV:60

HENRY DEAN'S TURNPIKIN' FRIENDS: Before EDDIE DEAN met Roland, he, his brother, Henry, and a bunch of their friends would get seriously goobered, pile into BUM O'HARA's Chrysler, and go up I-95 or the Taconic Parkway, feeling the wind and listening to music. Luckily, the driver stayed relatively straight. IV:90

    CORBITT, SANDRA: IV:90

    O'HARA, BUM: IV:90

    POLINO, JIMMIE: *See* HENRY DEAN'S KA-TET, *listed above*

DEAN, MRS. (EDDIE'S MOTHER)
Mrs. Dean was EDDIE, HENRY, and poor dead GLORIA's mother. She was a single parent and so often left Eddie in Henry's care. (Not a good idea.) Mrs. Dean made Eddie feel like he owed his life to his older brother, who could have been great had he not had Eddie to watch out for. This was a complete family lie.

    II:171–74, II:156 *(parents dead)*, II:206 *(indirect)*, II:239, III:22, III:28, III:60, III:76, III:179, III:185, III:187, III:188, III:207, III:235, V:98, V:140 *(mother)*, V:179 *(ma)*, V:182 *(mother)*, V:187 *(mother)*, V:215 *(ma)*, V:245, V:368, V:510, V:540, V:622, VI:28, VI:32, VI:137 *(exclamation)*, VI:195

DEAN, SUSANNAH (DETTA WALKER, ODETTA HOLMES, LADY OF SHADOWS, LADY BLACKBIRD, BLACKBIRD MOMMY, SUSANNAH-MIO)
ODETTA HOLMES (the first of Susannah Dean's personalities) was the only child of the wealthy black dentist and inventor DAN HOLMES, founder of the incredibly successful and lucrative HOLMES DENTAL INDUSTRIES. She was named after the town of ODETTA, ARKANSAS, the place where her mother, ALICE, was born. Odetta lived in the penthouse of GREYMARL APART-

MENTS on FIFTH AVENUE and Central Park South. In the early 1960s, she was the only black resident at that exclusive address. At the age of five, Odetta was hit on the head by a brick dropped out of a window by JACK MORT and slipped into a coma. As a result, her second personality, that of DETTA WALKER, gained life. Detta remained a small part of Odetta until August 19, 1959, when Jack Mort once again entered Susannah's life by pushing Odetta/Detta in front of an approaching A train at CHRISTOPHER STREET STATION. As a result, both of her legs were amputated just above the knee. After the accident, Detta had more and more waking time.

Odetta was a vocal supporter of the Civil Rights Movement and often took part in protests. In fact, some racist rednecks in OXFORD TOWN actually imprisoned her and some of her Movement friends during their time in the South. Unlike Odetta, Detta didn't believe in any movements but was full of rage against white oppression. In fact, her rage often pushed her into committing dangerous and bizarre acts.

Roland entered the mind of Odetta/Detta in the *when* of 1964, and brought her (complete with wheelchair) into MID-WORLD. It was in Mid-World that Detta and Odetta were forced to face each other. From their battle and eventual union arose the stronger and more vibrant third of Susannah Dean, EDDIE DEAN's lover and then wife. Despite the creation of Susannah Dean, both Odetta and Detta continue to play an important role in the final three books of the Dark Tower series, as does Susannah's susceptibility to multiple personality disorder.

At the beginning of *Wolves of the Calla,* we find out that Susannah Dean is pregnant (something she suspected as early as *The Waste Lands*), but within the first hundred pages we begin to fear (as does Roland) that the child she carries is not human at all, but the offspring of the DEMON she trapped in a sexual vise while Roland and Eddie drew JAKE CHAMBERS into the SPEAKING RING, located on the great plains of RIVER BARONY. While trying to keep his suspicions a secret, Roland follows Susannah on her nocturnal feeding prowls through the forests and bogs of the BORDERLANDS, as much to keep her safe as to try to discern the nature of her carry.

Quite soon, Roland discovers that Susannah is not the only mother of her child. Her body now contains yet another personality, that of MIA, whose name (in High Speech) means "mother." Over the course of both *Wolves of the Calla* and *Song of Susannah,* we learn that Mia (unlike Susannah's previous personalities) is not a part of Susannah's psyche at all, but an invading spirit whose sole purpose is to feed and protect the CHAP, which Susannah's body harbors. Unlike Susannah, who lost her legs from the knee down, Mia can walk. Susannah can use those legs when she travels TODASH or when her psyche is completely dominated by Mia, as it is in 1999 NEW YORK. In *Song of Susannah,* we also find out that Mia is white, which does not sit too well with Detta Walker.

In many ways, this schism between Susannah and Mia propels the action of *Song of Susannah.* At the end of *Wolves,* Mia hijacks Susannah's body and travels through the UNFOUND DOOR to 1999, where SAYRE and the other WARRIORS OF THE SCARLET EYE await her and her soon-to-be-born offspring. Hoping to outsmart Susannah's *ka-tet,* Mia takes BLACK THIRTEEN with her, essentially locking this magic door behind her so that no one can follow.

Not surprisingly, Mia underestimates both Susannah and her friends. With the help of the MANNI, our *tet*-mates Jake, OY, and PERE CALLAHAN track SUSANNAH-MIO to the DIXIE PIG, which also happens to be a den of TYPE ONE VAMPIRES. Although Callahan is killed by vampires and LOW MEN, Jake and Oy follow Susannah's back trail to the FEDIC DOGAN, where Mia has just given birth to her were-spider baby, MORDRED. Although Susannah manages to kill her captors and escape to the New York/Fedic door, where she awaits the arrival of the rest of her *ka-tet*, she only manages to clip off one of Mordred's legs with a bullet. She is not able to save Mia, who is sucked dry by her offspring.

After the deaths of Eddie and Jake, Susannah becomes a member of a new *ka-tet*—one that is bound by hate as well as love. This new group consists of herself, Roland, and Mordred—the *dan-tete*, or little god, whose coming has been prophesied for generations. Wherever Susannah and Roland go, Mordred—child of Mia and the CRIMSON KING as much as he is the child of his "White Daddy" Roland and his "Blackbird Mommy" Susannah—is never far behind. From the wastelands of the DISCORDIA (where Susannah contracts a blood tumor above her lip) through the WHITE LANDS OF EMPATHICA, Mordred tracks his human parents, searching for a method of attack. With Susannah, he never gets the chance. Through a pair of stolen binoculars, he watches as the mute artist PATRICK DANVILLE removes Susannah's tumor and then literally draws the Unfound Door into END-WORLD so that Susannah can escape before Roland reaches his ultimate destination.

Susannah Dean is the only member of Roland's *ka-tet* to survive. However, *ka* is not always completely unkind. When Susannah passes through the Unfound Door, she finds herself in an alternative version of New York, where both Eddie and Jake are still alive (albeit under the names Eddie and Jake TOREN). Although Eddie no longer remembers his life in Mid-World, he has dreamed about Susannah, and he knows (as do we) that he's going to fall in love with her all over again. Susannah's gunslinging days are over. As if to symbolize this, she finds that Roland's gun (which she accidentally brought with her through the Unfound Door) seems absolutely ancient. Since it is plugged and unable to fire, Susannah throws it away.

Like EDDIE DEAN, JAKE CHAMBERS, and Jake's bumbler OY, Susannah plays a small part in *The Wind Through the Keyhole*. In that novel (which takes place just before *Wolves of the Calla*), Roland and his American *tet* are journeying southeast along the PATH OF THE BEAM. Along the way they cross the RIVER WHYE (meeting the friendly ferryman BIX), and then must hide up in the abandoned village of GOOK to wait out a STARKBLAST. During that terrible storm, Susannah and the others listen to two of Roland's tales. (These tales form the major adventures of the novel.) Roland's first story tells of his adventure with JAMIE DeCURRY when the two of them went hunting for a shape-changing SKIN-MAN in the village of DEBARIA. Roland's second story is a folktale called "The Wind Through the Keyhole," and it is from this story that the novel takes its name.

I:130 *(as Lady of Shadows)*, II:180–81 *(Lady of Shadows)*, II:185–203 *(Detta/Odetta in 1964 New York; 201 Roland and Eddie see her through door)*, II:204–9 *(discussed by Roland and Eddie)*, II:211–12 *(discussed by George Shavers)*, II:214–20 *(George Shavers remembers)*, II:220–23, II:225–96 *(on*

*beach. 235–38 remembers brick accident; 247–77 Detta takes over; 277–96
Odetta takes over), II:297, II:298, II:299, II:300–305 (these and previous
pages—Eddie and Roland discuss), II:305–7 (Detta), II:308–12 (discussed),
II:315, II:316 (Lady), II:318, II:320–24, II:324–26 (Detta), II:327–38 (Detta),
II:339, II:357, II:359–60, II:367, II:379–80, II:385–90 (Roland makes Detta
and Odetta face each other), II:393–99, III:11–19, III:23, III:24–25, III:26,
III:29–51 (from 37, Roland's story; 43 says Susannah from 1963), III:54–77,
III:78–86, III:96, III:97 (Lady), III:136 (Lady), III:149, III:151–52, III:158–65,
III:170–76 (171 says she is twenty-six years old), III:178–82, III:189–90 (draw-
ing Jake), III:193–94, III:196–98 (Detta's sex wars), III:201–3, III:206–13,
III:221–54, III:256–67, III:268, III:269, III:273–81, III:283–85, III:286–301
(Gasher), III:302–4, III:308–12, III:316–25, III:329, III:331–34, III:340–50
(345 says she's from 1963), III:356, III:361–65, III:372–73, III:377, III:378,
III:382–85, III:393–420, IV:3–10, IV:13–42 (riddling; 30 Edith Bunker blunder; 31–35 Falls of the Hounds), IV:44–70 (58–59 crash; 60 leave Blaine; 64
thinny's sound and saw player in Central Park "sounds Hawaiian"; 69 pains in
belly and dangers of demon contact), IV:70–112 (Topeka train station; 72–77*
Topeka Capital Journal *and superflu; 79 Beam disappears; 81 dead of Topeka
and crip spaces; 82 new wheelchair for Susannah; 87 Charlie the Choo-Choo
in Topeka; 91 sign of the Crimson King; 92 bullets in ears; 95 enter thinny; 97
Oz in distance; 106–12 Roland tells story), IV:335–37 (interlude in Kansas),
IV:570, IV:615–25 (end of Roland's story; back in Topeka), IV:626–68 (626
ruby cappies; 632 Green Palace; 634 gate like Wizard's Rainbow; 646 Tick-
Tock; 648 Flagg; 652 Roland's matricide), V:8 (strangers from Out-World),
V:29–31 (gunslingers), V:35, V:36, V:37, V:38–47, V:70, V:71–87 (Mia hunts),
V:87–119, V:120–37, V:139, V:140 (Detta/Odetta), V:142–60, V:162, V:165,
V:167–69, V:172–86 (181—Odetta), V:189–91, V:193–98, V:201–39, V:241,
V:242, V:243, V:244, V:245, V:246–49 (Roland and Eddie discuss), V:250,
V:251–53, V:257 (listening to Pere Callahan), V:258 (listening), V:260 (lis-
tening), V:262 (listening), V:266–71 (listening), V:273–74 (listening), V:282
(listening), V:284 (listening), V:285 (listening), V:290 (listening), V:291–96
(listening), V:301–2 (listening), V:309–12, V:318, V:321, V:322, V:325, V:329
(Detta), V:341, V:343–46, V:351–56, V:358, V:359 (indirect), V:365–66, V:368,
V:369, V:376–80, V:381–82, V:383, V:386, V:388, V:390–91, V:392, V:393,
V:394, V:395, V:396–406, V:408 (indirect, "other two"), V:412 (ka-mates),
V:413, V:417–20, V:421–23, V:428–30, V:437–38, V:442–45, V:448–49,
V:452–54, V:457, V:466–72, V:476, V:478–83, V:485, V:487, V:488–505,
V:507, V:513, V:519, V:535, V:539 (Odetta Holmes), V:555, V:563, V:575
(brownie), V:581–90, V:597 (Odetta), V:601–17, V:620, V:628–29, V:639–40,
V:641, V:652, V:654, V:658, V:659, V:662–74, V:679–91, V:695–705 (as
Mia), VI:3, VI:4, VI:5, VI:6, VI:7 (indirect), VI:9, VI:10–11, VI:12, VI:13,
VI:14, VI:16, VI:17, VI:21–22, VI:24–26, VI:32 (indirect), VI:35, VI:36,
VI:37, VI:43, VI:48–52, VI:53–125, VI:143, VI:147, VI:150, VI:163, VI:168,
VI:171, VI:173, VI:190, VI:194, VI:200, VI:205, VI:210, VI:216, VI:219–61,
VI:267 (sweetheart), VI:271, VI:284, VI:287, VI:297, VI:299, VI:311, VI:316,
VI:319, VI:320, VI:321, VI:322, VI:325, VI:334, VI:339, VI:340–41, VI:343,
VI:347–85, VI:399, VI:400, VI:408, VII:3, VII:4 (Susannah-Mio), VII:13
(Detta), VII:19, VII:21–22, VII:24, VII:25, VII:27 (indirect), VII:34, VII:35,*

VII:36 *(wife)*, VII:38 *(indirect)*, VII:47, VII:48, VII:52, VII:55–80, VII:81, VII:84 *(oops—feet!)*, VII:86, VII:87–88, VII:89, VII:91, VII:92 *(indirect)*, VII:110, VII:111, VII:112, VII:114–15, VII:120, VII:121, VII:126, VII:136–38, VII:141–59, VII:161, VII:162, VII:163, VII:168, VII:169, VII:173, VII:177 *(indirect)*, VII:182, VII:183, VII:186 (ka-tet*)*, VII:187, VII:188, VII:189–220, VII:239, VII:247–61, VII:262 *(indirect)*, VII:265–73, VII:276 *(indirect)*, VII:279–309 *(297–303 listening to Ted's story)*, VII:315, VII:316, VII:317, VII:318–24, VII:325, VII:328, VII:329–42, VII:349–51, VII:361, VII:363–67, VII:373, VII:374, VII:381–85, VII:387, VII:388–90 *(on 389 she grows feet!)*, VII:395, VII:396–97, VII:401–4, VII:407, VII:408–11, VII:413, VII:416, VII:417, VII:446, VII:448, VII:459, VII:485, VII:486–87, VII:488, VII:499, VII:502, VII:508–9, VII:513, VII:519–20, VII:531–42, VII:549–619 *(619— no feet to run!)*, VII:620, VII:621–22 *(indirect)*, VII:624–31 *(624 feet)*, VII:632–710, VII:711, VII:715–50, VII:751, VII:754 *(Blackbird Mommy)*, VII:756, VII:757, VI:758, VI:759, VII:761, VII:768, VII:769, VII:771, VII:773, VII:774, VII:780, VII:785, VII:789, VII:801, VII:802, VII:807–13 *(gun no longer works)*, VII:818, VII:819, W:3–31 *(4 Detta Walker; 20 Detta Walker)*, W:303–7

SUSANNAH DEAN'S OTHER SELVES:

HOLMES, ODETTA: Odetta Holmes was the birth name of Roland's *ka-tet* mate SUSANNAH DEAN. Odetta was the only child of the dentist/ inventor DAN HOLMES and was sole heir to the HOLMES DENTAL INDUSTRIES fortune. At the age of five, Odetta was hit on the head by a brick dropped by the psychopath JACK MORT, and her personality fractured, resulting in the birth of DETTA WALKER, who shared Odetta's body if not her opinions.

Odetta Holmes was a socially conscious young woman who was active in the Civil Rights Movement of the early 1960s. However, Detta Walker had a very different way of dealing with the oppression she faced from an unjust, prejudiced society. Her angry reaction was to take personal vengeance upon white boys (whenever the opportunity arose), and at the white world, by shoplifting from stores such as Macy's.

Detta and Odetta lost their legs from the knee down in 1959, when Jack Mort once again entered their shared life. At that time, Mort pushed them in front of an A train at CHRISTOPHER STREET STATION, in NEW YORK CITY. After this tragedy, an angry Detta Walker gained more and more waking time.

For years, Detta and Odetta lived their separate lives, each unaware of the existence of the other. They were finally united by Roland, who (while occupying Jack Mort's body in our world) forced Mort to commit suicide in front of the very train which had severed Detta/Odetta's legs. Witnessing this event through one of the magical BEACH DOORS while simultaneously seeing each other reflected in Roland's borrowed gaze forced the two women to confront each other. They united to create the much stronger personality of Susannah Dean, wife of EDDIE DEAN. *For page references, see* DEAN, SUSANNAH, *listed above*

SUSANNAH-MIO: While traveling TODASH, our *tet* sees this piece of graffito written on the fence around the Vacant LOT in NEW YORK

CITY: "Oh Susannah-Mio, divided girl of mine, Done parked her RIG in the DIXIE PIG, in the year of '99." Although our *tet* does not yet know it, Susannah-Mio refers to the combined personalities of Susannah Dean and MIA, daughter of none. *For page references, see* DEAN, SUSANNAH, *listed above*

WALKER, DETTA: The angry, vindictive personality of Detta Walker gained life when five-year-old ODETTA HOLMES was hit on the head by a brick dropped by the psychopath JACK MORT. She and Odetta lost their legs from the knee down in 1959, when Mort once again attacked, pushing their shared body in front of an A train at CHRISTOPHER STREET STATION in NEW YORK CITY. This second tragic event gave angry Detta more waking time than she had previously enjoyed and allowed her to do what she liked best—tempt, tease, and torture white boys as well as shoplift from white-owned businesses such as Macy's.

Although they shared a body, Detta and Odetta were completely different women. While Odetta was both wealthy and educated, streetwise Detta took pride that she "didn't go to Morehouse or *no* house." While Odetta believed in social justice and was an active participant in the Civil Rights Movement of the early 1960s, Detta had little faith in the justice meted out by white society and figured she'd be better off creating her own. This usually resulted in aggressive acts against those who angered her, or who she felt had treated her unfairly.

Although Roland succeeded in uniting Detta and Odetta at the end of *The Drawing of the Three,* creating the much more stable personality of SUSANNAH DEAN, Detta continues to make appearances throughout the last three books of the Dark Tower series. In fact, when it comes to facing the demon-spirit MIA, Detta proves to be as great an ally to Susannah and her *ka-tet* as she once was an enemy to Roland and EDDIE during their long travels along LOBSTROSITY Beach. *For Detta's page references, see* DEAN, SUSANNAH, *listed above*

SUSANNAH'S PRESENT ASSOCIATES:

BELLMAN: VI:94

BUSKER: Susannah-Mio sees and hears this busker on her way to the DIXIE PIG. He is playing "Man of Constant Sorrow," a song which inundates Susannah's mind with memories of her days as ODETTA HOLMES, a Civil Rights activist. The busker's music, combined with Susannah's memories, touches MIA's heart and fortifies what good exists inside her. VI:334, VI:338–39, VI:340, VI:347–57

CABBIE (GIVES SUSANNAH/MIA A LIFT TO THE DIXIE PIG): *See* TAXI DRIVERS: TAXI DRIVER NUMBER THREE

CHAP: *See* MORDRED, *listed separately*

DAMASCUS, TRUDY: *See* GUTTENBERG, FURTH, AND PATEL: DAMASCUS, TRUDY

EXOTIC HOTEL RECEPTIONIST: *See* PLAZA–PARK HYATT CHARACTERS: RECEPTIONISTS

GIRL SCOUTS: Like MATHIESSEN VAN WYCK, these two Girl Scouts are mesmerized by SUSANNAH/MIA's SCRIMSHAW TURTLE. Susannah makes them move on, since they are not as useful to her as Mats. VI:87

JAPANESE TOURISTS AT THE PLAZA: *See* PLAZA–PARK HYATT CHARACTERS: JAPANESE TOURISTS

MIA: *See* MIA, *listed separately*

RAT, MR.: *See* MIA, *listed separately*

VAN WYCK, MATHIESSEN (MATS): Mats is the second assistant to the Swedish ambassador. He is also the first person SUSANNAH DEAN mesmerizes with her SCRIMSHAW TURTLE. Mats pays for SUSANNAH-MIO's room at the PLAZA–PARK HYATT hotel. He also gives her all of his cash. In return, Susannah uses hypnotic suggestion to assure his regular bowel movements (one of Mats's problems) and to make him cease worrying about his wife's affair. VI:83–89, VI:93, VI:94 *(indirect)*, VI:256, VI:349, VII:143

   SWEDISH AMBASSADOR: VI:85, VI:88

   WIFE (UNNAMED): She is having an affair, and this causes Mats tremendous grief. VI:85, VI:88

      HER LOVER: VI:85, VI:88

   WOMAN WITH STROLLER: VI:75

DETTA WALKER'S ASSOCIATES:

DETTA/ODETTA'S "A TRAIN" ACCIDENT ASSOCIATES:

   ELDERLY WHITE BUSINESSMAN: This man gave his belt to the OLD BLACK WOMAN who was trying to save Detta/Odetta's legs. II:216

   ESTEVEZ, JULIO: An ambulance worker who helped to save Detta/Odetta's life after her legs were amputated by the A train at CHRISTOPHER STREET STATION. He was deeply disturbed by her split personality. Julio belonged to the bowling team **THE SPICS OF SUPREMACY.** II:211–12, II:214–20 *(present)*

      BASALE, MIGUEL: One of the guys on Julio Estevez's bowling team. II:211

   OLD BLACK WOMAN: This elderly lady jumped onto the tracks to make tourniquets around Detta/Odetta's bleeding thighs, thereby saving her life. She was later given a Medal of Bravery by the mayor. The only other people to help in the rescue effort were a white kid who called for an ambulance and an old businessman who loaned his belt. II:215–16

   PARAMEDICS (THE BOBBSEY TWINS): II:211, II:217–20 *(present)*

   SHAVERS, GEORGE: The intern from SISTERS OF MERCY HOSPITAL who was part of the "Emergency Ride" program. He helped to keep Detta/Odetta alive during her ambulance ride. Like JULIO ESTEVEZ, he knew that there was something profoundly wrong with DETTA/ODETTA's mind. II:211–20

   YOUNG WHITE GUY: This young man called for an ambulance while most of the A train commuters just stood and stared. II:215

DETTA'S MACY'S ASSOCIATES: Detta Walker liked to shoplift from this department store.

   FLOORWALKER: II:221, II:222, II:223

   HALVORSEN, JIMMY: Halvorsen was the Macy's store detective who caught Detta shoplifting. His jiggling belly resembled a sack of potatoes. II:221–23, II:227

SALESGIRL #1: II:202–3, II:208
SALESGIRL #2: II:208
DETTA'S OTHER ASSOCIATES:
   FRAT BOY: He was one of the many white boys cock-teased by vengeful Detta. II:195–96
   HORNY BOYS IN ROADSIDE PARKING LOTS: VI:237
ODETTA HOLMES'S ASSOCIATES:
   BEASLEY, JESSICA: Jessica Beasley was Odetta's mother's friend. She suffered the indignity of two false pregnancies. V:121
   BLUE LADY: *See* SISTER BLUE, *listed below*
   CARVER, MOSES (POP MOSE): *See* TET CORPORATION: FOUNDING FATHERS
   CYNTHIA: Odetta's friend. IV:626
   FEENY, ANDREW: Odetta's chauffeur. II:185–93, II:197, II:242, II:294, III:258, VI:219, VII:555
   FOLK CLUB BOYFRIEND: This young man introduced Odetta to the folk music she grew to love. II:199
   FREEMAN, NATHAN: Nathan Freeman took sixteen-year-old Odetta Holmes to the Spring Hop. VI:101
   GIRL AT COLUMBIA UNIVERSITY (STORYTELLER): At a college hen party, this girl told a story about a young woman on a long car trip who was too embarrassed to tell her friends that she needed to stop and pee. Her bladder burst and she died. VI:62
      GIRL WHOSE BLADDER BURST: VI:62
   GRANDMOTHERS (MATERNAL AND PATERNAL): VII:643
   HOLMES, ALICE (MOTHER): *See* HOLMES, ALICE, *listed separately*
   HOLMES, DAN (FATHER): *See* HOLMES, DAN, *listed separately*
   HOLMES DENTAL: *See* HOLMES DENTAL INDUSTRIES, *listed separately*
   HOWARD: Doorman, Greymarl Apartments. II:190–93
   LEON: Odetta's friend. He was with her in the OXFORD TOWN prison. The guards called him a pinko fag. III:15
   MURRAY, PROFESSOR: Professor Murray taught medieval history at COLUMBIA UNIVERSITY. In this class Susannah learned the story of KING ARTHUR and his betraying son/nephew, MORDRED. VI:107
   OVERMEYER, PROFESSOR: Professor Overmeyer taught Psych 1 at COLUMBIA UNIVERSITY. Odetta took his class as an undergraduate. VI:68
   PIMSY: Odetta's beloved childhood pet. VII:123–24, VII:519
   SISTER BLUE (BLUE LADY): Sister Blue (often called Blue Lady) was ODETTA HOLMES's maternal aunt. Her real name was Sophia, but she earned her nickname thanks to her fondness for the color blue. After attending Aunt Blue's wedding, Odetta was hit on the head by a brick thrown by the psychopathic JACK MORT. Mort's brick cracked her skull and gave birth to Odetta's second personality, that of nasty DETTA WALKER. For some reason, Detta blamed Aunt Blue for her accident and as a result developed a particular abhorrence for both her aunt and the beautiful white-and-blue wedding plates that Aunt Blue received from the Holmes family.

The Blue Lady's white-and-blue china *forspecial* plates play an important part in *Wolves of the Calla*. First, they are identical to the plates from which MIA eats in her magical BANQUETING HALL. Second, they bear an uncanny resemblance to the plates thrown by the SISTERS OF ORIZA. However, unlike Sister Blue's *forspecial* plates, the deadly weapons thrown by the Sisters are made of titanium and are honed to a murderous sharpness. While in the Calla we also find out that the delicate blue webbing found on the plates actually resembles the young rice plants called ORIZAs, named after the goddess of the rice. II:194, II:235–36, II:277, II:324, II:388, III:266, IV:650, V:76 *(Blue Lady)*, V:84 *(Blue Lady)*, VI:375

VAN RONK, DAVE: Dave Van Ronk was a white blues-shouter. ODETTA saw him perform in GREENWICH VILLAGE in the early 1960s. He must have been pretty good, since Susannah remembered some of his songs. V:168

ODETTA HOLMES AND THE CIVIL RIGHTS MOVEMENT:

FREEDOM RIDERS: In 1961, seven black and six white members of the Congress of Racial Equality (CORE) left Washington, D.C., on two public buses bound for the Deep South. They wanted to test the Supreme Court ruling which stated that segregation on interstate buses and rail stations was unconstitutional. Although they suffered terrible treatment at the hands of racists (one of their buses was burned and many of the Freedom Riders were brutalized), the protests continued. In fact, by the end of the summer, protests had spread to airports and train stations throughout the South. In November, the Interstate Commerce Commission issued rules prohibiting segregated transportation facilities. The Freedom Riders' aim—to desegregate public transportation in the South—had succeeded. II:227, VI:256

ODETTA'S "MOVEMENT" ASSOCIATES: In 1964, the Congress of Racial Equality (CORE) led a massive voter registration and desegregation campaign in MISSISSIPPI. They called it the Freedom Summer. Odetta Holmes took part in the voter registration movement. VI:351, VI:353, VI:355

> **ANDERSON, DELBERT:** Delbert Anderson was a guitar player involved in the voter registration movement. VI:352, VI:353
>
> **BAIL BONDSMAN:** VI:220, VI:221
>
> **BAMBRY, JOHN:** He was the pastor of the FIRST AFRO-AMERICAN METHODIST CHURCH in OXFORD, MISSISSIPPI. VI:352
>
> **BAMBRY, LESTER:** Lester Bambry was the brother of JOHN BAMBRY. He owned the BLUE MOON HOTEL, where Odetta and her friends stayed while registering black voters in MISSISSIPPI. VI:352
>
> **DARRYL:** Darryl was a white boy who became Odetta's lover during her time in the voter registration movement. VI:354–55
>
> **OXFORD TOWN COPS:** VI:220

VOTER REGISTRATION BOYS: These three young men (historical figures, every one) were killed while registering black voters in MISSISSIPPI in 1964. Their deaths mark one of the true low points of American history.

> **CHANEY, JAMES:** James Chaney was born in May of 1943 and was a native of Meridian, MISSISSIPPI. In 1963 he joined CORE (Congress of Racial Equality) and was an active participant in the voter

registration movement. On June 21, 1964, Chaney and two white activists—ANDREW GOODMAN and MICHAEL SCHWERNER— were attacked and killed by the Ku Klux Klan. VI:351, VI:352, VI:354, VI:355, VI:356, VI:357

GOODMAN, ANDREW: Andrew Goodman, from MANHATTAN, was twenty when he died on the Rock Cut Road. He had been in MISSISSIPPI for only one full day. VI:351, VI:352, VI:354, VI:355, VI:356, VI:357

SCHWERNER, MICHAEL: The rednecks of OXFORD, MISSISSIPPI, called Schwerner the "Jewboy." To the Klan members of NESHOBA COUNTY, he was known as "goatee." Schwerner was the most hated Civil Rights worker in Mississippi. His "elimination" was ordered by the Klan's imperial wizard. ANDREW GOODMAN and JAMES CHANEY died with him. VI:351, VI:352, VI:354, VI:355, VI:356, VI:357, VI:361

DEAN, WENDELL (EDDIE DEAN'S FATHER)
EDDIE DEAN's mom claimed that Eddie's father's name was Wendell. Since Eddie couldn't remember the guy, he had to take his mother's word for it.
   III:68, III:174, V:215, VI:188 *(saying)*

DEARBORN, WILL
This was young Roland's alias in HAMBRY. It is used throughout much of *Wizard and Glass*. Since Roland is the main character in the Dark Tower series, his presence is implied in all other entries. For specific information about Roland's adventures, look up the other characters or places involved. For example, page references for his love affair with Susan Delgado are listed under DELGADO, SUSAN. *See also* DESCHAIN, ROLAND, *later in this section*

DEATHFLY
This is the fly that the young JAKE CHAMBERS is certain will buzz around his corpse.
   VII:95, VII:96

DEBARIA CHARACTERS
The first of the interlocking tales which Roland tells in *Wind Through the Keyhole* is an autobiographical story about his adventures with JAMIE DeCURRY in the town of DEBARIA, where STEVEN DESCHAIN had sent the two young gunslingers to hunt down a shapeshifting SKIN-MAN. Located on the edge of the ALKALI FLATS, ten or twelve wheels from the women's retreat of SERENITY, the dusty, hide-smelling railhead town of Debaria shipped their two main products—cattle and block salt—south, east, and north, in other words in every direction other than the one where JOHN FARSON's rebellion raged. In Roland's grandfather's days, Debaria had been a fine little city, but by the time our story takes place, the town's two lifelines—the mines and the railroad—are both failing. STEVEN DESCHAIN thought that Debaria would soon dry up and blow away like so many others in Mid-World, but when Roland and Jamie traveled there it was still a lively (if decaying) town.

According to Roland's father, many of Debaria's residents were drinkers, whores, gamblers, and confidence men, but there were still a few honorable citizens left among the rabble. First and foremost among these good men was HIGH SHERIFF HUGH PEAVY, whom Roland and Jamie were told to seek out as soon as they arrived in the town via the small train known as SMA' TOOT. It turns out that many years previously, when Peavy was still a deputy, he helped Steven Deschain hunt down the nasty CROW GANG. From Peavy, Roland learned that the dimple-like scar on his father's forearm was from one of PA CROW's bullets.

During his days in Debaria, Roland discovered just how widespread the influence of the glorified harrier, JOHN FARSON, had become. According to Peavy's not-so-good deputy, STROTHER, many people in Debaria were so sick of the riffraff in town that they were ready to throw in their lot with Gileads' greatest enemy.

GENERAL: W:39, W:42, W:45, W:54, W:61 (*sheriff discusses whoremasters, gamblers, ranchers, drifters*), W:62 (*sheriff discusses drunk cowpunchers and farmhands*), W:270–77 (*watching*), W:278 (*three dozen dead*), W:294 (*women*)

ALORA FARM CHARACTERS: *See* SKIN-MAN: SKIN-MAN'S VICTIMS

BLACKSMITH: Debaria's blacksmith plays a small but important role in Roland's plan to defeat the flesh-eating SKIN-MAN. Despite the hot wind blowing across town (and the fact that Debaria no longer has a fire department), this blacksmith agrees to fire up his forge so that he can construct the only weapon that will kill a shapeshifter—a silver bullet. The blacksmith's diligence is probably encouraged by the three gold knuckles that Roland shakes into his palm. However, his admiration for Roland's weaponry could also be a factor. (When Roland tells the blacksmith that a shell from his gun holds fifty-seven grains of gunpowder, the smith is shocked. "Gods!" he says. "It's a wonder the barrel of your revolver don't bust when'ee pull the trigger!") W:98–99, W:100, W:101, W:283, W:285

DA': When the blacksmith's da' was a boy, Debaria still had a fire department. W:99

CROW GANG: When HIGH SHERIFF HUGH PEAVY was still a deputy, the people of Debaria and the surrounding area lived in fear of the predations of the murderous CROW GANG. Led by PA CROW, the gang robbed ranches, citizens, and trains, but their main business was the coward's crime of kidnapping for ransom.

According to Peavy, at the apogee of the gang's nefarious activities, STEVEN DESCHAIN happened to be doing his gunslinger rounds in the area. Hence he was in town the day after the Crows had stolen a rancher's wife named BELINDA DOOLIN. Leading a posse of seven, plus Peavy and the old High Sheriff, Deschain followed the Crows' trail north through the hardpan toward the abandoned salt-houses where the Crows had their hideout. Rather than approaching the hideout directly, Steven Deschain wanted to circle to the east so that the posse could come at the gang from the HIGH PURE, but the old High Sheriff, PEA ANDERSON, would have none of it. Saying that *sai* Doolin would be dead by the time they arrived, he set off along the straightest path, his posse in tow. Within half an hour, Deschain and Peavy heard gunshots. PA CROW had seen the sheriff's men coming, and from the high rocks of AMBUSH ARROYO, he and his gang had poured lead on Anderson and his possemen.

Figuring that the Crows would be celebrating their apparent victory, Peavy and the elder Deschain circled in from the east, and the two lawmen ambushed the gang and rescued *sai* Doolin. Being honorable, *sai* Deschain woke up the gang before shooting them. "Wake up, Allan Crow," he said, "unless you'd go into the clearing at the end of the path with your eyes shut." The only member of the gang to survive Deschain's first fusillade was Allan Crow himself. Pa Crow only got off one shot before he died and the bullet went wild, but it richocheted against the wall and hit Steven Deschain just above the crook of his elbow. Hugh Peavy dug the slug out with his skinning knife. W:56–61, W:290

> **CROW, ALLAN (PA CROW):** Despite the fact that Allan Crow was a thief, a murderer, and rapist, he was very trig. A stroke had left one side of his face snarled up and frozen, but he could still move as fast as the devil. When STEVEN DESCHAIN arrived at the Crows' hideout to slaughter the gang, Pa Crow (still wearing his long johns) reached for the gun stuck in the top of his boot. Although he only got off a single round before Steven Deschain shot him dead, Pa Crow's bullet ricocheted against the wall and hit the gunslinger's *dinh* in the arm, just above the elbow. W:58, W:59–61 *(shot Steven Deschain)*

> **FOURTEEN-YEAR-OLD GUARD:** This guard was asleep when STEVEN DESCHAIN and HUGH PEAVY ambushed the Crow gang in their hide-out. Later Peavy saw him with a rope around his neck, a trapdoor under his feet, tears running out of his eyes, and a mess in his pants. Peavy didn't mourn the boy since he had raped *sai* DOOLIN along with the rest of the men, even though she was old enough to be his grandmother. W:58–59

DOOLIN, BELINDA: Belinda Doolin was kidnapped by the CROW GANG and then saved by STEVEN DESCHAIN and HUGH PEAVY. Unfortunately, she was raped by the gang before she was rescued. W:56, W:57, W:59, W:60

DOOLIN (RANCHER): After the CROW GANG kidnapped his wife, BELINDA DOOLIN, this rancher managed to untie himself and call the sheriff on the jing-jang. This was the Crows' undoing, since they didn't know how swiftly this telephone could send and receive messages.

HOSTLER: As the winds of the simoom picked up, Roland left his horse, and YOUNG BILL STREETER's mule, in this hostler's livery. Roland gave the man half a gold knuckle for his trouble. The hostler told Roland where to find the town BLACKSMITH. W:98

JEFFERSON RANCH CHARACTERS: Soon after ROLAND DESCHAIN and JAMIE DeCURRY reached Debaria, the SKIN-MAN struck again. This time he massacred the people of the Jefferson Ranch. All told, the monstrous shapeshifter killed sixteen proddies, the COOK (BILL STREETER), *sai* JEFFERSON, Jefferson's WIFE, and his two DAUGHTERS. The few members of the Jefferson Ranch who survived the skin-man's rampage are listed below. YOUNG BILL STREETER is listed separately. The rest of the characters are listed under SKIN-MAN: SKIN-MAN'S VICTIMS: JEFFERSON RANCH CHARACTERS.

> **ARN:** *See* CANFIELD, BILL: FRIENDS/TRAILMATES, *below*

CANFIELD, BILL (BILL CANFIELD OF THE JEFFERSON RANCH): When we first met Bill Canfield we thought he was a pokie—which is to say a wandering cowboy not signed to any particular ranch. However, we soon discovered that he had put his mark on Jefferson's wall the month before, and so he was a proddie, or steady ranch-hand.

At the time of the SKIN-MAN massacre, Canfield and his two mates, ARN and SNIP, were camping out on the PURE so that they could round up strays. In the middle of the night they were woken up by screams, snarls, and gunshots. The three men mounted up and galloped to the ranch.

Canfield arrived first, since he was riding a ranch horse and the other two men were riding mules. He began his investigations at the big house where he found the body of JEFFERSON'S WIFE. Following the bloody tracks outside, he discovered the two Jefferson DAUGHTERS, whose backs had been carved open right down to their spines. Next, Canfield went to the bunkhouse which had been turned into an abattoir by the skin-man. Unfortunately, Canfield and his friends had to shoot the two ranch dogs, ROSIE and MOZIE, since they were lapping up the blood and the brains of the victims. W:69, W:70–73 *(70–71 described)*, W:84, W:270–74 *(at Busted Luck)*, W:277–80 *(watching salties)*

> **FRIENDS/TRAILMATES:** W:70–73, W:85
>> **ARN:** Arn and Snip were camping out on the PURE with Canfield when the SKIN-MAN struck, so they survived the massacre. W:71 *(named)*, W:72–73 *(named)*, W:270–73
>> **SNIP:** Snip and Arn were camping out on the PURE with Canfield when the SKIN-MAN struck, so they survived the massacre. W:71 *(named)*, W:72–74 *(named)*, W:270–74, W:277–80

COOKIE (BILL STREETER, YOUNG BILL'S FATHER): *See* SKIN-MAN: SKIN-MAN'S VICTIMS: JEFFERSON RANCH

JEFFERSON FAMILY: *See* SKIN-MAN: SKIN-MAN'S VICTIMS: JEFFERSON RANCH

> **JEFFERSON (RANCHER):** *See* SKIN-MAN: SKIN-MAN'S VICTIMS: JEFFERSON RANCH
> **DAUGHTERS:** *See* SKIN-MAN: SKIN-MAN'S VICTIMS: JEFFERSON RANCH
> **SONS:** *See* SKIN-MAN: SKIN-MAN'S VICTIMS: JEFFERSON RANCH
> **WIFE:** *See* SKIN-MAN: SKIN-MAN'S VICTIMS: JEFFERSON RANCH

NUTTER, ELROD (FOREMAN): *See* SKIN-MAN: SKIN-MAN'S VICTIMS: JEFFERSON RANCH

ROSIE and MOZIE (dogs): Rosie and Mozie were the ranch dogs. CANFIELD, ARN, and SNIP shot them after they discovered the animals lapping up the blood and brains of the SKIN-MAN's victims. W:69, W:72

PRODDIES:
> **FREDDY TWO-STEP:** *See* SKIN-MAN: SKIN-MAN'S VICTIMS: JEFFERSON RANCH
> **ROSCOE:** *See* SKIN-MAN: SKIN-MAN'S VICTIMS: JEFFERSON RANCH

TINY BRADDOCK: *See* SKIN-MAN: SKIN-MAN'S VICTIMS: JEF-FERSON RANCH

UNNAMED COWBOY (face ripped off): *See* SKIN-MAN: SKIN-MAN'S VICTIMS: JEFFERSON RANCH

SNIP: *See* CANFIELD, BILL: FRIENDS/TRAILMATES

STREETER, BILL (COOKIE): *See* SKIN-MAN: SKIN-MAN'S VICTIMS: JEFFERSON RANCH

STREETER, YOUNG BILL: *See* STREETER, YOUNG BILL, *listed separately*

DEBARIA SALOON AND WHOREHOUSE CHARACTERS: According to KELLIN FRYE, DEBARIA's saloons were whore-holes and he didn't want his son to enter them. But compared to the saloons of LITTLE DEBARIA, Debaria's drinking holes were high-class establishments. Little Debaria was the destiny of whores who had grown too old or too diseased to work in Debaria. When the SALTIES were drunk on White Blind, they didn't care whether or not their women had noses as long as they had their sugar-purses. W:272

BIDDER-WEE: When the whores of DEBARIA's Bidder-Wee grew too old or diseased, they ended up in the wrecked saloons of LITTLE DEBARIA.

WHORES: W:62

BUSTED LUCK SALOON AND WHOREHOUSE: The Busted Luck was one of Debaria's saloons-cum-whorehouses. Although KELLIN FRYE disliked the place, it was a sight better than the saloons and whorehouses found in LITTLE DEBARIA. It was in the Busted Luck that Roland gave all the horse-riding SALTIES a final drink before making them take off their boots. (Roland wanted to discover how many had spent time in BEE-LIE STOCKADE.) W:272, 277–280

BARTENDER: When Roland asked the SALTIES to take off their boots so that he could see how many had BLUE RINGS around their ankles, the bartender couldn't take the smell. He left, holding his nose. W:279

WHORES: When Roland asked the SALTIES to take off their boots so he could see how many had BLUE RINGS around their ankles, the whores were driven away by the stench. W:62, W:272 *(whorehouse)*, W:277, W:279

CHEERY FELLOWS SALOON AND CAFE:

MAN IN FRONT OF THE CHEERY FELLOWS SALOON: When ROLAND and JAMIE DeCURRY arrived in DEBARIA, a WOMAN WITH A BASKET asked them if they'd come to kill the SKIN-MAN. Much to the merriment of the surrounding spectators, this fellow replied that the two boys weren't old enough to kill a bottle of rye. W:54

WHORES: Like the other whores in Debaria, these women had a short working life. When they grew old or diseased to attract customers, they were sent to the saloons in LITTLE DEBARIA. When the salties drank enough White Blind, they didn't care what their women looked like. W:62

LITTLE DEBARIA CHARACTERS: The poor and depressing town of LITTLE DEBARIA was situated in the foothills of the SALT ROCKS, northeast of DEBARIA. Although Debaria was a dusty, hide-smelling railhead town that had seen better days, compared to Little Debaria it was a rich and thriving settlement. Little Debaria's saloons, whorehouses, and company store served the needs of the dirt-poor SALTIES, or salt miners, who worked for the DEBARIA SALT COMBYNE. The Combyne was owned by big bugs in GILEAD, but the store, saloons, whorehouses, and even the skiddums (or shacks) where the miners lived were owned by a greedy crook named SAM SHUNT. Although the shapeshifting SKIN-MAN was actually a transformed saltie, he did not spare his fellows any more than he spared the other people of Debaria. *For page references, see individual entries listed below.*

LITTLE DEBARIA WHORES: When DEBARIA whores grew too old or diseased to attract custom in the big town's whorehouses, they ended up in the Little Debaria saloons, which served the poor SALTIES. When the salties were drunk on White Blind, they didn't care whether a whore had her nose, as long as she still had her sugar-purse. W:62, W:275, W:276, W:277

WHORES WHO ACT AS AMMIES: SAM SHUNT (or Shunt the Cunt) owned all of LITTLE DEBARIA except the mine itself. (That belonged to big bugs in GILEAD.) Twice a year, Shunt ran races for the miners to enjoy, though he paid for the event by taking entrance fees out of the miners' wages. When the SALTIES got injured during the games, some of the whores acted as AMMIES, or nurses. W:276

SALTIES: *See* SALT MINE CHARACTERS: SALTIES, *below*

SHUNT, SAM (SHUNT THE CUNT): Sam Shunt didn't own the LITTLE DEBARIA SALT COMBYNE—that belonged to big bugs in GILEAD—but he owned the company store, the bars, the whores, and the skiddums, (or shacks) where the miners slept. Twice a year, he set up races for the miners—footraces, obstacle course races, and horse races. He took the entrance fees out of the miners' wages to pay his expenses. The winners got a year's worth of debt forgiven at the company store. However, the interest was so high for the other miners that Sam never lost out. W:275–76

WEGG, WILL: Will Wegg was the constable in LITTLE DEBARIA. Thanks to his sand-colored handlebar mustache, yellow duster, and brass knuckle-dusters, he was easily recognizable. Wegg always bet on the SALTIES' biannual races, so he knew which miners could ride horses and which ones couldn't. This piece of information was critical when it came to rounding up SKIN-MAN suspects. (Roland and JAMIE DeCURRY knew that the saltie responsible for the skin-man murders could ride a horse.) When the skin-man was finally forced into revealing his identity, he turned into a man-sized POOKIE and bit Will Wegg on the arm. Wegg died from the poison. W:270–77, W:281–92 *(291 bitten)*, W:299

SADDLETRAMP (DRUNK): *See* WIDOW BRAILLEY, *below*

SALT MINE CHARACTERS:

MINE BOSSES: The men who owned the LITTLE DEBARIA SALT COMBYNE didn't come from DEBARIA; they were rich men from GILEAD. Unfortunately, these greedy men didn't care about their workers, only their profits. W:282

BANDERLY (FOREMAN): Banderly was the SALTIES' bull foreman. When an eerie, bitter green light was seen shining through a crack in the salt plug, the salties told Banderly about it. Banderly saw the light for himself—the way it shone bright then dim, like a heartbeat, and the way it seemed to beckon the miners to enter it—but he knew that the MINE

BOSSES would refuse to close the plug. Instead, he had the crew block up the crack with rocks. This was a mistake. The ancient evil artifact that gave off this light transformed OLLIE ANG into a *skin-man*. W:282

SALTIES (SALT HOUSE FOLKS, SALT MINERS, MINERS):
GENERAL: Long before ROLAND and JAMIE DeCURRY arrived in DEBARIA, the DEBARIA SALT COMBYNE was a thriving business. However, by the time our story takes place there were only about two hundred salt miners, or salties, left, all of whom worked in the company's single remaining plug. In the old days, the miners lived in the SALT-HOUSES, or cliff-face caverns that were part of the mining network. (Each of these caverns had tunnels in the back that led into the earth.) But in the time period of our tale the salties had an encampment of their own, a few wheels west of Little Debaria. Although bigwigs in GILEAD owned the Combyne, most of the salties were permanently indebted to a man named SAM SHUNT, who was not-so-affectionately known to the miners as Shunt the Cunt. Shunt owned Little Debaria's bars and whores. He even owned the skiddums, or shacks, where the miners slept. But worst of all he owned the company store, which meant that the miners were permanently indebted to him. In essence, Shunt owned the miners. To Roland, the salties' lot sounded little better than slavery. W:58, W:62 *(in Little Debaria)*, W:64 *(skin-man is one of them; woke a demon in new plug, 200 miners)*, W:65, W:67, W:76, W:78 *(they know skin-man is one of them; a saltie is not a proddie—not riders)*, W:83, W:84, W:85, W:86, W:101, W:104, W:267, W:270–94 *(all the salties who can ride horses; 274 into bar; subject of discussion until 277; 279 ten with blue rings)*
BLUE-RING SALTIES: Any saltie with a blue ring tattooed around his ankle had done time in BEELIE STOCKADE, and so was marked forever as a criminal. W:278–94 *(salties who can ride, all the salties with blue rings)*
    ANG, OLLIE: *See* SKIN-MAN, *listed separately*
    FRANE, BOBBY: This saltie was almost as old as STEG LUKA. He had a mangy white mustache, dirty gray hair that fell to his shoulders, and a sinister squint in one eye. Roland thought that this squint was probably caused by nearsightedness, not meanness. Roland was right, since when Bobby Frane paraded past BILL STREETER so that the boy could see his blue ankle-ring, he tipped his hat to the lad. W:286
    LUKA, STEG (OLD FELLA OF THE CREW, GRAYBEARD): Graybearded Steg Luka wasn't ashamed of spending time in BEELIE STOCKADE, since his crime was stealing a loaf of bread to feed his wife and children. (Sadly, his two children died anyway.) By the time Roland met him, Steg was so old that his Beelie Stockade ankle-ring had faded to a blue ghost, and his bare feet were as gnarled as old tree stumps. Despite his age and poor physical condition, Steg had an iron grip and was mighty trig. He was the only saltie to connect the strange, bitter green light in the NEW SALT PLUG with the OLD PEOPLE's evil artifacts, and with the sudden predations of DEBARIA's shapeshifting SKIN-MAN. As he confided to Roland, all of the miners had seen the light and had felt the pull of its seductive, whispered promises. Steg believed that one of his fellow miners had entered the crack when the

mine was officially closed and had been changed forever, and not for the better. When Steg found out that his theory was correct, and that his fellow saltie, OLLIE ANG, was actually the skin-man, he attacked Ang, calling the man a liar and a murdering trullock. But Ollie, ever blood-thirsty, transformed into a POOKY and jammed himself into Steg's mouth, killing him. W:278 *(stole a loaf of bread)*, W:279–91 *(281 Steg Luka; 282 something belonging to the Old People is in the plug 291 killed)*, W:292, W:293

> **OLD WOMAN AND TWO BABBIES:** Steg Luka stole a loaf of bread to feed his wife and two children. The children died anyway, and Steg was sent to BEELIE STOCKADE. W:278

MARSH, JAKE: Jake Marsh was one of the younger men to have spent time in BEELIE STOCKADE. When Jake paraded past BILL STREETER, his trousers rolled up to expose his ankles, he stuck his tongue out at the boy. His ugly tongue was stained yellow from bingo-weed tobacco. W:286

YOUNG SALTY: This young man didn't want to take off his boots so that Roland could inspect his ankles. He said that if Roland shot him, at least he wouldn't have to go down into the mine plug anymore. W:278

YOUNGEST SALTY: This young man was about Roland's age. According to him, salties were always afraid. W:278, W:286

SALTIES' FAMILIES: In the old days, salties and their families lived in the salt-houses, or caverns, in the SALT ROCKS. By the time Roland and JAMIE DeCURRY arrived in town, most of the salties lived in shacks, or skiddums, a few miles outside of Little Debaria. The shacks were far from ideal, but at least they weren't underground. W:58

SKIN-MAN: *See* SKIN-MAN, *listed separately*

SHERIFF'S OFFICE:

ANDERSON, PEA (HIGH SHERIFF-THAT-WAS): In the days before HUGH PEAVY wore Debaria's silver star upon his chest, Pea Anderson was Debaria's High Sheriff. It was during Anderson's stint as head law-man that the CROW GANG rampaged through Debaria, thieving, train-robbing, and kidnapping. Just after a rancher's wife named BELINDA DOOLIN was kidnapped, STEVEN DESCHAIN came to town. With the gunslinger's help, Pea Anderson, Hugh Peavy, and Anderson's POSSE tracked the Crows to their hideout in THE SALT ROCKS. Steven Deschain wanted to surprise the Crows by coming to their lair from the HIGH PURE to the east, but Pea Anderson wanted to march straight to their hideout. Flouting the elder Deschain's advice, Anderson took his posse and rode for the salt-houses. Unfortunately, the Crows saw them coming and slaughtered them at AMBUSH ARROYO. W:55–57 *(57 named)*, W:58, W:59

POSSE FOR CROW GANG: These seven men followed the old High Sheriff, PEA ANDERSON, when he, HUGH PEAVY, and STEVEN DESCHAIN tracked the CROW GANG to their lair. When Anderson and the gunslinger disagreed about how to approach the Crows' hideout, this posse followed Anderson rather than Steven Deschain. They paid for this mistake with their lives. W:57–58

DEPUTATION: Roland sent this group of men to LITTLE DEBARIA so that they could round up all of the SALTIES who could ride horses and who had also spent time in BEELIE STOCKADE. See PEAVY, HUGH *(above)*; CANFIELD, BILL *(JEFFERSON RANCH CHARACTERS, above)*; DeCURRY, JAMIE; FRYE, KELLIN *(below)*; FRYE, VIKKA *(below)*

FRYE, KELLIN: Kellin Frye was HUGH PEAVY's best deputy. He and his son, VIKKA, traveled to the JEFFERSON RANCH with ROLAND, JAMIE, and Hugh Peavy so that they could assess the carnage left by the SKIN-MAN. (During their rounds, Kellin Frye found *sai* JEFFERSON's lower jaw under a bunk, where the skin-man had thrown it after ripping it off *sai* Jefferson's face.) Later in our tale, Kellin and Vikka traveled with Jamie to LITTLE DEBARIA to round up all of the SALTIES who could ride horses. However, when Roland decided to take the suspects into the BUSTED LUCK SALOON, Kellin refused to let his son enter. He called Debaria's saloons whore-holes. W:63 *(best deputy)*, W:70–75, W:84, W:86, W:270–73 *(watching the salties' backs)*, W:277–93

> **FRYE, VIKKA:** Though Vikka Frye was just a boy, he played an impor-tant role in ROLAND's plan to catch the SKIN-MAN. Under Roland's instruction, Vikka told a boy named PUCK DeLONG that BILLY STREETER had seen the SKIN-MAN in his human shape. Roland wanted this untruth to reach the SKIN-MAN himself, so that he'd be easier to flush out. W:63 *(son)*, W:70–74, W:86, W:270–93 *(guards backdoor of the Busted Luck)*

>> **PUCK DeLONG:** VIKKA knew Puck from Reap Fairday, where they did the three-leg race together. Under Roland's instruction, Vikka told Puck DeLong that YOUNG BILL STREETER had seen the SKIN-MAN in his human shape. W:272–73

>> **DA:** According to Puck, his da wasn't an ordinary saltie. He was the foreman of the miners' night work crew. W:273

NOT SO GOOD DEPUTIES: HIGH SHERIFF HUGH PEAVY had one excellent deputy named KELLIN FRYE, and two not-so-good deputies. The not-so-good deputies were called PICKENS and STROTHER. W:83, W:95, W:100, W:102, W:105

> **PICKENS:** Pickens had an undershot jaw and thought that Roland was awfully high-handed for a shaveling. Despite his resentment, he treated the young gunslinger with equal amounts of care and distrust. This unpleasant fellow had fond memories of BEELIE STOCKADE. When he was a boy, his family used to take picnics to the hangings there. W:95, W:96, W:97, W:98, W:102–4 *(named, discusses Beelie Town and blue ankle tattoos)*, W:274, W:281

> **STROTHER:** Fat Deputy Strother wore a tall black hat decorated with a gaudy rattlesnake band. Like PICKENS, he thought that Roland threw his weight around the sheriff's office too much. Strother told Roland about both the fate of BEELIE TOWN (formerly the site at a militia outpost), and the BEELIE STOCKADE. (After the stockade closed and the militia departed, the town was overrun by harriers.) Strother didn't believe the gossip which stated that the harriers who destroyed Beelie worked for FARSON. In fact, we get the distinct

impression that Strother secretly supported the Good Man. W:95 *(described)*, W:96, W:97, W:98, W:102–4 *(named, discusses Beelie Town and blue ankle tattoos)*, W:274, W:281

PEAVY, HUGH (HIGH SHERIFF): Debaria's High Sheriff, Hugh Peavy, was a big-bellied man with long white hair and a droopy mustache. His face was deeply lined and careworn, which isn't surprising when you consider that he had seen his town deteriorate from a fine little city to a town filled with whores, gamblers, confidence-men, and poor, desperate SALTIES. According to STEVEN DESCHAIN, Hugh Peavy was one of the few good men left in Debaria. His confidence is not surprising since, many years previously, Peavy—then a deputy—had defied the old High Sheriff, PEA ANDERSON, and had stood with the elder Deschain against the wicked CROW GANG. (Peavy even dug PA CROW's bullet out of *sai* Deschain's arm.) According to Peavy, Steven Deschain had let him take most of the credit for defeating the gang and he'd been High Sheriff ever since.

When Steven Deschain sent ROLAND and JAMIE DeCURRY to Debaria to investigate tales of a murderous, rampaging SKIN-MAN, he told the two boys to report directly to Peavy. The sheriff was pleased to see the young gunslingers, but concerned that they had so few years between them. (He'd really hoped to see either PETER McVRIES or Steven Deschain himself.) However, when the two boys showed Peavy their *sigul* (a box containing the bullet he had dug out of the elder Deschain's arm), Peavy was satisfied with their qualifications, and with the faith that Steven Deschain had in the two young men. However, even as he explained the layout of the town to Roland and Jamie, and the details of the attacks, Peavy confided that this case would be his last. He'd had enough of blood and mysteries and he was ready to retire.

W:39, W:45, W:54–66 *(54 described, crow gang story, and Steven Deschain)*, W:67, W:68, W:69, W:70–75 *(Jefferson Ranch)*, W:80–84, W:85, W:86, W:95 *(Peavy's desk)*, W:100, W:101, W:270–94, W:294

> **GRANDDA:** When he was young, Sheriff Peavy used his grandda's barrel-shooter to kill two members of the CROW GANG. W:59
>
> **WIFE:** W:69, W:83

PICKENS: *See* NOT SO GOOD DEPUTIES, *above*

SALTY SAM: Salty Sam was an old drunk who often spent time in the sheriff's cells. He rarely woke up before sundown. W:62, W:67, W:96

> **STROTHER:** *See* NOT SO GOOD DEPUTIES, *above*

SISTERS OF SERENITY: *See* SERENITY, SISTERS OF, *listed separately*

STRINGY BODEAN (JUSTICE MAN): Before he decided to try his luck at raising horses in the CRESCENT, Stringy Bodean was DEBARIA's Justice Man. When WIDOW BRAILLEY slit the throat of a drunk saddletramp who tried to rape her in her own outhouse, Stringy Bodean declared her not guilty by reason of self-defense. W:66 *(declared Widow Brailey innocent)*

TIMBERSMITH FARM CHARACTERS: *See* SKIN-MAN: SKIN-MAN'S VICTIMS

UNDERTAKER: During the SKIN-MAN's reign of terror, DEBARIA's undertaker was kept very busy. After the JEFFERSON RANCH massacre, he had to organize a convoy to pick up the dead. W:83, W:85

WIDOW BRAILLEY: The Widow Brailley ran the last boardinghouse in DEBARIA. Two years before Roland and JAMIE DeCURRY arrived in town, a drunk saddletramp tried to rape her while she sat in the outhouse. She slit the man's throat. Although the Justice Man, STRINGY BODEAN, declared her not guilty of murder, she decided she'd had enough of Debaria and returned to GILEAD. W:66

> **DRUNKEN BUFFOON:** Two days after the Widow Brailley packed her bags and left for GILEAD, this drunken fool burned down her boardinghouse. W:66

> **DRUNK SADDLETRAMP:** This man tried to rape the Widow Brailley in her outhouse and she cut him a new smile—right across his throat. W:66

WOMAN WITH BASKET: When Roland and JAMIE DeCURRY arrived in DEBARIA, they were spotted by this woman as she came out of the mercantile with a basket over her arm. When she asked whether the two young gunslingers had come to kill the SKIN-MAN, a MAN IN FRONT OF THE CHEERY FELLOWS SALOON AND CAFE retorted that the boys weren't old enough to kill a bottle of rye. W:54

DEBORAH
See BIG COFFIN HUNTERS: DEPAPE, ROY

DECURRY, JAMIE (JAMIE RED-HAND)
Like CUTHBERT ALLGOOD and ALAIN JOHNS, Jamie DeCurry was one of Roland's early *ka*-mates. Jamie's nickname, Jamie Red-Hand, came from the fact that one of his hands looked as if it had been dipped in blood. Luckily this skin discoloration was a birthmark, not the result of an accident. When they were young, Jamie swore that Roland had eyes in his fingers and so could shoot blindfolded. Unlike his fellow apprentices whose chosen weapons would always be guns, Jamie preferred the bow and arrow as well as the bah (or crossbow) and bolt. In *Song of Susannah* we learn that Jamie was one of the gunslingers who survived the fall of GILEAD. Just after this horrific defeat of the WHITE, he, Roland, Cuthbert, and Alain experienced a BEAMQUAKE.

In *Wind Through the Keyhole*, we learn that—not long after the death of Roland's mother—Roland and Jamie traveled to DEBARIA at STEVEN DESCHAIN's request so that the boys could investigate murders supposedly committed by a shapeshifting SKIN-MAN. Just as Cuthbert and Alain each had unusual skills which helped Roland to deal with the challenges of his HAMBRY adventure, so Jamie DeCurry also had some exceptional talents that made him a valuable companion during Roland's search for the skin-man. Although he didn't like to read much, Jamie was an excellent tracker. When it came to following a trail—whether on a map or on the ground—Roland often relied upon his friend's superior skills. It was Jamie who, upon studying the pattern of attacks marked upon SHERIFF PEAVY's map, realized that the skin-man must have been one of Little Debaria's SALTIES, or salt miners (something that the sheriff already suspected).

Jamie's skill at deduction was truly remarkable. For example, by studying the transformation of the skin-man's tracks, Jamie discovered that the monster could morph from bear to bull to monstrous cat and then back to human form in a matter of seconds. It was Jamie who showed that the stealthy skin-man arrived at and departed from the Jefferson Ranch on horseback, proving the premeditated nature of the crimes committed there. It was because of Jamie that Roland was able to reduce the number of salties that he rounded up as murder suspects. As Jamie pointed out, salties weren't proddies, and only a few of them would be able to mount and ride a horse.

Roland often stated that his mind was cold, like that of his father STEVEN DESCHAIN, but after reading *The Wind Through the Keyhole*, CONSTANT READERS can tell that Jamie's heart was warm. When Roland decided to spread the story that YOUNG BILL STREETER could identify the skin-man in his human form, Jamie was dismayed. He did not approve of Roland using a young bereaved boy as trap-bait. When YOUNG BILL STREETER cried himself to sleep, it was Jamie, not Roland, who carried the boy upstairs so that he could rest in one of the JEFFERSON RANCH bedrooms.

Unlike CUTHBERT, who never stopped talking, Jamie was usually closed-mouthed. For him, a twitch of the lips was the equivalent of holding his belly, rolling around on the floor, and howling with glee. Jamie died at the battle of JERICHO HILL, where he was killed by a sniper. Roland thinks that his friend was murdered by either GRISSOM or his eagle-eyed son. Throughout the series, Jamie's last name is spelled in a variety of ways. It is listed as De Curry, de Curry, and DeCurry.

I:140, I:149–52 *(Dance)*, I:156–57, I:160, I:161–62, I:167–73 *(witnesses Roland's coming of age)*, I:174, III:41, III:417, IV:7, IV:649 *(birthmark)*, IV:658, E:158, V:78, V:169, V:170, V:182, V:248, VI:16, VII:497, VII:503, VII:552, VII:801, W:31, W:38, W:39, W:40–84 *(42 likes bow and bah)*, W:84–87, W:96, W:100, W:101 *(trailmate)*, W:104, W:270–83 *(rarely says anything)*, W:284–94, W:294–97, W:300

FATHER: Jamie's father made a special leather boot for Jamie's bah so that Jamie could travel with his two favorite weapons tied to his saddle. W:44

DEEPNEAU, AARON
See TET CORPORATION: FOUNDING FATHERS

DEEPNEAU, ED
Ed Deepneau was one of the major players in STEPHEN KING's novel *Insomnia*. Ed tried to crash an airplane into the DERRY Civic Center so that he could disrupt the pro-choice rally which was being held there. Ed thought his central target was the feminist Susan Day. However, Ed was just a pawn of the CRIMSON KING, whose actual goal was to assassinate four-year-old PATRICK DANVILLE. Luckily for Roland, the Crimson King failed. On the level of the DARK TOWER where the TET CORPORATION is formed, Ed Deepneau was a gentle bookkeeper who died in 1947. He was related to both AARON DEEPNEAU and NANCY DEEPNEAU.
VII:512–13, VII:514

DEEPNEAU, NANCY REBECCA
See TET CORPORATION

DEERE
See DEAN, EDDIE: DELTA FLIGHT 901 CHARACTERS

DEIRDRE THE MAD
Deirdre the Mad was Roland's grandmother. It was from her that he inherited his particular combination of dry pragmatism and wild intuition.
   III:361

DELEVAN, CARL
Carl Delevan was the overweight, cigarette-loving NEW YORK cop who patrolled the area around CLEMENTS GUNS AND SPORTING GOODS. He and his partner GEORGE O'MEARAH were fooled and then humiliated by Roland. Years later, Delevan died of a stroke while watching *The Terminator.* The reason? The Terminator reminded him of Roland.
   II:343, II:346, II:347–59 *(354 unconscious)*, II:368 *(indirect)*, II:371–77, II:378, II:380

DELGADO, CORDELIA
Cordelia Delgado was SUSAN DELGADO's skinny maiden aunt. She figured prominently in Roland's MEJIS adventures, described in *Wizard and Glass.* Susan's widowed father, PAT DELGADO, took Cordelia in when she had nowhere else to go, but this act of goodwill proved to be quite unwise. Within a few years Pat was dead—betrayed by one of his friends. His lands and possessions were stolen by the traitorous members of THE HORSEMEN'S ASSOCIATION and his daughter's maidenhead was essentially auctioned off by Cordelia. (Although Cordelia seemed prudish in many other ways, she had no qualms about acting as a kind of pimp for her niece.) It seems unlikely that Cordelia participated in the plot against her brother, but she most certainly knew about it.
   Over the course of *Wizard and Glass,* Cordelia's suppressed aggression flowered into a dangerous psychotic rage. When Susan defied her aunt by giving her maidenhead to Roland freely rather than saving it for Mayor THORIN's hard cash, Cordelia went mad and joined forces with the witch RHEA OF THE CÖOS. After Susan was burned on a Charyou Tree fire, Cordelia died of a stroke.
   IV:125, IV:126, IV:130, IV:131, IV:133, IV:135, IV:140, IV:151, IV:152 *(story of Susan's family "madness"),* IV:166–69 *(167 personality described),* IV:176–77 *(Jonas mentions),* IV:191–210 *(Thorin's party: 195–203 introduced; 197 described; 202–3 whispers to Susan; 206–8 sits next to Susan),* IV:211, IV:212, IV:235–39 *(235 described; 236 blouse incident),* IV:240, IV:241–43 *(242–43 described),* IV:244, IV:245, IV:249, IV:256, IV:278–79, IV:281, IV:287, IV:294, IV:303–4, IV:307, IV:308–14, IV:324, IV:328–31 *(with Jonas),* IV:336, IV:343, IV:356, IV:361–62, IV:364–66, IV:372–74 *(tells Jonas suspicions about Susan/Roland),* IV:375–76, IV:377–78, IV:397, IV:413, IV:426–28, IV:429, IV:459–60, IV:466–67 *(burns Susan in effigy),* IV:495–98 *(496 has horse teeth),* IV:503, IV:513, IV:515, IV:549–52 *(and Rhea),* IV:563–65, IV:605–8 *(Susan burns),* IV:624–25 *(dies of stroke),* VII:335

DELGADO, HIRAM
Hiram was SUSAN's grandfather as well as PAT and CORDELIA DELGADO's father.
    IV:551

DELGADO, LUPE
    See CALLAHAN, FATHER DONALD FRANK: CALLAHAN'S HOME SHELTER ASSOCIATES

DELGADO, PAT
Red-haired, red-bearded Pat Delgado was SUSAN DELGADO's "da." He also happened to be the best drover on the WESTERN DROP. By the time Roland and his first *ka-tet* arrived in HAMBRY, Pat had already been dead for five years. Unlike many of the important men of Hambry, Pat Delgado was loyal to the AFFILIATION. FRAN LENGYLL maintained that Pat was killed by his horse, **OCEAN FOAM**, but he was actually murdered for daring to stand up to Lengyll and CROYDON's plans to turn traitor. Though Pat was honorable in life, his memory was desecrated. The men who were supposed to be his friends stole his lands, and his money-hungry sister, CORDELIA DELGADO, tried to sell his only daughter's maidenhead to the highest bidder.
    IV:124–25, IV:135, IV:139, IV:140, IV:142, IV:143, IV:144, IV:146, IV:150–51, IV:156 *(remembered first appearance of thinny)*, IV:157–58, IV:168, IV:169, IV:202–3, IV:205, IV:207–8, IV:212, IV:235, IV:236, IV:237, IV:240, IV:251, IV:254–56 *(rolled on by his horse)*, IV:279, IV:282, IV:287 *(Susan thinks he was murdered)*, IV:293, IV:294 *(interest in Old People)*, IV:295, IV:301 *(friend of betrayer Brian Hookey)*, IV:309, IV:314, IV:315, IV:365, IV:457–60 *(Susan in his office)*, IV:466, IV:497, IV:504, IV:505, IV:507, IV:541, IV:551, IV:604

DELGADO, SUSAN
Although we hear of Susan Delgado, "the lovely girl at the window," as early as *The Gunslinger*, we don't find out much about her love affair with Roland until *Wizard and Glass*. Susan was Roland's only true love. He met her in HAMBRY, after he and his first *ka-tet* were sent east by their fathers, who wished to keep them far from the dangerous machinations of THE GOOD MAN, otherwise known as JOHN FARSON. At the time of their meeting, Roland was fourteen and Susan sixteen. Roland had just won his guns and had only recently lost his virginity. Susan, a drover's daughter, had lost her father and was about to lose her honor as well, thanks to her AUNT CORDELIA's financial deal with the randy mayor, HART THORIN.
    Susan was probably descended from the "FRIENDLY FOLK," a sect that seemed quite widespread in MID-WORLD before it moved on. Like them, she used the terms "thee" and "thou" in her speech. It's quite possible that the Friends were somehow related to the MANNI, though we do not know this for certain. Although she was an excellent horsewoman (her beloved horses, PYLON and FELICIA, are also characters in the book), Susan was uncomfortable with guns. This, too, may have been owing to her family's background.
    Roland first met Susan while she was on her way home from her disagree-

able and embarrassing meeting with the nasty old witch RHEA OF THE CÖOS. Rhea was to check Susan's "honesty"—in other words, her virginity. In order to fulfill her upcoming duty as Mayor Hart Thorin's jilly she had to be pure— unsullied by man or demon. Ostensibly she was to bear the mayor a child (his own wife was barren), but Thorin was actually much more interested in the planting than in the cultivation of his seed.

With her waist-length golden-blond hair and gray eyes, Susan is the most beautiful woman found in the Dark Tower series. She is also "honest" in every sense of the word and gives Roland her heart freely and completely, despite the fact that her prissy and hypocritical maiden aunt has already squirreled away much of the gold given for Susan's maidenhead.

Susan's devotion to Roland did not end happily. Branded a traitor, she was burned as a Charyou Tree sacrifice. Although she didn't know it, Roland had already abandoned her, though she was forced to witness her death while lost in the nowhere dreamtime of MAERLYN'S GRAPEFRUIT.

In the years following her death, Roland frequently dreamed of Susan, often in association with the rhyme: "bird and bear and hare and fish, give my love her fondest wish." Her scent of jasmine, rose, honeysuckle, and old sweet hay was evoked by the ORACLE OF THE MOUNTAINS when she wanted to seduce him.

In *Wolves of the Calla*, we learn that PERE CALLAHAN's beloved friend and coworker at the HOME shelter was named LUPE DELGADO, an unmistakable echo of Susan's name. Like Susan, Lupe was beautiful, and like her he suffered a tragic fate. In *The Dark Tower*, the final book of our series, we find out that SHEEMIE, the mildly retarded tavern boy from MEJIS who becomes a BREAKER in THUNDERCLAP, was also in love with Susan. Like Roland, Sheemie blamed himself for her death.

I:86, I:106, I:119–20, I:128, I:131, I:140, I:157, II:231, II:394, III:41, IV:65, IV:66–67, IV:68 *(physical description. ". . . bird and bear and hare and fish . . ."),* IV:79, IV:98, IV:116, IV:120, IV:122–38 *(and Rhea; 123 "Careless Love"; 123 heart vs. head; 127 sees Maerlyn's Grapefruit; 130–35 Rhea inspects her "honesty"; 133–34 Rhea's sexual touch; 134 invokes Thorin's name for protection and is ashamed; 137–38 Rhea puts spell on Susan),* IV:139–59 *(meets "Will Dearborn." He whistles "Careless Love"),* IV:162, IV:164–65 *(Roland thinks about her),* IV:166–70 *(and Cordelia. Won't lie with Thorin until Demon Moon),* IV:191, IV:191–210 *(Thorin's Party; 195 sapphire pendant, fog-colored eyes; 197–98 introduced to Roland, 208 Roland wants to shoot her; 209–10 Roland dances with her. A question of propriety),* IV:211–12, IV:213, IV:222–23 *(Roland and love/hate),* IV:233, IV:234–59 *(237–38 cheated of inheritance; 239 desire for Roland; 241 flowers from Roland; 247 Roland on Drop),* IV:277, IV:278–84, IV:285, IV:286, IV:287 *(suspects father was murdered),* IV:288–305 *(Citgo with Roland. Rhea spying),* IV:306–28 *(311–12 Thorin grabs; 316 loss of virginity; 326 Roland's rhyme to wake her from trance),* IV:329–31, IV:336, IV:342–45, IV:353, IV:356–60 *(subject of angry thoughts),* IV:361–62 *("lovely girl at the window"),* IV:364–67, IV:368, IV:370, IV:372, IV:373–74, IV:377–78, IV:388, IV:393, IV:399, IV:400, IV:401, IV:405, IV:406, IV:411–12, IV:413, IV:415, IV:416, IV:418–19, IV:426–44 *(with Roland, Cuthbert, Alain. 432 Roland's plan of attack; 435 hypnotized; 441–42 remembers Rhea and Maerlyn's Grapefruit),*

IV:449–50 *(stealing firecrackers with Sheemie)*, IV:452, IV:457–61 *(in father's office)*, IV:463–66 *(464 intuition that Roland will desert her)*, IV:466–67 *(Cordelia burns her in effigy)*, IV:474, IV:479, IV:480–83, IV:494–500, IV:502–13 *(507–13 rescues Roland's ka-tet)*, IV:514–19, IV:523–26, IV:529, IV:531, IV:533–34 *(Rhea tells Jonas her location)*, IV:536–46 *(taken by Jonas)*, IV:548–49, IV:549–52 *(subject of discussion between Cordelia and Rhea)*, IV:561–62, IV:564–65 *(Rhea and Cordelia lead crowds against her)*, IV:565–70 *(Sheemie follows)*, IV:571, IV:577, IV:578, IV:579–81 *(Roland decides to leave her)*, IV:581–83, IV:585–87, IV:594, IV:602–9 *(Roland sees her burn in* Wizard's glass*)*, IV:619, IV:622 *(Roland always dreams of her)*, IV:650, IV:653, IV:655, IV:664, E:160, E:165, E:168, E:169, E:195, V:35, V:46, V:174, V:181, V:210, V:211, V:411 *(bit o' tail)*, VI:234 *(indirect)*, VI:269, VI:277, VI:290, VI:294, VI:391, VI:404, VII:142, VII:219, VII:220, VII:468, VII:498, VII:695, VII:762, VII:802, VII:825, W:82, W:84, W:89

SUSAN DELGADO'S ASSOCIATES:

AMY (SUSAN'S CHILDHOOD FRIEND): IV:327

DELGADO, CORDELIA: *See* DELGADO, CORDELIA, *listed separately*

DELGADO, HIRAM: *See* DELGADO, HIRAM, *listed separately*

DELGADO, PAT: *See* DELGADO, PAT *listed separately*

GRAMMA: Susan inherited her singing voice from this grandmother. IV:123

MATERNAL GREAT-AUNT: She ran crazy, set herself on fire, and threw herself over the DROP. IV:152

MOTHER: The only thing we know about Susan's mother is that her maiden name was Manchester. IV:313

DELICIOUS RAIN
See NORTH CENTRAL POSITRONICS

DELONG, PUCK
See DEBARIA CHARACTERS: SHERIFF'S OFFICE: FRYE, KELLIN: FRYE, VIKKA

DEMON ELEMENTALS (DEMON ASPECTS OF THE BEAM)
According to the metaphysical map of MID-WORLD, which Roland drew in *The Waste Lands*, Mid-World is shaped like a wheel. The hub of the wheel is the DARK TOWER. Crossing at this nexus point are six BEAMS, which simultaneously hold the Tower in place and maintain the proper alignment of time, space, size, and dimension. The Beams both bind the macroverse together and separate the many worlds which spin about the great, smoky-colored linchpin of existence. The twelve termination points of the Beams are watched over by twelve animal totems known as GUARDIANS.

In *Song of Susannah*, we find out that—like the kabbalistic Tree of Life found in our world—Mid-World's metaphysical map has a darker side. Just as each Beam has two designated Guardians, each Beam is also overseen by a Demon Elemental. Although there are only six Demon Elementals, there are twelve demon *aspects*, since each demon has a male and a female self. The Guardians of the Beam watch over the mortal world, but the hermaphroditic Demon Elementals watch over the invisible world of speaking demons, ghosts, and ill-sicks—all those LESSER DEMONS OF THE PRIM, which remained in Mid-World after the magical tide of the PRIM (or GREATER DISCORDIA) withdrew from the land.

If some of the Guardians serve the WHITE, then at least some of the Demon Elementals serve the Outer Dark. In *Song of Susannah,* we find out that one such Demon Elemental tricked both Roland and SUSANNAH into helping the CRIMSON KING bring MORDRED RED-HEEL (the *dan-tete,* or little god) into being.

Posing as the ORACLE OF THE MOUNTAINS that we met in *The Gunslinger,* the demon's female aspect had sex with Roland in exchange for prophecy. Once collected, Roland's sperm was stored (probably in one of the GREAT OLD ONES' machines) until he and his *tet*-mates EDDIE and Susannah Dean arrived at the SPEAKING RING near LUD, where JAKE CHAMBERS was about to be reborn into Mid-World.

As Roland and Eddie brought Jake through the magical door labeled THE BOY, Susannah kept the sex-hungry, male SPEAKING-RING DEMON busy. Though our *tet* didn't know it, this was no ordinary speaking-ring demon but the male aspect of the Demon Elemental who had copulated with Roland earlier in our tale.

Roland's sperm must have been defrosted beforehand, because this demon—though sterile itself—shot our gunslinger's fertile seed into Susannah, seed which was (or soon would be) mixed with that of the Crimson King.

VI:112–14, VI:117, VI:242, VI:252 *(service for the King)*

ORACLE OF THE MOUNTAINS (SUCCUBUS): CONSTANT READERS met the Oracle of the Mountains in *The Gunslinger,* the first book of the Dark Tower series. This female demon haunts a circle of DRUIT STONES in the WILLOW JUNGLES of the CYCLOPEAN MOUNTAINS, where Roland and JAKE CHAMBERS travel while following the MAN IN BLACK. Like others of her kind, the Oracle feeds on desire. This weeping, sighing presence, who is described as a "demon with no shape, only a kind of unformed sexual glare with the eye of prophecy," first lures Jake into her cold embrace and then, when she is thwarted, takes Roland. (Roland is probably the one she wants anyway.)

Unlike Jake, Roland enters the Oracle's circle willingly, and with the aid of mescaline (what CORT once called the Philosopher's Stone) makes conscious contact with the haunting presence. Roland's desire is to force the spirit to prophesy, but in order to do this he has to have sex with this star-slut and whore of the winds. During their encounter, the Oracle takes on the voice and scent of Roland's dead love, SUSAN DELGADO. In the 2003 version of *The Gunslinger,* the Oracle warns Roland to watch for Roses and Unfound Doorways.

In *Song of Susannah* we learn that this demon was no run-of-the-mill demon sexpot but the female aspect of a Demon Elemental posing as a speaking-ring demon. She seduced Roland so that she could collect his sperm for the making of his nemesis, MORDRED. I:117, I:121–32, I:138, I:215, II:25, II:40, II:315, III:173, V:46, VI:112–13, VI:121–22, VI:241 *(indirect)*

SPEAKING-RING DEMON (JAKE'S ENTRY INTO MID-WORLD): Like the MANSION DEMON that Jake Chambers battles in *The Waste Lands,* this invisible male monster is a doorkeeper. Roland, EDDIE, and SUSANNAH have to outwit it in order to draw Jake from his version of our world into Mid-World. However, unbeknownst to our friends, this wraith is in actuality a Demon Elemental, the male facet of the ORACLE with whom Roland had sexual relations in *The Gunslinger.*

Like all such sexually charged Druit Stone spirits, this invisible creature's weakness is the same as its weapon. Hence, the only hope our *ka-tet* has of "drawing" Jake successfully is first to capture the doorkeeper and then to keep him in a sexual snare long enough for the boy to pass through.

As soon as our *ka-tet* enters the circle, this raging, hungry demon senses their presence and comes toward them, disturbing the grasses to the north as it rushes forward. Since Eddie is the one outlining the magical picture of the door itself (and hence the one transgressing that ancient law against passage between worlds), he is the lightning rod attracting the force. However, as the demon rushes toward him, Susannah Dean traps it, quite literally, between her legs. Though it is agonizingly painful, Susannah manages to hold the demon long enough for Jake to be "born."

Sex with such demons has its risks, as Roland is all too aware. As the novel progresses we find that Susannah is pregnant, but that the baby's father is not Eddie but this demon, whose engorged sex is compared to a giant icicle.

In retrospect, it seems that our *tet*'s tangle with this spirit was a setup designed by the followers of the CRIMSON KING. As the Oracle of the Mountains, this Demon Elemental took Roland's sperm so that it could be genetically fused with that of the Red King. This tainted seed was then planted inside Susannah so that she would give birth to Roland's ultimate nemesis, MORDRED. III:189–90, III:193–94, III:197–98, III:201–3, III:206–12, IV:69, IV:92, V:84, V:246, V:258, V:378, V:478, V:483, VI:106, VI:107, VI:113, VI:116

DEMONS/SPIRITS/DEVILS (LESSER DEMONS OF THE PRIM)

MID-WORLD is a desolate land littered with the ruined machinery and leaking poisons of the GREAT OLD ONES. However, it is also a landscape haunted by the magic of a more primitive but equally dangerous people—those who knew more about demonology than they did about technology.

In three of the first four novels, Roland and his friends encounter "thin" places—areas where the division between the spirit world and the physical world is almost nonexistent. These places—whether circles of DRUIT STONES or cellars where men have been murdered and their bodies hidden—are the sites of human sacrifice. Hence, they function as evil magic circles. Unfortunately for unwary travelers, it is not just the magician who can conjure demons and spirits in these "in-betweens." Because of their history of violence and blood, these evil places are PORTALS where thirsty demons can manifest whenever they scent possible prey.

Like the demons of our world, Mid-World demons seem to feed on human blood and human energy. Locked in the circles or buildings they haunt, they wait for unwary men and women to chance upon them. Drawn by the *khef,* or life force, of human beings, they come to drink. Lucky people chancing upon these beings will be able to entice a prophecy from them. Unlucky ones will lose their lives.

In the final books of the Dark Tower series, we learn the origin of Mid-World's demonic forces. Like the DARK TOWER itself, these negative energies arose from the primal magical soup of creation. When the magical tide of the PRIM receded from the Earth, it left behind the Tower and the BEAMS, as well as a flotsam and jetsam of demons, elemental spirits, oracles, and succubi. Some of these intangible beings (known collectively as the Lesser Demons of the Prim) strangled in this new element, but others adapted and thrived. Among the less savory of the Prim's survivors were sexual predators such as MIA and demonic beings such as the DEMON ELEMENTALS and the TYPE ONE VAMPIRES, also known as the GRANDFATHERS.

GENERAL REFERENCES: I:14 *(dust devils)*, I:16, I:22, I:44, I:48–52 *(Pittston's Interloper)*, I:55–56 *(Pittston's Interloper)*, I:58, I:59–62 *(Pittston's Interloper)*, I:85, I:88 *(spooks)*, I:90, I:91, I:124, I:154, I:205, II:25, II:34, II:40, II:44, II:73, II:114, II:362, II:367, III:20, III:35, III:315, IV:15, IV:63, IV:92 *(thinny as demon)*, IV:132, IV:157 *(thinny as demon)*, IV:321, IV:353 *(inside Maerlyn's glass)*, V:2 *(bogarts, speakies)*, V:150 *(bogarts)*, V:247 *(devil)*, V:341 *(ogres)*, V:350 *(devil)*, V:394 *(demon)*, V:577, VI:36, VI:106 *(Demons of the Prim)*, VI:112 *(Speaking Demons, general)*

SPECIFIC DEMONS:

CENTIPEDE MONSTER: *See* TODASH DEMONS, *listed below*

CHAP (MIA'S CHAP): *See* MORDRED, *listed separately*

DANDELO: *See* DANDELO, *listed separately*

DEMON CHILD: *See* MORDRED, *listed separately*

DEMONS OF HOUSE: VI:112, VI:117

DEMONS IN THE EARTH: In "The Skin-Man," the first of the two stories which Roland recounts in *The Wind Through the Keyhole*, we learn that the mines of Mid-World are populated by monsters very similar to the ones found in Desperation, Nevada. (See the novel *Desperation*.) According to HIGH SHERIFF HUGH PEAVY, the DEBARIA SALT COMBYNE dug too deep to reach their NEW SALT PLUG and in the process woke a demon of the earth, which he believes turned one of the miners into a flesh-eating SKIN-MAN. Roland, on the other hand, doesn't believe that a demon transformed a miner into a monster. Instead he blames one of the OLD PEOPLE's *artyfax*. Although we never learn exactly what transformed OLLIE ANG into a shape-shifting monstrosity, we are led to believe that the cause was a ghost (or in this case a demon) inside one of the Old People's machines. Hence, both Peavy and Roland prove to be correct. W:64 *(in plug, woken by miners)*

DEMONSTUFF, JAR OF: The people of FEDIC believed that the Red Death, the plague which wiped out their town, came from a jar of demonstuff that had been opened in CASTLE DISCORDIA. VI:244

DEVIL: VI:247, VI:259, VI:318 *(Satan)*, VI:319 *(Satan)*, VII:582 *(tempting)*, VII:590 *(tempting)*

DEVIL GRASS: Devil grass grows in the wastelands of Mid-World. In CALLA BRYN STURGIS, removing devil grass from the fields is New Earth's first chore. This weed—which is the first growth to appear on ruined ground and the last to disappear once land is poisoned—is also narcotic. However, as we saw in *The Gunslinger*, smoking weed leads to chewing weed, and chewing leads to death. Roland thinks that the devil powder (cocaine) of our world is very similar to devil grass.

When no other fuel is available, devil grass can be burned. However, burning it brings its own dangers. Devils dance in the greasy flickering flames and those who watch them can be drawn into the fire. I:12–13, I:15, I:23, I:28–29, I:34, I:35, I:36, I:39–40, I:44, I:51, I:118, I:119, I:138, II:40, II:65, II:73, II:100 *(devil powder)*, II:101 *(devil dust)*, II:141 *(devil powder)*, II:394, III:46, III:248, IV:268, V:3, V:403, VII:580, VII:588, VII:612, VII:829

DEVIL'S ARSE DEMONS/MONSTERS OF THE ABYSS: These telepathic demons are neither for the CRIMSON KING nor against him. However, it seems reasonable to assume that they are creatures of the Outer Dark. Although they were once contained in a crack in the earth located near the town of Fedic, they are slowly tunneling toward the underground chambers below both the FEDIC DOGAN and Castle Discordia. It seems likely that these creatures originated in TODASH and are the GREAT ONES which MORDRED says live in that terrible no-place between worlds. *See* TODASH DEMONS, *listed below.* VI:105, VII:539–40, VII:557, VII:567

DISCORDIA: *See* PRIM, *listed separately*

DUST-DEVILS: VI:642

GREAT ONES: *See* TODASH DEMONS, *listed below*

HOUSIES: Housies are a particularly nasty type of house-ghost. They can't hurt people but they can hurt small animals. You can often hear them whispering in the dark. VII:590

ILL-SICK DEMONS: Demons of disease. VI:112, VI:117

**INTERLOPER/SATAN/ANTICHRIST: The Bible-bashing lunatic SYL-VIA PITTSTON believed that Roland was the Interloper—in other words, Satan himself. In the 2003 version of *The Gunslinger,* Roland shares this dubious honor with his eventual nemesis, THE CRIMSON KING. I:49–52, I:59, I:62

MANSION DEMON/DOORKEEPER OF DUTCH HILL (PLASTER-MAN): In *The Waste Lands,* Jake Chambers leaves 1970s NEW YORK and enters Mid-World. However, in order to move between his level of the DARK TOWER and Roland's, he must confront this demon-of-place in BROOKLYN's DUTCH HILL MANSION. Not only is this demon the animating spirit of an evil house but it is also a doorkeeper, or a spirit that guards one of the lesser portals (or thin places), which lead out of our world and into Mid-World.

The Dutch Hill Mansion Demon is paired with the SPEAKING RING DEMON that Roland, SUSANNAH, and EDDIE encounter while traveling along the PATH OF THE BEAM toward LUD. Although both of these demonic doorkeepers are evil, they also serve a purpose. The Dutch Hill Demon keeps people from leaving our world; the Speaking Ring Demon stops them from entering Mid-World.

Because of these two demons, Jake Chambers's second entry into Mid-World is doubly dangerous. Luckily, he has his *ka-tet* to help him make the journey. III:190–92, III:194–96, III:198–201, III:203–11, III:219, III:234, III:263, III:265, IV:98, V:50, V:68, V:93, V:258, V:478, VII:144–45, VII:249, VII:592

MIA: *See* MIA, *listed separately*

MIND-SPIRITS: These spirits knock at your mind's door, seeking entrance. If you refuse to answer, they may try to gnaw their way through. (Rather unpleasant, when you think about it.) VII:593

MORDRED: *See* MORDRED, *listed separately*

ORACLE OF THE MOUNTAINS (SUCCUBUS): *See* DEMON ELEMENTALS, *listed separately*

PRIM: *See* PRIM, *listed separately*

SAITA: *See* ELD, ARTHUR, *listed separately*

SATAN: *See* DEVIL, *listed above*

SPEAKING DEMON (WAY STATION): In *The Gunslinger,* Roland descends into the Way Station's cellar and hears this demon moaning. The sound, which soon turns into labored breathing, comes from behind one of the cellar's crooked sandstone walls. Roland addresses the creature in High Speech and it responds in a low, dragging voice which resembles that of Roland's dead lover ALICE from the town of TULL. After hearing the demon's warning about the DRAWERS and about Jake ("Go slow past the Drawers, gunslinger. While you travel with the boy, the Man in Black travels with your soul in his pocket"), Roland punches the wall, reaches in, and pulls out a human jawbone. Though this action seems violent to us, it is one of the things Roland has been taught to do when dealing with demons. As the old Mid-World proverb states, "only a corpse may speak true prophecy." From the moment he heard that initial moan, Roland knew that a body lay behind the sandstone. Such corpses can be possessed by spirits and can prove to be powerful mojo when dealing with other demonic beings. I:122–26, I:132, I:139, III:44, III:46, III:48, III:97, III:136, VI:112 *(general)*

SPEAKING-RING DEMON (JAKE'S ENTRY INTO MID-WORLD): *See* DEMON ELEMENTALS, *listed separately*

SUCKERBATS: These strange creatures live in the WILLOW JUNGLES of the CYCLOPEAN MOUNTAINS. Many of them are vampire bats. Those bitten in the night do not wake to the world of the living. I:118

SUVIA: Suvia is a female demon with eight or nine arms. II:181

TENTACLED MONSTER: In "The Wind Through the Keyhole," one of the stories Roland tells in the novel of the same name, TIM ROSS comes across this horrific tentacled creature on his way to the NORTH FOREST KINNOCK DOGAN, three days after leaving the FAGONARD. This monster lives at the bottom of a narrow chasm that is a hundred feet deep. Its existence is masked by a drift of white flowers so thick that Tim originally mistakes them for a cloud that fell to earth. These flowers have a fantastically sweet scent, but we cannot help but think that the flowers are this predatory creature's lure.

While Tim is crossing the gorge's narrow rock bridge, long, leathery tentacles emerge from the billows of white flowers. The tentacles are slate-gray on top and as pink as burned skin underneath. They rise toward Tim in a wavery dance—first two, then four, then eight, then a forest of them. At first Tim thinks they cannot reach him, but as he closes in on the far side of the bridge, the tentacles thin out and stretch to extend their reach.

When he feels something caressing his boot, he throws himself forward with an inarticulate yell. He escapes. Fans of *The Lord of the Rings* will be struck by the similarities between this monster and the Watcher in the Water, found just outside of the Doors of Durin which lead into the Mines of Moria. W:230–31, W:232

THINNY: *See entry in* PORTALS

TODASH DEMONS: According to MORDRED, the nastiest demons inhabiting TODASH space are known as the GREAT ONES. I imagine that *todash* is filled with many unpleasant "lesser ones" as well. We see some glimmers of these terrible Great Ones (and many of the lesser ones) in STEPHEN KING's story "The Mist," which can be found in *Skeleton Crew*. VI:18, VI:248–49, VII:539, VII:557, VII:559, VII:567, VII:754

> **CHEWING MONSTER:** Roland and Susannah hear this monster behind an ancient ironwood door located beneath the Fedic Dogan. VII:560–61
>
> **THUDDING MONSTER:** The thudding monster (we never see it) is trapped behind one of the many doors found beneath Castle Discordia and the Fedic Dogan. It hasn't been able to escape. (Yet.) VII:562
>
> **TUNNEL DEMON (CENTIPEDE MONSTER):** This stinking, slithering demon tries to attack Roland and SUSANNAH DEAN as they travel through the dark tunnels beneath the Fedic Dogan and Castle Discordia. Although it may have originated in the DEVIL'S ARSE, that terrible crack in the Earth located beyond the nearby town of Fedic, Roland thinks that their pursuer is more likely a monster that has broken through from TODASH space. The tunnel demon/tunnel monster is one of the ugliest creatures we've met in the Dark Tower series (SLOW MUTANTS aside, of course). It resembles a giant fanged centipede, but one whose round lump of a face is covered with pink albino eyes and whose gaping, trapdoor-sized mouth is filled with squirming tentacles. Luckily for our friends, this particular demon is photosensitive. VII:564, VII:566, VII:567–76, VII:579, VII:658 *(indirect)*

ZOMBIE FACES: Susannah sees these dead faces staring at her from behind the strangely distorted windows and buildings of CASTLETOWN, the ruined habitations located near LE CASSE ROI RUSSE. VII:592

DEMULLET (DEMULLET'S COLUMN)
DeMullet's Column was an army fighting on the side of the AFFILIATION. FARSON'S MEN defeated them at the fateful battle of JERICHO HILL.
    V:170

DENBY, TOM
    See CHAMBERS, JAKE: JAKE'S FAMILY, FRIENDS, ASSOCIATES AND ALIASES

DENNIS
    See WALTER: WALTER'S ALIASES: FLAGG, RANDALL

DEPAPE, AMOS
    See BIG COFFIN HUNTERS: DEPAPE, ROY

DEPAPE, ROY
See BIG COFFIN HUNTERS

DESCHAIN, ALARIC
Alaric Deschain was Roland's grandfather. He was known as "him of the red hair." Alaric went to GARLAN to slay a dragon, but that dragon had already been slain by another king, one who was later murdered. Since Alaric Deschain was known by the TOREN family of our world, it seems likely that he—like Roland—traveled between different levels of the DARK TOWER. If this is true, it seems even likelier that the dragon he wished to slay was none other than the dragon slain by King Roland of DELAIN, one of the main characters found in *The Eyes of the Dragon. (For further reflections on the similarities between Mid-World and the world of* The Eyes of the Dragon, *see* APPENDIX V.)
VI:197

DESCHAIN, GABRIELLE
Born Gabrielle of Arten, Gabrielle Deschain was Roland's mother. Despite her standing as the wife of STEVEN DESCHAIN—the last Lord of Light and the direct descendant of ARTHUR ELD, King of ALL-WORLD—she broke GILEAD's code of honor and had an affair with the court enchanter, MARTEN BROADCLOAK. Gabrielle was quite a tragic character, since this affair was, at least in part, a trap set for her by the enemies of the AFFILIATION.

Despite her dislike of guns and her gentleness toward her son, Gabrielle had a dangerous side. In MAERLYN's glass, Roland saw his mother scratch his father with a poisoned knife. This terrible deed was to be done after Gabrielle falsely repented her affair and made love with her husband. Roland prevented this disaster, but later on, blinded by the glammer of Maerlyn's Grapefruit and the evil magic of RHEA OF the CÖOS Roland, committed matricide by shooting the woman who bore him.

In the 2003 version of *The Gunslinger,* we learn that Gabrielle's given name was GABRIELLE VERISS, and that she was the daughter of ALAN. She was also known as GABRIELLE OF THE WATERS. However, in the seventh book of the *Dark Tower* series we are told that she was the daughter of CANDOR THE TALL. Gabrielle's people came from ARTEN.

When Roland was a little boy sleeping in his nursery below the window of many colors (the spectrum of which represented the WIZARD'S RAINBOW), Gabrielle often sang the Baby-Bunting Rhyme to him. This little song becomes important at the end of the Dark Tower series, since one of the song's High Speech words, *chassit* (NINETEEN), is the verbal code which opens the DOOR-WAY BETWEEN WORLDS linking the DIXIE PIG to the FEDIC DOGAN.

Although we see very little of Gabrielle in the Dark Tower novels (she is, for the most part, either a memory or a haunting shadow), she plays an incredibly important role in the shaping—and misshaping—of Roland's destiny. In *Wizard and Glass,* Gabrielle's unfaithfulness was the spark which set the story in motion. Not only did her affair galvanize Roland's desire to take his test of manhood years too early, but his success in that test resulted in Steven Deschain sending Roland east to HAMBRY so that he could avoid MARTEN BROAD-CLOAK's assassins. In *The Wind Through the Keyhole,* Roland's memories of his mother, and his grief over his matricide, are the indirect catalysts for the tales which he recounts to his *ka*-mates while they shelter from the terrible winds of the STARKBLAST. In fact, in Roland's mind, Gabrielle and the winds of the starkblast are intrinsically linked. The reason? All that Roland knows about such storms—from the erratic behavior of bumblers to the warm weather which precedes the starkblast was told to him by Gabrielle. Hence it is not surprising that, at the beginning of the novel, all of Roland's knowledge about the stark-blast has been repressed. It is not until the starkblast's winds begin to blow that the doors of memory are opened and Roland recalls both the autobiographical story of the SKIN-MAN (which took place soon after Gabrielle's death) and his favorite childhood tale about the brave exploits of TIM STOUTHEART, which his mother often read to him before he fell to sleep.

The autobiographical story entitled "The Skin-Man," which Roland shares with EDDIE, SUSANNAH, JAKE, and OY near the beginning of *The Wind Through the Keyhole*, takes place shortly after Roland's accidental matricide. At the beginning of this tale, Gilead is still in mourning for the wife of their *dinh*. Men wear black mourning collars or black bands around their shirtsleeves, and women wear black nets on their hair. According to the publishment of her death, Gabrielle had died "while possessed of a demon which troubled her spirit." Among Gilead's nobility, that was the polite way of announcing that an individual had committed suicide.

The story of the skin-man begins with STEVEN DESCHAIN questioning Roland as to why he—a trained gunslinger—is acting like the nursemaid of his broken old teacher CORT. Roland replies that he is nursing Cort out of respect, but Steven suspects a much darker motivation: Roland is playing the part of AMMIE to pay penance for his murder of his mother. To take his son away from these self-imposed duties and away from the oppressive atmosphere of Gilead, Steven sends Roland and Roland's *ka*-mate, JAMIE DeCURRY, to DEBARIA so that they can investigate reports of a murderous shapeshifter, who has been terrorizing the people of that western land. Ironically, DEBARIA is also the site of SERENITY, the women's retreat where Gabrielle had been sent to repent her affair with Marten Broadcloak.

On the way to Debaria, Roland and Jamie stop at Serenity, where they meet the giant prioress, EVERLYNNE, and the disfigured FORTUNA, who had survived an attack by the skin-man. Although elsewhere in Mid-World Roland is addressed as "son of Steven," in woman-centered Serenity, Roland is called "son of Gabrielle." Toward the end of the novel, after Roland and Jamie have defeated the skin-man, Everlynne invites Roland into her private chamber so that she can share her knowledge of Gabrielle's final days. Through Everlynne, we learn that before Gabrielle left Serenity, Marten Broadcloak had come to the retreat, demanding to see the wife of Gilead's *dinh*. Showing him her knife, Everlynne had sent the evil magician away, but she was certain that Broadcloak had succeeded in gaining an audience with Gabrielle anyway.

Before returning to Gilead, Gabrielle had given Everlynne a note which she asked the prioress to hand to her son when he came to Debaria. Blotted and uneven, the writing was as disjointed and distraught as the mind of the woman who had penned it. Much to our surprise, Gabrielle's note proved that Roland's mother knew that she was destined to die at her son's hand, yet she returned to her home city anyway. Roland never shared this missive with his father, though he carried Gabrielle's dead letter with him for many years after the fall of Gilead and the disastrous battle at JERICHO HILL. Although most of Gabrielle's letter was in low speech, the final words were in High Speech. They said *I forgive you everything. Can you forgive me?* Roland traced these letters over and over until the paper fell apart and the wind took it.

I:71–72 *(71 mistake: should say mother not father)*, I:77, I:95, I:106, I:127, I:136, I:151–52, I:159–61, I:167, I:171, I:173, I:187, I:205, III:417, IV:7, IV:107, IV:110–11, IV:223 *(and Olive Thorin)*, IV:257, IV:317, IV:439, IV:594–95 *(Roland's memory of his parents, Lake Saroni; 595 Gabrielle of Arten)*, IV:619, IV:620, IV:652–58 *(Roland's matricide)*, IV:661–62, IV:665–66, E:195, V:36 *(Roland's mother)*, V:77 *(Roland's mother)*, V:188, V:193 *(indirect)*, V:410, V:415, V:605, V:659 *(mother)*, VII:22–23, VII:179, VII:529, VII:801, VII:820, VII:821, VII:822, VII:823, VII:829

GABRIELLE DESCHAIN'S ASSOCIATES:

**ALAN (GABRIELLE'S FATHER): In the 2003 version of *The Gunslinger*, we are told that Gabrielle's father's name was Alan.

CANDOR THE TALL: Gabrielle Deschain's father. VII:529

ROLAND'S CRADLE AMAH: Roland's childhood nurse. III:33, III:39, III:40, V:188, W:14, W:31 *(mother)*, W:35, W:36 *(mother)*, W:37, W:38, W:40, W:41 *(her people in Beesford-on-Arten)*, W:53, W:67, W:68 *(and starkblast)*, W:82–83 *(mother)*, W:89, W:99 *(indirect)*, 105, 106, 267 *(indirect)*, 268 *(indirect)*, 296–300 *(299 "last shreds of sanity" letter)*, W:305, W:306

DESCHAIN, HENRY (HENRY THE TALL)
Henry the Tall was STEVEN DESCHAIN's father and Roland's grandfather.
IV:270–71, W:35

DESCHAIN, HORN OF
See ELD, ARTHUR: HORN OF ELD

DESCHAIN, MORDRED
See MORDRED

DESCHAIN, ROLAND (THE GUNSLINGER, THE REALLY BAD MAN, OLD WHITE DADDY, WILL-DEARBORN-THAT-WAS, GABBY)
Roland Deschain began life in our world as a version of Sergio Leone's Man with No Name, a wandering Clint Eastwood–type character traveling across a desert wasteland littered with the weapons, poisons, and machinery of an extinct civilization. However, as so often happens with characters, he soon morphed beneath the pen of his creator, STEPHEN KING, shook off the paper pulp, and stepped into the room, a full-fledged being in his own right.

The Roland we have come to know so well over the Dark Tower series is MID-WORLD's last hereditary gunslinger and the final human descendant of ARTHUR ELD, the ancient King of ALL-WORLD. Born in the IN-WORLD BARONY OF NEW CANAAN before the world moved on, Roland witnessed the toppling of his civilization and the drowning of his family and friends in the wave of anarchy that followed. Although he still carries the sandalwood-handled guns of his forefathers—guns whose barrels were forged from EXCALIBUR, the blade of Arthur Eld—Roland is a king without a kingdom. However, as a Warrior of the WHITE, he still has a quest—he will travel to the DARK TOWER, that linchpin of the time/space continuum, and climb to the room at the top, where he will question the God or Force that resides there.

Although he does not realize it, Roland, Warrior of the White, is a version of the eternal hero. Like his enemies who serve the Outer Dark, Roland *darkles* and *tincts*. He will relive his quest over and over, saving both Tower and BEAMS again and again, until he comes to understand that success must not be won at the cost of either the heart or the soul. Only when he remains true to his actual destiny (symbolized by the HORN OF ELD, which he must sound at the edge of CAN'-KA NO REY) will the Tower grant him the peace he so desires.

Since Roland is the main character of the Dark Tower series, his presence is implied in all other entries. For specific information about Roland's various adventures, look up the other characters or places involved. For example, if you want to read about Roland's interactions with DANDELO and PATRICK DANVILLE, look up both of those characters in the CHARACTERS section of the *Concordance*. If you wish to learn more about the battle of JERICHO HILL, look up JERICHO HILL in the MID-WORLD PLACES section. If you wish to learn more about Roland's adventures in DEBARIA, where he and JAMIE DeCURRY searched for the shapeshifting SKIN-MAN, look up those references in the MID-WORLD PLACES and CHARACTERS sections.

 RING-A-LEVIO (RINGO): Ringo was Roland's pet dog. He died when Roland was three. VII:824

 YOUNG JOE (ROLAND'S HORSE): W:48 *(named here; riding longer)*

****DESCHAIN, STEVEN (ROLAND THE ELDER)**

Steven Deschain, the last Lord of Light, was twenty-ninth, on a side line of descent, from ARTHUR ELD, King of ALL-WORLD. (In other words, he was descended from one of Arthur's side-wives, or jillies.) Before Roland gained his guns at fourteen, Steven Deschain was the youngest apprentice to prove his manhood and win his weapons. (Steven bested CORT when he was sixteen.) After he was murdered, and after the final gunslingers were defeated at the battle of JERICHO HILL, the last vestiges of MID-WORLD's decaying civilization collapsed into complete anarchy.

Steven Deschain (also occasionally called Roland the Elder) was the leader of NEW CANAAN's gunslingers. Tall, painfully thin, and with a heavy handlebar mustache, the elder Deschain's gruff looks belied his actual nobility. Like all the gunslingers, he was an aristocrat, and it was in part this class division that turned many common people against the AFFILIATION and toward the cause of the traitorous GOOD MAN, JOHN FARSON. Like his fathers before him, Steven Deschain wore the true gunslinger's six-shooters—the ones with sandalwood grips—against the wings of his hips. He passed them on to Roland after the younger man proved himself in HAMBRY.

In the 2003 *Gunslinger*, we learn that during Roland's childhood his father managed to take control of his *ka-tet* (the *tet* of the Gun), and was on the verge of becoming *dinh* of Gilead, if not all of IN-WORLD. He was betrayed by the serpent in his bosom—his own counselor and sorcerer, MARTEN—who first seduced his wife and then raised the forces of anarchy in his lands. Although Steven didn't know it, Marten was actually a shape-shifter of multiple identities, known to CONSTANT READERS as WALTER O'DIM. In all of his incarnations, Walter/Marten/R.F. served the chaotic force of THE CRIMSON KING. Hence he opposed the WHITE and all who championed it.

Just as Steven Deschain's decision to send Roland, ALAIN, and CUTHBERT to HAMBRY set off the chain of events of *Wizard and Glass,* so Steven's decision to send Roland and JAMIE DeCURRY to DEBARIA initiated Roland's adventures with the SKIN-MAN, recounted in *Wind Through the Keyhole.* In both cases, Steven's decisions were motivated by his deep—although not always apparent—love and respect for his son. In *Wizard and Glass,* the elder Deschain wanted to keep Roland safe from Marten Broadcloak's assassins and so sent him east—as far from the Good Man's rebellions as he could. (He did not yet realize that Hambry had already fallen to the enemy.) In "The Skin-Man," Steven wanted to save Roland from himself. (In penance for murdering his mother, Roland had appointed himself as the nurse and AMMIE for his broken teacher, CORT.)

Unlike his wife, GABRIELLE, whose belief in love and romance proved to be her undoing, Steven Deschain was a hardheaded realist. Unlike Roland's teacher VANNAY, who realized that Debaria's skin-man was probably a shapeshifter as well as a shape-changer, Deschain secretly thought that the skin-man was no more than a murdering maniac dressed up in animal skins. Although Steven Deschain was wrong about the skin-man, his judgment of human character proved to be sound. Before sending Roland and Jamie to Debaria, Deschain told the boys to contact Debaria's High Sheriff, HUGH PEAVY, one of the few good men left in that western part of Mid-World. Years before, Peavy and the elder Deschain had joined forces to track down a slightly different form of demon—a band of outlaws known as the CROW GANG.

Although Steven Deschain died while still relatively young (he was stabbed by an unknown assailant), experience had transformed his face into one that was both hard and cruel. However, in the vision Roland had of him in one of the DARK TOWER's many rooms, his father's visage was still soft, and his eyes reflected his love for his only son.

I:71 *(mistake: says father, should say mother),* I:103–6, I:107, I:109, I:110, I:111, I:151–52, I:160, I:161, I:164, I:167, I:171, I:184, I:205, I:213, I:216, II:104–5, III:11, III:50, III:276, III:375, III:377, III:415, III:417, IV:19, IV:50, IV:108–12 *(grabs Roland from a whore's bed),* IV:144, IV:163–64 *(Roland as "son who had lived"),* IV:181, IV:183–84 *(twenty-ninth generation descended from Arthur Eld's side line),* IV:258, IV:262, IV:270–71 *(line of Arthur Eld, son of Henry the Tall),* IV:275–76 *(voice of Eyebolt Canyon thinny),* IV:285 *(father's son),* IV:286, IV:317, IV:436–39 *(tells of Maerlyn's Grapefruit and Maerlyn's Rainbow),* IV:443, IV:464, IV:499, IV:530, IV:531, IV:570, IV:594–95 *(Roland's memory of his parents, Lake Saroni),* IV:620–21 *(plot to kill him),* IV:650, IV:653, IV:655–56 *(Gabrielle plans to murder him),* IV:657, IV:665, E:195, E:206, V:85 *(Roland's father),* V:105 *(knew of glass balls),* V:193 *(indirect),* V:215, V:242 *(father),* V:392, V:400, V:410, V:415, V:481, V:482, V:541, V:579 *(father),* V:590, V:597 *(father),* VI:106, VI:162, VI:197,

VI:295, VII:23 *(indirect)*, VII:50, VII:111, VII:134, VII:178, VII:442, VII:473, VII:499, VII:529, VII:769, VII:801, VII:822, VII:823–24, VII:827, W:35–40, W:41, W:42, W:44 *(father)*, W:46 *(as possible trickster)*, W:54, W:55–61 *(and crow gang: 60 map of scars & crow gang scar)*, W:63, W:86 *(cold mind like Roland)*, W:97 *(swear in my father's name)*, W:98 *(guns)*, W:288, W:297, W:298, W:299, W:306

DESMOND
Desmond was one of Roland's original gunslinger companions. When Roland sees the neon sign for BALAZAR's headquarters, the LEANING TOWER, he calls out this old friend's name. For a moment, Roland believes that he has reached his final destination.
    II:121

DESTRY (FARMER DESTRY, OLD DESTRY)
    See TREE VILLAGE CHARACTERS

DESTRY, HUNTER
    See TREE VILLAGE CHARACTERS

DESTRY, RANDY
    See TREE VILLAGE CHARACTERS

DESTRY, STRAW WILLEM
    See TREE VILLAGE CHARACTERS

DETTA
    See DEAN, SUSANNAH

DEVAR-TOI CHARACTERS
    See WARRIORS OF THE SCARLET EYE

DEWEY
    See DEAN, EDDIE: EDDIE'S ASSOCIATES, PAST AND PRESENT: BUN-KOWSKI, DEWEY

DEWLAP
    See GRAYS: GRAY HIGH COMMAND: TICK-TOCK: TICK-TOCK'S FAM-ILY AND FORMER ASSOCIATES

DEWLAP
    See GRAYS: GRAY LEADERS: TICK-TOCK

DIANA'S DREAM
    See MID-WORLD FOLKLORE

DICK, GRAY
    See ORIZA, LADY

DILLON, MARSHALL
See DESCHAIN, ROLAND

DISCORDIA
See PRIM; see also DISCORDIA, in PORTALS

DISCORDIA, LORD OF
See CRIMSON KING

DIXIE PIG CHARACTERS
See WARRIORS OF THE SCARLET EYE: DIXIE PIG CHARACTERS/ FEDIC CHARACTERS

DOBBIE
See NORTH CENTRAL POSITRONICS

DOCTOR BUGS
See ELURIA CHARACTERS: CAM TAM (DOCTOR BUGS)

DOG GUARDIAN
See GUARDIANS OF THE BEAM

DOLLENTZ
See KATZ

DOLORES
See SERENITY, SISTERS OF

DOOLIN, BELINDA
See DEBARIA CHARACTERS

DOOLIN, EAMON
See CALLA BRYN STURGIS CHARACTERS: WOLF POSSE

DOOLIN, MINNIE
See CALLA BRYN STURGIS CHARACTERS: ROONTS

DOOLIN, MOLLY
See ORIZA, SISTERS OF

DOOM, DR.
See WOLVES

DORFMAN
See MORT, JACK

DORFMAN, STAN
See PIPER SCHOOL CHARACTERS

DORNING, JANE
  See DEAN, EDDIE: DELTA FLIGHT 901 CHARACTERS

DOROTHY
  See WIZARD OF OZ

DOUGLAS, SUSY
  See DEAN, EDDIE: DELTA FLIGHT 901 CHARACTERS

DRABNIK, CSABA
  See DEAN, HENRY: HENRY DEAN'S KA-TET

DRAGONS
Dragons are mentioned numerous times in the Dark Tower series. In *The Waste Lands,* Roland tells his *tet* about a place he knew as a boy called DRAGON'S GRAVE. It was a bottomless crack in the earth, named for the great bursts of steam that erupted from it every thirty to forty days. Although BLAINE'S CRADLE in LUD was decorated with images of the GUARDIANS OF THE BEAM, at the corners of the building were hideous stone dragons. In the ruins of CANDLETON, in the WASTE LANDS beyond LUD, there were mutant birds that looked like young dragonlets. The Kingdom of DELAIN, in EASTAR'D BARONY, was known derisively as DRAGON'S LAIR, though we are never told why. In *Song of Susannah,* we learn that Roland's grandfather, ALARIC, went to GARLAN to slay a dragon.

Since there are frequent references to dragons in the Dark Tower series, and since many important Mid-World buildings have dragon gargoyles, Constant Readers have always assumed that dragons once played an important role in Mid-World folklore. However, it is not until *Wind Through the Keyhole* that we learn more about Mid-World's association with these legendary monsters.

Wind Through the Keyhole's initial mention of dragons happens within the first few pages. "Hile, Sir Throcken," Roland says to the bumbler OY as he, EDDIE, SUSANNAH, and JAKE continue to walk along the PATH OF THE BEAM toward the RIVER WHYE. We soon learn that this saying comes from a book called *The Throcken and the Dragon,* which Roland's mother read to him when he was a child. Later on, Roland recounts another childhood tale entitled "Wind Through the Keyhole," in which the *ka* of the young hero, TIM STOUTHEART is intrinsically bound to the *ka* of these firebreathing reptiles.

  (**GENERAL**): III:37 *(Dragon's Grave)*, III:331 *(and Blaine's Cradle)*, IV:13, VI:197 *(Alaric)*, W:7 *(The Throcken and the Dragon)*, W:110, W:111, W:120, W:133 *(sound of indrawn breath)*, W:151 *(Garlan; a bonfire of dragons)*; 160 *(Tavares)*, W:218
  DRAGON OF THE FAGONARD: In the folktale "The Wind Through the Keyhole" (recounted in the novel of the same name), the young hero TIM ROSS (aka TIM STOUTHEART) had his life profoundly changed by two different dragons. The first of these huge reptiles—the dragon that supposedly incinerated his father—proved to be a nothing but a lie spun by the murdering cull BERN KELLS. However, the second dragon was extremely real. In fact, it almost roasted Tim alive.
  Tim's encounter with a live dragon happened in the FAGONARD Swamp,

while the boy was pursuing the pretty but wicked SIGHE, ARMANEETA. Fluttering flirtatiously ahead of young Tim, Armaneeta led him onto a dangerously isolated tussock and left him there. Much to Tim's horror, the tussock turned out to be the head of a submerged dragon.

If the dragon that Tim met in the Fagonard is anything to go by, Mid-World's fire-breathing reptiles are extremely impressive creatures. Although by nature dragons like to submerge themselves in mud and silt, when agitated they can rise out of the water and stand on their back legs, a stance they can maintain by fanning their wings. (The sound resembles drying sheets snapping in a brisk wind.) When they roar, green-orange fire belches from their mouths, sizzling any nearby reeds (or nearby boys). When they breathe, the gill, located between their plated breasts, flutters as they pull in air to stoke the furnace in their guts.

Luckily for Tim, the dragon he meets doesn't roast young boys on sight, and can be appeased by pleas and prayers. This is probably due to the fact that the MUDMEN of the Fagonard give her offerings. (Tim knows that the Fagonard dragon is female since she has a pink maiden's-comb on her head.) Sadly, the Fagonard dragon was not destined to survive. After the STARK-BLAST, Tim saw the dragon's vast, plated corpse floating on its side in the ice-choked waters of the swamp. Although she had fought the starkblast's cold with blasts of her own fiery breath, the storm took her just as it took everything else in the Fagonard. W:194–96 *(195 pink maiden't comb)*, W:197 *(firemaiden)*, W:198, W:201, W:204 *(appeasement)*, W:206, W:218, W:222, W:256–57

DRAGON THAT KILLED JACK ROSS: According to BIG KELLS, the pard of BIG ROSS, Jack Ross was burned to death by a she-dragon, probably one protecting an egg. However, as the story of "The Wind Through the Keyhole" progresses, we begin to realize that Big Kells was lying. According to the tax-collecting COVENANT MAN, not even a small dragon had nested close to civilization in almost a hundred years, never mind one as big as a house. Bern Kells was lying to hide the fact that he'd killed his partner in a jealous rage. He wanted Ross's wife, NELL, for himself. W:110, W:111, W:112, W:115–16 *(probably a she-dragon protecting her egg; sometimes swallow their fire and explode)*, W:120, W: 133, W:144, W:151 *(Garlan; a bonfire of dragons)*, W:158, W:160, W:173

DRETTO, 'CIMI
See BALAZAR, ENRICO: BALAZAR'S MEN

DRUNK IN CELL
See DEBARIA CHARACTERS: SHERIFF'S OFFICE

DUGAN, BISHOP
See CALLAHAN, FATHER DONALD FRANK: CALLAHAN'S OTHER PAST ASSOCIATES

DUGARELLI, FRANK
See DEAN, HENRY: HENRY DEAN'S KA-TET

E

EAGLE GUARDIAN
See GUARDIANS OF THE BEAM

EARNSHAW, DINKY
See BREAKERS

EARP, WYATT
See GUNSLINGERS (OUR WORLD)

EAST DOWNE, WALKING WATERS OF
See MID-WORLD FOLKLORE

EAST STONEHAM CHARACTERS
See MAINE CHARACTERS

EASTWOOD, CLINT
Clint Eastwood starred in a number of spaghetti Westerns, including *A Fistful of Dollars* and *For a Few Dollars More*. He also directed and starred in such great gothic Westerns as *Pale Rider* and *High Plains Drifter*. Roland looks a bit like Clint and is an even better shot.
    III:182

ECHEVERRIA
See CALLA BRYN STURGIS CHARACTERS: OTHER CHARACTERS

EDDIE
See DEAN, EDDIE

EISENHART, MARGARET
See ORIZA, SISTERS OF

EISENHART, TOM AND TESSA
See CALLA BRYN STURGIS CHARACTERS: RANCHERS: EISENHART, VAUGHN

EISENHART, VAUGHN
See CALLA BRYN STURGIS CHARACTERS: RANCHERS

EISENHART, VERNA
See CALLA BRYN STURGIS CHARACTERS: ROONTS

ELD, ARTHUR (THE ELD, LINE OF ELD, HORN OF ELD)
Arthur Eld—ancient King of ALL-WORLD and MID-WORLD's greatest mythical hero—was a warrior of the WHITE. Like the line of DESCHAIN, who were

descended from one of his forty jillies, the Eld was a Guardian of the DARK TOWER. Although history credits him with uniting the land, Arthur Eld's original kingdom lay in the western part of Mid-World, in the baronies destroyed by FARSON. Despite the glory associated with it, Arthur Eld's reign was a brutal time. In the days of Eld, people, not stuffy-guys, were sacrificed on Charyou Tree fires.

In story and tapestry, Arthur is often depicted as riding his white stallion, LLAMREI, and brandishing his great sword, EXCALIBUR. After his death and the dissolution of his kingdom, Arthur Eld's horse remained the *sigul* of IN-WORLD, and its image decorated the pennons of GILEAD. Although in *Wizard and Glass* we were told that Arthur Eld's unifying sword was entombed in a pyramid after the Eld's death, in the final book of the Dark Tower series we discover that it must have been the hilt that was entombed, since Roland's gun barrels were forged from the metal of that blade. As well as his guns, the young Roland carried another heirloom from the times of Eld—his ancestor's horn. Unluckily for him, Roland let his friend CUTHBERT ALLGOOD blow the Horn of Eld at the battle of JERICHO HILL, and Roland left it on the battlefield where it tumbled from Cuthbert's dead hand, an oversight which he later comes to regret.

All descendants of Arthur Eld, as well as their gunslinger-knights, are sworn to uphold the Way of the Eld (also known as the Way of Eld) at all costs. The Way of Eld designates the proper conduct of gunslingers. It refers to their rigorous physical and mental training as well as to their sense of honor and duty. According to the Way of Eld, gunslingers must help those in distress if it is within their power to do so. According to FATHER CALLAHAN's books, they were forbidden to take reward.

Sometime during his long and eventful life, Arthur Eld must have had sexual relations with a demon of some sort, since the CRIMSON KING is also his descendant. This is not so surprising, since Mid-World is full of SPEAKING RINGS, LESSER DEMONS OF THE PRIM, and wily DEMON ELEMENTALS, all of whom are able to cast powerful *glammer*. In the final three books of the Dark Tower series, we see the two bloodlines of the Eld—of GAN and Gilead, and of the PRIM and the AM—reunited in the body of MORDRED DESCHAIN, son of two fathers and two mothers.

Although the human line of Eld serves the White, the demonic line of Eld serves the Outer Dark. Both bloodlines are obsessed with the Tower, which is their birthright, yet while the line of Deschain is sworn to preserve it, the Red King and his son—the *dan-tete*, or little king—have pledged to destroy it.

It seems likely that the Eld's two bloodlines—destined to battle each other— have each developed their own distinct mythologies about their ancestor. While in her dream-version of CASTLE DISCORDIA's BANQUETING HALL, SUSANNAH-MIO sees a screen, which depicts a heroic Arthur Eld charging through a swamp with three of his knight-gunslingers behind him, the corpse of the dangerous snake SAITA around his neck. Yet in the DIXIE PIG, a blasphemous tapestry depicts Arthur Eld and his court feasting on human flesh.

Not only do Arthur Eld's two bloodlines present two different views of the Eld, but the people of Mid-World also seem to have two versions of their greatest hero. The mythical Eld was the first king to arise after the Prim receded, hence he predated the time of the GREAT OLD ONES. The historical Arthur Eld lived approximately seven hundred years—or thirty generations—before Roland's birth. Perhaps Mid-World's King Arthur was, like the ARTHUR of our world, both the once and future king. Although born in an ancient world, he never died but only lay sleeping. After the Great Old Ones' terrible disasters, his people needed him and so he returned.

IV:171 *(picture in Travellers' Rest. "ARGYOU NOT ABOUT THE HAND YOU ARE DEALT IN CARDS OR LIFE")*, IV:181, IV:183–84 *(and Steven Deschain)*, IV:194 *("he of the white horse . . .")*, IV:206 *(Excalibur and the Affiliation)*, IV:211 *(tapestry in Seafront. Sword entombed in a pyramid)*, IV:223 *(40 gillies)*, IV:251, IV:267–71, IV:302 *("fantastic pride" of his line)*, IV:317 *(Excalibur and crown of All-World)*, IV:350, IV:360 *(Jewels of Eld)*, IV:379, IV:382, IV:508, IV:558 *(Roland as Arthur Eld)*, IV:563, IV:580, E:206, V:30–31, V:73, V:110 *(line of Eld)*, V:128 *(line of)*, V:153, V:156 *(way of Eld)*, V:162 *(Eld's way)*, V:170 *(horn)*, V:171, V:172 *(horn)*, V:181 *(way of Eld)*, V:203, V:215 *(line of)*, V:216, V:236, V:238, V:240 *(horn)*, V:284 *(horn only)*, V:321, V:324, V:333, V:373, V:388, V:410, V:497, V:542, V:567, V:605, V:609, V:624, V:686, V:709, VI:15, VI:39, VI:110, VI:111 *(Arthur Eld)*, VI:135 *(Lost Beasts of)*, VI:177, VI:183, VI:197, VI:252, VI:371–73 *(tapestry)*, VII:26, VII:50, VII:51, VII:111, VII:168, VII:176, VII:199, VII:253, VII:322, VII:473, VII:499, VII:501, VII:512, VII:549, VII:608, VII:766, VII:780, VII:791, VII:799, VII:800, VII:801, VII:819 *(horn)*, VII:820, VII:821, VII:822, VII:825 *(horn)*, W:48, W:60, W:66, W:103, W:131, W:169, W:197, W:268

COUNCIL OF ELD: See GILEAD CHARACTERS

ELD OF THE ELD: Roland and his father Steven are the true descendants of Arthur Eld, hence they are the Eld of the Eld. W:60

ELD'S LAST FELLOWSHIP: A tapestry located in the DIXIE PIG depicts Eld's Last Fellowship. However, the feast it shows is a horrible parody of Eld and his knights' final meal. Instead of eating meat and drinking wine, Eld, his wife, and his followers are shown to be eating human flesh and drinking human blood. VII:6, VII:8, VII:10, VII:26 *(named)*, VII:28

EXCALIBUR: Like the blade carried by our world's mythical King Arthur, Arthur Eld's sword was called Excalibur. The barrels of Roland's sandalwood-handled guns were cast from the metal of this blade. VII:608

HORN OF ELD: The horn which has been passed from father to son from the time of Arthur Eld to the time of Roland Deschain. Unfortunately, Roland left the Horn of Eld (also called the Horn of Deschain) next to CUTHBERT ALLGOOD's dead body on the battlefield of JERICHO HILL. *(For page references, see main entry.)*

LLAMREI: Arthur Eld's white horse. Llamrei's image was the *sigul* of all IN-WORLD and decorated the pennons of GILEAD. In the office of RICHARD P. SAYRE, located in the FEDIC DOGAN, Roland and SUSANNAH come across a painting of a young boy (probably MORDRED) standing triumphantly over the dead body of Llamrei, his foot on the horse's corpse. VII:549, VII:550, VII:780

LOST BEASTS OF ELD: The Lost Beasts of Eld were flying creatures. They may have resembled dragons. VI:135

MAGIC TALES OF THE ELD: When Roland was a boy, he loved this volume of stories above all others. His mother, GABRIELLE DESCHAIN, often read it to him just before he went to sleep in his high tower bedroom. The book contained a dozen hand-colored woodcut illustrations, but Rolands' favorite was of six bumblers sitting on a fallen tree in the forest, beneath a crescent moon, their snouts raised. This story was from the tale "The Wind Through the Keyhole." W:14

ROWENA, QUEEN: Arthur Eld's lady-wife. In the blasphemous tapestry found in the DIXIE PIG, Queen Rowena is depicted drinking a goblet of blood. VI:371–73

SAITA: While MIA, daughter of none, searches for food in the deserted BANQUETING HALL located in her dream-version of CASTLE DISCORDIA, she sees a screen depicting Arthur Eld riding through a swamp with three of his knight-gunslingers behind him. Around his neck is Saita, the great snake, which he has just slain. V:373

SWORD OF ELD: See EXCALIBUR, *listed above*

THREE WIVES OF THE ELD: According to the COVENANT MAN of *The Wind Through the Keyhole,* Arthur Eld had three wives. These three women gave the Eld many sons, but there were moity-more born on the dark side of the blanket. (Arthur Eld was a busy man.) W:268

TRADITION OF THE ELD: The tradition of the Eld is the Way of the Gun, in which all apprentice gunslingers are trained. W:36

ELD, COUNCIL OF
See GILEAD'S COUNCIL OF ELD

ELI
See CHAMBERS, JAKE: CHARACTERS JAKE MEETS WHEN HE RUNS AWAY TO THE LOT, TO BROOKLYN, AND TO MID-WORLD

ELLEN
See SERENITY, SISTERS OF

ELURIA CHARACTERS
After the fall of GILEAD but before he managed to track down his enemy, the MAN IN BLACK, Roland traveled through Eluria, a small town located in the far west of MID-WORLD. Eluria is the setting for the story "The Little Sisters of Eluria."

Like so many Mid-World villages, Eluria resembles one of the tumbleweed towns of the Old West. When Roland arrived, it seemed to be deserted save for a CROSS DOG (also known as a JESUS DOG), a single corpse, some SLOW MUTANTS (called the GREEN FOLK), and some strangely disturbing singing insects. After being attacked by the Green Folk, an injured Roland finds himself in the hospital-tent of the *glammer*-throwing LITTLE SISTERS OF ELURIA— a tribe of female vampires posing as healers. Roland falls in love with SISTER JENNA, the youngest of these strange demonic women, and she, in turn, betrays her sisters in order to help him escape.

ELURIA CHARACTERS:

BOUNCER OF THE BUSTLING PIG: By the time Roland reaches Eluria, the only sign of this man is his nail-spiked club, wielded by one of the GREEN FOLK. E:154

CAM TAM (DOCTOR BUGS): The vampiric Little Sisters pose as a religious order of hospitalers. Hence, the doctor bugs—which are only a little smaller than fat honeybees—are an important part of their disguise.

Unlike the carrion-eating GRANDFATHER FLEAS, and despite the Little Sisters' evil habits, these insects are actually healers. Although ugly and disturbing to watch, the *cam tam* eat disease and knit broken bones. E:146, E:147–48, E:152, E:158, E:159, E:164, E:168, E:169–73, E:174, E:178, E:179, E:180, E:183, E:185, E:193, E:197, E:198–201, E:202, E:206, E:208–9, VI:234

CHAS: A freeborn cattle thief destined to be tried in Eluria. However, the Little Sisters get to the town first. E:151

CROSS DOG/JESUS DOG: The Cross Dog takes its name from the black cross upon its white chest fur. This coloration oddity saves its life, since the vampiric Little Sisters can't touch it. Despite its superficial relation to religious good, this crippled animal is a rather unpleasant creature. In fact, the first time Roland sees it, it is chewing on the bloated leg of dead JAMES NORMAN. At the end of the story, the Jesus Dog redeems itself by attacking the evil SISTER MARY. It kills her. E:151–53, E:155, E:156, E:159, E:160, E:182, E:204–5, E:207

GREEN FOLK: Like many other tribes of SLOW MUTANTS, the Green Folk are the descendants of human men and women exposed to the OLD ONES' toxic pollutants. In the case of the Green Folk, the poison was radium. In fact, Roland is fairly certain that the ones who attack him still hide from sunlight in the old radium mines.

Despite their unnerving color and their tallowy skin, these shuffling, snuffling, fluorescent green Slow Mutants have a more human shape than the group Roland and JAKE meet under the CYCLOPEAN MOUNTAINS. (Roland thinks of the latter tribe as both animate corpses and toadstools with brains.) Like other Slow Mutants, the Green Folk sometimes eat human flesh. For more information on Slow Mutants, see entry under MUTANTS. E:146, E:151, E:154–58, E:160, E:162, E:171, E:173, E:177, E:178–79, E:193, E:205

> **LUMPY BALD HEAD WITH RED SIZZLING SORES:** E:154–58
>
> **MALE WITH MELTED CANDLEWAX FACE:** E:154
>
> **MR. CLUB-WITH-NAILS:** This creature probably stole his nasty weapon from THE BUSTLING PIG'S dead BOUNCER. E:154–58, E:159
>
> **MR. TOAD:** Mr. Toad looks like a toad-mouthed troll. E:155–56 *(shot)*
>
> **RALPH:** One-eyed Ralph wears a bowler hat and red suspenders. He is one of the mutants who attacks Roland soon after his arrival in Eluria. While Roland is their patient/prisoner, the Little Sisters try to bribe Ralph into removing JOHN NORMAN's Christian medallion from around Roland's neck. It seems likely that Ralph is the leader of his tribe. E:155–58, E:179, E:190–92, E:193
>
> **RED VEST WOMAN:** Her saggy breasts are visible beneath her vest. E:155–58, E:179
>
> **SMASHER:** He gave Roland's guns to the Little Sisters without telling Ralph. E:192

TWO-HEADED MALE: This nasty creature sneaks up behind Roland and mounts a surprise attack. Roland shoots him. E:157 *(shot)*, E:174

LITTLE SISTERS OF ELURIA: *See* ELURIA, LITTLE SISTERS OF, *listed separately*

NORMAN, JAMES: James Norman was a young, towheaded cowboy of about fourteen to sixteen. He was the brother of JOHN NORMAN and the son of JESSE NORMAN. Roland comes across his drowned corpse early in his wanderings around Eluria. James wore a medallion that read "James, Loved of Family, Loved of God." SISTER JENNA places it around our gunslinger's neck and Roland continues to wear it throughout his time among the Sisters. They cannot bleed him while he wears it. E:146, E:151–58, E:162, E:164 *(medallion)*, E:172, E:176 *(Roland poses as James)*, E:177, E:178–79, E:184 *(Roland)*, E:185 *(Roland)*, E:188, E:189, E:193, E:194, E:196

NORMAN, JASON ("JASON, BROTHER OF JOHN"): The Little Sisters call Roland "Jason, Brother of John" to trick him into proving he is not really JAMES NORMAN. Roland doesn't fall for the trick. E:184

NORMAN, JESSE: Father of John and James. E:176, E:188

NORMAN, MRS.: Mother of John and James. Wife of Jesse. E:162, E:176, E:188

NORMAN, JOHN: John Norman is the brother of JAMES NORMAN, and occupies the bed next to Roland's in the LITTLE SISTERS' hospital tent. John warns Roland about the Sisters' evil natures. Like his brother James, John wears a Christian medallion around his neck. The Sisters eventually force one of the GREEN FOLK to tear it from him. E:162–64, E:168, E:172, E:176–80, E:181, E:183, E:184, E:186, E:187, E:188, E:190–92, E:193, E:194, E:196–97, E:199, E:202, E:205

SHERIFF: By the time Roland reaches Eluria, the sheriff had long since disappeared. Like everyone else in the town, he was probably drained dry by the Little Sisters. E:150, E:155

UNCONSCIOUS MAN: Roland sees this unconscious man dangling from a white sling in the LITTLE SISTERS' hospital tent. Like JAMES and JOHN NORMAN, this unfortunate fellow was attacked by the GREEN FOLK while protecting a long-haul caravan and was later given to the Little Sisters. This man never completely regains consciousness while under the Sisters' care. They drink his blood anyway. E:162–64, E:169–71, E:180–81, E:183, E:198

ELURIA, LITTLE SISTERS OF

This tribe of vampires poses as a holy order of hospital nuns. They dress in billowing white habits and their crones' faces are framed by white wimples. Hanging from the bands of silk imprisoning their hair are lines of tiny bells which chime when the Sisters move or speak. Upon the breast of each of their habits is embroidered a single, blood-red ROSE—the *sigul* of the DARK TOWER. Roland barely escapes the Sisters' deadly clutches. A few of their order are still wandering around MID-WORLD.

These strange sorceresses are not actually human. When Roland grabs SIS-

TER MARY by the throat he finds her flesh repellent. It doesn't feel like solid flesh at all but something both *various* and flowing.

In their true form, the Little Sisters look like the ghastly siblings of RHEA OF THE CÖOS, the ancient hag-witch we met in *Wizard and Glass*. Like Rhea, they are creatures of magic and can cast a *glammer* which makes them appear young and lovely. But this illusion fades quickly, especially when they are hungry. Like their own loveliness, the airy white silk pavilion in which they keep their victims—first to cure them, then to bleed them—is only a *glammer*. In reality it is a fraying canvas tent. The only truly beautiful creature ever existent in the dream-realm woven by the Little Sisters is SISTER JENNA, a twenty-one-year-old woman bound to these others by the cruelty of *ka*.

The Little Sisters are a strange order, and the reader cannot help but wonder whether they, like the mutants of Mid-World, were originally something good. The Rose the Sisters wear upon their habits is a *sigul* not only of the Dark Tower but of the WHITE. Similarly, their *cam tam* are healers, even though they are disturbing to watch.

As we know, not all things that serve a higher purpose are comfortable to contemplate. The dark bells which Sister Jenna wears, and which Roland thinks are the true *sigul* of the order, are described as *charry*. Since the High Speech root-word *char* means death, it seems likely that these quasi-mortal women were originally death-angels, or beings meant to help men avoid (or less painfully reach) death. Perhaps, as Sister Jenna says, before the world moved on, they really were an order of hospitalers, albeit supernatural ones. But sadly, the evil of the Great Old Ones poisoned not only the air and water of Mid-World, but the magic as well. Although they may have begun as creatures of the White, the evil Little Sisters now have cause to fear all religious *siguls*, even their own dark bells.
E:165–67, E:168, E:177–80, E:180–82, E:183, E:186 *(soup)*, E:188, E:190–92, E:193, E:195, E:200, E:202, E:205, E:206, VI:234

SISTER COQUINA: E:165–67, E:173–77, E:177 *(indirect)*, E:180–82, E:190–92, E:197–99

SISTER JENNA: Sister Jenna is a young black-haired beauty of twenty-one or twenty-two. Unlike that of her sisters, her youth is real, not the result of *glammer*. Although Jenna is a vampire and participates in her order's grisly meals, she wishes to rebel against her destiny.

Sister Jenna appears to be a kind of vampire royalty. Although the other sisters wear bells of bright silver, the ones Jenna wears looked as though they have been smoked over a fire. These dark bells—also called charry bells—are the true *sigul* of the order, and give Jenna special powers over the doctor bugs.

Jenna falls in love with Roland and betrays her sisters in order to help him escape, but human love is forbidden her. After she helps Roland flee from the hospital pavilion and then elude the evil clutches of SISTER MARY, Jenna's body becomes *cam tam*. E:159–61, E:162, E:165, E:166–73, E:174, E:175, E:177, E:179, E:180, E:184–88, E:189, E:194, E:195, E:197–209

JENNA'S MOTHER: Like her daughter, Jenna's mother tried to escape her fate. She deserted her order and bore a child, presumably to a human man, though it is possible these creatures reproduce by parthenogenesis. Unfortunately, escape was not possible. Without blood to sustain her, Jenna's mother began to sicken. She returned to her sisters along with her small child. Jenna's mother died, but the Little Sisters kept and raised Jenna. E:167, E:183, E:184, E:202, E:206

SISTER LOUISE: E:165–67, E:171, E:180–82, E:183–86, E:190–92, E:200–201, E:205

SISTER MARY/BIG SISTER: Sister Mary, also called Big Sister, is the head of the Little Sisters' order. Like the others of her kind, she is actually more shade than substance.

Although she does not wear the charry bells as does JENNA, Sister Mary's dominance over her order is complete. Whenever one of them disobeys her wishes, Sister Mary sends them to the nearby cave called THOUGHTFUL HOUSE. Sometimes she even has disobedient sisters whipped.

Out of love for Roland and despair over her fate, Jenna rebels against Big Sister. But outside the *glammer*-filled pavilion, not even the charry bells are strong enough to defeat her enemy. In the end, it is the *sigul*-bearing CROSS DOG—not Jenna or Roland—that destroys Sister Mary. E:165–67, E:169, E:175–76, E:177, E:180–82, E:183–86, E:187, E:190–92, E:193–95, E:196, E:197, E:201, E:202–4, E:205, E:208

SISTER MICHELA: E:165–67, E:171, E:180–82, E:188–89, E:190–92, E:200–201, E:205

SISTER TAMRA: E:165–67, E:171, E:176–77, 180–82, E:190–92, E:196, E:200–201, E:205

EMERSON, SONNY
   See TASSENBAUM, DAVID

ENGINEER BOB
   See CHARLIE THE CHOO-CHOO: ENGINEER BOB

ESTEVEZ, JULIO
   See DEAN, SUSANNAH: DETTA/ODETTA'S "A TRAIN" ACCIDENT

ESTRADA, DEELIE
   See CALLA BRYN STURGIS CHARACTERS: FARMERS (SMALLHOLD): ESTRADA, GEORGE

ESTRADA, GEORGE
   See CALLA BRYN STURGIS CHARACTERS: FARMERS (SMALLHOLD)

ETHELYN, AUNTIE
   See KING, STEPHEN: KING FAMILY

EURASIAN HOTEL CLERK
   See PLAZA–PARK HYATT CHARACTERS: RECEPTIONISTS: EXOTIC HOTEL RECEPTIONIST

EVANS, BERYL
   See CHARLIE THE CHOO-CHOO

EVERLYNNE OF SERENITY (PRIORESS)
See SERENITY, SISTERS OF

EXCALIBUR
See ELD, ARTHUR

EX LIBRIS, MR.
See TOWER, CALVIN

F

FAGONARD CHARACTERS
Deep in NORTH'RD BARONY's ENDLESS FOREST sat the great swamp known as the FAGONARD. Not even the people of TREE, who knew the forest better than any other people in Mid-World, dared to enter the swamp. Not only was the Fagonard full of natural dangers such as DRAGONS, but it also contained the deadly leavings of the OLD PEOPLE. Unlike the rest of the Endless Forest, which was filled with the grave, sweet-sour smell of ironwood trees, the Fagonard swamp stank of stagnant water and rotting vegetation. The Fagonard was home to a mutant tribe which TIM ROSS called the MUDMEN. Like the mutant CHILDREN OF RODERICK, the MUDMEN probably once gave their allegiance to ARTHUR ELD.
    CANNIBAL REPTILES: These hungry creatures have scaly, triangular heads, protruding eyes, and yawning jaws filled with triangular teeth. They have claws on the ends of their stubby front legs and tails which are blackish-green on top and white as a dead man's belly underneath. Above their snouts are nests of eyes that pulse and bulge. When their long jaws gnash, their teeth sound like stones driven together. The shortest of these beasts is ten feet long, but most are far longer. When Tim shoots one of these monsters (it is trying to eat him), he discovers that its blood is blackish-red. W:192, W:193–198 *(half dozen following Tim)*, W:198 *(circling)*, W:199 *(described, nest of eggs)*, W:201 *(shot)*, W:203, W:211 *(scaly)*, W:239
    DRAGON: See DRAGON, listed *separately*
    MUDMEN (PLANTMEN; FAGONARDERS; SWAMP PEOPLE): TIM ROSS first becomes aware of the mudmen of the FAGONARD while he is battling the CANNIBAL REPTILES that want to eat him for dinner. During this confrontation Tim suspects that his mutant onlookers are cheering for the hungry monster, but he soon comes to realize that they are cheering for him. As soon as Tim takes out WIDOW SMACK's four-shot revolver and shoots the alligator-like reptile that's lunging for him, the mudmen drop to their knees, place their fists against their foreheads, and speak the only word which they seem to know. That word is *hile*. Realizing that the mudmen mistake him for a young gunslinger, Tim decides to play the roll of a descendant of the ELD. "Hile, bondsman!" Tim cries to the mudmen on the bank. "I see

you very well! Rise in love and service!" Tim's role-playing works, since the mudmen subsequently row to the tussock where he is stranded and rescue him. However, we can't help but wonder whether the good-natured mudmen would have rescued him anyway.

Once he sees them up close, Tim realizes that the mudmen aren't really mudmen at all. They are plantmen. Although they are basically humanoid, with rounded shoulders and shaggy heads, long strands of green and brown moss hang from their arms, torsos, and faces. Shelf-mushrooms and other fungoid growths sprout from their bodies, and many sport festering sores. Though the mudmen are kind, their smell is earthy and enormous. Tim meets sixteen of the Fagonarders, and though he knows that the tribe must have some women as well, he doubts that there are any children. The mutant mudmen are becoming part of the swamp. They are a dying tribe.

As was stated earlier, the only word the mudmen seem to know is "hile," but they can palaver with one another in a mixture of grunts, clicks, chittering bird noises, and growls. In order to communicate with Tim, their HELMS-MAN (who seems to be their best actor) uses a series of gestures and signs. Although they are mutants, the mudmen of the Fagonard are extremely intelligent. Not only have they developed a relationship with the Fagonard DRAGON (they give her offerings of boarheads and other such delicacies) but they also have a sense of their own destiny. Sadly they know that they will die in the coming STARKBLAST.

As a parting gift, the Fagonarders give Tim the NORTH CENTRAL POSI-TRONICS Portable Guidance Module named DARIA, who becomes Tim's computerized guide as well as his friend. Given the mudmen's respect for gunslingers and the ELD, CONSTANT READERS cannot help but wonder whether the tribe took an oath to Arthur Eld in the longago, much like the mutant CHILDREN OF RODERICK. W:193, W:198–216, W:220, W:226–27, W:229, W:256

BLACK SILK TOP HAT/HELMSMAN: The helmsman of the mudmen's boat can be recognized by the black silk top hat he wears, the red ribbon of which is so long that it trails over one of his bare shoulders. Long strands of green and brown moss swing from his scrawny arms; more hangs from his cheeks and straggles from his chin. Tim thinks that if the helmsman had not been born in the Fagonard, he might have been handsome. He is broad-shouldered and sturdily built, and though his hands have six fingers, his eyes are bright with intelligence. Unfortunately, he *was* born in the Fagonard. Hence, he is afflicted by the skin diseases common there. Just above his right nipple is an enormous infected sore, which Tim sees burst in a spray of pus and blood. This wound births a spider the size of a robin's egg and a slick mass of throbbing eggs. Not surprisingly, Tim has to choke back a need to vomit as the helmsman tosses the spider away and scoops out the eggs that the spider had left inside of him.

Not only is Black Silk Top Hat the helmsman of the mudmen's boat, he is also the individual who calls up the Fagonard DRAGON to accept the tribe's offering of a boar's head. (They carry this offering on the boat's sail-less mast.) He beckons the beast with a sharp, hooting cry, followed by several rapid clicks. It is also the Helmsman who decides to give Tim the

NORTH CENTRAL POSITRONICS Portable Guidance Module named DARIA. W:204–16 *(207 described)*
CREW: These four men (along with their HELMSMAN), rescue TIM ROSS when he is trapped on a tussock in the watery land of the Fagonard. Although their boat is cobbled together from wood-scraps and rides low in the water, it floats well enough to take Tim across the swamp. Their paddles are made of an orange wood which Tim has never seen before. W:201
HEADMAN: The mudmen's headman is the tallest member of the tribe. He communicates to TIM that the tribe will die in the coming STARK-BLAST. W:203, W:212–213, W:256
TALL, BALD, AND TOOTHLESS: At the request of the HELMSMAN, Tall, Bald, and Toothless runs to the mudmen's camp. He brings back a waterskin and a small purse of the finest, smoothest leather Tim has ever seen. The Helmsman gives the purse to Tim. It turns out to be the NORTH CENTRAL POSITRONICS Portable Guidance Module DARIA. W:202–26 *(209 described)*
TWO TRIBESMEN WHOM HELMSMAN SENDS TO GET FOOD: W:209
SUCKERBUGS: These blood-drinking bugs swarm TIM as he travels through the FAGONARD. While Tim is following ARMANEETA, he is so mesmerized by her loveliness that he does not feel the insects' stings though they leave bloody splats on his skin. W:193

FANNIN, RICHARD
See WALTER: WALTER'S ALIASES: R.F.

FARADAY, GEORGE
See CALLA BRYN STURGIS CHARACTERS: ROONTS

FARADAY, GEORGINA
See CALLA BRYN STURGIS CHARACTERS: FARMERS (SMALLHOLD): FARADAY, NEIL

FARADAY, NEIL
See CALLA BRYN STURGIS CHARACTERS: FARMERS (SMALLHOLD)

FARDEN, WALTER
See WALTER

FARDO
See CORT

FARMER, HALF-MUTANT
See MUTANTS: HUMAN MUTANTS (MINOR MUTATIONS)

**FARSON, JOHN (THE GOOD MAN)
When Roland was a boy, the harrier and stage-robber John Farson began to gain followers in the west. Originally from either GARLAN or DESOY, the Good

Man opposed the inherited wealth and power of the aristocratic gunslingers as well as what he claimed were the unfair practices of the AFFILIATION, which supported them. Many were attracted to the Good Man's cause, including failed gunslingers, such as the BIG COFFIN HUNTER, ELDRED JONAS. In *The Gunslinger,* we saw GILEAD's head cook, HAX, hanged for his allegiance to Farson.

Despite his quasi-religious status, the Good Man was in actuality a madman who wanted nothing more than to bring death and destruction to MID-WORLD. A bandit who justified his thefts and murders with talk of democracy and equality, he had no intention of setting up a democratic government in place of Mid-World's reigning order. Like the CRIMSON KING, whose *sigul* he used and whom he ultimately served, Farson gloried in chaos, and chaos and destruction were exactly what he brought to the civilized lands Roland knew as a boy. At the beginning of *Wizard and Glass,* Farson had MAERLYN'S GRAPEFRUIT, one of Mid-World's magic seeing-spheres. Luckily for IN-WORLD, Roland stole it from him, though Roland paid a great price for this theft.

Despite the fact that Hax equated him with Jesus, there was little of the savior in the Good Man. According to HIGH SHERIFF HUGH PEAVY of DEBARIA, one of Farson's favorite tricks was kidnapping for ransom. His harriers were probably responsible for destroying the town of BEELIE after the militia closed their outpost there, though some of Debaria's inhabitants—including Deputy STROTHER—refused to believe that the Good Man was responsible for that particular evil. Late in his career Farson was known for his cruelty. According to ELDRED JONAS, the Good Man was dangerously insane. One of his favorite pastimes was playing polo with human heads as the balls.

Unlike the gunslingers, who knew that the OLD ONES' weapons were too dangerous to use, Farson and his men resurrected the Old People's weapons and tanks and planned to use them in their final battle against the Affiliation. Luckily, many of these pieces of machinery were destroyed by Roland, CUTHBERT ALLGOOD, and ALAIN JOHNS during their HAMBRY adventures. Ultimately, however, Farson and his men triumphed. At the battle of JERICHO HILL, they killed the last of Roland's gunslinger-companions, including our beloved Cuthbert Allgood.

One passage in *The Gunslinger* hints that Farson was actually STEVEN DESCHAIN's sorcerer, MARTEN BROADCLOAK, who in turn was none other than Roland's nemesis, WALTER O'DIM. However, by the end of the Dark Tower series we discover that Farson—though mad as the Crimson King himself—was not another incarnation of the demonic R.F., but one of his many pawns.

I:101–2, I:105, I:111, II:126, III:242, IV:110, IV:111, IV:142, IV:149 *(bandit who talks of "equality" and "democracy"),* IV:151 *(began as harrier/stage-robber in Garlan and Desoy),* IV:163 *(in Cressia. Speaks out against "class slavery"),* IV:164, IV:174–78, IV:183, IV:194, IV:196 *(and "Good Men"),* IV:199, IV:206, IV:262–63, IV:277, IV:302–3 *(brings Death),* IV:344 *(indirect reference),* IV:348, IV:351 *(attacks nobility, chivalry, ancestor worship. Will use robots),* IV:368, IV:378 *(insane, plays polo with human heads),* IV:386, IV:402, IV:404 *(eye sigul; Farson described and compared to Lord Perth),* IV:421, IV:422–25, IV:430–33, IV:438 *(and pink talisman),* IV:443, IV:470, IV:487–88, IV:489, IV:490, IV:496 *(Farson's soldiers),* IV:501, IV:518,

IV:519 *(and Horsemen's Association)*, IV:520, IV:522, IV:531, IV:538, IV:543, IV:580, IV:583 *(hand-clasping* sigul*)*, IV:584, IV:585, IV:589 *(his lieutenants)*, IV:590, IV:597, IV:601 *(the last of his men goes screaming into thinny)*, IV:609, IV:619, IV:621 *(Roland sees Farson's triumph in Wizard's glass)*, IV:623, IV:632, V:171, V:612 *(The Good Man)*, VII:135, VII:172, VII:174, VII:528, VII:550, W:36, W:37, W:39, W:40 *(land pirate)*, W:41, W:56, W:102, W:103, W:131 *(Good Man and the actions of the Covenanter)*

FARSON'S MEN:

> **FARSON'S NEPHEW:** Disguised as a wandering singer, this young man smuggled a poisoned knife into GILEAD. The knife was meant to kill STEVEN DESCHAIN. IV:621

> **GRISSOM/GRISSOM'S MEN/BLUE-FACED BARBARIANS:** Grissom was the leader of Farson's men during the battle of JERICHO HILL, where the AFFILIATION was defeated. Grissom's men are described as "blue-faced barbarians." V:169 *(Grissom's men)*, V:170, V:171 *(blue-faced)*, V:410 *(blue faces)*, VII:174 *(Walter fought with the "blue-faced barbarians")*

> > **GRISSOM'S SON:** V:169–70 *(eagle-eyed)*

> **HENDRICKS, RODNEY:** IV:590–93, IV:594 *(general)*, IV:596–98 *(present for battle; 598 swallowed by thinny)*

> **LATIGO, GEORGE:** One of Farson's chief lieutenants. IV:368, IV:371, IV:378 *(hired Big Coffin Hunters)*, IV:381, IV:404, IV:405, IV:421–25 *(blond, from Northern In-World)*, IV:470, IV:484, IV:501, IV:523, IV:528, IV:542, IV:583, IV:584, IV:589–91 *(589 we learn his first name)*, IV:592–94 *(and his men)*, IV:596–600 *(600 walks into thinny)*, IV:623, V:576 *(men)*

> **RAINES:** Bugler. IV:591, IV:596–98 *(not named, but present for battle)*

FARSON SUPPORTERS

> **BETWEEN GILEAD AND BEESFORD-ON-ARTEN (GENERAL):** In *The Wind Through the Keyhole,* we learn that in the scrubland towns beyond Gilead, many of the people are mutants, and many of them support The Good Man, John Farson. When they see Roland and JAIME DeCURRY riding by in the train SMA' TOOT, they point at an invisible eye at the center of their foreheads, indicating their support for the Good Man. Although some of GABRIELLE DESCHAIN's relatives still live in Beesford-on-Arten this does not increase the support for the gunslingers in the area. W:41

> **FAT MAN WITH ROCK:** Outside BEESFORD-ON-ARTEN, a fat man threw a rock at ROLAND and JAIME's train, SMA' TOOT. As the rock bounced off of the closed stable-car door, the man grinned, grabbed his crotch, and waddled away. W:41

FAT MAN WITH ROCK
See FARSON: FARSON SUPPORTERS

FEATHEREX (GRAND FEATHEREX)
The Grand Featherex is a winged being that supposedly lives in the mythical Kingdom of GARLAN. Like the stork, the Featherex brings babies. In *The Eyes of the Dragon,* we learn that this creature is related to the phoenix.
II:66, IV:151

FEDIC CHARACTERS

The unfortunate residents of FEDIC were annihilated by the Red Death more than two dozen centuries before the WOLVES began invading the BORDER-LAND CALLAS. SUSANNAH DEAN's demonic possessor, MIA (who haunted Fedic before she was incarnated in a human body by WALTER and his cohorts), describes the people of Fedic as stubborn. They must have been. Their town was caught between the haunted CASTLE DISCORDIA, the evil FEDIC DOGAN, and the DEVIL'S ARSE, a crack in the earth in which monsters bred. By the time Mia haunted Fedic, most of the women there were already giving birth to monsters, thanks to the poisons left by the GREAT OLD ONES. However, the one perfect baby born into that town—named MICHAEL—sowed the seeds of Mia's great child hunger and led to her Faustian pact with WALTER and the WARRIORS OF THE SCARLET EYE.

ANDY LOOK-ALIKE ROBOT: *See* NORTH CENTRAL POSITRONICS
BABY MICHAEL: *See* MIA
　FATHER: *See* MIA
　MOTHER: *See* MIA
DEAD ROBOT: *See* NORTH CENTRAL POSITRONICS
HUCKSTER ROBOT: *See* NORTH CENTRAL POSITRONICS
RESIDENTS OF FEDIC: VI:243, VI:244

FEEMALO
See WARRIORS OF THE SCARLET EYE: CASSE ROI RUSSE: HUMANS: FEEMALO/FIMALO/FUMALO

FEENY, ANDREW
See DEAN, SUSANNAH: ODETTA HOLMES'S ASSOCIATES

FELDON, AMY
See TULL

FELICIA
See DELGADO, SUSAN

FENNS
See MAINE CHARACTERS

FERMAN, ED
See KING, STEPHEN

FILARO, RUDIN
See WALTER: WALTER'S ALIASES: R.F.

FIMALO
See WARRIORS OF THE SCARLET EYE: CASSE ROI RUSSE: HUMANS: FEEMALO/FIMALO/FUMALO

FINLI
See TAHEEN: WEASEL-HEADED TAHEEN

FISH GUARDIAN
    See GUARDIANS OF THE BEAM

FLAGG, RANDALL
    See WALTER: WALTER'S ALIASES: R.F.

FLAHERTY, CONOR
    See WARRIORS OF THE SCARLET EYE: DIXIE PIG CHARACTERS/
FEDIC CHARACTERS: HUMANS

FLIP, MR.
    See CALLAHAN, FATHER DONALD FRANK: 'SALEM'S LOT CHARAC-
TERS

FOOT SOLDIERS OF THE CRIMSON KING
    See WARRIORS OF THE SCARLET EYE

FORCE, THE
    See MANNI: OVER, THE

FORT LEE REGISTER AMERICAN
    See CALLAHAN, FATHER DONALD FRANK: CALLAHAN'S HIDDEN
HIGHWAYS ASSOCIATES

FORTUNA
    See SERENITY, SISTERS OF

FORTY
Like NINETEEN and NINETY-NINE, forty is a magic number. In hobospeak, it
refers to the bus that will take you as far away as possible. If you live in NEW YORK
CITY and buy a ticket to FAIRBANKS, ALASKA, you are taking the forty bus.
    V:428

FOUNDING FATHERS
    See TET CORPORATION

FOYLE, FRANKIE
    See CALLAHAN, FATHER DONALD FRANK: 'SALEM'S LOT CHARAC-
TERS

FRANCESCA (AND ROBERT)
    See HAMBRY CHARACTERS: HAMBRY LOVERS

FRANK
    See PUBES; *see also* CALLAHAN, FATHER DONALD FRANK

FRANKS, JOANNE
    See PIPER SCHOOL CHARACTERS

FREDERICKS, TOMMY
See DEAN, HENRY: HENRY DEAN'S KA-TET

FREDDY TWO-STEP
See SKIN-MAN: SKIN-MAN'S VICTIMS: JEFFERSON RANCH

FREEDOM RIDERS
See DEAN, SUSANNAH: ODETTA HOLMES AND THE CIVIL RIGHTS
MOVEMENT

FREEMAN, NATHAN
See DEAN, SUSANNAH: ODETTA HOLMES'S ASSOCIATES

FRIENDLY FOLK
The Friends were a sect of the OLD PEOPLE. Like the MANNI, they spoke using
the terms "thee" and "thou." SUSAN DELGADO may have been descended from
them, since her family used these words in their daily speech. The Friendly Folk
remained in IN-WORLD throughout Roland's youth.
   IV:250

FRIGHTENED WOMAN
See WIND THROUGH THE KEYHOLE: CHARACTERS MET BETWEEN
GREEN PALACE AND RIVER WHYE

FRYE, KELLIN
See DEBARIA CHARACTERS: SHERIFF'S OFFICE

FRYE, VIKKA
See DEBARIA CHARACTERS: SHERIFF'S OFFICE: FRYE, KELLIN

FULCHER, ANDY
See KING, STEPHEN

FUMALO
See WARRIORS OF THE SCARLET EYE: CASSE ROI RUSSE: HUMANS:
FEEMALO/FIMALO/FUMALO

FURTH
See GUTTENBERG, FURTH, AND PATEL

G

GABBY

Gabby was the sarcastic nickname which the gunslinger apprentices' tutor, VAN-NAY, gave to Roland. The name came from Roland's childhood habit of being silent for prolonged periods.

VII:20–21

GAI COCKNIF EN YOM, MR.

See TET CORPORATION: FOUNDING FATHERS: DEEPNEAU, AARON

GALE, DOROTHY

See WIZARD OF OZ

GAMBLER AND WOMAN

See SKIN-MAN: SKIN-MAN'S VICTIMS

GAN (VOICE OF THE BEAM, SPIRIT OF THE DARK TOWER)

According to MID-WORLD's oldest legends, Gan arose from the magical soup of creation known as the GREATER DISCORDIA, or the PRIM.[4] From his navel, he spun the universe, and once it had spun into the shape he desired, he set it rolling with his finger. This forward movement was time. After creating the world, Gan moved on. The universe would have plunged into the void had not the great TURTLE caught it and balanced it upon his back. And it is here the universe still sits, poised upon the Turtle's shell.[5]

The great god Gan is actually the animating spirit of the DARK TOWER. Although this smoky-black edifice and its spiral of electric-blue windows may appear to be made of stone and glass, it is, in actuality, a huge living body. Just as the ancient myths of Mid-World maintain that the world spun from Gan's navel, so both the BEAMS and the red ROSES of CAN'-KA NO REY spun out from the Tower. Together, Tower, Beams, and Roses form a living, singing force field which sits at the heart of END-WORLD, and it is toward this energy field that Roland, the last of the line of ELD, is inevitably drawn.

Gan is the Mid-World god most closely linked to the voice of the WHITE. As JAKE CHAMBERS says while in a trance state, "So speaks Gan, and in the voice of angels. Gan denies the CAN-TOI; with the merry heart of the guiltless he denies the CRIMSON KING and Discordia itself." In the prayer which Roland utters over Jake Chambers's grave, Gan is called upon to raise the dead from the darkness of the earth and to surround them with light.

Although Gan is a god, and though (as the spirit of the Tower) he rules the destiny of the multiverse, he seems to have a particular interest in Roland and the line of Eld. When Roland mounts Gan's steps in the final book of the Dark

---

4. In some variations of the legend, Gan was said to rise from either the void or the sea.

5. Interestingly, in the novel *It,* the Turtle claims that he created the universe on a day he had a bellyache. Hence, all of the evils we experience are the result of trapped wind.

Tower series, what he sees in Gan's hundreds of rooms forces him to reflect upon his life, and how (if he gets the chance) he must choose to live differently.

In our world, the voice of Gan is often transmitted through artists and writers, who are called *kas-ka Gan,* which means one of the prophets, or singers, of Gan. For our *tet,* the most important of the KEYSTONE EARTH *kas-ka Gan* is the writer STEPHEN KING.

VI:294, VI:295 *("Gan bore the world and the world moved on"),* VI:298, VI:318 *("So speaks Gan along the Beam"),* VI:320, VI:321, VI:353 *(Gan the maker),* VI:380, VI:394, VII:4, VII:33 *(birthed universe from his navel),* VII:34 *(voice of Gan, voice of the Beam),* VII:129, VII:168, VII:291, VII:295 *(Wolf-Elephant is Gan's Beam),* VII:296 *(Beam),* VII:300 *(Beam),* VII:301 *(Beam),* VII:303 *(Beam),* VII:305, VII:306, VII:345, VII:348, VII:368, VII:371, VII:380, VII:388, VII:406, VII:447, VII:456, VII:457–58, VII:459, VII:474, VII:504, VII:505, VII:512, VII:513, VII:542, VII:543, VII:585, VII:607, VII:609, VII:638, VII:757 *(Gan's Gateway),* VII:798, VII:820, VII:821, VII:822, VII:823, VII:827, W:189, W:247 *(Gan's blood),* W:274

BLACK MAN IN JAIL CELL: While in 1999 NEW YORK, JAKE CHAMBERS has a vision of a black man in an OXFORD, MISSISSIPPI, jail cell. The man, who resembles a wizard in a fairy tale, has a toothbrush mustache, wears gold-rimmed glasses, and is listening to a radio, which is issuing a list of our world's dead. Jake thinks that this image was sent to him by the DARK TOWER, and that the man may be a human incarnation of Gan. However, the black man in question also resembles a younger version of MOSES CARVER, SUSANNAH DEAN's godfather, who is also a founding member of the TET CORPORATION. VI:320–21

GAN'S BEAM: Gan's Beam is the ELEPHANT-WOLF Beam. *For page references, see* GUARDIANS OF THE BEAM

GAN'S GATEWAY: The yellow hearts of the CAN'-KA NO REY ROSES (roses which are identical to a certain flower in NEW YORK CITY's Vacant LOT) are called Gan's Gateways. *For page references, see* ROSE

GANGLI, DR.
   See CAN-TOI

GAN'S BLACKBIRDS
   See APPENDIX I

GARBER
   See HAMBRY CHARACTERS: HORSEMEN'S ASSOCIATION

GARFIELD, BOBBY
   See BREAKERS: BRAUTIGAN, TED

GARFIELD, LIZ
   See BREAKERS: BRAUTIGAN, TED: GARFIELD, BOBBY

GARMA
   See MUTANTS: CHILDREN OF RODERICK

GARTON, WILLIAM
See CALLAHAN, FATHER DONALD FRANK: CALLAHAN AND THE HITLER BROTHERS

GARUDA
See GUARDIANS OF THE BEAM: EAGLE GUARDIAN

GASHER
See GRAYS: GRAY HIGH COMMAND

GASKIE
See TAHEEN: OTHER TAHEEN

GEE (JEY)
See TAHEEN: BIRDMEN

GERBER, CAROL
See BREAKERS: BRAUTIGAN, TED

GHOSTS IN THE MACHINES
See NORTH CENTRAL POSITRONICS: BLAINE

GILEAD CORPSES (FARMERS AND THEIR FAMILIES)
When Roland was a boy, STARKBLASTS used to sweep down upon the GREAT WOODS north of NEW CANAAN once or twice a year. Once he even saw cartloads of frozen bodies being drawn down GILEAD ROAD. (They had been frozen by the storm.) Roland assumed that these farming families didn't have BILLY-BUMBLERS to warn them of the impending disaster.
W:17

GILEAD'S COUNCIL OF ELD
In *The Wind Through the Keyhole*, WIDOW SMACK tells TIM ROSS that when the COVENANT MAN is not at his hobby of collecting taxes (a job which she states is no better than licking the tears from the faces of poor working folk) he's an advisor to the palace lords who call themselves the Council of Eld. The Widow does not believe that these men have any blood connection to ARTHUR ELD at all, although some of them are probably GUNSLINGERS. The Covenant Man's cruelty gives the Council of Eld a bad name, which is exactly what the Covenant Man wants. (He is, after all, another incarnation of WALTER O'DIM.)
W:169

GILEAD BIG BUGS (OWNERS OF DEBARIA SALT COMBYNE)
According to WILL WEGG, Debaria's salt mines were actually owned by big bugs in Gilead.
W:275

GILEAD LADY FRIENDLY WITH WIDOW SMACK
See WIDOW SMACK, *listed separately*

GILEAD, LORDS OF

According to the WIDOW SMACK, the evil tax-collecting COVENANT MAN serves both the lords and gunslingers of Gilead. We can assume that at least some of these lords are the cavaliers and perfumed diplomats that Roland speaks of so derisively in *The Gunslinger*. Unfortunately, some of them are also probably gunslingers.

I:159 *(2003 edition)*, I:116–17 *(2003 edition)*; W:170

GILEAD STABLEHAND

When Roland was a young boy, this man was badly burned in a kerosene fire. Like the patient-prisoners of the LITTLE SISTERS OF ELURIA, he was suspended above his bed rather than being placed directly upon the sheets. He eventually died, but only after two days of shrieking.

E:160

GILEAD'S WHITE AMMIES

The white ammies were the nurses who served Gilead palace. After Roland's old teacher CORT became confused and incontinent, they were responsible for his care. However, until he was sent to DEBARIA by his father, Roland insisted on nursing Cort himself.

W:36, W:38

GILEAD WHORE

After his coming-of-age battle with CORT, Roland went to one of GILEAD's brothels and lost his virginity to this prostitute.

I:174, IV:107–12, VII:824

GINELLI
See BALAZAR, ENRICO: BALAZAR'S MEN

GIRL SCOUTS
See DEAN, SUSANNAH: SUSANNAH'S PRESENT ASSOCIATES

GIRL WITH BODACIOUS TA-TAS
See CHAMBERS, ELMER

GLICK, DANNY
See CALLAHAN, FATHER DONALD FRANK: 'SALEM'S LOT CHARACTERS

GLUE BOY
See ALLGOOD, CUTHBERT

GODOSH
See PRIM

GODS OF CREATION
See GODS OF MID-WORLD

GODS OF MID-WORLD

Mid-World is home to many gods and goddesses, and it is from these older faiths that the MAN JESUS must win his followers. Although some, like LADY ORIZA, are described to us, most of these supernatural beings remain fascinating glimmers, half-seen, half-imagined. What follows is a list of the gods that are mentioned in the Dark Tower series. For additional information about Mid-World's folklore, see the following subentries: For Mid-World heroes and antiheroes, see ELD, ARTHUR, and CRIMSON KING. For demons and devils, see DEMON ELEMENTALS and DEMONS/SPIRITS/DEVILS. For figures from Mid-World's folklore, see MID-WORLD FOLKLORE.

V:10, V:313 *(Callahan calls Calla gods "second-rate")*, V:467 *(some listed)*, W:196

AMOCO, THE THUNDER GOD

ASMODEUS: E:147

APON: *See* OLD STAR, *listed below*

BAAL: E:147

BESSA: When things go according to plan, the people of Mid-World thank Bessa and GAN. We don't find out anything else about this god. VII:371

BIG SKY DADDY: Some tribes of SLOW MUTANTS call the father of the MAN JESUS "Big Sky Daddy." V:475

BUFFALO STAR: Buffalo Star is one of the many gods of Mid-World. Roland once killed a preacher of Buffalo Star. V:467

 PREACHER OF BUFFALO STAR: V:467

CAN-TAH: *See* CAN-TAH *and* GUARDIANS OF THE BEAM: TURTLE GUARDIAN

CASSIOPEIA: In one of Mid-World's folktales, Cassiopeia causes the breakup between OLD MOTHER (South Star) and OLD STAR (North Star). Old Mother (LYDIA) caught Old Star (APON) flirting with this sweet young thing. Cassiopeia found the whole affair quite humorous. III:36–37

CHLOE: According to a Mid-World prayer said over the bodies of the dead (a prayer translated either from High Speech or from the MANNI tongue), the goddess Chloe gives strength to those who have passed over. VII:474

FORCE, THE: *See* MANNI: OVER, THE

GAN: *See* GAN, *listed separately*

GODS OF CREATION: VI:12

GRAY DICK: *See* ORIZA, LADY, *listed separately*

GRENFALL, LORD: *See* ORIZA, LADY, *listed separately*

GUARDIANS OF THE BEAM: *See* GUARDIANS OF THE BEAM, *listed separately*

LYDIA: *See* OLD MOTHER, *listed below*

LYDIA'S DIPPER: *See* OLD MOTHER, *listed below*

MAN JESUS: This is a Mid-World term for Jesus. Although Christianity exists in Roland's universe, it is not the dominant religion. CALLA BRYN STURGIS is predominantly Christian thanks to the efforts of FATHER CALLAHAN, but in other towns Christianity has been blended with pagan faiths. Father Callahan likes to call Mid-World's other deities "second-rate gods." The women of SERENITY follow the Man Jesus. V:2, V:6, V:7, V:14, V:27,

V:39, V:143, V:146, V:224, V:311, V:318, V:325, V:376, V:398, V:475, V:477, V:484, V:601, V:647, VII:388, VII:617, W:49, W:164, W:231, W:274

MORPHIA: Morphia calls herself the Daughter of Sleep. Like SELENA, Daughter of the Moon, she is one of the female incarnations of Death. VII:460

NIS: Nis is both the dream-god of Mid-World and the name for the land of sleep and dreams. Nis is also the name of the CRIMSON KING's horse. V:500, V:549

**OLD MOTHER (LYDIA, SOUTH STAR): Old Mother is Mid-World's South Star and is an important fixture of the night sky. According to an old legend, Old Mother was married to APON, also known as OLD STAR. The universe was created when Old Mother and Old Star had a crockery-throwing fight over Old Star's flirtation with CASSIOPEIA. The other gods stepped in to break up the row but the two of them haven't spoken since. As a flirtatious gesture of respect, Roland calls AUNT TALITHA of RIVER CROSSING by this name. In the 2003 version of *The Gunslinger,* Roland looks up and sees Old Mother in the desert sky. III:12, III:36–37, III:86, III:181, III:231 *(Aunt Talitha),* III:232 *(Aunt Talitha),* III:239 *(Aunt Talitha),* III:250 *(Aunt Talitha),* IV:33, IV:98, IV:105, IV:154, V:234, VI:250, VII:723, VII:764, VII:765 *(brightest),* VII:766, VII:767, VII:770, VII:802, VII:826, W:91, W:215

LYDIA'S DIPPER: Mid-World's term for the Big Dipper. VII:724

**OLD STAR (NORTH STAR, APON): Old Star (also called North Star) is another name for the wickedly flirtatious husband of OLD MOTHER (South Star). The two of them had a knock-down-drag-out fight over his tête-à-tête with CASSIOPEIA. The universe was created from the crockery they threw at each other, but the two of them haven't spoken since. In the 2003 *Gunslinger,* Roland sees Old Star in the sky. III:12, III:36–37, III:86, III:179, III:181, IV:33, IV:98, IV:105, IV:166, IV:531, V:234, VI:250, VII:723, VII:802, VII:826, W:91, W:215

ORIZA, LADY: *See* ORIZA, LADY, *listed separately*

OVER, THE: *See* MANNI, *listed separately*

PRIM: *See* PRIM, *listed separately*

RAF: Raf is a magical being who has wings on his legs and/or feet. He seems to be similar to Mercury, the winged messenger of the Roman gods. V:173

SELENA: Selena calls herself the Daughter of the Moon. Like MORPHIA, the Daughter of Sleep, she is one of the female incarnations of Death. VII:460

SEMINON, LORD: *See* ORIZA, LADY, *listed separately*

S'MANA: According to a Mid-World death prayer (either translated from High Speech or from the MANNI tongue), the forgiving glance of S'mana heals the hearts of the dead. VII:474

SOUTH STAR: *See* OLD MOTHER, *listed above*

GOLDMAN, RICHARD
See GUTTENBERG, FURTH, AND PATEL: DAMASCUS, TRUDY: KIDZ-PLAY

GOLDOVER, SYLVIA
See DEAN, HENRY

GOOD MAN, THE
See FARSON, JOHN

GOODMAN, ANDREW
See DEAN, SUSANNAH: ODETTA HOLMES AND THE CIVIL RIGHTS
MOVEMENT: VOTER REGISTRATION BOYS

GOOD-MIND FOLK, THE
See TET CORPORATION

GOODMOUTH KING
See WARRIORS OF THE SCARLET EYE: CASSE ROI RUSSE: HUMANS:
FEEMALO/FIMALO/FUMALO

GRAHAM, TOMMY
See TOWER, CALVIN

GRANDFATHER FLEAS
See VAMPIRES: TYPE ONE (THE GRANDFATHERS)

GRANDFATHERS
See VAMPIRES: TYPE ONE (THE GRANDFATHERS)

GRAND FEATHEREX
See FEATHEREX

GRAN-PERE JAFFORDS
See JAFFORDS FAMILY

GRANT, DONALD
See KING, STEPHEN

GRAPEFRUIT, THE
See MAERLYN'S RAINBOW

GRAY DICK
See ORIZA, LADY

GRAYS
The Grays, whom we meet in *The Waste Lands,* are one of the two bands of
harriers warring over the city of LUD. They are the sworn enemies of the
PUBES. Although the Grays live in the mazes and old silos below the eastern
part of the city and the Pubes live aboveground in CITY NORTH, the Grays are
the more powerful. With the help of BLAINE, the city's mad computer brain,
they have convinced the Pubes that they have to appease the vindictive and flesh-
hungry GHOSTS IN THE MACHINES with a daily ritual of human sacrifice.
The Grays signal this horrid event by playing the god-drums (actually no more
than the backbeat of the ZZ Top song "Velcro Fly") over the city's loudspeakers.

Originally, the Grays were the city's besiegers. They were led by DAVID QUICK, the outlaw prince. In our story, the Grays are led by ANDREW QUICK, also known as TICK-TOCK, who is David Quick's great-grandson.

Tick-Tock and his band don't really understand why the god-drums work, but are eager to try to control more of Lud's computers. In the end, the computers (à la Blaine) destroy both of Lud's warring factions.

The easiest way to tell the difference between Pubes and Grays is by checking the color of their headscarves. The Pubes wear blue ones while the Grays wear yellow ones. The Grays also have a taste for young boys.

III:232, III:238, III:240, III:244–45, III:298, III:304, III:307, III:309, III:318, III:321, III:322, III:350–61 *(high command)*, III:362, III:365–72, III:373–82, III:388, III:403, III:411, IV:57, V:135, V:178, VI:152

GRAY HIGH COMMAND:

BLACK-HAIRED WOMAN: This unnamed woman has an annoying laugh, so TICK-TOCK throws a knife at her. The blade stabs her in the chest and she dies in front of JAKE. III:352–53, III:356

BRANDON: Brandon is a short, bandy-legged man. III:353–61, III:365–72, III:374, IV:646

COPPERHEAD: Copperhead is a tall, bespectacled man in a white silk shirt and black silk trousers. He looks like a college professor in a late-nineteenth-century *Punch* cartoon. III:313, III:365–74

GASHER: The first time Roland's *ka-tet* meets Gasher, he is wearing patched green velvet pants and looks like a dying, but dangerous, buccaneer. Since he is in the late stages of the nasty venereal disease known as mandrus, his face is covered with oozing sores. Gasher has gray eyes, and is bald except for a few black hairs that stick out of his head like porcupine quills. Gasher is responsible for kidnapping JAKE CHAMBERS on the city side of LUD BRIDGE. His former lover is named HOOTS. III:296–303 *(takes Jake)*, III:304–7, III:308, III:312–14, III:314–16 *(followed by Roland)*, III:323 *(indirect)*, III:325–28, III:328–31 *(followed by Roland)*, III:334–39, III:340, III:341, III:350–61, III:363, III:365–72, III:375, III:383, III:402, IV:23, IV:28, IV:88 *(indirectly compared to Charlie the Choo-Choo)*, IV:100–101 *(Eddie's bulldozer dream)*, IV:646, V:44, V:55, V:165, V:187, V:204, V:493, VI:184, VI:269, VI:337, VI:400, VII:502, W:3

    GASHER'S FATHER: When he died, he was so rotten with mandrus that the dogs wouldn't even eat him. III:355

HOOTS: Hoots is GASHER's former lover. When we see him in the CRADLE OF THE GRAYS, he is a tall skinny man in a black suit. He has a terrible, itchy rash on his face, caused by mandrus. III:338, III:352–61, III:365–72, IV:646, V:44, V:187, VI:269

QUICK, DAVID: Also known as the outlaw prince, David Quick was the original leader of the Grays. He was also the harrier who organized the sundry outlaw bands besieging the city of LUD. In *The Waste Lands*, Roland's *ka-tet* finds his giant, mummified body in a wrecked German Focke-Wulf airplane a few days' walk outside the city. David Quick was TICK-TOCK's great-grandfather. III:241, III:244, III:273–75, III:355–56, III:358 *(plane)*, III:381, III:410, IV:22 *(dead harrier)*, V:265, W:47

TICK-TOCK (ANDREW QUICK): Tick-Tock is the leader of the Grays at the time of Roland, JAKE, and OY's little visit to the CRADLE OF THE GRAYS. He is also the great-grandson of DAVID QUICK, the outlaw prince. Tick-Tock reminds Jake Chambers of the Morlocks from H. G. Wells's novel *The Time Machine*. This is probably due more to Tick-Tock's sense of cruelty than to his actual appearance. With his heavily muscled upper body, long dirty gray-blond hair, and green eyes, he is one of LUD's few healthy, vibrant inhabitants. In fact, Jake thinks he looks like a cross between a Viking and a giant from a child's fairy tale. Tick-Tock's name comes from the coffin-shaped clock around his neck. The clock runs backward. III:298, III:305, III:313, III:314, III:326, III:327, III:336, III:338–39, III:351–61, III:365–72, III:373, III:375, III:381, III:385–90, III:394, IV:28, IV:645–47 *(in Oz; killed by Roland's ka-tet)*, IV:663, V:36, V:44, V:55, V:187, V:204, V:535, V:573 *(as Morlock)*, VI:269, VII:502, W:3, W:31

TICK-TOCK'S FAMILY AND FORMER ASSOCIATES:

> **DEWLAP:** Once upon a time, a scrawny old man named Dewlap worked the cider presses located in a park on the far western side of LUD. In the later chaos of that city, even the cider houses were probably destroyed. By the time our tale takes place, Dewlap and his companions are no more than memories in the damaged brain of the injured Andrew Quick (Tick-Tock). III:386

> **FATHER:** After he was scalped by JAKE's bullet, Tick-Tock has a memory of his father taking him to see the cider presses of Lud. III:386

TILLY: Tilly is one of the two female members of the Grays High Command. (Unfortunately, Tick-Tock murders the other one.) She looks like a red-haired female truck driver. III:353–61, III:365–72, III:373–74, IV:646

OTHER GRAYS: After Blaine sets off the city's alarms, Roland and Jake see a number of unnamed Grays fleeing through the gang's kitchens. III:378

> **SCRUFFY MAN IN KITCHEN:** Blaine kills this man by dropping open an oven door and directing a blast of blue-white fire at his head. III:376

GREAT OLD ONES
See OLD ONES

GREAT ONES
See DEMONS/SPIRITS/DEVILS: TODASH DEMONS

GREATER DISCORDIA
See PRIM

GREEN FOLK
See ELURIA CHARACTERS

GREEN KING
See WALTER

GREENCLOAKS
See WOLVES

GRENFALL, LORD
   See ORIZA, LADY

GRISSOM
   See FARSON, JOHN: FARSON'S MEN

**GUARDIANS OF THE BEAM (TOTEMS OF THE BEAM)
In *The Waste Lands,* Roland drew a metaphysical map of MID-WORLD. The map was circular and looked like a clockface, but its circumference contained twelve X's rather than twelve numbers. Each X designated a PORTAL into, and out of, Mid-World. The twelve Portals were connected by six magnetic BEAMS. Each Beam, in turn, was guarded by two animal totems, or GUARDIANS. At the center of this map, in the place where all the Beams crossed, was the Thirteenth Gate or DARK TOWER, the linchpin of the macroverse.

During Roland's youth, many people maintained that the Beams and Portals were natural. However, when Roland was a little boy, HAX (the traitorous cook we met in *The Gunslinger*) told him a strange story about the framework of the universe. He believed that the Tower, Beams, and Guardians were man-made, not naturally or divinely created. They were the handiwork of the GREAT OLD ONES and were manufactured as a penance for the sins those ancient people had committed against the earth, and against each other. This latter tale explains why GILEAD's children were told that each Guardian had a thinking cap, or hat upon its head, which contained a second brain. This somewhat apocryphal story was based on the fact that all of the NORTH CENTRAL POSITRONICS Guardians had radar dishes coming out of their skulls.

When Roland was young, the Guardians were still revered. He sees them depicted outside HAMBRY'S MERCANTILE and then later upon the imposing CRADLE OF LUD, where they march along the roof in their Beam pairs. Many Mid-World sayings also invoke the Guardians, such as "Bird and Bear and Hare and Fish, Give my love her fondest wish."

In the final book of the Dark Tower series, we find out that the Tower, Beams, and Guardians are simultaneously magical and mechanical. Before the coming of the world of form, all that existed in the universe was the magical PRIM, or soup of creation. From this GREATER DISCORDIA arose GAN, the spirit of the Dark Tower. From his towering body he spun the Beams, the ROSES of CAN'-KA NO REY, and the physical substance of the multiple worlds, which the Beams bind together. Once the worlds were formed, the Prim receded, but the magic of Tower, Beams, and Guardians remained.

However, the Great Old Ones—those technological wizards who once ruled Roland's version of Earth—mourned the passing of the Prim. Although enough magic remained in Tower and Beams to last for eternity, the Old People used their technology to remake the supporting structures of the macroverse, and to create doorways into, and out of, as many *wheres* and *whens* as possible. As we saw as early as *The Waste Lands,* the outcome of this misconceived folly was disastrous. Not only were the manufactured Beams destined to become unstable and the Old Ones' doorways fated to be used by the evil followers of the CRIMSON KING, but the cyborg Guardians themselves—much like BLAINE, that other psychotic North Central Positronics creation—were fated to descend into a vicious, malfunctioning madness. When we meet the Bear Guardian (also known as SHARDIK, or MIR), he is coughing up white worms, a disease which (if we take a look at *The Talisman* by STEPHEN KING and Peter Straub) concurs with the breakdown of the time/space continuum.

By the time our *tet* reaches the DEVAR-TOI in the final book of the Dark Tower series, the Beams guarded by RAT and FISH, BAT and HARE, EAGLE and LION, and DOG and HORSE have all collapsed, and we can assume that their Positronics Guardians have already landed on the celestial junk pile. The only two guy-wires left holding the Tower in place are our *tet*'s Beam—the BEAR-TURTLE—and Gan's Beam—the ELEPHANT-WOLF.

Luckily for all of us, the remaining magical Guardians, though weakened, are far from helpless. Just as Gan, the spirit of the Dark Tower, aids those who serve the WHITE, the Prim's Guardians aid those who serve the Beams. In both *Wolves of the Calla* and *Song of Susannah,* the Turtle Guardian (in the form of a little CAN-TAH) takes an active role in assuring our *tet*'s success.

In *Song of Susannah,* we learn that the Tower, Beams, and Guardians have a shadow side as well. When the Prim receded, it left behind not only twelve Guardians to watch over the Beams, but also six mischievous, hermaphroditic DEMON ELEMENTALS. Just as the Guardians watch over the mortal world (including the world of men), these DEMON ASPECTS watch over the invisible world of spirits and demons. Although there are only six Demon Elementals, each of these demons has a male and a female aspect. Hence, there are twelve Demon Aspects, just as there are twelve Guardians. In the original version of *The Gunslinger,* we were told that a thirteenth Guardian, called the BEAST, guarded the Tower. If each of the Demon Elementals corresponds to one of the Guardians of the Beams, then the Crimson King, the polar opposite of Gan, must be (in his spider form at least) the Beast that guards the Tower. This would make perfect sense, since at least one of the Demon Elementals plays a large part in the Red King's plan to destroy both Tower and multiverse.

Throughout the Dark Tower series, our *tet* follows the Bear-Turtle Beam, specifically the Beam of the Bear, Way of the Turtle (sometimes called Path of the Bear, Way of the Turtle), which leads from Shardik's lair deep in the GREAT WEST WOODS to the Tower itself. Had our *tet* begun their journey on the same Beam, but from the Turtle's (or MATURIN's) end, they would have traveled along the Beam of the Turtle, Way of the Bear (Path of the Turtle, Way of the Bear).

GENERAL INFORMATION: III:29, III:33, III:37–40 *(40 thinking caps),* III:171, III:325, III:331, III:333, IV:222, IV:326, IV:328 *(Hambry's Mercantile),* IV:355 *(and Reap charms),* IV:424, IV:464, IV:529, IV:536, IV:571, IV:573, IV:606–8, IV:629, IV:667, IV:668, V:405, VI:112, VI:296, VI:297, W:234, W:250

BAT: III:39, IV:222 *(Hambry's Mercantile)*

BEAR (SHARDIK/MIR):

DESIGN 4 GUARDIAN
SERIAL # AA 24123 CX 755431297 L 14
TYPE/SPECIES: BEAR
SHARDIK

NRSUBNUCLEAR CELLS MUST NOT
BE REPLACED**NR**

Shardik was made in the dim, unknown reaches of OUT-WORLD, where we can assume the factories of NORTH CENTRAL POSITRONICS operated. Standing seventy feet high, Shardik was the largest creature ever to walk the GREAT WEST WOODS. He was so huge that he seemed to be a moving building or a shaggy tower rather than a bear. The primitive people who came across Shardik in the years following the destruction of the OLD ONES' world renamed the great bear Mir. In their language, Mir meant "the world beneath the world" (III:32). They believed him to be both a demon incarnate and the shadow of a god.

Although Shardik had roamed the woods for eighteen centuries before his encounter with our *ka-tet,* Roland believes that he is actually two or three thousand years old. By the time he attacks EDDIE DEAN at the beginning of *The Waste Lands,* this ancient cyborg has already been driven mad by the white worms tunneling through his body, and needs to be put out of his dangerous misery. (To save her husband Eddie, SUSANNAH DEAN kills Shardik by shooting the radar dish that spins on top of his head.) Though Shardik dies early on in our tale, his Beam still holds. This is probably due to the efforts of the magical TURTLE Guardian.

In *Wizard and Glass,* Eddie Dean has a dream-vision in which he and his friends stand before the fence surrounding the magic LOT. Written in dusky-pink letters upon the fence is the following rhyme:

> See the BEAR of fearsome size!
> All the WORLD'S within his eyes.
> TIME grows thin, the past's a riddle;
> The TOWER awaits you in the middle. (Eddie's Dream IV:100)

According to STEPHEN KING, the *kas-ka Gan* of our tale, Shardik's name comes from a Richard Adams novel. *(III:11–86 section title: Bear and Bone),* III:19–21, III:24, III:25–36 *(31 shot),* III:37, III:39, III:50–51 *(backtrail and portal),* III:53–77 *(58–65 following backtrail; 65–77 clearing and portal),* III:79, III:84, III:154, III:162, III:260, III:261, III:262, III:264, III:325, III:331, III:333, III:347, III:407, IV:42 *(Eddie remembers him),* IV:222 *(Hambry's Mercantile),* IV:326, IV:481, V:37, V:45, V:166, V:378, V:512, V:573, V:649, V:665, V:681, VI:14, VI:83, VI:112, VI:296, VI:297, VI:359, VII:21, VII:34 *(by Shardik),* VII:192, VII:232, VII:244, VII:272, VII:291, VII:295, VII:296, VII:301, VII:306, VII:307, VII:345, VII:409, VII:458, VII:466, VII:813

SERVOMECHANISMS (LITTLE GUARDIANS: TONKA TRACTOR, RAT, SNAKE, BLOCK, BAT): These nasty little mechanical creatures serve Shardik. Like the Guardians, they each have a radar dish on top of their heads. After Shardik's destruction, our *ka-tet* comes across their pathetic but dangerous little retinue walking round and round in a circle. When EDDIE lists these odd creatures in *Wolves of the Calla,* he names the snake, the Tonka tractor, the rat, and "some sort of mechanical bird" (it was a bat). The original retinue also contained a walking block. III:65–71,

III:72, III:153, III:260, V:378 (*snake, Tonka tractor, stainless steel rat, flying thing*), V:563 (*indirect*), V:665, V:681, VII:195

**BEAST, THE: In the original version of *The Gunslinger*, WALTER tells Roland that the DARK TOWER is guarded by a Beast, who stands watch over it. This Beast is the originator of all *glammer* and is an even more powerful force than MAERLYN. According to Walter, Roland will have to confront this Beast before he reaches the Tower.

In the 2003 version of *The Gunslinger*, Walter mentions neither the Beast nor Maerlyn. Instead he tells Roland that he will have to slay the AGELESS STRANGER, whose other name is LEGION, before he meets his final enemy, THE CRIMSON KING. Interestingly, in his spider shape the Red King bears an uncanny resemblance to this terrible monster. I:212, III:261, IV:464–65 (*and the wind*)

DOG: The Dog is paired with the HORSE Guardian. *See also* ROSE: UR-DOG ROVER. III:325, III:331, III:333

EAGLE/BIRD/HAWK/VULTURE (GARUDA): According to the NORTH CENTRAL POSITRONICS Guidance Module DARIA, the BEAM OF THE LION is also known as Way of the Eagle, the Way of the Hawk, and the Way of the Vulturine. The Eagle Guardian's name is GARUDA. In *The Dark Tower*, we find out that the BEAMQUAKE which our *tet* felt in CALLA BRYN STURGIS was caused by a snapping of the Eagle-Lion Beam. IV:222 (*Hambry's Mercantile*), IV:126–27 (*on gold coins*), VII:232, W:221, W:227, W:247, W:254, W:256

ELEPHANT: At the beginning of *The Dark Tower*, we find out that the only two BEAMS still intact are the BEAR-TURTLE Beam and the WOLF-Elephant Beam (also known as GAN's Beam). Together they form the only remaining guy-wires holding the TOWER in place. By the time Roland and his friends reach the DEVAR-TOI, the Devar's telemetry equipment has already picked up the first bends in the Bear-Turtle. Luckily for all of us in every world, our *ka-tet* defeats the CRIMSON KING's henchmen and the Beams are able to regenerate. VII:232, VII:295

FISH: The Fish is paired with the RAT Guardian. When JAKE runs through the CRADLE OF THE GRAYS (prodded ever onward by the malicious GASHER), he sees a huge chrome and crystal fish statue. Upon it is written a single word of High Speech. That word is DELIGHT. III:39, III:304, III:325, III:331, III:333, IV:222, IV:326, VI:16

HARE: IV:326

HORSE: The Horse is paired with the DOG Guardian. III:325, III:331, III:333

LION/TYGER/CAT: The Lion-Eagle Beam (also known as the BEAM of the CAT and the Beam of the TIGER) plays an important role in *The Wind Through the Keyhole*, since it runs from THE ENDLESS FOREST to the NORTH FOREST KINNOCK DOGAN, where the powerful magician MAERLYN is trapped in the shape of a TYGER. After leaving the MUDMEN in the FAGONARD swamp, TIM ROSS follows the LION-TIGER Beam for fifty miles (forty-five-point-forty-five wheels) despite the fact that his computerized friend DARIA (a NORTH CENTRAL POSITRONICS Guidance Module) warns him that she detects a strong disturbance along the Beam

Path, probably indicating deep magic. (DARIA reads the Beam electronically.) As we find out later, Daria is correct in her assessment of magical disturbances close to the North Forest Kinnock Dogan. Not only does she sense Maerlyn's White magic and the CRIMSON KING's black magic, but she also senses the chaotic energy of the STARKBLAST.

In *The Wind Through the Keyhole*, we learn that the Lion Guardian's is called ASLAN, a name he shares with the great lion king found in *The Chronicles of Narnia*. According to the NORTH CENTRAL POSITRONICS Guidance Module DARIA, Aslan lives in the LAND OF ENDLESS SNOWS. It is possible that the BLEEDING LION, which the taheen FINLI O'TEGO says has been seen stalking to the north, is none other than the Guardian Aslan. In *The Dark Tower*, we learn that the BEAMQUAKE which our *tet* felt in CALLA BRYN STURGIS was caused by the snapping of the Eagle-Lion Beam. (*For more information, see* MAERLYN *and* ASLAN *entries.*) III:39, IV:222 *(Hambry's Mercantile),* VII:232, W:221, W:234, W:250 *(lion)*

RAT: The Rat is paired with the FISH Guardian. III:325, III:331, III:333, VI:16

TURTLE (MATURIN): According to MID-WORLD's legends, GAN bore the world and moved on. However, if the Turtle hadn't been there to catch it on his back as it fell, all of the known worlds would have ended in the abyss.

The Turtle is one of the most important Guardians, and seems to be the major totem of the city of LUD. (The STREET OF THE TURTLE, with its sculptured Turtle, leads to BLAINE'S CRADLE.) Even before meeting him, we hear the following two poems about him:

> See the TURTLE of enormous girth!
> On his shell he holds the earth.
> His thought is slow but always kind;
> He holds us all within his mind.
> On his back all vows are made:
> He sees the truth but mayn't aid.
> He loves the land and loves the sea,
> And even loves a child like me. (III:40)

> See the TURTLE of enormous girth!
> On his shell he holds the earth
> If you want to run and play,
> Come along the BEAM today. (III:122)

(*For additional variations on the Turtle poem, see* APPENDIX III.)

The Turtle Guardian's name is Maturin. Unlike SHARDIK (Maturin's companion Guardian), the Turtle Guardian does not appear to be mad. In fact, he appears to be aiding our *ka-tet* in their search for the DARK TOWER.

In *Song of Susannah*, SUSANNAH-MIO finds a small SCRIMSHAW TURTLE in the lining of JAKE CHAMBERS's magical bowling bag (temporary home to BLACK THIRTEEN). This SKÖLDPADDA (as it is called by MATHIESSEN VAN WYCK) is actually one of the CAN-TAH, or little gods. Its good magic (probably derived from the Turtle Guardian, which it depicts) seems able to nullify some of the chaos wrought by Black Thirteen. Not only does it help Susannah/Mia to find shelter at the NEW YORK PLAZA–PARK HYATT, but it also later aids Jake and PERE CALLAHAN when they face the CAN-TOI, TYPE ONE VAMPIRES, and GRANDFATHERS at the DIXIE PIG. III:39–40, III:122, III:129, III:264, III:266, III:309 *(sculpture of and street of the)*, III:310 *(voice of the)*, III:312 *(street)*, III:316 *(street)*, III:325 *(street)*, III:331, III:332 *(street)*, III:333, III:341 *(street)*, IV:222 *(Hambry's Mercantile)*, IV:424 *("Bless the Turtle")*, IV:481 *("in the name of the turtle and the bear")*, IV:570–73 *(Roland hears the turtle's voice during his time trapped in Maerlyn's ball)*, V:97 *(Turtle Bay)*, V:99, V:165, *(cloud)*, V:183, V:188 *(Turtle Bay)*, V:405, V:618–19 *(indirect; Eddie feels scrimshaw in bottom of bag; we don't find out what it is until later book)*, VI:15 *(Maturin)*, VI:57 *(fountain)*, VI:66, VI:68, VI:71, VI:81–98 *(scrimshaw in Susannah/Mia's possession)*, VI:112, VI:124 *(scrimshaw)*, VI:230 *(scrimshaw)*, VI:256 *(scrimshaw)*, VI:259 *(scrimshaw)*, VI:295 *(world borne by Gan landed on Turtle's back)*, VI:296, VI:298, VI:299, VI:339–40 *(scrimshaw; indirect)*, VI:343 *(scrimshaw)*, VI:363 *(scrimshaw)*, VI:394, VI:398, VII:3 *(Maturin)*, VII:3–14 *(scrimshaw)*, VII:21, VII:25 *(can-tah)*, VII:26, VII:28, VII:51 *(can-tah)*, VII:143 *(scrimshaw)*, VII:144 *(scrimshaw)*, VII:147, VII:232, VII:244, VII:272, VII:291, VII:295, VII:409, VII:445, VII:446, VII:458, VII:488 *(New York sculpture)*, VII:489–90, VII:497, VII:513, VII:525–26 *(scrimshaw)*, VII:542, VII:813

SCRIMSHAW TURTLE (CAN-TAH): *For page references, see listing above; for more information about the* can-tah, *see* CAN-TAH, *listed separately*

WOLF: At the beginning of *The Dark Tower,* we find out that—thanks to the efforts of the BEAM BREAKERS—only two Beams are still intact. They are the BEAR-TURTLE Beam and the Wolf-ELEPHANT Beam (also known as GAN's Beam). Together they form the only remaining guy-wires holding the DARK TOWER in place. By the time Roland and his friends reach the DEVAR-TOI, the Devar's telemetry equipment has already picked up the first bends in the Bear-Turtle. Luckily for all of us in every world, our *ka-tet* defeats the CRIMSON KING's henchmen and the Beams are able to regenerate. IV:222 *(Hambry's Mercantile)*, VII:232, VII:295

GUNSLINGERS (MID-WORLD)

In the Foreword to *The Wind Through the Keyhole,* STEPHEN KING described Mid-World's gunslingers as a strange combination of knights errant and territorial marshals from the Old West. As we learn over the course of the Dark Tower series, the gunslingers of Mid-World were all this and more. Based in the city of GILEAD, Barony Seat of NEW CANAAN, in the heart of IN-WORLD, MID-WORLD's gunslingers were peace officers, messengers, accountants, diplomats, spies, and sometimes executioners. But most of all, gunslingers were highly trained fighting machines whose reflexes, memories, and powers of observation were honed to an incredible keenness. To become a gunslinger was to undergo a rigorous training of mind, body, and spirit unsurpassed in any of the worlds.

Descended from ARTHUR ELD, the ancient king of ALL-WORLD, and his many knights, Gilead's gunslingers were the aristocrats of their time. Armed with six-shot revolvers rather than swords, their job was to protect the enlightenment and knowledge of Elden times against the constant encroachment of the OUTER DARK. To a man who belonged to the tet of the gun, losing his life was preferable to losing his honor, since loss of honor reflected not just on himself but on all of his male ancestors. Among gunslingers, the saying "I have forgotten the face of my father" was the ultimate statement of remorse.

During Roland's youth, the gunslingers' greatest enemy was JOHN FARSON, also known as THE GOOD MAN. Despite his talk of equality and democracy, Farson was little more than a brutal, power-hungry harrier. He was also dangerously insane. Evidently, his favorite pastime was playing polo, but using human heads as the balls. Like MARTEN BROADCLOAK, Steven Deschain's treacherous sorcerer and advisor, Farson ultimately served the CRIMSON KING. *For more information, see* AFFILIATION *and* CORT (CORTLAND ANDRUS). *For information about individual gunslingers, see the entries for the characters listed under* INDIVIDUAL GUNSLINGERS, *below.*

APPRENTICE GUNSLINGERS: At the age of six, boys born to the line of ELD were taken from their parents (many of whom lived in Gilead's CENTRAL PLACE) and were made to sleep in the apprentices' BARRACKS, located above the munitions vault. The training of apprentices was undertaken by CORT, the gunslingers' teacher-at-arms. Strict as a sergeant, Cort trained generations of young men in the art of war. Not only did he instruct them in the use of a variety of weapons, but he also taught them to navigate by the sun and stars, and to keep a clock ticking inside their heads. Though he called them the very eye of syphilis, Cort's true hope was that each and every boy would one day earn his guns. Though Cort had a philosophical side, his lessons focused on the necessities and slyness of battle. For the subtle arts of the mind, the apprentices were taught by VANNAY THE WISE.

Drilled into each apprentice was the gunslinger's litany: "I do not aim with my hand; he who aims with his hand has forgotten the face of his father. I aim with my eye. I do not shoot with my hand; he who shoots with his hand has forgotten the face of his father. I shoot with my mind. I do not kill with my gun; he who kills with his gun has forgotten the face of his father. I kill with my heart." At approximately eighteen years of age, each gunslinger apprentice was expected to best Cort in a one-on-one battle in Gilead's SQUARE YARD, located behind the GREAT HALL. (They were to take Cort's ironwood staff from him.) Those who emerged triumphant from this all-or-nothing battle traded in their nickel and steel barrel-shooters for the six shooters of fully-fledged gunslingers. Those who failed were sent west, weaponless. Disgraced and outcast, they never returned to Gilead. Many ended up joining forces with JOHN FARSON. *See also* CORT *and* VANNAY, *listed separately*

I:110 *(2003 edition)*, I:169–186 *(Roland's coming-of-age battle, 2003 edition)*, II:16 *(Cort's teachings)*, II:36 *(training the memory)*, II:177, II:309 *(cleaning a gun)*, III:14, III:71, III:83, III:276 *(riddling)*, III:328 *(checking visual quadrants)*, IV:107, IV:109, IV:111, IV:112, IV:164, IV:232, IV:270, IV:350, IV:358, IV:574 *(waking a person from trance)*, V:29, V:78–81 *(lessons from Cort and Vannay)*, V:89 *(lessons about Manni)* V:225, V:235, V:388 *(Vannay)*, V:392 *(training)*, VI:203, VII:33 *(Cort's lessons)*, VII:34, VII:589, VII:778 *(Cort's teaching)*, W:36, W:40 *(baby gunslingers)*

APPRENTICES, SENT WEST: Like his father before him, CORT raised a moit of young men to the tradition of the ELD and the way of the gun. On the day of a young man's coming-of-age battle, in which an apprentice was required to take Cort's ironwood staff from him in a one-on-one fight, the apprentice entered Gilead's SQUARE YARD from the west end—the entrance used by boys. The teacher entered from the east end—the entrance used by men. Before the fighting began, teacher and pupil recited the following litany:

"Have you come here for a serious purpose, boy?"

"I have come for a serious purpose."

"Have you come as an outcast from your father's house?"

"I have so come."

"Have you come with your chosen weapon?"

"I have."

"What is your weapon?"

The final question always worked to the teacher's advantage, since he could adjust his plan of battle to the sling or spear or bah or bow. If the boy won the battle and took Cort's stick, he was allowed to exit by the east end. If he failed, he slunk out by the west entrance, a boy forever. Such young men were sent west in disgrace, into the very lands where JOHN FARSON's revolution raged. Many of these failed gunslingers—such as ELDRED JONAS—joined forces with Gilead's greatest enemy. Farson gave these broken boys weapons and encouraged them to vent their rage against the city of their fathers. *For page references, see* APPRENTICE GUNSLINGERS, *above.*

    INDIVIDUAL APPRENTICES SENT WEST: *See* BIG COFFIN HUNTERS: INDIVIDUAL BIG COFFIN HUNTERS: JONAS, ELDRED

COUNCIL OF ELD: *See* GILEAD'S COUNCIL OF ELD

INDIVIDUAL GUNSLINGERS:

    ALLGOOD, CUTHBERT: *See* ALLGOOD, CUTHBERT, *listed separately*

    ALLGOOD, ROBERT: *See* ALLGOOD, CUTHBERT: CUTHBERT'S FAMILY AND ASSOCIATES

    CALLAHAN, FATHER DONALD FRANK: *See* CALLAHAN, FATHER DONALD FRANK, *listed separately*

    CHAMBERS, JAKE: *See* CHAMBERS, JAKE, *listed separately*

    DEAN, EDDIE: *See* DEAN, EDDIE, *listed separately*

    DEAN, SUSANNAH: *See* DEAN, SUSANNAH, *listed separately*

    DeCURRY, JAMIE: *See* DeCURRY, JAMIE, *listed separately*

    DESCHAIN, ROLAND: *See* DESCHAIN, ROLAND, *listed separately*

    DESCHAIN, STEVEN: *See* DESCHAIN, STEVEN, *listed separately*

    JOHNS, ALAIN: *See* JOHNS, ALAIN, *listed separately*

    JOHNS, CHRISTOPHER: *See* JOHNS, ALAIN, *listed separately*

    McVRIES, PETER: When Roland and JAMIE arrived in DEBARIA to track the SKIN-MAN, the HIGH SHERIFF, HUGH PEAVY, admitted that he had hoped to see STEVEN DESCHAIN himself and perhaps PETER McVRIES. Roland told Peavy that McVries had died of a fever three years previously. (This fever was most likely induced by poison.) Peavy grieved McVries death, since he was a trig hand with a gun. W:54–55

    TAVARES POSSE: When TIM ROSS was twenty-one, three men wearing the hard calibers of gunslingers came to the village of TREE. They were bound for TAVERES and were hoping to raise a posse. Tim was the only young man who would go with them. Initially these gunslingers called Tim "the lefthanded gun" and later, after he'd proved himself to be both fearless and a dead shot, they called him *tet-fa*, or friend of the *tet*. Later, Tim actually became a gunslinger, one of the few of that *tet* not born to the line of ELD. W:268

GUNSLINGERS (OUR WORLD)

Individuals from our *where* and *when* who come in contact with Roland Deschain are often reminded of one or more gunslingers from the Old West of the late nineteenth and early twentieth centuries. Here is a short list of those gunslingers, including a brief bio of each.

BILLY THE KID: Billy the Kid (William H. Bonney) was one of the Old West's famous outlaws. Although he was born in New York, the Kid became one of the most notorious gunslingers involved in New Mexico's cattle wars. Legend has it that he killed twenty-one men before his twenty-first birthday. True to his nickname, the Kid died young. He never saw twenty-two. II:186

CASSIDY, BUTCH, AND THE SUNDANCE KID: Butch Cassidy was one of the most celebrated outlaws of the American West. Born Robert Leroy Parker, he took his last name from Mike Cassidy, a cowboy rustler who taught him the horse-thieving trade. His first name came from his stint working for a butcher in Wyoming.

Butch Cassidy and Harry Longbaugh (known as the Sundance Kid) formed the Wild Bunch Gang, also called the Hole in the Wall Gang. Cassidy was sometimes called a "gentleman bandit" because he claimed never to have killed anyone during his raids. II:358

EARP, WYATT: Wyatt Earp was one of the Old West's most famous lawmen and was a whiz with the six-shooter. He earned a reputation as a hard-caliber man in such towns as Tombstone and Dodge City. He and the other Earp brothers took part in the famous shoot-out at the OK Corral. (They fought the Clanton clan.) Earp actually wore the famous lawman's star for less than a decade. His other careers were as gambler, teamster, buffalo hunter, and railroad man. He was friends with the equally famous DOC HOLLIDAY. II:358

HOLLIDAY, DOC: Doc Holliday was born John Henry Holliday. Although he trained as a dentist, he moved west to try to ease the tuberculosis that was killing him. Unfortunately, the drier climate didn't help much and his constant coughing drove away his clientele. As a result, he took up a new profession—gambling—and was remarkably good at it. He eventually diversified and added train robbery, despite the fact that he was friends with the lawman WYATT EARP. (Interestingly enough, the Doc occasionally served as Earp's deputy.) Like so many of the other famous gunslingers of our world, Holliday was a deadly shot with the six-gun. However, in the end it was the TB, and not the gun, that killed him. Holliday died at age thirty-six. II:358

OAKLEY, ANNIE: Although Annie Oakley was a woman, she could shoot like Roland. From 1885 to 1902, she starred in Buffalo Bill's Wild West Show. Although she stood just under five feet tall, her aim could make a huge man tremble. As part of her act, Annie shot cigarettes from her husband's lips. She could even shoot through the pips of a playing card tossed in the air. Too bad she never met our *ka-tet*. II:368

GUTTENBERG, FURTH, AND PATEL
Guttenberg, Furth, and Patel is a NEW YORK CITY accountancy firm. TRUDY DAMASCUS works there.
VI:47, VI:52–54

DAMASCUS, TRUDY: Until the first of June 1999, Trudy Damascus prided herself on being a hardheaded, no-nonsense accountant. Her professional goal was to become a partner in the firm of Guttenberg, Furth, and Patel. However, while returning from lunch that fateful day, she witnessed SUSANNAH/MIA's materialization on SECOND AVENUE. Mia—desperate to find a *telefung* so that she could contact RICHARD P. SAYRE and the other WARRIORS OF THE SCARLET EYE who promised to let her bear her CHAP in safety—threatened Trudy and stole both her shoes and her *New York Times*. Trudy was never the same afterward. VI:47–58, VI:64 *(indirect)*, VI:65, VI:222

> **ANTASSI, OFFICER PAUL:** Officer Paul Antassi is the NEW YORK CITY police officer who arrives at Guttenberg, Furth, and Patel after Trudy Damascus reports being mugged on SECOND AVENUE. He is also the first person to hear Trudy's rather unlikely story about the abrupt appearance of SUSANNAH DEAN/MIA, daughter of none, into the New York of 1999. Like all the others who will listen later, Antassi refuses to believe Trudy's tale. VI:52–53, VI:54–55

GUTTENBERG, MITCH: Mitch Guttenberg is one of the partners of Guttenberg, Furth, and Patel. VI:54

KIDZPLAY: This company owes Guttenberg, Furth, and Patel a large sum of money. RICHARD GOLDMAN is the company's CEO. VI:47, VI:48

> **GOLDMAN, RICHARD:** Richard Goldman is the CEO for KidzPlay. Trudy Damascus is after his testicles. VI:48

H

HABER
See CAN-TOI

HACKFORD, DR. MORRIS
See TOPEKA CHARACTERS

HAGGENGOOD TWINS
See CALLA BRYN STURGIS CHARACTERS: OTHER CHARACTERS

HAGGERTY THE NAIL
See TREE VILLAGE CHARACTERS

HALF-MUTANT FARMER
  See MUTANTS: HUMAN MUTANTS (MINOR MUTATIONS)

HALVORSEN, JIMMY
  See DEAN, SUSANNAH: OTHER ASSOCIATES: MACY'S EMPLOYEES

HAMBRY CHARACTERS
In *Wizard and Glass,* Roland tells his *ka-tet* about his fourteenth year, and the months he spent in the town of HAMBRY after he won his guns. In Hambry, Roland lost his heart to SUSAN DELGADO, and what remained of his innocence and trust to the duplicitous followers of THE GOOD MAN. Under the false name of WILL DEARBORN, Roland and his two apprentice-gunslinger friends, CUTHBERT ALLGOOD (alias ARTHUR HEATH) and ALAIN JOHNS (alias RICHARD STOCKWORTH), discovered that the people of Hambry secretly supported JOHN FARSON. Roland and his friends destroyed the rebellion, whose forces were led by the BIG COFFIN HUNTERS and aided by the wicked witch RHEA OF THE CÖOS. They also stole John Farson's secret weapon, MAERLYN'S GRAPEFRUIT, for their fathers. Although Roland and his two friends survived, Roland (tricked by the *glammer* of Maerlyn's evil magic ball) deserted Susan and she was burned to death on a Charyou Tree fire.

  HORSEMEN'S ASSOCIATION: All of Hambry's important ranchers, stockliners, and livestock owners belonged to this local, but powerful, association. Many of the farmers belonged as well. FRAN LENGYLL—distant friend and later murderer of PAT DELGADO—was its president. Not surprisingly, SUSAN DELGADO thought them a cold lot. This association owned the BAR K RANCH, where Roland, CUTHBERT, and ALAIN stayed during their time in MEJIS. Although they pretended to be loyal to the AFFILIATION, the Horsemen's Association actually supported THE GOOD MAN. In reality, they were the FARSON Association. IV:188, IV:199, IV:211, IV:251–52 *(something is wrong),* IV:293, IV:381 *(all traitors),* IV:424, IV:519 *(as "Farson Association"),* IV:522, IV:541

  MEMBERS OF THE HORSEMEN'S ASSOCIATION:
  CROYDON, JOHN (PIANO RANCH): John Croydon owned the PIANO RANCH and a good part of THE DROP. He also owned some small orchards. IV:187, IV:188, IV:199, IV:204, IV:251, IV:341, IV:466, IV:470, IV:545 *(present 540–46),* IV:558 *(killed; present 553–58)*
  GARBER: This is the family that owned Bar K Ranch before it passed to the Horsemen's Association. IV:188, IV:251
  LENGYLL, FRANCIS (ROCKING B RANCH): Fran Lengyll, President of the Horsemen's Association, was a blocky man with pale eyes, a net of wrinkles, and wind-burned cheeks. His handshake was strong and quick.
  Lengyll owned the ROCKING B RANCH. He also owned the biggest Honda generator in Hambry. Although he pretended to be loyal to the AFFILIATION, he was one of the first of Hambry's residents that Roland caught lying in aid of FARSON's rebel forces.
  Lengyll's service to THE GOOD MAN extended to murder. According to Lengyll, PAT DELGADO—a loyal Affiliation man—was killed by his horse. However, this proved to be a lie. Lengyll killed him. IV:186, IV:187,

IV:188, IV:198–202, IV:204, IV:251, IV:254–56, IV:313–14, IV:355, IV:385, IV:447, IV:459, IV:460, IV:463, IV:466, IV:470, IV:473–80, IV:483, IV:484, IV:500–502, IV:522, IV:528, IV:535, IV:540–46, IV:548, IV:553–57 *(attacked by Roland's ka-tet; 557 killed)*, IV:566, IV:577, IV:582, IV:584 *(Alain has his machine gun)*, IV:589 *(machine gun)*, IV:592

RENFREW, HASH (LAZY SUSAN RANCH): Hash Renfrew, owner of the LAZY SUSAN RANCH, was a big boozer. Not surprisingly, he was even larger and blockier than FRAN LENGYLL. Renfrew's place was the biggest horse ranch in MEJIS. Like the other members of the Horsemen's Association, Renfrew was a secret supporter of THE GOOD MAN. Like Lengyll, Renfrew lied to Roland and his friends about the number of MUTIE horses born in the area. IV:187, IV:199, IV:203–8 *(206 mentions Excalibur)*, IV:222, IV:236, IV:254 *(lies about threaded stock)*, IV:255, IV:355, IV:421, IV:459, IV:522, IV:527–29, IV:532–35, IV:537–46 *(present for action)*, IV:556–57 *(557 killed)*

RIMER, LASLO: Laslo Rimer was KIMBA RIMER's older brother. He looked like a stony-hearted preacher. Laslo owned the ROCKING H RANCH, where he secretly kept oxen. They were for FARSON's use. IV:293, IV:561, IV:585–87

WERTNER, HENRY (BARONY STOCKLINER): Henry Wertner was the Barony's stockliner as well as a horse breeder in his own right. He took PAT DELGADO's job after he died. IV:187, IV:199, IV:204, IV:211, IV:341, IV:459, IV:545 *(present for action 540–46)*

WHITE, JAKE: White owned some of the apple orchards north of Hambry. IV:199, IV:251, IV:341, IV:473–80 *(present for arrest of Roland's ka-tet)*

HAMBRY LOVERS:

ROBERT AND FRANCESCA: Robert and Francesca were lovers who made it into Hambry's folklore. Francesca tried to end their affair, so Robert dashed out her brains and then clipped his windpipe. This murder/suicide supposedly happened in the town cemetery. IV:426

HAMBRY MAYOR'S HOUSE (SEAFRONT):

MORGENSTERN, CONCHETTA: A blade-faced seamstress. Her view of existence is that life is hard, so we'd all just better get used to it. IV:292, IV:310–11, IV:313 *(blade-faced)*, IV:426

RIMER, KIMBA: Kimba Rimer was HART THORIN's Chancellor. He was also the Barony's Minister of Inventory. Tall, thin, with skin pale as candle wax, Rimer reminded Roland of Doctor Death. His voice was that of either a politician or an undertaker.

According to OLIVE THORIN, Rimer looted Hambry's treasury, and what he didn't give to FARSON he kept for himself. But no matter how good he was at lining his own pockets, Rimer was even better at making enemies. Once, on account of CLAY REYNOLDS's swirling, silk-lined cloak, Rimer jokingly called the younger man *sai Manto,* an insult that also implied homosexuality. Reynolds never forgot it. Hence, when the time came to send Rimer on to the clearing at the end of the path, Reynolds took the job gleefully. IV:133, IV:139 *(relationship to Hart Thorin)*, IV:141, IV:153, IV:154, IV:175–78, IV:184 *(false papers for Roland's* ka-tet), IV:187, IV:191–210 (Hart Thorin's party. Rimer appears on the following pages: 192–93 [gaunt as Dr. Death], 195–201 [196 joke about "The Good Man"], 204, 208), IV:211, IV:212, IV:213, IV:250, IV:251, IV:257, IV:260, IV:301, IV:308, IV:347–53, IV:356, IV:358, IV:367–68, IV:373, IV:377, IV:381, IV:402, IV:405, IV:406, IV:425, IV:443, IV:453, IV:460, IV:470–71 (killed by Reynolds), IV:476, IV:482, IV:483, IV:488, IV:500–501, IV:519, IV:537, IV:564, IV:585, IV:664

THORIN, HART: Horny Hart Thorin was the Mayor of Hambry and the Chief Guard o' Barony. He was also CORAL THORIN's brother and OLIVE THORIN's husband. He and Coral co-owned Hambry's bar and brothel, the TRAVELLERS' REST. Thorin was anything but elegant, and often acted like a buffoon. In fact, the reader wonders why Olive continued to love this skinny and twitchy knuckle-cracker, especially since he couldn't wait to take on other women.

Though he was as gangly as a marsh bird, Hart Thorin conceived a passion for SUSAN DELGADO, a girl young enough to be his grand-daughter. By the beginning of *Wizard and Glass*'s MEJIS adventures, Thorin had already paid for Susan to become his jilly. Like other Hambry officials, Thorin allied himself with FARSON, though those he sold his soul to eventually murdered him. Thorin's dog was named WOLF. IV:116, IV:121, IV:125, IV:126, IV:129–30, IV:131, IV:133, IV:134, IV:135, IV:136, IV:139–41 (relationships with Susan and Rimer), IV:143, IV:153, IV:154, IV:168, IV:169, IV:172 (and Travellers' Rest), IV:176, IV:177, IV:184 (and Roland's false papers), IV:186–87, IV:188, IV:191–210 (Party. He appears on the following pages: 193, 195–202 [195–96 described]; 197 with Susan; 203, 205–8 [Susan as his Sheevin, or side-wife]; 209), IV:211–13, IV:223, IV:236 (and Susan's blouses), IV:237, IV:238, IV:242, IV:246, IV:250, IV:251–52, IV:278, IV:280, IV:285, IV:290, IV:299, IV:301, IV:303, IV:307, IV:308 (Wolf), IV:311–13 (lunges for Susan and loses his posh accent), IV:314, IV:317, IV:318, IV:331, IV:348 (involved with Farson affair), IV:351, IV:356, IV:360, IV:373, IV:377, IV:381, IV:405, IV:424, IV:426–27, IV:434, IV:461–62, IV:465, IV:471–73 (Depape kills him. Leaves Cuthbert's Lookout and Farson's sigul), IV:476, IV:482, IV:483, IV:492, IV:498, IV:500–501, IV:514, IV:519–20, IV:533, IV:537, IV:549, IV:561, IV:564, IV:569, IV:578, IV:585, IV:664

THORIN, OLIVE: Poor Olive Thorin was HART THORIN's long-suffering wife. She was a plump, good-natured woman with an artless smile, and was one of the few people in Hambry that Roland really liked. Olive grew up a fisherman's daughter and never forgot it. Even though her husband wanted SUSAN DELGADO as his jilly, when Susan needed to be rescued it was bighearted Olive who tried to help her. Olive was eventually killed by CLAY REYNOLDS. IV:191–210 (Thorin's party. She appears on the following pages: 191–92 [described], 193 [described], 194, 195, 205, 208 [sad about Thorin and Susan]), IV:211, IV:212 (John Haverty's daughter), IV:223 (parallel to Roland's mother), IV:238, IV:257, IV:259, IV:292, IV:324, IV:405, IV:428, IV:457, IV:461–62 (nightmare about Roc. Premonition of husband's death), IV:569–70, IV:577–78, IV:581–83, IV:585–86 (killed by Reynolds)

HAVERTY, JOHN: Olive Thorin's father. IV:212

TOMAS, MARIA: Susan's maid. IV:292, IV:306–8, IV:428, IV:457, IV:480–83, IV:537, IV:577–78, IV:581

TORRES, MIGUEL: A SEAFRONT servant. IV:405, IV:448, IV:481, IV:494–95, IV:522, IV:566–68, IV:578, V:166

HAMBRY SHERIFF'S OFFICE:

AVERY, HERK: Herk Avery was the High Sheriff of MEJIS and the Chief Constable of Hambry. He was a large, fat man "loose as a trundle of laundry" (IV:175). Like the other important men of Hambry, he had no real love for the AFFILIATION. SUSAN DELGADO shot him while trying to rescue Roland and his *ka-tet* from Hambry's jail. IV:155, IV:175, IV:179, IV:180, IV:181–90 *(181 described; 183–84 goes through Roland's false papers; 185 ice machines)*, IV:191, IV:192–93, IV:194, IV:197, IV:226–30 *(after standoff between Big Coffin Hunters and Roland's ka-tet)*, IV:251, IV:259–60, IV:273 *(and thinny)*, IV:295, IV:329, IV:359, IV:360, IV:362–64, IV:367, IV:423, IV:425, IV:432, IV:462–63, IV:473–80, IV:483, IV:502, IV:507, IV:508–13 *(511 Susan kills him)*, IV:517, IV:520, IV:521, IV:523, IV:564 *(Susan blamed for his murder)*

HERK'S DEPUTIES: IV:181–90

BRIDGER, TODD: IV:473–80 *(present for arrest of Roland's ka-tet)*, IV:508, IV:521

CLAYPOOL, FRANK: IV:329 *(named by Jonas. Broke his leg. Jonas standing in for him)*, IV:462, IV:605

HOLLIS, DAVE: Dave Hollis is often referred to as "Deputy Dave." Although he was only a few years older than SUSAN DELGADO, he was balding and wore a monocle. While she was attempting to rescue Roland and his friends, Susan accidentally killed him. IV:181–90, IV:192, IV:227–30, IV:259–60, IV:363–64, IV:367, IV:431–32, IV:462, IV:473–80 *(present for arrest of Roland's ka-tet)*, IV:508–13 *(510 Susan kills him)*, IV:521, IV:564 *(Susan blamed for his murder)*

HOLLIS, JUDY: Dave Hollis's wife. Her maiden name was JUDY WERTNER. IV:182, IV:185, IV:189, IV:287, IV:432, IV:512

RIGGINS, GEORGE: IV:259–60 *(name mentioned for the first time)*

TRAVELLERS' REST:

CALLAHAN, BARKIE: Saloon bouncer. IV:171, IV:172, IV:176, IV:218, IV:349, IV:451–52 *(at Citgo)*

CAPRICHOSO (CAPI): Caprichoso was the Rest's pack mule. SHEEMIE was the one who usually rode him. Caprichoso, in turn, liked to bite Sheemie. *For page references, see* BREAKERS: RUIZ, STANLEY (SHEEMIE)

COUNTESS JILLIAN OF UP'ARD KILLIAN: A whore who had royal pretensions. She maintained that she was from GARLAN. IV:214

MOGGINS, GERT: *See* BIG COFFIN HUNTERS: DEPAPE, ROY

PETTIE THE TROTTER: Pettie was one of the Rest's aging whores. She wanted to change professions and become a bartender. IV:171, IV:173, IV:176, IV:213–14, IV:216, IV:218, IV:224–25, IV:336, IV:382–83, IV:403, IV:468–69, IV:470, IV:563–65 *(present)*, IV:605, VII:220, VII:333

ROMP, THE: The Romp was the name of the two-headed MUTIE elk mounted on the wall behind the Rest's bar. He had a rack of antlers like a forest grove and four glaring eyes. IV:171–72, IV:176, IV:213, IV:214, IV:217, IV:382, IV:447, IV:468, IV:563, IV:570, IV:610, VII:220

RUIZ, STANLEY: Stanley Ruiz was the Travellers' Rest barkeep. He was also SHEEMIE RUIZ's father. When Roland and his *tet* meet Sheemie in the DEVAR-TOI in the final book of the Dark Tower series, Sheemie is using his father's name. VII:218, VII:220, VII:333, VII:391, IV:214, IV:215, IV:216, IV:217 *(Sheemie may be his son)*, IV:218, IV:242, IV:382, IV:396 *(Rhea mentions him as Sheemie's father)*, IV:397, IV:447, IV:467–69 *(His two clubs: The Calmer and The Killer)*, IV:470, IV:506, IV:563 *(562–65 present for action)*, IV:605

****SHEB (SHEB McCURDY):** Sheb played the piano in the Travellers' Rest. In the 2003 version of *The Gunslinger,* we find out that he later became a piano player in TULL. *See entry under* SHEB, *listed separately*

SHEEMER, DELORES: SHEEMIE'S mother. Before she died, she was probably one of the Rest's whores. IV:217

****SHEEMIE:** The mildly mentally retarded tavern boy who helped Roland, CUTHBERT, ALAIN, and SUSAN defeat the BIG COFFIN HUNTERS and the rest of FARSON'S MEN. In the final book of the Dark Tower series, we find out that Sheemie later became a BREAKER in THUNDERCLAP. *For more information, see* BREAKERS: RUIZ, STANLEY (SHEEMIE)

THORIN, CORAL: Morose Coral Thorin was the Madame of the saloon and whorehouse known as the Travellers' Rest. She and her brother, Mayor HART THORIN, jointly owned the place. Fifty-five-year-old Coral was a wild child in her youth and didn't get any better as she got older. She just became more mercenary about it. Although she was attractive in a large-eyed, weasel-headed way, she had a hard streak. Coral became ELDRED JONAS's lover. After he died and she fled Hambry, she became CLAY REYNOLDS's woman. The two of them turned to bank robbery and were eventually killed for it. IV:171, IV:172 *(described. Fifty-five years old)*, IV:178, IV:191–210 *(Thorin's party. She appears on the following pages: 191–92, 193, 194, 203–8 [we learn on 207–8 that she despises Susan])*, IV:228, IV:249, IV:341, IV:347, IV:351, IV:380–87, IV:388, IV:389–90, IV:420–25, IV:434, IV:447–48, IV:449, IV:460, IV:466, IV:468, IV:489, IV:500, IV:505–6, IV:515, IV:519–23, IV:527, IV:532, IV:537, IV:545, IV:561–62, IV:566, IV:623 *(Becomes Clay Reynolds's lover and a bank robber. They are killed.)*, VII:333

OTHER CHARACTERS:

ALVAREZ (LLEGLYL'S MAN): IV:476

ALVAREZ, MISHA: SUSAN DELGADO taught Misha Alvarez's daughter to ride a horse, but this didn't stop Misha from spitting on Susan as she was carted toward the Charyou Tree bonfire. IV:607

BEECH, MRS.: Hers was the first mailbox on the edge of town. IV:144, IV:155, IV:158

DELGADO, CORDELIA: *See* DELGADO, CORDELIA, *listed separately*

DELGADO, SUSAN: *See* DELGADO, SUSAN, *listed separately*

FARMER WITH LAMB SLAUGHTERER'S EYES: V:210, V:211

HOOKEY, BRIAN: He owned HOOKEY'S STABLE & SMITHY, also

known as HOOKEY'S STABLE AND FANCY LIVERY. IV:279–80, IV:282, IV:301 *(in on Farson plot)*, IV:330, IV:336, IV:377, IV:386, IV:390, IV:427, IV:501, IV:512, IV:545 *(present for 540–46)*, IV:556 *(556 killed; 553–56 present for action)*

HOOKEY, RUFUS: BRIAN HOOKEY's son. IV:427, IV:501

McCANN, JAMIE: This whey-faced boy was to be HART THORIN's stand-in during the Reap festivities. Thorin was too old to be the Reaping Lad. IV:292, IV:605

MEJIS COWPOKES: VII:455

OLD SOONY: He owned the hut in the BAD GRASS where SUSAN DEL-GADO and Roland made love, and where Susan was later captured by ELDRED JONAS. Old Soony joined the MANNI sect. IV:534

ORTEGA, MILLICENT: She was a gossip who stared at CORDELIA DELGADO and ELDRED JONAS from the window of ANN'S DRESSES. IV:328

O'SHYVEN, PETER: The husband of THERESA O'SHYVEN, he is described as "a vaquero of laughing temperament." IV:485

O'SHYVEN, THERESA MARIA DELORES: Wife of PETER O'SHYVEN, she sold rugs in Hambry's upper market. In her spare time, she licked corners in order to clean them. IV:485–86

QUINT, HIRAM: He worked at the PIANO RANCH. IV:451–52 *(at Citgo)*, IV:484, IV:527–29, IV:532–35, IV:558 *(557–58 present for action; flees scene of attack)*

HAMMARSKJÖLD PLAZA ASSOCIATION
See TET CORPORATION

HANDS FAMILY
See CALLA BRYN STURGIS CHARACTERS: OTHER CHARACTERS

HANSON, LUCAS
See PIPER SCHOOL CHARACTERS

HARE GUARDIAN
See GUARDIANS OF THE BEAM

HARLEM SCHOOL CHOIR (HARLEM ROSES)
At the end of the final book of the Dark Tower series, SUSANNAH DEAN travels through PATRICK DANVILLE's version of the UNFOUND DOOR and finds herself in an alternative version of NEW YORK CITY's CENTRAL PARK. There she hears the Harlem School Choir singing Christmas carols.

VII:807, VII:809, VII:818 *(indirect)*

HARLEY, MR.
See PIPER SCHOOL CHARACTERS

HARRIERS
See MID-WORLD ARGOT section

HARRIGAN, REVEREND EARL (CHURCH OF THE HOLY GOD-BOMB)
The Reverend Earl Harrigan is the preacher for the CHURCH OF THE HOLY
GOD-BOMB. Although the rev is from Brooklyn, he tends to preach in front of
the Vacant LOT on FORTY-SIXTH STREET and SECOND AVENUE. Harrigan,
who is the twinner of HENCHICK, leader of the MANNI in CALLA REDPATH,
is constantly harassed by OFFICER BENZYCK for parking his van illegally.

Harrigan is instrumental in helping CALLAHAN, JAKE, and OY when they
appear in 1999 NEW YORK. First, he silences a driver who threatens to report
Jake for drawing a gun in public. Second, he gives Callahan a pair of shoes (one
of the Pere's pair flew off during his flight through the UNFOUND DOOR). And
third, he passes on the psychic message he received from SUSANNAH, stating
that her *tet*-mates should go to the PLAZA–PARK HYATT before traveling on
to the DIXIE PIG.

VI:43 *(indirect)*, VI:258, VI:259–61, VI:307–20, VI:350, VII:90, VII:423,
VII:503

CROWD: VI:309–11 *(crowd grows when Jake freaks out)*, VI:315

> BLACK MAN IN GRAY FATIGUES: This man witnesses PERE CALLA-
> HAN's sudden appearance into NEW YORK, 1999. VI:308
> DRIVER NUMBER TWO (HORN HONKER): VI:310, VI:311, VI:312
> DRIVER NUMBER THREE (LINCOLN): This bossy Lincoln driver
> stands six foot three inches and has a big belly. He threatens to report
> JAKE for carrying a gun but Harrigan silences him. VI:312–15
> KID WITH HAT ON BACKWARD: VI:310
> SCARED WOMAN: VI:310
> SHOUTER: VI:309
> TAXI DRIVER WHO ALMOST HIT OY: *See* TAXI DRIVERS: TAXI
> DRIVER NUMBER ONE

HARRIGAN'S FATHER: Harrigan's father was also a preacher. (Are you
surprised?) VI:318

HASPIO, JIMMY
See BALAZAR, ENRICO: BALAZAR'S MEN

HATHAWAY, MISS
See DEAN, EDDIE: EDDIE'S ASSOCIATES PAST AND PRESENT

HATLEN, BURT
See KING, STEPHEN

HAUSER, FRED
See KING, STEPHEN

HAVERTY, JOHN
See HAMBRY CHARACTERS: HAMBRY MAYOR'S HOUSE (SEA-
FRONT): THORIN, OLIVE

HAWK GUARDIAN
See GUARDIANS OF THE BEAM

HAWK-HEADED MAN
See TAHEEN: BIRDMEN TAHEEN: JEY

**HAX
Hax was the GILEAD's castle head cook and the absolute ruler of the West Kitchen. He was a large, dark-skinned man with a gold hoop in his right ear. Although he loved children, he was a faithful follower of JOHN FARSON (THE GOOD MAN). To serve the cause of revolution, Hax was prepared to poison the men, women, and children of the town of FARSON. (In the 2003 version of *The Gunslinger,* Hax plots to poison the town of TAUNTON, not Farson.) Hax's plan was discovered by eleven-year-old Roland and his best friend CUTHBERT ALLGOOD. Hax was hanged for his crime and both Roland and Cuthbert were allowed to watch. Roland took a splinter from the gallows tree.

   I:100–106, I:107–11 *(hanged)*, I:137, I:158, I:159, II:105, III:37–38, III:39, III:40, III:41, IV:161, IV:302–3, IV:417, IV:656, V:590 *(indirect)*, VII:526, VII:585 *(cook)*, VII:748, VII:801
   HAX'S KITCHEN ASSOCIATES:
   MAGGIE: Maggie worked in the kitchens of GILEAD's castle. She was Hax's assistant cook. I:101

HAYCOX, LOUIS
See CALLA BRYN STURGIS CHARACTERS: FARMERS (SMALLHOLD)

HAYLIS OF CHAYVEN
See MUTANTS: CHILDREN OF RODERICK

HEATH, ARTHUR
See ALLGOOD, CUTHBERT

HEATH, GEORGE
See ALLGOOD, CUTHBERT

HENRY THE TALL
See DESCHAIN, HENRY

HEDDA JAFFORDS
See JAFFORDS FAMILY

HEDDON JAFFORDS
See JAFFORDS FAMILY

HEDRON
See MANNI

HENCHICK
See MANNI

HENRY THE TALL
See DESCHAIN, HENRY

HITLER BROTHERS
See CALLAHAN, FATHER DONALD FRANK: CALLAHAN AND THE
HITLER BROTHERS

HO FAT II
Ho Fat II is the rickshaw which the robot STUTTERING BILL gives to SUSAN-
NAH, Roland, PATRICK, and OY so that they can travel from THE FEDERAL
(located on the edges of the WHITE LANDS OF EMPATHICA) to the DARK
TOWER. Susannah christens it Ho Fat II after their previous vehicle.
    VII:720–24, VII:725–50, VII:756–65, VII:767–82

HO FAT III
Ho Fat III is the small electric scooter which STUTTERING BILL makes for
SUSANNAH DEAN so that she can ride the final miles toward the DARK
TOWER. In many ways, it is the perfect replacement for Susannah's Cruisin
Trike, which she left in the DEVAR-TOI. Susannah ends up taking Ho Fat III
through PATRICK DANVILLE's version of the UNFOUND DOOR and over
to an alternative version of NEW YORK CITY where everybody else is driving
Takuro Spirits.
    VII:720–50 *(742–43 Ho Fat III is named directly)*, VII:807–13

HO FAT'S LUXURY TAXI
Roland and SUSANNAH DEAN use this rickshaw while traveling through the
BADLANDS beyond CASTLE DISCORDIA.
    VII:579, VII:580–644 *(replaced by a travois in the snowlands)*, VII:697

HODIAK
See TREE VILLAGE, CHARACTERS

HODJI, WALTER
See WALTER

HOLDEN ("FAT JOHNNY" HOLDEN)
Stocky, black-haired "Fat Johnny" is the brother-in-law of JUSTIN CLEMENTS.
He works at CLEMENTS GUNS AND SPORTING GOODS.
    II:343–59, II:371–73, II:377
    MOTHER: II:356

HOLLIDAY, DOC
See GUNSLINGERS (OUR WORLD)

HOLLINGS, ERNEST "FRITZ"
See CALLAHAN, FATHER DONALD FRANK: CALLAHAN'S HIDDEN
HIGHWAYS ASSOCIATES

HOLLIS, DAVE
See HAMBRY CHARACTERS: SHERIFF'S OFFICE

HOLLIS, JUDY
See HAMBRY CHARACTERS: SHERIFF'S OFFICE

HOLMES, ALICE (SARAH WALKER HOLMES)
Alice Holmes (called Sarah Walker Holmes in *The Waste Lands* and ALLIE in *The Drawing of the Three*) was SUSANNAH DEAN's (ODETTA HOLMES's) mother. She was born in ODETTA, ARKANSAS, and christened her only child with the name of her hometown. One of Susannah's youthful memories is of borrowing her mother's White Shoulders perfume. Alice Holmes died before the accident which claimed her daughter's legs.

II:199–201 *(Alice)*, II:235–38, II:295, II:320–24 *(and Mort)*, III:15 *(Sarah Walker Holmes)*, V:101, V:121 *(mama)*, VI:80, VI:101, VI:237 *(white lie; this actually refers to Susannah/Odetta)*, VI:358 *(indirect)*, VI:361–63, VII:643 *(mother)*, VII:696 *(mother)*

HOLMES, DAN
Dan Holmes was ODETTA HOLMES's father and the founder of the extremely successful HOLMES DENTAL INDUSTRIES. He is described as a thin black man with gray hair and steel-rimmed spectacles. Born into a poor Southern family, Dan Holmes rose to success despite the prejudices of a hostile and racist society. Owing to unpleasant memories, he refused to discuss his early life with his daughter. However, these experiences probably fed his profound cynicism.

Dan Holmes was both a trained dentist and a talented inventor. He patented orthodontic and cosmetic procedures which made him extremely rich. However, despite his intelligence, resourcefulness, and resilience, his life was not without its tragedies. After the death of his wife and then the accident which claimed his daughter's legs, Dan Holmes suffered the first of a series of heart attacks for which his daughter, Odetta Holmes/SUSANNAH DEAN, felt personally responsible.

Until his health began to fail, Dan Holmes handled his business almost single-handedly. Then he turned financial responsibility over to his longtime friend MOSES CARVER. Carver continued to manage Holmes Dental after his friend's death in 1962.

In *The Dark Tower*, Moses Carver tells Roland that the Western writer BEN SLIGHTMAN JR., author of CALVIN TOWER's valuable misprinted book, *The Dogan*, wrote science fiction under the name Dan Holmes.

II:199–201, II:235–38, II:320–24 *(and Mort)*, II:389, III:258, III:310–11, III:394–96, V:100–101, V:103, V:122, V:181 *(father)*, V:597 *(father of Odetta)*, VI:268, VI:350, VI:361, VII:57, VII:497, VII:508, VII:534, VII:637, VII:657, VII:672, VII:732

MURDOCK, REVEREND: Minister of Grace Methodist Church. He once gave a sermon entitled "God Speaks to Each of Us Every Day." The subject made Dan Holmes laugh. Susannah's father believed that people put words into God's mouth and hear what they want to hear. III:311

HOLMES, ODETTA
See DEAN, SUSANNAH: SUSANNAH'S OTHER SELVES

HOLMES DENTAL INDUSTRIES
Holmes Dental Industries was founded by DAN HOLMES, father of SUSAN-
NAH DEAN. Begun with the money Dan Holmes earned from his innovative
dental-capping processes, Holmes Dental soon grew into a multimillion-dollar
business. Until his first heart attack in 1959, Dan Holmes managed the financial
aspects of his enterprise almost single-handedly. However, after this unfortunate event, he handed over financial responsibility to his close friend MOSES
CARVER. Pop Mose continued to manage the business for ODETTA HOLMES
(Susannah Dean's previous personality) after her father's death.

The success of Holmes Dental was a spectacular feat and speaks volumes for
the cleverness and tenacity of its founder. Born into a poor Southern family, Dan
Holmes became a dentist and built up both his practice and his business despite
the oppression of a racist society.

Under the leadership of Moses Carver, JOHN CULLUM, and AARON DEEP-
NEAU, Holmes Dental merged with the TET CORPORATION—the brainchild
of EDDIE DEAN—which was formed to protect the ROSE.

V:539, VI:188, VI:268 *(merger with Tet Corporation)*, VII:37, VII:40,
VII:125

HOLSTEN, RAND
See KING, STEPHEN

HOOKEY, BRIAN
See HAMBRY CHARACTERS: OTHER CHARACTERS

HOONIK, ZALIA
See ORIZA, SISTERS OF: JAFFORDS, ZALIA

HOONIK, ZALMAN
See CALLA BRYN STURGIS CHARACTERS: ROONTS

HOOTS
See GRAYS: GRAY HIGH COMMAND

**HORN OF DESCHAIN
See ELD, ARTHUR: HORN OF ELD

**HORN OF ELD
See ELD, ARTHUR: HORN OF ELD

HORSE GUARDIAN
See GUARDIANS OF THE BEAM

HORSEMEN'S ASSOCIATION
See HAMBRY CHARACTERS: HORSEMEN'S ASSOCIATION

HOSSA
See WARRIORS OF THE SCARLET EYE: DIXIE PIG CHARACTERS: HUMANS: JOCHABIM, SON OF HOSSA

HOSTLER (DEBARIA)
See DEBARIA CHARACTERS

HOT STOKES
See TREE VILLAGE CHARACTERS: STOKES, DUSTIN

HOTCHKISS, MR.
See PIPER SCHOOL CHARACTERS

HOUNDS OF THE FALLS
During their terrifying ride on BLAINE the Insane Mono, our *ka-tet* sees these magnificent stone statues jutting over a waterfall between RILEA and DASHER-VILLE. Although their bodies resemble those of enormous snarling dogs, their purpose is to gather the force of the BEAM and transform it into electricity. Blaine uses this energy to recharge his batteries. *See also* BLAINE'S ROUTE *in* MID-WORLD PLACES.
    IV:32–35, IV:41–42

HOWARD
See DEAN, SUSANNAH: ODETTA HOLMES'S ASSOCIATES

HUCKMAN, WARD
See CALLAHAN, FATHER DONALD FRANK: CALLAHAN'S LIGHT-HOUSE SHELTER ASSOCIATES

HUCKSTER ROBOT
See NORTH CENTRAL POSITRONICS: FEDIC ROBOTS

HUMMA O' TEGO
See TAHEEN: OTHER TAHEEN

HYPERBOREAN WANDERER
See CHAMBERS, JAKE

I

IL ROCHE
See BALAZAR, ENRICO

IMMORTAL TIGER
See ROSE

IMPERIUM
See NORTH CENTRAL POSITRONICS

INSIDE VIEW
Inside View is the kind of pseudo-news rag that prints stories about alligator-boys and Elvis sightings.
V:140

INTERLOPER
See TULL CHARACTERS: PITTSTON, SYLVIA *and* DEMONS/SPIRITS/DEVILS

IRONWOOD
Throughout the Dark Tower series, objects both sacred and profane are made of ironwood. The staff which CORT carried into GILEAD's SQUARE YARD, and which apprentice gunslingers were required to take from him in order to win their guns, was made of this strong and resilient wood. The boxes for both MAERLYN'S GRAPEFRUIT and BLACK THIRTEEN were made of ironwood, though the latter was created out of the rarer form known as black ironwood, or ghost wood. The three magic BEACH DOORS which Roland found in *Drawing of the Three* were made of ironwood, as were many of the DOORWAYS BETWEEN WORLDS located beneath the FEDIC DOGAN. The magical door within DOORWAY CAVE and the coff which held the MANNI's BRANNI BOB were also made of this enduring and sacred material. In *The Drawing of the Three* we were told that the grips of Roland's guns were made of ironwood rather than sandalwood (elsewhere they remain sandalwood), and in *The Wolves of the Calla* we discovered that the feast table in SUSANNAH-MIO's dream version of CASTLE DISCORDIA was also made of this sacred substance.

In *The Wind Through the Keyhole,* we find out much more about these strange trees that, once upon a bye, grew deep in the NORTH'RD BARONY's ENDLESS FOREST, north of NEW CANAAN. According to the COVENANT MAN, the ironwoods of the Endless Forest could think, and that was why woodsmen always cried the trees' pardon before beginning work. The old folken of TREE VILLAGE believed that when the winds came out of the north, the sweet-sour smell of the ironwood forest brought visions. For NELL ROSS, who had lost her beloved husband, JACK ROSS, to the ironwood forest, this scent was both bitter and sweet, like blood and strawberries.

The woodsmen of Tree both loved and feared the ironwood forest, which was wise. The forest fed and clothed the men's families, but like a living being it also needed to eat, and its food was often the woodsmen themselves. Despite the risks, cutting ironwood was a lucrative job. Both seaworthy and rot resistant (ironwood coffins would last a thousand years), this unusual wood fetched such a high price that it was paid for in silver rather than scrip. Still, many woodsmen contented themselves with harvesting the blossies that grew at the forest edge rather than attempting to cut the more valuable commodity. Only very brave and strong men—like Big Ross and his partner, BIG KELLS—dared to go deeper to where the good ironwood grew. And not even Ross or his treacherous partner dared to travel to the edge of the FAGONARD where ironwoods grew bigger than houses.

According to TIM ROSS, the ironwoods at the heart of the Endless Forest were as tall, straight, and solemn as Manni elders at a funeral. Although they were completely smooth for the first forty feet, above that their branches leaped skyward like upraised arms, tangling the narrow IRONWOOD TRAIL with a cobweb of shadows. Anyone foolish enough to wander off the trail or go beyond it quickly became lost in a maze.

Perhaps it was the dangerousness of the ironwood forest that inspired the people of Tree to link it to the afterlife. In DUSTIN STOKES burial parlor, there was a little room with forest scenes painted on the walls. In the center was an ironwood bier, an open space that represented the clearing at the end of life's path. *See also* NORTH'RD BARONY: IRONWOOD FOREST *in* MID-WORLD PLACES

I:56 *(2003 edition)*, I:178 *(2003 edition)*, I:179*(2003 edition)*, I:180 *(2003 edition)*, I:182 *(2003 edition)*, I:209 *(2003 edition)*, I:210 *(2003 edition)*, I:217 *(2003 edition)*, II:18, IV:117, IV:171, IV:178, IV:218, IV:519, V:73, V:81, V:131, V:294, V:313, V:352, V:409, V:411, V:612, VI:28, VII:194, VII:560, VII:679, VII:724, VII:779, W:47, W:109, W:110, W:111, W:114, W:115 *(forest)*, W:117, W:118 *(forest)*, W:119, W:122, W:125, W:127, W:129, W:133, W:136, W:139, W:145, W:146–64 *(Tim in the forest)*, W:168, W:172, W:175, 177 *(and clearing)*, W:181, W:182, W;183, W:189–255 *(Tim in forest, in Fagonard, at Dogan)*, W:257, W:285

ISRAEL
See MAINE CHARACTERS

ITTAWAY, DAVE
See BREAKERS

J

JAFFORDS FAMILY (KA-JAFFORDS)
The Jaffords clan of CALLA BRYN STURGIS owns a smallhold farm near the banks of the RIVER WHYE. Unlike the other Calla *folken*, they have consistently resisted the WOLVES of THUNDERCLAP. Seventy years before our story began, JAMIE JAFFORDS and a *moit* of friends fought the Wolves on the EAST ROAD. Jamie was the only one of the WOLF POSSE to survive, but thanks to him, Roland and his *tet* find out that the Wolves are actually robots produced by the sinister company NORTH CENTRAL POSITRONICS. TIAN JAFFORDS, Jamie's grandson, is the first in his village to suggest that the town should stand against the Wolves, paving the way for Roland's battle against the child-stealing villains of Thunderclap. ZALIA, Tian's wife, is one of the SISTERS OF ORIZA. She and the other Sisters of the Plate fight alongside Roland and his *tet* during the East Road battle.

V:1, V:3, V:8, V:321, V:340, V:343, V:353, V:380, V:394, V:396, V:401, V:488, V:492, VI:178 *(Jaffords's Rentals in Maine)*, VI:184 *(Jaffords's Rentals in Maine)*

HOONIK, ZALMAN: ZALIA JAFFORDS's ROONT brother, who lives with the Jaffords family. *See* CALLA BRYN STURGIS CHARACTERS: ROONTS

JAFFORDS, AARON: Aaron Jaffords is the two-year-old son of TIAN and ZALIA JAFFORDS. He is their youngest child, and a singleton. Unlike twins, singletons are safe from the WOLVES. V:9, V:10 *(children)*, V:14 *(indirect)*, V:15, V:25, V:143, V:146, V:162 *(indirect)*, V:344–46, V:351–56, V:379 *(indirect)*, V:380, V:397 *(indirect)*, V:488–92 *(present)*, V:494 *(baby)*

JAFFORDS, GRAN-PERE (JAMIE): Gran-pere Jaffords is the father of the deceased LUKE JAFFORDS and the grandfather of TIAN JAFFORDS. He is also the oldest person in the Calla. Although he is now toothless and spends most of his time dozing by the fire, in his youth he was full of thorn and bark. Seventy years before our story began, when Jamie was just NINETEEN years old, he and his friends MOLLY DOOLIN, EAMON DOOLIN, and POKEY SLIDELL formed a POSSE to defeat the WOLVES of THUNDERCLAP. Molly Doolin managed to kill one of the invaders with her ORIZA, but Jamie was the only human to survive the standoff.

Although Gran-pere lives with Tian and his family, he and his grandson have not spoken civilly for years. Their long feud began when Luke Jaffords allowed seventeen-year-old Tian to site the family well with a drotta, or dowsing stick, against Jamie's wishes. Tian found water, but when his father tried to dig the well, the ground collapsed under him and he was buried alive in the clay-filled water.

Like many of the people of the Calla, Gran-pere Jaffords wears a Jesus-tree. However, he doesn't seem particularly pious. During dinner grace he picks his nose. Despite his advanced years, Jamie Jaffords still has an eye for pretty ladies. He especially likes his granddaughter-in-law, ZALIA. V:1, V:10, V:11, V:12, V:13, V:14, V:25, V:27, V:162, V:236–37, V:322, V:346–48, V:352–69, V:377, V:396, V:401, V:405, V:419–20, V:485–86, V:484–92 *(present)*, V:494, V:509, V:530, V:601–17 *(present; mentioned directly on 601, 603, 608, 610, 611)*, V:621, V:664, V:679, VII:385

    GRAN-PERE'S GRAN-PERE: V:12

    GRAN-PERE'S TWIN: *See* CALLA BRYN STURGIS CHARACTERS: ROONTS

JAFFORDS, HEDDA: Hedda Jaffords is HEDDON JAFFORDS's twin. She and Heddon are the oldest of TIAN and ZALIA's five children. They are ten-year-old dark blonds. Hedda is the cleverer of the twins, but her brother is better-tempered. Tian describes her as good but plain-faced. V:9, V:10, V:12, V:13, V:14 *(children)*, V:15 *(children)*, V:23, V:144–45, V:146, V:162 *(indirect)*, V:344–46, V:351–56, V:357, V:379 *(indirect)*, V:380 *(indirect)*, V:397 *(indirect)*, V:488–92 *(present)*, V:494, V:601–17 *(present; mentioned directly on 603, 605)*, V:662–67 *(with children)*

JAFFORDS, HEDDON: Heddon Jaffords is HEDDA JAFFORDS's twin. He is not as clever as his sister but is more agreeable. He and Hedda are ten-year-old dark blonds. V:9, V:10, V:12, V:13, V:14 *(children)*, V:15 *(children)*, V:23,

V:144–45, V:146, V:162 *(indirect)*, V:344–46, V:351–56, V:357, V:379 *(indirect)*, V:380 *(indirect)*, V:397 *(indirect)*, V:488–92 *(present)*, V:494, V:601–17 *(present; mentioned directly on 603)*, V:662–67 *(with children)*, V:696

JAFFORDS, JAMIE: See JAFFORDS, GRAN-PERE, *listed above*

JAFFORDS, LIA: Lia is LYMAN JAFFORDS's twin. She is five years old. V:9, V:10, V:12, V:14 *(indirect)*, V:15 *(indirect)*, V:23, V:146, V:162 *(indirect)*, V:344–46, V:351–56, V:357, V:379, V:380 *(indirect)*, V:397 *(indirect)*, V:488–92 *(present)*, V:494, V:662–67 *(with children)*, V:693

JAFFORDS, LUKE: Luke Jaffords was the son of JAMIE JAFFORDS and the father of TIAN and TIA JAFFORDS. After Tia was taken to THUNDERCLAP and returned roont, Luke Jaffords doted on Tian. He even let his seventeen-year-old son site the family's new well, using a drotta, or dowsing stick, despite negative predictions by Jamie. Tian found the water they'd been searching for, but when his father dug the well, its clay sides collapsed and buried Luke alive. The grief and anger that resulted from this tragic and avoidable death set Tian and Jamie against each other forever after. V:8 *(Tian's father)*, V:15, V:24, V:123, V:347, V:368, V:485

JAFFORDS, LYMAN: He is LIA JAFFORDS's twin. He is five years old. V:9, V:10, V:12, V:14 *(indirect)*, V:15 *(indirect)*, V:23, V:146, V:162 *(indirect)*, V:344–46, V:351–56, V:357, V:379, V:380 *(indirect)*, V:397 *(indirect)*, V:488–92 *(present)*, V:494

JAFFORDS, TIA (ROONT): See CALLA BRYN STURGIS CHARACTERS: ROONTS

JAFFORDS, TIAN: Tian Jaffords is about thirty years old. He and his wife, ZALIA JAFFORDS, have five children—two sets of twins and one singleton. Tian is an anomaly in his village. Unlike most of the other smallhold farmers, he can read and write. He can also work with numbers. It is Tian Jaffords who calls the men of the Calla to meet at the TOWN GATHERING HALL so that they can try to save their children from the WOLVES. Tian and his GRAN-PERE have not spoken civilly in years. Each blames the other for LUKE JAFFORDS's death.

While Zalia Jaffords stands against the Wolves during the Calla's final battle, Tian acts as one of the CHILD-MINDERS. V:1–31, V:44 *(follows ka-tet)*, V:45 *(follows ka-tet)*, V:47 *(follows ka-tet)*, V:88 *(new friends)*, V:92 *(indirect)*, V:106 *(indirect)*, V:109 *(indirect)*, V:111–13, V:116, V:122–37, V:142–60, V:162, V:201–10 *(present; mentioned directly on 208)*, V:211–34 *(present; mentioned directly on 214, 216, 218, 222)*, V:236 *(indirect)*, V:237, V:319, V:343, V:344–57, V:359, V:360, V:368, V:376–77, V:379, V:380, V:397 *(indirect)*, V:398–99, V:419, V:485, V:486–92 *(present)*, V:494, V:572, V:587, V:589, V:601–17, V:629–35, V:641, V:644–50, V:652, V:654, V:662–67 *(present)*, V:686, V:689 *(folken)*, V:693–97 *(folken)*, VI:204, VI:373

MOTHER: Mentioned but unnamed. V:1

UNCLE: While trying to break ground in SON OF A BITCH, TIAN's uncle was attacked by MUTANT WASPS. V:1

JAFFORDS, ZALIA: See ORIZA, SISTERS OF

JAFFORDS RENTALS
See MAINE (STATE OF): EAST STONEHAM, *in* OUR WORLD PLACES

JAKE
See CHAMBERS, JAKE

JAKLI
See TAHEEN: BIRDMEN TAHEEN

JAMIE
See DeCURRY, JAMIE

JAVIER, ANNABELLE
See CALLA BRYN STURGIS CHARACTERS: FARMERS (SMALLHOLD):
JAVIER, BUCKY

JAVIER, BUCKY
See CALLA BRYN STURGIS CHARACTERS: FARMERS (SMALLHOLD)

JAVIER, BULLY
See CALLA BRYN STURGIS CHARACTERS: ROONTS

JAVIER, ROBERTA
See CALLA BRYN STURGIS CHARACTERS: FARMERS (SMALLHOLD):
JAVIER, BUCKY

JEFFERSON FAMILY
See SKIN-MAN: SKIN-MAN'S VICTIMS

JEFFERSON RANCH CHARACTERS
See SKIN-MAN: SKIN-MAN'S VICTIMS; *and* DEBARIA CHARACTERS:
JEFFERSON RANCH CHARACTERS. *See also* STREETER, BILL

JEFFY
See CALLAHAN, FATHER DONALD FRANK: CALLAHAN'S HOME
SHELTER ASSOCIATES

JEMMIN
See MANNI

JENKINS
See WARRIORS OF THE SCARLET EYE: DEVAR-TOI CHARACTERS:
UNKNOWN RACE

JENNA, SISTER
See ELURIA, LITTLE SISTERS OF

JESSERLING, PETRA
See PIPER SCHOOL CHARACTERS

JESUS DOG (CROSS DOG)
   See ELURIA CHARACTERS

JEY
   See TAHEEN: BIRDMEN TAHEEN; *see also* WARRIORS OF THE SCAR-
LET EYE: DIXIE PIG CHARACTERS: TAHEEN

JIM (UNCLE JIM)
   See BREAKERS: BRAUTIGAN, TED

"JIM CROW"
Jim Crow was a character in an early-nineteenth-century plantation song found
in our world. His name was given to the set of laws and social practices known
as segregation. During her time on our level of the DARK TOWER, SUSANNAH
DEAN and other Civil Rights activists fought to oust the Jim Crow policies
found in the South.
   II:234, II:235, II:236

J.J. THE BLUE JAY
   See BREAKERS: EARNSHAW, DINKY

JOCHABIM
   See WARRIORS OF THE SCARLET EYE: DIXIE PIG CHARACTERS:
HUMANS

JOHN LAWS
This bit of slang means "policeman."
   VI:65

**JOHNS, ALAIN (RICHARD STOCKWORTH)
Alain Johns was Roland's sworn brother and his fellow gunslinger. Although
he is mentioned earlier, we do not meet Alain until *Wizard and Glass,* when he
and CUTHBERT ALLGOOD accompany Roland to the OUTER ARC town of
HAMBRY.
   Alain was a big boy with a mop of unruly blond hair, bright blue eyes, and
a round face. Because of his looks, many people assumed he was a dullard (in
The Wind Through the Keyhole, STEVEN DESCHAIN derisively called the boy
Thudfood); however, he was actually both clever and sensitive. Like Roland's
later *ka-tet* mate JAKE CHAMBERS, Alain had "the touch." Perhaps because of
this mixture of empathy and psychic ability, Alain was much more stable than
volatile Cuthbert.
   While in Hambry, Alain's alias was Richard Stockworth. His horse was
named BUCKSKIN. In the original version of *The Gunslinger,* Alain was not
mentioned, though Roland spoke of a friend named ALLEN. In the 2003 version
of *The Gunslinger,* Allen's name is replaced with Alain's.
   After the fall of GILEAD, Alain, Roland, Cuthbert, and JAMIE DeCURRY
experienced one of MID-WORLD's BEAMQUAKES. Sadly, just before the battle

of JERICHO HILL, Alain was shot by Roland and Cuthbert. The shooting was accidental, but nevertheless deadly.

II:355 *(dies under Roland and Cuthbert's guns)*, II:394, III:15, III:33, III:41, III:60, III:262, III:276, III:279, III:280, IV:59, IV:119, IV:148 *(as Richard Stockworth)*, IV:151–53, IV:162, IV:163 *(Buckskin only)*, IV:164, IV:174, IV:179–80 *(Mayor Thorin's party; 179 Alain described)*, IV:181–89 *(Flashback to Sheriff Avery visit; 183–84 false papers. Richard Stockworth, Rancher's son, 184 described)*, IV:190–91 *(discussing Avery)*, IV:191–210 *(Mayor Thorin's party continued)*, IV:218–21 *(Travellers' Rest standoff)*, IV:224–30 *(standoff continued; 224 "the touch"; 226–30 with Avery)*, IV:241, IV:259–60 *("Little Coffin Hunters")*, IV:261–64 *(261 pigeons and message. 263 Susan's hair)*, IV:266–71 *(Depape finds out identities)*, IV:271–77, IV:280 *(gives message to Susan)*, IV:282, IV:283, IV:284–88, IV:291, IV:344–47, IV:357–61, IV:371, IV:388–89 *(the touch and premonitions)*, IV:392–93 *(the touch and senses trouble at Bar K)*, IV:398–402, IV:408–15, IV:426–42 *(428 described; 432 Roland's plan of attack; 436 speaks to Susan in her trance state; 436–39 Steven Deschain and Maerlyn's Grapefruit; 439 Christopher Johns [a.k.a. "Burning Chris"])*, IV:443 *("magic in his hands")*, IV:454–56, IV:463, IV:465, IV:474–80 *(ka-tet arrested)*, IV:482, IV:483, IV:487 *("boys")*, IV:503, IV:506, IV:508–13, IV:514–19, IV:523–24, IV:525 *(mentioned)*, IV:526, IV:529–32, IV:533–36, IV:538 *(reference)*, IV:540, IV:547–48, IV:549 *(indirect)*, IV:552–60 *(attacking Jonas's company)*, IV:561 *(indirect reference)*, IV:573–75, IV:579–81, IV:583–84, IV:587–602 *(driving Farson's men into thinny)*, IV:609–11 *(Roland unconscious due to Maerlyn's ball)*, IV:620, IV:658, IV:663, E:186, V:41, V:59, V:78, V:79, V:85, V:98, V:164, V:170, V:182, V:184, V:389, V:400 *(indirect)*, VI:16 *(lived through Beamquake)*, VI:279, VII:219, VII:220, VII:271, VII:497, VII:503, VII:552, VII:762, VII:801, W:38, W:39, W:41, W:65

> **ALAIN'S MOTHER:** IV:391 *(general)*, IV:399
>
> **BUCKSKIN:** Buckskin was the horse Alain rode while in HAMBRY. IV:163
>
> **JOHNS, CHRISTOPHER (BURNING CHRIS):** Alain John's father. In his youth he was known as "Burning Chris." IV:286, IV:436–39, IV:620, V:85 *(father)*, V:195 *(father)*

JOHNSON
See TULL CHARACTERS

JOLENE
See RITZY CHARACTERS

JONAS, ELDRED
See BIG COFFIN HUNTERS

JOSHUA
See WIDOW SMACK

K

KA-JAFFORDS
See JAFFORDS FAMILY

KA-TET OF NINETEEN
See NINETEEN

KA-TET OF NINETY-NINE
See NINETY-NINE

KA-TET OF THE ROSE
See TET CORPORATION

KAS-KA GAN
See KING, STEPHEN; *see also* APPENDIX I

KATZ
Katz was the forty-six-year-old owner of KATZ'S PHARMACY AND SODA FOUNTAIN. With his frail body, balding head, and yellow skin, he looked more like sixty-six. Katz hated his shop and never forgave his father for burdening him with it.
 II:333, II:362–70, II:374, II:375
KATZ SENIOR: Katz's deceased father. Katz curses him every day.
 II:363, II:365, II:366–67, II:375
 KATZ'S EMPLOYEES, CUSTOMERS, AND COMPETITORS:
  BRUMHALL, DR.: MRS. RATHBUN's doctor. He's a little too free handing out the Valium prescriptions. II:364–65
  DOLLENTZ: Katz's competitor in the pharmacy business. II:365
  GUY IN LEATHER JACKET: This guy tries to sneak up on MORT/ Roland with a knife. Roland shoots it out of his hand. II:368–69
  KATZ'S PIMPLE-FACED ASSISTANT: II:365–70
  LENNOX, RALPH: Security guard at Katz's. II:365–70
  RATHBUN, MRS.: She's a Valium addict who harasses Katz with outdated prescriptions until he refills them. II:363–65, II:366

KELLS, BIG BERN
Big Bern Kells was a character in the folktale "The Wind Through the Keyhole," which Roland recounted to YOUNG BILL STREETER while the two of them spent time in the DEBARIA JAIL. (Neither of them had done anything wrong. Young Bill was the only witness to the SKIN-MAN massacre at the JEFFERSON RANCH, so Roland was trying to keep the boy safe in the most secure environment possible.)
 At the beginning of our story, the woodsman Big Bern Kells was a forty-year-old widower with thinning hair and a black beard. Kells was the pard of BIG JACK ROSS, the father of eleven-year-old TIM ROSS, hero of the tale. Big Kells

and Big Ross worked the ROSS-KELLS STAKE, cutting valuable IRONWOOD which they then sold to the TREE SAWMILL.

Many years previously, Big Kells, Big Ross, and Ross's wife NELL had been childhood friends, and both Ross and Kells had vied for Nell's kisses. Ross had won Nell's hand, and though Kells had stood by Ross at the wedding and had slipped the silk around the new couple, in his secret heart he was eaten alive by jealousy. Although he was good-humored and laughing when he was sober, after Nell and Big Ross's wedding, Kells's habit of drunken violence grew worse. After a particularly nasty binge in which Kells destroyed most of the furniture in the local saloon before passing out, Big Ross told Kells that he had to stop. When he was sober he was good and dependable, but when he was drunk he was no more reliable than quickmud. Unless Kells quit the drink, Ross would look for a new cutting pard. Despite the fact that his living was in danger, Kells kept drinking, brawling, and bawding for a few months more. However, when he met MILLICENT REDHOUSE, he sobered up and married. Big Kells and Milly were married for six seasons, until Milly died giving birth. (The baby died soon after.) Milly's dying wish was that Kells stayed off the drink. He did, at least until his loneliness and desire for Nell Ross drove him to the vile act of murder.

In Tim Ross's eleventh year, Big Kells came out of the ENDLESS FOREST on his own. His skin was sooty and his jerkin was charred. There was a hole in the left leg of his homespun pants. Red and blistered flesh peeped through it. He claimed that he'd been singed by a DRAGON—a dragon that had incinerated his partner. Later on we discover that Kells's tale of a dragon was nothing more than a concocted alibi, and that all of his burns were self-inflicted. In truth, Kells had crept up on his partner and had struck him on the back of the head. Then he'd hidden Big Ross's dead body in a stream located on a fallow stub of the COSINGTON-MARCHLY STAKE.

Not long after Big Ross's death, Kells began courting Nell. Reluctantly—and for the most part out of fear of the Barony's tax-collecting COVENANT MAN—Nell agreed to slip the rope with her deceased husband's partner. Kells sold his own house to BALDY ANDERSON and moved into the Ross cottage. Although he managed to remain teetotal for a brief period, soon Kells's temper and his simmering resentment of Nell got the better of him. Blaming his new wife for all his ills (after all, if she hadn't tempted him with her good looks he wouldn't have killed his friend), he turned to drink. Kells—whose beard was now streaked with gray—began beating his wife and new stepson, and even made Tim give up his lessons at the WIDOW SMACK'S COTTAGE so that he could earn money at the Tree Sawmill. Kells's reputation in the village became so bad that he couldn't even get a new partner to replace Ross. Instead, he was forced to go cutting in the Ironwood Forest alone, which was a dangerous business indeed.

This unhappy situation was a perfect one for the wicked Covenant Man to exploit. While collecting taxes at the Ross house (now the Kells house), the Covenant Man gave Young Tim a key which would open any lock, hinting that Tim should look inside his stepfather's well-loved trunk. While Big Kells was drinking himself into unconsciousness at GITTY's, Tim used the key as the Covenant Man directed. Inside, among ragged clothing, rusty tools, and a picture of the deceased Millicent Kells, Tim found his father's lucky coin. Knowing that a real dragon would have melted the coin which his father always wore on a silver chain around his neck, Tim began to suspect his stepfather of murder. This suspicion was confirmed by the Covenant Man himself, who showed Tim his father's corpse floating six or eight inches below the surface of a stream. Using his magic SILVER BASIN, the Barony tax-collector also showed Tim an image of Kells smashing Nell on the forehead with a heavy ceramic jug and beating her into unconsciousness for the sin of opening his trunk.

Terrified for his mother's safety and enraged at his father's murder, Tim returned home where the Widow Smack was nursing blinded Nell. Tim informed PETER COSINGTON, ERNIE MARCHLY, and Baldy Anderson about his steppa's crimes, and the men gathered a posse to find the murderer. Now a wanted man, Kells stayed on the run, shivering out the STARKBLAST under a pile of hay in DEAF RINCON'S BARN. But when Tim returned from the Endless Forest with a magic potion to cure his mother's blindness, Kells was waiting. Having already slit the Widow Smack's throat, Kells waited near his trunk in the mudroom while Tim spoke with his ma in the bedroom. When Tim emerged, Kells grabbed the boy by the neck and began choking him. Once Tim's struggles weakened, Kells tossed aside Tim's four-shot gun so that he could throw Tim onto the fire. But before he could make good on his threat to burn Tim alive, Nell Ross buried the blade of her first husband's ax in Bern Kells's head, killing him. W:110, W:116–20, W:121, W:122, W:123–24 *(124 wedding day)*, W:125–27, W:128, W:129, W:130, W:131–38 *(138 hits Nell)*, W:139, W:140, W:141, W:142 (miser), W:143, W:144, W:145, W:146, W:153–54 *(in basin vision)*, W:155, W:158, W:160, W:161 *(murderer)*, W:162, W:165, W:166 *(beast)*, W:167–68, W:170, W:171 *(his evil told by Tim)*, W:172, W:173, W:175, W:176, W:178, W:190, W:196, W:206, W:221, W:238, W:241, W:246 *(indirect)*, W:262–64 *(263 ax in head)*, W:267

FATHER (MATHIAS): Big Kells's father, Mathias Kells, was killed in the ENDLESS FOREST by a vert, also known as a bullet-bird. The vert had bored a hole right through him with its stony beak. Bern Kells learned his habit of wife-beating from Mathias. (Nastiness ran in the family.) Kells's much-loved trunk once belonged to his father. W:125, W:126, W:129 *(died from Vert)*, W:133, W:135

> **WIFE (BERN'S MOTHER):** We don't learn anything about Bern Kells's mother except that her husband beat her. W:135

KELLS, MILLICENT (MILLICENT REDHOUSE): When TIM ROSS searched through his stepfather's trunk, he found a picture of Kells's first wife, Millicent Redhouse. Millicent was only five feet tall and had masses of dark hair that tumbled over her shoulders. She died giving birth to Bern Kells's child. W:117, W:119 *(Redhouse)*, W:122, W:139, W:143

> **BABY:** Bern Kells's only child died shortly after birth. W:119

LIMPING PETER (GRANDFATHER): W:133

MULES: Bern Kells's mules were as ill-tempered as their master. W:145

POSSE: After hearing about JACK ROSS'S murder from TIM ROSS, PETER COSINGTON, ERNIE MARCHLY and BALDY ANDERSON gathered this posse to find the murdering trull, Bern Kells. In the end, NELL ROSS (also known as Nell Kells) saved them the trouble. She buried an ax in Bern Kells's head. W:175

KELLS, MILLICENT
   See KELLS, BIG BERN

KELLS, NELL
   See ROSS, NELL

KELLY, TAMMY
   See WARRIORS OF THE SCARLET EYE: DEVAR-TOI CHARACTERS: HUMANS

KENNEDY, JOHN F.
John F. Kennedy, who was much admired by SUSANNAH DEAN, was the thirty-fifth President of the United States. During his three years in office he introduced the legislative program called the "New Frontier," which was supposed to extend Civil Rights. He was allegedly assassinated by **LEE HARVEY OSWALD** in November 1963, only about four months before Susannah entered MID-WORLD. Two days after the assassination, Oswald was shot at point-blank range by **JACK RUBY.** Kennedy's successor was Lyndon B. Johnson.
   II:185–87

KENNERLY
   See TULL CHARACTERS

KENOPENSKY, MARY LOU
   See DEAN, EDDIE: EDDIE'S PAST ASSOCIATES

KEYSTONE WORLD
   See entry in PORTALS

KEYSTONE YEAR
   See NINETEEN NINETY-NINE

KI'-DAM
   See WARRIORS OF THE SCARLET EYE: WARRIORS BY LOCATION: DEVAR-TOI CHARACTERS: HUMANS: PRENTISS, PIMLI

KID SEVENTY-SEVEN
   See CHAMBERS, JAKE

KIDZPLAY
   See GUTTENBERG, FURTH, AND PATEL: DAMASCUS, TRUDY

KILLINGTON
   See NORTH CENTRAL POSITRONICS: BLAINE

KING, STEPHEN (THE WRITER, KAS-KA GAN)
Like TED BRAUTIGAN, Stephen King—our favorite *kas-ka Gan*—is actually a facilitator. However, whereas Ted's special talent increases the psychic abilities

of those around him, *sai* King's special skill brings characters out of the PRIM and into the world of form. In more than two hundred short stories and more than forty novels, King has created hundreds of doorways leading into, and out of, KEYSTONE EARTH. No wonder there is such a problem with WALK-INS in his part of the world.

When seven-year-old King was on punishment duty sawing wood in his uncle's barn, he was approached by the CRIMSON KING, Lord of Discordia. The Red King wanted to make little Stevie into a bard of the Outer Dark, but he was destined to be thwarted in this endeavor. Steve King was saved by CUTH-BERT ALLGOOD and EDDIE DEAN, who convinced him to serve the cause of the WHITE instead. The Red King (never a good loser) has been gunning for King ever since.

Stephen King makes several guest appearances in the final books of the Dark Tower series. In *Song of Susannah,* King comes face-to-face with two of his "creations"—Roland of GILEAD and Eddie Dean of NEW YORK. King also plays a kind of deus ex machina by leaving JAKE CHAMBERS a key to SUSAN-NAH's room in the PLAZA–PARK HYATT so that Jake and PERE CALLAHAN can retrieve BLACK THIRTEEN. King plays this role again in *The Dark Tower,* when he warns Susannah Dean that the seemingly friendly JOE COLLINS is not what he seems. (He is actually the were-spider DANDELO.)

Although his characters form the TET CORPORATION to keep King and the ROSE safe, the *todanna,* or death-bag, which Roland and Eddie saw around the writer back in BRIDGTON, MAINE, is destined to have its day. In 1999—the KEYSTONE YEAR in the KEYSTONE WORLD—Stephen King is hit by a Dodge minivan driven by BRYAN SMITH. King's life is saved by Jake Chambers, who jumps between him and the oncoming vehicle. King survives the accident but Jake does not. As a badly hurt King lies on the side of SLAB CITY HILL, an angry Roland makes King promise to finish the Dark Tower series. True to his promise, King has done so.

> V:54, V:706, V:709, VI:167, VI:168–72, VI:207–8, VI:210 *(tale-spinner),* VI:211, VI:221, VI:270–303 *(294 possessed by Gan; his Beam is the Bear-Turtle Beam),* VI:322–24, VI:336, VI:350, VI:389–411 *(journal extracts and article about accident),* VII:17, VII:18, VII:33, VII:36, VII:39, VII:76, VII:120, VII:121, VII:125 *(writah),* VII:143–44 *(telecaster),* VII:145, VII:173–74, VII:266, VII:300, VII:301, VII:302, VII:303–7, VII:311, VII:312–14, VII:332, VII:336, VII:388, VII:405, VII:406, VII:409, VII:424, VII:434, VII:435, VII:436–39, VII:440, VII:441, VII:442, VII:444–62, VII:465, VII:467–68, VII:472, VII:475, VII:480, VII:485, VII:487, VII:505, VII:511–15, VII:524, VII:534, VII:542–45, VII:552, VII:601–13 *(uffis),* VII:614, VII:627, VII:680–81, VII:689 *(enters tale again),* VII:690–95 *(leaves poem),* VII:706, VII:728, VII:802

BACHMAN, RICHARD: See BACHMAN, RICHARD, *listed separately*

CALDERWOOD, FLOYD: A friend or acquaintance of King's, Floyd Calder-wood also makes a guest appearance in King's novel *It.* In that book, he appears in a flashback as a 1905 lumberjack who has a shady past. VI:276

CARLINER, MARK: VI:409

FAN MAIL/HATE MAIL: VI:401–3, VI:406

    SPIER, JOHN T.: VI:401

VELE, MRS. CORETTA: VI:402–3, VI:406 *(Vermont gramma)*

FERMAN, ED: Editor in chief of *Fantasy and Science Fiction.* VI:390–91

FULCHER, ANDY: Babysitter. VI:391, VI:395

GRANT, DONALD: The publisher who first put King's novel *The Gunslinger* into print. VI:392, VI:395, VI:396, VI:403

HATLEN, BURT: Steve King's professor and friend who teaches at the UNIVERSITY OF MAINE. Burt Hatlen arranged for King to be a writer in residence at the University of Maine at ORONO. VI:391

HAUSER, FRED: VI:407

HOLSTEN, RAND: VI:409

JONES, BETTY: OWEN KING's babysitter. VI:289, VI:301

KING FAMILY (GENERAL): VI:272, VI:273 *(kids)*, VI:280 *(kids)*, VI:295 *(kids)*, VI:391 *(kids)*, VI:396 *(kids)*, VI:405 *(kids)*, VII:436, VI:438

   AUNTIE ETHELYN: King's aunt. VI:292, VI:389

   KING, DAVE: Stephen King's brother. VI:278, VI:292, VI:389, VI:399

   KING, JOE: King's eldest son. VI:280, VI:281, VI:283, VI:287 *(indirect)*, VI:296, VI:297, VI:301, VI:302, VI:389, VI:390, VI:406, VI:407, VI:408, VI:409

      ETHAN (SON): VI:409

      WIFE: VI:406, VI:410

   KING, NAOMI: King's daughter. VI:280, VI:390, VI:393, VI:405, VI:410

   KING, OWEN: King's youngest son. VI:280, VI:289, VI:389, VI:391, VI:392, VI:393, VI:404, VI:407, VI:408, VI:410

   KING, TABITHA (TABBY): King's wife. VI:273, VI:280, VI:285, VI:286, VI:289, VI:295, VI:389, VI:390, VI:391, VI:394, VI:398, VI:403–4, VI:406, VI:407, VI:408–9

      FATHER: VI:280 *(poppa)*

      MOTHER: VI:280 *(nana)*, VI:389 *(nanna)*

   KING'S MOTHER: VI:278, VI:286

   UNCLE OREN: King's uncle. VI:292, VI:389

KOSTER, ELAINE: She worked for NAL. VI:393

MANSFIELD FAMILY (DAVIE, SANDY, MEGAN): VI:398

MARLOWE: King's dog, who resembles OY. VII:544–45

McCAULEY, KIRBY: King's agent. VI:390–91, VI:392, VI:393

McCAUSLAND, CHARLES (CHIP): *See* MAINE CHARACTERS, *listed separately*

McCUTCHEON, MAC: VI:276

McKEEN (GROUNDSKEEPER): Great-grandson of GARRETT McKEEN, who lived in the LOVELL area more than one hundred years before our story takes place. The present Mr. McKeen is the groundskeeper for the King's family home, CARA LAUGHS. Roland thinks of him as King's bondsman. VII:437–38, VII:441–42, VII:443

   McKEEN, GARRETT: Garrett McKeen lived in the Lovell area of Maine at the turn of the twentieth century. His great-grandson is Stephen King's groundskeeper. VII:439, VII:443

McLEOD, GEORGE: One of King's old drinking buddies from his UNIVERSITY OF MAINE days. VI:409

ROUTHIER, RAY (REPORTER): This reporter writes King's obituary, which appears at the very end of *Song of Susannah*. Luckily, our *tet* prevents this disaster from taking place. However, altering *ka* always has its price. King survives being hit by BRYAN SMITH's van, but Jake Chambers dies in his place. VI:410

SMITH, BRYAN: Bryan Smith (who, we are told, is SHEEMIE's twinner) has two Rottweilers, BULLET and PISTOL, and an extremely long list of motor vehicle offenses. In the KEYSTONE EARTH, Smith hits both Jake Chambers and Stephen King with his 1985 Dodge minivan. King survives the accident but Jake does not. VII:433–34, VII:440–41, VII:443–44, VII:447, VII:448–62, VII:463, VII:467–68, VII:472, VII:528, VII:543

  BULLET: VII:433–34, VII:441 *(indirect)*, VII:444, VII:448–49, VII:456, VII:461

  HIPPIES WITH DRUGS: VII:433

  PISTOL: VII:433–34, VII:441 *(indirect)*, VII:444, VII:448, VII:456, VII:461

SOYCHAK, MR.: King's algebra teacher. VI:289

THOMPSON, FLIP: King's old drinking buddy from his UNIVERSITY OF MAINE days. VI:409

VAUGHN, SAM: VI:393

VERDON, HENRY K.: The sociologist Henry K. Verdon authored the article on WALK-INS which Stephen King pasted into his journal. VI:397–98

VERRILL, CHUCK: Stephen King's New York editor. VII:448

ZOLTAN: *See* BORDER DWELLERS, *listed separately*

KING DANDO
See DANDO (KING DANDO)

KINGERY, MR.
See PIPER SCHOOL CHARACTERS

KING'S TOWN GIRL
This girl was one of the many that Roland loved and then left behind.
  I:158

KNOPF, MR.
See PIPER SCHOOL CHARACTERS

KOSTER, ELAINE
See KING, STEPHEN

KUVIAN NIGHT-SOLDIER
It seems likely that the Kuvian night-soldiers were a band of assassins.
  I:200

L

LADY BLACKBIRD
See DEAN, SUSANNAH

LADY OF SHADOWS
See DEAN, SUSANNAH

LADY OF THE PLATE
See ORIZA, LADY

LADY OR THE TIGER, THE
See MID-WORLD FOLKLORE: DIANA'S DREAM

LADY ORIZA
See ORIZA, LADY

LADY RICE
See ORIZA, LADY

**LAMERK INDUSTRIES (LAMERK FOUNDRY)
In the days of the GREAT OLD ONES, LaMerk Foundry built the long and rusty bridge leading to the city of LUD. It also manufactured Lud's manhole covers. According to SYLVIA PITTSTON in the 2003 version of *The Gunslinger,* the INTERLOPER (also known as THE CRIMSON KING) was responsible for LaMerk's nasty machines.

As we find out in EDDIE's dream about the destruction of JAKE's magic LOT on SECOND AVENUE and FORTY SIXTH STREET, LaMerk is connected to that enemy of the ROSE found in our world—MILLS CONSTRUCTION AND SOMBRA REAL ESTATE. In fact, it is probably part of the SOMBRA GROUP.

In one of the ALTERNATIVE AMERICAS that CALLAHAN travels through, a footbridge (just in the shadow of the GEORGE WASHINGTON BRIDGE) stretches across the HUDSON RIVER. This nineteenth-century bridge was repaired by LaMerk Industries during the bicentennial.

III:290, III:326, IV:100 *(Eddie's bulldozer dream),* V:5, V:132, V:292–93, V:460, V:578, V:633, V:650

LAMLA
See TAHEEN: STOAT-HEADED TAHEEN

LARS
See CALLAHAN, FATHER DONALD FRANK: CALLAHAN'S HIDDEN HIGHWAYS ASSOCIATES

LATIGO
See FARSON'S MEN

LATIGO, GEORGE
  See FARSON, JOHN: FARSON'S MEN

LAVENDER HILL MOB
According to SUSANNAH DEAN, in her *when* and *where* of early 1960s
GREENWICH VILLAGE, the term *Lavender Hill Mob* was an oblique reference
to homosexual men.
  VII:549

LEABROOK REGISTER
  See CALLAHAN, FATHER DONALD FRANK: CALLAHAN'S HIDDEN
HIGHWAYS ASSOCIATES

LEEDS, TANYA
  See BREAKERS

LEFTY ROSS
  See ROSS, TIM

**LEGION
  See AGELESS STRANGER

LENGYLL, FRANCIS
  See HAMBRY CHARACTERS: HORSEMEN'S ASSOCIATION

LENNOX, RALPH
  See KATZ

LESSER DEMONS OF THE PRIM
  See DEMONS/SPIRITS/DEVILS

LESTER THE LOBSTER
  See LOBSTROSITIES

LEWIS
  See MANNI

LIA JAFFORDS
  See JAFFORDS FAMILY

LIGHTHOUSE SHELTER WORKERS AND CLIENTS
  See CALLAHAN, FATHER DONALD FRANK: CALLAHAN'S LIGHT-
HOUSE SHELTER ASSOCIATES

LITTLE COFFIN HUNTERS
  See BIG COFFIN HUNTERS

LITTLE SISTERS OF ELURIA
  See ELURIA, LITTLE SISTERS OF

LITTLE SISTERS OF ELURIA
See ELURIA CHARACTERS

LINCOLN, MR.
See HARRIGAN, REVEREND EARL

LION GUARDIAN
See GUARDIANS OF THE BEAM; *see also* ASLAN

LIPPY
See DANDELO

LISA
See CALLAHAN, FATHER DONALD FRANK: CALLAHAN'S HOME SHELTER ASSOCIATES

LLAMREI
See ELD, ARTHUR

LOBSTROSITIES
These critters, which live on the beaches of the WESTERN SEA, look like a cross between scorpions and giant lobsters. They are four feet long, have bleak eyes on stalks, and sharp, serrated beaks. Every time a wave comes, they assume "The Honor Stance" by holding their claws up in the air. They maintain this position until the water crashes over them. Lobstrosities are most vicious at night, and are responsible for eating two of Roland's fingers and some of his toes. They constantly murmur *Dad-a-chum? Did-a-chick? Dum-a-chum? Ded-a-Chek?*
    II:15–21, II:26, II:28–29, II:31, II:32, II:44, II:55, II:93, II:94, II:99–101, II:107, II:135, II:139, II:140–41, II:161–65 *(Eddie and Roland eat them)*, II:167–68, II:206, II:228, II:230, II:238, II:245, II:248, II:253, II:254, II:258, II:267, II:273, II:283, II:286, II:293, II:294, II:297, II:359–60, II:387–90, II:394, III:13, III:52, III:78, III:79, III:150, IV:23, IV:63 *(indirect)*, IV:68, V:46, V:61, V:241, V:379, V:462 *(indirect)*, V:525, V:540, V:686, VI:10, VI:132, VI:295, VI:296, VI:395, VII:741, VII:797, VII:826

LONDON, JACK
See CAN-TOI

LORD GRENFALL
See ORIZA, LADY

LORD OF DISCORDIA
See CRIMSON KING

LORD OF THE SPIDERS
See CRIMSON KING

LORD PERTH
See MID-WORLD FOLKLORE

LORD SEMINON
   See ORIZA, LADY

LOS
   See CRIMSON KING

LOST BEASTS OF ELD
   See ELD, ARTHUR

LOUISE, SISTER
   See ELURIA, LITTLE SISTERS OF

LOVELL, MAINE, CHARACTERS
   See MAINE CHARACTERS

LOW MEN
   See CAN-TOI

LUD CHARACTERS
   See GRAYS *and* PUBES

LUDDITES
On our level of the TOWER, the Luddites were a group of nineteenth-century
textile workers in the English manufacturing districts who rioted and destroyed
the machines which they believed were stealing their jobs. Contemporary Luddites are people who are opposed to increased industry or new technology. In
MID-WORLD, the Luddites are the inhabitants of the city of LUD. Like their
namesakes in our world, their lives have been made unbearable by the totalitari-
anism of mad machines. *See also* GRAYS *and* PUBES.
   VI:287

LUNDGREN, DAHLIE
   See DEAN, EDDIE: EDDIE'S PAST ASSOCIATES

LUSTER
   See PUBES

LYDIA
   See GODS OF MID-WORLD

LYDIA'S DIPPER
   See GODS OF MID-WORLD: OLD MOTHER

LYMAN JAFFORDS
   See JAFFORDS FAMILY

M

MAD DOG OF GILEAD
EDDIE DEAN tells BLAINE the Insane Mono that Roland used to be called the Mad Dog of Gilead.
   III:415, IV:5

**MAERLYN (AGELESS STRANGER; ARTHUR ELD'S MAGE; MAERLYN OF THE ELD)
In the 1982 version of *The Gunslinger,* we were told that Maerlyn was also known as the AGELESS STRANGER, and that—before reaching the DARK TOWER—Roland would have to slay this unknown enemy. In that original version of our story, we were told that Maerlyn, like WALTER, was a minion of the Tower. He *darkled* and *tincted,* or lived in all times. The only being more powerful than Maerlyn was the BEAST—both the originator of all *glammer* and the keeper of the Tower.

In the 2003 edition of *The Gunslinger,* STEPHEN KING cut all references to Maerlyn. Obviously, *sai* King discovered that Maerlyn of the ELD, original keeper of the magic seeing spheres known as MAERLYN'S RAINBOW, had quite a different history than the one previously imparted to him by the sneaky Walter O'Dim. However this is not surprising, since we all know that Walter enjoys twisting the truth.

Throughout most of the Dark Tower series, Maerlyn remains an elusive and mysterious character. Yet in some regions of MID-WORLD, people have come to believe that the good magician Maerlyn and the wicked sorcerer Walter are the same being. In *The Wind Through the Keyhole,* we learn some of the apocryphal stories that explain how a magician serving the White could be turned to the Outer Dark. According to one tale, Maerlyn had once been court mage to ARTHUR ELD himself, but he had been poisoned by the evil glam of the Wizard's Rainbow, the keeping of which had been given to him in the days before the Elden Kingdom fell. Another version of the Maerlyn/Walter tale maintained that, during the mage's wanderings after the fall of Arthur Eld's kingdom, he had discovered certain artyfax of the OLD PEOPLE in the ENDLESS FOREST and his soul had become blackened by them. According to these sources, the wizard still kept a magic house in the Endless Forest, and in the environs of his house, time stood still.

However tempting it might be to think that Maerlyn and Walter are one being, we are given plenty of evidence throughout the series to refute this belief. At the end of *Wizard and Glass,* Walter himself (in the guise of RICHARD FANNIN) told a half-dead TICK-TOCK that he was not and never would be ARTHUR ELD's mage. And in *Wind Through the Keyhole,* we meet the wizard himself, and he assures us that he is the enemy of both the COVENANT MAN (Walter) and Walter's much more powerful master, the CRIMSON KING.

In *Wind,* the mythic Maerlyn becomes not only a living, breathing being, but the focus of TIM ROSS's quest to cure his mother's blindness. Ironically, Tim set out on his journey to find the wizard because of a vision he saw in a MAGIC PAIL of water, left for him by the treacherous Covenant Man. After his mother had been blinded by her cruel second husband, BERN KELLS, and after Tim had found the dead body of his father, JACK ROSS, in a stream in a fallow stub of the COSINGTON-MARCHLY STAKE, Tim stumbled across this bucket as well as the Covenanter's magic wand. The vision which Tim saw in the battered pail seemed innocent enough at first, and perhaps even helpful. In the clear water, Tim watched as a version of himself—water-Tim—visited the wizard in his many-gabled house in a clearing in the forest. Water-Maerlyn gave water-Tim a black silk blindfold which, when placed over Nell's eyes, restored her sight. Although this vision was the catalyst that set Tim on his journey, the reality of finding Maerlyn proved to be much more difficult. *In Song of Susannah,* MIA stated that when magic went away from the world Maerlyn left his many-gabled house and retired to a cave. But in *Wind Through the Keyhole,* we discover that it wasn't a cave that Maerlyn finally ended up in, but a *cage.*

When Tim finally located the real Maerlyn in the clearing of the NORTH FOREST KINNOCK DOGAN, located deep in the Endless Forest, he did not recognize the mage at all. This is not surprising since Maerlyn had been transformed into a huge green-eyed TYGER locked inside a rounded, steel-bar cage. In his tiger form, Maerlyn wore a silver collar around his neck. Hung from the collar were two objects. One looked like a playing card (it was actually a keycard to open the Dogan), and the other was a strangely shaped key. Facing a decision much like that found in the Mid-World legend of DIANA'S DREAM, Tim had to decide between using the cage key and facing the tyger so that he could retrieve the keycard for the Dogan and find shelter from the approaching STARKBLAST, or die in the impending storm.

Drawing his four-shot revolver, Tim opened the tyger's cage. Much to Tim's surprise and relief, the beast proved to be peaceful. In fact, since the Dogan was offline and could not be opened, the tyger saved Tim's life by directing the boy to a magic METAL BOX left by the Dogan's door. Opening the box with the tyger's second collar key, Tim discovered a magic napkin, or DIBBIN, which, when shaken out, became a storm-shelter big enough to cover both boy and beast. Once the storm passed, Tim fed the tyger drops of liquid from the MAGIC BROWN BOTTLE also located within the magic metal box. Upon swallowing the drops, the tyger magically transformed back into Maerlyn.

In his human form, Maerlyn was so thin that he appeared to be little more than a skeleton. (This is hardly surprising considering the amount of time he had been trapped inside a cage.) He had a white waist-length beard encrusted with rubies, emeralds, sapphires, and diamonds, and wore a white silk robe, the cuffs of which were covered in silver *siguls* of moons, stars, and spirals. On his head he wore a conical cap as yellow as the sun and on his feet he sported old black boots.

During his discussions with Tim, the grave but kindly sorcerer confided a truth which Tim had never suspected. Namely, that the evil Covenant Man was not half so powerful as he seemed, since his gifts were limited to long life and a little magic. Maerlyn also assured Tim that the Covenanter (whom Maerlyn called the Broad Cloak) would be punished by his true master—the Red King— for the foolish game he played with Tim's life. As for his own transformation into animal form, Maerlyn stated that a spell had been cast upon him by an emissary of the Red King. The emissary came to Maerlyn's cave pretending to be a wandering peddler. Although the peddler's magic wasn't as powerful as that of the old wizard, Maerlyn was drunk at the time and so the peddler got the better of him.

After their palaver, Maerlyn set Tim atop the folded dibbin, which was now the size of a flying carpet. Instructing the lad to hold the magic FEATHER (also found in the Dogan's metal box) the sorcerer told Tim to think of home. Tim did so, but before the boy zoomed off, Maerlyn gave him two final but urgent instructions. First, as soon as Tim returned home, he should place the last of the brown bottle's magic drops in his mother's eyes. Second, after restoring his mother's sight, he should hand her Jack Ross's ax. Luckily Tim obeyed both of Maerlyn's final commands. Not only did the magic drops cure his mother's blindness, but when Tim was attacked by his stepfather, Big Kells, Nell Ross was able to bury her former husband's ax in Kells's head.

W:169–70, W:183 *(Water Maerlyn)*, W:207, W:217 *(mage)*, W:222, W:223, W:249–50, W:250–55 *(254 Tyger; Tim sees once more)*, W:256 *(furry bedmate)*, W:259, W:261, W:269 *(as tiger)*
MAERLYN AS A TYGER: W:222, W:233–49, W:269

MAERLYN'S MAGICAL OBJECTS

TIM ROSS found these three magical objects in a METAL BOX located at the base of the NORTH FOREST KINNOCK DOGAN. The box was opened by a key attached to the collar of the caged TYGER who was actually none other than the mage of ELD, MAERLYN. Although we are never told directly, it is probable that these objects originally belonged to Maerlyn, since even in his tyger form, he knows about their existence and how to use them. In fact, if it weren't for Maerlyn's magical objects, Tim would never have survived the STARKBLAST, nor would he have been able to return home to the village of TREE.

W:239–64
METAL BOX: Tim found this box at the base of the NORTH FOREST KINNOCK DOGAN's door. (It reminded Tim of the box his mother used for trinkets and keepsakes, only it was made of metal rather than wood.) When Tim first discovered the box it was locked, though it had an odd-shaped keyhole that looked a little like a letter from High Speech. Engraved upon the box were letters from a language that Tim couldn't read. When he tried to lift it, the box felt as if it had been anchored to the ground by a powerful force.

Tim finally opened the box with a key attached to the collar of the caged TYGER he found in the Dogan's CLEARING. (He wouldn't have opened the box at all if the tyger—actually MAERLYN trapped in a tyger's shape by a powerful spell—hadn't insistently nuzzled it.) The box contained three magical objects which proved to be Tim's salvation: a BROWN BOTTLE of healing drops, a magic flying FEATHER taken from the wing of GARUDA, the EAGLE GUARDIAN, and a napkin that turned out to be the versatile magic DIBBIN. W:236–37, W:240–41, W:246

BROWN BOTTLE: This small brown bottle contained a powerful magical liquid. Not only did this liquid transform the magician MAERLYN from tyger shape back into human shape, but it restored sight to NELL ROSS's blinded eyes. W:241, W:247
FEATHER: This feather was taken from the tail of GARUDA, the EAGLE GUARDIAN. When TIM sat upon the magical DIBBIN and held the

feather, all he had to do was think of home and the dibbin flew him there. W:241, W:247, W:254, W:255

NAPKIN (DIBBIN): Although TIM ROSS originally mistook this dibbin for an ordinary napkin, it was anything but ordinary. Not only did it expand exponentially when it was shaken out, providing both Tim and Maerlyn with shelter from the raging STARKBLAST, but when used with the magic FEATHER, it became a flying carpet. W:241–47, W:252–55, W:256–57, W:258

MAERLYN'S RAINBOW (BENDS O' THE RAINBOW, WIZARD'S RAINBOW, MAERLYN'S MAGIC BALLS)

There are thirteen glass balls in the Wizard's Rainbow, one for each GUARDIAN and one for the TOWER itself. (In the original version of *The Gunslinger*, we were told that the final ball—BLACK THIRTEEN—corresponded to the BEAST that guards the Dark Tower.) Some of these magic balls look into the future; others look into the past or into alternative realities. Still others (chief among them being Black Thirteen) can act as doorways into other worlds. All of the balls are alive and hungry. A person begins by using them, but in the end, he or she is used by them and sucked dry.

The Wizard's Rainbow represents a corruption of the pure energy of the WHITE. If the White represents wholeness, and the best human beings can strive for in ideal and action, then the debased colors of the rainbow represent the baser emotions, or the fallen drives of a fallen world. For example, the Pink One resonates with sexual energy, but it is desire, possessiveness, and cruelty without the higher emotions that true love can instill in us. Not surprisingly, the gate of the sinister GREEN PALACE is made to resemble Maerlyn's Rainbow. The gate's two wings consist of six colored bars each; one for every bend. The central bar (which is broad instead of flat and round), is dead black.

Since the thirteen colored balls reflect the baser aspects of human nature, then it seems likely that they correspond not to the twelve Guardians and the Tower, but to the twelve aspects of the DEMON ELEMENTALS and the CRIMSON KING, the were-spider who wishes to bring the Tower crashing down.

When Roland was a boy, it was believed that only three or four of these magic balls were still in existence. In *The Dark Tower*, we realize there must have been more, since Roland has had temporary control of two of them (MAERLYN'S GRAPEFRUIT and Black Thirteen), and the Crimson King—until about halfway through *Wolves of the Calla*—owned six. (Never a good loser, the Red King smashed his once they foretold Roland's victories in both CALLA BRYN STURGIS and the DEVAR-TOI.)

GENERAL REFERENCES FOR ALL THE BALLS: IV:437–39 *(Steven Deschain describes)*, IV:442, IV:443, IV:452–53, IV:485–93 *(Jonas takes from)* IV:634–35 *(gate of Green Palace)*, V:79, V:80, V:89 *(glass balls)*, V:90, V:105, V:116, V:142, V:176, VI:8 *(bends o' the rainbow)*, VII:550, VII:606–7 *(Crimson King had six of them)*, VII:674, VII:770, W:169–70

BLACK THIRTEEN: According to Roland Deschain, Black Thirteen is the most terrible object left over from the days of ELD. In fact, Roland suspects that its wickedness even predates the time of his illustrious ancestor. If Roland is correct and the ancient magician MAERLYN is actually none other than our *tet's* nemesis, WALTER O'DIM, then this magic ball probably dates from the time of the GREAT OLD ONES, who tried, in their hubris, to unite magic and technology.

Although we don't see Black Thirteen until *Wolves of the Calla*, we hear of it through Roland's father STEVEN DESCHAIN as early as *Wizard and Glass*. According to the elder Deschain, it is unlucky to even speak of Thirteen, as it may hear its name called and roll the speaker away to unknown worlds.

Black Thirteen enters our tale directly via an unlikely person—namely FATHER CALLAHAN, formerly of 'SALEM'S LOT, MAINE. Before coming to rest beneath the floorboards of Callahan's church in CALLA BRYN STURGIS, Thirteen was in Walter's possession. In fact, it seems likely that the ball was in Walter's hands throughout much of *The Gunslinger*, since when that nasty multifaced magician forces Thirteen upon an unwilling Callahan in the WAY STATION between worlds, we catch a glimpse of Roland and JAKE distantly struggling up an incline toward the CYCLOPEAN MOUNTAINS.

Before we see the malevolence of Thirteen at work, we are told that it looks like the slick eye of a monster that grew outside of God's shadow. As Callahan removes it from its hidey-hole beneath his church floor and unwraps it from its altar boy's surplice, Roland feels the ball's low hum vibrating in his bones, a sound and sensation he compares to a swarm of angry bees. Once Callahan removes the surplice, Roland sees Thirteen's ghostwood box, upon which is carved a ROSE, a stone, a door, and the word *unfound*. With the exception of the Rose, the engraved images come from Thomas Wolfe's novel *Look Homeward, Angel*. (In Wolfe's book, the "rose" is actually a leaf, but within the context of the Dark Tower series, a rose is a more appropriate image.) The word *unfound* refers to the UNFOUND DOOR, which Black Thirteen inevitably opens.

It seems likely that Thirteen's box (like the altar boy's surplice that Callahan wraps it in) is meant to minimize the ball's evil vibrations. After Roland touches the magical ghostwood, his fingers smell of camphor, fire, and the flowers of the north country—the ones that bloom in the snow.

In both *Wolves of the Calla* and *Song of Susannah*, our *tet* carries Black Thirteen in a TODASH version of Jake's pink bowling bag. Although Jake's original bag bore the motto, "Nothing but Strikes at Mid-Town Lanes," the *todash* version reads, "Nothing but Strikes at Mid-World Lanes." Despite Thirteen's evil nature, our *tet* uses it to travel between Calla Bryn Sturgis and Calla NEW YORK. At the end of *Wolves of the Calla*, SUSANNAH DEAN (now under the control of her invading demon, MIA) uses Black Thirteen to escape through the Unfound Door to 1999, where Mia plans to give birth to her CHAP. With some help from STEPHEN KING, Jake and Callahan retrieve the magic ball from Susannah-Mio's room in the PLAZA–PARK HYATT before it can fall into the hands of the WARRIORS OF THE SCARLET EYE. The two of them store it in a locker located below the TWIN TOWERS. We can presume that the ball has since been destroyed.

Like the singing Rose, Thirteen's hum speaks of power, but it is the dangerous power of the void, a colossal malevolent emptiness which, if aroused, could send its unwary victims to all NINETEEN points of nowhere. Throughout the Dark Tower series, our *tet* believes that this nasty ball is the eye of the CRIMSON KING himself. Although the Red King may use Thirteen to spy upon our *tet*'s movements, by the final book of the Dark Tower series we realize that it is not his actual eye. Los's eyes are as red as the roses of CAN'-KA NO REY, and when we see him, shouting madly from the DARK TOWER's balcony, he has both his ruby orbs. In fact, once PATRICK DANVILLE erases the Red King from MID-WORLD, all that he leaves are the Lord of Discordia's floating eyes. IV:437–39 *(Steven Deschain describes)*, V:31 *(indirect)*, V:48–70 *(Eddie and Jake travel via* todash; *53–56 reality of Black Thirteen)*, V:114–16, V:117, V:142 *(worst of the bunch)*, V:172–97 *(traveling in it via* todash; *176 origins, 180, 196)*, V:235 *(indirect)*, V:238 *(indirect)*, V:252, V:271 *(thing in church)*, V:311, V:313–18 *(described)*, V:338, V:383 *(indirect)*, V:393, V:400, V:409 *(box)*, V:413 *(box)*, V:414, V:415, V:461–65, V:468–70, V:502–5, V:506–49 *(Eddie's New York trip; 507–8 keep Black Thirteen in* todash *bag)*, V:591–600 *(Callahan to our world)*, V:618–27 *(Callahan to Stoneham, Maine)*, V:688, V:697, V:704 *(indirect)*, V:705, VI:4, VI:7, VI:8 *(and* glammer, *the sum of all the bends o' the rainbow)*, VI:21 *(dark glass)*, VI:28, VI:49 *(in bag)*, VI:68 *(in box)*, VI:74–97 *(in bag)*, VI:178, VI:234, VI:300, VI:326–38, VI:342, VII:147, VII:302, VII:550, VII:689

THE BLUE: Fifty years before Roland's first *ka-tet* sets off for MEJIS, this Bend o' the Rainbow was in the possession of a desert tribe of SLOW MUTANTS called the TOTAL HOGS.

THE GREEN: This one is thought to be hidden in the city of LUD.

THE ORANGE: This ball was last seen in the ruined city of DIS.

MAERLYN'S GRAPEFRUIT (THE PINK ONE): Maerlyn's Grapefruit played a large part in Roland's MEJIS adventures, recounted in the novel *Wizard and Glass*. Until Roland and his friends stole the Pink One for the AFFILIATION, it was in the hands of FARSON's followers. (Through much of the novel it is held by the wicked witch RHEA OF THE CÖOS.) Like all of Maerlyn's magic glasses, the Grapefruit is hungry and feeds on the minds of those who use it. Roland was lucky to survive his travels within its pink glare. Like the other Bends o' the Rainbow, the pink ball is alive. On the lid of its box (now lost) was the High Speech motto I SEE WHO OPENS ME. The Grapefruit's energy is sexual, and its color is often described as labial pink. It is one of the balls that exposes people's secrets. IV:116–21, IV:122, IV:134, IV:141, IV:164, IV:290–91, IV:299, IV:319–20, IV:325–26, IV:335, IV:353–54, IV:356, IV:374–75, IV:378, IV:413, IV:424–25, IV:437–39 *(Steven Deschain describes)*, IV:442, IV:443, IV:452–53, IV:485–93 *(Jonas takes from Rhea)*, IV:528 *(voice of the ball)*, IV:532–33, IV:536, IV:542–44, IV:545–46, IV:558–60 *(Roland takes ball from Jonas)*, IV:570–75 *(Roland's vision; he's trapped within the glass)*, IV:579–81 *(Roland decides to leave Susan)*, IV:601–2, IV:604–11, IV:618–21, IV:634–35 *(gate of Green Palace)*, IV:648–58 *(650 the Grapefruit; 652 Roland's matricide)*, V:36, V:37, V:38, V:49, V:53 *(Wizard's Glass)*, V:79, V:116, V:176

MAGGIE
See HAX

MAGICAL WAND/MAGICAL BASIN/MAGICAL PAIL
For generations, the BARONY COVENANTER had been coming to the village of TREE to collect taxes. Mounted on top of his tall black stallion, his gaunt

black silhouette was a familiar, if unwelcome, sight. Just as familiar, if more puzzling, was the silver basin roped to the Covenant Man's *gunna*. No one seemed to know the purpose of this priceless basin which the Covenant Man claimed was a relic from GARLAN-that-was, but TIM ROSS was destined to find out.

After discovering his dead father's LUCKY COIN in his murderous stepfather's trunk (the magical skeleton key that Tim used had been a gift from the treacherous Covenanter), young Tim rode his father's mule into the ENDLESS FOREST to find the Barony tax collector. There, surrounded by ancient IRONWOODS, the Covenanter asked Tim to fill his basin with the nearby stream's putrid, bug-infested water. Once Tim collected the water (avoiding a dangerous POOKY as he did so), the Covenant Man twice waved a magic wand over the basin to clear away the flesh-eating bugs it contained. (The wand was actually the gearshift of an old Dodge Dart.) Once the water was pure, the evil magician waved his wand a third time, and the water in the basin became a kind of scrying mirror—one which showed both future events and events happening at a great distance. The image that the Covenant Man conjured was a cruel one—it was of Tim's steppa, BIG KELLS, beating Tim's mother, NELL, into unconsciousness for opening his precious trunk. Soon after, the Covenanter showed Tim an even more horrific sight—the body of his father, Big Ross, floating in a nearby stream.

Later in the folktale, after Tim informed the men of Tree where they could locate his father's corpse, Tim found yet another silver water-holder and magic wand. This time the scrying vessel was a battered silver pail, and the wand—which Tim discovered sticking out of the ground as if someone had plunged it into the dirt with amazing force—was of stainless steel and had a white tip that looked like ivory. Remembering the Covenant Man's words that, in the proper hand, any object could be magic, Tim used this bucket and gearshift to glimpse his destiny. In the magical water he saw a vision of the Covenant Man and a beautiful green female SIGHE beckoning him deep into the heart of the forest where the FAGONARD swamp lay. Beyond the swamp, he saw a version of himself—water-Tim—finding the home of the great magician MAERLYN who gave him a magic blindfold which would cure his mother's blindness.

Unfortunately, as with every other gift given by the Covenant Man, Tim's visions proved to be cruelly misleading. Although beautiful, the sighe named ARMANEETA turned out to be both faithless and treacherous, and Maerlyn was stuck in TYGER form, locked in a cage in the clearing of the NORTH FOREST KINNOCK DOGAN. The Covenant Man's silver pail played one final trick on Tim before the end of the tale. Tim discovered it sitting upside down in front of tyger-Maerlyn's cage. Beneath it was a mocking note from the wicked Covenanter.
W:137, W:141, W:150–60, W:165, W:167, W:169, W:181–84, W:188, W:194, W:206, W:237, W:242, W:247

MAGRUDER, GEORGE
See CALLAHAN, FATHER DONALD FRANK: CALLAHAN'S HOME SHELTER ASSOCIATES: MAGRUDER, ROWAN

MAGRUDER, ROWAN
See CALLAHAN, FATHER DONALD FRANK: CALLAHAN'S HOME SHELTER ASSOCIATES

MAGRUDER, ROWENA
See CALLAHAN, FATHER DONALD FRANK: CALLAHAN'S HOME
SHELTER ASSOCIATES: MAGRUDER, ROWAN: RAWLINGS, ROWENA
MAGRUDER

MAINE CHARACTERS

ANGSTROM, JUNIOR: Junior Angstrom is one of the many western Maine
residents who sighted a WALK-IN. Angstrom's walk-in was a naked man,
traveling up the center of ROUTE 5. *For more information on the supernatural walk-ins, those beings that "walk in" to our world from other worlds, see*
WALK-INS. VI:151

BARKER, GARY: Gary Barker has photographs of the bizarre weather patterns that affect KEZAR LAKE in LOVELL. VII:113

BARKER, JUNIOR: Junior Barker runs JOHN CULLUM's caretaking business whenever Cullum is out of town. VII:44

BECKHARDT, DICK/BECKHARDTS: Dick Beckhardt owns one of the
many beautiful houses located along TURTLEBACK LANE in LOVELL.
JOHN CULLUM is his caretaker. The Beckhardt cabin is the site of Cullum's
final palaver with Roland Deschain and EDDIE DEAN. The Beckhardts are
friends of the TASSENBAUMS. VII:117, VII:118, VII:120, VII:123, VII:126,
VII:432, VII:518

BEEMER, CHARLIE: He is the husband of RUTH BEEMER, one of the
women killed in the EAST STONEHAM GENERAL STORE shoot-out in
1977. VII:46

BEEMER, RHODA: She is CHARLIE and RUTH BEEMER's daughter and
is in the EAST STONEHAM GENERAL STORE when Roland and JAKE
return in 1999. VII:424, VII:431

BEEMER, RUTH: Ruth Beemer is one of the two elderly sisters killed by
BALAZAR'S MEN in the EAST STONEHAM GENERAL STORE shoot-out
in 1977. VI:130–31, VI:132, VI:193–94, VII:46, VII:425
   SISTER: VI:130–31, VI:132, VI:193–94, VII:46, VII:425 *(not named)*

CENTRAL MAINE POWER GUY: VII:17–18

CONVEIGH, REVEREND: A minister in the STONEHAM/LOVELL area
of Maine. VII:426

CROWELL, GARY: When JOHN CULLUM pretends to leave for VER-
MONT so that he can escape from JACK ANDOLINI and BALAZAR's other
hardboys, he tells his clients to contact Gary Crowell if they need any work
done on their properties. VII:44

CULLUM, JOHN: *See* TET CORPORATION: FOUNDING FATHERS

FENNS: The Fenns are one of the families that owns a house along TURTLE-
BACK LANE in LOVELL. VII:115

FIREBUG LADY: VI:165

ISRAEL: Israel is the surname of one of the families living along TURTLE-
BACK LANE in LOVELL, MAINE. VII:115

JOGGER: VII:49

McAVOY, CHIP: Owner of the EAST STONEHAM GENERAL STORE
in EAST STONEHAM, MAINE. During the East Stoneham General Store
battle, which takes place between Roland, EDDIE DEAN, and BALAZAR'S

MEN in 1977, Chip is wounded and his store is almost destroyed. Luckily, he has good insurance. After Eddie Dean's death in the DEVAR-TOI, Roland and JAKE CHAMBERS make a second trip to Chip's store (this time they're searching for the writer STEPHEN KING). Chip isn't too pleased to see them. V:621, VI:123, VI:132–45 *(faints)*, VI:148, VI:177, VII:128, VII:423–30, VII:431, VII:435, VII:442, VII:445, VII:449, VII:469

    FATHER: VII:424, VII:425

    SON: Chip's son fought in VIETNAM. VI:136

    UNNAMED SHOP PATRONS: VII:423–30 *(present)*, VII:431

McCAUSLAND, CHARLES (CHIP): Charles McCausland was a STONE-HAM man who was hit by a car while walking on ROUTE 7. VI:403–4

McCRAY FAMILY: The McCray family owned CARA LAUGHS, the house in LOVELL, MAINE, later purchased by STEPHEN KING. VII:116

McKEEN, GARRETT: *See* KING, STEPHEN, *listed separately*

PETERSON, REVEREND: Peterson is the reverend of the CHURCH OF THE WALK-INS, located in STONEHAM CORNERS. VII:435

PORTLAND SUNDAY TELEGRAM: On another level of the DARK TOWER, this paper carried STEPHEN KING's obituary. Praise GAN, the obituary wasn't needed. VI:410

POSTMISTRESS IN STONEHAM, MAINE: Although the postmistress of STONEHAM, MAINE, is never named, we know that she is in her late fifties or early sixties and has blue-white hair. V:622–24, V:627

ROYSTER, ELDON: Eldon Royster is the county sheriff for the area around EAST STONEHAM and LOVELL. VII:118

RUSSERT, DON: JOHN CULLUM's friend Don Russert is a retired history professor. Although his working life was spent at VANDERBILT COLLEGE, he presently lives in WATERFORD, MAINE. Like others living in the LOVELL/Waterford region, Russert has had firsthand experience of WALK-INS. In fact, Russert even managed to record one of them in his living room. Unfortunately, Russert couldn't decipher the language the man spoke, nor could his former colleagues in the Vanderbilt Languages Department. VI:151–53, VI:180–81, VI:200–201 *(indirect)*, VII:131

    PSYCHIC STUDIES PROFESSOR: This unnamed professor works at DUKE UNIVERSITY. One of Russert's friends at Duke contacted her about MAINE's WALK-IN activity. VI:153

SARGUS, JANE: Jane Sargus owns a small store called COUNTRY COLLECTIBLES, located near where the DIMITY ROAD branches off ROUTE 5 near EAST STONEHAM, MAINE. Jane sells furniture, glassware, quilts, and old books. Although he was supposed to be hiding from BALAZAR'S MEN, CALVIN TOWER went on a book-buying spree at her place, drawing unwanted attention to both himself and his companion, AARON DEEPNEAU. VI:165–66

SMITH, BRYAN: *See* KING, STEPHEN, *listed separately*

TASSENBAUM, DAVID: *See* TASSENBAUM, DAVID, *listed separately*

TASSENBAUM, IRENE: *See* TASSENBAUM, IRENE, *listed separately*

TOOTHAKER, ELVIRA: Elvira Toothaker attended VASSAR COLLEGE with her MAYBROOK, NEW YORK, friend JUSTINE ANDERSON. Elvira—now middle-aged—lives in LOVELL. She and Justine are out picking raspberries on ROUTE 7 when BRYAN SMITH careens by in his minivan. VII:439–41

    ANDERSON, JUSTINE: Justine Anderson is a friend of Elvira Toothaker of LOVELL, MAINE. They attended VASSAR together and have remained friends ever since. Justine and Elvira are picking raspberries along ROUTE 7 when they see BRYAN SMITH career past in his minivan. Justine recognizes the make of Smith's 1985 Dodge Caravan because her son once owned a similar vehicle. VII:439–41

      SON: VII:440

TRUCK DRIVER: VI:134–35

WIDOW: This woman sells used books in EAST FRYEBURG, MAINE. CALVIN TOWER buys books from her. VI:191

WILSON, TEDDY: Teddy Wilson lives on KEYWADIN POND in EAST STONEHAM, MAINE. He is the county constable and the game warden. VI:172

MAN IN BLACK
See WALTER

MAN JESUS
See GODS OF MID-WORLD

**MANNI (SEEKING FOLK)
The Manni are one of MID-WORLD's strange religious sects. Their worship seems to center, at least in part, on traveling between worlds. Roland suspects that his old teacher CORT held palaver with these people (a tribe of them once lived outside GILEAD) since he seemed to know something about jumping the time/space continuum. ELDRED JONAS also knew about Manni beliefs.

    In the 2003 version of *The Gunslinger,* we learn that Manni holy men can achieve a clinical detachment from their own bodies, attaining a complete division between the mind/spirit and the physical self. They can even watch their bodies die without becoming emotionally upset. Also in the new *Gunslinger,* we learn that a tribe of Manni-folk lived in the dens to the north of the MOHAINE DESERT. BROWN, the BORDER DWELLER who lived on the edge of the Mohaine, married a Manni woman and lived among them for a while. Although he left their settlement, he still retained their habit of using "thee" and "thou" in his speech.

    The first time we see the Manni of MANNI REDPATH, their village located north of CALLA BRYN STURGIS, they are crammed into a buckboard wagon drawn by a pair of MUTIE GELDINGS. Although in appearance they resemble both the Quakers and the Amish found in the America of our world, the Manni are not actually Christian. Their religion, which worships an entity called both THE FORCE and THE OVER, focuses on traveling between worlds via TODASH.

    To induce the necessary state of mind to travel *todash,* the Manni use both magnets and plumb bobs, which they store in large boxes, called coffs. The coffs are covered in moons, stars, and odd geometric shapes. The largest and most powerful of the bobs is called the BRANNI BOB. This plumb bob is so powerful that it is used only by HENCHICK, the Manni *dinh.* As you might expect, Manni magic is extremely powerful. The Manni help Roland's *ka-tet* open the

UNFOUND DOOR after MIA, SUSANNAH DEAN's demon possessor, leaves Mid-World, taking BLACK THIRTEEN—and Susannah's body—with her.

Manni men are easily recognized. They wear dark blue cloaks and round-crowned hats, and they use the terms *thee* and *thou*. Manni men also have extremely long fingernails, since they are allowed to cut them only twice a year. Not only does their appearance set them apart from the other people of Mid-World, but the Seeking Folk's culture is also radically different from that of their neighbors. Manni men marry multiple wives and live in cabins called *kras*. Those who leave their clan to marry outsiders (such as MARGARET EISEN-HART) are called the forgetful. As far as their former brethren are concerned, these deserters are damned and will spend eternity in the depths of NA'AR, which is like Hell.

When the name of ARTHUR ELD is mentioned, the Manni whisper, "The Eld!" and lift their hands, raising their first and fourth fingers in the air. The movement is a sign of respect. When a Manni covers his eyes with his hands, it is a signal of deep religious dread. When Manni folk shake their heads in negation, they do so slowly, sweeping their heads back and forth in wide arcs. The gesture is so common among them that Roland thinks it might well be genetic. As well as having their own philosophy, the Manni have their own poetic tradition. The lines "Beyond the realm of human range/ A drop of hell, a touch of strange" come from a Manni poem.

IV:34, IV:175 *(and Jonas)*, IV:534, V:6, V:14–31 *(Town Gathering Hall; present)*, V:79, V:80, V:89, V:105, V:115, V:158, V:211–34 *(present; mentioned directly on 218, 219, 223)*, V:236, V:335, V:337, V:399 *(Seeking Folk)*, V:406, V:407 *(have ways of knowing)*, V:411 *(elder Manni seek other worlds for enlightenment)*, V:412, V:414 *(as travelers)*, V:422, V:465, V:483, V:566, V:573, V:601–17 *(present; mentioned directly on 602)*, V:654, V:677, VI:5, VI:7, VI:8, VI:9, VI:17, VI:21, VI:24–43 *(cloak folk)*, VII:149, VII:335, VII:413, VII:540, VII:756, VII:798, VII:817, W:150

INDIVIDUAL MANNI:

ARRA: See CANTAB, *listed below*

BONY SHOULDERS, BALEFUL EYES: When the men of CALLA BRYN STURGIS meet in the TOWN GATHERING HALL to discuss what to do about the arrival of the WOLVES, this Manni states that they should have a festival for the children and then kill them. He thinks death is a more welcoming place for them than THUNDERCLAP. V:14–31 *(Town Gathering Hall; present but not mentioned until 16)*

BRANNI BOB: The Branni Bob is the largest and most potent of the magical plumb bobs that the Manni used to travel TODASH. It is kept in a four-foot-long ironwood coff, is about eighteen inches long, and looks a bit like a child's top, though it is made of a yellowish, greasy-looking wood. As EDDIE DEAN finds out, it is extremely powerful and becomes *dim* as it sways back and forth. The Branni Bob appears to have a will of its own. Perhaps this is why HENCHICK refers to it as a "he" rather than an "it." VI:28–43

CANTAB: When Roland asks FATHER CALLAHAN for the names of some adults that the children of the Calla trust implicitly, Callahan mentions Cantab of the Manni. Evidently, the children follow him as if he were the Pied Piper. Cantab and his wife, ARRA, are two of the CHILD-MINDERS during the final battle against the WOLVES. Cantab is also present when the Manni help Roland and the remains of his *ka-tet* open the UNFOUND DOOR. V:483, V:601–17 *(present; mentioned directly on 602, 603)*, V:662–67 *(present; mentioned directly on 666)*, V:677, V:689 *(folken)*, V:693–97 *(folken)*, VI:3–9, VI:24–43

> **ARRA:** Arra is Cantab's wife. Like him, she is one of the CHILD-MINDERS during the final battle against the WOLVES. Like the SISTERS OF ORIZA, Arra throws the dish, but belonging to the Manni prohibits her fellowship with the other Sisters. V:662–67 *(present; mentioned directly on 666)*, V:677, V:689 *(indirect)*, V:693–97 *(folken)*, VI:3 *(Henchick's granddaughter)*

ELDERS (GENERAL): VI:24–43, W:147

FORCE, THE: *See* OVER, THE, *listed below*

HEDRON: Hedron is a strong Sender. He is one of the Manni elders who helps HENCHICK open the UNFOUND DOOR for Roland and his *ka-tet* after their battle with the WOLVES. VI:41–43 *(present from 24, but not mentioned until 41)*

HENCHICK (SILKY WHITE BEARD): Henchick is the *dinh* of Manni Redpath. He is about eighty years old but is in marvelous physical shape, as Roland discovers when Henchick leads him up the steep incline to the DOORWAY CAVE. (Roland is fatigued by the exertion, but Henchick barely breaks a sweat.)

Like the other Manni, Henchick has multiple wives. (He has three.) MARGARET EISENHART (formerly Margaret of the Redpath clan) is either one of his daughters or one of his granddaughters. Bad blood still exists between them because Henchick opposed Margaret's marriage to a "heathen." Despite Margaret's having been with her husband, VAUGHN EISENHART, for more than twenty years, Henchick still believes she is destined for NA'AR.

In the end, Henchick proves to be one of Roland's greatest allies in CALLA BRYN STURGIS. He and his *ka-tet* help Roland, EDDIE, JAKE, and PERE CALLAHAN open the UNFOUND DOOR so that they can rescue SUSANNAH from the FEDIC DOGAN where MIA has escaped with her body.

Henchick has a twinner in our world. His name is REVEREND EARL HARRIGAN. V:17–31 *(Town Gathering Hall; present)*, V:211–34 *(present; mentioned directly on 223, 224 not yet named)*, V:236, V:335, V:336, V:338 *(Margaret's da)*, V:389, V:393, V:399, V:400, V:401, V:406–16, V:421, V:466, V:508, V:510, V:601–17 *(present; mentioned directly on 602, 605, 608, 610)*, VI:3–9, VI:12, VI:17, VI:21, VI:23–43, VI:258, VI:288, VI:307, VI:311, VII:540

JEMMIN: Jemmin and HENCHICK were the Manni elders who discovered CALLAHAN lying by the UNFOUND DOOR in DOORWAY CAVE. Jemmin eventually died of a heart attack. V:411–14, V:466

LEWIS: Like THONNIE, Lewis is one of the younger Manni men. He is a strapping fellow with a short beard and hair that is pulled back in a long braid. VI:28–43

MANNI COUPLE KILLED BY SKIN-MAN: *See* SKIN-MAN: SKIN-MAN'S VICTIMS

OVER, THE: This is the name for one of the GODS OF MID-WORLD, specifically the one worshipped by the Manni. The other names for the Over are THE FORCE and the PRIM. V:406 *(The Force, The Over)*, V:412, V:414, VI:26, VI:108 *(as Discordial/Prim)*

REDPATH CLAN: They are the Manni clan that lives near CALLA BRYN STURGIS. MARGARET EISENHART was born into this family. V:335, V:399 *(Manni Redpath)*, VI:3, VI:5, VI:6, VI:7 *(sixty-eight men)*, VI:9, VI:38 *(Manni kra; Redpath-a-Sturgis)*

THONNIE: Like LEWIS, Thonnie is one of the younger Manni men. He is a strapping young man with a short beard and hair that is pulled back in a long braid. VI:28–43

YOUNG AND BEARDLESS: He is one of the younger members of the Manni delegation that comes to CALLA BRYN STURGIS's meeting at the beginning of *Wolves of the Calla.* He does not believe that the adults should let any children be taken by the WOLVES. V:18–31 *(Town Gathering Hall; present)*

MANNI COUPLE KILLED BY SKIN-MAN
See SKIN-MAN: SKIN-MAN'S VICTIMS

MANPOWER
See CALLAHAN, FATHER DONALD FRANK: CALLAHAN'S HIDDEN HIGHWAYS ASSOCIATES

MANSFIELD FAMILY
See KING, STEPHEN

MANSION DEMON
See DEMONS/SPIRITS/DEVILS

MARCHLY, ERNEST
See TREE VILLAGE CHARACTERS: WOODSMEN

MARGARET OF THE REDPATH CLAN
See ORIZA, SISTERS OF: EISENHART, MARGARET

MARIA
See HAMBRY CHARACTERS: HAMBRY MAYOR'S HOUSE (SEAFRONT)

MARIAN
See ORIZA, LADY

MARK
See CORT

MARK CROSS BRIEFCASE BUSINESSMAN
See VAMPIRES: TYPE THREE

MARK CROSS PEN BUSINESSMEN
See CHAMBERS, JAKE: CHARACTERS JAKE MEETS WHEN HE RUNS AWAY TO BROOKLYN AND MID-WORLD

MARLOWE
See KING, STEPHEN

MARTEN BROADCLOAK
See WALTER

MARTIN, MR. RAYMOND
See CHARLIE THE CHOO-CHOO

MARY DAME
See MID-WORLD FOLKLORE

MARY, SISTER
See ELURIA, LITTLE SISTERS OF

MARYANNE
See DEAN, HENRY

MATURIN
See GUARDIANS OF THE BEAM: TURTLE

MAUDE AND JEEVES
See PUBES

McAVOY, CHIP
See MAINE CHARACTERS

McCAIN, LARRY
See DEAN, HENRY: HENRY DEAN'S KA-TET

McCANN, BIRDIE
See BREAKERS

McCAULEY, KIRBY
See KING, STEPHEN

McCAUSLAND, CHARLES (CHIP)
See MAINE CHARACTERS

McCOWAN, AL
See CALLAHAN, FATHER DONALD FRANK: CALLAHAN'S LIGHTHOUSE SHELTER ASSOCIATES

McCRAY FAMILY
See MAINE CHARACTERS

McCURDY, SHEB
See SHEB; *also see* HAMBRY CHARACTERS: TRAVELLERS' REST: SHEB

McCUTCHEON, MAC
See KING, STEPHEN

McDONALD, CAPTAIN
See DEAN, EDDIE: DELTA FLIGHT 901 CHARACTERS

McGURSKY, MRS.
See DEAN, EDDIE: EDDIE'S ASSOCIATES PAST AND PRESENT

McKEEN, GARRETT
See KING, STEPHEN: McKEEN (GROUNDSKEEPER)

McLEOD, GEORGE
See KING, STEPHEN

McVRIES, PETER
See GUNSLINGERS

MEARS, BEN
See CALLAHAN, FATHER DONALD FRANK: 'SALEM'S LOT CHARAC-
TERS

MEJIS CHARACTERS
See HAMBRY CHARACTERS

MELLON
See TREE VILLAGE CHARACTERS

MENSO THE ESP WONDER
See CALLAHAN, FATHER DONALD FRANK: CALLAHAN'S HIDDEN
HIGHWAYS ASSOCIATES

MERCY
See RIVER CROSSING CHARACTERS

MERLIN
Although the MAERLYN of Roland's world is different from the mythical Merlin of the Arthurian legends, in *The Gunslinger* Roland seems to be aware of
the existence of both these magicians. He even compares MARTEN, the wicked
magician of his father's court, to Merlin. *See also* MAERLYN.
    I:94, III:261, III:387

MEXICAN IMMIGRANTS
See CALLAHAN, FATHER DONALD FRANK: CALLAHAN'S HIDDEN
HIGHWAYS ASSOCIATES

MIA

In High Speech, *mia* means "mother," and there could be no more appropriate name for this invading spirit that hijacks SUSANNAH DEAN's body in *Wolves of the Calla*. Unlike Susannah's previous split personalities of DETTA WALKER and ODETTA HOLMES, Mia does not come from a deep psychological schism within her host, but attaches herself to Susannah once she has conceived the CHAP in the demon-haunted SPEAKING RING of the RIVER BARONY plains.

Originally, Mia was one of the disincarnate spirits left behind when the magical PRIM receded. In her wraith state, she was a sexual VAMPIRE who caused the deaths of many men, including AMOS DEPAPE, brother of the BIG COFFIN HUNTER ROY DEPAPE. For many years, Mia haunted the city of FEDIC. There, she saw and fell in love with a baby named MICHAEL. After the Red Death ravaged the city's populace and baby Michael was taken away by his parents, WALTER made the lovesick Mia a Faustian bargain. If she would give up her disincarnate immortality, Walter would give her a baby. Mia could not conceive (like all elemental beings, she was sterile), but if she could be given a body, then she could carry to term. After submitting herself to the horrid process of *becoming* (a technological and magical alchemy accomplished in the FEDIC DOGAN operating theater/torture chamber), Mia gained the necessary equipment for surrogate motherhood. All she needed was someone else's fertilized egg.

Mia's sole purpose is to nurture and bear the Chap, the demonic offspring of herself, Susannah Dean, Roland Deschain, and the CRIMSON KING. As a servant of the Outer Dark, the *dan-tete*, or little king, is destined to destroy his White Daddy (Roland) and rule after his Red one. Although the fetal MORDRED is slowly being "faxed" into Mia's body located in END-WORLD, at first it is Susannah who experiences pregnancy's strange cravings. As an early service to the Red King, Mia occasionally hijacks Susannah's body to feed it the binnie bugs, frogs, and raw piglets that Susannah (in her waking state) would not have been able to stomach. However, like Detta Walker, the longer Mia is inside of Susannah, the more control-time she seems to require. By the beginning of *Song of Susannah*, Mia has seized the reins of the physical form she shares with her host.

Unfortunately for Mia (who goes mad upon the delivery of her chap), she never gets to raise the child for whom she has sacrificed so much. No sooner does Mordred begin to suckle at his mother's breast than he turns into a werespider and sucks all the moisture from her body. All that is left of Mother-Mia is a giant dust bunny.

V:71–81 *(hunts in Susannah's body)*, V:127, V:173, V:174, V:181, V:183, V:184, V:196, V:198, V:241, V:248, V:249, V:251, V:311 *(baby's keeper)*, V:318, V:329, V:341, V:370–76, V:376–80 *(Eddie knows she is in Susannah)*, V:382, V:383, V:385, V:390 *(indirect)*, V:391, V:392 *(indirect)*, V:394, V:396, V:472, V:478, V:479–83, V:488, V:583, V:617, V:628, V:629, V:648 *(Susannah-Mio)*, V:659, V:674, V:688, V:697, V:699–705, VI:8, VI:48–52, VI:53–125, VI:150, VI:190, VI:194, VI:210, VI:216, VI:219, VI:223, VI:224, VI:225–61, VI:241–45 *(Mia as elemental)*, VI:287, VI:316–17, VI:319 *(indirect)*, VI:320, VI:321, VI:322, VI:325, VI:326, VI:327, VI:339, VI:343, VI:347–85, VII:3, VII:4 *(Susannah-Mio)*, VII:21–22, VII:35, VII:47, VII:52, VII:55–75 *(by 75 she is dried-out dust on a bed)*, VII:76, VII:81, VII:115, VII:141–42 *(a giant dust bunny)*, VII:145, VII:149, VII:160, VII:163, VII:168,

VII:169, VII:170, VII:173, VII:175, VII:176, VII:302, VII:303, VII:315, VII:398, VII:399, VII:487, VII:488, VII:531, VII:538, VII:539, VII:554, VII:578, VII:595, VII:620 *(lunatic mother)*, VII:689, VII:741 *(body-mother)*, VII:766 *(dust-mummy)*

MIA'S ASSOCIATES:

BABY MICHAEL: Michael was one of the few healthy babies born in the town of FEDIC before the onset of the Red Death. In her incorporeal state, Mia saw this baby and fell in love with him, realizing that her true destiny was motherhood. Mia's longing for motherhood, a desire kindled by observing the untouchable Michael, was later used by WALTER, servant of the CRIMSON KING. He offered Mia motherhood in exchange for her incorporeal immortality. Mia, to her own undoing, accepted this most Faustian of bargains. VI:243–44, VI:249, VI:251, VI:254

   MICHAEL'S FATHER: VI:243–44

   MICHAEL'S MOTHER: VI:243–44

CHAP: *See* MORDRED, *listed separately*

RAT, MR.: During one of her food-raids in her dream-version of CASTLE DISCORDIA, Mia kills Mr. Rat and steals his dinner. They are competing over a roasted suckling pig, which appears, momentarily, to be a human baby. Mr. Rat is the size of a tomcat, so Mia is a fairly fierce fighter. As always happens in the Dark Tower series, Mia's foe has a twinner in MID-WORLD. Mr. Rat is also the rat which SUSANNAH DEAN kills in the JAFFORDS's barn. V:373–75, V:376, V:381–82, V:390, VI:373

MICHAEL (BABY MICHAEL)
See MIA

MICHELA, SISTER
See ELURIA, LITTLE SISTERS OF

MID-WORLD FOLKLORE (HEROES, ANTIHEROES, MAGICAL FORCES, FAMOUS TALES)
For a list of Mid-World divinities, see GODS OF MID-WORLD

   AM: *See* PRIM, *listed separately*

   BEAMS: *See* BEAMS, PATH OF THE, *in* PORTALS

   BEAMS, GUARDIANS OF THE: *See* GUARDIANS OF THE BEAM, *listed separately*

   BIG SKY DADDY: *see* GODS OF MID-WORLD

   BLACK THIRTEEN: *See* MAERLYN'S RAINBOW, *listed separately*

   BRAVE BILL: In the story of "The Wind Through the Keyhole" (which is really a tale about a young gunslinger-to-be called TIM STOUTHEART), the WIDOW SMACK tells young Tim Ross that he should make himself a pallet behind the cottage door so that he can surprise his murderous steppa, BIG KELLS, if he comes home unexpectedly. She adds that this strategy isn't much like one Brave Bill of the stories would use. Tim replies that being hit from behind is all his bastard steppa deserves, since that was how he murdered BIG JACK ROSS.

Interestingly, Bill is also the name of YOUNG BILL STREETER, the boy to whom Roland recounts "The Wind Through the Keyhole." We can't help but wonder whether Roland chose the name "Brave Bill" to make his young companion feel brave in the face of everything he has seen, and everything he has yet to do. (Young Bill was the only witness to the SKIN-MAN murders at the JEFFERSON RANCH and had to identify the killer.) Just as Tim Ross grows up to be Tim Stoutheart despite the fact that he fears his cruel steppa, so Roland is secretly assuring Bill that he can grow up to be Brave Bill, despite the fact that he must identify the terrifying skin-man. W:168

CAM TAM: *See* ELURIA CHARACTERS: CAM TAM (DOCTOR BUGS)

CAN-TAH: *See* CAN-TAH *and* GUARDIANS OF THE BEAM, *both listed separately*

CHASSIT: *See* NINETEEN, *listed separately*

CHILDREN OF RODERICK: *See* MUTANTS: CHILDREN OF RODERICK

CRIMSON KING: *See* CRIMSON KING, *listed separately*

DAME MARY: *see* MARY DAME *below*

DEMON ELEMENTALS: *See* DEMON ELEMENTALS, *listed separately*

DEMONS: *See* DEMONS/SPIRITS/DEVILS, *listed separately*

DIANA'S DREAM: This is an old Mid-World story which is very much like "The Lady or the Tiger?" II:105–6, V:39, V:442

DRAGON: *See* DRAGON, *listed separately*

ELD, ARTHUR: *See* ELD, ARTHUR, *listed separately*

GAN: *See* GAN, *listed separately*

GODOSH: *See* PRIM, *listed separately*

GRANDFATHERS: *See* VAMPIRES: TYPE ONE

GREATER DISCORDIA: *See* PRIM, *listed separately*

GREEN DAYS, QUEEN OF: The Queen o' Green Days is probably a figure from IN-WORLD folklore. When Roland tracks MIA through the BORDER-LAND bogs, he mentions this figure. We don't learn anything else about her. V:81

GRENFALL, LORD: *See* ORIZA, LADY, *listed separately*

HORN OF ELD: *See* ELD, ARTHUR, *listed separately*

KAMMEN: *See* TODASH, *in* PORTALS

KELLS, BIG BERN: *See* KELLS, BIG BERN, *listed separately*

KELLS, MILLICENT: *See* KELLS, BIG BERN: KELLS, MILLICENT, *listed separately*

LLAMREI: *See* ELD, ARTHUR, *listed separately*

LOST BEASTS OF ELD: *See* ELD, ARTHUR, *listed separately*

MAERLYN (THE SORCERER): *See* MAERLYN, *listed separately*

MAERLYN'S GRAPEFRUIT: *See* MAERLYN'S RAINBOW, *listed separately*

MARY DAME: We never learn who Mary Dame is. However the phrase "haughty as Mary Dame" tells us a lot about her character. W:274

OLD MOTHER: *See* GODS OF MID-WORLD

OLD ONES (GREAT OLD ONES): *See* OLD ONES, *listed separately*

OLD STAR: *See* GODS OF MID-WORLD

ORIZA, LADY: *See* ORIZA, LADY, *listed separately*

PERTH, LORD: "So fell Lord Perth, and the countryside did shake with thunder." The story of Lord Perth comes from one of Mid-World's old poems and is very much like our world's biblical tale of David and Goliath. According to tradition, Lord Perth was a giant who went forth to war with a thousand men, but he was still in his own country when a little boy threw a stone at him and hit him in the knee. He stumbled, the weight of his armor bore him down, and he broke his neck in the fall. When eleven-year-old JAKE CHAMBERS mentions this story to the huge and wicked TICK-TOCK, Tick-Tock becomes enraged. He considers the story unlucky. This isn't surprising since it proves to be a foretelling of his own fate. III:274–75, III:356–57, IV:89, IV:90, IV:294, IV:404, IV:422, IV:452, IV:571, IV:647, V:10, V:39, W:48

ROSS, BIG JACK: *See* ROSS, BIG JACK, *listed separately*

ROSS, NELL: *See* ROSS, NELL, *listed separately*

ROSS, TIM: *See* ROSS, TIM, *listed separately*

ROWENA, QUEEN: *See* ELD, ARTHUR, *listed separately*

RUSTY SAM: Rusty Sam is the central character in one of Mid-World's folktales. In this story, Rusty Sam steals an old widow's best loaf of bread. VI:250

SAITA: *See* ELD, ARTHUR, *listed separately*

SEMINON, LORD: *See* ORIZA, LADY, *listed separately*

SIGHE: The sighe are Mid-World's fairyfolk. According to the WIDOW SMACK, they live in the deep woods of the ENDLESS FOREST. The sighe that TIM ROSS meets looks like a tiny, naked green woman with wings. She is beautiful but treacherous. *See* ARMANEETA, *listed separately* W:164, W:170, W:182–83

SKIN-MAN: *See* SKIN-MAN, *listed separately*

SMA' LADY MUFFIN ON HER TUFFIN: We never learn who Sma' Lady Muffin is, but we can assume that she is a lot like our world's nursery rhyme character, Little Miss Muffet who sat on her tuffet, eating her curds and whey. W:203

STUFFY-GUYS: Red-handed stuffy-guys, which can be found all over MID-WORLD, are a staple of Reaptide festivities. In the days of ARTHUR ELD, human beings were sacrificed during the autumn festival of REAP. However, by Roland's day, stuffy-guys, or human effigies, were burned instead. In Mid-World-that-was, stuffy-guys had heads made of straw, and their eyes were made from white cross-stitched thread, and their arms held baskets of produce. In the BORDERLANDS, their heads are often made of SHARPROOT. In *Wolves of the Calla,* Roland has the SISTERS OF ORIZA prove their skills by aiming their sharpened plates at stuffy-guys. IV:355, IV:361, IV:373, IV:415, IV:417, IV:446–47 *(propitiating old gods),* IV:449, IV:466–67 *(Cordelia burns Susan in effigy),* IV:501, IV:502, IV:505, IV:507, IV:605 *(Susan placed among them on the fire),* V:320, V:332–34, V:405

SWORD OF ELD: *See* ELD, ARTHUR, *listed separately*

TAHEEN: *See* TAHEEN, *listed separately*

TIM STOUTHEART: *See* ROSS, TIM, *listed separately*

TODASH: *See entry in* PORTALS

TREE VILLAGE CHARACTERS: *See* TREE VILLAGE CHARACTERS, *listed separately*

UFFIS: *Uffi* is an ancient term for a shape-changer. In LE CASSE ROI RUSSE, Roland and SUSANNAH come across three identical STEPHEN KINGs, who claim to be a single uffi. However, they are not FEEMALO/FIMALO/FUMALO as they pretend, but servants of the RED KING who have transformed themselves using *glammer.* Their leader is actually AUSTIN

CORNWELL, a servant of the Red King who hailed from upstate NEW YORK in one of the MULTIPLE AMERICAS. *For page references, see* WARRIORS OF THE SCARLET EYE: LE CASSE ROI RUSSE: HUMANS
VAGRANT DEAD: *See* VAGRANT DEAD, *listed separately*
VAMPIRES: *See* VAMPIRES, *listed separately*
WALKING WATERS OF EAST DOWNE: Roland met the Walking Waters of East Downe during his travels through Mid-World. We never learn anything more about this intriguing entity. VI:234
WIZARD'S RAINBOW: *See* MAERLYN'S RAINBOW, *listed separately*

MID-WORLD GODS
See GODS OF MID-WORLD

MID-WORLD MONSTERS
See DEMONS, SPIRITS, DEVILS (LESSER DEMONS OF THE PRIM)
See also POOKY

MID-WORLD RAILWAY CO.
See CHARLIE THE CHOO-CHOO

MIGUEL
See HAMBRY CHARACTERS: HAMBRY MAYOR'S HOUSE (SEAFRONT)

MILL, AUNT
See TULL CHARACTERS

MILLIE
See STREETER, YOUNG BILL

MILLS CONSTRUCTION AND SOMBRA REAL ESTATE
Along with NORTH CENTRAL POSITRONICS and LaMERK INDUSTRIES, Mills Construction and Sombra Real Estate are part of the SOMBRA GROUP, a corporate conglomerate which serves the CRIMSON KING. In our world, Mills Construction and North Central Positronics were jointly responsible for building the MIND-TRAP under the DIXIE PIG.

As JAKE CHAMBERS realized as far back as *The Waste Lands,* Sombra and its subsidiaries want to destroy both the magical Vacant LOT and the ROSE that grows there. In fact, if Roland's *ka-tet* hadn't stopped them, they would have built the TURTLE BAY LUXURY CONDOMINIUMS on the site of the Lot. *For more information, see* SOMBRA CORPORATION.

III:121, IV:100, V:96, V:188, VII:492

MINERS
See DEBARIA CHARACTERS: SALTIES

MINNIE
See CALLA BRYN STURGIS CHARACTERS: ROONTS: DOOLIN, MINNIE

MIR
> *See* GUARDIANS OF THE BEAM: BEAR GUARDIAN

MISLABURSKI, MRS.
> *See* DEAN, EDDIE: EDDIE'S PAST ASSOCIATES

MOGGINS, GERT
> *See* BIG COFFIN HUNTERS: DEPAPE, ROY: DEBORAH (GERT MOGGINS)

MOLLY (AUNT MOLLY)
> *See* BREAKERS: BRAUTIGAN, TED

MOLLY (RED MOLLY)
> *See* ORIZA, SISTERS OF

MONSTERS
> *See* MUTANTS; *see also* DEMONS/SPIRITS/DEVILS

MONTOYA, DR. APRIL
> *See* TOPEKA CHARACTERS

MOONS
> *See* DEMON MOON, GOAT MOON, HUNTRESS MOON, PEDDLER, *all in* APPENDIX I

MORDRED (THE CHAP, DAN-TETE, LITTLE RED KING, MORDRED DESCHAIN, MORDRED OF DISCORDIA, MORDRED RED-HEEL, MORDRED SON OF LOS, KING THAT WILL BE, SPIDER BOY)
As a father, Roland Deschain doesn't have much luck. His first child, conceived with SUSAN DELGADO in HAMBRY, died in the womb when Susan was burned upon a Charyou Tree fire. JAKE CHAMBERS, his adopted son, dies three times—first beneath the wheels of a Cadillac on FIFTH AVENUE, NEW YORK; second, beneath the CYCLOPEAN MOUNTAINS, where Roland let him drop into an abyss; and finally in our world's LOVELL, MAINE, where he steps in front of a van destined to kill the writer STEPHEN KING. Yet, however terrible the fates of these two children may be, the destiny awaiting Roland's third child is much more frightening to contemplate. He is the *dan-tete,* the "little savior" or "baby god" whose coming has been predicted for hundreds of years. Unlike the human line of ELD, from which he is (in part) descended, Mordred Deschain is a creature of the Outer Dark, and if his fate is fulfilled, he will destroy both the last of the gunslingers and all of the multiple worlds that spin like sequins upon the needle of the DARK TOWER.

For generations, the MANNI folk have prophesied the coming of Mordred Red-Heel, the were-spider who is the son of two fathers and two mothers. According to legend, this child—the last miracle spawned by the still-standing Dark Tower—will be half-human, half-god, and will oversee the end of humanity and the return of the PRIM, or GREATER DISCORDIA.

Like the creature whose coming is apprehensively awaited by the Manni, Mordred Deschain unites both the mortal and nonmortal worlds. Two of his parents—Roland Deschain and his *ka-tet* mate SUSANNAH DEAN—are human. However, his two other parents—the CRIMSON KING and MIA, daughter of none—are not. The nature of Roland and Susannah's relationship (that of *dinh* and bondswoman, or leader and his symbolic daughter) also fulfills a MID-WORLD prophecy, which tells us even more about the destiny of this *enfant terrible*: "He who ends the line of Eld shall conceive a child of incest with his daughter, and the child will be marked, by his red heel shall you know him. It is he, the end beyond the end, who shall stop the breath of the last warrior." Like the fate of his namesake from the Arthurian legends of our world, Mordred is to destroy what is left of the WHITE and then kill the mortal hero who sired him.

As the series progresses, we come to realize that Mordred's conception was not an accident, but a carefully staged event that has been planned for eons. With his multiple destinies, Mordred is a valuable tool, which can be used by both WALTER, the Crimson King's prime minister, and the Crimson King himself. Not only can Mordred kill the seemingly unstoppable Roland, but the red, hourglass-shaped widow's brand, which sits upon his belly, can unlock the door to the Tower. (The only other key to GAN's body is Roland's pair of guns.) If the Crimson King wants to beat Roland to the Tower (and if Walter wants to climb to its top to become God of All), then both of them need the key, which rests upon the *dan-tete*'s body.

In retrospect, we realize that all of the seemingly random sexual encounters of the series—from Roland's copulation with the ORACLE OF THE MOUNTAINS to the rape of Susannah Dean in the SPEAKING RING—were actually planned by the servants of the Red King so that they could collect Roland's sperm, mix it with that of their master, and then use it to fertilize Susannah's egg. However, although Mordred is both the Crimson King's heir apparent and a potential A-bomb of a BREAKER, those who brought him into being misjudged the human aspects of Mordred's nature, a nature which both foils the Crimson King's plans and proves to be Mordred's undoing.

From the moment he is born in the FEDIC DOGAN to his body-mother, Mia, until the second he dies under Roland's guns on the TOWER ROAD, Mordred is a creature of conflicting emotions. While his spider-self consists almost entirely of physical desires ("Mordred's a-hungry"), and although he seems to show no regret for either eating his birth mother just after emerging from her womb or cruelly devouring Walter O'Dim piece by piece, the small white node which connects Mordred's two selves is obviously capable of other modes of operating. No doubt, the black-haired, blue-eyed hume-Mordred is spiteful, cruel, and vicious, but his feelings for Roland combine hatred, jealousy, and rage with a sad and hungry love. Although he has several chances to arrange for Roland's demise (most notably he could have informed the guards of the DEVAR-TOI that their compound would soon be attacked), Mordred chooses instead to watch and wait. In this, he serves his own child-like curiosity, not the will of the Red King, who arranged for his arrival in the world. If Roland is to die, Mordred wants to be the one who kills him. However, Mordred does not choose to attack his White Daddy until he, himself, is dying of food poisoning. Perhaps he hopes to take Roland with him to the clearing at the end of the path? As unlikely as this may initially seem, we must remember the vision of Mordred which Roland sees within the Tower. This child is no monster, but a sad and lonely creature, one who never received any love at all.

V:71–87 *(fed by Mia)*, V:122, V:183 *(indirect)*, V:184, V:241 *(baby)*, V:370–76, V:377–78, V:382, V:383, V:391, V:393 *(baby)*, V:394, V:472 *(indirect)*, V:478, V:479–83 *(480 poison with a heartbeat)*, V:577, V:583–84 *(pregnancy)*, V:617, V:628–29 *(indirect)*, V:674, V:688, V:697, V:700–701, V:703, V:704, V:706, VI:5, VI:8, VI:10–11, VI:16, VI:50, VI:51–52 *(inside Susannah/Mia)*, VI:55, VI:56, VI:61–125, VI:194, VI:216, VI:222 *(as monster baby)*, VI:223 *(dream monster baby)*, VI:224 *(kid)*, VI:227 *(baby)*, VI:228, VI:229, VI:231, VI:233, VI:234, VI:235–56 *(Mia's pregnancy)*, VI:256–61 *(and trip to Dixie Pig)*, VI:297, VI:347–85, VI:408, VII:19 *(baby)*, VII:38 (dan-tete), VII:47 *(baby)*, VII:52 *(baby)*, VII:55–71 *(birth; 71 leg shot off)*, VII:76 *(monster—Jekyll and Hyde, twin with two fathers)*, VII:141 *(chap)*, VII:149–50, VII:157, VII:160–64, VII:166–88 *(Roland's blue bombardier's eyes)*, VII:192, VII:226, VII:238, VII:261–63, VII:301, VII:314–18, VII:332 *(were-spider)*, VII:399, VII:406, VII:518, VII:537, VII:540, VII:549, VII:550, VII:589, VII:593–94, VII:595, VII:615–16, VII:618, VII:619–24, VII:625, VII:626, VII:627, VII:631–32, VII:639, VII:640, VII:648–50, VII:653, VII:667, VII:671, VII:710 *(stays in Dandelo's but for two days; hears Tower sing in minor key)*, VII:721, VII:722, VII:725, VII:727, VII:730, VII:731, VII:741, VII:750, VII:751–56, VII:759, VII:762–63, VII:765–71 *(dual body's brain in white node; killed on 770)*, VII:774–75, VII:779, VII:822–23

MORGENSTERN, CONCHETTA
See HAMBRY CHARACTERS: HAMBRY MAYOR'S HOUSE (SEAFRONT)

MORKS
See BREAKERS

MORLOCKS
See GRAYS: GRAY HIGH COMMAND: TICK-TOCK

MORPHIA
See GODS OF MID-WORLD

MORT, JACK ("THE PUSHER")
Despite the fact that he was a professional CPA, the prim Jack Mort had a very nasty hobby. He liked to "depth-charge" people. In other words, he liked to kill them. Mort dropped the brick that hit five-year-old ODETTA HOLMES on the head. Years later, he pushed her in front of the A train at CHRISTOPHER STREET STATION.

Like WALTER, Mort is a man of many disguises. Dressed as a priest, he shoved JAKE CHAMBERS in front of a Cadillac on FIFTH AVENUE. Quite understandably, Mort is the human embodiment of the Death card found in Walter's tarot pack. He is also the destination of the magic door labeled "The Pusher."

Jack Mort divides the world into "Do-Bees" and "Don't Bees." Do-Bees get away with their crimes while Don't Bees get caught. This extremely unpleasant character (who also happens to come in his pants when he kills) keeps a scrapbook of his murders. His gold-rimmed glasses, blue eyes, and expensive address (he lives at 409 Park Avenue South) fool people into thinking he is not a psychopath. But not only is Mort psychologically imbalanced, he is also a fairly easy target for demons/demonic presences who want to use a mortal agent to do their dirty deeds. When Mort killed Jake, he was actually no more than the pawn of Walter, also known as the MAN IN BLACK. Underneath his business suits, Jack Mort wears women's underwear.

II:315–26, II:339–59 (Roland in control), II:360–86 (Roland in control. Mort dies), II:389, III:15, III:59–62 (62 dark hair. In Book II said to be blond), III:103–6 (and Jake's death), III:261, III:262, III:266, V:72 (indirect), V:479, V:597, VI:221, VI:232, VII:567

MORT'S ASSOCIATES:

BALD MAN WITH GLASSES: This guy works in Mort's office. II:326, II:339

CURD-FACED TEENAGE GIRL: After missing his opportunity to push JAKE in front of a car, a very angry Mort shoves this girl out of his way. II:317–18

DORFMAN: Jack Mort handles the difficult Dorfman account. II:326, II:340, II:350

FAT MAN WITH GLASSES: This man works in Mort's office. II:339–40

FRAMINGHAM, MR.: Mort's boss. II:382

MUCCI, TIMMY
See CHAMBERS, JAKE: JAKE'S FAMILY, FRIENDS, ASSOCIATES AND ALIASES

MUDMEN
See FAGONARD CHARACTERS

MUFFIN, BILL
See RIVER CROSSING CHARACTERS

MUNOZ, ROSALITA
See ORIZA, SISTERS OF

MURDOCK, REVEREND
See HOLMES, DAN

MURRAY, PROFESSOR
See DEAN, SUSANNAH: ODETTA HOLMES'S ASSOCIATES

MUSHROOMS, GIANT YELLOW
See MUTANTS: VEGETABLES

MUTANTS (MUTIES)
Although the GREAT OLD ONES and their destructive culture disappeared many generations before the rise of GILEAD, the poisons they left in soil, water,

and air remained. We cannot be certain whether these destructive ancients engaged in all-out chemical and biological warfare, but it seems probable. By the end of their reign over MID-WORLD, most of their women were already giving birth to monsters, as the people of FEDIC could testify.

By the time Roland was a young man, Mid-World was still full of genetically mutated beings which were commonly referred to as muties. As we learned in MEJIS, both domesticated and wild muties could be carefully bred to breed true. However, since this process was extremely slow, "threaded stock," or those that were born healthy and perfectly formed, were extremely valuable.

The most horrific mutants of Mid-World were actually the SLOW MUTANTS. These physically disgusting beings were once men and women, although they often bore little resemblance to their human forebears. The Slow Mutants that infested the old underground railway systems of Mid-World and the ruined kitchens of Gilead's castle had green, phosphorescent skin. Their mutations were as varied as they were horrible. Some had insect eyes, others had suckered tentacles. Many of them were nocturnal, preferring dark places to light ones. Although most Slow Mutants were ugly, stupid, and cannibalistic, some tribes (such as the CHILDREN OF RODERICK) retained their human dignity.

III:223, IV:13–14, (Candleton), IV:115 (men of Mid-World and mutant sperm), IV:140 (babies), IV:203, VI:372, VII:670

ANIMALS, BIRDS, REPTILES:

GENERAL: IV:14 (muties and threaded stock), IV:123 (werewolves), IV:203

ASSES (ALBINO): The MANNI own these beasts. VI:21, VI:23, VI:152

DEER (MUTANT DOE): VII:633

DEER, BLUE: TIM ROSS saw these mutant dwarf deer in the ENDLESS FOREST while traveling with the NORTH CENTRAL POSITRONICS guidance mechanism, DARIA. The deer were less than two feet high. W:228

DRAGON-BIRDS AND PTERODACTYLS: III:406, IV:13

ELK: See HAMBRY CHARACTERS: TRAVELLERS' REST: ROMP, THE

EROMOT: Rhea's poisonous pet snake. See RHEA OF THE CÖOS

HAMBRY MUTANT HORSES: IV:203, IV:254, IV:359 (muties)

MUSTY: Rhea's six-legged tomcat. See RHEA OF THE CÖOS

MUTANT DOE AND FAWNS: IV:14–15

MUTIE GELDINGS: The MANNI of CALLA BRYN STURGIS arrive at the TOWN GATHERING HALL in a buckboard drawn by a pair of mutie geldings. One of these muties has three eyes; the other has a pylon of raw pink flesh poking out of its back. V:14

RAVEN: IV:15

ROMP, THE: See HAMBRY CHARACTERS: TRAVELLERS' REST

SNAKES IN LUD'S WASTELANDS: III:413, IV:3

SUCKERBATS: See DEMONS/SPIRITS/DEVILS

TRIPOD-STORKS IN LUD'S WASTELANDS: III:407

WASTELAND MONSTROSITIES: Roland's ka-tet sees these whitish, leaping creatures while zooming through LUD'S WASTE LANDS in BLAINE's Barony Coach. III:407

WILD DOGS: Packs of these dogs are known to wander the BORDER-LANDS of MID-WORLD. They have no vocal cords so are silent preda-tors. V:397

HUMAN MUTANTS (MINOR MUTATIONS): Thanks to the poisons that the OLD PEOPLE left in MID-WORLD's air, soil, and water, Roland's level of the TOWER contained many human mutants. The most disfigured of these beings were known as SLOW MUTANTS, *see* SLOW MUTANTS, *listed later in this entry.*

> **HALF-MUTIE FARMER:** At the beginning of *The Wind Through the Keyhole,* Roland catches sight of this old farmer spying on his *tet* as they walk southeast along the PATH OF THE BEAM. The farmer has a jerking tentacle hanging from one corner of his mouth. W:5

> **MUTIES SUPPORTING FARSON:** In *Wind Through the Keyhole,* we learn that in the scrublands beyond GILEAD, many of the people are mutants, and many of them support the Good Man, JOHN FARSON.
> *For page references, see* FARSON: FARSON SUPPORTERS

INSECTS:

> **ALBINO BEES:** Roland's *ka-tet* comes across these mutant bees while on their way to LUD. These insects are truly terrible to see—they are sluggish, snowy white, and produce poisonous honey. Even their hive looked as if it had been melted by a blowtorch.

> Roland believes that the bees' mutation was a result of the Great Poisoning, which destroyed so much of Mid-World. (*See* GREAT POISONING *in* APPENDIX I.) III:283–84, III:286, III:311

> **GIGANTIC BEETLES:** These are found in the WASTE LANDS beyond LUD. III:413, IV:3, IV:13

> **SPIDERS:** Roland found these rather disgusting creatures in the cellar beneath the WAY STATION. They had eyes on stalks and as many as sixteen legs. I:89

> **WASPS:** Some of the fields in CALLA BRYN STURGIS contain nests of mutant wasps. The ones that attacked TIAN JAFFORDS's uncle had stingers the size of nails. V:1–2

SLOW MUTANTS (HUMAN MUTANTS): Mid-World's Slow Mutants are the direct descendants of those men and women who were exposed to and tainted by the poisonous fallout of the OLD PEOPLE's Great Cataclysm or Great Poisoning. Their appearances vary greatly—from shuffling humanoids to what can only be described as fungi with brains. Although many Slow Mutants (such as the GREEN FOLK of ELURIA and the mutants below the CYCLOPEAN MOUNTAINS) attack ordinary humans on sight, others, such as the CHILDREN OF RODERICK, have maintained their humanity and human dignity. A few have also retained their respect for the divine forces of the multiverse. For example, Roland has heard that some tribes of Slow Muties refer to the MAN JESUS as BIG SKY DADDY. I:137, I:157–58, I:175–80, II:379, III:33, III:171 *(subhuman things under mountains),* III:223, III:245, V:475, VI:152 *(Maine walk-ins as slow mutants),* VI:243, VII:25, VII:51

> **CHILDREN OF RODERICK (RODS):** The Children of Roderick are a band of wandering slow mutants who originated in the distant SOUTH PLAINS, a land beyond those known to the people of GILEAD. Before the world moved on, they gave their grace to ARTHUR ELD and so owe allegiance to the Eld's final human descendant, Roland Deschain. Despite their allegiance to the First Lord of Light, many of the Rods

now serve as the CRIMSON KING's groundskeepers in the DEVAR-TOI. Their dirty little village is located about two miles from THUN-DERCLAP STATION.

In appearance, the Rods resemble a cross between the radiation-sick slow mutants and a band of lepers. Boogers are their favorite tasty treats. According to FINLI O'TEGO, it is not good to touch the skin of a Rod since many of the diseases they carry are easily transmittable.

In DINKY EARNSHAW's opinion, the Rods are untrustworthy, since their mouths tend to run at both ends. However, the Rods still remember their allegiance to the Eld, and at least one of their number— HAYLIS OF CHAYVEN—is instrumental in the destruction of the Devar. Many of the WALK-INS sighted in western MAINE are actually Rods. VII:50, VII:51, VII:114, VII:130, VII:180, VII:216–17, VII:223, VII:225, VII:234, VII:256–57, VII:300, VII:319, VII:321, VII:322, VII:323, VII:324, VII:329, VII:330, VII:338, VII:340, VII:341, VII:346, VII:347, VII:348, VII:351, VII:357

CHEVIN OF CHAYVEN: Green-skinned, lyre-carrying Chevin of Chayven is the first of the Children of Roderick that Roland and EDDIE encounter on their way to LOVELL, MAINE. His one double-yolked eye, fang-like booger, talon-toed feet, and urine stench are quite a shock to Eddie.

When Roland first sees this grim-looking creature scurrying into the roadside growth, he calls the Rod forth saying, "So come forth, ye child of Roderick, ye spoiled, ye lost, and make your bow before me, Roland, son of STEVEN, of the line of ELD." Chevin, who among his own people is a minstrel, comes forth. After questioning him about FEDIC and the DEVAR-TOI, Roland cuts short the Rod's slow and painful half-life by shooting him. VII:48–50, VII:52 *(indirect)*, VII:114, VII:120, VII:130, VII:142, VII:216, VII:217, VII:329

HAMIL: Father of Chevin of Chayven. VII:51

GARMA: Garma is HAYLIS OF CHAYVEN's female friend. She does the "pokey-poke" with him when he gives her snotty tissues. Talk about a cheap date. VII:349

HAYLIS OF CHAYVEN (CHUCKY): Haylis of Chayven is a red-haired Rod whose nose has been eaten away by a large, strawberry-shaped sore. EDDIE thinks he looks like Chucky—a nasty killer-toy from a horror movie—but when Haylis smiles he seems sweet and child-like. Like the rest of his kind, Haylis owes allegiance to Roland. Because of this allegiance, he plants sneetches in the DEVAR-TOI, initiating THUNDERCLAP's final battle. VII:319–24, VII:329–35, VII:337–42, VII:346–49, VII:351, VII:357, VII:406

ONE-EYED WOMAN WITH DEAD CHILD: EDDIE DEAN sees this WALK-IN by the magical doorway of CARA LAUGHS. VII:130

CYCLOPEAN MOUNTAIN MUTANTS: The Slow Mutants living beneath the Cyclopean Mountains are some of the most hideously mis-shapen of all human muties. Their brains are also the most seriously damaged. Like the GREEN FOLK of ELURIA, their skins are greenly phosphorescent, but their appearance is much less humanoid. Many have developed insect-like eye-nodes and some have suckered tentacles instead of arms. Those that have retained hands tend to have webbed fingers. Roland and JAKE CHAMBERS are attacked by these mutants while they travel beneath the Cyclopean Mountain range in pursuit of the MAN IN BLACK. I:157–58, I:175–80

GREEN FOLK: *See* ELURIA CHARACTERS

MUDMEN: *See* FAGONARD CHARACTERS

SLOW MUTANTS OF GILEAD: When Roland returned to his home city more than twelve years after its fall to the GOOD MAN, he found Slow Mutants nesting in the ruined kitchens. I:137

TOTAL HOGS: This desert tribe of Slow Mutants held the Blue Bend of MAERLYN'S RAINBOW fifty years before Roland and his *ka-tet* arrived in HAMBRY. IV:437

WALK-INS: *See* WALK-INS, *listed separately*

VEGETABLES (MUTANTS)

GIANT YELLOW MUSHROOMS: In the fairy tale "The Wind Through the Keyhole," recounted in the novel of the same name, Young TIM ROSS saw these giant yellow mushrooms while he and the NORTH CENTRAL POSITRONICS guidance mechanism DARIA travelled in the region of the ENDLESS FOREST that sat just beyond the FAGONARD swamp. The mushrooms were four feet high and had caps the size of funeral umbrellas. Daria warned Tim not to touch them. Not only were they too poisonous to eat, but if he brushed their dust on his skin, he would die of seizures. W:228

RHEA'S MUTANT VEGETABLE GARDEN: *See* RHEA OF THE CÖOS, *listed separately*

MYSTERY NUMBER

See NINETEEN; *see also* NINETY-NINE

N

NASSAU CHARACTERS

See DEAN, EDDIE: DELTA FLIGHT 901 CHARACTERS

NEW YORK CUSTOMS

See DEAN, EDDIE: DELTA FLIGHT 901 CHARACTERS

NIGEL THE BUTLER

See NORTH CENTRAL POSITRONICS

**NINETEEN (CHASSIT, KA-TET OF NINETEEN)

One of the most immediately striking changes made to the 2003 version of *The Gunslinger* is the addition of three front pages. On the first is a quote from the novel *Look Homeward, Angel;* on the second is the lone number 19; and on the third is the single word RESUMPTION. These are all vital clues about the nature of Roland's quest, and about what he is going to find over the course of the three final books of the series.

In the 2003 *Gunslinger,* we also find out that the number nineteen is a magic number. After WALTER O'DIM resurrects the weed-eater NORT in the dried-up town of TULL, he implants a secret door in Nort's memory and imagination. That door, which holds back the secret horrors of the afterlife, is locked. But the lock has a key, and the key is nineteen. In a letter written to Roland's lover ALICE, Walter confides the nature of Nort's door, what Alice will find when she opens it, and the numerical key to the lock. Driven on by a maddening curiosity, Alice speaks the word *nineteen* and pays the price for it. Nineteen is the key to the Land of Death.

At the beginning of *Wolves of the Calla,* our *tet* refers to the number nineteen as the "mystery number." They find themselves gathering firewood in bundles of nineteen branches and even see its double digits take shape in the sky's passing clouds. Many of the important figures they meet or otherwise have dealings with—from DONALD FRANK CALLAHAN and CLAUDIA Y INEZ BACHMAN to RICHARD PATRICK SAYRE—have nineteen-letter names. When EDDIE DEAN questions ANDY, CALLA BRYN STURGIS's Messenger Robot, about how he predicts the WOLVES' cyclical invasions, Andy states that he cannot answer. The reason? Directive Nineteen. Directive Nineteen also plays an important part in *Wind Through the Keyhole.* In that book, Directive Nineteen fries the circuits of TIM ROSS's Portable Guidance System (and good friend), DARIA. Why? Because she offers restricted information to the young gunslinger-to-be.

And the coincidences continue. GRAN-PERE JAFFORDS was nineteen years old when he and his WOLF POSSE faced down the Greencloaks on the Calla's EAST ROAD. When Eddie saves CALVIN TOWER from BALAZAR's thugs (Calla NEW YORK's version of the Wolves), he discovers that Tower's great-great-great-grandfather wrote about Roland Deschain in his will, a document drawn up on March 19, 1846. Both Father Callahan and his friend ROWAN MAGRUDER end up in room 577 of Riverside Hospital after being attacked by the HITLER BROTHERS (5+7+7 = 19). When SUSANNAH DEAN and her demon-possessor, MIA, travel to 1999 New York, they stay in room 1919 of the PLAZA–PARK HYATT hotel.

Although nineteen plays an important role throughout *Wolves of the Calla* and *Song of Susannah,* not until the final book of the Dark Tower series do we learn the full significance of this curious number. *Chassit* (High Speech for "nineteen") is the password for the OLD ONES' DOOR, which connects our world's New York with END-WORLD's FEDIC. When nineteen (the *ka* of our world) joins with NINETY-NINE (the *ka* of Roland's world), they form 1999, which happens to be the KEYSTONE YEAR in the KEYSTONE WORLD. Nineteen ninety-nine is the year that MORDRED DESCHAIN is born, and on June 19, 1999, our *kas-ka Gan,* STEPHEN KING, is hit by a minivan in LOVELL, MAINE. Hence, it is in 1999 that the fate of the DARK TOWER is decided.

V:37–38, V:41, V:52, V:55, V:68, V:94, V:95, V:98, V:99, V:108, V:111, V:117, V:119, V:130, V:141, V:142, V:164, V:165, V:166–67, V:169, V:175, V:179, V:201, V:215, V:232, V:257, V:284 *(Nineteenth Street),* V:302, *(Route 19),* V:315, V:350 *(Directive Nineteen),* V:357 *(Jamie Jaffords),* V:360, V:367, V:423, V:428 *(room),* V:443, V:447 *(Nineteenth Nervous Breakdown),* V:449,

V:451 *(and Callahan's death)*, V:459, V:525, V:532, V:565, V:573, V:585, V:606, V:620, V:643, V:648, V:678, V:685, V:695, V:707, VI:48 *(time)*, VI:53 *(time)*, VI:84, VI:93, VI:95, VI:96, VI:118, VI:178, VI:184, VI:223, VI:225, VI:230, VI:270, VI:288, VI:325, VI:326, VI:328, VI:336 *(8+8+3 = 19)*, VI:338, VII:7 *(plates)*, VII:36, VII:130, VII:156 *(ka-tet of)*, VII:302 *(ka of)*, VII:303, VII:305, VII:399, VII:405, VII:418, VII:434, VII:436, VII:444, VII:453, VII:505, VII:551, VII:555, VII:556, VII:645, VII:665, VII:689, VII:761, VII:764, VII:821, VII:822, VII:825, VII:827, W:148, W:220, W:222, W:223, W:229, W:234 *(and Daria)*, W:237

NINETEEN NINETY-NINE (KEYSTONE YEAR IN THE KEYSTONE WORLD)

The year 1999 is considered the Keystone Year in the Keystone World. In it, the number NINETEEN (the *ka* of our world) joins with NINETY-NINE (the *ka* of Roland's world). It is a year of transformation, either for good or dis. On our level of the TOWER, it is the year that *sai* KING is hit by a Dodge minivan. It is also the year that JAKE CHAMBERS passes into the clearing while trying to save him. It is to 1999 NEW YORK that MIA, the bodyjacking mommy-bitch, takes SUSANNAH DEAN so that the two of them can give birth to MORDRED DESCHAIN, Roland's half-son and nemesis.

The fates of both the Dark Tower and the Dark Tower series depend upon what our *tet* can accomplish in this year. If they can save Stephen King and destroy Mordred, both Towers will survive. If they fail, then the multiverse will blink out of existence.

On the following pages, action takes place in the year 1999: V:648, V:695, VI:47–75, VI:66, VI:67, VI:72, VI:79–98, VI:86, VI:97, VI:119–25, VI:210, VI:219–34, VI:224, VI:256–61, VI:269, VI:307–85, VI:328, VI:333, VII:302, VII:303, VII:304, VII:305, VII:307, VII:405, VII:406, VII:418, VII:476, VII:485

NINETY-NINE (KA-TET OF NINETY-NINE)

Ninety-nine is another mystery number that continues to pop up throughout *Wolves of the Calla*. When he introduces himself to the *folken* of CALLA BRYN STURGIS, JAKE CHAMBERS claims to be of the *ka-tet* of ninety and nine. ANDY, the Calla's Messenger Robot (many other functions), will not disclose any information about his nasty programming until EDDIE DEAN recites his password, which is 1999. On the fence surrounding NEW YORK's Vacant LOT, our TODASH *ka-tet* sees a poem which reads, "Oh SUSANNAH-MIO, divided girl of mine, Done parked her RIG in the DIXIE PIG, in the year of '99."

Ninety-nine's true significance lies in that it is the *ka* of Roland's world, and of END-WORLD. It is also one-half of 1999, the KEYSTONE YEAR in the KEYSTONE WORLD, where the life of our *ka-tet*'s facilitator—STEPHEN KING—is in grave danger. It is also the year that Roland's nemesis MORDRED DESCHAIN is born.

V:215, V:565, V:567, V:570, V:643, V:648, V:654, V:677, V:695, VI:73, VI:289, VII:302 *(ka of Mid-World)*, VII:303, VII:473, VII:485

NIS

See GODS OF MID-WORLD

NORDITES

The blond people of Northern IN-WORLD are known as Nordites. Rumor has it that their chief sports are incest and reindeer fucking.

IV:422, IV:583

NORT

See TULL CHARACTERS; see also CALLAHAN, FATHER DONALD FRANK: CALLAHAN AND THE HITLER BROTHERS

**NORTH CENTRAL POSITRONICS

North Central Positronics was one of the nasty companies set up by the arrogant GREAT OLD ONES. This company and its affiliates created the technology that eventually destroyed MID-WORLD. They were responsible for the highly complex computers which controlled entire cities (as well as their stockpiles of weapons and poisons), and the cyborg GUARDIANS which guarded the PORTALS in and out of Mid-World. It seems highly likely that, through North Central Positronics, the Great Old Ones merged technology and magic. It seems even likelier that these arrogant ancestors believed that they could re-create the fabric of the multiverse and bend it to suit their fancy.

In the 2003 version of *The Gunslinger,* we learn more about North Central Positronics's unsavory history. One hundred generations before the world moved on, humanity made enough technological advances to chip a few splinters from the great pillar of reality. The company at the forefront of these discoveries was (of course) North Central Positronics. But these so-called technological advances, wondrous as they seemed, were accompanied by little or no insight into the true nature of the universe. Instead, they were seen only in the flat but false light of science. This was where both the Old People and their glorious company fell short. They had no perspective, only an arrogant and dangerous drive toward what they labeled "progress." The water pump in the WAY STATION may have been created by North Central Positronics, but so were the insane SHARDIK, the psychotic ANDY, and the murderous BLAINE, who liked to play evil god to the people of LUD.

Although North Central Positronics was founded by the Old Ones on Roland's level of the TOWER, this company seems to exist in the MULTIPLE AMERICAS as well. (The brainy Positronics folks probably designed the MIND-TRAP, which almost kills JAKE under the DIXIE PIG.) The TASSEN-BAUMS have a North Central Positronics magnet on their refrigerator, and DINKY EARNSHAW, one of the DEVAR-TOI's BREAKERS, originally worked for a Positronics subsidiary that hired psychic assassins. In conjunction with SOMBRA, North Central Positronics is also in the process of taking over the PLAZA–PARK HYATT, where SUSANNAH-MIO stays during her brief trip to 1999 NEW YORK.

No matter how beneficent the original NCP intended to be (after all, it seems likely that they were hired to redesign the Tower, BEAMS, and Guardians), under the directorship of the CAN-TOI, RICHARD P. SAYRE, it serves the purposes of the CRIMSON KING and the Outer Dark. Like the other subsidiaries of Sombra, they hope to destroy the ROSE and bring down the Dark Tower. Hence, it is little wonder that when EDDIE DEAN and Roland Deschain discuss the founding of the TET CORPORATION with JOHN CULLUM, they state that Tet must have three primary functions: save the Rose, protect STEPHEN KING, and sabotage both Sombra and North Central Positronics whenever possible. The future of all the worlds depends upon the destruction of this dangerous conglomerate. III:34, III:54, III:75, V:5, V:72, V:132, V:564, V:702, VI:11, VI:72, VI:91–92, VI:109, VI:219, VI:235, VI:237, VI:238, VI:248, VI:269, VI:270, VI:336, VI:348, VI:377, VI:381, VII:37, VII:75, VII:87–88, VII:125, VII:126, VII:343 *(not directly mentioned, but they probably made the booby-trapped robots)*, VII:470 *(and Tassenbaums)*, VII:471, VII:498, VII:517, VII:664–65, W:12, W:220, W:221, W:226, W:235

ANDY: Andy is CALLA BRYN STURGIS's seven-foot-tall Messenger Robot. To EDDIE DEAN, he looks like C3PO from the film *Star Wars*. However, unlike C3PO, Andy's skinny legs and arms are made from a silvery material and his head is stainless steel. (Only his body is gold.) His eyes are described as electric blue.

Like SHARDIK, the marauding man-made BEAR GUARDIAN, Andy bears the North Central Positronics stamp. Located on his chest, it reads as follows:

NORTH CENTRAL POSITRONICS, LTD.
IN ASSOCIATION WITH LaMERK INDUSTRIES
PRESENTS
ANDY
Design: MESSENGER (Many Other Functions)
Serial # DNF 34821 V 63

Although he is the last robot for wheels around, Andy never leaves the Calla. He wanders here and there, spreading gossip, singing songs, and telling horoscopes. (Despite his amazing strength, he rarely helps with any manual task more strenuous than cookery.) On the whole, the Calla *folken* consider Andy a nuisance; however, he does serve one important function. Each generation, he accurately predicts the coming of the WOLVES. No one has ever been able to find out how Andy knows this, since whenever they question him about it, he responds that he cannot answer unless they know the appropriate password. The reason? Directive NINETEEN.

In actuality, Andy works for the minions of the CRIMSON KING in THUNDERCLAP. Each generation, he finds a vulnerable adult who has parented only a single set of twins. Andy then infects one of the children with a deadly disease. (In the case of BENNY SLIGHTMAN's twin sister, the disease was hot-lung.) Once the parent has only one child left, Andy begins his emotional blackmail. If the parent acts as a spy for the Wolves, then his or her remaining child will be kept safe. Until the arrival of Roland and his *ka-tet*, Andy's ploy worked incredibly well. The people of the Callas felt powerless against the Greencloaks, since the child-snatchers seemed to predict their every act of resistance.

In the final book of the Dark Tower series, we learn that robots like Andy are called ASIMOV ROBOTS. Logic faults are quite common in such intelligent mechanical beings. However, whatever happened to make Andy such a traitorous monster seems to have less to do with logic faults and more to do with plain old meanness. V:1–2, V:3–8, V:10, V:15, V:18, V:25, V:29, V:31, V:129, V:131, V:132–33, V:134, V:137–42, V:144, V:150, V:151, V:154, V:155, V:161 *(indirect)*, V:168, V:207–8, V:211–34 *(present; mentioned directly on 218, 220)*, V:293, V:318, V:321–24 *(present with Jake and Benny)*, V:328, V:331, V:332, V:337, V:339, V:340, V:350–51, V:356, V:362, V:381, V:384–86, V:391, V:412, V:415, V:484, V:485, V:487, V:488, V:489–92, V:494–95, V:501, V:554, V:558, V:561, V:567–77, V:578, V:581, V:585, V:586–89, V:590, V:601–17 *(present; mentioned directly on 602, 603, 608, 610, 611)*, V:629, V:630–35, V:641, V:644–50, V:652, V:655 *(pard)*, V:656, V:658, V:659, V:660, V:678, V:702, V:704, VI:9, VI:67, VI:252, VII:65, VII:73, VII:146 *(indirect)*, VII:156 *(indirect)*, VII:157, VII:191, VII:708, VII:710, VII:722, W:16, W:17

ASIMOV ROBOTS: Intelligent robots created by North Central Positronics. They are prone to logic faults. In a working robot, such faults tend to be quarantined, like e-mail viruses that arrive on a computer protected by an anti-virus program. However, as we see in the case of NIGEL, this quarantining process doesn't always seem to work, especially in instances where a robot's less stable emotional programming is involved. VII:156

BLAINE:

Now, although the unthinkable machinery which maintained the Beams had weakened, this insane and inhuman intelligence had awakened in the rooms of ruin and had begun once more, although as bodiless as any ghost, to stumble through the halls of the dead.
(III:373)

Our *ka-tet*'s nasty adventure with Blaine the Insane Mono was prefigured by the story of CHARLIE THE CHOO-CHOO and also by JAKE CHAMBERS's crazed English essay entitled "My Understanding of Truth." This nasty, overly sophisticated train was created by the sinister North Central Positronics. He was therefore a distant cousin of SHARDIKand the other cyborg GUARD-IANS.

Despite superficial appearances, Blaine was not just a train. He was in fact the GHOST IN THE MACHINES—LUD's city-wide computer intelligence so feared by the PUBES and the GRAYS. This fear was not unfounded, since Blaine was completely psychotic. He suffered from a computerized form of split personality disorder (he was composed of nasty "Big Blaine" and terrified "Little Blaine"). While a horrified Little Blaine watched, Big Blaine committed terrible crimes such as destroying his companion mono PATRICIA (she was crying all the time) and gassing the residents of Lud. Big Blaine, whose logic and reasoning twisted long ago, agreed to take Roland and his friends southeast along the PATH OF THE BEAM to his termination point in TOPEKA. His price was a riddling contest. If the *ka-tet* won, Blaine would deliver them safely to their destination. If they lost, Blaine would kill them when he killed himself. Obviously, our *ka-tet* was at a severe disadvantage since Blaine had access to information on all levels of the DARK TOWER. However, EDDIE DEAN succeeded in defeating Blaine with the Eddie specialty—bad jokes. III:52, III:53, III:98, III:140, III:239, III:245–49 *(Blaine/Patricia)*, III:254,

III:255–56, III:263, III:267, III:286, III:288–89, III:303, III:309, III:322–25, III:332–34, III:340–50 *(cradle)*, III:361–65, III:372–85 *(373–82 voice in Cradle of the Grays with Roland and Jake)*, III:389, III:393–420, IV:3–10 *(Roland refuses to riddle, so Blaine turns on "visual" mode; 3–6 Roland challenges, 6–9 Roland bargains)*, IV:13–42, IV:44–63 *(45 transteel piers are yellow and black, like Portal of the Bear; 49 Eddie decides to piss off Blaine; 56 Blaine blows circuit; 58–59 crash; 61 leave Blaine; 62 standing on Blaine)*, IV:642–43, V:35, V:38, V:55, V:58, V:106, V:125, V:139, V:164 *(mono)*, V:220, V:258 *(indirect)*, V:291, V:478, V:508, V:565, V:567, V:572, V:573, V:639, VI:109, VI:117, VI:138, VI:244, VI:266, VI:269, VI:287, VI:358, VI:359, VI:404, VI:406, VII:19, VII:44, VII:160, VII:201, VII:407, VII:536, VII:645, VII:698, VII:808, VII:811, W:13, W:31

> **GHOSTS IN THE MACHINES:** Every time the PUBES of LUD heard the god-drums, they drew lots to see who among them should be sacrificed. The Pubes believed that there were ghosts living in the machines under the city. If these ghosts were not appeased, they would take over the bodies of the dead, rise up, and eat those left alive. As JEEVES of the Pubes said, "There are a great many machines under Lud, and there are ghosts in all of them—demonous spirits which bear only ill will to mortal men and women. These demon-ghosts are *very* capable of raising the dead . . . and in Lud, there are a great many dead to raise" (III:322). Although the Grays ran the god-drum machines that incited the Pube's frenzied sacrifice, they also believed that the city's computers were haunted by demonic spirits. When you think about it, they were right. III:322–23, III:336, III:347, III:364, III:373, III:400

> **IMPERIUM:** III:398

> **LITTLE BLAINE:** III:347–49, III:361, III:363, III:364, III:377 *(voice)*, III:398, III:409, III:413, IV:35, IV:52, IV:54, IV:55

> **PASSENGER KILLINGTON:** While he and SUSANNAH are in the CRA-DLE OF LUD, EDDIE DEAN imagines the station as it must once have been. He even imagines he hears a loudspeaker calling for this particular passenger. III:342

DARIA (NORTH CENTRAL POSITRONICS PORTABLE GUIDANCE MODULE DARIA, NCP-1436345-AN): In *The Wind Through the Keyhole,* the mutant MUDMEN of the FAGONARD swamp gave TIM ROSS this speaking guidance module to help him find his way through the ENDLESS FOREST and to the home of the magician MAERLYN. Unlike so many of the wicked technological objects created by the Old People, Daria had a kind and gentle mechanical heart and eventually became Tim's friend.

When Tim first saw Daria, he mistook her for a small purse of smooth leather with a metal seam running across her center. It was only when the Mudmen's HELMSMAN pulled a tab attached to this seam that the purse opened and Tim saw the brushed metal disc inside which was the size and thickness of a small dinner plate. Although Tim couldn't read the writing on top of the device, below the writing were three buttons. Pushing one of these buttons made the disk emit a low whining sound and forced a short metal stick to emerge from the plate. Pushing a second button made the disk beep and a red light come on. Once the stick was out and the red light was on, the guidance mechanism was ready to use. The person holding the mechanism had to then turn in a circle until the device beeped again and the light turned green, indicating the correct direction of travel.

Throughout his trip from the Fagonard to the NORTH FOREST KINNOCK DOGAN, where the enchanted magician MAERLYN waited in the form of a hungry TYGER, Daria proved to be a dependable guide and protector. Not only could she read the location and magical state of the magnetic BEAM which Tim followed, but upon request, she could supply a bright light. (The light made Tim think of burning phosphorus.) Throughout Tim's journey, Daria helped him avoid dangers, such as the poisonous GIANT YELLOW MUSHROOMS that Tim would otherwise have eaten and the TENTACLED DEMON that would have eaten Tim, if it had gotten the chance.

Although DIRECTIVE NINETEEN officially restricted the amount of information that she could give to Tim, Daria purposefully disobeyed it in order to help her young traveler. As a result, she was permanently shut down. W:210–32 *(216 talks)*, W:232–35 *(dies because of directive 19)*, W:237, W:239, W:256

DELICIOUS RAIN: Delicious Rain and the other D-line trains run south from the DEVAR-TOI to the poisoned DISCORDIA. VII:411

DEVAR-TOI ROBOTS (UNNAMED):

    SIX-ARMED ROBOT: This robot has six pincer-like arms, which he waves about as he tours the DEVAR-TOI. VII:343, VII:351–52

DOBBIE: Dobbie is a type of domestic robot known as a house elf. She does much of TAMMY KELLY's work in the DEVAR-TOI Master's house. VII:354

FEDIC ROBOTS AND UNNAMED FEDIC DOGAN ROBOTS:

    CLASS A CONDUCTOR ROBOT (FEDIC STATION): VII:201

    DEAD ROBOT: VI:235

    HUCKSTER ROBOT: This robot travels up and down FEDIC's main street advertising humie and cybie girls, even though all of the potential customers are dead. Although we don't see the North Central Positronics stamp on this electronic pimp's body, we can be fairly certain that he was made by them. VI:235, VI:244, VII:536

    HUNTER-KILLER ROBOTS IN DOGAN: VII:159–60

    MAINTENANCE DRONE: DINKY EARNSHAW places this fried maintenance drone near the FEDIC/THUNDERCLAP STATION door to disguise our *ka-tet*'s entrance into END-WORLD. VII:203, VII:222

    PLAYER PIANO: VI:235

    ROBOT THAT LOOKS LIKE ANDY: This robot is rusting in front of the FEDIC CAFÉ. VI:252

    STEEL BALL ON LEGS: SUSANNAH DEAN spots this mechanical foreman while the ASIMOV ROBOT NIGEL carries her through the FEDIC DOGAN. The foreman fried his boards eight hundred years earlier and all he can manage to say when they pass is "Howp! Howp!" VII:75

FIRE-RESPONSE TEAM BRAVO: Although they are officially the DEVAR-TOI's mechanical firemen, Fire-Response Team Bravo are actually better at running people over with their fire engines than they are at putting out fires. VII:363, VII:369, VII:371–73, VII:389, VII:393

NIGEL THE BUTLER (CHUMLEY): When MORDRED DESCHAIN is

due to be born in the FEDIC DOGAN, Nigel the Butler (DNK4932 DOMES-TIC) arrives in the EXTRACTION ROOM bearing an incubator. However, as soon as he sees Mordred turn into a spider and devour his birth mother, Nigel realizes that such precautions probably aren't necessary. During the fray which follows Mordred's birth, SUSANNAH DEAN shoots out Nigel's eyes (an aggressive but understandable act, since Nigel closely resembles ANDY, CALLA BRYN STURGIS's treacherous Messenger Robot). Although both Nigel and Andy are ASIMOV ROBOTS, Nigel has a much more sensitive nature. Whereas Andy seems to take a vengeful pleasure in betraying the people of the Callas, Nigel seems positively pleased to help feed and house our *tet* once they are reunited in the Fedic Dogan. In fact, he finds feeding small animals to Spider-Mordred so distressing that his circuits blow. VII:65–80, VII:111, VII:145–46 *(sleeping until next entry)*, VII:148–49, VII:150–59 *(Asimov Robots)*, VII:160, VII:161, VII:162, VII:163–64, VII:166–67, VII:169 *(indirect)*, VII:171, VII:172 *(indirect)*, VII:176, VII:189, VII:250, VII:541, VII:707

PATRICIA: Patricia was the twin of BLAINE the Insane Mono. She was blue and traveled northwest. Blaine fried her circuits because he was tired of hearing her cry all the time. Although back in *The Waste Lands* our *tet* saw the remains of her bright blue train body jutting out of the RIVER SEND near the city of LUD, in the distant past Patricia also embarked from the town of FEDIC in END-WORLD. III:245–49 *(speaking of Blaine, probably mean Patricia)*, III:288–89, III:342, III:346, III:410–11, III:412, IV:4, VI:237, VI:244, VI:269, VII:89, W:13

PHIL: When TED BRAUTIGAN first arrived at the DEVAR-TOI, Phil was his robot driver. His favorite saying was "My name's Phil, I'm over the hill, but the best news is I never spill." Not long after Ted met him, Phil ended up on the garbage dump. VII:289–90

SHARDIK: *See* GUARDIANS OF THE BEAM, *listed separately*

SPIRIT OF THE SNOW COUNTRY: Along with DELICIOUS RAIN, Spirit of the Snow Country is one of the D-line trains that run from the DEVAR-TOI to the DISCORDIA. VII:411

SPIRIT OF TOPEKA: The Spirit of Topeka is the atomic engine (also called a hot-enge) which runs from the DEVAR-TOI to FEDIC. Like BLAINE, it doesn't require a human driver. VII:531, VII:536–37

STUTTERING BILL: Stuttering Bill (whose official name is William, D-746541-M, Maintenance Robot, Many Other Functions) is the kindhearted robot that SUSANNAH and Roland meet after their terrible ordeal with DANDELO. Like the other ASIMOV ROBOTS we've met, Bill has rudimentary emotions. Hence, he is extremely happy to find out that our dwindling *tet* has freed PATRICK DANVILLE from his prison in Dandelo's basement. Stuttering Bill gives Roland, Susannah, and Patrick HO FAT II and HO FAT III to speed them along on their journey to the DARK TOWER. Roland fixes Bill's stutter using the power of suggestion. (It works, even though he doesn't have access to Bill's fix-it manual.) VII:661–62, VII:663, VII:664, VII:665, VII:670, VII:679, VII:705–10, VII:715–22, VII:753 *(indirect)*, VII:774 *(indirect)*, VII:801, VII:803

TURNIP-HEADED ROBOT: JAKE comes across this run-down robot in the passage between the DIXIE PIG and the FEDIC/NEW YORK doorway. Once he was a guard. Now all he can do is flash his eyes and croak. VII:89

NORTH STAR
See GODS OF MID-WORLD: OLD STAR

NORTON, SUSAN
See CALLAHAN, FATHER DONALD FRANK: 'SALEM'S LOT CHARAC-TERS

**NOT-MAN
When Roland was young, he saw a Not-Man, or an invisible man, hanged for the crime of rape. Evidently, he was very good at sneaking up on people.

NUTTER, ELROD
See SKIN-MAN: SKIN-MAN'S VICTIMS: JEFFERSON RANCH

O

OAKLEY, ANNIE
See GUNSLINGERS, *in* OUR WORLD

OCEAN FOAM
See DELGADO, PAT

ODETTA
See DEAN, SUSANNAH: SUSANNAH'S OTHER SELVES

**O'DIM, WALTER
See WALTER

OFFICER BOSCONI
See DEAN, EDDIE: EDDIE'S PAST ASSOCIATES

OLD FARTS OF THE APOCALPYSE
See TET CORPORATION: FOUNDING FATHERS

OLD FATTY
See TOWER, CALVIN

OLD FELLA
See CALLAHAN, FATHER DONALD FRANK

**OLD MOTHER (SOUTH STAR, LYDIA)
See GODS OF MID-WORLD

OLD ONES (GREAT OLD ONES, THE MAKERS, OLD PEOPLE)

The Old Ones (also known as the Great Old Ones) were the ancient people of MID-WORLD. Their era was long gone even by the time of ARTHUR ELD. The Old Ones had a god-like knowledge of technology and the workings of the universe but they were also a violently destructive people.

As a horrified SUSAN DELGADO said when she found out that FARSON was trying to resurrect the Old Ones' war machines, "The ways of the Old People are the ways of death" (IV:302). This certainly seems to be true. When BIX, the RIVER WHYE ferryman, went to fetch his steel crank from the UNDERGROUND DOGAN near the GREEN PALACE, he found miles of tunnels filled with the Old Ones' perfectly preserved artifacts, but the radiation of the place made him violently ill. (He lost his hair and teeth and puked for days.) It was also one of the Old People's leavings that was responsible for the SALTIE, OLLIE ANG, transforming into the violent shapeshifting SKIN-MAN. As far as we can tell, the computers and killing machines of this ancient race were responsible for the incredible catastrophe that originally poisoned Mid-World, just as their RED DEATH killed the people of FEDIC. Farson's resurrection of these instruments of war and death succeeded in destroying Mid-World's civilization a second time.

The company that the Old Ones founded (namely NORTH CENTRAL POSITRONICS) was responsible for the creation of BLAINE the Insane Mono, ANDY the Messenger Robot, and SHARDIK, the cyborg BEAR GUARDIAN. The Great Old Ones desired to replace the magical DARK TOWER and the BEAMS with technological replicas, and it was their wars, weapons, and pollutants which created Mid-World's many MUTANTS.

The Old People may have been technological wizards, but in the long run, little good came from their experiments with the time/space continuum. They may have created DOORWAYS BETWEEN WORLDS, but they also built the DOGANS, the sinister equipment found in the DEVAR-TOI, and the diseases (such as the Red Death) which destroyed the people of FEDIC. Unfortunately, the Great Old Ones could well be our own descendants. As Roland so wryly notes when he visits NEW YORK, 1999, that city looks like a young and vibrant LUD. Occasionally, the term *Old Ones* is used for the ancient vampires known as the GRANDFATHERS.

III:37–39, III:46 *(larger than men)*, III:73, III:240–41, III:244, III:245, III:246, III:284, III:288, III:297, III:342–43 *(faces on Blaine's Cradle)*, III:362, III:399, IV:23, IV:35 *(possible carvers of the Hounds of the Falls of the Hounds)*, IV:120, IV:294 *(called Old People by Susan)*, IV:295, IV:296, IV:302 *(their ways were the ways of death)*, IV:430 *(their weapons)*, IV:431, IV:484 *(as devils)*, V:100, V:108 *(Old People of the forest, not Great Old Ones)*, V:141, V:144, V:151, V:210, V:339, V:340, V:565, VI:252, VII:25, VII:77 *(indirect)*, VII:92, VII:100, VII:107, VII:108, VII:132, VII:152, VII:156, VII:238, VII:239, VII:537, VII:538, VII:566 *(mad)*, VII:825, W:12, W:64, W:110, W:180 *(and Dodge Dart)*, W:210, W:282

OLD PEOPLE
See OLD ONES

OLD PEOPLE OF THE WEST WOODS
Although the GREAT OLD ONES are sometimes called the Old People, the Old People of the West Woods were a much later and much more primitive culture— one which probably arose after the Great Old Ones destroyed most of MID-WORLD's cities. Roland and his *ka-tet* found the Old People's primitive remains while they camped in this mixed forest located east of the WESTERN SEA.

This forest-dwelling tribe hunted with bows and arrows and lived in awe of SHARDIK, the great BEAR GUARDIAN. Shardik thought of them as trap-setters and forest-burners, but they regarded him as both a demon and the shadow of a god. They called him MIR, which meant "the world beneath the world."
III:19–21, III:29

OLD SPLINT
See TREE VILLAGE CHARACTERS

**OLD STAR (NORTH STAR, APON)
See GODS OF MID-WORLD

OMAHA
A one-eyed gambler who died with a knife in his throat at a Watch Me table.
IV:72

O'MEARAH, GEORGE
O'Mearah was one of the NEW YORK cops who patrolled the area in front of CLEMENTS GUNS AND SPORTING GOODS. His partner's name was CARL DELEVAN. The two of them were hoodwinked by Roland while Roland was in JACK MORT's body.
II:343, II:346, II:347–59 *(354 unconscious),* II:368 *(indirect),* II:371–77, II:378, II:380

OPOPANAX
See APPENDIX I

ORACLE OF THE MOUNTAINS
See DEMON ELEMENTALS

ORIZA, LADY (LADY OF THE PLATE, LADY RICE)
In some parts of MID-WORLD, Lady Oriza is considered to be a mythical heroine. However, in the BORDERLANDS, she is the pagan goddess of the rice. According to local folklore, Oriza gave birth to the first man, and from this man's breath came the first woman. To honor Oriza's part in the creation of the human race, the old folks of the Calla still say, *"Can-ah, can-tah, annah Oriza,"* which translates as "All breath comes from the woman."

According to another old tale, Lady Oriza's father, LORD GRENFALL, was murdered by the infamous harrier GRAY DICK, and the beautiful Lady Oriza swore to take bloody vengeance. Cloaking her true motives in veils of seduction, she proposed that she and Dick share a conciliatory feast at WAYDON, her family castle. To prove her good intentions, she stated that they should each leave their weapons—and their clothes—at the door.

Not surprisingly, Dick accepted the offer. During the second toast, both Dicks stood at attention. "May your beauty ever increase," he said. To which Oriza replied, "May your first day in Hell last ten thousand years, and may it be the shortest." Then, flinging her specially sharpened dinner plate at him, she sliced off his head.

A female society called the SISTERS OF ORIZA was formed in honor of Lady Oriza's triumph. Although they may originally have been a sisterhood of warriors or priestesses, by the time our story begins, they are essentially a ladies' auxiliary that practices throwing their deadly, sharpened plates. Interestingly, their plates (known as Orizas) closely resemble DETTA WALKER's *forspecial* plate. However, the fine blue webbing which decorates the Orizas is in the form of the young oriza, or seedling rice plant. Two of the rice stalks cross at the edge of the plate, forming the great letter ZN, which means both "here" and "now." This segment of the rim is dull and slightly thicker so that the plate can be gripped without danger. The titanium Orizas are manufactured by the women of CALLA SEN CHRE and have a whistle underneath them so that they hum as they fly.

Like that of many gods and goddesses, Lady Oriza's vengeful nature surfaces frequently. Both she and her sister wished to marry LORD SEMINON, the god of the prewinter windstorms. However, Seminon preferred Oriza's sister and married her. Enraged that her love was rejected—and that a marriage between wind and rice would never take place—Oriza often blocks Seminon's passage over the RIVER WHYE. This pleases the people of the Calla since it protects them from Seminon's blasts.

V:313, V:321, V:325–27, V:329, V:330, V:331–37 *(throwing plate)*, V:338 *(plate)*, V:360 *(by 'Riza)*, V:361 *(Reap charm)*, V:398, V:467, V:491 *('Riza)*, V:492, V:495, V:500, V:572 *('Riza)*, V:576, V:582 *(indirect)*, V:604, V:631, V:642–43, V:644 *(plate)*, V:662 *(plate)*, V:663, V:680, V:685, V:686, V:689, VI:68 *(plates)*, VI:92, VI:95, VI:97, VI:333 *(plates)*, VI:335 *(plates)*, VII:10 *(plates)*, VII:25 *(plates)*, VII:35 *(plates)*, VII:82 *(plates)*, VII:85 *(plates)*, VII:87 *(plates)*, VII:89 *(plates)*, VII:111 *(plates)*, VII:173 *(plates)*, VII:255 *(plates)*, VII:352 *(plates)*, VII:491 *(plates)*, VII:535 *(plates)*, VII:557 *(plates)*, VII:558 *(plates)*, VII:567 *(plates)*, VII:634 *(plates)*, VII:708–9 *(plates)*, VII:726 *(indirect)*

GRAY DICK: Gray Dick was an infamous harrier who killed Lady Oriza's father, LORD GRENFALL. Oriza's revenge was both clever and seductive. Inviting her enemy to a meal at WAYDON, her family castle, she proposed that the two of them eat naked, to prove that they were each weaponless. Nevertheless, Oriza managed to decapitate Dick with one of her specially sharpened plates. V:325–27, V:332, V:398

GRENFALL, LORD: Lord Grenfall was Lady Oriza's father. Once he was known as the "wiliest lord in all the RIVER BARONIES," but when Oriza was still a young woman he was murdered by the infamous harrier GRAY DICK. Oriza decapitated her father's murderer. V:325, V:326, V:327 *(father)*

MARIAN: Marian was Lady Oriza's maid. After she left Oriza's service, she went on to have many of her own adventures. Unfortunately, we never hear about any of them. V:326

ORIZA'S SISTER: Lady Oriza and her sister both sought the love of LORD SEMINON, the BORDERLANDS' wind god, but Seminon preferred Oriza's sister and married her. Lady Oriza has never forgiven him. V:642–43

SEMINON, LORD: Lord Seminon is the personification of the prewinter winds that sweep across the RIVER WHYE and into CALLA BRYN STURGIS. According to one old story, Lord Seminon rejected Lady Oriza's love so that he could marry her sister. Out of spite, Oriza frequently refuses to let the harsh Seminon winds cross into the Callas. V:642–43

ORIZA, SISTERS OF (SISTERS OF THE PLATE)

The Sisters of Oriza, also known as the Sisters of the Plate, honor the goddess ORIZA's triumph over her enemy, the harrier GRAY DICK. Although in many ways the Sisters function as a ladies' auxiliary, they also practice throwing their deadly sharpened plates, known as Orizas. Seventy years before our story takes place, one of the Sisters—MOLLY DOOLIN—destroyed one of the Calla's child-stealing WOLVES. Unfortunately, she paid for the victory with her life.

The Sisters of Oriza are, by far, the fiercest fighters in the Calla. Three of them, MARGARET EISENHART, ZALIA JAFFORDS, and ROSALITA MUNOZ, stand with Roland's *ka-tet* against the final Wolf invasion. During that attack, Margaret Eisenhart is killed.

Like the mythical lady they are named for, the Sisters of Oriza are a multi-talented group of women. Not only are they the best fighters and cooks in the CRESCENT, but they also serve as the area's doctors and midwives.

V:331, V:338–39, V:358, V:489, V:493–94, V:496–500 *(competition),* V:509 *(Ladies of),* V:575, V:601–17 *(present; mentioned directly on 602, 607, 609, 611),* V:630, V:641, V:642, V:662–68 *(present),* V:674, V:679–97, VI:10

ADAMS, SAREY: Fat, jolly Sarey Adams is the wife of the rancher DIEGO ADAMS. Although Sarey is surprisingly light on her feet, Sarey's aim is not as accurate as that of the other Sisters. Hence, Roland thinks it is too risky to place her on the front line of the EAST ROAD battle against the invading WOLVES. Instead, he asks this Sister of Oriza to lead the CHILD-MINDERS, who hide the Calla's children in the rice paddies near the DEVAR-TETE WHYE. V:338, V:341, V:399, V:419, V:421, V:483, V:493–94, V:496–500, V:575, V:658, V:662–67 *(present),* V:667, V:689 *(folken),* V:693–97 *(folken)*

DOOLIN, MOLLY (RED MOLLY): Molly Doolin was the wife of EAMON DOOLIN and was the only woman to stand with GRAN-PERE JAFFORDS's WOLF POSSE against the GREENCLOAKS. Although Molly was seventy years dead by the time our *ka-tet* entered CALLA BRYN STURGIS, Gran-pere's memory of her flinging her plate at an oncoming Wolf—and destroying it—still burns bright. Molly died during her stand on the EAST ROAD, but what she managed to do with her Oriza inspired Roland to draft the Sisters of the Plate to join him in his own stand against those menacing, robotic horse-riders.

In life, Molly Doolin's fiery personality (not her blazing red hair) earned her the nickname Red Molly. She wore a silver Reap charm around her neck which was shaped like Lady Oriza raising her fist in defiance. When Molly flung her Wolf-destroying plate, she shouted the name of her twin, MINNIE, whom the Wolves had taken to THUNDERCLAP during their previous raid and had returned ROONT. V:358–63, V:365, V:390, V:485, V:611, V:665, V:679

EISENHART, MARGARET (MARGARET OF THE REDPATH CLAN):

Margaret Eisenhart was born Margaret of the Redpath clan. Although her family was MANNI, she left the fold to marry VAUGH EISENHART. According to her father (or grandfather) HENCHICK, she is destined for NA'AR because of it. Margaret is one of the three Sisters of Oriza that stand with Roland during the battle of the EAST ROAD. Sadly, she is decapitated by one of the WOLVES' light-sticks. We never find out whether she ends up in Na'ar. V:318 *(indirect)*, V:320 *(indirect)*, V:322–25, V:328–42 *(of Redpath clan)*, V:389, V:398, V:399, V:407–8, V:483, V:491, V:493–94, V:496–500, V:601–17 *(present; directly mentioned on 602, 607, 609)*, V:654, V:662–68, V:674 *(indirect)*, V:679–82 *(killed on 682)*, V:689, V:691–94, V:700, VI:3, VI:28, VI:73, VI:80, VI:205, VII:83

JAFFORDS, ZALIA (ZALLIE): Zalia Jaffords is the dark-skinned wife of TIAN JAFFORDS. The two of them have five children—two sets of twins and a singleton. Zalia's maiden name was HOONIK. Like the other people of the Calla, she lost a twin, ZALMAN, to the horrors of THUNDERCLAP. Though he was bright as polished agate when he was small, when Zalman returned from the dark lands of the east, he was ROONT.

Just as she stood by her husband in his decision to oppose the WOLVES, Zalia stands with Roland and his *ka-tet* during the Calla's final battle. Unlike her friend MARGARET EISENHART, Zallie survives. V:8–13, V:15, V:25, V:27, V:28, V:44 *(following* ka-tet*)*, V:45 *(following* ka-tet*)*, V:47 *(following* ka-tet*)*, V:88 *(new friends)*, V:92 *(indirect)*, V:106 *(indirect)*, V:109, V:111–13, V:116, V:122–37, V:142–60, V:162, V:201–10 *(present; mentioned directly on 207, 208)*, V:211–34 *(present; mentioned directly on 216, 218, 224)*, V:236–37, V:338, V:343–46, V:347 *(indirect)*, V:348 *(indirect)*, V:350, V:351–57, V:358, V:376–77, V:379, V:397–99, V:401, V:483, V:485, V:488–92 *(present)*, V:493–94, V:496–500, V:601–17, V:654, V:662–68, V:674 *(indirect)*, V:679–97, VI:205, VI:373

MUNOZ, ROSALITA (ROSITA, ROSA): Rosalita Munoz is PERE CALLAHAN'S housekeeper and (as EDDIE DEAN surmises) his executive secretary. Although Rosalita is a converted Catholic, this doesn't stop her from having an affair with Roland. Although she herself is childless, Rosalita's hatred of the WOLVES is ferocious, and she is one of the first people in the Calla to openly support Roland's *ka-tet* in their plan to resist these invaders from THUNDERCLAP. Not surprisingly, Rosalita is also one of the female warriors Roland chooses to be on the front line during the EAST ROAD battle.

Like many of the other Sisters, Rosalita is a healer as well as a fighter. Her cat-oil eases the pain of Roland's dry twist. She is also an accomplished midwife. V:236, V:242–44, V:245, V:250, V:251, V:252, V:281, V:293–94, V:310–12 *(present)*, V:320, V:331, V:338, V:341, V:399, V:417, V:418–19, V:420–21, V:438, V:442–51 *(present)*, V:467, V:475, V:476, V:477, V:480–83, V:484, V:493–94, V:496–500, V:584, V:589, V:601–17 *(present with Sisters of Oriza; mentioned on 602, 604, 609, 615)*, V:628, V:639, V:640–41, V:644, V:646–50, V:652, V:653, V:654, V:662–68, V:674 *(indirect)*, V:679–96, VI:4, VI:8, VI:9–10, VI:13–18, VI:24, VI:205, VI:281, VII:122, VII:152

ORTEGA, MILLICENT
See HAMBRY CHARACTERS: OTHER CHARACTERS

OUTER DARK
   See APPENDIX I

OUTWORLDERS
In *Wolves of the Calla,* outworlders are people who come from the lands west of the BORDERLANDS. Roland, EDDIE, SUSANNAH, JAKE, and OY are all considered outworlders.
   V:312, V:344, V:402, V:418

OVER, THE
   See MANNI

OVERHOLSER, ALAN
   See CALLA BRYN STURGIS CHARACTERS: FARMERS (LARGE FARMS): OVERHOLSER, WAYNE DALE

OVERHOLSER, WAYNE
   See CALLA BRYN STURGIS CHARACTERS: FARMERS (LARGE FARMS)

OVERHOLSER, WELLAND
   See CALLA BRYN STURGIS CHARACTERS: ROONTS

OVERMEYER, PROFESSOR
   See DEAN, SUSANNAH: ODETTA HOLMES'S ASSOCIATES

OXFORD TOWN COPS
   See DEAN, SUSANNAH: ODETTA HOLMES AND THE CIVIL RIGHTS MOVEMENT: ODETTA'S "MOVEMENT" ASSOCIATES

OY
Oy is JAKE CHAMBERS's pet BILLY-BUMBLER (or perhaps Jake is Oy's pet boy). Oy approached our *ka-tet* while they traveled along on the BEAM leading toward LUD. When Jake first found Oy—or when Oy first woke Jake by licking his face—the bumbler had some bites on his body. It seems likely that he was chased away from his own pack because he talked too much. Like the best billy-bumblers, Oy is intelligent and faithful. He can count, add, and communicate. He can also predict the coming of a STARKBLAST. Oy is completely devoted to Jake, and becomes a full-fledged member of Roland's *ka-tet.*
   Like all other bumblers, Oy looks like a cross between a raccoon, a wood-chuck, and a dachshund. He has expressive, gold-ringed eyes and a little squiggle of a tail. Although he is not human, Oy is extremely intelligent. Just as some kinds of terriers are bred to be ratters, in the days of old, billy-bumblers (also called THROCKENS) were kept to destroy GRANDFATHER FLEAS. Hence, by their very nature they serve the WHITE.
   In the seventh book of the series, we discover that Oy's devotion to our *tet's* quest, and his allegiance to Roland, are as profound as that of his young master. After Jake dies saving the writer STEPHEN KING, brave little Oy remains with

Roland rather than lying down and expiring upon his friend's grave. In fact, Oy makes it closer to the DARK TOWER than any other member of Roland's *ka-tet*.

Sadly, as was predicted back in *Wizard and Glass,* Oy dies impaled upon the branch of a tree. He is thrown there by MORDRED when he tries to foil the spider-boy's attempt to kill Roland.

III:219–22, III:224, III:226–54, III:255–67, III:273–81, III:283–85, III:286–300 *(294 almost falls off Send Bridge),* III:302, III:303, III:307–8 *(follows Jake),* III:314–16 *(follows Jake),* III:328–31 *(follows Jake),* III:339–40 *(follows Jake),* III:344, III:358–61, III:367–72, III:373–82, III:382–85 *(Blaine),* III:389, III:393–420, IV:3–10 *(afraid of Blaine's "visual mode"),* IV:13–42, IV:44–47 *(present for Blaine blowout),* IV:71–112 *(present for entry into Topeka. 88 Jake dreams about Oy and train),* IV:335–37 *(Interlude in Kansas),* IV:572 *(in Roland's vision, he is impaled upon a branch),* IV:615–25 *(back in Topeka),* IV:626–68 *(626 ruby booties; 632 Green palace; 634 gate like Wizard's Rainbow; 646 Tick-Tock; 648 Flagg; 652 Roland's matricide),* V:8 *(strangers from Out-World),* V:29–31 *(gunslingers),* V:35, V:36, V:38–47, V:48–70, V:77, V:78, V:80, V:81, V:87, V:88–119, V:125–37, V:138, V:139, V:142–60, V:176–86, V:189–91, V:193–98, V:201–34, V:238, V:318–24, V:381, V:383, V:384–87, V:400, V:402–5, V:417, V:418–19, V:444 *(sleeping),* V:467, V:470, V:488, V:490–96, V:553–80, V:581–90 *(present),* V:591 *(indirect),* V:601–17, V:636–38, V:652, V:685, VI:3–8, VI:11–43, VI:68, VI:143, VI:216, VI:307–44, VI:402, VII:5–11, VII:14, VII:26–27, VII:28, VII:81–104 *(100 changes places with Jake!),* VII:109–12, VII:141–59, VII:164–65, VII:168 *(circle),* VII:169, VII:177, VII:186 *(ka-tet),* VII:187, VII:188, VII:189–220, VII:247–61, VII:265–73, VII:276 *(indirect),* VII:279–324 *(297–302 listening to Ted's story),* VII:329–35, VII:337–42, VII:349 *(indirect),* VII:352, VII:362–63, VII:369–70, VII:382–85, VII:387–418 *(sitting with Jake during Jake's long flashback),* VII:421–33, VII:441–43, VII:444–45, VII:449–67, VII:472–90, VII:510, VII:513, VII:520–30, VII:532–42, VII:549–619, VII:620, VII:625–31, VII:632–44, VII:647–710, VII:716–24, VII:725, VII:737, VII:742–50, VII:752–53, VII:754 *(the mutt),* VII:756–65, VII:768–75 *(killed),* VII:780, VII:802, VII:818, W:3–31, W:303–7

TODDLER WHO SEES OY IN TODASH STATE: V:176

OZ, WIZARD OF
See WIZARD OF OZ

OZ THE GREEN KING
See WALTER: WALTER'S ALIASES

P

PADICK, WALTER
See WALTER

PANIC-MAN
When JAKE CHAMBERS enters an abandoned office closet in THUNDERCLAP STATION, he feels the fingers of the Panic-Man stroke his neck. In other words, Jake has claustrophobia.
VII:205

PAPPA DOC
See BORDER DWELLERS: BROWN

PATEL
See GUTTENBERG, FURTH, AND PATEL

PATRICIA
See NORTH CENTRAL POSITRONICS

**PAUL
The only thing we know about Paul is that Roland thinks of him while at the WAY STATION. Paul's name is cut from the 2003 version of *The Gunslinger.*
I:86

PEAVY, HUGH
See DEBARIA CHARACTERS: SHERIFF'S OFFICE

PERTH, LORD
See MID-WORLD FOLKLORE

PETACKI, PETE
See CALLAHAN, FATHER DONALD FRANK: CALLAHAN'S HIDDEN HIGHWAYS ASSOCIATES

PETER
See DEAN, EDDIE: DELTA FLIGHT 901 CHARACTERS

PETERSON, REVEREND
See MAINE CHARACTERS

PETRIE, MARK
See CALLAHAN, FATHER DONALD FRANK: 'SALEM'S LOT CHARACTERS

PETTIE
See HAMBRY CHARACTERS: TRAVELLERS' REST

PHIL
See NORTH CENTRAL POSITRONICS

PICKENS
See DEBARIA CHARACTERS: SHERIFF'S OFFICE

PIED PIPER
See MANNI: CANTAB; see also GERMANY: HAMELIN, in OUR WORLD PLACES

PIMSY
See DEAN, SUSANNAH: ODETTA HOLMES'S ASSOCIATES

PINK
See MAERLYN'S RAINBOW: MAERLYN'S GRAPEFRUIT

PINK BIRDS
While in the FAGONARD, TIM ROSS saw these beautiful pink-plumaged birds. Their long thin legs paddled the water as they fought to become air-bound. Their high, ululating cries sounded like the laughter of children who had lost their minds.
  W:203

PINKY PAUPER (PIGGY PECKER)
Pinky Pauper is the main character in a skip-rope rhyme sung by SUSANNAH DEAN while she's playing with the JAFFORDS FAMILY children. In the version that EDDIE DEAN sings, Pinky Pauper becomes Piggy Pecker.
  V:351–52

PIPER SCHOOL CHARACTERS
Before entering MID-WORLD, JAKE CHAMBERS attended Piper School—an exclusive NEW YORK CITY middle school. He hated it. Below is a list of Piper School students and employees. For more information about Piper, see PIPER SCHOOL in the OUR WORLD PLACES section.
  GENERAL: VII:332 (Piper kids), VII:395
  PIPER STAFF AND STUDENTS:
  AVERY, BONNIE: JAKE's English teacher. In The Waste Lands, she gave him an A+ on his very strange essay, "My Understanding of Truth." III:94–100, III:101, III:135–36, III:195, III:417, V:52, V:381, V:445, V:567, V:636, V:669, V:689
  BISSETTE, LEN: Len Bissette was a very kindhearted French teacher. III:91–93, III:99, III:101, III:131, III:134, III:135–36
  DORFMAN, STAN: A Piper student and one of Jake's "almost" friends. III:101
  FRANKS, JOANNE: Piper's school secretary. III:92, III:93, III:94, III:101
  HANSON, LUCAS: Lucas Hanson was another Piper School student. He tried to trip Jake whenever Jake walked past him. V:636
  HARLEY, MR.: Headmaster and teacher for spoken arts. III:93, III:94, III:101, III:131
  HOTCHKISS, MR.: Piper's school shrink. III:134
  JESSERLING, PETRA: Jake's classmate. She had a crush on him. III:96, V:636
  KINGERY, MR.: Science teacher. IV:82
  KNOPF, MR.: Geometry teacher. III:101, III:106

STEVENS, BELINDA: Student. III:101
SURREY, DAVID: Student. III:97, III:100
YANKO, MIKE: Student. V:636

PISTOL
See KING, STEPHEN: SMITH, BRYAN

**PITTSTON, SYLVIA
See TULL CHARACTERS: PITTSTON, SYLVIA

PLASTERMAN
See DEMONS/SPIRITS/DEVILS: MANSION DEMON

PLATE, LADY OF THE
See ORIZA, LADY

PLATE, SISTERS OF THE
See ORIZA, SISTERS OF

PLAZA–PARK HYATT CHARACTERS (NEW YORK)
The Plaza–Park Hyatt is the FIRST AVENUE hotel where MIA takes a captive SUSANNAH once they land in 1999 NEW YORK. (Mia needs to find a *telefung* so that she can contact the evil RICHARD P. SAYRE, servant of the CRIMSON KING, who has promised to help her deliver her CHAP.) Since neither Susannah nor Mia has any money, Susannah uses her little CAN-TAH (in the shape of the TURTLE GUARDIAN) to mesmerize MATHIESSEN VAN WYCK into paying for their room.

Susannah stores BLACK THIRTEEN in the room safe, and JAKE and CALLAHAN (with a little help from the *deus ex machina* STEPHEN KING) retrieve the ball from the safe so that they can stash it in NEW YORK's TWIN TOWERS.

DOORMEN: VI:228, VI:257, VI:321

HOTEL MAID: Like JAKE and CALLAHAN, this tiny, middle-aged Hispanic lady falls under the spell of BLACK THIRTEEN and remains hypnotized even after the evil ball falls back to sleep. A guilty Callahan robs her so that he and Jake have taxi fare. VI:330–32, VI:337

JAPANESE TOURISTS: VI:226–29, VI:231–32

   MAN AND WIFE WITH CAMERA: VI:226–27

   MAN WITH CAMERA: VI:228

   SHOPPING WOMEN: VI:227

   TWO WOMEN WITH CAMERA: VI:228

   WOMEN IN RESTROOM: VI:229, VI:231–32

PIANO PLAYER: VI:91, VI:93 *(indirect)*, VI:95, VI:227 *(indirect)*, VI:229

PRETTY WOMEN IN LOBBY: Despite his higher calling, PERE CALLAHAN enjoys watching these attractive ladies. VI:324

RECEPTIONISTS:

   EXOTIC HOTEL RECEPTIONIST: This beautiful Eurasian woman checks SUSANNAH/MIA into room 1919 *(see NINETEEN)* of the Plaza–Park Hyatt. Like MATHIESSEN VAN WYCK, she is hypnotized by Susannah's magical CAN-TAH, which looks like a scrimshaw version of the TURTLE GUARDIAN. VI:91–95, VI:109, VI:226, VI:257

JAKE'S RECEPTIONIST (DAD-A-CHUM, DAD-A-CHEE, NOT TO WORRY, YOU'VE GOT THE KEY!): When JAKE, OY, and CALLAHAN arrive at the Plaza–Park Hyatt, this hotel receptionist delivers a letter to them which is addressed to Jake. The letter is from STEPHEN KING and contains a key to room 1919 (*see* NINETEEN), where Susannah stored MAERLYN's evil magic ball, BLACK THIRTEEN. VI:322–24

OTHER RECEPTIONISTS: VI:226

WOMEN IN SHORT SKIRTS: SUSANNAH DEAN is as shocked to see 1999 hemlines as she is to see women with bra straps and bellies on display. In her *when* of 1964, such dressing would have been considered risqué and may even have landed the exposed ladies in jail. VI:90–91

POLINO, JIMMY
See DEAN, HENRY: HENRY DEAN'S KA-TET

POOKY
A pooky is a huge, reddish snake with a spade-shaped head as big as a cooking pot. It has amber eyes with black slit pupils, glittering fangs, and a ribbon-like tongue which is split into a fork. When the tongue snaps back into the snake's mouth, it makes a hungry, *slooping* sound. When a pooky is fair swole (meaning it has eaten not long before), it is less dangerous, but even under these circumstances it is best to avoid contact. (A pooky's bite paralyzes its victim, but does not kill it. Pookies like to eat their prey alive.) TIM ROSS has to face a pooky when he fetches water for the COVENANT MAN in the ENDLESS FOREST. At the end of *The Wind Through the Keyhole*, the SKIN-MAN transforms into a man-sized pooky.
    W:151, W:152, W:156, W:157, W:158, W:159, W:160, W:162, W:172, W:180, W:291 *(skin-man becomes one)*

POP MOSE
See TET CORPORATION: FOUNDING FATHERS: CARVER, MOSES

PORTLAND SUNDAY TELEGRAM
See MAINE CHARACTERS

POSELLA, FARREN
See CALLA BRYN STURGIS CHARACTERS: OTHER CHARACTERS

POSITRONICS
See NORTH CENTRAL POSITRONICS

POST, THE
See CALLAHAN, FATHER DONALD FRANK: CALLAHAN'S HIDDEN HIGHWAYS ASSOCIATES

POSTINO, TRICKS
See BALAZAR, ENRICO: BALAZAR'S MEN

POSTMISTRESS, EAST STONEHAM
See MAINE CHARACTERS

PRATT, GEORGIE
See DEAN, HENRY: HENRY DEAN'S KA-TET

PRENTISS, PIMLI (DEVAR MASTER)
See WARRIORS OF THE SCARLET EYE: DEVAR-TOI CHARACTERS: HUMANS

PRIM (AM, GADOSH, GREATER DISCORDIA)
In the final book of the Dark Tower series, we learn that MORDRED DESCHAIN, Roland's half-son and nemesis, was born of the joining of two worlds—the Prim and the *am*, the *gadosh* and *godosh*, GAN and GILEAD. *Prim, gadosh,* and *Gan* all refer to the primordial magical substance (or generating force) from which the multiverse arose. *Am, godosh,* and *Gilead* refer to the physical world, also known as the mortal world.

The people of MID-WORLD believe that, at the beginning of all things, there was only the Prim, or magical soup of creation. From the magical Prim arose Gan, the spirit of the DARK TOWER, whose body is the linchpin of existence. Gan spun the multiverse from his navel and then set it rolling with his finger. This forward movement was time. After the multiverse came into being, the Prim receded, leaving on the shores of existence not only the Tower and BEAMS but the DEMONS, DEMON ELEMENTALS, oracles, and succubi that haunt our world.

Like all magic, the Prim is neither good nor evil but contains the seeds of both. Hence, Gan, the magical creator, sired both the line of ELD (from which the DESCHAINs are descended) and the line of the CRIMSON KING.

According to the MANNI, Mordred Deschain's birth is intrinsically linked to the Prim. Their legends state that when this child, who is simultaneously half-human and half-god, descends into the world, humanity will be destroyed and the Prim will return. However, this particular apocalyptic view takes into consideration only the negative aspect of the Prim (that represented by the Crimson King in his Lord of Discordia guise). Ultimately, Mordred's birth—and early death—plays its part in the restoration of the Tower and the WHITE. Hence the good of the Prim, not its evil, ultimately triumphs.

VI:106, VI:108–14, VI:117, VI:242 *(and creatures of the Prim)*, VI:248, VI:249, VI:251, VII:25, VII:26, VII:35, VII:132, VII:168 (am, gadosh, godosh), VII:176, VII:249, VII:291, VII:303, VII:334, VII:406, VII:447, VII:504, VII:515, VII:755, VII:756 *(return of the Prim)*

PRISONER, THE
See DEAN, EDDIE

PUBES
The Pubes (short for pubescents) were the original defenders of LUD, although the sickly bunch we meet in *The Waste Lands* were probably descended from one of the later bands of harriers that overran the city. The Pubes' archenemies,

the GRAYS, live in underground silos beneath eastern Lud. The Pubes live aboveground in CITY NORTH, but are no healthier for it. You can tell a Pube from a Gray because the Pubes' headscarves are blue. (The Grays' are yellow.)

The Pubes are convinced that there are GHOSTS IN THE MACHINES below the city, and that if these demonic spirits aren't appeased they will animate the bodies of Lud's many dead and rise up to eat the living. Although the Grays also fear the machine ghosts, they use the god-drums (actually the backbeat of ZZ Top's song "Velcro Fly") to drive the Pubes into a paranoid frenzy of human sacrifice. The grisly method the Pubes use to choose their victims is reminiscent of Shirley Jackson's story "The Lottery."

SUSANNAH and EDDIE battle the Pubes on the STREET OF THE TURTLE. In the end, two of this gang (MAUD and JEEVES) reluctantly agree to lead them to BLAINE'S CRADLE. The Pubes believe that of all the ghosts in the machines, Blaine is the most terrible. Little do they know that psychotic Blaine is actually *all* of the ghosts in the machines.

III:229, III:230, III:238, III:240, III:244–45, III:254, III:270, III:308–12 *(dead)*, III:316–25, III:327, III:329, III:337, III:358, III:373, III:380, III:402, III:411, IV:57, V:135, VI:152

PUBE CHARACTERS:

ARDIS: He was electrocuted by BLAINE. III:323–24, III:344, III:346, III:348, III:361

BLONDE WOMAN WITH MANGE: III:320

FRANK: III:321, V:226

JEEVES: Eddie nicknames this guy Jeeves because of his bowler hat. Along with Maud, Jeeves leads Eddie and Susannah to BLAINE'S CRADLE. III:322–25, III:332–33, IV:75, IV:226, IV:621

LUSTER (DWARF): Luster reminds Eddie and Susannah of Little Lord Fauntleroy. III:317–18, III:321, IV:75, V:226

MAN IN SILK-LINED CAPE AND KNEE-BOOTS: III:319

MAN WITH BLUE ASCOT AND RED HAIR TUFTS: This fellow reminds Eddie of Ronald McDonald. III:319–20

MAN WITH HAMMER: III:319

MAUD: Maud is a heavyset woman who is very fond of WINSTON. She is one of the two who leads Eddie and Susannah to BLAINE'S CRADLE. III:318–20, III:321, III:322–25, III:332–33, III:334, IV:75, V:226

SPANKER/SPANKERMAN: Spanker was the leader of the Pubes, but when the god-drums started up, his stone was pulled from the hat and it was his turn to dance from the hangman's rope. III:317, III:321, IV:75

TOPSY THE SAILOR: III:321, V:226, VI:118

WINSTON: Winston wore a kilt and brandished a cutlass. He was killed by Eddie and Susannah. III:318–19, III:320, III:321, III:324, III:332, IV:75, V:226

PYLON
See DELGADO, SUSAN

Q

QUEEN OF BLACK PLACES
IV:493 *(Rhea of the Cöos compared to her)*

QUEEN O' GREEN DAYS
See MID-WORLD FOLKLORE

QUEEN ROWENA
See ELD, ARTHUR

QUICK, ANDREW
See GRAYS: GRAY HIGH COMMAND: TICK-TOCK

QUICK, DAVID
See GRAYS: GRAY HIGH COMMAND

QUINT, HIRAM
See HAMBRY CHARACTERS: OTHER CHARACTERS

R

RAF
See GODS OF MID-WORLD

RALPH
See ELURIA CHARACTERS: GREEN FOLK

RANDO THOUGHTFUL
See WARRIORS OF THE SCARLET EYE: CASSE ROI RUSSE: HUMANS:
FEEMALO/FIMALO/FUMALO: FIMALO

**RANDOLPH
Young Roland's friend. Randolph doesn't appear in the 2003 *Gunslinger*.
I:140

RANDOLPH, NORTON
See CALLAHAN, FATHER DONALD FRANK: CALLAHAN AND THE
HITLER BROTHERS

RASTOSOVICH, JOSEPH
See BREAKERS

RAT, MR.
  See MIA

RAT GUARDIAN
  See GUARDIANS OF THE BEAM

RATHBUN, MRS.
  See KATZ: KATZ'S EMPLOYEES, CUSTOMERS, AND COMPETITORS

RAVENHEAD, PIET
In *Wizard and Glass*, Piet Ravenhead signed identity papers stating that ALAIN
was actually RICHARD STOCKWORTH of PENNILTON.
  IV:183

RAWLINGS, ROWENA MAGRUDER
  See CALLAHAN, FATHER DONALD FRANK: CALLAHAN'S HOME
SHELTER ASSOCIATES: MAGRUDER, ROWAN

RED BIRDS
TIM ROSS saw thousands of these huge red birds flying above him while he trav-
eled through the ENDLESS FOREST with his NORTH CENTRAL POSITRON-
ICS guidance mechanism, DARIA. The birds covered the sky for almost an hour.
  W:228

RED EYE (FOLLOWS TIM ROSS)
  See WALTER: WALTER'S ALIASES

REDHOUSE, MILLICENT
  See KELLS, BIG BERN: KELLS, MILLICENT

RED KING
  See CRIMSON KING

REDPATH CLAN
  See MANNI

REED, JAMES
In *Wizard and Glass*, James Reed signed identity papers stating that Roland was
actually WILLIAM DEARBORN of HEMPHILL.
  IV:183

REFEREE KING
  See WARRIORS OF THE SCARLET EYE: CASSE ROI RUSSE: HUMANS:
FEEMALO/FIMALO/FUMALO: FIMALO

REGULATORS
In *Wolves of the Calla*, we find out that the term *Regulator* refers to the LOW
MEN, or CAN-TOI, who serve the CRIMSON KING. In *Wizard and Glass*, we

learned that the BIG COFFIN HUNTERS were also sometimes called Regula-tors. In RICHARD BACHMAN's book entitled *The Regulators,* the Regula-tors were a band of killers who were part cowboy and part *Motocops* cartoon characters. Their name came from a 1958 cowboy film about vigilantes on the rampage. Whereas STEPHEN KING's Regulators serve the Crimson King, Bach-man's Regulators ultimately serve a demon named Tak. Despite their formal differences, all Regulators serve the Outer Dark.

V:290–91

RENFREW, HASH
See HAMBRY CHARACTERS: HORSEMEN'S ASSOCIATION

RENT-A-COP
JAKE and PERE CALLAHAN see this police officer when they store BLACK THIRTEEN in the lockers below the TWIN TOWERS.

VI:335

REYNOLDS, CLAY
See BIG COFFIN HUNTERS: JONAS, ELDRED

**R.F.
See WALTER: WALTER'S ALIASES

**RHEA OF THE CÖOS
The nasty old witch Rhea of the Cöos was one of Roland's most formidable enemies during his time in the town of HAMBRY. This bad-smelling hag lived on Cöos Hill outside of town with her two mutant pets, ERMOT and MUSTY.

Like the men of the HORSEMEN'S ASSOCIATION, Rhea played a part in the defeat of the AFFILIATION. At the beginning of *Wizard and Glass*'s Hambry adventures, the BIG COFFIN HUNTERS entrusted the evil magic ball known as MAERLYN'S GRAPEFRUIT to Rhea's keeping. This magical ball was FARSON's prize and secret weapon, but it was also vampiric. Rhea used the ball to spy on people (including Roland), but in the end the ball made her even more crazily malicious than she was at the beginning of the tale. By the end of *Wizard and Glass,* Rhea is a sore-covered specter. However, she is still a formidable enemy.

Rhea was attracted to pretty young women, but even before her journeys in the pink BEND O' THE RAINBOW her desires had a malicious edge, especially when her advances were rebuffed. It was in large part Rhea's vindictiveness that landed pretty SUSAN DELGADO on the Charyou Tree fire. In the 2003 version of *The Gunslinger,* Roland bitterly remembers the part Rhea played in Susan's death. Rhea's mark looked like a pitchfork.

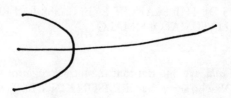

IV:65 *(indirect—"crone on the hill"),* IV:115–21 *(115 description of her hut and Cöos hill; 118 described),* IV:122–38 *(122 left side of her face is frozen; 130 inspects Susan's "honesty"; 133–34 touches Susan's clit; 137 parallel between Susan's sexuality and her hair; 137–38 spell on Susan to make her cut her hair),* IV:140–41, IV:146, IV:154, IV:157 *(and Susan),* IV:159, IV:166–70, IV:177 *(keeper of glass),* IV:202, IV:212, IV:228 *(cures),* IV:235, IV:246, IV:249, IV:290–91 *(sees Roland and Susan. She's being eaten by Maerlyn's ball),* IV:299, IV:300, IV:311, IV:319–20, IV:324, IV:325–26, IV:335, IV:343, IV:353–54 *(Susan must die),* IV:355–56, IV:374–75, IV:384 *(Rhea Dubativo),* IV:389–90, IV:394–98 *(repercussions of using Maerlyn's ball. Message for Cordelia),* IV:403, IV:411 *(note to Cordelia),* IV:413, IV:415–19, IV:420, IV:424–25, IV:426, IV:434, IV:436, IV:440–42, IV:443, IV:449, IV:452–53 *(aging because of Maerlyn's glass),* IV:485–93 *(493 as Queen of Black Places),* IV:495, IV:496, IV:498–99, IV:519, IV:527–29, IV:532–35, IV:536, IV:540, IV:541–44, IV:545, IV:546, IV:549–52 *(and Cordelia),* IV:563–65, IV:570, IV:571, IV:587, IV:602, IV:603–8 *(burning Susan),* IV:622, IV:628–29, IV:649, IV:650, IV:656–58, IV:662, IV:666, E:165, E:166, V:40, V:55, V:71, V:411, V:703, VII:179, VII:219, VII:550, W:37 *(witch),* W:38, W:84

RHEA'S MUTANT PETS:

ERMOT: Poisonous snake. Had four pairs of fangs. IV:115, IV:117, IV:290–91, IV:299, IV:356, IV:396–97, IV:417–18 *(killed by Roland),* IV:419, IV:452, IV:488, IV:492, IV:533, IV:602, IV:657, IV:658

MUSTY: A six-legged tomcat with a split tail. He had gray-green eyes which were the same color as Rhea's. IV:115–21 *(116 described),* IV:123, IV:124, IV:291, IV:320, IV:353–54, IV:356, IV:383–85, IV:452, IV:453, IV:485, IV:486

RHEA'S MUTANT VEGETABLE GARDEN: IV:415

RICE, LADY
See ORIZA, LADY

RIGGINS, GEORGE
See HAMBRY CHARACTERS: SHERIFF'S OFFICE

RIMER, KIMBA
See HAMBRY CHARACTERS: HAMBRY MAYOR'S HOUSE (SEAFRONT)

RIMER, LASLO
See HAMBRY CHARACTERS: HORSEMEN'S ASSOCIATION

RINCON, DEF
See TREE VILLAGE CHARACTERS

RING-A-LEVIO (RINGO)
See DESCHAIN, ROLAND

**RITTER, AILEEN
See AILEEN OF GILEAD

RITZY CHARACTERS

In *Wizard and Glass,* ROY DEPAPE passed through this miserable little mining village while riding Roland's backtrail. While here, he discovered Roland's true identity.

JOLENE: Whore. IV:267–68

OLD MAN: A weed-eater who told DEPAPE that Roland was descended from ARTHUR ELD. Depape killed him after he shared this information. IV:267–71

RIVER CROSSING CHARACTERS

Although River Crossing was once a very busy town, since the beginning of the LUD wars her aging citizens have lived in relative isolation. In order to disguise their town from passing looters, they hide their gardens behind clumps of weeds and let the façades of their buildings go to ruin. However, to friendly folk passing through, they are extremely generous.

By the time we meet them in *The Waste Lands,* most of the citizens of River Crossing are positively ancient. Their leader is the matriarch TALITHA UNWIN. Like Roland, Talitha speaks the High Speech. When she sees Roland she proclaims, "Behold ye, the return of the White! After evil ways and evil days, the White comes again! Be of good heart and hold up your head, for ye have lived to see the wheel of *ka* begin to turn once more" (III:232).

GENERAL REFERENCES (ALL CHARACTERS): III:257, III:258, III:270, III:276, III:284, III:288, III:385, V:55, V:78, V:110, V:134, V:192, VI:111, VI:117, VI:182, VII:120

    GENERAL CHARACTERS NOT LISTED BELOW: (unnamed women, man with crutch) III:233–36

    BILL AND TILL: *See* TUDBURY, BILL AND TILL, *below*

    MERCY: Mercy was one of the first people that Roland's *ka-tet* met in River Crossing. Like almost all of the other townspeople, Mercy is very old. Twenty-five years before the beginning of our tale she was blinded by harriers who said she was looking at em pert. Mercy is married to SI. III:229–36, III:246, III:247–51, III:288

    MUFFIN, BILL, AND HIS BOY: Bill Muffin and his son saw the bridge over the RIVER SEND. Bill eventually died of blood sickness. III:241, III:248

    SI: Si is MERCY's husband. He assures her that Roland and his friends are gunslingers, not harriers. He and his wife were the first two people Roland's *ka-tet* met in River Crossing. III:229–51, III:288

        GREAT GRAND'DA: III:243

    TALITHA, AUNT (TALITHA UNWIN): Aunt Talitha's full name is Talitha Unwin. She is the matriarch of River Crossing as well as its oldest citizen. Roland calls her OLD MOTHER. Talitha gives Roland her cross and asks him to lay it at the foot of the DARK TOWER. In the final book of the Dark Tower series, Roland does so. III:231–51, III:263, III:274, IV:14, V:192, VI:118, VII:50, VII:123, VII:124, VII:518, VII:519, VII:802, VII:820

        TALITHA'S GRANDFATHER AND GREAT-GREAT-GRAND-FATHER: III:232

    TUDBURY, BILL AND TILL: These two old twins are albino. III:231–51, III:252

RIVERLY
See TREE VILLAGE CHARACTERS

RIVERS, LUCAS
In *Wizard and Glass,* Lucas Rivers signed identity papers stating that CUTH-
BERT ALLGOOD was actually ARTHUR HEATH of GILEAD.
   IV:183

ROBERT AND FRANCESCA
See HAMBRY CHARACTERS: HAMBRY LOVERS

ROBERTSON, NELL
See ROSS, NELL

ROBESON
Robeson was one of GILEAD's guards. Like HAX, he was a traitor who sup-
ported FARSON.
   I:101–3, I:105 *(indirect)*

RODERICK, CHILDREN OF (RODS)
See MUTANTS: CHILDREN OF RODERICK

ROLAND
See DESCHAIN, ROLAND

ROLAND THE ELDER
See DESCHAIN, STEVEN

ROLL CALL
   See CALLAHAN, FATHER DONALD FRANK: CALLAHAN'S HIDDEN
HIGHWAYS ASSOCIATES

ROMP, THE
   See HAMBRY CHARACTERS: TRAVELLERS' REST

RONIN
   See WARRIORS OF THE SCARLET EYE

RONK, DAVE VAN
   See DEAN, SUSANNAH: ODETTA HOLMES'S ASSOCIATES

ROONT
   See CALLA BRYN STURGIS CHARACTERS: ROONTS

ROSALITA
   See ORIZA, SISTERS OF: MUNOZ, ROSALITA

ROSARIO, FREDDY
   See CALLA BRYN STURGIS CHARACTERS: FARMERS (SMALLHOLD)

ROSCOE
See SKIN-MAN: SKIN MAN'S VICTIMS: JEFFERSON RANCH

ROSE, THE
JAKE CHAMBERS discovered this magical dusky-pink rose in the Vacant LOT on SECOND AVENUE and FORTY-SIXTH STREET where it was growing amid a clump of alien purple grass. This magic flower hums like a great open chord, inexpressively lonely and inexpressibly lovely. It is full of faces and voices. Jake believes that it is the key to everything; Roland suspects that it is the DARK TOWER itself.

Throughout the Dark Tower books, roses are extremely significant. The Dark Tower of END-WORLD sits amid a sea of shouting red roses, the LITTLE SIS-TERS OF ELURIA wear an embroidered rose upon their white flowing habits, and a model of CHARLIE THE CHOO-CHOO sits in REINISCH ROSE GAR-DEN in the alternative version of TOPEKA that our *tet* visits in *Wizard and Glass*. As EDDIE states within the *glammer* of his dream-vision, "First the key, then the rose! Behold! Behold the opening of the way to the Tower!" (III:49).

According to the three STEPHEN KINGs that Roland and SUSANNAH meet at LE CASSE ROI RUSSE, the wild, dusky-pink rose growing in the Vacant Lot in NEW YORK CITY is, as Roland suspected, our world's incarnation of the Dark Tower. In other worlds, the Tower can resemble an IMMORTAL TIGER or an UR-DOG named Rover. Although we don't know whether this triple-bodied shape-shifting UFFI speaks truthfully (after all, the three Kings are not one creature at all but three separate servants of LOS, LORD OF DISCORDIA), we do know that the Rose, which Jake, Eddie, and Roland see in New York City's Vacant Lot, is almost identical to the beautiful red roses of CAN'-KA NO REY. Like them, it sings a song, which is simultaneously inexpressively lonely and inex-pressively lovely, and its sun-yellow center contains faces and voices. However, unlike the healthy rose-song, which Roland hears as he approaches the Tower, threading into the song of our world's Rose is a note of discord.

In *The Dark Tower*, we find out that the roses, which grow in such profusion at the heart of END-WORLD, are a light pink shade on the outside but darken to a fierce red on the inside, a shade which Roland believes is the exact color of heart's desire. Their centers, which are called GAN'S GATEWAYS, burn such a fierce yellow that they are almost too bright to look upon. However, this yellow is the yellow of light and love, not destruction. What Roland comes to realize as he travels through their midst is that the roses feed the BEAMS with their songs and their perfume, and that the Beams, in turn, feed them. Roses and Beams are actually a living force field, a giving and taking, all of which spins out of the Tower. Interestingly enough, the roses (when mixed with Roland's blood) are the exact color of the Crimson King's eyes. Though in the case of the Red King, the red becomes the color of evil and greed, not pure, living energy.

In *Wolves of the Calla* and *Song of Susannah*, Eddie Dean discovers a way to save our world's Rose from the evil machinations of the Crimson King's many destructive companies, collectively known as the SOMBRA GROUP. Under the name of the TET CORPORATION, Eddie and his friends buy the magic Lot from CALVIN TOWER, thus saving the Rose from being bulldozed by Sombra.

When Roland visits New York 1999, in the final book of the Dark Tower series, he sees that Eddie's idea has worked. The Tet Corporation—founded by JOHN CULLUM, AARON DEEPNEAU, and SUSANNAH DEAN's godfather, MOSES CARVER—has erected a great black building around the Rose and has protected that most important of flowers in a small indoor garden called the GARDEN OF THE BEAM. Roland believes that the people who work in that building live long, happy, and productive lives.

III:49 *(Eddie's vision in the jawbone fire)*, III:50, III:51, III:52–53 *(field of)*, III:54–55, III:56 *(field of)*, III:98, III:124–29, III:130, III:132, III:155, III:158, III:177, III:205, III:262, III:264–65, III:267, III:280 *(fire like roses)*, IV:48 *(hope compared to it)*, IV:83 *(Jake's reflections upon it)*, IV:86–87 *(Reinisch Rose Garden, Topeka)*, IV:100–101 *(Eddie's bulldozer dream)*, IV:102, IV:103, IV:429–30 *(Thorin mausoleum)*, IV:447 *(field of roses and Dark Tower)*, IV:552 *(Rhea dreams of it)*, IV:572 *(and Roland's vision)*, IV:667, E:165, E:175, V:51, V:58, V:59, V:97–106 *(how to save)*, V:174, V:177, V:179, V:181 *(begin to feel pull of it)*, V:182–85 *(183 effect described)*, V:187–89 *(effect described)*, V:190, V:191–94 *(Tower and rose)*, V:196, V:197, V:198, V:201 *(red as roses)*, V:249, V:291 *(Topeka roses)*, V:302 *(and lost worlds)*, V:314, V:315, V:317, V:335, V:377, V:389, V:393, V:513, V:528, V:531, V:539, V:555, V:594–95, V:598, V:706, VI:32 *(on knob)*, VI:35, VI:39, VI:40, VI:55–56, VI:73, VI:102, VI:171, VI:257, VI:265, VI:266, VI:267, VI:268, VI:270, VI:296, VI:308, VI:318 *(indirect)*, VI:319 *(still it sings)*, VI:324, VI:398–99 *(delivery to Stephen King)*, VII:121, VII:123, VII:125, VII:127, VII:143, VII:301, VII:409–10, VII:475, VII:483, VII:488, VII:491–95 *(Garden of the Beam)*, VII:497, VII:499, VII:520, VII:524, VII:535, VII:550 *(roses)*, VII:609, VII:616 *(roses)*, VII:663 *(field)*, VII:666 *(field)*, VII:713 *(field)*, VII:721 *(field)*, VII:756–60 *(first they come across; twin of rose in Vacant Lot)*, VII:795–800 *(a rose from Can'-Ka No Rey used to paint the Red King's eyes)*. For additional rose references, see CAN'-KA NO REY, in PORTALS

HIPPIE WITH ACNE: PERE CALLAHAN meets this long-haired young man near the Vacant LOT on FORTY-SIXTH STREET and SECOND AVENUE in 1977 NEW YORK. This hippie-in-a-cowboy-hat believes that the Rose's emanations have cleared up his acne. In 1999, TRUDY DAMASCUS meets the same hippie outside 2 HAMMARSKJÖLD PLAZA. V:594–95, VI:55–56
    DERMATOLOGIST: V:594
    FATHER: V:594
IMMORTAL TIGER: VII:609
UR-DOG ROVER: VII:609

ROSEANNA
    See SERENITY, SISTERS OF: EVERLYNNE OF SERENITY

ROSIE (ROSIE & MOSIE)
    See DEBARIA CHARACTERS: JEFFERSON RANCH CHARACTERS

ROSITA
    See ORIZA, SISTERS OF: MUNOZ, ROSALITA

ROSS, BIG JACK

The burly, good-tempered woodsman Big Jack Ross was the father of TIM ROSS (later, Tim Stoutheart), one of the few boys to become a gunslinger despite the fact that he was not born to the line of ELD. The story entitled "The Wind Through the Keyhole," which Roland recounts to YOUNG BILL STREETER in the days following the SKIN-MAN's massacre at the JEFFERSON RANCH in DEBARIA, tells the tale of Big Ross's betrayal and murder, and of his son Tim's struggle not only to bring his murderous stepfather to justice, but to undo the wrongs that had been done to himself and his mother. Not only does Tim's triumph over his father's murderer give Young Bill the courage to identify the shape-shifting monster that killed his own da, but Tim's luck at reversing his mother's blindness, and at eventually becoming a gunslinger despite his low birth, gives us all hope that the evils of the past can be transformed, and that *ka*, however subtly, can be shifted.

Like all folktales, "The Wind Through the Keyhole" begins in the land of "Once upon a bye." In this particular story, that land is the unexplored wilderness of the ENDLESS FOREST, and the little village of TREE which exists on its edge. At the outset of the tale, Big Jack Ross is alive and well, and is living in his cottage with his son, Tim, and his wife, NELL. Big Ross is proud of the fact that, though he doesn't have much in the world, he has four possessions to pass on to his son. Those are his sharp ax, his lucky coin (a rhodite double which hangs around his neck on a fine silver chain), his wood plot along the IRONWOOD TRAIL, and his home place, GOODVIEW COTTAGE, which is as good as the place of any king or gunslinger in Mid-World.

But, as so often happens in tales and in life, those good days aren't destined to last. When Tim is eleven, Big Ross and his partner, BIG KELLS, set off as usual for a day of cutting ironwood. However, only Kells returns, sooty and charred, and slumped on the seat of his wagon as if he were too weary to sit up straight. According to Kells, he and Ross had been set upon by a DRAGON, and Big Ross had been incinerated.

Although Nell, now widowed, accepts Kells's offer of marriage (though more out of fear of the tax-collecting COVENANT MAN than out of love for her deceased husband's partner), life soon goes tragically wrong. Soon after his wedding, Kells—who in his youth had been a drunken carouser—takes up the bottle again and begins to beat both his new wife and stepson. He even forces Tim to give up his lessons at the WIDOW SMACK'S COTTAGE, so that he can earn a little in scrip from the TREE SAWMILL. To make matters worse, after Big Ross's accident, the other woodsmen distrust Big Kells and refuse to partner him in the forest. In their eyes, without Big Ross's positive influence, Kells is little more than a drunken, raging lout.

Into this terrible situation comes the Barony tax collector, or Covenant Man. While collecting taxes at Goodview Cottage, the Covenanter slips Tim a key which will open any lock. Using it to open his steppa's trunk, Tim finds his father's lucky coin, proof that Jack Ross had been murdered, not incinerated by a dragon. Enraged, Tim sets off to find the Barony Covenanter. Later that night, in a stream running through the COSINGTON-MARCHLY STAKE, the Covenant Man shows Tim his father's corpse. The body lies six or eight inches below the water and is perfectly preserved. (According to Tree's old wives, neither the flesh-eating bugs of forest streams nor the hungry POOKIES of the woods will dare to eat the flesh of a virtuous man. In the case of Tim's father, the old tales are true.)

Upon returning home with his father's ax (Kells had tossed it as far across the stream as he was able, but the Covenant Man had fetched it back again), Tim informs PETER COSINGTON, ERNIE MARCHLY, and BALDY ANDERSON about his stepfather's crimes. The men not only fetch Big Ross's body home, but gather a posse to hunt down Kells. Tim's last sight of his father is in DUSTIN STOKES's burial parlor. There, in a little room painted with forest scenes, in an ironwood bier meant to represent the clearing at the end of life's path, Big Ross lies dressed in a fine white shroud. Holding his father's cold hand as he had when he was a sma' one, Tim bids his father goodbye.

W:106, W:109–10, W:111, W:112, W:113, W:114, W:115 *(indirect)*, W:116 *(indirect)*, W:117, W:118–19, W:126, W:127, W:129, W:131–32, W:133 *(death described)*, W:134, W:139, W:140, W:142–43, W:144, W:145, W:146, W:147, W:154, W:158, W:159–63 *(Tim finds body; 161 skull riven from behind; 162 body; 163 hand ax)*, W:166, W:167, W:168, W:171 *(ax)*, W:172, W:174, W:175, W:176, W:177–78, W:179, W:181 *(son of Jack)*, W:182, W:188 *(indirect)*, W:190, W:191 *(dead father's sign)*, W:201, W:202 *(da)*, W: 206, W:214 *(indirect, in dream)*, W:222, W:229, W:239, W:241, W:246, W:249, W:251 *(ax)*, W:252, W:254 *(son of)*, W:260 *(indirect)*, W:261 *(indirect)*, W:262 *(murdered)*, W:263

FLESH-EATING BUGS: These fat white bugs live in the sluggish stream that runs through the COSINGTON-MARCHLY STAKE. Their oversized black heads have eyes which sprout from stalks. These waterborne maggots are constantly at war, eating each other. However, like all flesh-eaters, they cannot eat the flesh of a virtuous man. Hence, when TIM ROSS finds his father's body, it is perfectly preserved. W:151–153, W:158, W:159, W:160–61 *(will not eat the flesh of a virtuous man)*

MULES: Big Jack Ross had two mules, MISTY and BITSY, which he had raised from guffins. They were both mollies—unsterilized females theoretically capable of bearing offspring—but Ross kept them for their sweetness of temper rather than for breeding. According to Big Ross, such mollies rarely gave birth to true-threaded offspring.

   MISTY: Unlike Bitsy, Misty liked to stop and nibble at every bush on the forest floor. Hence, Tim chose BITSY to share his adventures in the END-LESS FOREST. W:126, W:127, W:145–64, W:173, W:255

   BITSY: Bitsy was Tim's favorite mule. After discovering his father's lucky coin in BIG KELLS's trunk, Tim rode Bitsy into the ENDLESS FOREST to meet the COVENANT MAN. Later in the story he rode Bitsy to the IRONWOOD TRAIL again, this time to find the magician MAERLYN. Rather than risk Bitsy on this dangerous venture, Tim tied her to a bush at the side of the trail and scattered oats in front of her, confident that *sai* COSINGTON would come for her in the morning. W:126, W:127, W:145, W:173, W:184, W:189, W:190, W:255

ROSS, NELL (NELL ROBERTSON, NELL KELLS)
Nell Ross was a character in the folktale "The Wind Through the Keyhole," which Roland shared with YOUNG BILL STREETER in DEBARIA's JAIL. (Neither of them had done anything wrong. Young Bill was the sole survivor of

the JEFFERSON RANCH massacre and the only person who could identify the SKIN-MAN responsible for the attack. Hence, Roland wanted to keep him safe.)

Nell Ross (born Nell Robertson) was mother of TIM ROSS and the wife of the burly, good-tempered woodsman BIG JACK ROSS. After being widowed, she became the wife of Ross's former pard, BIG BERN KELLS. According to Roland's story, Nell Robertson, Jack Ross, and Bern Kells had been childhood friends. Both boys had fallen in love with the chestnut-haired Nell, but Nell chose Ross, who had the sweeter disposition and better temperament. Although Kells had stood by Ross at the wedding and had slipped the silk around the new couple, in his secret heart he was eaten alive by jealousy. After Nell and Big Ross's wedding, Kells's habit of drunken violence worsened. In fact, it was not until Kells met and married MILLICENT REDHOUSE that he reformed his behavior. Unfortunately, Millicent died giving birth six seasons after her marriage. After this, Kells's jealousy of Ross and his lust for Nell grew into a secret but murderous rage.

One day in Tim's eleventh year, Big Ross and Big Kells traveled into the wood together as they always did, but only Kells returned. Sooty, blistered, and charred, Kells claimed that he and his partner had been attacked by a she-DRAGON deep in the forest, and that Ross had been incinerated. A few months after Big Ross's death, Kells began courting Nell. Reluctantly—and for the most part out of fear of the Barony's tax-collecting COVENANT MAN—Nell agreed to slip the rope with her deceased husband's partner.

Although Kells managed to remain teetotal for a brief period, soon his temper and his simmering resentment of Nell got the better of him. Blaming his new wife for all the ills of his life (after all, if she hadn't tempted him with her good looks he wouldn't have killed his friend), he turned to drink. Kells—whose beard was now streaked with gray—began beating his wife on a regular basis, and even made Tim give up his lessons at the WIDOW SMACK'S COTTAGE so that he could earn money at the TREE SAWMILL. Hating Kells for his abusive behavior, Tim took a magic key from the evil Covenant Man, one that would open any lock. He used this to open his steppa's beloved trunk and to spy on what he kept there. Within the trunk, a horrified Tim discovered his father's lucky coin—the one Big Ross always wore around his neck on a fine silver chain. Now certain that Kells had murdered his da, Tim went in search of the wicked Covenanter. Unfortunately, while he was gone, drunken Kells blamed Nell for opening his trunk and smashed a ceramic jug against her forehead. He then beat her into unconsciousness. Nell was permanently blinded.

Upon returning to the cottage with his father's ax and certain knowledge of his father's horrible manner of death, Tim informed the men of Tree about his stepfather's crime. Then, egged on by false scrying visions seen in the Covenanter's MAGICAL SILVER PAIL, Tim set off for the Endless Forest, where he hoped to find the sorcerer MAERLYN who would be able to restore Nell's sight. Nell remained blind and bedridden, cared for by the WIDOW SMACK, until her son Tim returned from the forest with one of MAERLYN'S MAGICAL OBJECTS: a BROWN BOTTLE of liquid, drops of which cured Nell's blindness. Nell's first sighted act (after embracing her son) was to save Tim's life.

Unbeknownst to either Nell or Tim, by the time Tim returned with the magic drops for Nell's eyes, Kells was already hiding in the cottage's mudroom. When Tim exited Nell's bedroom and tried to wake the Widow Smack (who had already had her throat cut by Kells), Kells attacked. Choking his stepson, Kells tossed away Tim's gun and told him that he was going to throw him onto the fire to burn him alive. Kells never managed to fulfill his threat, since Nell buried her first husband's ax in his head. Years later, when Tim Ross became the gunslinger Tim Stoutheart, Nell became a great lady in GILEAD.

W:106, W:109, W:113–22, W:123–24 *(124 wedding day)*, W:125, W:126, W:127, W:128, W:129, W:130, W:131–41 *(141 remembers Covenant Man)*, W:145, W:146, W:148, W:150, W:153–54 *(in basin vision)*, W:155, W:156, W:157, W:158, W:161–62, W:163, W:164, W:167 *(she has been blinded; asleep part of this time)*, W:168, W:171, W:172, W:173, W:174, W:175–76, W:178, W:179, W:180, W:184 *(water Nell)*, W:185, W:188, W:195 *(mother's sheets)*, W:201, W:202, W:206, W:214 *(Tim's dream)*, W:221, W:223, W:236, W:238, W:239, W:250, W:251 *(drops in eyes, Tim gives her the ax)*, W:254 *(mama)*, W:255, W:258, W:259–64, W:267, W:268
FATHER: W:140, W:143, W:144, W:145

ROSS, TIM (TIM STOUTHEART, LEFTY ROSS)

Tim Ross, also known as Tim Stoutheart and Lefty Ross, was an important figure in Mid-World folklore. According to Roland, Tim was one of the very, very few men to become a gunslinger even though he was not descended from the proven line of ELD. When Tim was twenty-one years old, three gunslingers, bound for TAVARES, came through his home village of TREE. The gunslingers were hoping to raise a posse, but Tim was the only local man willing to go with them. At first the men called him "the lefthanded gun," for that was the way he drew. But he was both fearless and a dead shot, and so earned the name *tet-fa,* or friend of the *tet.* After a great battle on the shores of LAKE CAWN at which he proved his bravery, Tim gained his name Tim Stoutheart. Later, he became *ka-tet,* or a fully-fledged member of Gilead's *tet* of the gun.

In the novel *The Wind Through the Keyhole,* Roland tells YOUNG BILL STREETER the story of Tim Stoutheart's first adventure, when he (like Young Bill) was eleven years old. Like Young Bill Streeter, who was about to identify the shapeshifting SKIN-MAN who had murdered his father, Young Tim Stoutheart had to brave many perils in order to bring to justice the man who had murdered his father and blinded his mother.

At the opening of the tale, Tim lived happily with his mother, NELL ROSS, and his father, BIG JACK ROSS, in their cottage called GOODVIEW, in the village of Tree, located on the edge of the beautiful but dangerous ENDLESS FOREST. Big Ross was a woodcutter, partnered with his old friend BIG BERN KELLS. Together they worked the ROSS-KELLS STAKE, located far down the IRONWOOD TRAIL where the ironwood trees grew tall. However, one day in the year that Tim turned eleven, Big Kells came back from the forest alone. There was a hole in the left leg of his homespun pants, his skin was sooty and blistered, and his jerkin was charred. According to Kells, he and his partner had been set upon by a DRAGON and Big Ross had been incinerated.

Without Big Ross to support them, Tim and his mother fell on hard times. As Reaptide drew closer and the annual visit of the Barony COVENANT MAN, or tax collector, drew near, Nell began to fear that the two of them would be turned off the land. But just as Nell was certain that come the following Full Earth she and Tim would be following the crops with burlap rucksacks on their backs, Big

Kells came courting. He promised to sell his own place and pay the Covenant Man what Nell owed, if Nell would become his wife. Although Nell was terrified of losing her husband's plot and place to the Covenant Man, she hesitated before accepting Kells's offer. She had known Big Kells all of her life, but she also knew that he was a drinker and at times, violent. In the end her fear of the Covenant Man outweighed her misgivings, but her decision was one she came to regret.

As Nell had feared, soon after their marriage, Big Kells returned to drink and took up his father's pastime of wife-beating. He forced Young Tim to give up his lessons at the WIDOW SMACK'S COTTAGE—a pursuit that Tim dearly loved—so that he could earn scrip at the TREE SAWMILL. (Tim would have been happy to pursue his father's profession of woodcutting, but Big Kells said that he was, and always would be, too small to cut ironwood.) When the gales of Wide Earth came howling in from the west, and Tim began to think that life with Big Bern Kells had become too unbearable, the evil Barony Covenanter blew into Tree. While collecting the taxes at Goodview Cottage, the Covenant Man gave Tim a key which would open any lock. Secretly, Tim used the key to open his stepfather's trunk, which was exactly what the Barony Covenanter wanted him to do. Inside, below ragged old clothes, rusty tools, and a picture of Kells's first wife, MILLICENT, Tim found his father's lucky coin, a rhodite double. Tim knew that a dragon couldn't have incinerated his father, since Big Ross's coin had survived. There was only one answer—he had been murdered by his partner, Big Kells.

Mounting BITSY, his father's mule, Tim rode deep into the Endless Forest to find the Covenant Man's camp. There, in the waters of a MAGICAL SILVER BASIN, and using the gearshift of an old Dodge Dart as a magic wand, the Barony Covenanter showed Tim a terrible image—of Bern Kells smashing a ceramic jug into Nell Kells's face and then beating her into unconsciousness. After showing Tim the image of the Widow Smack tending to Nell's wounds (otherwise the boy would have galloped home immediately on Bitsy's back), the nasty Covenant Man showed Tim his father's dead body, floating in a stream which ran through a fallow stub on the COSINGTON-MARCHLY STAKE.

Returning home with his father's ax tucked into his belt (the Covenanter had found Big Ross's belongings in the forest), Tim told PETER COSINGTON, ERNIE MARCHLY, and BALDY ANDERSON about his stepfather's crimes. After bidding Big Ross goodbye in the Tree BURYING PARLOR, Tim set off for yet another journey into the depths of the forest. This time—egged on by a vision provided by yet another one of the treacherous Covenanter's scrying vessels— Tim was determined to find the magician MAERLYN, who he was certain could restore his mother's sight.

Wearing his father's lucky coin around his neck, scuffed shor'boots upon his feet, and his father's ax tucked into his belt by his right hip, Tim set off for the Widow Smack's cottage. He wanted the Widow to inform his ma about his travels, and also to send him on with a blessing. Unlike Tim, the Widow Smack did not trust the visions sent by the blackhearted Barony Covenanter. However, since she knew she could not stop Tim from taking his journey, she sent him on with a lamp, a loaf of bread, and a four-shot revolver which had belonged to her brother, JOSHUA. Tim lost the lamp while following the pretty but treacherous SIGHE named ARMANEETA through the FAGONARD (she led Tim right on top of a sleeping DRAGON, probably hoping that the boy would be eaten), but

Tim kept the gun. In fact, he used it to shoot one of the Fagonard's hungry CAN-NIBAL REPTILES that wanted to swallow him whole.

Holding a smoking gun but stranded on a grassy tussock deep in the watery Fagonard, Tim was eventually rescued by the MUTANT MUDMEN who mistook him for a young gunslinger. From these friendly if physically disgusting mutants Tim received the talking NORTH CENTRAL POSITRONICS guidance mechanism called DARIA. Daria led Tim along the PATH of the EAGLE-LION BEAM, past dancing BUMBLERS, GIANT YELLOW MUSHROOMS, MUTANT BLUE DEER, and a DEMON TENTACLED MONSTER, all the way to the NORTH FOREST KINNOCK DOGAN. Upon reaching the Dogan, and the deep magic which Daria detected there, Tim's North Central Positronics friend was forced to shut down for providing Tim with too much restricted information and hence violating Directive NINETEEN.

At the Dogan, Tim found not the magician Maerlyn, whom he had hoped to find, but a huge caged TYGER with two objects attached to its collar. One was a flat keycard; the other was a key shaped like a letter from High Speech. Beneath a silver pail located just outside the cage, Tim found a note from the Covenant Man along with the key to the tyger's cage. The note, which was signed RF/MB, dared Tim to open the cage, since around the tyger's neck hung the key to the nearby Dogan.

With the deadly winds of the STARKBLAST already blowing down the iron-woods of the forest, Tim felt he had little choice and so set the tyger free. Much to his surprise, the tyger did not try to eat him, but instead waited patiently for the boy to remove his collar. As the winds buffeted him, Tim tried to use the keycard, but unfortunately the Dogan was offline. However, just outside the Dogan's permanently locked door was the METAL BOX for which the tyger's second key was made. Inside that box were three MAGICAL OBJECTS: a large white FEATHER, a small BROWN BOTTLE, and a white dinner napkin that was actually a magical DIBBEN. As gale force winds blew Tim against the side of the Dogan, the tyger held the white dibben between his teeth and began shaking it out. The napkin, Tim soon realized, was enchanted and could expand exponentially. It was also windproof. Huddling beneath the expansive dibben with his furry companion, Tim found that he did not feel the wind at all, though the starkblast wreaked havoc all around them.

The next afternoon, after the starkblast had blown out most of its rage, Tim opened the brown bottle and placed a dropperful of its liquid into the tyger's mouth. To Tim's astonishment, the tyger transformed into none other than the magician Maerlyn! Finally freed from the enchantment cast upon him by one of the CRIMSON KING's servants, Maerlyn folded the dibben into a flying blanket. Telling Tim to hold the feather and think of home, Maerlyn sent Tim off to the village of Tree, but not before telling him to place the remaining contents of the brown bottle into his mother's blind eyes. He also warned Tim that he must hand his father's ax to Nell as soon as she could see again.

Tim did as the magician bid, and mighty thankful he must have been afterwards. Unbeknownst to Tim, his steppa had crept into the cottage before Tim's arrival and had murdered the Widow Smack, who had been caring for Nell during the starkblast. As soon as Tim emerged from his mother's bedroom, Big Kells grabbed him by the throat, intending to throw him into the fire, but before he could, Nell Kells buried her first husband's ax in Kells's thick skull.

W:46 *(Tim Stoutheart story)*, W:67 *(Tim Stoutheart)*, W:106–16 *parallel, when da killed)*, W:117, W:118, W:119 *(kiddie)*, W:120–24, W:124–30, W:131–45, W:145–W:170, W:170–190 *(182–83 Water Tim; 186 gun described)*, W:190–202 *(197—son of Gilead and the Eld; 201 as gunslinger)*, W:202–32 *(212 calls self "stupid gunslinger")*, W:232–64 *(almost shoots Maerlyn/Tyger)*, W:250–64, W:267, W:268 *(Lefty Ross, the left-handed gun, Tim Stoutheart)*, W:269 *(story about reaching the Tower)*, W:297 *(Tim Stoutheart)*

ROSSITER
See CALLA BRYN STURGIS CHARACTERS: FARMERS (SMALLHOLD): STRONG, GARRETT

ROSTOV, DANEEKA (DANI)
See BREAKERS

ROUTHIER RAY
See KING, STEPHEN

ROWENA, QUEEN
See ELD, ARTHUR

ROYSTER, ELDON
See MAINE CHARACTERS

RUBBERBAND AIRLINES
This is IRENE TASSENBAUM's airline of choice when she flies from NEW YORK CITY to MAINE.
VII:521

RUDEBACHER, DICKY
See CALLAHAN, FATHER DONALD FRANK: CALLAHAN'S HIDDEN HIGHWAYS ASSOCIATES

RUIZ, STANLEY (SHEEMIE)
See BREAKERS

RUIZ, STANLEY (THE ELDER)
See HAMBRY CHARACTERS: TRAVELLERS' REST

RUMBELOW, GRACE
See BREAKERS

RUSSERT, DON
See MAINE CHARACTERS

RUSTY SAM
See MID-WORLD FOLKLORE

RUTA
See CALLAHAN, FATHER DONALD FRANK: CALLAHAN'S HIDDEN HIGHWAYS ASSOCIATES

S

SACRAMENTO BEE
See CALLAHAN, FATHER DONALD FRANK: CALLAHAN'S HIDDEN HIGHWAYS ASSOCIATES

SAITA
See ELD, ARTHUR

'SALEM'S LOT CHARACTERS
See CALLAHAN, FATHER DONALD FRANK: 'SALEM'S LOT CHARACTERS

SALLOW BRITISH MAN
See BALAZAR, ENRICO: BALAZAR'S NASSAU CONNECTION

SALT HOUSE FOLKS
See DEBARIA CHARACTERS: SALTIES

SALT MINERS
See DEBARIA CHARACTERS: SALTIES

SALTY SAM
See DEBARIA CHARACTERS: SHERIFF'S OFFICE

SAM THE MILLER
See WALTER: WALTER'S ASSOCIATES

SARGUS, JANE
See MAINE CHARACTERS

SAYRE, RICHARD P.
See CAN-TOI

SCHWERNER, MICHAEL
See DEAN, SUSANNAH: ODETTA HOLMES AND THE CIVIL RIGHTS MOVEMENT: VOTER REGISTRATION BOYS

SCOWTHER
See WARRIORS OF THE SCARLET EYE: DIXIE PIG CHARACTERS: HUMANS

SCRIMSHAW TURTLE
  See GUARDIANS OF THE BEAM: TURTLE

SEEKING FOLK
  See MANNI

SEJ
  See BREAKERS

SELENA
  See GODS OF MID-WORLD

SEMINON, LORD
  See ORIZA, LADY

SERENITY, SISTERS OF (BLACK AMMIES)
GABRIELLE DESCHAIN, Roland Deschain's lady mother, was sent to the SERENITY RETREAT in DEBARIA to repent her affair with MARTEN BROADCLOAK, her husband's advisor and sorcerer. Perhaps this is why STEVEN DESCHAIN distrusted those convent-women so completely. "Serenity, what a joke. Those women are the black ammies. They'd flay you alive if you so much as trespassed their holy doors." According to the elder Deschain, most of the Sisters of Serenity preferred a longstick to a man. According to the engineer of SMA' TOOT, they ate men.

The Retreat of Serenity was located ten or twelve wheels beyond the town of Debaria along DEBARIA HIGH ROAD. It was the size of a Barony estate and was extremely well tended. The walls of its dazzling white haci were tall and topped with forbidding sparkles of broken glass, but the wooden gates stood open with invitation. Behind the haci, down a narrow creek, was a large green garden and a grape arbor. The women of Serenity served God and the MAN JESUS.

Serenity's Prioress was EVERLYNNE OF SERENITY, a six-and-a-half-foot-giantess who (according to Roland) was so tall and broad she could have mated with the legendary outlaw prince, DAVID QUICK. When Roland first saw her, sitting on what appeared to be an IRONWOOD throne in front of the retreat's open gates, her lap was full of needlework and she was dressed in white muslin with a hood of white silk that flared around her head like gullwings. Everlynne's body was as big as a barrel, and her breasts were so large that each of them could have shaded a baby from the sun. Her voice was rolling, and was almost (but not quite) as deep as a man's baritone. Her laughter was like moderate thunder, and her black eyes twinkled.

Despite the reputation of her retreat among the GUNSLINGERS of GILEAD, Everlynne greeted Roland and his *ka*-mate, JAMIE DeCURRY, very warmly. (In fact, she greeted Roland as "son of Gabrielle," an unusual epithet in father-centered Mid-World.) In Everlynne's opinion, her retreat had a bad name in Gilead because the men there distrusted women who dared to live on their own. But despite what Gilead might say about her, Everlynne was glad to see two young gunslingers who served the ELD and the WHITE, even if they were extremely young. After all, two of her women—FORTUNA and DOLORES—had been attacked by the SKIN-MAN that Roland and Jamie had come to hunt, and only Fortuna (badly mutilated) had lived to tell the tale. Everlynne thought the skin-man was a soulless skin-man monster from the DEEP CRACKS.

After Roland killed the skin-man, he returned to Serenity and was greeted by Everlynne with a kiss and a hug. (Roland noted that her aroma was sweet: a mixture of cinnamon and thyme and baked goods.) Everlynne and her women had a celebratory feast with the two young gunslingers. Afterwards, in a private meeting in her quarters, Everlynne told Roland about his mother's last days at the retreat, and how Marten Broadcloak had tried to visit her. Everlynne had sent the scoundrel away, but was fairly certain that he'd managed to meet with Gabrielle secretly. Shortly after this clandestine meeting, Gabrielle had quit the retreat, saying she had a duty to perform in Gilead and much to atone for. However, before she left, she gave the prioress a letter for Roland. She was certain that one day her son would visit Serenity. The letter, which Roland read while alone in Everlynne's chamber, was blotted and uneven. Roland was fairly certain that his mother was half-mad by the time she wrote it. However, the letter contained one extremely important line which haunted Roland, guilty as he was of matricide, for the rest of his life. That line was *I forgive you everything. Can you forgive me?*
W:38, W:39, W:41–42 *(and longstick/diddlestick)*, W:43–44 *(eat the mens)*, W:47–W:53 *(at the Priory; 49 named)* W:61, W:63, W:295

BRIANNA: Briana was one of the Sisters of Serenity. She, ELLEN, and CLEMMIE served food to Roland and JAMIE when they visited the Retreat on their way to DEBARIA to hunt the SKIN-MAN. W:49, W:53

CLEMMIE: Clemmie was one of the Sisters of Serenity. She served food when Roland and JAMIE stopped at the Retreat on their way to DEBARIA to hunt the SKIN-MAN. W:49, W:53

DOLORES: Dolores and FORTUNA were the two unlucky Sisters of Serenity to be attacked by DEBARIA's shapeshifting SKIN-MAN. A fortnight and a day before Roland and JAMIE came to the Retreat, the two women had been outside at dusk to close the gate and draw water for evening chores. Fortuna had held the bucket while Dolores had swung the gate closed. But as Dolores was swinging the gate, a creature knocked it wide, grabbed her, and bit her head from her shoulders with its long jaws. The creature had been taller than a man, with scales instead of skin, and a long tail that dragged behind it like a snake. Yellow eyes with slitted dark pupils glowed in its flat head. Its mouth was a trap filled with teeth, each as long as a man's hand. W:51, W:53

ELLEN: Like BRIANNA and CLEMMIE, Ellen was called by EVERLYNNE to serve food to Roland and JAMIE when they arrived at SERENITY. W:49

EVERLYNNE OF SERENITY (PRIORESS): According to HIGH SHERIFF HUGH PEAVY, Prioress Everlynne was so full of fire that she would spit in the devil's face if he came to call on her. And if that fork-tailed demon took her down to Nis, she'd be running the place in a month. There certainly seems to be truth in the sheriff's statement, since Everlynne was the only person other than Roland to shoot the monstrous SKIN-MAN and survive. (That shapeshifting nightmare was tearing at SISTER FORTUNA's face when Everlynne aimed and fired. The pellets tore away some of the knobs and scales on the monster's head.) Everlynne also turned away MARTEN BROADCLOAK at gunpoint when he came to call on GABRIELLE DESCHAIN, who at the time was a resident at the Retreat. (Sadly, "the Broad Cloak" as Everlynne calls him, managed to rendezvous with Gabrielle anyway.)

When Roland met the six-and-a-half-foot-tall prioress on his way to DEBARIA, he was shocked by her size. He thought her a giantess, one tall and broad enough to have mated with the legendary outlaw prince, DAVID QUICK. When Roland first saw her, sitting on what appeared to be an iron-wood throne in front of the retreat's open gates, her lap was full of needle-work, and she was dressed in white muslin with a hood of white silk which flared around her head like gullwings. Everlynne's body was big as a barrel, and her breasts were so large that each of them could have shaded a baby from the sun. Her voice was rolling, and was almost (but not quite) as deep as a man's baritone. Her laughter was like moderate thunder, and her black eyes twinkled. Despite her good nature and religious calling, the prioress was always willing to take up arms to defend herself. Strapped to the outside of her calf was a rawhide scabbard. Within that scabbard was a butcher's knife.

Although the gunslingers of GILEAD did not trust Everlynne or her women since they lived without men, Everlynne welcomed both Roland and JAMIE DeCURRY with open arms. Calling him "son of Gabrielle" (an epithet rarely used in father-centered Mid-World), Everlynne gave Roland a letter which she'd saved for him—a letter from his mother. (Gabrielle had entrusted Everlynne with the missive shortly before leaving the retreat.) Although the letter was disjointed and half-mad, it gave Roland—guilty of matricide—a sense of peace. Evidently, Gabrielle had known about her coming death at her son's hands and had accepted it. The letter's final words were *I forgive you everything. Can you forgive me?* W:47–W:53 *(described; 52 daughter of Roseanna)*, W:61, W:100 *(Roland wants to take Bill to her)*, W:268, W:293, W:295–99, W:300

> **CAT:** When Roland visited Prioress Everlynne's private quarters, this cat was asleep in a bar of sunlight that slanted onto her desk. That huge oaken desk was heaped high with papers. W:297

> **ROSEANNA (MOTHER):** Roseanna was Everlynne's mother. Everlynne refers to herself as "daughter of Roseanna." W:52

FORTUNA (FORTIE; ANNIE CLAY-THAT-WAS): Fortuna and DOLORES were the two Sisters of Serenity unlucky enough to be attacked by the SKIN-MAN. Only tiny Fortuna survived, but her wounds were horrendous. When Roland and Jamie met her, she was clad in a rough gray cotton robe, her arms were crossed over her scant bosom, and her hands were buried deep in her sleeves. She wore no hood, but half of her face was hidden beneath a thick swath of bandages. (A large section of the right side of her nose was gone; all that was left was a raw red channel.) At dusk, a fortnight and a day before, she and Dolores had come out to close the Retreat's gate and to draw water for the evening chores. Fortuna was the one with the bucket, and so she had lived—barely. After biting off Dolores's head, the skin-man lunged for Fortuna. Luckily for her, Everlynne heard the younger women's screams and so came running out with the Retreat's gun. According to Everlynne, the monster was set to rape Fortuna as well as eat her. W:49–53 *(wounded)*, W:61, W:63, W:88, W:291, W:295–96

SERGIO
   See TOWER, CALVIN

SERVOMECHANISMS (LITTLE GUARDIANS)
   See GUARDIANS OF THE BEAM: BEAR

SHANNIES
   See MID-WORLD ARGOT

SHARDIK
   See GUARDIANS OF THE BEAM: BEAR

SHARPTON, MR.
   See BREAKERS: EARNSHAW, DINKY

SHAVERS, GEORGE
   See DEAN, SUSANNAH: DETTA WALKER'S ASSOCIATES

SHAW, GRETA
   See CHAMBERS, JAKE: JAKE'S FAMILY, FRIENDS, ASSOCIATES AND ALIASES

**SHEB (SHEB McCURDY: PIANO PLAYER)
In the 2003 version of *The Gunslinger,* we find out that the two piano players named Sheb—one in TULL, one in HAMBRY—are actually the same man. In both stories he works in bars owned by women. (Though Tull's local honky-tonk bears his name, the place actually belongs to Sheb's former lover, ALICE.)
   Sheb of Hambry, and later of Tull, is described as a small, useless man with one gold tooth. He is in love with Alice though she thinks of him as a gelded dog. Jealous that Roland monopolizes Alice's attentions, he tries to assault Roland with a knife. Later, during the town's surprise attack on the gunslinger, Sheb uses Allie as a human shield. In the 2003 version of *The Gunslinger,* Roland recognizes Sheb as the man he met in MEJIS.
   I:26–29, I:34–38, I:40, I:45–47, I:47–52, I:58, I:59, I:60, II:126, III:42, IV:171–72, IV:213, IV:216, IV:218, IV:226, IV:349, IV:382–83, IV:403, IV:453, IV:468, IV:505, IV:563, IV:570, IV:628, VII:317, VII:333

SHEEMER, DELORES
   See HAMBRY CHARACTERS: TRAVELLERS' REST

SHEEMIE
   See BREAKERS

SHOE SHINE BOY
   See TOWER, CALVIN

SI
   See RIVER CROSSING CHARACTERS

SIGHE
See MID-WORLD FOLKLORE and ARMANEETA

SILICON VALLEY COKE-HEADS
These guys supply high-tech police equipment to BALAZAR'S MEN.
  II:125

SIMONS, FRANKIE
See TREE VILLAGE CHARACTERS

SISTER BLUE
See DEAN, SUSANNAH: ODETTA HOLMES'S ASSOCIATES

SISTER COQUINA
See ELURIA, LITTLE SISTERS OF

SISTER JENNA
See ELURIA, LITTLE SISTERS OF

SISTER LOUISE
See ELURIA, LITTLE SISTERS OF

SISTER MARY
See ELURIA, LITTLE SISTERS OF

SISTER MICHELA
See ELURIA, LITTLE SISTERS OF

SISTER TAMRA
See ELURIA, LITTLE SISTERS OF

SISTERS OF ORIZA
See ORIZA, SISTERS OF

SISTERS OF SERENITY (BLACK AMMIES)
See SERENITY, SISTERS OF

SISTERS OF THE PLATE
See ORIZA, SISTERS OF

SKANK, BANGO
Although we never meet Bango Skank, Roland's *tet* sees his graffiti on the MILLS CONSTRUCTION AND SOMBRA REAL ESTATE sign which they find in JAKE's magic LOT in NEW YORK CITY. While having a seizure in a TOPEKA JAIL CELL, Callahan also comes across Skank's signature, as does Jake in the tunnels leading from the DIXIE PIG to the MIND-TRAP, which guards the New York/FEDIC DOORWAY BETWEEN WORLDS. SUSANNAH comes across Bango's writing when she and MIA visit one of the stalls in the women's bath-

rooms located in the PLAZA–PARK HYATT hotel. This last bit of graffiti reads, "Bango Skank awaits the King."

III:121, V:189, V:447, V:619, VI:233 *(Bango Skank awaits the King)*, VI:256 *(Bango Skank awaits the King)*, VII:89

SKIN-MAN (OLLIE ANG)

In *The Wind Through the Keyhole* we meet one of the most terrifying monsters of the Dark Tower novels. The creature is called a skin-man. According to the reports received by STEVEN DESCHAIN, this legendary monster was massacring the people of DEBARIA. The elder Deschain was not certain whether this demon was real or whether it was a human maniac dressed up in animal skins, but he did know for certain that many people had been killed. As a result, he sent Roland and Roland's *ka*-mate, JAMIE DeCURRY, to investigate.

Before setting off from Gilead, Roland visited his old tutor VANNAY, who had been collecting reports about the attacks. According to the missives that Vannay had received from HIGH SHERIFF HUGH PEAVY, twenty-three people had been torn to pieces by the monster. (That number was soon to mount much higher.) In two cases, whole clans had been massacred. Worryingly, the descriptions of the beast were inconsistent. Some witnesses stated that the creature looked like a wolf but ran upright like a man. Others described it as a lion; still others as a tyger. Based upon what he'd read, Vannay believed the creature was both a shape-*shifter* and a shape-*changer*. The old tutor had come across other such beasts in Gilead's old records, and assumed that it was a type of mutant that had worked its way out of the true thread. The truth turned out to be much more terrible.

Roland and Jamie's first sight of one of the skin-man's victims came when they visited the Women's Retreat of SERENITY, on their way to Debaria. There they met SISTER FORTUNA, who had lost half her face to the hungry beast. According to Sister Fortie, the creature had been taller than a man, with scales instead of skin, and a long tail that dragged behind it like a snake. Its yellow eyes had slitted dark pupils that glowed in its flat head. Its mouth had been a trap filled with teeth, each as long as a man's head. PRIORESS EVERLYNNE (who managed to shoot some of the knobs and scales off the beast's head with the pellets of her shotgun) added an even more disturbing piece of information: while attacking Fortuna, the beast had an erection. Everlynne was certain that, if she hadn't chased it off with her shotgun, the creature would have raped Sister Fortie as it ate her.

Upon reaching Debaria, Roland and Jamie met with Sheriff Peavy to discuss who the skin-man might be when in human form. Based upon the pattern of attacks, the three decided the perpetrator was probably one of the SALTIES, or salt miners, based near LITTLE DEBARIA. They also came to realize that though the monster only struck at night, the phase of the moon seemed to have little effect upon its powers. (It attacked Sister Fortuna at Full Peddlar, but at TIMBERSMITH farm it struck at the dark of the moon.) Roland and Jamie had been in Debaria less than twenty-four hours when the skin-man struck again. This time the massacre was at the JEFFERSON RANCH, where he killed sixteen proddies, the COOK (BILL STREETER), *sai* JEFFERSON, Jefferson's WIFE, and his two DAUGHTERS. While following the monster's backtrail (and tracking its morphs from eight-hundred-pound bear, to giant bull, to monstrous cat), Roland and Jamie realized that the skin-man's killing spree had been premeditated. (It rode to the ranch in human form, and only morphed into a monster when it was ready to kill.)

During their search of the ranch, the two young gunslingers discovered YOUNG BILL STREETER hiding in a pile of old tack in a disused hostelry. The boy had been sleeping under the stars when the skin-man attacked, but had been woken by screams. He'd run down to the ranch and had witnessed the slaughter in the bunkhouse. Later, while hiding under the pile of tack, Young Bill had seen the skin-man transform back into a human being. Unfortunately, he only saw the man's lower legs and feet. However, he did give Roland one important piece of information: the skin man had a broken blue ring tattooed around his ankle.

The evidence that Roland and Jamie discovered at the ranch allowed them to deduce the following: the skin-man was a saltie who could ride a horse, and who had done time in the BEELIE STOCKADE. (The blue ankle ring was tattooed on anyone who did time in the stockade.) Roland sent Jamie, Sheriff Peavy, the deputy KELLIN FRYE, and Kellin's son VIKKA to round up all the salties who fit that description. He also gave young Vikka a more sinister job. He wanted the boy to spread the word that Young Bill had seen the skin-man in human form, and would be able to identify him. Roland hoped that this exaggeration might help to flush out the murderer.

While Jamie and the others went to LITTLE DEBARIA to round up all the suspects, Roland locked Young Bill in Debaria's JAIL to keep him safe. Before returning to the cell to keep Bill company, Roland had the local blacksmith cast a very special bullet, the only kind which, according to legend, could kill a skin-man. That bullet was cast from pure silver.

Thanks to the knowledge of WILL WEGG, Little Debaria's constable, Jamie and the others returned with twenty-one suspects who could ride horses. In the BUSTED LUCK saloon, Roland has the miners roll up their trouser legs to show whether or not they'd been marked at the stockade. Ten had been. One of these men, an old graybeard called STEG LUKA, confided an important piece of information. He told Roland that deep in the SALT PLUG there was a CRACK with a green light shining through, bright then dim, like a heartbeat. According to Luka, the light had a bitter voice which called the miners to come to it. Most wanted the crack plugged up, but Luka believed that one of the men had listened to the call, entered the crack between midnight and 6 A.M. when all was quiet, and had been transformed into a shapeshifting monster. Luka was certain that both light and voice belonged to one of the OLD PEOPLE's artifacts. In the end, he proved to be right.

As Young Bill waited in his protective cell, the salt miners lined up according to age and paraded past. Steg Luka passed by, as did BOBBY FRANE, JAKE MARSH, and OLLIE ANG, a thin, balding, bookish-looking fellow whose arms were nevertheless slabbed with muscle, and who wore a strange wrist-clock with a rusty string-mended band. At Young Bill's request, all the men walked by a second time, but this time with their pants legs hiked up so that the boy could see their ankles. Bill recognized OLLIE ANG's blue ankle ring, which was broken by a thick line of white scar tissue which ran all the way up to Ang's knee.

What next transpired happened so quickly that neither Roland nor any of the others were able to prevent it. Steg Luka grabbed Ang by the shoulders and bore him back against the bars across from the drunk-and-disorderly cell. Spitting in Ang's face, Steg called the man a murdering, skin-changing bastard. But even as Steg Luka attacked, Ang transformed into a giant snake and rammed his body into Steg's mouth and then tore his way out through the nape of Steg's neck. Next, the snake battened down on Constable Wegg's arm, injecting him with poison. As it lunged at Roland, our gunslinger shot his silver bullet into the creature's yawning mouth. In death, the skin-man transformed once again into his human form. After midnight, Roland, Jamie, and Sheriff Peavy doused Ang's body with coal oil and burned it.

W:40, W:42, W:44–47 *(attacks described: 45 wolf that runs upright; lion; 46 tyger)*, 48 *(monster from deep cracks)*, W:48–53 *(attack on Fortuna and Delores)*; W:54, W:55, W:56, W:57 *(looked like a wolf)*; W:61, W:62, W:63–83 *(62–63: victim list and map; 66 moon phases; 69–83 Jefferson attack reported and investigated; 72 bear; 75 eight hundred pounds running on hind legs; 76 ull-shape, cat shape; 78 knows what he is and rides a horse)*, W:85 *(as saltie)*, W:86, W:91–97 *(Bill Streeter's memory)*, W:99, W:100, W:248 *(legend)*, W:268, W:271–93 *(he is among the salties who can ride; mentioned directly on 274, 276, 289, 283; on 289 we learn his name)*, W:294, W:297–98 *(possibly as Walter's work? He cursed Serenity)*

SKIN-MAN'S VICTIMS: All of the skin-man's victims were torn to pieces. Many of them were also partially eaten. W:45

    ALORA FARM VICTIMS: The skin-man killed seven people at the Alora Farm. W:63

    COWPUNCHERS (WITNESSES): Two cowpunchers camped on DEBARIA STREAM heard the screams of a young MANNI COUPLE on marriage retreat and rode toward the sound. They saw the killer loping off with the woman's lower leg in its jaws. They swore the beast ran upright like a man. W:45–46 *(witnesses)*, W:46 *(as rope-swingers)*, W:46–47 *(drunk or not)*

    DOLORES OF SERENITY: *See* SERENITY, SISTERS OF

    FORTUNA OF SERENITY: *See* SERENITY, SISTERS OF

    GAMBLER AND WOMAN: This man had been caught cheating at Watch Me in one of the local pits. He and his moll had been given a Bill of Circulation and were told to leave town by nightfall or be whipped. They were headed for either the rail tracks or LITTLE DEBARIA when they were beset by the beast. The man fought, which gave the woman just enough time to get clear. She hid in some rocks until the skin-man was gone. According to her testimony, the monster looked like a lion. W:45, W:64

    JEFFERSON RANCH CHARACTERS: *See also* STREETER, BILL, *listed separately*; DEBARIA CHARACTERS: JEFFERSON RANCH CHARACTERS: CANFIELD, BILL; DEBARIA CHARACTERS: JEFFERSON RANCH CHARACTERS: CANFIELD, BILL: ARN; DEBARIA CHARACTERS: JEFFERSON RANCH CHARACTERS: CANFIELD, BILL: SNIP; DEBARIA CHARACTERS: JEFFERSON RANCH CHARACTERS: ROSIE & MOZIE

        COOKIE (BILL STREETER, YOUNG BILL STREETER'S FATHER): Bill Streeter—cook at the JEFFERSON RANCH—was YOUNG BILL STREETER's beloved father. According to VIKKA FRYE, Cookie was very proud of his son. When Billy won the Goose Dash at Reap Fairday, the elder Streeter cheered loud enough to bust his throat. Cookie died beside his stove, his rent and bloodstained apron thrown over his face like a shroud. W:69 *(dead)*, W:75, W:80, W:81, W:82, W:83, W:84, W:86, W:87, W:88, W:90, W:91, W:95, W:96, W:97, W:100, W:101, W:106, W:268 *(da)*, W:285 *(indirect)*, W:286 *(indirect)*

JEFFERSON FAMILY: *sai* Jefferson, his lady wife, and his two daughters were slaughtered by the skin-man. His two sons survived, since they were in GILEAD when the attack took place. W:69 *(dead)*, W:93 *(womenfolk)*, W:97 *(womenfolk)*

    JEFFERSON (RANCHER): *sai* Jefferson faced the skin-man (in the shape of a bear) ten feet in front of the bunkhouse. The rancher got off a few rounds before the monster tore the gun from his hands and bent the barrel. Then the skin-man picked *sai* Jefferson up and threw him into the bunkhouse. Inside the bunkhouse, Roland and JAMIE DeCURRY found Jefferson's body, which had been torn limb from limb. His severed head stared up at the rafters with a fearful grin that showed only his top teeth. The skin-man had ripped the rancher's lower jaw right out of his mouth. KELLIN FRYE found it under a bunk. W:69 *(dead)*, W:70–72, W:74 *(rancher)*, W:75 *(torn limbless)*, W:81, W:83, W:92, W:93, W:101

    DAUGHTERS: The bodies of *sai* Jefferson's two daughters were found in the dirt between the house and the barn. One had gotten three or four dozen running steps ahead of her sissa, but they were both equally dead, with their nightdresses torn off and their backs carved open right down to their spines. W:70, W:72 *(killing described)*, W:73 *(indirect)*, W:74, W:75, W:93 *(womenfolk)*, W:97 *(womenfolk)*

    SONS: *sai* Jefferson's two sons were attending auctions in Gilead when the attacks took place. Hence, they survived. W:74

    WIFE: Jefferson's lady-*sai*'s body was found under the kitchen table. Her half-eaten head had rolled up against the pantry door. W:70, W:72, W:73 *(indirect)*, W:74, W:93 *(womenfolk)*, W:97 *(womenfolk)*

NUTTER, ELROD (FOREMAN): Elrod Nutter was the foreman of the Jefferson Ranch. He was an excellent rider and roper, but when he was in drink he got mean. According to YOUNG BILL STREETER, Elrod once twirled the bunkhouse cat by her tail and she never came back. When he was drunk, Elrod liked to drag Young Bill around by his boots. (According to SHERIFF PEAVY, Elrod had been in lockup numerous times because of his wicked drunken temper.) Elrod kept a knife in his boot, but as Young Bill pointed out, neither Elrod's temper nor his knife saved him from the skin-man. (When Elrod was cornered by the bunkhouse's back door he'd turned to fight off the skin-man with his knife. But as he'd stabbed at the monstrous bear-shape, the creature grabbed his arm and tore it off his shoulder. It then hit Elrod with his own arm and bit into his neck.) W:81 *(nasty in drink)*, W:91, W:92 *(death)*, W:94, W:97

PRODDIES: A number of the proddies—or permanent hands—at the Jefferson Ranch were friends with YOUNG BILL STREETER. W:69, W:75 *(16 killed)*, W:80, W:93, W:100, W:101

FREDDY TWO-STEP: Freddy Two-Step had promised to teach YOUNG BILL STREETER how to brand in the fall. Sadly, he didn't live long enough to fulfill his promise. W:81

ROSCOE: Before he died, Roscoe was teaching YOUNG BILL STREETER the bow. W:81

TINY BRADDOCK: Before he was killed by the skin-man, Tiny Braddock taught YOUNG BILL STREETER how to make a lasso. W:81

UNNAMED COWBOY: This unnamed cowboy had his face ripped off by the skin-man. W:75

MANNI COUPLE: This young couple was on their marriage retreat when they were attacked by the skin-man. Two COWPUNCHERS who went to investigate the screaming saw the skin-man loping off with the woman's lower leg in its jaws. W:45–46

SALTIES: A number of salties were torn up by the skin-man, although we're not told about these attacks in detail. W:64

SHEPHERD VICTIM (YON CURRY): This sheepherder was killed by something that looked like a wolf, but ran upright like a man. His two dogs were torn to pieces by the monstrous attacker. W:45, W:57, W:63, W:64

SHEPHERD WITNESS: This shepherd saw his partner attacked by the skin-man. The man's two dogs, who tried to protect their master, were torn apart too. According to this witness, the attacking monster looked like a wolf but ran upright like a man W:45

TIMBERSMITH FARM: Nine people were killed at the Timbersmith farm. SHERIFF PEAVY also found a little boy's head stuck onto a pole. There were tracks all around it. The tracks were those of a big cat, but when Peavy's posse followed the tracks, they changed into hoofs, then into the prints of a giant human being. Finally, they became the prints of a small man. W:63

BOY: The skin-man stuck this young boy's head on pole. The boy's skull was smashed and his brain was scooped out. W:45, W:47, W:63

SKÖLDPADDA
See GUARDIANS OF THE BEAM: TURTLE

SLEEPY JOHN'S
See CALIFORNIA (STATE OF): SACRAMENTO: SLEEPY JOHN'S, *in* OUR WORLD PLACES

SLIDELL, POKEY
See CALLA BRYN STURGIS CHARACTERS: WOLF POSSE

SLIGHTMAN, BEN
See CALLA BRYN STURGIS CHARACTERS: RANCHERS: EISENHART, VAUGHN

SLIGHTMAN, BENNY
See CALLA BRYN STURGIS CHARACTERS: RANCHERS: EISENHART, VAUGHN

SLIGHTMAN, EDNA
See CALLA BRYN STURGIS CHARACTERS: RANCHERS: EISENHART, VAUGHN: SLIGHTMAN, BEN (EISENHART'S FOREMAN)

SLOW MUTANTS
See MUTANTS

SMACK, ARDELIA
See WIDOW SMACK

SMA' LADY MUFFIN
See MID-WORLD FOLKLORE

S'MANA
See GODS OF MID-WORLD

SMASHER
See ELURIA CHARACTERS: GREEN FOLK

SMA' TOOT
When Roland was a boy, Sma' Toot was a special two-car train that ran along MID-WORLD'S WESTERN LINE. Once the Western Line ran a thousand wheels or more to the MOHAINE DESERT, but in the years before GILEAD fell, it ran to DEBARIA and no farther. Beyond that, many tracklines had been destroyed by washouts and ground-shakers. Others had been taken up by harriers and roving bands of outlaws.

To the people of Gilead, Sma' Toot looked like little more than a steam-driven toy, and they laughed to see it puffing over the bridge to the west of the PALACE. However, the small train with its isinglass windows and velveteen seats that folded out into uncomfortable beds did serve an important purpose. It brought Roland and JAMIE to Debaria, where they investigated the vicious murders committed by the SKIN-MAN.
W:40–44, W:48, W:51, W:62, W:63, W:294, W:303

ENGINEER TRAVIS (ENG, ENJIE): Sma' Toot's engineer was a broad-shouldered, bow-legged plug of a man. After Sma' Toot went off her rails, Roland and JAMIE DeCURRY rode to get help. But before they left, Engineer Travis warned the boys not to stop at the women's retreat of SERENITY. The Eng maintained that the SISTERS OF SERENITY ate men. (Obviously, he was wrong.) Engineer Travis made another brief appearance later in our tale. He traveled with SHERIFF PEAVY, KELLIN FRYE, VIKKA FRYE, Roland, and Jamie to the JEFFERSON RANCH, just after the massacre. He didn't have the stomach for all the blood he saw there. W:43–44, W:48, W:62, W:63, W:70–74 *(present at Ranch; mentioned on 70, 72; 74 says "seen enough")*, W:294

FIXING CREW: W:44 *(mentioned)*, W:63, W:294

SERVANT: This old man served Roland and JAMIE their meals while they traveled on Sma' Toot toward DEBARIA. When the train derailed he was flung all the way back to the door between the car and his little kitchen. His false teeth flew out of his mouth and into his lap. W:41, W:42–43, W:62, W:63

WIFE: After Sma' Toot derailed, the old servant decided to quit his job. Otherwise he feared he wouldn't outlive his nag of a wife. W:43

SMITH, BRYAN
See KING, STEPHEN

SNEETCHES
See APPENDIX I

SNIP
See DEBARIA CHARACTERS: JEFFERSON RANCH CHARACTERS

SNUGGLEBUT
See CALLAHAN, FATHER DONALD FRANK: CALLAHAN'S PRESENT ASSOCIATES

SOBIESKI, MARY JEAN
See DEAN, EDDIE: EDDIE'S PAST ASSOCIATES

SOLDIERS OF THE CRIMSON KING
See WARRIORS OF THE SCARLET EYE

SOMBRA CORPORATION (SOMBRA GROUP)
NORTH CENTRAL POSITRONICS, LaMERK INDUSTRIES, and MILLS CONSTRUCTION AND SOMBRA REAL ESTATE are all part of the Sombra Group, a corporate conglomerate which serves the CRIMSON KING. Like its subsidiary North Central Positronics, Sombra has been a leader in mind-to-mind communication since the ten thousands. Mills Construction and North Central Positronics were responsible for building the MIND-TRAP under the DIXIE PIG. They are also refurbishing the PLAZA–PARK HYATT hotel where SUSANNAH-MIO stays during her trip to 1999 NEW YORK.

Incorporated in NASSAU, Sombra is a closed corporation that deals in technology, real estate, and construction. This dangerous conglomerate is after both the Vacant LOT and the magical ROSE which grows there. As CALVIN TOWER realizes when he hesitates at selling the Vacant Lot to them, if Sombra can't appeal to a person's greed, they will resort to terrorizing them. Just as the servants of the Red King use the WOLVES of END-WORLD to steal the children of the BORDERLANDS, the Red King's men use BALAZAR and his thugs to intimidate those who stand in their way in our world.

Not only are Sombra's employees determined to destroy the DARK TOWER, the Lot, and the Rose, but they also bear grudges against those who hunt down the VAMPIRES who serve the Outer Dark. When the vampire-killer FATHER CALLAHAN is working at the LIGHTHOUSE SHELTER in DETROIT, the Sombra Corporation lays a trap for him. Telling Callahan and his associates that their shelter has been awarded a million dollars, they lure the unsuspecting men to the TISHMAN BUILDING (982 Michigan Avenue), so that they can pick up their check. However, rather than receiving the money, Callahan finds himself in the hands of the evil RICHARD P. SAYRE, the LOW MAN who is also Sombra's executive vice president. Rather than submitting to the bites of Sayre's AIDS-infected TYPE THREE VAMPIRES, Callahan jumps out the window. He awakes in MID-WORLD's WAY STATION.

V:68–69, V:95–106 *(and rose)*, V:188 *(Mills Construction and Sombra)*, V:451, V:453–57, V:503, V:522, V:527, V:528, V:539, V:550, VI:91–92, VI:109, VI:202, VI:219, VI:269, VI:336, VI:359, VI:381, VII:37, VII:48, VII:75, VII:125, VII:127, VII:492

SAYRE, RICHARD P.: *See* CAN-TOI, *listed separately*

SKANK, BANGO: *See* SKANK, BANGO, *listed separately*

SOMBRA ESCORT: V:451

SOMBRA SECRETARIES: V:454

SOMBRA SUBSIDIARIES:

   LaMERK INDUSTRIES: *Listed separately*

   MILLS CONSTRUCTION AND SOMBRA REAL ESTATE: *Listed separately*

   NORTH CENTRAL POSITRONICS: *Listed separately*

SONESH, TASSA OF

See WARRIORS OF THE SCARLET EYE: DEVAR-TOI CHARACTERS: HUMANS

SOO LINES

Once upon a time, the Soo Line trains ran to the DEVAR-TOI. By the time our *tet* reaches THUNDERCLAP, the line no longer runs. However, one of their boxcars is still stalled on the tracks just southwest of the Devar's fence. Roland, JAKE, and EDDIE hide behind this stalled car (as well as some of the others) while they are waiting to attack the Devar.

VII:340

SOOBIE

See TULL CHARACTERS: KENNERLY, JUBAL

SOPHIA (SISTER BLUE)

See DEAN, SUSANNAH: ODETTA HOLMES'S ASSOCIATES

SOUTH AMERICAN SEABEES

According to FRANK ARMITAGE, one of the humes who recruits BREAKERS to work in END-WORLD, back in 1946 a consortium of wealthy South American businessmen hired U.S. engineers, construction workers, and roughnecks to work for them. These workers were known as the South American Seabees. The consortium gave the North Americans four-year contracts. The workers were extremely well paid, but were not allowed to go home during their term of employment. Like the South American Seabees, Armitage explains, the workers that he hires also have to remain in their place of employment until their contracts expire. However, what this servant of the CRIMSON KING neglects to tell TED BRAUTIGAN and the other recruits is that their term of service in the DEVAR-TOI will not expire until the (literal) end of the world.

VII:284

SOUTH STAR
  See GODS OF MID-WORLD: OLD MOTHER

SOYCHAK, MR.
  See KING, STEPHEN

SPALTER
  See CALLA BRYN STURGIS CHARACTERS: OTHER CHARACTERS

SPEAKING-RING DEMON
  See DEMON ELEMENTALS

SPICS OF SUPREMACY
  See DEAN, SUSANNAH: DETTA WALKER'S ASSOCIATES

SPIDERS, LORD OF THE
  See CRIMSON KING

SPIER, JOHN T.
  See KING, STEPHEN: FAN MAIL/HATE MAIL

SPINELLI, FRANK
  See CALLAHAN, FATHER DONALD FRANK: CALLAHAN'S HOME SHELTER ASSOCIATES

SPIRIT OF THE SNOW COUNTRY
  See NORTH CENTRAL POSITRONICS

SPIRIT OF TOPEKA
  See NORTH CENTRAL POSITRONICS

SPLINTER HARRY
  See TREE VILLAGE CHARACTERS

SPOT HUNTER
  See TREE VILLAGE CHARACTERS

STARKBLAST
A starkblast is a type of powerful, fast-moving storm which is unique to Mid-World. Its features include steep and sudden drops in temperature accompanied by strong winds. It has been known to cause great destruction and loss of life in civilized portions of the world. In primitive areas, entire tribes are often wiped out by it. When Roland was a boy, starkblasts used to come down on the GREAT WOODS north of NEW CANAAN once or twice a year, though luckily for the people living in GILEAD, the storms usually rose into the air and dispersed before reaching the city. Unfortunately, those living farther north were not so lucky. Roland remembers seeing cartloads of frozen bodies being drawn down GILEAD ROAD soon after a starkblast. He assumed that the corpses were those

of farming families that didn't have BILLY-BUMBLERS to warn them about the coming storm.

Most starkblasts originate in the northernmost reaches of Mid-World, where the snows never end and New Earth never comes. When warm southern air reaches that northerly clime, a great funnel begins to form. This funnel breathes like a lung, sucking up the frigid air from below, which in turn makes it swirl faster, creating a self-sustaining energy pump. Soon enough, this funnel-like storm finds the nearest PATH OF THE BEAM and begins to travel along it toward human habitations.

Days before a starkblast is due to blow, the weather becomes unseasonably warm. To those without bumblers to alert them to the approaching danger, it might seem pleasantly balmy. However, those with bumblers will begin to notice their furry companions' strange behavior. First of all, the bumblers will sit very still, their noses lifted to the coming storm, their eyes bright and dreamy, and their little corkscrew-like tails tucked around their bodies. As the storm comes closer, the excited bumblers will begin to turn in circles. In fact, some (like JAKE's pet bumbler OY) will become so mesmerized by the approaching storm that they will not seek shelter. (Luckily, Jake grabbed Oy and carried him into the safety of the GOOK Meetinghouse before the storm could freeze him and sweep him away.)

When the starkblast finally descends it hits full force. In less than an hour, the temperature falls as much as forty limbits below freezing. Ponds freeze in an instant, with a sound like bullets breaking window-panes. Birds turned to ice-statues and fall from the sky like rocks. Grass turned to glass. Yet the cold is only part of the horror. The winds of a starkblast are gale-force, snapping the frozen trees like straws. Such storms often roll for three hundred wheels before lifting off into the sky as suddenly as they came.

Strong winds, especially the winds of the starkblast, unify the three inter-linked stories of *The Wind Through the Keyhole*. At the beginning of the novel, ROLAND, EDDIE, SUSANNAH, Jake, and Oy are traveling along the Path of the Beam toward CALLA BRYN STURGIS, completely unaware of the trouble about to beset them. Thanks to Oy's strange behavior, and also the observations of the ancient WHYE ferryman BIX, Roland's *tet* has enough forewarning to hide up in the MEETING HALL of a deserted village called Gook. They collect firewood and get a fire blazing just in time.

As the freezing winds rage outside of the building, Roland tells his *tet* a story from his youth. Just after the death of his mother, GABRIELLE DESCHAIN, Roland and his *ka*-mate, JAMIE DeCURRY, were sent to the town of DEBARIA to investigate murders committed by a shapeshifting monster known as a SKIN-MAN. While protecting the only living witness to one of the skin-man's massacres—a young blond boy named BILL STREETER—the younger Roland also recounted a story. Serenaded by the winds of a simoom, Roland told Young Bill a tale called "The Wind Through the Keyhole," which told the story of a boy named TIM ROSS. While on a quest to find the wizard MAERLYN, Young Tim was faced with the horrors of a starkblast.

W:4 *(Oy's behavior)*, W:5 *(Oy)*, W:13–15, W:16, W:17–31 *(storm is coming)*, W:46, W:67, W:68, W:166, W:173, W:220 *(throcken)*, W:224–27 *(throcken,*

Fagonard tribe), W:232–47, W:252, W:254, W:255, W:256–57, W:258, W:305–6

STAUNTON, ANDREW
A NEW YORK CITY foot patrolman. His partner is NORRIS WEAVER.
II:380–84, III:262 *(indirect)*

STEVENS, BELINDA
See PIPER SCHOOL CHARACTERS

STOCKWORTH, RICHARD
See JOHNS, ALAIN

STOKES, DUSTIN
See TREE VILLAGE CHARACTERS: STOKES, DUSTIN

STONEHAM, MAINE, CHARACTERS
See MAINE CHARACTERS

STOUTHEART, TIM
See ROSS, TIM

STRAW WILLEM
See TREE VILLAGE CHARACTERS

STRAKER
See VAMPIRES: TYPE ONE: BARLOW, KURT

STRAW
See CAN-TOI

STREET ANGEL
See CALLAHAN, FATHER DONALD FRANK: CALLAHAN'S HOME
SHELTER ASSOCIATES: MAGRUDER, ROWAN

STREETER, BILL (COOKIE)
See SKIN-MAN: SKIN-MAN'S VICTIMS: JEFFERSON RANCH

STREETER, OLD BILL
See STREETER, YOUNG BILL

STREETER, YOUNG BILL (YOUNG BILL OF THE JEFFERSON)
Young Bill Streeter was the only witness to the massacre at the JEFFERSON
RANCH, a crime committed by the shapeshifting SKIN-MAN whom Roland
and JAMIE DeCURRY were trying to hunt down during their stay in the railhead town of DEBARIA. Roland and Jamie found Young Bill while following
the skin-man's bloody backtrail through the ranch. As the two young gunsling-

ers stood outside an abandoned TACK SHED and hostelry, they heard moaning. They ran inside the shed, only to see a heap of old tack heaving up and down as if it were breathing. As they watched, the tangle of hames, bridles, cinch straps, and reins tumbled away to either side, birthing a terrified blue-eyed boy. The boy wore jeans and an old, unbuttoned shirt. His white-blond hair stuck out in all directions. In a trembling voice, the lad asked whether the monster was gone. As soon as Roland assured him that it was, the boy passed out.

Before the skin-man's killing spree, Young Bill (son of the ranch's cook) had been the ranch's bunkhouse boy. He'd been responsible for making bunks, coiling rope, cinching bedrolls, polishing saddles, and setting the gate at the end of the day after the horses were turned in. This was a lot of responsibility for a lad who was probably not yet eleven years old. Other than the psychopathic ranch foreman, ELROD NUTTER, who liked to pick on anyone smaller than himself, most of the proddies and pokies at the ranch were fond of Billy. TINY BRAD-DOCK taught him how to make a lasso, and Roscoe was teaching him the bow. If he'd survived, FREDDY TWO-STEP would have shown him how to brand. Sadly, the skin-man's murders left Billy not only friendless but also orphaned. Bill's da, COOKIE, numbered among the dead.

Under a willow tree which grew to one side of the Jefferson house, Roland, Jamie, and SHERIFF PEAVY questioned Bill about the night of the attack. Other than stating that he had been camping out beyond the corral, Billy could remember almost nothing. The sheriff thought that the boy's mind had been scrubbed clean by shock, but Roland knew better. Since Roland, Jamie, and Peavy knew that the skin-man was most probably a salt miner—but one who could sit a horse—Roland sent his *ka*-mate and the sheriff to LITTLE DEBARIA to round up the SALTIES who could ride. Deputy KELLIN FRYE and Kellin's son VIKKA went with them. To Vikka, Roland gave a very specific job. He was to spread the rumor that Young Bill Streeter had seen the skin-man in his human form. Roland hoped that this rumor would help to flush out the killer.

While the other lawmen and Vikka were occupied with their own job, Roland took Billy back to Debaria. On the way our gunslinger used the *howken*—or the play of a shell over his quickly moving fingers—to hypnotize Billy. While in this trance-state, Young Bill remembered the night of the murders in great detail. Since Elrod had gotten hold of a bottle and was bound to turn mean, Billy had taken his blanket and his shaddie so that he could sleep under the stars. Hours later he was awoken by screams, roars, and fighting sounds issuing from the bunkhouse. Running to the bunkhouse's grease-paper window, he peered inside. Amid rivers of blood, he saw an enormous bear tearing off the arm of Elrod Nutter and hitting him with it before biting off the man's head. Young Bill ran for the big house, but when *sai* Jefferson accidentally shot at him, Billy ran for the old hostelry and hid under the tack. Unaware of Young Bill's presence, the beast—now in the form of a giant cat—entered the hostelry, where it soon transformed into a screaming human. From his hiding place, Bill saw the skin-man's feet, and noticed that there was a blue ring tattooed around one of his ankles, and that the ring was broken by a white mark of some kind. (Roland did not realize the significance of this white mark until much later in the tale.)

After drawing forth memories from Young Bill's deep mind, Roland took the lad back to the sheriff's office in Debaria and put him in the lockup to keep him safe. He then visited Debaria's smithy, where he requested the smith to forge a silver bullet for him—the only kind of bullet that could kill a skin-man. Returning to the JAIL, Roland joined Billy in Debaria's drunk-and-disorderly cell. There, serenaded by the raging winds of a simoom and eating stew and candy, Roland told Young Bill the story of "The Wind Through the Keyhole," and of the heroic young lad named TIM ROSS, also known as Tim Stoutheart. Like Young Bill, Tim Ross's father had been murdered, and Tim was destined to identify his killer.

When Jamie DeCurry, Sheriff Peavy, Constable WILL WEGG, Deputy Frye, and Frye's son Vikka returned from Little Debaria with all the salties who could ride, Roland took the men into the BUSTED LUCK saloon. After giving the miners a drink, he rounded up the ten tattooed salties who had done time in the BEELIE STOCKADE. These fellows he took back to the jail. As Young Bill (pretending to be Tim Stoutheart) waited in his protective cell, the salt miners lined up according to age and paraded past. At Young Bill's request, the salties walked by a second time, but with their pants legs hiked up to show their ankles. At that point Bill recognized OLLIE ANG's blue ankle ring, which was broken by a thick line of white scar tissue which ran all the way up to Ang's knee.

What happened next transpired so quickly that neither Roland nor any of the others were able to prevent it. STEG LUKA, the oldest of the miners, grabbed Ang by the shoulders, spit in his face, and called him a murdering, skin-changing bastard. But even as Steg Luka attacked, Ang transformed into a giant snake, first ramming his body into Steg's throat and out the back of his neck, and then battening down on Will Wegg's arm, injecting him with deadly poison. As Billy screamed, the snake lunged at Roland, but before he could strike, our gunslinger shot his silver bullet into the creature's yawning mouth. In death, the skin-man transformed once again into its human form.

At the end of the tale, we are told that the orphaned Billy Streeter would be cared for by the SISTERS OF SERENITY until he came of age.
> W:79–83 *(79 described; 81 bunkhouse boy)*, W:84, W:85, W:86, W:87–97, W:98, W:99–102, W:104–6, W:267–70, W:273, W:280 *(indirect)*, W:281–82, W:283–94 *(284 Tim Stoutheart)*, W:295, W:296

MILLIE (MULE): Millie the mule was Young Bill's special friend. According to Billy, Millie was solid as a dromedary. When ROLAND took Young Bill back to the SHERIFF'S OFFICE and DEBARIA JAIL to keep him safe, the boy rode Millie. Bill's feet came almost to the ground. W:87, W:88, W:98

STREETER, BILL (COOKIE): *See* SKIN-MAN: SKIN-MAN'S VICTIMS: JEFFERSON RANCH

STREETER, OLD BILL: Young Bill's granther, or grandfather. He went into the Clearing two years before the story of the SKIN-MAN took place. W:80

STRONG, GARRETT
See CALLA BRYN STURGIS CHARACTERS: FARMERS (SMALLHOLD)

STROTHER
See DEBARIA CHARACTERS: SHERIFF'S OFFICE

STUFFY-GUYS
See MID-WORLD FOLKLORE

STUTTERING BILL
See NORTH CENTRAL POSITRONICS

SUCCUBUS
See DEMONS/SPIRITS/DEVILS

SUCKERBATS
See DEMONS/SPIRITS/DEVILS

SULLIVAN, JOHN (SULLY JOHN)
See BREAKERS: BRAUTIGAN, TED

SUNSHINE
See WIDOW SMACK

SURREY, DAVID
See PIPER SCHOOL

SUSAN
See DELGADO, SUSAN

SUSANNAH
See DEAN, SUSANNAH

SUSANNAH-MIO
See DEAN, SUSANNAH; see also MIA

SWEDISH AMBASSADOR TO THE UNITED NATIONS
See DEAN, SUSANNAH: SUSANNAH'S PRESENT ASSOCIATES: VAN WYCK, MATHIESSEN

SWORD OF ELD
See ELD, ARTHUR: EXCALIBUR

T

**TAHEEN
The *taheen* servants of the CRIMSON KING have the heads of either beasts or birds but the bodies of men. Although JAKE, CALLAHAN, and SUSANNAH see several of these bizarre creatures while in NEW YORK CITY's DIXIE PIG, most of the *taheen* work in END-WORLD. (There, at least, they don't have to pass for human.) Unlike the rat-headed CAN-TOI (or low men), the *taheen* do not hide their beaks and snouts behind humanoid masks, nor do they believe that they are *becoming* human. Consistent with their appearance, the voices of mammal-headed *taheen* sound like yelps and growls. Although the *taheen* can speak and

reason, their brains must be drastically different from ours, since their thoughts cannot be read by the psychic BREAKERS. (Any psychic trying to prog one of these creatures will only hear white noise.)

According to Roland, the *taheen* arose from neither the PRIM nor the natural world, but rather from somewhere in between. They are sometimes called the third people, though we are never told exactly what this means. Those *taheen* employed as guards at the DEVAR-TOI tend to man the watchtowers, since they have sharper eyes than either their hume or *can-toi* comrades.

If you thought the CHILDREN OF RODERICK's taste for snotty tissues was hard to stomach, you'll find *taheen* delicacies even worse. If you want to form an alliance with one of these creatures, offer him some pus. You'll make a friend for life, since the *taheen* think that pus is as sweet as candy. Unfortunately, they can't take advantage of the pimples and rashes that plague their human charges in THUNDERCLAP, since the dark land's emanations poison all human body fluids. *Taheen* don't get such blemishes themselves; however, those who work in the Devar do find that their skins tend to crack and ooze and their noses (or snouts) tend to bleed spontaneously.

The *taheen* are found in the 2003 version of *The Gunslinger,* but not the original version. In the new *Gunslinger,* Roland sees a *taheen* with a man's body but a raven's head wandering in the MOHAINE DESERT. According to the BORDER DWELLER BROWN, the *taheen* is searching for a place called ALGUL SIENTO.

V:26 *(indirect),* V:150, V:660, VII:25, VII:126, VII:129–30, VII:200, VII:201, VII:204, VII:207, VII:209, VII:221, VII:223, VII:224, VII:225, VII:226, VII:229, VII:230, VII:231, VII:235, VII:239, VII:241, VII:244, VII:269, VII:281, VII:289, VII:292–93, VII:300, VII:326, VII:337, VII:352, VII:356–82 *(Devar-Toi battle),* VII:392, VII:393, VII:394, VII:448, VII:554, VII:808

BEAR-HEADED TAHEEN: A *taheen* employed at the DEVAR-TOI. VII:381

BEAVER-HEADED TAHEEN: This *taheen* guards the DEVAR's east watchtower. He's shot by our *ka-tet* mate SUSANNAH DEAN. VII:350, VII:364

BIRDMEN TAHEEN:

CANARY/CANARYMAN/MEIMAN/TWEETY BIRD/WASEAU-TAHEEN: Meiman (who is called Canary by his friends, Canaryman by SUSANNAH DEAN, and Tweety Bird by JAKE CHAMBERS) has a feathered, dark yellow head, eyes like drops of liquid tar, and talon-hands. He is one of the first true *taheen* which Susannah Dean (and later Jake Chambers and PERE CALLAHAN) encounters in the DIXIE PIG.

Like the other true *taheen,* Canary does not wear a humanoid mask, even when he is in CALLA NEW YORK. However, he seems to like human clothing. When we encounter him in the Dixie Pig, Canary is wearing jeans and a plain white shirt, like any ordinary American.

Canary appears to be a fairly high-ranking WARRIOR OF THE SCARLET EYE. However, this does not prevent him from being mesmerized by the magical SCRIMSHAW TURTLE (or CAN-TAH) which Callahan uses to paralyze his enemies at the Pig. Unluckily for Jake and Callahan, Canary and his *can-toi* friends manage to break out of their paralysis. However, Callahan manages to shoot this nasty bird-man (as well as one of his *can-toi* accomplices) before turning his gun on himself. VI:366, VII:6–15, VII:26, VII:28, VII:104

JAKLI: This raven-headed *taheen* works at the DEVAR-TOI and is often in the company of FINLI O'TEGO and the Devar Master, PIMLI PRENTISS. Jakli has residual wings, which he flaps when he is excited or upset. We can assume that he has arms as well (otherwise he'd have a hard time wielding weapons). Like most of his comrades at the Devar, he is killed by our *tet*. VII:241, VII:352, VII:358–59, VII:362, VII:371–74, VII:379–82

JEY (GEE, HAWK-HEADED MAN): Hawk-headed Jey is one of the WARRIORS OF THE SCARLET EYE who accompany SUSANNAH DEAN and MIA from the DIXIE PIG to the FEDIC DOGAN, where the two of them are destined to give birth to MORDRED of DISCORDIA. In the chaotic battle which transpires after Mordred's birth (and after the *dan-tete*'s first meal, which happens to be his mother, Mia), Susannah shoots Jey. VI:370–84, VII:22, VII:55–69, VII:71

ROOSTER-HEADED TAHEEN (FOGHORN LEGHORN): This *taheen* works at the DEVAR-TOI. Roland's *tet* doesn't kill him, but old Foghorn finds the thought of life outside of his THUNDERCLAP home extremely daunting. VII:392–93, VII:394

CAT ON LEGS (HOUSE-CAT TAHEEN, DISHWASHER NUMBER ONE): JAKE CHAMBERS decapitates this nasty, hissing dishwasher in the kitchens of the DIXIE PIG. VII:82

RAT-HEADED TAHEEN:

ALIA (NURSE): Although Alia has the head of a rat, she does not wear a humanoid mask. Hence, it seems likely that she considers herself *taheen* rather than CAN-TOI. As servants of the RED KING go, Alia doesn't seem so bad. While MIA groans with labor pains in the EXTRACTION ROOM of the FEDIC DOGAN, Alia offers what comfort she can. During the Fedic Dogan battle which takes place after Mordred's birth, Alia is wounded in the knee. She flees the fray and so survives. We never learn what happens to her. VI:378–84, VII:21, VII:22, VII:56–69, VII:75

ANDREW: *See* CAN-TOI

HABER: *See* CAN-TOI

SAYRE, RICHARD P.: *See* CAN-TOI

STRAW: *See* CAN-TOI

TIRANA: *See* CAN-TOI

STOAT-HEADED TAHEEN:

LAMLA OF GALEE: Lamla has the head of a stoat and narrow feet with thorn-like nails. He, his hume companion FLAHERTY, and several LOW MEN pursue JAKE through the MIND-TRAP located below the DIXIE PIG. Although he survives Flaherty's murderous temper tantrum (which takes place just after Jake manages to elude their posse by slipping through the NEW YORK/FEDIC DOORWAY), Lamla is brought down by Roland's guns. VII:104–9, VII:111 *(posse)*, VII:112, VII:129, VII:133–35, VII:528

WARTHOG TAHEEN:

DIXIE PIG CHEF: JAKE CHAMBERS encounters this imposing creature in the steamy kitchens of the DIXIE PIG. Warthog—dressed in a chef's whites—stands seven feet tall and speaks a dialect which is only marginally comprehensible. After Jake kills his HOUSE-CAT TAHEEN dishwasher,

Warthog insists that Jake take up dish-scrubbing. Jake resumes his special art of dish-throwing instead and slices off Warthog's head. VII:81–83, VII:86

WEASEL-HEADED TAHEEN:

FINLI O'TEGO (FINLI OF THE TEGO CLAN, THE WEASEL, THE WEASE): Three-hundred-year-old Finli O'Tego is head of security at the DEVAR-TOI. He stands over seven feet tall, which is damn big, even by *taheen* standards. PIMLI PRENTISS, the Devar Master, thinks Finli would make a great basketball player. He is probably right, since a *taheen* like Finli could run up and down a basketball court for hours and not even get winded.

True to his nickname, "the Wease" has the head of a weasel complete with fur, large black eyes, and needle-sharp teeth. Like many of the other *taheen* at the Devar-Toi, Finli likes to wear lots of gold chains. At some point in the past he even docked his tail, a fashion statement he regrets since the act will probably ultimately land him in the HELL OF DARKNESS.

Although Finli is *taheen* and the Devar Master is hume, the two are close friends. In fact, when EDDIE DEAN puts a wounded Finli out of his misery by shooting him in the head, the dying Pimli Prentiss shoots Eddie. Our *tet*-mate dies from the resulting head wound. V:573–76, V:610, V:611, V:660, V:702, VII:200, VII:203, VII:204, VII:205, VII:207, VII:212, VII:215, VII:220–27, VII:230–45, VII:261, VII:272, VII:292, VII:297, VII:298–99, VII:300, VII:325, VII:341, VII:343–48, VII:358–59, VII:361–62, VII:371–74, VII:377, VII:380–82, VII:383–84, VII:385

OTHER TAHEEN (NOT DESCRIBED):

GASKIE O'TEGO: Gaskie is the DEVAR-TOI's deputy security chief—second only to FINLI O'TEGO. Since the two of them share the same clan name, it seems likely that they are related. During the Devar's final battle, Gaskie is shot by SUSANNAH DEAN. VII:300, VII:356–57, VII:362, VII:371–74

HUMMA O'TEGO: Humma was the Devar-Toi Master who sentenced the CAN-TOI rapist CAMERON to death. Humma lost his job (and possibly his life) after TED BRAUTIGAN escaped the BREAKER prison. VII:286, VII:297, VII:326, VII:343

TALITHA UNWIN
   See RIVER CROSSING CHARACTERS

TAMRA, SISTER
   See ELURIA, LITTLE SISTERS OF

TASLEY, HOWARD
   See TREE VILLAGE CHARACTERS

TASSA
   See WARRIORS OF THE SCARLET EYE: DEVAR-TOI CHARACTERS: HUMANS

TASSENBAUM, DAVID SEYMOUR

David Tassenbaum is married to IRENE TASSENBAUM. According to his wife, David and his egghead friends created the Internet. Since Tassenbaum is associated with NORTH CENTRAL POSITRONICS (at least we see a Positronics magnet on his refrigerator), we can assume that the "information highway" is an incredibly sinister cultural force. (Hence, be wary of your keyboard.) Both David and Irene are staunch Republicans.

VII:423, VII:425 *(indirect)*, VII:429 *(indirect)*, VII:431, VII:435, VII:469, VII:470–71 *(North Central Positronics)*, VII:482, VII:486, VII:487, VII:490, VII:521, VI:522

EMERSON, SONNY: Sonny Emerson is David Tassenbaum's friend. They like to go fishing together. VII:470

TASSENBAUM, IRENE (IRENE CANTORA, DAUGHTER OF ABRAHAM)

Middle-aged Irene Tassenbaum, a staunch Republican, was born Irene Cantora in STATEN ISLAND, NEW YORK. Her computer-wiz husband, DAVID, helped to create the Internet. The two of them are extremely wealthy.

Although they live most of the year in MANHATTAN, Irene and David spend their summers in the old CULLUM cabin on KEYWADIN POND, located in EAST STONEHAM, MAINE. Hence, Irene is in the EAST STONEHAM GENERAL STORE when Roland and JAKE appear there in 1999. Although she seems an unlikely heroine, Irene Tassenbaum plays her own small but important part in the Dark Tower saga.

Kidnapped by Roland, Jake, and OY, Irene drives our three *tet*-mates first to STEPHEN KING's house in LOVELL, Maine, then to SLAB CITY HILL, where King is about to be run down by a Dodge minivan. Thanks to her, our *tet* arrives just in time to save the writer, but since *ka* always demands that a blood-price be paid if a blood-price be owed, Jake dies in King's place. While driving bereaved Roland and Oy to New York City so that Roland can meet with the TET CORPORATION, Irene becomes Roland's lover. At the end of her adventure, Irene returns to her husband. However, she seems to be a changed person; the WHITE has touched her life.

VII:423–33, VII:434–38, VII:441–43, VII:444–45, VII:449–65, VII:469–71, VII:475–90, VII:504, VII:510, VII:520–25, VII:535, VII:573

TAVERY, FRANCINE
See CALLA BRYN STURGIS CHARACTERS: OTHER CHARACTERS

TAVERY, FRANK
See CALLA BRYN STURGIS CHARACTERS: OTHER CHARACTERS

TAXI DRIVERS

TAXI DRIVER NUMBER ONE: When JAKE, CALLAHAN, and OY are propelled through the UNFOUND DOOR into 1999 NEW YORK, this dashiki- and fez-wearing driver almost hits Oy. Jake threatens to shoot him. VI:309–13, VI:322

TAXI DRIVER NUMBER TWO: This Jamaican cabbie takes CALLAHAN and JAKE to the TWIN TOWERS. They don't tip him very well. VI:333–34

TAXI DRIVER NUMBER THREE: SUSANNAH/MIA's driver takes them to Sixtieth and Lexington, close to the DIXIE PIG. VI:347–49

TAXI DRIVER NUMBER FOUR: This driver drops JAKE and CALLAHAN off near the DIXIE PIG. VI:338

TELFORD, GEORGE
See CALLA BRYN STURGIS CHARACTERS: RANCHERS

TENTACLED MONSTER
See DEMONS/SPIRITS/DEVILS (LESSER DEMONS OF THE PRIM)

TET CORPORATION (KA-TET OF THE ROSE)
In *Wolves of the Calla*, the Tet Corporation is nothing more than a white lie fabricated by EDDIE DEAN. Although the lie is for a good cause (Eddie wants CALVIN TOWER to sell the Vacant LOT to his spontaneously incorporated *ka-tet* so that they can save the magical ROSE from the destructive SOMBRA CORPORATION), it is nonetheless an untruth. No Tet Corporation exists, and although SUSANNAH DEAN is an heiress in her own *where* and *when*, the newly formed Tet has no way to access her HOLMES DENTAL INDUSTRIES fortune to pay for the expensive SECOND AVENUE plot which they wish to buy.

However, sometimes *ka*'s will works through such odd twists of chance (and through the seemingly silly utterances that escape the mouth of a *ka-mai*). Although in 1977 (when Eddie spins his tale in the back room of the MANHATTAN RESTAURANT OF THE MIND) Tet is no more than a pipe dream, by 1999 (the KEYSTONE YEAR in the KEYSTONE WORLD) the Tet Corporation is a powerful reality.

Through the efforts of JOHN CULLUM (the *dan-tete* that Roland and Eddie meet in EAST STONEHAM, MAINE, in 1977), the lawyerly skills of Calvin Tower's friend AARON DEEPNEAU, and the financial clout of MOSES CARVER, Susannah Dean's godfather, Tet takes form in our world. When Roland visits the corporation in 1999, it is housed in 2 HAMMARSKJÖLD PLAZA, a towering black building located on the former Vacant Lot. Just inside the building's lobby is a small, protected garden called the GARDEN OF THE BEAM. In it grows the sacred Rose. Just as Eddie and Roland had envisioned and hoped back in 1977, when they held their final long palaver with John Cullum in LOVELL, Maine, Tet has accomplished its three major tasks. It has protected the Rose; it has watched out for the writer STEPHEN KING; and it has screwed Sombra Corporation whenever possible.

When Roland holds palaver with Moses Carver, MARIAN CARVER, and NANCY DEEPNEAU in Tet's headquarters in 1999, they give our gunslinger a Patek Philippe pocket watch engraved with three symbols—a key, a Rose, and a Tower. According to the psychic GOOD-MIND FOLK whom Tet employs, the watch will either stop or run backward once Roland gets close to the DARK TOWER. These three leaders of the Tet Corporation also give our gunslinger a copy of the book *Insomnia* and return AUNT TALITHA's gold crucifix to him (the one Roland gave to John Cullum and which spoke to Moses Carver in the voice of Susannah Dean). The book is the only one of the three gifts which Roland does not take on his journey. (He leaves it with IRENE TASSENBAUM.)

True to the Good-Mind Folk's prediction, the Patek Philippe runs backward once Roland reaches the end of his journey. V:527, V:538, VI:189, VI:201, VI:202, VI:267–70 *(merger with Holmes Dental)*, VI:319, VII:37, VII:48, VII:123, VII:125, VII:146, VII:479, VII:490, VII:496–520, VII:586, VII:812

CALVINS, THE: The Calvins (who took their name in honor of the grumpy bibliophile CALVIN TOWER) are a group of researchers hired by the Tet Corporation to read all of STEPHEN KING's books. These scholars spend their working time cross-referencing King's novels by character, setting, and theme. They also trace any of King's characters who live or may once have lived on KEYSTONE EARTH.

According to the Calvins, the novel *Insomnia* is of central importance to Roland's quest since it contains a direct reference to the CRIMSON KING, and since it predicts that the artist PATRICK DANVILLE may play an important part in Roland's future. VII:509, VII:511–14

CARVER, MARIAN ODETTA: Marian Odetta Carver was born when her father, MOSES CARVER, was seventy. She is a tall, stately black woman with the beautiful but hard face of a warrior. (She stands six foot six.) Marian has been president of the Tet Corporation since her father retired in 1997, at the age of ninety-eight. VII:498–520

CARVER, MOSES: See FOUNDING FATHERS, *listed below*

CULLUM, JOHN: See FOUNDING FATHERS, *listed below*

DEEPNEAU, AARON: See FOUNDING FATHERS, *listed below*

DEEPNEAU, ED: See DEEPNEAU, ED, *listed separately*

DEEPNEAU, NANCY REBECCA: Nancy Rebecca Deepneau is the granddaughter of AARON DEEPNEAU's older brother. She is also a high-ranking member of the Tet Corporation. According to Roland, she is a green-eyed beauty. VII:492–520

FOUNDING FATHERS (KA-TET OF THE ROSE, OLD FARTS OF THE APOCALYPSE, THREE TOOTHLESS MUSKETEERS): VII:496–98, VII:499

  CARVER, MOSES ISAAC (DADDY MOSE, POP MOSE): Moses Carver (called Pop Mose by his goddaughter, SUSANNAH DEAN) was DAN HOLMES's accountant and friend. After Dan Holmes's first heart attack, Moses handled the financial side of HOLMES DENTAL INDUSTRIES.

  Moses Carver is one of the three men that Roland and EDDIE choose to found the Tet Corporation. By the time Roland arrives in 1999 NEW YORK, one-hundred-year-old Moses is the only living member of the original founding fathers. He has officially retired, but his daughter, MARIAN ODETTA CARVER, runs the corporation. V:43, V:101, V:102, V:103, VI:268, VI:270, VII:36, VII:37, VII:38, VII:48, VII:119, VII:123, VII:124, VII:125–27, VII:141, VII:496–520, VII:579, VII:654, VII:656

  CULLUM, JOHN (*SAI* YANKEE FLANNEL SHIRT, JOHN OF EAST STONEHAM): John Cullum, called John of East Stoneham by Roland, is the elderly bachelor who becomes Roland and EDDIE's ally when they fight BALAZAR'S MEN at the EAST STONEHAM GENERAL STORE in EAST STONEHAM, MAINE, in 1977. At first, Eddie refers to him as Mr. Flannel Shirt, but by the end of their acquaintance Cullum has won the respect of both gunslingers. Though he is far from young, Cullum is tough and resilient. A caretaker by trade, he eventually becomes (at least on our level of the DARK TOWER) one of the most important guardians of the ROSE. Although Cullum helps Roland and Eddie defeat Balazar's men, his role in the larger war between Light and Dark is sizable. It is Cullum who shows Eddie and Roland CARA LAUGHS, the magic door spun from the substance of the PRIM. It is also Cullum whom Eddie and Roland name as executive vice president of the Tet Corporation, the company formed to protect the Rose. Cullum dies of a gunshot wound in 1989. VI:130–82, VI:186, VI:200, VI:209, VI:210, VI:215, VI:270, VI:271, VI:274, VI:285, VI:301, VII:18, VII:19, VII:20, VII:24, VII:31, VII:34, VII:38–48 *(38 Waterford* dan-tete*?)*, VII:52, VII:114, VII:115–31, VII:141, VII:305, VII:414, VII:423, VII:428, VII:429, VII:432, VII:434, VII:438, VII:469, VII:487, VII:496–98 *(498 died in 1989 of a gunshot wound)*, VII:499, VII:519

> **AIDAN (YOUNG NEPHEW):** John Cullum's grandnephew. In 1977, he is three years old and full of questions. VI:180
>
> **FATHER:** VI:158 *(folks)*
>
> **GRANDPARENTS:** VI:158
>
> **MOTHER:** VI:158 *(folks)*, VI:160 *(ma)*
>
> **NEPHEW (UNNAMED SMOKING NEPHEW):** In John Cullum's opinion, his nephew is too young to smoke, so he gives the boy's stale cigarettes to Roland. Since Roland isn't used to filters, he thinks that people on our level of the DARK TOWER like to inhale murky air. VI:160
>
> **NIECE:** VII:41
>
> **RUSSERT, DONNIE (FRIEND):** *See* MAINE CHARACTERS, *listed separately*
>
> **VERMONT FRIEND:** Cullum used to work with this man at the Maine State Prison. VI:181, VI:182

DEEPNEAU, AARON (CHEMOTHERAPY KID, AIRY, MR. GAI COCKNIF EN YOM, VOICE NUMBER TWO): Aaron Deepneau made his first appearance in the Dark Tower series back in *The Waste Lands*. In that book he met JAKE CHAMBERS in the MANHATTAN RESTAURANT OF THE MIND, a bookshop owned by his anally retentive friend CALVIN TOWER. Aaron explained Samson's riddle to Jake, and also informed him about the intellectual importance of riddling. Not only was Aaron a fan of riddles and of Existentialism (when Jake met him he was reading *The Plague*), but he was also a pretty good folksinger. According to Calvin Tower, Deepneau was hanging around BLEECKER STREET before Bob Dylan could blow more than an open G on his Hohner.

Although he is about seventy years old and ill with cancer when we meet him again in *Wolves of the Calla*, Aaron has no shortage of healthy courage. When BALAZAR'S MEN threaten Tower's life because he will not sell the magical Vacant LOT to the SOMBRA CORPORATION, Aaron escapes with his friend to MAINE. Later, and despite Tower's protests, Aaron writes up the "selling papers," which bestow ownership of the Lot upon Roland, EDDIE, and the newly created Tet Corporation, a company which he then helps to develop. (On a humorous note, Deepneau draws up the contract on a piece of paper that has a cartoon of a beaver on it and the caption "Dam Important Things to Do.")

In *Wolves of the Calla*, we learn that Deepneau and Tower are destined to save FATHER CALLAHAN's life when he is attacked by the HITLER BROTHERS in the TURTLE BAY WASHATERIA in 1981. During this adventure, Deepneau and Tower keep their identities secret. Callahan calls Deepneau both "Voice Number Two" and "Mr. Gai Cocknif En Yom." (The latter name comes from the Yiddish insult which Deepneau screams at the Hitler Brothers. It means "Go shit in the ocean.")

When Roland visits Tet's headquarters in 1999, he meets Aaron's grandniece, NANCY REBECCA DEEPNEAU. Unfortunately, Aaron succumbed to his cancer in 1992. III:115–18, III:155–56, III:279, IV:28, IV:46, V:56, V:58, V:62–64, V:100, V:168–69, V:437–42 *(as calvary, as Voice Number Two, and as Mr. Gai Cocknif En Yom)*, V:447–48 *(cavalry)*, V:471, V:518, V:528, V:530, V:537, V:538, V:542, V:544, V:545, V:550, V:584–85, V:600 *(friend)*, V:623–24, V:626–28, V:703–4, V:705, V:706, V:709, VI:35, VI:36, VI:81, VI:142, VI:163–68, VI:177, VI:183–212, VI:214–16, VI:269, VI:270, VII:18, VII:19, VII:34, VII:37–38, VII:39, VII:48, VII:122, VII:123, VII:125, VII:126, VII:128, VII:141, VII:495, VII:496–98 *(lived until 1992)*, VII:499, VII:513

MOTHER (UNNAMED): VI:202

SISTER AND TWO BROTHERS: V:538

GOOD-MIND FOLK: Like the CALVINS, the Good-Mind Folk are a group of researchers hired by the Tet Corporation. Whereas the Calvins are scholars, the Good-Mind Folk are psychics. Their headquarters are located on a ranch in TAOS, NEW MEXICO. Although they squabble a lot, the Good-Mind Folk and the Calvins work together. VII:507–8, VII:510, VII:517, VII:586 *(watch)*

FRED TOWNE: Fred is the most talented of the Good-Mind Folk. His predictions are many and they are rarely wrong. Fred is the Tet employee who states that Roland's Patek Philippe watch will either stop or run backward once he nears the DARK TOWER. VII:517, VII:518

GUARD AT DIXIE PIG: VII:523

HAMMARSKJÖLD PLAZA ASSOCIATION: VII:505

LIMOUSINE DRIVER: VII:520–21

OLD FARTS OF THE APOCALYPSE: See FOUNDING FATHERS, *listed above*

SECRETARY: VII:504

SECURITY GUARDS AT HEADQUARTERS: VII:495 *(rose)*, VII:496 *(Tet headquarters)*, VII:505 *(Tet headquarters)*

THREE TOOTHLESS MUSKETEERS: See FOUNDING FATHERS, *listed above*

THINNY
See entry in PORTALS

**THOMAS OF GILEAD (THOMAS WHITMAN)
The Dark Tower series contains references to two different characters named Thomas. One was a gunslinger companion of Roland's youth who witnessed Roland's coming-of-age battle against CORT. The second was a young man from the novel *Eyes of the Dragon*. This second Thomas (who met Roland only

briefly) was in pursuit of RANDALL FLAGG. (For pages including references to Flagg's pursuer, see entry under R.F.) In the 2003 version of *The Gunslinger*, we learn that Roland's friend Thomas had the last name Whitman.

I:162 *(Roland's childhood friend)*, I:167–73 *(witnesses Roland's coming of age)*

THOMPSON, FLIP
See KING, STEPHEN

THONNIE
See MANNI

THORIN, CORAL
See HAMBRY CHARACTERS: SEAFRONT

THORIN, HART
See HAMBRY CHARACTERS: SEAFRONT

THORIN, OLIVE
See HAMBRY CHARACTERS: SEAFRONT

THREE TOOTHLESS MUSKETEERS
See TET CORPORATION: FOUNDING FATHERS

THROCKEN
See BILLY-BUMBLERS; *see also* OY
BABY THROCKEN: Under extreme duress, NIGEL, the robotic butler we meet in the FEDIC DOGAN, gives this baby billy-bumbler to MORDRED so that the spider-boy can suck it dry. Softhearted Nigel suffers a complete mechanical meltdown because of it. VII:163–64, VII:166, VII:180, VII:182

THROCKEN AND THE DRAGON
See DRAGON

TIA JAFFORDS
See CALLA BRYN STURGIS CHARACTERS: ROONTS

TIAN JAFFORDS
See JAFFORDS FAMILY

TICK-TOCK
See GRAYS: GRAY HIGH COMMAND

TIGER, IMMORTAL
See ROSE

TILLY
See GRAYS: GRAY HIGH COMMAND

TIM STOUTHEART
See ROSS, TIM

TIMBERSMITH FARM CHARACTERS
See SKIN-MAN: SKIN-MAN'S VICTIMS

TINY BRADDOCK
See SKIN-MAN: SKIN-MAN'S VICTIMS: JEFFERSON RANCH

TIRANA
See CAN-TOI

TODASH DEMONS
See DEMONS/SPIRITS/DEVILS

TOMAS, MARIA
See HAMBRY CHARACTERS: HAMBRY MAYOR'S HOUSE (SEAFRONT)

TOOK, EBEN
See CALLA BRYN STURGIS CHARACTERS: OTHER CHARACTERS

TOOK, OLD
See CALLA BRYN STURGIS CHARACTERS: OTHER CHARACTERS

TOOK FAMILY
See CALLA BRYN STURGIS CHARACTERS: OTHER CHARACTERS

TOOK (TOOK'S OUTLAND MERCANTILE)
See *WIND THROUGH THE KEYHOLE:* CHARACTERS MET BETWEEN
GREEN PALACE AND RIVER WHYE

TOOTHAKER, ELVIRA
See MAINE CHARACTERS

TOPEKA CHARACTERS
At the beginning of *Wizard and Glass,* Roland and his *ka-tet* journey on
BLAINE the Insane Mono and crash into an alternative version of TOPEKA,
KANSAS. According to Roland, Topeka is where MID-WORLD ends and END-
WORLD begins. It is also where the first part of our *tet's* quest is completed.
Although this alternative version of Kansas is much like the state found in the
KEYSTONE WORLD, this version of Topeka has been devastated by the super-
flu virus, a disease that killed off most of America's population in STEPHEN
KING's related novel, *The Stand.*
    CORCORAN, JOHN: *Topeka Capital Journal* correspondent. IV:74
    HACKFORD, DR. MORRIS: Doctor at Topeka's St. Francis Hospital and
Medical Center. He reports on superflu. IV:74
    MONTOYA, DR. APRIL: Doctor at Stormont-Vail Regional Medical Center.
She reports on superflu. IV:74

TOPSY
Roland's horse in "Little Sisters of Eluria."
E:146–54

TOPSY THE SAILOR
See PUBES

TOREN, CALVIN
See TOWER, CALVIN

TOREN, EDDIE
See DEAN, EDDIE

TOREN, JAKE
See CHAMBERS, JAKE

TOREN, STEPHAN
Stephan Toren was CALVIN TOWER's great-great-great-grandfather. His will (written on March 19, 1846) included a piece of paper addressed to *ROLAND DESCHAIN, OF GILEAD/THE LINE OF ELD/GUNSLINGER.* Although the will itself no longer remains, the piece of paper addressed to Roland survives, as does the dead letter's envelope. The envelope bears the symbols for "unfound," symbols which also appear on BLACK THIRTEEN's box and upon the UNFOUND DOOR.
V:541–42, V:546, VI:187, VI:195

TORRES, MIGUEL
See HAMBRY CHARACTERS: SEAFRONT

TOTAL HOGS
See MUTANTS: SLOW MUTANTS

TOTEMS OF THE BEAM
See GUARDIANS OF THE BEAM

TOWER, CALVIN (CALVIN TOREN, MR. EX LIBRIS, OLD FATTY, VOICE NUMBER ONE)
Calvin Tower (born Calvin Toren) is the owner of the MANHATTAN RESTAURANT OF THE MIND, located on SECOND AVENUE. In *The Waste Lands*, he sold *Charlie the Choo-Choo* and *Riddle-De-Dum* to JAKE CHAMBERS. The Toren family (a Dutch name which means "tower") were the original custodians for the Vacant LOT, located on FORTY-SIXTH STREET and Second Avenue, and for the wild, dusky-pink ROSE which grows there. Not surprisingly, the Toren family are linked to the DESCHAIN family, who are custodians for the DARK TOWER. In fact, there is a good chance that one of Calvin's ancestors met one of Roland's forefathers, or perhaps even met Roland himself. When EDDIE DEAN visits the Manhattan Restaurant of the Mind in 1977 to convince Tower to sell the Lot to the TET CORPORATION instead of to the CRIMSON KING's

evil SOMBRA CORPORATION, Calvin shows him the envelope in which his great-great-great-grandfather kept his will. Although the dead letter has long disappeared, a single brittle sheet of paper remains, and that sheet is addressed to Roland Deschain, of GILEAD, the line of ELD.

Just as Eddie Dean saves Calvin Tower from BALAZAR's thugs when they try to force him to sell the Lot to Sombra, Tower and his friend AARON DEEP-NEAU are destined to rescue FATHER CALLAHAN as he is being attacked by the HITLER BROTHERS in the TURTLE BAY WASHATERIA in 1981. Since Deepneau and Tower try to keep their identities secret during this escapade, Callahan can only identify Tower as "Voice Number One" and "Mr. Ex Libris," the latter name derived from the words engraved on the signet ring he wears.

In *Song of Susannah,* a reluctant Tower agrees to sell both Vacant Lot and Rose to Roland and Eddie. Although Tower has little to do with the Tet Corporation once it is formed, he does make one extremely valuable contribution. Borrowing an idea he found in a science-fiction novel written by BEN SLIGHTMAN JR. (who wrote sci fi under the name DANIEL HOLMES), he tells Aaron Deepneau and the other FOUNDING FATHERS to hire precogs and telepaths to help them battle their archenemies (the Sombra Corporation) and to protect their two charges (the Rose and STEPHEN KING). These psychic GOOD-MIND FOLK prove to be extremely useful. However, another group of more ordinary researchers—hired to catalogue and index the works of Stephen King—are the ones who acknowledge Tet's debt to Tower the most openly. They christen themselves the Calvins in honor of this grumpy old bibliophile. Calvin Tower dies of a heart attack in 1990.

III:114–18, III:119, III:277, III:281, V:54, V:55–58, V:62–70, V:92, V:93, V:94–106 *(rose and Sombra),* V:118, V:168–69, V:196, V:338, V:437–42 *(as cavalry, as Voice Number One, and as Mr. Ex Libris),* V:447–48 *(cavalry),* V:471, V:503–5, V:517, V:518–50, V:584–85, V:591, V:593, V:595, V:597, V:599, V:600, V:618, V:622–24, V:626–28, V:703–4, V:705, V:706, V:709, VI:7, VI:35, VI:36, VI:81, VI:84, VI:136–37, VI:139, VI:140, VI:141, VI:142, VI:154 *(indirect),* VI:163, VI:171, VI:177–80, VI:183–212, VI:214–16, VI:269, VI:334, VII:19, VII:37–38, VII:39, VII:122 *(indirect),* VII:123, VII:128, VII:495, VII:507–8, VII:509, VII:821

BRICE, MR.: One of Calvin Tower's clients. V:543

FATHER (UNNAMED): VI:195

FIRST WIFE: V:530–31

GRAHAM, TOMMY: He owned TOM AND JERRY'S ARTISTIC DELI, which once sat on the Vacant LOT located on SECOND AVENUE and FORTY-SIXTH STREET. When the deli went bust, Tower paid for it to be torn down. V:531

GRANDFATHER (UNNAMED): VI:195

HARRIED-LOOKING WOMAN: V:593–94

MIDDLE-AGED COUPLE: V:596

SERGIO: Shop cat. He lives at the MANHATTAN RESTAURANT OF THE MIND. V:67, V:525, V:543, V:548, V:549

SHOE SHINE BOY: V:593

TOREN, STEPHAN: *See* TOREN, STEPHAN, *listed separately*

TOWNE, FRED
See TET CORPORATION: GOOD-MIND FOLK

TRAINS
See CHARLIE THE CHOO-CHOO

TRAMPAS
See CAN-TOI

TREE VILLAGE CHARACTERS
In the novel *The Wind Through the Keyhole,* Roland told YOUNG BILL STREETER the story of another brave young boy, TIM ROSS (later Tim Stoutheart), a lad who not only had to face the terrors of a STARKBLAST but (like Billy) had to identify his father's murderer. In Tim's case, the murderer was his father's best-friend and woodcutting partner, BERN KELLS.

Most of the folktale "The Wind Through the Keyhole" took place in or near Tim's home village of TREE, which was located at the farthest reaches of NORTH'RD BARONY, at the edge of an unexplored wilderness called the ENDLESS FOREST. Most village men were woodcutters, like Tim's father, BIG JACK ROSS, and his evil stepfather, Big Bern Kells. But much as the villagers loved the forest, they also feared it, and for good reason. Ten wheels beyond where the BLOSSIE GROVES ended and the IRONWOOD trees began, lay an unexplored wilderness of virgin forest and impassable swamp. According to local belief, the area contained not only the deadly leavings of the OLD PEOPLE but mythical creatures such as DRAGONS.

> **GENERAL:** W:110–11, W:112 *(stories about Widow Smack),* W:115 *(smell of forest),* W:131 *(villagers),* W:244, W:257, W:264 *(Widow Smack's burial)*
> **ANDERSON, RUPERT (BALDY ANDERSON):** In order to pay his own tax and that owed by his new wife, the widow NELL ROSS, BIG BERN KELLS sold his land to Baldy Anderson, on of Tree's big farmers. (He was originally going to sell his land to FARMER DESTRY.) Since Anderson knew Kells was desperate for money, he didn't give him full price for either his house or land. Kells remained bitter about it. W:125–26, W:133, W:171–73
>> **BOYS:** W:172
> **BALDY ANDERSON:** *See* ANDERSON, RUPERT, *above*
> **CONSTABLE HOWARD:** *See* TASLEY, HOWARD, *below*
> **COSINGTON, ADA:** *See* WOODSMEN: COSINGTON, PETER, *below*
> **COSINGTON, PETER:** *See* WOODSMEN, *below*
> **DESTRY (FARMER DESTRY, OLD DESTRY):** In order to marry NELL ROSS and pay off both their taxes, BIG BERN KELLS decided to sell his place to Farmer Destry. Old Destry had hard coin, and wanted Kells's land because it sat next to his east field. Although Destry seemed fairly honest (when TIM ROSS cut hay for him, Destry paid him in scrip, and also gave him a sack of his goodwife's sweet peppers and busturd tomatoes), Kells decided to sell to RUPERT ANDERSON instead. He regretted the decision, since Anderson was tight. W:114, W:116, W:117, W:120, W:123, W:144 *(Tim asks about dragons),* W:186 *(picture of rifle)*
>> **DESTRY BOYS:** Farmer Destry's sons. W:127

HUNTER (SPOT HUNTER): Spot Hunter got his nickname because of his freckles. Hunter and his brother, STRAW WILLEM, helped Tree's posse search for the murderer BIG BERN KELLS. W:175

RANDY: Randy was Straw Willem and Spot Hunter's big brother. He was one of the first people to see BIG BERN KELLS get drunk after his marriage to NELL ROSS. W:128

STRAW WILLEM: Straw Willem got his nickname because of his nearly colorless hair. He worked at the TREE SAWMILL with TIM ROSS. Straw Willem was the first person to tell Tim that his stepfather, BIG BERN KELLS, was drinking again. He enjoyed sharing this ugly piece of news. W:127–28, W:129, W:170, W:175, W:255

WIFE: Destry's goodwife gave a sack of sweet peppers and tomatoes to TIM ROSS after he cut hay for her husband. W:120

HAGGERTY THE NAIL: When TIM ROSS broke into his steppa BERN KELLS's trunk, he discovered a toolbox and five extra ax-heads. Tim was enraged, since Kells could have sold these rusty tools to Haggerty the Nail. Even after paying his taxes, he would have had money left over and Tim wouldn't have had to give up his lessons at the WIDOW SMACK'S COTTAGE. W:142

HODIAK (BARONY BUYER): Twice a year, Hodiak, the barony buyer, came to Tree Village sawmill to buy IRONWOOD. Ironwood commanded a high price, since it was used to make seagoing vessels. (Although Blossie wood was good for lake boats, it wasn't strong enough for sea travel.) W:111

KELLS, BIG BERN: *See* KELLS, BIG BERN, *listed separately*

KELLS, MILLICENT: *See* KELLS, BIG BERN: KELLS, MILLICENT, *listed separately*

MARCHLY, EARNEST (SLOW ERNIE MARCHLY): *See* WOODSMEN, *below*

MELLON: BERN KELLS fell off the wagon while he was talking to Mellon about the man's new stake. Kells started out with a ginger-beer, but when someone put a glass of jackaroe in front of him, he drank it without thinking and then he was off. W:128

POSSE: *See* KELLS, BIG BERN, *listed separately*

RINCON, DEF: While hiding from the POSSE that wanted to arrest him for murder, BERN KELLS spent two nights shivering in Def Rincon's barn. W:262, W:263

RIVERLY: The COVENANT MAN told TIM ROSS about Riverly's dead cows. W:158

ROSS, BIG JACK: *See* ROSS, BIG JACK, *listed separately*

ROSS, NELL: *See* ROSS, NELL, *listed separately*

ROSS, TIM: See ROSS, TIM *listed separately*

SIMONS, FRANKIE: The COVENANT MAN told TIM ROSS that Frankie Simons broke his leg. W:157–58

SPLINTER HARRY (OLD SPLINT): Splinter Harry was one of the codgers who worked part-time at the TREE SAWMILL. Old Splint was half foolish and liked to babble nonsense, pretending it was High Speech. He liked nothing better than talking about the men from Gilead who carried the big irons and went forth on quests. When Tim met the MUDMEN of the FAGONARD and pretended to be a young gunslinger, he used the phrases that Old Splint had taught him. W:202, W:205

STOKES, DUSTIN (HOT STOKES): Dustin Stokes, also known as Hot Stokes, ran a burying parlor behind his smithy. This was where the murder victim, BIG JACK ROSS, was finally laid out. W:173, W:176–78, W:179

TASLEY, HOWARD (CONSTABLE HOWARD): According to BALDIE ANDERSON, when it came to prosecuting criminals, Constable Howard wasn't worth a fart in a high wind. He spent too much time in TAVARES, either looking for poachers or visiting the woman he kept there. W:166–67, W:172

VENN, RUPERT (SAWMILL FOREMAN): Although he was TIM ROSS's foreman at the TREE SAWMILL, Tim thought that Rupert Venn was a decent *sai*. He told Tim and STRAW WILLEM that they might get more work at the mill if the season's snowfall was light. W:129

WIDOW SMACK: *See* WIDOW SMACK, *listed separately*

WOMEN OF TREE (LADIES OF TREE, NELL'S FRIENDS): After Nell was blinded by her second husband, BIG BERN KELLS, these women came to her aid. (However, none nursed Nell as devotedly as the WIDOW SMACK.) W:124 *(view Nell with pity on her wedding day)*, W:173, W:174, W:175, W:176, W:179, W:252

WOODSMEN: W:110–11, W:122, W:179

> **COSINGTON, PETER (PETER "SQUARE FELLA" COSINGTON, SQUARE FELLA COSSIE):** Square Peter Cosington and SLOW ERNIE MARCHLY cut wood on the COSINGTON-MARCHLY STAKE. Both men were friends of the Rosses. According to BIG JACK ROSS, neither Cosington nor Marchly was willing to go into the deep wood, near the FAGONARD, where the densest ironwood could be found.
>
> Before Big Ross's death, a tree fell across *sai* Cosington's back, laying him up for eight weeks. This accident, and the fact that a POOKY had taken up residence in one of their STUBS, meant that the Cosington-Marchly stake was deserted for a good stretch of time. BIG BERN KELLS took advantage of this and hid the body of his murdered partner there. When TIM ROSS told Peter Cosington, Ernie Marchly, and Baldy Anderson that Kells had thrown his father's corpse in their stream, Cosington wanted to kill Kells for the insult as well as the crime. Square Fella Cosington was one of the POSSEMEN who went after Kells. W:149, W:150, W:157 *(stake)*, W:158, W:159, W:160, W:162, W:168, W:171–73, W:176 *(found Big Ross)*, W:176–77, W:178–79, W:189 *(stake)*, W:190, W:257 *(stake)*
>
> **COSINGTON, ADA:** Ada Cosington was one of NELL ROSS's friends. After the WIDOW SMACK saved Nell's life, Ada and several other women traveled to the Ross-KELLS house to help out. W:173–74, W:175

> **KELLS, BIG BERN:** *See* KELLS, BIG BERN, *listed separately*

> **ROSS, BIG JACK:** *See* ROSS, BIG JACK, *listed separately*

> **MARCHLY, ERNEST (SLOW ERNIE MARCHLY):** Slow Ernie Marchly was SQUARE FELLA COSINGTON's cutting partner. The two of them cut the COSINGTON-MARCHLY STAKE. After a tree fell on Peter Cosington's back, laying him up for eight weeks, Ernie Marchly did not go cutting alone. Hence, his stub was deserted long enough for BIG BERN

KELLS to hide Jack Ross's body there, in a stub where a POOKY had taken up housekeeping. (Because of the pooky, the stub was left fallow even after Cosington's recovery.) Both Ernest Marchly and Peter Cosington were incensed that Kells dared to leave Ross's body on their stake. Along with BALDY ANDERSON, these two men drummed up the posse that set out to bring Bern Kells to justice. However, in the end it was Tim Ross and his mother NELL who ended Kells's evil life. W:149, W:150, W:157 *(stake)*, W:158, W:160, W:162, W:168, W:171–73, W:189 *(stake)*, W:257 *(stake)*

> WIFE: W:173

WYLAND: While doing his tax-collecting rounds, the COVENANT MAN discovered that the Wylands' baby had milk-sick. W:158

> WYLAND'S BABY: W:158

TRELAWNEY
See CAN-TOI

TRISTUM, DR. GANGLI
See CAN-TOI

TUBTHER, MR.
See DEAN, EDDIE: EDDIE'S PAST ASSOCIATES

TUDBURY, BILL AND TILL
See RIVER CROSSING CHARACTERS

TULL CHARACTERS
At the beginning of *The Gunslinger*, Roland traveled through the dying town of Tull, located on the edges of the MOHAINE DESERT. Here he battled the crazed followers of SYLVIA PITTSTON, who was herself an acolyte of the MAN IN BLACK. By the time the battle was over and Roland pushed on into the desert, Tull's entire population, which consisted of thirty-nine men, fourteen women, and five children, lay dead. Roland even accidently killed his lover ALICE. The only person Roland didn't slaughter was the weed-eater NORT. (Poor Nort had already been crucified by the townsfolk.) According to STEPHEN KING, the town of Tull was named after the rock band Jethro Tull.

I:23–24, I:26–29 *(barflies)*, I:33, I:34–39 *(barflies)*, I:40 *(barflies)*, I:47–52 *(barflies and others at Pittston's revival)*, I:58–65 *(attack Roland)*, I:78

INDIVIDUAL TULL CHARACTERS:

> ALICE (ALLIE): *See* ALICE OF TULL (ALLIE), *listed separately*
>
> BALD MAN WITH KNIFE: This man tried to attack Roland in SHEB's bar. I:27–28
>
> **BOYS PLAYING MARBLES: In the 2003 *Gunslinger*, these boys are described. One has a scorpion's tail poking out of his hatband, one has a bloated and sightless eye, and the youngest has a large cold sore on his lip. The youngest one is named CHARLIE and is scorned by his companions for giving directions to Roland. I:24, I:25–26
>
> CASTNER: He owned Tull's Dry Goods emporium. I:47–52
>
> > SLAT-SIDED WIFE: I:47–52

**FELDON, AMY: One of Tull's barflies. At NORT's wake, ZACHARY threw Amy's skirts over her head and drew zodiacs on her knees. In the 2003 *Gunslinger,* we find out that Amy was a whore and that Zachary drew Reap charms on her knees, not zodiacs. I:34–39, I:61

JONSON: Jonson was one of the born-again sinners attending PITTSTON'S revival. I:51–52

**KENNERLY, JUBAL: Kennerly was a skinny, incestuous livery owner who was plagued with daughters. In the 2003 *Gunslinger,* we learn that he buried two wives and that his first name was Jubal. I:24–25, I:33, I:40, I:42–45, I:47–52, I:57–58, I:61, I:64

   DAUGHTERS (GENERAL): I:33 *(second-eldest),* I:43–45, I:47–52, I:58, I:61

      BABY GIRL: I:43, I:44

      KENNERLY, SOOBIE: One of Kennerly's overly sensual daughters. She liked to suck her thumb. I:43–45, I:57–58, I:61

   KENNERLY'S FATHER: I:44

LADIES IN BLACK SLACKS: I:24

MILL, AUNT: She was a barfly who had a broad belly and a quavery voice. She sang at NORT's funeral. Mill was one of PITTSTON's followers. Like everybody else in Tull, she was killed by Roland. I:34–39, I:61

**NORT: Nort was Tull's resident weed-eater. Once he had a honey wagon, but drink and then weed killed off his desire to do anything but chew his way to oblivion. Before his first death, Nort already resembled a walking corpse. He looked like a man made of coat hangers and had green-coated teeth—as green and as smelly as his stinking pants. By the time Roland arrived in town, Nort had already died of weed and had been resurrected by the MAN IN BLACK. Thanks to the magic of the Man in Black, the resurrected Nort addressed Roland in High Speech. Nort's second death was a crucifixion. In the 2003 *Gunslinger,* WALTER (the Man in Black) places a locked door in Nort's imagination. Behind this door lurk the secrets of the afterlife. The key to the door is the number NINETEEN. I:18–19, I:20 *(indirect),* I:26–30, I:31–41 *(Nort's story),* I:42, I:63, II:40, III:42, V:253, VI:284, VII:826 *(weed-eater mentioned. Reference actually refers to Brown, the border dweller; see BROWN, listed separately).*

OLD MAN WITH STRAW HAT: This man was the first person Roland saw when he entered Tull. I:24, I:62

**PITTSTON, SYLVIA: Sylvia Pittston was Tull's psychotic Bible-bashing preacher. Before the events of *Wizard and Glass* took place, Pittston traveled through HAMBRY. Originally a DESERT DWELLER, she came to Tull from the dry wastes on the edge of the MOHAINE DESERT. When Roland confronted her in Tull, she was living in a shack behind her church. Pittston wore the burlap dress of a penitent.

   Pittston was a huge but sexually alluring woman. She weighed about three hundred pounds but had large dark eyes and rich brown hair. Pittston's revivals were so intense that they were almost erotically ecstatic. ALICE believed that Pittston had a hoodoo on the town and that her religion was evil. Roland believed that when the MAN IN BLACK (WALTER) passed through Tull, he had sex with this preacher and left a demon inside of her. Roland's theory proves to be right.

When Roland visited Pittston's shack, she was sitting in her rocker waiting for him. She believed that Roland was Satan (the INTERLOPER) and that the Man in Black was an angel. Roland removed Pittston's demon by making her come with the barrel of his gun, but in revenge, Pittston set the townspeople on him. Roland ended up killing everyone in Tull.

In the 2003 version of *The Gunslinger,* Roland has an eerie sense of déjà vu when he hears Pittston preach, almost as if he had heard her preach before. In this version, Walter once again comes to Pittston pretending to be an angel, but this time he admits that he serves THE CRIMSON KING, the very evil being that Pittston pretends to preach against. Pittston allows Walter to implant the Red King's child inside of her, but Roland removes it in the same way that he removed the demon in the earlier version of the novel. In the new *Gunslinger,* as in the old, Pittston dies under Roland's guns. I:47–52, I:53, I:54–56, I:58–63, I:124, I:131, III:42, IV:381–82 *(she came through Hambry)*

SHEB (PIANO PLAYER): Sheb was Tull's piano player. Although the local honky-tonk bore his name the place actually belonged to ALICE. Sheb was also once a piano player in the HAMBRY saloon called the TRAVELLERS' REST. *See* SHEB, *listed separately*

YOUNG BOY AND GIRL: I:24

**ZACHARY: One of the barflies at SHEB's. He liked to draw zodiacs on girls' knees, although in the 2003 version of *The Gunslinger,* he draws Reap charms instead of zodiacs. I:34–39

TUNNEL DEMON
See DEMONS/SPIRITS/DEVILS: TODASH DEMONS

TURTLE GUARDIAN
See GUARDIANS OF THE BEAM

TYGER GUARDIAN
See GUARDIANS OF THE BEAM

TYGER IN FOREST
See GUARDIANS OF THE BEAM *and* MAERLYN

U

UFFIS
See WARRIORS OF THE SCARLET EYE: CASSE ROI RUSSE: HUMANS; *see also* APPENDIX I

UNCLE JIM
See BREAKERS: BRAUTIGAN, TED

UNWIN, TALITHA
See RIVER CROSSING CHARACTERS

UPS GUY
See CHAMBERS, JAKE: JAKE'S ASSOCIATES

UR-DOG ROVER
See ROSE

V

VAGRANT DEAD (VAGS)
When our *ka-tet* travels to NEW YORK CITY via TODASH at the beginning of *Wolves of the Calla,* they see a number of these forlorn creatures wandering around the city. A vag (or one of the vagrant dead) is a person who died so suddenly that he or she does not yet comprehend that he or she is dead. Sooner or later the vag will pass on, but seeing one walking around with his or her death wounds still oozing is disconcerting (to say the least). A vag who died in a frontal collision walks the streets bleeding, his head split like a melon. One who died on an operating table may still have his or her incisions hanging open. When Roland was a boy, BURNING CHRIS (father of ALAIN JOHNS) warned him that traveling *todash* meant such meetings were possible.
   V:195, V:284, V:285, V:286, V:288, V:289, V:290, V:297 *(walking dead),* V:302 *(bewildered dead people),* V:304 *(dead folks),* V:506, V:516, VI:147
   BURNED WOMAN MISSING ARM AND LEG: Seen by FATHER CALLAHAN on Park Avenue. V:284
   DEAD WOMAN: Seen by SUSANNAH DEAN in TODASH NEW YORK. She has a white face, empty, black eye sockets, and a black, moss-splotched dress. V:186, V:190, V:194
   LITTLE GIRL: Seen by SUSANNAH DEAN and then by her *ka-tet* in TODASH NEW YORK. She died in a car accident. V:194–95, V:196
   MAN WITHOUT EYES: Seen by FATHER CALLAHAN while on Park Avenue. V:284
   NAKED MAN: Seen by SUSANNAH DEAN and then by her *ka-tet* in TODASH NEW YORK. V:191, V:194, V:196, V:197

VAMPIRES
In *Wolves of the Calla,* the people of CALLA BRYN STURGIS state that THUNDERCLAP is a land of vampires. They call these bloodsuckers "brokenhelm undead ronin" or the "WARRIORS OF THE SCARLET EYE." Although we later learn that END-WORLD is actually populated by CAN-TOI and TAHEEN—animal-headed creatures who serve the CRIMSON KING—MID-WORLD and End-World contain plenty of vampires, though not all of them subsist on blood alone. In the short story "The Little Sisters of Eluria," we met the vampiric LITTLE SISTERS, a tribe of blood- and semen-drinking wraiths that wandered

the land posing as a religious sect of healers. In *The Gunslinger* and *The Waste Lands,* we learned about the Speaking-Ring spirits that required a sexual payment from any human who dared to pause within the circumference of their enchanted circles. (While in her wraith form, MIA, SUSANNAH's demon possessor, was a similar type of sexual vampire.) And finally, in *The Dark Tower,* we encounter DANDELO, a giant were-insect who feeds upon human emotion.

However, even if we narrow our present category so that it includes only the bloodsucking variety of vamps, we can still add three more types of vampires to our list. They are called (quite appropriately) TYPE ONE vampires, TYPE TWO vampires, and TYPE THREE vampires (*see below*).

V:26, V:150, V:256–57, V:266, V:269–71, V:273, V:285, V:289, V:297, V:299, V:302, V:306, V:423, V:430, V:452, V:610, VI:22, VI:64, VI:122, VI:172, VI:231, VI:253, VI:293, VI:303, VI:320, VI:326, VI:337, VI:364–84 *(Dixie Pig),* VII:5, VII:55–70 *(in birth room),* VII:104–9 *(following Jake),* VII:111 *(posse),* VII:133–35, VII:146, VII:147, VII:259, VII:332, VII:473, VII:526

TYPE ONE (THE GRANDFATHERS): According to FATHER CALLAHAN, there are only about a dozen Type One vampires in the world. They live extremely long lives and can survive periods of up to two hundred years in deep hibernation. These creatures, also known as Grandfathers, were some of the nastiest demons to survive once the magical PRIM receded. When JAKE and Callahan travel to the DIXIE PIG in NEW YORK CITY, they discover approximately a dozen of these monsters feeding behind a blasphemous tapestry depicting ARTHUR ELD and his court taking part in a cannibals' feast.

The Grandfathers do not just drink blood. They eat human flesh as well, and their appearance is as revolting as their appetites. Their evil, shriveled, apple-doll faces are twisted by age, and their mouths are filled with huge numbers of teeth, which are so pronounced and so numerous that they cannot close their lips. Their eyes are black and oozing, and their skin is yellow, scaled with teeth, and covered with patches of diseased-looking fur. Their auras are of a poisonous violet so dark that they appear almost black. When Type One vampires feed on humans, they create TYPE TWO vampires. V:261, V:269–70, V:292, V:396, V:708, VI:365, VI:372–73, VI:376, VII:8 *(not seen),* VII:11–16, VII:26, VII:28, VII:32, VII:86, VII:145, VII:166, VII:168

BARLOW, KURT: Kurt Barlow, the bloodsucker who spread his infection throughout the town of 'SALEM'S LOT, MAINE, is an example of a Type One vampire. (See STEPHEN KING's novel *'Salem's Lot.*) Although Barlow was not quite as ugly as the Type Ones that JAKE and CALLAHAN meet in the DIXIE PIG, he was every bit as dangerous. When a much younger Father Callahan challenged Barlow in the PETRIE family kitchen back in Maine, he found that his faith in the WHITE was not strong enough to defeat this servant of the Outer Dark. Barlow broke the arms of Callahan's cross and forced him to drink his contaminated blood. Despite this victory, Barlow was eventually destroyed by Callahan's companion BEN MEARS. V:257, V:258–61, V:266, V:268, V:269, V:270 *(vampire-demon),* V:271, V:275 *(vampire-demon),* V:280, V:283 *(indirect; blood taste),* V:291, V:292 *(indirect),* V:306, V:423, V:437, V:451, V:456, V:463, V:465, V:591 *(filthy bloodsucker),* V:706 *(vampire),* V:708, VI:329, VI:330, VII:12, VII:16, VII:28 *(indirect)*

STRAKER: Straker was Barlow's half-human accomplice. V:258

CROSS OF MALTA VAMPIRE: This vile creature looks like a deformed skeleton in a moss-encrusted dinner suit. Around its neck it wears an ancient award, which CALLAHAN believes is the Cross of Malta.

The Cross of Malta Vampire is the first of the Grandfathers to attack Callahan during the DIXIE PIG battle. As the vamp attacks, Callahan stabs the end of his crucifix into the creature's forehead and burns through the flesh. The vampire's vile aura whiffs out like a candle, leaving nothing but liquefying flesh spilling out of his dinner jacket and pants. VII:12

GRANDFATHER FLEAS: These horrible insects, which are roughly the size of mice, accompany the Grandfathers and feed upon their leftovers. They are the parasites of parasites and are both blood-drinkers and camp followers. BILLY-BUMBLERS hunt them the way some terriers hunt rats. Whenever you see Grandfather Fleas, you can be sure that the Grandfathers are close. (Watch your neck.) VI:366, VI:381, VII:8–16, VII:26

TYPE TWO: Type Two vampires are created by TYPE ONE vampires. They are more intelligent than zombies, but not much. Though they can't go out in daylight, they make up for it at night by feeding voraciously. Thanks to their unquenchable hunger and diminished intellect, Type Twos rarely survive for long. V:269–70, V:396

TYPE THREE: Type Three vampires are like mosquitoes. They are made by TYPE TWO vampires but don't seem to be able to create more of their kind. However, they feed voraciously and are dangerous. Type Threes are more intelligent than Type Twos (perhaps because they retain a bit more of their humanity). Hence, they can pass for human. Like ordinary mortals, they withstand daylight and can eat food. However, psychic individuals (such as FATHER CALLAHAN) can identify them by their burned-onion smell and by the blue haze which surrounds them.

While they feed, Type Threes secrete an enzyme, which simultaneously numbs the skin and keeps the blood flowing freely. It also seems to create a temporary amnesia that prevents their victims from remembering the attack. Type Three vampires can spread HIV. Also, once a person has been bitten by a Type Three, they become a magnet for more bloodsuckers. V:266, V:269–70, V:273, V:274–79, V:280–81, V:284, V:286, V:289, V:290, V:291, V:301, V:303, V:304 *(bloodsucking folks)*, V:444, V:451, V:455–57, VII:5, VII:14–16, VII:55–70 *(in birth room)*, VII:104–9 *(following Jake)*, VII:111 *(posse)*, VII:133–35

INDIVIDUAL TYPE THREE VAMPIRES AND THEIR VICTIMS:

BATTERY PARK VAMPIRE: PERE CALLAHAN stabbed this vampire four times—once in the kidneys, once between the ribs, once in the back, and once in the neck. V:287

DOMINICAN TEENAGER (VICTIM): V:287–88

DIXIE PIG VAMPIRE GUARDS (GUARDING SUSANNAH/MIA): VI:364–66, VI:368, VI:377–84, VII:8–16

DIXIE PIG VAMPIRES: VI:365–71

EAST VILLAGE VAMPIRE: V:274–75

VICTIM: V:275

MARK CROSS BRIEFCASE BUSINESSMAN: He attacked LUPE DEL-GADO outside the HOME shelter. V:276–79, V:281

DELGADO, LUPE: *See* CALLAHAN, FATHER DONALD FRANK: CALLAHAN'S HOME SHELTER ASSOCIATES

MOTORCYCLE MESSENGER: PERE CALLAHAN killed this vampire and then took his boots. V:288

OLD WOMAN FEEDING SQUIRRELS: CALLAHAN encountered this Type Three in a NEW YORK CITY park. V:285–86, V:287

PETE PETACKI'S VAMPIRE GIRL: CALLAHAN saw this seventeen-year-old girl while he was working as a grave digger in rural KENTUCKY. His fellow worker PETE PETACKI thought she was hot. He was wrong. She was probably cold. Callahan killed her before she could cause any damage. Pete Petacki never found out. V:302

SOMBRA CORPORATION VAMPIRES: These Type Threes work for RICHARD P. SAYRE. Some of them are HIV-positive. V:455–57

TIMES SQUARE MOVIE THEATER VAMPIRE (YOUNG MAN): The Times Square movie theater vampire was the first Type Three that CALLA-HAN encountered. Although the vamp and his victim first appeared to be lovers, Callahan saw the telltale blue light hovering around both of them. V:268–69, V:270–71 *(homosexual)*, V:276 *(indirect)*

VICTIM (OLDER MAN): V:268–69, V:270–71 *(homosexual)*, V:276 *(indirect)*

WOMAN IN MARINE MIDLAND BANK: This Type Three flirted with CALLAHAN. V:275, V:288, V:289

VAN RONK, DAVE
See DEAN, SUSANNAH: ODETTA HOLMES'S ASSOCIATES

VAN WYCK, MATHIESSEN
See DEAN, SUSANNAH: SUSANNAH'S PRESENT ASSOCIATES

**VANNAY, ABEL (VANNAY THE WISE)
Vannay was one of Roland's tutors. He was often called Vannay the Wise. Gentle, limping Vannay told Roland that a boy who could answer riddles was a boy who could think around corners. While CORT taught apprentice gunslingers how to fight, Vannay believed that violence often caused more problems than it solved. Vannay gave Roland the sarcastic nickname GABBY because—as a young boy—Roland was given to prolonged silences. In the 2003 version of *The Gunslinger,* we find out that Vannay taught his students about the poisons used by the OLD ONES. Vannay had a son named WALLACE, who died of the falling sickness.

Although in most of the Dark Tower novels Cort was presented as Roland's most important teacher, in *The Wind Through the Keyhole* it was Vannay, not Cort, who proved to be Roland's most important tutor. While Cort lay in his bed, barely able to recognize his former pupil, Vannay was still actively researching, trying to help STEVEN DESCHAIN solve the many problematic mysteries that IN-WORLD faced during its last days. It was Vannay who collected SHERIFF PEAVY's reports about the SKIN-MAN terrorizing Debaria. Unlike the elder Deschain, who thought that the skin-man was probably just a maniac dressed up in animal skins, Vannay knew from Gilead's records that such anomalies sometimes existed. Although he assumed that the skin-man was a MUTANT rather than a product of the OLD ONES' poisonous magical technology, he did realize that the monster was both a shapeshifter, or a human being who could change to animal form, and a shapechanger, or a being who could adapt multiple forms. When faced with skepticism about his theories, Vannay replied, "When facts speak, the wise man listens." As Roland added, twenty-three people torn to pieces made a moit of facts.

III:276, IV:326, IV:650, IV:664, E:195, V:78–80 *(described)*, V:81, V:86, V:89, V:90, V:204, V:388, V:392, VII:20–21, VII:33, VII:589, VII:742, VII:801 *(Vannay the Wise)*, VII:829, W:37, W:40, W:42, W:44, W:46, W:47, W:54, W:65–66 *(indirect)*, W:98, W:285, W:288

VANNAY'S FAMILY AND ASSOCIATES:

**WALLACE: Wallace, son of Vannay, was one of Roland's childhood friends. We learn about Wallace's existence in the 2003 version of *The Gunslinger*. (We don't learn his name until *Wolves of the Calla*.) Like the TAVERY twins, Wallace was a child prodigy. While still a boy, he died of the falling sickness, also known as King's Evil. V:78–79

VAUGHN, SAM
    See KING, STEPHEN

VECHHIO, RUDY
    See BALAZAR, ENRICO: BALAZAR'S MEN

VELE, MRS. CORETTA
    See KING, STEPHEN: FAN MAIL/HATE MAIL

VENN, RUPERT
    See TREE VILLAGE CHARACTERS

VERDON, HENRY
    See KING, STEPHEN

VERONE, TIO
    See BALAZAR, ENRICO

VERRILL, CHUCK
    See KING, STEPHEN

VI CASTIS COMPANY
This is the name of the corrupt mining company that destroyed all of the freehold mines north of RITZY. The BIG COFFIN HUNTERS were part of this conspiracy.
    IV:265

VINCENT, COL
    See BALAZAR, ENRICO: BALAZAR'S MEN

VOICE NUMBER ONE
See TOWER, CALVIN

VOICE NUMBER TWO
See TET CORPORATION: FOUNDING FATHERS: DEEPNEAU, AARON

VOICE OF THE BEAM
See GAN

VOTER REGISTRATION BOYS
See DEAN, SUSANNAH: ODETTA HOLMES AND THE CIVIL RIGHTS
MOVEMENT: VOTER REGISTRATION BOYS

VULTURE GUARDIAN
See GUARDIANS OF THE BEAM

W

WALKER, DETTA
See DEAN, SUSANNAH: SUSANNAH'S OTHER SELVES

WALKIN' DUDE
See WALTER: WALTER'S ALIASES

WALKING WATERS OF EAST DOWNE
See MID-WORLD FOLKLORE

WALK-INS
Walk-ins are people (and sometimes animals) that seem to *walk in* to our world
from other *wheres* or *whens*. Often they are dressed in old-fashioned clothes and
speak indecipherable languages. Some of these walk-ins are disfigured (JOHN CUL-
LUM calls them ROONT, or ruined) and are probably either SLOW MUTANTS
or CHILDREN OF RODERICK. Others have a bleeding hole in the center of their
forehead and appear to be CAN-TOI servants of the CRIMSON KING.
    In *Song of Susannah,* we find out that the towns near LOVELL, MAINE, are
plagued by walk-ins. In the final book of the Dark Tower series, we discover that
these walk-ins are entering our world through the doorway of CARA LAUGHS,
the home which the writer STEPHEN KING is destined to buy. Obviously, our
kas-ka Gan uses his imagination to create DOORWAYS BETWEEN WORLDS,
doorways which the walk-ins can use.
    VI:151–54, VI:161, VI:170–71, VI:172, VI:180–81 *(center)*, VI:182,
    VI:285, VI:301, VI:397–98, VI:407, VI:409, VII:46, VII:49, VII:50, VII:116,
    VII:129–30 *(taheen)*, VII:131, VII:173, VII:305, VII:433, VII:434, VII:438
    BIRDS: VI:153
    CHEVIN OF CHAYVEN: *See* MUTANTS: CHILDREN OF RODERICK

ONE-EYED WOMAN WITH DEAD CHILD: *See* MUTANTS: CHILDREN OF RODERICK
WOMAN WITH BALD HEAD AND BLEEDING EYE IN FOREHEAD: VI:153, VI:171

WALK-INS, CHURCH OF THE
See MAINE (STATE OF): OXFORD COUNTY: STONEHAM: STONEHAM CORNERS: LOVELL-STONEHAM CHURCH OF THE WALK-INS, *in* OUR WORLD PLACES

WALLACE
See VANNAY

**WALTER (THE DARK MAN, THE MAN IN BLACK, WALTER OF ALL-WORLD, WALTER OF END-WORLD, WALTER O'DIM, THE CRIMSON KING'S PRIME MINISTER, WALTER PADICK, WALTER HODJI, WALTER FARDEN, WALTER THE BLIND)
As far back as *The Gunslinger,* Walter O'Dim (also known as the Man in Black) has been Roland's nemesis. Under the name MARTEN BROADCLOAK, he served as STEVEN DESCHAIN's betraying sorcerer, the man who seduced Roland's mother and shamed Roland into taking his test of manhood years too early. While in the service of JOHN FARSON, he helped to bring down GILEAD, the last bastion of civilization, in a tide of blood and murder.[6] Under the name RUDIN FILARO, he fought with the BLUE-FACED BARBARIANS at JERICHO HILL and shot CUTHBERT ALLGOOD through the eye with an arrow.

An accomplished sorcerer and a devoted servant of the Outer Dark, Walter has many infernal skills. In the first book of the Dark Tower series, we saw him restore the weed-eater NORT to life. In *The Drawing of the Three* we learn that in his incarnation as RANDALL FLAGG, he is able to change men into dogs.

Although a sorcerer, Walter often functions as a kind of trickster, leading Roland into the darkest regions of his own soul. It is Walter who tempts Roland to let JAKE fall into the abyss below the CYCLOPEAN MOUNTAINS, and it is often Walter's taunting voice that Roland hears in his head, mocking and deriding his desire to live—and pursue his quest—honorably.

Among Walter's infernal skills is that of prophecy. In the bone-strewn wastes of the GOLGOTHA, located near the shores of the WESTERN SEA, he reads Roland's future with a stacked deck of tarot cards. During this reading he foretells the drawing of the Three, and tells Roland the perils he will have to face on his way to the DARK TOWER. Walter also gives our gunslinger an overwhelming vision of the universe, and a sense of the immensity of the Tower itself. At the end of the first book of the series, Roland wakes up from a short sleep to find that he has aged a decade and that Walter is only a pile of bones. Roland takes Walter's jaw as a talisman. Later on in the series we learn that, although Walter

6. In *The Gunslinger,* Stephen King hints that the Good Man may be just another of Walter's aliases. However, by the time we reach *The Dark Tower,* Walter tells us that this bit of information was a red herring. John Farson and Walter are separate beings. Farson was one of Walter's many pawns.

pretended to die in the golgotha, he did not actually travel to the clearing at the end of the path. Oh, no. He is too much of a survivor to meet such a simple end.

Changing both his name and his face, Walter can travel through time and between worlds, spreading destruction and disaster like plague or poison. As MOTHER ABAGAIL states in the related novel *The Stand,* whereas ordinary mortals wish to live and create, dark creatures such as Walter (aka Randall Flagg) only want to uncreate or destroy. Wherever goodness or hope exists, or wherever tragedy has taken place and the forces of the WHITE are needed to rebuild human society, Walter will turn up, dragging his shadow of chaos behind him.

In the provinces south of GARLAN, Walter was known as Walter Hodji, the latter word meaning both "dim" and "hood." When Roland and his *tet* met him in the GREEN PALACE back in *Wizard and Glass,* he claimed to be both OZ THE GREEN KING and Randall Flagg, the demonic sorcerer whose nefarious deeds are recorded in STEPHEN KING's novels *The Eyes of the Dragon* and *The Stand.*

Although CONSTANT READERS have long been familiar with Walter and his multiple masks (many of which begin with the initials R.F.), not until the seventh book of the Dark Tower series do we find out the true identity of this multifaced sorcerer. Born Walter Padick, the son of a simple miller in DELAIN, a town located in the EASTAR'D BARONY of a world much like Roland's, Walter chose at a young age to avoid the path most humans travel. At the age of thirteen he ran away from home and refused to return even after being raped by a fellow wanderer. Instead, he pursued his dark destiny, using and abusing his magical powers so that he gained a kind of quasi-immortality. Despite having belonged to numerous cliques and cults through the ages, often espousing conflicting causes, Walter, like Roland, has only ever had one ultimate goal. He longs to climb to the top of the Dark Tower and enter the room at its summit. However, whereas Roland wants to hold palaver with whatever god controls that linchpin of existence, Walter secretly hopes to take up residence there and become God of All.

By the time our series begins, Walter has taken up another cause in pursuit of his own secret ambition and has become the prime minister of the mad CRIMSON KING. In the name of the Lord of Discordia, Walter convinces MIA to give up her immortality so that she can give birth to MORDRED, who (according to legend) is destined to murder Walter's longtime enemy and ultimate rival, Roland. However, in creating Mordred (whose amputated foot he hopes to use to unlock the Tower), Walter finally overplays his hand. Once Mordred realizes Walter's true intentions, he eats him.

One of the most interesting ideas added to Walter's palaver with Roland in the 2003 version of *The Gunslinger* is the theme of RESUMPTION, a word which we see on one of the new opening pages of the revised volume. Roland believes that his quest for the Tower has been continuous, but Walter implies that it has not. Roland has been repeating the same quest over and over, he just never recalls it. At the end of the Dark Tower series, we learn that Walter is right. Roland is caught in a time loop, constantly reliving the period from the fall of Jericho Hill (or perhaps from his time in the MOHAINE DESERT) to his reaching the Dark Tower. Walter implies that Roland is damned to repeat his own history over and over because he never remembers and never learns. In the final book of the series, Roland proves his nemesis wrong.

I:11–14, I:16–17, I:20–21, I:23, I:29, I:30, I:33–39 *(Nort's story)*, I:42, I:54–56

(Pittston), I:58, I:64, I:73–74, I:76–77, I:78–79, I:82–84, I:86, I:87, I:90, I:93, I:94, I:95, I:112–13, I:119, I:122, I:130, I:131, I:136, I:137, I:138, I:139, I:140, I:142–43, I:149, I:174, I:176–77, I:184, I:186, I:190–216, II:15, II:16, II:20, II:25, II:30, II:31, II:36, II:40, II:55, II:101, II:104, II:316, II:318, II:319, II:324, II:397, III:38, III:41, III:42, III:43, III:46–47, III:48, III:59–62, III:94, III:103–6, III:107, III:172, III:226, III:261, III:417, IV:7, IV:65, IV:106, IV:404–8, IV:421, IV:423 *(and The Good Man)*, IV:597, IV:624 *(the dark man in the west)*, E:146, E:209, V:314, V:410, V:412 *(as Maerlyn/Marten/Flagg)*, V:460–65 *("I am what* ka *and the King and the Tower have made me")*, V:470, V:702, VI:239–40, VI:245–55 *(prime minister of the Crimson King)*, VI:282, VI:283, VI:284, VI:288, VI:337, VI:405, VII:13 *(O'Dim)*, VII:106, VII:107, VII:141 *(Crimson King's chancellor)*, VII:148, VII:171–87, VII:188, VII:192, VII:250, VII:442, VII:515, VII:518, VII:531, VII:535, VII:762, VII:829, VII:830

WALTER'S ALIASES:

**BROADCLOAK, MARTEN: Although Marten Broadcloak was STEVEN DESCHAIN's sorcerer, he was actually an enemy of the AFFILIATION. In a carefully orchestrated bit of treachery, Marten seduced Roland's mother, GABRIELLE, and then exposed the shameful affair so that Roland—raging that his father had been cuckolded and dishonored—would face his test of manhood years too early. Marten's hope was that Roland would fail his test and be sent west, into exile. To Marten's chagrin, Roland succeeded in besting his teacher CORT and won his guns at the unheard-of age of fourteen.

In *Wizard and Glass,* we learn that Gabrielle conspired to kill her husband, Steven Deschain. It seems most likely that her poisoned knife came from Marten. This plot also failed, though at the eventual cost of Gabrielle's life. (Not long after this event, Roland shot her.) In *The Gunslinger,* we learn that Marten was delivered into Roland's hands by the Man in Black posing as a sorcerer named Walter. However the person delivered to Roland must have been an imposter, since later in the series we learn that Marten and Walter are the same man.

In the 2003 *Gunslinger,* Marten's identity takes a further twist. Marten is still Steven Deschain's sorcerer, but he is now also his foremost counselor. But unbeknownst to the elder Deschain, Marten is simultaneously his many-faced enemy.

As JOHN FARSON's wizard, Marten is actually the force behind the revolutions tearing MID-WORLD's Affiliation apart. (In the early books of the series KING implies that Marten and Farson may be the same creature, but later this proves not to be true.) Walter is simultaneously the penitent Walter that Roland knew in his youth, and Walter O'Dim, otherwise known as the Man in Black. Hence, like all of his alter egos, Marten is an evil agent of the CRIMSON KING. I:86, I:94, I:95, I:106 *(as the good man)*, I:125, I:131, I:140 *(killed)*, I:151–52, I:159–61, I:164, I:167, I:172, I:173, I:175, I:205–6 *(possessed by Walter)*, I:213, II:103, II:250, II:362, III:41, III:44, III:124, III:417, IV:7, IV:65, IV:107, IV:110–12, IV:163, IV:164, IV:165, IV:223, IV:258, IV:275 *(and voice of thinny in Eyebolt Canyon)*, IV:436, IV:619 *(with Farson)*, IV:647–49 *(claims to be Flagg)*, IV:652–56, IV:665, V:36, V:412 *(as Walter/Maerlyn/Flagg)*, VII:178,

VII:184, VII:822, VII:824, W:37, W:250–51, W:297–98, W:299, W:300, W:306 *(son of a bitch)*

COVENANT MAN (BARONY COVENANTER): The Covenant Man, also known as the Barony Covenanter, was the official tax collector for the BARONY of NEW CANAAN as well as the NORTH'RD BARONY, where the village of TREE was located. He had been the tax collector in those parts for as long as anyone could remember. Every year he arrived on his tall black horse, dressed in his flapping black cloak and black gloves. Tied to his saddle (which was inscribed with silver *siguls* and was worth more than a woodcutter made in a lifetime of risking his neck) was a BASIN of pure silver. The Covenanter looked as thin as Old Scrawny Death, but this didn't stop him from marking a new fence here, a cow or three added to a herd there. The money he collected was taken in the name of GILEAD, and those who could not pay had their plots repossessed and were turned out on the land, also in the name of Gilead.

The Covenanter's physical presence was as abhorrent as his calling. His body smelled of old sweat and his breath was rank. His husky voice—which sounded like a deaf man trying to sing a lullaby—issued from a mouth full of large white teeth. The man's eyes didn't blink and his lips were as red as those of a woman who had painted her mouth with madder.

As TIM ROSS realized soon after the Covenant Man gave him a magic key to open his stepfather's trunk (a key that would only work once, which meant that Tim's spying would inevitably be discovered), the Covenanter liked to play with people, but he was the kind of person who enjoyed breaking his toys. Thanks to the Covenanter's gift, Tim found his father's lucky coin in BERN KELLS's trunk (proof that BIG ROSS hadn't been incinerated by a DRAGON as Kells claimed, but murdered by his partner), but it also set off the chain of events which led to NELL ROSS (now Nell Kells) being beaten into blindness by her cruel and drunken second husband.

As the WIDOW SMACK stated so eloquently, the Covenanter left only ruin and weeping in his wake. Any help he gave—from showing Tim his father's corpse floating in a stream on the COSINGTON-MARCHLY STAKE to giving the boy glimpses of his future in one of his silver scrying vessels—was always double-edged. Although the vision Tim had of meeting the magician MAERLYN eventually came true, as did Maerlyn's gift which restored Nell's sight, the way these events unfolded was nothing like what Tim had foreseen when he waved the Covenanter's magic wand (probably made from the gear shift of an old Dodge Dart) over a battered silver PAIL. Tim's quest to find Maerlyn—which led him through the heart of the ENDLESS FOREST and into the FAGONARD swamp—was fraught with danger, and those beings that the Covenanter implied would help (such as the SIGHE ARMANEETA) turned out to be treacherous. Even Maerlyn, who Tim found near the NORTH FOREST KINNOCK DOGAN, was under a spell that made him look like a man-eating tyger rather than a wise magician. (Luckily, Tim did not shoot the mage with his four-shot pistol.)

We can't help but think that the Covenanter's true skill was wrapping just enough truth in a web of dangerous lies, and of making his cruel play appear to be altruism. No matter what the circumstances, the Covenanter's goal was always the same—to trap the unwary and destroy them. It was only luck that saved Tim from the jaws of a dragon, and then again from the certain death of the STARKBLAST. Or then again, perhaps it was *ka*. After all, despite his low birth, Tim was destined to become TIM STOUT-HEART, one of Mid-World's finest gunslingers.

One of the most interesting aspects of Tim Ross's story is that—although it is a fairy tale and takes place in the land of *once upon a bye*—the Covenanter's true identity turns out to be none other than that of Roland's longtime face-shifting enemy, WALTER O'DIM/MARTEN BROADCLOAK. Although when we read the tale we take the Covenant Man's identity at face value—after all, we know that O'Dim can travel to different levels of the TOWER and has lived far longer than one human lifetime—it is also important to contemplate the possibility that Roland *inserted* his enemy into the tale, and by so doing, made a conscious critique of the political situation of his time.

The grown-up Roland who travels with EDDIE, SUSANNAH, JAKE and OY has encountered O'Dim in many different guises, and knows that the sorcerer served both JOHN FARSON and the CRIMSON KING. Yet even as a young man, Roland knew that Broadcloak's forked tongue was responsible not only for his own personal tragedy, but also for the hatred and suspicion with which so many people regarded the *tet* of the gun. Hence, it is little surprise that young Roland, like the older Roland, chose to cast Broadcloak as the evil Barony Covenanter—the man who made the good people of Tree resent Gilead so deeply.

Although "The Wind Through the Keyhole" is a fairy tale, it is also history in disguise. Just as Broadcloak betrayed the gunslingers he was supposed to serve, so the Covenant Man poisoned the name and reputation of Gilead by squeezing taxes out of the people of Tree in the name of the ancient Covenant they held with Arthur ELD. Even in the land of fairy tale, people whispered that the Covenanter's taxes weren't fair, and that, even if Arthur Eld *had* existed, he was long dead and the Covenant had been paid a dozen times over, in blood as well as silver. Like Broadcloak, the Covenanter knew full well that he was creating a situation in which people were longing for someone like John Farson to appear and actively challenge the rule of In-World. W:112, W:113, W:114, W:117, W:120, W:123, W:126 (old You Know Who), W:131–37 *(sowing bad will; 136 foul breath)*, W:138, W:139, W:140, W:141 *(never ages)*, W:144 *(indirect)*, W:145–48 *(Tim goes in search of him)*, W:148–64 *(153 magic wand, magic basin; 160 wanting to know secrets is his vice)*, W:167 *(chary man)*, W:168–69 *(poisoning the name of Eld as Maerlyn)*, W:170, W:172 *(found Big Ross's corpse)*, W:173, W:175 *(great description)*, W:179, W:180–83 *(leaving Dodge Dart stick, pail)*, W:184, W:185, W:187 *(Widow Smack gives Tim a gun, calls Covenant Man a devil)*, W:188, W:189, W:191, W:192 W:195, W:196, W:198, W:200, W:206, W:207 *(indirect)*, W:223 *(indirect)*, W:226, W:236 *(indirect)*, W:237–38, W:239 *(man in black)*, W:241, W:242, W:247–49, W:250–51, W:258, W:259, W:264

   BLACKIE: Blackie was the Covenant Man's horse. W:131–37, W:138, W:150, W:160, W:195

GREEN KING, THE: Oz, otherwise known as Oz the Great and Terrible, was the sorcerer of the Emerald City in the children's book *The Wizard of Oz*. Walter occasionally uses this disguise as well. VII:173

PADICK, WALTER: Walter's birth name was Walter Padick. He was the son of SAM THE MILLER and grew up on a farm in DELAIN, located in EASTAR'D BARONY. At thirteen, Walter was raped by another wanderer, but refused to return home. Instead, he pursued his dark destiny. VII:184

R.F.: As we discovered in the first four novels of the Dark Tower series, Roland's multifaced archenemy often uses pseudonyms whose initials are R.F. This nasty being occasionally uses other initials to disguise himself as well, including W.O. (Walter O'Dim) and M.B. (Marten Broadcloak). In the first books of the series King hints that John Farson (J.F.) may also be an incarnation of Walter, but by the end of the series we come to realize that this is not so. Whatever his real name, R.F. is an agent of Chaos (but we are much nicer in our female incarnations). IV:663–64, IV:666, VII:194

WALTER'S ALIASES BEGINNING WITH R.F.:
The first time we come across the initials R.F. in the Dark Tower series is at the end of *Wizard and Glass*, after our *tet* has left the GREEN PALACE. While drinking Nozz-A-La Cola, EDDIE DEAN discovers a piece of paper flapping by. It turns out to be a note written on the back of *The Oz Daily Buzz*. Surrounded by smile faces is the message:

Next time I won't leave. Renounce the

Tower. This is your last warning.

And have a <u>great</u> day!

The note is signed R.F. Beneath those initials is a small drawing of a cloud and lightning bolt.

The note that the Covenant Man left for TIM ROSS at the NORTH FOREST KINNOCK DOGAN was signed with the letters R.F./M.B. Constant Readers are familiar with R.F. (after all, many of Walter O'Dim's aliases begin with those initials), but the letters M.B. could stand for either the Man in Black, or Marten Broadcloak. W:3

    FANNIN, RICHARD: In his form as Richard Fannin, R.F. is described as being inhuman. He has blue-green eyes but blue-black hair that looks like a raven's feathers. Fannin must be a fairly imposing figure, since even TICK-TOCK, leader of the murderous GRAYS, is afraid of him.

    Fannin's hand has no lines on it, which makes us wonder if he is mortal at all. He claims not to be MAERLYN, but he is obviously a sorcerer of extreme power. Like all of R.F.'s selves, Fannin glories in destruction. III:385–90, VII:184

    FILARO, RUDIN: Walter fought at JERICHO HILL under this name. VII:174, VII:184

    FLAGG, RANDALL: Under the name of Randall Flagg, Walter played a major role in both *The Eyes of the Dragon* and *The Stand*. In the first of these two books, he framed Peter (King Roland's eldest son) for his father's murder and placed the king's weaker-willed younger son, Thomas, on the throne. (Walter hoped to bring the kingdom to ruin by manipulating Thomas.) In *The Stand*, Flagg becomes a truly demonic force. After more than 99 percent of America's population dies of the superflu, Flagg gathers the dregs of the survivors to him in Las Vegas. There, he accumulates both technological and biological weapons so that he can annihilate those people who live in the Free Zone and who still honor the WHITE. In this novel Flagg is referred to as the Walkin' Dude, an epithet that Roland's *ka-tet* sees spray-painted on a road sign in the alternative TOPEKA which they pass through at the beginning of *Wizard and Glass*. Although in his *Stand* incarnation Walter/Flagg seems almost as powerful as the CRIMSON KING himself, his ambitions are ultimately thwarted.

In *The Drawing of the Three*, Roland describes Flagg as a demon posing as a man, and says that he is capable of transforming men into dogs. Roland also tells us that Flagg is being pursued by two desperate and grim young men named Dennis and Thomas. Both of these characters come from *Eyes of the Dragon*. II:362, IV:648–50, V:36, V:37, V:187, V:412 *(also Walter, Maerlyn)*, VI:246, VI:249, VI:251, VI:337, VI:405, VII:43, VII:125, VII:148, VII:172, VII:173, VII:176, VII:178, VII:184, VII:185, VII:250

WALKIN' DUDE: This epithet was used by RANDALL FLAGG in STEPHEN KING's novel *The Stand*. V:291

WALTER'S ASSOCIATES

    CRIMSON KING, THE: *See* CRIMSON KING, *listed separately*

    FARSON, JOHN: *See* FARSON, JOHN, *listed separately*

    SAM THE MILLER: Walter's father. He was from EASTAR'D BARONY. VII:184

WARRIORS OF THE SCARLET EYE (MEN OF THE EYE)

The Warriors of the Scarlet Eye are the FOOT SOLDIERS OF THE CRIMSON KING. Like their master, they oppose the WHITE and serve the Outer Dark. *See also* BIG COFFIN HUNTERS, CAN-TOI, NORTH CENTRAL POSITRONICS, REGULATORS, SOMBRA CORPORATION, TAHEEN, VAMPIRES, WOLVES.

    V:26 *(Broken-helm undead ronin)*, VI:64 *(indirect)*, VI:73 *(indirect)*, VI:74 *(indirect)*, VI:75 *(indirect)*, VI:114–15, VI:117, VI:233, VI:244–45, VI:246–47 *(indirect)*, VI:248, VI:326, VI:364–84 *(Dixie Pig)*

WARRIORS BY LOCATION:

    CASSE ROI RUSSE: Le Casse Roi Russe is the palace of the CRIMSON KING. Roland and SUSANNAH pass it on their way to the DARK TOWER.

    HUMANS (HUMES):

        BRASS: *See* FEEMALO/FIMALO/FUMALO: FEEMALO, *listed below*

        COMPSON: *See* FEEMALO/FIMALO/FUMALO: FUMALO, *listed below*

        CORNWELL, AUSTIN: *See* FEEMALO/FIMALO/FUMALO: FIMALO (RANDO THOUGHTFUL), *listed below*

        FEEMALO/FIMALO/FUMALO (UFFIS): Roland and SUSANNAH meet these three STEPHEN KING look-alikes on the stone moat-bridge of Le CASSE ROI RUSSE. At first the three Stephen Kings claim to be one being—an uffi, or shape-changer—who was once employed as the CRIMSON KING's court jester. However, in reality they are three separate men, all servants of the Red King. Their names are BRASS (Feemalo), COMPSON (Fumalo), and RANDO THOUGHTFUL (Fimalo). The most important of these three is Fimalo/Rando Thoughtful.

According to this false, three-faced uffi, once the Crimson King discovered that Roland and his *tet* would defeat both the WOLVES of CALLA BRYN STURGIS and the DEVAR-TOI guards in THUNDERCLAP, he realized that the BEAMS would regenerate and that all of his dreams of murder and mayhem were destined to fail. Being an extremely bad loser, the Red King threw a temper tantrum. First he forced his castle servants to swallow rat poison, then he smashed the six BENDS O' THE WIZARD'S RAINBOW which were in his possession, and finally he killed himself by swallowing a sharpened spoon. Once he was undead, he galloped toward the DARK TOWER so that he could (he hoped) prevent Roland from achieving his life's goal.

Pretending to be conciliatory (since they alone had survived the Red King's pique), the triple uffi offers Roland, Susannah, and OY two wicker baskets, which appear to contain warm clothes and food. Not surprisingly, the real contents (disguised by *glammer*) are much more disgusting. What the uffis offer are poisonous snakes and human body parts.

Susannah and Roland shoot Feemalo and Fumalo but leave Fimalo (who—once the *glammer* is broken—looks like an extremely ill old man) to confront the were-spider MORDRED, who is following them. The bodies of both Feemalo and Fumalo rot unnaturally fast.

FEEMALO (BRASS/GOODMOUTH KING/EGO): As well as being called Goodmouth King, Feemalo is also referred to as STEPHEN KING Number Two and Right-Hand Stephen King. Unlike Fumalo, he is polite. He claims to be the uffi's ego. VII:600–613, VII:614, VII:615, VII:619

FIMALO (RANDO THOUGHTFUL, AUSTIN CORNWELL/ REFEREE KING/SUPEREGO): During his years as the CRIMSON KING's minister of state, Fimalo (who originally claims to be the uffi's superego) was called Rando Thoughtful. Rando (who is actually an ordinary hume) was born AUSTIN CORNWELL in one of the MULTIPLE AMERICAS' upstate NEW YORKs. Once upon a time, he ran the NIAGARA MALL. He also had a successful career in advertising. (He proudly tells our *tet* that he worked for both the Nozz-A-La and the Takuro Spirit accounts.)

Once his *glammer* disperses, Austin Cornwell looks like a very ill old man. His skull is covered in peeling eczema and his face is lumped with pimples and open, bleeding sores. Roland and Susannah choose not to kill him. Instead, they leave him to greet MORDRED, who arrives soon after they leave. Mordred feeds Austin's eyes to the castle rooks and then eats the rest of him. VII:600–617, VII:619–24, VII:627, VII:632

CORNWELL, ANDREW JOHN: Austin Cornwell's father from TIOGA SPRINGS, NEW YORK. VII:616

FUMALO (COMPSON/BADMOUTH KING/ID): Fumalo, also called STEPHEN KING Number One, Left-Hand Stephen King, and Badmouth King, is supposed to be the uffi's id. VII:600–613, VII:614, VII:615, VII:619

DEVAR-TOI CHARACTERS: The Devar-Toi is the BREAKER prison located in THUNDERCLAP.

BREAKERS: *See* BREAKERS, *listed separately*

CAN-TOI (LOW MEN): *See the following entries under* CAN-TOI, *listed separately*

    ALEXANDER, BEN
    CAGNEY, JAMES
    CAMERON
    CONROY
    LONDON, JACK
    TRAMPAS
    TRELAWNEY
    TRISTUM, DR. GANGLI

HUMANS (HUMES):

ARMITAGE, FRANK: Frank Armitage is a hume who recruits BREAK-ERS from the parallel Earths. Real humans have to do this work since the CAN-TOI (despite their aspirations) don't make very convincing men and women. VII:281, VII:283–90, VII:297

BURKE, DAVID: A stupid human guard who was lobotomized for throwing peanut shells at BREAKERS working in the STUDY. VII:241

KELLY, TAMMY: Tammy Kelly is PIMLI PRENTISS's housekeeper. She has a large bottom. VII:347, VII:348, VII:352–55, VII:358, VII:361, VII:371, VII:381

PRENTISS, PIMLI (DEVAR MASTER, KI'DAM): Pimli Prentiss (formerly Paul Prentiss of RAHWAY, NEW JERSEY) is the Master of the DEVAR-TOI. Among the more discontented BREAKERS, he is known as the Devar-Toi's *ki'-dam* or "shit-for-brains." *Sai* Prentiss stands six foot two inches, has an enormous sloping belly, long legs, and slab thighs. He is balding and has the turnip nose of a veteran drinker. When he arrived at the Devar-Toi, he was a former prison warden and approximately fifty years old. He still looks the same age, though he has been in END-WORLD for decades. Although he is working to bring about the end of all the worlds, Pimli spends every Mother's Day in tears. (He misses his ma.) Prentiss (who took a TAHEEN name) is good friends with the *taheen* security chief, FINLI O'TEGO.

During the final battle at the Devar-Toi, Roland shoots Prentiss and leaves him for dead. However, the prostrate and bleeding Devar Master still has enough life left to shoot EDDIE DEAN in the head. Roland quickly dispatches Prentiss, but Eddie dies. VII:197, VII:207, VII:212, VII:215, VII:221–46, VII:261, VII:262, VII:270, VII:271, VII:275, VII:292, VII:295, VII:298–99, VII:325, VII:340, VII:341, VII:343–48, VII:352–53, VII:354 *(indirect)*, VII:358–59, VII:361–62, VII:371–75, VII:377, VII:380–81 *(shot)*, VII:383–90, VII:396, VII:398 *(indirect)*

    GRANDFATHER: VII:232

    MOTHER: VII:228, VII:229, VII:235, VII:246

PROCTOR OF CORBETT HALL: We never meet the proctor of COR-

BETT HALL, but EDDIE DEAN, who has been shot in the head, dies in his rooms. JAKE believes that SUSANNAH used the proctor's nail-care gadget to clean Eddie's fingernails before she buried him. VII:409

SONESH, TASSA OF: Tassa of Sonesh is PIMLI PRENTISS's houseboy. He is slim and willowy and likes lipstick. He and TAMMY KELLY (Prentiss's housekeeper) do not get along at all. (Tammy dislikes homosexual men.) Tassa is one of the few servants of the CRIMSON KING to survive the DEVAR-TOI battle. VII:299, VII:352–55, VII:358, VII:366, VII:371, VII:375, VII:400, VII:407

ROBOTS: *See the following entries under* NORTH CENTRAL POSI-TRONICS, *listed separately*
DOBBIE
FIRE-RESPONSE TEAM BRAVO
PHIL
SIX-ARMED ROBOT

TAHEEN: *See the following entries under* TAHEEN, *listed separately*
FINLI O'TEGO CLAN (HEAD OF SECURITY)
GASKIE O'TEGO
HUMMA O'TEGO
JAKLI

UNKNOWN RACE:
JENKINS: Jenkins is the DEVAR-TOI's chief technician. We don't know whether he is TAHEEN, CAN-TOI, or hume. VII:343–44, VII:345

DIXIE PIG CHARACTERS/FEDIC CHARACTERS: After the EAST ROAD battle in CALLA BRYN STURGIS, MIA, daughter of none, steals SUSAN-NAH DEAN's body so that she can keep her appointment with RICHARD P. SAYRE at the Dixie Pig restaurant in NEW YORK CITY. Sayre has prom-ised to help Mia deliver her CHAP. When Susannah/Mia enters the Pig, they are met by approximately fifty men and seventy-five women. Most of these guards are LOW MEN, though some are also TYPE THREE VAMPIRES. In a separate dining room (located behind a tapestry depicting ARTHUR ELD partaking in a cannibal's feast) are a group of ancient TYPE ONE vampires.

Below the Dixie Pig is a DOORWAY, which leads from our world to the FEDIC DOGAN. Here, in the Dogan's EXTRACTION ROOM, Mia gives birth to MORDRED. VI:365–84

CAN-TOI (LOW MEN): *See the following entries under* CAN-TOI, *listed separately*
ANDREW
DOORMEN
HABER
STRAW
TIRANA

HUMANS (HUMES):
FLAHERTY, CONOR (HUME FROM BOSTON): Along with a TAHEEN named LAMLA and a number of LOW MEN, Conor Flaherty pursues JAKE CHAMBERS through the MIND-TRAP which lies beneath the Dixie Pig. VII:93 *(indirect)*, VII:104–9, VII:111 *(posse)*, VII:112, VII:129, VII:133–35, VII:528

FATHER: VII:106

JOCHABIM, SON OF HOSSA (DISHWASHER NUMBER TWO):
This young boy originally came from LUDWEG, a town north of the
city of LUD. He now works in the kitchens of the Dixie Pig. Jochabim
is none too bright; however, he does manage to warn JAKE about the
MIND-TRAP he will encounter on his way to the NEW YORK/FEDIC
DOOR. VII:82–86, VII:99, VII:526

   HOSSA: VII:84

LIMO DRIVERS: VI:341–42

SCOWTHER (DOCTOR): Scowther is the impudent hume doctor
who delivers baby MORDRED. He is described as a stoutish man with
brown eyes, flushed cheeks, and hair combed back against his skull.
He wears a scarlet cravat decorated with the red eye of the CRIMSON
KING. VI:378–84, VII:22, VII:55–68 *(shot by Susannah)*, VII:71 *(automatic)*, VII:149, VII:152

ROBOTS: *See the following entry under* NORTH CENTRAL POSI-
TRONICS, *listed separately*
   NIGEL THE BUTLER (DNK4932 DOMESTIC)

TAHEEN: *See the following entries under* TAHEEN, *listed separately*
   ALIA (NURSE)
   CANARYMAN (MEIMAN)
   DIXIE PIG CHEF (WARTHOG)
   JEY
   LAMLA

VAMPIRES: *See the following entries under* VAMPIRES, *listed separately*
   TYPE ONE (GRANDFATHERS)
      GRANDFATHER FLEAS
   TYPE THREE

WOLVES: *See* WOLVES, *listed separately*

WAVERLY
   See BREAKERS

WEASEL, THE
   See TAHEEN: WEASEL-HEADED TAHEEN

WEAVER, NORRIS
NEW YORK CITY foot patrolman. His partner is ANDREW STAUNTON.
   II:380–84, III:262 *(indirect)*

WEED-EATER
   See TULL CHARACTERS: NORT

WEGG, WILL
   See DEBARIA CHARACTERS: LITTLE DEBARIA CHARACTERS

WERE-SPIDER
   See MORDRED

WERTNER, HENRY
 See HAMBRY CHARACTERS: HORSEMEN'S ASSOCIATION

**WHEELER'S BOY
Like many of the figures from Roland's past, we don't know much about this gunslinger apprentice. The only bit of information we're given is that STEVEN DESCHAIN thinks he is brighter than Roland. This character is cut from the 2003 version of *The Gunslinger.*
 I:105

WHITE AMMIES
 See GILEAD'S WHITE AMMIES

WHITE, JAKE
 See HAMBRY CHARACTERS: HORSEMEN'S ASSOCIATION

WHITE, THE
The White is the force of good. It is akin to faith in God, but it is both larger and more elemental than a belief in any particular religion or creed. To the beleaguered inhabitants of MID-WORLD, the aristocratic gunslingers are knights of the White. Although the ancient hero ARTHUR ELD is often associated with the White, the term is not limited to a particular political faction, allegiance, or social class. Its true meaning relates back to the philosophy of wholeness and unity embedded in the language of High Speech. Like white light and white magic, the White contains all colors within its balance and is the opposite of the evil Outer Dark. *(Page references for Volumes I–IV not included. See APPENDIX I.)*
 V:101, V:104, V:605, V:709, VII:4, VII:6, VII:10, VII:12, VII:13, VII:27, VII:127, VII:607, VII:748

WHITMAN, THOMAS
 See THOMAS OF GILEAD

WIDOW SMACK (ARDELIA SMACK)
The Widow Smack was TREE's beloved schoolteacher. Despite her shakes and the veils she wore to hide the ruin of her face, the Widow was a highly respected member of the village. Just as CORT instructed generations of boys in the art of war, so the Widow Smack—once a great lady in the Barony Estate—taught the children of Tree how to read, how to practice the art of mathmatica, and how to *think*. Although physically frail, the widow was a fearsomely smart woman who took no guff. On most days she was tireless. However, on occasion she was overcome by trembling fits and headaches and sent the children home. There must have been an unhappy love affair early in her life, because during these fits she would urge the students to remind their parents that she regretted nothing, least of all her beautiful prince. Sadly, the bloodsores that had eaten off half her face had also stolen her ability to cry. Her only remaining eye was unable to weep.
 Although TIM ROSS's stepfather, BIG KELLS, forced Tim to give up schooling at the WIDOW'S COTTAGE so that he could earn scrip at the TREE SAWMILL, the widow remained Tim's closest ally. Not only did she continue to give Tim

books to read and mathematical problems to solve, but when she saw Tim riding past her house one night, heading for the ENDLESS FOREST where he was secretly meeting the evil COVENANT MAN, she was alerted to danger. With the help of her little burro SUNSHINE, the Widow traveled to the Ross cottage, GOODVIEW, where she found Nell, who had been beaten into unconsciousness by her husband. The Widow's nursing probably saved Nell's life, if not Nell's sight.

The Widow Smack was the first person Tim told about his father's murder and that the murderer had been his own stepfather, Big Kells. The Widow Smack told Tim that he must relay the news to SQUARE PETER COSINGTON and SLOW ERNIE MARCHLY, in whose stake the body lay. They would fetch the body home but also drum up a posse to catch Kells. But the Widow also told the boy to beware of the wicked Covenant Man, who she stated was a pestilence incarnate. Alone among the people of Tree, the Widow knew the Covenanter's true identity—that when he wasn't at his hobby of collecting taxes and licking the tears off poor folks' faces, he was an advisor to the LORDS OF GILEAD.

Later, when Tim decided to travel into the Endless Forest again (this time to find MAERLYN, who he believed could restore his mother's sight), the Widow did not approve. (After all, Tim's information had come from the trickster Covenanter.) Nevertheless, she gave Tim a lamp and a loaf of bread, and a warning to watch for THROCKEN dancing in the moonlight, for they would presage the coming of a STARKBLAST. But most importantly, she gave Tim her brother's four-shot revolver.

While Tim was gone, and the starkblast stormed upon the village of Tree, it was the Widow who watched over blind Nell. Sadly, while she slept in the big rocker by the Ross's fire, Bern Kells sneaked back into the cottage and slit the Widow's throat. Her death was avenged by Nell, who put her first husband's ax in Kells's thick skull.

W:112–13 *(112 bloodsores that ate half her face)*, W:115, W:126 *(veils and shakes)*, W:127, W:130, W:142, W:147, W:155–56, W:164–70, W:171, W:173–75 *(174 saves Nell's life)*, W:184–89 *(degenerative disease, 189 harsh country accent)*, W:190, W:104 *(lamp)*, W:196, W:199, W:202, W:207, W:212 *(cotton sack)*, W:215 *(sack)*, W:221, W:225–26, W:246, W:255 *(cottage)*, W:258–62 *(asleep; 262 dead)*, W:263, W:264, W:267

GILEAD LADY FRIENDLY WITH WIDOW SMACK: Long ago, after the Barony's COVENANT MAN took part in some foul business in the village of TREE, the WIDOW SMACK wrote to a great lady she once knew in GILEAD. That lady was a woman of discretion and beauty, and replied to the Widow's inquiries promptly, though she begged her friend to burn the letter and the information it contained. According to this lady, collecting taxes was merely the Covenant Man's hobby. In truth he was a great mage, and an advisor to the Gilead's palace lords who call themselves the COUNCIL OF ELD. W:169, W:170

JOSHUA: Joshua was Widow Smack's brother. He died in the ENDLESS FOREST twenty years before the events of "The Wind Through the Keyhole" took place. Joshua bought a gun from a roving peddler and showed his sister how to use it. Joshua must have been very wise. He said, "a gun must never be pointed at a person unless you want to hurt or kill him, for guns have eager hearts." Widow Smack gave Joshua's gun to TIM ROSS.

PEDDLER: This peddler sold JOSHUA his four-shot revolver. W:186

SUNSHINE (BURRO): Sunshine was the Widow's burrow. W:155, W:164, W:166, W:174, W:258

WILSON, TEDDY
See MAINE CHARACTERS

WILSON, WILLIAM
See BALAZAR, ENRICO: BALAZAR'S NASSAU CONNECTION

***WIND THROUGH THE KEYHOLE* CHARACTERS MET BETWEEN GREEN PALACE AND RIVER WHYE:**
FRIGHTENED WOMAN: This frightened woman peeks at ROLAND, EDDIE, SUSANNAH, JAKE, and OY as they travel along the PATH OF THE BEAM toward the RIVER WHYE. She has her arms around two children and carries a baby in a sling around her neck. W:5
HALF-MUTIE FARMER: *See* MUTANTS: HUMAN MUTANTS (MINOR MUTATIONS)
TOOK (TOOK'S OUTLAND MERCANTILE): In *The Wind Through the Keyhole,* Roland and his American *tet* pass by this deserted store. Its sign is barely readable. W:4

WINKLER
See CALLA BRYN STURGIS CHARACTERS: OTHER CHARACTERS

WINSTON
See PUBES

WIZARD OF OZ (DOROTHY, TOTO, TIN WOODSMAN)
The Wizard of Oz, which tells the tale of Dorothy, Toto, the Cowardly Lion, and the Tin Woodsman, is mentioned quite often in the Dark Tower series. Like JAKE, SUSANNAH, and EDDIE, Dorothy Gale was blown from a world much like ours to one where witches and magic are real. However, had *The Wizard of Oz* taken place in MID-WORLD, the Tin Woodsman would have been manufactured by NORTH CENTRAL POSITRONICS, and the Cowardly Lion would have been a MUTIE of some sort. In *Wizard and Glass,* our *ka-tet* actually visits an emerald palace where the evil wizard RANDALL FLAGG poses as the Great and Terrible Oz.
II:229 *(Dorothy),* III:59, III:408, IV:629–30, IV:643–46, V:166
DOROTHY: V:567
TOTO: V:296

WIZARD'S GLASS
See MAERLYN'S RAINBOW

WIZARD'S RAINBOW
See MAERLYN'S RAINBOW

WOLF POSSE
See CALLA BRYN STURGIS CHARACTERS: WOLF POSSE

WOLVES (GREENCLOAKS)

Once every generation, the CALLAS of MID-WORLD's BORDERLANDS are invaded by giant, green-cloaked horse-riders from THUNDERCLAP. These servants of the CRIMSON KING steal one of each pair of prepubescent twins and deliver them en masse to their masters in the dark land. Although the people of the Callas don't know exactly what happens to their young children once they are kidnapped, they do know that those who survive the journey home upon the train-pulled flatcars come back ROONT, or mentally and physically ruined.

Although the Wolves' coming is always foretold by ANDY, CALLA BRYN STURGIS's one remaining Messenger Robot, before the arrival of our gunslinger *tet* the *folken* have never successfully rebuffed an attack. As they so morosely state during their meeting at the TOWN GATHERING HALL, they are a village of farmers, not fighters, and the Greencloaks who come galloping across the RIVER WHYE, bearing their terrible light-sticks and sneetches, are more than a match for a bunch of clod-turners.

By anyone's standards, the Wolves (named for the gray wolf masks they wear) are truly terrifying. As they gallop through the town on their huge gray steeds, wearing their green, swirling cloaks and black, cruel-looking boot spurs, they seem unassailable. No weapon penetrates the armor they wear beneath their clothes, and the ones they wield are the deadly technological creations of the GREAT OLD ONES. Their light-sticks burn the skin black and stop the heart, and their flying metal buzz-balls strip a man of skin in five seconds.

In truth, the Wolves are neither men nor beasts but robots manufactured by NORTH CENTRAL POSITRONICS. However, by the time our *tet* rides into Calla Bryn Sturgis on their borrowed horses, only one of the Calla's *folken* knows the true nature of the town's terrible adversaries. This person— GRAN-PERE JAFFORDS—has guarded his secret for years, afraid that he will be disbelieved by his fellows or (worse yet) killed by Andy and whatever other traitors lurk in the town. Because, as becomes clear in *Wolves of the Calla*, the Calla always contains traitors—adults willing to sell information to Thunderclap as long as their own children are guaranteed safety.

At the EAST ROAD battle, which takes place at the end of *Wolves of the Calla*, our *tet* defeats these terrible invaders and ends a cycle of violence which has been playing out for six generations. They kill these monsters not by shooting them through the heart, but by destroying the small radar dishes, or thinking caps, which revolve above their heads, but which are hidden by the hoods of their cloaks. (In this one vulnerability, they resemble SHARDIK, the cyborg BEAR GUARDIAN, which SUSANNAH killed at the beginning of *The Waste Lands*.) When EDDIE and JAKE remove the mask from one of their metallic enemies, they discover that he looks much like DR. DOOM from the *Spider-Man* comic books. He has lenses for eyes, a round mesh grille for a nose, and two sprouted microphones for ears.

V:5–31 *(coming to Calla)*, V:113, V:117, V:132, V:135, V:139, V:142–60 *(149—described)*, V:161, V:163, V:164, V:207, V:214, V:217, V:220, V:221–22, V:224, V:236, V:237, V:247, V:257–91, V:295, V:318, V:319, V:321, V:322, V:328, V:339, V:340, V:341, V:342, V:347–49, V:350, V:356, V:357–69, V:382, V:383, V:390 *(killed)*, V:393, V:394, V:396, V:397, V:413, V:416, V:420, V:434 *(Hitler Brothers and Wolves)*, V:479, V:481, V:483,

V:484, V:490, V:491, V:492, V:494, V:501, V:509, V:536 (*Balazar's men as*), V:537 (*Wolves of our world*), V:554, V:555, V:561, V:567, V:572, V:574, V:575, V:580, V:581, V:582, V:584, V:586, V:590, V:602, V:603, V:604, V:606, V:607–17, V:629, V:632–35, V:636–38, V:642, V:645, V:650, V:656, V:658, V:659, V:661, V:663–97, V:700, VI:4, VI:6, VI:10, VI:23–26, VI:27, VI:61, VI:64, VI:81, VI:237, VI:238 (*horses*), VI:243, VI:245, VI:246, VI:247, VI:248, VI:337, VI:365, VII:21, VII:43, VII:81, VII:149, VII:151–53, VII:173, VII:179, VII:191, VII:192, VII:193–94, VII:206, VII:214, VII:232, VII:233, VII:234, VII:239, VII:252, VII:272, VII:407, VII:538, VII:540

WORTHINGTON, FRED
See BREAKERS

WYLAND (WYLAND BABY)
See TREE VILLAGE CHARACTERS

Y

YANKO, MIKE
See PIPER SCHOOL CHARACTERS

YOUNG AND BEARDLESS
See MANNI

Z

ZACHARY
See TULL CHARACTERS

ZALIA JAFFORDS
See ORIZA, SISTERS OF

ZALMAN HOONIK
See CALLA BRYN STURGIS CHARACTERS: ROONTS

ZOLTAN
See BORDER DWELLERS

ZOMBIS
In *Wolves of the Calla*, Roland must hide his knowledge of the WOLVES' true nature from whatever traitors lurk in CALLA BRYN STURGIS. He does this by telling the *folken* that the Greencloaks are zombis (spelled without the usual *e*), not robots.
V:610, V:616

MID-WORLD PLACES
AND BORDERLAND PLACES[1]

For the gunslinger it had been a stranger death yet—the endless hunt for the man in black through a world with neither map nor memory.

I:140*

My world is like a huge ship that sank near enough shore for most of the wreckage to wash up on the beach. Much of what we find is fascinating, some of it may be useful, if ka allows, but all of it is still wreckage. Senseless wreckage.

Roland Deschain, IV:71

Eddie slept. There were no dreams. And beneath them as the night latened and the moon set, this borderland world turned like a dying clock.

V:239

**ALGUL SIENTO
See ALGUL SIENTO, *in* PORTALS

ALKALI FLATS
See DEBARIA, BARONY OF

---

1. **NOTE ON MID-WORLD DIRECTIONS:** In the original version of *The Gunslinger*, Roland follows WALTER (the MAN IN BLACK) due south through the MOHAINE DESERT and the CYCLOPEAN MOUNTAINS. In the 2003 edition of the book, Roland follows Walter southeast, both of them drawn toward the force of the BEAR-TURTLE BEAM. For a detailed account of how this alters MID-WORLD's geography, see MID-WORLD MAPS located in Appendix VII of this *Concordance*.

* This line comes from the 1982 version of *The Gunslinger*. It was cut from the revised 2003 edition.

ALL-WORLD

In the time of Roland's semi-mythical ancestor, ARTHUR ELD, all of the kingdoms of the land—whether part of IN-WORLD, OUT-WORLD, or MID-WORLD—were united under one high king who wore the crown of All-World upon his brow. This king was Arthur, Warrior of the White and the first Lord of Light. Like the great King Arthur of our world, Arthur Eld wielded a magical sword called EXCALIBUR. Arthur reigned during a kind of Golden Age that came (we believe) after the nuclear and chemical destruction wreaked by the OLD ONES.

Even in Roland's youth, when the In-World Baronies still stood and the gunslingers maintained relative peace by exerting their strength through the fragmenting AFFILIATION, the unity of Arthur Eld's All-World was only a myth. FARSON (who we believe was the pawn for an even greater destructive force) warred in the west, drawing over to his side many of the embittered, failed gunslingers originally sent to the western lands in disgrace. In *Wizard and Glass*, we learned that Arthur Eld's original kingdom (known as the ancient land of Eld) was located in the northwest. Ironically (or perhaps quite pointedly) these western baronies were the first to fall to THE GOOD MAN during Roland's youth.

IV:317, V:486, VI:251

ALORA FARM
See DEBARIA, BARONY OF

AMBUSH ARROYO
See DEBARIA, BARONY OF

APPLE, THE BIG
See NEW YORK CITY, *in* OUR WORLD PLACES

ARC
See BORDERLANDS: GRAND CRESCENT

**ARROYO COUNTRY
See BORDERLANDS: CALLA BRYN STURGIS

ARTEN
Roland's lady-mother, GABRIELLE DESCHAIN, was originally from Arten.
W:37, W:306
BEESFORD-ON-ARTEN: The town of Beesford-on-Arten was located west of GILEAD along the WESTERN LINE which ran from NEW CANAAN to DEBARIA. In stark contrast to the fertile lands of Gilead, Beesford-on-Arten was a land of scrub and struggling ranches. A few of GABRIELLE DESCHAIN'S relatives still lived in Beesford-On-Arten, but we can't tell whether or not they were loyal to the AFFILIATION, since many people in Arten supported JOHN FARSON. W:41

ATCHISON
See ATCHISON, TOPEKA, AND SANTA FE RAILROAD *in* OUR WORLD PLACES

B

BACK COURTS
   See NEW CANAAN, BARONY OF: GILEAD

BAD GRASS
   See MEJIS, BARONY OF

BADLANDS
   See CALLA BADLANDS *and* DISCORDIA, *both in* PORTALS

BANQUETING HALL
   See CASTLE DISCORDIA, *in* PORTALS

BAR K RANCH
   See MEJIS, BARONY OF: HAMBRY

BAYVIEW HOTEL
   See MEJIS, BARONY OF: HAMBRY

BEACH (LOBSTROSITY BEACH)
   See WESTERN SEA

BEACH DOORS
   See DOORWAYS BETWEEN WORLDS: MAGICAL DOORWAYS, *in* POR-
TALS

BEAM ROAD
Roland and his *tet* follow this road from the GREEN PALACE to the RIVER
WHYE, where they meet the ferryman, BIX.
   TOOK'S OUTLAND MERCANTILE: Roland's *tet* passed this abandoned
   store while walking toward the RIVER WHYE. Inside they found cobwebs
   and the skeleton of an animal that might have been a BILLY-BUMBLER.
   W:4

BEAMS
   See BEAMS, PATH OF THE, *in* PORTALS

BEELIE TOWN (BEELIE STOCKADE)
   See DEBARIA, BARONY OF

BEESFORD-ON-ARTEN
   See ARTEN

BIDDER-WEE SALOON
   See DEBARIA, BARONY OF

BIG EMPTY
In the town of RIVER CROSSING, the elderly residents refer to the wastelands beyond LUD as the Big Empty. SUSANNAH DEAN thinks that all of MID-WORLD's barren lands are a "Big Empty," and confronting that desolation turned Roland in on himself. *See also* WASTE LANDS *and* DRAWERS, *in* PORTALS.
III:226, III:243

BIG RIVER
See BORDERLANDS: RIVER WHYE

BIX'S BOATHOUSE
See BORDERLANDS: RIVER WHYE

BLAINE'S ROUTE
Our desperate *ka-tet* boarded the slo-trans mono BLAINE in LUD, just after EDDIE and SUSANNAH's shoot-out with the PUBES and JAKE's escape from TICK-TOCK, leader of the GRAYS. Blaine's track led southeast, roughly along the PATH OF THE BEAM, in the direction of the DARK TOWER. Although Blaine claimed that he could take our group closer to their final destination, none of them was certain whether they would be able to disembark this Barony Coach alive.

Although probably originally endowed with a polite personality by the GREAT OLD ONES (who in retrospect were much less than great), over the centuries Blaine's personality fragmented into its component parts, finally evincing some of the cruelty of his Makers. The resulting monstrosity—which our *ka-tet* battled in a life-or-death riddling contest—consisted of a frightened Little Blaine as well as a nasty Big Blaine, who seemed to believe he served the people of Lud best by killing them.

Blaine's route led through the surreal WASTE LANDS and terminated in an alternative version of our world's TOPEKA, one afflicted by the terrible superflu found in STEPHEN KING's novel *The Stand.*

Blaine was obviously created to transport the Great Old Ones onto other levels of the Tower, and is an example of the sinister technology created by NORTH CENTRAL POSITRONICS. For more discussion on the subject of trains between worlds, see the ATCHISON, TOPEKA, AND SANTA FE RAIL-ROAD, in OUR WORLD PLACES.

CANDLETON: This was the first official stop on Blaine's route. Luckily for our *ka-tet* the train didn't actually stop here; otherwise they would have been exposed to the killer radiation levels still pulsing from a nearby Ground Zero.

Although described as "a poisoned and irradiated ruin," Candleton is not completely dead. Trundling along the corridors of the CANDLETON TRAVELLERS' HOTEL are turtle-sized beetles, birds that look more like small dragons, and blind, bloated, mutant rats. III:404, III:416, IV:13–14, IV:15

CANDLETON FOUNTAIN: IV:13–14

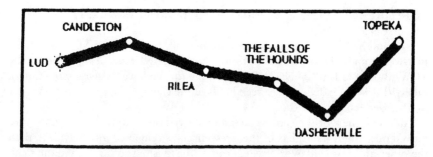

CANDLETON TRAVELLERS' HOTEL: IV:13–14
ELEGANT BEEF AND PORK RESTAURANT: IV:13
DASHERVILLE: Dasherville was the stop before TOPEKA on Blaine's run.
III:404, IV:36
FALLS OF THE HOUNDS: The Falls of the Hounds was actually a torrential
waterfall guarded by two giant stone sculptures shaped like ferocious dogs.
(The dogs actually protruded from a point about two hundred feet below the
place where the torrential, brawling river tumbled over its drop.)

It was at the Falls of the Hounds that Blaine switched to battery power.
His batteries were fired up by the electric-blue energy zapping from the giant
hounds' eyes. III:404, IV:31–33, IV:34–35, IV:41, IV:643, IV:653
RILEA: Rilea was the stop after Candleton on Blaine's run. III:404, IV:15,
IV:16, IV:22, IV:26, IV:643
TOPEKA: Topeka was Blaine's termination point. It also happened to be
located in an alternate version of our world's KANSAS. *See* KANSAS, *in* OUR
WORLD PLACES

BLOSSIE GROVES
See NORTH'RD BARONY: ENDLESS FOREST; *see also* NEW CANAAN,
BARONY OF

**BLUE HAVEN/BLUE HEAVEN
See DEVAR-TOI, *in* PORTALS

BLUFFS
See MEJIS, BARONY OF

BOG
See MID-FOREST (MID-FOREST BOG)

BOOM-FLURRY HILL
See CALLA BADLANDS, *in* PORTALS

BORDER (BORDER DWELLERS)
The Border Dwellers live in this transitional desert area bordering the waterless
wasteland of the MOHAINE DESERT. This region was one of the first in which
time grew soft.
BROWN'S HUT: I:15–22, I:64–65, I:72

BORDERLANDS (THE RIM, ARC O' THE BORDERLANDS, THE CRESCENT)

The Arc o' the Borderlands is the crescent of land that separates MID-WORLD-that-was from END-WORLD, location of both THUNDERCLAP and the DARK TOWER. In CALLA BRYN STURGIS (setting for the novel *Wolves of the Calla*), the RIVER WHYE divides the green lands of the Callas from the desolate wastes of Thunderclap.

Although the world has most definitely moved on, and the borderlands have moved on with it, the Callas of the Crescent have remained more civilized than the other areas of Mid-World which our *tet* has visited so far. Unlike the mad, warring citizens of LUD (whom we learned about in *The Waste Lands*), the Calla *folken* have roads, law enforcement, and a system of government reminiscent of the democratic process found in New England town meetings. Perhaps the borderlands have managed to hold on to an older way of life because—even before IN-WORLD fell to JOHN FARSON—life in the Rim was always strange.

Despite having remained civilized, the people of the Callas have had to face a menace which those towns farther from the dark land of Thunderclap have never had to contemplate. Every generation, for the past six generations, masked riders have galloped over the River Whye and entered the Callas to steal one of every pair of prepubescent twins. (In the Callas, most children are born as twins, not as singletons.) These GREENCLOAKS, or WOLVES, deliver the children to the servants of the CRIMSON KING, who cull their brains for the chemical which causes twin-telepathy. When the children are returned to their homes (and most are sent back), they are ROONT, or ruined.

V:11, V:113, V:135, V:386, VI:7, VI:122, VII:21, VII:214, VII:716 *(Arc o' the Borderlands)*

ARC, THE: *See* GRAND CRESCENT, *listed below*

ARC QUADRANT: According to the rusted steel plate of the CALLA DOGAN, the area of the borderlands which our *tet* visits was once known as the Northeast Corridor Arc Quadrant. *See also* DOGAN, *in* PORTALS. V:564, V:565

BIG RIVER: *See* RIVER WHYE, *listed below*

BOG: *See* MID-FOREST (MID-FOREST BOG), *listed separately*

BOOM-FLURRY HILL: *See* CALLA BADLANDS, *in* PORTALS

CALLA (CALLAS): According to SUSANNAH DEAN, the word *Calla* means street or square. In the borderlands, Callas are towns. There are approximately seventy Callas in the borderlands. They form a mild arc, known locally as the GRAND CRESCENT. This crescent is approximately six thousand miles from tip to tip. As you travel north, toward the lands where snow falls, the towns are smaller. The people who live in them wear wooden shoes and make good cheese. They tend to farm and raise sheep. CALLA BRYN STURGIS (situated approximately one-third of the way down the Crescent) is a farming and ranching Calla. Farther south, the Callas consist of vast tracks of ranchland. There are mining Callas, manufacturing Callas, and pleasure Callas. All of the Callas near Calla Bryn Sturgis are attacked by the WOLVES of THUNDERCLAP once each generation. V:135–36 *(Callas in a mild arc, north and south of Calla Bryn Sturgis)*, V:332, VI:88, VI:377, VII:21, VII:52,

VII:142, VII:152, VII:232, VII:233 *(Calla-bound)*, VII:300, VII:412, VII:558, VII:594, W:10

CALLA AMITY: Located north of CALLA BRYN STURGIS, Calla Amity is a farming and ranching Calla. V:135, V:397

CALLA BOOT HILL: We never learn where Calla Boot Hill is located. However, if EDDIE DEAN ever got the chance, he would slap leather and blow EBEN TOOK all the way to Calla Boot Hill. V:402

CALLA BRYN BOUSE: This Calla consists mainly of ranches. V:135

CALLA BRYN STURGIS: Calla Bryn Sturgis is located approximately one-third of the way down the GRAND CRESCENT. A town has existed on this site for more than one thousand years, though its citizens have only been losing their children to THUNDERCLAP's green-cloaked WOLVES for about six generations. In the novel *Wolves of the Calla,* Roland and his *tet* defeat these robotic child-stealers. In the final EAST ROAD battle, where the horse-riders from Thunderclap are defeated, three members of the SISTERS OF ORIZA fight beside Roland and his friends.

The people of Calla Bryn Sturgis ride donkeys and burros. The men dress in white pants, long, colorful shirts, and dusty sombreros. Both women and men wear the clodhoppers known as shor'boots. There are approximately 140 men in the Calla, if one does not count either ROONTS or the very old. Since some of these men are unmarried farmhands, the female population is probably somewhat smaller. At the time our story takes place, approximately NINETY-NINE prepubescent children are in the town.

At times, Calla Bryn Sturgis is reminiscent of HAMBRY, the setting for *Wizard and Glass,* but at other times it bears a strong resemblance to STONEHAM, MAINE, and even 'SALEM'S LOT, MAINE. Perhaps they are all variations of the same town, just ones that exist on different levels of the DARK TOWER. The accent found in Calla Bryn Sturgis is similarly mixed. Some Calla words sound almost Scottish; others are reminiscent of Maine's Yankee dialect.

CALLA BRYN STURGIS DIRECTLY NAMED ON THE FOLLOWING PAGES: V:2, V:4, V:5, V:11, V:20, V:24, V:27, V:28, V:29, V:31, V:106, V:109 *(Calla)*, V:111, V:113, V:114, V:115, V:119, V:123–24, V:128, V:129, V:142, V:143, V:147, V:148, V:151, V:153, V:154, V:156, V:158, V:159, V:160, V:161 *(Calla-folk)*, V:166, V:174, V:180, V:188, V:201, V:204, V:206–7 *(ka-tet's first view)*, V:208, V:210–34 *(pavilion)*, V:237, V:296, V:321, V:339, V:340, V:359 *(indirect)*, V:362, V:382, V:385, V:393, V:398, V:406, V:442, V:467, V:469, V:479, V:481, V:489, V:490, V:493, V:497, V:498, V:499, V:502, V:516, V:547, V:551, V:552, V:555, V:557, V:561, V:562, V:572, V:577, V:580, V:581, V:584, V:592, V:601, V:602, V:606, V:607, V:618, V:623, V:625, V:627, V:637, V:641, V:642, V:648, V:650, V:654, V:655, V:658, V:679, V:686, V:700, V:703, V:707, V:708, VI:3–43 *(setting)*, VI:63, VI:67, VI:81, VI:84, VI:88 *(Calla)*, VI:92, VI:103, VI:115, VI:122, VI:131, VI:178, VI:179, VI:184, VI:185, VI:187, VI:203, VI:222, VI:237, VI:247, VI:248, VI:252, VI:268, VI:272, VI:273, VI:281, VI:329, VI:339, VI:350, VII:4, VII:14, VII:26, VII:44, VII:73, VII:75, VII:81, VII:120, VII:126, VII:143, VII:146, VII:150, VII:152, VII:153, VII:156, VII:173, VII:207, VII:339, VII:398, VII:404, VII:423, VII:428, VII:473,

VII:493, VII:518, VII:540, VII:602, VII:606, VII:627, VII:703, VII:708, VII:710, VII:722, VII:726, VII:743, VII:744, VII:748, W:17; W:307

ARRA'S SMALLHOLD PATCH: V:361

ARROYO COUNTRY (COMMALA DRAWS, MAGNETIC HILLS, BATTLE SITE): The arroyo country is the hilly land located northeast of Calla Bryn Sturgis. Here, in a worn-out garnet mine located at the end of a long dead-end canyon, Roland proposes that the Calla *folken* hide their children while he and his *tet* ambush the green-cloaked, child-stealing WOLVES. (Roland doesn't really plan to hide the children in such a dangerous place, but the Calla has too many informants for him to reveal his true strategy.)

The hills above the Calla are magnetic. Not only are they full of old garnet mines, but they are also riddled with many DOORWAYS BETWEEN WORLDS. The DOORWAY CAVE, where the MANNI found an unconscious PERE CALLAHAN, is located deep in the arroyo country. The EAST ROAD battle, where Roland, his *tet*, and the SISTERS OF ORIZA make a final stand against the Wolves, is located on a stretch of road that also winds north into this hilly land. V:340–42, V:406–9, V:508–9, V:548–52, V:575–76, V:662–97, V:700, VI:23–27, VI:30. *See also* MAGNETIC HILLS *and* DOORWAY CAVE, *both in* PORTALS

> **GLORIA MINE and REDBIRD TWO MINE:** These two mines are located at the far end of a dead-end canyon. Roland tells the Calla *folken* that they should hide their children here when the WOLVES attack the town. (In actuality, Roland plans to hide the children in the rice paddies located near the RIVER WHYE.) V:508, V:575–76, V:608, V:615–16, V:663–97

UNFOUND DOOR: *See* DOORWAY CAVE, *in* PORTALS

UNFOUND DOOR (PATH TO THE): As HENCHICK warns Roland, this long, twisty path which leads through the arroyo country to the UNFOUND DOOR is rather "upsy." Despite this, the going is clear (and contains some spectacular views). However, the mouth of the DOORWAY CAVE is blocked by a large boulder. Anyone who wishes to enter this cave must first ease himself or herself around this rock. Unfortunately, the bit of free ledge is so small that a visitor's boot heels will have to dangle free over a two-thousand-foot drop as he or she inches toward the cave mouth. (Ten feet farther down, where EDDIE DEAN almost falls, the drop from path to ground reduces to a mere seven hundred feet!) V:406–9, V:508–9, V:548–52, V:699–703, VI:6, VI:8, VI:23–27, VI:33, VI:41, VI:63–64

BADLANDS: *See* CALLA BADLANDS, *in* PORTALS

BLUFF: The bluff is located near a bend in the RIVER WHYE. JAKE and BENNY SLIGHTMAN go camping here. Not far from this spot, Jake overhears SLIGHTMAN THE ELDER having a suspicious conversation with ANDY, the Calla's traitorous Messenger Robot. V:323, V:380–87 *(camping)*, V:558 *(tenting place)*

BOOM-FLURRY HILL: *See* CALLA BADLANDS, *in* PORTALS

BUCKHEAD RANCH: This is GEORGE TELFORD's ranch. V:553

CAUSEWAY: *See* CALLA BADLANDS, *in* PORTALS

CAVE OF VOICES: *See* DOORWAY CAVE, *in* PORTALS

CAVERRA HOUSE: Home of the Caverra family. V:15

COMMALA DRAWS: *See* ARROYO COUNTRY, *listed above*

DOGAN: *See* DOGAN, *in* PORTALS

DOORWAY CAVE: *See* DOORWAY CAVE, *in* PORTALS

EAST ROAD: East Road is Calla Bryn Sturgis's major artery. Although for most of its length it runs from the west to the east, once it approaches the western shore of the RIVER WHYE, it turns and heads roughly north-northeast. (During his trip to the CALLA DOGAN, JAKE CHAMBERS discovers that the East Road originally continued east into THUNDER-CLAP. For quite obvious reasons, the Calla *folken* no longer use this section and it has fallen into disrepair.)

Many years before our story takes place, JAMIE JAFFORDS and his WOLF POSSE killed a Wolf on the East Road. (Unfortunately, all of the human fighters, save for Jamie, died as well.) In *Wolves of the Calla*, the East Road is the site of our *tet*'s final stand against Thunderclap's child-stealers. V:237 *(says west, should say east)*, V:348, V:360–65 *(Wolf posse)*, V:390–96, V:399–402, V:487, V:492 *(main road)*, V:508, V:561–62 *(continues into Thunderclap)*, V:629–35 *(junction with River Road)*, V:638–44 *(directly mentioned on 641)*, V:654–97, V:703, VI:5, VI:6, VI:10, VI:21–27, VI:31, VI:67, VII:126, VII:142, VII:558

GARNET MINES: *See* ARROYO COUNTRY, *listed above*

GATHERING HALL: *See* TOWN GATHERING HALL, *listed below*

GLORIA MINE: *See* ARROYO COUNTRY, *listed above*

HIGH STREET: During his brief but terrifying visit to the CALLA DOGAN, JAKE CHAMBERS discovers that either BEN SLIGHTMAN SR. or ANDY the Messenger Robot planted two spy cameras along the Calla's High Street. (However, it is also possible that an earlier spy planted these cameras.) V:9, V:10, V:13, V:210–12, V:213, V:234, V:238, V:618 *(two cameras)*, VII:423

JAFFORDS'S LAND (JAFFORDS'S BARN, JAFFORDS'S HOME, RIVER FIELD, ROADSIDE FIELD, SON OF A BITCH): The JAFFORDS FAMILY home place is located on RIVER ROAD. As well as their house and barn, the Jaffordses own three fields. River Field grows rice; Roadside Field grows sharproot, pumpkin, and corn; and Son of a Bitch produces nothing but rocks, blisters, and busted hopes. This final bit of information is hardly surprising, since Son of a Bitch sits on loose ground. (Bogarts probably live below it.) V:1–13, V:343–69, V:376–80 *(barn)*, V:396–99, V:401, V:488–92, V:649

LIVERY: V:159, V:210

MAGNETIC HILLS: *See* ARROYO COUNTRY, *listed above; see also* DOORWAY CAVE *and* DOORWAYS BETWEEN WORLDS, *both in* PORTALS

MANNI CALLA (MANNI REDPATH, REDPATH KRA-TEN, RED-PATH-A-STURGIS): Manni Calla, home of the local MANNI sect, is located approximately two hours north of Calla Bryn Sturgis. In the CALLA DOGAN, JAKE discovers that someone planted two spy cameras in Manni Calla. V:6 *(indirect)*, V:213, V:399, V:566 *(two cameras)*, VI:3, VI:5, VI:6, VI:7, VI:9, VI:35 *(indirect)*, VI:38

HENCHICK'S KRA (CABIN): Henchick's home. He lives here with his three wives. V:466

TEMPA (MANNI MEETING HALL): The MANNI's Tempa is equivalent to the Calla's TOWN GATHERING HALL. VI:6

OLD CALLA ROAD: Although the Old Calla Road used to look like a true road, by the time Roland, EDDIE, SUSANNAH, JAKE, and OY come across it, the road looks more like a little lane. Like so many of MID-WORLD's roads, it follows the PATH OF THE BEAM. The village of GOOK lies along this road. W:14

GOOK, VILLAGE OF: According to Roland, a gook is a deep well which any traveler can drink from without let or penalty. When Roland discovered that a STARKBLAST was about to thunder along the PATH OF THE BEAM, he asked the WHYE ferryman, BIX, if there was a place where he and his *tet* could hide up and wait for the storm to pass. Bix told them about the village of GOOK, which still had a strong stone meeting hall that could probably withstand the starkblast's powerful but frigid winds. It also contained a large fireplace where they could keep warm.

Besides the stone TOWN MEETING HALL, which sat at the southern end of the high street, and the deep well from which the town took its name, the abandoned settlement of Gook was completely dilapidated. Along the village high street was a sad cluster of empty, tumbling buildings that ran on for about a quarter mile. Some had been houses, some stores, but in their state of decay it was impossible to tell which had been which. Our *tet* used the remains of Gook's timber buildings as firewood so that they could remain warm during the storm. W:14–15, W:17 *(deserted village)*, W:18–31, W:303–5

GOOK WELL: Gook's well was located on the far side of the TOWN MEETING HALL, in what EDDIE assumed had once been the town common. Eddie and SUSANNAH went to the well so that Susannah could clean the town meeting hall's chimney soot from her body. W:21–23, W:30

TOWN MEETING HALL: Gook's town meeting hall was the only building in the abandoned village which remained intact. Located at the southern end of the town, where the village high street forked, the hall was a squat blockhouse-like building constructed of gray fieldstone. It stood hip-deep in overgrown shrubbery and was partly concealed by young fir trees.

Although swallows (or bin-rusties) had found their way into the second floor, the large downstairs central hall was still sound. Although the hall's windows were glassless, Roland, Eddie, and Jake were able to use the building's many tables and benches as makeshift shutters. (They covered the windows on the northwest wall from the outside, so that STARKBLAST's strong wind would press the shutters tighter.) Rolling her wheelchair into the fireplace, Susannah Dean opened the flue, and was rewarded by a heavy rain of black soot. (Her colorful response was pure DETTA WALKER.)

While the starkblast raged outside, our *tet* remained by the fire, listening to Roland's two intertwining stories. The first of these was the autobiographical tale of Roland's adventures in DEBARIA, where he and his *ka*-mate, JAMIE DeCURRY, hunted down a shapeshifting SKIN-MAN. The second story was a MID-WORLD folktale entitled "The Wind Through the Keyhole." This story told of the early exploits of TIM ROSS (later known as Tim Stoutheart), a young boy who became a gunslinger, despite the fact that he was not born to the line of ELD. "The Wind Through the Keyhole" was Roland's favorite childhood tale. W:15, W:18–21, W:23–31, W:303–7

OUR LADY OF SERENITY (CHURCH, CHURCH RECTORY, and ROSALITA'S COTTAGE): Our Lady of Serenity is FATHER CALLAHAN's church. Locally, it is also known as the MAN JESUS Church. As well as a house of worship, the church grounds contain Callahan's rectory, his small garden, and ROSALITA's cottage. Like many other places in the Calla, Pere Callahan's living room contains a spy camera. (This camera must have been placed by either BEN SLIGHTMAN SR. or ANDY, since Our Lady of Serenity was built relatively recently.)

Although the spies for THUNDERCLAP probably don't know it, Callahan's modest wooden church contains a secret. Under its floorboards sleeps BLACK THIRTEEN, the most evil of all MAERLYN's magic spheres. V:8, V:27 *(indirect)*, V:128 *(indirect)*, V:158 *(indirect)*, V:221 *(indirect)*, V:234 *(indirect)*, V:235–53 *(setting)*, V:254–309 *(Callahan tells his story here)*, V:309–17, V:337 *(indirect, bedroom)*, V:338, V:381, V:383, V:402, V:415, V:417–72 *(428–65 Callahan's story)*, V:475–86, V:487, V:488, V:494, V:496–505, V:506–8, V:566 *(one camera in church and one in rectory)*, V:584, V:589, V:598, V:617, V:628–29 *(privy)*, V:639–41, V:644–50, V:653 *(indirect)*, V:685, VI:3–18 *(setting)*, VI:67, VI:336

PAVILION and TOWN COMMON: All of the Calla's outdoor festivities are held on the town's common. When our *tet* first arrives in the village, the *folken* hold a welcoming party for them here, and Roland dances the Commala on the pavilion's bandstand. On Wolf's Eve (the night before the WOLVES are due to raid the town), Roland requests that all of the Calla's children come here to camp. One of the DOGAN's spy cameras records all that goes on in this place. Luckily, Roland and his *tet* know it and so only spread misleading information. V:13, V:204, V:205, V:208, V:209, V:211–34, V:238, V:322, V:331, V:403, V:566 *(camera)*, V:567, V:581–90 *(palaver)*, V:601–17 *(green and musica)*, V:638, V:641, V:650–53, V:662 *(common)*, VI:12 *(common)*, VI:21 *(common)*, VI:67, VI:339

PEABERRY ROAD: V:360

RANCH ROAD: V:487

REDBIRD MINE TWO: *See* ARROYO COUNTRY, *listed above*

RIVER ROAD: River Road branches off the EAST ROAD. Many of the smallhold farms (including the JAFFORDS FAMILY home) are located here. V:343, V:345, V:360, V:603, V:629–35 *(junction with East Road)*

RIVER STREET: River Street is located in the central part of Calla Bryn Sturgis. V:585

ROCKING B RANCH: The Rocking B Ranch, situated south of Calla Bryn Sturgis, is owned by VAUGHN EISENHART. The traitorous BEN

SLIGHTMAN SR. is Eisenhart's foreman. JAKE's friend BENNY lives at the Rocking B. V:13, V:153, V:203, V:205, V:223, V:234, V:294, V:318–42, V:385, V:388, V:407, V:487, V:491, V:495, V:500, V:552, V:553–58, V:569, V:578, V:579–80, V:636–39, VI:17

SEVEN MILE: This is OVERHOLSER's farm. It is the largest in the Calla. V:157, V:213

TOOK'S GENERAL STORE (TOOKY'S): EBEN TOOK, owner of Took's General Store, is one of the most important men in Calla Bryn Sturgis. He is also one of the richest. Many years before the events of *Wolves of the Calla* take place, Tooky's was burned flat because some of the townsfolk tried to hide children there. Now the Tooks are too afraid of the WOLVES (and of lost profits) to stand up to the monsters of THUNDERCLAP.

According to both PERE CALLAHAN and Roland, Tooky's closely resembles the EAST STONEHAM GENERAL STORE located in EAST STONEHAM, MAINE. (Perhaps the biggest difference is that, at Tooky's, you can pay for your purchases with garnets as well as coins.) Like so many of the other gathering places of the Calla, Tooky's contains a hidden camera, probably planted by either BEN SLIGHTMAN SR. or ANDY the Messenger Robot.

In the STEPHEN KING story "Return to 'Salem's Lot," Tooky's is the name of a bar. V:13, V:14, V:19, V:147, V:150, V:211, V:359–60, V:400, V:401, V:402–6 *(mercantile and grocery)*, V:417, V:418, V:487, V:497, V:502 *(mercantile)*, V:534, V:545, V:566 *(camera)*, V:585, V:621, VI:67, VI:130, VI:162, VII:423

TOWN COMMON: *See* PAVILION, *listed above*

TOWN GATHERING HALL: All of Calla Bryn Sturgis's town meetings are held in the Town Gathering Hall, which stands at the end of HIGH STREET, beyond TOOK'S GENERAL STORE. Only men attend these gatherings. When one of the townsmen wants to call a meeting, he sends round the opopanax feather. If enough men touch the feather, the meeting is called. V:12, V:13–31, V:135, V:150, V:210, V:214, V:225, V:311, V:331, V:354, V:582, V:604, V:620

TRAVELERS' REST: This boardinghouse and restaurant is owned by the TOOK family. Unlike the TRAVELLERS' REST found in HAMBRY, the Calla's Travelers' Rest is spelled with only one *l*. *See also* MEJIS, BARONY OF: HAMBRY, TOWN OF: TRAVELLERS' REST. V:158 *(indirect)*, V:210

CALLA DIVINE: This Calla is located south of CALLA BRYN STURGIS. We know that the SISTERS OF ORIZA have members here too, since they buy ORIZAS from the women of CALLA SEN CHRE. V:332 *(as far south as the Orizas travel)*

CALLA LOCKWOOD: This Calla is located just south of CALLA BRYN STURGIS. It consists of farms and ranches. V:27, V:135, V:207, V:397

CALLA SEN CHRE: The people of this Calla farm and raise sheep. The women also make the titanium plates thrown by the SISTERS OF ORIZA. V:135, V:331–32 *(plates made here)*

CALLA SEN PINDER: The people of this Calla are farmers and sheep breeders. V:135

CALLA STAFFEL: This Calla consists mainly of ranchland. V:135

EASTERN PLAIN: *See* CALLA BADLANDS, *in* PORTALS

GRAND CRESCENT (ARC, ARC QUADRANT, MIDDLE CRESCENT, RIM): The Grand Crescent, also known as the Arc, contains all of the borderland Callas. It stretches for six thousand miles. CALLA BRYN STURGIS is located one-third of the way down the Crescent. V:135 *(indirect),* V:143, V:149, V:158, V:211, V:322, V:328, V:360, VII:300. *See also* OUTER ARC, *listed separately*

GREAT ROAD: *See* MEJIS, BARONY OF

MIDDLE CRESCENT: *See* GRAND CRESCENT, *listed above*

MID-FOREST: *See* MID-FOREST (MID-FOREST BOG), *listed separately*

RIVER WHYE (BIG RIVER, DEVAR-WHYE, DEVAR-TETE WHYE): Northwest of CALLA BRYN STURGIS, the River Whye divides into two branches. The western branch, located close to where the borderlands meet MID-WORLD-that-was, is known as the Devar-Whye. During the town meeting which takes place at the beginning of *Wolves of the Calla,* BUCKY JAVIER suggests that the Calla *folken* try to escape the WOLVES by heading in this direction. The eastern branch of the River Whye is known as the Devar-Tete Whye, or the Little Whye. The Devar-Tete Whye divides Calla Bryn Sturgis from the dead lands of THUNDERCLAP. The River Whye (which runs roughly north-south) is an important trade route for the people of the borderlands. Lake-boat marts often travel along it. Both branches of the River Whye empty into the SOUTH SEAS. V:18, V:136, V:153 *(river),* V:206, V:211, V:238, V:242 *(river),* V:311, V:322 *(indirect),* V:331, V:338 *(indirect),* V:377, V:381, V:495, V:496, V:553, V:557, V:558–61, V:562, V:566, V:611, V:632, V:641, V:642, V:643, V:655, V:659, V:665–67, V:672, V:702, VI:10 *(riverbank),* VI:23, VI:24, VI:64 *(should say east side of Whye),* VI:67, VI:72, VII:151, VII:191, VII:203, VII:412, W:6–17, W:20

   BIX'S BOATHOUSE: The ferryman BIX had two boathouses. The more impressive of them sat on the northwestern bank of the RIVER WHYE. It was a barnlike building painted a green so bright that it almost seemed to yell. Its mouth jutted over the water on pilings painted a similar green. Docked to two of these pilings by thick hawsers was Bix's sixty-foot by sixty-foot raft. The ferry itself was painted in alternating stripes of red and yellow. A tall wooden pole that looked like a sail-less mast jutted from the center. Several wicker chairs sat in front of the pole, facing the closest shore.

   In order to move the ferry, Bix attached a ringbolt to the top of the ferry post, then hooked the ringbolt to the steel cable which spanned the river. To crank the ferry across, he used a large metal crank shaped like a block Z. Not surprisingly, the crank was stamped with the NORTH CENTRAL POSITRONICS logo. According to Bix, both the steel cable and the crank were at the ferry when he took his job more than ninety years previously. He thought that the equipment had come from an underground bunker or DOGAN, located near the GREEN PALACE. Bix had visited it once. He said that the underground area went on for miles, and that it was full of things that had belonged to the OLD PEOPLE. Strange, tooth-rattling music still played from overhead speakers. Unfortunately, after visiting the place he broke out in sores, puked, and started to lose his teeth.

   On the southeastern bank of the river sat Bix's second dock and boathouse. From a distance our *tet* could see that the boathouse was far less grand. (For one thing, it was unpainted.) However, once they came close, they realized that it was actually on the verge of collapse. W:6–12, W:14, W:15

BUSTED LUCK SALOON
See DEBARIA, BARONY OF

C

CAIN
We don't know where Cain is located. However, we do know that it figures prominently in a song sung by the servants of the CRIMSON KING as they chase JAKE CHAMBERS and OY through the passage located beneath the DIXIE PIG:

> We don't care how far you run!
> We'll bring you back before we're done!
> You can run to Cain or Lud!
> We'll eat your balls and drink your blood!
> VII:109

CALLA
For all Callas and Calla entries, see BORDERLANDS

CALLA BRYN STURGIS
See BORDERLANDS

CANDLE, THE
See MEJIS, BARONY OF: HAMBRY: CITGO

CANDLETON
See BLAINE'S ROUTE

CAUSEWAY (DEVIL'S CAUSEWAY)
See CALLA BADLANDS, *in* PORTALS

CAVE OF VOICES
See DOORWAY CAVE, *in* PORTALS

CENTRAL PLACE
See NEW CANAAN, BARONY OF: GILEAD

CHASM OF WHITE FLOWERS
See NORTH'RD BARONY

CHEERY FELLOWS SALOON AND CAFÉ
See DEBARIA, BARONY OF

CHURCH OF THE BLOOD EVERLASTING
See RIVER BARONY: RIVER CROSSING

CITGO
See MEJIS, BARONY OF: HAMBRY

CLEAN SEA
In *Wizard and Glass,* we learned that the Clean Sea is located east of HAMBRY. In *Wolves of the Calla,* Roland tells us that JERICHO HILL lies at least five hundred miles farther north along the Clean Sea's shores.
    IV:145, IV:151, IV:164, IV:231–32, IV:233, IV:341, IV:441, IV:479, IV:521–22, V:170

CLEARING AMID THE IRONWOODS
See NORTH'RD BARONY

CLEARING WITH ENORMOUS TOWER
See DOGAN: NORTH FOREST KINNOCK DOGAN *in* PORTALS

**COACH ROAD
This is the two-rut track that Roland follows during *The Gunslinger.* It runs from PRICETOWN (though it probably began much farther back) through TULL, past BROWN's hut and then into the wastes of the MOHAINE DESERT. Before the world moved on, this road was one of MID-WORLD's highways. The deserted WAY STATION, where Roland meets JAKE, was once a stopping place for the coaches that traveled along this artery.
    Like most of the amenities of organized culture, by the time the events of *The Gunslinger* take place, Mid-World's coach service has almost disappeared. A few still run between Pricetown and Tull, but none venture into the deadly regions of the desert. In the 2003 version of *The Gunslinger,* we find out that bucka waggons also use this road. In this version of the story, the Coach Road runs southeast, like the BEAR-TURTLE BEAM, not due south.
    I:11–16 *(Roland on it),* I:22–24

COMMALA DRAWS
See BORDERLANDS: CALLA BRYN STURGIS: ARROYO COUNTRY

CONSTABLE HOWARD'S HOUSE
See NORTH'RD BARONY

CÖOS
See MEJIS, BARONY OF: HAMBRY

COSINGTON COTTAGE
See NORTH'RD BARONY

COSINGTON-MARCHLY STAKE
See NORTH'RD BARONY

COSINGTON-MARCHLY STORAGE SHED
See NORTH'RD BARONY

COVENANT MAN'S CAMP
See NORTH'RD BARONY

CRADLE OF LUD
See RIVER BARONY: LUD

CRAVEN'S UNDERTAKING PARLOR
See MEJIS, BARONY OF: HAMBRY

CRESCENT
See BORDERLANDS: GRAND CRESCENT; *see also* DEBARIA, BARONY OF

CRESSIA
Cressia was one of the baronies located west of GILEAD. Its barony seat was INDRIE, a city burned to the ground by FARSON'S harriers. Fearful for their lives and afraid to join the thousands already slaughtered by THE GOOD MAN (including Indrie's mayor and high sheriff, who were beheaded by the rebel forces), Cressia repudiated the AFFILIATION and bowed to Farson. It later became one of his strongholds.

When Roland challenged CORT and underwent an early test of manhood against his father's wishes, he thought that his father was far away in this distant barony searching for one of MAERLYN's glass balls. He was wrong. Cressia was famous for one of its sayings: "If ye'd steal the silver from the dining room, first put the dog in the pantry" (IV:175). Many of the gunslinger apprentices who failed their coming-of-age test against either CORT or his father FARDO went west to Cressia, where they joined forces with the GOOD MAN, JOHN FARSON.

IV:110, IV:163, IV:164, IV:175, IV:619 *(Marten joins Farson here)*, W:36
INDRIE: IV:163

CYCLOPEAN MOUNTAINS[2]
The first foothills of the Cyclopean Mountain Range can be seen from the dry wastes of the MOHAINE DESERT. The WILLOW JUNGLE, where JAKE and Roland encounter the demonically sexual ORACLE OF THE MOUNTAINS, is located here among the first tumbling rises of granite and grasses.

These mountains are one of the many physical barriers which Roland and Jake have to traverse in order to pursue the MAN IN BLACK, also known as

---

2. For *The Drawing of the Three* I only listed direct references to the Cyclopean Mountains. However, whenever action takes place on LOBSTROSITY BEACH, which borders the WESTERN SEA, these mountains are on the horizon.

WALTER. At first, their path winds through a much more hospitable landscape than the desert which Roland traversed earlier in *The Gunslinger*. Trees grow here, and there are rabbits to hunt and eat. However, as their experience with the sexual demon of the SPEAKING RING shows, Roland's world contains sinister magic, much of it manipulated by the very sorcerer they pursue.

As Jake and Roland climb higher toward the mountain pass, following the burned-out ideograms left by their elusive and dangerous quarry, the way becomes steeper and less accessible, at times no more than a narrow V cut into the mica- and quartz-veined granite. Just before the mountains rise to their most inaccessible icy heights, the path zigzags into a canyon. There, our two friends follow a taunting Walter into the black cleft of a waterfall cave. Little do they know it, but they are eagerly awaited by the band of SLOW MUTANTS who nest in the deserted mountain subway system left by the OLD ONES.

I:11, I:44, I:56, I:65, I:72, I:92, I:112–34 *(foothills)*, I:134–44, I:149–58 *(Gilead story 149–52)*, I:174–216, II:31, II:32, II:168, II:177, II:231, II:232, II:242 *(foothills)*, II:275 *(hills)*, II:286 *(brakes)*, II:291–97 *(they reach beach)*, II:300–312, II:315 *(abyss)*, II:327, II:367, II:379, II:394, III:36, III:42, III:48, III:97, III:109, III:180, III:195 *(indirect)*, III:223, III:260, III:407, V:462 *(indirect)*

D

DARK TOWER
See entry in PORTALS

DASHERVILLE
See BLAINE'S ROUTE

DEAF RINCON'S BARN
See NORTH'RD BARONY

DEBARIA, BARONY OF (DEBARIA OUTERS)
The Barony of Debaria included the towns of DEBARIA, LITTLE DEBARIA, BEELIE, SALLYWOOD, and the Women's Retreat of SERENITY.
  GENERAL REFERENCES: IV:619, IV:620, IV:655, W:85
  ALKALI FLATS: The alkali flats were located west of the town of DEBARIA, and south of the abandoned SALT-HOUSES. Beyond them, at the base of the high rocks known as AMBUSH ARROYO, were the foothill meadows known as the LOW PURE. W:39, W:57 *(flats)*, W:67
  ALORA FARM: The skin-man killed seven people at the Alora Farm. W:63
  AMBUSH ARROYO: The high rocks of Ambush Arroyo don't exactly constitute an arroyo. However, the name was given to this area after the CROW GANG slaughtered the old High Sheriff, PEA ANDERSON, and his POSSE there. Ambush Arroyo was located in the hardpan north of Debaria, east of the ALKALI FLATS, and west of the HIGH PURE. W:57

BEELIE TOWN (BEELIE STOCKADE): Beelie Town was located west of DEBARIA. Five years before our story takes place, harriers rode through Beelie and left it a ghost town. (Some folks said it was FARSON's men who destroyed Beelie.) In its heyday, Beelie had been the home of a militia outpost, and the Beelie Stockade had been their place of business. The circuit judge sent thieves, murderers, card cheats, cannibals, witches, and warlocks to the stockade. Anyone who did time at the stockade had a blue ring tattooed around his ankle. Watching the Beelie hangings was a favorite pastime in Debaria. Families would pack lunches to watch criminals dance the dead-man's jig. W:102–4, W:278–93 *(blue rings)*

CRESCENT: We don't know exactly where the Crescent is, but we do know that after the Justice Man STRINGY BODEAN retired, he decided to raise horses in the Crescent. W:66

DEBARIA HIGH ROAD: Debaria High Road ran along a ridge close to the rails of the WESTERN LINE. It ran past SERENITY WOMEN'S RETREAT, and all the way to the town of DEBARIA. W:43, W:63, W:95

DEBARIA RAIL LINE: *See* WESTERN LINE, *listed separately*

DEBARIA STREAM: Two COWPUNCHERS were camped out here near a MANNI COUPLE on marriage retreat. They heard screams and went to investigate. They saw a tyger-like creature, but one which ran upright like a man, loping off with the Manni woman's lower leg in its jaws. W:45

DEBARIA, TOWN OF: The town of Debaria was located on the edge of the ALKALI FLATS, in the lands far west of GILEAD. It was a dusty, hide-smelling railhead town where cattle and block salt were shipped south, east, and north—in every direction except the one where FARSON's harriers ruled. Although STEVEN DESCHAIN believed that Debaria would soon dry up, when Roland and JAMIE visited it in search of the murderous SKIN-MAN, it was still a lively place full of saloons, whoredens, gamblers, and confidence men. Luckily there were still a few good men there, including the HIGH SHERIFF, HUGH PEAVY.

Debaria was also the location of the women's retreat where Roland's mother, GABRIELLE DESCHAIN, secluded herself while Roland was in HAMBRY. Supposedly she went to the retreat to pray for Roland's safe return, but—in *The Wind Through the Keyhole*—we come to understand that she was sent there by Roland's father, Steven, to pay penance for her betrayal. Earlier in the Dark Tower series we were led to believe that Gabrielle met her lover, MARTEN BROADCLOAK, while in Debaria, and that she was schooled in the ways of deceit while there. (Steven Deschain certainly never trusted the Sisters of Serenity afterwards.) However, despite whatever part Gabrielle played in Broadcloak's plot to overthrow the aristocratic gunsling-ers, and to assassinate her husband, it seems that Lady Deschain's mind was unhinged by the time she reached this far western land. Hence, she cannot be fully blamed for her actions. IV:619, IV:620, IV:655, W:38, W:39, W:40, W:42, W:43, W:44, W:53–106, W:267–300

DELIGHTFUL VIEW: Delightful View was DEBARIA's only hotel. The view wasn't delightful, and the beds were full of bugs as big as toad's eye-balls. SHERIFF PEAVY told Roland that if he wanted to sleep at Delightful View, he should wear a full suit of ARTHUR ELD's armor. W:66

HIGH STREET: DEBARIA's High Street was wide and paved, though the pavement was already crumbling away to the hardpan underneath. (Luckily, the High Street also had boardwalks.) Roland thought that the remains of the pavement would be entirely gone within a few years. Nonetheless, there was a good deal of commerce on that road and the saloons were busy. W:53–54, W:98, W:270, W:274

> **BIDDER-WEE SALOON:** When the whores of DEBARIA's Bidder-Wee grew too old or diseased, they ended up in the wrecked saloons of LITTLE DEBARIA. W:62
>
> **BLACKSMITH'S SHOP:** The blacksmith's shop was located across the street from DEBARIA's LIVERY. It was here that Roland had the silver bullet made that would eventually kill the SKIN-MAN terrorizing the town. W:98–99
>
> **BUSTED LUCK SALOON:** The Busted Luck was one of DEBARIA's saloons-cum-whorehouses. Although KELLIN FRYE disliked the place, it was a sight better than the saloons and whorehouses found in LITTLE DEBARIA. It was in the Busted Luck that Roland gave all the horse-riding SALTIES a final drink before making them take off their boots. (Roland wanted to discover how many had spent time in BEELIE STOCKADE.) W:62, W:272, W:273, W:277–80, W:286, W:294
>
> **CHEERY FELLOWS SALOON AND CAFÉ:** When the woman from DEBARIA's MERCANTILE asked Roland whether he and Jamie had come to kill the SKIN-MAN, a man standing in front of this saloon retorted that the boys didn't look old enough to kill a bottle of rye. W:54
>
> **HIGH SHERIFF'S OFFICE AND JAIL:** HIGH SHERIFF HUGH PEAVY's office was a little wooden building attached to the much larger stone-built town jail. The jail was in the shape of a T. There were eight big cells down the central aisle and a dozen small ones on the cross quarter. One of the smaller ones was the drunk-and-disorderly cell, where Roland stayed with YOUNG BILL STREETER to keep him safe from the SKIN-MAN. W:54–69, W:95–96, W:98–106, W:267–74, W:274, W:281–94
>
> **LIVERY:** When SMA' TOOT went off her rails, Roland promised the ENJIE, TRAVIS, that he and JAMIE would ride to DEBARIA's livery and get help. The livery was located on the far end of the HIGH STREET. W:44, W:98
>
> **MERCANTILE:** When Roland and JAMIE first road into DEBARIA, a woman came out of the town mercantile and asked the boys whether they had come to kill the SKIN-MAN. W:54
>
> **RACEY'S CAFÉ:** There were only two restaurants in Debaria, and Racey's was the better of them. W:99, W:279, W:294

WIDOW BRAILEY'S BOARDING HOUSE: The WIDOW BRAILLEY ran the last boardinghouse in DEBARIA. Two years before Roland and JAMIE arrived, a drunk saddletramp tried to rape her while she sat in the outhouse. She slit the man's throat. Although the Justice Man, STRINGY BODEAN, declared her not guilty of murder, she decided she'd had enough of Debaria and returned to GILEAD. W:66

DOOLIN RANCH: The Doolin Ranch was located north of DEBARIA. BELINDA DOOLIN, wife of Rancher DOOLIN, was kidnapped by the CROW GANG and taken to the SALT HOUSES where the gang had their hideout. W:56

HIGH PURE: The High Pure was the high meadowland located northeast of the ALKALI FLATS and AMBUSH ARROYO. W:57

JEFFERSON RANCH: Soon after ROLAND DESCHAIN and JAMIE DeCURRY reached DEBARIA, the SKIN-MAN struck again. This time he massacred the people of the Jefferson Ranch. All told, he killed sixteen prod-dies, the COOK (BILL STREETER), *sai* JEFFERSON, Jefferson's WIFE, and his two DAUGHTERS. The Jefferson Ranch was located ten wheels due north of the town of Debaria. It had a wide stock gate with JEFFERSON posted over it in white birch letters. Near the entrance was the shakepole fence of a horse corral, which stood near to the big house. A half mile or so north, standing atop a little hill, was the bunkhouse. W:69–87, W:91–95 *(Young Bill's hypnosis vision)*, W:270, W:278, W:280

> **BIG HOUSE:** The SKIN-MAN killed *sai* JEFFERSON'S WIFE in the kitchen of the big house. Her body was under the table and her half-eaten head was by the pantry door. Jefferson's two DAUGHTERS lay halfway between the house and the barn. Roland and SHERIFF PEAVY questioned YOUNG BILL STREETER under the big house's willow tree. W:69–87, W:91–95 *(Young Bill's hypnosis vision)*

> **BUNKHOUSE:** The Jefferson Ranch bunkhouse was located on a little hill a half mile north of the big house. By the time ROLAND, JAMIE, SHERIFF PEAVY, KELLIN FRYE, VIKKA FRYE, and TRAVIS (the ENJIE of SMA' TOOT), arrived at the Jefferson Ranch, the bunkhouse door was unlatched and was swinging back and forth in the alkali-wind. Most of the SKIN-MAN's carnage was discovered in the bunkhouse. The dismembered bodies of *sai* JEFFERSON, COOKIE, and sixteen PRODDIES were found there. W:69–87, W:91–95 *(Young Bill's hypnosis vision)*, W:268

> **TACK SHED (ABANDONED HOSTELRY):** Roland and JAMIE found YOUNG BILL STREETER hiding in this abandoned tack shed under a pile of old tack. (Many years previously, this tack shed had been a hostelry and a jackleg veterinary.) Located on an uphill lane north of the bunkhouse, it was the perfect place for the SKIN-MAN to tether his horse before he transformed into a monster. After slaying almost everyone at the ranch (and becoming injured in the process), the flesh-eating shapeshifter staggered into this tack shed. It was here that Young Bill spied the killer's feet and ankles as he transformed back into a human being. Although Billy didn't see the skin-man's human face, he *did* see the blue ankle ring that he had tat-tooed around his ankle as well as the scar that bisected it. This proved to be the skin-man's undoing. W:78–87, W:91–95 *(Young Bill's hypnosis vision)*

LITTLE DEBARIA: The poor and run-down town of Little Debaria served the needs of the SALTIES, or salt miners, who mined salt from the nearby SALT ROCKS. (Little Debaria was located in the foothills of the Salt Rocks.) There were two saloons in Little Debaria, and they were both nasty places. When the whores who served DEBARIA's whorehouses became too old or diseased, they ended up in Little Debaria. (When the salties were drunk on

White Blind, they didn't care if a woman had a nose, as long as she had her sugar-purse.) Although the DEBARIA SALT COMBYNE was owned by rich men from GILEAD, the company store (and most of little Debaria) was owned by a nasty character called SAM SHUNT. W:45 *(indirect)*, W:55, W:62, W:64, W:85, W:270, W:275–77 *(and Shunt the Cunt)*, W:289

> **COMPANY STORE:** The DEBARIA SALT COMBYNE's company store belonged to a man named SAM SHUNT (known as Shunt the Cunt to the miners). As well as the company store, Shunt owned the bars, the whores, and the skiddums, or shacks, where the miners slept. Twice a year, he set up races for the miners—footraces, obstacle course races, and horse races. He took the entrance fees out of the miners' wages to pay his expenses. The winners got a year's worth of debt forgiven at the company store. However, Shunt charged the other miners such high interest rates that he never lost out. W:275–76
>
> **DEBARIA SALT COMBYNE:** The men who owned the DEBARIA SALT COMBYNE didn't come from DEBARIA; they were rich men from GILEAD. Unfortunately, these greedy men put profit before safety. If they had shut the mine long enough to seal the crack in the salt plug where one of the OLD PEOPLE's *artyfax* was hidden, the SKIN-MAN would never have come into being. W:282
>
> **ROAD TO LITTLE DEBARIA:** A GAMBLER and his Moll were attacked here. W:45
>
> **SALOONS:** Little Debaria's saloons were nasty places. When the SALTIES were drunk on White Blind, they didn't care if a woman had a nose, as long as she had her sugar-purse W:62
>
> **SALTIES ENCAMPMENT (SALTIE TOWN):** The SALTIES had an encampment a few wheels west of Little Debaria. W:85, W:87

LONG SALT SWAMPS: We don't know exactly where the Long Salt Swamps were located, but we do know that there were alligators there. W:66

LOW PURE: In DEBARIA, the foothill meadow located below the SALTHOUSES was known as the Low Pure. The Low Pure was located east of the ALKALI FLATS and north of AMBUSH ARROYO. The sheepherder YON CURRY was killed there. W:45, W:57, W:63, W:71

RANCHLAND NORTH OF DEBARIA: Much of Debaria's ranchland was located north of the town. W:56, W:62–63, W:70

SALLYWOOD: The settlement of Sallywood was located to the south of Debaria. Although Debaria's jing-jang used to be able to call all the way to GILEAD, by the time Roland and JAMIE arrived in town it could only reach north to the JEFFERSON RANCH, northeast to LITTLE DEBARIA, and south to SALLYWOOD. W:55

SALT HILLS (SALT ROCKS): The high hills located north of Debaria were known as the Salt Rocks. The DEBARIA SALT MINES were located in these hills. W:45, W:56–60, W:64, W:70, W:272

> **DEBARIA SALT MINES (SALT-HOUSES):** To the people of Debaria, the local salt mines were also known as the salt-houses. The salt-houses were caverns in the cliff faces of the SALT ROCKS. (The mining tunnels went down into the earth from the backs of the salt-house caverns.) In the past, miners and their families lived in the salt-houses, though by the time our

story takes place, the salties had their own encampment a short distance from LITTLE DEBARIA. When SHERIFF HUGH PEAVY was a deputy, the CROW GANG had their hideout in the abandoned salt-houses. At that time, all of the salt plugs had worn out, so the mines were empty. Twenty years before Roland and JAMIE arrived in Debaria, the DEBARIA SALT COMBYNE discovered a new plug. Unfortunately, this plug was a lot deeper than the others, and the company drilled too close to some of the OLD ONES' evil artifacts. As a result, one of the miners who came in contact with the Old Ones' leavings transformed into the cannibalistic SKIN-MAN. W:45, W:56–60, W:64, W:289

> NEW SALT PLUG: The only active mine in Debaria's Salt Rocks was opened twenty years before Roland and JAMIE arrived in the dusty railhead town. This plug was a lot deeper than the others, and came too close to some of the OLD PEOPLE's artifacts. As the old SALTIE, STEG LUKA, told Roland, deep in the new plug, the miners had found a crack in the salt with a green light shining through, an ugly light that pulsed like a heartbeat and spoke with a bitter voice, calling the men to enter. Although the men told their foreman about the light and he saw it for himself, he refused to close the plug. (He knew that the big bugs in Gilead would never agree to cease operaions and lose their profits.) Instead, he had the crew close the crack with rocks. Steg Luka was certain that one of the miners had been tempted to go back and reopen the crack. He turned out to be correct. OLLIE ANG had entered the green light and had been transformed into the SKIN-MAN. W:64, W:278, W:281–82

SERENITY WOMEN'S RETREAT: Although GABRIELLE DESCHAIN went to the women's retreat of Serenity to atone for her sin of adultery, STEVEN DESCHAIN did not trust the secluded sisters who gave her shelter. He called them the black ammies, and said they'd flay a man alive if he so much as trespassed their holy doors. When Roland visited Serenity, he found that it was very different from his father's description. Not only did he befriend the prioress, EVERLYNNE OF SERENITY, but he found the retreat itself to be very beautiful. Located ten or twelve wheels beyond the town of Debaria along DEBARIA HIGH ROAD, the retreat was the size of a Barony estate and was extremely well tended. The walls of its dazzling white haci were tall and topped with forbidding sparkles of broken glass, but the wooden gates stood open with invitation. Behind the haci, down a narrow creek, was a large green garden and a grape arbor. Unfortunately, neither the broken glass atop the haci walls nor the large wooden gates kept the SKIN-MAN from attacking two of the sisters, FORTUNA and DOLORES. IV:619, IV:620, IV:655, W:38, W:39, W:41, W:43, W:47–53, W:63, W:66, W:269, W:291, W:293, W:295–300

SHEEPHERDER'S LEAN-TO: This lean-to was located about halfway between the JEFFERSON RANCH and DEBARIA. Roland hypnotized YOUNG BILL STREETER here. W:88–95

TIMBERSMITH FARM: The SKIN-MAN killed nine people at the Timbersmith Farm, which was located on the HIGH PURE. Among those dead was a young boy whose skull had been smashed so that his brains could be scooped out. SHERIFF PEAVY found the boy's head stuck onto a pole. There were tracks all around it. Initially the tracks were those of a big cat, then they transformed into hoofmarks, then into the prints of a giant human being. Finally, they became the prints of a small man. W:45, W:47, W:63

DEBARIA HIGH ROAD
See DEBARIA, BARONY OF

DEBARIA RAIL LINE
See DEBARIA, BARONY OF

DEBARIA SALT COMBYNE
See DEBARIA, BARONY OF

DEBARIA SALT MINES
See DEBARIA, BARONY OF

DEBARIA STREAM
See DEBARIA, BARONY OF

DEBARIA, TOWN OF
See DEBARIA, BARONY OF

DELAIN
See EASTAR'D BARONY

DELIGHTFUL VIEW
See DEBARIA, BARONY OF

DESATOYA MOUNTAINS
The town of ELURIA is located in the Desatoya Mountains. Like so many of the landscapes found in the Dark Tower series, both the mountains and the towns dotted through them resemble the landscape of the American Southwest.
   E:146

DESOY
FARSON began his career as a harrier in GARLAN and Desoy.
   IV:151

DESTRY FARM
See NORTH'RD BARONY

DIS
The orange ball of MAERLYN'S RAINBOW is reputed to be in Dis.
   IV:437

DOGAN
See entry in PORTALS

DOOLIN RANCH
　　See DEBARIA, BARONY OF

DOORWAY CAVE
　　See entry in PORTALS

DOORWAYS BETWEEN WORLDS
　　See entry in PORTALS

DOWNLAND BARONIES
　　See GREATER KINGDOMS OF THE WESTERN EARTH

DRAGON'S GRAVE
The Dragon's Grave was a bottomless crack in the earth named for the great
bursts of steam that erupted from it every thirty to forty days. Roland knew of it
as a boy, so it is most likely located near GILEAD-that-was.
　　III:37

DRAGON'S LAIR
　　See EASTAR'D BARONY: DELAIN

DRAWERS
　　See DRAWERS, *in* PORTALS

DROP, THE
　　See MEJIS, BARONY OF: HAMBRY

DRUIT STONES
　　See STONE CIRCLES, *in* PORTALS

E

EAST DOWNE
East Downe was one of the many lands Roland traveled through during his years
as a MID-WORLD wanderer. In East Downe, there are walking waters. Unfortunately, they are never described.
　　VI:234

EAST ROAD
　　See BORDERLANDS: CALLA BRYN STURGIS

EASTAR'D BARONY
　　VII:184
　　DELAIN: JOHN NORMAN, the young man Roland meets while imprisoned
by the LITTLE SISTERS OF ELURIA, comes from Delain. This kingdom is

derisively known as Dragon's Lair, Liars' Heaven, and the home of tall tales. It also happens to be the setting for the novel *Eyes of the Dragon*. According to *The Dark Tower*, WALTER was born in Delain. E:188, VII:184

EASTERN PLAIN (CALLA BADLANDS)
See CALLA BADLANDS, *in* PORTALS

ELD, LAND OF (ELDEN KINGDOM)
Eld was the name of the ancient land ruled by Roland's ancestor, ARTHUR ELD, who later became King of ALL-WORLD. Eld was located northwest of GILEAD, in the northwesternmost reaches of the AFFILIATION. By the time of Roland's trials in HAMBRY, those ancient lands were already being burned and looted by FARSON and his men.
 IV:181, W:170

ELURIA
Eluria is a small town located in the DESATOYA MOUNTAINS. It is also the setting for the short story "The Little Sisters of Eluria." Like many of the places in MID-WORLD, it looks like a town out of the old American West. Along its High Street are quite a few wooden shop fronts, including a mercantile, a smithy, a Gathering Hall, a church (complete with bell tower), a livery, a market, and a sheriff's office. It also has a single hotel (**GOOD BEDS HOTEL**), and two saloons, one of which is called **THE BUSTLING PIG**. When Roland arrives during the heat of Full Earth, the place has been deserted for about two weeks. The only living (or once living) beings Roland finds are the CROSS DOG, a single corpse, and some singing insects.
 Although there are no people to be seen, the town's gates are still strung with garlands of dried flowers and the church doorway with tiny silver bells—decorations which Roland finds both disturbing and eerie. Soon after his arrival he discovers that the town is not completely deserted after all. It is inhabited by the mutant GREEN FOLK and the vampiric LITTLE SISTERS OF ELURIA.
 E:146–58, E:159, E:166, E:173, E:178–79, E:181, E:190, E:193, E:201, E:205, E:209, VI:234
> **HOSPITAL (RUN BY LITTLE SISTERS):** *See* LITTLE SISTERS' HOSPITAL, *in* PORTALS
> **LEXINGWORTH:** This is where Eluria's citizens hang criminals. E:151
> **RADIUM MINES:** The foul-looking muties known as the GREEN FOLK inhabit the radium mines outside Eluria. E:154
> **RUINED HACIENDA:** This is where the Little Sisters live during their time in Eluria. E:200, E:201
> **THOUGHTFUL HOUSE:** In "The Little Sisters of Eluria," the tyrannical SISTER MARY tells Roland that Thoughtful House is a "home for contagion," a place where the sick are brought to recover. But like so much that is said in the white tents of the sinister Little Sisters, this is a lie. Thoughtful House is not a house at all but a small hillside cave where Sister Mary sends disobedient members of her order to endure a kind of solitary confinement. The lovely and rebellious SISTER JENNA is forced to spend much time here. E:175, E:185, E:194, E:201, E:206

ENDLESS FOREST
  See NORTH'RD BARONY

END-WORLD
  See END-WORLD, *in* PORTALS

EYEBOLT CANYON
  See MEJIS, BARONY OF

F

FALLS OF THE HOUNDS
  See BLAINE'S ROUTE

FAGONARD
  See NORTH'RD BARONY

FARMING VILLAGES OF THE MIDDLES
  See NORTH'RD BARONY

**FARSON (TOWN OF)
In the original version of *The Gunslinger*, we learn that the AFFILIATION's enemy JOHN FARSON (also known as THE GOOD MAN) planned to poison this town when Roland was still a boy. Given the fact that this rather nasty character bears the town's name, it seems likely that he—or his ancestors—originated here. In the 2003 version of *The Gunslinger*, the town of Farson is replaced by the town of TAUNTON.
  I:101, I:102, I:105, I:108

**FARSON ROAD
Farson Road is the name given to the coach road that runs between GILEAD and the town of FARSON. GALLOWS HILL is located here. In the 2003 *Gunslinger*, the Farson Road becomes the TAUNTON ROAD.
  I:106–11

FIELD OF GIANT YELLOW MUSHROOMS
  See NORTH'RD BARONY

**FOREST O' BARONY
  See NEW CANAAN, BARONY OF

FOREST TREES
  See PASS O' THE RIVER

G

GADDISH FEEDS
See: KANSAS: TOPEKA, in OUR WORLD PLACES

GAGE BOULEVARD
See KANSAS: TOPEKA, in OUR WORLD PLACES

GALLOWS HILL
Gallows Hill is located on the FARSON ROAD. HAX, Gilead's traitorous head cook, is hanged here.
   I:106–11, IV:161

**GARLAN, BARONY OF
Garlan is a distant kingdom which seems almost mythical to many of the people we meet in the Dark Tower series. According to AUNT TALITHA of RIVER CROSSING, the people of Garlan have brown skin. According to the COVENANT MAN, there are dragons in this Barony. It is also supposed to be the home of that strange baby-bearing bird, the GRAND FEATHEREX. ELDRED JONAS—Roland's enemy in *Wizard and Glass*—received a terrible whipping in Garlan. In *Song of Susannah,* we discover that Roland's grandfather ALARIC went to Garlan to slay a dragon, though that dragon had already been slain by another king. In the 2003 version of *The Gunslinger,* we are told that this kingdom is located west of GILEAD, and that it is a tobacco-growing region.
   Garlan also has more sinister associations. According to the novel *Eyes of the Dragon,* the nasty sorcerer RANDALL FLAGG once lived in this land famed for its poisons. In fact, it seems likely that he lived there twice, once under the initials R.F. and once (according to *The Dark Tower*) under the name WALTER HODJI. Not surprisingly, the poison coating the knife intended to kill Roland's father came from this kingdom.
   II:66, III:231, III:242, IV:214, IV:480 *(Jonas scarred here),* IV:621 *(poison from here),* VI:197, VII:39, VII:183, W:151

GARNET MINES
See BORDERLANDS: CALLA BRYN STURGIS: ARROYO COUNTRY

GATEWAY OF OUT-WORLD
See DOGAN: NORTH FOREST KINNOCK DOGAN in PORTALS

GATHERING HALL
See BORDERLANDS: CALLA BRYN STURGIS: TOWN GATHERING HALL

GAUNTLET
See GREAT ROAD, THE

GILEAD
See NEW CANAAN, BARONY OF

GILEAD, BARONY OF
See NEW CANAAN, BARONY OF

GITTY'S SALOON
See NORTH'RD BARONY

GLASS PALACE
See GREEN PALACE, *in* PORTALS

GLENCOVE
See TAVARES

GLORIA MINE
See BORDERLANDS: CALLA BRYN STURGIS: ARROYO COUNTRY

GOLGOTHA, THE
See entry in PORTALS

GOODVIEW COTTAGE
See NORTH'RD BARONY

GOOK, VILLAGE OF
See BORDERLANDS

GRAND CRESCENT
See BORDERLANDS

GRAYS' CASTLE/GRAYS' MAZE
See RIVER BARONY: LUD

GREAT CANYON
See NORTH'RD BARONY

GREAT HALL
See NEW CANAAN, BARONY OF: GILEAD

GREAT ROAD
There are many Great Roads in MID-WORLD. Like the Roman roads of our world, they are the leftovers of an earlier civilization, namely that of the OLD ONES. Although these byways were once major highways, by the time of *The Gunslinger* their broken surfaces are covered with years of dirt. However, many of them still have intact subterranean drainage systems. Most of the Great Roads follow the PATH OF THE BEAM.
    IV:653
    GREAT ROAD TO LUD: III:159–65, III:170–76, III:178–82, III:189–90,

III:223–32 *(directly mentioned on 224, 225, 226, 228, 230)*, III:240, III:243, III:273–89 *(ka-tet on it; 273 Quick's airplane; directly mentioned on 283, 286, 287)*

   GAUNTLET: This is the term JAKE uses for the fortifications around the Great Road just outside LUD. III:286–89

THROUGH HAMBRY: One of MID-WORLD's Great Roads runs from the BARONY OF NEW CANAAN to the BARONY OF MEJIS. Along its course it passes through the town of Hambry. It runs east-west. IV:182 *(runs from New Canaan to Mejis)*, IV:266, IV:271, IV:375, IV:377, IV:379 *(leads to Citgo)*, IV:402–3, IV:498, IV:610, V:210

GREAT WEST WOODS (SHARDIK'S WOODS)

The Great West Woods of OUT-WORLD are located north of the CYCLO-PEAN MOUNTAINS and just east of the WESTERN SEA. Roland, EDDIE, and SUSANNAH recover here after their long journey along LOBSTROSITY BEACH, a trial we read about in *The Drawing of the Three*. These woods are the home of the GUARDIAN SHARDIK, also known as MIR. It is the home of the PORTAL OF THE BEAR and the place where our *ka-tet* picks up the PATH OF THE BEAM. In the SHOOTING GALLERY (a clearing in the woods), Roland teaches both Eddie and Susannah the WAY OF ELD.

   II:395–99, III:11–21, III:23–51 *(setting)*, III:53–86, III:149–53 *(Eddie's Dream)*, III:158–65, III:170, III:247, III:347, V:37, V:110, V:512 *(clearing)*, V:563 *(clearing)*, V:573 *(Shardik's woods)*, VII:466 *(indirect)*

   SHOOTING GALLERY: III:11–19, III:36, III:163

GREAT WOODS

See NORTH'RD BARONY

GREATER KINGDOMS OF THE WESTERN EARTH

When Roland was a boy he saw a map of the Greater Kingdoms of the Western Earth. It depicted GILEAD, the DOWNLAND BARONIES (which were overrun by riot and civil war the year after he won his guns), and showed the hills, the desert, and the mountains which stretched all the way to the WESTERN SEA. At the time the map was made, one thousand miles lay between Gilead and the Western Sea. However, as the BEAMS disintegrated, distances within MID-WORLD shifted and grew. It took Roland many years to cross that distance.

   III:74

GREEN HEART

See MEJIS, BARONY OF: HAMBRY

GREEN PALACE

See entry in PORTALS

H

HALL OF THE GRANDFATHERS
See NEW CANAAN, BARONY OF: GILEAD

HAMBRY
See MEJIS, BARONY OF

HAMBRY CEMETERY
See MEJIS, BARONY OF: HAMBRY

HAMBRY CREEK
See MEJIS, BARONY OF: HAMBRY

HAMBRY POINT
See MEJIS, BARONY OF: HAMBRY

HAMBRY POST OFFICE
See MEJIS, BARONY OF: HAMBRY

HANGING ROCK
See MEJIS, BARONY OF

HATTIGANS
See RITZY

HEMPHILL
Hemphill was a small town located near GILEAD-that-was. Roland's HAMBRY
alter ego, WILL DEARBORN, supposedly grew up there.
    IV:148, IV:183, IV:201

HENDRICKSON (TOWN)
Hendrickson was one of the many towns attacked by THE GOOD MAN.
    I:104

HIGH PURE
See DEBARIA, BARONY OF

HIGH SHERIFF'S OFFICE AND JAIL
See DEBARIA, BARONY OF

HILL OF STONE FACES
See JERICHO HILL

HOOKEY'S STABLE AND SMITHY
See MEJIS, BARONY OF: HAMBRY

I

IL BOSQUE
Il Bosque is a forest west of MEJIS. Roland, CUTHBERT, and ALAIN travel through it after SUSAN's death and after Roland's disastrous magical journey through MAERLYN'S GRAPEFRUIT.
IV:610–11

IMPERIUM
See NORTH CENTRAL POSITRONICS, *in* CHARACTERS

INDRIE
See CRESSIA, BARONY OF

**IN-WORLD (INNER BARONIES/IN-WORLD BARONIES, INNER ARC)
When the author STEPHEN KING refers to the whole of Roland's version of Earth, he uses the term MID-WORLD. However, when he refers to specific regions of Mid-World, he uses the terms *In-World, Out-World, Mid-World,* END-WORLD, and the BORDERLANDS.

When Roland was growing up in GILEAD, the world was often described as having two parts, In-World and Out-World. These terms were relative to each other. The term *In-World* was used to refer to those baronies which sat at the center of human culture, where the old civilized ways still held and where some of the old electrical machinery still worked. In-World was ruled by the elite gunslingers from the walled city of Gilead, barony seat of NEW CANAAN. The *sigul* of In-World was ARTHUR ELD's horse, LLAMREI. An image of Llamrei decorated Gilead's pennons. Throughout *Wizard and Glass,* Roland and his youthful *ka-tet* are stationed in the Out-World barony of MEJIS. Hence they are often resentfully referred to as the "In-World boys."

The terms *In-World* and *Out-World* may also be metaphorical references to the metaphysical map of Mid-World which Roland draws in *The Waste Lands.* According to this map, Mid-World is shaped like a circle, with the DARK TOWER at its center and the BEAMS radiating out from it and terminating in twelve PORTALS. Just as the Tower is the center of the Universe, Gilead and the In-World Baronies are the centers of human culture. Backwaters such as Mejis are on the Outer Crescent of the "civilized" world. In the 2003 version of *The Gunslinger,* Roland refers to himself as being from In-World.
III:375, IV:145 *(Roland's ka-tet),* IV:183, IV:192, IV:207, IV:347, IV:363, IV:379, IV:388, IV:422 *(Northern In-World and reindeer fucking),* IV:503, IV:506, IV:557, IV:583 *(and Nordites),* V:11, V:13, V:94, V:243, V:604 *(In-World-that-was),* VI:97, VI:247, VII:210, VII:549 *(Llamrei, Arthur Eld's horse, is the* sigul *for all In-World),* VII:550, VII:594, VII:607, VII:664, W:14, W:48, W:120
INNER ARC: Home of the Inner Baronies. IV:196
INNER BARONIES: IV:145, IV:295

INNER CRESCENT: IV:302
INNERS: IV:360

IRONWOOD FOREST
See NORTH'RD BARONY

IRONWOOD TRAIL
See NORTH'RD BARONY

J

JAFFORDS LAND
See BORDERLANDS: CALLA BRYN STURGIS

JEFFERSON RANCH
See DEBARIA, BARONY OF

**JERICHO HILL (NEAR THE HILL OF STONE FACES)
The last great battle between the tattered remnants of the AFFILIATION and the remains of FARSON's army took place on Jericho Hill. CUTHBERT ALLGOOD died here, shot through the eye by an arrow aimed at him by Roland's old enemy WALTER O'DIM. JAMIE DeCURRY was also brought down here, though he was killed by a sniper (probably GRISSOM's eagle-eyed son). Roland (the only gunslinger to survive) saved his skin by hiding in a cart filled with the dead. He crept out of the slaughter pile at sundown, just before the whole works were set alight.

The east side of Jericho Hill was a shale-crumbly drop to the CLEAN SEA. Its western edge, known as the Hill of Stone Faces, was a long, sloping field filled with great gray-black, sculptured visages. Roland's horn, the HORN OF ELD, was dropped on Jericho Hill by a dying Cuthbert. Roland never retrieved it, which he regrets greatly by the time he reaches the DARK TOWER.

V:153, V:169–72, V:173, V:240, V:284, V:347, V:410, VI:134, VI:219, VII:144, VII:174–75, VII:465, VII:552, VII:748, VII:762, VII:819, VII:825, VII:829, W:300

JIMTOWN
See RIVER BARONY

K

KAMBERO
This is one of the villages located in the far western regions of MID-WORLD. It is probably even farther west than ELURIA.
  E:193

KANSAS
  See KANSAS, *in* OUR WORLD PLACES

KASHMIN, BARONY OF (KASHAMIN, BARONY OF)
Before the complete destruction of the AFFILIATION and of culture as Roland knew it, the Kashmin province was famous for its rugs. Sumptuous Kashmin carpets adorned the halls of GILEAD. They also lined the floors of the CRADLE OF THE GRAYS.
  III:350 *(Kashmin)*, IV:654 *(rugs from Province of Kashamin)*

KELLS COTTAGE
  See NORTH'RD BARONY

KING'S TOWN
This is one of the hundreds of towns Roland traveled through on his search for the DARK TOWER. Twelve years before he met JAKE (and not long after the fall of GILEAD), Roland had a girl here. She was one of the many he deserted in order to pursue his quest.
  I:158

KUNA
When EVERLYNNE OF SERENITY sweeps toward Roland with her arms wide, the huge woman reminds him of the vast trucks that used to run at the oilfields near Kuna.
  W:295

L

LAKE CAWN
Once upon a bye, a great battle took place on the shores of Lake Cawn. During this battle, TIM ROSS proved his bravery and was given the name TIM STOUT-HEART. Tim was one of the few gunslingers not born to the line of ELD.
  W:268

LAMERK FOUNDRY
  See LaMERK INDUSTRIES, *in* CHARACTERS

LAND OF ENDLESS SNOWS
ASLAN lives in the land of endless snows. It is here, in the northernmost reaches of MID-WORLD, that the STARKBLASTS begin. Before he met MAERLYN, TIM ROSS thought that perhaps the wizard lived in the land of endless snows.
W:217, W:220, W:234

LANDING, THE
See RIVER BARONY

LAZY SUSAN RANCH
See MEJIS, BARONY OF: HAMBRY

LEXINGWORTH
See ELURIA

LIARS HEAVEN
See EASTAR'D BARONY: DELAIN

LITTLE DEBARIA
See DEBARIA, BARONY OF

LOBSTROSITY BEACH
See WESTERN SEA

LONG SALT SWAMPS
See DEBARIA, BARONY OF

LOW PURE
See DEBARIA, BARONY OF

LUD
See RIVER BARONY

LUDWEG
See RIVER BARONY

M

MAERLYN'S HOUSE
See NORTH'RD BARONY

MANNI CALLA (MANNI REDPATH)
See BORDERLANDS: CALLA BRYN STURGIS

MARCHLY COTTAGE
See NORTH'RD BARONY

MEJIS, BARONY OF

Mejis (more specifically, the barony seat of HAMBRY) is the setting for most of *Wizard and Glass*. Mejis's barony color is a deep orange-red, as can be seen on the official sash worn by Mayor HART THORIN. Located east of GILEAD and on the edge of the desert, Mejis is considered one of the quiet backwaters of the OUTER ARC, or OUTER CRESCENT. Like much of MID-WORLD, it resembles areas of the American West. Its citizens breed horses and, in the areas closest to the sea, they also fish.

STEVEN DESCHAIN, Roland's father, sends Roland and his two friends to Mejis in order to keep them safe from JOHN FARSON, who is destroying the lands farther west. Little does he know that THE GOOD MAN's poison has spread as far as the Outer Arc. Mejis is no longer loyal to the AFFILIATION, and the final battle of Mid-World is destined to take place in this quiet barony. Within two years of Roland's trials in Mejis, the light of the IN-WORLD BAR-ONIES will be snuffed out and the world, as Roland's forefathers knew it, will no longer exist. (Below are some of the direct references to Mejis's character, customs, etc.)

IV:68, IV:99 *(east of Gilead)*, IV:144, IV:149, IV:151, IV:161, IV:162 *(end of the world)*, IV:164 *(Steven Deschain thinks it's safe)*, IV:179 *(the smells of it. Loyal to the Affiliation)*, IV:180, IV:187, IV:193, IV:195, IV:201, IV:206, IV:214, IV:221, IV:232, IV:244, IV:256, IV:269, IV:271, IV:316, IV:336, IV:341, IV:342 *(orchards north of Hambry)*, IV:351, IV:355 *(and Reap)*, IV:391, IV:410, IV:414, IV:423, IV:426, IV:431, IV:434, IV:436, IV:445, IV:447 *(Out-World Barony)*, IV:451, IV:456, IV:461, IV:471, IV:473–74, IV:480, IV:485, IV:486, IV:500, IV:502, IV:506, IV:507, IV:521, IV:546, IV:547, IV:555, IV:605, IV:620, IV:624, IV:627, IV:650, E:160, V:35, V:85, V:92, V:116, V:117, V:166, V:170, V:181, V:195, V:202, V:210, V:211, V:341, V:400, V:405, VI:184, VI:242, VI:279, VI:404 *(and Mexico)*, VII:84, VII:175, VII:219, VII:270, VII:271, VII:317, VII:321, VII:331, VII:333, VII:455, VII:468, VII:524, VII:552, VII:651, VII:695, VII:802, W:37, W:38, W:55, W:73, W:84, W:86

BAD GRASS AND AREAS WEST OF HAMBRY:

BAD GRASS: This is the freeland west of Hambry and is located on the edge of the desert wastelands. Although it smells sweet, the bad grass poisons grazing animals. IV:271, IV:324, IV:343, IV:344, IV:394, IV:474, IV:499, IV:523–26 *(setting)*, IV:529–35 *(setting)*, IV:536–49, IV:552–60

BLUFFS: The bluffs are six miles beyond the long grassy DROP at the edge of HAMBRY. HANGING ROCK is located here. IV:272

CÖOS: The Cöos is a ragged hill five miles from the town of Hambry, ten miles from EYEBOLT CANYON. To the northwest of it is the desert, the BAD GRASS, HANGING ROCK, and EYEBOLT CANYON. RHEA, the weirdling of the Cöos, has her hut here below the crest of the hill. IV:115–38, IV:166, IV:168, IV:246, IV:290, IV:299, IV:343, IV:394–98, IV:414, IV:415–19 *(setting)*, IV:420, IV:448, IV:449, IV:452–53 *(setting)*, IV:657, IV:662, V:40, V:55, V:71, V:703, VII:179, VII:219

EYEBOLT CANYON: A short, steep-walled box canyon shaped like a chimney lying on its side. A thinny has eaten its way into the far end of it. Roland destroys his enemies by laying a trap for them in Eyebolt Canyon.

IV:115, IV:118 *(and thinny)*, IV:156 *(described)*, IV:272–76 *(described)*, IV:324, IV:351, IV:394–95 *(described)*, IV:422, IV:431, IV:432, IV:454–56, IV:470, IV:547, IV:580, IV:590–602 *(Latigo's men are trapped here)*, IV:622–23, V:341, V:508, V:576, VII:524

HANGING ROCK: Hanging Rock is located about three-quarters of the way between the DROP and the BLUFFS, or about four miles from the Drop and two miles from the Bluffs. This jutting upthrust of rock is the only real geographical feature in the area and resembles a finger bent at the first knuckle. Below it is a small, boomerang-shaped green sward. The green is due to a freshwater spring located at the rock's base. IV:272, IV:324, IV:368, IV:371 *(Latigo's men come here)*, IV:386, IV:394, IV:407, IV:422, IV:432, IV:456, IV:484, IV:503, IV:522, IV:530, IV:532, IV:536, IV:547, IV:555, IV:573, IV:579, IV:583, IV:584, IV:589–91 *(setting)*

HAMBRY (BARONY SEAT OF MEJIS): Hambry is a beautiful town located on the edge of the CLEAN SEA. From High Street you can see the bay, the docks, and the many-colored boathouses. The newer buildings are adobe; the older ones are brick and are reminiscent of GILEAD's Old Quarter. Hambry has two markets—an upper and a lower. The lower market smells fishy but is cheaper.

Roland associates Hambry with the smell of sea salt, oil, and pine. Its citizens are fishermen and horse breeders. Although Hambry is picturesque, it is full of hidden dangers. The thinny of EYEBOLT CANYON is the most visible; however, other dangers lurk. As Roland soon realizes, "in Hambry, the waters on top and the waters down below seem to run in different directions" (IV:205). Although they declare their allegiance to the AFFILIATION, the politically powerful men of the town have (metaphorically speaking) sold their souls to FARSON, also known as THE GOOD MAN. Although the gunslingers of NEW CANAAN do not know it, the destruction of their world will begin here, in a barony they can barely recall.

In Hambry, Roland faces the first true trials of his manhood. He also discovers MAERLYN's GRAPEFRUIT, the pink sphere of MAERLYN's RAINBOW.

GENERAL PAGES: IV:115–331, IV:341–611

SPECIFIC REFERENCES: IV:65, IV:79 *(and thinnies)*, IV:115, IV:142, IV:144 *(mailboxes)*, IV:145, IV:153 *(dinner of state)*, IV:180–89 *(180–81 description of bay; 182 five hundred miles from In-World; 183 and "old ways"; 186 four hundred wheels from Gilead)*, IV:190, IV:193, IV:200, IV:205, IV:206, IV:219, IV:220, IV:238, IV:239 *(beauty of it)*, IV:244, IV:254 *(few muties in Outer Baronies)*, IV:261, IV:263, IV:267, IV:271, IV:276, IV:282 *(upper and lower markets)*, IV:284, IV:293 *(and game of Castles)*, IV:300, IV:305, IV:402, IV:426, IV:430, IV:446, IV:451, IV:453 *(lower market)*, IV:461, IV:467 *(lower market)*, IV:484, IV:504, IV:506, IV:521, IV:550, IV:569, IV:570, IV:584, IV:603, IV:605

LOCATIONS IN THE TOWN OF HAMBRY:

ANNE'S DRESSES: IV:328

BAR K RANCH: A deserted spread of land northwest of town. It was once owned by the GARBER family; now it belongs to the HORSEMEN'S ASSOCIATION. Roland's *ka-tet* stays in Bar K's bunkhouse during their time in Hambry. IV:175, IV:188, IV:199, IV:211, IV:233, IV:260–64 *(260 described)*, IV:274, IV:276, IV:277, IV:286, IV:288, IV:294, IV:305, IV:352, IV:357–60, IV:368, IV:378, IV:388–89, IV:390–92, IV:393–94 *(Jonas is there)*, IV:398–402 *(Roland's ka-tet finds Jonas's mess)*, IV:403, IV:431, IV:450, IV:473–80, IV:484, IV:502, IV:574

BAYVIEW HOTEL: Located on High Street. IV:447, IV:502

CITGO: An oil patch filled with 200 steel towers, 19 of which still ceaselessly pump oil. They have existed for more than six centuries. IV:135, IV:145–48, IV:157, IV:159, IV:176 *(Jonas tells Depape to cover tankers)*, IV:185, IV:186, IV:214 *(Reynolds and Depape camouflage)*, IV:281, IV:285, IV:289–304 *(289 orange grove nearby; 295 "the candle")*, IV:300–301 *(tankers)*, IV:319, IV:345, IV:363, IV:378–80, IV:385–86, IV:390, IV:395, IV:411, IV:421, IV:430, IV:432, IV:451, IV:480, IV:483–85, IV:515–19

  CANDLE, THE: The gas-pipe of Citgo. IV:295, IV:363.

CLEAN SEA: *See* CLEAN SEA, *listed separately*

CRAVEN'S UNDERTAKING PARLOR: IV:381

DROP, THE (WESTERN DROP): This long, grassy slope stretches for thirty wheels toward the sea. It is used as a horse meadow, though much of it belongs to JOHN CROYDON. Part of it is known as TOWN LOOK-OUT. SUSAN DELGADO's house is visible from here (IV:284). IV:125, IV:133, IV:140, IV:153, IV:160–65, IV:170, IV:188, IV:191, IV:205, IV:234, IV:239–40, IV:246–59 *(too many horses)*, IV:261, IV:271–72, IV:276, IV:281, IV:284, IV:288, IV:293, IV:301, IV:311, IV:324, IV:346, IV:352, IV:358, IV:361, IV:368, IV:371, IV:378, IV:400, IV:402, IV:414, IV:423, IV:427, IV:446, IV:459, IV:502, IV:503, IV:522, IV:525, IV:529, IV:532, IV:548, IV:566, IV:568, IV:608, IV:635, V:202, VI:184, VII:762

  RIM: *See also* BORDERLANDS: GRAND CRESCENT. VI:184

GREAT ROAD: *See* GREAT ROAD, *listed separately*

GREEN HEART (also PAVILION, MANAGERIE, RED ROCK): Green Heart is a pavilion located on HILL STREET, fifty yards from the jail and TOWN GATHERING HALL. It is the site of the Reap Dance. The stone wall at the back contains the red rock where Roland and SUSAN agree to leave notes for each other. Susan is eventually burned here. IV:147, IV:327, IV:343 *(red rock)*, IV:351, IV:355, IV:370, IV:371, IV:372–74 *(Jonas and Cordelia)*, IV:381, IV:434, IV:462, IV:505, IV:507, IV:605–8 *(Susan burned)*

HAMBRY CEMETERY: Hambry Cemetery is the site of the famous murder/suicide of ROBERT AND FRANCESCA. Roland, CUTHBERT, ALAIN, and SUSAN DELGADO meet to palaver here. IV:426, IV:428–36, IV:495, IV:514–15

HAMBRY CREEK: *See also* WILLOW GROVE, *below.* IV:311

HAMBRY JAIL: *See* SHERIFF'S OFFICE, BARONY JAIL, *below*

HAMBRY MERCANTILE STORE: Located on south High Street. The porch has a line of carved totems depicting seven of the twelve GUARD-IANS OF THE BEAM. They are BEAR, TURTLE, FISH, EAGLE, LION, BAT, and WOLF. People often hang Reap charms from them. IV:222, IV:245, IV:328, IV:342 *(rattlesnake skins)*, IV:355 *(Reap charms hang from the Guardians)*, IV:447

HAMBRY POINT: The point is located two miles from the TRAVEL-LER'S REST. IV:216

HAMBRY POST OFFICE: Although it is an OUT-WORLD Barony, Hambry has a postal service. IV:181

HOOKEY'S STABLE AND SMITHY/HOOKEY'S STABLE AND FANCY LIVERY: IV:279–80, IV:282, IV:330, IV:344, IV:376, IV:512, IV:514–15

LAND OFFICE: IV:181

LAZY SUSAN RANCH: This ranch belongs to RENFREW and is the largest one in Mejis. IV:187, IV:205, IV:208, IV:355, IV:421

MENAGERIE: *See* GREEN HEART, *above*

MILLBANK, THE: Food is served here. IV:259

ORANGE GROVE: *See* CITGO, *above*

PIANO RANCH: Owned by CROYDEN. IV:187, IV:191, IV:215 *(Her Nibs is here),* IV:344, IV:451, IV:558

ROADS:

    CAMINO VEGA: Crosses HIGH STREET. IV:329

    GREAT ROAD (runs east-west): *See* GREAT ROAD, *listed separately*

    HIGH STREET: The TRAVELLERS' REST is located here. IV:171, IV:180, IV:189, IV:224, IV:329, IV:381, IV:447, IV:505

    HILL STREET: GREEN HEART and the SHERIFF'S OFFICE are located here. IV:180, IV:327, IV:371, IV:507, IV:605

    SEACOAST ROAD (BARONY SEA ROAD): IV:271, IV:370, IV:402, IV:581

    SILK RANCH ROAD: IV:602, IV:603, V:210

ROCKING B RANCH: Owned by LENGYLL. IV:186 *(generator),* IV:187, IV:199, IV:355

ROCKING H RANCH: This is LASLO RIMER's place. IV:262 *(has oxen),* IV:293

SEAFRONT: This is Mayor HART THORIN's house. "Come in peace" is inscribed above the door. IV:153, IV:158, IV:162, IV:179–80, IV:191–210 *(193–94 interior described),* IV:222, IV:234, IV:278, IV:279, IV:292, IV:306–8, IV:310–13, IV:328, IV:350, IV:367, IV:376, IV:391, IV:403, IV:405, IV:420, IV:428, IV:443, IV:448–49, IV:453, IV:457, IV:460, IV:468, IV:480–83 *(action here),* IV:494–95 *(action here),* IV:496, IV:498, IV:499, IV:506, IV:519–23 *(setting),* IV:537, IV:542, IV:552, IV:561–62, IV:566–70, IV:577–78, IV:579, IV:582, V:166

SEVEN-MILE ORCHARD: IV:370

SHERIFF'S OFFICE, BARONY JAIL: This dual-purpose building is located on HILL STREET, overlooking the bay. IV:180–90 *(descriptions of office. Sheriff goes through Roland's false papers),* IV:226, IV:259–60, IV:327 *(jail),* IV:329, IV:362–64, IV:367–68, IV:371, IV:501, IV:502, IV:507, IV:508–13, IV:520, IV:523, IV:537

TOWN GATHERING HALL: IV:181, IV:185, IV:227–30, IV:500–502 *(setting),* IV:562

TOWN LOOKOUT: Located on THE DROP. IV:284

TRAVELLERS' REST: Located on HIGH STREET, the Rest is Hambry's bar and whorehouse. It is owned by CORAL THORIN and her brother,

HART THORIN. Hart never sets foot in the place, but Coral runs it. The Travellers' Rest is the site of a showdown between Roland's *ka-tet* and the BIG COFFIN HUNTERS. In *Wizard and Glass*, SHEEMIE RUIZ worked here doing odd jobs. In the final book of the Dark Tower series, Sheemie (now a BREAKER in THUNDERCLAP) meets the BEAM BOY in a dream-version of the Travellers' Rest. *See also* BORDERLANDS: CALLA BRYN STURGIS: TRAVELLERS' REST. IV:144, IV:170–78, IV:190, IV:213–22, IV:224–26, IV:232, IV:241–42, IV:244–45, IV:286, IV:287, IV:342 *(and rattlesnake skins)*, IV:347–53, IV:355, IV:366, IV:367, IV:380–87, IV:389, IV:403–5, IV:420–25, IV:447 *(cotton gillies)*, IV:451, IV:500, IV:502, IV:505, IV:506, IV:512, IV:527, IV:562–65 *(setting)*, VII:219, VII:220, VII:271 *(indirect)*, VII:333, VII:336

WILLOW GROVE: Roland and SUSAN DELGADO make love here. It is Susan's favorite place, and eerily prefigures the WILLOW JUNGLE in which Roland later encounters the succubus, or ORACLE OF THE MOUNTAINS. IV:311, IV:315–19, IV:321–23, IV:343, IV:435, IV:436, IV:537

ONNIE'S FORD: IV:306, IV:311

ORCHARDS NORTH OF HAMBRY: IV:341

SANTA FE: There is a sign for this city at BLAINE's termination point in TOPEKA. However, there is also a Santa Fe in Mejis. For more information on the significance of Santa Fe to the series, see ATCHISON, TOPEKA, AND SANTA FE RAILROAD, in OUR WORLD PLACES. IV:68

WASTE LANDS: There are wastelands beyond Hambry. But later on, when Roland and his new *ka-tet* reach the city of LUD, they find much nastier ones. IV:271

MIA'S CASTLE
See CASTLE DISCORDIA, *in* PORTALS

MID-FOREST (MID-FOREST BOG)
The wooded region which our *tet* travels through at the beginning of *Wolves of the Calla* is known as Mid-Forest. It marks the beginning of the BORDER-LANDS. While following the PATH OF THE BEAM through this fairy-tale wood, Roland and his *ka-tet* are tracked by FATHER CALLAHAN and the other representatives from CALLA BRYN STURGIS. Our *tet* makes their first trip to NEW YORK, via TODASH, from their Mid-Forest campsite.

V:38–47 *(traveling through; mentioned on 41, 45)*, V:66–68 *(Roland follows Susannah)*, V:80–169 *(setting)*, V:197–206 *(setting)*, V:246 *(woods)*, V:406, V:604 *(named)*, V:681, VI:30, VII:594

BOG: While Roland's *ka-tet* travels through Mid-Forest, MIA, daughter of none, takes over SUSANNAH DEAN's body so that she can feed her CHAP in the Mid-Forest bogs. Although she is actually eating frogs and binnie bugs, Susannah-Mio dreams that she is dining in CASTLE DISCORDIA's BAN-QUETING HALL. V:82–86, V:88

**MID-WORLD
When the author STEPHEN KING refers to the whole of Roland's version of Earth, he uses the term *Mid-World*. However, when he refers to specific regions

of Mid-World, he uses the terms IN-WORLD, OUT-WORLD, *Mid-World*, END-WORLD, and the BORDERLANDS. In the Mid-World version of Earth which our *tet* travels through in the Dark Tower series, both time and directions are in drift. Hence, ANDY (CALLA BRYN STURGIS's Messenger Robot) often refers to it as Mid-World-that-was.

In *The Waste Lands,* Roland drew a metaphysical map of Mid-World, which was meant to encompass all the known lands of his reality. According to this map, Mid-World was shaped like a sequin impaled upon a central needle. The center of the needle—or the hub of the Earth-wheel—was the DARK TOWER, or the nexus of the time/space continuum. Radiating out from the Tower were the BEAMS, those invisible high-tension wires which simultaneously held all of the universes together and maintained the divisions between them. According to this map, End-World (home of the Dark Tower) sat at the center of everything, like a bull's-eye, and In-World (the hub of human civilization when Roland was a boy) didn't even appear on the map. Although the terms *End-World* and *In-World* are confusing when viewed in this manner, readers must remember that Roland's map was meant to be figurative, not literal. It was a teaching tool used to explain universal forces, not actual geography. (For an explanation of why In-World was called In-World, see the IN-WORLD entry, listed separately.)

Although the term *Mid-World* is usually used in its most general form, the word originally applied to a specific kingdom—one which tried to preserve culture and knowledge in a time of darkness. Mid-World's ancient boundaries stretched from a marker near the edge of the GREAT WEST WOODS to MID-FOREST, the wooded area which abuts the borderlands, to TOPEKA, the city where BLAINE the Insane Mono terminated his run. The city of LUD (which our *tet* traveled through in *The Waste Lands*) was Mid-World's largest urban center. Since King often implies that Lud is a future version of our world's NEW YORK, and since the BEAR-TURTLE BEAM runs through both New York and Lud, it seems likely that the ancient kingdom of Mid-World was (geographically at least) more closely linked to the northeastern part of the United States than to the Southwest, which it resembles.

In Roland's youth, the great city of GILEAD tried to keep Mid-World's traditions alive and in many ways thought of itself as Mid-World's successor. Hence, Roland sometimes refers to his world as Mid-World, a term which includes both the IN-WORLD BARONIES, such as NEW CANAAN, and the farthest reaches of Out-World, including forgotten ruins such as ELURIA. In the 2003 version of *The Gunslinger,* we learn that Roland has been searching for the old Kingdom of Mid-World for a very long time. He has heard rumors that green lands still exist there, but he finds it hard to believe. Interestingly, the term *Mid-World* is reminiscent of both Middle Earth—Tolkien's magical world—and Midgard, the realm inhabited by human beings in both Norse and Anglo-Saxon mythology.

III:153 *(Mid-World Railway)*, III:154, III:163–64, III:177, III:256, III:266, III:267, III:334, III:347, III:375, III:410, III:419, III:420, IV:66 *(Mid-World ends near Topeka)*, IV:71, IV:445, IV:447, E:147, E:165, E:198, V:4, V:13, V:18, V:25 *(the Mids)*, V:31, V:35, V:39, V:44 *(term for Roland's world)*, V:48, V:49 *(term for Roland's world)*, V:51 *(term for Roland's world)*, V:56, V:58, V:61, V:71, V:89, V:100, V:108, V:111 *(term for Roland's world)*, V:137, V:138 *(Mid-World-that-was)*, V:165, V:202, V:214, V:478, V:501, V:631, VI:7, VI:30,

VI:40, VI:67, VI:84, VI:122, VI:148, VI:247, VI:403, VI:404, VI:405, VI:407, VII:12, VII:37, VII:51, VII:84, VII:103, VII:141, VII:234, VII:260, VII:262, VII:300, VII:336, VII:382, VII:395, VII:398, VII:555, VII:580, VII:594, VII:598, VII:601, VII:607, VII:668, VII:669, VII:670, VII:715, VII:802, VII:810, VII:817, W:11, W:13, W:15, W:19, W:20, W:25, W:109, W:110, W:162, W:220, W:245

MID-WORLD LANES
See MID-WORLD LANES, in PORTALS

MID-WORLD RAILWAY
See MID-WORLD RAILWAY, in PORTALS

MILLBANK, THE
See MEJIS, BARONY OF: HAMBRY

**MOHAINE DESERT
In *The Gunslinger,* Roland crosses this desert in pursuit of WALTER. The Mohaine is described as "the apotheosis of all deserts, huge, standing to the sky for what might have been parsecs in all directions. White; blinding; waterless; without feature save for the faint, cloudless haze of the mountains which sketched themselves on the horizon and the devil grass which brought sweet dreams, nightmares, death." It is a harsh and unforgiving place that steals youth and sucks moisture from the very soul. The town of TULL is located near the desert and BORDER DWELLERS live on the edges of this wasteland, but nothing can live within its desiccated heart.

In pursuit of the MAN IN BLACK, Roland crosses this desert on foot, making his way along the old COACH ROAD, which winds through PRICETOWN and Tull. He stops briefly at BROWN's hut (the final human habitation), then travels across the hardpan until he reaches the WAY STATION, where he meets JAKE. The final leg of this journey (from Brown's hut to the Way Station) almost kills him. Much of MID-WORLD has been reduced to desert, but the Mohaine seems to be, by far, the worst. In the 2003 version of *The Gunslinger,* we find out that the Mohaine is haunted by at least one TAHEEN—a hybrid creature with a raven's head and a man's body.

In *The Wind Through the Keyhole* we learn that, long ago, the WESTERN LINE ran trains from NEW CANAAN to the Mohaine Desert. However, in the years before Gilead fell, the train line ran to DEBARIA and no farther. When TIM ROSS rode on the magical DIBBIN, he felt like a prince of the Mohaine on an elephaunt.

I:11–22, I:30, I:31, I:42, I:44, I:45, I:52, I:65–81 *(72–81 Way Station),* I:83–95 *(83–92 Way Station),* I:119, I:124, I:127, I:134–35, I:209, II:40, III:43, III:101, VI:180 *(indirect),* VI:283 *(not directly named),* VI:288, VII:175, VII:515, VII:594, VII:827–30, W:40, W:256

N

NA'AR
See entry in PORTALS

NEW CANAAN, BARONY OF
The Barony of New Canaan, ruled by the gunslinger descendants of ARTHUR ELD, shares its name with the biblical land of milk and honey. Before the fall of the AFFILIATION, New Canaan (and its barony seat of GILEAD) was the hub of IN-WORLD. Like the ancient kingdom of MID-WORLD (the kingdom for which Roland's version of Earth is named), New Canaan tried to keep alive the ideals of hope, knowledge, and light. Roland remembers his home city of Gilead as a jewel set amid New Canaan's green-gold fields and serene blue rivers. Unlike many of the OUT-WORLD baronies, New Canaan still had working electricity.
I:136, IV:108, IV:148, IV:153, IV:182, IV:190, IV:199, IV:266–67, IV:289 *(apple orchards)*, IV:350

FORESTS OF NEW CANAAN:

BABY FOREST: The Baby Forest was located west of Gilead's castle. In it took place one of the apprentice gunslingers' tests of manhood, overseen by none other than the infamous CORT. Cort maintained that neither clocks nor sundials could be depended upon all of the time, so his students had to learn to keep a timepiece ticking inside of their minds. Summer evening after summer evening, the apprentices were sent out to spend an uncomfortable night in the forest until they could return to the yard behind the GREAT HALL at exactly the moment that Cort specified. As Roland testified to SUSANNAH, it took a great while to get that internal clock ticking, but once it did, it ran true. Roland lost this ability when the BEAMS began collapsing, but after the battle at the DEVAR-TOI, the skill returned. VII:587

BLOSSWOOD FOREST (BLOSSIE FARM): While he and his *ka-tet* are trying to explain to the people of CALLA BRYN STURGIS why it is important to fight the WOLVES, even at the risk of losing everything, Roland tells the story of the Blosswood Forest, which he knew and loved as a boy. The thousand-acre Blosswood Forest tree farm was located in the eastern part of the Barony of New Canaan. The blossies were farmed and so stood in neat rows, which were overseen by the barony forester. Blosswood was strong, yet so light that a thin piece could practically float on the air. Hence, it was the best possible wood for making boats. The rule of the foresters was always the same—for every two trees harvested, three must be planted. That way, the barony was assured a good crop for all time.

However, during Roland's youth, a terrible plague fell upon the Blosswood Forest. Spiders spun white webs in their crowns of the trees, killing the upper branches and rotting them. Most of the trees fell before the plague could reach their roots. Seeing what was happening, the foresters ordered that all the trees be cut down, to save what wood was still usable. Within a year, the Blossie Forest no longer existed. In Roland's opinion,

the Wolves are like the foresters. Since end-times are so close, the Wolves will take *all* the children when they next arrive, not just one of every pair of twins. *See also* NORTH'RD BARONY: ENDLESS FOREST. V:612–13
FOREST O' BARONY: The warped pines that grow here are used to make gallows trees.

GREAT WOODS: *See* NORTH'RD BARONY: ENDLESS FOREST

GILEAD: At the time fourteen-year-old Roland set out for HAMBRY, Gilead was MID-WORLD's last great living city. Ancient and walled, it was the baronly seat of New Canaan, one of the INNER BARONIES of western Mid-World. Gilead was known as the green land, and its city was divided into two separate towns. The filthy maze-like streets of LOWER TOWN (frequented by CORT) contained brothels. From the high, pennon-fluttering battlements of the castle, you could view the vendors of the brick and wrought-iron Old Quarter. The color of Gilead's royal court was dark blue. LLAMREI, who was both ARTHUR ELD's horse and the *sigul* of all IN-WORLD, decorated the city's pennons. I:94, I:96–111, I:149–52, I:158–74, III:152, III:207, III:242, III:349, III:375, III:410, III:411, III:414, III:415, III:416, III:417, III:418, III:419, IV:6–9, IV:15, IV:48, IV:49, IV:50, IV:93 *("green land")*, IV:107–12 *(brothels of lower town. Roland visits a whore)*, IV:119 *(western barony)*, IV:164, IV:194, IV:201 *(and outlying towns of Hemphill and Pennilton)*, IV:213, IV:219, IV:266, IV:289, IV:350, IV:357, IV:388, IV:389, IV:402, IV:405, IV:415, IV:436, IV:464, IV:474, IV:499, IV:536, IV:547, IV:564, IV:570, IV:584, IV:587 *(Roland of Gilead)*, IV:603, IV:611, IV:621 *(Roland sees its fall in Wizard's glass)*, IV:624, IV:644, IV:651, IV:652, IV:653, E:159, E:170, E:171, E:172, E:195, E:198, E:202, V:30, V:49, V:50, V:85, V:94 *(most inner of inner baronies)*, V:109, V:124, V:128, V:143, V:153, V:162, V:171, V:175, V:182, V:195, V:214, V:215, V:218, V:221, V:230, V:243, V:318, V:321, V:322, V:392, V:406, V:416, V:500, V:527, V:528, V:542, V:604, V:605 *(low-town)*, V:612, V:641, V:654, V:679, VI:16, VI:17, VI:63, VI:106, VI:129, VI:149, VI:183, VI:197, VI:234, VI:271, VI:275, VI:277, VI:279, VI:299, VI:319, VI:328, VI:370, VI:395, VI:396, VII:24, VII:35, VII:43, VII:50, VII:111, VII:122, VII:134, VII:135, VII:159, VII:166, VII:168, VII:172, VII:174, VII:176, VII:178, VII:179, VII:199, VII:219, VII:266, VII:270, VII:317, VII:322, VII:323, VII:333, VII:349, VII:381, VII:382, VII:384, VII:393, VII:411, VII:415, VII:439, VII:443, VII:487, VII:492, VII:494 *(Great Letters)*, VII:496, VII:499, VII:516 *(dark blue is the royal color)*, VII:549 *(Llamrei on pennons)*, VII:552, VII:601, VII:607, VII:651, VII:657, VII:711, VII:727, VII:749, VII:759, VII:801, VII:802, VII:821, VII:824, VII:828, W:4, W:8, W:30, W:40, W:41, W:49, W:55, W:57, W:66, W:69, W:73, W:74, W:76, W:99, W:103, W:120, W:131, W:169, W:170, W:179, W:197, W:202, W:268, W:269, W:271, W:294, W:299, W:300, W:301, W:306

BRIDGE WEST OF THE PALACE: The small, steam-driven train known as SMA' TOOT puffed across this bridge on its way to DEBARIA. W:40

CENTRAL PLACE AND GILEAD PALACE: This ancient part of Gilead consisted of one hundred stone castles. Gilead's central palace must have sat among them. By the time Roland was a young man, Gilead's central palace was not a happy place. Its shadowy rooms were full of whispers of intrigue, and the whole of it was heavy with a pervasive sense that darkness and anarchy were coming and nothing could stop them. The world would move on, but Gilead would not move on with it. I:71–72, I:137, I:158, III:37, IV:111, IV:161, IV:164, IV:436, IV:439, IV:619, IV:621, IV:652, W:35, W:39 *(Roland wants to escape it)*, V:171, W:40

BACK COURTS AND FIELDS: Women played Points in the main castle's Back Courts. These courts seemed to be adjacent to the fields where CORT trained young gunslingers in archery and falconry. I:96–100, I:137

BARRACKS: This was where young gunslinger apprentices lived, away from their parents. The apprentices' nickel guns (given once they passed their coming-of-age battle against CORT) were stored in the vaults below. I:171

CORT'S COTTAGE: After GABRIELLE DESCHAIN's death, Roland spent much time in Cort's cottage, tending to his old teacher. STEVEN DESCHAIN thought that this was Roland's self-imposed penance for committing matricide. I:162–64, I:170, I:172, W:35–36

EXERCISE YARD: I:161

GABRIELLE'S APARTMENTS: I:159–61, IV:654–58

GATHERING FIELDS: E:160

**GREAT HALL (CENTRAL HALL, HALL OF THE GRAND-FATHERS, WEST'RD HALL): The Spring Ball, also known as **the Sowing Night Cotillion, was held in Gilead's Great Hall. It was a grand place with great balconies and a central dancing area illuminated by electric flambeaux. Roland saw his mother dance with the traitorous MARTEN BROADCLOAK here. In the 2003 version of *The Gunslinger*, Roland calls it the West'rd Hall. I:137, I:150–52, I:156, I:164, I:166, III:276, III:417–18, IV:7–8, IV:150 *(electric lights)*, IV:178, IV:193–94, IV:405, IV:436, IV:547, E:160, V:50, VII:587

> **YARD BEHIND THE GREAT HALL:** Here, CORT awaited those apprentice gunslingers who had spent the night in the BABY FOREST. VII:587

GREAT HOUSE KITCHENS (WEST KITCHENS): This was HAX's domain. I:100–103, I:109, I:137, E:187

LOWER TOWN: the filthy, maze-like streets of this quarter of the city were filled with brothels and taverns. IV:107–12

MAIN RECEIVING HALL: I:103–6

NORTH FIELD: Apprentice gunslingers practiced bow-shooting in North Field. V:248

ROLAND'S NURSERY (ROOM OF MANY COLORS): As a young child, Roland slept in a circular bedroom at the top of a tall stone tower. The windows of this nursery were made of stained glass colored to represent the BENDS O' THE RAINBOW. Whenever Roland heard the word *chassit,* he had a vivid memory of this room, and of his mother singing the Baby-Bunting Rhyme to him. *(For the words to the Baby-Bunting Rhyme, see* APPENDIX III.*)* In *The Wind Through the Keyhole,* we learn that GABRIELLE DESCHAIN also read him *The Magic Tales of Eld* here. Roland associates this room with his mother. I:71–72, VII:22, VII:23, VII:329, W:68, W:267, W:305

ROYAL COURT GARDENS: II:300

SQUARE YARD: Apprentice gunslingers proved themselves here. The square yard sat just east of the Great Hall, and was the site of Fair-Day Riddling. I:164, I:166–74, IV:436 *(east of Great Hall)*, IV:436–39

STEVEN DESCHAIN'S STUDY: Steven Deschain's study was located in the north wing of the palace. It was a small, cold room with slit windows and high shelves of books that were worth a fortune, though the elder Deschain never read them. Steven rarely called for his fire to be lit, even on the coldest days. W:35–40

WEST-TOWN: This was the merchant area in the western part of Gilead. I:159

GILEAD ROAD: This road ran from the GREAT WOODS, north of New Canaan, to GILEAD. Once, after a STARKBLAST had hit the Great Woods, Roland saw a cart full of frozen bodies being drawn down this road. W:17

LANDS WEST OF GILEAD: West of Gilead, along the rails of the old WEST-ERN LINE, Gilead's green and forested land gave way to dirty scrub, a few struggling ranches, and herders' huts. There were a few towns in this area, but many of the inhabitants were MUTANTS, and even more supported the GOOD MAN, JOHN FARSON. GABRIELLE DESCHAIN's family came from ARTEN, which was located between Gilead and DEBARIA. W:41

LAKE SORONI: This lake was located in the northern part of the Barony. When Roland was still a small child, his parents brought him here. IV:595

NONES
See NONES, *listed in* PORTALS

NORTH CENTRAL POSITRONICS (FACTORY)
See NORTH CENTRAL POSITRONICS, *in* CHARACTERS

NORTH'RD BARONY
Both the ENDLESS FOREST and the village of TREE were located north of NEW CANAAN in North'rd Barony.

GENERAL REFERENCES: W:111, W:170

BARONY ESTATES: Once the WIDOW SMACK had been a great lady in the Barony Estates. W:112

ENDLESS FOREST (GREAT WOODS): The Endless Forest (also known as the Great Woods) was an unexplored wilderness located north of NEW CANAAN, in North'rd Barony. Once or twice a year, this woodland was struck by STARKBLASTS. Although the storms never reached GILEAD, the effect they had on the country folk was devastating. Once Roland saw some carts loaded with frozen bodies drawn down GILEAD ROAD. The people hadn't had any BILLY-BUMBLERS to warn them that the storm was coming.

The village of TREE, setting for the folktale "The Wind Through the Keyhole," sat on the edge of the Endless Forest. Most of the men in Tree Village were woodcutters, and earned their daily bread by cutting the BLOSSWOOD that grew at the edges of the forest as well as the more valuable IRONWOOD trees that grew deeper in. No one living today has ever seen the likes of the Endless Forest. From above, the forest looked like a giant green dress so dark it was almost black. This dark green was the foliage of the ironwood trees. Along the bottom of the dress was a hem of lighter green. This paler shade was the foliage of the blossies. Just below the blossies, at the farthest edge of North'rd Barony, was the village of TREE.

Like all wild places, the Endless Forest was dark and full of dangers, and not even the woodsmen of Tree Village, who knew it better than anyone in MID-WORLD, could say what lived or grew beyond where the IRONWOOD TRAIL ended. But according to gossip, the depths of the forest were littered with the dangerous leavings of the OLD PEOPLE. That shadowy realm was also the home of strange animals and plants, stinking weirdmarshes, throckets of wild bumblers, and even bonfires of DRAGONS.

According to the COVENANT MAN, the ironwoods of the Endless Forest could think, and that was why woodsmen always cried the trees' pardon before beginning work. The old *folken* of Tree believed that when the winds came out of the north, the sweet-sour smell of the ironwoods brought visions. For NELL ROSS, who had lost her beloved husband JACK ROSS to the Endless Forest, this scent was both bitter and sweet, like blood and strawberries.

The woodsmen of Tree both loved and feared the ironwood forest, which was wise. The forest fed and clothed the men's families, but like a living being it also needed to eat, and its food was often the woodsmen themselves. Despite the risks, cutting ironwood was a lucrative job. Both seaworthy and rot resistant (ironwood coffins would last a thousand years), this unusual wood fetched such a high price that it was paid for in silver rather than scrip. Still, many woodsmen contented themselves with harvesting the blossies that grew at the forest edge rather than attempting to cut the more valuable commodity. Only very brave and strong men—like Big Ross and his partner BIG KELLS—dared to go deeper to where the good ironwood grew. And not even Ross or his treacherous partner dared to travel to the edge of the FAGO-NARD where the ironwoods grew bigger than houses.

Perhaps it was the dangerousness of the ironwood forest that inspired the people of Tree to link it to the afterlife. In DUSTIN STOKES's burial parlor, there was a little room with forest scenes painted on the walls. In the center was an ironwood bier, an open space that represented the clearing at the end of life's path. *See also* IRONWOOD, listed in CHARACTERS *section.* W:17, W:67, W:73, W:106, W:109, W:110–11, W:115, W:117, W:118, W:119, W:120, W:122, W:123, W:127, W:146–64, W:170, W:174, W:184, W:185, W:186, W:187, W:191–257

BLOSSIE GROVES: Most of Tree's woodsmen went no deeper into the forest than the pale green fringes where the blossie groves grew. But even there, dangers could arise. Snakes, such as POOKYS, were the worst. But there were also dog-sized poisonous rodents called wervels, and verts, also known as bullet-birds. Many men had been lost in the blossies over the years, but on the whole, cutting blossie was worth the risk. It was a lovely fine-grained wood, golden in color and almost light enough to float on air. It made fine lake and rivercraft but was not good for sea travel. Even a moderate gale would tear apart a boat made of blossie. *See also* NEW CANAAN, BARONY OF FORESTS OF NEW CANAAN: BLOSSWOOD FOREST. W:109 W:110, W:119, W:149, W:172

CHASM OF WHITE FLOWERS: TIM ROSS discovered this chasm while traveling with his NORTH CENTRAL POSITRONICS companion, DARIA, through the ENDLESS FOREST. This narrow chasm fell away for a thousand feet or more. He could not see the bottom, because it was filled with a drift of sweet-smelling white flowers so thick that Tim at first mistook them for a cloud that had fallen to earth. Spanning the gorge was a narrow rock bridge. On the opposite side of the gorge the bridge passed through a waterfall. Although Tim did not wish to cross the bridge late at night (he wanted to wait until morning), Daria urged speed. It was a good thing she did, since the beautiful white flowers hid a TENTACLED MONSTER. Beyond the waterfall was a little rock cave. Written on one wall, in paint that might once have been red, was this cryptic notation:

JOHN 3:16
FEER HELL HOPE FOR HEVEN
MAN JESUS

Beyond that was a short stone staircase, to one side of which was a litter of tin cans and bits of broken machinery. On the other side of the staircase was a grinning skeleton. W:228–32

CLEARING AMID THE IRONWOODS: TIM ROSS saw a throcket of BILLY-BUMBLERS dancing in this clearing. The sight was beautiful, but it was also a sure sign that a STARKBLAST was on its way. W:224–27

COSINGTON-MARCHLY STAKE: BIG BERN KELLS hid the body of BIG JACK ROSS in a sluggish stream on the Cosington-Marchly Stake. He knew that particular stub would be deserted for a goodish while, since a POOKY had taken up housekeeping there. W:148–64, W:168, W:172, W:189, W:257

> **COVENANT MAN'S CAMP:** The Covenant Man set up his camp on the COSINGTON-MARCHLY STAKE, very near the sluggish stream where BIG ROSS's body floated just under the water. He wanted to show the corpse to TIM ROSS. W:148–64

FAGONARD: Beyond the IRONWOOD TRAIL, which led through the ENDLESS FOREST, lay the great swamp known as the FAGONARD. Unlike the Endless Forest, which was filled with the grave, sweet-sour smell of the ironwoods, the Fagonard had the less pleasant stench of stagnant water and rotting vegetation. As Tim realized when he was lured there by the wicked little SIGHE named ARMANEETA, this swampy world was more liquid that solid.

The Fagonard was the hunting ground for the CANNIBAL REPTILES that attacked TIM ROSS during his travels through the swamp, but it was also home to the MUDMEN who saved Tim's life and who gave him the NORTH CENTRAL POSITRONICS portable guidance module, DARIA. In addition, it was the dwelling place of the DRAGON that the MUTANT Mudmen appease with their offering of a boar's head. W:110 *(weird-marshes)*, W:149, W:160, W:182, W:191–216, W:218, W:220, W:226, W:227, W:238, W:245, W:250, W:256–57

FIELD OF GIANT YELLOW MUSHROOMS: TIM ROSS discovered this grove of four-foot-high bright yellow mushrooms while traveling through the ENDLESS FOREST in search of the magician MAERLYN. At first Tim thought that they might be good to eat, but his companion, DARIA, warned him that if the mushroom dust so much as brushed his skin, he would die of seizures. W:228

GREAT CANYON: The Great Canyon sat at the end of the NORTH FOREST KINNOCK DOGAN's clearing, deep in the ENDLESS FOREST. It was at least a hundred wheels across. W:233–55 *(present during this time, occasionally mentioned)*

IRONWOOD FOREST: According to TIM ROSS, the ironwoods at the heart of the Endless Forest were as tall, straight, and solemn as Manni elders at a funeral. Although they were completely smooth for the first forty feet, above that their branches leaped skyward like upraised arms, tangling the narrow IRONWOOD TRAIL with a cobweb of shadows. Anyone foolish enough to wander off the trail or go beyond it quickly became lost in a maze. Only the strongest and bravest men went beyond the forest's fringe of blosswood groves to cut ironwood in the deep forest, but the rewards for doing so were great. Ironwood brought a high price from HODIAK, the Barony buyer who came twice a year to the TREE SAWMILL. It was ironwood that gave the Endless Forest its green-black hue. W:109, W:111, W:119, W:146–64, W:172, W:189–257, W:257

IRONWOOD TRAIL: The Ironwood Trail was the narrow track that led from Tree Road (also called Main Road) into the Endless Forest. At the very end of the trail, before the FAGONARD began, was the ROSS-KELLS STAKE. W:110, W:114, W:115, W:117, W:122, W:127, W:129, W:133, W:136–37, W:139, W:146–64, W:168, W:172 W:173, W:175, W:182, W:188, W:189–90, W:206, W:245

MAERLYN'S HOUSE: According to some *folken* in MID-WORLD, the sorcerer MAERLYN and the evil COVENANT MAN of GILEAD were one and the same person. According to these gossips, the once-good wizard had been turned evil by some of the artifacts of the OLD PEOPLE that he found in the ENDLESS FOREST. These artifacts blackened him to the bottom of his soul. Such folk said that Maerlyn kept a magic house in the forest forever after, and that time stood still there. While staring into the Covenanter's magic silver pail, Tim saw a vision of Maerlyn's house. It was a tall building with many gables and many chimneys. However, we can't be certain whether Maerlyn's house actually ever existed. When Tim met the wizard, the sorcerer was trapped in the shape of a TYGER and was living in a cage near the NORTH FOREST KINNOCK DOGAN. Later, the wizard hinted that he lived in a cave with nothing but a single table and a pallet. The only thing we can be certain of is that Maerlyn and the Covenanter were not the same person. In fact, they were enemies. W:170, W:183, W:207

ROSS-KELLS STAKE: BIG JACK ROSS and BIG BERN KELLS had four or five small stakes just off the IRONWOOD TRAIL. At least one of these was the last stub before the FAGONARD swamp. (In fact, the end of the Ironwood Trail was marked by a sign written by Ross: IRON-WOOD TRAIL ENDS HERE. BEYOND LIES FAGONARD. TRAVELER, BEWARE!) Ross and Kells cut ironwood on their remote stake, where the trees were big. Unfortunately, it was also on one of these stakes that Big Kells murdered his partner, though he hid the body on a fallow stub of the COSINGTON-MARCHLY STAKE. W:110, W:133, W:182

FARMING VILLAGES OF THE MIDDLES: The avaricious COVENANT MAN collected taxes in these villages before he visited TREE. W:114

TREE VILLAGE: The fairy-tale village of Tree was the last town in what was then considered civilized country. It was located on the very edge of NORTH'RD BARONY, nestled close to the ironwood-rich ENDLESS FOR-EST. There were only two locks in Tree. One was on the JAIL. The other was on GITTY'S SALOON. W:110, W:111–146, W:164–89, W:204, W:206, W:210, W:224, W:228, W:245, W:251, W:252, W:255, W:257–64, W:268

 CEMETERY: W:255

 CONSTABLE HOWARD'S HOUSE: After BERN KELLS beat his wife NELL into blindness, it was impossible to find the constable. Unfortu-nately for Nell, Kells committed his crime while the COVENANT MAN was in town. Whenever the Covenant Man came to TREE, Constable Howard made himself scarce. W:166–67

 COSINGTON COTTAGE: Before the death of BIG ROSS, the Ross family frequently ate meals at the Cosington Cottage. W:149, W:178

 COSINGTON-MARCHLY STORAGE SHED: W:171–72

 DEAF RINCON'S BARN: The murderer BIG BERN KELLS waited out the STARKBLAST in Deaf Rincon's barn. W:262, W:263

 DESTRY FARM: Farmer Destry was one of the biggest farmers in Tree. Not long after his father died, TIM ROSS got two weeks work cutting hay on this farm. Destry's east field sat next to BERN KELLS's place. Hence, he wanted to buy it. (Kells sold to Baldy Anderson instead.) Destry had a framed picture of a rifle in his parlor. W:116–17, W:120, W:172, W:186

 GATHERING HALL: When TIM ROSS returned home to TREE after his adventures in the Endless Forest, he hoped that one of the local people had rescued his mother from the dangers of the STARKBLAST and had brought her to the village Gathering Hall. Instead, he found his mother in their cottage, where she was being cared for by the good WIDOW SMACK. W:258

 GOODVIEW COTTAGE (ROSS COTTAGE): The Rosses' cottage, Good-view, sat less than a wheel from the edge of the ENDLESS FOREST. The house was tiny but cozy. (The sitting room was so small that when BIG JACK ROSS stood in the middle and stretched out his arms, he could touch the opposite walls.) After NELL ROSS was widowed and married BIG BERN KELLS, Goodview became the Kellses' cottage. W:109, W:110, W:112, W:113–24, W:131, W:149, W:153–56, W:164–71, W:173–74, W:175, W:178, W:180, W:181, W:251, W:254, W:255, W:258–64

 GITTY'S SALOON: Gitty's Saloon was one of only two buildings in Tree Village to have a lock on it. The other was the Tree JAIL. It was at this saloon that the COVENANT MAN discovered that BIG BERN KELLS had slipped the rope with his partner's widow. At that point, the Covenanter knew that Kells was guilty of murder. All that remained was for him to find the incriminating evidence, namely Ross's dead body. W:118, W:119, W:127–28, W:129, W:136, W:139 *(indirect)*, W:141, W:161, W:173

 JAIL: Tree's jail was one of only two buildings in the village to have a lock. The other was the SALOON. BIG KELLS spent time in both of these buildings. In his younger days (and especially after his friend BIG JACK ROSS married NELL ROSS), Bern Kells often ended up in jail for his drunken and disorderly behavior. W:118, W:136, W:168

KELLS COTTAGE: BERN KELLS sold his cottage to BALDY ANDERSON so that he could pay the COVENANT MAN the taxes due for both himself and his new wife, NELL ROSS. (Kells didn't get a very good price for his old home.) W:117, W:125–26, W:133

MAIN ROAD (TREE ROAD, HIGH STREET): In order to get to the IRONWOOD TRAIL, Tree's woodsmen had to travel down Tree's Main Road, or high street. (Farther from the town, this street was called Tree Road.) W:110, W:126, W:146, W:174, W:175, W:179, W:255

MARCHLY COTTAGE: Before BIG ROSS's death, the Ross family frequently ate meals at the Marchly cottage. W:149, W:173

STAPE BROOK: Stape Brook originated in the clear spring that welled up between the ROSS COTTAGE and barn. W:180, W:257–58

STOKES BURYING PARLOR AND SMITHY: Stokes Burying Parlor was located behind his smithy. At the back of the parlor was a little room with forest scenes painted on the walls. In the center was an ironwood bier for the dead. This open space represented the clearing at the end of life's path. W:173, W:176–78, W:255

TOWN STORE (MERCANTILE): When TIM ROSS cut hay for FARMER DESTRY, he was paid in scrip for the town store. W:120

TREE RIVER: When the STARKBLAST blasted into Tree, it blew the town sawmill into this river. W:257

TREE SAWMILL: At his steppa's insistence, TIM ROSS worked at the Tree Sawmill for a while. The STARKBLAST blew the mill into TREE RIVER. W:111, W:127, W:129, W:130, W:172, W:202, W:206, W:257

WIDOW SMACK'S COTTAGE: Widow Smack's cottage doubled as the Tree schoolhouse. It was located at the end of the high street, where the woodland scents were stronger. W:112, W:146, W:164, W:173–75, W:184–89, W:255

NORTHWEST BARONIES

BLAINE's twin mono PATRICIA headed to the Northwest Baronies. We are not told any of their names.

III:342

O

OAKLEY

CLAY REYNOLDS and CORAL THORIN escaped the carnage of HAMBRY and set off to become outlaws. They became lovers and formed a gang of bank robbers and coach thieves. They were eventually killed by the sheriff of Oakley.

IV:623

OLD CALLA ROAD
See BORDERLANDS

ONNIE'S FORD
See MEJIS, BARONY OF

ORACLE OF THE MOUNTAINS
See STONE CIRCLES, *in* PORTALS

ORANGE GROVE
See MEJIS, BARONY OF: HAMBRY

OUR LADY OF SERENITY
See BORDERLANDS: CALLA BRYN STURGIS

OUTER ARC
In *Wizard and Glass,* we learned that geographical terms such as *Outer Arc* were metaphorical rather than literal. During Roland's youth, backwater baronies such as MEJIS, which existed far from the civilized hub of the IN-WORLD baronies, were known as OUT-WORLD baronies or Outer Arc baronies. These relative terms of *in, out,* and *outer* make sense when you consider them in terms of the metaphysical map of MID-WORLD which Roland drew in *The Waste Lands.* On that map, the DARK TOWER sat at the center of the world-circle, and the PORTALS (watched over by the GUARDIANS) sat at its periphery. If this metaphor of the world-circle is applied to the human world, then In-World, and the In-World baronies such as NEW CANAAN, sit at the center of the map, since they form the hub of civilization. Cultural backwaters, which are both physically and psychically distant from the hub, are considered part of the Outer Arc. In *Wolves of the Calla,* we learn that most of Mid-World's coffee was grown in the southern reaches of the Outer Arc.
  V:89

OUT-WORLD
In *Wizard and Glass,* we learned that, during Roland's youth, geographical terms such as *Out-World* were more metaphorical than literal. To the IN-WORLD citizens of GILEAD (barony seat of NEW CANAAN), those baronies located far from the hub of civilization were part of Out-World. They existed "out there," on the OUTER ARC of human culture. In *Wolves of the Calla,* the same metaphorical use of terms applies, but the center, or hub, of the world changes. To the people of CALLA BRYN STURGIS, the Callas of the BORDERLANDS form the hub of the known world. Hence, any people who travel to the borderlands from other parts of MID-WORLD are considered *outworlders.*

  The terms *In-World* and *Out-World* may also be metaphorical references to the metaphysical map of Mid-World which Roland drew in *The Waste Lands.* According to this map, Mid-World is shaped like a circle, with the DARK TOWER at its center and the BEAMS radiating out from it and terminating in twelve PORTALS. Just as the Tower is the center of the Universe, Gilead and the In-World baronies are the centers of human culture. Backwaters such as MEJIS are on the Outer Crescent of the "civilized" world. *See also* MID-WORLD, *listed in this section, and* END-WORLD, *in* PORTALS

During Roland's youth, the people of Gilead considered the western lands, once served by the WESTERN LINE, to be part of Out-World. By the time Roland won his guns this area was overrun with harriers and roving bands of outlaws who called themselves land-pirates. It was essentially the lawless kingdom of JOHN FARSON, who was himself no more than a glorified land-pirate. The town of DEBARIA sat on the edge of Out-World. In fact, Roland thought of HIGH SHERIFF HUGH PEAVY as the High Sheriff of the Debaria Outers.

IV:213, IV:295, IV:350 *(Crescent)*, IV:359 *(Outer Crescent)*, IV:436, IV:447, IV:506, IV:653, V:8, V:312 *(outworlders)*, V:344 *(outworlders)*, V:402 *(outworlders)*, V:418 *(outworlders)*, VII:176, W:41, W:55, W:237

OUTWORLD, GATEWAY OF
See DOGAN: NORTH FOREST KINNOCK DOGAN, *in* PORTALS

P

PASS O' THE RIVER (TOWN)
A MID-WORLD town whose bar, **FOREST TREES,** had a female bartender.
IV:382

PEABERRY ROAD
See BORDERLANDS: CALLA BRYN STURGIS

PENNILTON
Mr. RICHARD STOCKWORTH (ALAIN's alias in HAMBRY) was supposed to have come from this town.
IV:148, IV:183

PIANO RANCH
See MEJIS, BARONY OF: HAMBRY

PORLA
The people of RIVER CROSSING believe that the civil wars of MID-WORLD began in either this land or in GARLAN.
III:242

PORTALS
See DOORWAYS BETWEEN WORLDS *and* BEAMS, PATH OF THE, *both in* PORTALS

PRICETOWN
Roland passes through Pricetown on his way to TULL. He buys a mule here.
I:22, I:23, III:42

R

RACEY'S CAFÉ
See DEBARIA, BARONY OF

RADIUM MINES
See ELURIA

RAILROAD
SUBWAY: In *The Gunslinger,* JAKE and Roland were attacked by SLOW MUTANTS in this underground subway system that ran beneath the CYCLO-PEAN MOUNTAINS. I:154–58 *(following tracks)*, I:174–92 *(following tracks)*
WESTERN LINE: Once the Western Line ran a thousand wheels or more, from NEW CANAAN to the MOHAINE DESERT. However, in the years before GILEAD fell, it went to DEBARIA and no farther. Beyond there, many tracklines had been destroyed by washouts and ground-shakers. Others had been taken up by harriers and roving bands of outlaws who called themselves land-pirates. Running along the little bit of remaining track was the special two-car train known as SMA' TOOT. Roland and JAMIE DeCURRY took Sma'Toot all the way to Debaria, where they investigated the SKIN-MAN murders. W:40–44 *(Roland, Jamie, and Sma' Toot)*

REDBIRD TWO MINE
See BORDERLANDS: CALLA BRYN STURGIS: ARROYO COUNTRY

REDPATH KRA-TEN
See BORDERLANDS: CALLA BRYN STURGIS: MANNI CALLA

REDPATH-A-STURGIS
See BORDERLANDS: CALLA BRYN STURGIS: MANNI CALLA

RILEA
See BLAINE'S ROUTE

RIM, THE
See BORDERLANDS: GRAND CRESCENT

RIMROCKS
A few days before the final gunslinger battle of JERICHO HILL, Roland's reinforcements (DEMULLET'S COLUMN) were ambushed and slaughtered here. ALAIN JOHNS heard the news, but when he galloped back to camp after midnight to inform his friends about the disaster, he was accidentally shot. Alain died under Roland and CUTHBERT's guns.
   V:170

RITZY

The down-and-out town of Ritzy is located four hundred miles west of MEJIS. It is a one-road mining village on the eastern slope of the VI CASTIS MOUNTAINS, fifty miles from the VI CASTIS CUT. Once there were freehold mines in the foothills, but they were regulated out by the VI CASTIS COMPANY.

IV:265–271, IV:348, IV:391, IV:527, IV:545

BEAR AND TURTLE MERCANTILE & SUNDRIE ITEMS: IV:265

HATTIGAN'S SALOON: IV:266, IV:267–69

SIX ROARING BARROOMS: IV:265

TOWN GATHERING HALL/JAILHOUSE: IV:265

VI CASTIS COMPANY STORE: IV:265

VI CASTIS CUT: IV:265 *(fifty miles from Ritzy)*

VI CASTIS MINES: IV:265–66

VI CASTIS MOUNTAINS: IV:265, IV:527

VI CASTIS (TOWN): FARSON will refine CITGO oil here. IV:431

RIVER BARONIES (AND WAYDON CASTLE)

According to the stories Roland heard as a child, LADY ORIZA, the rice goddess, was born in Waydon Castle near the RIVER SEND. However, in the BORDERLANDS Oriza is associated with the RIVER WHYE. Although Lady Oriza is always associated with a river (rice only grows in flooded paddies), the particular river barony she rules may vary from region to region and from folktale to folktale.

V:325–26 *(Waydon Castle)*

RIVER BARONY

River Barony, which our *ka-tet* traveled through in *The Waste Lands*, took its name from the RIVER SEND, which flowed through it. According to some MID-WORLD folktales, LADY ORIZA came from River Barony.

III:240, III:379 (West River Barony)

BARONY CASTLE AND VILLAGE: III:242–43

GREAT PLAINS OF RIVER BARONY: III:170 *(not named yet)*, III:281, III:407

JIMTOWN: A village near RIVER CROSSING. III:228, III:240, III:309, III:346

**LUD: Lud, which our *ka-tet* travels through in *The Waste Lands*, was once the major city of River Barony. For many years after River Barony erupted in civil war, Lud held out against its besieging harriers. However, as the years passed, the difference between the besiegers and the besieged began to disintegrate. By the time our *tet* arrives, both sides are mad.

When our story begins, Lud has been torn apart by constant warfare for more than a hundred years. The major players in this ongoing battle are the PUBES, who are the descendants of the besieged artisans who stayed in Lud to defend their homes, and the GRAYS, who are the great-great-grandchildren of the attacking harriers. The Pubes practice human sacrifice to appease the god-drums operated by the Grays (with the help of Lud's sadistic computer BLAINE) and the Grays have dwindled to a gang of murderous, disease-ridden lechers hiding like rats in mazes below the city.

Children, especially boys, are sought out in the decaying and decadent city of Lud. They can be trained as fighters and can be used for sexual gratification. In the 2003 version of *The Gunslinger,* we learn that two thousand years before our story takes place, Lud looked a lot like NEW YORK CITY. Later in the series, we discover that Lud is actually MID-WORLD's version of this great metropolis. III:164, III:170–72, III:181 *(drums),* III:195, III:222–23 *(drums),* III:226, III:228, III:233, III:238, III:239–45, III:240, III:242, III:248, III:254–55 *(drums),* III:256–57, III:263, III:267, III:268 *(drums),* III:269–70, III:274, III:281, III:282 *(drums),* III:285, III:287, III:289–302 *(cross bridge),* III:302–404 *(drums 312, 313, 314, 315, 316, 317; land of drums, 321, 329, 332–33, 411; 404 leaving on Blaine),* III:405, III:406, III:408, III:410, III:411, IV:16, IV:23, IV:25, IV:28, IV:34, IV:35, IV:62, IV:66, IV:75 *(drums),* IV:76 *(drums),* IV:663, V:35, V:135, V:141, V:165 *(and Mid-World),* V:166, V:178–79 *(and New York),* V:225, V:246, V:319 *(The Great City),* V:377, V:379, V:512, V:565, V:610, VI:14, VI:67, VI:91, VI:118, VI:152, VI:184, VI:206, VI:244, VI:287, VII:84, VII:109, VII:120, VII:160, VII:502, VII:521, VII:558, VII:590, VII:594, VII:725, W:10–11, W:13, W:31

APPLE PARK: TICK-TOCK, leader of the GRAYS, remembers visiting this park on the west side of Lud when he was a child. His father took him there to see the cider house and apple press. III:386

CITY NORTH: The PUBES occupy City North. It is here that they practice human sacrifice in response to the god-drums. III:308–12, III:316–25 *(321 named)*

CRADLE OF LUD/BLAINE'S CRADLE: The Cradle of Lud is a magnificent structure of blinding white stone. Despite the fact that its builders died off hundreds of generations before, the walls still clean themselves with endless streams of water. Marching around the Cradle's roof are the GUARDIANS OF THE BEAM, two by two. The roof's corners are guarded by dragons, but on its peak, towering sixty feet above an already imposing edifice, is a golden statue of a gunslinger.

The Cradle of Lud—which was the GREAT OLD ONES' equivalent of GRAND CENTRAL STATION—is the home of BLAINE the Insane Mono. Praise the Imperium! III:303, III:316, III:322–25 *(Eddie and Susannah make Pubes bring them here),* III:329, III:331–34, III:340–50, III:360–65, III:372–73, III:381, III:382–85, III:393–400, IV:67, IV:71, IV:75, V:38, VII:77, VII:492

GRAYS' CASTLE/GRAYS' MAZE/CRADLE OF THE GRAYS: This winding mess below the city looks more like a trash midden than the headquarters of the GRAYS. In order to build it they dragged old cars, old computers, and even sculptures and fountains from other parts of the city. This varied pile acts as a kind of barrier, but one full of trip wires and booby traps. Located in the eastern part of Lud, the Cradle of the Grays is essentially the kingdom of the very nasty ANDREW QUICK, also known as TICK-TOCK. From here the Grays operate the god-drums, whose frenzied beat drives the PUBES to sacrifice each other. III:304–8, III:312–16, III:325–31, III:334–40, III:350–61 *(357 named),* III:365–72, III:373–78, III:378–82, III:385–90, IV:647

GREAT ROAD TO LUD: *See* GREAT ROAD

GREAT WALL OF LUD: III:405

HANGING FOUNTAIN: III:313–14, III:328–29

LUD BRIDGE: *See* SEND RIVER: SEND RIVER BRIDGE

LUDWEG: The town of Ludweg is located north of Lud. JOCHABIM, the hume dishwasher whom JAKE CHAMBERS meets in the kitchens of the DIXIE PIG, originally came from Ludweg. VII:84

PLAZA OF THE CRADLE: III:331–34, III:341

SEND BASIN NUCLEAR PLANT: Lud computers control this area as well. III:379

STREET OF THE TURTLE: *See also* GUARDIANS OF THE BEAM, *in* CHARACTERS. III:309–12, III:316–25, III:331–34, III:341

RIVER CROSSING: River Crossing is the last outpost of civilization in River Barony. Its citizens are ancient but this does not stop them from trying to keep the old ways alive. Over the years they have had to keep their gardens and well-tended homes and meeting places secret from the harriers who pass through, burning, killing, and blinding as they go. River Crossing is ruled by the matriarch AUNT TALITHA. The old folks of this town tell our *ka-tet* everything they know about the lay of the land, give them a wonderful meal, and then send them on their way toward Lud. Talitha gives Roland her silver cross and asks him to lay it at the foot of the DARK TOWER. III:225–45, III:245–51, III:253, III:254, III:257, III:258, III:270, III:276, III:284, III:288, III:309, III:310, III:329, III:383, IV:14, IV:31, IV:52, V:55, V:78, V:110, V:134, V:192, VI:111, VI:117, VI:118, VI:182, VII:50, VII:120, VII:126 *(a forgotten town)*, VII:473, VII:802

CHURCH OF THE BLOOD EVERLASTING: III:227, III:232–45, III:232–49

LANDING, THE: III:227, III:240

RIVER ROAD: III:228

SEND RIVER: The Send River flows through RIVER BARONY. Roland's *ka-tet* travels along the Send River through much of *The Waste Lands* and then crosses it in order to enter LUD. (Below are some specific references.)

III: 170–71, III:176, III:223, III:241, III:256, III:283, III:285, III:288–302, III:310, III:311, III:363, IV:28, IV:31, IV:53, IV:100, V:325

SEND RIVER BRIDGE (CROSSING TO LUD): In *The Waste Lands,* our *tet* had to cross this dilapidated bridge to enter the city of LUD. Unfortunately, the child-snatcher GASHER was waiting for them on the far side. EDDIE and SUSANNAH think that the Send River Bridge resembles the GEORGE WASHINGTON BRIDGE in NEW YORK CITY. This bridge was made by LaMERK FOUNDRY. III:241–42, III:256–57, III:268, III:285, III:287, III:288–303, III:380, VII:502

TOM'S NECK: A town located near River Crossing. III:240

WEST RIVER BARONY: BLAINE (who is actually the computer-brain behind all of Lud's computers) controls this area. III:379

RIVER CROSSING
See RIVER BARONY

RIVER FIELD
See BORDERLANDS: CALLA BRYN STURGIS: JAFFORDS LAND

RIVER ROAD
See BORDERLANDS: CALLA BRYN STURGIS

RIVER SEND
See RIVER BARONY

RIVER STREET
See BORDERLANDS: CALLA BRYN STURGIS

ROADSIDE FIELD
See BORDERLANDS: CALLA BRYN STURGIS: JAFFORDS LAND

ROCKING B RANCH
See MEJIS, BARONY OF, *and* BORDERLANDS: CALLA BRYN STURGIS

ROCKING H RANCH
See MEJIS, BARONY OF: HAMBRY

ROSALITA'S COTTAGE
See BORDERLANDS: CALLA BRYN STURGIS: OUR LADY OF SERENITY

ROSS-KELLS STAKE
See NORTH'RD BARONY

S

SALLYWOOD
See DEBARIA, BARONY OF

SALT HILLS
See DEBARIA, BARONY OF

SALT-HOUSES
See DEBARIA, BARONY OF

SALTIE TOWN
See DEBARIA, BARONY OF

SANTA FE
See MEJIS, BARONY OF

SEAFRONT
  See MEJIS, BARONY OF: HAMBRY

SEND BASIN NUCLEAR PLANT
  See RIVER BARONY: LUD

SERENITY WOMEN'S RETREAT
  See DEBARIA, BARONY OF

SEVEN MILE
  See BORDERLANDS: CALLA BRYN STURGIS

SEVEN-MILE ORCHARD
  See MEJIS, BARONY OF: HAMBRY

SHARDIK'S WOODS (SHARDIK'S LAIR)
  See GREAT WEST WOODS; *see also* BEAMS, PATH OF THE, *in* PORTALS

SHAVÉD MOUNTAINS
The Shavéd Mountains are located northwest of GILEAD. FARSON intended to
battle the AFFILIATION here.
  IV:378, IV:430, IV:465

SHEB'S
  See TULL

SILK RANCH ROAD
  See MEJIS, BARONY OF

SON OF A BITCH
  See BORDERLANDS: CALLA BRYN STURGIS: JAFFORDS LAND

SOUTH PLAINS
The MUTANT minstrel CHEVIN OF CHAYVEN—one of the CHILDREN
OF RODERICK—once called the South Plains his home. Although his tribe
originated in lands far from those Roland ever knew, Chevin's people gave their
grace to Roland's ancestor ARTHUR ELD in the days before the world moved
on. EDDIE DEAN assumes that the South Plains are in MID-WORLD, so I have
placed them here as well.
  VII:51

SOUTH SEAS
The RIVER WHYE, which runs through the BORDERLANDS, eventually flows
into the South Seas.
  V:136

SPEAKING RINGS
See DOORWAYS BETWEEN WORLDS, *in* PORTALS

SQUARE YARD
See NEW CANAAN, BARONY OF: GILEAD

STAPE BROOK
See NORTH'RD BARONY

STOKES BURYING PARLOR AND SMITHY
See NORTH'RD BARONY

STONE CIRCLES
See DOORWAYS BETWEEN WORLDS, *in* PORTALS

SUBURB OF NOWHERE
This is EDDIE DEAN's term for the area northwest of the RIVER WHYE, where he, ROLAND, SUSANNAH, JAKE, and OY travel at the beginning of *The Wind Through the Keyhole*. Other than BIX, the RIVER WHYE ferryman, most of the people in this area stay well hidden. However, Roland does catch sight of a frightened woman with two children and a MUTANT farmer with a jerking tentacle attached to one corner of his mouth.
    W:4

SWAMP
See MID-FOREST (MID-FOREST BOG)

T

**TAUNTON
In the 2003 version of *The Gunslinger,* it is the people of Taunton, and not the people of FARSON, that HAX and THE GOOD MAN's followers try to poison.

**TAUNTON ROAD
In the 2003 version of *The Gunslinger,* GALLOWS HILL is located on the Taunton Road. Taunton Road replaces the FARSON ROAD.

TAVARES
Tavares was a town located up the coast from HAMBRY. One of its bars (GLEN-COVE) had a female bartender who eventually died of the pox. In *Wind Through the Keyhole,* we learn that Tavares was located forty wheels east of the ENDLESS FOREST. Tales of BIG JACK ROSS's death-by-dragon reached there quickly. The gunslinger posse that eventually accepted TIM ROSS as one of their own was headed for Taveres. IV:382, W:160, W:171, W:172, W:264, W:268, W:268

TEJUAS

Tejuas is an unincorporated township located two hundred miles west of ELURIA. The NORMAN brothers were headed here when their caravan was attacked by the GREEN FOLK.

E:178, E:193

TEMPA

See BORDERLANDS: CALLA BRYN STURGIS: MANNI CALLA

TEPACHI, BARONY OF

People from Tepachi have an accent similar to that of the people in the nearby Barony of MEJIS.

IV:269

TERRITORIES

The Territories are mentioned by CALVIN TOWER in *The Waste Lands* as he sells JAKE CHAMBERS both *Charlie the Choo-Choo* and *Riddle-De-Dum!* "Consider it my gift to a boy wise enough to saddle up and light out for the territories on the last real day of spring." The Territories, which are a parallel world to our Earth, are found in *The Talisman*, and in *Black House*, novels cowritten by STEPHEN KING and Peter Straub. Every human being in our world has a "twinner" in the territories.

III:116

THINNIES

See THINNY, *in* PORTALS

THOUGHTFUL HOUSE

See ELURIA

THUNDERCLAP

See entry in PORTALS

TIMBERSMITH FARM

See DEBARIA, BARONY OF

TOM'S NECK

See RIVER BARONY

TOOK'S GENERAL STORE

See BORDERLANDS: CALLA BRYN STURGIS

TOOK'S OUTLAND MERCANTILE

See BEAM ROAD

TOPEKA

See KANSAS: TOPEKA, *in* OUR WORLD PLACES

TOWER
See DARK TOWER, in PORTALS

TOWN COMMON
See BORDERLANDS: CALLA BRYN STURGIS

TOWN GATHERING HALL
See BORDERLANDS: CALLA BRYN STURGIS; see also MEJIS, BARONY
OF: HAMBRY

TRAVELERS' REST/TRAVELLERS' REST
See BORDERLANDS: CALLA BRYN STURGIS; see also MEJIS, BARONY
OF: HAMBRY

TREE RIVER
See NORTH'RD BARONY

TREE SAWMILL
See NORTH'RD BARONY

TREE VILLAGE
See NORTH'RD BARONY

**TULL
The sand-colored, pitted buildings of Tull are located south of PRICETOWN
and just north of the MOHAINE DESERT. The town consists of four roads—the
COACH ROAD and the three that cross it. Since Tull is located on the line of the
Coach Road, we can assume that it was once more prosperous. Now it consists
of a boarded-up grocery, a livery, a tailor, a church, a barber, a dry goods emporium, and a bar called SHEB'S.

Like so many of MID-WORLD's towns, Tull—located on the floor of a circular, bowl-shaped hollow—is reminiscent of the Old West. It is in Tull that Roland
meets his lover ALICE. It is also where he meets the formidable (and dangerously
crazy) SYLVIA PITTSTON. Thanks to Pittston's treachery, Roland ends up killing everyone in the town, including Allie. In the 2003 version of The Gunslinger,
we find out that there's an old train yard near Tull.

I:15, I:18–19, I:20–21, I:22–64, I:77, I:78, I:86, I:90, I:118, I:124, I:131, I:143,
I:156, II:40, II:126, II:145, III:42, III:44, IV:72, IV:628, V:253, VI:283, VI:284,
VI:288

SHEB'S: Sheb's is Tull's single honky-tonk. Despite its name, it actually
belongs to ALICE. Within its bat-wing doors it has a sawdust floor, spittoons,
and tipsy-legged tables. The bar is a plank resting on sawhorses. At the back
people play interminable games of Watch Me while SHEB bangs away on his
piano. I:22, I:23, I:26–43, I:45–47, I:52–54, I:58, I:61, I:63, I:64, II:40, II:126,
II:145, II:264

TURTLE, STREET OF THE
See RIVER BARONY: LUD

U

UNFOUND DOOR
See DOORWAY CAVE, *in* PORTALS

UNFOUND DOOR (PATH TO THE)
See BORDERLANDS: CALLA BRYN STURGIS: ARROYO COUNTRY

V

VI CASTIS CUT
See RITZY

VI CASTIS MOUNTAINS
See RITZY

W

WASTE LANDS
See WASTE LANDS, CALLA BADLANDS, *and* DISCORDIA, *all in* POR-
TALS

WAY STATION
See entry in PORTALS

WAYDON
See RIVER BARONIES

WEST RIVER BARONY
See RIVER BARONY

WEST-TOWN
See NEW CANAAN, BARONY OF: GILEAD

WEST WOODS
See GREAT WEST WOODS

WESTERN LINE
See NORTH'RD BARONY

WESTERN PLAINS
See BORDERLANDS

**WESTERN SEA AND LOBSTROSITY BEACH
Throughout *The Gunslinger,* Roland pursues the MAN IN BLACK south and then southwest through the MOHAINE DESERT and the CYCLOPEAN MOUNTAINS (in the 2003 *Gunslinger,* he follows his enemy southeast). At the end of his journey Roland finds himself at the GOLGOTHA, just three miles from the Western Sea, which is the setting for the next book in the series. The Western Sea is a terrible, barren place. Its waters are the color of dirty undergarments and its yellow, gross-grained beaches are littered with no-color shells and rocky protrusions. The tide line crawls with man-eating LOBSTROSITIES and its horizons seem endless and hopeless. The sea's Lobstrosity Beach is a terrible place, but it is through the magical BEACH DOORS, found here, that Roland draws EDDIE DEAN and SUSANNAH DEAN into his world. In the 2003 version of *The Gunslinger,* we find out that the Western Sea is the edge of the world.
I:44, I:214, II:15–21, II:26–36, II:44, II:55–56, II:62–63, II:72–74, II:76–78, II:79–82, II:92–94, II:99–105, II:135–43, II:154 *(indirect),* II:156–57, II:161–82, II:201–9, II:225–312, II:327–38, II:359–60, II:371, II:387–90, II:393–94, III:12, III:47, III:261, III:407, IV:42, IV:96, V:77, V:105, V:409, V:445, V:701, VI:132, VI:284, VI:295, VI:395, VII:177 *(shore),* VII:339, VII:594, VII:723, VII:741, VII:749
LOBSTROSITY BEACH: II:15–21, II:26–36 *(setting),* II:44, II:54, II:55–56, II:62–63, II:72–74, II:76–78, II:79–82, II:92–95, II:99–105, II:135–43, II:154 *(indirect),* II:156–57, II:161–82, II:201–9, II:225–312, II:327–38, II:359–60, II:387–90, II:393–94, III:13, III:36, III:316

**WEST'RD HALL
See NEW CANAAN, BARONY OF: GREAT HALL

WHYE
See BORDERLANDS: RIVER WHYE

WIDOW BRAILEY'S BOARDING HOUSE
See DEBARIA, BARONY OF

WIDOW SMACK'S COTTAGE
See NORTH'RD BARONY

WILLOW GROVE
See MEJIS, BARONY OF: HAMBRY

WILLOW JUNGLE
The Willow Jungle, located in the foothills of the CYCLOPEAN MOUNTAINS, was the home of the ORACLE OF THE MOUNTAINS. (It is sometimes also called the WILLOW GROVE, although the main Willow Grove is in HAMBRY.) After the dry hardpan of the desert, the Willow Jungle's wet lushness is a relief.

However, this dangerous jungle is the home of vampiric SUCKERBATS and the demonic Oracle of the Mountains. In *The Gunslinger*, Roland gained prophecy from this oracle, but her price was sexual intercourse. Although Roland didn't know it at the time, this creature was no mere wraith but the female aspect of a DEMON ELEMENTAL. Once she collected Roland's sperm, she gave it to the servants of the CRIMSON KING, who used it to create MORDRED.

I:117–34, III:172–73, V:46 *(indirect)*

WIND
Wind is a town even less ritzy than RITZY. It is located fifty miles from Ritzy and the VI CASTIS MOUNTAINS.

IV:266

X

XAY RIVER
ALAIN JOHNS, CUTHBERT ALLGOOD, and Roland Deschain crossed the Xay River while returning to GILEAD from HAMBRY. To cross the Xay, Roland and his friends had to clamber across a rope bridge. To make sure that no enemies followed, Alain severed the rope after they used it, and the remains of the bridge fell into the water a thousand feet below. Despite there being no bridge to cross, SHEEMIE managed to follow Roland's *tet* all the way back to Gilead. In *The Dark Tower*, we find out that Sheemie (a powerful BREAKER) teleported himself.

VII:271

OUR WORLD PLACES
AND THE MULTIPLE AMERICAS[3]

Go then. There are other worlds than these.
Jake Chambers, I:191

Maybe instead of forty-two continental United States on the other side of the Hudson, there are forty-two hundred, or forty-two thousand, all of them stacked in vertical geographies of chance.

And he understands instinctively that this is almost certainly true. He has stumbled upon a great, possibly endless, confluence of worlds. They are all America, but they are all different. There are highways which lead through them, and he can see them.
V:298–99

Look, there are a billion universes comprising a billion realities. . . . Those realities are like a hall of mirrors, only no two reflections are exactly the same. I may come back to that image eventually, but not yet. What I want you to understand for now—or simply accept—is that reality is organic, reality is alive.
VII:270

A

AKRON
See OHIO (STATE OF)

ALABAMA (STATE OF)
In SUSANNAH DEAN's *when* of 1964, Alabama cops were more than willing to sic dogs on black marchers protesting for voting rights. The world might be moving on, but some things have improved.
V:75, VI:109
BIRMINGHAM/BOMBINGHAM: V:75

3. For definitions of the terms *Multiple Americas* and *Alternative Americas,* see APPENDIX I, MID-WORLD DIALECTS. Also see the entry MULTIPLE AMERICAS, in this section of the *Concordance.*

> MONTGOMERY: II:199
>   WOOLWORTH'S: II:199

ALASKA (STATE OF)
V:428, VII:41, VII:229
ACHIN' ASSHOLE: Believe it or not, EDDIE DEAN made this place up.
II:396
FAIRBANKS: The FORTY bus is hobo-speak for the bus that will take you as far away as possible. If you're living in NEW YORK CITY, the forty bus will probably drop you off somewhere near Fairbanks, Alaska. V:428, VII:41

ALBUQUERQUE
See NEW MEXICO (STATE OF)

ALDERSHOT
See ENGLAND

ALTERNATIVE AMERICAS (ALTERNATE AMERICAS)
See MULTIPLE AMERICAS, *below in this section; see also* ALTERNATIVE AMERICAS, *in* APPENDIX I

AMHIGH
See DRAWERS: DETTA'S SEX HAUNTS, *in* PORTALS

APPALACHIAN TRAIL
The Appalachian Trail is a continuous footpath that runs from Mount Katahdin in central Maine to Springer Mountain in Georgia, a distance of approximately 2,160 miles. EDDIE DEAN imagines that the trail is overrun by bomber-joint-smoking hippies carrying packsacks like Roland's.
II:77

AQUINAS HOTEL
See BAHAMAS

ARCTIC
JAKE CHAMBERS doesn't envy people who live in arctic countries, since they have to deal with long periods of darkness each year. He thinks such a life would be even worse than one spent under the artificial sun of THUNDERCLAP.
VII:256

ARIZONA (STATE OF)
V:57, V:118, V:305
BLACK FORK: In the kind of Western novels which CALVIN TOWER likes to read, heroes always blow into places like Black Fork, Arizona, clean up the town, then blow on like tumbleweeds. III:115, V:57, V:118
GRAND CANYON: VI:241
PHOENIX: V:305

ARKANSAS

ODETTA: ODETTA HOLMES's mother, ALICE HOLMES, was born here. Hence Odetta (later called SUSANNAH DEAN) was christened with this name. II:199

ATCHISON

See KANSAS (STATE OF); see also ATCHISON, TOPEKA, AND SANTA FE RAILROAD below

ATCHISON, TOPEKA, AND SANTA FE RAILROAD

The Atchison, Topeka, and Santa Fe Railroad Company (originally called the Atchison and Topeka Railroad Company) was founded in 1859 by Colonel Cyrus K. Holliday of KANSAS, one of the founders of the town of TOPEKA. The railroad changed its name in 1863 because of its planned expansion. By 1887 the railroad extended all the way to Los Angeles. Known as "The Atchison" in the East and as "The Santa Fe" in the West, it was one of the major railroads serving the Southwest United States.

Our *ka-tet* stumbles across a sign for the Atchison, Topeka, and Santa Fe at BLAINE's terminating point in an alternative version of our world's Kansas. Roland assumes—quite rightly—that the three names designate three towns. However, because he does not know the history of railroads in our *where* (or in this Topeka's alternate *when*) he does not understand the full significance of these places or of the towns he sees listed on the departures board, namely DEN-VER, WICHITA, and OMAHA.

All of the listed towns were linked—directly or indirectly—by the AT&SF. Obviously, Atchison, Topeka, and Santa Fe were part of the service's main run. Denver was also served by the Atchison line, and Wichita could be reached by one of the railroad's branch lines. Although Omaha was actually accessible by the Union Pacific Railroad, the Union Pacific and the Atchison, Topeka, and Santa Fe were linked in 1881, completing the second transcontinental railroad.

Hence, what we learn from Roland's sojourn in the alternative Topeka is that not only do the GREAT ROADS of MID-WORLD follow the BEAM but so do the great railroads. Also, it seems that these railroads can be used not only to cross continents, but to jump from one level of the DARK TOWER to another. Blaine and his fellow locomotives and slo-trans engines are PORTALS every bit as much as the other doorways in and out of Mid-World. The GREAT OLD ONES, aided by the technology of their sinister company, NORTH CENTRAL POSITRONICS, learned how to bridge the time/space continuum.

IV:68

ATLANTIC CITY

See NEW JERSEY (STATE OF)

ATTICA STATE PRISON

See NEW YORK (STATE OF)

AUSCHWITZ

See POLAND

AUSTRIA

VIENNA: Sigmund Freud, author of *Ego and Id* (1923), studied medicine in Vienna and joined the staff of the Vienna General Hospital in 1882. In *Ego and Id,* Freud discussed his theories concerning the division of the unconscious mind into the id, the ego, and the superego. AUSTIN CORNWELL and his fellow fake UFFIS must have read this book. VI:231 *(Viennese)*

B

BABYLON
VI:319

BACK BAY
See MASSACHUSETTS (STATE OF)

BAHAMAS
EDDIE DEAN'S little trip to the Bahamas almost ends in disaster and incarceration. Although he is dressed like a college kid, Eddie goes to NASSAU so that he can smuggle packages of cocaine for the drug king ENRICO BALAZAR. At this point in our story (namely, at the beginning of *The Drawing of the Three*), Eddie is a heroin addict under the thumb of his older brother, the great sage and eminent junkie HENRY DEAN. Roland saves Eddie's bacon three times: first by helping him evade the CUSTOMS police, second by coming to his aid against Balazar and his thugs, and finally by spiriting Eddie off to LOBSTROSITY BEACH. There, on the shore of the WESTERN SEA, Eddie comes down off the Horse, only to become addicted to ODETTA HOLMES (aka DETTA WALKER/ SUSANNAH DEAN) and another potent drug—Love.
II:42, II:86, II:87, II:112, II:176, V:453, VI:212, VII:19

NASSAU (AQUINAS HOTEL): Eddie goes to Nassau to pick up Balazar's cocaine. While there he stays at the Aquinas Hotel. II:47, II:47–51 *(hotel),* II:57 *(flashback to hotel),* II:58, III:346, V:453, V:524, VII:19

BALAZAR'S OFFICE
See NEW YORK CITY: MANHATTAN: LEANING TOWER

BANGOR
See MAINE (STATE OF): PENOBSCOT COUNTY

BARCELONA LUGGAGE STORE
See NEW YORK CITY: MANHATTAN: SECOND AVENUE

BEAMS
See BEAMS, PATH OF THE, *in* PORTALS

BECKHARDT COTTAGE
See MAINE (STATE OF): OXFORD COUNTY: LOVELL: TURTLEBACK LANE

BEIRUT
See LEBANON

BERGEN-BELSEN
See GERMANY

BERMUDA
LAMLA, a TAHEEN servant of the CRIMSON KING, likes to wear Bermuda shorts (close-fitting shorts which reach the knees). I don't know what connection Bermuda shorts have to Bermuda, but I figure it's worth mentioning.
VII:104

BERMUDA TRIANGLE
See entry in PORTALS

BERNIE'S BARBER SHOP
See NEW YORK CITY: BROOKLYN

BLACK FORK
See ARIZONA (STATE OF)

BLACK HOLE OF CALCUTTA
See INDIA

BLACK TOWER (2 HAMMARSKJÖLD PLAZA)
See LOT, THE: 2 HAMMARSKJÖLD PLAZA, *in* PORTALS

BLACKSTRAP MOLASSES CAFÉ
See NEW YORK CITY: MANHATTAN

BLEECKER STREET
See NEW YORK CITY: MANHATTAN

BOGOTÁ
See COLOMBIA

BOLIVIA
Back in *The Drawing of the Three,* EDDIE DEAN tried to smuggle cocaine into NEW YORK CITY for ENRICO BALAZAR. This high-grade white powder originated in Bolivia. Eddie refers to it as Bolivian marching powder.
V:525

BONDED ELECTROPLATE FACTORY
See NEW YORK CITY: BROOKLYN

BOSTON
See MASSACHUSETTS (STATE OF)

BRAZIL
According to FRANK ARMITAGE, secret servant of the CRIMSON KING, most of the South American businessmen who hired the SOUTH AMERICAN SEABEES were Brazilian.
VII:284
RIO: VII:285

BRENDIO'S (SHOP)
See NEW YORK CITY: MANHATTAN

BRIDGTON
See MAINE (STATE OF): CUMBERLAND COUNTY

BROOKLYN
See NEW YORK CITY: BROOKLYN

BROOKLYN BRIDGE
See NEW YORK CITY: BROOKLYN

BRYCE
See COLORADO (STATE OF)

BUCHENWALD
See GERMANY

C

CAIRO
See EGYPT

CALIFORNIA (STATE OF)
During his years traveling along the HIGHWAYS IN HIDING, PERE CALLAHAN spent quite a bit of time in California. His longest drunken period (four full days) took place in this state. While in SACRAMENTO, Callahan discovered that his old friend ROWAN MAGRUDER had been attacked by the HITLER BROTHERS.

Callahan's twinner, TED BRAUTIGAN, applied for his *job of a lifetime* while in California. He got the position, but it ended up being a life sentence as a BREAKER in THUNDERCLAP.
III:284, V:179, V:305, V:306–309, V:424, VI:13, VI:211, VII:707
DEATH VALLEY: V:461
DISNEYLAND: II:169, V:152, VII:369

FORT ORD: V:101

HOLLYWOOD: V:451, V:640, VII:207

LOS ANGELES: V:451

SACRAMENTO: CALLAHAN spent the spring of 1981 in Sacramento. He read about ROWAN MAGRUDER's terrible injuries in the *Sacramento Bee*. V:296 *(Bee)*, V:306–9, V:422, VII:281, VII:283

> **CRAZY MARY'S:** FATHER CALLAHAN and his Mexican workmates liked the enchiladas made at this take-out restaurant. V:307

> **SLEEPY JOHN'S:** FATHER CALLAHAN worked here while living in Sacramento. V:307

SAN BERDOO: V:102

SAN FRANCISCO: In the back of an out-of-business dance studio, surrounded by filmy pink tutus, FRANK ARMITAGE, a hume servant of the CRIMSON KING, offered TED BRAUTIGAN the *job of a lifetime*. The job turns out to be a life sentence in the DEVAR-TOI of THUNDERCLAP. V:255, V:451, VI:188, VII:7, VII:211, VII:281, VII:283, VII:285, VII:286, VII:289, VII:657

> **MARK HOPKINS HOTEL:** VII:286

> **SANTA MIRA:** A door here leads from our world to THUNDERCLAP. VII:287–89, VII:297

> **SEAMAN'S SAN FRANCISCO BANK:** VII:285, VII:287, VII:289

SANTA MONICA: VII:471

> **SANTA MONICA ASPCA:** IRENE and DAVID TASSENBAUM began their romance here amid the howls and yaps of homeless pets. Irene arrived looking for a kitten; David came to drop off a stray dog. Irene may not have found her kitten, but she did find a beau. VII:471

YOSEMITE: VI:242

CALTECH

DAVID TASSENBAUM attended CalTech. According to his wife, IRENE, David and his CalTech friends invented the Internet.

> VII:429

CANADA

> VII:94

> **MONTREAL:** One of the little old ladies on EDDIE DEAN'S disastrous Delta flight from NASSAU to NEW YORK was headed to Montreal. II:78–79, VII:94

CANNIBAL ISLANDS

See entry in PORTALS

CAPE CANAVERAL

See FLORIDA (STATE OF)

CARA LAUGHS

See DOORWAYS BETWEEN WORLDS, *in* PORTALS

CASTLE AVENUE
See NEW YORK CITY: BROOKLYN

CENTRAL PARK
See NEW YORK CITY: MANHATTAN

CHEW CHEW MAMA'S
See NEW YORK CITY: MANHATTAN: SECOND AVENUE

CHICAGO
See ILLINOIS (STATE OF)

CHINA
III:287, V:561

CHRISTOPHER STREET STATION
See NEW YORK CITY: MANHATTAN

CHURCH OF THE HOLY GOD-BOMB
See NEW YORK CITY: BROOKLYN

CHURCH OF THE WALK-INS
See MAINE (STATE OF): OXFORD COUNTY: STONEHAM

CITY HALL
See NEW YORK CITY: MANHATTAN

CLEMENTS GUNS AND SPORTING GOODS
See NEW YORK CITY: MANHATTAN

CLEMSON UNIVERSITY
Clemson University is located in Clemson, SOUTH CAROLINA. DAMLI
HOUSE of the DEVAR-TOI would look at home on the Clemson campus.
    VII:230

CLEVELAND
See OHIO (STATE OF)

COHOES STREET
See NEW YORK CITY: BROOKLYN

COLOMBIA
    BOGOTÁ: II:58

COLORADO (STATE OF)
    IV:32, V:192, VII:283, VII:811
    BRYCE: The BREAKER TANYA LEEDS was born and raised in Bryce.
    VII:283

DENVER: One of the towns that could be reached by the ATCHISON, TOPEKA, AND SANTA FE RAILROAD. *(See also* ATCHISON, TOPEKA, AND SANTA FE RAILROAD.*)* IV:72, V:192

COLUMBIA UNIVERSITY

ODETTA HOLMES attended this university. During a late-night college hen party, she heard the story of a girl on a road trip who was too shy to tell her friends that she had to stop and pee. As a result, her bladder burst in the car. (Messy!)

During her college years, Odetta (later Susannah) took Psych I with PROFESSOR OVERMEYER. In this class she learned the fantastic visualization technique which helps her see, and enter, her internal DOGAN. While at Columbia, she also took a medieval history course with PROFESSOR MURRAY. Professor Murray taught his students the story of KING ARTHUR and his betraying son/ nephew MORDRED.

VI:62, VI:116, VI:221

CONEY ISLAND

See NEW YORK CITY: BROOKLYN

CONNECTICUT (STATE OF)

When TED BRAUTIGAN escaped from the DEVAR-TOI through a door made for him by his fellow BREAKER, SHEEMIE, he landed in Connecticut. The story of Ted's Connecticut adventure—and of his friendship with BOBBY GARFIELD—is the subject of the short story "Low Men in Yellow Coats," which can be found in the STEPHEN KING book *Hearts in Atlantis.*

In the recorded tale which our *ka-tet* listens to in their camp on STEEK-TETE in THUNDERCLAP, Ted confides that he was born in MILFORD, Connecticut, in 1898. However, in *Hearts in Atlantis,* he tells Bobby Garfield that he was born in Teaneck, NEW JERSEY. (In the latter case, Ted must have been talking about a parallel version of himself.)

VI:389, VII:212, VII:233, VII:234, VII:270, VII:273, VII:297, VII:298, VII:304, VII:326, VII:339, VII:357, VII:376, VII:415

BRIDGEPORT: This is where the LOW MEN caught TED BRAUTIGAN at the end of his Connecticut adventure. They dragged him back to the DEVAR-TOI. For more information about Ted's little vacation in Connecticut, see *Hearts in Atlantis.* VII:376

HARTFORD: V:263, VII:274–76, VII:282, VII:297

   EAST HARTFORD HIGH: During World War One, TED BRAUTIGAN visited a recruitment office here. He was rejected because of health problems but *also* because he was a telepath. His uncanny abilities frightened the doctors. VII:275

HARWICH: VII:483

   MOTEL 6: VII:483

MILFORD: In the final book of the Dark Tower series, TED BRAUTIGAN tells our *tet* that he was born in Milford in 1898. VII:212, VII:273, VII:415

MYSTIC: III:32

NORWICH: PATRICK DANVILLE's pencils (complete with erasers) were bought in a Norwich Woolworth's in 1958. Hence, Norwich played its own small but significant part in Roland's ultimate triumph over the CRIMSON KING. VII:800

SEDONVILLE: Somewhere in this town, buried under a chicken house, is an Irishman shot dead for blowing down one of BALAZAR's card houses. II:117

WESTPORT: V:544, VI:185

CO-OP CITY
See NEW YORK CITY: BROOKLYN

COPIAH
See MISSISSIPPI (STATE OF)

COSTA DEL SOL
See SPAIN

CROSS BRONX EXPRESSWAY
See NEW YORK CITY: BRONX

CUBA
JANE DORNING—one of the stewardesses on EDDIE's Delta flight from NASSAU to JFK—harbors a fear of being hijacked by Cubans.
    II:54, VII:599

CULLUM'S CABIN
See MAINE (STATE OF): OXFORD COUNTY: EAST STONEHAM: KEYWADIN POND

CUSTOMS, NEW YORK
See NEW YORK CITY: QUEENS

CUYAHOGA RIVER
See OHIO

D

DAHLIE'S (DAHLBERG'S)
See NEW YORK CITY: BROOKLYN

DALE'S FANCY BUTCHER SHOP
See OHIO (STATE OF): AKRON

DEAN FAMILY APARTMENT
See NEW YORK CITY: BROOKLYN

DELAWARE (STATE OF)
During his years traveling along the HIGHWAYS IN HIDING, PERE CALLA-HAN worked for a while as an apple-picker in Delaware.
V:302
ROUTE 71: V:302

DENBY'S DISCOUNT DRUG
See NEW YORK CITY: MANHATTAN: TIMES SQUARE

DENMARK
See also MAINE (STATE OF): OXFORD COUNTY
VII:603

DENMARK, MAINE
See MAINE (STATE OF): OXFORD COUNTY

DENNIS'S WAFFLES AND PANCAKES
See NEW YORK CITY: MANHATTAN: CHEW CHEW MAMA'S

DENVER
See COLORADO; see also ATCHISON, TOPEKA, AND SANTA FE RAIL-ROAD

DES MOINES
See IOWA (STATE OF)

DETROIT
See MICHIGAN (STATE OF)

DETTA'S SEX HAUNTS
See DRAWERS, in PORTALS

DIMITY ROAD
See MAINE (STATE OF): OXFORD COUNTY: EAST STONEHAM

DISNEYLAND
See CALIFORNIA (STATE OF)

DISNEY WORLD
See FLORIDA (STATE OF)

DIXIE PIG
See entry in PORTALS

DODGE
See KANSAS

DOORS: NEW YORK TO MID-WORLD
See DOORWAYS BETWEEN WORLDS, *in* PORTALS

DRAWERS
See entry in PORTALS

DUBLIN
See IRELAND

DUKE UNIVERSITY
Duke University has a department of Psychical Research. According to JOHN
CULLUM, one of the subjects they study is WALK-IN activity.
   VI:152

DUTCH HILL
See NEW YORK CITY: BROOKLYN

DUTCH HILL MANSION
See DOORWAYS BETWEEN WORLDS, *in* PORTALS

DUTCH HILL PUB
See NEW YORK CITY: BROOKLYN

DUTCH HILL USED APPLIANCES
See NEW YORK CITY: BROOKLYN

E

EAST CONWAY VILLAGE
See NEW HAMPSHIRE (STATE OF)

EAST FRYEBURG
See MAINE (STATE OF): OXFORD COUNTY

EAST STONEHAM
See MAINE (STATE OF): OXFORD COUNTY

EASTER ISLAND
   III:24

ECUADOR
   IV:86

EGYPT
   VII:115

CAIRO: V:140
PYRAMIDS: VII:115

**ENGLAND
In *The Gunslinger,* WALTER O'DIM claims that he lived in England hundreds (or perhaps a thousand) years before the GREAT OLD ONES crossed the ocean to the land that Roland now inhabits. In the 2003 version of *The Gunslinger,* the direct reference to England is cut. In the final book of the Dark Tower series we find out that GRACE RUMBELOW, an incredibly annoying BREAKER, came from ALDERSHOT.
I:211, VI:390, VII:394
HAMPSHIRE: VII:394
    ALDERSHOT: VII:394
LONDON: IV:34, V:91, V:506, VII:242
STONEHENGE: VII:777

ETHIOPIA
VII:732

EVEREST
See MOUNT EVEREST

F

FIFTH AVENUE AND FORTY-THIRD STREET
See NEW YORK CITY: MANHATTAN

FLORIDA (STATE OF)
V:305, VI:408, VII:570, VII:674
BUSCH GARDENS: RIVER CROSSING's garden (located behind the CHURCH OF THE BLOOD EVERLASTING) reminds EDDIE of Busch Gardens. III:233
CAPE CANAVERAL: When SUSANNAH sees the missiles lining the GREAT ROAD leading to LUD, she thinks about the Redstones fired from Cape Canaveral. III:287
DISNEY WORLD: II:334, III:73, III:91
FLORIDA KEYS: II:227

FORD ORD
See CALIFORNIA (STATE OF)

FORMOSA (TAIWAN)
Originally known by its aboriginal name, Pakan, this island was renamed Formosa when an early Dutch navigator (sailing on a Portuguese ship) saw it and

exclaimed, "Ilha formosa," or "beautiful island." The contemporary name *Taiwan* is an adaptation of the word *tayouan,* which means "terrace bay."
VII:115

FOUR FATHERS RESTAURANT
See NEW YORK CITY: BROOKLYN: GINELLI'S PIZZA

FRANCE
VII:275, VII:276
PARIS: VI:242
    LOUVRE: VII:242
    NOTRE DAME CATHEDRAL: V:595

FRENCH LANDING
See WISCONSIN (STATE OF)

FRYEBURG
See MAINE (STATE OF): OXFORD COUNTY

G

GAGE PARK
See KANSAS (STATE OF): TOPEKA

GAIETY
See NEW YORK CITY: MANHATTAN: TIMES SQUARE

GARDEN OF THE BEAM
See LOT, THE, *in* PORTALS

GEORGIA (STATE OF)
II:198

GERMANY
VII:276
BERGEN-BELSEN: A Nazi concentration camp located in northwest Germany, near the village of Belsen. VII:698
BUCHENWALD: A Nazi concentration camp located in eastern Germany, near the village of Buchenwald. VII:698
HAMELIN: In *Wolves of the Calla,* EDDIE DEAN compares ANDY, CALLA BRYN STURGIS's duplicitous Messenger Robot, to the Pied Piper of Hamelin. Eddie draws this comparison because the children of the Calla love Andy and follow him everywhere, but another, more sinister meaning is behind Eddie's statement. According to the old folktale, the town of Hamelin was afflicted by a plague of rats, and the people of the town could not get rid of

the terrible, flea-bitten rodents. However, just as they were about to go out of their minds, along came a piper in a parti-colored suit who agreed to solve their problem as long as they paid him what he wanted. The Pied Piper and the townsfolk agreed on an amount, but once the rats were gone, the stingy *folken* refused to honor their pledge. The Piper left, only to return the following Saint John's Day. This time when he played his pipe, he charmed the children away. None of them were ever seen again. Only two little children remained in the village—one who was blind and could not see the Piper to follow him, and one who was lame and could not keep up with his playmates. Like the Pied Piper, Andy steals children. He doesn't do it himself—the WOLVES of THUNDERCLAP do it for him—however, he is every bit as guilty as they are. V:586–87

GINELLI'S PIZZA (FOUR FATHERS RESTAURANT)
See NEW YORK CITY: BROOKLYN

GRAND ARMY PLAZA
See NEW YORK CITY: BROOKLYN

GRAND CANYON
See ARIZONA (STATE OF)

GRAND COULEE DAM
See WASHINGTON (STATE OF)

GRAND RIVER MEN'S WEAR
See MICHIGAN (STATE OF): DETROIT

GRANT PARK
See NEW YORK CITY: BROOKLYN

GREAT PLAINS
III:171

GREAT SMOKIES
SUSANNAH DEAN/ODETTA HOLMES's AUNT BLUE had her honeymoon in these mountains.
II:236

GREEN BAY
See WISCONSIN (STATE OF)

GREENWICH VILLAGE
See NEW YORK CITY: MANHATTAN

GREYMARL APARTMENTS
See NEW YORK CITY: MANHATTAN

GUTTENBERG, FURTH, AND PATEL
See NEW YORK CITY: MANHATTAN

GUYANA
The Reverend Jim Jones established the People's Temple in Jonestown, Guyana. Almost one thousand people committed suicide there by drinking poisoned Kool-Aid. While they downed their final drinks, the reverend stood on his porch and, holding a bullhorn to his lips, recounted stories about his mother.
    III:378, VII:211

H

HAITI
    II:58, II:186

HAMELIN
See GERMANY

HAMMARSKJÖLD PLAZA (2 HAMMARSKJÖLD PLAZA)
See NEW YORK CITY: MANHATTAN: SECOND AVENUE

HAMPSHIRE
See ENGLAND

HARRIGAN'S STREET CORNER
See NEW YORK CITY: MANHATTAN: SECOND AVENUE

HARVARD
TED BRAUTIGAN attended Harvard.
    VII:212, VII:273, VII:276
    HARVARD BUSINESS SCHOOL: VII:126

HAWAII (STATE OF)
    V:48, V:89

HENRY'S CORNER MARKET
See NEW YORK CITY: BROOKLYN: DUTCH HILL

HIDDEN HIGHWAYS/HIGHWAYS IN HIDING
See HIDDEN HIGHWAYS, *in* PORTALS

HOBOKEN
See NEW JERSEY (STATE OF)

HOME

Home was a wet shelter for homeless people located on FIRST AVENUE and FORTY-SEVENTH STREET in MANHATTAN, NEW YORK. The owner and chief supervisor was PERE CALLAHAN's friend ROWAN MAGRUDER. Unlike many of New York City's shelters, Home accepted both men and women and allowed in people who were drunk as well as sober. At Home, the drunks weren't locked up, the booze was. If somebody came in suffering from the d.t.'s, he or she would be given a shot of liquor, and probably a sedative chaser to keep him or her quiet. Despite—or more probably because of—its unusual policies, Home became one of the city's most successful, and highly regarded, shelters. In 1977, Mother Teresa visited it, and in 1980, Magruder was named Man of the Year by New York City's Mayor Ed Koch. (Magruder even made the cover of *Newsweek.*)

After his terrible encounter with the VAMPIRE BARLOW, Pere Callahan traveled to New York and ended up at this shelter. Although he began as a resident, he ended up as an employee. Pere worked for Home from October of 1975 until June of 1976. However, in June of 1976, just after his friend and fellow Home employee LUPE DELGADO died from AIDS (contracted through the bite of a TYPE THREE VAMPIRE), a distraught Callahan went back on the booze. Pere left Home and—bottle in hand—began his inebriated journeys along America's HIGHWAYS IN HIDING.

V:106, V:266–68, V:271–82, V:287, V:292, V:308–9 *(Magruder and Hitler Brothers)*, V:422, V:424 *(flophouse)*, V:425, V:426, V:427, V:428–29, V:443, V:445, V:452, V:466, VI:332

HUDSON RIVER
See NEW YORK (STATE OF)

HUNGRY I
See NEW YORK CITY: MANHATTAN

I

ILLINOIS (STATE OF)

CHICAGO: V:423

GREENTOWN: To Ray Bradbury fans, Greentown is a well-known and well-loved place. Based upon Bradbury's hometown of Waukegan, Illinois, it represents all that is best in small-town America. However, in the Dark Tower series, Greentown becomes a sinister place.

According to SUSANNAH DEAN, the DEVAR-TOI (or BREAKER prison) is reminiscent of Bradbury's idealized Midwestern town. Its cozy Main Street and nearby college campus look like snapshots out of an album of Americana—places where there is no crime, where girls wearing dresses with hemlines safely below the knee kiss their boyfriends a chaste goodnight and then return to their college dorms early so that their dormitory moms (as well as their actual mothers) will think well of them. Its low buildings and friendly streets make the viewer daydream about a time before the world *moved on*— an era predating world wars and cold wars, when the sun always shone and old folks sat happily on their porches, drinking lemonade.

However, as our *tet* knows all too well, the apparent friendliness of THUNDERCLAP's Greentown is an illusion. The sun is an artificial spotlight, run by a technological egg timer. The town is surrounded by barbed wire and all of the citizens are prisoners who have become so accustomed to their lot that they no longer question the terrible job that they have been brought here to do. In truth, the psychic residents of the Devar-Toi are eroding the BEAMS so that the DARK TOWER—the linchpin of existence—will collapse. The instability of the multiverse is being generated from this outpost owned by the CRIMSON KING.
VII:209

INDIA
CALCUTTA:
BLACK HOLE OF CALCUTTA: In the annals of imperialist history, the Black Hole of Calcutta is infamous. Following the capture of Calcutta by Siraj-ud-Dawalah, nawab of Bengal, in 1756, 146 British defenders were placed in this narrow, airless dungeon, twenty feet by twenty feet. According to the story, only 23 survived the night. The actual details of the event remain controversial, and many historians believe that the true number of Englishmen jailed was probably smaller. However, as SUSANNAH DEAN discovers when she is imprisoned by MIA, the Black Hole of Calcutta remains a fairly accurate description of the horror and desperation a person feels when she is imprisoned without hope of escape or rescue. VI:124
NEW DELHI: VII:127

IOWA (STATE OF)
V:192
DES MOINES: VII:279

IRELAND
II:371, V:465
DUBLIN: The crucifix which FATHER CALLAHAN used to stave off the VAMPIRE BARLOW in 'SALEM'S LOT, MAINE, originally came from Dublin. Callahan's mother bought it in a souvenir shop, probably at a scalper's price. During his confrontation with Barlow, Callahan learned that the trappings of religion have no intrinsic worth if the one wielding them does not have faith. V:459

ISRAEL
JERUSALEM: *See* also MAINE (STATE OF): JERUSALEM'S LOT. V:192

ISSAQUENA COUNTY
See MISSISSIPPI (STATE OF)

ITALY
II:133 *(Old Country)*
PISA:
LEANING TOWER OF PISA: The Leaning Tower of Pisa, whose official name is Torre Pendente di Pisa, is an Italian bell tower which was built between A.D. 1173 and 1350. As can be deduced from its name, it lists to one side, a problem that architects through the ages have not been able to rectify.

The Dark Tower series refers to this famous tower in two different contexts. First, in *The Drawing of the Three,* we learn that the neon sign marking BALAZAR's bar and headquarters is in the shape of this historic monument. Much to EDDIE DEAN's alarm, the first time Roland sees this sign he thinks he has arrived at his destination—the DARK TOWER itself.

The next time we see the Leaning Tower it takes the form of a pho-tograph (or as Roland would say, a *fottergraf*) pasted to the last page of JAKE CHAMBERS's English Comp essay entitled "My Understanding of Truth." Though he didn't realize it at the time, the Leaning Tower (which he had covered in black crayon scribbles) was his unconscious mind's version of the Dark Tower. *See also* NEW YORK CITY: MANHATTAN: LEANING TOWER (BALAZAR'S OFFICE). II:121, V:56
SICILY: II:114

J

JAFFORDS RENTALS
See MAINE (STATE OF): OXFORD COUNTY: EAST STONEHAM

JAPAN
SAPPORO: VI:226

JERUSALEM
See ISRAEL; *see also* MAINE (STATE OF): ALTERNATIVE AMERICAS AND THE STATE OF MAINE: JERUSALEM'S LOT

JERUSALEM'S LOT
See MAINE (STATE OF): ALTERNATIVE AMERICAS AND THE STATE OF MAINE: JERUSALEM'S LOT

JFK AIRPORT
See NEW YORK CITY: QUEENS

JOHN CULLUM'S CABIN
See MAINE (STATE OF): OXFORD COUNTY: EAST STONEHAM

JONESTOWN
See GUYANA

K

KANSAS (STATE OF)

The state of Kansas (initial setting for *The Wizard of Oz*) plays an important part in the Dark Tower series. At the beginning of *Wizard and Glass,* BLAINE the Insane Mono crashed into an alternative version of our world's TOPEKA. The Kansas that our *tet* is forced to travel through is both subtly and not so subtly different from our Kansas. Unlike the Kansas of our world, this Kansas seems still to use the old ATCHISON, TOPEKA, AND SANTA FE RAILROAD. Its former residents drove Takaru Spirits and ate at Boing Boing burgers—cars and fast-food joints we've never heard of—but worse yet, they've all been wiped out by the superflu, the same disease that killed most of America's population in STEPHEN KING's novel *The Stand.*

Like HAMBRY—the MID-WORLD town where Roland, CUTHBERT ALL-GOOD, and ALAIN JOHNS battled the BIG COFFIN HUNTERS and the other traitors to the AFFILIATION—this alternative Topeka contained a THINNY. The sight and sound of this warbling DOORWAY BETWEEN WORLDS enticed Roland to tell his new friends about the trials he faced in Hambry, and about his ill-fated love affair with the beautiful young SUSAN DELGADO. Also in this alternative version of Kansas, our *tet* entered the GREEN PALACE and confronted OZ the Great and Terrible—a wizard who turned out to be none other than Roland's longtime nemesis, WALTER (aka RANDALL FLAGG).

Kansas continues to play a significant role in the final books of the Dark Tower series. In late winter of 1982, PERE CALLAHAN reeled drunkenly through the city of Topeka and landed in a JAIL CELL there. While incarcerated, he had an alcohol-related seizure. Although Callahan joined Alcoholics Anonymous and managed to sober up, he was not destined to settle in this state. In the fall of that year, Callahan saw the first of the LOW MEN's "lost pet" posters advertising for information about his whereabouts. Callahan left Topeka for DETROIT.

II:229 *(Dorothy),* III:139–45 *(Charlie the Choo-Choo),* III:258, III:287 *(concrete silos),* IV:62–112, IV:335–37, IV:615–51, IV:658, IV:660, V:35, V:106, V:296, V:447, V:456, VI:298, VI:401

ATCHISON: Atchison is a town in Kansas famous for being the birthplace of both Amelia Earhart and the ATCHISON, TOPEKA, AND SANTA FE RAILROAD. IV:68

DODGE: In the late nineteenth and early twentieth centuries, Dodge had a reputation as a rowdy frontier town. III:258, III:373, VII:811

KANSAS MUSEUM OF NATURAL HISTORY: IV:75

LAWRENCE: VI:401

PHILLIP BILLARD: IV:75

TOPEKA: In the children's story *Charlie the Choo-Choo,* Topeka is the MID-WORLD RAILWAY's final destination. It also happens to be BLAINE'S destination as well as the place where Mid-World ends and END-WORLD begins. *See entry under* ATCHISON, TOPEKA, AND SANTA FE RAILROAD. III:139–45, III:199, III:266, III:400, III:404, III:409, III:411, III:413,

III:419, IV:62–112, IV:335–37, IV:615–25, V:36, V:106, V:440, V:445–49, VI:25, VI:103, VII:531

BERRYTON ROAD: IV:74

BOING BOING BURGERS: IV:92, IV:617

CRADLE OF TOPEKA: Like an outdoor LUD. Looks Western. IV:67, IV:72

FORBES: IV:75

    FORBES FIELD: IV:74

GADDISH FEEDS: Grain-storage tower. IV:95

GAGE BOULEVARD: IV:83, IV:84

    GAGE BOULEVARD AMTRAK STATION: IV:75

GAGE PARK: IV:86–91, V:291, V:449, VII:335

HEARTLAND LANES: IV:92

HEARTLAND PARK RACE TRACK: Disposal pit for superflu dead. IV:74

JAIL CELL: FATHER CALLAHAN was held here for assaulting an officer. While incarcerated, he had an alcohol-related seizure. V:445–49

KANSAS CITY: V:36

KANSAS TURNPIKE (I-70): IV:62, IV:63, IV:71, IV:91–112 *(ka-tet follows. Directly mentioned on 92, 94, 104)*, IV:623, IV:625, IV:629, IV:635, IV:660, V:35, V:36, V:291, V:516

OAKLAND BILLARD PARK: Disposal plant for superflu dead. IV:74

REINISCH ROSE GARDEN: In Reinisch Rose Garden (home of the infamous toy version of CHARLIE THE CHOO-CHOO) PERE CALLAHAN saw some of the LOW MEN's "lost pet" posters, offering a reward to anyone who could disclose his whereabouts. Callahan left Kansas in a hurry. IV:86, IV:87–89 *(and* Charlie the Choo-Choo*)*, V:449

SOUTHEAST SIXTY-FIRST STREET: IV:74

ST. FRANCIS HOSPITAL AND MEDICAL CENTER: IV:74

STORMONT-VAIL REGIONAL MEDICAL CENTER: IV:74

TOPEKA STATE HOSPITAL: IV:92

TOPEKA ZOO: IV:89

WAMBEGO: IV:75

    KAW RIVER NUCLEAR PLANT (KAWNUKE): IV:75

WICHITA: A town in Kansas accessed by a branch line of the ATCHISON, TOPEKA, AND SANTA FE RAILROAD. Roland sees a sign for it in the alternative TOPEKA that he and his *ka-tet* travel through in *Wizard and Glass. See entry under* ATCHISON, TOPEKA, AND SANTA FE RAILROAD. IV:72

KANSAS CITY BLUES
See NEW YORK CITY: MANHATTAN

KANSAS ROAD
See MAINE (STATE OF): CUMBERLAND COUNTY: BRIDGTON

KATZ PHARMACY AND SODA FOUNTAIN (SUNDRIES AND NOTIONS FOR MISSES AND MISTERS)
See NEW YORK CITY: MANHATTAN

KENTUCKY
While traveling along the HIGHWAYS IN HIDING, CALLAHAN worked as a grave digger in Kentucky. His shovel-buddy was a digger named PETE PETAKI. Pete had a taste for seventeen-year-old jailbait. However, the girl who caught his eye turned out to be a TYPE THREE VAMPIRE. Callahan destroyed her before she could sink her teeth into Petaki's all-too-willing throat.
  V:302
  ROUTE 317: V:302

KEYSTONE EARTH/KEYSTONE WORLD
  See KEY WORLD/KEYSTONE WORLD, *in* PORTALS

KEYWADIN POND
  See MAINE (STATE OF): OXFORD COUNTY: EAST STONEHAM

KEZAR LAKE
  See MAINE (STATE OF): OXFORD COUNTY: LOVELL

KIDZPLAY
  See GUTTENBERG, FURTH, AND PATEL, *in* CHARACTERS

KING'S CHILDHOOD BARN
  See entry in PORTALS

KING'S HOUSE IN LOVELL
  See DOORWAYS BETWEEN WORLDS: CARA LAUGHS, *in* PORTALS

KLATT ROAD
  See MAINE (STATE OF): OXFORD COUNTY: FRYEBURG

KOREA
  VII:280

L

LA GUARDIA AIRPORT
  See NEW YORK CITY: QUEENS

LAS VEGAS
  See NEVADA (STATE OF)

LAWRENCE
  See KANSAS (STATE OF)

LEANING TOWER (BALAZAR'S OFFICE)
  See NEW YORK CITY: MANHATTAN

LEANING TOWER OF PISA
  See ITALY

LEBANON
  BEIRUT: IV:87

LEWISTON
  See MAINE (STATE OF): ANDROSCOGGIN COUNTY

LIGHTHOUSE SHELTER
CALLAHAN worked at this wet shelter (located in DETROIT) from the late autumn of 1982 until December of 1983. According to Pere, it was an almost exact replica of the HOME shelter he'd worked at in NEW YORK CITY, although one without ROWAN MAGRUDER to manage it. Callahan's workmates at Lighthouse were WARD HUCKMAN and AL McCOWAN. In early December of 1982, Ward received a letter from the SOMBRA CORPORATION, saying that Lighthouse had been awarded a million-dollar grant. However, when the three men arrived at Sombra's corporate headquarters to discuss the details of their windfall, they discovered that the whole thing was a setup. Huckman and McCowan were knocked unconscious by electrical stunners, and Callahan was left to face the evil RICHARD P. SAYRE and the other servants of the CRIMSON KING alone. Rather than submit to the bites of Sayre's HIV-infected TYPE THREE VAMPIRES, Callahan jumped out the window of the TISHMAN BUILDING. He died in our world only to awake in MID-WORLD's WAY STATION.
  V:270, V:449, V:450–57 *(up to Sayre's trickery)*, V:466

LONDON
  See ENGLAND

LOS ZAPATOS
  See MEXICO

LOT, THE
  See LOT, THE, *in* PORTALS

LOUISIANA (STATE OF)
  NEW ORLEANS: V:305, V:621

LOVELL
  See MAINE (STATE OF)

LOWELL
  See MASSACHUSETTS (STATE OF)

M

MACY'S
See NEW YORK CITY: MANHATTAN

MADISON SQUARE GARDEN
See NEW YORK CITY: MANHATTAN

MAGIC SHOP
See NEW YORK CITY: MANHATTAN

MAINE (STATE OF)
Maine is the home state of our *kas-ka Gan,* STEPHEN KING. It is also the set-ting for several scenes in *Wolves of the Calla* and significant stretches of *Song of Susannah.* When CALVIN TOWER flees NEW YORK CITY to escape from BALAZAR'S MEN, he and his sidekick, AARON DEEPNEAU, take up tempo-rary residence in EAST STONEHAM, Maine. When Roland and EDDIE DEAN travel through CALLA BRYN STURGIS's UNFOUND DOOR to find the anally retentive bibliophile, they land in front of the EAST STONEHAM GENERAL STORE, where Balazar's men already lie in wait for them.

In Maine, Roland and Eddie meet JOHN CULLUM, their *dan-tete.* Cullum leads them to Calvin Tower (from whom they finally buy the Vacant LOT), and also directs them to the home of Stephen King, where these two members of our *tet* finally meet their maker. In addition, Cullum brings Roland and Eddie to CARA LAUGHS, the magical DOORWAY BETWEEN WORLDS, which is the center of western Maine's WALK-IN activity.

When Roland and JAKE CHAMBERS return to Maine in 1999 to save Ste-phen King from the Dodge minivan which is destined to hit him, Jake dies. He is buried on a Maine roadside. Over his grave, IRENE TASSENBAUM promises to plant a ROSE. *For further information about walk-in activity, see also* NEW HAMPSHIRE (STATE OF).

V:106, V:256, V:537, V:598, V:627, VI:4, VI:35, VI:123, VI:130–54, VI:158–216, VI:265–303, VI:397, VI:408, VII:17–53, VII:113–32, VII:266, VII:421–79, VII:521, VII:522, VII:559

ALTERNATIVE AMERICAS AND THE STATE OF MAINE: The following towns don't exist on KEYSTONE EARTH, hence we cannot assign them to specific counties. However, they do exist on other levels of the TOWER, and in a number of other STEPHEN KING novels.

JERUSALEM'S LOT ('SALEM'S LOT): In one of the ALTERNATIVE AMERICAS, Jerusalem's Lot is located in CUMBERLAND COUNTY. Jerusalem's Lot (usually referred to as 'Salem's Lot) was the VAMPIRE-infested setting for STEPHEN KING's novel *'Salem's Lot.* Our good friend PERE CALLAHAN, whom we meet in *Wolves of the Calla,* was the Lot's boozing Catholic priest.

Although initially skeptical, Callahan eventually joined forces with BEN MEARS, MATTHEW BURKE, JAMES CODY, and MARK PETRIE to destroy the TYPE ONE VAMPIRE, BARLOW, who initiated all of the Lot's problems. Although Callahan managed to save Mark Petrie (if not the boy's parents) from this servant of the Outer Dark, the priest's faith ultimately proved too weak to stand up against his enemy. Callahan was forced to drink Barlow's blood, and though it did not turn him into a vampire, it disgraced him in the eyes of God. Outcast from the WHITE, Callahan fled 'Salem's Lot for NEW YORK CITY. V:31, V:106, V:109, V:119, V:234, V:256–62, V:269, V:270, V:291, V:298, V:299, V:454, V:468, V:470, V:706, VI:171, VI:177, VI:211, VI:271, VI:280, VI:307, VI:329, VII:3, VII:15, VII:28, VII:593, VII:802

MARSTEN HOUSE: The evil Marsten House was built by Hubie Marsten, the president of a 1920s trucking company that specialized in running Canadian whiskey into Massachusetts. Hubie and his wife, Birdie, settled in the Lot in 1928, but they lost most of their money in the stock market crash of 1929. In the ten years between the disaster of 1929 and the rise of Adolf Hitler, Hubie and his wife became hermits, and Hubie went mad. In 1939, one of the Lot's residents smelled something foul issuing from the building and so entered the house through the back door. He found booby traps (set for unwanted visitors) all over the place. He also found the body of Birdie sprawled on the kitchen floor (her husband had shot her in the head), and the remains of Hubie himself dangling from a rafter. When the VAMPIRE BARLOW and his servant STRAKER decided to take up residence in 'Salem's Lot, they chose this scene of a murder-suicide as their abode. V:257, V:291–92 *(indirect)*

PETRIE HOUSE AND KITCHEN: MARK PETRIE's home. The fateful confrontation between PERE CALLAHAN and the VAMPIRE BARLOW took place here. V:258–61, V:280, VII:11

SAINT ANDREW'S CHURCH: CALLAHAN's church. After drinking BARLOW's blood, Callahan was too polluted to enter this sacred space. V:261

    RECTORY: VI:307

SPENCER'S DRUGS: Spencer's Drugs doubled as the town's bus station. V:261, V:262

DERRY: STEPHEN KING's version of BANGOR, MAINE. Like JERUSALEM'S LOT, it exists on one of the other levels of the DARK TOWER. Many of King's novels (including *Insomnia* and *It*) take place in Derry. VII:412

EAST OVERSHOE: East Overshoe is EDDIE DEAN's humorous nickname for the town of EAST STONEHAM. V:627

'SALEM'S LOT: *See* JERUSALEM'S LOT, *above*

ANDROSCOGGIN COUNTY:

    AUBURN: VII:118

    CENTRAL MAINE GENERAL HOSPITAL: STEPHEN KING was taken to this hospital after being hit by BRYAN SMITH's Dodge minivan. VII:480, VII:485 *(indirect)*

    LEWISTON: VI:403, VII:480, VII:485

    LISBON:

        LISBON HIGH: VI:289

CUMBERLAND COUNTY:

BRIDGTON: In 1977, STEPHEN KING and his family lived in this town, which is located twenty-five miles from EAST STONEHAM. In *Song of Susannah*, EDDIE and Roland meet King here. Like many other western Maine towns, Bridgton is plagued by WALK-INS. VI:151, VI:170, VI:172, VI:207, VI:209, VI:211, VI:265–303, VI:389, VI:391, VI:411, VII:17, VII:20, VII:24, VII:33–48 *(Eddie and Roland on road)*, VII:119, VII:123, VII:159, VII:435, VII:457, VII:476, VII:573

   BRIDGTON HIGH STREET: VII:40
   BRIDGTON PIZZA AND SANDWICHES: VII:41
   BRIDGTON SHOPPING CENTER: VI:265, VI:267, VII:41
   DEPARTMENT STORE (RENY'S): VII:41
   DRUGSTORE: VI:265, VII:41
   HIGHLAND LAKE: VII:40
   KANSAS ROAD: VI:266–67, VII:19, VII:24, VII:32–40
   KING HOUSE: Roland and EDDIE visit STEPHEN KING here, in his family home. King is so shocked to see them that he tries to run into the nearby lake. Afterward, he faints. VI:273–300, VI:301–2, VI:350 *(bedroom)*, VII:17, VII:36
   LAUNDRY: VI:265
   LONG LAKE: VI:276, VII:24
   MAGIC LANTERN (MOVIE THEATER): VII:41
   NORTH CUMBERLAND MEMORIAL HOSPITAL: VII:411
   SLAB CITY HILL: *See* ROUTE 7
HARRISON: VI:280, VII:40, VII:433
NORTH WINDHAM: VI:392
   DISCOUNT BEVERAGE: VI:392
PORTLAND: V:598, VI:409, VI:410, VII:521
   BOOKLAND: VI:169, VI:208
RAYMOND: VI:172
   SEBAGO LAKE (BIG SEBAGO): VI:172
WINDHAM: VI:172
KENNEBEC COUNTY:
KING'S CHILDHOOD BARN: *See entry in* PORTALS
KING'S HOME: *See* BRIDGTON, *under* CUMBERLAND COUNTY; LOVELL, *under* OXFORD COUNTY; *and* ORRINGTON, *under* PENOBSCOT COUNTY
WATERVILLE: VI:389
   THE SILENT WOMAN RESTAURANT: VI:389
KNOX COUNTY:
MAINE STATE PRISON: Until it closed its doors in 2002, the Maine State Prison was located in Thomaston, Knox County. Hence, within the state it was known simply as Thomaston. VI:181
OXFORD COUNTY: VII:18
DENMARK: Like many of the towns in its immediate vicinity, Denmark was plagued by WALK-INS during the 1970s. This strange phenomenon may still be going on. VI:151
EAST FRYEBURG: VI:181, VI:191

EAST STONEHAM: East Stoneham is a small town located forty miles north of PORTLAND. This is where CALVIN TOWER and AARON DEEPNEAU go to hide from BALAZAR'S MEN. It is also where Roland and EDDIE are ambushed by these WOLVES of NEW YORK. In 1999, Roland and JAKE return to East Stoneham in search of STEPHEN KING, whose life they wish to save. With the help of IRENE TASSENBAUM, they find King walking down ROUTE 7 in LOVELL. Our dwindling *tet* manages to save King from being killed by BRYAN SMITH's Dodge minivan, but at the cost of Jake's life. V:598, V:620–24, V:627, VI:123, VI:130–54, VI:158–216, VI:265, VII:17–18, VII:24, VII:39, VII:123, VII:124, VII:465

> **COUNTRY COLLECTIBLES:** JANE SARGUS owns this shop. VI:165
> **DIMITY ROAD:** Dimity Road branches off of ROUTE 5. CALVIN TOWER and AARON DEEPNEAU stay near here on the ROCKET ROAD. VI:165, VI:167, VI:171, VI:178
> **EAST STONEHAM GENERAL STORE:** The East Stoneham General Store, owned by CHIP McAVOY, is the site of Roland and EDDIE's battle with BALAZAR'S MEN in 1977. In 1999, it is the site of JAKE and Roland's entrance into our world. They meet IRENE TASSENBAUM here. V:621, V:624–25, V:707, VI:130–47, VI:162, VII:46, VII:87, VII:124, VII:128, VII:417, VII:421–29, VII:431, VII:437, VII:438, VII:442 *(indirect)*, VII:468 *(indirect)*, VII:479
> **EAST STONEHAM POST OFFICE:** V:621, V:622–24 *(one mile from General Store)*, VI:133, VI:166, VI:177
> **EAST STONEHAM TOWN GARAGE:** VI:132
> **EAST STONEHAM TOWN OFFICE:** VI:132
> **EAST STONEHAM VOLUNTEER FIRE DEPARTMENT:** VI:158
> **KEYWADIN POND:** JOHN CULLUM's cabin is located on Keywadin Pond. VI:148–54, VI:161, VI:163, VI:169, VI:179, VII:44, VII:423, VII:469, VII:470
>> **CULLUM'S CABIN (SUNSET COTTAGE):** JOHN CULLUM's cabin is a tidy little bachelor pad located on the shores of Keywadin Pond. It reminds EDDIE DEAN of a hobbit hole. Years later, after Cullum leaves Maine to become one of the FOUNDING FATHERS of the TET CORPORATION, the cabin is bought by IRENE AND DAVID TASSENBAUM. They rename it Sunset Cottage. VI:149, VI:158–73, VII:39, VII:44, VII:469–71
> **ROCKET ROAD:** TOWER and DEEPNEAU's cabin (number NINETEEN of JAFFORDS RENTAL CABINS) is on this small dirt road which branches off DIMITY ROAD. VI:178, VI:184, VI:194, VI:216
>> **JAFFORDS RENTAL CABINS:** During their brief but eventful stay in East Stoneham, CALVIN TOWER and AARON DEEPNEAU stay in number NINETEEN of these lakeside cabins. Here Deepneau draws up the bill of sale which transfers ownership of NEW YORK's magic LOT from Tower to the TET CORPORATION. VI:166, VI:167, VI:178–216, VII:128

FRYEBURG: Home of the annual Fryeburg Fair. VI:166, VI:181, VI:407, VI:410, VII:40, VII:446

YOUR TRASH, MY TREASURE: During his stay in Maine, CALVIN TOWER goes book hunting here. VI:166

KLATT ROAD: VII:422

LOVELL: Lovell is one of the many Maine towns plagued by WALK-IN activity. CARA LAUGHS (a home located on TURTLEBACK LANE in Lovell) is the DOORWAY BETWEEN WORLDS through which the walk-ins enter our world. Not surprisingly, this house is destined to be the home of STEPHEN KING. VI:151, VI:165, VI:180, VI:181, VI:210, VI:285, VI:394, VI:397, VI:398, VI:404, VI:405, VII:17, VII:18, VII:34, VII:35, VII:40, VII:45, VII:46, VII:47, VII:48–53, VII:115, VII:127, VII:142, VII:329, VII:339, VII:414, VII:422, VII:424, VII:428, VII:429, VII:432, VII:434, VII:439, VII:441–43, VII:520

BERRY HILL: VII:446

CENTER LOVELL STORE: BRYAN SMITH loves the Mars bars that are sold here. VII:433

KEZAR LAKE: The KING family home is located on beautiful Kezar Lake. According to locals, Kezar is famous for its bizarre weather patterns. A section of its shoreline is also the center of western Maine's WALK-IN activity. VI:181, VII:113, VII:117, VII:120, VII:128, VII:132, VII:438, VII:443

SCHINDLER PLACE: VII:438

TURTLEBACK LANE: Turtleback Lane is the center of western Maine's WALK-IN activity. The lane is a loop which runs off ROUTE 7 and follows the shores of Kezar Lake. STEPHEN KING's house, CARA LAUGHS, is located on this lane. VI:180, VI:210, VI:285, VI:301, VI:394, VI:397, VI:403, VI:404, VI:405, VI:407, VI:408, VI:409, VII:17, VII:34, VII:35, VII:46, VII:47, VII:49, VII:53, VII:113–32, VII:173, VII:304, VII:428, VII:429, VII:432, VII:434, VII:436–39, VII:441–43, VII:444, VII:445, VII:446, VII:542

BECKHARDT COTTAGE: JOHN CULLUM is the caretaker for the Beckhardt Cottage. He, Roland, and EDDIE hold their final palaver here. VII:115, VII:117–27, VII:518

CARA LAUGHS (KING HOUSE): *See* DOORWAYS BETWEEN WORLDS, *in* PORTALS

FENN COTTAGE: VII:115

ISRAEL COTTAGE: VII:115

LOVELL-STONEHAM CHURCH OF THE WALK-INS: *See* STONEHAM, *below*

MILLION DOLLAR BRIDGE: This rickety wooden bridge spans the water near the MILLION DOLLAR CAMPGROUND. Hippies often come here to sell drugs. VII:433

MILLION DOLLAR CAMPGROUND: This campground is located just over the Lovell/STONEHAM town line. BRYAN SMITH stays here with his two Rottweilers, BULLET and PISTOL. VII:432, VII:433, VII:434, VII:443

SLAB CITY HILL: *See* ROUTE 7

WARRINGTON ROAD: This road leads to ROUTE 7. VII:441, VII:443, VII:446, VII:447, VII:449

NORWAY: VI:166, VI:185

HOSPITAL: Despite CALLAHAN's written warning stating that CALVIN TOWER and AARON DEEPNEAU should keep a low profile, Tower refuses to sleep in his rental cabin's boathouse. He says that the damp there will land his wheezy friend Deepneau in Norway's shitpot little hospital. VI:185

NOTIONS: Although he should be in hiding, CALVIN TOWER insists on going book hunting here. VI:166

OXFORD: VI:407, VII:425

VIKING MOTORS: "The Boys with the Toys." They sell Jet-Skis here. CHIP McAVOY has ordered some. VII:425

ROUTE 5: JUNIOR ANGSTROM saw a naked WALK-IN on this road. VI:151, VI:165, VI:178

ROUTE 7 (OLD FRYEBURG ROAD): Route 7 is a dangerous place to walk. In July of 1994, a Stoneham man named CHARLES McCAUSLAND was struck by a car and killed here, an event which foreshadows STEPHEN KING's accident. King's accident (and JAKE CHAMBERS's death) takes place on the section of tarmac known as SLAB CITY HILL. In 1977, Roland and EDDIE meet CHEVIN OF CHAYVEN, a CHILD OF RODERICK, while they are driving along this road. VI:181, VI:403, VI:406, VI:410, VII:46, VII:48–53 *(Roland and Eddie see Child of Roderick)*, VII:113, VII:422, VII:424, VII:430–33 *(driving)*, VII:439–41, VII:443, VII:444, VII:446, VII:447, VII:449–68, VII:472–75

MELDER'S GERMAN RESTAURANT AND BRATHOUSE: VII:440

SLAB CITY HILL: This section of Route 7 is extremely dangerous because of its short sight lines. Worse yet, there is nowhere to jump if a car goes off the road and ends up on the shoulder. Slab City Hill is the place where STEPHEN KING is hit by BRYAN SMITH's Dodge minivan. VI:403, VI:406, VI:411, VII:446, VII:451–68, VII:472–75

WOODS OFF ROUTE 7: JAKE CHAMBERS manages to save the life of STEPHEN KING by grabbing King around the waist and using his own body to shield the writer from BRYAN SMITH's oncoming Dodge minivan. Although King survives, Jake is killed. Roland buries his adopted son in the woods off Route 7. VII:465–68, VII:472–75

ROUTE 93 (BOG ROAD): VII:17

SOUTH PARIS: VI:302

SOUTH STONEHAM: VII:45

SOUTH STONEHAM SHOE: VII:45

STONEHAM: Like DENMARK, EAST CONWAY, EAST STONEHAM, LOVELL, SOUTH STONEHAM, and SWEDEN, the town of Stoneham in western Maine is plagued by WALK-IN activity. *(See also EAST STONEHAM, above.)* VI:151, VI:165, VI:180, VI:280, VI:403, VI:404, VII:422, VII:432

FIRST CONGREGATIONAL CHURCH: This church is located on the corner of ROUTE 7 and KLATT ROAD. VII:422, VII:423

STONEHAM CORNERS: VII:435

LOVELL-STONEHAM CHURCH OF THE WALK-INS: Given the number of WALK-INS in this part of Maine, it's not surprising that a church has grown up around the phenomenon. The Church of the Walk-Ins is located in Stoneham Corners. Its pastor is REVEREND PETERSON. The church's sign reads, "We Seek the Doorway to Heaven—Will You Seek With Us?" VII:422

STONEHAM FIRE AND RESCUE: VI:132

SWEDEN: Sweden is another Maine town plagued by WALK-INS. VI:151, VI:181, VII:40, VII:433

WATERFORD: Waterford is one of the many Maine towns plagued by WALK-INS. VI:151 *(walk-ins)*, VI:165, VI:181, VII:40, VII:433

  DON RUSSERT'S HOUSE: Don Russert, a friend of JOHN CULLUM's, is a retired history professor who once worked at VANDERBILT COLLEGE. Don actually interviewed a WALK-IN in his living room. VI:151–52

PENOBSCOT COUNTY:

BANGOR: TABITHA KING's family lives in Bangor. VI:280, VI:389 *(Nanatown)*, VI:398, VI:404, VII:512, VII:513, VII:545

ORONO:

  PAT'S PIZZA: A pizza joint located close to the UNIVERSITY OF MAINE. They make great pizza. (The beer is good too.) I especially recommend the jalapeño-and-garlic pizza—it's guaranteed to keep vampires away. (Unfortunately, it will probably drive away most of your friends as well.) VI:409

  UNIVERSITY OF MAINE: *See* MAINE, UNIVERSITY OF, *listed separately*

ORRINGTON: STEPHEN KING lived in this town while teaching at the UNIVERSITY OF MAINE. VI:391

SAGADAHOC COUNTY:

TOPSHAM: VI:290, VI:399

UNIVERSITY OF MAINE: *See* MAINE, UNIVERSITY OF, *listed separately*
WHITE MOUNTAINS: *See* WHITE MOUNTAINS, *listed separately*

MAINE, UNIVERSITY OF
STEPHEN KING attended the University of Maine located in ORONO. Thanks to BURT HATLEN, he also taught creative writing there for a year.
  VI:283, VI:391

MAJESTIC THEATER
  See NEW YORK CITY: BROOKLYN

MAMARONECK
  See NEW YORK (STATE OF): WESTCHESTER

MANHATTAN RESTAURANT OF THE MIND
  See NEW YORK CITY: MANHATTAN: SECOND AVENUE

MANSION, THE
  See DOORWAYS BETWEEN WORLDS, *in* PORTALS

MARKEY ACADEMY
  See NEW YORK CITY: BROOKLYN: MARKEY AVENUE

MARKEY AVENUE
  See NEW YORK CITY: BROOKLYN

MARINE MIDLAND BANK
  See NEW YORK CITY: MANHATTAN

MARSTEN HOUSE
  See MAINE (STATE OF): ALTERNATIVE AMERICAS AND THE STATE OF MAINE: JERUSALEM'S LOT

MASS GENERAL
  See MASSACHUSETTS (STATE OF): BOSTON, *below*

MASSACHUSETTS (STATE OF)
  V:254, VII:479
  BOSTON: II:348, V:254, V:255, VI:166, VI:200, VI:408, VII:104, VII:115, VII:134
    BACK BAY: CONOR FLAHERTY, a servant of the CRIMSON KING, has a Back Bay accent. VII:108
    FILENE'S: VII:612
    HARVARD: *See* HARVARD, *listed separately*
    HYATT HARBORSIDE: VI:408
    MASS GENERAL (MASSACHUSETTS GENERAL HOSPITAL): VI:402
    MUSEUM OF SCIENCE: II:348
  LOWELL: V:254, V:255, V:593, VI:200
  SEA BREEZE INN: During their trek from MAINE to NEW YORK CITY, Roland, OY, and IRENE TASSENBAUM stay at this roadside motel. Although we don't know exactly where the Sea Breeze is located, we do know that it sits somewhere off Route I-95. As far as Roland can tell, there are no sea breezes at the Sea Breeze. VII:479–83

MELDER'S GERMAN RESTAURANT AND BRATHOUSE
  See MAINE (STATE OF): OXFORD COUNTY: ROUTE 7

MERCURY LOUNGE
  See NEW YORK CITY: MANHATTAN

MERRITT PARKWAY
  VII:297, VII:298

MEXICO
  V:236, V:469. *Also see* TODASH: MEXICO, *in* PORTALS
  LOS ZAPATOS: While in the TODASH state, PERE CALLAHAN attended the funeral of BEN MEARS here. V:236, V:469

MICHIGAN (STATE OF)
II:169, V:53, V:106
DETROIT: PERE CALLAHAN's five years traveling along America's HIGH-
WAYS IN HIDING finally led him to the LIGHTHOUSE SHELTER in
Detroit. Callahan worked at Lighthouse from the late fall of 1982 until
December of 1983. On December 19 of that year, Callahan and his two
Lighthouse workmates—WARD HUCKMAN and AL McCOWAN—were
tricked by RICHARD SAYRE of the SOMBRA CORPORATION into enter-
ing the company's local headquarters on MICHIGAN AVENUE. Huckman
and McCowan were rendered unconscious, but Callahan was forced to face
the wrath of Sayre's HIV-infected TYPE THREE VAMPIRES. Rather than
submit to their bites, Callahan threw himself out a window. V:106, V:270,
V:449, V:450–57, V:464, VI:122

> **GRAND RIVER MENSWEAR:** In anticipation of his meeting with SOM-
> BRA, CALLAHAN actually bought a suit here. All things considered, it
> turned out to be a waste of money. V:456, V:458
> **HOLY NAME HIGH SCHOOL:** The LIGHTHOUSE SHELTER held its
> annual Thanksgiving Day festivities in this Catholic high school located on
> West Congress Street. V:450–51
> **JEFFERSON AVENUE:** V:452
> **LIGHTHOUSE SHELTER:** See LIGHTHOUSE SHELTER, listed sepa-
> rately
> **MICHIGAN AVENUE:** V:453–57 (setting), V:466
>> **TISHMAN BUILDING:** The Tishman Building was the Detroit head-
>> quarters of the CRIMSON KING's SOMBRA CORPORATION. When
>> CALLAHAN was attacked here by the Red King's TYPE THREE VAM-
>> PIRES, he jumped out the window. V:453–57
> **WEST FORT STREET:** V:452

MID-TOWN LANES
See NEW YORK CITY: MANHATTAN

MIDTOWN TUNNEL
See NEW YORK CITY: MANHATTAN

MID-WORLD LANES
See entry in PORTALS

MILLION DOLLAR BRIDGE
See MAINE (STATE OF): OXFORD COUNTY: LOVELL

MILLION DOLLAR CAMPGROUND
See MAINE (STATE OF): OXFORD COUNTY: LOVELL

MILLS CONSTRUCTION AND SOMBRA REAL ESTATE
See entry in CHARACTERS

MISSISSIPPI (STATE OF)

Back in 1964, ODETTA HOLMES (one of SUSANNAH DEAN's previous personalities) spent three days in an OXFORD, Mississippi, jail. She was incarcerated for her participation in the Civil Rights Movement. In *Song of Susannah,* we learn that Susannah was part of the voter registration campaign which took place in this state during the summer of '64, nicknamed Freedom Summer. On June 21, 1964, three VOTER REGISTRATION BOYS—JAMES CHANEY, ANDREW GOODMAN, and MICHAEL SCHWERNER—were attacked and killed by the Ku Klux Klan.

During his travels along the HIGHWAYS IN HIDING, PERE CALLAHAN spent some time in Mississippi. His experiences in the state were much better than Susannah's.

II:188, III:220, IV:67, V:305, V:403, V:445, VI:256, VI:321, VI:350, VI:351–55, VI:361, VII:62, VII:76, VII:145, VII:587, VII:716

ADAMS COUNTY:
  NATCHEZ: V:304
COPIAH COUNTY: V:304
  SHADY GROVE: V:305
ISSAQUENA COUNTY: V:303, V:445
  ROUTE 3: V:303–5
LAFAYETTE COUNTY:
  OXFORD: Oxford was made famous (or infamous) by the Bob Dylan song "Oxford Town" and by the events upon which the song was based. In 1962, there were riots on the University of Mississippi campus based on the university's forced acceptance of its first black student, James Meredith. Meredith, whose acceptance at the university had been rescinded once it was discovered that he was dark-skinned, had fought for reacceptance for more than a year before the Fifth U.S. Circuit Court of Appeals ruled that the state could not deny him admission based on color. Meredith was escorted to campus by federal marshals but the city of Oxford erupted in violence. Before the National Guard could arrive, two students were killed.

  SUSANNAH DEAN's three-day incarceration in a Mississippi jail (which she refers to as a short season in hell) came about because of her participation in the nonviolent Civil Rights Movement. Like Meredith's antagonists, Susannah's captors were racists abusing their legal power. II:187–90, II:193, II:233–34, II:236–37, II:238, II:241, II:242, II:243, II:258, III:15, V:445, VI:11, VI:219–22 *(jail cell),* VI:223, VI:256, VI:321, VI:350, VI:351, VI:352–55, VI:356, VI:361, VII:62, VII:76, VII:145, VII:259

    BLUE MOON MOTOR HOTEL: ODETTA HOLMES and her VOTER REGISTRATION friends stayed in the Blue Moon Motor Hotel during their time in Mississippi. VI:352, VI:353, VI:355, VI:357
    JOHN BAMBRY'S CHURCH (FIRST AFRO-AMERICAN METHODIST CHURCH): VI:352
    OLE MISS: *See* MISSISSIPPI, UNIVERSITY OF, *listed separately*
NESHOBA COUNTY: VI:356
  LONGDALE: VI:351, VI:354, VI:355
  PHILADELPHIA: VI:351, VI:352, VI:355

UNIVERSITY OF MISSISSIPPI (OLE MISS): *See* MISSISSIPPI, UNIVERSITY OF (OLE MISS), *listed separately*
YAZOO COUNTY:
   YAZOO CITY: V:303, V:304

MISSISSIPPI, UNIVERSITY OF (OLE MISS)
Ole Miss was the site of the 1962 riots which Bob Dylan immortalized in his song "Oxford Town." The riots were the result of the university's forced acceptance of its first black student, James Meredith. We are told that DAMLI HOUSE, located in the DEVAR-TOI in END-WORLD, would look at home on the campus of Ole Miss.
   VI:354, VII:230

MISSOURI (STATE OF)
In the children's story *Charlie the Choo-Choo,* the talking train CHARLIE travels through the state of Missouri, tooting his horn.
   III:255, III:256, V:308
   MISSOURI PLAINS (THE BIG EMPTY): III:140, III:255, III:383
   ST. LOUIS: III:139–45, III:255

MONTANA (STATE OF)
   V:532, V:534

MONTGOMERY
   See ALABAMA (STATE OF)

MONTREAL
   See CANADA

MOREHOUSE
Founded in 1867, Morehouse College is a highly respected private liberal arts college for African-American men. Morehouse is located three miles from downtown Atlanta and has strong ties with Spelman College (also located in Atlanta), a prestigious private liberal arts college for African-American women.
   V:76, V:85, V:375, VI:106, VI:116, VI:150, VI:221, VI:230, VI:363

MORNINGSIDE HEIGHTS
   See NEW YORK CITY: MANHATTAN

MOROCCO
   TANGIERS: VII:115

MOUNT EVEREST
   VII:244

MOZAMBIQUE
   V:179

MULTIPLE AMERICAS (ALTERNATIVE AMERICAS)

Although the DARK TOWER contains only one KEYSTONE EARTH, and that Keystone Earth contains only one United States, other levels of the Tower contain alternative versions of the North American superpower. These multiple Americas are subtly different from the United States that we know. In some, people drive Takuro Spirits and drink Nozz-A-La cola. In at least one of them, more than 99 percent of the American population was wiped out by the superflu virus. As PERE CALLAHAN discovers during his five years along the HIGHWAYS IN HIDING, which connect these various United States, politics also vary from one version of America to another. While in one *where*, Jimmy Carter may have been elected president, in two other *wheres* (but the same *when*) Ronald Reagan and George Bush were elected instead of him.

Landscapes and town names also change from one Alternative America to another. In one version, FORT LEE sits across the HUDSON RIVER from NEW YORK CITY, yet in a different America, a town named LEABROOK sits in its place. In *Song of Susannah*, a somewhat disturbed EDDIE DEAN discovers that he is not from the Keystone World at all, but from one of these Alternative Americas. (In his version of the Big Apple, CO-OP CITY is located in BROOK-LYN, not the BRONX.)

At the end of *The Dark Tower*, SUSANNAH DEAN decides to abandon her quest for the Tower and goes to live in one of these alternative versions of America. The reason? Even though her beloved husband, Eddie, died in the DEVAR-TOI, in this other *where* and *when* he is alive and well, though his name isn't Eddie Dean anymore but Eddie TOREN. Unlike the former junkie Eddie Dean, Eddie Toren doesn't have a bullying big brother named HENRY, but a wonderful kid brother named JAKE. *See also* MAINE (STATE OF): ALTERNA-TIVE AMERICAS AND THE STATE OF MAINE

V:298–310, V:423 *(indirect)*, V:456, V:463 *(prisms of America)*, V:543, VI:199–200 *(Eddie discovers Co-Op City is in the Bronx)*, VI:204 *(Co-Op City)*, VI:271 *(Co-Op City)*, VII:807–13 *(Susannah in an alternative New York)*, W:153 *(and Dodge Dart)*

N

NASSAU
See BAHAMAS

NATCHEZ
See MISSISSIPPI (STATE OF)

NATHAN'S
See NEW YORK CITY: MANHATTAN

NATIONAL GRAMOPHONE INSTITUTE
See NEW YORK CITY: MANHATTAN: SECOND AVENUE

NEBRASKA (STATE OF)

In *Wizard and Glass* we find out that ABAGAIL—the champion of the WHITE found in King's novel *The Stand*—lives in an alternate version of Nebraska. *(See also* ROCKY MOUNTAINS)

    IV:624, V:149

    BUTTFUCK: Believe it or not, this place doesn't really exist. EDDIE DEAN just pretends it does. III:331

    OMAHA: A town in Nebraska served by the Union Pacific Railroad. The Union Pacific was joined with the ATCHISON, TOPEKA, AND SANTA FE in 1881, creating the second transcontinental railroad. *See* ATCHISON, TOPEKA, AND SANTA FE RAILROAD. IV:72, VII:657

NEEDLE PARK

    See NEW YORK CITY: MANHATTAN: GREENWICH VILLAGE

NETWORK, THE

    See NEW YORK CITY: MANHATTAN

NEVADA (STATE OF)

Beneath the mountains of this state there are concrete bunkers containing ICBMs.

    III:287, V:305

    ELKO: V:305

    LAS VEGAS: EDDIE DEAN thinks that "Roland the Hypnotist" could make a fortune in Vegas plying his trade. V:59, VII:94

    RAINBARREL SPRINGS: V:305

    RENO: III:241

NEW DELHI

    See INDIA

NEW ENGLAND

    V:135, V:256, V:537, V:538, V:544, V:584, VI:207, VI:208, VI:265, VII:487

NEW GUINEA

    PAPUA: VI:52

NEW HAMPSHIRE (STATE OF)

Some New Hampshire towns located just over the border from western MAINE are also prone to WALK-IN activity.

    V:537, VI:181, VI:397

    EAST CONWAY VILLAGE: Like many of the towns located in OXFORD COUNTY, MAINE, East Conway is plagued by the sinister WALK-INS. VI:153

    NORTH CONWAY: VI:397, VI:406

    PORTSMOUTH: VII:435

NEW JERSEY (STATE OF)
During his travels through the MULTIPLE AMERICAS, PERE CALLAHAN
spends much time flipping between two versions of New Jersey. In the KEY-
STONE version of this state, he lives in FORT LEE and works at the FORT
LEE HOMESTYLE DINER. In an alternative version of New Jersey, he lives
in LEABROOK and works at the LEABROOK HOMESTYLE DINER. In both
cases, his boss is named DICKY RUDEBACHER. PIMLI PRENTISS, the Master
of the DEVAR-TOI, was originally from one of the New Jerseys. We don't know
if he hailed from the Keystone World or not.
   II:115, III:55, V:264, V:292, V:296–301 *(Callahan is there)*, VI:165, VII:212,
   VII:225, VII:239, VII:297, VII:324, VII:362
   ATLANTIC CITY: II:131, III:316, V:181–82, V:537
   ELIZABETH: When ODETTA HOLMES (later SUSANNAH DEAN) was
   a child, her AUNT BLUE got married in Elizabeth, New Jersey. Five-year-
   old Odetta went to the wedding, but on the way to the train station JACK
   MORT (who was hiding in an abandoned building at the time) dropped a
   brick on her head. Odetta went into a coma for three weeks and her second
   personality—that of the venomous DETTA WALKER—was born. II:234–38,
   II:320–24, III:266
   FORT LEE: During his travels through the MULTIPLE AMERICAS, PERE
   CALLAHAN spends time in Fort Lee. However, sometimes he wakes up in
   the morning to find himself in LEABROOK instead. V:296, V:298, V:299,
   V:427
      FORT LEE HOMESTYLE DINER: DICKY RUDEBACHER owns this
      diner. (He owns its LEABROOK twinner as well.) V:302
      SUNRISE HOTEL: One of the ways that PERE CALLAHAN can fig-
      ure out whether he has awoken in Fort Lee (in the Sunrise Hotel) or in
      LEABROOK (in the SUNSET MOTEL) is to examine the color of his
      bedspread. In Fort Lee, it's orange. V:300
   HACKENSACK: V:297
   HOBOKEN: V:524, VI:141
   LEABROOK: On another level of the DARK TOWER, FORT LEE is called
   Leabrook. V:296–301
      LEABROOK HOMESTYLE DINER: An alternative version of DICKY
      RUDEBACHER owns this diner. (The KEYSTONE WORLD Dicky lives
      in Fort Lee.) V:299–301
      LEABROOK TWIN CINEMA: V:301
      MAIN STREET: V:299
      SUNSET MOTEL: In the Sunset Motel, PERE CALLAHAN has a pink
      bedspread. (His alternative bed, located in FORT LEE, has an orange
      spread.) V:300
   **LEEMAN/LEIGHMAN/LEE-BLUFF/LEE PALISADES/LEGHORN VIL-
   LAGE:** These are all versions of FORT LEE. V:298
   MEADOWLANDS: Eddie once saw a concert here. III:55
   NEWARK AIRPORT: VI:226
   NEW JERSEY TURNPIKE: I:180
   NUTLEY: *See* DRAWERS, *in* PORTALS

PERTH OIL AND GAS: When he was in high school, EDDIE DEAN went on a field trip to this oil refinery. The smell was so terrible that two of the visiting girls, and three of the visiting boys, puked. Evidently, the defunct factories located south of the DEVAR-TOI smell a bit like Perth Oil and Gas. VII:324–25

RAHWAY: PAUL PRENTISS (who later becomes PIMLI PRENTISS, the Devar Master) originally came from Rahway. VII:225, VII:226, VII:227, VII:229

TEANECK: In one of the MULTIPLE AMERICAS, the War of Kites takes place in Teaneck. V:297

NEW MEXICO (STATE OF)

V:305, VII:497, VII:510, VII:514, VII:517

ALBUQUERQUE: VII:287

SANTA FE: Santa Fe was one of the stops on the ATCHISON, TOPEKA, AND SANTA FE RAILROAD. It is also the name of a town in Roland's world. *See* MEJIS, BARONY OF: SANTA FE, *in* MID-WORLD PLACES, *and* SANTA FE, *in* PORTALS. IV:68

TAOS: The FOUNDING FATHERS of the TET CORPORATION sometimes held executive retreats in Taos. (The company owns a ranch there.) Tet's GOOD-MIND FOLK—a group of psychics who rival the CRIMSON KING's BREAKERS—have their headquarters at this ranch. VII:497, VII:507, VII:509

NEW ORLEANS

See LOUISIANA (STATE OF)

NEW YORK (STATE OF)

V:68, VII:614 *(upstate)*, VII:615 *(upstate)*

ATTICA STATE PRISON: II:372, VII:229

HUDSON RIVER: V:292, V:296–99, V:427, V:522

LONG ISLAND SOUND: EDDIE DEAN's plane from the BAHAMAS flies over Long Island Sound before landing at JFK AIRPORT. II:58

NEW YORK CITY: *See* NEW YORK CITY, *below*

NIAGARA FALLS: IV:32, VII:237

NIAGARA MALL: We don't know exactly where the Niagara Mall is located, just that it is situated in upstate New York in one of the ALTERNATIVE AMERICAS. (In other words, you won't find it in the KEYSTONE WORLD, where we live.) VII:614

STATEN ISLAND: IRENE TASSENBAUM was born on Staten Island. VII:430

TIOGA SPRINGS: RANDO THOUGHTFUL, the CRIMSON KING's minister of state, was born Austin Cornwell, son of ANDREW JOHN CORNWELL. Andrew Cornwell came from Tioga Springs. VII:616

UTICA: In the children's story *Charlie the Choo-Choo*, CHARLIE's replacement, a BURLINGTON ZEPHYR, was built in Utica. III:141

VASSAR COLLEGE: *See* VASSAR COLLEGE, *listed separately*

WHITE PLAINS: When SUSANNAH DEAN abandons her quest for the DARK TOWER and departs MID-WORLD via the magical DOOR drawn for her by PATRICK DANVILLE, she enters one of the ALTERNATIVE AMERICAS. Although her *tet*-mates EDDIE DEAN and JAKE CHAMBERS are both dead (one passed on in the DEVAR-TOI and the other entered the clearing on ROUTE 7 in MAINE), in her new America both are alive and well. These alternative versions of Eddie and Jake are the TOREN brothers, and they hail from White Plains. Although Susannah knows that this *where* is not the KEYSTONE WORLD (people drive Takuro Spirits and drink Nozz-A-La cola), nevertheless she is overjoyed to be there with her resurrected loved ones. VII:812

WOODSTOCK: V:527

NEW YORK CITY (CALLA NEW YORK, THE BIG APPLE)

The city of New York plays a central role in the Dark Tower series. All three of Roland's human companions—EDDIE DEAN, SUSANNAH DEAN, and JAKE CHAMBERS—come from this late-twentieth-century metropolis. Although they all hail from New York, each of our friends was drawn from a slightly different version of the city. Roland brought Susannah from the New York of 1964; he took Jake from that of 1977, and Eddie from 1987. Although our *tet*-mates were drawn from their home places through magical DOORWAYS BETWEEN WORLDS (doors which were, in one way or another, derived from the magical substance of the PRIM), in the final book of the Dark Tower series, we learn that the city is absolutely lousy with mechanical doorways as well. These mechanized portals, which Roland often refers to as the OLD ONES' doors, lead to multiple time periods and multiple worlds, and at least a score of them open onto parallel versions of New York City itself. Unfortunately, most of these mechanical portals are controlled by the servants of the CRIMSON KING.

New York City is important for other reasons as well. It is the home of the magical ROSE, which is the KEYSTONE WORLD's manifestation of the Dark Tower. It is also the home of the TOREN family (custodians for the Rose), and the future corporate headquarters of the TET CORPORATION, the company whose job it is to guard that most sacred of flowers.

Although the New York City we know is alive and well, the Dark Tower series hints that it may have a less than happy future. In *The Gunslinger,* the subway system beneath the CYCLOPEAN MOUNTAINS reminds Jake of New York's subways. Later, in LUD, the bridges and buildings of that war-torn city make our *ka-tet* think of Manhattan. If Lud provides a glimpse of what New York will look like in about two thousand years, then the technological and biochemical disasters which almost destroyed Roland's world may yet happen to ours.

ACTION TAKES PLACE IN NEW YORK CITY ON THE FOLLOWING PAGES: I:79–84, I:123 *(Jake's when of 1977),* II:45, II:50 *(see JFK Airport entries),* II:90–99, II:105–22, II:123–57, II:172–76 *(Susannah's when of 1964),* II:185–201, II:202–9 *(Susannah's 1964),* II:211–20 *(Susannah's 1959),* II:220–23 *(Susannah's when),* II:230, II:237–38, II:315–26 *(New York 1977),* II:339–59, II:360–86, III:11 *(indirect),* III:22 *(state of),* III:43, III:45, III:51, III:72, III:89–146, III:154–58, III:164, III:165–70, III:171, III:176–78, III:182–88, III:190–92, III:220, III:225, III:238, III:261, III:336, III:340, III:349, III:350, III:355, III:361, III:363, III:365, III:375, III:376, III:377, III:402, III:409, III:417 *(Barony of),* III:419, IV:7 *(Barony of),* IV:9–10, IV:20,

IV:22, IV:36, IV:45, IV:46, IV:47, IV:48, IV:51, IV:52, IV:53, IV:63, IV:77, V:48–70 *(todash)*, V:172–97 *(todash)*, V:264–93 *(Callahan's story)*, V:423–43 *(Callahan's story)*, V:515–47 *(through door)*, V:592–98 *(through door)*, VI:47–58, VI:73–98, VI:119–25, VI:225–34, VI:256–61, VI:307–63 *(characters move to the* DIXIE PIG—*entries in* PORTALS*)*, VII:3–5 *(characters move to the* DIXIE PIG—*entries in* PORTALS*)*, VII:485–525, VII:724–25 *(Susannah's dream)*, VII:807–13

DIRECT REFERENCES: V:40, V:47, V:48–70 *(todash)*, V:97, V:98, V:101, V:103, V:105 *(New York in all its multiples)*, V:106, V:108, V:110 *(Big A)*, V:131 *(Calla New York)*, V:135, V:138 *(Calla York)*, V:141, V:167, V:172–97 *(todash, 179 as Lud)*, V:201, V:221, V:223, V:231, V:247, V:260, V:263, V:264–93 *(Callahan's story)*, V:296, V:298, V:308, V:309, V:314, V:321, V:338, V:352, V:360, V:377, V:382, V:383, V:393, V:394, V:395, V:400, V:427, V:494, V:502, V:503, V:508, V:509, V:511, V:512, V:513, V:514–48, V:549, V:550, V:558, V:561, V:573, V:593, V:622, V:631, V:633, V:646, V:648, V:649, V:687, VI:11, VI:12, VI:13, VI:14, VI:28, VI:31, VI:35, VI:42, VI:43, VI:47–61, VI:64, VI:65–98 *(67–72 Susannah's dogan)*, VI:102, VI:104, VI:107, VI:108, VI:117, VI:118–25, VI:147, VI:149, VI:163, VI:165, VI:180, VI:185, VI:188, VI:210, VI:223, VI:225–34, VI:238, VI:239, VI:243, VI:248, VI:256–61, VI:275, VI:288, VI:296, VI:300, VI:307–63, VI:405, VI:407, VII:3–5, VII:21 *(todash)*, VII:36, VII:47, VII:56, VII:84, VII:87, VII:90, VII:93 *(under it)*, VII:104, VII:105, VII:110, VII:111, VII:119, VII:121, VII:122, VII:133, VII:135, VII:146, VII:201, VII:208, VII:266, VII:297, VII:309, VII:325, VII:381, VII:396, VII:398, VII:399, VII:405, VII:424 *(Jew York)*, VII:443, VII:477, VII:478, VII:485–525 *(502—City of Lud in its prime; 526, 527, 521—young and vital Lud)*, VII:550, VII:555, VII:559, VII:586, VII:591, VII:601, VII:604, VII:652, VII:657, VII:676, VII:687, VII:689, VII:724–5 *(Susannah's dream)*, VII:728, VII:743, VII:747, VII:762, VII:802, VII:807–13, VII:818, W:4, W:8, W:19, W:306

BRONX: In the KEYSTONE WORLD, CO-OP CITY is located in the Bronx. However, in EDDIE DEAN's New York, it is located in BROOKLYN. II:110, VI:43, VI:199, VI:200 , VI:204, VI:271, VII:812

    CO-OP CITY: In our *where* and *when*, Co-Op City is an ethnically diverse housing cooperative located in the northeasternmost corner of the Bronx. In Eddie's version of New York, Co-Op City is located in BROOKLYN. (On II:110 it is said to be in the Bronx.)

    CROSS BRONX EXPRESSWAY: V:264

BROOKLYN: For many years EDDIE DEAN lived in CO-OP CITY, which— in his version of New York—is located in Brooklyn. As he points out to JAKE when the two of them meet in a dream version of New York, Brooklyn also contains his world's version of the portal of the BEAR. The mobster ENRICO BALAZAR also hails from Brooklyn. III:154, III:165, III:168, III:169, III:170, III:176–78, III:179, III:182–88, III:190–92, III:265, V:50, V:62, V:65, V:162, V:203, V:207, V:443, V:512, V:525, V:527, V:537, V:544, V:548, V:637, VI:150, VI:153, VI:154, VI:199, VI:200, VI:204, VI:206, VI:214, VI:271, VI:277, VI:312, VII:17, VII:305, VII:381, VII:668, VII:807, VII:812

    BERNIE'S BARBER SHOP: BALAZAR plays poker here. V:537

BROOKLYN AVENUE: *See also* BROOKLYN AVENUE BEAT *and* MAJESTIC THEATER, *both below*. III:190

BROOKLYN AVENUE BEAT: BOSCO BOB, a slightly mad officer of the law, patrolled this beat when EDDIE DEAN was a boy. V:140

BROOKLYN BRIDGE: VI:96

BROOKLYN VOCATIONAL INSTITUTE: III:179

CASTLE AVENUE: JAKE travels along Castle Avenue while looking for MARKEY AVENUE. He thinks that his doorway into MID-WORLD will be there. It's not, but it does lead him to the MAJESTIC THEATER and a thirteen-year-old EDDIE DEAN. III:176–78

CASTLE AVENUE MARKET: VII:102

CHURCH OF THE HOLY GOD-BOMB: Although the Reverend EARL HARRIGAN lives in Brooklyn, he often preaches on SECOND AVENUE in MANHATTAN. VI:312

COHOES STREET: Home of the BONDED ELECTROPLATE FACTORY. II:172

   BONDED ELECTROPLATE FACTORY: EDDIE and HENRY DEAN smoked here. II:172

CONEY ISLAND: II:117 *(mirror maze)*, II:169, III:350, III:372, V:37, V:443, V:701, VI:90, VI:157

CO-OP CITY: In EDDIE DEAN's version of New York, Co-Op City is located in Brooklyn rather than the BRONX. (This is one of the many time/space variations found on different levels of the TOWER.) Eddie and his brother, HENRY, lived in this big cooperative located between CASTLE and BROOKLYN AVENUES. II:95, II:105–13, II:241, III:23, III:154, III:170, III:176–78, III:179, III:182–88 *(Dean family apartment 187, 188)*, III:190–92 *(Dean family apartment 192)*, V:203, VI:199, VI:200, VI:204, VI:214, VI:271, VI:277, VII:17, VII:102, VII:305, VII:807

DAHLIE'S (DAHLBERG'S): Dahlie's, a shop located in EDDIE DEAN's old neighborhood, was owned by Dahlie Lundgren. Dahlie's sold great fried dough as well as Popsicles and hoodsie rockets, and its comic books were fairly easy to steal. The Dean brothers and their friends used to smoke cigarettes behind Dahlie's back door. III:76, III:187, IV:43, IV:54, IV:60, V:187, V:257

DEAN FAMILY APARTMENT: VI:157

DUTCH HILL: Dutch Hill was the site of the infamously evil DUTCH HILL MANSION. When EDDIE DEAN was a boy, he was afraid of this place, and for good reason. Its reputation rivaled that of the MARSTEN HOUSE, found in 'SALEM'S LOT, MAINE. In *The Waste Lands*, JAKE CHAMBERS had to travel to this demon-infested house to reenter MID-WORLD. III:161–62, III:189, III:191–92, III:262, III:344, V:50, V:93, V:104, V:204, V:258, V:476, VII:143, VII:144–45, VII:249, VII:592

   DUTCH HILL LITTLE LEAGUE FIELD: III:204

   DUTCH HILL PUB: III:204

   DUTCH HILL USED APPLIANCES: III:192, III:204–5

   HENRY'S CORNER MARKET: III:204

   RHINEHOLD STREET: The terrible haunted MANSION (which

JAKE enters in order to find his doorway into MID-WORLD) is located on this street. III:75, III:189, III:190, III:192, III:195, III:204, III:344

MANSION IN DUTCH HILL (DUTCH HILL MANSION): *See* DOORWAYS BETWEEN WORLDS, *in* PORTALS

GINELLI'S PIZZA (FOUR FATHERS RESTAURANT): Ginelli's is a front for BALAZAR's illegal empire. II:91

GRAND ARMY PLAZA: New York has two Grand Army Plazas—one in MANHATTAN and one in Brooklyn. Midtown Manhattan's Plaza is located on Fifth Avenue, between Fifty-eighth and Sixtieth Streets. Brooklyn's Grand Army Plaza is located at the main entrance to Prospect Park, near the main branch of the Brooklyn Public Library. Brooklyn's Grand Army Plaza is best known for the Soldiers and Sailors Memorial Arch, which is Brooklyn's rival to Paris's Arc de Triomphe.

In *Wolves of the Calla,* EDDIE DEAN saves CALVIN TOWER's bacon by telling JACK ANDOLINI that if he and his nasty boss, BALAZAR, don't leave Tower alone, Eddie will fill Grand Army Plaza with dead gangsters from Brooklyn. Whichever Grand Army Plaza Eddie is talking about, that's a lot of carnage. V:528, V:536, VI:193

MAJESTIC THEATER: The Majestic movie theater is located on the corner of MARKEY and BROOKLYN AVENUES. EDDIE DEAN used to watch Westerns here. His brother, HENRY, liked to tease the ticket girl. III:182–84, V:152, V:209, V:257, VI:285

MARKEY AVENUE: On his travels through Brooklyn, JAKE travels along Markey Avenue. III:161, III:165, III:178

MARKEY ACADEMY: This place doesn't actually exist. III:167, III:177–78

MARKEY AVENUE PLAYGROUND: EDDIE and HENRY used to play basketball here. It has since been replaced by the JUVENILE COURT BUILDING. III:161, III:165, III:185–88, VII:336

JUVENILE COURT BUILDING: III:161

NORWOOD STREET: Some kids from this street were mysteriously killed at the DUTCH HILL MANSION. III:187

PROJECTS: EDDIE, HENRY, and their mom lived in the projects when Eddie and Henry were young. II:68

RINCON AVENUE: Once upon a time there was a candy store on Rincon Avenue. EDDIE and HENRY DEAN filched comic books from it. II:172

ROOSEVELT ELEMENTARY SCHOOL: This was EDDIE DEAN's elementary school. V:352

WOO KIM'S MARKET: V:140

EAST RIVER: III:102

EAST RIVER DRIVE: III:301

MANHATTAN: II:345, III:23, III:122, III:171, III:345, V:48–70 *(todash, mentioned directly on 62, 68),* V:93, V:96, V:97, V:99, V:172–97 *(todash),* V:264–93 *(Callahan's story),* V:297, V:299, V:308, V:422, V:423–43 *(Callahan's story),* V:451, V:512, V:515–47 *(door),* V:592–98 *(door),* VI:57, VI:225–34 *(setting),* VI:256–61 *(setting),* VI:307–63 *(setting—directly mentioned on 338),* VII:3–5 *(setting),* VII:33, VII:240 *(Manhattan Project),* VII:430, VII:486–525

ALPHABET CITY: VI:11

    AVENUE B: VI:43

AMERICANO BAR: This is where PERE CALLAHAN fell off the wagon, even though he'd managed to stay sober during his months of employment at the HOME shelter, located on FIRST AVENUE. Despite the strain LUPE DELGADO's death placed on him, Callahan did not return to the bottle until he saw some VAGS (or VAGRANT DEAD) walking along PARK AVENUE. V:285, V:444

BARCELONA LUGGAGE STORE: *See* SECOND AVENUE, *below*

BATTERY PARK: V:287

BELLEVUE: II:176, II:241

BLACK TOWER (2 HAMMARSKJÖLD PLAZA): *See* LOT, THE: 2 HAMMARSKJÖLD PLAZA, *in* PORTALS

BLACKSTRAP MOLASSES CAFÉ: The Blackstrap Molasses Café is located on Sixtieth Street and Lexington, not far from the DIXIE PIG. The young BUSKER who plays "Man of Constant Sorrow" for SUSAN-NAH DEAN and MIA, daughter of none, sits in front of this café. VI:350

BLARNEY STONE: V:283, V:444

BLEECKER STREET: As well as being known for its music, Bleecker Street houses one of New York's many DOORWAYS BETWEEN WORLDS. This particular door connects the MULTIPLE AMERICAS to one another. In some versions of New York City, the door is located in an abandoned warehouse. In other New Yorks, it is located in an eternally half-completed building. III:118, III:155, V:169, VII:105

BLIMPIE'S: V:175, V:515

BLOOMINGDALE'S: III:45, III:103, III:106, III:107, V:53

BORDERS: During her lunch hour, TRUDY DAMASCUS carries her good shoes in a canvas Borders bag. Unfortunately for her, shoeless MIA (who is in control of SUSANNAH DEAN's body) mugs her on SECOND AVENUE. She steals Trudy's bag, shoes, and *New York Times*. VI:50, VI:65, VI:87, VI:97

BRENDIO'S: *See* FIFTH AVENUE, *below*

BROADWAY: V:283, VII:405

CENTRAL PARK: As she and Roland near the DARK TOWER, SUSAN-NAH DEAN begins to have repeating dreams about her two dead *ka-tet* mates, EDDIE and JAKE. The scenario she sees is always the same. Eddie and Jake stand in Central Park wearing two woolly hats, one of which says "Merry" and one of which says "Christmas." Although they can't give her many clues about how she can manage the transition, they want her to leave MID-WORLD and join them. (Otherwise, she will probably die like all of Roland's previous companions.)

Traveling through the magical UNFOUND DOOR which PATRICK DANVILLE draws for her, Susannah abandons the quest. Riding HO FAT III, she idles into Central Park, where the HARLEM ROSES sing Christmas carols in the snow. As in her dreams, Eddie is there to greet her, a cup of hot chocolate in hand. II:187, II:189, II:200, II:237, IV:64, IV:67, V:290 *(Central Park, west side of the Ramble)*, VII:208, VII:554, VII:555, VII:559,

VII:581, VII:645–46, VII:724–25, VII:728, VII:743, VII:749, VII:807–13 *(Susannah arrives in 1987)*, VII:818

CHEW CHEW MAMA'S (DENNIS'S WAFFLES AND PANCAKES): *See* SECOND AVENUE, *below*

CHRISTOPHER STREET STATION: In SUSANNAH DEAN's version of New York (yet another level of the DARK TOWER) the fabled A train stops at Christopher Street Station. Unfortunately, ODETTA HOLMES/ DETTA WALKER happened to be waiting at this stop at the same time as the evil JACK MORT. Mort pushed her in front of the train. Luckily Susannah (and her many selves) survived; however, her legs (or what was left of them) had to be amputated just above the knee. II:215–17, II:380–86, VI:221, VI:232 *(indirect)*

CITY HALL: V:517, V:520, VI:256

CITY LIGHTS BAR: After LUPE DELGADO's death, but before he began to be actively hunted by the LOW MEN, PERE CALLAHAN spent a lot of time in this bar. It was located on Lexington Avenue. V:290

CLEMENTS GUNS AND SPORTING GOODS: This shop is located on Seventh Avenue and Forty-ninth Street. While occupying JACK MORT's body, Roland visits Clements so that he can restock his dwindling supply of live rounds. Besides buying ammo, Roland causes general havoc. II:342–59, II:371–73

COLUMBIA UNIVERSITY: *See* COLUMBIA UNIVERSITY, *listed separately*

DENBY'S DISCOUNT DRUG: *See* TIMES SQUARE, *below*

DENNIS'S WAFFLES AND PANCAKES: *See* SECOND AVENUE: CHEW CHEW MAMA'S, *below*

DIXIE PIG: *See entry in* PORTALS

DUNHILL'S: This shop sells expensive lighters. II:382

EMPIRE STATE BUILDING: III:350, V:286, V:321, VII:18, VII:47

FIFTH AVENUE: V:271, VI:41, VII:724, VII:811

> **BRENDIO'S:** JAKE passes Brendio's on his way to school. Some of the mannequins in the window are dressed in Edwardian clothes. Others are "barenaked." I:82, III:103, VII:811
>
> **BRENTANO'S BOOKSTORE:** VII:811
>
> **FIFTH AVENUE AND FORTY-THIRD STREET/THE PUSHING PLACE:** On one level of the DARK TOWER, JAKE is killed here by a 1976 Sedan de Ville. JACK MORT (who pushed Jake in front of oncoming traffic) dubs it "The Pushing Place." II:315–18, III:104–6
>
> **PLAZA HOTEL:** During the day, LUPE DELGADO worked as part of the maintenance crew at the Plaza Hotel. However, his real calling was working with homeless people at the HOME shelter. V:271, V:280

FIRST AVENUE: V:266, V:429, V:433, V:531, VI:57, VI:74, VI:86

> **FIRST AVENUE POLICE SHOOTING RANGE:** III:157
>
> **NEW YORK PLAZA–PARK HYATT (U.N. PLAZA, U.N. PLAZA HOTEL, REGAL U.N. PLAZA):** The Plaza–Park Hyatt is the First Avenue hotel where MIA takes a captive SUSANNAH once they land in 1999 New York. (Mia needs to find a *telefung* so that she can contact the evil RICHARD P. SAYRE, servant of the CRIMSON KING, who

has promised to help her deliver her CHAP.) Although neither Mia nor Susannah has any money to pay for their room, Susannah uses her little CAN-TAH to mesmerize MATHIESSEN VAN WYCK into paying for their stay. She also uses it to hypnotize the EXOTIC HOTEL RECEPTIONIST into giving her the room key even though she has no identification. Later on in *Song of Susannah,* JAKE CHAMBERS and PERE CALLAHAN travel to the Plaza–Park Hyatt to retrieve BLACK THIRTEEN from the hotel room safe where Susannah has hidden it. According to the sign located in the Plaza–Park's lobby, as of July 1, 1999, SOMBRA REAL ESTATE and NORTH CENTRAL POSITRON-ICS are going to rename the hotel the Regal U.N. Plaza. V:595, VI:57, VI:74, VI:86, VI:89, VI:90–98, VI:107, VI:109, VI:118–25, VI:219, VI:223–34, VI:251, VI:256–57, VI:297 *(U.N. Plaza Hotel),* VI:317, VI:320–33, VII:67, VII:143 *(indirect),* VII:145, VII:303, VII:689

FORTY-EIGHTH STREET: *See* SECOND AVENUE: EIGHT MAGIC BLOCKS, *below*

FORTY-FIFTH STREET: *See* SECOND AVENUE: EIGHT MAGIC BLOCKS, *below*

FORTY-SEVENTH STREET: *See* SECOND AVENUE: EIGHT MAGIC BLOCKS, *below*

FORTY-SIXTH STREET: *See* SECOND AVENUE, *below, and* LOT, THE, *in* PORTALS

FOUR SEASONS RESTAURANT: II:191

GAIETY: *See* TIMES SQUARE, *below*

GEORGE WASHINGTON BRIDGE: The George Washington Bridge is our world's version of LUD BRIDGE. III:256, III:292, V:292, V:297, V:298, V:444, VII:503 *(Lud Bridge)*

> **FOOTBRIDGE (LaMERK INDUSTRIES):** According to PERE CALLAHAN, in one of the ALTERNATIVE AMERICAS a footbridge (not far from the George Washington Bridge) crosses the HUDSON RIVER. The footbridge was manufactured by LaMERK INDUSTRIES. V:292–93, V:296–99, V:444

GIMBEL'S: II:191, III:45

GRACE METHODIST CHURCH: The REVEREND MURDOCH preached here. SUSANNAH's father didn't agree with his sermons. III:311

GRAND ARMY PLAZA: There are two Grand Army Plazas, one in BROOKLYN and one in Manhattan. *See entry in* BROOKLYN *subsection.*

GRAND CENTRAL STATION: III:331, VII:77, VII:201, VII:537

GREENWICH VILLAGE: II:190, II:199, II:211, II:378, III:350 *(East Village),* V:89, V:168, V:169, V:275 *(East Village),* V:276, V:290, V:544, VII:653

> **NEEDLE PARK (WASHINGTON SQUARE PARK):** Washington Square Park was one of PERE CALLAHAN's hangouts during his drunken vagrant days. When he first arrived in the Big Apple (just after his terrible confrontation with the VAMPIRE BARLOW), he slept on one of its benches. He became a Needle Park vagrant once more after the death of his friend LUPE DELGADO and after the shock of seeing the VAGRANT DEAD wandering around the city.

In Needle Park, Callahan discovered the first of the LOW MEN's "lost pet" posters advertising for information about him. The writing, spray-painted across the back of one of the benches, said, "He comes here. He has a burned hand." As a result, Callahan had to leave the city in a hurry.

It's not surprising that Washington Square Park became a haunt for the low men, given its less than savory history. Before the park was built in 1826, it was a burial ground and then an execution site (public gallows were situated here). During the 1980s, when Callahan would have frequented it, it was a well-known drug-dealing center (hence its nickname). It has cleaned up its act since then, but (as Roland and his *ka*-mates know all too well) the dead of such places don't rest easy. V:89, V:265, V:289, V:290

GREYMARL APARTMENTS: The Greymarl Apartments are a Victorian block of flats located on FIFTH AVENUE and Central Park South. ODETTA HOLMES (one of SUSANNAH DEAN's earlier selves) lived in the penthouse apartment. II:189–93, II:200, II:226 *(Odetta's apartment)*, II:255 *(Odetta's apartment)*

GUTTENBERG, FURTH, AND PATEL: The accountant TRUDY DAMASCUS works for this firm. VI:47, VI:52–54 *(setting)*

HAMMARSKJÖLD PLAZA: See LOT, THE: 2 HAMMARSKJÖLD PLAZA, *in* PORTALS

HARLEM: VII:807, VII:809

HOME (WET SHELTER): See HOME, *listed separately*

HUDSON RIVER: See NEW YORK (STATE OF)

HUNGRY I: A café that ODETTA HOLMES frequented. A lot of folk musicians performed here during the early 1960s. II:218, VI:351, VII:533

JAKE CHAMBERS'S APARTMENT: The Chambers family apartment is located on FIFTH AVENUE, three and a half blocks farther up than the PUSHING PLACE. Hence it is probably on Fifth and Forty-sixth or Fifth and Forty-seventh. I:81, III:102, III:107–8, III:129–46, III:155–58, III:165, V:565–66 *(Elmer's study)*

KANSAS CITY BLUES: A midtown saloon located on Fifty-fourth Street, just around the corner from SECOND AVENUE. When Jake travels TODASH to New York City at the beginning of *Wolves of the Calla*, he finds himself standing in front of this bar. V:49

KATZ PHARMACY AND SODA FOUNTAIN (SUNDRIES AND NOTIONS FOR MISSES AND MISTERS): Katz Pharmacy is located at 395 West Forty-ninth Street, and has been at that address since 1927. (It was founded by the present owner's father.) While searching for Keflex, Roland causes complete havoc here. As KATZ says, Roland commits the first penicillin holdup in history. II:333, II:358, II:360, II:361–70, II:373–77

KIDZPLAY: See GUTTENBERG, FURTH, AND PATEL: DAMASCUS, TRUDY, *in* CHARACTERS

LEANING TOWER (BALAZAR'S OFFICE): Although ENRICO BALAZAR is one of BROOKLYN's resident thugs, his head offices are in a midtown saloon known as the Leaning Tower. The first time Roland saw the sign for this den of iniquity (back in *The Drawing of the Three*), he assumed that the sign depicted the DARK TOWER itself. EDDIE DEAN informed him that it was merely a picture of the LEANING TOWER OF PISA. II:91, II:107, II:112, II:113–22, II:123–57 *(135–43 Western Sea as well)*, II:204, II:205, II:309, II:369, III:67, III:68, III:99, III:100, III:180, III:262, III:340, V:61, V:92, V:104, V:164, VI:134, VI:139, VI:334

LEXINGTON AVENUE (AND THE DIXIE PIG): *See* DIXIE PIG, *in* PORTALS

LEXINGTON AVENUE AND SIXTIETH STREET: In *Song of Susannah*, SUSANNAH and MIA stop to listen to a BUSKER performing on this street corner. VI:338–39, VI:347–57

LOT, THE (FORTY-SIXTH STREET AND SECOND AVENUE): *See entry in* PORTALS

MACY'S: II:99, II:196, II:202–9, II:221–23, II:226, II:227, II:228, II:243, II:255, II:336, III:45, V:174, V:703

MADISON SQUARE GARDEN: VI:311

MAGIC SHOP: *See* SECOND AVENUE, *below*

MANHATTAN RESTAURANT OF THE MIND: *See* SECOND AVENUE, *below*

MARINE MIDLAND BANK: V:275, V:288, V:289 *(indirect)*

MERCURY LOUNGE: V:183

METROPOLITAN MUSEUM OF ART: The Met appears to exist in all the New Yorks on all levels of the DARK TOWER. It is located on FIFTH AVENUE. III:166–67

MIDTOWN: VI:73

****MID-TOWN LANES:** The bowling alley that JAKE CHAMBERS frequented while he lived in New York. It is also mentioned in the 2003 version of *The Gunslinger*. While traveling to New York via TODASH, Jake and his *tet*-mates discover a version of his Mid-Town Lanes bowling bag in the Vacant LOT on SECOND AVENUE. (It is the perfect size for carrying BLACK THIRTEEN.) However, whereas Jake's original bag said, "Nothing but Strikes at Mid-Town Lanes," the bag he finds while in the *todash* state says, "Nothing but Strikes at Mid-World Lanes." III:107, III:168, V:198, V:694, VI:49, VI:73, VI:97, VII:143

MILLS CONSTRUCTION AND SOMBRA REAL ESTATE: *See entry in* CHARACTERS

MISS SO PRETTY (SHOP): III:166

MORT'S HOME: 409 Park Avenue South. II:349

MORT'S OFFICE: Mort's accountancy firm is located on Sixth Avenue, also known as the Avenue of the Americas. II:324–26, II:339–41

NATHAN'S HOT DOGS: V:46

NATIONAL GRAMOPHONE INSTITUTE: *See* SECOND AVENUE, *below*

NEEDLE PARK (WASHINGTON SQUARE PARK): *See* GREENWICH VILLAGE, *listed above*

NETWORK, THE: JAKE's father, ELMER CHAMBERS, is a high-powered executive at this TV network, where he is an acknowledged master of "The Kill." The Network offices are located at 70 Rockefeller Plaza. I:81, I:82, III:90, III:91, III:102, III:168, IV:32, VII:95, VII:299, VII:398

NEW YORK GENERAL HOSPITAL: *See also* RIVERSIDE HOSPITAL. V:282
NEW YORK HARBOR: III:90
NEW YORK PUBLIC LIBRARY: V:596, V:598 *(indirect)*, V:619–23, V:621
NEW YORK UNIVERSITY: II:115, II:174, V:424
NINETEENTH STREET: V:284
PARK AVENUE: V:283, V:284 *(vags)*
PAUL STUART (SHOP): III:166
PENN STATION: VII:194
PIPER SCHOOL: *See* PIPER SCHOOL, *listed separately*
PLAZA HOTEL: *See* FIFTH AVENUE, *listed above*
PLAZA–PARK HYATT: *See* FIRST AVENUE, *listed above*
POCKET PARK: *See* SECOND AVENUE, *below*
PORT AUTHORITY: II:42, V:264, V:428
PUSHING PLACE: *See* FIFTH AVENUE: FIFTH AVENUE AND FORTY-THIRD STREET, *listed above*
RADIO CITY MUSIC HALL: III:122, III:350, V:183, VI:53, VII:47
REFLECTIONS OF YOU: *See* SECOND AVENUE, *below*
REGENCY TOWER: II:41
RIVERSIDE HOSPITAL, ROOM 577 (NEW YORK GENERAL HOSPITAL): Both ROWAN MAGRUDER and PERE CALLAHAN end up in this hospital room after being attacked by the HITLER BROTHERS. (Quite appropriately, if you add up the room's digits, they equal NINETEEN.) V:422, V:423–27, V:442, V:443
SAINT ANTHONY'S: II:359
SAINT PATRICK'S CATHEDRAL: VI:90
SAKS: II:191
SECOND AVENUE: According to EDDIE DEAN and JAKE CHAMBERS, the eight Second Avenue blocks which stretch from Forty-sixth Street to Fifty-fourth Street function as a kind of magic portal. This area contains both the MANHATTAN RESTAURANT OF THE MIND and the magic LOT, home of the ROSE. III:51–53, III:77–78, III:79, III:118–20, V:47, V:49–70 *(todash)*, V:174–97, V:284 *(and Nineteenth Street)*, V:429–33 *(setting)*, V:502, V:511, V:514, V:515–48 *(setting)*, V:590, V:592–96 *(setting)*, VI:43, VI:47–52, VI:53, VI:54–58, VI:68, VI:65–69 *(pocket park)*, VI:189 *(buying Vacant Lot)*, VI:195 *(Vacant Lot)*, VI:308–20, VII:423 *(Harrigan)*
  EIGHT MAGIC BLOCKS (FIFTY-FOURTH STREET TO FORTY-SIXTH STREET): V:49–50 *(we learn that these are the "magic blocks" later)*, V:57, V:58, V:95, V:173, V:175, V:178, V:181, V:182, V:502–3 *(magic blocks and key world)*, V:592, V:594–96
    BARCELONA LUGGAGE STORE: V:49 *(todash)*
    BLACK TOWER: *See* LOT, THE: 2 HAMMARSKJÖLD PLAZA, *in* PORTALS
    CHEW CHEW MAMA'S (DENNIS'S WAFFLES AND PANCAKES): Chew Chew's is located at Second Avenue and Fifty-second Street. In *The Waste Lands*, both EDDIE DEAN and JAKE CHAMBERS pass by this address—Eddie in a dream, and Jake on his way to see

the ROSE. Both of them see ENRICO BALAZAR here, dressed as a bum. (However, in Eddie's dream, Chew Chew's is disguised as a MAGIC SHOP.) In *Wolves of the Calla,* our entire *ka-tet* strolls past this restaurant while traveling to New York City via TODASH.

Not surprisingly, PERE CALLAHAN also has a connection to Chew Chew's. During his days at the HOME shelter, he and some of his friends would occasionally eat there. After visiting ROWAN MAGRUDER in RIVERSIDE HOSPITAL, Callahan decided to return to Chew Chew's for one final bite before leaving New York. When he is attacked by the HITLER BROTHERS, it is a Swissburger from Chew Chew's that Callahan vomits onto his clothing.

In 1994, Chew Chew's changed its name to Dennis's Waffles and Pancakes, but still managed to retain its central significance to our *ka-tet*'s story. After eating at Dennis's, TRUDY DAMASCUS witnesses SUSANNAH/MIA suddenly appear on the corner of Second Avenue and Forty-sixth Street, and Mia promptly confiscates her shoes.

As we all know from the earlier books of the series, Chew Chew's isn't an entirely benevolent place. *Chew Chew* sounds a lot like *Choo-Choo,* as in *Charlie the Choo-Choo,* a sinister storybook starring CHARLIE, the nasty train. III:119, V:60, V:178, V:429, V:432, V:503, V:514, VI:47, VI:52, VI:313

DENNIS'S WAFFLES AND PANCAKES: *See* CHEW CHEW MAMA'S, *listed above*

FORTY-SIXTH STREET: The corner of Forty-sixth Street and Second Avenue is an important place. On one side of the road is the magical Vacant LOT. On the other (at least in 1999) there is a POCKET PARK, which contains a fountain and a statue of the TURTLE GUARDIAN (*see* POCKET PARK, *below; and* LOT, THE, *in* PORTALS). VI:47–51, VI:53, VI:54–58, VI:65–89, VI:90, VI:104, VI:189, VI:195

HAMMARSKJÖLD PLAZA (2 HAMMARSKJÖLD PLAZA, THE BLACK TOWER): *See* LOT, THE, *in* PORTALS

GARDEN OF THE BEAM: *See* LOT, THE: 2 HAMMAR-SKJÖLD PLAZA, *in* PORTALS

POCKET PARK: This little pocket park is located across the street from 2 HAMMARSKJÖLD PLAZA, the 1999 home of the ROSE. Inside the park is a fountain containing a metal sculpture of the TURTLE GUARDIAN. In this park SUSANNAH DEAN enters her internal DOGAN so that she can delay the birth of baby MORDRED. Here also she charms MATHIESSEN VAN WYCK with her little CAN-TAH. In the final book of the Dark Tower series, IRENE TASSENBAUM waits for Roland in this peaceful place while he visits the TET CORPORATION across the street. Those visiting the pocket park sometimes hear singing reminiscent of the Rose's song. For all who go there, it is a refreshing place. VI:57–58, VI:65–89 *(in dogan—67–77),* VII:488–91, VII:497

HARRIGAN'S STREET CORNER (SECOND AND FORTY-SIXTH STREET): The Reverend EARL HARRIGAN likes to preach on this corner. VI:257–61, VI:308–20, VII:423

LOT, THE: *See entry in* PORTALS

MAGIC SHOP (HOUSE OF CARDS): This magic shop exists only in EDDIE DEAN's dream version of New York. He imagines it sits on Second Avenue and Fifty-second Street, the location of CHEW CHEW MAMA'S. In Eddie's sleep vision, ENRICO BALAZAR sits in front of the store dressed as a bum. In the window is a sign that reads "House of Cards." Quite appropriately, the window display is of a tower built of tarot cards. III:51–52

MANHATTAN RESTAURANT OF THE MIND: The Manhattan Restaurant of the Mind is located on Second Avenue and Fifty-fourth Street. It's run by CALVIN TOWER, probably with a little help from his sidekick, AARON DEEPNEAU. Back in *The Waste Lands,* JAKE bought *Riddle-De-Dum!* and *Charlie the Choo-Choo* here. In *Wolves of the Calla,* EDDIE visits the Manhattan Restaurant of the Mind and arrives just in time to save Tower from BALAZAR'S MEN. After Eddie beats up Balazar's thugs, telling them that Tower will not sell the Vacant LOT to them, the WOLVES of New York burn this shop down. Luckily, Tower isn't there when they do it. We don't know whether the shop cat, SERGIO, survives the blaze. III:112–18, III:119, III:128, III:155, IV:18 *(as bookstore),* IV:46, V:51, V:54–70 *(todash),* V:91, V:92–100 *(discussed),* V:177, V:178, V:503, V:516, V:518–48, V:592–93, V:709, VI:35 *(indirect),* VI:84 *(indirect),* VI:139, VI:140, VI:183 *(indirect),* VI:192 *(indirect),* VI:196 *(indirect),* VI:399, VII:495

NATIONAL GRAMOPHONE INSTITUTE: This place doesn't really exist. EDDIE DEAN makes it up to show that any old institution can exist on the Vacant LOT as long as the ROSE is protected from harm. VI:270

PAPER PATCH: III:120

POCKET PARK: *See* FORTY-SIXTH STREET, *listed above*

REFLECTIONS OF YOU: This shop's display window is full of mirrors. In his dream-vision of New York, EDDIE sees himself reflected in these mirrors but his image is actually dressed like JAKE. Later, on his way to find the ROSE, Jake also sees himself reflected in these mirrors. III:77, III:119

STATION SHOES AND BOOTS: Located on Second Avenue and Fifty-fourth Street. V:517, V:593

TOM AND JERRY'S ARTISTIC DELI: *See* LOT, THE, *in* PORTALS

TOWER OF POWER RECORDS: As JAKE passes by this shop on his way to the ROSE (which he actually hopes is a portal to Roland), "Paint It Black" is belting out of the doorway. Not surprisingly, the lyrics are about doors. III:119, V:60, V:178, V:179, V:186, V:515, V:518, V:593

TURTLE BAY: *See* TURTLE BAY, *listed below*

TURTLE BAY LUXURY CONDOMINIUMS: *See* TURTLE BAY, *listed below*

SIR SPEEDY CAR PARK: Located on Sixty-third Street. When in New York, the TASSENBAUMs park their cars here. VII:486

SISTERS OF MERCY HOSPITAL: II:211–12, II:214–20

SIXTIETH STREET: VI:41

SIXTY-FIRST STREET (DIXIE PIG ENTRANCE): *See* DIXIE PIG, *in* PORTALS

SPARKS: A restaurant that EDDIE and HENRY like to go to. II:47

STATION SHOES AND BOOTS: *See* SECOND AVENUE, *listed above*

STATUE OF LIBERTY: I:79, III:349, V:321, VII:18

TASSENBAUM APARTMENT: VII:486

TENTH STREET: V:283

THIRTIETH STREET: V:283

TIMES SQUARE: While searching for a doorway into MID-WORLD, JAKE stops here to rest and is accosted by an officer of the law. He uses his magic key to mesmerize the cop and escape. III:167–69, V:268, V:321, VI:157, VII:405, VII:682

> **CLARK MOVIE THEATER:** VII:682
>
> **DENBY'S DISCOUNT DRUG:** This shop is located in Times Square. JAKE sits across the street from it during his search for a doorway into Mid-World. Denby is part of the pseudonym Jake gives to the policeman he mesmerizes with his magic key. III:169
>
> **GAIETY MOVIE THEATER:** PERE CALLAHAN saw his first TYPE THREE VAMPIRE here. V:268–69, V:274

TOM AND JERRY'S ARTISTIC DELI: *See* LOT, THE, *in* PORTALS

TOOKER'S WHOLESALE TOYS: III:104 *(exact location not mentioned)*

TOWER OF POWER RECORDS: *See* SECOND AVENUE, *listed above*

TURTLE BAY: JAKE's magic LOT is located in an area of Manhattan once known as Turtle Bay. Since the Turtle is one of the GUARDIANS OF THE BEAM, it seems that this area of New York—and the magical ROSE that lives here—is protected by the TURTLE. III:122, V:96, V:97, V:98, V:540, VI:91

> **SECOND AVENUE, EIGHT MAGIC BLOCKS:** *See* SECOND AVENUE, *listed above*

TURTLE BAY LUXURY CONDOMINIUMS: The Turtle Bay Condos are a project planned by MILLS CONSTRUCTION AND SOMBRA REAL ESTATE, an evil company that has no interest in building housing. What they really want to do is own the magic LOT so that they can destroy the ROSE that grows there. III:121, III:264, IV:100, V:96

TURTLE BAY WASHATERIA: Just after visiting ROWAN MAGRUDER in RIVERSIDE HOSPITAL, CALLAHAN was attacked by the HITLER BROTHERS and dragged to this deserted laundromat, located on Forty-seventh Street, between SECOND and FIRST AVENUES. Luckily, CALVIN TOWER and AARON DEEPNEAU saved him from the disgusting duo. V:434–42, V:448, VI:198

TWEENITY (SHOP): III:166

TWIN TOWERS (WORLD TRADE CENTER): In the *when* of 1999, JAKE and CALLAHAN store BLACK THIRTEEN in a locker below the Twin Towers. III:350, V:321, VI:300 *(double towers)*, VI:334–38, VII:147
UNITED NATIONS: III:124,V:266, VI:83, VI:85, VII:405
UNITED NATIONS PLAZA HOTEL: *See* FIRST AVENUE: PLAZA-PARK HYATT HOTEL, *above*
VACANT LOT: *See* LOT, THE, *in* PORTALS
WALL STREET: III:402
  STOCK EXCHANGE: III:350
WORLD TRADE CENTER: *See* TWIN TOWERS, *listed above*
ZABAR'S: Zabar's is a specialty food store. III:297, V:42
QUEENS: III:168, III:265, V:265, V:436, V:443, VII:807

JFK AIRPORT: In order to deliver his cocaine packages to the nefarious BALAZAR, EDDIE has to pass through CUSTOMS at JFK airport. He manages to do so, but only because of Roland's intervention. *(Please note: On the following pages, JFK is mentioned. I have also listed pages where Eddie's plane is sitting on a JFK runway.)* II:57, II:68, II:70–76, II:78–79, II:80, II:81, II:82–84, II:85–90, II:91, II:92, II:96–99, II:118–19, II:127, III:161, V:185, V:525, VI:226, VII:46, VII:119

  CUSTOMS: The Customs officials found in *The Drawing of the Three* suspect that EDDIE DEAN is carrying drugs, so they search for them in rather personal places. Since the packages are on LOBSTROSITY BEACH, they can't arrest him. *(For Customs page references, see the listings under* EDDIE DEAN, *in* CHARACTERS. *For* CUSTOMS *located at Forty-third Street, see* II:118, II:119, and II:127.)
LA GUARDIA AIRPORT: VI:226
REHAB CENTER: V:443
QUEENS MIDTOWN TUNNEL: V:525
RIKERS ISLAND: Rikers Island is the United States's largest penal colony. There are ten jails on the island. Had EDDIE DEAN been caught carrying BALAZAR's coke, he would have ended up at Rikers. II:112
TRIBOROUGH BRIDGE: The Triborough Bridge is a major New York City traffic artery. It connects MANHATTAN, Queens, and the BRONX. III:171, III:292
WESTCHESTER: II:345
MAMARONECK: VII:103

NEWARK
  See NEW JERSEY (STATE OF)

NIAGARA FALLS
  See NEW YORK (STATE OF)

NIAGARA MALL
  See NEW YORK (STATE OF)

NORTH CONWAY
  See NEW HAMPSHIRE (STATE OF)

NORTH WINDHAM
See MAINE (STATE OF): CUMBERLAND COUNTY

NORWAY
See MAINE (STATE OF): OXFORD COUNTY

NORWICH
See CONNECTICUT (STATE OF)

NOTIONS
See MAINE (STATE OF): OXFORD COUNTY: NORWAY

NOTRE DAME
See FRANCE: PARIS

NUTLEY
See DRAWERS, *in* PORTALS

O

ODETTA
See ARKANSAS (STATE OF)

OHIO (STATE OF)
V:255, VI:336, VII:673
AKRON: In Akron, Ohio, in 1935, TED BRAUTIGAN became a murderer. As Ted stood on the corner of STOSSY AVENUE, a brown bag containing a pork chop in his hand, a mugger ran past, drove Ted face-first into a telephone pole, and stole his wallet from his pocket. Enraged, Ted threw a mind-spear at the man. He dropped dead. VII:277, VII:376, VII:657
  STOSSY AVENUE: VII:277–78
    DEFUNCT CANDY STORE: VII:277, VII:283
    MR. DALE'S FANCY BUTCHER SHOP: Ted bought his pork chop here. He never ate it. VII:277
  CLEVELAND: VI:336, VII:669, VII:673, VII:674, VII:676
    JANGO'S NIGHT CLUB: JOE COLLINS (who is actually the were-insect DANDELO) tells Roland and SUSANNAH that he performed his comedy act in this club. VII:669, VII:673, VII:674
  CUYAHOGA RIVER: VII:674
  DAYTON: V:255
  SPOFFORD: V:255

OKLAHOMA (STATE OF)
V:309
ENID: V:309

OLD FRYEBURG ROAD
See MAINE (STATE OF): OXFORD COUNTY: ROUTE 7

OLE MISS
See MISSISSIPPI, UNIVERSITY OF

OMAHA
See NEBRASKA (STATE OF); *see also* ATCHISON, TOPEKA, AND SANTA FE RAILROAD

OREGON (STATE OF)
V:305
FOSSIL: During his years traveling the HIGHWAYS IN HIDING, PERE CALLAHAN passed through Fossil. V:305

ORONO
See MAINE (STATE OF): PENOBSCOT COUNTY

ORRINGTON
See MAINE (STATE OF): PENOBSCOT COUNTY

OXFORD, MAINE
See MAINE (STATE OF)

OXFORD TOWN
See MISSISSIPPI (STATE OF)

P

PACIFIC
VII:286

PAPUA
See NEW GUINEA

PARIS
See FRANCE

PARK ON SECOND AVE
See NEW YORK CITY: MANHATTAN: SECOND AVENUE

PARKLAND MEMORIAL HOSPITAL
See TEXAS: DALLAS

PECOS RIVER
VII:325

PENN STATION
See NEW YORK CITY: MANHATTAN

PENNSYLVANIA (STATE OF)
PHILADELPHIA: Known to those who live there as Philly, this city figures prominently in a song JAKE CHAMBERS sings to scare away the GHOSTS IN THE MACHINES. It goes, "My girl's a dilly/She comes from Philly."
III:336
PITTSBURGH: VII:668
WILKES-BARRE: VII:285

PENTAGON
See WASHINGTON, D.C.

PERTH OIL AND GAS
See NEW JERSEY (STATE OF)

PERU
II:371, V:561

PHILADELPHIA
See PENNSYLVANIA (STATE OF)

PIPER SCHOOL
This was JAKE CHAMBERS's exclusive middle school, located on East Fifty-sixth Street, between Park and Madison Avenues, in MANHATTAN. It was Private and Nice and most of all, White. Jake hated it.
I:81, I:82, III:89–102, III:106, III:110, III:119, III:126, III:131 *(indirect)*, III:134, III:135, III:136, III:156, III:183, III:225, III:358 *(Jake calls it a "Cradle of the Pubes")*, IV:30 *(Piper and Blaine)*, IV:62, IV:626, V:51, V:52, V:502, V:669, V:689, VI:40, VII:85, VII:332, VII:395

PITTSBURGH
See PENNSYLVANIA

PLAZA HOTEL
See NEW YORK CITY: MANHATTAN: FIFTH AVENUE

PLAZA–PARK HYATT
See NEW YORK CITY: MANHATTAN: FIRST AVENUE

POCKET PARK
See NEW YORK CITY: MANHATTAN: SECOND AVENUE

POLAND
AUSCHWITZ: A Nazi concentration camp located near the town of Auschwitz. VII:698

PORTALS
See entry in PORTALS

PORT AUTHORITY
See NEW YORK CITY: MANHATTAN

PORTLAND
See MAINE (STATE OF): CUMBERLAND COUNTY

PUSHING PLACE
See NEW YORK CITY: MANHATTAN

Q

QUEENS
See NEW YORK CITY

QUINCON
II:58

R

RAHWAY
See NEW JERSEY (STATE OF)

RAYMOND
See MAINE (STATE OF): CUMBERLAND COUNTY

RED WINDMILL, THE
See DRAWERS, *in* PORTALS

REFLECTIONS OF YOU
See NEW YORK CITY: MANHATTAN

REINISCH ROSE GARDEN
See KANSAS (STATE OF)

RHODESIA
V:179

RIDGELINE ROAD
See DRAWERS, *in* PORTALS

RIKERS ISLAND
See NEW YORK CITY

RINCON AVENUE
See NEW YORK CITY: BROOKLYN

RIVERSIDE HOSPITAL
See NEW YORK CITY: MANHATTAN

ROCKET ROAD
See MAINE (STATE OF): OXFORD COUNTY: EAST STONEHAM

ROCKY MOUNTAINS (ROCKIES)
The Rocky Mountains stretch from the U.S. border with Mexico to the Yukon
Territory in northern Canada. Their peaks form the backbone of the Conti-
nental Divide, separating the Great Plains from the Pacific Coast. This range
also separates the rivers which flow eastward into the Atlantic from those
which flow westward into the Pacific. JAKE thinks that the mountains beyond
THUNDERCLAP must look like the Rocky Mountains. In actuality, the peaks
of the DISCORDIA resemble the WHITE MOUNTAINS of MAINE and NEW
HAMPSHIRE.
V:149

ROUTE 5
See MAINE (STATE OF): OXFORD COUNTY

ROUTE 7
See MAINE (STATE OF): OXFORD COUNTY

ROUTE 88
See DRAWERS, *in* PORTALS

RUSSIA
III:31, VI:274, VII:290, VII:598

S

SACRAMENTO
See CALIFORNIA (STATE OF)

SAINT ANDREW'S CHURCH
See MAINE (STATE OF): ALTERNATIVE AMERICAS AND THE STATE
OF MAINE: JERUSALEM'S LOT

'SALEM'S LOT
See MAINE (STATE OF): ALTERNATIVE AMERICAS AND THE STATE OF MAINE: JERUSALEM'S LOT

SAN BERDOO
See CALIFORNIA (STATE OF)

SAN FRANCISCO
See CALIFORNIA (STATE OF)

SANTA FE
See MEJIS, BARONY OF: SANTA FE, in MID-WORLD PLACES; see also NEW MEXICO and ATCHISON, TOPEKA, AND SANTA FE RAILROAD, above

SAPPORO
See JAPAN

SCANDINAVIA
VI:84–85

SEATTLE
See WASHINGTON (STATE OF)

SEBAGO LAKE
See MAINE (STATE OF): CUMBERLAND COUNTY: RAYMOND

SECOND AVENUE PARK
See NEW YORK CITY: MANHATTAN: SECOND AVENUE: EIGHT MAGIC BLOCKS: FORTY-SIXTH STREET: POCKET PARK

SHADY GROVE
See MISSISSIPPI (STATE OF)

SILENT WOMAN, THE
See MAINE (STATE OF): KENNEBEC COUNTY: WATERVILLE

SLAB CITY HILL
See MAINE (STATE OF): OXFORD COUNTY: LOVELL

SLEEPY JOHN'S
See CALIFORNIA (STATE OF): SACRAMENTO

SMILER'S MARKET
See NEW YORK CITY: MANHATTAN

SOMBRA REAL ESTATE
See SOMBRA CORPORATION, in CHARACTERS

SOUTH AMERICA
The SOUTH AMERICAN SEABEES were a group of North American engineers, construction workers, and roughnecks hired to work in South America for a group of South American businessmen.
VII:284

SOUTH CAROLINA (STATE OF)
V:232

SOUTH DAKOTA (STATE OF)
V:262
HOT BURGOO: After the bloody Eucharist served to him by BARLOW the VAMPIRE in 'SALEM'S LOT, MAINE, FATHER CALLAHAN was so desperate to leave town that he claims he would even have fled to Hot Burgoo, if he could have hopped on a bus heading in that direction. I don't know whether this place exists, but I can define *burgoo* for you. A burgoo is a hot soup made from chicken, beef, and vegetables. It is cooked for several hours so that the flavors blend and the consistency becomes stew-like. According to the burgoo Web site (yes, there is one), burgoo was probably originally just a thin gruel served by sailors in the seventeenth century. Early burgoos probably also included such tantalizing ingredients as squirrel. V:262

SOUTH PARIS
See MAINE (STATE OF): OXFORD COUNTY

SPAIN
"The rain in Spain falls mainly on the plain." This rhyme is heard in both our world and MID-WORLD, although Mid-World's version is quite a bit longer.
I:71, I:73
COSTA DEL SOL: The Costa del Sol is a resort region located on southern Spain's Mediterranean coast. At the beginning of *Wolves of the Calla*, JAKE CHAMBERS believes that MOSES CARVER (SUSANNAH DEAN's godfather) probably funneled all of Susannah's HOLMES DENTAL INDUSTRIES fortune into his own accounts and moved to the Costa del Sol. (After all, that's the kind of thing that happens in mystery novels.) However, as we learn in the final book of the Dark Tower series, Pop Mose did no such thing. V:102

STATION SHOES AND BOOTS
See NEW YORK CITY: MANHATTAN: SECOND AVENUE

STONEHAM
See MAINE (STATE OF): OXFORD COUNTY

STONEHAM FIRE AND RESCUE
See MAINE (STATE OF): OXFORD COUNTY: EAST STONEHAM

STONEHENGE
See ENGLAND

STOSSY AVENUE
See OHIO (STATE OF): AKRON

STOWE
See VERMONT (STATE OF)

SUNNYVALE SANITARIUM
This is where we will probably all end up one day. JAKE has an especial fear of it.
   III:91, III:92, III:93, III:99

SUNSET COTTAGE
See MAINE (STATE OF): OXFORD COUNTY: EAST STONEHAM: CUL-LUM'S CABIN

SWEDEN (TOWN OF)
See MAINE (STATE OF): OXFORD COUNTY

SWEDEN
   III:100, VI:85, VI:88

SWITZERLAND
   VI:213

T

TANGIERS
See MOROCCO

TENNESSEE (STATE OF)
MEMPHIS: VII:78

TEXAS (STATE OF)
The band ZZ Top was originally from Texas.
   II:396, III:254, V:31, V:305, VII:697
   DALLAS: V:468
      PARKLAND MEMORIAL HOSPITAL: While being driven through Dallas, Texas, in an open car in November of 1963, President JOHN F. KENNEDY was shot by an assassin. He was rushed to Parkland Memorial Hospital, but could not be saved. Two days later, the alleged assassin, Lee Harvey Oswald, was shot at point-blank range by Jack Ruby. In the vivid dream which SUSANNAH DEAN experiences while locked inside the body she shares with MIA, Susannah hears Walter Cronkite announce the president's death. VI:219
   LUFKIN: V:305

THERMOPYLAE
The pass of Thermopylae is located in Greece; it leads between mountains and the sea. Although much wider now, in ancient times it was (at its narrowest) only twenty-five feet across. In 480 BC, the pass of Thermopylae was the site of a famous confrontation between the Greeks and the Persians. Although they were vastly outnumbered, the Greek defenders held the pass against a huge army of invaders. Eventually, all the Greeks were betrayed and killed, but their stand was heroic. JAKE's DIXIE PIG battle strategy is based on the Greek plan used at Thermopylae. Luckily, Jake doesn't die.
VII:85, VII:86, VII:110

TIMES SQUARE
See NEW YORK CITY: MANHATTAN

TISHMAN BUILDING
See MICHIGAN (STATE OF): DETROIT

TOM AND JERRY'S ARTISTIC DELI
See LOT, THE, *in* PORTALS

TOOKER'S WHOLESALE TOYS
See NEW YORK CITY: MANHATTAN

TOPEKA
See KANSAS (STATE OF); *see also* ATCHISON, TOPEKA, AND SANTA FE RAILROAD

TOWER OF POWER RECORDS
See NEW YORK CITY: MANHATTAN: SECOND AVENUE

TRIBOROUGH BRIDGE
See NEW YORK CITY

TURTLE BAY, MANHATTAN
See NEW YORK CITY: MANHATTAN

TURTLE BAY CONDOMINIUMS
See NEW YORK CITY: MANHATTAN

TURTLE BAY WASHATERIA
See NEW YORK CITY: MANHATTAN

TURTLEBACK LANE
See MAINE (STATE OF): OXFORD COUNTY: LOVELL

TWIN TOWERS
See NEW YORK CITY: MANHATTAN

U

UNITED NATIONS
See NEW YORK CITY: MANHATTAN

UNITED NATIONS PLAZA–PARK HYATT
See NEW YORK CITY: MANHATTAN: FIRST AVENUE

UNITED STATES CUSTOMS (U.S. CUSTOMS)
See NEW YORK CITY: QUEENS

UNIVERSITY OF MAINE AT ORONO
See MAINE, UNIVERSITY OF

USSR
III:287

UTAH (STATE OF)
V:305

V

VACANT LOT
See LOT, THE, in PORTALS

VANDERBILT COLLEGE
JOHN CULLUM's friend DON RUSSERT was a history professor at Vanderbilt College before he retired and moved to WATERFORD, MAINE.
VI:151, VI:152, VI:180

VASSAR COLLEGE
JUSTINE ANDERSON and ELVIRA TOOTHAKER, the two women who see BRYAN SMITH careering along ROUTE 7 in LOVELL, MAINE, met at Vassar College.
VII:439–40

VERMONT (STATE OF)
JOHN CULLUM once worked at the MAINE STATE PRISON with a man who later moved to Vermont. When Roland states that it is no longer safe for Cullum to stay in EAST STONEHAM, MAINE (after all, he helped our *tet* battle BALAZAR'S MEN, and those folks aren't exactly forgiving), John says that he will go visit his friend and former coworker. Not surprisingly, Cullum never makes it across the state border. Instead, he helps EDDIE and Roland find CARA

LAUGHS, a magical DOORWAY BETWEEN WORLDS. Roland calls the state of Vermont "Vermong."
> V:308, VI:181, VI:182, VI:211, VII:38 *(Vermong)*, VII:39, VII:41, VII:45, VII:47, VII:128
> **MONTPELIER:** VII:46
> **STOWE:** VI:402

VIENNA
> *See* AUSTRIA

VIETNAM
EDDIE DEAN's bossy older brother, HENRY DEAN, fought in Vietnam. He returned home with a bad knee and a worse drug habit.
> II:169, II:174, II:207, II:239, II:242, II:337–38, V:254, V:264, V:468, VI:136, VI:285, VI:407, VI:409, VII:173

W

WASHINGTON (STATE OF)
> **GRAND COULEE DAM:** The Grand Coulee Dam is located on the Columbia River in central Washington. It is the largest concrete structure in the United States. VI:241, VI:242
> **SEATTLE:** VI:241

WASHINGTON, D.C.
> II:114, VII:116
> **GEORGETOWN:** II:114
> **PENTAGON:** VI:41

WATERFORD
> *See* MAINE (STATE OF): OXFORD COUNTY

WATERVILLE
> *See* MAINE (STATE OF): KENNEBEC COUNTY

WEST VIRGINIA (STATE OF)
> V:302
> **ROUTE 19:** V:302

WESTPORT
> *See* CONNECTICUT (STATE OF)

WHITE MOUNTAINS
New England's White Mountains, located in northern NEW HAMPSHIRE and southwestern MAINE, are part of the Appalachian system. The White Moun-

tains of our world parallel the dry, poisoned mountains of the DISCORDIA in END-WORLD.
VI:397, VII:117

WICHITA
See KANSAS (STATE OF); *see also* ATCHISON, TOPEKA, AND SANTA FE RAILROAD

WILKES-BARRE
See PENNSYLVANIA (STATE OF)

WINDHAM
See MAINE (STATE OF): CUMBERLAND

WISCONSIN (STATE OF)
BELOIT: V:425, V:426, VII:183
FRENCH LANDING: French Landing, Wisconsin, is the setting for the KING/Straub novel *Black House*. Evidently, the nasty WALTER traveled there to get his "thinking cap." Unfortunately for him, the thinking cap (so effective in the DEVAR-TOI) cannot keep baby MORDRED from spying on his thoughts. VII:183
GREEN BAY: V:102

WOOLWORTH'S
See also ALABAMA (STATE OF)
II:64

WORLD TRADE CENTER
See NEW YORK CITY: MANHATTAN

WYOMING (STATE OF)
IV:32

Y

YAZOO
See MISSISSIPPI (STATE OF)

YOSEMITE
See CALIFORNIA (STATE OF)

Z

ZABAR'S
See NEW YORK CITY: MANHATTAN

ZION
VI:319

PORTALS, MAGICAL PLACES, AND END-WORLD PLACES

Beyond the reach of human range
A drop of hell, a touch of strange . . .
Line from a Manni poem, I:127

All is silent in the halls of the dead. All is forgotten in the stone halls
of the dead. Behold the stairways which stand in darkness; behold
the rooms of ruin. These are the halls of the dead where the spiders
spin and the great circuits fall quiet, one by one.
III:76–77

This is a place between . . . a place where shadows are canceled and
time holds its breath.
VI:240

A

ABYSS
According to the *Oxford English Reference Dictionary*,[1] the word *abyss* has several related meanings. They are: 1. A deep or seemingly bottomless chasm. 2a. An immeasurable depth (as in *an abyss of despair*). 2b. A catastrophic situation as contemplated or feared *(his loss brought him a step nearer the abyss)*. And finally, when preceded by the word *the* (as in *the abyss*): 3. Primal chaos, or Hell.

In the Dark Tower series, all of these definitions apply. When Roland first touches the ghostwood box containing BLACK THIRTEEN, the voice of MAERLYN's evil magic ball warns him that if he is not careful, his mind, body, and soul could all be swallowed by its dark magic. "Do you see how little it all matters?" it says. "How quickly and easily I can take it all away, should I choose to do so? Beware gunslinger! Beware shaman! The abyss is all around you. You float or fall into it at my whim."

1. *Oxford English Reference Dictionary*, 2nd ed., rev. (Oxford: Oxford University Press, 2002).

CASTLE DISCORDIA, which abuts the town of FEDIC, is also known as the Castle on the Abyss. The abyss for which it is named is actually a great crack in the earth, located just beyond its adjoining town. This abyss is filled with terrible monsters that cozen, diddle, and plot to escape. Although we cannot be completely certain, it seems likely that these creatures originated in the TODASH darkness located between worlds.

According to MID-WORLD folklore, GAN bore the world and then moved on. If the great TURTLE had not caught the plummeting universe on his back, all of the worlds would have landed in yet another version of the abyss.

Finally, in *The Gunslinger*, JAKE CHAMBERS died for the second time when his adopted father, Roland, let him fall into an abyss located below the CYCLO-PEAN MOUNTAINS. While he fell, Jake uttered the famous phrase "There are other worlds than these." In Jake's case, perhaps the abyss turned out to be yet another DOORWAY BETWEEN WORLDS.

V:317, VI:105 *(Castle on the Abyss)*, VI:295 *(and Turtle)*, VI:299 *(and Jake)*

AFTERLIFE, PLANET
See PLANET AFTERLIFE

**ALGUL SIENTO
See DEVAR-TOI

ALL-A-GLOW
The All-A-Glow is the magical kingdom which children inhabit. As adults, we spend years trying to return to this place.
VII:23

ALLURE
See CASTLE DISCORDIA

ALTERNATIVE AMERICAS
See MULTIPLE AMERICAS, *in* OUR WORLD PLACES; *see also* ALTERNATIVE AMERICAS *and* MULTIPLE AMERICAS, *in* APPENDIX I

ARC 16 EXPERIMENTAL STATION (FEDIC DOGAN)
See DOGAN: FEDIC DOGAN

ARC 16 STAGING AREA
See DOGAN: FEDIC DOGAN

ATCHISON
See KANSAS, *in* OUR WORLD PLACES; *see also* ATCHISON, TOPEKA, AND SANTA FE RAILROAD, *also in* OUR WORLD PLACES

AVEN KAL
See APPENDIX I; *see also* BEAMS, PATH OF THE, *below*

AYJIP
According to the Book of the MANNI, when the Angel of Death passed over
Ayjip, he killed the firstborn in every house where the blood of a sacrificial
lamb hadn't been daubed on the doorposts. The Book of the Manni sounds very
much like the Bible, and this story, which the Manni recount in CALLA BRYN
STURGIS's TOWN GATHERING HALL, is similar to one found in the Book
of Exodus. According to Exodus, God imposed ten plagues upon the Egyptians
because Pharaoh would not release the Israelites from captivity. The smiting of
the firstborn was the tenth of these plagues.
   V:16

B

BADLANDS (CALLA BADLANDS)
   See CALLA BADLANDS

BADLANDS (THE BADS)
   See DISCORDIA

BADLANDS AVENUE
   See DISCORDIA: BADLANDS AVENUE

BANQUETING HALL, THE
   See CASTLE DISCORDIA

BEACH DOORS
   See DOORWAYS BETWEEN WORLDS

BEAM, GARDEN OF THE
   See LOT, THE: GARDEN OF THE BEAM

BEAM PORTALS
   See BEAMS, PATH OF THE, *and* PORTALS OF THE BEAM, *below*

BEAMQUAKE
   See BEAMS, PATH OF THE

**BEAMS, PATH OF THE (BEAM PORTALS, BEAMQUAKE)
In *The Waste Lands*, Roland draws a metaphysical map of his world. According
to this map, MID-WORLD is shaped like a wheel. At the hub of this Earth-wheel
sits the DARK TOWER, the linchpin of the time/space continuum. The spokes
radiating out from this hub are BEAMS. Each end of a Beam terminates in a
PORTAL, which is a doorway leading into, and out of, Mid-World. The twelve
Portals are watched over by twelve animal GUARDIANS.

The six Beams, which connect opposite Portals and which pass through the nexus of the Dark Tower, are like invisible high-tension wires. Their energy can be felt by those who pass close to them, and their stream-like paths can be detected in the movement of nearby clouds. As well as affecting gravity and the proper alignment of time, space, size, and dimension, the Beams hold the Dark Tower in place. Their purpose is to bind the multiverse together while simultaneously holding the separate worlds—which spin upon the Tower like sequins upon a needle—apart. As the Beams break down, and as the Tower becomes unstable, the effects are felt in all worlds. The coherence of the time/space/size continuum weakens and THINNIES appear.

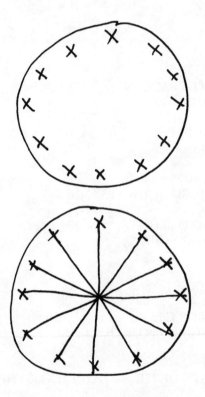

Although the Beams may not be visible in all worlds, they affect all of them. In *The Waste Lands*, JAKE follows the path of the Beam to the MANHATTAN RESTAURANT OF THE MIND and later to the DUTCH HILL MANSION. While Jake follows the Beam in his version of Earth, Roland, EDDIE, and SUSANNAH follow the same Beam from its origin at SHARDIK'S LAIR through the GREAT WEST WOODS and finally on to the GREAT ROAD, which leads southeast toward the decaying and dangerous city of LUD. Along the Path of the Beam, Roland, Susannah, and Eddie use a magical SPEAKING RING—one of the places where the divisions between worlds are thin—to draw Jake into their *where* and *when*. Perhaps the fact that they are on the path of the BEAR-TURTLE Beam makes this drawing easier. In the 2003 version of *The Gunslinger*, Roland follows WALTER (the MAN IN BLACK) southeast. Both of them are drawn in the direction of the Bear-Turtle Beam.

In *Wolves of the Calla*, Roland and his *tet* discover just how far the crazed CRIMSON KING has progressed in his desire to destroy both the Beams and the Tower. For approximately 140 years, the servants of the Red King have been sending robotic WOLF-masked horse-riders into Mid-World's BORDERLANDS to steal one of every pair of prepubescent twins born there. From the brains of these innocent victims, the workers in the FEDIC DOGAN withdraw the chemical which causes twin-telepathy. This chemical is then fed to the psychic BREAK-ERS, whose wild talents are being used to erode the Beams.

Although Roland has experienced only two Beamquakes in his life (Beamquakes are similar to earthquakes, but are caused by the snapping of a Beam), many more must have taken place over the centuries. By the time our *tet* reaches the DEVAR-TOI, the Beams guarded by RAT and FISH, BAT and HARE, EAGLE and LION, and DOG and HORSE have all collapsed. The only two Beams left to hold the Tower in place are our *tet*'s Beam (the Bear-Turtle) and GAN's Beam (the ELEPHANT-WOLF). These two remaining Beams are in place, but they are not healthy, as the wounded and disfigured BEAM BOY can attest. Luckily, Roland and his *tet* manage to destroy the Devar-Toi and stop the terrible erosion of the macroverse's framework before the whole thing comes crashing down. We readers are also assured that the future of the Tower is secure. Either the collapsed Beams will regenerate, or the two existing Beams will generate more Beams to support the macroverse's linchpin.

In the seventh book of the Dark Tower series, we learn that Tower, Beams, and the red ROSES of CAN'-KA NO REY (the Red Fields of None in which the Tower sits) are all part of one living force field. The song and perfume of the Roses feed the Beams, and the Beams, in turn, feed the Roses. Both Roses and Beams spin out from Gan, the living body of the Dark Tower. As Roland approaches his life's goal, he sees two jutting steel posts atop the Tower. The Beams emanate from these posts.

In the novel *The Wind Through the Keyhole*, TIM ROSS follows the LION-EAGLE BEAM from the ENDLESS FOREST to the NORTH FOREST KIN-NOCK DOGAN. This is the same Beam that passes near GILEAD. In *Wind Through the Keyhole* we learn that STARKBLASTS like to follow the Beam Paths. *(For information about the AVEN KAL, or tidal wave along the Beam, see APPENDIX I.)*

III:39, III:73–77, III:80–86, III:122, III:130, III:149–52, III:155, III:158–65 *(following the Beam. Direct references on 158, 164)*, III:166, III:170–76, III:178–82, III:191, III:194, III:219–32 *(following. Directly mentioned on 232)*, III:238, III:243, III:253–70 *(following the Beam. Directly mentioned on 262, 264, 266, 269)*, III:273–301 *(leave the Beam. Directly mentioned on 285)*, III:309 *(Street of the Turtle corresponds to Beam)*, III:310–12, III:331, III:337 *(Grays tunnel follows it)*, III:349, III:350, III:400–420 *(Blaine follows path of the Beam. Directly mentioned on 404)*, IV:3–61 *(Blaine follows path of the Beam. Directly mentioned on 14, 34 electricity at Falls of the Hounds, 49)*, IV:62–78 *(ka-tet follows Beam through Topeka. Directly mentioned on 72)*, IV:79 *(ka-tet falls off the Beam)*, IV:96, IV:659–68, V:8, V:29, V:31, V:36, V:37–47 *(following; 38 near it but not on it, 39)*, V:72, V:93, V:97,

V:99, V:101–69 *(on or near Path; directly mentioned on 101, 110, 121–22, 126, 129, 160)*, V:183, V:192 *(indirect)*, V:193, V:539, V:562, V:563, V:604, V:638, V:660, V:661, VI:3, VI:12–18 *(Beamquake; 14 Beam portals; 16 fish and rat)*, VI:21, VI:33, VI:40, VI:83, VI:108, VI:109–144 *(discussed)*, VI:117, VI:118, VI:148, VI:211, VI:265–303 *(heart of the Beam; 265, barrel of the Beam and King's house)*, VI:318, VI:319, VI:336, VI:353, VI:359, VI:394, VII:17, VII:20–28 *(aven kal—Beamquake; 21 Bear-Turtle Beam; 22 voice of the Beam)*, VII:32 *(Beamquake)*, VII:33, VII:34, VII:40, VII:77, VII:92, VII:117, VII:121, VII:148, VII:150 *(Beamquake)*, VII:188 *(Beamquake)*, VII:195 *(Shardik's portal)*, VII:208, VII:212, VII:214, VII:232 *(Bear-Turtle, Eagle-Lion, Wolf-Elephant)*, VII:234, VII:237, VII:244 *(Shardik/Maturin)*, VII:251, VII:272 *(Bear-Turtle)*, VII:291 *(Bear-Turtle)*, VII:292 *(Wolf-Elephant)*, VII:295 *(Bear-Turtle is Shardik's Beam; Elephant-Wolf is Gan's Beam)*, VII:296, VII:297, VII:300, VII:301 *(Shardik's/Gan's)*, VII:304, VII:305, VII:306 *(Gan, Shardik)*, VII:317, VII:330, VII:333–36 *(Beam Boy)*, VII:360, VII:378, VII:381, VII:387–88 *(Gan's)*, VII:389, VII:391, VII:392, VII:401, VII:406, VII:409 *(Bear/Turtle)*, VII:428 *(Beamquake)*, VII:438, VII:442, VII:455, VII:458, VII:476, VII:477, VII:505, VII:506, VII:518 *(Beamquake)*, VII:551 *(following it toward place of Turtle)*, VII:574, VII:577–803 *(Roland and his companions follow the Beam through the badlands, the White Lands of Empathica, and all the way to the Tower. Page numbers that follow are for direct references)*, VII:582, VII:587, VII:592, VII:593, VII:594, VII:606, VII:609, VII:610, VII:617, VII:620, VII:624, VII:647, VII:658, VII:661, VII:663, VII:670, VII:691, VII:705, VII:706, VII:757, VII:780, VII:782, VII:786, VII:813, VII:819, VII:825, W:3–17 *(Roland and his tet follow)*, W:23–24 *(and starkblast)*, W:220, W:221–55, W:307

BERMUDA TRIANGLE
EDDIE thinks that DAVID QUICK's Nazi airplane arrived from our world via a time/space warp similar to the Bermuda Triangle. Eddie calls this huge doorway between worlds the Roland Zone. The THINNIES, found in both the alternative KANSAS where BLAINE terminates and in the HAMBRY of Roland's youth, also make Eddie think of the Bermuda Triangle. As is purported to happen in the Triangle, people, animals, and machinery can disappear into a thinny and never be seen again.
   III:275, IV:86

BLACK THIRTEEN
   See MAERLYN'S RAINBOW, *in* CHARACTERS

BLUE HEAVEN
   See DEVAR-TOI

BLUETOWN
   See DEVAR-TOI

BOG
   See MID-FOREST (MID-FOREST BOG), *in* MID-WORLD PLACES

BOOM-FLURRY HILL
  See EASTERN PLAIN (CALLA BADLANDS)

BREAKER U
  See DEVAR-TOI

BRIDGE OVER THE ABYSS
  See CASTLE DISCORDIA *and* FEDIC

C

CALLA BADLANDS (EASTERN PLAIN)
Located east of the RIVER WHYE, the dry wastes of the Eastern Plain form a border zone between CALLA BRYN STURGIS and THUNDERCLAP. The CALLA DOGAN is situated here. Although the Calla *folken* maintain that they could once see mountains beyond the Eastern Plain, by the time our *tet* reaches the BORDERLANDS, all that is visible beyond the plain is a vast darkness. The train which returns ROONT children must cross this desert land before it reaches the banks of the Whye.
  V:149, V:153 *(plains)*, V:207, V:386, V:445, V:574 *(region leading to Thunderclap)*, VI:72
  BOOM-FLURRY HILL: The giant, carnivorous, cactus-like BOOM-FLURRY guard this wrecked section of the EAST ROAD, which leads from the RIVER WHYE to the CALLA DOGAN. V:561–62, V:567–68, V:571, V:577
  CALLA DOGAN (NORTH CENTRAL POSITRONICS NORTHEAST CORRIDOR ARC QUADRANT OUTPOST 16): *See* DOGAN, THE, *listed separately*
  DEVIL'S CAUSEWAY: The Devil's Causeway is the train bridge which crosses the RIVER WHYE. The CALLA's ROONT children cross it in flatcars once they are released from THUNDERCLAP. V:562

CALLA DOGAN
  See DOGAN: CALLA DOGAN (NORTH CENTRAL POSITRONICS NORTHEAST CORRIDOR ARC QUADRANT OUTPOST 16)

CAN CALYX
  See DARK TOWER

CAN STEEK-TETE
  See DEVAR-TOI: STEEK-TETE

CANDY HOUSE
  See GINGERBREAD HOUSE

CAN'-KA NO REY
See DARK TOWER

CANNIBAL ISLES
According to EDDIE DEAN, the people of the BORDERLANDS are so civilized that they make the city of LUD, with its warring GRAYS and PUBES, look like the Cannibal Isles in a boy's sea story.
V:135

CARA LAUGHS
See DOORWAYS BETWEEN WORLDS

CASSE ROI RUSSE (LE CASSE ROI RUSSE, LE CASSE ROI ROUGE, COURT OF THE CRIMSON KING, FORGE OF THE KING, RED KING'S CASTLE, CASTLE OF THE KING)
According to the old legends, the CRIMSON KING's castle is called Le Casse Roi Russe. When SUSANNAH DEAN first sees its pulsing crimson glow from the ALLURE of CASTLE DISCORDIA, MIA tells her not to stare at the Forge of the King, since the Lord of Discordia can fascinate, even at a distance.

By the time Susannah, OY, and Roland reach its cobbled forecourt, the forge has been extinguished and the Red King has galloped toward the DARK TOWER, but the castle is not completely deserted. Left to greet the remaining members of our *tet* is an UFFI, or shape-shifter, who has split himself into three and taken on the form of our *kas-ka Gan*, STEPHEN KING (albeit in triplicate). In the end, this false uffi proves not to be a shape-shifter at all, but three servants of the Red King (AUSTIN CORNWELL, BRASS, and COMPTON) disguised by *glammer*.

The Crimson King's wide cobbled forecourt is painted with the king's *sigul*, a staring crimson eye, and is guarded by two deserted watchtowers. Before this outer courtyard is an unpleasant-smelling river (which serves as a moat), and beyond the moat, an inner courtyard. Beyond the courtyard, the castle rises in a jumble of towers, turrets, and walkways, which remind Susannah of turnpike entrances and exits. However, the center of the castle, from which this mind-boggling architecture sprouts, is quite plain, its only decoration being the staring eye carved into the keystone of the main entrance's arch.

As its name suggests, Le Casse Roi Russe is built of deep red stone, which, over the years, has darkened to near black. The sills of its oddly narrow windows are haunted by castle rooks (birds known to feed from bodies of hanged men). Crossing the castle's yellow-foamed moat-river is a humped stone bridge. Here, the false uffis await our friends, and it is here that two of them die under Roland and Susannah's guns.

V:236, V:470, VI:13 *(Court of the Crimson King)*, VI:102 *(Forge of the King)*, VI:105 *(King's Eye)*, VII:47, VII:150, VII:173, VII:300, VII:559, VII:580, VII:581, VII:585 *(Roi Rouge)*, VII:589, VII:590, VII:592, VII:595 *(described)*, VII:599–617 *(600, described)*, VII:618, VII:619–24, VII:625, VII:703, VII:823 *(indirect)*

CASSE ROI RUSSE RIVER: This foul-smelling river flows around a number of fangy black rocks. Its foam is yellow instead of white. VII:597, VII:600

CASTLE TOWN: This evil town surrounds Le Casse Roi Russe. The cottages are narrow and steep-roofed; the doorways are thin and abnormally high. Many of the buildings are haunted by *housies*. VII:590 *(ruined city near castle)*, VII:591, VII:592–600, VII:619, VII:624 *(named)*, VII:630, VII:631, VII:703

CASTLE DISCORDIA (CASTLE ON THE ABYSS, THE LAST CASTLE, MIA'S CASTLE, ROOMS OF RUIN)

The first time SUSANNAH DEAN hears the name of this castle is when it is spoken by her demon possessor, MIA. However, even before she and Mia wander along the castle's ALLURE, Susannah (possessed by Mia) had journeyed to the castle's phantom BANQUETING HALL so that she could feed the CHAP growing inside her. (At the time, we knew of this imposing architectural nightmare only as Mia's castle.) Although throughout much of *Wolves of the Calla* we assume that this castle is a dream place which Susannah-Mio visits to fool herself into thinking that the bog frogs and binnie bugs she eats are actually succulent roasts and caviar, in *Song of Susannah* and *The Dark Tower,* we discover that Castle Discordia is a real place, located deep in END-WORLD.

The version of Castle Discordia which Susannah visits to feed her chap is illuminated by electric flambeaux and has long stone corridors floored with black and red marble. It contains the Rooms of Ruin, which we already know about from EDDIE DEAN's poem fragment, recited first at SHARDIK's portal and then later on his deathbed in the PROCTOR'S SUITE of the DEVAR-TOI. Beneath the castle lie crypts, as well as some slo-trans engines created by NORTH CENTRAL POSITRONICS. From the Allure, or wall-walk around the inner keep, one can see southeast to the FORGE OF THE CRIMSON KING.

In its heyday, Castle Discordia would have been well defended. Behind its inner keep is a terrible drop leading to the huge, needle-like rocks of the DISCORDIA. On the other side of the ruined keep are two towers (one of them broken), and beyond the towers is the deserted village of FEDIC. Beyond the village is an outer wall, and beyond the outer wall is the DEVIL'S ARSE, a great crack in the earth filled with monsters that cozen, diddle, increase, and plot to escape. The bridge that once crossed this abyss exists no longer.

Like Fedic, Castle Discordia is located on the far side of THUNDERCLAP, on the PATH OF THE BEAM, on V SHARDIK, V MATURIN. It is the last castle (besides that of the RED KING himself) before reaching the soot-colored DARK TOWER, which rises in its field of shouting red ROSES. According to NIGEL THE BUTLER, Castle Discordia and the FEDIC DOGAN are connected by underground passages. Together, they contain 595 operational DOORWAYS BETWEEN WORLDS. At least one of these doors leads to TODASH SPACE. Another leads to THUNDERCLAP STATION.

V:71–77 *(Mia is there)*, V:370–76, V:385, V:390, V:391, V:478, VI:79, VI:101–18 *(on the Allure)*, VI:124, VI:229, VI:230, VI:232 *(Allure)*, VI:236, VI:240 *(Allure)*, VI:243, VI:247 *(passages)*, VI:248 *(Rooms of Ruin)*, VI:249, VI:254, VI:255 *(Allure)*, VI:364, VI:371, VI:373, VI:374–76 *(walkway)*, VII:52, VII:67, VII:151, VII:158, VII:531 *(Allure)*, VII:539, VII:540, VII:549, VII:554, VII:560–76 *(tunnels beneath)*, VII:577, VII:580, VII:590, VII:595 *(Allure)*, VII:619, VII:658, VII:808

BANQUETING HALL: For MIA and SUSANNAH, the Banqueting Hall is the most important room in Castle Discordia. Here, the dreaming pair comes to feed the CHAP growing inside their shared womb. The Banqueting Hall is forty yards wide, seventy yards long, and is illuminated by brilliant electric torches in crystal sheaths. It also contains a vast ironwood table laden with delicacies both hot and cold. Before each of the several hundred chairs is a white plate with delicate blue webbing. These plates resemble both the deadly weapons flung by the SISTERS OF ORIZA and the *forspecial* plate given by ODETTA HOLMES's mother to SISTER BLUE. Standing before the Banqueting Hall where Mia/Susannah feasts is a statue of ARTHUR ELD. It is made of chrome and rose-colored marble. Somewhere in this castle stands an old throne drenched in ancient blood. V:71–77, V:83, V:85, VI:174, VI:198, V:370–76, V:478, V:659, V:674, VI:79
DOOR TO TODASH DARKNESS: *See* DOORWAYS BETWEEN WORLDS: MAGICAL DOORWAYS
PASSAGES BENEATH DOGAN AND CASTLE: VII:151, VII:553–54, VII:558–76 *(tunnels beneath)*
ROOMS OF RUIN: V:72, V:371, VI:248, VII:397
ROTUNDA: *See* DOGAN: FEDIC DOGAN
WOLF STAGING AREA: *See* DOGAN: FEDIC DOGAN

CASTLE OF OZ
See OZ

CASTLE OF THE KING
See CASSE ROI RUSSE

CATACOMBS
See DEVAR-TOI

CAVE OF VOICES
See DOORWAY CAVE

CHAYVEN
See RODERICK, CHILDREN OF, *in* CHARACTERS

CLEARING AT THE END OF THE PATH
See entry in APPENDIX I

COFFAH
Coffah is another term for Hell and is a particularly potent Hell for men like Roland. Unlucky adventurers fall into this pit by following the white-robed bitch-goddess who beckons them forward, always assuring them that the goal they seek will be attained. She lures them on and on, and then, once the goal is in sight, she tricks them into the black pit where they must spend eternity—forever seeing, but not reaching, their desire. According to Roland, this goddess will be laughing when the world finally comes to an end.
    VII:265

COURT OF THE CRIMSON KING
See CASSE ROI RUSSE

D

DANDELO'S HOUSE
See EMPATHICA, WHITE LANDS OF

**DARK TOWER (CAN CALYX, HALL OF RESUMPTION)
As every CONSTANT READER knows, the Dark Tower, located deep in END-WORLD, is the focus of Roland Deschain's lifelong quest. (It could also be argued that it is the focus of STEPHEN KING's creative quest as well, since he has been writing about it, in one guise or another, for more than thirty years.)

Sitting in the red field of ROSES known as CAN'-KA NO REY, this looming gray-black edifice rears six hundred feet into the sky. (When one enters it, however, it grows exponentially taller.) Narrow, slit windows emitting an eldritch blue glow decorate its barrel in an ascending spiral. The oriel window at its top blazes with many colors, though its black glass center peers at those who approach like the very eye of TODASH. Two steel posts jut from the Tower's top; the two working BEAMS flow away from their tips, making a great X shape in the sky. The Tower's door is a steel-banded slab of black ghostwood, upon which is the ancient symbol for UNFOUND.

As the linchpin of the time/space continuum, the Tower contains all worlds and all parallel realities within its many levels. Its stairs murmur with the voices of the lost (or damned) souls trapped within it. Throughout the first six books of the series we are left to wonder whether the room at the top contains God or if it's empty.

The line of ELD, of which Roland is the last, is sworn to protect the Tower. Yet a terrible illness affects this structure, one that is often compared to a cancer. As this cancer spreads, THINNIES appear and the divisions between worlds soften.

The Tower is held in place by a network of magical magnetic force-rays known as Beams. There are six Beams that terminate in twelve PORTALS. Each Portal has an animal GUARDIAN. Although some believe that the Tower, Beams, Portals, and Guardians were magical things that preceded the destructive technology of the GREAT OLD ONES, it seems fairly certain that the Old Ones re-created the world according to their own laws, seeking to replace outmoded magic with machinery. Yet machinery, like Man, is mortal. Hence the Beams, Portals, and mechanical Guardians are breaking down. If the weakening Beams collapse and the Tower falls, all creation will blink out of existence.

TOWER ROAD, which follows the course of the BEAR-TURTLE Beam through the WHITE LANDS OF EMPATHICA, leads directly to this most important of edifices. In fact, Tower Road leads directly onto the circular road which encircles the Dark Tower—a road which appears white against the red of the surrounding rose field. Like both Beams and Roses, the Tower sings in a thousand voices. Its song is a musical tapestry weaving together the names of all the worlds.

When Roland approaches the Tower at the end of the final book of the Dark Tower series, the CRIMSON KING (in his human form) has taken possession of one of its many balconies. There he waits with his piled boxes of sneetches, hoping to keep Roland from achieving his life's dream. However, *ka* has other plans. With the help of PATRICK DANVILLE, the young artist whom he and SUSANNAH DEAN rescued from the were-spider DANDELO, Roland *uncreates* the Red King, leaving nothing but his red eyes floating above the balcony's waist-high railings. Once Roland lays AUNT TALITHA's cross, along with his ancient six-shooter, at the Tower's base, the word *Unfound*, written upon its door, becomes *Found*. Roland enters.

Although the Dark Tower appears to be made of gray-black stone, it is actually the body of GAN the creator, initiator of *ka,* and the first being to rise out of the PRIM. However, when Roland enters the Tower and climbs its spiral staircase, what he sees in room after room is not the incarnations of the macroverse's many worlds, but the story of his own life. It seems that the Tower—which welcomed him in its wind-like voice as the son of both GILEAD and Eld—has a lesson to teach him, a lesson which Roland has been slow in learning.

Like the Crimson King, Roland *darkles* and *tincts*. He is eternal and can live in all worlds and all times. However, although he was born to serve the WHITE, at many times Roland has not fulfilled his obligation to the code of Eld. Due to his lack of foresight as well as his ambitious heart and preternaturally fast hands, he has often, unintentionally, served the death-drive of Discordia rather than the cause of life.

The revelation which awaits Roland in the room located at the apex of the Tower is that he has reached the Tower not just once but at the end of many, many long journeys. He is caught in a loop. Each time his hand touches the knob of the Tower's final door—the one marked Roland—he does so without memory, without recall. Yet invariably, this door does not lead him to that silent place where the God of All resides, but to the beginning of his own unquestioning pursuit of the MAN IN BLACK across the wastes of the MOHAINE DESERT.

Like so many of us, Roland is caught in a trap. To escape that trap, Roland must first understand that it is of his own creation. According to Gan, Roland's journey must endlessly repeat because he does not have the HORN OF ELD with him. (He left it on the battlefield of JERICHO HILL next to the body of his dead childhood friend CUTHBERT ALLGOOD.) This lack of foresight, and Roland's inability, at times, to see the long-term consequences of his actions, is one personal fault which Roland must correct before he can reach the true end of his quest.

The second lesson that Roland has to learn before he finds peace is that life itself, not just the blind pursuit of the quest, is valuable. We often think that the ends justify the means, but what Roland finds when he reaches his life's goal is that the means can taint the end. Each Tower room represents an event from Roland's life, but each one contains a loss and a betrayal. What Roland begins to realize as he ascends toward the Tower's top is that every floor is a place of death, but they are like this only because his fast hands and single-mindedness have made them so.

What Roland must learn, if the Tower's topmost door is to lead him to a place of final redemption, is forethought and respect for life. And these are the very two lessons which, over the Dark Tower series, he has struggled to learn. Gone is the man who let JAKE CHAMBERS fall into the abyss below the CYCLOPEAN MOUNTAINS, and who killed all the people of TULL, even his lover ALICE, without guilt. And although Gan will not let Roland's journey end quite yet (*ka* is never so merciful) he acknowledges our gunslinger's progress by allowing him to resume his journey with the horn of his fathers at his hip. To an extent at least, Roland has learned forethought, has learned mercy, has learned (once more) to love. Hence, he has regained the right to wear yet another powerful symbol of the White. Perhaps, then, the story we read in the Dark Tower series is Roland's penultimate journey to the Tower. Maybe, if he is careful, Roland's next journey to End-World will be his last.

I:80–81, I:113, I:130, I:136, I:140, I:151, I:184, I:191, I:200, I:201, I:202, I:204, I:205, I:206, I:207, I:209, I:212, I:213, I:214, I:216, II:30, II:40, II:55, II:101, II:113, II:120–21, II:155, II:156, II:166, II:170, II:177, II:206, II:231, II:307, II:308, II:310, II:311, II:332, II:333, II:362, II:393, II:395–99, III:39, III:40–41, III:49, III:52–53, III:56, III:70, III:71, III:72, III:73–77, III:78, III:82, III:83, III:155, III:158, III:172, III:176, III:191, III:212, III:232, III:238, III:250, III:252, III:262, III:264, III:267, III:268, III:285, III:349, III:389, III:400, III:409, III:410, III:411, IV:9, IV:17, IV:19, IV:27 *(image of Tower's many levels)*, IV:30 *(worlds as levels of the Tower)*, IV:63, IV:66, IV:78–79 *(and thinnies)*, IV:86 *(structural weakness and thinnies)*, IV:86 *(destiny)*, IV:102–3 *(and roses)*, IV:164 *(Roland as a boy, thinking it is the center of all things)*, IV:437, IV:447, IV:552 *(Rhea dreams of it)*, IV:572–73 *(great description)*, IV:580–81, IV:588, IV:601, IV:617, IV:618, IV:621, IV:624, IV:635, IV:648, IV:649, IV:651, IV:658, IV:664, IV:666, IV:667, IV:668, E:157, E:161, E:165, E:207, V:36, V:53, V:56, V:72, V:93, V:105, V:110, V:163, V:170, V:171, V:192–94 *(described)*, V:410, V:413, V:463, V:464, V:465, V:481, V:525 *("along this track of possibility"—on this level of the Tower)*, V:533, V:539, V:555, V:626, V:634, V:660, V:686, V:689, V:706, V:708, VI:13, VI:15, VI:16, VI:17, VI:18, VI:35, VI:38, VI:43, VI:50 *(black tower)*, VI:83, VI:89, VI:91, VI:95, VI:103, VI:106, VI:109–14 *(discussed)*, VI:118, VI:132, VI:147, VI:148, VI:199, VI:200, VI:210, VI:266, VI:269–70, VI:271, VI:275, VI:278, VI:279, VI:280, VI:281, VI:282, VI:283, VI:289, VI:293 *(tower-pent)*, VI:298, VI:302 *(title)*, VI:303 *(title)*, VI:321, VI:339, VI:378, VI:389 *(title)*, VI:390 *(title)*, VI:391 *(title)*, VI:392 *(title)*, VI:393 *(title)*, VI:394 *(title)*, VI:396 *(title)*, VI:398 *(title)*, VI:399 *(title)*, VI:404 *(title)*, VI:407, VI:408 *(title)*, VI:409, VII:16, VII:25, VII:32, VII:37, VII:40, VII:51, VII:76, VII:77, VII:111, VII:112, VII:116, VII:127, VII:138, VII:147, VII:148, VII:150, VII:159, VII:161, VII:169, VII:173, VII:174, VII:175, VII:176, VII:177, VII:179, VII:210, VII:224, VII:228, VII:229, VII:232, VII:238, VII:244, VII:250, VII:253, VII:259, VII:262, VII:266, VII:270, VII:271, VII:279, VII:292, VII:294, VII:296, VII:305, VII:332, VII:338, VII:387, VII:406, VII:410, VII:442, VII:446, VII:447, VII:452, VII:456, VII:483, VII:486, VII:488, VII:506, VII:511, VII:512, VII:513, VII:514, VII:517, VII:519, VII:535, VII:545, VII:550, VII:551, VII:552, VII:555, VII:559, VII:586, VII:588, VII:589, VII:595, VII:606, VII:607, VII:608, VII:609, VII:610, VII:615, VII:616, VII:617, VII:618,

VII:626, VII:630, VII:650, VII:655, VII:662–66 *(painting of it)*, VII:670, VII:672, VI:695, VII:706, VII:710, VII:711, VII:717, VII:718 *(100 miles/120 wheels from the Federal)*, VII:719, VII:720, VII:721, VII:725, VII:727, VII:728, VII:729, VII:740, VII:741, VII:745, VII:747, VII:750, VII:752, VII:753, VII:754, VII:755, VII:756, VII:759, VII:760, VII:762, VII:767, VII:771, VI:772, VII:775, VII:777, VII:779–803 *(begin to see it)*, VII:813, VII:817, VII:818–28, VII:830, W:3, W:31, W:162, W:245, W:253, W:269, W:304

CAN'-KA NO REY (THE RED FIELDS OF NONE; FIELD OF SHOUTING RED ROSES): Can'-Ka No Rey is the great sea of ROSES which grows at the heart of END-WORLD, around the base of the Dark Tower. The single Rose which grows in the Vacant LOT of our world's NEW YORK CITY is an exact replica of one of these roses. However, whereas the song sung by our world's Rose contains a note of discord (or at least it did before our *tet* saved both BEAMS and Tower by destroying the DEVAR-TOI), the song sung by the roses of Can'-Ka No Rey is sweet and pure.

Like the Lot's Rose, the roses which grow in such profusion at the heart of End-World are a light pink shade on the outside but darken to a fierce red on the inside, a shade which Roland believes is the exact color of heart's desire. Their centers, which are called GAN'S GATEWAYS, burn such a fierce yellow that they are almost too bright to look upon. However, this yellow is the yellow of light and love, not destruction. What Roland comes to realize as he travels through their midst is that the roses feed the Beams with their song and perfume, and that the Beams, in turn, feed them. Roses and Beams are actually a living force field, a giving and taking, all of which spins out of the Tower. Interestingly enough, the roses (when mixed with Roland's blood) are the exact color of the CRIMSON KING's eyes. Though in the case of the Red King, the red becomes the color of evil and greed, not pure, living energy. *See* ROSE, *in* CHARACTERS. *For the representation of this field in* KEYSTONE WORLD, *see* GARDEN OF THE BEAM. III:52–53 *(Eddie's dream)*, III:54–55, III:78, III:83, III:267, E:207 *(implied)*, VII:127, VII:447, VII:483, VII:486, VII:488 *(indirect)*, VII:513, VII:550, VII:551, VII:663, VII:666, VII:721, VII:756–57 *(first rose described)*, VII:759, VII:760–81 *(roses begin to grow densely)*, VII:782–803 *(786, they speak)*, VII:818–20, VII:824

LEVEL NINETEEN OF THE DARK TOWER: According to EDDIE DEAN, the KEYSTONE WORLD is level NINETEEN of the Dark Tower. V:525

TOWER KEYSTONE: *See* KEYSTONE WORLDS, *listed separately*

DEEP CRACKS

PRIORESS EVERLYNNE OF SERENITY believed that the SKIN-MAN had divested himself of any remaining humanity. By the time he began slaughtering the people of DEBARIA, he had become nothing more than a monster from the Deep Cracks.

W:48

DERRY

See MAINE (STATE OF): ALTERNATIVE AMERICAS AND THE STATE OF MAINE, *in* OUR WORLD PLACES

DERVA

What little we know about the Derva comes from NIGEL THE BUTLER, a friendly robot who unfortunately looks much like ANDY, CALLA BRYN STURGIS's Messenger Robot. According to Nigel, the FEDIC DOGAN is deserted because most of its workers have moved on to the Derva. He can't explain what the Derva is or what purpose it serves, since such information is classified.

VII:76

DEVAR-TETE

See DOGAN: FEDIC DOGAN

**DEVAR-TOI (ALGUL SIENTO, BLUE HEAVEN, PLEASANTVILLE, BREAKER U, ELMVILLE, THUNDERCLAP STATION)

In the 2003 version of *The Gunslinger*, we see a TAHEEN bird-man in the MOHAINE DESERT. According to the BORDER DWELLER named BROWN, he is looking for a place called Algul Siento. In the final book of the Dark Tower series we find out that Algul Siento means Blue Heaven, but that Blue Heaven's other name is the Devar-Toi, or Big Prison. The Devar-Toi (whose other translation means BREAKER prison) is located in the desert wastes of THUNDERCLAP, the first, sunless region of END-WORLD. It lies on the SHARDIK/MATURIN BEAM and is six miles from Thunderclap Station.

To anyone looking down upon its cheerful blue roofs from the nearby butte, STEEK-TETE, the Devar-Toi looks like a delightful slice of Americana set amid the dry, dead lands of End-World. Half of the Devar is modeled upon a quiet American college campus, and the other half resembles the Main Street of an old-fashioned Midwestern town, complete with a local movie theater and a drugstore/soda fountain.

However, despite its idyllic appearance, the Devar-Toi is a horrible place. Its ground and air are poisonous, a lingering toxicity left over from the deadly gas set off by the mad CRIMSON KING generations before. All who live here—hume, *taheen,* or CAN-TOI—suffer from skin irritations, frequent infections, and general bad health. Since Thunderclap itself has no real sunlight (a permanent darkness left over from the mad king's gas), the daylight which illuminates the compound is artificially generated by an electric (or perhaps atomic) sun. Like everything else in MID-WORLD and End-World, the machinery that runs this false sun is wearing down, hence days usually last more than twenty-four hours and are often disrupted by moments of complete darkness, like a foretaste of the Void.

True to its real name, the Devar-Toi is a prison, not a holiday camp. It employs 180 full-time personnel, all of whom serve the Crimson King and his ultimate goal of destroying the macroverse. Surrounding the campus and town are three runs of electric fence (guarded by humes) and six watchtowers (guarded by armed *taheen*). Both campus and Main Street are watched over by wandering *can-toi* guards, known as floaters.

The purpose of the Devar-Toi is to house (and cage) the psychic Breakers, whose powers are enhanced by the twin-telepathy chemicals culled from the brains of the BORDERLANDS' prepubescent children. Whether they want to or not, the Breakers are forced to use their powerful minds to weaken the BEAMS, which hold the DARK TOWER in place. Unfortunately, few of the Breakers have the moral integrity needed to stand up against their captors' desires. Most are in complete denial, but even those who suspect what they are doing are unwilling to rock the proverbial boat. The food is good, the sim sex is excellent, and most of them were outcasts in the hume world anyway, so why should they care if the universe ends in fire or in ice? However, luckily for our *tet*, a few of the Breakers (including TED BRAUTIGAN, DINKY EARNSHAW, and SHEEMIE RUIZ) find the job they do morally reprehensible. They help Roland and his friends destroy the Devar, saving the Tower, and the macroverse, from almost certain annihilation.

V:573, VII:151, VII:152, VII:153, VII:178, VII:181, VII:207–16, VII:221–46, VII:250, VII:254–59 *(map)*, VII:261, VII:266, VII:272, VII:292–302, VII:309, VII:312, VII:323, VII:325 *(indirect)*, VII:326, VII:329, VII:331, VII:340–42, VII:343–416, VII:421, VII:455, VII:535 *(Blue Heaven)*, VII:559, VII:560, VII:606 *(Algul)*, VII:627 *(algul)*, VII:629 *(dorms)*

BREAKER U: The section of the Devar that resembles a college campus. The BREAKERS' luxurious accommodations are located here, as are the INFIRMARY and the all-important STUDY. VII:209, VII:257

CORBETT HALL (DORMS, PROCTOR'S SUITE): Corbett Hall is one of the Breaker dorms. (SHEEMIE lives here.) After he is fatally wounded, EDDIE DEAN is brought to Corbett's Proctor's Suite. He dies here. VII:267, VII:366, VII:378, VII:387, VII:394, VII:395, VII:396, VII:399, VII:400–404, VII:408–16, VII:411–14

PROCTOR'S SUITE: EDDIE DEAN dies here. VII:394, VII:395–97, VII:400, VII:401–404, VII:408–10

DAMLI HOUSE (HEARTBREAK HOUSE): This large Queen Anne–style house is home to both the CAN-TOI and TAHEEN guards. It also contains the STUDY, the INFIRMARY, and the CAFETERIA. All of the Devar's deep telemetry equipment (which measures psychic activity, among other things) is located here. On Roland's instructions, HAYLIS OF CHAYVEN (a CHILD OF RODERICK) plants two sneetches in Damli. VII:201, VII:209, VII:230, VII:231, VII:232, VII:233, VII:234, VII:235–45, VII:256–57, VII:258, VII:293, VII:300, VII:345, VII:347, VII:349, VII:356–57, VII:358, VII:359, VII:361, VII:362, VII:363 *(indirect)*, VII:366, VII:367–68, VII:370, VII:371, VII:372, VII:373, VII:374, VII:375, VII:389, VII:395, VII:414, VII:577

INFIRMARY: The infirmary is located on the third floor of Damli and is overseen by the much feared DR. GANGLI. V:367–68

THE STUDY: This plush room, which looks much like a richly endowed Victorian gentlemen's club, is located in the center of Damli House. It is a long, high, oak-paneled room decorated with Turkish rugs, Tiffany lamps, and expensive art. Through its glass ceiling, the BREAKERS can see THUNDERCLAP's false sun.

Any guard in a bad mood will jump at the chance to take a stroll onto the Study's third-floor balcony. Watching the Breakers work in their sumptuous room is pleasurable. However, this pleasure doesn't arise from the beauty of the room itself but from the "good mind" vibe which the Breakers exude while they're working. VII:236, VII:239, VII:241–45, VII:272, VII:290, VII:291, VII:295, VII:337, VII:343, VII:353, VII:357, VII:359–61, VII:364

FEVERAL HALL: This Breaker dorm is located directly behind DAMLI HOUSE. Roland instructs HAYLIS OF CHAYVEN, a CHILD OF RODERICK, to plant a sneetch here. VII:349, VII:356, VII:357–58, VII:359, VII:362, VII:371, VII:389

MALL: The Mall is the large green lawn located at the center of the campus section of the Devar-Toi. DAMLI HOUSE and SHAPLEIGH HOUSE both overlook the Mall. VII:224, VII:230–34, VII:236, VII:241, VII:245, VII:343, VII:352, VII:358, VII:371, VII:372, VII:393, VII:400, VII:404–8, VII:411, VII:414, VII:416–17

SHAPLEIGH HOUSE (DEVAR MASTER'S HOUSE, WARDEN'S HOUSE, SHIT HOUSE): This tidy Cape Cod belongs to PIMLI PRENTISS and sits on the opposite side of the MALL from DAMLI. The BREAKERS call it SHIT HOUSE. HAYLIS OF CHAYVEN plants the last of his sneetches in Shapleigh. VII:221–30, VII:245–46, VII:256, VII:258, VII:299, VII:343–49, VII:352–55, VII:358, VII:361, VII:371, VII:377, VII:389, VII:400

PLEASANTVILLE (ELMVILLE): Pleasantville (which our *tet* originally calls Elmville) is the town section of the Devar-Toi. It looks like an old-fashioned Main Street taken from small-town-anywhere, USA. VII:209, VII:255, VII:257, VII:293, VII:299, VII:310–11, VII:327, VII:351, VII:362, VII:363, VII:381, VII:387, VII:399, VII:491

CLOVER TAVERN: Located at the end of Main Street in Pleasantville. After the Devar's final battle (and after EDDIE DEAN is mortally wounded), JAKE CHAMBERS waits here until it is time for him to go to Eddie's deathbed. VII:387–99 *(Jake waits here for Roland's call; his flashback happens here)*

GAY PAREE FASHIONS: VII:370, VII:380

GEM THEATER: VII:210, VII:272, VII:293, VII:370, VII:382

HAIR TODAY: VII:370, VII:381

HENRY GRAHAM'S DRUG STORE AND SODA FOUNTAIN: VII:272, VII:369

MAIN STREET: VII:208, VII:293, VII:299, VII:327, VII:352, VII:369, VII:374, VII:378, VII:379, VII:380, VII:382, VII:387, VII:391

PLEASANTVILLE BAKESHOP: VII:378, VII:380

PLEASANTVILLE BOOKSTORE: VII:369

PLEASANTVILLE HARDWARE: This shop also contains Pleasantville's robotic firemen. VII:363, VII:369

PLEASANTVILLE SHOES: VII:370, VII:380

STORAGE SHEDS: These empty sheds are located north of the Devar, just beyond the electric fence. SUSANNAH hides behind them at the beginning of our *ka-tet*'s attack upon the Breaker prison. V:341, V:349

ROD VILLAGE: The CHILDREN OF RODERICK live in this small, dirty village located about two miles beyond THUNDERCLAP STATION. The Rods do grounds work at the Devar. VII:216

STEEK-TETE (CAN STEKE-TETE): In English, *Can Steek-Tete* means "The

Little Needle." Steek-Tete is a butte located about six or eight miles from THUNDERCLAP STATION. While planning their attack on the Devar-Toi, Roland's *ka-tet* stays in one of the butte's many caves. This hideout was prepared for them by TED BRAUTIGAN and his comrades. VII:203–20 *(setting)*, VII:247–342 *(setting; our* ka-tet *listens to Ted's tapes here)*

THUNDERCLAP STATION: Thunderclap's deserted train station, located approximately six miles from the Devar-Toi, is a green-roofed structure adjacent to a huge, glass-roofed switching yard. Although we do not actually see Thunderclap Station until the final book of the Dark Tower series, it is an ominous, unseen presence as early as *Wolves of the Calla*.

To reach the CALLAS of the BORDERLANDS, the robotic, child-stealing WOLVES travel through a MECHANICAL DOORWAY (located beneath the FEDIC DOGAN) and come out in Thunderclap Station. It is from here that they gallop toward the Callas on their child-stealing mission. After they are made ROONT in the Fedic Dogan's EXTRACTION ROOM, the Callas' ruined children pass through this same door so that they can be loaded onto one of Thunderclap Station's remaining flatcars. This train returns the children to the borderlands so that they can live out the remainders of their brief (and painful) shadow-lives. VII:151, VII:152, VII:153, VII:200–205, VII:206, VII:207, VII:208, VII:213, VII:214, VII:215, VII:221–22, VII:225–26, VII:261, VII:288, VII:297, VII:300, VII:411, VII:531

DEVIL'S ARSE
See FEDIC

DISCORDIA, THE (BADLANDS, THE BADS, NOWHERE LANDS)
The Discordia badlands, located deep in END-WORLD, lie between the southeastern side of CASTLE DISCORDIA and the northwestern edge of the WHITE LANDS OF EMPATHICA. When SUSANNAH DEAN first sees the broken rocks and gaping crevices of the Discordia from Castle Discordia's ALLURE, she thinks it is the most forbidding landscape she has ever seen. Unfortunately for her, she and her *dinh*, Roland, are destined to travel through these poisoned lands on their way to LE CASSE ROI RUSSE, castle of the CRIMSON KING. According to Roland, the badlands were poisoned by the Crimson King himself.

The dead, needle-like mountains of the Discordia are the twinners of our world's beautiful WHITE MOUNTAINS. Interestingly, the term *Greater Discordia* is sometimes used for the PRIM, the magical, chaotic soup from which all life arose.

VI:93, VI:95, VI:98, VI:101–18 *(near castle)*, VI:219, VI:221, VI:222, VI:229, VI:232, VI:234, VI:244, VI:254, VI:290, VI:291, VI:294 *(and Dis)*, VI:295 *(and Dis)*, VI:318, VI:352, VI:353, VI:354, VI:357, VI:374, VI:384, VI:408, VI:409, VII:51, VII:52, VII:76, VII:96, VII:97, VII:127, VII:144, VII:150, VII:223 *(lands beyond Fedic)*, VII:246, VII:259, VII:300, VII:303, VII:378, VII:406, VII:411, VII:533, VII:539, VII:554, VII:577, VII:580–627 *(Badlands Avenue; 588, Nowhere Lands)*, VII:644, VII:658, VII:670, VII:677, VII:709, VII:710, VII:746

BADLANDS AVENUE (KING'S WAY): Badlands Avenue is SUSANNAH DEAN's name for the path which winds through the Discordia. Badlands

Avenue follows the PATH OF THE BEAM. As it nears LE CASSE ROI RUSSE, it is also known as King's Way. VII:580–99 *(591 named King's Way)*, VII:617–19, VII:624–27

DISCORDIA (CASTLE OF)
See CASTLE DISCORDIA

DISCORDIA CHECK-POINT DOGAN
See DOGAN: DISCORDIA CHECK-POINT DOGAN

DIXIE PIG
The first time we hear a reference to the Dixie Pig is when Roland's entire *ka-tet* travels to NEW YORK CITY via TODASH. Written on the fence surrounding the Vacant LOT, located on FORTY-SIXTH STREET and SECOND AVENUE, is the following rhyme: "Oh, SUSANNAH-MIO, divided girl of mine, Done parked her RIG in the Dixie Pig, in the year of '99." Our second hint that the Pig will play an important part in our tale comes while Mia hunts for food in CASTLE DISCORDIA's deserted BANQUETING HALL (a dining room which is, in reality, just the JAFFORDS FAMILY barn). While Mia struggles with *sai* RAT over a suckling pig, we see that she is wearing a Dixie Pig T-shirt.

In *Song of Susannah,* we learn that the Dixie Pig is a restaurant located on LEXINGTON AVENUE and SIXTY-FIRST STREET in New York City. According to a *todash* version of *Gourmet* magazine, they have the best ribs in town. Unfortunately, the ribs are human, and the high-class clientele are actually the GRANDFATHERS, those hideous TYPE ONE VAMPIRES left over by the receding PRIM. Besides its two dining rooms (the second of which is secreted away behind a blasphemous tapestry depicting ARTHUR ELD's court partaking in a cannibal feast), the Dixie Pig contains a kitchen, a pantry, and an underground tunnel containing a MIND-TRAP. Beyond the mind-trap is a MECHANICAL DOORWAY leading to the FEDIC DOGAN.

V:183, V:376 *(Lexington and Sixty-first)*, V:648, VI:120 *(Sixty-first and Lexington)*, VI:125, VI:143, VI:227, VI:229, VI:254, VI:255, VI:256, VI:317, VI:320, VI:327, VI:333, VI:334, VI:337, VI:339, VI:340–44 *(Jake and Callahan outside)*, VI:360–78 *(through door!)*, VI:382, VII:3, VII:4–16, VII:23 *(via aven kal)*, VII:25–28 *(via aven kal)*, VII:32, VII:34, VII:81–112 *(86—mind-trap; 87–112—tunnel beneath Dixie Pig)*, VII:133–38 *(tunnel beneath Dixie Pig)*, VII:145, VII:146, VII:147, VII:152, VII:297, VII:303, VII:309, VII:522–29, VII:531, VII:538

MIND-TRAP: To guard the NEW YORK/FEDIC DOOR, the GREAT OLD ONES fitted the Dixie Pig's subterranean tunnel with a mind-trap, which, when activated, will (quite literally) stop unwanted visitors dead in their tracks. This mind-trap accesses a person's deepest and oldest fears, then makes those fears manifest. Of course, the vision is an illusion, but the body reacts to the visual stimuli as if they were real and the victim dies of heart failure. When JAKE and OY travel through the mind-trap, Jake sees the dinosaur-infested landscape of a film entitled *The Lost Continent.* Oy saves Jake's life by switching places with him. Taking over Jake's body, Oy carries his friend (who is hiding in his own furry skin) to safety. VII:81–112

DOGAN, THE

The first time we encounter the term *Dogan,* it is merely a misprinted title on the cover of one of CALVIN TOWER's rare books. (*The Dogan,* which is supposed to read *The Hogan,* was a Western novel written by our world's version of BEN SLIGHTMAN JR.) Although, in our world, the word *Dogan* is no more than a typing error, in END-WORLD it has a particular and sinister meaning.

End-World's Dogans are a series of military-like control centers and are shaped like Quonset huts. (As any CONSTANT READER knows, STEPHEN KING's Quonset huts are invariably nasty places.[1]) In these Dogans, technology still works. Some of these Dogans (such as the CALLA DOGAN) are used as spy centers for the CRIMSON KING's followers in THUNDERCLAP. In others, such as the FEDIC DOGAN, magic and technology can be merged. The series of Dogans which run along the BEAR-TURTLE BEAM were built by the OLD ONES' sinister company NORTH CENTRAL POSITRONICS. V:532 *(Tower's rare book),* V:533 *(rare book),* V:552 *(rare book),* V:553 *(chapter title),* VI:32

CALLA DOGAN (NORTH CENTRAL POSITRONICS NORTHEAST CORRIDOR ARC QUADRANT OUTPOST 16): The Northeast Corridor Arc Quadrant Dogan is the END-WORLD control center located on the THUNDERCLAP side of the DEVAR-TETE WHYE. JAKE CHAMBERS and his pet BILLY-BUMBLER, OY, discover it when they follow BEN SLIGHTMAN SR.'s backtrail through the CALLA BADLANDS. (Jake and Oy had seen Ben senior and ANDY, the CALLA's devious Messenger Robot, holding a suspicious conversation near the Whye.)

What Jake discovers is that CALLA BRYN STURGIS is full of secret cameras, and that all of these images are projected onto monitor screens in the Dogan. From this Northeast Corridor Arc Quadrant Outpost, Ben Slightman and Andy report useful information about hidden children to FINLI O'TEGO, chief of security at the DEVAR-TOI. Obviously, Finli then feeds this information to the invading WOLVES. V:561–78, V:582 *(indirect),* V:656, V:678, V:702–3, VI:64 *(should say on east side of River Whye),* VI:67, VI:171, VI:247 *(Jake's Dogan),* VII:151, VII:191

DISCORDIA CHECK-POINT DOGAN: SUSANNAH DEAN and Roland Deschain discover this Quonset hut in the wastelands of the DISCORDIA. (It sits next to the crumbling hillside arch where CASTLE DISCORDIA's subterranean tunnels exit into the open air.) This Quonset hut looks similar to the ARC 16 Experimental Station found across the WHYE from CALLA BRYN STURGIS, only it is smaller and in even worse shape. The roof of the Discordia Check-Point Dogan is covered with rust, and piles of bones are scattered in a ring around its front. Both Roland and Susannah think that it was the site of a terrible battle. VII:577–80, VII:620

FAGONARD SWAMP CHARGING STATION: According to DARIA, the NORTH CENTRAL POSITRONICS Portable Guidance Module, there is no Dogan in the Fagonard, but there is a Charging Station. W:222

FEDERAL OUTPOST 19: TOWER WATCH (THE FEDERAL): Federal

---

1. In the novel *Desperation,* Diablo Mining has its headquarters in a Quonset hut in the Nevada desert. The military experiment stations, where the superflu virus was developed in *The Stand,* were Quonset huts.

Outpost 19 (which the robot STUTTERING BILL refers to as the Federal) sits on the edge of the WHITE LANDS OF EMPATHICA. Like all the other Dogans, it is a lonely-looking Quonset hut. The Federal is located 120 wheels from the DARK TOWER. Until the CRIMSON KING took up residence on one of the Tower's balconies and blew the observation cameras, one of the Federal's TV surveillance screens projected images of that linchpin of the worlds. VII:709, VII:715, VII:717–22, VII:801, VII:803

FEDIC DOGAN (NORTH CENTRAL POSITRONICS LTD, FEDIC HEAD-QUARTERS, ARC 16 EXPERIMENTAL STATION; THE DOGAN OF ALL DOGANS): According to MIA, the Fedic Dogan is the Dogan of all Dogans. Located deep in the heart of END-WORLD, it was once the Fedic headquarters of NORTH CENTRAL POSITRONICS. Just as we readers have long suspected, the GREAT OLD ONES' company learned how to fuse the magic of the PRIM with their own rancid technology, and the Fedic Dogan was a center for such dangerous research. Once there may have been many such magical/technological Dogans in IN-WORLD, MID-WORLD, and End-World, but by the time our story begins, the Fedic Experimental Station is the only outpost of its kind left. To Mia, it is a place both wonderful and terrible.

As the followers of the CRIMSON KING know all too well, at the Fedic Dogan, magic and technology can still be merged. This Dogan's technological magic made possible Mia's transformation from spirit to flesh. This Dogan's technological magic also made the conception and birth of MORDRED (child of four parents) possible.

Although we do not know the original purpose of the Fedic Dogan, like most of the other wreckage left by the Old Ones, it is now being used for evil ends. Several centuries after the Red Death decimated Fedic's human population, the Crimson King's servants began to use this experimental station to extract the twin-telepathy enzyme from the children of the BORDERLAND CALLAS. They did this in the EXTRACTION ROOM, which is also the room in which Mia gives birth to Mordred. Roland calls this place *devar-tete* or "little torture chamber."

The Fedic Dogan is connected to CASTLE DISCORDIA by a series of subterranean tunnels. According to NIGEL THE BUTLER, the Fedic Dogan and the adjacent castle contain 595 operational DOORWAYS BETWEEN WORLDS. At one time, 30 one-way doors connected Fedic to NEW YORK CITY, but after Door #7 (leading to the Extraction Room) burns out, all that is left is Default Door #9, located in the ROTUNDA. VI:237–38, VI:244–45, VI:247, VI:249, VI:251, VI:378–84, VII:21–23 *(Extraction Room via aven kal)*, VII:27, VII:55–80 *(77–80 Rotunda)*, VII:141–96 *(141–58 Extraction Room setting)*, VII:206, VII:222, VII:232, VII:532, VII:537–40, VII:549–52 *(kitchen, pantry, office)*, VII:553, VII:557, VII:558–70 *(tunnels under Discordia; 559 Rotunda; 563 Main Street)*, VII:591, VII:708

> **CONTROL CENTER ("THE HEAD"):** The Arc 16 Experimental Station's nerve center is located four levels down from the EXTRACTION ROOM. During his short stay in the Fedic Dogan, baby MORDRED installs himself here so that he can view the Dogan's many monitors. (He uses them to spy on Roland's *ka-tet*.) Mordred kills and eats WALTER here. VII:159–64, VII:166–86

EXTRACTION ROOM: According to Roland, the Extraction Room's true name is the *devar-tete,* or "little torture chamber." The NEW YORK/ FEDIC door (#7), which SUSANNAH is dragged through at the end of *Song of Susannah,* leads directly to this room. The Extraction Room gained its terrible name from the awful procedures done on its many beds. The BORDERLANDS children were brought to this room so that the twin-telepathy chemical could be extracted from their brains. MORDRED was also born here. VI:378–84, VII:21–23, VII:27 *(indirect),* VII:55–75, VII:141–58

NIGEL'S QUARTERS: Nigel's three-room apartment is located near the Fedic Dogan's kitchen. It contains no bedroom, but it does have a living room and a butler's pantry full of monitoring equipment. It also contains a book-lined study. Nigel is a big fan of STEPHEN KING's novels. VII:158–59, VII:164–66, VII:189–90, VII:538

ROTUNDA: Deep below the Fedic Dogan and CASTLE DISCORDIA is a Rotunda, whose shape reminds SUSANNAH DEAN both of GRAND CENTRAL STATION in NEW YORK CITY and of BLAINE'S CRADLE in LUD. Around the circumference of this rotunda are a series of doors that lead to other *wheres* and *whens.* Among them are portals labeled SHANGHAI/FEDIC, BOMBAY/FEDIC, DALLAS (NOVEMBER 1963)/ FEDIC, and NEW YORK/FEDIC. All these doors are one-way. *(For more information, see DOORWAYS BETWEEN WORLDS, listed separately.)* VII:77–80, VII:559

STAGING AREA: Deep in the entrails of the Fedic Dogan, our *tet* finds a hangar-sized door marked *To Horses.* Beyond this is a door marked *Staging Area.* When our *tet* enters this staging area, they find that it is thick with hanging WOLVES awaiting repair, as well as the utility bays used to fire them up. To the left of the utility bays is the DOORWAY leading to THUNDERCLAP STATION. VII:192–96, VII:207, VII:232

JAKE'S MIND-DOGAN: While trying to escape the CRIMSON KING's gunbunnies in the tunnels below the DIXIE PIG, Jake feels an unseen hand fiddling with his mind's control center. He slams all doors shut, but the damage has been done. By the time Jake realizes what has happened, the OLD ONES' MIND-TRAP has already located a memory which it can use to scare Jake to death. (The memory is of a dinosaur film called *The Lost Continent.*) The only way Jake survives the mind-trap is by switching bodies with OY. Oy's mind-Dogan isn't affected by the Old Ones' machinery. In fact, he finds the controls of Jake's mind-Dogan to be much more mesmerizing. Luckily, he ignores them. VII:88 *(mind-trap),* VII:101 *(Oy)*

NORTH FOREST KINNOCK DOGAN (NORTHERN AERIE, GATEWAY OF OUT-WORLD): The Dogan closest to the FAGONARD swamp was the North Forest Kinnock Dogan. When the NORTH CENTRAL POSITRON- ICS guidance module, DARIA, located it for TIM ROSS, the Dogan was already off-line. Although Daria recommended detouring around the Dogan (she detected a magical disturbance at that location as well as a Changed Life form), Tim decided to visit it. Luckily he did, since he found the magician MAERLYN there (albeit in the form of a caged TYGER), and shelter from the approaching STARKBLAST.

The round, metal-roofed Dogan sat in a large clearing amid a stand of IRONWOOD trees, at the base of a huge tower made of metal girders. Atop the tower was a blinking red light. Small windows, made of very thick glass, marched around the building's sides at the height of Tim's head. The door was made of metal, but had no knob or latch, only a slot like a narrow mouth. Above the slot, on a rusting steel plate, were the following words, written in a strange mixture of High and Low Speech:

NORTH CENTRAL POSITRONICS, LTD.
North Forest Kinnock
Bend Quadrant
OUTPOST 9
Low Security
USE KEYCARD

Scrawled below this was a single phrase: ALL HERE ARE DEAD. At the base of the door was a box that looked like a metal version of NELL ROSS's trinket box. The box was locked, and was so heavy that Tim could not lift it. The box's keyhole was shaped like the High Speech letter for "S." Engraved on the box top were words in a language that Tim could not read.

The Dogan's clearing ended in a rocky precipice a hundred wheels wide, but the clearing was crossed by a path paved in a smooth dark material so bright that it reflected the trees and the clouds. To the left of the metal road, about three yards from the place where the world dropped off into nothingness, there stood a round cage made of steel bars. Inside the cage was an enormous green-eyed TYGER. Around the tyger's neck was a silver collar from which hung a keycard and a key. Beneath a silver bucket, located just in front of the cage, was a note from the wicked COVENANT MAN, and a key to the tyger's cage. The keys to both the Dogan and the box hung from the tyger's collar. Although faced with a decision as awful as that in the folktale, DIANA'S DREAM, Tim decided to open the tyger's cage. His kindness paid off, as the tyger's key opened the metal box, and the tyger himself showed Tim how to use the magic DIBBIN within to create a shelter from the approaching starkblast. After the storm passed and Tim helped the tyger transform back into his wizard-shape, the sorcerer gave Tim magic drops to restore his mother's sight. W:222, 232–55

CLEARING WITH ENORMOUS TOWER AND BLINKING BEACON (NORTH FOREST KINNOCK DOGAN CLEARING): Soon after escaping the TENTACLED MONSTER in the CHASM OF WHITE FLOWERS, TIM ROSS saw this enormous clearing ahead of him, at the end of a long upslope. From three wheels distant, the most prominent feature of this clearing was its tall tower, made of metal girders, which was topped by a blinking red light. Later, when he drew closer, he realized that the tower and clearing were both part of the NORTH FOREST KINNOCK DOGAN. W:232

SUSANNAH'S MIND-DOGAN: This Dogan, which actually exists within SUSANNAH DEAN's mind, is a version of the CALLA DOGAN, which JAKE CHAMBERS entered in *Wolves of the Calla*. (Susannah uses a visualization technique to create it.) Susannah's Dogan acts as a kind of inner control room. From this place she can see the CHAP growing inside her body, and can control (or at least regulate) the birth contractions racking her body. She can also use this control room to send urgent psychic messages to EDDIE DEAN. Much to Susannah's dismay, some of the Dogan's machinery is stamped with the NORTH CENTRAL POSITRONICS insignia. VI:62, VI:64, VI:67–72, VI:82, VI:89, VI:107, VI:124, VI:150, VI:171, VI:210, VI:222–29 *(Susannah in it)*, VI:247, VI:259–60, VI:321, VI:348, VI:351 *(gulag)*, VI:357–61, VII:142, VII:182, VII:239

UNDERGROUND TUNNELS OF THE OLD ONES: According to the ferryman BIX, this maze of tunnels between the GREEN PALACE and the RIVER WHYE stretched for miles. Although we can't say for certain, it seems likely that these underground tunnels were once a type of bunker or Dogan. When Bix visited the tunnels, he saw hundreds of *artyfax* that had belonged to the OLD PEOPLE and heard strange, tooth-rattling music playing from overhead speakers. Unfortunately, after visiting the place Bix broke out in sores, puked, and started to lose his teeth. W:12

WALTER'S MIND-DOGAN: According to baby MORDRED, the controls in Walter's mind-Dogan are similar to the ones in SUSANNAH'S MIND-DOGAN. However, instead of switches labeled *Emotional Temp* and the *Chap*, Walter's switches control functions such as ambulation. Mordred turns this latter switch off. VII:182.

WAYPOINT NINE: According to DARIA, the NORTH CENTRAL POSI-TRONICS Portable Guidance Module that the MUTANT FAGONARD TRIBE gave to TIM ROSS so that he could find the sorcerer MAERLYN, Waypoint Nine was located in the FAGONARD swamp. We never discover exactly what Waypoint Nine might be, but it was definitely related to the Dogans. (According to Daria, there was no Dogan in Fagonard swamp, but there was a charging station.) W:222

YOUNG THROCKEN'S MIND-DOGAN: According to baby MORDRED, the machinery inside a young BILLY-BUMBLER's mind-Dogan is no more complicated than a series of granny knots. OY might disagree. VII:164, VII:182

DOORWAY CAVE (CAVE OF VOICES, KRA KAMMEN)
CALLA BRYN STURGIS's Doorway Cave, high in the garnet-veined hills of the BORDERLAND'S ARROYO COUNTRY, plays a major part in *Wolves of the Calla* and *Song of Susannah*. Located about three hours north of Calla Bryn Sturgis and an hour north of MANNI CALLA, this cave contains two significant magical features. The first, situated about twenty feet from the cave's mouth, is the freestanding UNFOUND DOOR *(for more information about the Unfound Door, see DOORWAYS BETWEEN WORLDS, listed below)*. The second, placed much deeper in the cave, is the noxious-smelling Pit of Voices. Before the sudden appearance of the magical Unfound Door (which came to the Calla at the same time as FATHER CALLAHAN), this nasty cavern was known to the people of Calla Bryn Sturgis as the Cave of Voices. To the MANNI folk, it was Kra Kammen, or the House of Ghosts.

As HENCHICK, the Manni *dinh*, warns Roland, the twisting arroyo PATH which leads to Doorway Cave is "rather upsy." The cave itself is not much more welcoming. Its ragged mouth, measuring nine feet by five feet, is partially blocked by a fallen boulder, so to enter it a seeker must ease his way around this huge stone, letting his heels hang over a two-thousand-foot drop. Once inside, the seeker is assailed by the Pit's noxious fumes, as well as the terrible voices which rise from it, accusing him of any misdeed (real or imaginary) which he has ever committed.

The chasm known as the Pit of Voices functions as a kind of distorted psychic mirror. It is almost as if the cave (or some entity or mechanical device haunting the cave) can hear the voices that play through an individual's mind. When a person stands in the cave, all of his ghosts scream up from the depths of the pit, accusing him of all his most painful failings and awful wrongdoings.

Despite the horror of the Pit of Voices and the dangers of using BLACK THIR-TEEN (MAERLYN's evil magic ball, which opens the otherwise locked Unfound Door), in *Wolves of the Calla* and *Song of Susannah*, every member of our *tet* travels to this cavern. EDDIE uses the Unfound Door to travel to NEW YORK CITY, circa 1977. Pere Callahan travels through it to visit both New York City and EAST STONEHAM, MAINE. At the end of *Wolves of the Calla*, SUSAN-NAH DEAN (controlled by her demon, MIA) wheels her way up to the cave so that Mia can escape through the door to 1999 New York, where she is destined to bear her CHAP. (In this final instance, Mia takes Black Thirteen with her.)

At the beginning of *Song of Susannah*, Roland, Eddie, JAKE, OY, and Calla-han travel to the Doorway Cave once more. Although the door initially seems to have lost its magic, and though the voices in the Pit of Voices seem to have tipped over into complete insanity, our *tet* (with quite a bit of help from the Manni) manage to use the Unfound Door two more times. Jake, Oy, and Callahan are propelled to 1999 New York, to pursue Susannah-Mio. Roland and Eddie are sent to East Stoneham, Maine (circa 1977), to track down CALVIN TOWER.

V:335, V:399–400, V:407 *(indirect)*, V:408–16 *(two thousand feet up; 408–10 described; 411 previously Cave of Voices)*, V:421, V:458–65 *(Unfound Door only)*, V:466, V:468, V:505, V:508, V:509–48 *(Roland waiting there)*, V:549, V:550–51 V:573, V:584, V:590–600 *(door)*, V:618–27, V:642, V:687, V:699, V:702, V:703–9, VI:3–8 *(under discussion)*, VI:12, VI:21, VI:26 *(cave)*, VI:28–43 *(34 kra kammen means "house of ghosts")*, VI:49 *(indirect)*, VI:64, VI:80–82, VI:122 *(Unfound Door)*, VI:124, VI:129, VI:142, VI:164, VI:167, VI:307, VI:308, VII:36 *(Cave of Voices)*, VII:88 *(Cave of Voices)*, VII:123 *(Unfound Door)*, VII:143, VII:196, VII:239, VII:416, VII:447 *(inside sai King's head)*, VII:540, VII:743

DOORWAYS BETWEEN WORLDS

Both MID-WORLD and KEYSTONE EARTH contain numerous doorways between worlds. These doorways can be divided into two types—MAGICAL and MECHANICAL. Magical doorways can be formed either from the same sub-stance as the PRIM (the magical soup of creation), or from the magical tension between two people. STEPHEN KING's home, CARA LAUGHS, is an example of the first type of magical door. The BEACH DOORS through which Roland drew EDDIE and SUSANNAH DEAN are examples of the latter. Most magical doors are two-way. Others (such as the UNFOUND DOOR found in the BOR-

DERLANDS) are doors to anywhere. What world or time period they open onto depends completely upon the mind-set, and desire, of the user.

Unlike Magical Doorways, Mechanical Doorways are *dedicated*. In other words, they always open onto the same location, if not the same time period. The majority we see in the Dark Tower series were created by the GREAT OLD ONES' sinister company NORTH CENTRAL POSITRONICS. Few are in good working order. Unlike Magical Doorways, most Mechanical Doorways are one-way only. Both NEW YORK CITY and the subterranean tunnels joining the FEDIC DOGAN with CASTLE DISCORDIA are lousy with Mechanical Doorways.

GENERAL REFERENCES: III:43, III:52 *(Eddie's dream door—Tom and Gerry's)*, III:62 *(Walter's door)*, III:261, III:275, V:72 *(indirect)*, V:89, V:97, V:102, V:104, V:105–6 *(doors you can aim in time)*, VI:40–41 *(Jake must imagine them)*, VI:147 *(need to find one)*, VI:247–48, VI:251 *(Mia's doorway to mortality)*, VII:73–74 *(595 doorways in Castle Discordia and Fedic Dogan)*

MAGICAL DOORWAYS:

ARTIST'S DOOR (UNFOUND DOOR, EBERHARD-FABER DOOR): *See* UNFOUND DOOR, *below*

BEACH DOORS (WESTERN SEA): In *The Drawing of the Three*, Roland Deschain encountered three magical Beach Doors. These doors, located on the LOBSTROSITY-infested beach of the WESTERN SEA, were the result of the magical tension that existed between Roland and his nemesis WALTER. The first door, labeled *The Prisoner*, led him to heroin-addicted EDDIE DEAN. The second, labeled *The Lady of Shadows*, opened into the mind of ODETTA HOLMES/DETTA WALKER. The final door, named *The Pusher*, led to the exceedingly seedy personality of the sociopath JACK MORT. (At different times, Mort tried to kill both Susannah Dean and JAKE CHAMBERS. Hence, he was tied to Roland's *ka-tet*.) All three of these doors were made of ironwood and stood six and a half feet tall. None had any visible support. III:38, III:62, IV:44, V:105, V:409, V:410 *(indirect)*, V:411, V:478, V:479, V:597, VII:177, VII:560, VII:724, VII:741

> **DOOR #1 (THE PRISONER):** II:32, II:33–40, II:44, II:54, II:55, II:62–63, II:72 *(72–82 it is present)*, II:82, II:92–95, II:99, II:100–102, II:135–43, II:156–57, II:259, II:268–69, III:41
>
> **DOOR #2 (THE LADY OF SHADOWS):** II:178 *(Roland sees)*, II:179–82, II:245, II:256–57, II:259, II:268–69, II:306, III:41
>
> **DOOR #3 (THE PUSHER):** II:259, II:268–69, II:286–96 *(looking for it)*, II:300–312, II:325, II:328, II:329, II:332, II:385–87

BEAM PORTALS: *See* BEAMS, PATH OF THE, *listed separately*

BLACK THIRTEEN: *See* MAERLYN'S RAINBOW, *in* CHARACTERS

CARA LAUGHS: Cara Laughs is the name of the house located at 19 TURTLEBACK LANE in LOVELL, MAINE. In 1979, two years after JOHN CULLUM takes EDDIE and Roland there so that they can transport themselves to the subterranean tunnels below the 1999 DIXIE PIG, STEPHEN KING purchases it. Obviously, either King has a nose for magic, or magic has a nose for him.

Like the BEACH DOORS, Cara Laughs is a magical doorway. However, unlike them, it is created not by the magical tension between two people but from the pure, undifferentiated magic of the PRIM. The Cara Laughs Doorway is the source of the many WALK-INS found throughout western Maine and northern NEW HAMPSHIRE. The name *Cara Laughs* is very similar to SARA LAUGHS, the summer home of Mike Noonan, the main character of *Bag of Bones*. VI:394–95, VI:397, VI:403, VI:405, VI:408, VI:410, VII:116–17, VII:129–32, VII:304, VII:435–39, VII:441–43, VII:444, VII:446, VII:453, VII:463 *(indirect),* VII:542–45

CHEWING DOOR: This doorway (and its hidden chewing monster) is located in the tunnels beneath the FEDIC DOGAN and CASTLE DISCORDIA. VII:560–61

DOOR TO EVERYWHERE: *See general entry for* DOORWAYS BETWEEN WORLDS, *listed above*

DOOR TO TODASH DARKNESS: This door is located beneath CASTLE DISCORDIA. The CRIMSON KING sends his worst enemies through it to be devoured by TODASH's many hideous monsters. VI:248–49

DOORWAY CAVE: *See* DOORWAY CAVE, *listed separately*

GREEN PALACE: *See* GREEN PALACE, *listed separately*

JAKE'S DOOR (DOOR #4: THE BOY): *See* MANSION DOOR, *below, and* STONE CIRCLES (SPEAKING RINGS): SPEAKING RING ALONG THE PATH OF THE BEAM, *listed separately*

MAERLYN'S RAINBOW (THE BENDS O' THE RAINBOW): *See* MAERLYN'S RAINBOW, *in* CHARACTERS

MANSION DOOR (JAKE'S DOOR): Located on RHINEHOLD STREET in DUTCH HILL, BROOKLYN, this haunted Mansion sits only one mile from where EDDIE DEAN grew up in CO-OP CITY. It also happens to sit on the PATH OF THE BEAM. Like many magical places, the Mansion is not really a mansion at all but a portal between worlds that shifts shape from reality to reality and TOWER level to Tower level. In JAKE's world it most certainly looks like an imposing building, but in Roland's world it is the haunted force within a SPEAKING RING. All that Eddie has to do to let Jake pass through this portal—and be born into MID-WORLD—is to connect these two thin places with a drawn door. Unfortunately, the door is locked and both Eddie and Jake need copies of the key.

Just as the PORTALS OF THE BEAM are protected by GUARDIANS, all other portals, in our world or Mid-World, are protected by demons. In order to cross over into Mid-World and join Roland's *ka-tet*, Jake must face the Mansion's demon. The Mansion's demon is the animating spirit of the house, a spirit of place, and parallels the demon which SUSANNAH battles sexually in the Speaking Ring. *See also* STONE CIRCLES, *this section,* and DEMONS/SPIRITS/DEVILS *and* DEMON ELEMENTALS, *in* CHARACTERS. III:75–76, III:161–62, III:185, III:187–88, III:189, III:190–92, III:194–96, III:198–201, III:203–4, III:205–6, III:207, III:208–9, III:210–11, III:262, III:344, III:348, III:399, IV:98, V:50 *(indirect),* V:93, V:104, V:246 *("pulling Jake through" and demon of the stone circle),* V:258 *(stone-circle demon/doorkeeper in Dutch Hill),* V:478 *(stone-circle demon/doorkeeper in Dutch Hill),* VII:143, VII:144–45, VII:249

JAKE'S DOOR (MANSION VERSION): *See also* STONE CIRCLES. III:200–204, III:205–12, III:219

PORTALS OF THE BEAM: *See* PORTALS OF THE BEAM *and* BEAMS, PATH OF THE, *listed separately. See also* GUARDIANS OF THE BEAM, *in* CHARACTERS

SHARDIK'S LAIR: *See* PORTALS OF THE BEAM *and* BEAMS, PATH OF THE, *listed separately. See also* GUARDIANS OF THE BEAM, *in* CHARACTERS

SHEEMIE'S MAGIC DOORS: Although teleportation is a talent forbidden in THUNDERCLAP's DEVAR-TOI, Roland's old friend SHEEMIE RUIZ can make Doorways with his mind. When Roland was young, Sheemie used this skill to follow our gunslinger and his original *ka-tet* to GILEAD. Sheemie used this ability again to help TED BRAUTIGAN escape the Devar-Toi and return to his home state of CONNECTICUT. Unfortunately, when Sheemie uses this skill (as he does several times to help our *tet*), he has tiny strokes. *See* BREAKERS: RUIZ, STANLEY (SHEEMIE), *in* CHARACTERS

SPEAKING RINGS: *See* STONE CIRCLES (SPEAKING RINGS), *listed separately*

STONE CIRCLES: *See* STONE CIRCLES, *listed separately*

THINNY: *See* THINNY, *listed separately*

TODASH: *See* TODASH, *listed separately*

TRAINS BETWEEN WORLDS: *See* BLAINE'S ROUTE *in this section. See also* NORTH CENTRAL POSITRONICS: BLAINE, *in* CHARACTERS, *and* ATCHISON, TOPEKA, AND SANTA FE RAILROAD COMPANY, *in* OUR WORLD PLACES

UNFOUND DOOR: In the Dark Tower series, the Unfound Door has three manifestations. The first time we see it, it is a freestanding ironwood door located in DOORWAY CAVE, high in the ARROYO COUNTRY of the BORDERLANDS. In this incarnation, it bears a strong resemblance to the BEACH DOORS, through which Roland drew EDDIE and SUSANNAH DEAN into MID-WORLD. Like the portals Roland found on the shores of the WESTERN SEA, the Unfound Door stands six and a half feet high and has no visible support, its hinges apparently fastened to nothing. However, whereas the Beach Doors were marked with the High Speech words for *The Prisoner, The Lady of Shadows,* and *The Pusher* (the final of these being the door which led Roland to the evil JACK MORT), the Unfound Door is marked with hieroglyphs. These hieroglyphs mean *Unfound* and also appear on the ghostwood box containing BLACK THIRTEEN. Etched upon the Unfound Door's crystal knob is a ROSE.

By the time our *tet* arrives in CALLA BRYN STURGIS, the Unfound Door has been in Doorway Cave as long as PERE CALLAHAN has been in the Calla (probably between five and ten years). In fact, the two of them appeared together in that cavern, which, before their arrival, had been known as the Cave of Voices. Callahan, the Unfound Door, and Black Thirteen were transported to the arroyo cave from the MOHAINE DESERT's WAY STATION. The magician who did the transporting was Roland's old nemesis WALTER. Since the Unfound Door had not previously existed in the Way Station (otherwise Roland and JAKE would have seen it during their sojourn there), we can assume that Walter conjured it from another *where* and *when*. This would be completely consistent with the Unfound Door's later appearances in the series.

While in the Cave of Voices/Doorway Cave, the Unfound Door is locked. Although it has no keyhole, it does have a key. That key is MAER-LYN's most dangerous magic ball, Black Thirteen. Despite the many risks involved in waking Thirteen, our *tet* uses it to open the door so that they can travel to other *wheres* and *whens*. With Roland's help, Eddie uses ball and door to travel to NEW YORK CITY, 1977. With Roland and Eddie's aid, Pere Callahan uses them to travel to New York and to STONEHAM, MAINE. At the end of *Wolves of the Calla,* MIA, Susannah's demon possessor, opens the door for what she hopes will be a final time. Taking Black Thirteen with her, she escapes to New York City, 1999, where the servants of the CRIMSON KING await her arrival.

However, the Unfound Door's job in the Callas is not over yet. With the help of the MANNI, our remaining *tet*-mates reopen the door so that they can complete their quest. Callahan, Jake, and OY travel to New York City, 1999, to pursue Susannah-Mio. Roland and Eddie travel to Stoneham, Maine, circa 1977, to track down CALVIN TOWER (owner of the Vacant LOT) and to meet our *kas-ka Gan,* STEPHEN KING.

We next encounter the Unfound Door in the final book of the Dark Tower series. Only three members of our *tet*—Roland, Susannah, and Oy—still struggle onward toward their goal. Although Eddie and Jake are dead, Susannah begins to dream about them. In her dream, Eddie and Jake are in a snowy CENTRAL PARK. Behind them is the Unfound Door. This ironwood dream-door looks exactly like the Unfound Door in Doorway Cave, only below the hieroglyphs for *Unfound* are the words *The Artist.* The knob is no longer crystal but solid gold, and filigreed with the shape of two crossed pencils—#2's whose erasers have been cut off. When they are but a few days' journey from the Tower, PATRICK DANVILLE, the artist whom Susannah and Roland rescued from DANDELO in the WHITE LANDS OF EMPATHICA, draws this second version of the Unfound Door so that Susannah can escape Mid-World. Although the door he draws does not have *The Artist* written upon it, and though the knob is of a plain shiny metal, not filigreed gold, it bears the necessary hieroglyphs and so works perfectly well. Susannah leaves Mid-World through this ironwood portal and joins her beloved *ka-tet* mates (who in this particular ALTER-NATIVE AMERICA are named Eddie and Jake TOREN) in a wintertime Central Park.

The final time we encounter the Unfound Door is at the base of the DARK TOWER itself. Roland's long journey ends at a ghostwood door banded with black steel. Upon it, engraved three-quarters of the way up, is the hieroglyphic *sigul* meaning *Unfound.* As Roland lays AUNT TALITHA's cross and his final remaining six-gun at the Tower's base, the hieroglyphs change. The door which Roland has been seeking all of his life transforms from Unfound to Found. Through this, the Found Door, Roland enters the Tower.

UNFOUND DOOR AND DOORWAY CAVE/CAVE OF VOICES:
V:335, V:399–400, V:407 *(indirect),* V:408–16 *(two thousand feet up;*

408–10 described; 411 previously Cave of Voices), V:421, V:458–65 (Unfound Door only), V:466, V:468, V:505, V:508, V:509–48 (Roland waiting there), V:549, V:550–51, V:573, V:584, V:590–600 (door), V:618–27, V:642, V:687, V:699, V:702, V:703–9, VI:3–8 (under discussion), VI:12, VI:21, VI:26 (cave), VI:28–43 (34—kra kammen means "house of ghosts"), VI:49 (indirect), VI:64, VI:80–82, VI:122 (Unfound Door), VI:124, VI:129, VI:142, VI:164, VI:167, VI:307, VI:308, VII:36 (Cave of Voices), VII:88 (Cave of Voices), VII:123 (Unfound Door), VII:143, VII:196, VII:239, VII:416, VII:447 (inside sai King's head), VII:540, VII:743

UNFOUND DOOR DRAWN BY PATRICK DANVILLE (ARTIST'S DOOR, EBERHARD-FABER DOOR): VII:724–25, VII:729, VII:738–50, VII:751–52

UNFOUND DOOR TO THE DARK TOWER: VII:820–21

WIZARD'S RAINBOW (MAERLYN'S MAGIC BALLS): *See* MAERLYN'S RAINBOW, *in* CHARACTERS

MECHANICAL DOORWAYS (OLD ONES' DOORWAYS): Both our world and MID-WORLD are riddled with mechanical doorways left over by the GREAT OLD ONES. At one time, 595 working mechanical doors existed below CASTLE DISCORDIA and the FEDIC DOGAN alone. More than thirty of them were one-way ports leading from NEW YORK CITY to FEDIC. Unlike magical doors, mechanical doorways are *dedicated*. In other words, they always open onto the same place.

The Great Old Ones (who, as we all know, learned to merge technology and magic) built doorways to other *wheres* and *whens* for mere entertainment. For example, anyone wishing to witness the assassination of President JOHN F. KENNEDY had merely to enter the ROTUNDA portal (located below Castle Discordia and the Fedic Dogan) marked DALLAS (NOVEMBER 1963)/FEDIC. Anyone wishing to see the Lincoln assassination had only to go through the door marked FORD'S THEATER. Like the cyborg GUARDIANS, ANDY the Messenger Robot, and BLAINE the Insane Mono, the mechanical doorways between worlds were manufactured by NORTH CENTRAL POSITRONICS. VII:73–74, VII:200

BOMBAY/FEDIC DOOR: VII:78

DALLAS (NOVEMBER 1963)/FEDIC DOOR: VII:78, VII:538

DOOR TO TODASH DARKNESS: According to MIA, below CASTLE DISCORDIA is a door that goes TODASH, or to the no-place between worlds. Although this door was probably created by mistake, the CRIMSON KING uses it to punish his worst enemies. Anyone unfortunate enough to be pushed through this door will wander, blind and insane, until eaten by one of *todash*'s many monsters. VI:248–49, VII:562

FEDIC/THUNDERCLAP STATION DOOR: This doorway leads from the ARC 16 WOLF STAGING AREA to THUNDERCLAP STATION, six miles from the DEVAR-TOI. Although the robotic WOLVES have been using it for decades, this portal is in terrible shape. Any human unlucky enough to pass through it feels as though he or she is being turned inside out. Once on the other side, he/she is overcome with a terrible, gut-spewing nausea. Unlike the other magical and mechanical doorways we have encountered so far, this one is made of steel, not ironwood. It is painted green and bears a *sigul* which resembles a cloud with a lightning bolt. VII:151–52, VII:179, VII:187–88 *(marked with a cloud and lightning sigul)*, VII:190, VII:194–200, VII:203

FORD'S THEATER DOOR: This door leads to Ford's Theater, in WASHINGTON, D.C. We can also assume that it always opens onto April 14, 1865—the day on which President Lincoln was assassinated. (He was killed while attending the play *Our American Cousin.*) VII:538, VII:561, VII:562

FORTY-SEVENTH STREET DOOR (BLEECKER STREET, NEW YORK CITY): Like the NINETY-FOURTH STREET door, NEW YORK CITY's Forty-seventh Street door links both the MULTIPLE AMERICAS and the multiple New Yorks. In all of its manifestations, this door is located on BLEECKER STREET, between FIRST and SECOND AVENUES. However, in some versions of New York, the door stands in an empty warehouse. In other versions of the city, it stands in an eternally half-completed building. VII:105

NEW YORK #7/FEDIC DOOR: This door leads from the tunnels below the DIXIE PIG to the EXTRACTION ROOM in the ARC 16 EXPERIMENTAL STATION in FEDIC. It is made of ghostwood. After SUSANNAH DEAN is dragged through this door by SAYRE and his *closies,* it burns out. Hence, when our other *tet*-mates travel from the Dixie Pig to Fedic, they are rerouted to a default door (NEW YORK #9/FEDIC), located in the ROTUNDA below CASTLE DISCORDIA and the FEDIC DOGAN. SUSANNAH has the robot NIGEL carry her from the Extraction Room to the Rotunda so that she can meet her friends. VI:373 *(indirect)*, VI:377–79, VII:74

NEW YORK#9/FEDIC/FINAL DEFAULT DOOR: At one time, more than thirty one-way portals led from NEW YORK CITY to FEDIC. However, after the FEDIC DOGAN's EXTRACTION ROOM door (NEW YORK #7/FEDIC) burns out, only #9 Final Default remains. All operational doors leading from New York to Fedic now transport to this doorway. VII:74, VII:78–80, VII:110 *(New York side)*, VII:133–38, VII:146, VII:529, VII:538

NINETY-FOURTH STREET DOOR (NEW YORK CITY): This doorway connects alternative versions of NEW YORK CITY. Unfortunately, it is usually on the blink. VII:105

SANTA MIRA/THUNDERCLAP DOOR: TED BRAUTIGAN and his fellow BREAKERS—TANYA LEEDS, JACE McGOVERN, DAVE ITTAWAY, and DICK of the forgotten last name—were all brought to END-WORLD through this door. VII:287–89, VII:297

SHANGHAI/FEDIC DOOR: VII:78

DRAWERS

According to SUSANNAH DEAN (previously ODETTA HOLMES/DETTA WALKER), the Drawers are places that are spoiled, useless, or both. However, they are also places of power. In many ways they resemble psychic trash middens. The Drawers are a kind of WASTE LAND.

I:90, II:327, III:44–46, III:82, III:264, III:347, III:377, III:407, VII:733

DETTA AND *FORSPECIAL* PLATE: II:194–96

DETTA'S SEX HAUNTS: These locations (RIDGELINE ROAD outside NUTLEY, ROUTE 88 outside AMHIGH, and THE RED WINDMILL) were places where Detta Walker vented her rage against white men. The negative force of her emotion, and the experiences she had in these places, transformed them into a kind of psychic Drawers. III:196–97

E

EASTERN PLAIN (CALLA BADLANDS)
See CALLA BADLANDS

ELMVILLE
See DEVAR-TOI

EMPATHICA, WHITE LANDS OF (WESTRING, SNOWLANDS)
The White Lands of Empathica are the snow-laden lands located southeast of the DISCORDIA BADLANDS. Unlike the Badlands, which were poisoned by the CRIMSON KING, the White Lands still contain living creatures. After their terrible encounter with the false UFFI at LE CASSE ROI RUSSE, Roland, SUSANNAH, and OY travel into the hilly White Lands, where they hunt deer, make themselves some winter clothes, and build a travois. (Susannah even makes snowshoes for Roland.)

However, from the beginning, the careful reader realizes that something is fishy about any land called Empathica. When you empathize with someone, you identify completely with that person's mind-set and emotions. In a place called Empathica, someone or something is using this power. On ODD'S LANE, our threesome meets the empath living in Empathica. However, he is anything but empathetic.

DANDELO, the were-insect who uses *glammer* to disguise himself as a cheery old man named JOE COLLINS, eats other people's emotions. For years he has been milking fear and laughter out of PATRICK DANVILLE, a young artist whom Dandelo keeps in his basement. Dandelo tries to feed from Roland, but SUSANNAH (warned by the deus ex machina STEPHEN KING) kills him first.
VII:545, VII:607, VII:609 *(pass into them)*, VII:611, VII:612, VII:618, VII:625, VII:647–711 *(action takes place here)*, VII:715, VII:746
CAMPSITE WHERE HIDES ARE PREPARED: Roland and SUSANNAH prepare deer hides here. They use the "brain-tanning" method. Gross but effective. VII:636–45
FEDERAL, THE (FEDERAL OUTPOST 19): *See* DOGAN: FEDERAL OUTPOST 19
ODD LANE (ODD'S LANE): Three weeks after entering the White Lands of Empathica, SUSANNAH, Roland, and OY emerge from a snowy tract of upland forest and see, below them, an inverted *T* carved in the snow. Much to their delight, they realize that this letter is actually the crossing point of two roads. The long body of the *T,* which continues over the hump of the horizon,

is TOWER ROAD, but the relatively short cross-arm is Odd's Lane, home of JOE COLLINS and his horse, LIPPY.

The self-proclaimed "Odd Joe of Odd's Lane" seems as friendly and welcoming as his house is cozy. However, in the White Lands of Empathica, not everything is as it seems. In reality, Odd Joe is none other than the dangerous were-spider DANDELO. Dandelo disguises his appearance (as well as the run-down façade of his cottage) using *glammer*. In actuality, Dandelo is a vampire, but one who drinks human emotion. Fearful that our *tet* will discover that *Odd Lane* is an anagram of *Dandelo,* this tricky were-spider painted an *S* onto the end of his lane's name. (It doesn't work.) VII:651–60 *(corner),* VII:661, VII:666, VII:671, VII:680, VII:682, VII:683, VII:690, VII:696, VII:707, VII:710 *(intersection),* VII:751

DANDELO'S HOUSE: VII:652–711, VII:731, VII:755

DESERTED VILLAGE: VII:652

STONE'S WARP: According to the improvised life's tale which the false JOE COLLINS spins for our *tet,* Joe awoke in an END-WORLD town called Stone's Warp after being beaten up by three NBA-size men in our world's CLEVELAND. VII:670

TOWER ROAD: Tower Road runs from DANDELO's house, in the White Lands of Empathica, all the way to the DARK TOWER itself. VII:651–60 *(corner),* VII:664, VII:671, VII:682, VII:705, VII:707, VII:709, VII:710 *(intersection),* VII:711, VII:715–17, VII:718 *(discuss traveling along it),* VII:726–27 *(on it),* VII:729–803 *(on it; 777, 779, 781—description of road near Tower)*

**END-WORLD

In the first four books of the Dark Tower series we learn that End-World is the fey region that exists beyond MID-WORLD. It contains both THUNDERCLAP and the DARK TOWER. According to the LITTLE SISTERS OF ELURIA, the ashes of the dead blow out toward this dream place. Once, hundreds of years before our *ka-tet* traveled in his Barony Coach, BLAINE had monitoring equipment in End-World. However, it has been down for more than eight centuries. When Roland and his friends reach the border between Mid-World and End-World, the first part of their journey is complete.

In the 2003 version of *The Gunslinger,* SYLVIA PITTSTON states that when God casts out the unrepentant from his palaces, he will send them to the burning place beyond the end of End-World. End-World must be a terrible place. Even the sorcerer WALTER states that to speak of things in End-World is to speak of the ruination of one's own soul. In *Wolves of the Calla,* we discover that the RIVER WHYE marks the end of Mid-World and the beginning of the BORDER-LANDS, that strange region that sits on the lip of End-World.

From *The Waste Lands* through to *The Dark Tower,* Roland's dwindling *ka-tet* travels southeast along the PATH OF THE BEAM. As they do so, they travel through the following End-World regions: Thunderclap (containing the CALLA DOGAN, the DEVAR-TOI, and THUNDERCLAP STATION), the DISCORDIA (containing FEDIC, CASTLE DISCORDIA, the DISCORDIA BADLANDS, and LE CASSE ROI RUSSE), the WHITE LANDS OF EMPATHICA (containing DANDELO's house and the FEDERAL), and finally CAN'-KA NO REY, the red ROSE fields containing the Dark Tower.

ACTION TAKES PLACE IN END-WORLD ON THE FOLLOWING
PAGES: VI:379–84, VII:55–80, VII:137–418, VII:531–803, VII:827–28
END-WORLD DIRECTLY NAMED ON THE FOLLOWING PAGES:
III:412, IV:66, IV:580, E:184, V:558, VI:13, VI:103, VI:247, VI:251, VI:406,
VI:407, VII:176, VII:407, VII:555, VII:594, VII:696, VII:715, VII:798,
VII:800, VII:818, W:10 *(the great darkness)*
END-WORLD PLACES, MOVING SOUTHEAST ALONG THE PATH OF
THE BEAM, FROM THE BORDERLANDS TO THE DARK TOWER:
   CALLA BADLANDS (EASTERN PLAIN): *See* CALLA BADLANDS,
   listed separately
      BOOM-FLURRY HILL: *See* CALLA BADLANDS, *listed separately*
      DEVIL'S CAUSEWAY: *See* CALLA BADLANDS, *listed separately*
      CALLA DOGAN (NORTH CENTRAL POSITRONICS NORTH-
      EAST CORRIDOR ARC QUADRANT OUTPOST 16): *See* DOGAN,
      THE, *listed separately*
   CAN'-KA NO REY: *See* DARK TOWER, *listed separately*
   CASSE ROI RUSSE, LE: *See* CASSE ROI RUSSE, *listed separately*
   DARK TOWER, THE: *See* DARK TOWER, *listed separately*
   DISCORDIA (BADLANDS): *See* DISCORDIA, *listed separately*
      KING'S WAY (BADLANDS AVENUE): This is the coach road between
      CASTLE DISCORDIA and LE CASSE ROI RUSSE.
   REGION OF THE UNDERSNOW: *See* EMPATHICA, WHITE LANDS
   OF, *listed separately*
   THUNDERCLAP: *See* THUNDERCLAP, *listed separately*
      BRIDGE OVER THE ABYSS: *See* FEDIC: DEVIL'S ARSE and FALLEN
      BRIDGE
      CAN-STEKE-TETE (STEKE-TETE): *See* DEVAR-TOI, *listed separately*
      CASTLE DISCORDIA: *See* CASTLE DISCORDIA, *listed separately*
         BANQUETING HALL: *See* CASTLE DISCORDIA, *listed separately*
      DEVAR-TOI (ALGUL SIENTO, BLUE HEAVEN): *See* DEVAR-TOI,
      listed separately
      DEVIL'S ARSE: *See* FEDIC: DEVIL'S ARSE and FALLEN BRIDGE,
      listed separately
      FEDIC: *See* FEDIC, *listed separately*
         FEDIC DOGAN: *See* DOGAN, *listed separately*
      THUNDERCLAP BADLANDS: *See* THUNDERCLAP, *listed separately*
      THUNDERCLAP STATION: *See* DEVAR-TOI, *listed separately*
   WHITE LANDS OF EMPATHICA: *See* EMPATHICA, WHITE LANDS
   OF, *listed separately*
      ODD LANE (ODD'S LANE): *See* EMPATHICA, WHITE LANDS OF,
      listed separately
         DANDELO'S HOUSE AND BARN: *See* EMPATHICA, WHITE
         LANDS OF, *listed separately*
         FEDERAL, THE: *See* EMPATHICA, WHITE LANDS OF, *listed sepa-
         rately*

EXTRACTION ROOM
   See DOGAN: FEDIC DOGAN, *above*

F

FEDERAL, THE (FEDERAL OUTPOST 19)
See DOGAN: FEDERAL OUTPOST 19

FEDIC (FEDIC O' THE DISCORDIA)
The deserted village of Fedic (also known as FEDIC O' THE RED DEATH and Fedic o' the Discordia) lies on the far side of THUNDERCLAP, on the PATH OF THE SHARDIK-MATURIN BEAM. Fedic sits within the outer wall of the CASTLE ON THE ABYSS (also known as CASTLE DISCORDIA). It consists of a single street, which terminates against the castle's inner wall. The town contains several deserted shops as well as a number of bars and brothels. (Before the Red Death obliterated its population, boozing and prostitution were popular distractions on this far-flung edge of the world.) In the days of the GREAT OLD ONES, PATRICIA, BLAINE's twin mono, terminated at FEDIC STATION. Beyond both village and outer castle wall is a great fissure in the earth called the DEVIL'S ARSE. Demons breed here. Long ago, a bridge crossed this crack, but by the time Roland and SUSANNAH visit the town, the bridge is long gone.
Fedic also contains one extremely sinister building, which is still in use. This place is the FEDIC DOGAN, which MIA calls the Dogan of all Dogans. Within the walls of the Fedic Dogan is the ARC 16 EXPERIMENTAL STATION, which is run by the minions of the RED KING. The Fedic Dogan is unique, since it is one of the few places where magic and technology have been integrated successfully.
   VI:105, VI:229, VI:234–55, VI:382, VII:13, VII:51, VII:52, VII:89, VII:106, VII:110, VII:111, VII:146, VII:149, VII:150, VII:152, VII:153, VII:158, VII:167, VII:206, VII:207 *(staging area)*, VII:223, VII:246, VII:297, VII:300, VII:306, VII:407, VII:409, VII:477 *(Faydag)*, VII:485, VII:520, VII:531–42, VII:553, VII:554, VII:556–58, VII:559, VII:590, VII:594
DEVAR-TETE: *See* DOGAN: FEDIC DOGAN
DEVIL'S ARSE AND FALLEN BRIDGE: The Devil's Arse is a great crack in the earth located just northeast of the town of Fedic. It contains horrific monsters that cozen, diddle, and plot to escape. According to TED BRAUTI-GAN and the other BREAKERS who travel to Fedic with SUSANNAH, the monsters from the Devil's Arse have been tunneling through to the catacombs beneath CASTLE DISCORDIA and the FEDIC DOGAN for years, and they are close to breaking through. VI:105 *(not yet named)*, VI:243 *(not yet named)*, VI:244, VII:536, VII:539, VII:557, VII:567
EXTRACTION ROOM: *See* DOGAN: FEDIC DOGAN
FEDIC CAFÉ: VI:252
FEDIC DOGAN: *See* DOGAN, *listed separately*
FEDIC GOOD-TIME SALOON AND DANCE EMPORIUM: VI:235, VI:245 *(where Mia met Walter)*, VII:557 *(saloon next door to hotel)*
FEDIC HOTEL: VI:235, VII:534, VII:553, VII:556–58
FEDIC STATION: Although it appears somewhat derelict, Fedic Station plays its own small but important role in the plans of the CRIMSON KING. After

the WOLVES arrive in THUNDERCLAP with the CALLAS' kidnapped children, they and their prisoners board a train at THUNDERCLAP STATION. This train terminates at Fedic Station. From here, the children are brought to the FEDIC DOGAN's EXTRACTION ROOM, where a twin-telepathy chemical is extracted from their brains, leaving them ROONT. Once upon a time (before she threw herself into the RIVER SEND), BLAINE's twin, the blue mono called PATRICIA, ran from LUD to Fedic Station. VI:237, VII:531, VII:537

GAIETY BAR AND GRILLE: VII:536
GIN PUPPY SALOON: VI:239–55 *(sitting outside)*, VII:149, VII:532
LIVERY: VI:235
MILLINERY AND LADIES WEAR (FEDIC MILLINERY AND LADIES WEAR): VI:239, VI:534
SERVICE'S MALAMUTE SALOON: VI:235–36

FEDIC DOGAN
  See DOGAN: FEDIC DOGAN

FIELD O' END-WORLD
  See DARK TOWER: CAN'-KA NO REY

FIELD OF RED ROSES
  See DARK TOWER: CAN'-KA NO REY

FORGE OF THE KING
  See CASTLE DISCORDIA *and* CASSE ROI RUSSE

FOUND DOOR
  See DOORWAYS BETWEEN WORLDS: MAGICAL DOORS: UNFOUND DOOR

G

GAGE PARK
  See KANSAS (STATE OF), *in* OUR WORLD PLACES

GALEE
  See TAHEEN: STOAT-HEADED TAHEEN, *in* CHARACTERS

GARDEN OF THE BEAM
  See LOT, THE, *below*

GEM THEATER
  See DEVAR-TOI

GINGERBREAD HOUSE

The Gingerbread House, where TED BRAUTIGAN, DINKY EARNSHAW, and SHEEMIE RUIZ go to escape the constant surveillance of the DEVAR-TOI guards, was actually created by Roland's old friend Sheemie. Unlike any of the other Breakers, Sheemie can create fistulas in time, which are like balconies on the DARK TOWER. Since the Gingerbread House exists outside the time/space continuum, our rebel Breakers can spend many hours recuperating here and yet return to the Devar at the same instant in which they left. Hence, no one ever detects their absence.

Like the edible witch's cottage in *Hansel and Gretel,* Sheemie's Gingerbread House is made entirely of sweets. The walls are of green, yellow, and red candy. The stairs are chocolate; the banister is a candy cane. VII:266–302 *(Ted Brautigan tells his story here)*

TWIZZLER AVENUE: Although it is impossible to step outside the Gingerbread House and onto this licorice-like street, you can see it from the Gingerbread House window. The cars that drive along Twizzler Avenue look suspiciously like bonbons. VII:267

GLASS PALACE

See GREEN PALACE

GOLGOTHA, THE

Roland and the MAN IN BLACK (WALTER) hold palaver here in this ancient killing ground located on the western slopes of the CYCLOPEAN MOUNTAINS. To Roland, the golgotha is "the place of the skull." Its floor is dusty with bonemeal and contains the skeletal remains of many small animals. It is here that Walter tells Roland's fortune, and it is here that Roland experiences a ten-year-long night as well as a tremendous vision of the multiverse.

I:197–216, II:20, III:47 *(indirect),* III:48, V:314, VI:284, VII:176–77 *(indirect)*

GREEN PALACE (GLASS PALACE)

This palace, which FANNIN/FLAGG maintains is in OZ, is actually located along the I-70 THINNY in the ALTERNATIVE TOPEKA, which Roland's *ka-tet* travels through at the end of *Wizard and Glass.* R.F. probably created it as a kind of practical joke. Like the buildings of Oz's Emerald City, it is entirely green.

The Green Palace's gate is made of twelve colored bars (six on each gate wing). They represent the twelve bends of MAERLYN'S RAINBOW. The central bar (which is broad instead of flat and round) is dead black. All of the bars contain strange little life-forms. The Green Palace hums like a thinny, but the sound isn't as unpleasant.

While here, our *tet* travels through MAERLYN'S GRAPEFRUIT back to GILEAD, where they witness Roland's matricide. At the beginning of *Wolves of the Calla,* we find out that just before our *tet* arrived in the BORDERLANDS, a green palace appeared and then disappeared near the western branch of the RIVER WHYE. The novel *The Wind Through the Keyhole* begins just after Roland's *tet* leaves the Green Palace.

IV:97 *(in distance),* IV:103–5, IV:626, IV:632–51 *(632 hums),* IV:659, IV:660, IV:662, IV:666, V:18, V:36, V:121, V:166, VI:290, VII:173 *(Castle of Oz),* W:3, W:12, W:31

GREY HAVENS
In Tolkien's *Lord of the Rings,* the Grey Havens was an Elvish port. According to STEPHEN KING, tired characters go to the Grey Havens to rest.
VII:817

H

HALL OF RESUMPTION
See DARK TOWER

HAUNTED MANSION
See DOORWAYS BETWEEN WORLDS

HEAD, THE
See DOGAN: FEDIC DOGAN: CONTROL CENTER

HEARTBREAK HOUSE
See DEVAR-TOI

HELL OF DARKNESS
This is where bad TAHEEN go after death, especially ones who have had their tails docked.
VII:224

HENRY GRAHAM'S DRUG STORE AND SODA FOUNTAIN
See DEVAR-TOI: PLEASANTVILLE

HIDDEN HIGHWAYS (HIGHWAYS IN HIDING, TODASH TURNPIKES, SECRET HIGHWAYS, DARKSIDE ROADS)
Although the DARK TOWER contains only one KEYSTONE EARTH and that Keystone Earth contains only one North America and one United States, other levels of the Tower also contain ALTERNATIVE AMERICAS, or alternative versions of North America and of the United States. These Alternative Americas are linked by hidden highways. Often, the hidden highways lead us to our destinies. JAKE CHAMBERS followed one of these from his apartment door to CO-OP CITY in BROOKLYN and then to the haunted DUTCH HILL MANSION. Each BEAM is also a kind of hidden highway.

The hidden highways are not just bridges between worlds. They are darkside roads where people can lose themselves, their memories, and their identities. To ordinary people, these roads are *dim,* or almost invisible, but to those in need of their slightly poisonous freedom, they are an escape route. After the death of his dear friend LUPE DELGADO in NEW YORK CITY, PERE CALLAHAN traveled these highways for five years. In *The Stand,* we find out that RANDALL FLAGG follows America's hidden highways as well.
III:83, III:122, III:158, V:260, V:263–64, V:289, V:292–93, V:299 *(and multiple Americas),* V:300–310 *(302 and Rose),* V:444, V:461, V:543

HIGHWAYS IN HIDING
See HIDDEN HIGHWAYS

HOGAN HOUSE
See DEVAR-TOI

J

JAKE'S DOOR
See DOORWAYS BETWEEN WORLDS

JAKE'S MIND-DOGAN
See DOGAN

JERUSALEM'S LOT
See MAINE (STATE OF): ALTERNATIVE AMERICAS AND THE STATE OF MAINE, in OUR WORLD PLACES

K

KANSAS
See KANSAS (STATE OF), in OUR WORLD PLACES

KEYSTONE EARTH
See KEYSTONE WORLDS

KEYSTONE WORLDS
KEY WORLD, KEYSTONE EARTH, REAL WORLD: The Keystone World is the version of Earth that STEPHEN KING inhabits and is the one in which he writes his books. (I assume it is also the world in which you and I read them.) Keystone Earth has many twinners—EDDIE DEAN and TED BRAUTIGAN both come from such parallel realities—but Keystone World is the only true version of Earth. On Keystone, time flows in one direction only, and what is done there can't be undone. In other words (to quote Dorrance Marstellar, one of my favorite characters from the novel *Insomnia*), on Keystone, what's "done-bun can't be undone."

Keystone Earth is the true twin of Roland's world, which is also known as TOWER KEYSTONE. The *ka* of Keystone Earth is NINETEEN. VI:200, VI:270 *(no do-overs)*, VI:271 *(only world that matters)*, VII:121 *(twin of Roland's world)*, VII:174 *(indirect)*, VII:242 *(Keystone Earth)*, VII:280 *(Keystone Earth)*, VII:300 *(Real World)*, VII:302-3, VII:304, VII:304, VII:307,

VII:339, VII:400 *(Real World)*, VII:405, VII:416, VII:488, VII:493, VII:511, VII:528, VII:627 *(Stephen King's world)*, VII:728, VII:773, VII:807

TOWER KEYSTONE: Tower Keystone is Roland's world (MID-WORLD). It is the true twin of KEYSTONE EARTH. Tower Keystone takes its name from the DARK TOWER, which exists here in its true form, not disguised as a ROSE, as it is on Keystone Earth. The *ka* of Tower Keystone is NINETY-NINE. VII:121 *(called key world)*, VII:609, VII:773

KING'S CHILDHOOD BARN

The first time STEPHEN KING saw the CRIMSON KING, he was seven years old and sawing wood in his uncle and aunt's barn. (He and his brother were on punishment duty because they had tried to run away.) This barn was also the site of our author's first meeting with CUTHBERT ALLGOOD and EDDIE DEAN.
VI:292–93, VI:389

KING'S HOUSE IN LOVELL

See DOORWAYS BETWEEN WORLDS: CARA LAUGHS

KING'S WAY

See DISCORDIA

KRA KAMMEN

See DOORWAY CAVE

L

LAND OF DARKNESS

See THUNDERCLAP

**LAND OF DEATH (LAND OF NINETEEN)

This is the place that the weed-eater NORT of TULL journeyed to. Unlike most people, he came back again. After the sorcerer WALTER raised Nort from the dead, he sealed Nort's memories of the Land of Death behind an imaginary door, or blockade. This door could only be opened—and Nort's memories released—by uttering the word NINETEEN. ALICE of TULL is the unlucky person who does so. What she learns drives her mad. The Land of NINETEEN is also the land of bizarre coincidences. Sometimes it seems to be the land of failed plans as well. *See* NINETEEN, *in* CHARACTERS
V:169, VII:36

LAND OF THE DRUMS

The PUBES of LUD believe that they must sacrifice one of their own each time they hear the god-drums pounding out over the city's loudspeakers. If they don't give a life, the GHOSTS IN THE MACHINES will animate the city's many corpses and rise up to eat the living. It is thought that once a Pube is sacrificed, he or she journeys to the Land of the Drums. We can assume that the Land of the Drums isn't a very nice place, since the Ghosts must be there, hungrily beating their instruments.

Although the Pubes don't know it, the god-drums are actually no more than the backbeat of the ZZ Top song "Velcro Fly." They are operated by the city's rival gang, the GRAYS, with a little help from BLAINE the insane computer brain.

III:317

LAND OF UNDERTABLE
A strange kingdom of wet mud and scampering feet. It exists below the feast-laden table of MIA's BANQUETING HALL. (Although Mia dreams she is in CASTLE DISCORDIA, in actuality Mia's Banqueting Hall is nothing but a BOG.)

V:74

LE CASSE ROI RUSSE
See CASSE ROI RUSSE

LICORICE AVENUE
See GINGERBREAD HOUSE

LITTLE SISTERS' HOSPITAL
When Roland awakes in the Little Sisters' Hospital he believes he is in a vast and airy pavilion of white silk, one hung with tiny silver bells. However, like the beauty of the LITTLE SISTERS OF ELURIA, the pavilion's loveliness is no more than a *glammer*. In reality it is an old, fraying canvas tent so thin and worn in places that it lets in the light of the Kissing Moon.

E:158–99, E:200–201

LOS ZAPATOS
See MEXICO, *in* OUR WORLD PLACES

LOT, THE (VACANT LOT)
"The Lot" refers to the magical Vacant Lot, located on the corner of FORTY-SIXTH STREET and SECOND AVENUE in NEW YORK CITY. The Lot contains the magical singing ROSE, which is our world's version of the DARK TOWER. It was also once the home of TOM AND JERRY'S ARTISTIC DELI. The Lot (also known as LOT #298, BLOCK #19, in MANHATTAN) is owned by CALVIN TOWER (also known as Calvin TOREN).

In 1977, SOMBRA REAL ESTATE (secret servants of the CRIMSON KING) approached Calvin Tower about buying the Lot. In fact, they paid him $100,000 for first right of sale. Luckily, their plans to buy the Lot and bulldoze the Rose are foiled by EDDIE DEAN, our *ka-mai*, whose brilliant flash of intuition leads him to spontaneously create the TET CORPORATION while palavering with Calvin Tower in the back room of his bookshop.

By 1999, the Lot is no longer vacant, but the site of 2 HAMMARSKJÖLD PLAZA, headquarters of Eddie's spontaneously incorporated corporation. Tet, whose major purpose is to protect the Rose, has done its job well. This most important flower still grows, and sings, in its original locale. The only difference is that the Rose now grows in an indoor garden called the GARDEN OF THE BEAM.

III:121–29, III:264, IV:83 *(Jake's vision of empty lot)*, IV:100–101 *(Eddie's dream)*, V:51, V:58 *(Second Avenue and Forty-sixth)*, V:66–67, V:68 *(Lot #289, Block #19)*, V:69 *(indirect)*, V:95, V:96, V:98, V:174, V:177, V:181, V:182–97, V:312, V:316, V:431, V:432 *(hears Rose)*, V:502, V:503, V:504, V:507, V:517, V:522, V:527, V:528, V:530, V:531, V:538–42 *(Eddie and Tower discuss selling)*, V:544–45, V:584, V:594, V:706, VI:35, VI:47, VI:56, VI:147, VI:171, VI:187, VI:189, VI:195–216 *(and bill of sale)*, VI:267, VI:270, VI:297, VII:26, VII:33, VII:36, VII:37, VII:122, VII:143, VII:487, VII:492, VII:495, VII:526, VII:756, VII:757

HAMMARSKJÖLD PLAZA (2 HAMMARSKJÖLD PLAZA, THE BLACK TOWER, HOUSE OF THE ROSE): This tall black building was erected by the TET CORPORATION on what was once the Vacant Lot. It serves as Tet's headquarters and is the home of the ROSE. VI:47, VI:50, VI:51, VI:53, VI:54–56, VI:89, VI:91–92, VI:257, VI:308, VI:315, VI:318, VII:487, VII:488, VII:489, VII:490–520

> **GARDEN OF THE BEAM:** When he visits 1999 NEW YORK, near the end of *The Dark Tower*, Roland sees this small garden shrine on the ground-floor lobby of 2 HAMMARSKJÖLD PLAZA. The Garden of the Beam is surrounded by ropes of wine-dark velvet. At its center, separate from the dwarf palm trees and Spathiphyllum plants which surround it, is the ROSE. In front of this garden is a small brass sign bearing the following dedication: "Given by the Tet Corporation, in honor of Edward Cantor Dean and John 'Jake' Chambers. Cam-a-cam-mal, Pria-toi, Gan delah" ("White over Red, thus Gan wills ever" or "God over evil, this is the will of God"). Before Eddie and Jake died, the plaque read, "Given by the Tet Corporation, in honor of the Beam family, and in memory of Gilead." Like the Rose, this sign is magical. No matter what language a person speaks, the plaque translates itself so that its message can be understood. VII:491–95, VII:503–5, VII:520

TOM AND JERRY'S ARTISTIC DELI: Before the Vacant Lot became vacant, it was the home of this deli. In JAKE's *when*, Tom and Jerry's has already been demolished. However, the magical ROSE grows in the Vacant Lot left behind. Tom and Jerry's was run by TOMMY GRAHAM, though the ground landlord was CALVIN TOWER. III:52, III:77–78, III:79, III:119–20, III:123, III:177, III:262, III:264, IV:83 *(Jake's vision)*, IV:100–101 *(Eddie's dream)*, V:51, V:61 *(deli)*, V:99, V:266, VI:47, VI:297, VI:318 *(indirect)*

M

MAERLYN'S GRAPEFRUIT
See MAERLYN'S RAINBOW, *in* CHARACTERS

MAERLYN'S RAINBOW
See MAERLYN'S RAINBOW, *in* CHARACTERS

MAGICAL DOORS
See DOORWAYS BETWEEN WORLDS

MAGNETIC HILLS
See BORDERLANDS, *in* MID-WORLD PLACES

MALL
See DEVAR-TOI; *see also* NEW YORK (STATE OF): NIAGARA MALL, *in* OUR WORLD PLACES

MANSION, THE
See DOORWAYS BETWEEN WORLDS

MECHANICAL DOORS
See DOORWAYS BETWEEN WORLDS

MEXICO
See MEXICO, *in* OUR WORLD PLACES; *see also* TODASH, *below*

MIA'S CASTLE
See CASTLE DISCORDIA

MID-WORLD AMUSEMENT PARK
In the children's story *Charlie the Choo-Choo*, the talking train CHARLIE is given a nice retirement taking children round and round on a track located in CALIFORNIA's Mid-World Amusement Park. The Mid-World Amusement Park doesn't exist on KEYSTONE EARTH. However, a version of it exists in the alternative TOPEKA that Roland's *ka-tet* reaches after their catastrophic ride on BLAINE the Insane Mono. In the alternative Topeka, a rather sinister Charlie resides in the REINISCH ROSE GARDEN.
   III:145

MID-WORLD LANES
When JAKE CHAMBERS lived in NEW YORK CITY, he liked to go bowling at MID-TOWN LANES. When he and his *tet* travel TODASH to the magical Vacant LOT at the beginning of *Wolves of the Calla*, Jake finds a twinner of his old bowling bag amid the trash and weeds growing near the singing ROSE. This *todash* bag looks almost exactly like his New York bowling bag, except his New

York bag said, "Nothing but Strikes at Mid-Town Lanes," while his *todash* bag reads "Nothing but Strikes at Mid-World Lanes." Our *tet* uses this bag to carry BLACK THIRTEEN. Back in *The Waste Lands,* Jake was accosted by an officer of the law in TIMES SQUARE. (Jake was on his way to DUTCH HILL's haunted MANSION.) When the policeman asked him for identification, Jake offered to show his Mid-World Lanes membership card. *See also* NEW YORK: MANHATTAN: MID-TOWN LANES, *in* OUR WORLD PLACES.

III:168, V:198, V:316, V:506, V:704, VI:329, VI:335, VII:143

MID-WORLD RAILWAY (KANSAS-TO-TOPEKA LINE)

We first learn about the Mid-World Railway through the children's book *Charlie the Choo-Choo,* which JAKE CHAMBERS finds in the MANHATTAN RESTAURANT OF THE MIND. Despite the fact that it was written for kiddies, Jake finds the story (and the main character, a talking train) extremely sinister. Jake senses that CHARLIE is a force of destruction, and that the Mid-World Railway has only one ultimate destination—the LAND OF DEATH.

Jake's vision of a killer train on a death-track prefigures the actual Mid-World Railway that exists on Roland's level of the TOWER. In Roland's world, Charlie is replaced by the talking mono BLAINE, though their routes are very similar. In Roland's world, *char* means "death." Hence, Charlie (like Blaine) is literally a killer train. Roland, Jake, and their *ka-tet* survive Blaine only to find a toy version of Charlie's railway in the alternative TOPEKA. *For more information on the children's book, see entry under* CHARLIE THE CHOO-CHOO, *in* CHARACTERS

BLAINE'S VERSION: III:267
CHARLIE THE CHOO-CHOO VERSION: III:139–46, III:266

MIND-TRAP

See DIXIE PIG, *above*

MORDOR

This realm of darkness and death can be found in J. R. R. Tolkien's famous trilogy, *The Lord of the Rings.* SUSANNAH thinks about Mordor and the Cracks of Doom as she rides through the WASTE LANDS beyond LUD.

III:406

MULTIPLE AMERICAS (ALTERNATIVE AMERICAS)

See entry in OUR WORLD PLACES

N

**NA'AR

When WALTER reads Roland's cards in the 2003 version of *The Gunslinger,* he calls him the Hanged Man, plodding ever onward toward his goal over the pits of Na'ar. In *Wolves of the Calla* we find out that Na'ar is the MANNI equivalent of Hell. Roland wonders whether the voices issuing up from the PIT OF VOICES (located in the DOORWAY CAVE) are actually the voices of the damned rising out of Na'ar. According to the Manni, all of the Forgetful Folk (those who leave their tribe to marry heathens) are doomed to spend eternity in Na'ar.

V:408, V:511, VII:384, W:227

NEW YORK, TODASH
See NEW YORK CITY, *in* OUR WORLD PLACES; *see also* TODASH, *below*

NIS
Nis is the name of Mid-World's dream god. It is also the name of his realm of sleep and dreams. The CRIMSON KING's horse is named Nis. In *The Wind Through the Keyhole*, Nis is sometimes used interchangeable with NA'AR. (People often use the exclamation "What in Nis," as in "What in Nis are you talking about?")

V:500 *(god)*, V:549, VII:601 *(Land of sleep and dreams, also Red King's horse)*, W:138, W:217

NONES
The Moon Peddler comes from the Nones bearing his sack of squealing souls.
IV:274

NORTH CENTRAL POSITRONICS NORTHEAST CORRIDOR ARC QUADRANT OUTPOST 16
See DOGAN: CALLA DOGAN

NOWHERE LANDS
See DISCORDIA

O

ODD LANE (ODD'S LANE)
See EMPATHICA, WHITE LANDS OF

ORACLE OF THE MOUNTAINS
See STONE CIRCLES (SPEAKING RINGS)

OUTER DARK
See entry in APPENDIX I

OZ
Oz is the magical land which the cyclone-blown Dorothy visited in the famous book-turned-film *The Wizard of Oz*. At the end of *Wizard and Glass*, our *tet* visits a version of Oz's GREEN PALACE.

V:70, V:166 *(Wizard of)*, V:567, VI:223, VI:308, VII:173, W:3

P

PALACE OF GREEN GLASS
See GREEN PALACE, THE

PATH OF THE BEAMS
See BEAMS, PATH OF THE

PINK ONE, THE
See MAERLYN'S RAINBOW, *in* CHARACTERS

**PLACE OF BURNING DARKNESS
See END-WORLD

PLANET AFTERLIFE
This is PERE CALLAHAN's term for death. After he falls from the window of
SOMBRA CORPORATION's headquarters in DETROIT, Callahan wonders
whether he's landed on Planet Afterlife. He hasn't. He's landed in the MOHAINE
DESERT's WAY STATION.
   V:458

PLEASANTVILLE
See DEVAR-TOI

POCKET PARK
See NEW YORK CITY: MANHATTAN: SECOND AVENUE, *in* OUR
WORLD PLACES

PORTALS
See DOORWAYS BETWEEN WORLDS *and* BEAMS, PATH OF THE

PORTALS OF THE BEAM
In *The Waste Lands,* Roland draws a metaphysical map of MID-WORLD.
This map is shaped like a wheel. At the center of the wheel is the DARK
TOWER, also known as the THIRTEENTH GATE. The twelve power points
on the rim of this wheel are known as PORTALS. These Portals are actually
twelve doorways leading into and out of Mid-World. The six BEAMS, which
connect opposite Portals and which pass through the nexus of the Dark Tower,
are like high-tension wires that maintain the proper alignment of time, space,
size, and dimension. They can be seen and felt by those who pass near them.
   According to HAX, when the GREAT OLD ONES re-created the world, they
made twelve Guardians to watch over the twelve Portals. These GUARDIANS
OF THE BEAM, also known as TOTEMS OF THE BEAM, had animal shapes.
Although we met MIR/SHARDIK, the cyborg Bear Guardian, it seems highly
likely that the Beams, Guardians, and Dark Tower existed before the technology
of the Great Old Ones came into being.

The portals are not the only doorways into and out of Mid-World, but they are the most powerful ones. Their health is intrinsically tied to the health of the Dark Tower, the Beams, and the time/space continuum. As the alterations the Old Ones made to the fabric of reality begin to unravel, THINNIES appear. Thinnies are like extremely nasty portals. We don't know where they lead, but it seems likely that they transport their victims to the demon-haunted emptiness between worlds. Like BLAINE's termination point in TOPEKA, the Portals of the Beam are marked with yellow and black stripes. *See also* BEAMS, PATH OF THE, *and* GUARDIANS OF THE BEAM, *in* CHARACTERS, *and* GREAT WEST WOODS, *in* MID-WORLD PLACES.

III:37–40, III:51, III:65–77 *(one of six paths to the Dark Tower),* III:78 *(bone-littered clearing),* III:81, III:84, III:153, III:154, III:162, III:260, III:262, III:264, III:394, III:407, IV:42 *(Eddie's memory)*

PRIM
See entry in CHARACTERS

Q

QUONSET HUT
See DOGAN

R

RED KING'S CASTLE
See CASSE ROI RUSSE

RED ROSES, FIELD OF
See DARK TOWER: CAN'-KA NO REY

REINISCH ROSE GARDEN
See KANSAS (STATE OF): TOPEKA: GAGE PARK, *in* OUR WORLD PLACES

ROOMS OF RUIN
See CASTLE DISCORDIA

ROTUNDA
See DIXIE PIG; *see also* CASTLE DISCORDIA *and* DOGAN: FEDIC DOGAN

S

'SALEM'S LOT
See MAINE (STATE OF): ALTERNATIVE AMERICAS AND THE STATE OF MAINE, *in* OUR WORLD PLACES

SHARDIK'S LAIR
See BEAMS, PATH OF THE *and* PORTALS OF THE BEAM; *see also* GREAT WEST WOODS, *in* MID-WORLD PLACES, *and* GUARDIANS OF THE BEAM, *in* CHARACTERS

SNOWLANDS
See EMPATHICA, WHITE LANDS OF

SOUTH PLAINS
See entry in MID-WORLD PLACES

SPEAKING RINGS
See STONE CIRCLES (SPEAKING RINGS)

STAGING AREA (WOLF STAGING AREA)
See DOGAN: FEDIC DOGAN

STEEK-TETE
See DEVAR-TOI

STONE CIRCLES (SPEAKING RINGS, DRUIT STONES)
MID-WORLD contains many ancient stone circles. These circles (also known as Speaking Rings) are the haunts of spirits and oracles. In these demonic places, the boundaries between the visible and invisible worlds are thin.

The first Speaking Ring we see is the ORACLE OF THE MOUNTAINS, found in *The Gunslinger*. The second one we see is in *The Waste Lands*, along the PATH OF THE BEAM. It is through this second Speaking Ring that our *ka-tet* draws JAKE CHAMBERS into Mid-World.

We don't know who created the Stone Circles, or whether they predate the technological rule of the GREAT OLD ONES, or came during the postapocalyptic dark age that followed. However, we do know that Roland sees them as ancient, mysterious, and dangerous—hence they must precede the rise of GILEAD and the IN-WORLD BARONIES by many hundreds of years. Although we do not know who lifted these heavy stones and made them reach toward the sky, we do know that human sacrifice was often practiced within them, and possibly contributed to their sinister energy.

GENERAL REFERENCES: II:367 *(Druit Stones)*

ORACLE OF THE MOUNTAINS: The Oracle of the Mountains is the name Roland gives to the Speaking Ring succubus that he and JAKE encounter in the WILLOW JUNGLE located in the foothills of the

CYCLOPEAN MOUNTAINS. Although this demoness originally tried to draw Jake into her circular lair, Roland thwarted her, saving Jake from almost certain death. In the end, Roland offers himself to this hungry succubus so that he can force her to make a prophecy. Roland uses mescaline, a drug which CORT once called the Philosopher's Stone, to draw the demon, but after he has extracted information from her he must pay her sexual price. The oracle uses *glammer* to conjure the scent and voice of Roland's lost love, SUSAN DELGADO.

In *Song of Susannah,* we learn that this oracle was no run-of-the-mill demon sexpot. In fact, she was the female aspect of a DEMON ELEMENTAL and had been sent to her Speaking Ring specifically to collect Roland's sperm for the servants of the CRIMSON KING. (Our gunslinger's seed was then used to create MORDRED DESCHAIN.) I:121–22, I:124, I:126–32, I:134, I:138, II:315, III:172–73, IV:68, VI:112–13 *(Place of the Oracle)*

SPEAKING RING ALONG THE PATH OF THE BEAM (JAKE'S DOOR): In *The Waste Lands,* Roland, EDDIE, and SUSANNAH drew JAKE CHAMBERS into MID-WORLD through a door which Eddie sketched on the ground of this Speaking Ring. This magical door could be opened only by a key which Eddie carved while traveling along the GREAT ROAD (which followed the PATH OF THE BEAM) toward LUD. Eddie's magical door is actually a portal connecting Mid-World to the haunted DUTCH HILL MANSION, located in a part of BROOKLYN no more than a mile or so from Eddie's old family apartment. Hence, Eddie is drawing Jake from the world of his own childhood every bit as much as he draws him from a real city.

Like all portals between worlds, these two connected doorways are not unguarded. While Eddie and Roland help Jake battle the DUTCH HILL MANSION DEMON, who tries to block Jake's passage from our side, Susannah keeps the Speaking Ring's male demon trapped in a sexual vise. Unfortunately, this demon impregnates her.

In *Song of Susannah,* we discover that Susannah's pregnancy is no accident, but had long been planned by the servants of the CRIMSON KING. The demon who shot seed into Susannah's core was none other than the male aspect of the DEMON ELEMENTAL who had collected Roland's sperm many years before as the ORACLE OF THE MOUNTAINS. III:173, III:181, III:182, III:189–90, III:193–94, III:195–98, III:202–3, III:206, III:207–8, III:209–10, III:211–13, III:258, III:262, IV:69, V:46, V:246 *("pulling Jake through" and demon of the stone circle),* V:258 *(stone-circle demon/doorkeeper in Dutch Hill),* V:478 *(stone-circle demon/doorkeeper in Dutch Hill),* VI:113, VI:116 *(demon of the ring),* VI:253

JAKE'S DOOR (DOOR #4: THE BOY): Like all portals, THE BOY (DOOR #4) has a different form in each world. In our world, it appears to be a haunted house called THE MANSION. In MID-WORLD, it exists within a Speaking Ring. (The Mid-World version of the door is actually drawn by EDDIE within the Speaking Ring.) Obviously, places of sinister power in one world are also places of sinister power in all of the others. III:202, III:205–12, III:219

STONE'S WARP
See EMPATHICA, WHITE LANDS OF

STUDY, THE
See DEVAR-TOI

SUSANNAH'S MIND-DOGAN
See DOGAN

T

THINNY, THINNIES
Thinnies are places where the fabric of existence has almost entirely worn away. These cancerous "sores on the skin of existence" have increased in number since the DARK TOWER began to fail. Thinnies can exist only because the multiverse itself is sickening. In fact, as thinnies spread over the earth, disease spreads among humans and other creatures.

Thinnies look like silvery, shimmering water and make a nauseating, atonal squalling. In many ways they seem like fluidly animate demons, especially since they have both a kind of body and a definite, malign presence. Sometimes their liquefying element spreads, develops arms, and snatches birds out of the air. These liquid/ether demons are like monstrous sirens, singing hungrily, always willing to whisper our secret fears to us so that they can lure us into their dead embrace.

Roland first encountered a thinny in the town of HAMBRY, when he was fourteen years old. (This thinny had a green hue.) Our *tet* stumbles across another one in the ALTERNATIVE TOPEKA which they travel through in *Wizard and Glass*. The monster-filled fog which David and Billy Drayton have to face in STEPHEN KING's short story "The Mist" is a cross between a thinny and TODASH space.

IV:64 *(sounds Hawaiian, doesn't it?)*, IV:66 *(wastelands beyond Lud are another kind of thinny)*, IV:67, IV:68 *(parallel between thinnies, lobstrosities, and god-drums)*, IV:70 *(hear it)*, IV:78 *(thinnies as doors)*, IV:92 *(enter thinny)*, IV:93, IV:95 *(enter it and feel nauseated)*, IV:96 *(like an entombment, an unclean purgatory)*, IV:118 *(Eyebolt Canyon)*, IV:155–57 *(voice)*, IV:261, IV:272–76 *(Roland and his ka-tet face it)*, IV:281, IV:336, IV:371, IV:395, IV:422, IV:432, IV:433 *(Roland's war plans against Farson)*, IV:454–56 *(voice of thinny)*, IV:595–601 *(Farson's men driven into it)*, IV:622–23, IV:632, IV:634, IV:660, V:36, V:48, V:130–31, V:341, V:508, V:516, V:597

THUNDERCLAP (THE LAND OF DARKNESS, THE DARK LAND)
In *Wizard and Glass* we learn that the fey realm of Thunderclap sits on the lip of END-WORLD. It is described as a land of dead fields, deserted villages, blasted trees, and dead soldiers. From here come the pale warriors; all clocks run backward in this land of death, and the graveyards vomit out their dead. Roland will

have to pass through Thunderclap on his way to the TOWER, and it is here that Roland and his friends will have to meet their enemy FLAGG once more.

In *Wolves of the Calla,* we discover that the dark land of Thunderclap sits just east of the BORDERLANDS, which in turn sit on the eastern edge of MID-WORLD-that-was. Beyond Thunderclap is CASTLE DISCORDIA and the arid DISCORDIA BADLANDS. In Thunderclap, the world has already ended. It is described as "a great darkness, like a rain cloud on the horizon." Despite the rain-cloud analogy used by the CALLA *folken,* Thunderclap is a dry, rainless desert.

Thunderclap is the home of the DEVAR-TOI, or Big Prison, where the CRIMSON KING keeps the psychic BREAKERS. The Breakers (who are human) are forced to use their wild talents to erode the BEAMS so that the foundering DARK TOWER will collapse, causing the macroverse to blink out of existence. Long before our story began, the insane Red King released poison gas over the whole of this area. Hence, the Breakers, as well as their CAN-TOI and TAHEEN guards, are plagued by skin diseases and other illnesses. (It seems likely that they suffer some of the effects of radiation sickness as well.) In Thunderclap, even the most minor skin abrasions can turn septic and deadly.

Since there is no sun in Thunderclap, the Devar-Toi's residents are dependent upon a mechanical (or atomic) sun, which runs on what might as well be the world's largest egg timer. Unfortunately for them, it is wearing down and occasionally goes on the blink, creating pseudo-eclipses and general depression and panic.

IV:570–73, IV:580, IV:628, IV:666, V:5, V:6, V:7, V:12, V:16, V:22, V:26, V:113, V:117, V:136–37, V:144, V:149, V:150 *(vampires, bogarts, taheen),* V:152, V:182, V:207, V:225, V:226, V:249, V:291, V:312, V:368, V:390, V:401, V:413, V:422, V:452 *(dark land is root of association between vampires and low men),* V:481, V:484, V:509, V:557, V:562, V:574, V:586, V:601, V:610, V:615, V:655, V:659, V:703, VI:13, VI:246, VI:247, VI:248, VII:51, VII:52, VII:58, VII:148, VII:152, VII:178, VII:190, VII:195, VII:200–416 *(setting; individual references are as follows: 200, 203, 210, 215, 223, 230, 247, 258, 261, 266, 282, 288, 289, 290, 306, 333, 337, 356, 357, 404, 416),* VII:485, VII:494, VII:507, VII:510, VII:514, VII:531, VII:536, VII:559, VII:563, VII:581, VII:594, VII:736, W:3, W:10 *(great darkness),* W:307

CAUSEWAY, THE: *See* CALLA BADLANDS, *listed separately*
DEVAR-TOI: *See* DEVAR-TOI, *listed separately*
DOGAN, THE: *See* DOGAN, *listed separately*
THUNDERCLAP STATION: *See* DEVAR-TOI, *listed separately*

THUNDERCLAP STATION
  See DEVAR-TOI

TODASH

In *Wolves of the Calla,* we are told that traveling *todash* is similar to the state of lucid dreaming. However, unlike lucid dreaming, both body and mind travel *todash.* As we see when EDDIE and JAKE travel to NEW YORK CITY via *todash* at the beginning of *Wolves of the Calla,* the body of a person in the *todash* state fades out of existence in a series of jerky pulses and is replaced by a dull gray glow. Those not traveling, but sleeping or sitting near a *todash* traveler, may hear a kind of low crackling or electrical buzzing. Entry into the *todash* state is signaled by the chiming of the *kammen,* or the *todash* CHIMES.

The blue-cloaked MANNI are well acquainted with traveling *todash.* Many (such as the Manni *dinh,* HENCHICK) have even seen the *todash tahken,* or the holes in reality. Some spheres of MAERLYN'S RAINBOW also facilitate traveling via *todash.* Most notorious of these is BLACK THIRTEEN. A desperate person can also travel *todash* without the aid of any magical instrument. During the five years following the death of his beloved friend LUPE DELGADO, FATHER CALLAHAN traveled along the *todash* turnpikes of America, also known as the HIGHWAYS IN HIDING.

Although traveling *todash* is practiced by the magnet- and plumb bob–wielding Manni, it is not without risks. *Todash* space is the void place between worlds, or the equivalent of the monster-filled hollows between the walls and floors of the DARK TOWER. Below CASTLE DISCORDIA is a doorway that leads directly to *todash* space. Although the OLD ONES considered this door a mistake, the CRIMSON KING makes good use of it. He has his bitterest enemies thrown into the null lands, so that they will wander in that nothingness, blind and mad, until they are devoured by *todash*'s many monsters.

According to MORDRED DESCHAIN, the nastiest of the *todash* monsters are known as the Great Ones. CONSTANT READERS familiar with STEPHEN KING's short story "The Mist" will probably recognize these *todash* monsters. In that tale, the military personnel responsible for the Arrowhead Project ripped a hole in reality. What leaked through was a cross between *todash* space and the horror of a monster-infested THINNY.

V:48–70 *(New York),* V:78–81 *(described),* V:84, V:88–97 *(89 Manni; 90 Wizard's Rainbow; 91–97 Eddie and Jake describe),* V:105 *(holiest of rites, most exalted of states),* V:110, V:114–16, V:139, V:165 *(like being stoned),* V:166, V:172–97 *(New York),* V:201, V:236, V:257, V:271, V:275, V:284, V:314, V:469, V:470, V:502, V:505, V:507, V:511, V:515, V:516, V:539, V:546, V:549, V:558, V:599, V:709, VI:12, VI:18, VI:37, VI:81, VI:82, VI:119, VI:131, VI:248–49 *(doors to* todash *darkness or* todash *space),* VI:251, VI:265 *(Beams as anti*todash*),* VI:281, VI:301, VI:307, VI:326 *(can get lost forever there),* VI:328–31 *(Black Thirteen brings* todash *darkness; it disappears when Thirteen sleeps),* VI:375, VI:378, VII:20, VII:21, VII:23 *(chimes),* VII:32, VII:38, VII:196, VII:407, VII:531, VII:539, VII:542 *(writing as a benign* todash*),* VII:557, VII:559, VII:567, VII:582, VII:711, VII:747 *(todash space),* VII:749, VII:754, VII:779

CHIMES, THE (KAMMEN): In the MANNI tongue, *kammen* means "ghosts." Hence, the DOORWAY CAVE is known as *kra kammen,* or "house of ghosts," because of the voices that echo within it. Those traveling *todash* are assailed by the beautiful but bone-vibrating sound of the *kammen,* or *todash* bells. Their painful music is reminiscent of the warble of the THINNY. Evidently, when the box containing BLACK THIRTEEN is opened, the *kammen* begin to chime. The sound is both overwhelming and maddening. V:48, V:53, V:65, V:67, V:68, V:69, V:90, V:139, V:167–68 *(bells),* V:171, V:174, V:184, V:196, V:197, V:268–69, V:275, V:283, V:299, V:317, V:413, V:414, V:432, V:457, V:458, V:459, V:462, V:515, V:516, V:540, V:546, V:591, V:592,

V:597, VI:81, VI:98, VI:307, VI:326, VI:327, VI:328, VI:378, VII:20, VII:21, VII:23, VII:28, VII:36, VII:288, VII:539, VII:540, VII:562, VII:564

DOOR TO TODASH DARKNESS: *See* CASTLE DISCORDIA

END-WORLD (VIA BLACK THIRTEEN): *See* END-WORLD, *listed separately*

> **CASTLE OF THE KING (VIA BLACK THIRTEEN):** *See* CASSE ROI RUSSE, *listed separately*

MAINE (VIA BLACK THIRTEEN): *For page references, see* MAINE (STATE OF), *in* OUR WORLD PLACES

> **EAST STONEHAM:** East Stoneham is a small town forty miles north of PORTLAND. This is where CALVIN TOWER and AARON DEEPNEAU go to hide from BALAZAR'S MEN. PERE CALLAHAN visits East Stoneham courtesy of Black Thirteen and the UNFOUND DOOR. This town is also the site of Roland and EDDIE's battle with Balazar's thugs. *For page references, see* MAINE (STATE OF): OXFORD COUNTY: STONEHAM, *in* OUR WORLD PLACES
>
> > **EAST STONEHAM GENERAL STORE:** *For page references, see* MAINE (STATE OF): OXFORD COUNTY: STONEHAM, *in* OUR WORLD PLACES
> >
> > **METHODIST MEETING HALL:** *For page references, see* MAINE (STATE OF): OXFORD COUNTY: STONEHAM, *in* OUR WORLD PLACES
> >
> > **POST OFFICE:** *For page references, see* MAINE (STATE OF): OXFORD COUNTY: STONEHAM, *in* OUR WORLD PLACES

MEXICO (VIA BLACK THIRTEEN):

> **LOS ZAPATOS (VIA BLACK THIRTEEN):** In the years before our *tet* reached CALLA BRYN STURGIS, FATHER DONALD CALLAHAN traveled here, propelled by BLACK THIRTEEN. Los Zapatos is also the village where we find BEN MEARS and his eleven-year-old companion, MARK PETRIE, at the beginning of *'Salem's Lot.* (The body of the novel is told in retrospect.) *Los zapatos* means "the shoes." *For page references, see* MEXICO: LOS ZAPATOS, *in* OUR WORLD PLACES

NEW YORK (VIA BLACK THIRTEEN): *For page references, see* NEW YORK CITY, *in* OUR WORLD PLACES

> **DIXIE PIG:** *See* DIXIE PIG, *listed separately*
>
> **GEORGE WASHINGTON BRIDGE:** *For page references, see* NEW YORK CITY, *in* OUR WORLD PLACES
>
> > **FOOTBRIDGE (LaMERK INDUSTRIES):** *For page references, see* NEW YORK CITY, *in* OUR WORLD PLACES
>
> **LOT, THE (FORTY-SIXTH STREET AND SECOND AVENUE):** *See* LOT, THE, *listed separately; see also* ROSE, THE, *in* CHARACTERS
>
> **SECOND AVENUE—FORTY-SIXTH STREET TO FIFTY-FOURTH:** According to EDDIE DEAN and JAKE CHAMBERS, these eight blocks function as one large DOORWAY BETWEEN WORLDS. *For page references, see* NEW YORK CITY, *in* OUR WORLD PLACES

TODASH HOSPITAL (ROOM NINETEEN): V:423

TODASH TAHKEN: The holes in reality. V:413

TODASH TURNPIKES (USA): *See* HIDDEN HIGHWAYS, *listed separately*

TOPEKA
See KANSAS, *in* OUR WORLD PLACES

TOWER
See DARK TOWER

TOWER KEYSTONE
See DARK TOWER *and* KEY WORLDS/KEYSTONE WORLDS

TOWER ROAD
See EMPATHICA, WHITE LANDS OF

U

UNDERSNOW
See EMPATHICA, WHITE LANDS OF

UNFOUND DOOR
See DOORWAYS BETWEEN WORLDS: MAGICAL DOORS: UNFOUND DOOR; *see also* DOORWAY CAVE

UNFOUND DOOR TO LAND OF MEMORY
Inside each of us there is an UNFOUND DOOR, and memory is the key which opens it. When we find that door, we find forgotten parts of ourselves.
    VI:352–53, VI:362

UPLANDS
See EMPATHICA, WHITE LANDS OF

V

VACANT LOT
See LOT, THE

W

WALTER'S MIND-DOGAN
See DOGAN

WASTE LANDS

The Waste Lands are those desolate lands located beyond LUD. These horrible areas—too poisoned to support life as we know it but full of mutants and monsters—are man-made. It seems that they were the result of one of the GREAT OLD ONES' wars. We already know that BLAINE, the computer mind of LUD, has access to chemical and biological weapons, but what was loosed upon the Waste Lands was worse than these. It was, Blaine assures EDDIE, even worse than a nuclear catastrophe. *See also* DRAWERS.

III:109 *(little "w")*, III:248, III:405–20 *(travel through via Blaine)*, IV:3, IV:13–14 *(and Candleton)*

WASTE LANDS EAST OF THE RIVER WHYE

See CALLA BADLANDS

**WAY STATION

The Way Station, where Roland finds JAKE, was once a stopping point for the Coach lines that ran across the MOHAINE DESERT. By the time our story takes place it has been deserted for years. The station consists of two buildings (a stable and an inn) surrounded by a fallen rail fence whose wood is so fragile that it's rapidly thinning into desert sand. Luckily for both Jake and Roland, the station's water pump still works. (In the 2003 version of *The Gunslinger,* we find out that this pump was made by NORTH CENTRAL POSITRONICS.) In the building's cellar, Roland faces down the SPEAKING DEMON.

Both Jake Chambers and FATHER CALLAHAN end up in the Mohaine Desert's Way Station after they "die" in our world. According to Roland's longtime nemesis WALTER, this Way Station is "a little rest stop between the hoot of [our] world and the holler of the next." When Callahan arrives in the Way Station, Walter is waiting for him. Walter gives Callahan BLACK THIRTEEN, then forces him to enter the UNFOUND DOOR. When Callahan regains consciousness, he finds himself with the MANNI of CALLA BRYN STURGIS.

I:72–81, I:83–92, I:93, I:122, II:319, III:43–46, III:47, III:48, III:59, III:60, III:62, III:91, III:106–7, III:128, III:132, III:263, IV:106, V:458–65 *(460 hoot and holler)*, V:470, VI:290, VI:327, VI:389, VI:391, VI:399, VII:826
CELLAR: I:87–88

WAYDON CASTLE

See RIVER BARONIES, *in* MID-WORLD PLACES

**WEST END OF THE WORLD

The West End of the World is an almost unreachable place. Hence the expression "Where else would I be? The West End of the World?" At the end of the 2003 version of *The Gunslinger,* we learn that the WESTERN SEA is the western edge of the world.

III:339

WESTRING

See EMPATHICA, WHITE LANDS OF

WHITE LANDS OF EMPATHICA
See EMPATHICA, WHITE LANDS OF

WIZARD'S GLASS
See MAERLYN'S RAINBOW, *in* CHARACTERS

WOLF GARAGE
See DOGAN: FEDIC DOGAN *and* CASTLE DISCORDIA

WOLF STAGING AREA
See DOGAN: FEDIC DOGAN *and* CASTLE DISCORDIA

NORTH CENTRAL
POSITRONICS
LTD.

MAXIMUM SECURITY

verbal entry code required

APPENDIX I
MID-WORLD DIALECTS

CONTENTS

INTRODUCTION

High Speech (also called the "Tongue") was the ancient, ritualized language of Mid-World. Low speech—also called the common tongue or the vulgate—was the speech of everyday interaction, but High Speech was the language of gunslingers. It was also the language of ritual and magic.

Although not confined to the court of Gilead (Sylvia Pittston of Tull and Aunt Talitha of River Crossing both speak the Tongue), it was, primarily, bound to the hierarchies and courtly codes of In-World. While we can assume that Fair-Day Riddling was conducted in low speech, and while the common tongue contained many fascinating terms and phrases, the spiked letters of High Speech carried the heart of Roland's culture. With one notable exception (explained in the pages that follow), each word in the Tongue had multiple meanings. These meanings were so varied that they were (and are) difficult to explain to those born outside of Mid-World.

Like other sacred languages, the words and phrases of High Speech imply an entire philosophy of life, and the speaking of it was ritualized. Gunslinger apprentices were not allowed to utter its words publicly until after they had won their guns. To do so before proving themselves in the yard behind the Great Hall was considered an affront to all that their culture held sacred. As was said earlier, High Speech was the language of gunslingers, but it was also the language used to address spirits, demons, and *dinhs*. If the glorious history of Roland's world is now no more than the wreckage of a sunken ship, then High Speech is one of the sacred relics that washed up on the shores.

A BRIEF NOTE ON THE USE OF APPENDIX I

For each word or phrase listed in this appendix, I have provided at least one page reference so that you can view the relevant word, object, or phrase in the context of the Dark Tower series. My hope, in so doing, is to enrich your enjoyment of Mid-World's diverse dialects. In instances where the word or phrase under discussion receives a lengthier description elsewhere in the *Concordance,* I direct you to the entry and section where an in-depth discussion of the subject is available. A word in all capitals within an entry indicates that word has an entire entry devoted to it within Appendix I. If a word or phrase comes from the 2003 version of *The Gunslinger* but does not appear in the 1982 edition, then I have marked that entry with a double asterisk (**).

Since in Mid-World, as in our world, dialects often share words and expressions, some terms could be placed with equal validity in more than one subsection. In such cases, I have tried to place the questionable term in the most general category. For example, if a word is used in Calla Bryn Sturgis but is also used elsewhere in Mid-World, it can be found in the "Mid-World Argot" subsection. Similarly, if a word is used by the Manni but is also related to a High Speech term, then the word will be found in the "High Speech" subsection.

If you are unsure where to find a particular word or phrase, then the following guidelines may help. For words and phrases that sound similar to ones from our world, begin in "Mid-World Argot." If you don't find what you're searching for there, move to "Calla Bryn Sturgis Dialect." Finally, try "End-World Terms." For words and phrases that are definitely in High Speech or a similar language, begin searching in "High Speech," then proceed to "Manni Terms." Last of all, try "End-World Terms." If you are searching for a hand motion or gesture which Roland uses, begin with "Mid-World Gestures."

I apologize to those Constant Readers who would have preferred a single, straightforward alphabetical listing of all the unusual words and phrases found in the Dark Tower series. That was one organizational option, but in the end, I decided that it would be more enjoyable—both for me and for you—if I tried to capture at least a bit of Mid-World's magic, a *glammer* cast as much by the variety of cultures we encounter there as by the story line itself.

HIGH SPEECH TERMS AND SYMBOLS

ᗝᛞᗧᗣ ᗝᗡᔓ: This scrollwork means UNFOUND. VII:739, VII:820

ᛞᗧᗣ ᗝᗡᔓ: This scrollwork means FOUND. VII:820

CR: This scrollwork means WHITE. It was Arthur Eld's DINH mark and is found near the muzzle of Roland's guns. VII:501

ꝗ: This letter sounds like S in the Low Speech. However, it seems likely that the letter itself is in High Speech. (In the earlier draft of *The Wind Through the Keyhole*, it was listed as a High Speech letter.) W:236

⟨scrollwork symbols⟩

C-X: These lines are taken from the note that Gabrielle Deschain left for her son at the women's retreat of Serenity. The words mean: *I forgive you everything. Can you forgive me?* W:309

⟨scrollwork symbols⟩: Roland believes that these words, written in High Speech, are the most beautiful in any language. They mean *I forgive*. W:309

AM: *See* PRIM, *in* CHARACTERS

ANRO CON FA; SEY-SEY DESENE FANNO BILLET COBAIR CAN: These words are spoken by Chevin of Chayven, a CHILD OF RODERICK, to Roland of Gilead. The words are never translated. Here is Chevin's complete statement: "Anro con fa; sey-sey desene fanno billet cobair can. I Chevin devar dan do. Because I felt sad for dem. Can-toi, can-tah, can Discordia, aven la cam mah can. May-mi. Iffin lah vainen eth—" His words are cut short by Roland's guns. Roland considers this a mercy killing. VII:50–51

AN-TET: The term *tet* refers to people linked by the same destiny or goals. *An-tet* implies intimacy of all kinds. To speak *an-tet* to someone is to be completely honest and open, to share all. It also means to sit in council. Roland and his trailmates are both *ka-tet* and *an-tet*. *An-tet* can also imply sexual intimacy. In *Wizard and Glass,* Roland refers to the first time he and Susan made love as the first time they were together *an-tet*. Given the profound link between Roland and Susan (she appears and reappears to him in dreams and visions throughout the Dark Tower series), the term *an-tet* is appropriate. A mere sexual encounter does not necessarily imply *an-tet*. IV:439, V:115, V:216, V:394, V:472, VII:22

ANTI-KA: The force that works against one's *ka*, or destiny. It is a counterforce which tries to stop a person from fulfilling his or her life-mission. The anti-*ka* which works against Roland's *ka-tet* was set in motion by the Crimson King. VII:266

AVEN KAL: An *aven kal* is a kind of tidal wave that runs along the path of the Beam. Literally translated, *aven kal* means "lifted on the wind" or "carried on the wave." The use of *kal* rather than the more usual form *kas* implies a natural force of disastrous proportions. In other words, not a hurricane but a tsunami. VII:20

AVEN-CAR: A hunting term which refers to carrying the kill and preparing to make it into something else. VII:635

BONDSMAN: *See entry in* MID-WORLD ARGOT

CAM-A-CAM-MAL, PRIA-TOI, GAN DELAH: "White over Red, Thus God Wills Ever." This is written on the plaque in front of the Garden of the Beam. It also translates as "Good over evil, this is the will of God." VII:504

CAN CALAH: The *can calah* are angels. VI:318

CAN-AH, CAN-TAH, ANNAH, ORIZA: "All breath comes from the woman." This is a saying repeated in Calla Bryn Sturgis, though it is probably used throughout Mid-World. Although mortal woman was made from the breath of mortal man, the first man came from Lady Oriza. V:631

CANDA: The distance (never the same in any two situations) which a pair of outnumbered gunslingers must keep between them to assure they will not be killed by a single shot. VII:25

CAN STEEK-TETE: The Little Needle. Can Steek-Tete (also called Steek-Tete) is a butte located near the DEVAR-TOI. VII:205

CAN-TAH: According to Roland, the tiny scrimshaw turtle which Susannah Dean finds hidden in a pocket of Jake Chambers's bowling bag is one of the *can-tah*, or little gods. Constant Readers have met the *can-tah* before, namely in Stephen King's novel *Desperation*. In *Desperation*, the little *can-tah* were tiny demonic sculptures depicting the *can-toi*—coyotes, snakes, etc.—that served Tak the Outsider. (*Tak* is short for *can-tak*, which means "big god.") *See also* CAN-TAH, *in* CHARACTERS

CAN-TOI: *Can-toi* is another term for the low men. The *can-toi* are rat-headed beings who wear humanoid masks. (The masks are grown and so are made of a living substance.) Unlike the TAHEEN, the *can-toi* worship the human form and believe that they are slowly transforming into humans themselves. They call this process "becoming." In the novel *Desperation*, the *can-toi* were the coyotes, spiders, snakes, and other dangerous creatures that obeyed the will of Tak the Outsider. (*Tak* is short for *can-tak*, which means "big god.") *See also* CAN-TOI, *in* CHARACTERS

CAN-TOI-TETE: Roland uses the term *can-toi-tete* to refer to the desert dogs of Thunderclap. *Can-toi-tete* translates roughly as "little *can-toi*" or "tiny *can-toi*." In Stephen King's novel *Desperation*, the *can-toi* were the coyotes, spiders, snakes, and other dangerous creatures that obeyed the will of Tak the Outsider. (*Tak* is short for *can-tak*, which means "big god.") *See also* CAN-TAH, *above*. VII:255, VII:261

CHAR: Most words in High Speech have multiple meanings. However, *char* is an exception to this general rule. *Char* has one meaning only, and that is death. *Char* is the root of many Mid-World terms, including Big Charlie Wind and CHARYOU TREE. III:382

CHARY (YOU CHARY MAN): As we all know, the High Speech term *char* means "death." Hence, a chary man is one who courts death, brings death, or deals death. Think of him as the Grim Reaper's deputy. V:335, V:612

CHARY-KA: This insult is thrown at Roland by one of the Crimson King's TAHEEN just before Roland kills him. It most likely means somebody who is one of death's *ka*-mates, or one whose *ka* is aligned with death. It may also imply that although the *chary-ka* is destined to deal death, he is also destined to suffer from death's nasty sense of humor. VII:135

CHARYOU TREE: Charyou Tree was the ritual bonfire made on the Festival of REAP. In the days of Arthur Eld, people were burned on this fire. By Roland's day, STUFFY-GUYS were burned instead. The term *Charyou-tree* means "Come Reap." IV:447, V:124, V:210 *(Reap fair of the Old People)*, VI:219

CHASSIT (CHUSSIT, CHISSIT, CHASSIT): *Chussit, chissit, chassit* are the numbers seventeen, eighteen, and nineteen. They are used in the BABY-BUNTING RHYME, one of Mid-World's childhood rhymes. *See entries in* MID-WORLD ARGOT *and* APPENDIX III. VII:22, VII:23, VII:57

CHILDREN OF RODERICK: *See entry in* MID-WORLD ARGOT

COFFAH: This is another term for Hell. VII:265 *See entry in* PORTALS

**COMMALA: *Commala* is a Mid-World term for rice. In the 2003 version of *The Gunslinger*, we are told that it is also an alternative name for the festival dance known as the Sowing Night Cotillion. The Commala is the courting rite of New Earth, a festival also known as Sowing and Fresh Commala. *See entry in* CALLA BRYN STURGIS DIALECT

COMMALA DAN-TETE: The coming of the little god. VII:61

**COTILLION (SOWING NIGHT COTILLION): *See* COMMALA, *above*

**DAN-DINH: The term *dan-dinh* has many meanings. To speak *dan-dinh* is to open your heart and your mind to another. This term also means Little Leader. In the 2003 version of *The Gunslinger*, Roland feels the urge to speak to Jake *dan-dinh* after his encounter with the Oracle of the Mountains.

In *Wolves of the Calla*, we learn that the literal interpretation of this term is "May I open my heart to your command." Roland's tutor Vannay maintained that the phrase predated Arthur Eld by centuries. To ask your leader a question *dan-dinh* means to seek your leader's advice on an emotional problem. However, when you turn to your DINH in this way, you agree to do exactly as the *dinh* advises, immediately and without question. Men and women usually address their leader *dan-dinh* about love-affair problems, but in *Wolves of the Calla*, Jake speaks to Roland *dan-dinh* about the problem of Susannah/Mia and her chap. V:388

DAN SUR, DAN TUR, DAN ROLAND, DAN GILEAD: We are never given a translation of this phrase. However, since Roland tells Ted Brautigan to say it to one of the mutant CHILDREN OF RODERICK, we know it must refer to the vow of allegiance which that race once swore to the line of Eld. VII:216

DAN-TETE: (The second part of this word is pronounced *tee-tee*.) *Dan-tete* means "little savior" or "baby god." Mordred is End-World's *dan-tete*. Roland calls John Cullum his KA-TET's *dan-tete*. VI:182, VII:38

DARKLES and TINCTS: In the 1982 edition of *The Gunslinger*, we were told that Maerlyn (also known as the Ageless Stranger) *darkles* and *tincts*. In other words, he lives backward in time and can live simultaneously in all times. In *The Dark Tower*, we learn that the Crimson King also *darkles* and *tincts*. This makes it difficult for the artist Patrick Danville to draw him. At the very end of this seventh book of the Dark Tower series, we learn that Roland also *darkles* and *tincts*. Roland will not die but will go on forever, repeating his journey to the Tower over and over, until he learns the lessons *ka* wishes him to learn. I:212, VII:789

DASH-DINH: A *dash-dinh* is a religious leader. Henchick of the Manni is a *dash-dinh*. V:389

DEATH PRAYER: Roland translates this prayer for us and recites it over Jake's grave:

> Time flies, knells call, life passes, so hear my prayer.
> Birth is nothing but death begun, so hear my prayer.
> Death is speechless, so hear my speech.
> This is Jake, who served his ka and his tet. Say true.
> May the forgiving glance of S'mana heal his heart. Say please.
> May the arms of Gan raise him from the darkness of the earth. Say please.
> Surround him, Gan, with light.
> Fill him, Chloe, with strength.
> If he is thirsty, give him water in the clearing.
> If he is hungry, give him food in the clearing.
> May his life on this earth and the pain of his passing become
> as a dream to his waking soul, and let his eyes fall upon
> every lovely sight; let him find the friends that were lost to him,
> and let every one whose name he calls call his in return.
> This is Jake, who lived well, loved his own, and died as ka would have it.
> Each man owes a death. This is Jake. Give him peace.
> VII:474

DEH: Pronunciation of the letter *D* in High Speech. V:130

DELAH: Many. V:148, V:598, V:642, VI:268, VI:294, VII:50

DELAH GESTURE: *See* MID-WORLD GESTURES *section.*

DEVAR: Prison. VII:142

DEVAR-TETE: Little prison or torture chamber. VII:142

DEVAR-TOI: *See entry in* END-WORLD TERMS

DINH: A *dinh* is a leader or a king. It can also mean father, as in "father of his people." Roland is the *dinh* of his *ka-tet.* In *Wizard and Glass,* Roland asks whether the Wizard of Oz was a great *dinh*—a baron or king. IV:558, IV:630, V:31, V:203, V:368, VI:252

FAN-GON: The exiled one. This term is used to describe Eddie Dean when he returns to New York via the Unfound Door. VII:515

FIN-GAN: Literally speaking, this means *the first word.* According to the Manni, the first word, or *fin-Gan,* was *hile.* According to their beliefs, the word *hile* set the world spinning. W:201

GODOSH: *See* PRIM, *in* CHARACTERS

GUNNA (GUNNA-GAR): All of one's worldly possessions. In the case of a traveler, it is what he or she carries. IV:103, V:404, VI:33, VI:73, VII:134

GUNSLINGER LITANY: *See* GUNSLINGER LITANY, *in* MID-WORLD ARGOT

HAD HEET ROL-UH, FA HEET GUN, FA HEET HAK, FA-HAD GUN?: This is a phonetic translation of something which Calvin Tower says to Roland. We know that these words are probably in the Tongue, but we never find out what they mean. VI:197

HILE: Hile is one of the few words that is exactly the same in both low and High Speech. It is the one that the Manni called *fin-Gan,* or the first word; the one that set the world spinning. In low speech, *hile* is used as a formal greeting. It can also be used to call animals. IV:21, IV:261, V:107, W:201, W:202

HILE, BONDSMEN! I SEE YOU VERY WELL! RISE IN LOVE AND SER-VICE: It seems likely that this phrase is translated from High Speech. This is what gunslingers say when people kneel before them and raise their fists to their foreheads. *See also* MID-WORLD GESTURES. W:202

HODJI: *Hodji* means both "dim" and "hood." In the southern provinces of Mid-World, Walter O'Dim was known as Walter Hodji. He was given this nickname for two reasons—first for the hooded cloak he often wore and second for his ability to make himself DIM so that he could move unnoticed. VII:183

HOUKEN: *Houken* is a descriptive term. If someone comments on your *sad houken's eyes* they are talking about your waif eyes, or your melodramatically sad eyes. When Mordred calls Oy a "little furry *houken,*" he's calling him a sad little furry waif. VI:753

**HOWKEN: The act (and art) of hypnotizing someone, usually using a bullet as a focusing point. In the 2003 version of *The Gunslinger,* Roland twirls a bullet *howken* to hypnotize Jake.

IRINA: The healing madness that comes after terrible loss. VII:466

JIN-JIN: Quickly. As in "Get me a piece of chalk and do it *jin-jin.*" VII:149, W:69

KA: Like many words in High Speech, *ka* has multiple meanings and so is difficult to define precisely. It signifies life force, consciousness, duty, and destiny. In the vulgate, or low speech, it also means a place to which an individual must go. The closest terms in our language are probably *fate* and *destiny,* although *ka* also implies karma, or the accumulated destiny (and accumulated debt) of many existences. We are the servants of *ka,* but we are also its prisoners. *Ka's* one purpose is to turn, and we turn with it, albeit sometimes under different names and in different bodies. In the final volume of the Dark Tower series, *ka* is compared to a train hurtling forward, one which may not be sane. The *ka* of our world is NINETEEN. The *ka* of Roland's world is ninety-nine. II:178, V:31, V:91, VI:293, VI:341, VII:169, VII:302, VII:307

**KA-BABBIES: Young KA-TET mates. In the 2003 version of *The Gunslinger,* Cort warns Roland that if he takes his test of manhood and fails, he may never see his father, mother, or *ka*-babbies again. *See entry in* CALLA BRYN STURGIS DIALECT

KA-DINH: Oy believes that Jake is his *ka-dinh.* VII:92

KA-GAN: Gan himself. Writers and artists are KAS-KA-GAN. VII:458

KA-HUMES: *See entry in* END-WORLD TERMS

KA-MAI (KA-MAIS): *Ka's* fool, or destiny's fool. Roland uses this term to describe both Eddie Dean and Cuthbert Allgood. The servants of the Crimson King call Jake and Callahan *Gilead's ka-mais.* Those who are designated *ka-mais* are often safe from harm, or at least until *ka* tires of their antics and swats them out of the world.

The term *ka-mai* has other connotations as well. As has already been stated, it implies a constant joker (the kind Roland is obviously drawn to and easily angered by), yet the addition of *ka* adds another dimension to this term. One must remember that in Shakespeare's plays, it is often the fool who speaks the most profound truths. Sometimes jest is serious, or cuts to the heart of a matter which otherwise could not be addressed at all. Cuthbert and Eddie, both referred to as *ka-mai,* often have insights that Roland would neither grasp nor face on his own. It is Eddie, alone among the *ka-tet* traveling to the Tower, who realizes that Roland's potential for treachery and betrayal still exists. He jokes about it, yet he states it clearly enough, and directly to Roland. The gift of *ka-mai* is a necessary one on the road to the Tower. It is as necessary as the gift of the touch. IV:42, IV:282, V:527 *(opposite of* ka-me*),* VI:358, VII:6, VII:427

**KA'S BOOK: The Book of Destiny. Roland mentions this book when he meets his lover Alice in the 2003 version of *The Gunslinger.*

KA-MATES: Your *ka*-mates are those people whose fates (or destinies) are entwined with your own. It is another term for the members of your KA-TET. V:405

KA-ME: Wisely. It is the opposite of KA-MAI, which means foolishly. V:527

KAMMEN: The TODASH chimes, or the bells that you hear when you travel *todash.* This word has special significance for the Manni, since they travel between worlds so frequently. *See* TODASH: KAMMEN, *in* PORTALS

KA-SHUME: This rue-laden term does not have an exact translation. It describes the dark emotion one feels when a break in one's KA-TET looms. *Ka-tets* can only be broken by death or betrayal. Some argue, however, that these things are also aspects of KA. If this is the case, then *ka-shume* implies a sense of approaching disaster involving the members of a *ka-tet*. *Ka-shume* is the price paid for attempting to change or divert *ka*. VII:247, VII:250, VII:259, VII:307

KAS-KA GAN: Prophets of Gan or singers of Gan. All artists—whether they are writers, painters, sculptors, poets, or composers—are *kas-ka Gan*. VII:458

KA-TEL: A *ka-tel* is a class of apprentice gunslingers. Roland was the youngest of his *ka-tel*, yet he was the first to win his guns. IV:106

KA-TET: *Ka-tet* means "one made from many." *Ka* refers to destiny; *tet* refers to a group of people with the same interests or goals. *Ka-tet* is the place where men's lives are joined by fate. *Ka-tet* cannot be changed or bent to any individual's will, but it can be seen, known, and understood. The philosophers of Gilead stated that the bonds of *ka-tet* could be broken only by death or treachery. However, Roland's teacher Cort maintained that neither death nor treachery is strong enough to break the bonds of *ka-tet*, since these events are also tied to *ka*, or fate. Each member of a *ka-tet* is a piece of a puzzle. Each individual piece is a mystery, but when put together, the collective pieces form a greater picture. It takes many interwoven *ka-tets* to weave an historical tapestry. *Ka-tets* overlap, often sharing members. Individuals can also be partial members of a *ka-tet*, as Roland states when he pursues Jake through the underground mazes of Lud. Unlike the billy-bumbler Oy, who follows Jake by instinct as much as by sense of smell (members of the same *ka-tet* are drawn to one another), Roland believes he is not a complete member of Jake's destiny-bound group. He can share thoughts, but his destiny is slightly different from those of his companions. This may be because Roland is from a different world, but this explanation is not complete. After all, Oy is also from a different world, and is part of a different species.

A *ka-tet* is not always bound by love, affection, or friendship. Enemies are also *ka-tet*. Although usually referred to as positive or at least inevitable, the forces of *ka* and *ka-tet* can cast a sinister shadow over our lives. As Roland says to his friends when the shadow of KA-SHUME falls over their lives, "We are *ka-tet* . . . we are one from many. We have shared our water as we have shared our lives and our quest. If one should fall, that one will not be lost, for we are one and will not forget, even in death" (VII:260). For Jake, Eddie, Susannah, and Roland, the *ka-tet* holding them together also binds them to the Dark Tower and the Vacant Lot on Forty-sixth Street and Second Avenue. This place, where Tom and Jerry's Artistic Deli once stood, is the "secret heart" of their *ka-tet*. III:259, III:264, V:108, V:149, VI:341

KES: Pronounced like *kiss*. A person's *kes* is linked to his or her vitality. Even the Beams have *kes*. VII:334

KHEF: Literally speaking, *khef* means "the sharing of water." It also implies birth, life force, and all that is essential to existence. *Khef* can only be shared by those whom destiny has welded together for good or ill—in other words, by those who are KA-TET.

At the beginning of the original *Gunslinger*, we learn that one can progress through the *khef*. When we meet Roland, he has "progressed through the *khef* over many years, and had reached the fifth level." Those who attain the higher levels of *khef* (levels seven and eight) are able to have a clinical detachment from their bodies. The physical self may thirst, but the mind remains separate, a spectator.

Khef is both individual and collective. It implies the knowledge a person gains from dream-life as well as his or her life force. *Khef* is the web that binds a *ka-tet*. Those who share *khef* share thoughts. Their destinies are linked, as are their life forces. Behind the multiple meanings of this word lies a philosophy of inter-connectedness, a sense that all individuals, all events, are part of a greater pattern or plan. It also implies that through rigorous training (similar to that endured by gunslingers) the self can progress upward, rising tier to tier, until the body, if not one's ultimate destiny, is under the control of mind and will.

An individual's *khef* is often more complex than he or she realizes. In psychological terms, *khef* accounts for all parts of ourselves, even those aspects we wish not to see. It may also account for our other selves, those "twinners" (to borrow a term from *The Talisman*) who are our manifestations in other realities, or on other levels of the Dark Tower. Our fates, for good or for evil, are the result of both our own and our shared *khef*. Like Roland, who must face the fact that betrayal of those he loves is part of his destiny, we must realize that we are capable of both good and evil actions. Susannah Dean—the woman who emerged from the dual personalities of Detta Walker and Odetta Holmes—experiences this firsthand. While riding through the blasted lands beyond the city of Lud, "the dark side of her personality, that side of her *khef* which was Detta Walker" drank in the vision of complete destruction. Her other personalities—Susannah Dean and Odetta Holmes—reject the hateful horrors shown by Blaine's sadistic "visual mode," but Detta rejoices in them. The part of her that has experienced rage and pain identifies with the violence of it, and is somehow pleased by it. III:260, III:407, IV:29, V:15, V:92, V:98, V:149, V:296, VI:7, VI:341, VII:259

KI'BOX: *See entry in* CALLA BRYN STURGIS DIALECT

KI'COME: *See entry in* CALLA BRYN STURGIS DIALECT

KI'DAM: *See entry in* END-WORLD TERMS

MA'SUN: A war chest. Roland uses this word to describe the cave in STEEK-TETE where Ted Brautigan, Sheemie Ruiz, and Dinky Earnshaw have stored weapons for his KA-TET. VII:253

MIA: Mother. V:248

MIM: Mother Earth. VII:798

POL-KAM: The *pol-kam* is a dance, faster and lighter than a waltz, danced in the Great Hall of Gilead. Roland associates it with the courtesans, the jewel-like eyes of his lover Aileen, and the bright, shining electric lights of Gilead. I:137

PRIM: The Prim is the original magical Discordia, or soup of creation, from which the MULTIVERSE arose. *See also entry in* CHARACTERS

PROPHECY: In High Speech, prophecy is the information a person gains by having intercourse with a supernatural being. The term does not necessarily imply sexual intercourse, although, as we saw in *The Gunslinger,* many demons will not give prophecy unless a sexual price is paid. Prophecy is, as its name implies, prophetic. It describes events—in the distant future, a distant past, or in a distant place—which the seeker could learn about in no other manner. To seek prophecy is dangerous and should not be embarked upon lightly. VI:112

PROPHECY FOR THE LINE OF ELD: Mordred Deschain's birth fulfills an ancient prophecy which foretold the destruction of the last gunslinger:

> He who ends the line of Eld shall conceive a child of incest with his sister or his daughter, and the child will be marked, by his red heel shall you know him. It is he who shall stop the breath of the last warrior.

As we know from the Dark Tower series, Roland was tricked into conceiving a child with his KA-TET mate Susannah Dean. Roland's sperm was taken by a Demon Elemental (posing as the Oracle of the Mountains), which then turned itself into a male and impregnated Susannah in the Speaking Ring where she, Roland, and Eddie drew Jake Chambers into Mid-World. Although Roland is not actually Susannah's father, he is her DINH, or leader, and so is the father of their *ka-tet.* VI:252

RODERICKS (CHILDREN OF RODERICK, RODS): *See entry in* MID-WORLD ARGOT

SAI: Although used in low speech, *sai* appears to be a form of address that originated in High Speech. (Nort, Tull's weed-eater, used this term when he spoke to Roland in the Tongue.) *Sai* is a term of respect and can be roughly translated as "sir" or "madam." IV:143, IV:145

SEE-LAH: We aren't given a translation of this term, which is used by the Reverend Harrigan of our world. VI:318, VI:319

SEPPE-*SAI*: *Seppe-sai* was the name Roland's mother gave to the pie seller in the low-town of Gilead. It meant death-seller. During the heat of summer, his pies often became poisonous. V:605

SHUME: Shame and sorrow. W:11

SH'VEEN: A jilly, or mistress. V:120

**SILL: To desire or to yearn. If used patronizingly, it means that the yearner longs for something childish. It is a word with many subtle innuendos.

SO SPEAKS GAN, AND IN THE VOICE OF THE CAN CALAH, WHICH SOME CALL ANGELS: In its entirety, this quote reads as follows: "So speaks Gan, and in the voice of the can calah, which some call angels. Gan denies the can-toi; with the merry heart of the guiltless he denies the Crimson King and Discordia itself." Jake utters these words in a trance state. It seems likely that they are translated from the Tongue. VI:318

SOH (YOUNG SOH): The people of the MID-WORLD seem to use the term *soh* rather than *sai* when they are addressing a young person. Hence they often call Jake *Jake-soh*. V:150, V:417, V:489, W:272

STEEK-TETE: *See* CAN STEEK-TETE, *above*

TAHEEN: The *taheen* are creatures that belong neither to the natural (physical) world nor to the magical PRIM. According to Roland, they are misbegotten creatures from somewhere between the two. The *taheen* have the bodies of men but the heads of beasts. They are also known as the third people or the CAN-TOI. The *can-toi* (or low men) are rat-headed *taheen* that believe they are becoming human. *See entry in* CHARACTERS

TELAMEI: This term means to gossip about someone you shouldn't gossip about. V:389

TELEMETRY: *See entry in* END-WORLD TERMS

TET: A group of people with the same interests and goals. *Tet* is often joined with other terms, such as in the words *ka-tet, tet-ka can Gan*, etc. III:259

TET-FA: Friend of the *tet*. Before Tim Ross became a member of the *tet* of the gun, he was called *tet-fa*. W:268

TET-KA CAN GAN: The navel. When babies were born in the In-World baronies, the umbilical cord was cut and a cedar clip was placed just above the newborn's *tet-ka can Gan,* or navel. The clip would be wrapped in blue silk if the baby was a boy, or pink if the baby was a girl. VII:821

THROCKEN: This is an old term for a billy-bumbler. In Mid-world-that-was bumblers were bred to hunt down Grandfather Fleas and to predict the coming of STARKBLASTS. *See* BILLY-BUMBLER, *in* MID-WORLD ARGOT

TODANA: The term *todana* is a variation of the word *todash*. *Todana* means "death-bag." Eddie and Roland see one around Stephen King when they visit him in Bridgton in 1977. We also encounter death-bags in Stephen King's novel *Insomnia*. VI:290, VI:301

TODASH: *Todash* is a state similar to that of lucid dreaming. However, unlike in lucid dreaming, both the body and the mind travel *todash*. The sounding of the chimes, or KAMMEN, signal entry into the *todash* state. The blue-cloaked Manni often travel to other worlds via *todash*. Some of Maerlyn's magic balls can also send the unwilling into this place between worlds. Traveling via *todash* is not without risks. Many monsters live in the crevices between realities. *See entry in* PORTALS

TODASH TAHKEN: The holes in reality. V:413

TRIG DELAH: *See entry in* MID-WORLD ARGOT

TRUM: *See entry in* MID-WORLD ARGOT

TWIM: This means "two." It can also refer to a twin. VI:35, VI:39, VI:319, VII:141

URS-KA GAN: The Song of the Bear. *Urs-A-Ka Gan* means the scream of the Bear. VII:458

VES'-KA GAN: The Song of the Turtle. VII:446, VII:458

**WURDERLAK: When Roland meets with Walter in the golgotha, he fears that his guilt over Jake's death has made him into a *wurderlak,* or a kind of shape-shifter. As he says, "He was a *wurderlak,* lycanthropus of his own making, and in deep dreams he would become the boy and speak in strange tongues." This term is cut from the 2003 version of *The Gunslinger* and is replaced with the word *werewolf.* I:192

Zn: The Great Letter *Zn* stands for both "eternity" and "now," but it also means "come," as in *come-commala.* The green rice tendrils which decorate the ornate plates thrown in honor of Lady ORIZA take the shape of this letter. V:372

MID-WORLD GESTURES
(Hand motions, bows, throat taps, etc.)

ATTEND ME: This is a hand gesture that we have in our world too. If you look at someone and raise your index finger, it means *listen to me, or pay attention.* W:207

COME TO ME: This is actually an arm gesture. (It is the same beckoning gesture that we use in our world.) Roland uses it frequently. V:116

DELAH GESTURE: You can make the *delah* gesture by swinging your arms skyward. It is almost as if your arms are encompassing the whole world. (If someone asks you what you love about a place and you want to reply "everything," just make the *delah* gesture.) If you fling your arms skyward in an exaggerated *delah* gesture, it means *Who knows?* W:209

FIST TO FOREHEAD: To be polite to a new Mid-World acquaintance, you should raise your fist to your forehead. If you want to be extra polite, bow over your bended leg as you hold your fist to your forehead. If you are in an extremely formal situation, you should stretch one leg out in front of you, and while you keep your heel planted on the ground, bow forward while raising your fist to your forehead. If you must pay homage to a gunslinger, then kneel when you make your fist-to-forehead. This fist-to-forehead gesture can also be used as a military salute. VII:105, VII:130, VII:175, VII:236, VII:442

FORKED FINGERS: Forking your fingers at someone, something, or in a particular direction, is a way of warding off the evil eye.

    1. TO INDICATE AN EVIL PLACE, OR A PLACE YOU PERCEIVE AS EVIL: When Roland Deschain tells Talitha Unwin that he and his *tet* go in search of the Dark Tower, she recoils and forks the sign of the evil eye to the southeast, along the Path of the Beam. "I'm sorry to hear it!" she cries. "For no one who ever went in search of that black dog ever came back!" III:232.

    2. TO WARD OFF A DEMON: In *The Gunslinger,* a speaking ring oracle lures Jake away. When Roland pursues the boy, the demon tries to blind him with its sensual *glammer*. To break the spell, Roland holds the magical jawbone he found at the way station before his own eyes, and he holds his other arm out stiffly, the first and last fingers poked out in the ancient sign that wards off the evil eye. I:129 (2003 edition)

    3. FORKED FINGERS AND MAGIC: When Walter (the Man in Black) wants to use magic to create a fire, he lifts his hand skyward and shakes back his sleeve. Then he brings his hand down rapidly, index and pinkiey finger forked in the ancient sign of the evil eye, until his fingers point at the pile of wood to be burned. There is a flash of blue flame, and the fire lights. I:210 *(2003 edition)*

GIVE YOU PEACE: A short blessing, or prayer, to be said over the bodies of the dead. It should be accompanied by a simple gesture—pronging the fingers and drawing them down over the face of the corpse. Roland performs this ritual over the remains of Chevin of Chayven, a CHILD OF RODERICK. VII:51

HAND TWIRLING GESTURE: A somewhat impatient gesture. Roland frequently uses it. It means "carry on" or "hurry up." V:701

HILE GUNSLINGER. I SALUTE THEE: This honorary greeting made to a gunslinger is usually accompanied by dropping to one knee and placing a fist to the center of the forehead. *See* FIST TO FOREHEAD, *earlier in this section.* W:8

I SEE YOU VERY WELL: In some instances, when words cannot be exchanged, Roland places his fist to his forehead and bends his leg. Then he touches the corner of his eye and points to the person with whom he is communicating. This says, without words, "I see you very well." VII:131

I TELL YOU TRUTH: This is actually a hand gesture made by laying the fore-finger of the left hand across a circle made by the thumb and pinkie of the right. VII:311

MAKE HASTE: This sign language is used in the village of Tree. You raise one hand in a semi-circle above your head, scissoring the first two fingers as you do so. W:183.

POINTING TO THE CENTER OF YOUR FOREHEAD: Pointing to the center of your forehead, as if to an invisible eye, means you stand for John Farson. W:41

SALUTE FOR THE GOOD MAN/ SIGUL OF THE GOOD MAN (USED BY JOHN FARSON'S FORCES): This is a sigul, a greeting, and a salute. When two followers of the Good Man meet each other, they do the following:. They clasp their hands to their chests, left above right, then hold out both hands to the person being greeted. (The hands remain clasped.) As they make this motion, they say "Hile Farson!" IV:583--84

STAY PUT: This bit of sign language was used by the Fagonard tribe to commu-nicate with Tim Ross. The headman turned to Tim and held out both his hands (probably palm downwards). We have a very similar type of wordless communi-cation in our world. W:203

THROAT TAPS/CHEST TAPS: Throat tapping and chest tapping are important customs in Mid-World. For examples of different types of taps, see below. V:205, V:356, VI:148

    1. FORMAL GREETING WHEN A GUNSLINGER IS INTRODUCED TO A WOMAN OF IMPORTANCE: When Roland meets Talitha Unwin, the ancient matriarch of River Crossing, she speaks to him in the High Speech. "Hail, Gunslinger!" she says. "Welcome to River Crossing!" In reply, Roland removes his hat, bows, and with his right hand, rapidly taps his throat three times. (He bows as he taps.) "Thankee-*sai*, Old Mother," he says. This throat tapping expresses his respect for Talitha. III:231.

    2. COURTLY BOWS AND THROAT TAPS: When Roland meets Susan Delgado on the road to Hambry, he introduces himself and bows to her. "Will Dearborn at your service," he says as he doffs his hat and extends a foot on one boot heel and bows as they do in the Inner Baronies. Susan is embarrassed by such courtliness amid the wilds, but she curtsies and replies, "Susan Delgado at yours." Roland then taps his throat with the fingers of his right hand. "Thankee-*sai*, Susan Delgado," he says. "We're well-met, I hope." (NOTE: Roland's eagerness, and his extreme solicitous-ness, have to do with his youth and Susan's beauty. He falls in love with her as soon as he meets her.)

Roland asks permission to walk with Susan into Hambry. Susan says he can accompany her as far as the edge of town. Roland is so pleased that he taps his throat three times again and makes another bow with his leg held out stiffly before him, heel planted in the dirt. "Thankee Miss Delgado!" he says. IV:144–145

3. WOMEN AND BREASTBONE TAP (FORMAL GREETING WHEN A WOMAN IS INTRODUCED TO A MAN): When Susannah Dean introduces herself to Blaine the insane Mono, she taps her throat rapidly three times with the fingers of her right hand. Roland corrects her. When a woman greets a man, she must use the fingers of her left hand to tap her breastbone.

4. FOR LUCK: For luck, a man will tap his chest above his heart and then kiss his palm. IV:517

TWIRLING HAND: A somewhat impatient gesture which we have in our world too. Roland frequently uses it. It means "carry on" or "hurry up." V:701

YOU ARE SAFE: If you need to tell someone that he is safe, but you cannot speak out loud, this is what you should do: Cup your hands together and point them at the person who is in danger. This lets the individual know that you can and will help him. W:59

MID-WORLD ARGOT, ROLAND'S VERSIONS OF OUR WORDS, AND TERMS USED IN THIS CONCORDANCE

A BOY WHO CAN READ IS A TREASURE TO THE BARONY: This is one of the Covenant Man's sayings. W:157

A GUN MUST NEVER BE POINTED AT A PERSON UNLESS YOU WANT TO HURT OR KILL HIM. FOR GUNS HAVE EAGER HEARTS. This saying came from the Widow Smack's brother. He was very wise. W:187

A LADY'S ROSES: A light menstrual period. V:121

A MAN CAN'T PULL HIMSELF UP BY HIS OWN BOOTSTRAPS NO MATTER HOW HARD HE TRIES: This is one of Cort's sayings. Roland doesn't agree with it. VII:33

A ONE-EYED MAN SEES FLAT: This was one of Cort's sayings. It means that a person must use both eyes to gain a true perspective. In other words, it is best to try to see a situation from several angles before judging it. V:204

A ROPE SLIPPED IN CHURCH CAN'T BE UNSLIPPED: Marriage is permanently binding. W:123

A RUSTIE JUST WALKED OVER MY GRAVE (A RUSTIE HAD JUST WALKED OVER HIS GRAVE): *See* RUSTIE WALKED OVER MY GRAVE, *below*

A SOFTENING OF TIME: In Mid-World, time is no longer constant. It runs erratically. A day is no longer twenty-four hours, the sun doesn't always rise in the east, etc. V:105

A TALE FOR ANOTHER DAY: The full saying is, *But all those things are a tale for another day.* This comes at the end of a folktale, when people ask for more information, or when the talespinner wants his audience to return at a later date to hear more yarns. W:268

A WORD TO TUCK BENEATH YOUR HATS: Here's something to think about, or to remember. V:336

ABBA KA DABBA: This is the only magical saying that Tim Ross knows. It is a lot like *abracadabra* in our world. W:180

ABOUT THE GREAT MATTERS, YOU HAVE NO SAY: In other words, sometimes it is fate, and not the individual, who decides which events are to take place. All we mere mortals can do is hope and pray. This phrase is often used along with THERE WILL BE WATER IF GOD WILLS IT. V:87

ACHES AND MOLLIES: Aches and pains. VII:314

ADELINA SAYS SHE'S RANDY-O: This is part of a Mid-World drinking song. VII:520

AFTER A WHILE TALK SICKENS: There's only so much to say before you need to stop discussing a matter. V:142

AGE OF MAGIC/AGE OF MACHINES: According to the ancient history of Mid-World, the universe spun from Gan's navel, but Gan himself arose from the magical soup of creation called the PRIM. Eventually, the magical tide of the Prim receded, but it left on the shores of the mundane worlds the demons and spirits which human beings occasionally encounter, as well as the Dark Tower and the Beams, which hold the multiverse together. Although the Prim left enough magic to uphold both Tower and Beams for eternity (and enough demons and spirits to give mankind trouble for ages to come), human beings suffered a great loss of faith and sought to replace the magical Beams with manufactured machinery. Unfortunately, machines—like the men who make them—are mortal. Hence, the Age of Magic began the universe, but it seems likely that the Age of Machines will end it. VI:108–12

AIM TIME LIKE A GUN (TO AIM TIME LIKE A GUN): To time-travel, but to do so with a specific date in mind. V:116

AIM WITH THE EYE, SHOOT WITH THE MIND, KILL WITH THE HEART: This is the essence of the gunslinger litany, or what a gunslinger must learn to do to become an accomplished killer. V:110

ALL MY GODS ON THE HILL: This is the equivalent of *Oh my God!* When Roland ulters this phrase, he thumps his forehead with his reduced right hand. W:14

ALL THINGS SERVE KA AND FOLLOW THE BEAM: A phrase similar to ALL THINGS SERVE THE BEAM. In other words, all things work in harmony with the greater tides of fate. V:706

ALL THINGS SERVE THE BEAM: All things work in harmony with the greater tides of fate. All events serve a greater purpose, even if we can't understand what that purpose might be. V:93, VI:266, VII:304

ALL-A-GLOW: This is a Mid-World term for the imaginative and magical kingdom which children inhabit. VII:23

ALLEYO (PLANNING ALLEYO): Someone who is planning alleyo is planning to run away. V:395

ALLURE: The name given to a castle wall-walk. VI:103

ALTERNATE (OR ALTERNATIVE) AMERICAS: Many levels of the Dark Tower contain versions of the United States, but each version is unique. Hence, when I refer to the many incarnations of America (the versions that are similar to the one found on KEYSTONE EARTH but which are not exactly the same), I use this term. *See* MULTIPLE AMERICAS, *below*

ALWAYS CON YOUR VANTAGE: This was Cort's rule. In other words, always stop and examine your whereabouts. VII:778

AMERICA-SIDE: When our *tet*-mates use the term "America-side," they are usually referring to New York City, the metropolis where Eddie, Jake, and Susannah lived before entering Mid-World. However, this term could just as easily refer to part of the United States in any of the MULTIPLE AMERICAS. VII:758

AMMIES (WHITE AMMIES): Nurses. W:36

AMOCO: In Mid-World, AMOCO: LEAD FREE is a legend of unknown meaning. Roland once met a hermit who gained a religious following by placing an Amoco gasoline hose between his legs and preaching wild, guttural, sullen sermons. Amoco became the totem of a thunder god who was worshipped with a half-mad slaughter of sheep. I:154

AND MAY YOU HAVE TWICE THE NUMBER: *See* MAY YOUR DAYS BE LONG UPON THE EARTH, *below*

**ANIMALS THAT TALK BE TOUGH: Don't eat anything that can answer you back. Their flesh isn't pleasant.

ANTI-TODASH: According to Roland and Eddie, the heightened reality of our world is like an anti-*todash* force. Our world exists at the heart of the Beam, probably because Stephen King, the creator of Mid-World and the Beams, lives here. VI:265

ANY RO': Anyhow. V:407, VI:33, VII:239

AR'EE READY?: Are you ready? W:12

ARGYOU NOT ABOUT THE HAND YOU ARE DELT IN CARDS OR IN LIFE: This pithy phrase was written on a sign in the Travellers' Rest. IV:171

ARTYFAX: Artifacts, usually left by the Old People of Mid-World. W:64, W:170

ASSUME MAKES AN ASS OUT OF U AND ME: This particular phrase comes from Eddie Dean of New York. Basically, it means that if you assume something, there's a good chance that you'll be proven wrong, and in an embarrassing fashion. V:583

ASTIN: Roland's pronunciation of the word *aspirin*. II:98, II:102, V:104, VI:209, VII:41

ATTEND ME: *See* MID-WORLD GESTURES

AUTO-CARRIAGE: A car. V:518

AVEN-CAR: *See entry in* HIGH SPEECH

AYE: Yes. Can be used at the end of a sentence. For example, *take heed, aye?* V:161, W:13

AY-YI: An explanation of surprise or shock. Like "Oh my God" or "JEEZ." W:47

BABY-BUNTING RHYME:

> Baby-bunting, baby-dear,
> Baby, bring your berries here.
> Chussit, chissit, chassit!
> Bring enough to fill your basket.

When Roland was a little boy, his mother sang this song to him. *Chussit, chissit, chassit* are the High Speech words for the numbers seventeen, eighteen, and NINETEEN. VII:23

BAD TIMES ARE ON HORSEBACK: Bad times are coming quickly. I:163

BAG-FOLKEN: Bag-people. Unfortunately, many bag-people sleep rough in the cities of our world. VI:80

BAH AND BOLT: The bah is a crossbow. (It shoots bolts instead of arrows.) Like the people of Calla Bryn Sturgis, Roland's old friend Jamie DeCurry favored bah and bolt. V:20, V:204, V:324

BAH-BO: A bah-bo is a baby. It is a term of endearment. VII:149, VII:487

BANNOCK: Bannocks are herd beasts. They look like buffalo. VII:734, VII:745

BARN RUSTIES: *See* RUSTIES, *below*

BARREL OF THE BEAM (HEART OF THE BEAM): The energy that flows through the center of the Beam. If you are caught in the barrel of the Beam, you are in the heart of that ceaseless, powerful current. Your hair will probably be standing on end! VI:265, VI:269

BARREL-SHOOTERS: A type of gun. Vaughn Eisenhart owns two of them. Roland and his childhood friends called these firearms barrel-shooters because of their oversize cylinders. Unlike the cylinders of many other handguns, the cylinder of a barrel-shooter must be revolved by hand after each shot. V:319

BASTED IN A HOT OAST: A Mid-World saying which basically means "our goose is cooked." Roland likes to use it. VII:195

BATTLES THAT LAST FIVE MINUTES SPAWN LEGENDS THAT LIVE A THOUSAND YEARS: This is one of Roland's sayings. VII:5

BEAM BREAKERS: The Beam Breakers are powerful psychics who were kidnapped by the Crimson King and brought to End-World. The Red King stationed them in the DEVAR-TOI—a kind of luxurious prison—and set them to the task of destroying the Beams and bringing down the Dark Tower. Although a few of the Breakers rebel against their fate, most of them are pretty comfortable doing their job. Sad but true. *See* BREAKERS (BEAM BREAKERS), *in* CHARACTERS

BEAMQUAKE: A Beamquake feels like an earthquake, but it is a tremor felt in all of the worlds. A Beamquake takes place when one of the Tower's support Beams snaps. *See also* AVEN KAL, *in* HIGH SPEECH. VI:14

BEANS, BEANS, THE MUSICAL FRUIT. THE MORE YOU EAT, THE MORE YOU TOOT: We have this saying in our world too. The raven Zoltan was very fond of it. I:16

BEFORE VICTORY COMES TEMPTATION. AND THE GREATER THE VICTORY TO WIN, THE GREATER THE TEMPTATION TO WITHSTAND: This was one of Vannay's sayings. He called it "the one rule with no exceptions." VII:589, VII:601

BEHOLD YE, THE RETURN OF THE WHITE! AFTER EVIL WAYS AND EVIL DAYS, THE WHITE COMES AGAIN! BE OF GOOD HEART AND

HOLD UP YOUR HEAD, FOR YE HAVE LIVED TO SEE THE WHEEL OF KA BEGIN TO TURN ONCE MORE: Aunt Talitha of River Crossing utters this pronouncement. III:232

BIDE: Where you bide is where you live. W:38, W:66

BIG CHARLIE WIND: The Big Charlie Wind is a death wind. Mercy, from River Crossing, refers to the Big Charlie Wind that "came and almost blew the steeple off the church." III:248

BIG-HAT STOCK: Good, threaded stock. IV:206

BIG SKY DADDY: Some tribes of slow mutants call God "Big Sky Daddy." V:475

BILL OF CIRCULATION: A Bill of Circulation is a warrant or order. Often, a Bill of Circulation is an order to get out of town. W:45

BILLY-BUMBLER (BUMBLER, THROCKEN): A billy-bumbler (also called a throcken) looks like a cross between a raccoon, a woodchuck, and a dachshund. Bumblers' eyes are gold-black and they wag their little corkscrew tails like dogs. Bumblers are intelligent. In the days they lived with men, they could parrot the words they heard, and some could even count and add. Few wild ones seem to remember how to speak, although Jake's pet, Oy, does. Originally, Bumblers were bred to keep down vermin, including the nasty Grandfather Fleas. They were also kept to predict the coming of STARKBLASTS. If Oy is anything to go by, they are devoted to those they love and fiercely protective of them. According to the ferryman Bix, bumblers' ability to predict starkblasts is their BRIGHT, or special talent. *See also* OY, *in* CHARACTERS

BIN-RUSTIES: Bin-rusties are swallows. W:19, W:20

BINGO-WEED: In Mid-World, people chew bingo-weed. It stains the tongue yellow. W:286

BINNIE BUGS: These bugs hover over the swamps of Mid-Forest. While she is possessed by Mia, Susannah snatches them out of the air and gobbles them to feed her chap. (Yum.) V:82

BIT O' TAIL: "Bit of ass." A man's bit o' tail is his woman on the side, or his mistress. V:411

BLACK COLLAR OF MOURNING: After Gabrielle Deschain's death, every man in Gilead wore either a black mourning collar or a black band around his shirtsleeve. Women wore black nets over their hair. This continued for six months. W:35

BLACK THIRTEEN: Black Thirteen is the last and worst of Maerlyn's evil seeing spheres which are collectively known as Maerlyn's Rainbow. According to Roland, it is the most terrible object left over from the days of Arthur Eld, although it probably even predates Roland's illustrious and semimythical ances-tor. *See also* MAERLYN'S RAINBOW, *in* CHARACTERS

BLACKMOUTH: Cancer. Or as Roland pronounces it, *can't sir.* VII:141

BLOODSORES: A terrible degenerative disease that can eat away a person's face. The Widow Smack contracted bloodsores many years before Tim Ross knew her. Hence her face was terribly disfigured. W:112

BLOSSIES (BLOSSWOOD TREES): When Roland was young, Blossie trees were grown on a farm east of Gilead. Blossie was a lovely fine-grained wood, golden in color and almost light enough to float on air. Blossie wood could be used to build lakecraft, but it wasn't strong enough to build seafaring vessels. When Roland was a boy, the Blossie farms were wiped out by plague. However, Bloss-ies still grew in North'rd Barony's Endless Forest, north of Gilead. V:612, W:111

BLOW-WEED: Tobacco. VII:310

BLUE CAR SYNDROME: According to Susannah Dean, a person develops Blue Car Syndrome when he or she buys a blue car and then suddenly begins to see blue cars everywhere. Our *ka-tet* doesn't have Blue Car Syndrome but "Nineteen Syndrome." V:98

BLUEBACKS: Roland's term for police officers. VII:463, VII:472

**BOCKS: Dollars. It is the currency used in Tull.

BONFIRE OF DRAGONS: Just as a gathering of crows is called a murder, a gathering or group of dragons is called a bonfire. W:150

BOLA: A Mid-World weapon. According to Mid-World mythology, the harrier Gray Dick thought that his enemy, Lady ORIZA, would try to murder him with a bola. She killed him with a sharpened dinner plate instead. V:326

**BOLT AND BAH: Crossbow and bolt. Although Roland's KA-TEL trained with the bolt and bah, this weapon tends to be used by those without access to guns.

BONDSERVANT: A servant. VII:437

BONDSMAN: One who is bound to serve the DINH of his or her KA-TET. VII:258

BOOBYRIGGED: This is a term from Lud and is used by Tick-Tock. It means booby-trapped. III:354

BOOGERY HOT: Extremely hot. W:47

BORDER DWELLERS: Border Dwellers are the men and women who live on the edges of the Mohaine Desert. They burn devil grass and live in huts with sod roofs. Their diet consists of corn, beans, and peas. *See also* BORDER DWELL-ERS, *in* CHARACTERS

BOUGIE: A reanimated corpse. VII:764

BRAIN-STORM: A stroke. IV:625

BRAKES: The Brakes are those tangled areas of mixed vegetation and woody bushes that exist in the low hills near the Western Sea. II:286, II:296

BRIGHT: A person's bright is his talent. (A BUMBLER's bright is predicting the arrival of a STARKBLAST.) W:14

**BUCKA (BUCKA WAGGON, BUCKBOARD): A buckboard wagon is a horse-drawn vehicle whose body is formed by a plank of wood fixed to the axles. The ones driven by the Manni have rounded canvas tops. In the 2003 version of *The Gunslinger,* we learn that Buckas once followed the Great Road through the Mohaine Desert. V:14, V:21, V:477, V:654, VI:62

BUGGER-MAN: This is the Mid-World term for the Bogeyman. II:286

BUGS WON'T EAT THE FLESH OF A VIRTUOUS MAN: This is an old wives' saying repeated in the Endless Forest. It seems to hold true, since no flesh-eating insects marred the body of Big Jack Ross, though for many months he floated six inches below the bug-infested water of a sluggish forest stream. W:160–61

BULLDINK: This term is used in River Crossing and is the equivalent of "bullshit." III:248

BUMBLER: *See* BILLY-BUMBLER, *above*

BUMBLER GOT YOUR TONGUE?: Mia uses this term during her PALAVER with Susannah. It translates as "Cat got your tongue?" In other words, why are you so quiet? III:327, VI:246

BUMHUG: *Bumhug* is an amusing word that Jake and Eddie made up. Although we don't hear it as often in the final books of the Dark Tower series, we still occasionally come across it. A bumhug is a jerk, a poop-head, etc. VII:144, VII:173

BUMP-CRIBS: The small rooms or stalls where prostitutes do their business. W:277

BUX: Roland-speak for dollars (bucks). II:345

BY SHARDIK: This is the equivalent of saying "By God!" VII:34

CAMISAS: Spanish for shirts. Used in Hambry. IV:237

CANDA: *See entry in* HIGH SPEECH

CAN'EE SEE HOWGIT ROSEN-GAFF A TWEAK IT BETTER: Roland utters this phrase while talking to Patrick Danville about one of the roses of Can'-Ka No Rey. Basically, it means "Can you see that-there goddamn rose a little better?" VII:759

CARTOMOBILE: This is Roland's word for a car. VI:166, VII:426

CARVERS (BEER BARRELS): Five-shot revolvers. IV:393

CASTLE ROOKS: *See* GAN'S BLACKBIRDS, *below*

CASTLES: A game similar to chess. V:530

CAT'S PAW: When you PULL A COZY, or do a sting operation, you need someone to be your cat's paw, or your front-man or pawn. W:86

CATACLYSM: *See* GREAT POISONING, *below*

CHAFE: To chafe someone about something they've done is to upbraid them about it. W:186

CHANGED LIFE: According to Daria, the North Central Positronics Portable Guidance Module, a Changed Life is a creature that has been changed from its original form into that of a different type of creature. When Tim Ross first meets Maerlyn in *The Wind Through the Keyhole,* Maerlyn is a Changed Life. (He is in the form of a tyger.) W:222

CHASSIT: *See entry in* HIGH SPEECH

CHEFLET: Roland's pronunciation of the antibiotic Keflex. II:157, VII:635

CHERT: A stone much like quartz, which can be used to scrape hides. Hunters say it breaks lucky. VII:636, VII:638

CHILDREN OF RODERICK (RODS): The Children of Roderick (also known as Rods) are a band of mutants who swore allegiance to Arthur Eld in the long-ago. They are from lands beyond those known to Roland. *See* MUTANTS: CHILDREN OF RODERICK, *in* CHARACTERS

**CLAN-FAMS: Extended family units, or clans. In the 2003 version of *The Gunslinger,* we learn that many of these inbred groups live on the borders of the Mohaine Desert. *See also* END-WORLD TERMS

CLEARING AT THE END OF THE PATH (THE CLEARING AT THE END OF THE PATH): This is the place we all go to in the end, though each of us arrives there by a different route. The clearing at the end of the path is death—the snip at the end of the life-cord. III:380, V:374, VI:34, VI:243, VI:259

CLOAK FOLK: This is Eddie Dean's term for the Manni. VI:24

CLOBBERS/CLUMPETS: Straw hats worn by working men. W:270

CLOUTS: A clout is a cloth that can be used for cleaning, as in a dish-clout, or for diapering a BAH-BO. IV:127, IV:448, VII:22, VII:91

COME FORWARD, GOOD STRANGER, AND TELL US OF YOUR NEED: Come forward and speak. V:107

COME TO ME: *See* MID-WORLD GESTURES

COME-COME-COMMALA: *See* COMMALA, *in* CALLA BRYN STURGIS DIALECT

**COMMALA: A Mid-World dance also known as the Sowing Night Cotillion. *See entries in* HIGH SPEECH *and* CALLA BRYN STURGIS DIALECT

CONVERSATIONAL: A Conversational is a political event. In every barony of Mid-World, the week leading up to Fair-Day is full of Conversationals, which are like political luncheons. Important people come from all corners of a barony to meet and PALAVER. The main Conversational takes place on Fair-Day itself. IV:456–57

COOL AS A BLESSING: Water on a burn is cool as a blessing. W:260

COOZEY: Jonas calls Roland a "coozey little brat." IV:484

CORPSE-LAMPS: This is the name Roland gives for the lights he sees floating in the underground river located below the Cyclopean Mountains. I:153

CORSE: Corpse. W:172

CORVETTE: In the Barony of Mejis, a corvette is a small leather purse, big enough for a few coins. It tends to be carried by women rather than men, but men occasionally use them as well. Literally speaking, corvette means "little packet." As can be seen, however, a more practical definition is "little purse." IV:283

COSY: This term is from Lud. Gasher tells Jake "you've got a cosy look about you." Cosy seems to mean clever or full of guile. III:299

COTTON-GILLIES: *Cotton-gilly* is a fancy term for a common whore. A gilly (or sheevin) is a side-wife taken by a man who already has a legal wife. She is a mistress, but one who will be faithful to the man she serves. A cotton-gilly goes with whoever has enough ready cash. Gert Moggins of the Travellers' Rest uses this term for herself and the other girls. IV:447

COTTONWOOD: This is a tree that grows near the desert beaches of the Western Sea. Eddie makes a travois out of it in order to drag Roland north. II:167

COVENANT: A Covenant was sworn between Arthur Eld and the people of In-World. The people of In-World would pay taxes and the Eld and his men would protect them. The evil Covenant Man/tax collector (who was none other than Walter O'Dim in disguise) took advantage of this situation and charged exceedingly high taxes. The people came to resent Gilead, which was exactly what the Covenant Man wanted. W:113, W:133

COWPUNCHERS: Cowboys. W:45

COZEN (COZENING, COZENING BASTARDS): To cozen is to deceive. A cozening bastard is a deceitful bastard. V:647, VI:74, W:186

CRADLE: A station or homeport. It can also mean headquarters. III:303, III:316

CRADLE-AMAH: A nanny or childhood nurse. V:188

CRADLE-STORY: Nursery tale. V:341

CRIP SPACES: This term is actually used by Eddie, king of good taste. It refers to the handicapped spaces in a parking lot. IV:81

CROSSTREE: Gallows tree from which men are hanged. I:111

CRUNK: Dialect spoken by Mejis *vaqueros*. IV:575

CRY OFF: Renege. Stop. IV:40

CRY YOUR PARDON (CRY PARDON): I ask (or beg) your forgiveness. V:157, V:226, V:471, VI:22

CRY YOUR PARDON, BUT . . . NO MORE: I'm sorry, but that is no longer the case. W:28

CUCHILLLO: Spanish for knife. The term is used in Hambry. IV:365

CUJO: Although King fans may associate this word with mad dogs, in Mejis, *cujo* means "sweet one." VII:468

CULLIES (CULLY): In Mid-World, the word *cully* can be used positively. So much so that it seems roughly equivalent to the British term *lad*. However, you can also use the term *cully* or *cullies* to refer to a callow youth, or to foolish young men. In our world, a cully is someone who is easily duped or deceived. We hear this term in Lud and then again in Hambry. When Roland pulls his revolver on Gasher, Gasher replies, "Put it away, my cully . . . Put it away, my dear heart. Ye're a fierce trim, ay, that's clear, but this time you're outmatched." Susan Delgado calls Cuthbert "cully" when she gives him a CORVETTE with a note in it for Roland. Later, Coral Thorin uses the term when she addresses her lover, Eldred Jonas. It can be used negatively as well. Rhea calls Roland a "murdering cull" after he shoots Ermot, her pet snake. IV:418, V:44, V:362, VII:84

CUNNING: As in "a cunning little baby." Sweet, clever, amazing, perfectly made. IV:140

CUPPING YOUR HANDS TOGETHER: *See* MID-WORLD GESTURES

DAB HAND: If you have a dab hand at an activity, you are good at it. Susannah Dean proves to have a dab hand at throwing ORIZAS. IV:182, V:491

DANCE OF THE EASTERLING: *See* MID-WORLD HOLIDAYS, *in* APPENDIX IV

DANDY-O BALL: Although we are not given an exact definition, we know that a dandy-o ball is similar to the white silk of a milkweed. After Mordred sucks all of the moisture out of his second mother, Mia, we are told that her head looks like a dandy-o ball. It seems likely that a dandy-o ball is the fluffy seedhead of a dandelion. VII:141

DARK SIDE OF THE BLANKET: A child conceived on the dark side of the blanket is an illegitimate child, or one born outside of marriage. W:268

DEAD LETTER: A will. V:319

DEAD-LINE: A dead-line is a line that you cannot cross. The Crimson King set a dead-line around his castle walls so that none of his servants could leave. VII:605

DEAR: Often dropped into speech, as when Sheriff Peavy is describing how sharp Steven Deschain's sight was: ". . . your father had eyes like you wouldn't believe. Hawks ain't even in it, dear, or eagles, either." W:56

DEAR HEART: A term of affection. W:68

DELAH: *See entry in* HIGH SPEECH

DEMON MOON: The Demon Moon is the demonic, red-faced moon that rises during the season of REAP. *See also* REAP MOON, *below, and* MID-WORLD MOONS *at the beginning of this* Concordance. VII:659

DEUCIES: This term is used by the Pubes of Lud. It is a negative term and seems to imply that the person being described is either cowardly or foolish. III:319

DEVIL DUST/DEVIL POWDER: This is Roland's term for cocaine. It reminds him of devil grass. *See* DEMONS/SPIRITS/DEVILS, *in* CHARACTERS

DEVIL GRASS: Devil grass is a narcotic weed that grows in the wastelands of Mid-World. It is both poisonous and addictive. Those who become addicted to the grass are usually too poor to afford alcohol. They begin by smoking this nasty weed and end up chewing it. Chewers have green teeth and a rank stench. Devil grass gives its users dreams, nightmares, then death. It kills faster than liquor. Border Dwellers use devil grass for fuel since they have little else to burn. It gives off a greasy light and many believe that beckoning devils dance in the flames. *See* DEMONS/SPIRITS/DEVILS: DEVIL GRASS, *in* CHARACTERS

DIANA'S DREAM: Diana's Dream is a folktale similar to our story "The Lady or the Tiger?" *For page references, see* MID-WORLD FOLKLORE, *in* CHARACTERS

DIBBIN: A magical cloth that looks a little bit like a napkin, but its uses are many. When it is shaken out, it grows exponentially larger, and can act as a shelter from any storm, even a STARKBLAST. When folded and used with a magic feather from the tail of the Eagle Guardian, Garuda, it can act as a flying carpet. W:253

DIDDLESTICK: The whores in Gilead's Lower Town use this term. It probably means a dildo. W:42

DIED WHILE POSESSED OF A DEMON WHICH TROUBLED HER SPIRIT: In Gilead, this is what was said when a person of high blood committed suicide. W:37

DIG OUT THY EARS AND LISTEN: Listen well. W:160

DIM: *Dim* has several meanings. Sorcerers and witches can make themselves *dim,* or difficult to see. When a person is *dim* he or she is not invisible, merely shadowy. *The dim* is like déjà-vu. When Susan Delgado meets with Roland she feels the *dim,* or the sense that she has met him before, and feels faint. When Henchick of the Manni was close to BLACK THIRTEEN, Maerlyn's evil magic ball, he began to feel *dim*. In this latter case, *dim* implies going TODASH, or slipping between worlds. IV:256, IV:416, V:414, VI:31

DINH: *See entry in* HIGH SPEECH

DIPOLAR: As we learned in *The Waste Lands,* Lud's computers ran on either dipolar or unipolar circuits. In fact, it seems as though Mid-World's technology was based on slo-trans engines as well as dipolar and unipolar circuitry. III:355, V:72, V:563

DIRECTIVE NINETEEN: This phrase is often used by North Central Positronics robots and mechanisms when they are not allowed to share additional information. (In order to bypass Directive Nineteen, you have to use a password. Occasionally, you may even be asked to spell the password.) Often Directive Nineteen is an excuse to withhold information which could help an individual on his quest or perhaps even keep him safe from danger. We can't help but wonder whether Directive Nineteen was programmed into North Central Positronics mechanisms by the servants of the Crimson King. W:220, W:222

DISTRESSAL OF A LADY: In Eluria, this is a legalistic euphemism for rape. E:151

DIT-DAH WIRE: A telegraph. In Debaria, they have a dit-dah wire and several JING-JANGS. W:55

DJINNI: An evil genie. III:315

DO BUMBLERS LEARN TO SPEAK BACKWARD? NO MORE THAN CATS CHANGE THEIR SPOTS: In other words, people don't change. IV:251

**DO THAT I BEG YA: Please do it.

DO YER KEN: This is a term Gasher uses for "do you know." III:297

DO YOU CALL ME DINH? WILL YOU SHARE KHEF WITH ME AND DRINK THIS WATER?: Once they feel the impending weight of KA-SHUME upon them, Roland's KA-TET performs this ritual to reaffirm the bonds between them. Roland asks each of his *ka-tet* mates, in turn, these two questions. They answer in the affirmative and then share KHEF with him, symbolized by a sip of water. VII:258

DO YOU COME FOR AID AND SUCCOR?: *See* WILL YOU OPEN TO US IF WE OPEN TO YOU?, *below*

**DO YOU KENNIT?: Do you understand?

DO YOU SEE US FOR WHAT WE ARE, AND ACCEPT WHAT WE DO?: *See* WILL YOU OPEN TO US IF WE OPEN TO YOU?, *below*

**DO YOU SEE YOUR SISTER'S BUM?: This was one of Cort's sayings. It means "What are you staring at?"

DO YOU SET YOUR WATCH AND WARRANT ON IT?: Do you guarantee it? VI:283

DO YOU SWEAR ON YOUR WATCH AND WARRANT?: Do you swear it is true? W:46

DO'EE KEN: Do you know. *(More entries can be found in the* CALLA BRYN STURGIS *section.)* W:15

DOCKER'S CLUTCH: Roland's term for a gunholder. He uses this term for both hidden gunholders (such as the one under the counter at Clements Guns and Sporting Goods) and shoulder holsters. II:351, III:13, V:490, V:559

DOCKEY: Chicory. In River Crossing, they make coffee from Dockey. III:237

DOES THEE ASK IF I PLAY THE TOADY?: This phrase has several possible meanings. It could translate as "Are you calling me a liar?" but it seems more likely that it means "Do you really think I'm sucking up to you?" V:416

DOLINA: A kind of blanket found in Hambry. IV:282–83

DON'T MAKE THE MISTAKE OF PUTTING YOUR HEART NEAR HIS HAND: Don't leave yourself emotionally vulnerable. II:104

DON'T SHILLY-SHALLY: Don't mess about; don't waste time. V:116

DOUBLE-STEEL: Rail lines. W:294

'DOWNERS: One of Gilead's mealtimes. Marten (a secret glutton) put sugar in his coffee in mornings and at 'Downers. II:103

DRAWERS: The Drawers are places that are spoiled or useless or both. However, they are also places of extreme power, like psychic trash middens. VII:733

DROGUE AND FORWARD: Mid-World cowboys hired to protect caravans will ride drogue-and-forward to protect their convoy. In other words, they will ride before and behind. E:178

DROMEDARY: A camel. Young Bill Streeter's da' liked to say that their mule, Millie, was as solid as a dromedary. VI:160, W:88

DRY TWIST (OLD BONE-TWIST MAN): Arthritis. V:241, V:243, VI:10, VI:273

DUDS: Clothes. W:48

DUST-DEVILS: Dust that rises up in little tornado-like shapes. Dust-devils appear to be animated by evil spirits. Roland encounters dust-devils on the hardpan of the Mohaine Desert, and then again in the borderland town of Calla Bryn Sturgis. I:14, V:642

ELAPHAUNTS: Roland heard of these great creatures when he was a child. They are supposed to bury their own dead. II:29

EFDAY: Efday and Ethday were the two days of the week when Debaria's jail was filled with drunken cowpunchers and farmhands. They are probably Saturday and Sunday. W:62

ELD (THE WAY OF ELD, THE WAY OF THE ELD, ELD'S WAY): "It's no trick," Roland said. "Never think it. It's the Way of the Eld. We are of that an-tet, khef and kin, watch and warrant." The Way of the Eld signifies the way in which true gunslingers must conduct themselves. Gunslingers must protect the weak if it is at all within their power to do so. *For additional discussion and page references, see* ELD, ARTHUR, *in* CHARACTERS

ELD OF THE ELD: One of Arthur Eld's true descendants. W:60

ELD'S LAST FELLOWSHIP: The tapestry in the Dixie Pig depicts Arthur Eld's last fellowship. However, in that tapestry, Eld's rite is blasphemed, as it shows Arthur, his lady, and his knights taking part in a cannibal's feast. VII:26

ELEPHAUNT: An elephant. W:256

ELE-VAYDORS: Roland's word for elevators. VII:494

ENJIE: The engineer, or driver, of a train. W:62

ETHDAY: Efday and Ethday were the two days of the week when Debaria's jail was filled with drunken cowpunchers and farmhands. They are probably Saturday and Sunday. W:62

FAIR AND TRUE: If you say Roland and his KA-TET are gunslingers "fair and true," you mean that they are—without a doubt—true gunslingers. V:230

FAIR-DAY GOOSE: In Roland's world, a person won the Fair-Day goose if he or she won a Fair-Day riddling contest. In *Song of Susannah*, we find out that this phrase has a special significance for Stephen King. When he and his brother finished all their chores and did them well, his mother would tell them both that they'd won the Fair-Day goose. III:276–77, VI:277–78

FAIR-DAY RIDDLING: In Gilead-that-was, riddling was taken very seriously. Riddling contests were held during each of the seasonal festivals, especially during the festivals of Wide Earth and Full Earth. Riddles were considered to be full of power and were thought to make the crops grow stronger. III:276–77, III:416–17

FAIR-DAY SHOOTING CONTEST: A shooting gallery found at fairs both in our world and Mid-World. The usual targets are clay birds. The usual prize (in our world at least) is a stuffed toy. In Mid-World, you might win a FAIR-DAY GOOSE. VI:146

FAKEMENT: It can mean an event or a scene. It can also mean a falsehood. III:317, III:337

FALLING SICKNESS (KING'S EVIL): This is the disease that killed Roland's childhood friend Wallace. Wallace was the son of Vannay, Roland's tutor. V:78

FAN-GON: *See entry in* HIGH SPEECH

FAR ON THE OTHER SIDE OF TIME'S HORIZON: Long, long ago. VI:162

FARO: One of the games (along with Watch Me) damned by Sylvia Pittston during her Tull sermons. I:50

FASHED: Riled up. V:571. *See also* BOOM-FLURRY, *in* CALLA BRYN STURGIS DIALECT

FATHER, GUIDE MY HANDS AND HEART SO THAT NO PART OF THE ANIMAL WILL BE WASTED: A hunter's prayer. IV:93

FAULT ALWAYS LIES IN THE SAME PLACE—WITH HIM WEAK ENOUGH TO LAY BLAME: This is one of Cort's sayings. II:174

FEAR ME NOT, BUT HEAR ME WELL: Don't be afraid, but listen well to what I have to say. V:250

**FEAST OF JOSEPH FAIRTIME: People could buy captive tubes of swamp gas at this fair. The swamp-gas tubes looked something like neon. In the 2003 version of *The Gunslinger,* it is renamed the Feast of Reaptide Fair. I:186

FILL (THIS IS NOT OUR FILL): Your fill is your territory. If a place is not your fill, it is not your territory and is not your responsibility. W:61

FIN DE AÑO: The end-of-the-year celebration. Reap Night. IV:136

FIREDIM: A sparkling jewel that reflects light. They come in a variety of colors. Some are red, like rubies; some are green, like emeralds. Tick-Tock's eyes sometimes glow like firedims. II:39–40, III:359

FIREDIM TUBES: In Lud, they call neon tubes "firedim tubes." III:366

**FIRST BLOOD! FIRST BLOOD TO MY BOSOM: In the 2003 version of *The Gunslinger,* Cuthbert says this when Roland begins to best Cort. It's what is said when the first blood is drawn during a coming-of-age battle.

FIRST THE SMILES, THEN THE LIES. LAST COMES GUNFIRE: Both Roland's father and Cuthbert Allgood's father followed this rule when maneuvering in potentially hostile territory. It shows that the gunslingers had to use guile as well as diplomacy. V:590

FIST TO FOREHEAD: *See* MID-WORLD GESTURES

FIVE MINUTES' WORTH OF BLOOD AND STUPIDITY: Roland's description of battle. V:679

FLOWER (TO FLOWER): When disease grows, it flowers. Irene Tassenbaum had a lump removed from her breast before cancer could flower. VII:482

FOLKEN: Folks, or ordinary people. VII:242, VII:350

FOOD AND PALAVER DON'T MIX: Food and heavy discussion don't mix. V:134

FOO-LIGHTS: *See* HOBS, *below*

FOOL NOT YOUR MOTHER 'LESS SHE'S OUT OF FACE: In other words, don't lie. E:183

FOOLS ARE THE ONLY FOLK ON EARTH WHO CAN ABSOLUTELY COUNT ON GETTING WHAT THEY DESERVE: Fools always get what they deserve. IV:160

FOR A PRETTY: This doesn't have a direct translation. You often ask someone to do something "for a pretty." It seems to sometimes mean "please." It can also be a rhetorical statement added on to the end of a sentence. I:29, I:198

FOR THESE ARE MINE, SURE AS I AM THEIRS. WE ARE ROUND AND ROLL AS WE DO: Essentially, this means "We are family." V:110

FOR YOUR FATHER'S SAKE: Roland often uses this phrase. It means "Do it for your honor's sake." In Mid-World, or at least in the In-World baronies, culture was patriarchal. A gunslinger did not just bring honor (or disgrace) upon himself, but upon his father and all of his father's fathers. IV:22, IV:129, V:91, V:245

FORSPECIAL (FORSPECIAL PLATE): The plate which Odetta Holmes/ Susannah Dean's mother gave to Susannah's aunt (Sister Blue) as a wedding present. Soon after the wedding, little Odetta was hit on the head by a brick dropped by the psychopath Jack Mort, giving birth to Odetta's second personality, Detta Walker. For some reason, Detta Walker blamed Sister Blue for her accident and so broke the *forspecial* plate. The *forspecial* bore a marked resemblance to the flying ORIZAs hurled by the Sisters of the Plate in the borderland CALLAS. V:74, V:329, V:370

**FOT-SULS: Roland's version of Jake's word for the phosphorescent man-made "fossils" embedded in the rock below the Cyclopean Mountains. It probably refers to neon tubing.

FOTTERGRAFS (FOTERGRAFFS, FOTTERGRAFFS): Technically speaking, this is not a Mid-World term at all but Roland's rather garbled version of our word "photograph." II:344, II:345, IV:74, V:104, VII:41, VII:496

FOUR-SHOT: A four-shot revolver. The one that the Widow Smack gave to Tim Ross was about a foot long. The gripping handle was made of wood, the trigger and barrels were of dull metal. It had four barrels bound together by a band of what looked like brass. The holes at the end, where the bullets came out, were square. W:186–87

**FRESH COMMALA: Another term for the season of Sowing, also known as New Earth. *See* COMMALA, *in* HIGH SPEECH, GILEAD FAIR-DAYS, *at the beginning of this* Concordance, *and* MID-WORLD HOLIDAYS, *in* APPENDIX IV.

FRESH EYES SEE CLEAR: This is actually Susannah Dean's saying. It means that a person seeing a situation for the first time has a clearer understanding because he or she isn't bogged down by small details. VII:121

FULL EARTH: Full Earth is the season which comes after MID-SUMMER but before REAP. It is the time of ripening. According to Andy, the Calla Bryn Sturgis's duplicitous Messenger Robot, it is a propitious time for finishing up old business and meeting new people. The red HUNTRESS MOON is a Full Earth moon. *See also* GILEAD FAIR-DAYS, *at the beginning of this* Concordance. V:2, V:6, W:121

FULL OF HOT SPIT AND FIRE: Full of life and energy, but in this case, the energy is like lightning. VII:509

GAMRY BOTTLED GAS: The Old People used this fuel to fire up their talking grills. Our KA-TET is forced to use some while hunkering down in a campsite on Can-Steek-Tete, near the DEVAR-TOI. Eddie Dean finds the talking grill exceptionally annoying. VII:318

GAN BORE THE WORLD AND THE WORLD MOVED ON: A saying often used in Mid-World. Gan gave birth to the world from his navel, then tipped it with his finger and set it rolling. This forward movement is what we perceive to be time. *For more information about Gan, see* GAN, *in* CHARACTERS. VI:295

GAN'S BLACKBIRDS (CASTLE ROOKS): Gan's blackbirds are scavenger birds which feed upon the bodies of the dead. Often called Castle Rooks (though never Royal Rooks), they haunt execution yards. Le Casse Roi Russe is home to many, many of these sinister birds. Their cry sounds like "Croo, croo!" VII:585

GAN'S BLOOD: This is an exclamation equivalent to *My God* or *By God*. W:247

GENTLE FELLOWS: Gentlemen; wellborn men. W:44

GHOSTS ALWAYS HAUNT THE SAME HOUSE: This explains why ghosts don't take vacations. A person who dies in a place under unhappy circumstances remains there, quite possibly because he or she does not understand that he or she is dead. Roland uses this term to explain why the VAGS (or vagrant dead) always remain close to the places where they died. V:288

GHOSTWOOD: Ghostwood is another name for black ironwood, which is heavier than the usual ironwood. Black Thirteen's box is made of ghostwood. V:316, VI:83

GILLY: *See* JILLY, *below*

GIVE YOU PEACE: *See* MID-WORLD GESTURES

GIVE'EE: To give thee, or to give you. (I wish I had more food to give'ee.) W:16

GLAMMER: Magic or enchantment. Susannah Dean thinks that *glammer* has its own rules. Unfortunately, we mere mortals rarely comprehend them. *See entry under* MANNI TERMS. I:211, V:469, VII:690

GLEEP: To have a gleep is to have a long look, a stare, a gape, etc. W:54, W:279

GOAT MOON: Also known as "Goat with beard." In our world, it would be the February moon. It is the moon under which Eddie Dean was born. V:138, V:530

GOBBLE O'CLOCK: This is an Eddie Dean saying for, *it's dinnertime!* W:7

GOD-DRUMS: As we learned in *The Waste Lands,* the Grays of Lud broadcasted the god-drums throughout the city so that their enemies, the Pubes, would kill each other. The Pubes believed that the god-drums were the voices of the ghosts in the machines, which demanded human sacrifice. If they didn't ritually sacrifice one of their band each time the drums began, the dead would rise up and devour the living. In actuality, the Grays only thought they played the god-drums. The whole sadistic scenario was the creation of Blaine, Lud's mad computer brain. (Lud's Blaine was the same as Blaine the Mono.) Sadly, the god-drums were nothing more than the backbeat of ZZ Top's song "Velcro Fly." As Eddie Dean wryly observed, the Pubes killed each other for a song that never even made it as a single. VI:205

GODS-A-GLORY: "Oh my God" or "Oh my gosh!" V:332

GOLGOTHA: A place of the skull, or a dead place. I:197

GOMPA HOLE: A horse that steps in a gompa hole will probably break his leg. W:92

GONE DAYS: Those days are gone, and you can't do anything to change them or to bring them back. V:101, W:31

GONE WORLD, THE: This phrase refers to the world from which our own world has "moved on." It is equivalent to "the olden days." For the people of Mid-World and the borderlands, the gone world was a better world. Gilead is part of the gone world, hence Roland himself is also part of the gone world. V:214

GONICKS: This is Mia's word. We are not given a translation. VII:64

GOOD RIDDANCE TO BAD SWILL: The Pubes of Lud use this term instead of "Good riddance to bad rubbish." III:324

GOOK: A deep well. Common law says that any traveler may drink from a gook without let or penalty. W:18

GOOSE JUST WALKED OVER YOUR GRAVE (A GOOSE JUST WALKED OVER YOUR GRAVE): This phrase is equivalent to "A cat just stepped on my grave." In other words, you had a sudden eerie, inexplicable chill. VII:315

GORMLESS: Stupid or foolish. W:134

GRAF: An apple beer that seems to be a specialty of Mid-World. It is offered to Roland, Susannah, Eddie, and Jake when they visit the elderly people of River Crossing. It is also served in Hambry. Mid-World is full of orchards (both Roland and Tick-Tock have memories of them), so it makes sense that the Mid-World drink of choice should be a kind of hard cider. III:234, V:127, W:123

GRANDFATHER FLEAS (LITTLE DOCTORS): Grandfather Fleas are the parasitic bugs which feast on the GRANDFATHERS' leftovers. If you see Grandfather Fleas, you know that the Grandfathers can't be far away. *For more information, see* VAMPIRES: TYPE ONE: GRANDFATHER FLEAS, *in* CHARACTERS

GRANDFATHERS: The Grandfathers are TYPE ONE VAMPIRES. They are the nastiest of the demons that the receding PRIM left stranded upon the shores of Mid-World. The Grandfathers are monstrous-looking creatures. They have shriveled faces and black, oozing eyes. They have so many teeth that they can't close their lips, and even their skin is scaled with teeth. These Type Ones don't just drink human blood—they eat human flesh as well. *For more information, see* VAMPIRES: TYPE ONE, *in* CHARACTERS

GRANTHER: Grandfather. W:80

GRASS-EATERS, GRASS-EATING LOOK: Roland thinks that most civilians look more like grass-eaters, or sheep, than people. VI:131, VII:39

GRAYS: *See* GRAYS, *in* CHARACTERS

GREAT DARKNESS: The End-World region of Thunderclap. W:10

GREAT FIRE: *See* GREAT POISONING, *below*

GREAT GROTTING IDIOT: A Mid-World insult. If you call someone a great grotting idiot you are telling them they are a big dummy. W:69

GREAT LETTERS: The letters of High Speech. V:93, VII:494

GREAT POISONING (OLD WAR, THE GREAT FIRE, THE CATACLYSM): This horrific event took place more than a thousand years before the grandparents of the River Crossing folks were born. It caused the animal, plant, and human populations of Mid-World to give birth to muties, and it made great swaths of land turn into wasteland. It was the beginning of all Mid-World's troubles. III:284–85

GREATER DISCORDIA: *See* PRIM, *below*

GREEN CORN A-DAYO: *See entry in* CALLA BRYN STURGIS DIALECT

GREENSTICKING: To put pressure on someone, or "to twist an arm." V:92

GREEZY: This is Lud-speak for "greasy." III:327

GROUND-SHAKERS: Many of the railroad tracks of the Western Line have been destroyed by washout and ground-shakers, in other words by floods and earthquakes. W:40

**GROW BAG: A grow bag is a magical purse that grows money. Roland's grow bag was given to him by his father, Steven Deschain. Roland's purse can be emptied three times, as we see in Calla Bryn Sturgis when Roland gives money to his three KA-TET mates. The first time the purse spills silver, the second time it spills gold, and the third time it spills garnets. We don't know whether the grow bag always grows the same riches or whether it responds to the needs of the receiver. At the end of the 2003 version of *Gunslinger,* while he holds palaver with Walter in the golgotha, Roland hints that his grow bag can grow tobacco as well as money and gems. V:401

GUARD, THE: This is a gun-holding position used by gunslingers. In the guard position, the gun barrel rests on the hollow of the left shoulder. VII:192

GUARD O' THE WATCH: An officer of the law. Roland uses this term for both the guards of his world and the police of ours. I:109, VI:258, VII:463

GUIJARROS: In Spanish this means cobbles or pebbles. Both the stone walls and the cracked *guijarros* of Rhea's roof are slimed with mold. IV:394

GULLYWASH: This is Gasher-speak and is probably part of Lud's slang. It seems to mean penis. III:298

GUNBUNNY: A gunbunny is a gunman. W:272

GUNNA: *See entry in* HIGH SPEECH

GUNNIE (YOUNG GUNNIE): Young gunslinger. W:49

GUNSLINGER BURRITOS: The vegetarian wraps which Roland makes for his KA-TET while they are traveling. Eddie Dean prefers meat. V:134, W:7

GUNSLINGER LITANY: Every gunslinger must learn to recite the following litany: "I do not aim with my hand; he who aims with his hand has forgotten the face of his father. I aim with my eye. I do not shoot with my hand; he who shoots with his hand has forgotten the face of his father. I shoot with my mind. I do not kill with my gun; he who kills with his gun has forgotten the face of his father. I kill with my heart." III:14, III:68, V:155–56

GUNSLINGER QUESTIONS: *See* WILL YOU OPEN TO US IF WE OPEN TO YOU?

HACI: Short for *hacienda* or house. IV:191, W:47

HAI: This is the term Roland uses to call his hawk, David. I:169

HARD BISCUIT: If you pay for something in hard biscuit, you are paying in silver or gold, not SCRIP. W:101

HARD COIN: Money, not SCRIP. W:114

HARD RAIN MAKES FOR QUEER BEDFELLOWS AT THE INN (A HARD RAIN MAKES FOR QUEER BEDFELLOWS AT THE INN): We have a version of this saying in our world too: "Necessity makes for strange bedfellows." VII:791

HARRIERS: Bandits or outlaws. The harriers of Mid-World rob, loot, murder and destroy. The Grays are harriers, as are the Big Coffin Hunters. Harriers blinded Mercy of River Crossing with a branding iron because, they said, she was "looking at em pert." III:226, III:230, V:92, VI:131, W:10

HAVE YOU THUDBRAINS NOT KENNED EVEN YET WHO'S IN CHARGE OF THIS RAREE?: Haven't you stupid men realized yet who is in charge of this operation? W:274

HE KEPT HIS FACE WELL: His face didn't betray his emotions. V:205

HE'S MADE OF LIES FROM BOOTS TO CROWN: This is the Widow Smack's assessment of the evil Covenant Man. W:175

HEAD CLEAR. MOUTH SHUT. SEE MUCH. SAY LITTLE: Roland's advice to Jake when the boy is about to go and stay at Eisenhart's ranch. V:205

HEADKNOCKER: A kind of club or nightstick used by Sheriff Peavy and other sheriffs. Headknockers are usually made of IRONWOOD. W:285

HEAR HIM VERY WELL: Listen to what he's saying. VI:193

HEART OF THE BEAM: *See* BARREL OF THE BEAM, *above*

HEART-STORM: *See* BRAIN-STORM

HERE WE ARE, AND KA STANDS TO ONE SIDE AND LAUGHS. WE MUST DO AS IT WILLS OR PAY THE PRICE: Sometimes it is fate, and not free will, which decides our destinies. If we try to buck fate, we will be punished for it. V:395

HIDE UP: To haul up, as in to haul up somewhere and wait out a storm. W:14

HIDE UP: When you hide up in a place you take refuge there. W:14

HIGH PURE: The Low Pure was the foothill meadow below the salt-houses in Debaria. The High Pure was the meadow on higher ground, located to the east of the salt-houses. W:63

HILE: Unlike most words, *hile* is used in both low and High Speech. The Manni call it *fin-gan*, or the first word. They believe that the word *hile* set the world spinning. In low speech, hile is a formal greeting. Roland greets Blaine by saying "Hile, Blaine." Blaine returns with "Hile, Gunslinger." This verbal exchange makes Susannah Dean think of Hitler, but it is actually a formal Mid-World greeting. This term is also used to call animals. *See entry in* HIGH SPEECH. IV:21, IV:261, V:107, W:201, W:202

HILE AND MERRY-GREET-THE-DAY: A form of "Good morning." The response is "Merry see, merry be." VII:310

HILE GUNSLINGER. I SALUTE THEE. This honorary greeting made to a gunslinger is usually accompanied by dropping to one knee and placing a fist to the center of the forehead. W:8

HILE SIR THROCKEN: This saying comes from *The Throcken and the Dragon,* W:7

HIS KA'S GONE INTO THE CLEARING, BUT WHAT'S LEFT IS HERE: His spirit has passed on, but here are his mortal remains. W:177

HOBS (FOO-LIGHTS): A hob is like a will-o'-the-wisp. Susannah sees these orange lights swirling while she and Roland travel through the White Lands of Empathica. A hob is also a kind of demon. Roland calls the Crimson King a hob. VII:630, VII:730, VII:799

HODJI: *See entry in* HIGH SPEECH

HOLD YOUR GABBER: Be quiet. W:272

HOLLERED LIKE AN OWL: This is Roland's phrase. It expresses disapproval of those who aren't stoic enough to withstand pain. VII:191

HOLLOW CHAMBER, THE: Roland's gentle tutor, Vannay, taught his pupils that violence worsened problems more often than it solved them. He called violence the hollow chamber where all true sounds become distorted by echoes and can no longer be clearly understood. V:78–79

HONOR STANCE: This is the term Cort uses for a boxer's opening stance. The lobstrosities that live on the shores of the Western Sea stand like this whenever there is an approaching wave. II:16

HOO-HOO BIRD: A nocturnal bird, probably an owl. VII:164

HORROR'S A WORM THAT MUST BE COUGHED OUT BEFORE IT BREEDS: This saying comes from the Prioress of Serenity, Everlynne. W:51

HORSEAPPLES: Horse droppings. W:79

HOSS-CLINKUM: A bridle-ring. W:94

HOT-ENJ: This is the Old People's term for an atomic locomotive. VII:531, VII:678

HOT-LUNG: *See entry in* CALLA BRYN STURGIS DIALECT

HOUKEN: *See entry in* HIGH SPEECH

HOUSIES: Ghosts or whispering voices that murmur in the shadows. Housies are quite nasty, and although they can't usually hurt humans, they can harm small animals like BILLY-BUMBLERS. VII:590

HOWLERS: This is Roland's term for sirens. II:153

HUBBERWOMEN: Hubberwomen are magical or fey women. E:177

HUMES: *See entry in* END-WORLD TERMS

HUMPIES: Roland uses this term for the cowboys that work Eisenhart's ranch. V:489

HUNCH-THINK: To go on a hunch. VII:217

HUNKER (TO HUNKER): To crouch down or squat. V:509

HUNTRESS MOON: The red Huntress Moon is the first moon of FULL EARTH. It marks the end of summer. *See also* MID-WORLD MOONS *at the beginning of this* Concordance. V:4, V:138

I CAN'T FORK HAY WITH A SPOON: I can't do this; what I'm being asked to do is impossible. W:237

**I CRY YOUR FAVOR: I ask for a favor.

I CRY YOUR PARDON: I beg your forgiveness. III:177, III:269, V:154

I HAVE FORGOTTEN THE FACE OF MY FATHER: This is a term often used by Roland. It is a phrase of shame. When one has forgotten the face of one's father, it means that one has behaved dishonorably. Mid-World is patriarchal, a cultural structure that is older than either the aristocracy of gunslingers (the Barons of Mid-World), or the kingship of Arthur Eld. When Eddie and Susannah visit the Cradle of Lud, they see the sculpted visages of "stern men with the harsh faces of executioners who are happy in their work" (III:343). We do not know whether these men were judges, justices, politicians, or legendary forefathers, but their sculpted faces, somehow reminiscent of busts of Roman senators, tell us something about both the pride and the unrelenting harshness of the Great Old Ones. Like the Romans, or our own culture, they were guilty of *hubris*. I:97

I HAVE JUST BEEN CASTLED: "I've just been stumped" or "I've just been outdone." It's similar to saying "touché" or "checkmate." V:482

I ONLY DO AS KA WILLS: I do only what fate demands of me, and what honor demands of me. V:336

I PULLED YOUR SNOUT: I pulled your leg. W:155

I'M JUST WHAT COMES IN THE SAME SADDLEBAG: I just come with the rest of the package. W:121

IN THE PROPER HAND, ANY OBJECT CAN BE MAGIC: This is one of the Covenant Man's sayings. He is evil, but this statement is true enough. W:242

I SEE YOU VERY WELL: "I see you," but it also implies a deeper and more profound focus upon the person being viewed. This phrase seems to imply that the speaker sees the whole person—their past and present, their needs and desires. *See also* MID-WORLD GESTURES VII:115

I SET MY WATCH AND WARRANT ON IT: I bet my life on it. V:30, V:538, VI:7

I SWEAR ON THE FACE OF MY FATHER: I swear upon all I hold sacred. VI:188

I TELL YOU TRUTH: *See* MID-WORLD GESTURES

I WILL SET MY WATCH AND WARRANT ON IT: I'll bet on it, or I'll guarantee it. It's damn true. III:332, III:353

I WON'T WORRY THAT OLD KNOT: I won't go back and dig up that old business. V:477

I WOT: "I believe so" or "I reckon so." IV:104

I WOULD SPEAK TO YOU AN-TET: I would speak to you in private, of important matters, etc. When you speak AN-TET, you speak honestly and intimately. V:117

IF IT'S KA, IT WILL COME LIKE THE WIND: If it's meant to be, it will be. IV:157

IF KA WILL SAY SO, LET IT BE SO: This was one of Steven Deschain's phrases. VII:442, VII:516

IF—THE ONLY WORD A THOUSAND LETTERS LONG: The word *if* encompasses a thousand possibilities. V:109

IF YE'D STEAL THE SILVER FROM THE DINING ROOM, FIRST PUT THE DOG IN THE PANTRY: A famous saying from the Barony of Cressia. IV:175

I'LL HAVE YOUR WORD, SWORN UPON THE FACE OF YOUR FATHER: If you ask someone to swear in this way, it's like asking them to swear an oath upon a sacred book. V:481

ILL-SICK VAPORS: According to Roland, tobacco keeps away ill-sick vapors. In other words, it chases away all those nasty viruses and diseases. Eddie Dean doesn't think that the Surgeon General would believe such a statement. VI:299

IRINA: *See entry in* HIGH SPEECH

IRONWOOD (BLACK IRONWOOD): Ironwood trees grow in many of Mid-World's forests, most famously the Endless Forest of North'rd Barony. Their wood is hard and durable. In fact, it's too hard to burn. Many of the doors between worlds (including the Beach Doors) are made of ironwood. Black Thirteen's box is made of black ironwood, a type which is also known as GHOST-WOOD. In "The Little Sisters of Eluria," we are told that this tree is also known as the seequoiah. Cort's stick was made of this durable material. *See also* IRON-WOOD *in* CHARACTERS *section* E:151, V:74, V:81, V:316

IT'S ALL THE SAME JOLLY FAKEMENT TO ME: This is a Lud term for "It's all the same to me." III:297

IT'S LONG SINCE I WAS WEANED: I wasn't born yesterday. W:49

IT'S THE WAY OF THE ELD. WE ARE OF THAT AN-TET, KHEF AND KA, WATCH AND WARRANT: Roland uses this phrase. In other words, he and his KA-TET are descended from the Eld and follow the Way of Eld in this life and every life. V:156

I-WANT LINES: The lines that carve their course from the sides of the nose down to the chin. V:122

JACKAROE: A strong alcoholic drink. W:128

JACKS POP UP: A card game played by children. W:105

JAKES: Toilet or outhouse. W:36

JESUS DOG (CROSS DOG): This is the term used to describe dogs with a cruciform shape upon their chest fur. As Roland finds out when he faces the Little Sisters of Eluria, they can prove extremely useful when confronting vampires. *See also* ELURIA CHARACTERS, *in* CHARACTERS

**JILLY: The term *jilly* is another spelling of the word *gilly,* which was used frequently in *Wizard and Glass.* Whichever way you spell it, *jilly* means concubine or mistress. This particular use of *jilly* should not to be confused with the jilly of Punch and Jilly (a Mid-World version of Punch and Judy). Its plural form is gillies or jillies. Arthur Eld had forty jillies, and it is from one of these women that Roland is descended. Although many great men of Mid-World had jillies and many more were born of jillies, there is a certain disgrace attached to this state of being. In Mid-World, where mutations abound and where sterility is common, jillies are seen as necessary if not necessarily respectable. Roland is shocked to find out that Susan Delgado will soon be Hart Thorin's jilly. Susan receives disapproving stares from the women of Hambry because of the "service" she is about to render the town's mayor. IV:207, V:7, V:632

**JILLY-CHILD: A young jilly or gilly. *See* JILLY, *above*

**JILLY-COME-LATELY: A sarcastic comment about youth. An old woman can also look like a jilly-come-lately when compared with a much older woman.

JIN-JIN: *See entry in* HIGH SPEECH

JING-JANG: An old-fashioned telephone. In Debaria, their jing-jangs used to be able to call all the way to Gilead. Now the telephone lines only reach as far as the Jefferson Ranch to the north, Sallywood in the south, and Little Debaria to the northeast. W:54

JIPPA: To go jippa is to go crazy. This is an unpleasant term that people in Tree Village use for someone who has lost his mind. W:219

JUGWEED: A weed that grows in the alkali ranchlands north of Debaria. W:74

KA HAS NO HEART OR MIND: *Ka* does what it must do without considering the emotions of mere mortals. VI:16

KA IS A WHEEL: *Ka* is a wheel. Its purpose is to turn and to bring us back to where we started, or to an equivalent place. W:60

KA LIKE A WIND: *Ka* comes with a force of its own. V:31

KA SPEAKS AND THE WIND BLOWS: *Ka* is the force behind all events. VII:305

KA WAS A WHEEL, ITS ONE PURPOSE TO TURN, AND IN THE END IT ALWAYS CAME BACK TO THE PLACE WHERE IT HAD STARTED: This is another Mid-World truism. What you do comes back to haunt you. What goes around comes around. III:394

KA WAS OFTEN THE LAST THING YOU HAD TO RISE ABOVE: *Ka* doesn't always bring what we want it to bring. It can bring death and failure too. V:661

KA WORKS AND THE WORLD MOVES ON: Roland utters this phrase in anger after Ben Slightman apologizes for supplying information to the WOLVES of Thunderclap and their masters. Roland's exact response is "Balls to your sorry. *Ka* works and the world moves on." V:658

KA WOULD TELL. IT ALWAYS DID: In the end, *ka* has the final say over our fates. V:160

KA-DADDY: A slang term for one's boss. VI:144

KA-DINH: *See entry in* HIGH SPEECH

KAFFIN TWINS: Identical twins who are joined at the body. In our world, we often use the term "Siamese twins." V:675

KA-MATE: Your *ka*-mate is your tet-mate, or a person bound to you by *ka*. W:31

KAMMEN: *See entry in* HIGH SPEECH

KA-SHUME: *See entry in* HIGH SPEECH

KEEP EM WELL, DO: Keep them safe. W:15

KEN (TO KEN) To know. *See also* CALLA BRYN STURGIS DIALECT. W:17

KENNIT: *See entry in* CALLA BRYN STURGIS DIALECT

KEY WORLD: Our world is the key world because Stephen King, the key maker, lives in it. *See also* KEYSTONE EARTH, *in* END-WORLD TERMS. VI:200

KI'BOX: *See entry in* CALLA BRYN STURGIS DIALECT

KI'COME: *See entry in* CALLA BRYN STURGIS DIALECT

KI'-DAM: *See entry in* END-WORLD TERMS

KING'S EVIL: *See* FALLING SICKNESS, *above*

KINKMAN: The kinkman is the showman who stands outside a carnival tent and tries to entice people in. W:58

KISSIN DON'T LAST; COOKIN DO: So say the Manni-folk. W:150

KISSING MOON: The full moon of FULL EARTH is known as the Kissing Moon. In *Wizard and Glass,* Roland meets Susan Delgado under this perfect disk of silver. *See also* MID-WORLD MOONS, *located at the beginning of this* Concordance. IV:115

KNUCKLES (GOLD KNUCKLES, SILVER KNUCKLES, GOLD KNUCKS): Used as money in the Mid-World of Roland's youth. W:44

**KUVIAN NIGHT-SOLDIER: It seems likely that the Kuvian night-soldiers were a band of assassins. This term does not appear in the 2003 version of *The Gunslinger.* I:200

LADY OF THE PLATE: *See entry in* CALLA BRYN STURGIS DIALECT

LADY-*SAI*: A formal term of address for a woman. W:49

LAND-PIRATES: Mid-World's roving bands of harriers gave themselves this name. Farson was essentially a land-pirate with pretensions. W:40

LAST TIMES: This is Sylvia Pittston's term for the End of the World. I:50

LEAD US NOT INTO TEMPTATION: This phrase is another one of the raven Zoltan's sayings. In our world, it can be found in the Lord's Prayer. I:20

LEMON JUICE WON'T TAKE THE STAIN OUT OF A LADY'S REPUTA-TION: It's not easy to lose a bad rep. IV:143

LET BE WHAT WILL BE, AND HUSH, AND LET KA WORK: Roland learned this saying from his mother, Gabrielle Deschain. VII:729

LET EVIL WAIT FOR THE DAY ON WHICH IT MUST FALL: This saying comes from Gilead. It means that you shouldn't borrow trouble from the future since it will arrive soon enough. V:162

**LET'S SHAKE A MILE: Let's get moving.

LET YOUR SHADOW GROW. LET IT GROW HAIR ON ITS FACE. LET IT BECOME DARK: Wait until you're older. I:172

LIFE FOR YOU AND FOR YOUR CROP: A Mid-World greeting. V:72

LIFE FOR YOUR CROP: This is a Mid-World greeting. Roland uses it when he meets Brown, the Border Dweller. I:15

LIFE IS A WHEEL AND WE ALL SAY THANKYA: Life, like KA, is a wheel. We seem to move forward, but in the end we find ourselves back just where we began. VII:4

LINEOUT: This is Roland's word for an outline. VI:285

LINIMENT AND STINKUM: The Jefferson Ranch's deserted tack shed contained dust-covered jugs of liniment and stinkum. W:77

LOAD (THE LOAD): *See entry in* CALLA BRYN STURGIS DIALECT

LOG OF EASE: The log which campers sit on to dump the proverbial dinner. I suppose some people find it easier than squatting to poop. VII:635

LONG AGO (THE LONG AGO): The time before the world moved on. VII:9, VII:161, VII:178

LONG DAYS AND PLEASANT NIGHTS: A Mid-World greeting. The proper response is "May you have twice the number." In Calla Bryn Sturgis, this greeting is accompanied by three taps to the throat. IV:197, V:3, VI:149

LONGSTICK: Steven Deschain stated that the women of Serenity preferred a longstick to a man. In other words, they would rather take pleasure from a fake phallus than lie with a man. W:38

LOOK NOT LONG AT WHAT'S OFFERED, FOR EVERY PRECIOUS THING HAS WINGS AND MAY FLY AWAY: This saying comes from the West'rds. In other words, take an opportunity when it appears—it may soon be gone. W:118

LOOKS: *See* THREE LOOKS TO THE HORIZON, *below*

LORD PERTH: Mid-World's story of Lord Perth bears a strong resemblance to our biblical tale of David and Goliath. *See also* MID-WORLD FOLKLORE, *in* CHARACTERS. V:39

LOS ÁNGELES: This Mejis term describes fat, white, fair-weather clouds. VII:455, VII:477

LOUTKIN: A lout; an ill-mannered person. VI:180

LOVE STUMBLES: This is Roland's mother's phrase. It is roughly equivalent to our saying "love is blind." V:77

LOW PURE: The foothill meadows below the salt-houses in Debaria. W:57

MACROVERSE: A term often used in Stephen King's fiction for all the known worlds that spin about the Tower. I use it frequently in this *Concordance*, even though Stephen King doesn't use it in the Dark Tower series. *See also* MULTI-VERSE

MADAME DEATH: Lady Death. In decks of cards, she is often represented by the Queen of Spades. VI:18

MAGDA-SEEN (MAGDA-SEENS): This is Roland's misinterpretation of the word *magazine,* and it doesn't make any sense to him. He can't figure out what Magda must have seen. II:61, V:677, VII:494

MAGIC TALES OF THE ELD: When Roland was a child, this was his favorite book. It contained the story entitled "The Wind Through the Keyhole." W:14

MAKE HASTE: *See* MID-WORLD GESTUES

MAKE WATER (TO MAKE WATER): To urinate. V:86

MALHABLADA: This is a Spanish word which means "woman who speaks badly," or, in the case of Susan Delgado, a woman who uses bad words. IV:237

MANDRUS: Mandrus's common name is "whore's blossoms." It is a venereal disease (endemic in cities such as Lud) that appears to have quite a lot in common with syphilis. The oozing sores apparent in the later stages of the disease are particularly horrific. III:297

MANTO: In Hambry, a manto is a cloak. In other places, it is a slang term for a homosexual. Kimba Rimer once jokingly called Clay Reynolds *"sai* Manto," referring to his cloak, but Reynolds later murdered him for doing so. IV:471

**MANY AND MANY-A: A long time ago. V:131, V:328

MARMAR: Mother. W:103

MARRY IN HASTE, REPENT AT LEISURE: This is another saying used by the old folks in the Endless Forest. If you marry too quickly you may regret it. W:162

MAY IT SERVE THEM VERY WELL: May it make them healthy, or may it make them prosper. V:74

MAY THE SUN NEVER FALL IN YOUR EYES: Good luck to you. V:402

MAY WE BE WELL-MET ON THE PATH: *See* WELL-MET, *below*

MAY WE MEET IN THE CLEARING AT THE END OF THE PATH WHEN ALL WORLDS END: May we meet after death. May we meet again in the next world. VII:801

MAY YOU DO WELL: May you prosper. VI:182

MAY YOU HAVE TWICE THE NUMBER: *See* LONG DAYS AND PLEASANT NIGHTS, *above*

MAY YOUR BEAUTY EVER INCREASE/AND MAY YOUR FIRST DAY IN HELL LAST TEN THOUSAND YEARS, AND MAY IT BE THE SHORTEST: This testy interchange is part of the story of Lady ORIZA and her suitor/enemy Gray Dick. *See* ORIZA, LADY, *in* CHARACTERS

MAY YOUR DAYS BE LONG UPON THE EARTH: A Mid-World greeting. The proper reply to this is "And may you have twice the number." V:123

MAY YOUR FIRST DAY IN HELL LAST TEN THOUSAND YEARS: *See* MAY YOUR BEAUTY EVER INCREASE, *above*

MAYHAP: Perhaps. V:328, W:29

MAYHAP SOME OF THE OLD WAYS STILL HOLD: Perhaps some of the old ways have survived. V:126

MEGRIMS: Fears. Fantasies. As Susan walks to Rhea's hut for the first time, she sings to keep "the worst of her megrims away." IV:123

MERRY SEE, MERRY BE: *See* HILE AND MERRY-GREET-THE-DAY, *above*

MESCALINE: We have this in our world too. Cort called mescaline the Philosopher's Stone and maintained that the old gods pissed over the desert and made this hallucinogen. The use of drugs (usually to communicate with speaking demons) was part of a gunslinger's training. *See* APPENDIX IV: MID-WORLD MISCELLANY. I:124–25, I:127

METALED/METAL: A metaled road is a paved road. III:287, V:291

MICKLE (USELESS MICKLE): Useless junk. W:163

MID-SUMMER: The season of Mid-Summer marks the hottest part of the year. Mid-Summer was also one of Gilead's FAIR-DAYS. *See* APPENDIX IV: MID-WORLD MISCELLANY. V:2

MIM: *See entry in* HIGH SPEECH

MIND (TO MIND): To watch out for something, as in "mind the step." W:16

MIND-SPEAR: A mind-spear is a focused thought which can kill the person at whom it is aimed. The BREAKER Ted Brautigan is especially good at throwing mind-spears. VII:278, VII:376

MOIT: A group of five or six. It is also part of an expression: "Surely you've got a moit more guts than that." V:237, V:358, VII:808 *(expression)*

MOITY'MORE: Many more. W:268

MOLLIES: Unsterilized female mules, usually kept for their good tempers rather than for breeding. Such creatures rarely give birth to true-threaded offspring. W:145

MORE THAN ONCE-UPON-A: More than once. V:367

MORTATA: *See entry in* CALLA BRYN STURGIS DIALECT

MOTHER-ROOT: Umbilical cord. III:175

MOZO: Spanish for porter. Used in Hambry for male servants. IV:278

MOUTH'S HUNG IN THE MIDDLE AND RUNS AT BOTH ENDS (MY MOUTH'S HUNG IN THE MIDDLE AND RUNS AT BOTH ENDS): I talk too much, or I say things I shouldn't. W:122

MUCH TALK IS JUST LA-LA-LA: Much talk is just nonsense. W:42

MUFFIN-BALLS: Although they look like mushrooms, muffin-balls are actually a kind of edible ground berry. V:42

MULTIPLE AMERICAS: Although the Tower contains only one Keystone Earth and that Keystone Earth contains only one North America and one United States, other levels of the Tower also contain alternate Americas, or alternate versions of North America and of the United States. These alternative Americas are subtly different from ours. (For example, in some of those other Americas people drive TAKURO SPIRITS and drink NOZZ-A-LA cola.) When I refer to the many Americas, including the one found on Keystone Earth, I use the term *Multiple Americas. See also entry in* OUR WORLD PLACES

MULTIVERSE: A term I often use in this *Concordance* when I am referring to the many worlds which spin around the Dark Tower.

MUMBLETY-PEG: A game in which players throw or flip a jackknife in various ways so that the knife sticks in the ground. We play this game in our world too. V:227

MUSICA: In Calla Bryn Sturgis, a musica is a bandstand on a town green. In other parts of Mid-World, a wandering musica is a wandering musician. V:210, VII:51

MUTIE: A mutant. Mutants are common in Mid-World. *See* MUTANTS, *in* CHARACTERS

MY LIFE FOR YOU: Richard Fannin makes Tick-Tock repeat this sinister saying. III:389

MY TONGUE TANGLES WORSE THAN A DRUNK'S ON REAP-NIGHT: Roland's way of saying that he isn't good with words. V:216

NAR: NO. W:63

NASTY LOT OF WORK (THEY WERE A NASTY LOT OF WORK); They were a nasty bunch of men/women. W:56

NAUGHT BE ZERO, NAUGHT BE FREE, I OWE NOT YOU, NOR YOU OWE ME: Nothing has been decided yet, and no one owes anyone else anything, at least as yet. V:110

NAWP: No. W:103

NECK-POPPED: Hanged. I:105–6

NE'MINE: Never mind. VI:50

NEN: A drink used by the Covenant Man to make Tim Ross feel like an icy visitor inside his own head. Nen isn't alcoholic but it must have some drug-like properties. W:161

NEVER IN LIFE: Not on your life. V:403

NEVER MIND SPLITTING NAILS TO MAKE TACKS: Don't split hairs. The gist of whatever is being said is correct. V:167

NEVER SAY SO. FOR 'TIS BLASPHEMY: Never say so, since it is a sin against God. W:52

NEVER SPEAK THE WORST ALOUD: This was one of Cort's sayings. Don't speak your worst fears. VII:589

**NEW EARTH: New Earth is the spring plowing season. Mother Nature is just waking from her long sleep. *See also* APPENDIX IV: MID-WORLD MISCEL-LANY. V:3

NINETEEN: Nineteen is the number which haunts our KA-TET throughout the last three books of the Dark Tower series. *See* NINETEEN, NINETY-NINE, *and* NINETEEN NINETY-NINE, *all in* CHARACTERS

NIS: Nis is another name for Na'ar, or Hell. W:61

NO FRET: Don't worry. W:65

**NO ONE EVER REALLY PAYS FOR BETRAYAL IN SILVER; THE PRICE OF ANY BETRAYAL ALWAYS COMES DUE IN FLESH: The cost of betrayal is dear.

NO QUARTER: *See* WE WILL ACCEPT NO QUARTER, *below*

NOON (TO NOON): To noon in the saddle is to spend noontime (or the after-noon) riding. You can also "noon with" someone, which means to spend the afternoon with them. V:205

NOT BY MY WARRANT: Not if it's up to me. V:47

NOT JUST ONE POINT OF WHEN: Not just one point in time, but more than one. V:103

NOW WHILE WE BIDE: Now while we stay here. V:230

NOZZ-A-LA: The Great Old Ones must have preferred Nozz-A-La cola to either Coke or Pepsi, since some of the cans are still kicking around End-World.

Nozz-A-La may also be found in many of the ALTERNATIVE AMERICAS. V:36, V:560, VII:724

NUB (TO HAVE THE NUB OF IT) To have the essence of it. W:42

NUMMORE: No more. W:91

NUMMORE THAN: No more than. W:58

OAST: *See* BASTED IN A HOT OAST, *above*

OGGAN: *See entry in* CALLA BRYN STURGIS DIALECT

OH BITE IT!: This was Pat Delgado's favorite cuss. IV:239

OLD BONE-TWIST MAN: *See* DRY-TWIST, *above*

OLD ONES: The Old Ones (also called the Old People or the Great Old Ones) were the technologically advanced inhabitants of Mid-World. By Roland's time, they were long gone, and all that remained of them were their weapons and dangerous, half-fried technology. *See* OLD ONES, *in* CHARACTERS

OLD ONES' DOOR: This is Roland's term for a mechanical door made by the Old Ones. Unlike the magical doors left over from the PRIM, or the enchanted doors created by KA or art, the Old Ones' doors are dedicated and always come out at the same place. Few are in good condition, so passing through them can make a person physically sick. *See also* DOORWAYS BETWEEN WORLDS, *in* PORTALS. VII:35

OLD RED FURY (THE OLD RED FURY): Battle fury. V:171

OLD WAR: *See* GREAT POISONING, *above*

OLLIE KNOT: A sloppy kind of knot used to secure things to the back of a wagon, etc. W:126

ONCE UPON A BYE, BEFORE YOUR GRANDFATHER'S GRANDFATHER WAS BORN: In Mid-World, this is how folktales and fairy tales begin. It is equivalent to our "Once upon a time." W:105

ONE TO WATCH AND ONE TO WORK. PULL TOGETHER AND NEVER APART: According to the old-timers of Tree Village, this was how woodcutting partners had to work. It was too dangerous to go into the Endless Forest alone. W:117

ONLY A FOOL BELIEVES HE'S DREAMING BEFORE HE WAKES UP: Don't ignore the situation, deal with it! Also, hope for the best and expect the worst. III:59

ORIZA: *See entry in* CALLA BRYN STURGIS DIALECT

OTHER WHERE-AND-WHEN: On some other level of the Dark Tower. In some other *where*-and-*when*, Lud is a version of New York City. V:179

OUTER DARK: Chaos. Evil. The Crimson King serves the Outer Dark. Roland and his fellow gunslingers serve the WHITE. V:115

OUTLANDERS: To the Pubes, outlanders are people not from Lud. III:321, III:322

PAIN RISES, FROM THE HEART TO THE HEAD: This is one of Roland's sayings. Eddie has a strange feeling that he's heard similar sentiments in cowboy flicks. When Roland removes a bullet from Eddie's leg, he tells Eddie to bite down on a belt so that he can catch the pain as it rises. The trick seems to work. VI:203

PALAVER: To hold palaver is to hold counsel. *Palaver* tends to imply the exchange of important ideas. I:197, V:108, V:158, VI:66, VI:183, W:7

PAÑUELO: Handkerchief. A Spanish term used in Hambry. IV:374

PARD: Short for "pardner." We use this term in our world too. It means partner or comrade. W:77, W:119

PASSING FINE (I'M PASSING FINE): I'm fine. W:175, E:179, W:77, W:198

PARTI: A brand of cigarettes once smoked by the inhabitants of End-World. V:560

PASEAR: To take a little pasear around town is to take a short tour of the town, or a short wander around the town. V:584

**PASS-ON-BY COUNTRY: Ugly country. The land between Pricetown and Tull is pass-on-by country.

PATH OF THE BEAR, WAY OF THE TURTLE: The section of the Bear-Turtle Beam which leads from Shardik's portal to the Dark Tower. Once the Dark Tower is reached and you begin to travel toward Maturin's portal, you're on the Path of the Turtle, Way of the Bear. In the final book of the Dark Tower series, the Path of the Bear, Way of the Turtle is called Beam of the Bear, Way of the Turtle. VI:15, VII:295

PATRONO: A term used in Hambry which means employer or boss. It is very similar to the Spanish word "patrón." IV:237

PEAK SEAT: The seat at the front of a BUCKA WAGGON, where the driver sits. V:655

PEDDLER (PEDDLER'S MOON): The late-summer moon. When the moon is full, you can see the squint-and-grin of the Peddler upon its face. This moon is also called Old Cheap Rover Man's moon. *See also* MID-WORLD MOONS, *at the beginning of this* Concordance. V:37, VII:165

PEELED OFF: Turned off, or left the path. V:42

PEEP: A peep is an eye. W:36

PENNY FOR EM, DIMMY-DA: Penny for your thoughts. VII:316

PENNY, POSY, JACK'S A NOSY! DO YA SAY SO? YES, I DO-SO! HE'S MY SNEAKY, PEEKING DARLING BAH-BO!: This bit of "cradle nonsense" was sung to children in Mid-World. Roland would have known it well. VII:171

PERT: Impertinent or impertinently. (Mercy of River Crossing is blinded with a branding iron for looking "pert" at some harriers.) However, it can also mean smart, leaning toward "smart-ass." Coming from the right person, however, it can be meant somewhat admiringly. Gasher refers to Jake as "pert," implying that he has a smart mouth but is also quick-witted and gutsy. III:328, III:351, III:356–57, VI:104

PETTIBONE: An alcoholic drink. IV:251

PIG-BACK: Roland's term for "piggyback." III:57

PLUG: A plug in a mine is a fresh deposit, one that can be dug out for profit. W:56–57, W:64

POINTING TO THE CENTER OF YOUR FOREHEAD: *See* MID-WORLD GESTURES

POINTS (WICKETS): A Mid-World game much like baseball. In Mid-World it was played with croquet balls. I:96, V:236

POISONING, THE: *See* GREAT POISONING, *above*

POISONTHORN: A poisonous bush that people avoid. A person can also behave like a poisonthorn. W:122

POKE: A small bag for carrying meat, tobacco, or other substances. We use this term in our world as well. I:21

**POKEBERRIES: Waxy-skinned berries that taste like sweet cranberries. Like corn, this is one of the crops grown between Tull and Pricetown. V:245, VI:102, VII:716

POKIE: A wandering cowboy not signed to any particular ranch. W:70

POOKY: A pooky is huge, reddish snake with a spade-shaped head as big as a cooking pot. It has amber eyes with black slit pupils, glittering fangs, and a ribbon-like tongue which is split into a fork. A pooky's bite paralyzes its victim, but does not kill it. (Pookies like to eat their prey alive.) *For more page references, see* POOKY *in the* CHARACTERS *section.* W:151

POPKIN: A sandwich. II:45, V:175, VII:42, VII:503

POSSE: A strong force, a company of men. II:342, VI:51

POUR DOWN LEAD: To shoot a lot of bullets. W:58

POXY WHORE: Nasty term for anything female. W:44

PRAYER AFTER A SUCCESSFUL HUNT: Roland recites this prayer after he and Susannah successfully hunt down deer. The prayer is addressed to the head of a dead deer.

> We thank you for what we are about to receive.
> (Father, we thank thee.)
> Guide our hands and guide our hearts as we take life from death.
> (VII:636–37)

PRIM: The magical soup of creation from which all life arose. It is sometimes called the Greater Discordia or the OVER. *See also entry in* CHARACTERS

PRINK-A-DEE: A trinket. V:661

PRODDIE: A proddie is a cowboy, or hired hand, assigned to a particular ranch. At the Jefferson Ranch, when a man signed on, he put his mark on the wall. W:70

PROVING HONESTY: A physical exam used to verify physical and spiritual purity. The examiner checks virginity and looks for suck marks (left by demons). IV:132

PUBES: A Pube is a young person. In Lud, which our KA-TET had to pass through during their *Waste Lands* journeys, the Pubes were the descendants of the city's original inhabitants. Originally, the term *Pube* had been short for "pubescent"; however, by the time Roland and his *ka-tet* arrived in the city, the original Pubes had grown older than GAN and had marched to the CLEARING AT THE END OF THE PATH. Like their enemies the Grays, the descendants of the Pubes were riddled with diseases and were half-mad. They also played a game of chance in which the winner was lynched to please the demonic GOD-DRUMS. *For more information about the Pubes, see entry in* CHARACTERS. VII:84

PULER: A young man. Cort uses this term to address Roland. We hear it again in Hambry. I:163

PULING: Crying, moaning, and making a fuss. II:155, III:173

PULL A COSY: To tell a half-truth, or to trick. Very similar to "pull a fast one." W:86

PRAY FOR RAIN ALL YOU LIKE, BUT DIG A WELL WHILE YOU DO IT: This was one of Big Jack Ross's sayings. Basically, hope for the best but prepare for the worst. W:172

PURSE: Roland's scuffed swag-bag. V:45

PUT ON YOUR THINKING CAP: As in our world, people in Mid-World tell puzzled children to put on their thinking caps. The story stems from the belief that the Guardians each carried an extra brain on the outside of their heads. They kept these brains in a hat. Actually, the "hats" were radar dishes. III:40

QUESA: A dance similar to a simple reel. IV:209

QUICKENED: A child quickens in the womb when it begins to move. V:480

QUICKPIT: Pit of quicksand. III:251

QUIRT: A whip. W:185

RAIN, HEALTH, EXPANSION TO THE SPIRIT: This is a blessing used by Brown, the Border Dweller. I:19

RAISED TO THE GUN: Gunslingers are raised to the gun, or trained to be fighters. W:36

RANCHER'S DINNER: A big dinner, which is meant to fill you up for your chores. V:134

REAP: Reap is both the season and the festival of harvest. In the days of Arthur Eld it was celebrated with human sacrifice, but by the time Roland was born, STUFFY-GUYS were thrown onto Reap bonfires instead of people. During the season of Reap, people decorate their houses, and their stuffy-guys, with Reap charms. Reap charms can also be painted on the body or worn like pendants. Although it is followed by the Year's End festival, Reap is the true closing of the year. *See* STUFFY-GUYS, *in* CHARACTERS, MID-WORLD HOLIDAYS, *in* APPENDIX IV, *and* GILEAD FAIR-DAYS, *at the beginning of this* Concordance. V:13

REAP CRACKERS: REAPTIDE firecrackers. V:226

REAP MOON: The Reap Moon is the DEMON MOON. VII:229

REAPTIDE: The time of REAP. V:202

RED DEATH: The Red Death can be found in Edgar Allan Poe's famous tale "Masque of the Red Death." In Poe's story we learn the symptoms of this awful plague. First, the sufferer complains of sharp pains, then of a sudden dizziness, and finally he or she begins to bleed profusely from all pores. The entire seizure—from first symptom until death—takes one-half hour. The people of Fedic were decimated by this terrible disease. VI:105, VI:243, VI:244

RED PLAGUE: The Red Plague is probably the same as the RED DEATH. VII:429

REDEYE: A strong intoxicating liquor. Also a tavern or bar. W:119

REMEMBER THE FACE OF YOR FATHER. HE WATCHES YOU FROM THE CLEARING: Remain honorable because your ancestors are watching you. W:285

REMUDA: A remuda is a corral. V:321, V:336, W:85

RHEUMATIZ: Rheumatoid arthritis. *See also* DRY TWIST, *above.* V:240

RHODITE: Big Jack Ross wore a lucky rhodite coin, or rhodite double, around his neck. However, knuckles of rhodite can be used as money. W:133

RICE SONG: *See* RICE SONG *and* COMMALA, *both in* CALLA BRYN STURGIS DIALECT

RIDE THE HANDSOME: To Ride the Handsome is a Lud euphemism for dying. III:300

RIDING DROGUE: Riding behind. V:128

RITUAL OF RENUNCIATION: I CURSE THEE WITH THE ASHES! I CURSE THEE TO DARKNESS! YE LOST AND RENOUNCED!: Cordelia Delgado performs this ancient ritual when she utters these words and smears her niece Susan with ashes. It is meant to dishonor Susan and brand her as an outcast. IV:497

ROCK-CATS: *See entry in* CALLA BRYN STURGIS DIALECT

RODERICK, CHILDREN OF: *See* CHILDREN OF RODERICK, *above*

ROLL IN (WHERE DID YOU ROLL IN?): Where did you sleep? W:82

ROLLERS AND CHOCKER-TWISTS: Mid-World candy. The chocker-twists are chocolate twists. W:100

ROOST ON (TO JUST ROOST ON): To remain in place. It implies pointless waiting and a sense of futility. V:172

ROPE-SWINGERS: Cowboys. W:46

ROSILLO: Susan Delgado calls her horse Pylon a *rosillo*. IV:239

ROT, THE: A disease which often affects the Border Dwellers of the Mohaine Desert. It sounds a bit like leprosy. People suffering from this disease are called "rotters." I:18

RUN YOUR GUMS: To run at the mouth. To talk endlessly and uselessly. W:272

RUSSEL: A slang term that means to take a woman by force. II:46

RUSTIES (BARN RUSTIES): A large Mid-World blackbird. The bird's name derives from its harsh squalling cry, a call slightly shriller than that of a crow. V:7, V:154, V:162, VI:23, VII:193 *(barn rusties)*, VII:793

RUSTIE WALKED OVER MY GRAVE (A RUSTIE HAD JUST WALKED OVER HIS GRAVE): "A cat stepped on my grave." These kinds of phrases describe the deep chill or shiver we feel when someone's statement (or something we experience) resonates with a deep, internal foreboding. V:103

SADDLE BRIGHTWORK: The metal pieces on a saddle that catch the sun. W:58

SAI: See entry in HIGH SPEECH

SALIG: A salig looks like a crocodile or alligator and lives in the swamps of Mid-World. IV:70

SALLY: Humorous reply, a riposte. W:54

SALT-HOUSES: In Debaria, this is the term people use for the caverns in the cliff faces of the Salt Rocks or Salt Hills. In the past whole families lived in these places. The tunnels that went down into the earth from the backs of these caverns led to the salt mines. W:56, W:58.

SALT-MOLE: A saltie, or salt miner. W:276

SALTIE: one of the salt miners in Debaria. W:64

SANDAY: In Mejis, this is the traditional cowboys' day of rest. IV:282, IV:287

SANDITCH: Roland's pronunciation of *sandwich*. VII:42

SAWBONES' BAG: A doctor's bag. VII:468

SAWGRASS: A type of grass that grows in the Fagonard swamp. The blades are so sharp that they will cut you if you grab them. W:195

SAWSEE: This is Roland's confused term for "seesaw." III:38

SCREW YOU AND THE HORSE YOU RODE IN ON: This is another one of Zoltan's favorite sayings. I:16

SCRIP: Scrip has several definitions. 1. A lawyer. (VI:186). 2. Scrip is payment, but payment that isn't in hard coin. If you're paid in scrip, you're essentially paid in a voucher for a certain shop, for example a company store or town mercantile. W:277

SECRET CODE: This code is used by gunslingers when they communicate by carrier pigeon. The phrase below means "Farson moves east . . . Forces split, one big, one small. Do you see anything unusual." IV:262

SEE ME! SEE ME VERY WELL: Look at me. *See also* I SEE YOU VERY WELL, *earlier in this section, and* I SEE YOU VERY WELL *in* MID-WORLD GESTURES. V:172, VII:115

SEE THE TURTLE OF ENORMOUS GIRTH: This is the first line of a well-known and well-loved Mid-World poem which invokes the spirit of the Turtle Guardian. Although there are many variations, Rosalita Munoz's version goes like this:

> See the Turtle of enormous girth!
> On his shell he holds the earth,
> His thought is slow but always kind;
> He holds us all within his mind.
> On his back the truth is carried,
> And there are love and duty married.
> He loves the earth and loves the sea,
> And even loves a child like me. (VI:15)

For more information and for page references, see GUARDIANS OF THE BEAM, *in* CHARACTERS

SEEN THE BOAT SHE CAME IN: *See entry in* CALLA BRYN STURGIS DIALECT

SELLIAN DIALECTS: Roland used to speak the Sellian dialects, but he has forgotten all but the curses. III:259

SEND YOU WEST WITH THE BROKEN ONES WHO HAVE FORGOTTEN THE FACES OF THEIR FATHERS (TO SEND YOU WEST): In In-World-that-was, failed gunslingers were sent west in disgrace. Hence, this saying arose. V:568

'SENERS: Keroseners, or kerosene lights. V:438, V:506, V:561, VI:14

SEPPE-*SAI*: *See entry in* HIGH SPEECH

SERAPE: Worn in Mejis and New Canaan by both men and women. It is a bit like a poncho or cape. IV:282, IV:365

SET MY WATCH AND WARRANT ON IT: You bet. I know it's true. V:214

SEVEN DIALS OF MAGIC: Vannay, Roland's tutor, taught him about the Seven Dials of Magic. We have not, as yet, found out what they are. V:79

SHADDIE: A bit of canvas used by cowboys in Debaria when they sleep under the stars. It won't keep off the rain, but it will keep the cowboy from getting damp after dewfall. W:81

SHAKING HIS KNEE: Pulling someone's leg, teasing them, joking with them or lying to them. W:41

SHANNIES: The pink-fleshed fish that live in the RIVER WHYE. (They are very tasty.) W:9

SHARPROOT: This is one of Mid-World's crops. V:1, V:151

SHAVELING: A young man. W:97

SHEEVIN (SH'VEEN): Literally speaking, *sheevin* means "quiet little woman." In practice it means side-wife or mistress. IV:207, V:120

SHEPPIE: A shepherd. W:105

SHINNARO: In the alternative America where Eddie Dean is actually Eddie Toren, Shinnaro cameras are popular. VII:728

SHIPMATE'S DISEASE: This malady is caused by nutritional deficiencies brought on by a lack of fruit and greens. In *The Drawing of the Three*, Roland and Eddie begin to suffer from this even though they are on dry land. II:268

**SHOOT-UP MONEY: Money gained from the gun. It can be money earned by a hired gunman.

SHOOTING-IRON: A gun. V:20, V:319, VII:47

SHOR'BOOTS: Short boots. W:230

SHORT BEER: *See entry in* CALLA BRYN STURGIS DIALECT

SHORTS: Half-sized smokes. VII:310

SHUCKIES: Corn shucks used to roll smokes. VI:299

**SHUT YOUR QUACK: Shut up.

SIDE LINE OF DESCENT: Descended from a jilly. The line of Deschain is a side line of descent. In other words, Roland's ancestor was born to one of Arthur Eld's side-wives. IV:184

SIGHE: The sighe are Mid-World's fairyfolk. They are tiny people with green skin and wings. They are beautiful but treacherous. W:164, W:170, W:182–83

SIGUL: A *sigul* is a sign, symbol, or insignia which is secret but full of meaning. It often has religious, political, or magical significance. John Farson's *sigul* is the same as that of the Crimson King—a staring red eye. III:353, VI:14, VI:65, VI:327, VII:26

**SILFLAY: To graze. This term comes from the novel *Watership Down*.

SILK-ARSE GENNELMAN: This is a crass Lud-term for somebody who is well-bred. III:354

SILVA COMPASS: This is a kind of compass used in Roland's world. In *The Gunslinger,* one of the Border Dwellers gives Roland a stainless-steel Silva compass and bids him give it to Jesus. I:15

SILVER METAL: What you paint on warts to make them go away. V:479

SIMOOM: A kind of windstorm that blows over Debaria during the simoom season. PRODDIES and POKES hate them, because if they're out on the range they have to sleep rough and can't light a fire since the flames could easily spread. W:83, W:100

SINGLETS: In our world, a singlet is an undershirt or vest worn under other clothes. Cort wears a singlet when he battles the apprentices. I:167, V:403

**SISSA: Sister.

SKIDDUMS: These are the shacks in Little Debaria where some of the miners sleep. The skiddums aren't much, but at least they aren't underground. W:275

SKIN-MAN: Skin-men are shapeshifters, or beings that can change from human to animal form. They are also shapechangers, or creatures that can assume multiple forms. Although skin-men were thought to be legendary creatures, the out-world town of Debaria was stalked by one. Hence Steven Deschain sent Roland and his friend Jamie DeCurry to hunt it down. The skin-man turned out to be a SALTIE who had been exposed to one of the Old People's ARTYFAX. In his myriad bestial forms, the skin-man had a taste for human flesh and human brains. *See also* SKIN-MAN *in the* CHARACTERS *section.* W:40

SKIN-TURNER: A skin-man, or shapechanger. W:274

SKIT: To skit in the wind is to become skittish. Some mules skit in the wind. W:88

SKÖLDPADDA: A turtle. *See* GUARDIANS OF THE BEAM: TURTLE GUARDIAN, *in* CHARACTERS

SLEWFEET: Roland's term for noisy trackers. V:44

SLINKUM: A strap-style undershirt. VII:518. W:6

SLIP THE SILK (TO SLIP THE SILK or TO SLIP THE ROPE): To marry. W:116

SLO-TRANS ENGINES: Mid-World's technology was one of unipolar circuits, dipolar circuits, and slo-trans technology. Blaine's engines are slo-trans engines. Slo-trans technology was supposed to be immune to malfunction, but this is obviously not the case, since Blaine himself admits that he is going mad. IV:14, V:72, V:371

SLOW MUTANTS: Slow Mutants are creatures damaged by radiation poisoning. They were the result of the Old Ones' disastrous wars. *See* MUTANTS: SLOW MUTANTS, *in* CHARACTERS

SLOWKINS FROM THE EYBROWS UP: If you're called a slowkins from the eyebrows up, someone is implying that you are slow or a bit thick. (Not very nice.): W:288

SLUGGARDLY: Slow. W:126

SLUMGULLION: This is a derogatory term for a man. III:249

SLUT OF THE WINDS: Roland's term for the female spirits who have sex (consensual or not) with traveling men. Often, these demonic sluts are deadly. VI:370

SMA': Small. W:64

SMA' ONE: A young one. A child. W:14

SMALLHOLDS: *See entry in* CALLA BRYN STURGIS DIALECT

SNICK: Smart, clever, wily. W:276

SNIVELMENT: To snivel is to show weak or tearful resentment. It can also imply hypocrisy. A young snivelment is a sniveler. *Snivelment* can also be used as a noun, as in "stop your snivelment." VI:29, VI:295

SNOOD: A head covering worn by women in Mid-World, especially when they are in formal attire. IV:194

SO FELL LORD PERTH, AND THE COUNTRYSIDE DID SHAKE WITH THAT THUNDER: "So Fell Lord Perth" is a line from a longer poem. The story is very similar to that of David and Goliath. According to the tale, Lord Perth was a giant who went forth to war with a thousand men, but he was still in his own country when a little boy threw a stone at him and hit him in the knee. He stumbled, the weight of his armor bore him down, and he broke his neck in the fall. Tick-Tock, the giant-sized leader of the Grays, thinks this story is unlucky. (He identifies with Lord Perth.)

SOFT: Go forward carefully, slowly. Keep your emotions under control. III:278, IV:67

SOH: *See entry in* HIGH SPEECH

SOLID AS A DROMEDARY: Very dependable. W:88

SOMBRERA/SOMBRERO: The wide-brimmed hats worn in Hambry. IV:365

SOME THINGS DON'T REST EASY EVEN WHEN THEY'RE DEAD: Some things come back to haunt you. IV:98

SOMETIMES YOU CAN PULL A SMALL THREAD AND UNRAVEL A WHOLE GARMENT: Sometimes a small clue can solve a big mystery. W:68

SONG OF THE TURTLE, CRY OF THE BEAR: Roland tells a hypnotized Stephen King that whenever he hears the Song of the Turtle or the Cry of the Bear he must turn his attention back to the Dark Tower series and continue writing it. VI:296

SONGS: *See* APPENDIX III

SOWING: One of Gilead's Fair-Days. It is also known as NEW EARTH and FRESH COMMALA. *See* GILEAD FAIR-DAYS, *at the beginning of this* Concordance. *See also* MID-WORLD HOLIDAYS, *in* APPENDIX IV.

SOWING NIGHT COTIL': *See* COMMALA

SPARE NOT THE BIRCH SO YOU SPOIL NOT THE CHILD: Saying from the Great Book. Recounted by Roland. III:13

SPARK-A-DARK, WHO'S MY SIRE?: Roland repeats this old catechism whenever he sets a campfire alight. It goes, "Spark-a-dark, who's my sire? Will I lay me? Will I stay me? Bless this camp with fire." VII:761

**SPARK-LIGHTS: Spark-lights (also known as filament lights) are electric flambeaux or electric lights. It is a Hambry term. In the 2003 version of *The Gunslinger,* we find out that the Coach Road leading from Pricetown to Tull was once lined with spark-lights. By the time Roland passes through, they are all dead. IV:150, V:90, V:561

SPARK MY COURAGE: To gather your courage: W:213

SPARKPOWER: Electricity. W:240

SPATHIPHILIUM: A plant that grew in Gilead. It also grows in the Garden of the Beam. VII:492

SPEAK QUIET, BUT SPEAK PLAIN: Speak quietly, but state what you mean. V:43

SPEAKIE: Another name for the jing-jang, or telephone. W:70

SPECIE: A form of money. W:44

SPEED-SHOOTER: A machine gun. VI:130, VI:228, W:58

SPIRIT-MAN: The spirit that lingers near the body after death. VII:474

SQUAT ON YOUR HUNKERS: To hunker down. To squat on your heels. To sit on your heels. W:57

SQUEAMY: Squeamish. W:60

SQUINT: We hear this term in both Lud and Hambry. Like "cully," it is usually used when talking to—or about—young men. However, it seems more pejorative. This term can also have sexual connotations. In boy-loving Lud, Gasher tells Roland that he must hand over the squint, meaning Jake. III:298

SQUIREEN: Owner of a small landed property. Also a knight's attendant. V:383

STAKE: In the Endless Forest, many woodcutters had stakes, or bits of woodland which they laid claim to cut. W:172

STAND TRUE: Remain true to your mission, your beliefs, etc. V:163

STAR WHISKEY: This is the best whiskey found in Tull. I:41

STARKBLAST: A starkblast is a type of powerful, fast-moving storm which is unique to Mid-World. Its features include steep and sudden drops in temperature accompanied by strong winds. Starkblasts have been known to cause great destruction and loss of life in civilized portions of the world. In primitive areas, entire tribes have been wiped out by them. When Roland was a boy, starkblasts used to descend upon the GREAT WOODS north of NEW CANAAN once or twice a year, though luckily for the people living in GILEAD, the storms usually rose into the air and dispersed before reaching the city. Unfortunately, those living farther north were not so lucky. Roland remembers seeing cartloads of frozen bodies being drawn down GILEAD ROAD soon after a starkblast. He assumed that the corpses were those of farming families that didn't have BILLY-

BUMBLERS to warn them about the coming storm. *See entry in* CHARACTERS *section.* W:14

STAY PUT: *See* MID-WORLD GESTURES

STEADY AS SAND THROUGH A GLASS: Steady, dependable, reliable. W:118

STEM: A stem is a man of affairs. VI:268

STEPPA: Stepfather. W:122

STICKS AND STONES WILL BREAK MY BONES YET TAUNTS SHALL NEVER WOUND ME: This is a variation on a saying from our world. III:17

STRAWBERRY COSY: A tasty dessert. V:134

STUB: To the woodsmen of the Endless Forest, a stub was a short side-trail which branched off of the main path through the wood, know as the Ironwood Trail. Every woodsman's stake would contain several stubs. W:149

STUFFY-GUYS: Red-handed stuffy-guys can be found all over Mid-World and are a staple of REAPTIDE festivities. In the days of Arthur Eld, human beings were sacrificed during the festival of REAP. However, by Roland's day, stuffy-guys, or human effigies, were burned instead. In Mid-World-that-was, stuffy-guys had heads made of straw, and their eyes were made from white cross-stitched thread. In the BORDERLANDS, their heads are often made of SHARPROOT. *See also entry in* CHARACTERS

SUCH WOULD PLEASE ME EVER: Yes, that would make me happy. VII:137

SUCKERBUGS: The biting, blood-drinking insects that swarm in the ENDLESS FOREST. W:193

SULPHUR MATCHES: In Mid-World, they use the old-fashioned kind of matches that you can light with a thumbnail. W:146

SUMMA LOGICALES: Roland studied this subject with Vannay. We don't know what it is, but its theories encompassed both the anatomy of the Beams and the Bends o' the Rainbow. VII:33

SUMMAT: Something. W:60

SUPERFLU: The genetically engineered disease that killed off more than 99 percent of the human population in Stephen King's novel *The Stand*. This disease also wiped out the citizens of the alternative Topeka, which Roland, Eddie, Susannah, Jake, and Oy traveled through in *Wizard and Glass*. The superflu is also called Captain Trips. IV:74–76, VI:110

SURELY YOU'VE GOT A MOIT MORE GUTS THAN THAT: Surely you've got more guts than that. VII:808

SWABBIES AND SLINKUM: In hot weather, Young Roland slept in his swabbies and SLINKUM, which probably means he slept in his underpants and undershirt. W:68

SWAG-BAG: Another name for Roland's scuffed old purse. V:512

SWAMP-GAS TUBES: These tubes looked a bit like neon. They were sold at Feast of Joseph fairtime. I:186

SWEETCHEEKS BERRY: This is Gasher's term for a boy-virgin. III:325

SWEETMEATS: This is a Lud term for testicles. III:354

SWOLE: When a POOKY is fair swole, it has recently eaten, so it isn't quite so dangerous. W:151

TACK-SEES: Roland's word for taxis. II:341, V:104, V:172, VII:426

TAHEEN: End-World creatures that have the bodies of men but the heads of birds or beasts. *See entry in* HIGH SPEECH; *see also entry in* CHARACTERS

TAKE HEED: Be careful. W:13

**TAKE THE DEAD FROM THE DEAD: ONLY A CORPSE MAY SPEAK TRUE PROPHECY: We hear this saying in the Way Station's cellar, where Roland hears the Speaking Demon and then finds human remains in the wall. Speaking Demons may only manifest where there has been a death, or where there are the remains of the dead. The phrase listed above comes from the 2003 version of *The Gunslinger.* In the original *Gunslinger,* this proverb has a slightly different form. It is "The dead from the dead; only a corpse may speak." I:91

TAKE THE KING'S SALT (TO TAKE THE KING'S SALT): To make a deal with someone and to be in their pay. When you take the Crimson King's salt, you make a bargain with the devil. V:550

TAKURO (TAKURO SPIRIT): A Takuro Spirit is a type of car found in some of the alternative versions of America. Takuro (along with North Central Positronics and Honda) manufactured the Cruisin Trike that Susannah Dean uses during the attack on the DEVAR-TOI. VII:250, VII:724

TALE-SPINNER: A storyteller. VI:210, VI:275

TATI JACKETS: Jackets worn by musicians in Hambry. They can be found in our world too. IV:194

TEARS OF MY MOTHER: Roland utters this phrase when he and Susannah discover tongueless Patrick Danville in a prison cell below Dandelo's house. The only other time Roland uttered this phrase (within Susannah's presence at least) was when the two of them stumbled upon a deer that had fallen in the woods and broken its legs. The flies had eaten its still-living eyes. VII:697–98

TELEFUNG: This is Mia's mispronunciation of the word *telephone.* VI:73

THANKEE-*SAI* WE ALL SAY THANKEE: Thankee-*sai* is the polite term for thank you. Its equivalent is "thank you, sir," or "thank you, madam." In Mid-World, these words are often accompanied by three brisk taps upon the throat with the fingers of the right hand. At the beginning of *Wizard and Glass* we learn that when addressing men, one should use the left hand and tap the breastbone. However, this seems to be extremely formal. When Roland and his young friends are in Hambry, they use their right hands and tap their throats when thanking elders of either sex. *See also* MID-WORLD GESTURES. II:52, IV:21, V:28, W:15

THAT WAS: This phrase is often added on to the end of a word, to indicate past tense. For example, Cort can be called Roland's teacher-that-was; Roland lived in Gilead-that-was, etc. W:35

THAT'S AS CLEAR AS EARTH NEEDS: This phrase was used by Cort and by Roland's father, Steven Deschain. It means "that's as clear as we need" or "that's obvious." VII:473

THAT'S AS KA WILLS: Whether it happens depends on fate's decree. V:167

THAT'S NONNIES TO YOU: That's none of your business. W:283

THE FOREST GIVES TO THEM THAT LOVE IT: This was one of Jack Ross's sayings. Basically, the Endless Forest provides for those who love it and respect it. W:114

THE LUCK OF THE GALLOWS: This is why Roland takes a piece of the hangman's tree when he sees Hax killed. I:109

THE ONLY STUPID QUESTION, MY CULLIES, IS THE ONE YOU DON'T ASK: This was one of the Widow Smack's sayings. In other words, it's foolish *not* to ask a question. W:207

THE QUICKEST WAY TO LEARN ABOUT A NEW PLACE IS TO KNOW WHAT IT DREAMS OF: This is one of Roland's truisms. III:59

THE SALT YOU TAKE IS THE SALT YOU MUST PAY FOR: We all must pay for our deeds, good and bad. W:59

THE SMELL OF THE FOREST WHEN THE WIND'S OUT OF THE NORTH BRINGS VISIONS: The old *folken* of the Endless Forest believed that this was true. When the north wind blew the scent of the ironwoods to the village, people had visions. W:115

THE SUN IS GOING DOWN ON THE WORLD: This is Aunt Talitha's saying. It means the end of the world is coming. The world is dying. III:237

THE WAY OF KA IS ALWAYS THE WAY OF DUTY: Basically, duty comes first. V:181

THE WHEEL OF KA TURNS AND THE WORLD MOVES ON: III:403

THE WISE MAN DOESN'T POKE A SLEEPING BEAR WITH A STICK: The wise man doesn't make a bad situation worse. Also, you shouldn't awaken dangerous forces—they may turn against you. V:316

THE WISE THIEF ALWAYS PROSPERS: The wise thief does well. III:45

THE WORLD HAS MOVED ON: This phrase is used throughout the Dark Tower series. It means that things have changed, and that the world is now profoundly different from what it once was. The change has not been for the better. III:73, III:310, III:411, IV:426, V:126

THE WORLD'S TILTED, AND THERE'S AN END TO IT: Good things often hurt. This is an oldtimers saying. W:106

THE WORLD WON'T MOVE ON TOMORROW: This was a term used in Gilead before the world really did move on. It means that there's time yet. I:173

THEE'LL BE PASSING FINE: You'll be fine. W:190

THERE ARE OTHER WORLDS THAN THESE: Jake Chambers's famous saying. In the final three books of the Dark Tower series, we learn just how true this statement is. V:105

THERE WILL BE WATER IF GOD WILLS IT (THERE WOULD BE WATER IF GOD WILLED IT): What is meant to happen will happen. III:26, V:81, V:87, V:113, V:569, W:21, W:293

THIN: When something feels thin, it feels dangerous, or full of tricks. A thin place is one where the fabric of reality has almost worn through and other worlds are close. The word *thin* is related to the word *thinny*, that nasty demonic entity which Roland encountered in Eyebolt Canyon in Mejis, and then again in the alternative Topeka. VII:114, VII:524

THINKING CAPS: In Roland's world, as in our world, children are sometimes told to put on their thinking caps. On Roland's level of the Tower this is based on a story about the Guardians. Supposedly, each Guardian carried an extra brain on the outside of its head, in a hat. This apocryphal tale had a true basis. The

Guardians have radar dishes sticking out of their skulls. *See also* END-WORLD TERMS. III:40

THOSE WHO DO NOT LEARN FROM THE PAST ARE CONDEMNED TO REPEAT IT: Vannay often repeated this maxim. VII:829

THREADED (THREADED STOCK): Threaded stock is normal stock, or animals born without mutations. MUTIES abound in Mid-World, so threaded stock is extremely valuable. Threaded stock can be bred with other threaded stock to keep the bloodlines pure, but threaded stock can also be born from late-generation muties. In Mid-World-that-was, they called this latter process "clarifying." IV:14, IV:203, V:2, V:613

THREE IS A NUMBER OF POWER: This particular belief is held in our world as well. V:110

THREE LOOKS TO THE HORIZON: This is a saying used to describe distance, as in "You should travel at least three looks to the horizon." Three looks is roughly equivalent to one hundred WHEELS. VI:151

THROAT TAPS: *See* MID-WORLD GESTURES

THROCKEN: *See* BILLY-BUMBLER, *above*

THROCKET OF BUMBLERS: Many bumblers is a throcket. W:151

TIGHT AS A VIRGIN'S COOCHIE: This is Big Bern Kells way of saying that someone is tight with their money. W:125–26

TIME HAS SOFTENED (TIME HAD BEGUN TO SOFTEN, TIME HAD GROWN SOFT): In Mid-World, time does not flow evenly but moves forward erratically. Like the points of the compass, time itself is in drift. IV:266, V:23, V:35, V:318

TIME IS A FACE ON THE WATER: Mejis proverb. Time is an illusion. IV:445, V:35, W:8

TIME IS SHORT ON THIS SIDE OF THE DOOR: The Whye ferryman, Bix, says this. In other words, life is short. W:10

**TIME IS THE THIEF OF MEMORY: This is one of Vannay's sayings.

TIME O' THE GOAT: Time of the Goat Moon, which is equivalent to the month of February in our world. Eddie Dean was born during Goat Moon. V:140

TINY SHINING SPLINTER OF KA: This is the soul. W:212

TO COME TO THE CLEARING AT THE END OF YOUR PATH: To die. IV:124

TODASH: *See entry in* HIGH SPEECH

TODASH TAHKEN: *See entry in* HIGH SPEECH

****TO DRAW THE BLACK STONE:** This is how gunslingers of old chose who would have to act as hangman.

TOOTER FISH: This is Roland's term for tuna fish. He thinks it's tasty. II:45–46

****TO PULL LEATHER:** To draw your gun.

TOUCH (THE TOUCH): The ability to read minds, also to see into the past and the future. It is similar to ESP and is half-empathy, half-telepathy. Jake is strong in the touch. IV:224, IV:388, V:296, V:381, V:389, VI:71, VII:190

TRAIL-FRAYED: This was Cuthbert Allgood's description of someone who has been on the road so long that he or she looks thin and worn. You treat this disorder with sassafras and salts. VII:758

TRAINING, THE: All apprentice gunslingers must undergo "the Training." In Roland's time, Cort was in charge of this arduous process. Before Cort, his father, Fardo, taught the apprentices (IV:407). For the most part, apprentice gunslingers were the sons of gunslingers. In other words, they belonged to the aristocracy of Mid-World. However, it is entirely possible that very young boys who showed promise were allowed to enter this small elect group.

The Training culminated in a rite of passage, enacted in the Square Yard, just beyond the Great Hall of Gilead. Eighteen was the usual age for this passage of an apprentice into manhood, although it could happen as late as twenty-five. Those who had not faced the all-or-nothing test by that age usually slipped into obscurity as freeholders. The litany and ritual of this rite were strictly observed, and had not changed for centuries. The apprentice entered the yard by the west entrance, which faced the barbarian forests. The teacher entered from the east, which faced the Great Hall and all of its symbolic civilization. The apprentice and his teacher faced each other from opposite ends of the yard and engaged in a ritual colloquy:

> "Have you come here for a serious purpose, boy?"
> "I have come for a serious purpose, teacher."
> "Have you come as an outcast from your father's house?"
> "I have so come, teacher."
> "Have you come with your chosen weapon?"
> "I have so come, teacher."
> "What is your weapon?"

The final twist in this traditional interplay was intended to give the teacher a slight advantage. He could adjust his battle plan by knowing his student's method of attack. It also meant that in order to move from childhood into manhood, the student had to be both wily and quick.

Only those who bested their teacher were permitted to exit through the east gate. Those who failed (and many did) were sent west, as exiles. In the end, the all-or-nothing aspect of the Training proved to be one of the Affiliation's weaknesses, since embittered failures, such as Eldred Jonas, took up the cause of John Farson, Gilead's great enemy.

The apprentice who won his guns was not yet entitled to the sandalwood-handled firearms of a true, mature gunslinger. Instead, he was given an apprentice's guns, which were less ornate than those he would wear later in life. I:100

TRAVOIS: We have this word in our world too. The travois was originally used by Native Americans. It was a means of transport composed of two poles, joined by a frame, which would then be drawn by an animal or a human. W:46

TRIG/TRIGGERS/TRIGGIE: Clever. *Trig* implies craftiness, and can also imply untrustworthiness. III:327, V:114, V:575

TRIG COVE: A clever bastard. Believe it or not, this term can be used as a compliment. For example, Gasher calls Tick-Tock a trig cove. III:298, III:356, VII:121

TRIG DELAH: Extremely clever. VII:176

TRIG HAND WITH A GUN: A good shot. W:54

TRUCKOMOBILE: A truck. VII:426

TRUE AS EVER WAS: True as ever. This statement is also uttered when an ORIZA flies true to its mark. V:334

TRUE AS THE TURTLE THAT HOLDS UP THE WORLD: As true as true can be. W:250

TRUE MEN OF THE GUN: True gunslingers. W:10

TRUE THREAD, THE: This is Cort's phrase. It refers to a person's most basic and fundamental skills. A gunslinger's true thread is his ability to use weapons. VII:250

TRUM: In the CALLAS, a person is trum when he or she can convince other people to do dangerous things. However, a "big and painful trum" is a terrible disease, like cancer. V:348, VII:413

TURN YOUR MIND BACK: Think back. W:90

TURNED A BAD APPLE OUT OF THE BASKET: If you've turned a bad apple out of the basket, you've shown the true nature of an evil person. W:173

TWINNER: The term *twinner* actually comes from the novels *The Talisman* and *Black House,* which Stephen King co-wrote with Peter Straub. Although King doesn't use this term in the Dark Tower series, I frequently use it in this *Concordance* to describe the "twin" phenomenon, which occurs so frequently in the Dark Tower books. A person's twinner is the version of that person that exists in another world, or on another level of the Dark Tower. For example, Eddie Dean dies in Mid-World, but Susannah Dean meets one of his twinners—Eddie Toren—in an alternative version of New York. Places can have twinners too. For example, Mid-World's Lud is the twinner of our world's New York, albeit in a distant future where terrible disasters have taken place.

TWIRLING HAND: A somewhat impatient gesture. Roland frequently uses it. It means "carry on" or "hurry up." V:701

UFFIS: This ancient term means shape-changer. VII:602

UNDERMIND: The unconscious mind. VII:513

UNIPOLAR CIRCUITS: *See* DIPOLAR CIRCUITS, *above*

UNIVERSAL TRUTHS, THE: Cort gave his apprentices lectures on what he called "the universal truths." We are not told what they are. V:78

VAGS: Vagrant dead. *See* VAGS, *in* CHARACTERS

VAQUERO (VAQ): Spanish for cowboy. This term is used in Hambry. IV:507

VURT: A nasty flying creature, also known as a bullet-bird. With its stony beak, it could bore a hole right through a person with its stony beak. W:118, W:129

WAITING WON'T MAKE IT ANY PRETTIER: Waiting won't make it any easier. W:74

WALK-INS: Certain parts of western Maine are plagued by walk-ins, or beings that enter our world from other worlds. *See* WALK-INS, *in* CHARACTERS

**WARE THE MAN WHO FAKES A LIMP: This was one of Cort's sayings. In other words, don't trust somebody who wants to be caught.

WASHOUTS: Many of the tracks of the Western Line had been destroyed by washout and ground-shakers, or floods and earthquakes. W:40

WATCH AND WARRANT: *See* DO YOU SET YOUR WATCH AND WARRANT ON IT?, *listed earlier in this section*

WATCH ME: A Mid-World card game. People usually place bets, so it can be rather dangerous. (One type of Watch Me game is a penny-it, three-to-stay.) Players are often killed at Watch Me tables. The phrase "Watch Me" can mean "You have a deal." III:278, III:366, IV:17, V:559, VI:17, W:287

WATCH ME CHIP (A WATCH ME CHIP): A Watch Me chip is like a poker chip. V:627

WATCH ME FACE: A Watch Me face is like a poker face. It is a face devoid of expression—one that can't be read because it doesn't expose emotion. The person behind the Watch Me face guards his or her secrets well. VI:38

**WAY OF THE GUN: This is another term for gunslinger training. W:36

WE ARE AT PEACE, YOU AND I: We are at peace. There is no argument between us. V:111

WE ARE KA-TET, WE ARE ONE FROM MANY: We are joined by fate, and our destinies are woven together. *See* KA-TET, *in* HIGH SPEECH. V:581, W:29

WE DEAL IN LEAD: A statement made by Steve McQueen in *The Magnificent Seven*, but Roland also uses it. Gunslingers are fighters first and foremost, but they are not mere hired guns. They are lawmakers and lawmen, and the bullet is the tool of their trade. V:115

WE MAY BE CAST ON . . . BUT NO MAN MAY CAST US BACK: Once we begin, we cannot be stopped. V:111

WE SPREAD THE TIME AS WE CAN, BUT IN THE END THE WORLD TAKES IT ALL BACK: We do what we can during a life, but in the end the world takes our lives along with everything we've accomplished. V:244

WE WILL ACCEPT NO QUARTER (NO QUARTER): We will neither accept nor give mercy. V:171, V:679

WEE SHIM: A small child. IV:458

WEDDIKEN: A burlap apron. W:116

WEEBEE: A small child. W:166

WEED-EATER: Somebody addicted to chewing devil grass. I:26, I:35

WE'LL HAVE TO MOVE VERY FAST, OR WE'LL FIND OURSELVES BASTED IN A HOT OAST: In other words, our goose will be cooked. II:136

WE'LL KEEP HIM VERY WELL: We'll take care of him. VI:37

WELL-MET (WE WERE WELL-MET, MAY WE BE WELL-MET ON THE PATH): We met, and that is important. Good has come from our meeting (implying an element of fate). "May we be well-met" means "Let good come of this meeting." IV:158, V:107, V:215, V:229, VI:9, VI:181

WELL-MET OR ILL, IT MAY BE YOU WILL FIND WHAT YOU SEEK: Whether good or evil comes of our meeting, you may find what you originally set out to find. V:107

WENBERRY: Wenberries are like strawberries. III:279

WERVELS: Poisonous rodents the size of dogs. They lived in the Endless Forest. W:111

WERY: This is Gasher's way of pronouncing "very." III:299

WESTERN LINE: The Western Line was one of Mid-World's train lines. Once, the Western Line ran from New Canaan to the Mohaine Desert. By Roland's youth, it only ran from Gilead to Debaria. W:40

WHAT I KEN: What I understand. V:205

WHATEVER THE GODS MAY BE, THEY HAVE FAVORED THIS PLACE: Similar to saying "God has favored this place," but it makes allowances for Mid-World's many deities. V:208

WHEELS: An archaic form of measurement still used throughout Mid-World and the BORDERLANDS. In *The Waste Lands,* Blaine tells us that a distance of eight thousand wheels is roughly equivalent to seven thousand miles. In that case, there are about 1.143 wheels to a mile. However, in *Wizard and Glass,* tricky Blaine tells us that 900 mph is the same as 530 wheels per hour. In this instance, one wheel is equal to 1.7 miles. In *The Dark Tower* (the final volume of the Dark Tower series), we are told that 120 wheels is roughly equivalent to 100 miles, hence a wheel equals about .83 of a mile, but slightly later we are told that twelve wheels is equal to nine or ten miles, hence a wheel is approximately .75 of a mile. Obviously, wheels, like the points of the compass, are in drift. IV:148, V:4, VII:718–19

WHEN FACTS SPEAK, THE WISE MAN LISTENS: This was one of Vannay's sayings. W:45

WHEN YOU ARE UNSURE, YOU MUST LET KA ALONE TO WORK ITSELF OUT: If you are unsure about what to do, leave the decision in the hand of God, the gods, or Lady Fate. V:392

WHERE AND WHEN (THIS WHERE AND WHEN): Your *where* and *when* refers to the specific level of the Dark Tower you are on (or which world you are in), and what time period you are inhabiting. Each *where* has many *whens,* and each *when* has many *wheres.* VII:36

WHERE ELSE WOULD I BE? THE WEST END OF THE WORLD?: This is a Lud saying. III:339

WHICH SIDE OF THE BISCUIT YOUR HONEY GOES ON: If you know which side of the biscuit your honey goes on, you know who pays your bills and so you do what they need you to do. W:72

WHITE: In our world, the White is an elemental force akin to faith and can mean faith in God or in a just universe. Before he lost his calling, Father Callahan knew the White well, and that energy was returned to him at the end of his life. To the beleaguered inhabitants of Mid-World and the BORDERLANDS, the White is the force of good and is the opposite of the OUTER DARK—that force of chaos and destruction championed by the Crimson King. When Aunt Talitha of River Crossing learns that Roland is a gunslinger, she says to her companions, "Behold ye, the return of the White! After evil ways and evil days, the White comes again! Be of good heart and hold up your heads, for ye have lived to see the wheel of *ka* begin to turn once more!" (III:232) To the beleaguered inhabitants of Mid-World, the aristocratic gunslingers are the knights of the White. In an unstable and violent present, they represent a stable and peaceful past, a kind of golden age. Roland's father, Steven Deschain, is often referred to as the last Lord of Light. Both the Affiliation and the ancient hero Arthur Eld represent the White, and yet the term means more than a particular political faction, allegiance, or social class.

The true meaning of the White relates back to the philosophy embedded in the Old Tongue, or High Speech, a philosophy of wholeness which seems to bear some resemblance to the Neoplatonic vision of the One. Just before Jake sees the Rose in the deserted Lot at Forty-sixth Street and Second Avenue, he hears the voice of the White, which he finds indescribably beautiful:

> The humming grew. Now it was not a thousand voices but a million, an open funnel of voices rising from the deepest well of the universe. He caught names in that group voice, but could not have said what they were. One might have been Marten. One might have been Cuthbert. Another might have been Roland—Roland of Gilead.
>
> There were other names; there was a babble of conversation that might have been ten thousand entwined stories; but above all that gorgeous, swelling hum, a vibration that wanted to fill his head with bright white light. It was, Jake realized with a joy so overwhelming that it threatened to burst him to pieces, the voice of *Yes;* the voice of *White;* the voice of *Always*. It was a great chorus of affirmation, and it sang in the empty lot. It sang for him. (III:124)

The White is wholeness and unity. It is the tapestry woven from many interlocking KA-TETS. It contains both good and evil, yet seen in the greater context of the White there is no gray or black, only whiteness. Like white light, the White contains all colors within its balance. Maerlyn's Rainbow is a breaking-up of this whiteness into a spectrum, many colors of which are troublesome. For example, the hungry, semisexual energy of Maerlyn's Grapefruit (the Pink One) proves disastrous for any who stare into its depths. V:101, V:104, V:115, VI:270, VII:4

WHITE BLIND: The poor salt miners of Debaria get drunk on White Blind. W:62

WHITE TEA: A refreshing, non-alcoholic drink. We have white tea in our world too. It is made from the young leaves of the tea plant. IV:184

WHY DON'T YOU STOP BEATING YOUR BREAST AND GET STARTED: Stop pulling your hair out and begin. V:559

WHY IS A CROOKED LETTER AND CAN'T BE MADE STRAIGHT . . . NEVER MIND WHY: This is one of Cort's sayings. In other words, don't bother asking. I:135

WHY LOOK FOR STORMS THAT ARE STILL OVER THE HORIZON? Why look for problems that haven't arisen yet. W:155

WICKETS: *See* POINTS, *above*

WIDE EARTH: One of Gilead's Fair-Days. It takes place in late winter/early spring. Wide Earth was famous for its riddling contests. *See* GILEAD FAIR-DAYS, *at the beginning of this* Concordance. *See also* MID-WORLD HOLI-DAYS, in APPENDIX IV. V:687, VII:64

WIDOWER'S HUMP: An older man's curved spine. VII:427

WIDOWMAKER: A gun. VII:49

WILL IT PLEASE YA: Used like "please" at the end of a sentence. For example, "Send word to my mother, will it please ya." W:185

WILL YOU DRINK TO THE EARTH, AND TO THE DAYS WHICH HAVE PASSED UPON IT? WILL YOU DRINK TO THE FULLNESS WHICH WAS, AND TO FRIENDS WHO HAVE PASSED ON? WILL YOU DRINK TO GOOD COMPANY, WELL MET?: This toast is made by Roland in River Crossing. III:234

WILL YOU NOT SEND ME ON WITH A WORD: Won't you speak to me? VII:760

WILL YOU OPEN TO US IF WE OPEN TO YOU?: If you ask a gunslinger to defend you in the name of the WHITE, he will ask you three questions. This is the first of them. The next questions is "Do you see us for what we are and accept what we do?" The final question is "Do you seek aid and succor?" V:109, V:230, V:397, VI:275, W:65

WILL YOU STAND WITH ME: Will you stand with me and fight? W:58

WISH YOU JOY OF IT: I hope it makes you happy, or *go for it.* W:227

WINE-BIBBER: A boozer. III:61

WINTER: One of Gilead's Fair-Days. *See* MID-WORLD HOLIDAYS, in APPENDIX IV.

WINTER'S SNOW IS FULL OF WOE, WINTER'S CHILD IS STRONG AND WILD: A Mid-World saying. V:138

WIT GREEN WIT: A canned drink, which Eddie tastes in the Fedic Dogan. He finds it utterly foul. VII:155

WITCHGRASS: Grass that grows in the foothills of the Cyclopean Mountains. I:118

WITCHLIGHT: In the tunnels beneath Castle Discordia, the puddles glow with what might be either radiation or witchlight. VII:562

WOODS TEA: Tea Roland brews from forest plants. V:107

WOODSMAN'S LUNCH: The filling lunch that a woodsman carries into the forest to sustain him while he works. W:209

WORDSLINGER: A writer. Roland calls Stephen King a wordslinger. VI:300

WORK-STOOP: A Gilead term for a porch located behind the main house and which faces both barn and fields. V:318

WORLD NEXT DOOR (THE WORLD NEXT DOOR): Those worlds which are similar to ours but which are not exactly the same. Eddie must come from one of the worlds next door, since in his version of New York, Co-Op City is in Brooklyn, not the Bronx. V:106

WOT (I WOT): I believe. W:5, W:10

WOULD'EE HAVE THE PEACE OF THE CLEARING?: Would you like to pass on to the next world? VII:50

WRISTBANDS: Handcuffs. II:356

WRIT OF TRADE: A legal document conveying ownership. VII:37

**YAR: Yes. VI:179, VII:83

YE CHARY GUNSTRUCK MAN: *See* CHARY, *in* HIGH SPEECH

YEAR END GATHERING: Year End Gathering is one of Mid-World's Fair-Days. Although REAP is the year's true end and marks the beginning of winter, Year End marks the end of the calendar year. V:21

YEAR'S END: One of Gilead's Fair-Days. *See* GILEAD FAIR-DAYS, *at the beginning of this* Concordance. *See also* MID-WORLD HOLIDAYS, in APPENDIX IV.

YE'RE A FIERCE TRIM: This is a Lud term for "you're a tough guy." III:297

YESTEREVE: Yesterday evening. V:410

YONDER: Over there. W:43

YOU HAVE DONE ME FINE: You have done well by me. W:251

YOU HAVE FORGOTTEN THE FACE OF YOUR FATHER: Gunslinger culture was patriarchal, and a man was expected to uphold the honor of his father, and his father's fathers, at all costs. V:661, VI:144

YOU MIGHT AS WELL TRY TO DRINK THE OCEAN WITH A SPOON AS ARGUE WITH A LOVER: There's no dissuading someone who is in love. II:304

YOU MUST NEVER DRAW UNTIL YOU KNOW HOW MANY ARE AGAINST YOU, OR YOU'VE SATISFIED YOURSELF THAT YOU CAN NEVER KNOW, OR YOU'VE DECIDED THAT IT'S YOUR DAY TO DIE: This rather bleak statement comes from Roland. VII:55

YOU NEEDN'T DIE HAPPY WHEN YOUR DAY COMES, BUT YOU MUST DIE SATISFIED, FOR YOU HAVE LIVED YOUR LIFE FROM BEGINNING TO END AND KA IS ALWAYS SERVED: This is another of Roland's sayings. VII:5

YOU RUN WITHOUT CONSIDERATION AND FALL IN A HOLE: One of Cort's sayings. IV:286

YOU SAY TRUE, I SAY THANKYA: *See entry in* CALLA BRYN STURGIS DIALECT

YOU WIN THE FAIR-DAY GOOSE: *See* FAIR-DAY GOOSE, *above*

YOUNG EYES SEE FAR: IV:174

YOUR FILL: Your territory. Debaria was Sheriff Peavy's fill. W:57

YOUR HEART SURELY SAID TRUE: Your heart guided you well. V:316

ZN: *See entry in* HIGH SPEECH

MANNI TERMS

ANYROA' (ANY RO'): *See entry in* MID-WORLD ARGOT

BAYDERRIES: Batteries. V:415

BEFORE THE SUN GOES ROOFTOP: Before the sun is high. VI:7

BOOK OF THE MANNI: The Manni's sacred book. It seems to be a version of the Bible. V:16

BRANNI BOB AND BRANNI COFF: The Branni Bob is the most powerful of the magical plumb bobs used by the Manni of Calla Redpath. As the Branni Bob swings, it gains weight and the space it passes through becomes DIM. The Branni Bob is carried in the Branni Coff. *See* MANNI: BRANNI BOB, *in* CHARACTERS

COFFS: Coffs are the boxes in which Manni carry their plumb bobs and magnets. They are large wooden boxes covered in stars, moons, and odd geometric shapes. The undersides of the coffs are fitted with long metal sleeves, which house long wooden rods. The rods can then be placed on the shoulders so that the coffs and their contents can be carried like coffins. VI:26

DIM: *See entry in* MID-WORLD ARGOT

FIN-GAN: The first word. According to the Manni, the first word, or fin-Gan, was *hile*. According to their beliefs, Hile was the first word, the one that set the world spinning. W:201

FORCE, THE: *See* OVER, THE, *below*

FORGETFUL, THE (THE FORGETFUL FOLK): Those who have left the Manni tribe to marry heathens. They will spend the rest of eternity in NA'AR, or the Manni Hell. V:407, VI:6, VI:28

GLAMMER: Although *glammer* is a term found throughout Mid-World, it has particular importance for the Manni, whose religion makes use of magic to travel between worlds. As the Manni say, "Magic and *glammer,* both are one, and they do unroll from the back. From the past, do'ee ken." VI:5

IN TIME OF LOSS, MAKE GOD YOUR BOSS: A Manni song. V:6

KAMMEN: *See entry in* HIGH SPEECH

KAVEN: The persistence of magic. The greater the magic, the longer it persists. Magic unrolls from the back, which means from the past. Hence, even when an object or a place seems to have lost its magic, a seed of that magic remains and can be awakened by those (like the Manni) who know how. VI:4, VI:26

KRA: A Manni cabin. Manni men live in a kra with all of their wives and offspring. When a Manni speaks of the "men of his kra," he means the men of his village, who are probably all kinsfolk. V:466, VI:34

KRA KAMMEN: This is the Manni term for the Doorway Cave. Jake thinks it means "house of bells," but it actually means "house of ghosts." To the Manni, the KAMMEN (TODASH chimes) are ghost bells. VI:34

MAGS AND BOBS: The magical tools which the Manni use to travel between worlds. *For more information, see* BRANNI BOB, *above, and* MANNI, *in* CHARACTERS. VI:7

MANNI KRA REDPATH-A-STURGIS: The Manni clan that lives in a village near Calla Bryn Sturgis. It is also the name of that village. VI:38

MANNI MANNERISMS: The Manni have many mannerisms which are as unique to their sect as are their blue cloaks, thick beards, and long fingernails. When a Manni covers his face with his hands, it is a gesture of deep religious dread (V:413). When Manni men have lost face, they tug their beards (VI:21). When Manni folk say "The Eld," they raise their fists in the air with the first and fourth fingers pointed (V:31). Finally, when Manni folk shake their heads, they do so in long, sweeping arcs (V:414).

MANNI REDPATH: Another name for Manni Calla, the Manni village located two hours north of Calla Bryn Sturgis. V:399

NA'AR: The Manni term for Hell. V:408

NAY: No. V:411

OVER, THE: Manni term for the divine force. According to Mia, the Over is identical to the PRIM, or the primordial soup of creation. *For page references, see* MANNI: OVER, THE, *in* CHARACTERS

OVER-SAM KAMMEN! CAN-TAH KAMMEN! CAN-KAVAR KAMMEN! OVER-CAN-TAH!: This is the praise-prayer Henchick gives when the Unfound Door opens. We are not given a translation. VI:42

OVER-SAM, OVER-KRA, OVER-CAN-TAH: A Manni prayer. We are not given a translation. VI:26

PASS OVER (TO PASS OVER): To time-travel or to travel between worlds. V:115

REDPATH KRA-TEN: Another term for Manni Calla, or the Manni village. VI:6, VI:7

SEEKING FOLK: Another descriptive term for the Manni. They are called seeking folk, far-seers, and far travelers because they travel between worlds. V:399

SENDERS: The senders are the most powerful of the Manni psychics and travelers. When Henchick and his followers reactivate the magic of the Unfound Door, they use the psychic strength of their strongest senders. VI:7, VI:39

SNIVELMENT (YOUNG SNIVELMENT): This is a Manni insult. Henchick calls Eddie Dean a young snivelment when he questions the power of the BRANNI BOB. *See entry in* MID-WORLD ARGOT. VI:29

TEMPA: The Tempa is the Manni Meeting Hall. VI:6

'TIS A GOOD NAME, AND A FAIR: Henchick says this to Roland. It is a way of saying that his name is good and honorable. V:416

TODASH: *See entry in* HIGH SPEECH

TODASH TAHKEN: *See entry in* HIGH SPEECH

WE ARE FAR-SEERS AND FAR TRAVELERS. WE ARE SAILORS ON KA'S WIND: This is how Henchick, the DINH of the Manni, describes his people. VI:38

CALLA BRYN STURGIS DIALECT

A HARD PULL THAT'D BE (THAT'D BE QUITE A PULL): That will be a tough one to pull off. V:224

A MAN WHO CAN'T STAY A BIT SHOULDN'T APPROACH IN THE FIRST PLACE: A man who can't spend the time to finish a conversation (or a visit) should have the sense not to begin one. V:477

A STONE MIGHT DRINK, IF IT HAD A MOUTH: This statement comes from Rosa Munoz, and is equivalent to "If pigs had wings, they would fly." VI:8

ADDLED (HE AIN'T HALF-ADDLED): Confused. *Addled* can also imply senility. V:346

ALL GODS IS ONE WHEN IT COMES TO THANKS: In other words, it doesn't matter which of Mid-World's gods you thank, as long as you thank one of them. V:206

AND MAY YOU HAVE TWICE THE NUMBER: *See* PLEASANT DAYS, AND MAY THEY BE LONG UPON THE EARTH, *below. See also* MAY YOUR DAYS BE LONG UPON THE EARTH, *in* MID-WORLD ARGOT

AND WITH THE BLESSING, WHAT AIN'T FINE WILL BE: With God's blessing, what isn't right will be put right. V:346

ANT-NOMIC: The people of the CALLA use this word instead of *atomic*. V:151, V:340

ANY RO': *See entry in* MID-WORLD ARGOT

ARC: *See* GRAND CRESCENT, *below*

ARMYDILLO: Armadillo. V:578

ASK PARDON: I beg your pardon. V:123

BABBIES: Children. V:611

BABY BANGERS (LITTLE BANGERS): Small fireworks or Reap-crackers set off during festivals or holidays. Children love them. V:227

BAH AND BOLT: *See entry in* MID-WORLD ARGOT

BARREL-SHOOTERS: *See entry in* MID-WORLD ARGOT

BEG-MY-EAR?: This phrase is equivalent to "Excuse me?" or "Pardon me?" V:124

BIDE (TO BIDE): To bide is to stay. V:322

BIG-BIG: Very much. It is usually heard in the context of "thankya big-big." It can also mean "a lot" or "a lot of." V:312, V:368

BLOODMUCK: Blood poisoning. V:651

BOAT, THE: *The boat* is a CALLA term for the rear part of a cowboy's saddle, or the place where bedrolls are tied. V:557

BOLA: *See entry in* MID-WORLD ARGOT

BOOM-FLURRY: *Boom-flurry* is the CALLA term for the nasty cacti which live in the desert dividing Calla Bryn Sturgis from Thunderclap. Boom-flurry eat humans. When they get all riled up (usually because a potential meal is passing by), they are said to be FASHED. V:571

BORDERLANDS: Calla Bryn Sturgis and the other CALLAS of the GRAND CRESCENT are located in the area known as the borderlands. The borderlands sit between Mid-World-that-was and End-World. *For page references, see entry in* MID-WORLD PLACES

BRIGHT OR DIM, THAT'S A LOT OF MEAT IN MOTION: Tian's da, Luke Jaffords, coined this phrase. He used it to describe his daughter Tia (Tian's twin), who was taken to Thunderclap by the Wolves and returned ROONT. Like the other roonts, Tia is a giantess, but her mental capabilities are extremely limited. V:8

BROWNIE: Eben Took uses this nasty phrase to describe Susannah Dean. (Gran-pere Jaffords uses it too, but Susannah doesn't take offense in Gran-pere's case, probably because he is so old and ADDLED that she figures he doesn't know any better.) Although many people in the CALLAS are dark-skinned, the term *brownie* refers specifically to a person who (in terms of our world's geography) is of African, or Afro-Caribbean, descent. V:359, V:405

BUCKA WAGGONS: *See entry in* MID-WORLD ARGOT

BUCKBOARD: *See entry in* MID-WORLD ARGOT

BUMPER: A bumper is a brimful glass of wine or beer. V:219

BUZZ-BALLS: *See* SNEETCHES, *below*

CALLA: According to Susannah Dean, the word *calla* means street or square. All of the villages in the BORDERLANDS are called callas. *For more information, see* BORDERLANDS, *in* MID-WORLD PLACES

CALLUM-KA: A callum-ka is a simple pullover worn by both the men and the women of the BORDERLANDS when the weather turns chilly. It looks like a boatneck. VI:229

CAN-AH, CAN-TAH, ANNAH, ORIZA: *See entry in* HIGH SPEECH

CAT-OIL: Rosa Munoz makes this arthritis rub. It contains mint and spriggum from the swamp, but its secret ingredient is ROCK CAT bile. It's potent stuff. V:242–43

CAVE OF VOICES: The Cave of Voices is located high in the arroyo country north of Calla Bryn Sturgis. Its name comes from the deep, noxious-smelling pit it contains—a pit that echoes with horrid, accusatory voices. What voices are heard depends upon who is there to hear them. Essentially, the demon of the cave (or its animating mechanism) taps into a listener's most guilty memories and then plays back the sobbing or angry voices of all those whom the listener believes he or she has wronged. Once Pere Callahan entered the Calla, the Cave of Voices was renamed Doorway Cave. This renaming came about because the freestanding magical door which Callahan used to enter the Calla (or was forced to use to enter the Calla) became a permanent fixture of the Cave. The door itself is known as the Unfound Door. *For more information, see* DOORWAY CAVE, *in* PORTALS

CHARY (YOU CHARY MAN): *See entry in* HIGH SPEECH

CHRIST AND THE MAN JESUS: The people of the CALLA are a little con-fused about whether the Man Jesus is the same as Christ. V:6

COMMALA: The Commala is another name for the RICE SONG, which was known and sung throughout Mid-World, In-World, and the BORDERLANDS.

On our KA-TET's first night in Calla Bryn Sturgis, Roland dances the Commala and wins the hearts (if not the trust) of the Calla FOLKEN.

In the borderlands, the term *commala* has more meanings than anywhere else in Roland's world. Here is a fairly complete collection of those definitions: 1. A variety of rice grown at the farthermost eastern edge of All-World. 2. Sexual intercourse. 3. Sexual orgasm (Q: Did'ee come commala? A: Aye, say thank ya, commala big-big.) 4. The commencement of a big, joyful feast. 5. A fork. 6. Schmoozing. 7. TO STAND COMMALA: literally speaking, this means to stand belly-to-belly. It is a slang term which translates as "to share secrets." 8. COME STURGIS COMMALA or COME BRYN COMMALA: literally speaking, to stand belly-to-belly with the entire community. 9. TO WET THE COMMALA: to irrigate the rice in a dry time. It can also mean to masturbate. 10. COMING COMMALA: a man who is losing his hair. 11. DAMP COMMALA: putting animals out to stud. 12. DRY COMMALA: gelded animals. 13. GREEN COMMALA: a virgin. 14. RED COMMALA: a menstruating woman. 15. SOF' COMMALA: a man who can no longer get an erection. 16. THE COMMALA DRAWS: the rocky arroyos north of Calla Bryn Sturgis. 17. COME-COME-COMMALA: the Rice Dance. 18. LOW COMMALA: *see* KI'BOX. 18. FUCK-COMMALA: a curse. 19. COMMALA-MOON: to stare aimlessly, or to be inattentive; to moon about. 20. STRONG COMMALA: a hard boy, or potentially dangerous man. V:208, V:230–33, V:325, V:484, V:486–87, V:489, V:587–89 *(words for the Commala)*, V:699, VI:229 *(Commala-moon)*

COOL EYES SEE CLEAR: A person who has an emotional distance from a situation will be able to see it in a more balanced way. V:323

COSY (A GOOD COSY, I HAVE A COSY FOR HIM): In our world, a cosy is a canopied corner seat for two. When Rosa Munoz says she has a "cosy" where Roland can sleep, she means she has a cot or a bed for him in a corner of her cabin. However, the sexual connotations of this phrase are fairly obvious. V:359, V:467

COWARDLY CUSTARDS: Cowards. V:360, V:362

COZENING BASTARDS: *See entry in* MID-WORLD ARGOT

CROSS-WAY: A person who holds to the Cross-way is a Christian. In other words, he or she follows the teachings of the crucified God. V:477

CRUSIE-FIX: *See* JESUS-TREE, *below*

CRY PARDON (CRY YOUR PARDON): *See entry in* MID-WORLD ARGOT

CULLIES: *See entry in* MID-WORLD ARGOT

DAIRTY: Dirty. V:402

DEEP HAIRCUT (A DEEP HAIRCUT): Margaret Eisenhart's term for the damage that can be done by an ORIZA. VII:83

DEVIL GRASS: *See entry in* MID-WORLD ARGOT; *see also* DEMONS/ SPIRITS/DEVILS: DEVIL GRASS, *in* CHARACTERS

DINH: *See entry in* HIGH SPEECH

DIVE DOWN: Like *yer bugger, dive down* is an exclamation often heard in the CALLA. V:223

DO YA (IF IT DOES YA; DO YA, I BEG; MAY IT DO YA): This is one of the CALLAS' all-purpose terms. It is often used rhetorically. Depending on the circumstances, it can mean "if you want," "if you know what I mean," or "Beg pardon?" V:22, V:129, V:209, V:353, V:477

DO YA EITHER WAY: This term translates loosely as "It's up to you" or "Do whichever you feel like doing." V:310

DO YA FINE: *See* MAY IT DO YA FINE, *below*

DO YA KEN: *See* KEN, *below*

DO YA TAKE NO OFFENSE, I BEG: "No offense intended." It can also mean "please." V:123, V:139

DO YE, I BEG: This is a polite way to demand what you want. For example, if you are in the Town Gathering Hall and the speaker is saying something with which you strongly disagree, you might demand the OPOPANAX feather by saying, "I'd have the feather, do ye, I beg!" V:22

DO'EE: "Do you." V:154

DO'EE FOLLER?: Do you follow what I'm saying? V:360

DON'T HURT A BOY TO SEE A WOMAN DO WELL: It's good for a boy to see a woman succeed. V:332

DOORWAY CAVE: *See* CAVE OF VOICES, *above*

DROTTA STICK: Dowsing stick. V:368

DRY-TWIST: *See entry in* MID-WORLD ARGOT

DUSTER: A duster is a kind of coat or rain-poncho. V:557

EARTHSHAKE: An earthquake. V:22

'EE (TO TELL 'EE): You (to tell you). V:417

EVEN HAND/ODD HAND: This is a way to take turns. For example, when Jake and Benny share Benny's room, Jake gets the bed on "odd hand" nights and Benny gets it on "even hand" nights. V:554

FAR-SEER: A telescope. V:573

FASHED: *See entry in* MID-WORLD ARGOT

FER GOOD OR NIS (FOR GOOD OR DIS): For good or ill. V:603

FOLKEN: *See entry in* MID-WORLD ARGOT

FOR GOOD OR DIS: *See* FER GOOD OR NIS, *above*

FOR THAT WE ALL SAY THANKYA: For that we are all grateful. V:350

FUCK-COMMALA: *See* COMMALA, *above*

FULL EARTH: *See entry in* MID-WORLD ARGOT

GALOOT: We have this word in our world too. It means a clumsy person. V:703

GARN (GARN, THEN): Go on. V:319, V:325, V:344

GET: When a man speaks of his get, he is referring to his begotten children. V:21

GITS: This word is used in our world too, especially in Britain. It translates loosely as "jerk." Neil Faraday calls Roland, his *tet,* and the townies who support them "numb gits" for thinking that they can defeat the WOLVES. V:612

GIVE YOU EVERY JOY OF THEM: May you enjoy them. V:173

GONE WORLD, THE: *See entry in* MID-WORLD ARGOT

GOODISH WANDER: Andy the Robot's term for a long walk. V:3

GRAF: *See entry in* MID-WORLD ARGOT

GRAND CRESCENT: The Grand Crescent (also known as the Arc, the Middle Crescent, and the Rim) is a mild arc of land located in the BORDERLANDS. It stretches for approximately six thousand miles and contains seventy CALLAS, or towns. Many of the Callas of the Crescent suffer from the predations of the WOLVES. Calla Bryn Sturgis, setting for *Wolves of the Calla,* is located about one-third of the way down from the Arc's northern tip. *See* BORDERLANDS: GRAND CRESCENT, *in* MID-WORLD PLACES

GRAN-PERE: Grandfather. V:251

GREEN CORN A-DAYO, THE: A popular song often sung in the CALLA. It has twenty or thirty verses. V:5

GUT-TOSSERS: Doctors. V:630

HE NEVER HAD NO SHORTAGE OF THORN AND BARK: He never had a shortage of guts. V:348

HEAR ME, I BEG (HEAR, I BEG; HEAR ME WELL, DO YA, I BEG): If you're staying in the CALLA and want people to listen to what you're about to say, or to contemplate what you've just said, then use this phrase. It can loosely be translated as "Hey" or "Listen up." The stock response (whether your listeners agree with you or not) is "We say thankee-*sai*." V:15, V:111, V:113, V:131, V:213, V:229

HOT-LUNG: This disease killed Benny Slightman's twin sister. Jake thinks hot-lung is similar to pneumonia. V:385

HOW FROM HEAD TO FEET, DO YA, I BEG?: This is the CALLA way of saying "How are you doing?" The stock response is "I do fine, no rust, tell the gods thankee-*sai*." V:113

HOWGAN: Hogan or home. V:612

HUNTRESS MOON: *See entry in* MID-WORLD ARGOT

I BEG: *I beg* is a term which, in the CALLA, is often tacked on to the end of sentences. *See* DO YA (DO YA, I BEG), *above*

I DO FINE, NO RUST, TELL THE GODS THANKEE-*SAI*: *See* HOW FROM HEAD TO FEET, DO YA, I BEG?, *above*

I SET MY WATCH AND WARRANT ON IT: *See entry in* MID-WORLD ARGOT

I WISH YOU JOY OF HIM: "I hope you enjoy dealing with him." Although this statement sounds pleasant enough, it is usually used sarcastically. In other words, "I hope you like dealing with the old bastard more than I do." V:347

I'D DO THAT MUCH, GODS HELP ME, AND SAY THANKEE: I'd do that much. V:128

IF IT DO YA FINE: This is another rhetorical statement. It can be used to mean "if that's all right by you," "if you want to," etc. V:127

IN THE END THE GROUND CURES ALL: In the end, death puts an end to all suffering. V:630

IT SPLIT THROG: It split three ways. V:359

IT'S TRIG AS A COMPASS: It sure is clever. V:130

JESUS-TREE: A Jesus-tree is a crucifix. Pere Callahan makes crucifixes (or "crusie-fixes") for the Christian converts of the CALLA. V:2

JILLY: *See entry in* MID-WORLD ARGOT

KA-BABY (KA-BABBY, KA-BABBIES): This term can be used for little brothers and sisters or for young KA-TET mates. It can also be used to insult a person who appears to be too young for the title he or she holds. For example, George Telford refuses to acknowledge Jake as a gunslinger. Instead, he refers to him as Eddie's *ka*-babby. V:9, V:223

KAFFIN TWINS: *See entry in* MID-WORLD ARGOT

KEN (AS YE KEN, DO YE KEN, DO YA KENNIT, I KEN, I DON'T KENNIT, YE KEN): To ken is to know. "Do ye ken?" is the equivalent of both "Do you know?" and "You know what I mean?" V:23, V:131, V:158, V:347, V:659

KI'BOX: Tian Jaffords explains human motivation to Eddie Dean in terms of a man's (or a woman's) body parts. Tian states that a human being consists of three boxes—a HEADBOX (also called a thoughtbox), a TITBOX (also called a heartbox), and a SHITBOX (also known as a ki'box). A person strives highest when he or she is motivated by the head or the heart. Nastiness, selfishness, lust, etc., all come from the ki'box. Actions motivated by the ki'box are LOW COM-MALA, or base actions born of base desires. V:630–31

KI'COME: Jake Chambers learned this term from his CALLA friend Benny Slight-man. *Ki'come* means "utter nonsense." It is probably related to KI'BOX. VII:396

KILLIN (YE FOOLISH KILLIN): Gran-pere Jaffords calls his grandson Tian a "foolish killin" for proposing that the men of the CALLA stand up and fight the WOLVES. (According to Gran-pere, drunken men will stand up and fight, but sober men are cowards.) Although we are not given a literal translation of *killin,* we know that Gran-pere thinks Tian's idea is admirable but unfeasible. Stephen King tells us that *killin* is a harsh word, but it can obviously be used in sadness as well. V:13

LADY OF THE PLATE: The Lady of the Plate is no other than Lady ORIZA, the rice goddess. Although the story of Lady Oriza was known throughout Mid-World-that-was, the tale of her confrontation with the harrier Gray Dick has special significance in the BORDERLANDS. In honor of Lady Oriza's clever revenge against her father's murderer, many of the CALLA's women practice throwing sharpened plates. Their deadly aim helps Roland's KA-TET win their battle against the WOLVES. *See* ORIZA, LADY *and* ORIZA, SISTERS OF, *both in* CHARACTERS

LADY ORIZA: *See* LADY OF THE PLATE, *above, and* ORIZA, *below*

LAKE-BOAT MART: The lake-boat marts are wide flatboats that are paddle-wheel-driven and gaily painted. They are covered with shops and float down the River Whye, selling wares. According to Gran-pere Jaffords, some of the women who work on these boats are as dark-skinned as Susannah Dean. V:211

LAST TIME PAYS FER ALL: Gran-pere Jaffords uses this term to express his desire for vengeance against the WOLVES. When the Wolves descend this last time, he says, the people of the CALLA will pay them back for all their previous attacks. V:369

LEG-BREAKERS (LEG-SMASHERS): These are the holes found in LOOSE GROUND. Leg-breakers are often nestled in innocent-looking weeds and high grass, so they can easily trap unwary or hurried people. Animals fall foul of them as well. There are many leg-breakers in Son of a Bitch, Tian Jaffords's worthless field. V:2, V:347

LEGBROKE: If you are lying on the ground legbroke, you have broken your leg. V:1

LEG-SMASHER: *See* LEG-BREAKERS, *above*

LIGHT-STICKS: These are the fire-hurling weapons used by the WOLVES. They look like the light sabers used in the *Star Wars* films. V:26, V:151

LOAD (THE LOAD): This term describes the stance taken by a woman (or boy) about to throw two ORIZAS at once. The stance was invented by Susannah Dean, but it was named by Margaret Eisenhart. VII:83

LONG DAYS AND PLEASANT NIGHTS: *See entry in* MID-WORLD ARGOT

LOOK HERE AT US, DO YA, AND SAY THANKEE: "Look at this" or "Look at what we've done." V:156

LOOSE GROUND: This term is used by the old folks of Calla Bryn Sturgis to describe ground riddled with holes and underground caves. The holes are called LEG-BREAKERS. Some of the Calla FOLKEN believe that bogarts live in the caves under loose ground. V:2

LOW COACHES: Like BUCKA WAGGONS, a low coach is a type of horse-drawn vehicle used in the CALLAS. *(For BUCKA WAGGON, see entry in* MID-WORLD ARGOT.) V:21

LOW COMMALA: *See* KI'BOX *and* COMMALA, *both above*

MADRIGAL: Tian Jaffords wants to grow this valuable crop in his field known as Son of a Bitch. But like PORIN, which his mother dreamed would grow in this rock-strewn waste-ground, it will probably die. The only thing that Tian is likely to grow in Son of a Bitch is a good crop of blisters. V:1

MAN JESUS: This is the CALLAS' term for Jesus. It can also be used as a curse. V:6

MANY AND MANY-A: *See entry in* MID-WORLD ARGOT

MAY I SPELL YE A BIT?: Shall I take a turn? V:129

MAY IT DO YA FINE: This can be used in place of "you're welcome." V:133, V:219, V:320, V:373

MAY THE SUN NEVER FALL IN YOUR EYES: *See entry in* MID-WORLD ARGOT

MAYHAP: *See entry in* MID-WORLD ARGOT

MIDS, THE: Another term for Mid-World, which lies to the west of the BORDERLANDS. V:25

MID-SUMMER: *See entry in* MID-WORLD ARGOT

MILK-SICK: This disease affects milk cows. It can kill them. V:8

MOIT: *See entry in* MID-WORLD ARGOT

MORTATA: Literally speaking, the mortata is the death dance. It is the opposite of the RICE DANCE (or COME-COME-COMMALA), which celebrates the fecundity of the rice. Some of the Calla FOLKEN suspect that Roland dances the mortata even better than he dances the commala. They have a point. V:607

MUMBLETY-PEG: *See entry in* MID-WORLD ARGOT

MUSICA: *See entry in* MID-WORLD ARGOT

NAR: No. V:332

NAY (NAYYUP): No. V:225, V:402

NEW EARTH: *See entry in* MID-WORLD ARGOT

NOBBUT (HE WON'T HAVE NOBBUT TO DO WITH ME): Nothing (he won't have anything to do with me). V:346

NUMMORE: No more, or no longer. V:322

NUP: No. V:209

OGGAN: This is the smooth-packed dirt used to make roads. V:654, VI:25, VI:272

OPOPANAX: Whenever a male resident of Calla Bryn Sturgis has something important to share with the FOLKEN, he sends around the opopanax feather. If enough men touch the feather, then a meeting is held at the Town Gathering Hall. The feather is a rust-red, ancient plume. In our world, the opopanax is not a kind of bird but a gum resin used in perfumery. In the novel *Black House*, the word *opopanax* becomes a sinister mantra for the main character, Jack Sawyer. As he states near the beginning of the book, "I'm falling apart. Right here and now. Forget I said that. The savage opopanax has gripped me in its claws, shaken me with the fearful opopanax of its opopanax arms, and intends to throw me into the turbulent Opopanax River, where I shall meet my opopanax." V:20–21

ORIZA: An Oriza is a plate made from a light metal alloy, probably titanium. Unlike most plates, Orizas aren't made for dining but for flinging. In fact, the deadly Orizas—which are manufactured by the ladies of Calla Sen Chre and thrown by the SISTERS OF ORIZA—are the deadliest weapons found in any of the CALLAS.

The Sisters of Oriza practice plate-throwing in memory of Lady Oriza, Goddess of the Rice, who invited her father's murderer over to dinner and then sliced off his head by flinging her specially made plate at him. Orizas are decorated with a delicate blue webbing which depicts the seedling rice plant. Two of the rice stalks on the edge of the plate cross, forming the Great Letter ZN, which means both "here" and "now." Luckily, the letter *Zn* also marks the one edge which is safe to hold. (Otherwise, an unwary person might absentmindedly pick up a plate and slice off a finger.) Beneath the plate is a small whistle, so the plate sings as it flies through the air. Interestingly enough, the Orizas bear a strong resemblance to a plate once owned by Susannah Dean's maternal aunt, Sister Blue. Detta Walker broke this *forspecial* plate in a fit of temper. *For page references, see* ORIZA, SISTERS OF, *in* CHARACTERS

OTTEN ELSE (I NEVER CONSIDERED OTTEN ELSE): Anything else (I never considered anything else). V:615

OUT-WORLD: To the people of Calla Bryn Sturgis, Out-World refers to the area west of the BORDERLANDS, close to Mid-World-that-was. V:8

PARD: Pardner, partner, or comrade. V:655

PEAK SEAT: *See entry in* MID-WORLD ARGOT

PLEASANT DAYS AND MAY THEY BE LONG UPON THE EARTH: This greeting is a variant of MAY YOUR DAYS BE LONG UPON THE EARTH, a phrase heard all over Mid-World. If someone greets you in this manner, your response should be "And may you have twice the number." V:3

PLOW-BREAKER (PLOW-BUSTER): A large fieldstone. V:2, V:349

POISON FLURRY: Poison flurry is a lot like poison ivy—the bane of Boy Scouts. If you find yourself needing to squat in Mid-Forest, make sure you don't wipe with this particular plant. Otherwise, you will develop a rash in a very uncomfortable place. V:137, V:644

PORIN: This is a spice of great worth. Tian Jaffords's mother thought it would grow in the family field known as Son of a Bitch. Unfortunately, the only things able to grow in that field are rocks, blisters, and busted hopes. V:1

PULLS: Corn-shuck wraps used for rolling tobacco. V:320

REAP: *See entry in* MID-WORLD ARGOT

RICE SONG/RICE DANCE: The Rice Song and the Rice Dance (jointly known as the COMMALA) are sung, danced, and loved throughout Mid-World. They celebrate the planting of rice and are (in essence) a fertility rite. *For page references, see* COMMALA, *above*

RIM: *See* GRAND CRESCENT, *above*

'RIZA (BY 'RIZA): Lady ORIZA is the rice goddess, who is worshipped all over Mid-World. *By 'Riza* is equivalent to *by God.* It can also be used in a stronger fashion. If you cry out because your "by 'Riza" eyes have been hurt, you mean your "goddamned eyes" have been hurt. Also, when the SISTERS OF ORIZA throw their sharpened plates (known as ORIZAS), they often cry "'Riza!" as they fling. V:360, V:572

ROCK CAT: *Rock cat* is the CALLA term for the wild cats that live in the desert east of the River Whye. Roland thinks they are probably pumas or cougars. Rock cat bile is the secret ingredient in Rosa Munoz's arthritis rub. V:340

ROONT: In Calla Bryn Sturgis, as in the other CALLAS of the CRESCENT, twins are the norm and singletons are rarities. Once a generation, the green-cloaked WOLVES sweep out of Thunderclap to kidnap one of every pair of prepubescent twins. Most of the children are returned, but they are returned roont, or ruined.

A roont child is a mentally handicapped child. Few of them can speak. Some cannot be toilet-trained. No matter how bright children were before being taken to Thunderclap, they return mentally challenged and with a central part of themselves missing. The roonts grow to prodigious size, but they die young. For roonts, both growing and dying is excruciatingly painful. *For page references, see* CALLA BRYN STURGIS CHARACTERS: ROONTS, *in* CHARACTERS

RUSTIES: *See entry in* MID-WORLD ARGOT

SALIDE: Although we're not told exactly what a salide is, it seems likely that it's either a blanket or cloak. V:234

SAUCY SUSAN: Saucy Susan is a flower with a lemony, faintly astringent smell. Rosa Munoz keeps a few sprigs of Saucy Susan in her privy. V:475

SAY SORRY: Sorry. VI:209

SAY THANKYA (SAY THANKEE, SAY THANKYA BIG-BIG): "Thank you," "Thanks," or "Thanks a lot!" V:124, V:130, V:143, V:265

SAY TRUE?: Do you mean it? Really? V:583, VII:129

SEEN THE BOAT SHE CAME IN: Although Roland thinks about this phrase in New York, it originates in Calla Bryn Sturgis. It comments on striking family resemblances. VII:493

SEMINON: This is the name given to the CALLA's late-autumn windstorms, the ones that come just before true winter. In the Calla they say, "Seminon comin', warm days go runnin'." Lord Seminon is also the name of a God whom Lady ORIZA wanted to marry. However, Lord Seminon preferred Oriza's sister, and Oriza never forgave him. *See SEMINON, LORD, and ORIZA, LADY, both under ORIZA, LADY, in CHARACTERS*

'SENERS: *See entry in* MID-WORLD ARGOT

SET US ON WITH A WORD: Say grace for us. *See also* WILL YOU NOT SET ME ON WITH A WORD, *in* MID-WORLD ARGOT. V:354

SHARPROOT: *See entry in* MID-WORLD ARGOT

SHOOTING-IRON: *See entry in* MID-WORLD ARGOT

SHOR'BOOTS: The heavy clodhoppers, or short boots, worn in the CALLA. V:14, V:18, V:21, V:136

SHORT BEER: In Calla Bryn Sturgis, a short beer is a beer served in a small water glass. V:656

SINCE TIME WAS TOOTHLESS: A great phrase that basically means "since before anyone can remember" or "forever." V:360

SINGLETON: A child born without a twin. In Calla Bryn Sturgis, singletons, and not twins, are the rarities. V:21, V:113, V:344

SINGLETS: *See entry in* MID-WORLD ARGOT

SISTERS OF ORIZA: The Sisters of Oriza are a female society, or network, found throughout the CALLAS of the BORDERLANDS. Although they function like a ladies' auxiliary—catering for town events, gossiping, etc.—their true purpose is to practice throwing sharpened, plate-like ORIZAS in honor of Lady ORIZA, goddess of the rice. The deadly skills of the Sisters help Roland and his KA-TET defeat the WOLVES in the final showdown on East Road. *For page references, see* ORIZA, SISTERS OF, *in* CHARACTERS

SLAGGIT!: A curse. It must be a bad one, since Gran-pere Jaffords's use of it at the dinner table makes the children giggle. V:355

SMALLHOLDS: The small family-run farms of the CALLA. Most of them are located on the fertile banks of the River Whye. V:208

SMALL-SMALL (SAY ANY SMALL-SMALL, AN' SNAY DOWN SMALL-SMALL): Very small. V:347, V:353, V:361

SMOKEWEED: Tobacco. V:403

SNEETCHES (BUZZ-BALLS, STEALTHIES): These flying metal balls are some of the most fearsome weapons used by the invading WOLVES against the people of the CALLAS. The sneetches seek their targets, and once they lock on, they put forth whirling blades that are as sharp as razors and can strip a man of flesh in five seconds. As Jake Chambers and Eddie Dean find out when they take a close look at one of these weapons, they are based upon the snitches found in the *Harry Potter* novels. Although neither Eddie nor Jake know who Harry Potter is (they left our world too early), both would have been interested to find out that the original snitches are little gold balls used in the game of Quidditch and aren't dangerous at all. (That is, unless you fall out of the sky while chasing one.) V:26, V:151, VI:25

SNUG: A snug is a small cottage. VI:13

SO I DO: This is yet another of the rhetorical phrases used in the CALLA. People tack it on the end of sentences. For example, someone might look at a dying fire and maintain, "I see a few sparks yet, so I do." V:127

SO IT IS: This is another phrase which the Calla FOLKEN tack on the end of sentences. It emphasizes what a person has just uttered. This phrase can also mean "you're right." V:226

SOF' CALIBERS: Sof' calibers are guns which are too old or too rusty to shoot. Given that *sof' commala* refers to a man who can no longer make iron at the proverbial feminine forge, you'd better be pretty damn sure that a man's calibers *are* sof' before you tell him they are. Otherwise, he might be so insulted that he shoots you. V:20

SPEAK A WORD O'BEGGARY: If you speak a word o' beggary to someone, you're crossing them, defying them, or arguing with them. V:359

SPEAK YOU WELL: This can either mean "you speak well" or be a request that you "speak well." V:216

SPEAKIES: A breed of demon found in the caves beneath LOOSE GROUND. V:2

SPELL YE (MAY I SPELL YE ON THAT CHAIR A BIT?): *See* MAY I SPELL YE, *above*

SPRIGGUM: Rosalita Munoz puts spriggum from the swamp into her CAT-OIL (her arthritis rub). We're not told what spriggum is, but we know it must be potent. V:243

SQUABBOT: This is part of a phrase uttered by an angry Neil Faraday during one of the Town Gathering Hall meetings held in Calla Bryn Sturgis. When Roland and his *tet* try to convince the townsfolk to stand up to the WOLVES, a cynical Faraday responds, "'Ay'll take 'een babbies anyroa' and burn 'een squabbot town flat." Roland and his friends find Faraday's accent almost incomprehensible, but it's obvious that he thinks that the Wolves, and not our *tet,* will triumph. Luckily, he's wrong. V:611

STEALTHIES: *See* SNEETCHES, *above*

STUBBORN AS A STICK: Incredibly stubborn. V:329

STUFF YOUR PRATTLE: Shut up. V:572

STUFFY-GUYS: *See entry in* MID-WORLD ARGOT

SURELY YOU'VE GOT A MOIT MORE GUTS THAN THAT: *See entry in* MID-WORLD ARGOT

SWARD (GREENSWARD): A sward is an expanse of short grass. Hence, a greensward is an expanse of short green grass. V:614

TA'EN: Taken. V:149

TELL GODS THANKEE (TELL THE GODS THANKEE): "Thank God" or "praise be to God" or "thankfully." V:149, V:206

TELL IT ANY OLD WAY IT DOES YA FINE: This is a soothing and reassuring phrase which is meant to set a person at ease so that he or she can tell the tale that needs telling. V:265

TELL ME, I BEG: Tell me. V:225

THANKEE-*SAI*: *See entry in* MID-WORLD ARGOT

THANKYA BIG-BIG: "Thank you very much!" V:312

THAT BEATS THE DRUM! DON'T IT JUST: This saying is equivalent to a rather strange phrase found in our world—"that just takes the cake." V:353

THE JIMMY JUICE I DRANK LAST NIGHT: A song sung in the CALLA. Andy the Messenger Robot likes to sing it. V:141

THOSE WHO HOLD CONVERSATION WITH THEMSELVES KEEP SORRY COMPANY: In other words, you shouldn't talk to yourself. V:207

THROAT-TAPPING: *See entry in* MID-WORLD ARGOT

THROG: *See* IT SPLIT THROG, *above*

TIME HAS SOFTENED: *See entry in* MID-WORLD ARGOT

TO LEAD US ALL TO BLUNDER WI' NO WAY BACK: To lead us into imminent danger with no way out. V:133

TODASH: *See entry in* HIGH SPEECH

TONGUE-WHIPPING: A tongue-lashing. V:572

TRIG: Clever. *Trig* implies an ability to read and understand other people's thoughts and motivations. It can also imply slyness. V:656

TRUE AS EVER WAS: Absolutely true. V:367

TRUM: *See entry in* MID-WORLD ARGOT

'TWERE: "It was." For example, "'Twere his eyes that frightened me." V:131

TWIN-TELEPATHY: *Twin-telepathy* describes the telepathy—or thought-sharing—which twins often experience. In the later books of the Dark Tower series, we find out that the WOLVES steal twins so that the servants of the Crimson King can harvest the brain chemical which causes twin-telepathy. They then feed this chemical (in pill form) to the BREAKERS working in the DEVAR-TOI. V:580

UNFOUND DOOR: An Unfound Door has the symbol for "unfound" written upon it. The magical portal in the CAVE OF VOICES bears this mark. *For page references, see* DOORWAY CAVE *and* DOORWAYS BETWEEN WORLDS: THE ARTIST'S DOOR, *both in* PORTALS

WEIRDLING WEATHER: Strange or ominous weather. V:601

WELL-MET: *See entry in* MID-WORLD ARGOT

WHAT IS IT FASHES AND DIDDLES THEE S'SLOW, OAFING: What is it that upsets you and makes you so slow? V:603

WILL IT DRAW WATER?: Will it work? V:491

WITTLES AND RATIONS: Food. V:358

WOLF'S EVE: The night before the WOLVES attack. V:608

WOLVES: The green-cloaked predators who come sweeping out of Thunderclap every generation to steal one of each pair of prepubescent twins born into the CALLAS of the GRAND CRESCENT. The Wolves ride gray horses and wear masks which look like the faces of snarling wolves, yet their bodies resemble those of giant men. At the end of *Wolves of the Calla,* we find out that the

Wolves are actually robots, and beneath their clothing they look a lot like Andy, Calla Bryn Sturgis's treacherous Messenger Robot. *For page references, see* WOLVES, *in* CHARACTERS

YAR: Yes. V:131

YE: You. V:411

YE DARE NOT: You wouldn't dare. V:411

YEAR END GATHERING: *See entry in* MID-WORLD ARGOT

YER BUGGER: The equivalent of "You bet your ass." V:149, V:151, V:222–23

YON: "Over yonder." V:207

YOU SAY TRUE AND I SAY THANKYA (YOU SPEAK TRUE AND I SAY THANKEE): "You speak truth and I say thank you." Also, "I agree with you." V:310

ZN: *See entry in* HIGH SPEECH

END-WORLD TERMS

ALGUL SIENTO: *See* DEVAR-TOI, *below*

ASIMOV ROBOTS: Intelligent robots, such as Nigel and Andy, built by North Central Positronics. Logic faults are quite common in these models. VII:156

BASCOMB: A type of wicker basket that has a lid and handles. It is a TAHEEN word. VII:347

BECOMING: For Mia, "becoming" was the process of becoming human, or for transforming from a creature of the PRIM into a being of flesh and blood. The bizarre surgery which made this transformation possible took place in the Fedic Dogan. *Becoming* is also the term that the CAN-TOI use for their own process of becoming human. However, despite all their efforts, the only thing that the *can-toi* are becoming is uglier. It is probably almost impossible for the *can-toi* to become human since they can't comprehend true human emotion. Hence, their humanoid faces—made from a kind of living latex—will never be more than masks to cover their lice-infested rat snouts. VI:251, VII:235, VII:293

BHST: Blue Heaven Standard Time. This is the way they measure time in the DEVAR-TOI. VII:271

BLUE HEAVEN: *See* DEVAR-TOI, *below*

BREAKERS (BEAM BREAKERS): The Beam Breakers are a group of psychics who were tricked by servants of the Crimson King into taking the perfect "job of a lifetime." It certainly turns out to be a lifetime job, since none of them can leave the DEVAR-TOI, or Breaker prison, until the universe collapses. Each day, the Breakers go to the Devar-Toi STUDY, where they focus their special skills on eroding the weakened Beams. *For page references, see* BREAKERS, *in* CHARACTERS

CHILDREN OF RODERICK: *See entry in* MID-WORLD ARGOT

CLAN-FAM: *Clan-fam* denotes a CAN-TOI clan family. The clan-fam gives a low man or low woman a human name as part of their process of BECOMING. The clan-fam name is a maturity-marker. VII:293, VII:617

CLOSIES: A term used by a washerboy in the Dixie Pig who warns Jake Chambers about Sayre and his "closies" or henchmen. VII:84

CRAZY, THE: This form of madness afflicts many in Thunderclap, especially the RODS. VII:300

CUT-EM-UP-MAN: A coroner. VII:106

DARKS: A dark is a unit of expelled psychic energy and is used to describe units of Breaker Force. In other words, it is a way to measure the amount of psychic energy which the BREAKERS emit at any one time—a force which is trained to erode the Beams. Ted Brautigan's talent as a facilitator means that he raises the Breaker Force exponentially every time he enters the STUDY where the Breakers do their work. With Ted around, the Breaker Force radiating from this room can jump from fifty breaks an hour to five hundred breaks an hour. VII:236, VII:295

DEEP TELEMETRY: *See* TELEMETRY, *below*

DESERT DOGS: This is the End-World term for coyotes. VII:289

DEVAR-TETE: *See entry in* HIGH SPEECH

DEVAR-TOI: The BREAKER prison located in End-World. *For page references, see entry in* PORTALS

DON'T WORRY ABOUT THE EGGS UNTIL YOU'RE ALMOST HOME: This phrase was originally used by the grandfather of Pimli Prentiss, the Devar Master. VII:232

EAR-STYKE: Like boils, eczema, headaches, and nosebleeds, this is one of the many ailments that can affect people in Thunderclap. VII:494

EATING SICKNESS: A nasty cancer that moves quickly and painfully through the body. The RODS often suffer from it. VII:300

END-TIMES: According to those who work in the DEVAR-TOI, End-Times are almost upon us. This is because the Tower and the Beams are almost ready to collapse. VII:226

ENJOY THE CRUISE, TURN ON THE FAN, THERE'S NOTHING TO LOSE, SO WORK ON YOUR TAN: This saying is popular among the BREAKERS. Rather disturbing when you consider that they are working to destroy all the known universes. VII:289

FACILITATOR: A facilitator is a psychic whose gift includes the ability to increase the power of other psychics. Ted Brautigan is a facilitator. VII:243

FLOATERS: CAN-TOI guards that roam about the DEVAR-TOI. VII:293

GMS: GMS stands for the General Mentation Systems found in North Central Positronics robots. There are two such systems—rational and irrational. VII:155–56

GOOD MIND: Good Mind is what rises from the BREAKERS when they work. It is a kind of psychic happy-gas. Not only does it dispel depression and pique, but it also increases the telepathic abilities of ordinary HUMES. VII:242

HINKY (HINKY-DI-DI): This is a term used by Finli O'Tego. (He picked it up from the HUME crime novels which he likes to read.) When something feels hinky-di-di, it means that it doesn't feel quite right. Trouble is on the wind. VII:226, VII:239

HUME: This term refers to humans. The CAN-TOI, who believe they are BECOMING human, find it demeaning. VII:9, VII:235

I TELL YOU TRUTH: This TAHEEN gesture is similar to the one used by Roland. The *taheen* (assuming he has hands) lays his right forefinger over a circle made by his left thumb and index finger. VII:238

KA-HUME: A term used by the GRANDFATHERS for human beings. VII:9

KEYSTONE EARTH: Keystone Earth, also called Keystone World, is our world—the one where Stephen King writes his books and where we read them. Keystone Earth is the only world in which time flows in a singular direction, or where (in the words of Dorrance Marstellar, a character from Stephen King's novel *Insomnia*) things that are "Done-bun-can't-be-undone." Keystone Earth is real in the same way that Mid-World was real before the Beams began to weaken. The KA of our world is NINETEEN. The *ka* of Mid-World/End-World is ninety-nine. When the two come together, as in the year 1999, cataclysmic events can take place. *For page references, see* KEYSTONE WORLDS, *in* PORTALS

KI'CAN: Shit-people or shit-FOLKEN. This is Ted Brautigan's term for the guards at the DEVAR-TOI. VII:286

KI'-DAM: Shit-for-brains. This is Dinky Earnshaw's term for *sai* Prentiss, the Devar Master. VII:197, VII:207, VII:262

LIGHT-STICKS: *See entry in* CALLA BRYN STURGIS DIALECT

MAKERS: The term that the ASIMOV ROBOTS use for the Old Ones. VII:156

MOMPS: A HUME disease. VII:356

MORKS: This is another term for a BREAKER. It comes from the 1970s American sitcom *Mork & Mindy*. Like the alien Mork of the series, Breakers don't have the same emotional makeup as other human beings. They tend to be disconnected from their fellow humans and so cannot form the emotional bonds that others feel. As a result, many of them are sociopaths. According to Ted Brautigan, most morks are selfish introverts masquerading as rugged individualists. Ted Brautigan, Dinky Earnshaw, and Sheemie Ruiz are three exceptions to this rule. VII:268–69

OTHER-SIDE WORLDS: To the Warriors of the Scarlet Eye living in End-World, our world is one of many other-side worlds. VII:300

PRECOG/POSTCOG: Precogs are psychics who see events before they happen. Postcogs are psychics who pick up on events that have already taken place. VII:238, VII:271

PROG: Dinky Earnshaw's word for reading thoughts. VII:292

REAL WORLD: Keystone Earth. VII:300

RED DEATH: *See entry in* MID-WORLD ARGOT

SHEEP GOD ('HEEP GOD): The GRANDFATHERS' term for the Christian God. VII:12

SHUFFLEFOOT BAH-BO: This is Pimli Prentiss's term for the CHILD OF RODERICK named Haylis. VII:346

SIM SEX: The kind of sex which most of the BREAKERS end up having. You can have sim sex with anyone you like. The only problem is that it's an illusion. The other person will seem real enough, but if you blow on them, the part your breath touches disappears. (Not a very nice thought.) In essence, sim sex is a fancy form of masturbation. VII:210–11

SNEETCHES: *See entry in* CALLA BRYN STURGIS DIALECT

STUDY, THE: The room in the DEVAR-TOI where the BREAKERS work on breaking the Beams. It looks like a library in a nineteenth-century men's club. *See* DEVAR-TOI, *in* PORTALS

SWING-GUARDS: The guards of the DEVAR-TOI. The term probably refers to either a particular rotation on the compound or to the changing of the guards. VII:237

TELEMETRY: Telemetry (or Deep Telemetry) is the machinery used in the DEVAR-TOI to detect psychic bursts. No one is sure exactly what this machinery was originally made to measure, but one suspects it was to detect telepathy, teleportation, or even deep tremors in the fabric of reality. VII:344

TELEPATH: Someone who can read other people's thoughts. VII:275

TELEPORTS: Teleports are psychics who can teleport, or move from one place to another using mind energy. Teleportation is the one wild talent that the DEVAR staff fear. VI:238–39

THINKING CAPS: The thinking caps are, in actuality, anti-thinking caps. The HUME and CAN-TOI guards at the DEVAR-TOI wear them so that the BREAKERS can't read their thoughts. The small radar dishes located on top of the heads of the robotic WOLVES are also called thinking caps. VII:171, VII:288

VAI, VAI, LOS MONSTROS PUBES, TRE CANNITSEN FOUNS: These words (which are never translated) are spoken by a huge warthog-headed chef at the Dixie Pig just before Jake Chambers cuts off its head with an ORIZA. The quote continues, "San Fai, can dit los! . . . Can foh pube ain-tet can fah! She-so pan! Vai! And eef you won'd scrub, don'd even stard!" VII:82

WE MUST ALL WORK TOGETHER TO CREATE A FIRE-FREE ENVIRON-MENT: These signs are posted all over the DEVAR-TOI. VII:236

WILD TALENT: A pulp-fiction term for psychic ability. Wild talents can manifest as precognition, telepathy, or even teleportation. VII:238–39, VII:277

LANGUAGE OF THE LITTLE SISTERS OF ELURIA

Roland doesn't hear much of the Little Sisters' language, but what he does hear he cannot identify. It is neither low speech nor High Speech, and it sounds like no other language or dialect he has ever heard. Since the Little Sisters are not human, it seems likely that theirs is a demon-tongue. The following phrases are uttered by Sister Mary (Big Sister) when she and the others of her vampiric order feed on the unconscious, unnamed man in the Sisters' hospital tent in Eluria. The words are never translated. E:180–81

CAN DE LACH, MI HIM EN TOW
RAS ME! ON! ON!
HAIS!

APPENDIX II
A BRIEF HISTORY OF MID-WORLD[1]
(ALL-WORLD-THAT-WAS)
AND OF ROLAND DESCHAIN,
WARRIOR OF THE WHITE

In the beginning there was only the Prim, the magical soup of creation. From the Prim arose Gan, spirit of the Dark Tower, who spun the physical universe from his navel. Gan tipped the world with his finger and set it rolling. This forward movement was Time.

The magical tide of the Prim receded from the earth but left behind it the Tower and the Beams, the fundamental structures which hold the macroverse together. Enough magic was left in Tower and Beams to last for eternity, but the Great Old Ones, in their hubris, decided to remake Beams and Tower using their technology. Magic is eternal, but machinery (like the men who build it) is mortal. Hence, the great technological advances of the Old People made possible not just the destruction of one level of the Tower but the obliteration of all of them.

The Great Old Ones had the knowledge of gods, and so, like reckless demiurges, they assumed that they had the right to manipulate reality with impunity. For their own decadent entertainment, they created doorways that led from their world to other *wheres* and *whens* on every level of the Tower. They built great cities where centralized computers and Asimov robots catered to their every need.

But still, it wasn't enough. The Old People designed Dogans, where magic and technology could be joined. Here, their scientists/alchemists created new diseases, such as the Red Death, and terrible weapons which they launched against their enemies, poisoning earth, air, and water. Soon every living creature on the surface of the Earth became contaminated. Animals and humans gave birth to mutants, and Mid-World was reduced to a great poisoned wasteland.

The time of the Great Old Ones was almost over. But before they disappeared from their level of the Tower, the Old People made a final act of atonement. To make amends for their atrocities and to pay penance for the sins they had committed against the earth and against each other, they built twelve giant mechani-

1. As readers of the Dark Tower series know, Mid-World was originally the name of an ancient kingdom, one that tried to preserve culture and knowledge during a great age of darkness. However, throughout the series Stephen King also uses *Mid-World* as a general term for Roland Deschain's level of the Tower. I have followed this practice.

cal Guardians to watch over the twelve entrances into, and out of, Mid-World. These Guardians—Bear and Turtle, Elephant and Wolf, Rat and Fish, Bat and Hare, Eagle and Lion, Dog and Horse—were cyborg versions of the twelve immortal animal totems left by the Prim to guard the Beams.

Yet even this final act of atonement proved misguided. The fabric of reality, rewoven by the Great Old Ones, was destined to fray. Less than three thousand years after being built in the farthest reaches of Out-World, the giant cyborg Bear Guardian, Shardik, ran mad. The mechanical Beams (already eroded) began—one by one—to topple. The computers and robots built by the ancient company North Central Positronics (a leader in mind-to-mind communications since the ten thousands) became dangerously psychotic and either murdered their masters' descendants or joined forces with the Crimson King, that ancient Lord of Chaos. And as the Old Ones' technological web collapsed, whole worlds were destroyed by plagues like the superflu.

But life is striving to be life, and against all odds it will defy the Outer Dark. The Tower had more than a little of its old magic left, and from its ancient gray-black foundations deep in the red rose-fields of End-World, it sent out a call. From In-World-that-was, it drew forth the world's last gunslinger—final descendant of Arthur Eld, King of All-World-that-was, Warrior of the White, and Guardian of the Tower. Although this gunslinger believed that his only ambition was to climb to the top of the Tower to meet whatever being resided there, *ka* had greater plans for him.

Like his enemy the Red King, Lord of Discordia, Roland Deschain of the White both *darkles* and *tincts*. Leaping from one level of the Dark Tower to another, he pursues his vision and his quest. With the help of a *ka-tet* drawn from other levels of the Tower (ones where the great city of Lud is called New York, and where North Central Positronics and the Sombra Corporation have not yet poisoned the ambitions of their culture), he opposes Discordia and fulfills the will of the White.

What began, in *The Gunslinger,* as the journey of a goal-obsessed loner becomes, in *The Dark Tower,* a great journey of redemption and sacrifice. End-World lies ahead, and the Tower waits.

TIMELINE FOR THE DARK TOWER SERIES

Books I–VII and "The Little Sisters of Eluria"

B.R.B.—Before Roland's Birth
A.R.B.—After Roland's Birth

2,700–1,700 B.R.B.

The Great Old Ones, rulers of All-World-that-was, create the cyborg Guardians to atone for their sins against the earth and against each other.[2]

---

2. III:33—Shardik is two thousand to three thousand years old when our *ka-tet* finds him in the Great West Woods. III:38—Creating the cyborg Guardians was the Great Old Ones' final act of atonement for the harm they had done to the earth, and to each other.

2,200 B.R.B.

Due to radiation poisoning and other types of fallout, most humans are already sterile. Women who can conceive give birth to mutants.[3]
Although rumor states that Castle Discordia, in End-World, is haunted again, a few stoic individuals continue to occupy End-World's towns and villages. They will soon regret it.
A jar of the Great Old One's demonstuff cracks open, loosening plague. The Red Death wipes out the people of Fedic.[4]

1,800 B.R.B.

The Great Old Ones finally destroy themselves.
They disappear from the Earth.[5]
Human society fragments, and the old knowledge is forgotten.
Mutants roam the wastelands.
Mid-World's Dark Age begins.

690 B.R.B.

Arthur Eld rises to power and rules the Kingdom of All-World.[6]
The people practice human sacrifice as part of the Charyou Tree Festival of Reap.

To pinpoint a timeline date, I counted backward from our *ka-tet*'s adventures in the Great West Woods. At that point, Roland is approximately 336 years old. (I explain Roland's age in Footnote 27.) Since Shardik's age is approximate, I thought this date should be approximate also. 3,000–336 A.R.B. = 2,664 B.R.B. 2,000–336 A.R.B. = 1,664 B.R.B., or approximately 2,700 B.R.B. to 1,700 B.R.B.

3. VI:243—The Red Death affected Fedic two dozen centuries, or twenty-four hundred years, before the coming of the Wolves. Most people were already birthing monsters. Mid-World's many mutants came into being thanks to the Great Old Ones' disastrous wars. For more information, see MUTANTS, in CHARACTERS.

4. VI:243—The Red Death may have come out of the deep crevice beyond Fedic, called the Devil's Arse, but given the name of the disease (taken from a fictional plague created by Edgar Allan Poe), and the terrible practices of the Great Old Ones, it seems most likely that it was created by biological engineers and accidentally released.

5. III:38—See Footnote 2. For date on the timeline, I counted backward. The Great Old Ones disappeared two thousand years before the Wolves began raiding the Callas (V:339). In *Wolves of the Calla*, we find out that the Wolves have been preying on the children of the borderlands for six generations (V:339). In the Calla, one generation is twenty-three years (V:15). Six generations equals 138 years. If Roland is approximately 336 at the time that *Wolves of the Calla* takes place, he was 198 when the Wolves started raiding (198 A.R.B.). I counted back from this date.

6. There appear to be two Arthur Elds—the mythical Arthur Eld, who was the first king to arise after the Prim receded and who was the ancestor of both the line of Deschain and the Crimson King (VII:176), and the historical Arthur Eld, forefather of Steven Deschain. Steven Deschain was twenty-ninth, on a sideline of descent, from the historical Arthur Eld. Roland, then, is thirtieth. If a generation is approximately twenty-three years (see V:15), and if Steven Deschain was approximately twenty-three when Roland was born, then 30 x 23 = 690.

464 B.R.B.

The Great Old One's technological web—supporting Beams and Tower—
continues to decay.
Blaine's computerized monitoring equipment in End-World collapses.[7]

464–64 B.R.B.

The Kingdom of All-World fragments and is replaced by a loose Affiliation
of baronies.
The In-World Barony of New Canaan is the Affiliation's hub.
New Canaan, and its barony seat of Gilead, is ruled by the gunslingers,
who are the descendants of Arthur Eld and his knights.

64 B.R.B.–36 A.R.B.

Civil War erupts in the distant baronies of Garlan and Porla.
Wars continue for a hundred years.[8]
The Affiliation begins to destabilize.

ROLAND IS BORN

John Farson, a harrier from Garlan and Desoy, gains power in the lands west
of New Canaan. His followers call him the Good Man.
Farson resurrects the Great Old One's killing machines so that he can
overthrow the Affiliation and the aristocratic gunslingers.
Failed gunslingers from Gilead and the In-World baronies, sent west
in disgrace, begin to join Farson's cause.

11 A.R.B.

Roland's father, Steven Deschain, is on the verge of becoming *dinh* of Gilead,
and possibly *dinh* of all In-World.[9]
Roland and his friend Cuthbert Allgood discover that Gilead's head cook, Hax,
is poisoning people for John Farson. They tell their fathers.
Hax is hanged for treason. Roland and Cuthbert witness his hanging.[10]

14 A.R.B.

West of Gilead, near the edge of the civilized world, fighting breaks out
between Farson's rebels and the Affiliation.[11]
Roland finds out that his mother is having an affair with his father's sorcerer
(Marten Broadcloak/Walter O'Dim), who also happens to be a secret

7. III:412—At the time *The Waste Lands* takes place, eight hundred years have passed
since Blaine's monitoring equipment went down in End-World. If Roland is 336 years old
when he and his *tet* riddle with Blaine, 800–336 = 464 B.R.B.

8. III:242—Civil war erupts in Garlan/Porla three hundred to four hundred years
before our *ka-tet* reaches River Crossing.

9. I(2003):160.

10. I(1988):159, I(2003):170—Roland is fourteen when he finds out that Marten
Broadcloak is having an affair with his mother. Roland challenges his teacher, Cort, and
wins his guns. Hax hanged by the neck three years before Roland's test of manhood.

11. I(2003):169.

supporter of the Good Man. Needing guns to exact revenge, Roland goes
for his test of manhood five years too early.
Roland succeeds.

14–14.5 A.R.B.
Roland and his two friends Cuthbert Allgood and Alain Johns
are sent east to Hambry, in the Barony of Mejis, to keep them safe
from Farson's treachery.[12]
They discover a plot against the Affiliation and defeat some
of the Good Man's forces.
They find Maerlyn's Grapefruit, the Pink One of the Wizard's Rainbow,
and steal it for their fathers.
Roland is captivated by the Pink One's *glammer* and gazes into its depths.
He sees his pregnant lover, Susan Delgado, burned to death
on a Charyou Tree fire.[13]

14.5 A.R.B.
Roland and his friends return to Gilead.
Roland is given his father's guns.
Gabrielle Deschain, lately back from a retreat in Debaria,
is still in Marten Broadcloak's power. She secretly plans to kill her husband,
but Roland prevents it.[14]
Roland accidentally shoots his mother.[15]

16 A.R.B.
Much of In-World falls to the Good Man.
Roland's father is murdered.[16]

19 A.R.B.
Roland's *ka-tel* (or graduating class) of gunslingers load their guns
for the first time.
Only thirteen remain out of a class of fifty-six.
Cort is too ill to attend the Presentation Ceremony.
Nine weeks later, Cort dies of poisoning.[17]

---

12. See Footnote 10. I(1988):163—Roland goes for his test five years too early. Steven Deschain sent Roland east because he thought that the Good Man and his followers were in the west. IV:112.

13. Events of *Wizard and Glass*.

14. IV:655–56.

15. Ibid.

16. I(2003):118—The land falls to Farson five years after Hax's hanging. Roland's father is dead by this time. I(2003):161—Steven Deschain was killed by a knife.

17. I(1988):163—Roland won his guns five years too early. He was fourteen at the time. Hence, the average age for gunslingers to win their guns is nineteen. II:177—We are told that Cort dies of poison nine weeks after the gunslinger apprentices' Presentation Ceremony.

21 A.R.B.

Two years after Cort's death, the red slaughter reaches Gilead,
the last bastion of civilization.
The final civil war begins.[18]

24 A.R.B.

The battle of Jericho Hill is fought.[19]
Cuthbert Allgood dies, shot through the eye by Rudin Filaro
(aka Walter O'Dim).[20]
Roland is the only gunslinger to survive.[21]
Roland leaves the Horn of Deschain (the Horn of Eld)
on Jericho Hill.

24–36 A.R.B.

Roland casts about for Walter's trail.[22]
He visits the ruins of Gilead, now overrun with timothy and wild vines.
The old castle's kitchens are infested with Slow Mutants.[23]
Roland travels to Eluria, is captured by the Green Folk, and ends up
in the clutches of the vampiric Little Sisters of Eluria.
He escapes.[24]

36 A.R.B.[25]

Roland is hot on the trail of the Man in Black.
He enters Tull and is besieged by the followers of the mad preacher
Sylvia Pittston, servant of the Crimson King and lover of the Man in Black
(aka Walter O'Dim).
Roland kills everyone in Tull, including his lover, Alice.
Roland crosses the Mohaine Desert and at the Way Station
and meets Jake Chambers.
In the Cyclopean Mountains, Roland sees the Man in Black
for the first time in twelve years.
Roland allows Jake to fall into an abyss below the mountains,
then enters the golgotha with Walter.

18. II:177.

19. V:347—Cuthbert was twenty-four when he died at Jericho Hill. If he and Roland were approximately the same age, then Roland must have also been about twenty-four when this battle was fought.

20. VII:174.

21. VII:174–75.

22. I(2003):152—Roland catches sight of Walter, presumably after the battle of Jericho Hill, and then does not see him again for twelve years, or until he and Jake enter the passages beneath the Cyclopean Mountains. Twenty-four years plus twelve years equals thirty-six years.

23. I(2003):146.

24. Events of "The Little Sisters of Eluria."

25. Events from *The Gunslinger*. For explanation of Roland's age, see Footnote 22.

Roland and Walter enter a fistula of time and Roland has a vision
of the Tower's many levels.[26]
When he awakes, Roland has aged ten years, but three hundred years have
passed in Mid-World-that-was.[27]
While Roland dreams, the remains of Mid-World collapse.

140 A.R.B.

River Barony Castle (near the town of River Crossing) falls to harriers.[28]

198 A.R.B.

The Wolves begin invading the Callas of Mid-World's borderlands.[29]
The Crimson King's followers are feeding a twin-telepathy
chemical (extracted from the brains of prepubescent twins) to the Breakers
of End-World so that these telepaths can speed the destruction of the Beams
and the collapse of the Dark Tower.

246 A.R.B.

David Quick, the outlaw prince, leads an attack on the city of Lud.
This city (Mid-World's version of New York) is caught in a constant cycle
of warfare.
Quick dies trying to use one of the Old Ones' flying machines.[30]

266 A.R.B.

Patricia (Blaine's twin mono) stops running.[31]

336 A.R.B.

Roland awakens in the golgotha and travels to the Western Sea,
where two of his right fingers and one of his toes are eaten by lobstrosities.

26. VII:176–77.

27. I(2003):230–31—Roland appears to be ten years older when he wakes. II:47—At least one hundred years pass while Roland is in the golgotha. III:375—According to Blaine, by the time our *ka-tet* reaches Lud, it has been three hundred years since any gunslinger walked either In-World or End-World. Since Roland is the last gunslinger, Roland must have disappeared for about three centuries. Roland was approximately twenty-four at the battle of Jericho Hill. (See Footnote 19.) He was approximately thirty-six when the events of *The Gunslinger* took place. (See Footnote 22.)

28. According to Si of River Crossing, the last tribute was sent to River Barony Castle in the time of his great-grand-da, but they found the castle in ruins. Si is at least seventy by the time he tells his story.

29. V:339—By the time *Wolves of the Calla* takes place, the Wolves have been invading the Calla for six generations, or 138 years. On V:15, we learn that a generation is approximately twenty-three years.

30. III:244—Ninety years before our *ka-tet* reached River Crossing, Quick rode into Lud with his harriers. III:273–75—Our *ka-tet* finds the remains of both Quick and the flying machine.

31. III:246—The mono under discussion stopped running seventy years before our *ka-tet* reached the town of River Crossing. On this page, our *tet* seems to think that the stalled mono is Blaine. Later in the story they realize that Patricia stopped running, not Blaine.

He draws forth Eddie Dean and then Odetta Holmes
(along with Odetta's second personality, the nasty Detta Walker).
Roland forces Odetta and Detta to unite, and they become
Eddie Dean's great love, Susannah Dean.
In the Great West Woods, our *tet* finds the Bear-Turtle Beam
and follows it to the ancient kingdom of Mid-World.
Jake is drawn, once more, onto Roland's level of the Tower.
While drawing Jake, Susannah becomes pregnant by the demon
of the Speaking Ring (actually a Demon Elemental) and conceives
"the chap."
Oy joins the *ka-tet*.
Our *tet* travels to River Crossing, then to Lud, and finally boards Blaine
the Insane Mono on his mad hurtle toward Topeka.
Blaine says he will kill them all, and himself, unless they can beat him
in a riddling contest.
Eddie defeats Blaine with the illogic of his bad jokes.
Blaine crashes, destroying himself, but our *ka-tet* survives.
They enter an alternative version of our Kansas and encounter a thinny.
There, by the warble of the thinny, Roland recounts the story of his time
in Mejis and of his love affair with Susan Delgado.
Our *tet* enters the Green Palace and faces down the infamous R.F.
(aka Walter O'Dim).
They awake in a clearing of white winter grass, once more
on the Path of the Beam.

336–337 A.R.B.[32]

Our *tet* journeys along the Path of the Beam and enters the borderlands.
Susannah, pregnant with the chap, develops another personality,
that of Mia (High Speech for "mother").
Roland and his companions enter Calla Bryn Sturgis and battle the Wolves,
saving the Calla's twins from being made "roont" in End-World.
The Crimson King foresees our *ka-tet*'s victory, so kills himself
and all but three of his followers.
Undead, the Crimson King rides to End-World and positions himself
on a balcony of the Dark Tower.
After the battle with the Wolves, Mia takes control of Susannah's body
and escapes through the magical portal of the Doorway Cave.
She travels to the Dixie Pig in New York, 1999, so that she can rendezvous
with the servants of the Crimson King and bear her demonic chap.
In the Extraction Room of the Fedic Dogan, Mordred Red-Heel is born.
Mordred immediately eats his body-mother, Mia.
Susannah Dean kills her captors and shoots off one
of Mordred's eight spider legs.
Jake, Oy, and their new *tet*-mate, Father Donald Callahan,

---

32. Throughout *Wolves of the Calla*, we are told that Jake is twelve years old. In the previous books he was eleven. Hence, a year (or a good part of a year) must pass between the events of *The Waste Lands/Wizard and Glass* and *Wolves of the Calla*.

track Susannah to the Dixie Pig in the *where* of New York City
and the *when* of 1999.
Pere Callahan is killed.
Pursued by the henchmen of the Crimson King, Jake and Oy
reach the New York/Fedic Door.
Roland and Eddie pass through the Unfound Door to Maine, 1977.
After battling Balazar's thugs, they track down Calvin Tower
and Aaron Deepneau.
Calvin Tower sells Roland and Eddie the magical Vacant Lot,
home of the Rose.
Roland and Eddie meet their maker, Stephen King, in the *when* of 1977
and the *where* of Bridgton, Maine.
With the help of John Cullum, Roland and Eddie
form the Tet Corporation to protect the Rose in our world.
Our *tet* is reunited in the Fedic Dogan and passes through
the Wolves' Door to Thunderclap Station.
Mordred eats Walter O'Dim and follows them.
Our *ka-tet* defeats the servants of the Crimson King in the Devar-Toi.
Eddie is shot by the Devar Master and dies.
Roland, Jake, and Oy travel through a magic door made by the Breakers
to Maine, 1999.
They save the life of their maker, Stephen King.
Jake dies.
Roland meets the executives of the Tet Corporation and sees the Rose.
Roland, Oy, and Susannah are reunited in Fedic.
They travel through the Discordia to Le Casse Roi Russe.
Mordred follows.
Roland, Oy, and Susannah destroy the were-insect Dandelo
and free the mute artist Patrick Danville.
On the road to the Tower, Patrick draws the Unfound Door for Susannah.
Susannah abandons the quest and enters an alternative version of New York.
Mordred—dying of food poisoning—attacks Roland.
Oy dies defending Roland.
Mordred dies under the gun of his White Daddy.
Roland and Patrick reach the Tower, but the Red King is waiting for them.
Patrick uses his magical drawing skills to draw, and then erase,
the Crimson King.
Roland climbs the Tower and finds . . . himself.
Commala come-come,
The journey's never done.
Or is it?
The man in black fled across the desert, and the gunslinger followed.
But this time, Roland has his horn, and he will sound it when he reaches
the distant fields of Can'-Ka No Rey, and the Tower which calls him.

APPENDIX III
MID-WORLD RHYMES, SONGS, PRAYERS, AND PROPHECIES

I: RHYMES

**1. BABY-BUNTING RHYME

When Roland was a little boy, his mother sang this song to him. *Chussit, chissit, chassit* are the High Speech words for the numbers seventeen, eighteen, and nineteen. (VII:23, VII:767)

> Baby-bunting, darling one,
> Now another day is done.
> May your dreams be sweet and merry,
> May you dream of fields and berries.
> Baby-bunting, baby-dear,
> Baby, bring your berries here.
> Chussit, chissit, chassit!
> Bring enough to fill your basket.

2. BREAKER RHYME

This little rhyme is popular among the Breakers of End-World. I suppose it helps them justify their part in the destruction of the macroverse. (VII:289)

> Enjoy the cruise,
> turn on the fan,
> there's nothing to lose,
> so work on your tan.

3. ORIZA RHYME

We learn this High Speech rhyme in Calla Bryn Sturgis. In the Calla they believe that mortal woman was made from the breath of mortal man, but that the first man came from Lady Oriza. The translation is "All breath comes from the woman." (V:631)

> Can-ah,
> can-tah,
> annah,
> Oriza

4. PENNY POSY

This bit of "cradle nonsense" was sung to children in Mid-World. Roland would have known it well. (VII:171)

Penny, posy,
Jack's a-nosy!
Do ya say so?
Yes I do-so!
He's my sneaky, peeky, darling bah-bo!

5a. RAIN IN SPAIN (Original Version)

The rain in Spain falls mainly on the plain.
There is joy and also pain
but the rain in Spain falls mainly on the plain.
Pretty-plain, loony-sane
The ways of the world all will change
and all the ways remain the same
but if you're mad or only sane
the rain in Spain falls mainly on the plain.
We walk in love but fly in chains
And the planes in Spain fall mainly in the rain. (I:71)

**5b. RAIN IN SPAIN (Version #2)

In the 2003 version of *The Gunslinger,* the second verse is replaced by the following:

Time's a sheet, life's a stain
All the things we know will change
and all those things remain the same,
but be ye mad or only sane,
the rain in Spain falls mainly on the plain.

6. SEE THE TURTLE OF ENORMOUS GIRTH

This well-known and well-loved Mid-World poem invokes the spirit of the Turtle Guardian. Each region repeats a slightly different version, but despite this, the poem remains essentially the same. *For more information and for page references, see GUARDIANS OF THE BEAM, in CHARACTERS.*

BORDERLANDS VERSION (VI:15)

See the Turtle of enormous girth!
On his shell he holds the earth,
His thought is slow but always kind;
He holds us all within his mind.
On his back the truth is carried,
And there are love and duty married.
He loves the earth and loves the sea,
And even loves a child like me.

IN-WORLD VERSION (VII:490)

See the Turtle of enormous girth!
On his shell he holds the earth,
His thought is slow but always kind;
He holds us all within his mind.
On his back all vows are made;
He sees the truth but mayn't aid.
He loves the earth and loves the sea,
And even loves a child like me.

7. SEMINON RHYME

Seminon is the name given to the Calla's late-autumn windstorms, the ones that come just before true winter. Lord Seminon is also the name of a god whom Lady Oriza wanted to marry. However, Lord Seminon preferred Oriza's sister, and Oriza never forgave him. (V:632) *See* SEMINON, LORD, *and* ORIZA, LADY, *under* ORIZA, LADY, *in* CHARACTERS.

Seminon comin',
warm days go runnin'.

**8. SPARK-A-DARK, WHO'S MY SIRE

Roland repeats this old catechism whenever he sets a campfire alight. In the 2003 version of *The Gunslinger,* he says it before lighting his devil grass fire. (VII:761)

Spark-a-dark, who's my sire?
Will I lay me?
Will I stay me?
Bless this camp with fire.

II: SONGS

Throughout the Dark Tower series, we learn about many of Mid-World's popular songs. Some of them are versions of songs found in our world (reinforcing the belief that Mid-World is one of our Earth's many possible futures). However, quite a few have never been heard in our world. Below are listed those songs which appear in the Dark Tower series.

1. ADELINA SAYS SHE'S RANDY-O

We never learn the words to this Mid-World drinking song. (VII:520)

2. A HUNDRED LEAGUES TO BANBERRY CROSS

Roland considers this to be one of Mid-World's old songs. We never learn the words. (I:120)

3. BUY ME ANOTHER ROUND YOU BOOGER YOU

Pere Callahan sings this song on the night of the Calla's welcoming fiesta, put on in honor of Roland and his *ka-tet*. We never learn the words. (V:228)

4. CARELESS LOVE

"Careless Love" has special significance, since we associate the song with Roland's first and only true love, Susan Delgado. Although "Careless Love" is mentioned in the final three books of the Dark Tower series, the extract we have comes from *Wizard and Glass*. (I:86, IV:121)

> Love, O love, O careless love,
> Can't you see what careless love has done?

5. CAPTAIN MILLS, YOU BASTARD

We never learn the words to this song. All we know is that Deputy Dave Hollis of Hambry played it very badly. (IV:508)

6. COME ON OVER BABY

Pettie the Trotter, who was an aging whore at Hambry's Travellers' Rest, bawled this song out when she was drunk. The lyrics are from "Whole lotta shakin' going on." (IV:213–14)

> Come on over baby, we got chicken in the barn
> What barn, whose barn, my barn!
> Come on over, baby, baby
> Got the bull by the horns . . .

7. THE COMMALA SONG

The Commala Song is probably one of the most important songs found in Mid-World. It is sung in the Calla, but it was also sung in In-World during Roland's youth. The Commala Song, and its many variants, can be found in Appendix IX.

8. EASE ON DOWN THE ROAD

This is another one of Mid-World's old songs. We never learn the words to it, though the title is shared by a song from our world taken from the musical *The Wiz*. (I:120)

9. GOLDEN SLIPPERS

Back when he lived in Mejis, Sheemie Ruiz liked to sing this song. We are never given the words. (IV:244)

10. THE GREEN CORN A-DAYO

We never hear this song, though we do learn that Andy likes to sing all twenty or thirty verses of it. It may be yet another version of the Commala Song. (V:5)

11. HEY JUDE

"Hey Jude" exists in our world too. The major difference between the Mid-World version and the Beatles' version is that Mid-World's begins "Hey Jude, I see you, lad." (I:22–23, I:26, V:39)

12. I AM A MAN OF THE BRIGHT BLUE SEA

Mejis's fishermen sing this song. (IV:445–46)

> I am a man of the bright blue sea,
> All I see, all I see,

I am a man of the Barony,
All I see is mine-o!
I am a man of the bright blue bay,
All I say, all I say,
Until my nets are full I stay
All I say is fine-o!

13. IN TIME OF LOSS, MAKE GOD YOUR BOSS
Andy the Messenger Robot (Many Other Terrible Functions) learned this song from the Manni. We never get to hear him sing it. (V:6)

14. THE JIMMY JUICE I DRANK LAST NIGHT
This is an amusing song sung in the Calla. (We never hear it.) Since Andy the Messenger Robot offers to sing it to Eddie not long after Eddie almost wipes his bottom with poison flurry, I can't help but wonder whether Jimmy juice is a bit like prune juice. (V:141)

15. MAID OF CONSTANT SORROW
This song comes from our world; Susannah Dean sings it at the Calla fiesta. It goes down well. (V:228)

16. ONWARD, CHRISTIAN SOLDIERS
The drunken customers at Sheb's bar in Tull liked to sing a version of this song. (I:34)

17. PLAY LADIES, PLAY
We never learn the words to this song, though we know the customers of Hattigan's in the run-down town of Ritzy like to sing it. (IV:268)

18. SHALL WE GATHER AT THE RIVER
The crazed parishioners of Sylvia Pittston's church in Tull sing this hymn. (I:48)

Shall we gather at the river,
The beautiful, beautiful,
The river;
Shall we gather at the river,
That flows by the Kingdom of God.

19. STREETS OF COMPARA
A pair of nine-year-old twins sings this song at the Calla fiesta. Since the Calla *folken* believe that the better part of one of the girl's brains is destined to be made into Breaker food, it's not surprising that the song makes them cry. We never learn the words. (V:227)

20. WE ALL SHINE ON
This is the refrain of John Lennon's song, "Instant Karma." Stephen King quotes it in the 1982 edition of *The Gunslinger*." (I:191)

21. WOMAN I LOVE
The customers at Hattigan's in Ritzy sing this song. We only learn the following lyr-ics: "Woman I love . . . is long and tall . . . She moves her body . . . like a cannonball." In our world, these lyrics come from the song "Come on in my kitchen." (IV:268)

III. BOOKS

1. *THE THROCKEN AND THE DRAGON*
Roland's mother read him this book when he was a small boy. The line he remembers best of all is "Hile Sir Throcken." It was in the pages of this book that Roland first discovered the term *throcken,* which was the ancient word for a billy-bumbler. W:7

2. *MAGIC TALES OF THE ELD* ("The Wind Through the Keyhole")
When Roland was a child and his mother read him to sleep in his tower bed-room, his favorite book was *Magic Tales of the Eld.* The book contained a dozen hand-colored woodcut illustrations, but Roland's favorite was of six bumblers, their snouts raised, sitting on a fallen tree in the forest beneath a crescent moon. This illustration belonged to the story "The Wind Through the Keyhole," from which the Dark Tower novel, *The Wind Through the Keyhole* takes its name. The original story tells the early adventures of Tim Ross, a woodcutter's son, who identifies his father's murderer and then goes on a quest into the Endless Forest so that he can find the magician Maerlyn. (He wants the magician to restore his mother's sight.) Later in life, Tim became a gunslinger. According to some tales, he even made it to the Dark Tower. W:14

V: PRAYERS/RITUALS

1. DEATH PRAYER
Roland translates this prayer for us and recites it over Jake's grave. (VII:474)

Time flies, knells call, life passes, so hear my prayer.
Birth is nothing but death begun, so hear my prayer.
Death is speechless, so hear my speech.
This is Jake, who served his ka and his tet. Say true.
May the forgiving glance of S'mana heal his heart. Say please.
May the arms of Gan raise him from the darkness of the earth. Say please.
Surround him, Gan, with light.
Fill him, Chloe, with strength.
If he is thirsty, give him water in the clearing.
If he is hungry, give him food in the clearing.
May his life on this earth and the pain of his passing become
as a dream to his waking soul, and let his eyes fall upon
every lovely sight; let him find the friends that were lost to him,
and let every one whose name he calls call his in return.

This is Jake, who lived well, loved his own, and died as ka would have it. Each man owes a death. This is Jake. Give him peace.

2. GUNSLINGER LITANY
Every gunslinger must learn to recite the following litany. (V:155–56)

I do not aim with my hand; he who aims with his hand has forgotten the face of his father. I aim with my eye. I do not shoot with my hand; he who shoots with his hand has forgotten the face of his father. I shoot with my mind. I do not kill with my gun; he who kills with his gun has forgotten the face of his father. I kill with my heart.

3. MANNI PRAYER (I)
This is the praise-prayer Henchick gives when the Unfound Door opens. We are not given a translation. (VI:42)

Over-sam kammen!
Can-tah, can-kavar kammen!
Over-can-tah!

4. MANNI PRAYER (II)
The Manni repeat this short prayer after Henchick prays to the Over in front of the Unfound Door. Henchick's prayer to the Over is for safe passage and success of endeavor with no loss of life or sanity. He also begs the Over to enliven their mags and bobs, and for *kaven,* or the persistence of magic. We are not given Henchick's words, nor are we given a translation of the short prayer, listed below. (VI:26)

Over-sam,
Over-kra,
Over-can-tah.

5. PRAYER AFTER A SUCCESSFUL HUNT
Roland recites this prayer after he and Susannah successfully hunt down deer. The prayer is addressed to the head of a dead deer. (VII:636–37)

We thank you for what we are about to receive.
(Father, we thank thee.)
Guide our hands and guide our hearts as we take life from death.

6. A SHORT PRAYER SAID OVER THE BODIES OF THE DEAD
"Give you peace," or "I give you the peace of the clearing." This prayer is accompanied by a benedictory gesture—pronging two fingers of the right hand and drawing them downward in front of the dead person's face. VII:51

7. A SHORT PRAYER FOR THE ROSE
This short prayer is written on a plaque by the garden of the Rose, located in the lobby of the Tet Corporation's headquarters:

Cam-a-cam-mal
Pria-Toi,
Gan Delah

The translation is "White over Red, Thus God Wills Ever," or "Good over evil, this is the will of God." VII:504

8. WHEN YOU MUST BID SOMEONE A FINAL FAREWELL

"May we meet in the clearing at the end of the path when all worlds end."
VII:801

9. RITUAL TO PREPARE THE DEAD TO ENTER THE CLEARING (NORTH'RD BARONY)

This ritual comes from the village of Tree, located in North'rd Barony. Although most of the folk in Tree preferred to see to their own dead (interring them on their own land with a wooden cross, if they followed the Man Jesus, or a slab of roughly carved stone), the town still had a burying parlor.

The newly dead person was washed and anointed with oils. A piece of birch bark inscribed with the names of the dead man's family was placed in his right hand. A blue spot was put on his forehead and he was wrapped in a fine linen shroud. Finally, he would be placed in a coffin of ironwood, which would keep his mortal remains very well for a thousand years or more. The body was placed in a little room with forest scenes painted on the walls. The ironwood bier in the center—that open space that represented the clearing at the end of life's path—was where the coffin was placed. (This was where a person's *ka* traveled after death.) In Tree, it was customary to wear white for the dead.
W:176–77, W:179

10. RITUAL FOR THE DEATH OF A WELL-BORN PERSON IN GILEAD

After the death of Roland's mother, Gabrielle Deschain, every man in Gilead wore a black collar of mourning or a black band around his shirtsleeve. Women wore black nets on their hair. This went on until Gabrielle had been six months in her tomb. W:35

11. RITUAL FOR A PERSON WHO HAS COMMITTED SUICIDE

When someone of high blood committed suicide in Gilead, the publishment of her death declared that she had died while possessed of a demon which troubled her spirit. W:37

V: PROPHECIES

1. PROPHECY ABOUT THE CRIMSON KING

When Roland was a boy, he heard a bit of doggerel which predicted the death of the Crimson King. According to this prophecy, the Red King would kill himself with a spoon. The second part of the prophecy stated that Los the Red could be killed by Roland's guns, since their barrels were made from Arthur Eld's great sword, Excalibur. However, by swallowing the sharpened spoon, the Crimson

King made himself Undead, and so safe from even Roland's guns. It's a shame we never get to hear the actual prophecy. (VII:607–8)

2. PROPHECY FOR THE LINE OF ELD

Mordred Deschain's birth fulfills an ancient prophecy which foretells the destruction of the last gunslinger—Roland Deschain. As we know from the Dark Tower series, Roland was tricked into concciving a child with his *ka-tet* mate Susannah Dean. Roland's sperm was taken by a Demon Elemental (posing as the Oracle of the Mountains), which then turned itself into a male and impregnated Susannah in the Speaking Ring where she, Roland, and Eddie drew Jake Chambers into Mid-World. Although Roland is not actually Susannah's father, he is her *dinh*, or leader, and so is the father of their *ka-tet*. (VI:252). The prophecy reads as follows:

> He who ends the line of Eld shall conceive a child of incest with his sister or his daughter, and the child will be marked, by his red heel shall you know him. It is he who shall stop the breath of the last warrior.

APPENDIX IV
MID-WORLD MISCELLANY

MID-WORLD DANCES

**Commala (Sowing Night Cotillion or Sowing Night Cotil'): This was the name of Gilead's Spring Dance. The geometric steps of this dance were meant to mimic a courting ritual. We learn about it in the 2003 version of *The Gunslinger.*

Pol-kam: This dance was popular in Gilead. It was lighter and faster than a waltz. I:137

Quesa: A simple sort of reel danced in Hambry. IV:209

Waltz: Waltzing was popular in Gilead. I:137

MID-WORLD DISEASES

Blood-sickness: This one sounds a bit like blood-poisoning, but it could also be another blood-related illness. III:248

Mandrus: A venereal disease found in Lud. It's also called Whore's Blossoms. III:297

Mutation: Mid-World's many mutations were caused by the Great Poisoning. *See* MUTANTS, *in* CHARACTERS. *See also* MID-WORLD ARGOT: THE GREAT POISONING, *in* APPENDIX I.

Rabies: We have this one in our world too. III:296

Rot: This disease affects the Border Dwellers of the Mohaine Desert. It is a lot like leprosy. I:15, I:18

Superflu: This one actually affects the alternative Topeka, not Mid-World. It is also known as Captain Trips and Tube-Neck. IV:73

Wasting Disease: IV:307

MID-WORLD DRUGS

Alder-bark: Helps bad breath. II:363

Graf: Strong apple beer.

Mescaline: A hallucinogen that helps gunslingers see and communicate with demons. I:125, I:127

Pettibone: An alcoholic drink. IV:251

Sugar: Good for energy bursts. II:103–4

MID-WORLD GAMES

Castles: A game very much like Chess. IV:191

**Croquet and Points: These games were popular among Gilead's ladies. In the 2003 version of *The Gunslinger,* we find out that Points is played with ninepins. It sounds a bit like bowling. I:88, I:96

Faro: This is probably a betting card game, since Sylvia Pittston makes her followers repent playing it. I:50

**Gran-Points: In this game you hold a bat and wait for a rawhide bird to be pitched. It sounds a bit like baseball.

Jacks Pop Up: A card game for children. W:105

**Mother Says: This children's game is similar to Simon Says.

Watch Me: This is one of Mid-World's card games. People tend to bet, and the games can get rather dangerous. I:26–27

MID-WORLD HOLIDAYS AND CARNIVALS

All-Saints Eve: I:32

Baron's Year-End parties: III:50

Dance of Easterling: This great party marked the end of the Wide Earth and the advent of Sowing. IV:194

Easter Night: In the 2003 version of *The Gunslinger,* the Easter Night Dance is replaced by the **Sowing Night Cotillion. I:150, I:156

Fair-Day Riddling: Riddling was an extremely important game in Mid-World-that-was. Riddling was believed to hold incredible power. A good Fair-Day Riddling contest would ensure that the crops grew well. III:281

Fair-Days: Here is a list of Mid-World's seasonal Fair-Days. III:416
  Winter
  Wide Earth
  Sowing (New Earth or Fresh Commala)
  Mid-Summer
  Full Earth
  Reaping
  Year's End

**Feast of Joseph fairtime: In the 2003 version of *The Gunslinger,* this holiday is renamed the Feast of Reaptide Fair. I:186

Glowing Day: Cuthbert liked this holiday because of the fireworks and the ice. IV:185

MID-WORLD MUSICAL INSTRUMENTS

Fiddles: I:145

Guitars: IV:194

Way-Gog Music: This instrument, which is a bit like a bagpipe, isn't actually from Mid-World. It is played on the upper levels of the Tower. III:409

MID-WORLD RELIGIONS

In *The Little Sisters of Eluria,* we're told that in Mid-World, faith—like everything else—had moved on. As far as Roland was concerned, the God o' the Cross was just another religion which taught that love and murder were inextricably bound together. In the end, all gods drank blood. E:147

> For a list of Mid-World gods, see GODS OF MID-WORLD and GUARDIANS OF THE BEAM, both listed in the CHARACTERS section. Also see MID-WORLD FOLKLORE.

Christian (general): In Mid-World, Christians are called "followers of the Jesus-man" or of the God o' the Cross. E:147

  Methodism: I:34

Guardian Totems: IV:222

Pagan Religions: *See* GODS OF MID-WORLD *in* CHARACTERS

MID-WORLD SIGULS

Christian Medallions: A Christian medallion saves Roland from the Little Sisters of Eluria. E:182

Coffins and Blue Coffin Tattoos: These tattoos adorn the hands of the Big Coffin Hunters. Tick-Tock of the Grays wears a coffin-shaped clock around his neck. In *Wolves of the Calla,* we find out that the low men also bear coffin–shaped tattoos. IV:155

The Dark Bells: The Dark Bells are the *sigul* of the Little Sisters of Eluria. E:184

The Eye: This is the *sigul* of John Farson, but it is also the *sigul* of the Crimson King. IV:91

Fist and Thunderbolt: This is a lot like Mid-World's version of the swastika. III:275

Jesus-Man *Sigul:* A crucifix. E:153

Rose: The Little Sisters of Eluria wear an embroidered rose on their habits. It is the *sigul* of the Dark Tower. E:165

APPENDIX V
THE TOWER, THE QUEST,
AND *THE EYES OF THE DRAGON*

A question recently arose on the Stephen King Web-site message board concerning the relationship between the Dark Tower books and *The Eyes of the Dragon*. The Constant Reader who posted the query wanted others to share their thoughts about where *The Eyes of the Dragon* should be placed on the Dark Tower timeline. Does *Eyes* take place before or after the rule of Roland's illustrious ancestor Arthur Eld? Is our Roland a descendant of King Roland? And, by extension, is the house of Delain related to the house of Deschain? Having just completed a Dark Tower timeline (it should be posted on-site soon), I found this question really interesting, so I thought I'd throw in my own two cents' worth of commentary.

My first job was to reread *Eyes*. I too had always assumed that *The Eyes of the Dragon* took place in Roland's world, albeit in the distant past. However, once I took a good long look at my timeline, at Volume I of my *Concordance*, and at the many, many notes and maps spread about my workroom, I realized that I had a very big problem. Namely, *The Eyes of the Dragon* doesn't fit into the history of Roland's world. Before you reach for your six-gun to shoot me, hear me out. Then decide what you think. As you read, keep in mind that familiar phrase, the essence of which I will return to at the end of my entry: *There are other worlds than these.* As Jake Chambers so eloquently stated before his free fall into the abyss below the Cyclopean Mountains, no world stands alone. A universe consists of many worlds, and the Dark Tower contains all of them. Some levels of the Dark Tower may be unique, some may be dangerous or downright deadly, but the majority of them seem like slightly distorted echoes of each other.

As we've seen over and over in the Dark Tower series, the multiverse is almost like a rabbit warren, with many secret entrances and byways leading from one "Earth" or "Mid-World" to another. As the Manni know so well, unwary travelers must beware. If you dare to click the heels of your ruby slippers together (or in the case of the Manni, set your plumb bob swinging), there is no guarantee that you will be able to return to the world that you left. There may only be one Keystone Earth, but there are many variants of that Earth. Eddie Dean may think that he comes from the same New York City as Calvin Tower, but in Eddie's world, Co-Op City is in Brooklyn. In Calvin's, it's in the Bronx.

As Callahan discovered during his five years traveling along the highways in hiding, and as our *ka-tet* found out in the alternative Kansas, the worlds-next-door may look the same as ours, but upon close scrutiny they prove to be subtly, but significantly, different. Though their landscapes are almost identical, and though they seem to share our history and culture, at some point in time those worlds, and ours, diverged. In *Wolves of the Calla*, Pere Callahan recounts his travels through the multiple Americas, which he calls the vertical geographies of chance (V:298). In Callahan's version of Earth, as in ours, Fort Lee sits on the far side of the George Washington Bridge, yet during his travels through the alternative Americas, he leaves New York City via the G.W. only to find himself in a town called Leabrook, where the face of someone named Chadborne decorates the ten-dollar bill and a politician named Earnest "Fritz" Hollings is elected president (V:300, V:305). Similarly, Susannah, Eddie, and Jake disembark from Blaine the Insane Mono into what they think is our world's Kansas, only to find that the Takuro Spirit–driving and Nozz-A-La-cola-drinking inhabitants have all been killed off by a disease called superflu.

Certainly, what holds true for our world also holds true for Roland's. We live on Keystone Earth, the template for all of the alternative Earths, but Roland comes from Tower Keystone, the template for all of the multiple Mid-Worlds. If there are many worlds similar to ours spinning about the central needle of the Dark Tower, then surely there are alternative versions of Roland's world to be found there as well. However, even by stating this obvious fact, I leave out a very important point. Related worlds can have differences that are as arresting as their similarities. After all, as Eddie Dean states in *The Dark Tower*, Roland's world and our world are also twins. Despite their divergent histories and apparent differences, they are protected by the same divine forces and are attacked by the same enemies.

As we all know, there *are* many striking similarities between the world depicted in *The Eyes of the Dragon* and the one we travel in during the Dark Tower series. In both tales, *Roland* is a royal name. The halls of the rich and powerful are adorned with Kashamin rugs, and the weapons of kings are made of sandalwood. In Delain, as in Gilead, Old Star shines in the night sky. People wonder about the semimythical Grand Featherex, and magicians (both good and evil) have the power to make themselves *dim*. Those born to aristocratic families are said to be of High Blood, and records are written, and read, using the Great Letters. Gunpowder is rare, and extremely valuable.

In both Delain and Gilead, the distant (and somewhat sinister) land of Garlan is well known for its poisons. Both the Dragon Sand used to kill King Roland of Delain and the poisoned knife meant to murder Steven Deschain of Gilead originated in Garlan. John Norman, whom we met in the Dark Tower novella "The Little Sisters of Eluria," was born in Delain (a land also known as Dragon's Lair and Liar's Heaven), which also seems to imply that *The Eyes of the Dragon* and the Dark Tower series both take place on the same level of the Tower.

But even the similarities between *The Eyes of the Dragon* and the Dark Tower series raise their own problems. For example, both Delain and Gilead are referred to as In-World baronies, yet how can this be so if Roland Deschain seems unaware of the places so frequently mentioned in *The Eyes of the Dragon*—the Sea of Tomorrow, the Far Forests, the Northern, Eastern, Western, and Southern Baronies? Wouldn't they have appeared on the map Roland saw as a boy, the one which depicted the Greater Kingdoms of the Western Earth? And why is the Delain that we learn about in "The Little Sisters of Eluria" closer to Eluria—an Out-World town—than to Gilead? And if the worlds of *The Eyes of the Dragon* and the Dark Tower series are the same, why are their gods so dissimilar? The people of King Roland's Delain worship at the Church of the Great Gods; the Man Jesus, and his Father, seem unknown. Yet the medallion worn by James Norman (of Mid-World's Delain) specifically mentions the One God, and it is this *sigul* which saves our gunslinger, Roland, from the bloodthirst of the Little Sisters.

And the questions continue. If the great city of Delain is part of In-World, why is it unaffected by the Great Old Ones' mutations and horrible munitions? And why are the Beams, the Guardians, and the Dark Tower never mentioned? The only hint given to us, suggesting that the people of *The Eyes of the Dragon* know of the Tower, is the existence of the Needle, a three-hundred-foot-tall stone prison located in the center of Delain's Plaza. And if all this can be explained away by temporal distance, by "long, long ago," how then did Dennis and Thomas, two of the main characters from *The Eyes of the Dragon,* make their way to Gilead during Roland Deschain's youth, and just after that great city's fall? How, except through some kind of magic door—the kind of magic door favored by their quarry, the magician Randall Flagg?

To any Constant Reader, Randall Flagg is a familiar, if slippery, figure. His name changes, as does his face, but his purpose always remains the same. Whether he calls himself Walter, Marten, or one of the many variations of "R.F.," his Chaotic Calling remains unchanged. He must search out lands where the White flourishes and bring them to ruin. His attempt to reduce Delain to anarchy failed, but in Roland's world, he triumphed. Somehow, he leapt from the In-World of *The Eyes of the Dragon* to the In-World of Roland's youth, dragging his shadow of darkness and anarchy with him. Dennis and Thomas, two Warriors of the White who helped to halt Flagg's machinations in Delain, were unable to stop him in Gilead. Perhaps they failed because it was not their world, or perhaps because their Flagg was as different from Mid-World's enemy as Jake '77 was from Mid-World Jake, though the two boys crossed paths (or one boy crossed his own path) on Second Avenue, New York, at the beginning of *Wolves of the Calla.*

Like the Crimson King, who in the novel *Insomnia* tried to destroy the town of Derry, Maine (twinner of our world's Bangor, Maine), Flagg travels through the multiverse, leaping from Earth to Earth and from Mid-World to Mid-World, spreading chaos and disaster like a plague or a poison. Yet each world he tries to destroy gives birth to its own heroes, its own Warriors of the White. And whether these warriors fight with sandalwood-handled six-shooters or arrows with sandalwood bolts, their purpose is the same—to champion that ancient, resilient, yet humble force that has redeemed humankind again and again and again. It is the force that begets life and that makes the Beams, and the Tower, stand true.

APPENDIX VI
POLITICAL AND CULTURAL FIGURES
OF OUR WORLD MENTIONED
IN THE DARK TOWER SERIES

ACTORS, DIRECTORS, AND STAGE PERSONALITIES: Abbott and Costello, Woody Allen, Fred Astaire, Jack Benny, Harry Blackstone, Humphrey Bogart, Walter Brennan, Yul Brynner, Horst Buchholz, James Cagney, George Carlin, George Clooney, Gary Cooper, David Copperfield, Tom Cruise, Robert Culp, Olivia de Havilland, James Dean, Cecil B. DeMille, Clint Eastwood, Emilio Estevez, Frederico Fellini, Henry Fonda, Clark Gable, Judy Garland, James Garner, John Gielgud, Whoopi Goldberg, Robert Goulet, Ty Hardin, Rondo Hatton, Dave Henning, Alfred Hitchcock, Harry Houdini, Rock Hudson, Nicole Kidman, Akira Kurosawa, Charles Laughton, Robin Leach, Sergio Leone, Jerry Lewis, Rich Little, Rob Lowe, George Lucas, Dean Martin, Harpo Marx, Butterfly McQueen, Marilyn Monroe, Paul Newman, Sidney Poitier, Claude Rains, Robert Redford, Jerry Reed, Burt Reynolds, Cesar Romero, George Romero, Winona Ryder, Mort Sahl, Adam Sandler, Peter Sellers, Jean Stapleton, Rod Steiger, Jimmy Stewart, John Sturges, Spencer Tracy, John Travolta, Lee Van Cleef, Van Heflin, Clint Walker, John Wayne, Jack Webb, Raquel Welch

FILMS AND PLAYS: *Armageddon; Blood Work; Child's Play; The Craft; The Dark Crystal; Death Valley Days; Dr. Jekyll and Mr. Hyde; Dopes at Sea; The Exorcist; Fail-Safe; Forbidden Planet; Girl, Interrupted; Gone With the Wind; Halloween; In the Heat of the Night; The Invisible Man; The Last Starfighter; The Lost Continent; The Magnificent Seven; Mandingo; Midnight Cowboy; Night of the Living Dead; Old Yeller; One Flew Over the Cuckoo's Nest; The Other Side of Midnight; Our American Cousin; Phantasm; Psycho; The Purple Rose of Cairo; Rambo; Rebel Without a Cause; Return to the O.K. Corral; Robocop; The Seven Samurai; The Shining; Smokey and the Bandit; The Snake Pit;* spaghetti Westerns; *Stalag 17; Star Wars; The Ten Commandments; The Terminator; Three Faces of Eve; Top Hat; War of the Zombies; White Heat; Yankee Doodle Dandy;* **Zorro

BIBLICAL FIGURES AND RELIGIOUS FIGURES FROM AROUND THE WORLD: Abednego, Adam and Eve, Buddha, Cain, Daniel, David and Bathsheba, David and Goliath, Devil (Interloper), Druids, Eve and the Serpent, Good Samaritan, Isaac, Jacob, Jeremiah, Jesus, Jesus on the Mount, Jezebel and

King Ahaz, Joseph, Lazarus, Mary, Mesach, Moses, Muhammad, Noah, Saint Matthew, Saint Paul, Saint Peter, Pontius Pilate, the Pope, Samson and Delilah, Shadrach, Star Wormwood

CULTURAL AND HISTORICAL FIGURES: Alfred Adler, Attila the Hun, Black Panthers, Bonnie and Clyde, Daniel Boone, John Wilkes Booth, Buffalo Bill, Ted Bundy, Bull Connor, John Dillinger, Albert Einstein, The Elks, Eratosthenes, Sigmund Freud, Bill Gates, Donald Grant, Ulysses S. Grant, Howard Hughes, I.B.M., Incas, Reverend Jim Jones and the People's Temple, Jackie Kennedy, John Kennedy Jr., Elisabeth Kübler-Ross, The Luddites, "Dougout" Doug MacArthur, Manhattan Project, Christa McAuliffe, Microsoft, Mother Teresa, Lee Harvey Oswald, Wily Post, Punxsutawney Phil *(he's a groundhog but I thought I would include him anyway),* Jack Ruby, Queen Elizabeth II, Anna Sage, Albert Schweitzer, Alan Shepard, The Shriners, Socrates, Jimmy Swaggart, Donald Trump

>   **CIVIL RIGHTS ACTIVISTS:** James Chaney, Medgar Evers, Freedom Riders, Andrew Goodman, Coretta Scott King, Martin Luther King, NAACP, Rosa Parks, Michael Schwerner

MAGAZINES AND NEWSPAPERS: *Fantasy and Science Fiction, Lewiston Sun, Look,* Marvel Comics, *New York Post, New York Sun, New York Times, Newsweek, Playboy, Portland* (Maine) *Press Herald, Publishers Weekly*

MUSICIANS AND BANDS: Allman Brothers, Andrews Sisters, Anthrax, Joan Baez, The Beatles, Big Bopper (Jay Perry Richardson), Hoagy Carmichael, Johnny Cash, Perry Como, Creedence Clearwater Revival, Reverend Gary Davis, Irene Day, Del-Vikings, Bob Dylan, Duke Ellington, The Four Seasons, Marvin Gaye, Andy Gibb, Merle Haggard, George Harrison, Billie Holiday, Buddy Holly, Michael Jackson, Wanda Jackson, The Jackson Five, Mungo Jerry, Elton John, Kiss, Led Zeppelin, John Lennon, Little Richard, Lovin' Spoonful, Madonna, The McCoys, Megadeth, Wayne Newton, Olivia Newton-John, Phil Ochs, Tony Orlando and Dawn, Ozzy Ozbourne, Elvis Presley, Joey Ramone, Lou Reed, Martha Reeves and the Vandellas, The Rivieras, Rolling Stones, David Lee Roth, Sex Pistols, Troy Shondell, Ralph Stanley, Steely Dan, Dodi Stevens, Barbra Streisand, Donna Summer, The Tokens, Jethro Tull, Richie Valens, Dave Van Ronk, Charlie Watts, Stevie Wonder, ZZ Top

>   **SONGS:** "Amazing Grace," "Blowin' in the Wind," "Born to Run," "Bridge over Troubled Water," "Buffalo Gals," "Buy Me Another Round You Booger You," "California Sun," "Careless Love," "Clinch Mountain Breakdown," "Come Go with Me," "Crazy Train," "Darlin Katy," "Dr. Love," "Double Shot (of My Baby's Love)," "Drive My Car," "Gangsta Dream 19," "Hang On Sloopy," "A Hard Rain's a-Gonna Fall," "Heat Wave," "Hesitation Blues," "Hey Jude," "Hey Nineteen," "The Hippy Hippy Shake," "Honky Tonk Woman," "I Ain't Marchin' Anymore," "I Left My Heart in San Francisco," "I Shall Be Released," "In the Summertime," "John Henry," "Knock Three Times," "The Lion Sleeps Tonight," "Love to Love You, Baby," "Maid of Constant Sorrow,"

"Moonlight Becomes You," "Night and Day," "Nineteenth Nervous Breakdown," "Ninety-nine Bottles of Beer on the Wall," "Oxford Town," "Paint It Black," "Sharp Dressed Man," "She Loves You," "Silent Night," "Someone Saved My Life Tonight," "Stardust," "Stormy Weather," "Streets of Campara," "Sugar Shack," "That's Amore," "This Time," "Tube Snake Boogie," "Velcro Fly," "Visions of Johanna," "Walk on the Wild Side," "What Child Is This?"

NOVEL, CARTOON, FILM, TV, FOLKTALE, AND MYTHICAL CHARACTERS: Ali Baba, Alice (of Wonderland), Barbara Allen (folksong), Archie, King Arthur, Frodo Baggins, Bambi, Beowulf, Bobbsey Twins, James Bond, Charlie Brown and Lucy, Buckwheat, Edith Bunker, C3PO, Captain America, Carrie, Pa Cartwright (Adam, Hoss, and Little Joe), Casper the Friendly Ghost, Hopalong Cassidy, Misery Chastain, Cheshire Cat, Mr. Chips, Chucky, Claribel the Clown, George M. Cohan, Barnabas Collins, Creature from the Black Lagoon, Croesus, Cujo, Daisy Mae, Marshal Dillon, Donald Duck, Doctor Doom, Dorothy (of Oz) and Aunt Em, Dracula, Excalibur, Falstaff, The Fantastic Four, Faust, Ferdinand the Bull, Huck Finn (Miss Watson and Widow Douglas), Foghorn Leghorn, Frankenstein, Samwise Gamgee, Goldilocks and the Three Bears, Flash Gordon, Prince Hal, Hamlet, Hansel and Gretel, Mina Harker, Mars Henry, Sherlock Holmes, Howdy Doody, The Incredible Hulk, Humpty Dumpty, Icarus, Jack and the Beanstalk (and the Giant), Janus, John Henry (folksong), Jove, Jughead, Keebler Elves, Clark Kent, Keystone Kops, King Arthur, Lois Lane, Little Lord Fauntleroy, Little Nell, Little Red Riding Hood, Jacob Marley, Philip Marlowe, Silas Marner, Miss Marple, Harpo Marx, Perry Mason, Maturin, Ronald McDonald, Travis McGee, Merlin the Magician, Minotaur, Mordred, Mork, Morlocks, Mickey Mouse, Minnie Mouse, Mutt and Jeff, Mr. Mxyzptlk, Narcissus, Annie Oakley, Oedipus, Old Yeller, Olive Oyl, Peter Pan and Captain Hook, Popeye, Pied Piper, Hercule Poirot, Popeye, Porky Pig, Harry Potter, Sergeant Preston and his dog King, Professor Peabody, Puck, Rambo, Rastus "Coon," Regulators, Ratso Rizzo, Robbie the Robot, Santa Claus, Scheherazade, Ebenezer Scrooge, The Shadow, Shane, Shardik, Sheena Queen of the Jungle, Paul Sheldon, Luke Skywalker, Speedy Gonzales, Spider-Man, Greg Stillson, Superman, Sylvester the Cat, Thor, Tin Woodman, Tinker Bell, Tony the Tiger, Trampas, Toto, Tweedledee and Tweedledum, Tweety Bird, Ulysses, Darth Vader, Vulcans, Lucy Westenra, White Rabbit, Annie Wilkes, William Wilson, Wimpy, Witch Hazel, Wizard of Oz, Yogi Bear, Yorick

POLITICAL FIGURES (PAST AND PRESENT): George Bush (Sr.), Jimmy Carter, Fidel Castro, CIA, Bill Clinton, Diem brothers (Ngo Dinh Nhu, Ngo Dinh Diem), Papa Doc Duvalier, Herman Goering, Al Gore, Ulysses S. Grant, Alexander Hamilton, Adolf Hitler, Andrew Jackson, Lyndon Johnson, John F. Kennedy, Robert Kennedy, Ed Koch, Nikita Khrushchev, General MacArthur, Abraham Lincoln, Henry Cabot Lodge, Nazi Party, Lee Harvey Oswald, Richard Nixon, Ytzhak Rabin, Ronald Reagan, Nelson Rockefeller, Harry S. Truman, United Nations, George Washington.

RADIO, TELEVISION, AND SPORTS PERSONALITIES: Mel Allen (sports announcer), Muhammad Ali, Braves, George Brett, David Brinkley, Bill Buckner,

Roger Clemens, Howard Cosell, Walter Cronkite, Bill Cullen, Joe DiMaggio, Bobby Doerr, Dwight Evans, Alan Freed, Dave Garroway, Dwight Gooden, Lefty Grove, Howdy Doody, Chet Huntley, Michael Jordan, Sugar Ray Leonard, Frank Malzone, Frank McGee, Mets, Joe Namath, Don Pardo, Mel Parnell, Walter Payton, John Pesky, Red Sox, Jackie Robinson, Royals, Babe Ruth, Buffalo Bob Smith, Ed Sullivan, Texas Rangers, Ted Williams, Yankees, Carl Yastrzemski

TV PROGRAMS: *All in the Family, Bonanza, The Brady Bunch, Cheyenne, Concentration, Danger UXB, Dark Shadows, Dragnet, The Ed Sullivan Show, Flash Gordon, General Hospital, The Guiding Light, Hollywood Squares, Howdy Doody, The Huntley-Brinkley Report, Journey to the Center of the Earth, Kingdom Hospital, Little Rascals, Maverick, Miami Vice, Million Dollar Movie, Mork & Mindy, Peter Gun, The Price Is Right, The Rifleman, Rose Red, Roseanne, Sergeant Preston of the Yukon, Star Search, Star Trek, Sugarfoot, The Twilight Zone, Warner Brothers Cartoons, Yogi Bear*

WRITERS, POETS, PLAYWRIGHTS, AND ARTISTS: Ansel Adams, Richard Adams, Charles Addams, Poul Anderson, Clark Ashton-Smith, Isaac Asimov, W. H. Auden, L. Frank Baum, Thomas Hart Benton, Clay Blaisdell, William Blake, William Peter Blatty, Hieronymus Bosch, Ray Bradbury, Max Brand, Elizabeth Barrett Browning, Robert Browning, Edgar Rice Burroughs, Thomas Carlyle, Lewis Carroll, Miguel de Cervantes, Raymond Chandler, Agatha Christie, William Cowper, Lee Brown Coye, Stephen Crane, Rodney Crowell, Salvador Dali, Charles Dickens, Emily Dickinson, Gordon Dickson, Walt Disney, Allen Drury, T. S. Eliot, Harlan Ellison, Ralph Ellison, William Faulkner, F. Scott Fitzgerald, John Fowles, Robert Frost, Chester Gould, Donald M. Grant, Zane Grey, Alex Haley, Thomas Hardy, Nathaniel Hawthorne, Robert E. Howard, Shirley Hazzard, Robert Heinlein, Ernest Hemingway, William Hope Hodgson, Ray Hogan, Robert E. Howard, Aldous Huxley, John Irving, Shirley Jackson, James Joyce, Stephen King, Roy Krenkel, Murray Leinster, Elmore Leonard, C. S. Lewis, Jack London, H. P. Lovecraft, John D. MacDonald, Archibald MacLeish, Norman Mailer, Henri Matisse, Ed McBain, Mary McCarthy, Grace Metalious, Michelangelo, Patrick O'Brian, Frank O'Hara, George Orwell, Wayne D. Overholser, John D. MacDonald, Charles Palliser, Maxwell Perkins, Edgar Allan Poe, David Rabe, Rembrandt, Frederick Remington, Charles Schulz, William Shakespeare, Irwin Shaw, John Steinbeck, Rex Stout, Algernon Swinburne, Henry David Thoreau, James Thurber, J. R. R. Tolkien, Mark Twain, John Updike, Vincent van Gogh, H. G. Wells, Owen Wister, Thomas Wolfe, Virginia Woolf, Herman Wouk, W. B. Yeats

BOOKS, STORIES, POEMS, AND PAINTINGS: *Alice's Adventures in Wonderland; The Bachman Books;* Bible; *The Bridge of San Luis Rey; The Caine Mutiny; Canterbury Tales; Carrie; Catch-22;* "The Charge of the Light Brigade"; *A Christmas Carol; The Collector; Complete Poetical Works of Robert Browning; The Dead Zone; Desperation; The Door into Summer; Dracula;* "Epistle to Be Left in the Earth"; "Fall of the House of Usher"; *Fahrenheit 451;* "Fra Lippo Lippi"; *The Garden of Earthly Delights* (painting); *Gormenghast; Hearts in Atlantis; The Hobbit, How the Grinch Stole Christmas;*

Huckleberry Finn; Insomnia; Invisible Man; The Island of Dr. Moreau; It; "The Lady or the Tiger"; *The Lion, the Witch and the Wardrobe; Little Lord Fauntleroy; Look Homeward Angel; Lord of the Flies; The Lord of the Rings;* "The Lottery"; "The Love Song of J. Alfred Prufrock" (quoted by Blaine); *The Magus; Marjorie Morningstar;* "Masque of the Red Death"; *Mike Mulligan and His Steam Shovel; Misery; Moby-Dick; The Mystery of Edwin Drood; On Writing; Pet Sematary; Peter Pan; The Plague; Punch* (magazine); *The Quincunx; Roads to Everywhere; Roots; 'Salem's Lot;* "The Second Coming"; *Seven Steps to Positive Thinking; Shardik; The Shining; Sign of the Four; The Stand; A Study in Scarlet; Tess of the D'Urbervilles; A Thousand and One Nights; Tom Saywer; The Troubled Air;* "Tyger"; *Ulysses; The Virginian;* "The Waste Land"; *Watership Down; We Have Always Lived in the Castle; The Wizard of Oz;* "The Wreck of the Hesperus"; *Yankee Highways; You Can't Go Home Again*

APPENDIX VII
MAPS OF MID-WORLD, END-WORLD, AND OUR WORLD

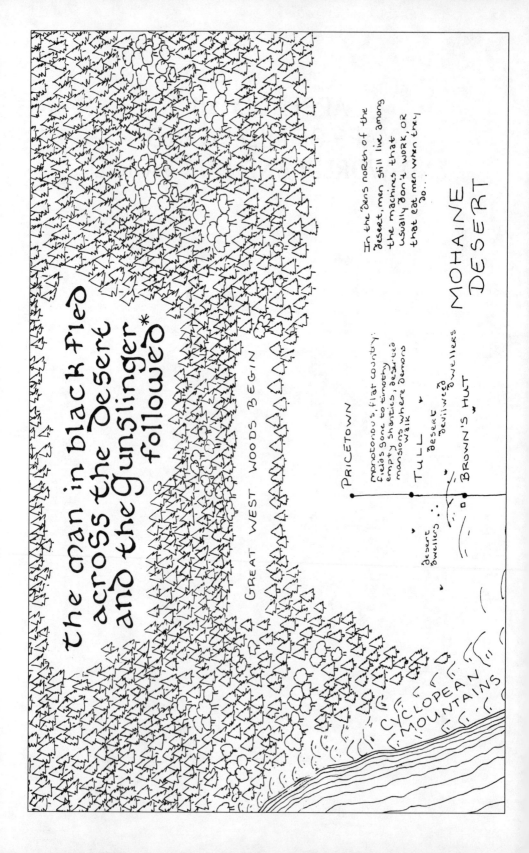

the man in black fled
across the Desert
and the gunslinger*
followed

GREAT WEST WOODS BEGIN

PRICETOWN

monotonous, flat country:
fields gone to timothy
empty shanties, deserted
mansions where Demons
walk

TULL

desert
Devilweed dwellers

BROWN'S HUT

desert
dwellers

In the dens north of the
desert, men still live among
the machines that
usually don't work, or
that eat men when they
do...

MOHAINE
DESERT

CYCLOPEAN
MOUNTAINS

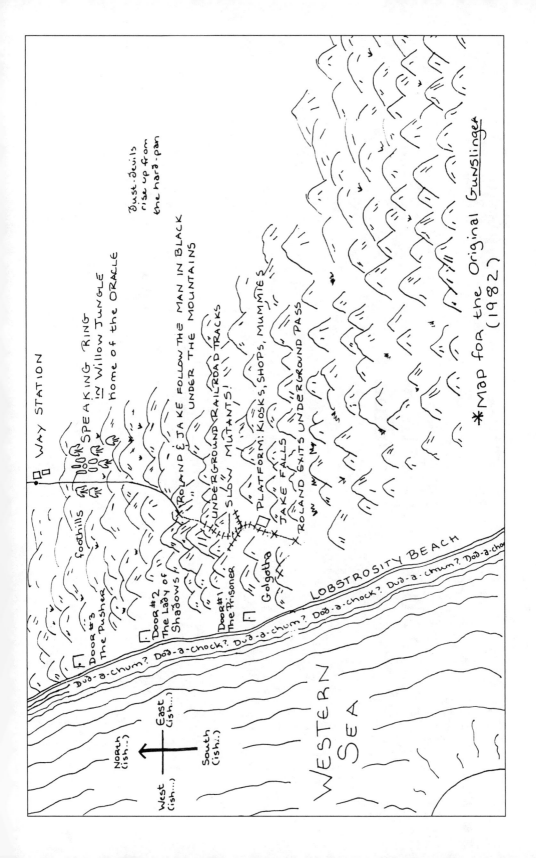

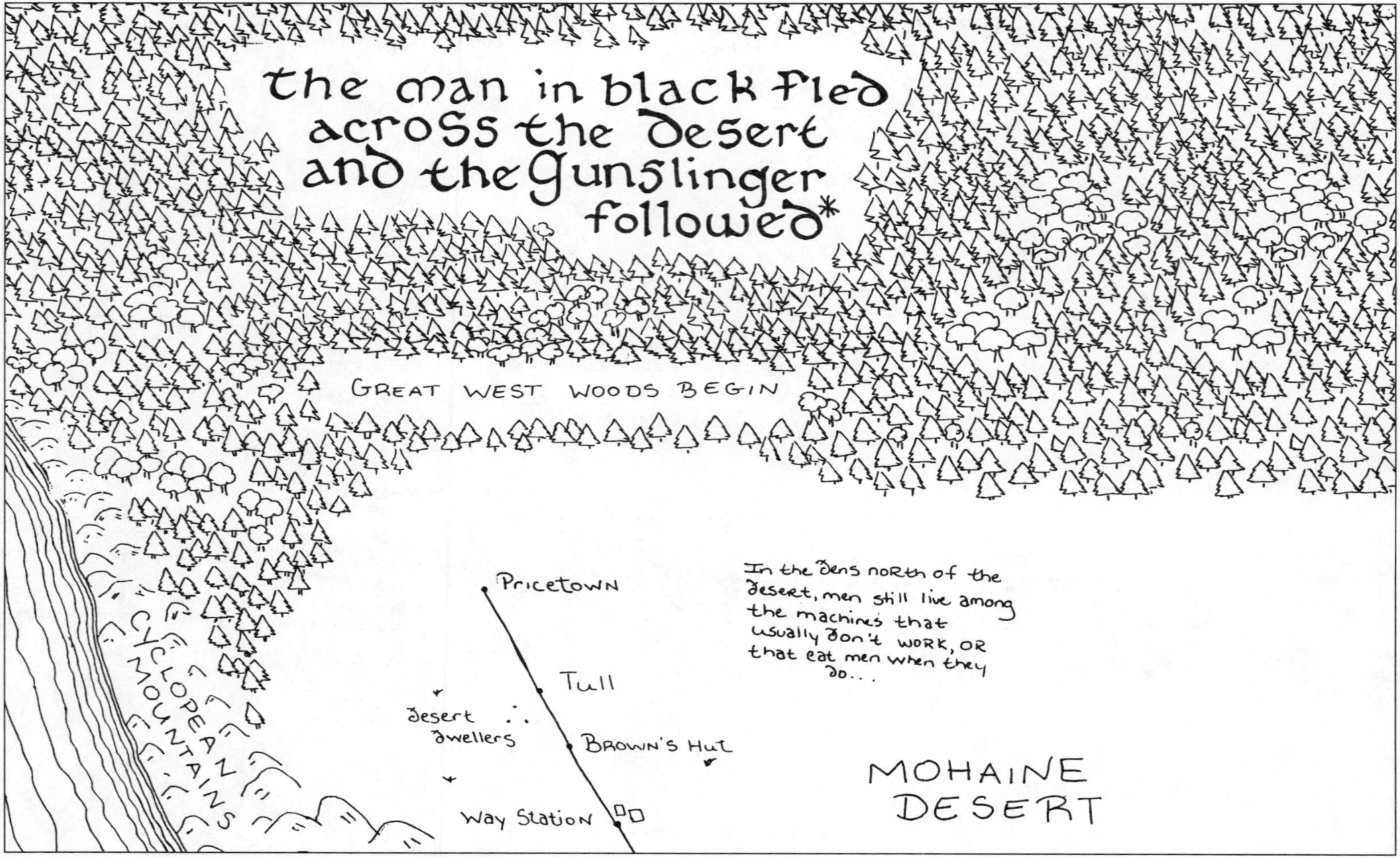

the man in black fled
across the desert
and the gunslinger
followed*

GREAT WEST WOODS BEGIN

In the Dens north of the
desert, men still live among
the machines that
usually don't work, or
that eat men when they
do....

MOHAINE
DESERT

Pricetown

Tull

Brown's Hut

desert
dwellers

Way Station

CYCLOPEAN
MOUNTAINS

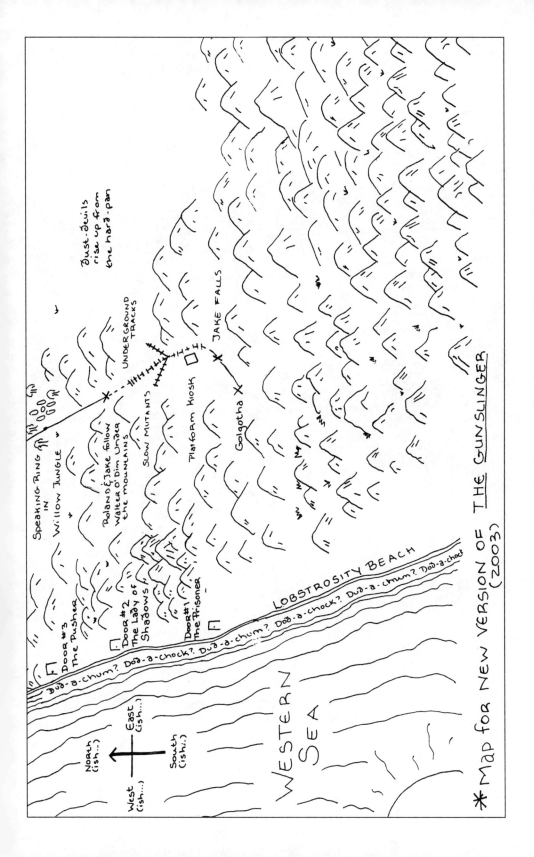

Speaking-Ring in Willow Jungle

Dust-devils rise up from the hard-pan

UNDERGROUND TRACKS

JAKE FALLS

Roland & Jake follow Walter o' Dim Under the mountains

SLOW MUTANTS

Platform Kiosk

Golgotha

Door #3 The Pusher

Door #2 The Lady of Shadows

Door #1 The Prisoner

LOBSTROSITY BEACH

Dud-a-chum? Dod-a-chock? Dud-a-chock? Dod-a-chum? Dud-a-chum? Dod-a-chock? Dud-a-chum? Dod-a-chock

North (ish...)
West (ish...)
East (ish...)
South (ish...)

WESTERN SEA

✱ MAP FOR NEW VERSION OF THE GUNSLINGER (2003)

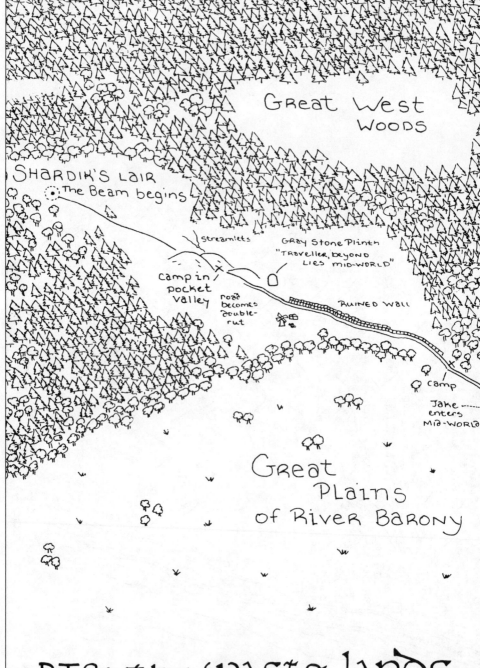

GREAT WEST
WOODS

SHARDIK'S LAIR
·The Beam begins

Streamlets

GRAY STONE PLINTH
"TROVELLER, BEYOND
LIES MID-WORLD"

camp in
pocket
valley

road
becomes
double-
rut

RUINED WALL

camp

Jake
enters
Mid-World

GREAT
PLAINS
of RIVER BARONY

DT3: the waste lands

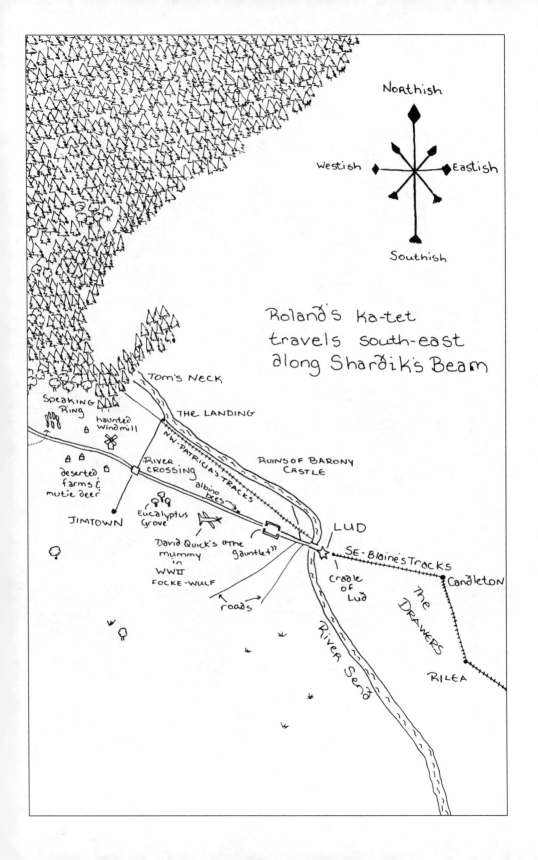

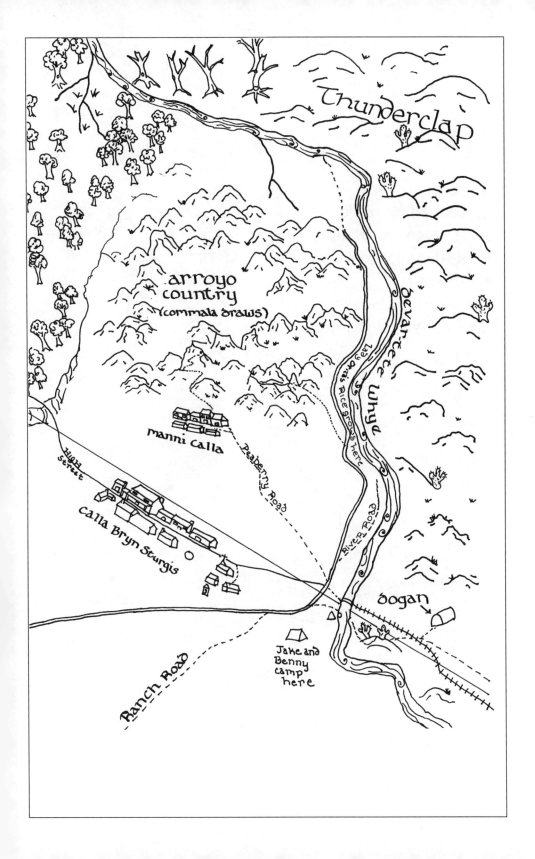

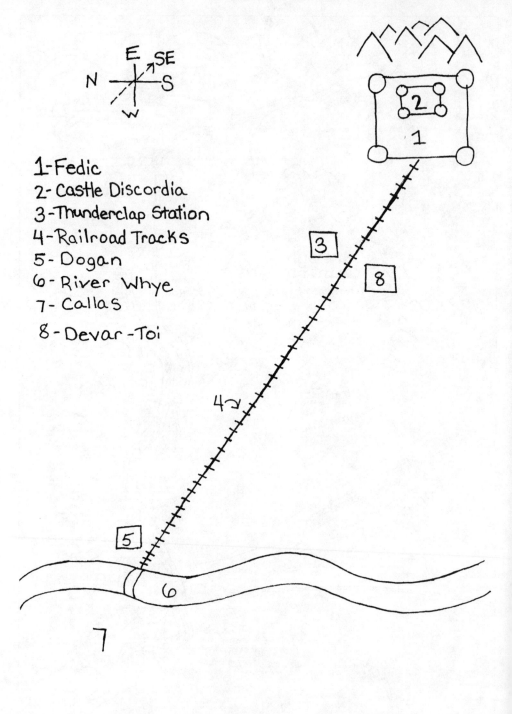

N — E — SE — S — W (compass)

1-Fedic
2- Castle Discordia
3-Thunderclap Station
4-Railroad Tracks
5- Dogan
6- River Whye
7- Callas
8- Devar-Toi

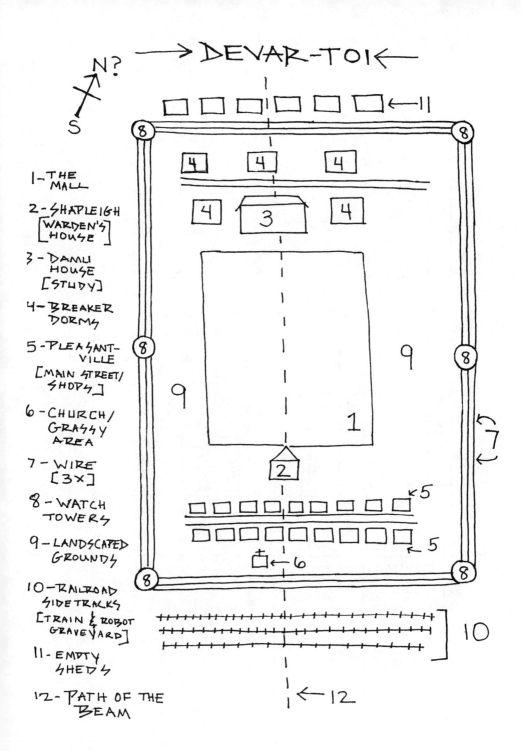

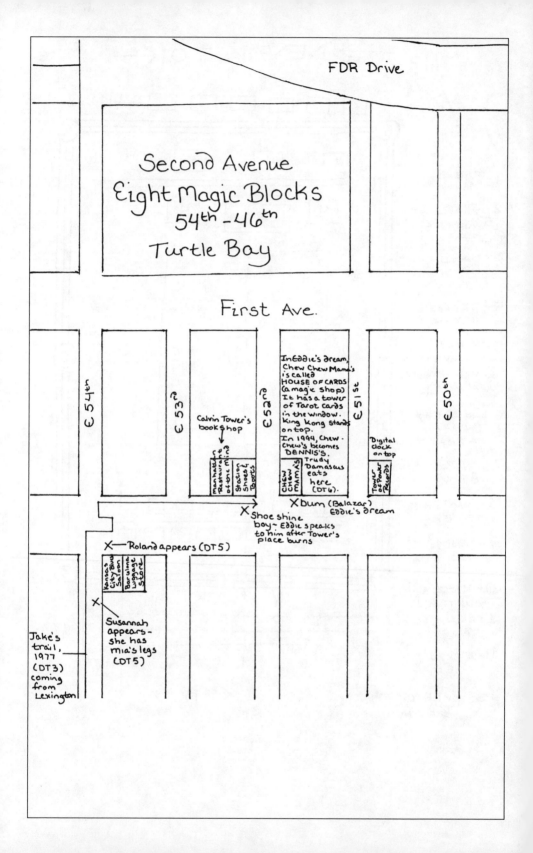

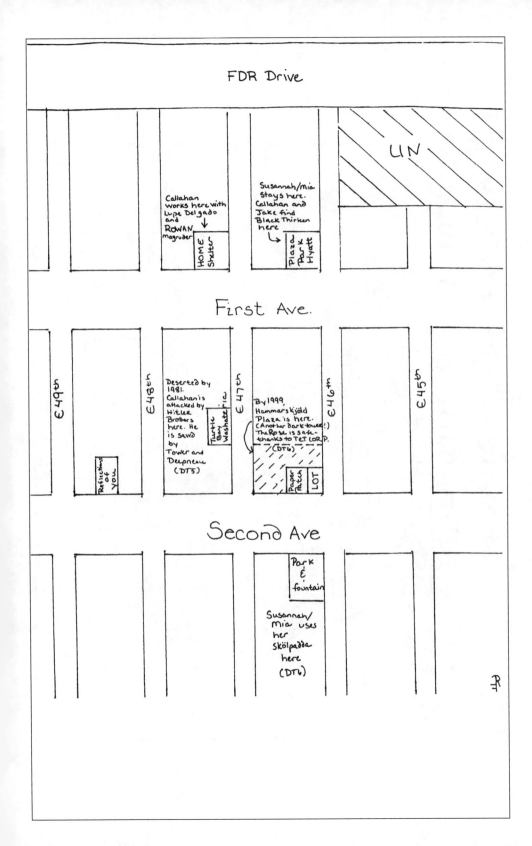

Sheriff Peavy's Map of Debaria and the Skin-man's attack pattern

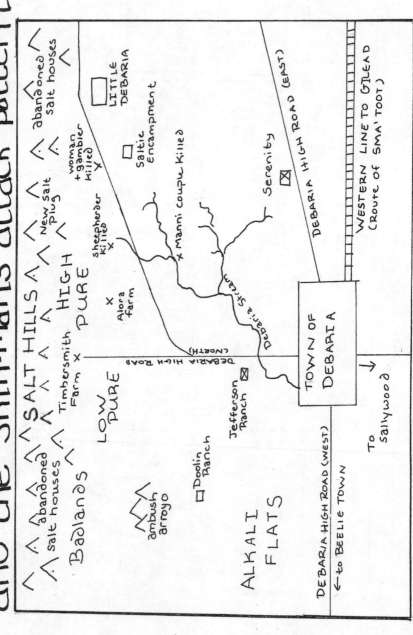

SALT HILLS

Abandoned salt houses

New salt Plug

Abandoned salt houses

Badlands

HIGH PURE

Timbersmith Farm ×

LOW PURE

× Alora farm

shepherder killed ×

woman + gambler killed ×

Saltie Encampment

LITTLE DEBARIA

× Manni couple killed

Serenity

ambush arroyo

□ Doolin Ranch

Jefferson ⊠ Ranch

DEBARIA HIGH ROAD (NORTH)

Debaria St. (MAIN)

DEBARIA HIGH ROAD (EAST)

ALKALI FLATS

TOWN OF DEBARIA

DEBARIA HIGH ROAD (WEST)

←to BEELIE TOWN

To Sallywood

WESTERN LINE TO GILEAD (ROUTE OF SMA' TOOT)

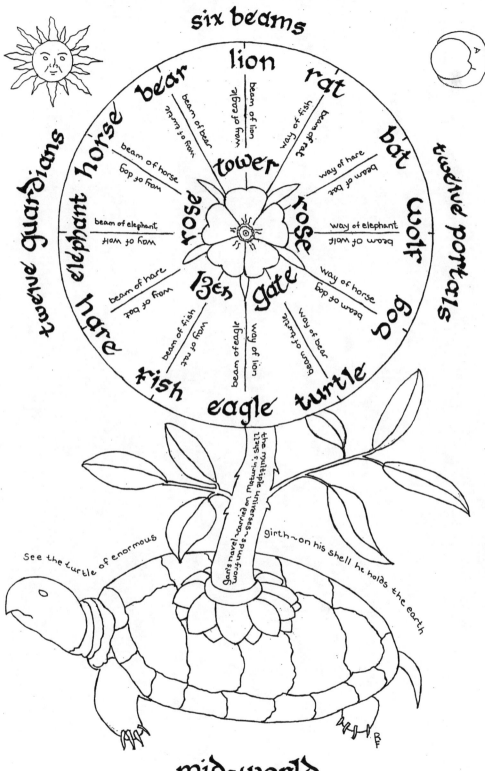

APPENDIX VIII
READING GROUP GUIDES

The Wind Through the Keyhole

1. In the novel *The Wind Through the Keyhole,* we discover that the book takes its title from a Mid-World folktale with the same name. This folktale, in turn, was part of a collection of stories entitled *Magic Tales of the Eld.* What is the literal significance of this title? What is the symbolic significance of this title? Why do you think Stephen King chose to name his novel after this folktale? Once you discovered where this title came from, did it affect how you read or interpreted the novel's three intertwined narratives?

2. *The Wind Through the Keyhole* is composed of three intertwined narratives. What are these three narratives? How do they relate to one another? How does Stephen King manage to link them together so that the stories transition smoothly, one into another?

3. All of the Dark Tower novels are told predominately in the third person, through the voice of a narrator. However, in *The Wind Through the Keyhole,* Roland becomes the narrator. In "The Skin-Man," Roland recounts an autobiographical tale in the first person, and then in "The Wind Through the Keyhole," he narrates a folktale. How does this switch to first person in "The Skin-Man" affect how you perceive Roland? Do you feel you have learned more about his personality? His soul? Roland is often presented to us as distant, reserved, and emotionally cool. Does this first-person narrative alter this perspective? Does Roland's narration of a folktale affect how we see him? What about the circumstances under which he narrates this folktale?

4. Roland refers to Jamie DeCurry as his *ka*-mate. What is the significance of this term? What is its literal definition? What does it say about Roland and Jamie's friendship? What does it tell us about the relationship between gunslingers?

5. Over the course of the Dark Tower novels, Roland Deschain changes tremendously. In *The Gunslinger,* he was depicted as an emotionally distant, goal-obsessed loner who was willing to sacrifice anyone—including Jake Chambers—in order to fulfill his quest. By the time he reaches the Dark Tower in the seventh book of the series, he is a man who has reclaimed his compassion and humanity. How would you describe the adult Roland we meet in *The Wind Through the Keyhole*? How does he compare to the young Roland we meet in *The Wind Through the Keyhole*? In what ways can you see the adult man in the boy? What parts of the boy have been lost by the man?

6. "The Skin-Man" begins after the death of Roland's mother. How was Gabrielle's death explained publicly? How does this compare to the truth? Why do you think Steven Deschain chose to explain his wife's death the way he did? Do you think it was the right thing to do? How do you think word of Gabrielle's death in places such as Arten affected the position of the gunslingers? How might it have affected people's support for John Farson?

7. In Roland's mind, what is the relationship between Gabrielle Deschain and the starkblast? Why does Roland associate them?

8. Although Roland's mother is dead and never appears as a character in our tale, she is a haunting presence throughout the narrative. How does Roland's mother haunt young Roland? How does she affect his behavior at the beginning of "The Skin-Man"? How does she haunt his time in Debaria? What about how she haunts the adult Roland? What new light did this novel shed upon Roland's relationship with his mother? Did anything about that relationship surprise you?

9. What does the young Roland have in common with the Young Bill Streeter? What does Young Bill Streeter have in common with Tim Ross?

10. Although the story "The Wind Through the Keyhole" is a fairy tale, the evil figure of the Covenant Man turns out to be none other than Marten Broadcloak/Walter O'Dim, who is Roland's enemy. Although it is tempting to take the Covenant Man's identity at face value (after all, we know that Roland's nemesis is an ageless sorcerer who can change his identity at will), it is important to contemplate the deeper reasons why both young Roland and adult Roland might have chosen to cast Broadcloak as the evil Covenanter. What personal grudge does the young Roland have against Broadcloak? What grudge does the older Roland have against O'Dim? Do you think that the tide of opinion against the gunslingers and in favor of John Farson, affected young Roland's decision to cast Broadcloak as the villain of the tale?

11. What is a skin-man? Does this figure remind you of any other monsters in Stephen King's fiction? (HINT: Think about the novel *Desperation*.)

12. "The Wind Through the Keyhole" is a fairy tale. How would you define a fairytale? Why does this story have a special place in Roland's heart? Although as a fairytale it takes place in the land of "Once upon a bye," it has particular relevance to Roland and his *ka-tet*. Why? Do you think that such fairy tales—in Mid-World and in our world—serve a greater purpose? Do you think the figure of Tim Ross—the lowborn lad who eventually becomes a gunslinger—is especially important in the context of our three intertwined tales? If so, why?

13. The wind is an extremely important force in *Wind Through the Keyhole*. How does the wind bind the three tales together? What is its symbolic significance?

14. How do the emotions and actions found in Tim Ross's story—jealousy, murder, grief, regret, questing, and redemption—relate to Roland's story? What about how they relate to Young Bill Streeter's story?

15. Who is Maerlyn? How does his depiction in this novel change how we view him?

16. At the end of "The Skin-Man," Roland tells us that he kept his mother's final letter for many years, tracing the words over and over. He says:

I traced them until the paper fell apart and I let the wind take it—the wind that blows through time's keyhole, ye ken. In the end, the wind takes everything, doesn't it? And why not? Why other? If the sweetness of our lives did not depart, there would be no sweetness at all.

What do you think Roland means? Do you think these words would be spoken by a younger character, and written by a younger author, or do you think that this perspective comes from maturity? Do you agree with what Roland says?

17. Why is it so significant that *The Wind Through the Keyhole* ends with Roland's dead mother telling her son that she forgives him and asking for his forgiveness in return? Does this affect how you see Gabrielle? Does it affect how you see Roland?

The Dark Tower I: The Gunslinger, Revised Edition, 2003

1. Who is Roland of Gilead? What is his ancestry? How does his personal history reflect the history of his land?

2. In many ways, Roland reminds us of the semimythical gunslingers of the late-nineteenth-century American West. Like them, he is simultaneously part lawman and part outlaw. Are there any figures from folklore, history, or film that remind you of Roland? How is he similar to them and how is he different? Would you call Roland a hero or an antihero?

3. Why does the term *Man in Black* have such emotional impact? What images do we automatically associate with such a figure? Do you believe that Walter is actually human? Is he demonic? What role does the demonic play in Roland's world?

4. One of Roland's favorite phrases is "the world has moved on." What does this mean? What do you think Roland's world was like before it moved on?

5. Throughout *The Gunslinger,* we are struck by the number of similarities between our world and Roland's world. The townsfolk of Tull know the words to the Beatles' song "Hey Jude," and they use *bocks* (bucks, or dollars) as their currency. Jake's description of New York (recounted while he is under hypnosis) reminds Roland of the mythical city of Lud, and the tunnels beneath the Cyclopean Mountains contain the ruins of a subway system that remind Jake of home. How do you explain these similarities? What is the relationship between Roland's world and our world?

6. Although Sylvia Pittston claims to be a woman of God, she is actually one of the most actively destructive characters found in *The Gunslinger.* As Roland's lover Allie says, Pittston's religion is poison. What role does Pittston play in the novel? Have you come across Pittston-like characters in any of King's other fiction? How do you explain the discrepancy between Pittston's professed role as a preacher and her actual allegiance to the Man in Black and the Crimson King? What are the divisions between good and evil in Roland's world?

7. Nort, the weed-eater Roland meets in Tull, suffers a terrible fate. After being poisoned by the addictive devil grass, he is resurrected by the sinister Man in Black, only to be later crucified by Sylvia Pittston and her followers. The

terms *resurrection* and *crucifixion* automatically make us reflect upon the biblical account of Jesus' crucifixion and resurrection, and the belief that, come Judgment Day, the dead will rise and be held accountable for the good and evil of their lives. Why do you think King includes these references? Why do you think Nort is crucified *after* being resurrected, a direct reversal of the biblical events?

8. Nort is not the only sacrificial figure found in *The Gunslinger*. Why does the Man in Black call Jake Roland's "Isaac"? What does this tell us about Roland, about his relationship to the Man in Black, and his relationship to the Dark Tower?

9. When do the characters of *The Gunslinger* use High Speech? Would it be justified to call this a sacred language? What languages, in our world, are associated with religious ceremonies, ritual, and magic? What makes them special? Can these same attributes be said to belong to High Speech?

10. In literature, settings often serve a symbolic purpose. Throughout *The Gunslinger,* the landscapes Roland traverses are described as hostile, dry "purgatorial wastes." Even relatively lush environments, such as the willow jungle, are full of dangerous forces, both mortal and demonic. In terms of its history, why is Roland's land so dangerous and desolate? What is the symbolic significance of this harshness?

11. Although the setting of the Dark Tower series reminds us of a cowboy Western, King's Tower novels draw from many other literary genres, including gothic fiction, science fiction, horror, and medieval Romance. Can you identify these elements in *The Gunslinger*?

12. One of Stephen King's central inspirations for writing *The Gunslinger* was Robert Browning's poem "Childe Roland to the Dark Tower Came." The Victorians who first read "Childe Roland" saw it as a story of heroism and duty. For them, it was a Romance in which a brave knight attempted to make a pilgrimage even though all before him had failed. More recent critics, however, have read the poem in much more psychological terms. They interpret the landscape that Browning's Roland traverses as a reflection of the character's fears, terrors, and preoccupations—in other words, as a reflection of his internal state. In this interpretation, the knight's search for the Dark Tower ultimately leads him to the center of himself, and to the truth of self-awareness. Do you think that either of these interpretations can be applied to *The Gunslinger,* in all or in part? Is Roland's story a heroic tale of a knight on a quest, or can Roland's travails be read as an allegory for the decisions, strivings, successes, failures, and personal betrayals we all face?

13. Ancient warrior cultures developed strict codes of honor and duty, which we now refer to as *heroic codes*. Great heroes were expected to be courageous, fearless, and headstrong. They had little or no regard for personal safety and in fact often acted rashly. What a warrior's peers thought of him mattered above all else, and he thought little or nothing about personal conscience (in the modern sense) or the well-being of the soul. The warrior did not aim to enter Heaven, but to become legendary. Personal honor, family honor, and/or loyalty to the king or chieftain were what made a man worthwhile. Did the gunslingers of Gilead obey a Christian code or a heroic code? What about Roland? Is there a shift between these two codes as the novel progresses?

14. Judeo-Christian culture is primarily a guilt-based culture. In other words, people believe that God alone has the right to judge sins, and that He knows our guilt or our innocence, no matter what the world thinks of us. If an individual is innocent, he (in theory at least) can hold his head high, even though his reputation has been ruined. What matters is personal conscience. Hence, by the same token, if an individual believes he has committed a crime, he will be consumed by guilt, even if no one else ever discovers what has been done. Warrior cultures, on the other hand, were often shame-based cultures. In shame-based cultures, an individual must avoid "losing face," since the disgrace he or she accrues reflects not only on the individual, but upon the family and the lineage. What a person thinks of himself matters less than what society thinks of him. Did Cort train apprentice gunslingers using guilt or shame? What does this tell us about gunslinger culture? At his hanging, does Hax show either guilt or shame? Why? What kind of culture does he seem to reflect? Does Roland primarily experience guilt or shame? Does this change over the course of the novel? Why, in terms of Roland's personal development (or lack of it), might this happen?

15. Take a look at the tarot reading Walter does for Roland in the golgotha. How many of these cards are from the traditional tarot deck? Are there any others that seem to be versions of traditional cards? Which cards did King create anew? Which ones actually come from other sources? (Hint: Take a look at T. S. Eliot's poem "The Waste Land.") What is your interpretation of this reading? Why do you think Walter burns the card of Life?

16. At the front of the revised edition of *The Gunslinger* (2003), King adds a quote from Thomas Wolfe's novel *Look Homeward, Angel*. (This quote did not appear at the front of the previous edition.) What emotions does this quote arouse in us? Why do you think King added it? Does it affect your interpretation of the novel?

The Dark Tower II: The Drawing of the Three

1. How does King's writing style change between *The Gunslinger* and *The Drawing of the Three*? What about his storytelling process? What are the strengths of each approach?

2. In the prologue of *The Drawing of the Three*, Roland has a dream in which he becomes the human embodiment of Walter's tarot card the Sailor. Why does he consider this a good dream? What is actually happening to him, and with what results? Do you believe that this is an existential punishment for his previous actions, a violent joke played upon him by the Man in Black, or simply a chance event?

3. What is *ka*, and how does it affect Roland's life? Does it seem to imply predestination? Are human beings trapped by *ka*, or do we retain free will?

4. Describe the three magic doors. How do they work? Does *ka* have anything to do with their existence?

5. What disembodied voices echo inside Roland's mind? What part do they play in Roland's internal monologue/dialogue? Are they forces for good or for ill? In turn, how does Roland *become* a voice in the minds of other people? Does this affect your interpretation of the voices inside Roland's consciousness?

6. Unlike the action of *The Gunslinger*, which takes place in Roland's world, much of the action of *The Drawing of the Three* takes place in our world. In fact, many of Eddie's problems, and most of Detta/Odetta's problems, have their roots in U.S. culture and U.S. history. What social, economic, and cultural problems of 1980s America touched Eddie Dean's life? What long-range effect did the Vietnam War have upon Henry Dean and, in turn, upon Eddie? How did racial hatred, segregation, and then the Civil Rights Movement affect Odetta Holmes's life? What about Detta Walker's?

7. Why is Eddie Dean willing to put his life at risk for his brother, Henry? Does Henry deserve this kind of loyalty?

8. What, in Roland's treatment of Eddie, shows that Roland comes from a warrior culture, not our culture? What part does patriarchal lineage play in gunslinger culture? Why would this be especially alien to Eddie?

9. Some warriors cultivate battle frenzy, using this altered state of consciousness to achieve feats that would otherwise be almost impossible. A famous historical example of this phenomenon can be found in the Norse berserkers. What is Roland's battle frenzy like? What about Eddie's? Is *frenzy* the right word?

10. Why did Odetta's father refuse to tell her about his past? What metaphor does King use to describe Dan Holmes's protective silence? How does Dan Holmes's treatment of his past contribute to Odetta's fragmentation?

11. How does Roland help to cure Odetta? Why is his timing so significant?

12. Were Jack Mort's attacks upon Odetta racially motivated?

13. How does Roland assess the people of our world—both those he sees on the plane and those he deals with while controlling Jack Mort's body? What does this say about the difference between a world that has "moved on" and one that has not?

14. The second section of *The Drawing of the Three* (the one immediately following "The Prisoner") is entitled "Shuffle." One of the images that King is conjuring is that of a cardsharp, shuffling a deck of cards. Why does King use this image? What kind of deck is being shuffled? What event, from *The Gunslinger*, does this remind us of? Why is the final section of the book entitled "Final Shuffle"?

15. The verb *to draw* has many meanings and can be used in many contexts. Roland, Eddie, and Detta all draw guns. Roland draws his two companions into his world. However, the verb *to draw* can also be used to describe the action of drawing poison from a wound so that the wound can heal. What role does this kind of drawing play in *The Drawing of the Three*?

16. What role does Jake play in this novel? Why is this so significant in terms of Roland's development?

The Dark Tower III: The Waste Lands

1. Between the end of *The Drawing of the Three* and the beginning of *The Waste Lands*, the relationships among Roland, Susannah, and Eddie shift. Describe these changes. What causes them? Does Eddie now trust Roland? Does Susannah?

2. What is the gunslinger litany? What worldview does it imply—from what a gunslinger should honor to how he/she should attack his/her enemies?

3. In what ways are Roland's new friends much like his deadly old friends? What happened to those old friends? Do you think the same fate awaits Roland's new friends?

4. What is *ka-tet*? How do the forces of *ka-tet* bind individuals together, and how do they ultimately bind a society together?

5. Describe the metaphysical map that Roland draws at the beginning of the novel. What is its linchpin? What sits upon its circumference? What forces hold the world together? What part did the Great Old Ones play in the devising of this map? Do you think that the forces described there pre-date them? Why or why not? Does this map describe the actual origins of the world or of the linked worlds? What role did North Central Positronics play in the making of this world, or in the remaking of it?

6. What are the Drawers? Are they objective places—places that you could find on a map—or is their existence more subjective? Have you encountered any such places in your life? If so, what are they? Do you have a special term for such places?

7. What paradox tears Roland's mind apart at the outset of the novel? What causes it? What eases his suffering? Why is this significant?

8. What voices does Jake hear in the Vacant Lot, just before he sees the Rose? What happens to him when he actually sees this flower? How does Jake's vision of the Rose differ from Eddie's vision of the Tower amid its sea of roses?

9. What is the White?

10. While contemplating the rose, Jake sees that it grows out of alien purple grass. Roland sees the same purple grass during his vision in the golgotha, at the end of *The Gunslinger*. Why does King seem to want us to compare these otherwise dissimilar visions? What is he telling us about the nature of the Rose?

11. What is the difference between Jake's door, labeled *The Boy*, and the beach doors?

12. The scene in which Roland and his new *ka-tet* cross the bridge into Lud eerily echoes the passage in *The Gunslinger* where Jake falls to his death. Compare these two scenes. What do they tell us about the changes happening within Roland?

13. The third book of the Dark Tower series takes its title from T. S. Eliot's long poem "The Waste Land." Two themes that thread through Eliot's poem are fragmentation and alienation—the fragmentation of modern culture and its inevitable loss of meaning, and the sense of alienation that individuals experience in reaction to this. (It must be remembered that "The Waste Land" was written in the aftermath of World War I, when Europe was still in shock over the death and destruction caused by modern weaponry.) How does King's novel reflect these themes? How does this fragmentation extend to the psyches of the characters themselves, and even to the computerized personalities of machines?

14. In his notes on "The Waste Land," T. S. Eliot stated that he was extremely influenced by the Grail legend. What is the legend of the Grail? Do you think it influenced Stephen King when he wrote *The Waste Lands*?

15. Eleven dimensions, worlds made out of vibrating strings, parallel universes

that contain alternative versions of you . . . sounds like another Dark Tower book? It's not, but it does seem as though the scientific community is finally taking Jake Chambers seriously. There *are* other worlds than these. For a fascinating description of string theory (and as a way to begin discussing the similarities between contemporary physics and the multiple worlds of the Dark Tower series), visit the following Web sites: www.pbs.org/nova/elegant (a terrific introduction), www.bbc.co.uk/science/horizon/2001/parallelunitrans.shtml (another great introduction), http://superstringtheory.com (for brave folks who are used to technical language), www.scientific american.com (in the "search" section, type *Parallel Universes*).

The Dark Tower IV: Wizard and Glass

1. Why, do you think, did the Great Old Ones build Blaine? What purpose did he serve in their world? What do you imagine the Old Ones' world was like?
2. While riding in Blaine, Eddie thinks to himself, *Not all is silent in the halls of the dead and the rooms of ruin. Even now some of the stuff the Old Ones left behind still works. And that's really the horror of it, wouldn't you say? Yes. The exact horror of it.* How does Eddie's statement prefigure the coming action? Does his observation hold true for the first three novels of the series?
3. What is a thinny? What effect does it have on those near it? Is it alive? How does the image of the thinny help to bridge the two parts of *Wizard and Glass*—the section that takes place in Topeka and the one that takes place in Hambry?
4. Why does Roland say that in Hambry "the waters on top and the waters down below seemed to run in different directions"?
5. *Ka* is a wheel; its one purpose is to turn and (inevitably) repeat. In what ways have we seen the wheel of *ka* turn so far in the series?
6. What is the story of Lord Perth, which we learned about in *The Waste Lands*? How did that myth play out in the novel? How does it continue to resonate throughout *Wizard and Glass*? Do you think the theme of the Lord Perth tale is also one of the themes of the Dark Tower series?
7. Who is Rhea of the Cöos? What role does she play in the novel? How does she compare to Roland's other major enemies—the Man in Black and Sylvia Pittston? If Rhea had been a male character, would she have been as convincing or as formidable? Why or why not?
8. What is the Wizard's Rainbow? What do we know about it? How many of the balls are still in existence, and why are they said to be alive and hungry? What is the relationship between the White, which Roland and the other gunslingers serve, and the spectrum of colors that make up the Wizard's Rainbow?
9. The imagery surrounding Maerlyn's Grapefruit is often sexual; even its color is described as "labial pink." Why does King use this imagery? What is the relationship between the Grapefruit and emotions such as desire, jealousy, and vengeance? How do these emotions drive the action of Roland's Hambry adventure? How did they begin his journey into manhood, even down to the early winning of his guns?
10. How does Roland's experience of Maerlyn's Grapefruit differ from that of

the other people who have it in their possession? Why do you think this is so? What visions does Roland have while the ball is in his possession? How does the ball lead to his downfall?

11. The tale of Hambry begins under a Kissing Moon and ends under a Demon Moon. Why is this significant? How does the transition from one of these moons to the other reflect the darkening of the novel's atmosphere?

12. At the beginning of the Hambry portion of *Wizard and Glass,* Susan Delgado must "prove" her honesty. What does this mean? In what other ways does Susan continue to prove her honesty throughout the book? What other characters prove themselves to be honest? Which characters prove to be dishonest?

13. *For if it is* ka, *it'll come like a wind, and your plans will stand before it no more than a barn before a cyclone.* In what ways have we seen Pat Delgado's description of *ka* hold true, both in this novel and in the three preceding ones?

14. How would you describe Cuthbert Allgood? What does Roland love about him? What about him angers Roland? In what ways is he like Eddie? Is this similarity also *ka*?

15. What do you think the relationship is between Walter (also known as the Man in Black), Marten, Flagg, Fannin, and Maerlyn? What part do these nasty characters play in this novel?

16. In what ways does gunslinger culture actually inflame the rebellion led by Farson?

17. When Roland first meets Susan Delgado, King tells us, "Roland was far from the relentless creature he would eventually become, but the seeds of that relentlessness were there—small, stony things that would, in their time, grow to trees with deep roots . . . and bitter fruit." Why does King tell us this? Do you agree with this assessment of Roland's character?

18. Where do we see the *sigul* of the open, staring eye? Why is it so sinister? How does it connect Hambry, Topeka, and the Green Palace? What does it tell us about Roland's world?

The Dark Tower V: Wolves of the Calla

1. In his author's note, Stephen King acknowledges the influence that several films and film directors have had upon the Dark Tower series. Most notably, he mentions Sergio Leone's spaghetti Westerns starring Clint Eastwood *(A Fistful of Dollars; For a Few Dollars More; The Good, the Bad, and the Ugly),* and Akira Kurosawa's classic *The Seven Samurai.* He also gives credit to John Sturges's 1960 Western (a remake of the Kurosawa film), *The Magnificent Seven.* Can you describe the influence that any or all of these films have had upon the Dark Tower series as a whole and upon *Wolves of the Calla* in particular?

2. At the beginning of Chapter I of *Wolves of the Calla,* Eddie Dean reflects upon the old Mejis saying *Time is a face on the water.* Do his theories explain why time passes differently in our world and in the borderlands? Why or why not? Do his observations hold true for you, personally? Have you ever experienced such time-dilation or time-contraction?

3. Why are Eddie, Jake, Susannah, and Roland so wary of Andy when they first meet him? Why is this significant, both in terms of our *ka-tet*'s history and in terms of the history of Roland's world?

4. What is happening to Susannah Dean's personality? How did this come to pass? Do you think this process is part of her *ka*? Given her condition, what do you think will happen to our *ka-tet* in the final two books of the series?

5. Who are the roonts? How did they become roont? Do you think that the roonts understand what has happened to them? What, from the text, makes you say this?

6. What power do the Wolves ultimately serve? Why are the people of the Calla so afraid to fight them? Can you understand their fear?

7. What mythical event do the Sisters of Oriza honor? What purpose do they serve in terms of plot? Do you think that King is trying to make us reexamine traditional ideas about men and women?

8. Describe Black Thirteen. What is its history? What role does it play in the book? How does it compare to Maerlyn's Grapefruit, which figured prominently in *Wizard and Glass*?

9. What is *todash*? Why is it dangerous to travel *todash*? Who are the Manni? Why do they believe that *todash* is "the holiest of rites and most exalted of states"?

10. What role does the number 19 play in *Wolves of the Calla*? Where have we seen it before? (Hint: You'll need a 2003 edition of *The Gunslinger* to answer the second part of this question.)

11. Describe the Cave of Voices (also known as Doorway Cave). What is its function? Is it magical or mechanical? What voices do the various characters hear when they are inside the cave? In what way does the "demon" or "mechanism" of this cave expose unconscious fear or guilt? If you were suddenly transported to the Cave of Voices, who would come to speak to you?

12. What is the meaning of the term *commala*? Why would the Commala Song be so important in a rice-growing community? Does the Commala Song—and its accompanying dance—remind you of any ceremonies from our world?

13. Compare the tale of Lady Oriza to the story of Lord Perth, which we learned about in *The Waste Lands*. What do they have in common? How do they differ? What themes do they share with the Dark Tower series as a whole?

14. Where, in King's fiction, have we met Father Callahan before? Why do you think King decided to link a non–Dark Tower book so closely to the Dark Tower series?

15. As we all know from experience, few people are completely good or completely evil. Even the most annoying individual can surprise us with a selfless act, and an otherwise admirable person can sometimes shock us with an angry word or an unfair judgment. The same goes for well-drawn, believable characters. Make a list of the most important characters we meet in Calla Bryn Sturgis. Who is "good"? Who is "bad"? Who would you say is "brave" and whom would you call "cowardly"? Now take a look at any scenes where these characters exhibit unexpected, opposite tendencies. How does the author make us sympathize with the wicked or feel disappointment with the opinions and actions of the "good"? How does King let us see both the savory and unsavory traits of each character?

16. Roland's world contains both machinery and magic. Most of the machinery we've encountered so far has been hostile, but the magic is more ambiguous. In *Wolves of the Calla,* the most potent magical objects are the Rose and Black Thirteen. Is one completely good and the other completely evil? Why or why not? What greater forces do these objects represent? Do you think that they symbolize a struggle found in our world as well?

17. Both fans and reviewers often refer to King's large body of work as "the Stephen King Universe" or "the Stephen King Multiverse." How do you interpret these terms? What part does the Dark Tower play in this universe? What part does our world play in this universe? Do you think that Stephen King's realistic fiction should also be classed as part of the "Stephen King Universe"?

18. Human beings have always craved magical, supernatural tales. In fact, many of the earliest and greatest of our stories—*The Epic of Gilgamesh, Beowulf,* and *The Odyssey,* to name just a few—tell about man's interaction with the unseen worlds. Although "official" culture denies that telepathy, spirit worlds, and magic exist, such ideas still thrive as part of modern folklore. Why do you think that magical and supernatural tales are still popular? Do you think their appeal has grown over the past few years? Why? Do these kinds of tales serve a particular purpose, either socially or personally? Do you think the appeal of the Dark Tower series lies in the way it successfully weaves together both technology and magic?

The Dark Tower VI: Song of Susannah

1. Stephen King placed two unusual facing pages at the beginning of *Song of Susannah.* At the center of the left-hand page (which is otherwise blank) is the word REPRODUCTION. At the center of the right-hand page is one large number—19. However, in the bottom left-hand corner of the right-hand page is the tiny number 99. What effect is King striving for? What effect do these pages have upon you as a reader?

2. How does King shift our mood from one of elation, when the Wolves are defeated near the end of *Wolves of the Calla,* to one of anxiety at the beginning of *Song of Susannah*? What series of tragedies—and inexplicable events—takes place?

3. What is a Beamquake? What effect does it have on the borderlands? What is its significance, as far as our characters' quest is concerned?

4. Who, or what, is Mia? How does her appearance (and disappearance) drive the action of *Song of Susannah*? In what ways does her history intertwine with Roland's?

5. When the Manni help Roland, Eddie, Jake, and Callahan open the Unfound Door, they all expect that it will open onto New York City in 1999, and then onto Stoneham, Maine, in 1977. Eddie and Roland are supposed to follow Susannah into the Big Apple, and Jake and Callahan are supposed to pursue Calvin Tower in Maine. What goes wrong? What series of unexpected events takes place? In your opinion, who or what is behind this change of plan?

6. What is Susannah's can-tah? How do you think it came to Susannah? With what force is it aligned? Have you ever encountered a similar type of object

in any of King's other fiction? (Hint: Take a look at the novel *Desperation*.) If so, how does it differ from Susannah's can-tah? What does this say about the forces of the White and the Outer Dark in the Stephen King universe?

7. What is Susannah's Dogan? What part does it play in *Song of Susannah*? How does it link this novel with *Wolves of the Calla*? Is Susannah's Dogan completely imaginary? Is the machinery within it completely under Susannah's control? Why or why not?

8. What are Demon Elementals? What role do they play in our *tet*'s adventures? Why do you think that King waited until *Song of Susannah* to tell us about them? How do they affect your view of the Guardians? How do they affect your vision of Roland's world?

9. What role does John Cullum play in *Song of Susannah*? Do you think that his appearance is linked to *ka*? If so, what part does *ka* play in the battle between the White and the Outer Dark? Does it always play the same role?

10. Unlike most novels, *Song of Susannah* is divided not into chapters but into stanzas, a term we usually associate with songs and poems. Does this name change affect how we read the novel? Does it affect our expectations? At the end of each chapter/stanza, King includes a short rhymed section containing a stave and a response. What do these terms mean, both in and of themselves and in the context of the novel?

11. What is the significance of Susannah's dream at the beginning of the tenth stanza? What visions does she have? What future do they foretell? Can this future be altered, even though the visions show future events in the Keystone World?

12. In stanza eleven, Roland says that Stephen King is the twin of the Rose. Earlier in the Dark Tower series, we were told that the Rose is the twin of the Dark Tower. How do you explain the relationship between King, the Rose, and the Tower?

13. What is the nature of the black shadow that Eddie Dean sees hovering around *sai* King? What is its possible significance, both in terms of King's life and our *tet*'s quest?

14. Why—according to *sai* King—did he stop writing the Dark Tower series? What about Roland, in particular, disturbed him? Do you agree or disagree with his assessment of our gunslinger? In your opinion, has Roland changed since King first started writing about him? Were there any other forces that contributed to King's ceasing work on the Dark Tower series?

15. In stanza eleven, King describes his writing process. Does this description surprise you? Why or why not?

16. At the end of *Song of Susannah*, Stephen King includes a section entitled "Coda: Pages from a Writer's Journal." According to the *Oxford English Reference Dictionary*, a coda is a concluding event or series of events. More specifically, it tends to refer to the concluding passage of a piece of music (or of a movement within a piece of music), usually one that acts as an addition to the basic structure. In ballet, the term *coda* refers to the concluding section of a dance. Why do you think King chose to call this section a coda? What does this say about the structure of *Song of Susannah*? What specific event in *Wolves of the Calla* is King consciously echoing?

The Dark Tower VII: The Dark Tower

1. Of all the books in the Dark Tower series, *The Dark Tower* is probably the most action-packed. What are the major crisis points within the novel? How does King create this dramatic tension? How do you think King goes about planning such a plot? Does the story line just evolve naturally from the characters he imagines?

2. What do Jake and Callahan find in the Dixie Pig? In what ways do the forces of the Outer Dark mock the White? Since the Crimson King is also descended from Arthur Eld, is there some hidden significance in this mockery? If so, what does this say about the nature of the White? What about the nature of the Tower?

3. How does Pere Callahan's death, at the beginning of *The Dark Tower,* refer back to his experiences in *'Salem's Lot*? What does this say about Callahan's *ka*?

4. What is an *aven kal*? How is it similar to, or different from, *todash*?

5. What kind of "walk-in" do Eddie and Roland meet along Route 7 in Lovell? How did this creature enter our world? What connection does King make between walk-ins, the Prim, and the creative imagination?

6. What is the difference between a magical door, which links worlds, and a mechanical one? Where do the different types come from? Is one aligned with the White and one with the Outer Dark? Can such simple labels be put on them? Why?

7. The Breaker prison in Thunderclap is known as the Devar-Toi to the prisoners and Algul Siento to the *can-toi* and *taheen* guards. How do these two names express different perspectives on the duties being performed there?

8. The three Breakers who initially aid Roland, Eddie, Susannah, and Jake all come from other places in King's fiction—either from earlier parts of the Dark Tower series or from other stories or novels. Where do these characters come from? Why does King choose these characters? What does this say about the Dark Tower itself, and about the interconnectedness of the "Stephen King Universe"?

9. To describe Pimli Prentiss, Master of the Devar-Toi, Stephen King compares him to Jim Jones, the leader of the People's Temple in Guyana, who convinced his followers to commit mass suicide. What effect does this have upon us? Is King making a wider social statement when he draws this comparison?

10. What is *ka-shume*? How does this force manifest in the *ka* of our *ka-tet*? Can a person escape *ka-shume*?

11. Although it has its own stark beauty, Roland's world has been devastated by mutations, plagues, and ruinous technology. Now that you've finished the series, how do you think Mid-World relates to our world? Does the company North Central Positronics have any symbolic significance? Is King commenting on contemporary culture? If so, what is he saying? Is his vision completely positive, completely negative, or something in between?

12. In the final two books of the Dark Tower series, King enters the tale directly. In fact, at one point King calls himself the deus ex machina, or the "god out of a machine." What is your reaction to King's appearance in the Dark Tower series? What place does the fictional Stephen King have in the Dark Tower universe? What about the real Stephen King?

13. According to the people of the Tet Corporation, there is a direct link between the Dark Tower series and King's other fiction. What is it? Do you view King's various novels as pieces of a giant jigsaw puzzle, with the Dark Tower novels at the center? Why or why not? If you don't see King's fiction in this way (or if you haven't read many of King's other books), think about any King films you've seen, or any episodes of his various TV series. Are there any themes that seem to repeat?

14. What are the *can-toi*? What are the *taheen*? How are they the same and how are they different? King compares the *taheen* to the monstrous figures found in Hieronymus Bosch's famous triptych, *The Garden of Earthly Delights,* painted circa AD 1500. Take a look at this painting. (It's fairly easy to find. Just type *Hieronymus Bosch,* and *Garden of Earthly Delights,* into your search engine.) As you will see, when the triptych is closed, its outer shutters depict the creation of the world. When the triptych is open, the left panel depicts Adam and Eve and the earthly paradise, the center panel illustrates the world engaged in sinful pleasures, and the right panel (where our *taheen*-like creatures appear) represents Hell. How are King's creations similar to these painted figures? By drawing this comparison, what other, unspoken comments is King making about End-World, the Devar-Toi, and the Crimson King?

15. At the beginning of *The Dark Tower,* Jake reflects upon one of Roland's sayings. According to our gunslinger, "You needn't die happy when your day comes, but you must die satisfied, for you have lived your life from beginning to end and *ka* is always served." What does this statement mean? Do you agree or disagree with the philosophy it expresses? Take a look at each member of Roland's *ka-tet*: Eddie, Susannah, Jake, Oy, Callahan, and even Roland himself. Do any or all of them remain true to this vision?

16. At the beginning of *Wolves of the Calla,* Stephen King includes a section entitled "The Final Argument." According to this introductory piece, each of the seven novels of the Dark Tower series has a subtitle. Moving, in order, from *The Gunslinger* to *Song of Susannah,* these subtitles are "Resumption," "Renewal," "Redemption," "Regard," "Resistance," and "Reproduction." In terms of Roland's quest, what is the meaning of each of these subtitles?

17. Although each of the first six novels of the Dark Tower series has a single-word subtitle, *The Dark Tower* (the final book of the series) has a four-word subtitle. It is "Reproduction, Revelation, Redemption, Resumption." How does this subtitle reflect the action of the novel? How does it interact with the subtitles of the previous novels? If you sit and contemplate the meaning of each of the words in *The Dark Tower*'s subtitle, does it affect your interpretation of the novel's ending? How does it affect your interpretation of Roland's quest?

APPENDIX IX
VERSIONS OF THE COMMALA SONG

The Commala Song is probably one of the most important songs found in Mid-World. It is sung in the Calla, but it was also sung in In-World during Roland's youth. The version which the Calla *folken* sing during their welcoming fiesta (and to which Roland dances at the beginning of *Wolves of the Calla*) is listed below. Following it you will find some of the Commala's variants, found throughout the rest of the series.

COMMALA
(THE RICE SONG)

CALLA BRYN STURGIS VERSION
Song and Dance in Honor of Lady Oriza, Lady of the Rice.

SINGER/DANCER: Do I not give you joy from my joy,
and the water I carried with the strength of my arm and my heart?
CHORUS: Give you to eat of the green-crop.
SINGER/DANCER: Give you joy of the rice.
CHORUS: Come! . . . Come! . . . Come!
Come-come-commala
Rice come a-falla
I-sisser 'ay-a-bralla
Dey come a-folla
Down come-a rivva
Or-i-za we kivva
Rice be a green-o
See what we seen-o
Seen-o the green-o
Come-come-commala!
Come-come-commala
Rice come a-falla
Deep inna walla
Grass come-commala
Under the sky-o
Grass green n high-o
Girl n her fella
Lie down togetha
They slippy 'ay slide-o

Under 'ay sky-o
Come-come-commala
Rice come a-falla!
CHORUS: COMMALA!

CALLA CHILDREN'S VERSION

Roland's tet overhears the Calla's prepubescent twins singing this version while they march behind Andy the Messenger Robot. (V:587–88)

Commala-come-one!
Mamma had a son!
Dass-a time 'at Daddy
Had d'mos' fun!
Commala-come-come!
Daddy had one!
Dass-a time 'at Mommy
Had d'mos' fun!
Commala-come-two!
You know what to do!
Plant the rice commala,
Don't ye be . . . no . . . foo'!
Commala-come-two!
Daddy no foo'!
Mommy plant commala
cause she know jus' what to do!
Commala-come-t'ree!
You know what t'be
Plant d'rice commala
and d'rice'll make ya free!
Commala-come-t'ree!
Rice'll make ya free!
When ya plant the rice commala
You know jus' what to be!

EAST ROAD BATTLE VERSION

The people of the Calla add this verse to the Commala Song after the battle of the East Road. It honors Lady Oriza for hiding the Calla's children in her rice. (V:689)

Come-come-commala
Rice come a-falla
I-sissa 'ay a-bralla
Dey come a-folla
We went to a-rivva
'Riza did us kivva.

SONG OF SUSANNAH VERSION

One stave and response from this version of the Commala Song can be found at the end of each Stanza section in *Song of Susannah*. (VI:18, VI:43–44, VI:58, VI:75, VI:98, VI:154, VI:173, VI:216, VI:261, VI:303, VI:344, VI:384–85, VI:411)

STAVE

Commala-come-come
There's a young man with a gun.
Young man lost his honey
When she took it on the run.

RESPONSE

Commala-come-come!
She took it on the run!
Left her baby lonely but
Her baby ain't done.

STAVE

Commala-come-coo
The wind'll blow ya through.
Ya gotta go where ka's wind blows ya
Cause there's nothing else to do.

RESPONSE

Commala-come-two!
Nothin' else to do!
Gotta go where ka's wind blows ya
Cause there's nothing else to do.

STAVE

Commala-come-key
Can ya tell me what ya see?
Is it ghosts or just the mirror
That makes ya want to flee?

RESPONSE

Commala-come-three!
I beg ya, tell me!
Is it ghosts or just your darker self
That makes ya want to flee?

STAVE

Commala-come-ko
Whatcha doin at my do'?
If you doan tell me now, my friend,
I'll lay ya on de flo'.

RESPONSE

Commala-come-fo'!
I can lay ya low!
The things I done to such as you
You never want to know.

STAVE

Commala-gin-jive
Ain't it grand to be alive?
To look out on Discordia
When the Demon Moon arrives.

RESPONSE

Commala-come-five!
Even when the shadows rise!
To see the world and walk the world
Makes ya glad to be alive.

STAVE

Commala-mox-nix!
You're in a nasty fix!
To take the hand in a traitor's glove
Is to grasp a sheaf of sticks!

RESPONSE

Commala-come-six!
Nothing there but thorns and sticks!
When you find your hand in a traitor's glove
You're in a nasty fix.

STAVE

Commala-loaf-leaven!
They go to Hell or up to Heaven!
When the guns are shot and the fire's hot,
You got to poke em in the oven.

RESPONSE

Commala-come-seven!
Salt and yow' for leaven!
Heat em up and knock em down
And poke em in the oven.

STAVE

Commala-ka-kate.
You're in the hands of fate.
No matter if you're real or not,
The hour groweth late.

RESPONSE

Commala-come-eight!
The hour groweth late!
No matter what the shade ya cast
You're in the hands of fate.

STAVE

Commala-me-mine
You have to walk the line.
When you finally get the thing you need
It makes you feel so fine.

RESPONSE

Commala-come-nine!
It makes ya feel fine!
But if you'd have the thing you need
You have to walk the line.

STAVE

Commala-come-ken
It's the other one again.
You may know her name and face
But that don't make her your friend.

RESPONSE

Commala-come-ten!
She is not your friend!
If you let her get too close
She'll cut you up again.

STAVE

Commala-come-call
We hail the One who made us all,
Who made the men and made the maids,
Who made the great and small.

RESPONSE

Commala-come-call!
He made the great and small!
And yet how great the hand of fate
That rules us one and all.

STAVE

Commala-come-ki,
There's a time to live and one to die.
With your back against the final wall
Ya gotta let the bullets fly.

RESPONSE

Commala-come-ki!
Let the bullets fly!
Don't 'ee mourn for me, my lads
When it comes my day to die.

STAVE

Sing your song, O sing it well,
The child has come to pass.

RESPONSE

Commala-come-kass,
The worst has come to pass.
The Tower trembles on its ground;
The child has come at last.

FINAL VERSE

Commala-come-come,
The battle's now begun!
And all the foes of men and rose
Rise with the setting sun.

SUSANNAH'S DREAM VERSION

Susannah Dean hears this version of the Commala Song in her dream version of Central Park. (VII:724)

Rice be a green-o,
Seen what we seen-o,
Seen-o the green-o,
Come-come-commala!